Travel to Germany

in a matter of seconds with the

Komm mit! Video Programs

(Levels 1-3) and **Expanded Video Programs** (Levels 1 and 2)! These on-location videos motivate your students as they meet German-speaking people, experience the culture, and learn German in context. **Integrated** with the Pupil's Editions, both video programs set the theme, dramatize the *Los geht's* dialogues, and close with cultural interviews. In addition, the Expanded Video Programs set the cultural scene and offer extended *Los geht's* dialogues, more cultural interviews, and authentic German television footage. Video Guides provide activity sheets, scripts, and teaching suggestions to *support your curriculum.* Order your video today! **Mail the postage-paid card,** or **fax** it to **(800) 874-6418,** or call **(800) 225-5425.**

See you there!

GY?

achers what they
nd advice became

ts available
th the curriculum.
at deal about
sult for teachers:
o mix and match.

since 1866, we
he technology.
ound your
d value that
s part of an

y and see for
n the student and

eo Program —

ent to fit your

the
cripts and

ople, experience
Programs or
er fax or mail it

HOLT
RINEHART
WINSTON

22H94A10
9-99-707544-7

Komm mit!

HOLT GERMAN LEVELS 1, 2, AND 3

SO SAGT MAN DAS!

Asking someone to take a position; asking for reasons; expressing opinions

When having a discussion, you use certain communication strategies. Here are some ways to help you encourage a discussion in German.

To ask someone to take a position on a subject you could say:

Möchtest du mal dazu Stellung nehmen?
Wer nimmt mal dazu Stellung?

To ask for reasons

Kannst du das

To express an opinion

Meiner Meinung
Ich finde, daß wi

A ROAD MAP TO PROFICIENCY

Komm mit!'s **functionally driven scope and sequence** gives students reasons to communicate. As a result, they develop proficiency in the four language **skills** (listening, speaking, reading, and writing) and build their critical-thinking skills.

Plus, **Komm mit!** presents **grammar** in context to support the functions, enhancing your students' ability to communicate with accuracy and confidence.

HOLT FOREIGN LANGUAGES

DESTINATION: COMMUNICATION

T1

JOURNEY AT A REALISTIC PACE

Komm mit!'s **manageable chapters** set a realistic pace, so you and your students can complete each level of this three-level program in one year—without sacrificing language development.

Komm mit!'s **spiraling** of functions, vocabulary, and grammar increases your students' retention of newly acquired language and presents opportunities for using the language in various situations. And, with only 70 to 80 active **vocabulary** words per chapter, your students can use the core vocabulary with greater ease, yet still personalize their own communication.

Best of all, **Komm mit!**'s variety of activities, strategies, and supplementary materials **meets individual student needs**—ensuring the success of all students.

Ein wenig *G*rammatik

Ordinal numbers
In order to use numbers as adjectives, as in the sentence "I am in the tenth grade", you need to know the ordinal numbers. The first three, as in English, are irregular.

Das ist mein **erst**er Wagen.
Ich würde mir den Film ein **zweit**es Mal ansehen.
Nein, ich meine die **dritt**e Straße rechts.

After that, add a **t** to the end of the cardinal number and then the correct adjective ending.

Ich bin in der **zehnt**en Klasse.
Meine Schwester hat am **achtzehnt**en Juli Geburtstag.

Remember, as adjectives, these numbers follow all the rules for adjective endings. For a list of the ordinal numbers, see the Grammar Summary.

WORTSCHATZ

auf deutsch erklärt

<u>ausgefallen</u> angezogen
interessante Klamotten tragen, die nicht jeder hat
<u>bei</u> anderen <u>gut ankommen</u>
wenn dich andere Leute mögen
Ich <u>pass'</u> <u>mich</u> meinen Freunden <u>an</u>. Ich möchte so sein, wie meine Freunde, und machen, was sie machen.
Er trägt <u>den</u> <u>letzten</u> <u>Schrei</u>. Er trägt, was gerade Mode ist.
in der Zeitung <u>herumblättern</u>
die Zeitung nicht lesen, sondern nur Seite für Seite ansehen

auf englisch erklärt

Ich <u>lasse</u> <u>mich</u> <u>von</u> der Mode <u>beeinflussen</u>. *I let myself be influenced by fashion.*
Aber ich <u>mache</u> nicht <u>mit</u> der Mode <u>mit</u>. *But I don't go along with fashion.*
Man <u>drückt</u> sich durch Kleidung <u>aus</u>. *You can express yourself with clothes.*
Ich <u>gebe</u> schon <u>zu</u>, daß ich einige Menschen <u>nach</u> ihrer Kleidung <u>beurteile</u>. *I admit that I judge some people by their clothes.*
Sagt das etwas <u>über</u> solche <u>Leute</u> <u>aus</u>? *Does that say something about such people?*

Sie näht gern.

Er spart Geld.

Sie zieht sich verrückt an.

EXPLORE CULTURE

Develop your students' appreciation of the German-speaking world with **Komm mit!**'s interviews, **authentic** dialogues, realia, photos, and videos. **Komm mit!**'s strong cross-cultural perspective enriches students' understanding of the **multicultural** nature of the German-speaking world.

Die verschiedenen Bildungswege in Deutschland

Helga, Klaus und Hassan sind im gleichen Alter und wohnen in derselben Nachbarschaft. Sie kennen sich schon Jahre lang. Als Kinder haben sie dieselbe Grundschule besucht, bis sie 10 Jahre alt waren. Danach hat jeder einen anderen Bildungsweg genommen. Jetzt sind sie 18 Jahre alt und sehen einander selten.

Hassan lernt jetzt für das Abitur. Er muß sehr gute Noten bekommen, weil er Psychologie an einer Universität studieren will.

Helga ist auch sehr fleißig und hat neulich ihre Lehre (*apprenticeship*) im Kaufhof als Verkäuferin begonnen. Sie geht zweimal die Woche in die Berufsschule; an den restlichen drei Tagen wird sie in den verschiedenen Abteilungen des Kaufhauses ausgebildet. Sie hat vor, eines Tages Abteilungsleiterin zu werden.

Klaus besucht jetzt die Fachoberschule und will danach eine Lehre als Krankenpfleger machen. Deshalb möchte er auch nach der Lehre nicht zur Bundeswehr, sondern Zivildienst in einem Krankenhaus machen.

A. 1. Schau dir die Tabelle an!
2. Welche Bildungswege sind Hassan, Klaus und Helga gegangen? Was fällt dir am deutschen Schulsystem auf? Diskutier über die Hauptmerkmale mit einem Klassenkameraden!
3.

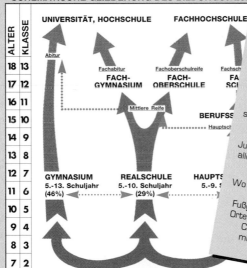

SCHEMATISCHE GLIEDERUNG DES BILDUNGSWESEN[S]

ALTER	KLASSE			
		UNIVERSITÄT, HOCHSCHULE	FACHHOCHSCHULE	
		Abitur		
18	13	Fachabitur	Fachoberschulreife	Fachs...
17	12	FACH-GYMNASIUM	FACH-OBERSCHULE	FA...SC...
16	11			
		Mittlere Reife		BERUFSS...
15	10			
14	9			Hauptsch...
13	8			
12	7	GYMNASIUM 5.-13. Schuljahr (46%)	REALSCHULE 5.-10. Schuljahr (29%)	HAUPTS... 5.-9. S...
11	6			
10	5			
9	4			
8	3			
7	2			
6	1	GRUNDSCHULE 1.-4. Schuljahr		

In manchen Bundesländern gibt es eine Orientierungsstufe (5. und 6. Klasse). Während dieser Zeit können die Schüler die Schulform wechseln.

Für Haupt- und Real[s]chüler gibt es die Möglichkeit, [...] gehen, wenn sie beim [...]chschnittliche Noten [ha]ben.

Studienwünsche männlicher Abiturienten 1992		Studienwünsche von Abiturientinnen 1992	
Fach	**Anteil (%)**	**Fach**	**Anteil (%)**
Wirtschaft	14	Wirtschaft	11
Maschinenbau	13	Jura	7
Elektrotechnik	11	Sozialwesen	6
Jura	5	Medizin	6
Informatik	5	Architektur	5
Bauingenieurwesen	4	Gestaltung	4
Architektur	4	Erziehungswissenschaft	4
Medizin	3	Germanistik	3
Physik	3	Biologie	3
Chemie	3	Psychologie	3

YOU'RE READY FOR ANYTHING!

Lesson plans, activities, strategies, scripts, and more highlight the **Teacher's Edition,** providing a **variety of instructional materials.**

Chapter Resource blackline masters—including realia, situation cards, and listening activities—are **organized by chapter** for ease of use. Students sharpen their language skills as they see and hear German in context via **integrated technology**: the high-interest audio and video programs enable them to have fun while they learn.

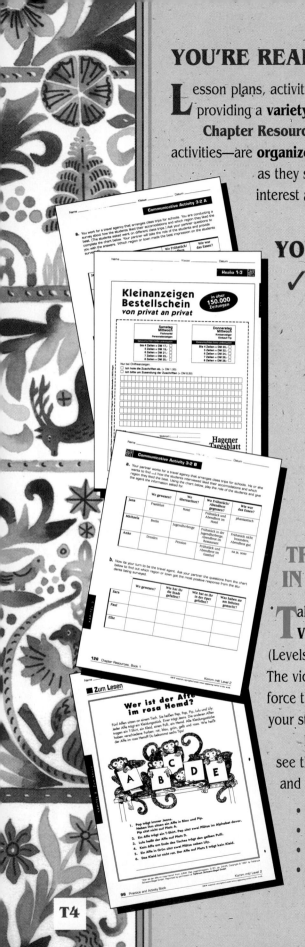

YOU'RE FULLY PREPARED!

✓ **Teaching Resources with Organizer**

    Chapter Teaching Resources, Books 1-4
- Communicative Activities
- Teaching Transparency Masters
- Additional Listening Activities
- Realia
- Situation Cards
- Student Response Forms
- Chapter Tests and Quizzes
- Answer Key for Practice and Activity Book

    Assessment Guide
    Video Guide

✓ **Practice and Activity Book, Pupil's Edition**

✓ **Audiocassette Program**

✓ **Teaching Transparencies: Situations and Maps**

✓ **Test Generator (IBM® PC and Compatibles and Macintosh®)**

✓ **Video Program (Levels 1-3)**

✓ **Expanded Video Program (Levels 1 and 2)**

TRAVEL TO GERMANY IN A MATTER OF SECONDS!

Take your students on a fun-filled trip to Germany with Komm mit! **Video Program** (Levels 1–3) and **Expanded Video Program** (Levels 1 and 2)— filmed **entirely** on location in German-speaking countries. The video programs—integrated with the Komm mit! **Pupil's Editions**—reinforce the language and culture presented in the **Pupil's Edition** by immersing your students in authentic German situations.

Reach **all** your students with these new, exciting video programs. And see their proficiency and confidence increase dramatically as they watch and listen to native German speakers in these locations:

- Potsdam/Brandenburg
- Wedel/Schleswig-Holstein
- München
- Bietigheim-Bissingen/ Baden-Württemberg
- Grünwald/Bayern
- Österreich
- Hamburg
- Stuttgart
- Berlin
- Die neuen Bundesländer
- Würzburg
- Frankfurt
- Dresden

Komm mit!

Holt German
Level 3

TEACHER'S EDITION

HOLT, RINEHART AND WINSTON
Harcourt Brace & Company

Austin • New York • Orlando • Atlanta • San Francisco • Boston • Dallas • Toronto • London

For permission to reprint copyrighted material, grateful acknowledgment is made to the following sources:

Alibaba Verlag GmbH, Frankfurt am Main: "Sabines Eltern" by Mustafa S. from *Wir leben hier!* edited by Ulrike Holler and Anne Teuter. Copyright © 1992 by Alibaba Verlag GmbH.

Baars Kaas Marketing GmbH: Advertisement, "Da haben wir den Salat...kein Leerdammer im Haus Kaas" from *freundin,* 14/94, June 6 1994, p. 149.

Heinrich Bauer Verlag: "Unsere heutige Jugend und ihre Sprüche" by Emily Reuter from *bella: für die moderne Frau,* no. 43, October 21, 1993. Copyright © 1993 by Heinrich Bauer Verlag.

Bayerisches Staatsministerium für Landesentwicklung und Umweltfragen, Rosenkavalierplatz 2, 81925 München, Germany: Graph, "Zusammensetzung der Abfälle," from *Der Abfall: Umweltschutz in Bayern.*

Burda Publications: "Liebe," "Lisa, 15," "Raver," and "Sprache" from *Bunte,* no. 22, May 26, 1994, pp. 39 & 42. Copyright © 1994 by Burda Publications.

Deutsche Bank: Table, "USA: Devisenkurse" published by Deutsche Bank.

Deutscher Sparkassenverlag GmbH: Advertisement, "Das Ticket zum Abheben," from *Popcorn,* no. 2, February 1992, p. 98.

Deutsches Jugendherbergswerk Hauptverband für Jugendwandern und Jugendherbergen e.V.: From "Willkommen!" from *DJH Willkommen.* From "Jugendgästehaus Weimar: Pauschalprogramm" from *Klassen Mobil: Schulfahrten und Schullandheimaufenthalte in Jugendherbergen 92/93: Region Ost.*

Reinhard Döhl: "Apfel" by Reinhard Döhl from *An Anthology of Concrete Poetry,* edited by Emmett Williams. Published by Something Else Press, New York, Villefranche, Frankfurt and Edition Hansjörg Mayer, Stuttgart. Copyright © 1965, 1966 by Reinhard Döhl. "menschenskind" by Reinhard Döhl from *Poem Structures in the Looking Glass* by Klaus Burkhardt and Reinhard Döhl. Copyright © 1969 by Reinhard Döhl.

Focus Magazin Verlag GmbH: Text and illustrations from "Verführt von dummen, mörderischen Sprüchen" from *Focus: das moderne Nachrichtenmagazin,* no. 20, May 16, 1994. Copyright © 1994 by Focus Magazin Verlag GmbH.

Fremdenverkehrsverband Rügen e.V.: From *Rügen: eine Liebeserklärung: Urlauberkatalog '93* by Günther Reymann. Copyright © 1993 by Fremdenverkehrsverband Rügen e.V.

Gerolsteiner Brunnen GmbH & Co.: Advertisement, "Guter Geschmack ist einfacher Natur....Gerolsteiner Sprudel," from *TV Spielfilm,* May 28, 1994, p. 135.

ACKNOWLEDGMENTS continued on page 395, which is an extension of the copyright page.

CONTRIBUTING WRITERS

Ulrike Puryear
Austin, TX
Mrs. Puryear wrote background information, activities, and teacher suggestions for all chapters of the *Teacher's Edition*.

Phyllis Manning
Vancouver, WA
Dr. Manning wrote teacher suggestions for the **Zum Lesen** pages.

CONSULTANTS

The consultants conferred on a regular basis with the editorial staff and reviewed all the chapters of the Level 3 *Teacher's Edition*.

Dorothea Bruschke
Parkway School District
Chesterfield, MO

Diane E. Laumer
San Marcos High School
San Marcos, TX

REVIEWERS

The following educators reviewed one or more chapters of the *Teacher's Edition*.

Nancy Butt
Washington and Lee High School
Arlington, VA

Frank Dietz
The University of Texas at Austin
Austin, TX

Connie Frank
John F. Kennedy High School
Sacramento, CA

Rolf Schwägermann
Stuyvesant High School
New York, NY

Jim Witt
Grand Junction High School
Grand Junction, CO

FIELD TEST PARTICIPANTS

We express our appreciation to the teachers and students who participated in the field test. Their comments were instrumental in the development of the entire **Komm mit!** program.

Eva-Marie Adolphi
Indian Hills Middle School
Sandy, UT

Connie Allison
MacArthur High School
Lawton, OK

Dennis Bergren
West High School
Madison, WI

Linda Brummett
Redmond High School
Redmond, WA

M. Beatrice Brusstar
Lincoln Northeast High School
Lincoln, NE

Jane Bungartz
Southwest High School
Fort Worth, TX

Devora D. Diller
Lovejoy High School
Lovejoy, GA

Margaret Draheim
Wilson Junior High School
Appleton, WI

Kay DuBois
Kennewick High School
Kennewick, WA

Elfriede A. Gabbert
Capital High School
Boise, ID

Petra A. Hansen
Redmond High School
Redmond, WA

Christa Hary
Brien McMahon High School
Norwalk, CT

Ingrid S. Kinner
Weaver Education Center
Greensboro, NC

Diane E. Laumer
San Marcos High School
San Marcos, TX

J. Lewinsohn
Redmond High School
Redmond, WA

Linnea Maulding
Fife High School
Tacoma, WA

Judith A. Nimtz
Central High School
West Allis, WI

Jane Reinkordt
Lincoln Southeast High School
Lincoln, NE

Elizabeth A. Smith
Plano Senior High School
Plano, TX

Elizabeth L. Webb
Sandy Creek High School
Tyrone, GA

PROFESSIONAL ESSAYS

Standards for Foreign Language Education
Robert LaBouve
Board Member,
National Standards in
Foreign Language Education
Austin, TX

Multi-Level Classrooms
Joan H. Manley
University of Texas at
El Paso, TX

Learning Styles and Multi-Modality Teaching
Mary B. McGehee
Louisiana State University
Laboratory School
Baton Rouge, LA

Higher-Order Thinking Skills
Audrey L. Heining-Boynton
The University of North
Carolina at Chapel Hill, NC

Teaching Culture
Nancy A. Humbach
Miami University
Oxford, OH

Dorothea Bruschke
Parkway School District
Chesterfield, MO

Using Portfolios in the Foreign Language Classroom
Jo Anne S. Wilson
Consultant
Glen Arbor, MI

AUTHOR

George Winkler
Austin, TX

Mr. Winkler developed the scope and sequence and framework for the chapters, created the basic material, selected realia, and wrote activities.

CONTRIBUTING WRITERS

Margrit Meinel Diehl
Syracuse, NY
Mrs. Diehl wrote activities to practice basic material, functions, grammar, and vocabulary.

Patricia Casey Sutcliffe
Austin, TX
Mrs. Sutcliffe wrote the process writing activities for the **Zum Schreiben** feature.

Carolyn Roberts Thompson
Abilene, TX
Mrs. Thompson was responsible for the selection of readings and for developing reading activities.

CONSULTANTS

The consultants conferred on a regular basis with the editorial staff and reviewed all the chapters of the Level 3 textbook.

Dorothea Bruschke
Parkway School District
Chesterfield, MO

Diane E. Laumer
San Marcos High School
San Marcos, TX

Phyllis Manning
Vancouver, WA

Ingeborg R. McCoy
Southwest Texas State University
San Marcos, TX

REVIEWERS

The following educators reviewed one or more chapters of the *Pupil's Edition*.

Nancy Butt
Washington and Lee High School
Arlington, Va

Joan Gosenheimer
Franklin High School
Franklin, WI

Carol Masters
Edison High School
Tulsa, OK

Linnea Maulding
Fife High School
Janesville, WI

Mike Miller
Cheyenne Mountain Junior High
Colorado Springs, CO

Doug Mills
Greensburg Central Catholic High School
Greensburg, PA

Rolf Schwägermann
Stuyvesant High School
New York, NY

Linda Wiencken
The Austin Waldorf School
Austin, TX

Scott Williams
The University of Texas at Austin
Austin, TX

Jim Witt
Grand Junction High School
Grand Junction, CO

FIELD TEST PARTICIPANTS

We express our appreciation to the teachers and students who participated in the field test. Their comments were instrumental in the development of the entire **Komm mit!** program.

Eva-Marie Adolphi
Indian Hills Middle School
Sandy, UT

Connie Allison
MacArthur High School
Lawton, OK

Dennis Bergren
West High School
Madison, WI

Linda Brummett
Redmond High School
Redmond, WA

M. Beatrice Brusstar
Lincoln Northeast High School
Lincoln, NE

Jane Bungartz
Southwest High School
Fort Worth, TX

Devora D. Diller
Lovejoy High School
Lovejoy, GA

Margaret Draheim
Wilson Junior High School
Appleton, WI

Kay DuBois
Kennewick High School
Kennewick, WA

Elfriede A. Gabbert
Capital High School
Boise, ID

Petra A. Hansen
Redmond High School
Redmond, WA

Christa Hary
Brien McMahon High School
Norwalk, CT

Ingrid S. Kinner
Weaver Education Center
Greensboro, NC

Diane E. Laumer
San Marcos High School
San Marcos, TX

J. Lewinsohn
Redmond High School
Redmond, WA

Linnea Maulding
Fife High School
Tacoma, WA

Judith A. Nimtz
Central High School
West Allis, WI

Jane Reinkordt
Lincoln Southeast High School
Lincoln, NE

Elizabeth A. Smith
Plano Senior High School
Plano, TX

Elizabeth L. Webb
Sandy Creek High School
Tyrone, GA

ACKNOWLEDGMENTS

We are very grateful to the German students who participated in our program and are pictured in this textbook. We wish to express our thanks also to the parents who allowed us to photograph these young people in their homes and in other places. There are many teachers, school administrators, and merchants whose cooperation and patience made an enormous difference in the quality of these pages; we are grateful to them as well.

YOUNG PEOPLE

Sonja Aßfalg, Monika Baumgartner, Markus Benck, Michael Drik, Stephan Edinger, Ulrika Engler, Michael Gipp, Isabel Hirt, Ralf Ibisch, Aileen Israel, Sandra Junghans, Michaela Kreutzer, Thomas Lutz, Anja Mayer, Thomas Mayer, Heiko Müller, Frieder Nollau, Kerstin Peuchof, Julia Pfaffenbichler, Christian Schmid, Michael Schneider, Katharine Sibeck, Philipp Tecklenburg, Stefan Voges, Juliane von Loesch, Victoria von Mutius, Michael Wagner, Stephan Wagner, Tanja Walloschke, Michaele Weber, Oliver Weisenseel, Sonja Zenner

TEACHERS AND FAMILIES

Eduard and Cordula Böhm, Fritz and Marianne Brunner, Burkhart and Edeltraut Ehrlich, Herr Passon, Karl-Heinz and Gisela Simon

SCHOOLS

Einstein-Gymnasium, München; Ellenthal-Gymnasium, Bietigheim-Bissingen; Markgräfler-Gymnasium, Müllheim

TEACHER'S EDITION

Contents

Komm mit!

Come along—to a world of new experiences!

Komm mit! offers you the opportunity to learn the language spoken by millions of people in several European countries and around the world. Let's find out more about these people and their culture.

KAPITEL 1
WIEDERHOLUNGSKAPITEL

Das Land am Meer 4

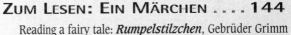

T15

T16

KAPITEL 8

Weg mit den Vorurteilen! 180

KAPITEL 9

Aktiv für die Umwelt! 204

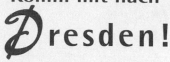

TEACHING SUGGESTIONS FOR THE DRESDEN
LOCATION OPENER.....227A–227B

Komm mit nach
Dresden!

LOCATION FOR KAPITEL 10, 11, 12....228

VISIT DRESDEN, THE CAPITAL
OF SAXONY, AND —

Find out what students do for
cultural entertainment • KAPITEL 10

Discuss educational plans
for the future • KAPITEL 11

Discuss your responsibility for
planning your life • KAPITEL 12

TEACHING SUGGESTIONS FOR KAPITEL 10...............231A–231R

KAPITEL 10

Die Kunst zu leben 232

Cultural References

MAPS

MEDIA

MILITARY

MODERN ISSUES

MONEY

To The Teacher

*S*ince the early eighties, we have seen significant advances in modern foreign language curriculum practice: (1) a redefinition of the objectives of foreign language study involving a commitment to the development of proficiency in the four skills and in cultural awareness; (2) a recognition of the need for longer sequences of study; (3) a new student-centered approach that redefines the role of the teacher as facilitator and encourages students to take a more active role in their learning; (4) the inclusion of students of all learning abilities.

The new Holt, Rinehart and Winston foreign language programs take into account not only these advances in the field of foreign language education but also the input of teachers and students around the country.

PRINCIPLES AND PRACTICES

As nations become increasingly interdependent, the need for effective communication and sensitivity to other cultures becomes more important. Today's youth must be culturally and linguistically prepared to participate in a global society. At Holt, Rinehart and Winston, we believe that proficiency in a foreign language is essential to meeting this need.

The primary goal of the Holt, Rinehart and Winston foreign language programs is to help students develop linguistic proficiency and cultural sensitivity. By interweaving language and culture, our programs seek to broaden students' knowledge of other languages while at the same time deepening their appreciation of other cultures.

We believe that all students can benefit from foreign language instruction. We recognize that not everyone learns at the same rate or in the same way; nevertheless, we believe that all students should have the opportunity to acquire language proficiency to a degree commensurate with their individual abilities.

By appealing to a variety of learning styles, the Holt, Rinehart and Winston foreign language programs are designed to accommodate all students.

We believe that effective foreign language programs should motivate students. Students deserve an answer to the question they often ask, "Why are we doing this?" They need to have goals that are interesting, practical, clearly stated, and attainable.

The Holt, Rinehart and Winston foreign language programs promote success. They present relevant content in manageable increments that encourage students to attain achievable functional objectives.

We believe that proficiency in a foreign language is best nurtured by programs that encourage students to think critically and to take risks when expressing themselves in the language. We also recognize that students should strive for accuracy in communication. While it is important that students have a knowledge of the basic structures of the language, it is also important that they go beyond simple manipulation of forms.

Holt, Rinehart and Winston's foreign language program reflects a careful progression of activities that guides students from comprehensible input of authentic language through structured practice to creative, personalized expression. This progression, accompanied by consistent re-entry and spiraling of functions, vocabulary, and structures, provides students with the tools and the confidence to express themselves in their language.

Finally, we believe that a complete program of foreign language instruction should take into account the needs of teachers in today's increasingly demanding classrooms.

At Holt, Rinehart and Winston we have designed programs that offer practical teacher support and provide multiple resources to meet individual learning and teaching styles.

Standards for Foreign Language Education

National Standards and School Reform

In 1989, educational reform in the United States took on an entirely different look when state and national leaders reached consensus on six national educational goals for public schools. In 1994, a new law, *Goals 2000: Educate America Act,* endorsed these six goals and added two more. The most important national goal in the law for foreign language educators is Goal 3, which establishes a core curriculum and places foreign languages in that core. As a result of this consensus on national goals, the Federal government encouraged the development of high standards in the core disciplines. While the federal government does not have the authority to mandate the implementation of foreign language standards locally, it will encourage their use through leadership and projects funded by the U.S. Department of Education.

We must first define "standards" in order to fully understand the rationale for their development. Content standards ask: What should students know and be able to do? Content standards are currently under development by foreign language professionals. Performance standards ask: How good is good enough? Opportunity-to-learn standards ask: Did the school prepare all students to perform well? There is a growing consensus that states and local districts should address the last two types of standards.

Progress Toward National Foreign Language Standards

A task force of foreign language educators began work on the standards in 1993 by establishing specific foreign language goals. They then set content standards for each goal. The task force sought feedback from the foreign language profession through an extensive dissemination program and produced a draft of the standards document for introduction at a number of sites around the United States during the 1994-1995 school year.

The target publication date for a final document is late 1995. The final version will incorporate suggestions from the sites where the standards were introduced and reactions from volunteer reviewers and the field in general. While the standards should be world-class, they must also be realistic and attainable by most students. The task force also realizes that the general set of goals and standards will have to be made language specific in a curriculum development process and that continu-ing staff development will be essential.

Proposed Foreign Language Standards

The proposed goals and standards in the draft document describe a K-12 foreign language program for all students, presenting languages, both modern and classical, as part of the core curriculum for every student, including those whose native language is not English. Five broad goals establish the basic framework of the language program. The proposed content standards set for these goals describe what students should know and be able to do in a language. The chart on page T45 shows how the standards are arrayed alongside the goals.

The first two goals in this expanded language program describe today's typical school language program. The last three are often identified by teachers as important, but are not always implemented. The standards-based program moves beyond an emphasis on skills to a redefinition of the content of a language program itself.

Sample benchmark tasks will be provided for Grades 4, 8, and 12 as examples of what students can do to meet the standards and accomplish the goals of the language program. A higher level or performance will be expected as students progress from one benchmark grade to another.

Impact of the Standards

While there is an assumption that national foreign language goals and standards will have a great impact upon the states and local districts, the standards themselves are voluntary. Clearly, the standards will influence instruction and curriculum development in districts that choose to align their language programs with the national standards. Assessment programs will most likely begin to reflect the influence of the standards. The standards will also have an impact on the preparation of future teachers and on staff development for teachers now in the classroom.

A curriculum based on the standards will encourage students to take responsibility for their learning by making the language curriculum coherent and transparent to them. Students will know from the beginning what they should be able to do when they exit the program and they will be able to judge for themselves how they are progressing, especially at established benchmarks, i.e., Grades 4, 8, and 12.

Proposed National Foreign Language Goals and Standards

Goal One	Communicate in languages other than English	**Standard 1.1** Students will use the target language to participate in social interactions and to establish and maintain personal relationships in a variety of settings and contexts. **Standard 1.2** Students will use the target language to obtain, process, and provide information in spoken or written form on a variety of topics of academic, personal, cultural, and historic interest. **Standard 1.3** Students will use language for leisure and personal enrichment.
Goal Two	Gain knowledge of other cultures	**Standard 2.1** Students will demonstrate knowledge of the components of the target culture.
Goal Three	Acquire information and connect with other disciplines.	**Standard 3.1** Students will use the target language to gain access to information and perspectives that are only available through the target language or within the target culture. **Standard 3.2** Students will use the target language to reinforce and further their knowledge of other cultures.
Goal Four	Develop insight into own language and culture	**Standard 4.1** Students will recognize that different languages use different patterns to communicate. **Standard 4.2** Students will recognize that cultures view situations from varying perspectives and evolve different patterns of interaction.
Goal Five	Participate in multilingual communities and global society	**Standard 5.1** Students will use the language both within and beyond the school setting with representatives of the target culture in a variety of ways.

The standards will also have a significant impact on the demand for sequential, cross-disciplinary instructional materials for a K-12 language program. Another challenge will be the development of new technologies that increase learning in order to meet high standards.

To those of us who feel that foreign language education is basic education for all students, the national standards document will become a strong advocate for languages in the curriculum of every school and for the extended sequences of study presented by the goals and standards. The standards document will make it easier for language educators to present a solid rationale for including foreign languages in the curriculum.

To receive the most up-to-date version of the standards document, please contact the project office: National Standards Project, c/o ACTFL, 6 Executive Plaza, Yonkers, NY 10701, (914) 963-8830.

Komm mit! supports *the proposed National Foreign Language Goals and Standards* in the following ways:

The Pupil's Edition
▶ Addresses all five proposed National Foreign Language Goals.

▶ Encourages students to take responsibility for their learning by providing clearly defined objectives at the beginning of each chapter.

The Teacher's Edition
▶ Provides a broad framework for incorporating the goals ans standards into the curriculum and for making the foreign language program accessible to all students.

The Ancillary Program
▶ Offers multiple options for practicing and assessing performance.

Multi-Level Classrooms

There are positive ways, both psychological and pedagogical, to make this situation work for you and your students.

So you have just heard that your third-period class is going to include both Levels 2 and 3! While this is never the best teacher, there are positive ways, both psychological and pedagogical, to make the multi-level classroom work for you and your students.

Relieving student anxieties

Initially, in a multi-level cllass environment, it is important to relieve students' anxiety by orienting them to their new situation. From the outset, let all students know that just because they "did" things the previous year, such as learn how to conjugate certain verbs, they may not yet be able to use them in a meaning ful way. Students should not feel that it is demeaning or a waste of time to recycle activities or to share knowledge and skills with fellow students. Second-year students need to know they are not second-class citizens and that they can benefit from their classmates' greater experience with the language. Third-year students may achieve a great deal of satisfaction and become more confident in their own language skills when they have opportunities to help or teach their second-year classmates. It is important to reassure third-year students that you will devote time to them and challenge them with different assignments.

Easing your own apprehension

When you are faced with both Levels 2 and 3 in your classroom, remind yourself that you teach students of different levels in the same classroom every year, although not officially. After one year of classroom instruction, your Level 2 class will never be a truly homogeneous group. Despite being made up of students with the same amount of "seat time," the class comprises multiple layers of language skills, knowledge, motivation, and ability. Therefore, you are constantly called upon to make a positive experience out of a potentially negative one. Your apprehension will gradually diminish to the extent that you are able to…

- make students less dependent on you for the successful completion of their activities.
- place more responsibility for learning on the students.
- implement creative group, pair, and individual activities.

How can you do this? Good organization will help. Lessons will need to be especially well-planned for the multi-level class. The following lesson plan is an example of how to treat the same topic with students of two different levels.

Teaching a lesson in a multi-level classroom

Lesson objectives:

Relate an incident in the past that you regret.

- Level 2: Express surprise and sympathy.
- Level 3: Offer encouragement and make suggestions.

Lesson plan

1. **Review and/or teach the past tense.**
   Present the formation of the past tense. Model its use for the entire class or call upon Level 3 students to give examples.

2. **Practice the past tense.**
   Have Level 3 students who have mastered the past tense teach it to Level 2 students in pairs or small groups. Provide the Level 3 student instructors with several drill and practice activities they may use for this purpose.

3. **Relate your own regrettable past experience.**
   Recount a personal regrettable incident—real or imaginary—to the entire class as a model. For example, you may have left your automobile lights on, and when you came out of school, the battery was dead and you couldn't start your car. Or you may have scolded a student for not doing the homework and later discovered the student had a legitimate reason for not completing the assignment.

4. **Prepare and practice written and oral narratives.**
   Have Level 2 students pair off with Level 3 students. Each individual writes about his or her experience, the Level 3 partner serving as a resource for the Level 2 student. Partners then edit each other's work and listen to each other's oral delivery. You might choose to have students record their oral narratives.

5. **Present communicative functions.**
   A. Ask for a volunteer to recount his or her own regrettable incident for the entire class.
   B. Model reactions to the volunteer's narrative.
      (1) Express surprise and sympathy (for Level 2): "Really! That's too bad!"
      (2) Offer encouragement and make suggestions (for Level 3): "Don't worry!" "You can still...."

6. **Read narratives and practice communicative functions.**
   Have Level 2 students work together in one group or in small groups, listening to classmates' stories and reacting with the prescribed communicative function. Have Level 3 students do the same among themselves. Circulate among the groups, listening, helping, and assessing.

7. **Assess progress.**
   Repeat your personal account for the entire class and elicit reactions from students according to their level. Challenge students to respond with communicative functions expected of the other level if they can.

Every part of the above lesson plan is important. Both levels have been accommodated. The teacher has not dominated the lesson. Students have worked together in pairs and small groups, while Level 3 students have helped their Level 2 classmates. Individual groups still feel accountable, both within their level and across levels.

Any lesson can be adapted in this way. It takes time and effort, but the result is a student-centered classroom where students share and grow, and the teacher is the facilitator.

Komm mit! addresses the *multi-level* classroom in the following ways:

The Pupil's Edition
▶ Provides creative activities for pair and group work that allow students at different levels to work together and learn from one another.

The Teacher's Edition
▶ Offers practical suggestions for *Projects* and *Cooperative Learning* that engage students of different levels.
▶ Provides a clear, comprehensive outline of the functions, vocabulary, and grammar that are recycled in each chapter. The *Chapter Overview* of each chapter is especially helpful to the teacher who is planning integrated or varied lessons in the multi-level classroom.

The Ancillary Program
▶ Provides a variety of materials and activities to accommodate different levels in a multi-level classroom.

Learning Styles and Multi-Modality Teaching

*I*ncorporating a greater variety of teaching and learning activities to accommodate the learning styles of all students can make the difference between struggle and pleasure in foreign language learning.

The larger and broader population of students who are enrolling in foreign language classes brings a new challenge to foreign language educators, calling forth an evolution in teaching methods to enhance learning for all our students. Educational experts now recognize that every student has a preferred sense for learning and retrieving information: visual, auditory, or kinesthetic. Incorporating a greater variety of teaching and learning activities to accommodate the learning styles of all students can make the difference between struggle and pleasure in foreign language learning.

Accommodating Different Learning Styles

A modified arrangement of the classroom is one way to provide more effective and more enjoyable learning for all students. Rows of chairs and desks must give way at times to circles, semicircles, or small clusters. Students may be grouped in fours or in pairs for small group work, cooperative work, or peer teaching. It is important to find a balance of arrangements, thereby providing the most comfort in varied situations.

Since auditory, kinesthetic, and visual learners will be present in the class, and also because every student's learning will be enhanced by a multi-sensory approach, lessons must be directed toward all three learning styles. Any language lesson content may be presented auditorially, visually, and kinesthetically.

Visual presentations and practice may include the chalkboard, charts, posters, television, overhead projectors, books, magazines, picture diagrams, flash cards, bulletin boards, films, slides, or videos. Visual learners need to see what they are to learn. Lest the teacher think he or she will never have the time to prepare all those visuals, Dickel and Slak (1983) found that visual aids generated by students are more effective than ready-made ones.

Auditory presentations and practice may include stating aloud the requirements of the lesson, oral questions and answers, paired or group work on a progression of oral exercises from repetition to communication, tapes, CDs, dialogues, and role-playing. Jingles, catchy stories, and memory devices using songs and rhymes are good learning aids. Having students record themselves and then listen as they play back the cassette allows them to practice in the auditory mode.

Kinesthetic presentations entail the students' use of manipulatives, chart materials, gestures, signals, typing, songs, games, and role-playing. These lead the students to associate sentence constructions with meaningful movements.

A Sample Lesson Using Multi-Modality Teaching

A multi-sensory presentation on greetings might proceed as follows. As the teacher begins oral presentation of greetings and introductions, he or she simultaneously shows the written forms on transparencies, with the formal expressions marked with an adult's hat, and the informal expressions marked with a baseball cap. The teacher then distributes cards with the hat and cap symbols representing the formal or informal expressions. As the students hear taped mini-dialogues, they hold up the appropriate card to indicate whether the dialogues are formal or informal. On the next listening, the students repeat the sentences they hear. A longer taped dialogue follows, allowing students to hear the new expressions a number of times. The students next write from dictation several sentences containing the new expressions. They may work in pairs, correcting each other's work as they "test" their own understanding of the lesson at hand. Finally, students respond to simple questions using the appropriate formal and informal responses cued by the cards they hold.

For additional kinesthetic input, members of the class come to the front of the room, each holding a hat or cap symbol. As the teacher calls out situations, the students play the roles, using gestures and props appropriate to the age group they are portraying. Non-cued, communicative role-playing

BY MARY B. McGEHEE

with props further enables the students to "feel" the differences between formal and informal expressions.

Helping Students Learn How to Use Their Preferred Mode

Since we require students to perform in all language skills, part of the assistance we must render is to help them develop strategies within their preferred learning modes to carry out an assignment in another mode. For example, visual students hear the teacher assign an oral exercise and visualize what they must do. They must see themselves carrying out the assignment, in effect watching themselves as if there were a movie going on in their heads. Only then can they also hear themselves saying the right things. Thus, this assignment will be much easier for the visual learners who have been taught this process, if they have not already figured it out for themselves. Likewise, true auditory students, confronted with a reading/writing assignment, must talk themselves through it, converting the entire process into sound as they plan and prepare their work. Kinesthetic students presented with a visual or auditory task must first break the assignment into tasks and then work their way through them.

Students who experience difficulty because of a strong preference for one mode of learning are often unaware of the degree of their preference. In working with these students, I prefer the simple and direct assessment of learning styles offered by Richard Bandler and John Grinder in their book *Frogs into Princes,* which allows the teacher and student to quickly determine how the student learns. In an interview with the

student, I follow the assessment with certain specific recommendations of techniques to make the student's study time more effective.

It is important to note here that teaching students to maximize their study does not require that the teacher give each student an individualized assignment. It does require that each student who needs it be taught how to prepare the assignment using his or her own talents and strengths. This communication

between teacher and student, combined with teaching techniques that reinforce learning in all modes, can only maximize pleasure and success in learning a foreign language.

References

Dickel, M.J. and S. Sleek. "Imaging Vividness and Memory for Verbal Material." *Journal of Mental Imagery 7*, i(1983):121-6

Bandler, Richard, and John Grinder. *Frogs into Princes,* Real People Press, Moab, Utah. 1978

Komm mit! accommodates *different learning styles* in the following ways:

The Pupil's Edition
▶ Presents basic material in video, audio, and printed format.
▶ Includes role-playing activities and a variety of multi-modality activities.

The Teacher's Edition
▶ Provides suggested activities for auditory, visual, and kinesthetic learners.
▶ Offers Total Physical Response activities.

The Ancillary Program
▶ Meets individual needs of students with additional reinforcement activities in a variety of modes.

Higher-Order Thinking Skills

*I*ntroduce students to the life skills they need to become successful, productive citizens in our society.

Our profession loves acronyms! TPR, ALM, OBI, and now the HOTS! HOTS stands for **h**igher-**o**rder **t**hinking **s**kills. These thinking skills help our students listen, speak, read, write, and learn about culture in a creative, meaningful way, while providing them with necessary life skills.

What Are Higher-Order Thinking Skills?

Higher-order thinking skills are not a new phenomenon on the educational scene. In 1956, Benjamin Bloom published a book that listed a taxonomy of educational objectives in the form of a pyramid similar to the one in the following illustration:

Bloom's Taxonomy of Educational Objectives

Evaluation
Synthesis
Analysis
Application
Comprehension
Knowledge

Knowledge is the simplest level of educational objectives, and is not considered a higher-order thinking skill. It requires the learner to remember information without having to fully understand it. Tasks that students perform to demonstrate knowledge are recalling, identifying, recognizing, citing, labeling, listing, reciting, and stating.

Comprehension is not considered a higher-order thinking skill either. Learners demonstrate comprehension when they paraphrase, describe, summarize, illustrate, restate, or translate.

Foreign language teachers tend to focus the most on knowledge and comprehension. The tasks performed at these levels are important because they provide a solid foundation for the more complex tasks at the higher levels of Bloom's pyramid. However, offering our students the opportunity to perform at still higher cognitive levels provides them with more meaningful contexts in which to use the target language.

When teachers incorporate **application**, **analysis**, **synthesis**, and **evaluation** as objectives, they allow students to utilize **higher-order thinking skills.**

Application involves solving, transforming, determining, demonstrating, and preparing.

Analysis includes classifying, comparing, making associations, verifying, seeing cause and effect relationships, and determining sequences, patterns, and consequences.

Synthesis requires generalizing, predicting, imagining, creating, making inferences, hypothesizing, making decisions, and drawing conclusions.

Finally, **evaluation** involves assessing, persuading, determining value, judging, validating, and solving problems.

Most foreign language classes focus little on higher-order thinking skills. Some foreign language educators mistakenly think that all higher-order thinking skills require an advanced level of language ability. Not so! Students can demonstrate these skills by using very simple language available even to beginning students. Also, higher-order thinking tasks about the target culture or language can be conducted in English. The use of some English in the foreign language classroom to utilize higher cognitive skills does not jeopardize progress in the target language.

Higher-order thinking skills prepare our students for more than using a foreign language. They introduce students to the life skills they need to become successful, productive citizens in our society. When we think about it, that *is* the underlying purpose of education.

Why Teach Higher-Order Thinking Skills?

There is already so much to cover and so little time that some teachers may question the worth of adding this type of activities to an already full schedule. Yet we know from experience that simply "covering" the material does not help our students acquire another language.

Incorporating higher-order thinking skills in the foreign language classroom can help guide students toward language acquisition by providing meaningful experiences in a setting that can often feel artificial.

Also, we now know that employing higher-order thinking skills assists all students, including those who are at risk of failing. In the past, we felt that at-risk students were incapable of higher-order thinking, but we have since discovered that we have been denying them the opportunity to experience what they are capable of doing and what they need to do in order to be successful adults.

Sample Activities Employing Higher-Order Thinking Skills

There are no limitations to incorporating higher-order thinking skills into the foreign language classroom. What follows are a few sample activities, some of which you may already be familiar with. Use *your* higher-order thinking skills to develop other possibilities!

Listening

HOTS: Analysis
Tasks: Patterning and sequencing
Vocabulary Needed: Three colors
Materials Required: Three colored-paper squares for each student

After reviewing the colors, call out a pattern of colors and have the students show their comprehension by arranging their colored pieces of paper from left to right in the order you give. Then have them finish the pattern for you. For example, you say: **rot, grün, blau, rot, grün, blau, rot, grün,...** now what color follows? And then what color?

This is not only a HOTS activity; it also crosses disciplines. It reviews the mathematical concept of patterning and sequencing. You can have the students form patterns and sequences using any type of vocabulary.

Reading

HOTS: Synthesis
Tasks: Hypothesizing and imagining
Vocabulary Needed: Determined by level of students
Materials Required: Legend or short story

After the students have read the first part of the story, have them imagine how the story would end based on the values of the target culture.

Speaking

HOTS: Evaluation
Tasks: Assessing and determining value
Vocabulary Needed: Numbers 0-25, five objects students would need for school
Materials Required: Visuals of five school-related objects with prices beneath them

Tell students that they each have twenty-five dollars to spend on back-to-school needs. They each need to tell you what they would buy with their money.

Writing

HOTS: Analysis
Tasks: Classifying
Vocabulary Needed: Leisure activities
Materials Required: Drawings of leisure activities on a handout

From the list of activities they have before them, students should write the ones that they like to do on the weekend. Then they should write those that a family member likes to do. Finally, students should write a comparison of the two lists.

Commitment to Higher-Order Thinking Skills

Teaching higher-order thinking skills takes no extra time from classroom instruction since language skills are reinforced during thinking skills activities. What teaching higher-order thinking skills does require of teachers is a commitment to classroom activities that go beyond the knowledge/comprehension level. Having students name objects and recite verb forms is not enough. Employing HOTS gives students the opportunity to experience a second language as a useful device for meaningful communication.

Komm mit! encourages *higher-order thinking* in the following ways:

The Pupil's Edition
▶ Develops higher-order thinking skills through a variety of activities.

The Teacher's Edition
▶ Includes the feature *Thinking Critically* that requires students to draw inferences, compare and contrast, evaluate, and synthesize.

The Ancillary Program
▶ Incorporates higher-order thinking skills in activities that help students use the language in a creative, meaningful way.

Teaching Culture

We **must integrate culture and language in a way that encourages curiosity, stimulates analysis, and teaches students to hypothesize.**

Ask students what they like best about studying a foreign language. Chances are that learning about culture, the way people live, is one of their favorite aspects. Years after language study has ended, adults remember with fondness the customs of the target culture, even pictures in their language textbooks. It is this interest in the people and their way of life that is the great motivator and helps us sustain students' interest in language study.

That interest in other people mandates an integration of culture and language. We must integrate culture and language in a way that encourages curiosity, stimulates analysis, and teaches students to hypothesize and seek answers to questions about the people whose language they are studying. Teaching isolated facts about how people in other cultures live is not enough. This information is soon dated and quickly forgotten. We must attempt to go a step beyond and teach students that all behavior, values, and traditions exist because of certain aspects of history, geography, and socio-economic conditions.

There are many ways to help students become culturally knowledgeable, and to assist them in developing an awareness of differences and similarities between the target culture and their own. Two of these approaches involve critical thinking, that is, trying to find reasons for a certain behavior through observation and analysis, and relating these observations to larger cultural patterns.

First Approach: Questioning

The first approach involves *questioning* as the key strategy. At the earliest stages of language learning, students learn ways to greet peers, elders, strangers, as well as the use of **du, ihr,** and **Sie.** Students need to consider questions such as: How do German-speaking people greet each other? Are there different levels of formality? Who initiates a handshake? What's considered a good handshake? Each of these questions leads students to think about the values that are expressed through words and gestures. They start to "feel" the other culture, and at the same time, understand how much of their own behavior is rooted in their cultural background.

Magazines, newspapers, advertisements, and television commercials are all excellent sources of cultural material. For example, browsing through a German magazine, one finds an extraordinary number of advertisements for health-related products. Could this indicate a great interest in staying healthy? To learn about customs involving health, reading advertisements can be followed up with viewing videos and films, or by interviewing native speakers or people who have lived in German-speaking countries. Students might want to find answers to questions such as: "How do Germans treat a cold? What is their attitude toward fresh air? Toward exercise?" This type of questioning might lead students to discover that some of the popular leisure-time activities, such as **einen Spaziergang machen** or **eine Wanderung machen,** are related to health consciousness.

An advertisement for a refrigerator or a picture of a German kitchen can provide an insight into practices of shopping for food. Students first need to think about the refrigerator at home, take an inventory of what is kept in it, and consider when and where their family shops. Next, students should look closely at a German refrigerator. What is its size? What could that mean? (Smaller refrigerators might mean that shopping takes place more often, stores are within walking distance, and people eat more fresh foods.)

Food wrappers and containers also provide cultural insight. For example, in German-speaking countries, bottled water is preferred to tap water even though tap water is safe to drink in most places. Why, then, is the rather expensive bottled water still preferred? Is it a tradition stemming from a time when tap water was not pure? Does it relate to the Germans' fondness of "taking the waters," i.e., drinking fresh spring water at a spa?

Second Approach: Associating Words with Images

The second approach for developing cultural understanding involves *forming associations of words with the cultural images they suggest.* Language and culture are so closely related that one might actually say that language is culture. Most words, especially nouns, carry a cultural connotation. Knowing the literal equivalent of a word in another language is of little use to students in understanding this connotation. For example, **Freund** cannot be translated simply as *friend,* **Brot** as *bread,* or **Straße** as *street.* The German word **Straße,** for instance, carries with it such images as people walking, sitting in a sidewalk café, riding bicycles, or shopping in specialty stores, and cars parked partly over the curb amid dense traffic. There is also the image of **Fußgängerzone,** a street for pedestrians only.

When students have acquired some sense of the cultural connotation of words—not only through explanations but, more importantly, through observation of visual images—they start to discover the larger underlying cultural themes, or what is often called deep culture.

These larger cultural themes serve as organizing categories into which individual cultural phenomena fit to form a pattern. Students might discover, for example, that Germans, because they live in much more crowded conditions, have a great need for privacy (cultural theme), as reflected in such phenomena as closed doors, fences or walls around property, and shutters on windows. Students might also discover that love of nature and the outdoors is an important cultural theme as indicated by such phenomena as flower boxes and planters in public places, well-kept public parks in every town, and people going for a walk or hiking.

As we teach culture, students learn to recognize elements not only of the target culture but also of their American cultural heritage. They see how elements of culture reflect larger themes or patterns. Learning what makes us Americans and how that information relates to other people throughout the world can be an exciting discovery for a young person.

As language teachers, we are able to facilitate this discovery of our similarities with others as well as our differences. We do not encourage value judgments about others and their culture, nor do we recommend adopting other ways. We simply say to students, "Other ways exist. They exist, just as our ways exist, due to our history, geography, and what our ancestors have passed on to us through traditions and values."

Komm mit! develops *cultural understanding and cultural awareness* in the following ways:

The Pupil's Edition
▶ Informs students about daily life in German-speaking countries through culture notes.
▶ Provides deeper insight into cultural phenomena through personal interviews in the **Landeskunde** section.
▶ Helps students associate language and its cultural connotations through authentic art and photos.

The Teacher's Edition
▶ Provides additional cultural and language notes.
▶ Suggests critical thinking strategies that encourage students to hypothesize, analyze, and discover larger underlying cultural themes.

The Ancillary Program
▶ Includes realia that develops cultural insight by serving as catalyst for questioning and discovery.
▶ Offers activities that require students to compare and contrast cultures, as well as to find reasons for certain behavior.

Using Portfolios in the Foreign Language Classroom

Portfolios offer a more realistic and accurate way to assess the process of language teaching and learning.

The communicative, whole-language approach of today's foreign language instruction requires assessment methods that parallel the teaching and learning strategies in the proficiency-oriented classroom. We know that language acquisition is a process. Portfolios are designed to assess the steps in that process.

What is a Portfolio?
A portfolio is a purposeful, systematic collection of a student's work. A useful tool in developing a student profile, the portfolio shows the student's efforts, progress, and achievements for a given period of time. It may be used for periodic evaluation, as the basis for overall evaluation, or for placement. It may also be used to enhance or provide alternatives to traditional assessment measures, such as formal tests, quizzes, class participation, and homework.

Why Use Portfolios?
Portfolios benefit both students and teachers because they

•**Are ongoing and systematic.** A portfolio reflects the real-world process of production, assessment, revision, and reassessment. It parallels the natural rhythm of learning.

•**Offer an incentive to learn.** Students have a vested interest in creating the portfolios through which they can showcase their ongoing efforts and tangible achievements. Students select the works to be included and have a chance to revise, improve, evaluate, and explain the contents.

•**Are sensitive to individual needs.** Language learners bring varied abilities to the classroom and do not acquire skills in a uniformly neat and orderly fashion. The personalized, individualized assessment offered by portfolios responds to this diversity.

•**Provide documentation of language development.** The material in a portfolio is evidence of student progress in the language learning process. The contents of the portfolio make it easier to discuss student progress with the students as well with parents and others interested in the student's progress.

•**Offer multiple sources of information.** A portfolio presents a way to collect and analyze information from multiple sources that reflect a student's efforts, progress, and achievements in the language.

Portfolio Components
The foreign language portfolio should include both oral and written work, student self-evaluation, and teacher observation, usually in the form of brief, non-evaluative comments about various aspects of the student's performance.

The Oral Component
The oral component of a portfolio might be an audio- or video-cassette. It may contain both rehearsed and extemporaneous monologues and conversations. For a rehearsed speaking activity, give a specific communicative task that students can personalize according to their individual interests (for example, ordering a favorite meal in a restaurant). If the speaking activity is extemporaneous, first acquaint students with possible topics for discussion or even the specific task they will be expected to perform. (For example, tell them they will be asked to discuss a picture showing a sports activity or a restaurant scene.)

The Written Component
Portfolios are excellent tools for incorporating process-writing strategies into the foreign language classroom. Documentation of various stages of the writing process—brainstorming, multiple drafts, and peer comments—may be included with the finished product.

Involve students in selecting writing tasks for the portfolio. At the beginning levels, the tasks might include some structured writing, such as labeling or listing. As students become more proficient, journals, letters and other more complicated writing tasks are valuable ways for them to monitor their progress in using the written language.

Student Self-Evaluation
Students should be actively involved in critiquing and evaluating their portfolios and monitoring their own progress. The process and procedure for student self-evaluation should be considered in planning the contents of the portfolio.

BY JO ANNE S. WILSON

Students should work with you and their peers to design the exact format. Self-evaluation encourages them to think about what they are learning (content), how they learn (process), why they are learning (purpose), and where they are going in their learning (goals).

Teacher Observation

Systematic, regular, and ongoing teacher observations should be placed in the portfolio after they have been discussed with the student. These observations provide feedback on the student's progress in the language learning process.

Teacher observations should be based on an established set of criteria that has been developed earlier with input from the student. Observation techniques may include the following:

- Jotting notes in a journal to be discussed with the student and then placed in the portfolio

- Using a checklist of observable behaviors, such as the willingness to take risks when using the target language or staying on task during the lesson

- Making observations on adhesive notes that can be easily placed in folders

- Recording anecdotal comments, during or after class, using a cassette recorder

Knowledge of the criteria you use in your observations gives students a framework for their performance.

How are Portfolios Evaluated?

The portfolio should reflect the process of student learning over a specific period of time. At the beginning of that time period, determine the criteria by which you will assess the final product and convey them to the students. Make this evaluation a collaborative effort by seeking students' input as you formulate these criteria and your instructional goals.

Students need to understand that evaluation based on a predetermined standard is but one phase of the assessment process; demonstrated effort and growth are just as important. As you consider correctness and accuracy in both oral and written work, also consider the organization, creativity, and improvement revealed by the student's portfolio over the time period. The portfolio provides a way to monitor the growth of a student's knowledge, skills, and attitudes and shows the student's efforts, progress, and achievements.

How to Implement Portfolios

Teacher/teacher collaboration is as important to the implementation of portfolios as teacher/student collaboration. Confer with your colleagues to determine, for example, what kinds of information you want to see in the student portfolio, how that information will be presented, the purpose of the portfolio, the intended uses (grading, placement, or a combination of the two); and the criteria for evaluating the portfolio. Conferring among colleagues helps foster a departmental cohesiveness and consistency that will ultimately benefit the students.

The Promise of Portfolios

The high degree of student involvement in developing portfolios and deciding how they will be used generally results in renewed student enthusiasm for learning and improved achievement. As students compare portfolio pieces done early in the year with work produced later, they can take pride in their progress as well as reassess their work habits.

Portfolios also provide a framework for periodic assessment of teaching strategies, programs, and instruction. They offer schools a tool to help solve the problem of vertical articulation and accurate student placement. The more realistic and accurate assessment of the language learning process that is provided by portfolios is congruent with the strategies that should be used in the proficiency-oriented classroom.

Komm mit! supports the *use of portfolios* in the following ways:

The Pupil's Edition
▶ Includes numerous oral and written activities that can be easily adapted for student portfolios.

The Teacher's Edition
▶ Identifies activities in the *Portfolio Assessment* feature that may serve as portfolio items.

The Ancillary Program
▶ Includes in the *Assessment Guide* criteria for evaluating portfolios.

Professional References

The Professional References section provides you with information about many resources that can enrich your German class. Included are addresses of German government and tourist offices, pen pal organizations, subscription agencies, and many others. Since addresses change frequently, you may want to verify them before you send your requests.

PEN PAL ORGANIZATIONS

The Student Letter Exchange will arrange pen pals for your students. For the names of other pen pal groups, contact your local chapter of AATG. There are fees involved, so be sure to write for information.

Student Letter Exchange
630 Third Avenue
New York, NY 10017
(212) 557-3312

EMBASSIES AND CONSULATES

Embassy of the Federal Republic of Germany
4645 Reservoir Rd. N.W.
Washington, D.C. 20007-1998
(202) 298-4000

Consulate General of the Federal Republic of Germany
460 Park Avenue
New York, NY 10022
(212) 308-8700
(also in Atlanta, Boston, Chicago, Detroit, Houston, Los Angeles, San Francisco, Seattle)

Embassy of Austria
3524 International Court N.W.
Washington, D.C. 20008
(202) 895-6700

Austrian Consulate General
950 Third Avenue
New York, NY 10022
(212) 737-6400
(also in Los Angeles and Chicago)

CULTURAL AGENCIES

For historic and tourist information and audiovisual materials relating to Austria, contact:

Austrian Institute
11 East 52nd Street
New York, NY 10022
(212) 759-5165

Material on political matters is available from **Bundeszentrale für politische Bildung**, a German federal agency.

Bundeszentrale für politische Bildung
Berliner Freiheit 7
53111 Bonn, GERMANY
(0228) 5150

For free political, cultural, and statistical information, films, and videos, contact:

German Information Center
950 Third Avenue
New York, NY 10022
(212) 888-9840

For various materials and information about special events your classes might attend, contact the **Goethe Institut** nearest you. For regional locations, contact:

Goethe Haus, German Cultural Center
1014 Fifth Avenue
New York, NY 10028
(212) 439-8700

The **Institut für Auslandsbeziehungen** provides cultural information to foreigners. The institute offers books and periodicals on a limited basis as well as a variety of two- and three-week professional seminars which allow educators to learn about the people, education, history, and culture of German-speaking countries.

Institut für Auslandsbeziehungen
Charlottenplatz 17
70173 Stuttgart, GERMANY
(0711) 22250

Inter Nationes, a nonprofit German organization for promoting international relations, supplies material on all aspects of life in Germany (literature, posters, magazines, press releases, films, slides, audio and video tapes, records) to educational institutions and organizations abroad.

Inter Nationes
Kennedyallee 91-103
53175 Bonn, GERMANY
(0228) 8800

TOURIST BUREAUS

Write to the following tourist offices for travel information and brochures.

German National Tourist Office
122 East 42nd St., 52nd Floor
New York, NY 10168
(212) 661-7200
(also in Chicago and San Francisco)

Deutsche Zentrale für Tourismus e.V.
Beethovenstraße 69
60325 Frankfurt GERMANY
(0611) 75720

PROFESSIONAL ORGANIZATIONS

The two major organizations for German teachers at the secondary school level are

The American Council on the Teaching of Foreign Languages (ACTFL)
6 Executive Plaza
Yonkers, NY 10701
(914) 963-8830

The American Association of Teachers of German (AATG)
112 Haddontowne Court
Suite 104
Cherry Hill, NJ 08034
(609) 795-5553

PERIODICALS

Listed below are some periodicals published in German. For the names of other German magazines and periodicals contact a subscription agency.

Deutschland-Nachrichten, a weekly newsletter available in both German and English, is published by the German Information Center *(see address under Cultural Agencies).*

Goethe Haus *(see address under Cultural Agencies)* publishes **Treffpunkt Deutsch,** a magazine of information, bibliographies, and ideas for teachers.

Bundeszentrale für politische Bildung *(see address under Cultural Agencies)* publishes **Politische Zeitung (PZ),** a quarterly magazine covering issues of social interest.
The Austrian Press and Information Service publishes a monthly newsletter. Write to:
Austrian Information
3524 International Court N.W.
Washington, D.C. 20008

Juma classroom magazine is a free publication to which you can subscribe. You can order multiple copies.

Redaktion Juma
Frankfurter Straße 128
5000 Köln, GERMANY
(0221) 693061

SUBSCRIPTION SERVICES

German magazines can be obtained through subscription agencies in the United States. The following companies are among the many which can provide your school with subscriptions:

EBSCO Subscription Services
P.O. Box 1943
Birmingham, AL 35201-1943
(205) 991-6600

Continental Book Company
8000 Cooper Ave. Bldg. 29
Glendale, NY 11385
(718) 326-0572

MISCELLANEOUS

(ADAC) Allgemeiner Deutscher Automobil Club
Am Westpark 8
81373 München, GERMANY

For students who want to find a summer job in Germany, write to

Zentralstelle für Arbeitsvermittlung
Dienststelle 2122
Postfach 70545
60079 Frankfurt, GERMANY
(069) 71110
(Applicants must have a good knowledge of German.)

For international student passes and other student services contact:

CIEE Student Travel Services
205 E. 42nd Street
New York, NY 10018
(212) 661-1414
(has branch offices in several other large cities)

A Bibliography for the German Teacher

This bibliography is a compilation of many resources available to enrich your German class.

SELECTED AND ANNOTATED LIST OF READINGS

I. Methods and Approaches

Cohen, Andrew, D. *Assessing Language Ability in the Classroom*, 2/e. Boston, MA: Heinle, 1994.
Presents various principles to guide teachers through assessment processes, such as oral interviews, role-playing situations, dictations, and portfolio assessment. The discussions are fully accessible to novice teachers, and touch upon some innovative means of assessing reading ability, evaluation of written and oral portfolios, and computer-based tests.

Hadley, Alice Omaggio. *Teaching Language in Context 2/e.* Boston, MA: Heinle, 1993.
An updated edition reviewing past and present language acquisition theories and models as they apply to successful teaching in the second language classroom. Discusses the nature of language proficiency, how adult learners develop second language proficiency, and how technology affects language learning. Generally used for teacher training at the university level.

Krashen, Stephen, and Tracy D. Terrell. *The Natural Approach: Language Acquisition in the Classroom.* New York: Pergamon, 1983.
Provides a brief overview of Krashen's Optimal Input Theory and its applications to teaching in the second language classroom. Suggestions and examples for curriculum, classroom activities, oral communication development, and testing are applicable to high school classes.

Oller, John W., Jr. *Methods That Work. Ideas for Language Teachers, 2/e.* Boston, MA: Heinle, 1993.
A revised collection of teaching methods including extensive selections of current methods. Shows how to keep pace with the current changes in language and culture instruction. Addresses topics such as literacy in multicultural settings, cooperative learning, peer teaching, and CAI (computer-assisted instruction).

Shrum, Judith L., and Eileen W. Glisan. *Teacher's Handbook: Contextualized Language Instruction.* Boston, MA: Heinle, 1993.
Focuses on practical application of the most recent language teaching theory at the high school level, including teaching grammar, testing, using video texts, and cooperative learning. Contains microteaching situations, case studies, and observational episodes. Samples of unit plans, daily lessons, different types of tests, and cooperative tasks are contained in a useful appendix. The book features extensive references and a resource list. Used in many teacher training programs at universities and in school districts.

II. Second Language Theory

Krashen, Stephen. *The Power of Reading.* New York: McGraw, 1994.
Updates Krashen's Optimal Input Hypothesis—which originally focused on listening—by applying it to reading in the second language classroom. This is an important book to read, because it emphasizes authentic reading texts for developing efficient use of oral language. Contains many suggestions and strategies for more effective reading comprehension.

Liskin-Gasparro, Judith. *A Guide to Testing and Teaching for Oral Proficiency.* Boston, MA: Heinle, 1990.
Provides important historical and other background information about the oral proficiency interview. An application section features sample oral activities based on each level of the ACTFL Proficiency Guidelines. Extensive commentaries on the taped interviews offer detailed analysis of the speech samples and the interviewer's techniques. An excellent book for understanding the foundations of the current proficiency model for second language acquisition.

Rubin, Joan, and Irene Thompson. *How To Be a More Successful Language Learner 2/e.* Boston, MA: Heinle, 1993.
Presents the latest research about learner strategies and language learning including psychological, linguistic, and practical matters surrounding the successful development of a second language. Also includes discussions and samples of cognitive and metacognitive learner strategies.

III. Video and CAI

Altmann, Rick. *The Video Connection: Integrating Video into Language Teaching.* Boston: Houghton, 1989.
Contains valuable discussions about using video texts to support second language learning. Author explains why authentic video texts are necessary and how to present them successfully to students. Diverse strategies for students before and after viewing are offered as practical suggestions.

Dunkel, Patricia A. *Computer-Assisted Language Learning and Testing.* Boston, MA: Heinle, 1992.
Examines the effectiveness of CAI and computer-assisted language learning (CALL) in the foreign language classroom. Has a very clear format and provides an insightful overview of the computer's effect on foreign language.

Kenning, M.J., and M.M. Kenning. *Computers and Language Learning: Current Theory and Practice.* New York: E. Horwood, 1990.
Offers an array of theoretical discussions as well as practical suggestions. Excellent overview of how CAI (computer-assisted instruction) can support successful second language development.

IV. Professional Journals

Calico (Published by Duke University, Charlotte, N.C.)
Dedicated to the intersection of modern language learning and high technology. Research articles on videodiscs, using computer-assisted language learning, how-to articles, and courseware reviews.
Examples of articles:
Complain, Jean, Lise Duquette, and Michel Laurier. "Video and Software Self-Development Tools for the Language Teacher." Calico 10 (1992): 5-15.
Hendricks, Harold H. "Models of Interactive Videodisc Development." Calico 11 (1993): 53-67.

The Foreign Language Annals (Published by the American Council on the Teaching of Foreign Languages)
Consists of research and how-to-teach articles.
Examples of articles:
VanPatten, Bill. "Grammar Teaching for the Acquisition-Rich Classroom." FLA 26 (1993): 435-50.
Young, Dolly Jesusita. "Processing Strategies of Foreign Language Readers: Authentic and Edited Input." FLA 26 (1993): 451-68.

German Quarterly (Published by the American Association of Teachers of German)
Articles on literary interpretations of German-language literature. An example of a published article:
Mehigan, Tim. "Eichendorff's Taugenichts; or, The Social Education of the Private Man." German Quarterly 66 (1993): 60-70.

The IALL Journal of Language Learning Technologies, (Published by the International Association for Learning Laboratories)
Research articles as well as practical discussions pertaining to technology and language instruction.
Examples of articles:
Kuettner, D., J. Toth and K. Landahl, eds. "Report on IALL '93: Defining the Role for the Language Lab." IALL Journal 26 (1993): 9 17.
Salay, Susan. "Secondary School Update." IALL Journal 26 (1993): 141-44.

The Modern Language Journal
Primarily features research articles. Examples of articles:
DeKeyser, Robert M. "The Effect of Error Correction on L2 Grammar Knowledge and Oral Proficiency." MLJ 77 (1993): 501-14.
Glisan, Eileen W. and Victor Drescher. "Textbook Grammar: Does It Reflect Native Speaker Speech?" MLJ 77 (1993): 23-33.
Hulstijn, Jan H. "When do Foreign-Language Readers Look Up the Meaning of Unfamiliar Words? The Influence of Task and Learner Variable." MLJ 77 (1993): 139-51.
Riley, Gail L. "A Story Approach to Narrative Text Comprehension." MLJ 77 (1993): 417-32.

Die Unterrichtspraxis (published by the American Association of Teachers of German)
Articles about teaching German successfully.
Examples of articles:
Fraser, Catherine C. "What is Technology Really Doing for Language Teaching and Learning?" Die Unterrichtspraxis 26 (1993): 127-31.
Myers, Michael. "Production and Use of Slides for Language and Culture Classes." Die Unterrichtspraxis 25 (1992): 75-79.
Pentecost, Gislind, E. "Deutschlandspiegelvideos." Die Unterrichtspraxis 26 (1993): 196-99.
Saur, Pamela S. "Teaching the Adjective Endings in 1992: A Survey." Die Unterrichtspraxis 26 (1993): 56-61.

Scope and Sequence: German Level 1

VORSCHAU
- Das Alphabet
- Wie heißt du?
- Im Klassenzimmer
- Die Zahlen von 0 bis 20

KAPITEL 1   WER BIST DU?
Functions:
- Saying hello and goodbye
- Asking someone's name and giving yours
- Asking who someone is
- Talking about where people are from
- Talking about how someone gets to school

Grammar:
- Forming questions
- Definite articles der, die, das
- Subject pronouns and sein

Culture:
- Greetings
- Using der and die in front of people's names
- Map of German states and capitals
- Wie kommst du zur Schule?

Re-entry:
- Asking someone's name
- Numbers 0-20
- Geography of German-speaking countries

KAPITEL 2   SPIEL UND SPASS
Functions:
- Talking about interests
- Expressing likes and dislikes
- Saying when you do various activities
- Asking for an opinion and expressing yours
- Agreeing and disagreeing

Grammar:
- The singular subject pronouns and present tense verb endings
- The plural subject pronouns and verb endings
- The present tense of verbs
- Word order: verb in second position
- Verbs with stems ending in d, t, n, or -eln

Culture:
- Formal and informal address
- Was machst du gern?
- German weekly planner

Re-entry:
- Question formation
- Greetings
- Expressions stimmt/stimmt nicht used in a new context

KAPITEL 3   KOMM MIT NACH HAUSE!
Functions:
- Talking about where you and others live
- Offering something to eat and drink and responding to an offer
- Saying please, thank you, and you're welcome
- Describing a room
- Talking about family members
- Describing people

Grammar:
- The möchte-forms
- Indefinite articles ein, eine
- The pronouns er, sie, es, and sie
- The possessive adjectives mein, dein, sein, and ihr

Culture:
- The German preference for Mineralwasser
- Wo wohnst du?

Re-entry:
- Definite articles der, die, das
- Asking someone's name and age
- Asking who someone is
- Talking about interests

KAPITEL 4   ALLES FÜR DIE SCHULE!
Functions:
- Talking about class schedules
- Using a schedule to talk about time
- Sequencing events
- Expressing likes, dislikes, and favorites
- Responding to good news and bad news
- Talking about prices
- Pointing things out

Grammar:
- The verb haben
- Using Lieblings-
- Noun plurals

Culture:
- The German school day
- 24-hour time system
- The German grading system
- Was sind deine Lieblingsfächer?
- German currency

Re-entry:
- Numbers
- Likes and dislikes: gern
- Degrees of enthusiasm
- The pronouns er, sie, es, and sie

KAPITEL 5   KLAMOTTEN KAUFEN
Functions:
- Expressing wishes when shopping
- Commenting on and describing clothes
- Giving compliments and responding to them
- Talking about trying on clothes

Grammar:
- Definite and indefinite articles in the accusative case
- The verb gefallen
- Direct object pronouns
- Separable-prefix verbs
- Stem changing verbs nehmen and aussehen

Culture:
- Exchange rates
- German store hours
- German clothing sizes
- Welche Klamotten sind „in"?

Re-entry:
- Numbers and prices
- Colors
- Pointing things out
- Expressing likes and dislikes
- Asking for and expressing opinions
- The verb aussehen

KAPITEL 6   PLÄNE MACHEN
Functions:
- Starting a conversation
- Telling time and talking about when you do things
- Making plans
- Ordering food and beverages
- Talking about how something tastes
- Paying the check

Grammar:
- The verb wollen
- The stem changing verb essen

Culture:
- Clocks on public buildings
- Was machst du in deiner Freizeit?
- Tipping in Germany

Re-entry:
- Expressing time when referring to schedules
- Vocabulary: School and freetime activities
- Inversion of time elements
- Sequencing events
- Accusative case
- The verb nehmen
- Using möchte to order food

KAPITEL 7 ZU HAUSE HELFEN

Functions:
- Extending and responding to an invitation
- Expressing obligation
- Talking about how often you have to do things
- Asking for and offering help and telling someone what to do
- Talking about the weather

Grammar:
- The modals **müssen** and **können**
- The separable-prefix verb **abräumen**
- The accusative pronouns
- Using present tense to refer to the future

Culture:
- **Was tust du für die Umwelt?**
- German weather map and weather report
- Weather in German-speaking countries

Re-entry:
- Separable-prefix verbs
- Time clauses
- Vocabulary: Free-time activities
- Using numbers in a new context, temperature

KAPITEL 8 EINKAUFEN GEHEN

Functions:
- Asking what you should do
- Telling someone what to do
- Talking about quantities
- Saying you want something else
- Giving reasons
- Saying where you were and what you bought

Grammar:
- The modal **sollen**
- The **du**-commands
- The conjunctions **denn** and **weil**
- The past tense of **sein**

Culture:
- Specialty shops and markets
- **Was machst du für andere Leute?**
- Weights and measures
- German advertisements
- German recipes

Re-entry:
- The **möchte**-forms
- Numbers used in a new context, weights and measures
- Responding to invitations
- Vocabulary: Activities
- Vocabulary: Household chores

KAPITEL 9 AMERIKANER IN MÜNCHEN

Functions:
- Talking about where something is located
- Asking for and giving directions
- Talking about what there is to eat and drink
- Saying you do/don't want more
- Expressing opinions

Grammar:
- The verb **wissen**
- The verb **fahren**
- The formal commands with **Sie**
- The phrase **es gibt**
- Using **kein**
- The conjunction **daß**

Culture:
- The German **Innenstadt**
- **Was ißt du gern?**
- Map of a German neighborhood
- **Imbißstube** menu
- **Leberkäs**

Re-entry:
- Vocabulary: Types of stores
- **Du**-commands
- Vocabulary: Food items
- Indefinite articles: accusative case

KAPITEL 10 KINO UND KONZERTE

Functions:
- Expressing likes and dislikes
- Expressing familiarity
- Expressing preferences and favorites
- Talking about what you did in your free time

Grammar:
- The verb **mögen**
- The verb **kennen**
- **Lieber, am liebsten**
- The stem changing verb **sehen**
- The phrase **sprechen über**
- The stem changing verbs **lesen** and **sprechen**

Culture:
- The German movie rating system
- A German pop chart
- German movie ads
- **Welche kulturellen Veranstaltungen besuchst du?**
- German upcoming events poster
- German best-seller lists
- German video-hits list
- Popular German novels

Re-entry:
- Expressing likes and dislikes
- The verb **wissen**
- The stem-changing verb **aussehen**
- Vocabulary: Activities
- The stem-changing verbs **nehmen** and **essen**
- Talking about when you do things

KAPITEL 11 DER GEBURTSTAG

Functions:
- Using the telephone in Germany
- Inviting someone to a party
- Talking about birthdays and expressing good wishes
- Discussing gift ideas

Grammar:
- Introduction to the dative case
- Word order when you use the dative case

Culture:
- Using the telephone
- Saints' days
- German good luck symbols
- **Was schenkst du zum Geburtstag?**
- German gift ideas

Re-entry:
- Numbers 0-20
- Time and days of the week
- Months
- Accusative case
- Vocabulary: Family members

KAPITEL 12 DIE FETE (Wiederholungskapitel)

Functions (Review):
- Offering help and explaining what to do
- Asking where something is located and giving directions
- Making plans and inviting someone to come along
- Talking about clothing
- Discussing gift ideas
- Describing people and places
- Saying what you would like and whether you do or don't want more
- Talking about what you did

Grammar (Review):
- The verb **können**; the preposition **für**; accusative pronouns; and **du**-commands
- The verb **wissen** and word order following **wissen**
- The verbs **wollen** and **müssen**; word order
- Nominative and accusative pronouns; definite and indefinite articles
- Dative endings
- The nominative pronouns **er, sie, es,** and **sie** (pl); possessive pronouns
- The **möchte**-forms; **noch ein** and **kein ... mehr**

Culture:
- **Spätzle** and **Apfelküchle**
- **Mußt du zu Hause helfen?**
- German gift ideas
- Photos from furniture ads
- Menu from an **Imbißstube**
- Recipes

Scope and Sequence: German Level 2

For more detailed re-entry list, see overview chart in TE interleaf before each chapter.

KAPITEL 1 BEI DEN BAUMANNS
(Wiederholungskapitel)
Functions (Review):
- Asking for and giving information about yourself and others; describing yourself and others; expressing likes and dislikes; identifying people and places
- Giving and responding to compliments; expressing wishes when buying things
- Making plans; ordering food; talking about how something tastes

Grammar (Review):
- Present tense forms of **haben** and **sein**
- The possessive adjectives **mein, dein, sein,** and **ihr** (nominative)
- Regular verbs and stem changing verbs
- The third person pronouns
- The verb **wollen**
- The **möchte**-forms

Culture:
- Questionnaire: **Was für eine Person bist du?**
- Article: **Sebastian über seine Familie**
- Article: **Popstars machen Mode**
- **Und was hast du am liebsten?**
- Advertisements

KAPITEL 2 BASTIS PLAN
(Wiederholungskapitel)
Functions (Review):
- Expressing obligations; extending and responding to an invitation; offering help and telling what to do
- Asking and telling what to do; telling that you need something else; telling where you were and what you bought
- Discussing gift ideas; expressing likes and dislikes; expressing likes, preferences, and favorites; saying you do or don't want more

Grammar (Review):
- The present tense forms of **müssen, können, sollen,** and **mögen**
- The interrogative **warum**
- Clauses introduced by **weil** and **denn**
- Personal pronouns: accusative case
- The possessives **mein, dein, sein,** and **ihr** (accusative)
- The **du**-commands

- The past tense forms of **sein**
- The dative case of **mein, dein, sein,** and **ihr**
- **Noch ein**, nominative and accusative
- **Kein**, nominative and accusative

Culture:
- **Was nimmst du mit, wenn du irgendwo eingeladen bist?**
- Grocery advertisements
- German gift ideas
- What German students like and dislike about school

KAPITEL 3 WO WARST DU IN DEN FERIEN?
Functions:
- Reporting past events, talking about activities
- Reporting past events, talking about places
- Asking how someone liked something; expressing enthusiasm or disappointment, responding enthusiastically or sympathetically

Grammar:
- The conversational past
- The past tense of **haben** and **sein**
- **An** and **in** with dative-case forms to express location
- The definite article, dative plural
- Personal pronouns, dative case
- The dative-case forms of **ein**

Culture:
- Information on Dresden
- Information on **Frankfurt**
- **Was hast du in den letzten Ferien gemacht?**

Re-entry:
- Expressions of time/sequencing
- **Weil**-clauses
- Talking about likes and dislikes

KAPITEL 4 GESUND LEBEN
Functions:
- Expressing approval and disapproval
- Asking for information and responding emphatically or agreeing with reservations
- Asking and telling what you may and may not do

Grammar:
- The verb **schlafen** (**schläft**)
- **Für** + accusative
- Reflexive verbs (accusative)
- **Jeder, jede, jedes** (nominative)
- The accusative forms of **kein**
- The verb **dürfen**

Culture:
- Interviews of German teenagers
- **Was tust du, um gesund zu leben?**
- Survey on health habits
- **Bioläden** and **Reformhäuser**

Re-entry:
- Modals: **sollen/müssen**
- **Daß**-clauses
- Conjunctions **weil** and **denn**
- Expressions of place, time, frequency, and quantity
- Giving reasons
- **Kein**
- Responding to an invitation
- The irregular verb **essen**

KAPITEL 5 GESUND ESSEN
Functions:
- Expressing regret and downplaying; expressing skepticism and making certain
- Calling someone's attention to something and responding
- Expressing preference and strong preference

Grammar:
- The demonstrative **dieser**
- The possessives (summary)
- Verbs used with dative-case forms
- The interrogative **welcher, welche, welches**
- The prepositions **auf** and **zu**

Culture:
- **Was ißt du, was nicht?**
- Nutritious snacks for **Gymnasiasten**
- German meals and mealtimes

Re-entry:
- Talking about prices and quantities
- The possessives
- Talking about how food tastes
- Comparatives and superlatives
- Saying you want more
- The interrogative **was für**

KAPITEL 6 GUTE BESSERUNG!
Functions:
- Inquiring about someone's health and responding; making suggestions
- Asking about and expressing pain
- Asking for and giving advice; expressing hope

Grammar:
- Reflexive pronouns in dative
- The inclusive command (**wir-**

T44

command)
- Verbs used with dative case
- The verbs **sich (etwas) brechen, waschen, messen, weh tun**
- The dative case to express the idea of something too expensive, too large, too small for you

Culture:
- **Was machst du, wenn dir nicht gut ist?**
- The difference between an **Apotheke** and a **Drogerie**
- Article about sun exposure

Re-entry:
- The verb **sich fühlen**
- The accusative reflexive pronouns
- Expressing obligations
- The conversational past
- **Daß**-clauses

KAPITEL 7   STADT ODER LAND?

Functions:
- Expressing preference and giving a reason
- Expressing wishes
- Agreeing with reservations; justifying your answers

Grammar:
- Comparative forms of adjectives
- The verb **sich wünschen**
- Adjective endings following **ein**-words
- Adjective endings of comparatives

Culture:
- **Wo wohnst du lieber? Auf dem Land? In der Stadt?**
- Letter from a German pen pal

Re-entry:
- Talking about places to live
- Reflexive dative verbs
- Expressing opinions
- The verb **gefallen**

KAPITEL 8   MODE? JA ODER NEIN?

Functions:
- Describing clothes
- Expressing interest, disinterest, and indifference; making and accepting compliments
- Persuading and dissuading

Grammar:
- Adjective endings following **der**- and **dieser**-words
- The verbs **tragen** and **sich interessieren**
- Further uses of the dative case
- The verb **kaufen** with dative reflexive pronouns
- The conjunction **wenn**

Culture:
- **Was trägst du am liebsten?**
- Clothes typically worn by German-speaking youths

- Interviews about fashion
- Excerpts from a clothing catalog

Re-entry:
- Talking about what you bought
- Accusative reflexive verbs
- The preposition **für** + accusative
- Giving reasons
- Word order with subordinate conjunctions

KAPITEL 9   WOHIN IN DIE FERIEN?

Functions:
- Expressing indecision; asking for and making suggestions
- Expressing doubt, conviction, and resignation
- Asking for and giving directions

Grammar:
- **Er** endings with place names
- **Nach, an, in,** and **auf**
- **Ob**-clauses
- Expressing direction and location (Summary)
- Prepositions followed by dative
- The prepositions **durch, um, vor,** and **neben**

Culture:
- **Wohin fährst du in den nächsten Ferien?**
- Statistics on transportation
- Students talk about vacations
- **Stadtrundgang durch Bietigheim**

Re-entry:
- Inclusive commands
- The modal **können**
- The stem changing verb **fahren**
- Giving directions
- Inviting someone and responding to an invitation

KAPITEL 10   VIELE INTERESSEN!

Functions:
- Asking about and expressing interest
- Asking for and giving permission; asking for information and expressing an assumption
- Expressing surprise, agreement, and disagreement; talking about plans

Grammar:
- Verbs with prepositions
- **Wo**-compounds and **da**-compounds
- The verbs **lassen** and **laufen**
- The use of **kein** to negate a noun
- The future tense with **werden**

Culture:
- Television companies
- **Was machst du, um zu relaxen?**
- Statistics on television programs
- Getting a driver's license in Germany

Re-entry:
- The conjunctions **weil** and **daß**
- Word order with modals
- Time expressions
- The interrogative **was für**
- Expressing future events with present tense
- Making plans

KAPITEL 11   MIT OMA INS RESTAURANT

Functions:
- Asking for, making, and responding to suggestions
- Expressing hearsay
- Ordering in a restaurant; expressing good wishes

Grammar:
- The **würde**-forms
- Unpreceded adjectives
- The **hätte**-forms

Culture:
- **Für welche kulturellen Veranstaltungen interessierst du dich?**
- State-supported art in Germany
- International cuisine
- Menu

Re-entry:
- Cultural activities and sights
- The impersonal pronoun **man**
- Talking about favorites
- The modal **sollen**
- Saying what's available
- Ordering and asking for the bill

KAPITEL 12   DIE REINICKEN-DORFER CLIQUE (Wiederholungskapitel)

Functions (Review):
- Reporting past events; asking for, making, and responding to suggestions
- Ordering food, expressing hearsay and regret; persuading and dissuading
- Asking for and giving advice; expressing preference, interest, disinterest, and indifference

Grammar (Review):
- The past tense
- **Sollen** and the **würde**-forms
- Prepositions
- The command forms of strong verbs
- Adjective endings
- Comparative forms of adjectives

Culture:
- **Welche ausländische Küche hast du gern?**
- Etiquette in German restaurants
- Franziska van Almsick in Germany

Scope and Sequence: German Level 3

KAPITEL 1 DAS LAND AM MEER (Wiederholungskapitel)

Functions (Review):
- Reporting past events
- Asking how someone liked something; expressing enthusiasm or disappointment; responding enthusiastically or sympathetically
- Asking and telling what you may or may not do
- Asking for information
- Inquiring about someone's health and responding; asking about and expressing pain
- Expressing hope

Grammar (Review):
- Prepositions followed by dative-case forms
- Past tense
- Dative-case forms
- Forms of **dieser** and **welcher**
- Reflexive pronouns

Culture:
- **Insel Rügen**
- **Fit ohne Fleisch**
- **Währungen und Geld wechseln**

KAPITEL 2 AUF IN DIE JUGEND-HERBERGE! (Wiederholungskapitel)

Functions (Review):
- Asking for and making suggestions
- Expressing preference and giving a reason
- Expressing wishes
- Expressing doubt, conviction, and resignation
- Asking for information and expressing an assumption
- Expressing hearsay
- Asking for, making, and responding to suggestions
- Expressing wishes when shopping

Grammar (Review):
- Two-way prepositions (**So sagt man das!**)
- Word order in **daß**- and **ob**-clauses (**So sagt man das!**)
- Adjective endings
- The verb **hätte** (**So sagt man das!**)

Culture:
- Explanation of **Jugendherbergen**
- **Einkaufsliste**
- **Programm für eine 6-Tage-Reise nach Weimar**
- **Weimar im Blickpunkt**

KAPITEL 3 AUSSEHEN: WICHTIG ODER NICHT?

Functions:
- Asking for and expressing opinions
- Expressing sympathy and resignation
- Giving advice
- Giving a reason
- Admitting something and expressing regret

Grammar:
- **Da**- and **wo**-compounds (Summary)
- Infinitive clauses

Culture:
- **Die deutsche Subkultur**
- Teenagers talking about what they do to feel better

Re-entry:
- Expressing interest
- Sequencing events
- Expressing opinions
- Verbs requiring prepositional phrases
- Hobby and clothing vocabulary
- **Wo**- and **da**-compounds
- Responding sympathetically
- Asking for and giving advice
- Making suggestions
- Giving reasons
- Infinitives
- **Weil**-clauses

KAPITEL 4 VERHÄLTNIS ZU ANDEREN

Functions:
- Agreeing
- Giving advice
- Introducing another point of view
- Hypothesizing

Grammar:
- Ordinal numbers
- Relative clauses
- **Hätte** and **wäre**
- The genitive case

Culture:
- Importance of **Cliquen** for young people
- **Die verschiedenen Bildungs-wege in Deutschland**

Re-entry:
- Agreeing
- **Wenn-**, **weil-**, and **daß**-clauses
- Cardinal numbers
- Pronouns (nom., acc., and dat. case)
- Giving advice
- **Wenn**-phrases
- Subjunctive (**würde-**, **hätte-**, **wäre**-forms)
- The preposition **von** + dative

KAPITEL 5 RECHTE UND PFLICHTEN

Functions:
- Talking about what is possible
- Saying what you would have liked to do
- Saying that something is going on right now
- Reporting past events
- Expressing surprise, relief, and resignation

Grammar:
- The **könnte**-forms
- Further uses of **wäre** and **hätte**
- Use of verbs as neuter nouns
- The past tense of modals (the imperfect)

Culture:
- **Artikel 38/2. Absatz des Grundgesetzes**
- Cartoon
- **Gleichberechtigung im deutschen Militär?**
- **Wehrpflicht**

Re-entry:
- **Hätte**-forms and **wäre**-forms
- **Weil**-clauses
- Giving reasons
- The modals **können, wollen,** and **müssen**
- Reporting past events
- Expressing surprise
- Expressing resignation
- Expressing hearsay

KAPITEL 6 MEDIEN: STETS GUT INFORMIERT?

Functions:
- Asking someone to take a position
- Asking for reasons
- Expressing opinions
- Reporting past events
- Agreeing or disagreeing
- Changing the subject
- Interrupting
- Expressing surprise or annoyance

Grammar:
- Narrative past (imperfect)
- Superlative forms of adjectives

Culture:
- **Die TV-Kids**
- **Die Schülerzeitung**
- **Leserbriefe an die Redaktion der Pepo**

Re-entry:
- Talking about favorites

- Leisure-time activities
- Expressing opinions
- The conversational past
- Agreeing and disagreeing
- Television vocabulary
- Expressing surprise
- The comparative forms of adjectives
- Time expressions
- Words of quantity

KAPITEL 7 OHNE REKLAME GEHT ES NICHT!

Functions:
- Expressing annoyance
- Comparing
- Eliciting agreement and agreeing
- Expressing conviction, uncertainty, and what seems to be true

Grammar:
- **Derselbe, der gleiche**
- Adjective endings following determiners of quantity
- Relative pronouns
- Introducing relative clauses with **was** and **wo**
- **Irgendein** and **irgendwelche**

Culture:
- **Werbung—pro und contra**
- **Warum so wenig Unterbrecherwerbung?**
- Excerpt from *Frankfurter Allgemeine*
- Cartoon

Re-entry:
- Expressing annoyance
- The conjunctions **wenn** and **daß**
- Comparative and superlative
- Adjective endings
- Agreeing
- Relative pronouns
- Word order in dependent clauses
- Expressing conviction
- Expressing uncertainty

KAPITEL 8 WEG MIT DEN VORURTEILEN!

Functions:
- Expressing surprise, disappointment, and annoyance
- Expressing an assumption
- Making suggestions and recommendations; giving advice

Grammar:
- The conjunction **als**
- Coordinating conjunctions
- Verbs with prefixes (Summary)

Culture:
- Cartoon
- **Verständnis für Aüslander?**
- **Der sympathische Deutsche**

Re-entry:
- Expressing surprise
- Expressing disappointment
- **Daß**-clauses

- Narrative past
- Conversational past
- Coordinating conjunctions
- Expressing an assumption
- Prepositions followed by dative
- Separable prefix verbs
- Making suggestions
- Giving advice

KAPITEL 9 AKTIV FÜR DIE UMWELT!

Functions:
- Expressing concern
- Making accusations
- Offering solutions
- Making polite requests
- Saying what is being done about a problem
- Hypothesizing

Grammar:
- Subjunctive forms of **müssen, dürfen, sollen,** and **sein**
- The passive voice, present tense
- Use of a conjugated modal verb in the passive
- Conditional sentences

Culture:
- Environmental concerns
- **Ein unweltfreundlicher Einkauf**

Re-entry:
- Adjective endings
- **Daß-, wenn-** and **weil**-clauses
- **Hätte-, würde-,** and **könnte-** forms
- **Werden** and **sollen**
- Environmental vocabulary
- Subjunctive forms

KAPITEL 10 DIE KUNST ZU LEBEN

Functions:
- Expressing preference, given certain possibilities
- Expressing envy and admiration
- Expressing happiness and sadness
- Saying that something is or was being done

Grammar:
- Prepositions with genitive
- **Da-** and **wo-**compounds
- The passive voice (Summary)

Culture:
- **Aphorismen**
- **Kultur findet man überall!**

Re-entry:
- Expressing preference
- **Würde-**forms
- Genitive-case forms
- Prepositions
- **Da-** and **wo-**compounds
- Past participles
- Subjunctive forms of modals
- **Von** + dative case

KAPITEL 11 DEINE WELT IS DEINE SACHE!

Functions:
- Expressing determination or indecision
- Talking about whether something is important or not important
- Expressing wishes
- Expressing certainty and refusing or accepting with certainty
- Talking about goals for the future
- Expressing relief

Grammar:
- The use of **wo-**compounds to ask questions
- Two ways of expressing the future tense
- The perfect infinitive with modals and **werden**

Culture:
- German universities
- **Wie findet man eine Arbeitsstelle in Deutschland?**
- **Umfragen und Tests**

Re-entry:
- Reflexive verbs
- Expressing indecision
- Conversational past and conditional
- **Ob-** and **daß-**clauses
- **Um ... zu**
- **Wo-**compounds
- Expressing wishes
- **Wäre**
- Determiners of quantity
- Negation with **kein**
- Future tense formation

KAPITEL 12 DIE ZUKUNFT LIEGT IN DEINER HAND!
(Wiederholungskapitel)

Functions (Review):
- Reporting past events
- Expressing surprise and disappointment
- Agreeing; agreeing with reservations; giving advice
- Giving advice and giving reasons
- Expressing determination or indecision
- Talking about what is important or not important
- Hypothesizing

Grammar (Review):
- Narrative past
- The **würde-**forms
- Infinitive forms of verbs
- Direct and indirect object pronouns
- Subjunctive

Culture:
- **Kummerkasten**
- **Pauken allein reicht nicht**
- **Claudias Pläne für die Zukunft**
- **Textbilder**

The Pupil's Edition

Proficiency is the goal of language instruction in Komm mit! Every chapter begins with authentic interviews or discussions that model communicative needs common among young people. Through these texts students learn the functions, vocabulary, and grammar that support natural expression. They also become interested, involved, and responsive—in short, they answer the invitation to Komm mit! and to communicate.

An Overview

Komm mit! Level 3, opens with a two-chapter review of the functions, vocabulary, and grammar learned in Levels 1 and 2. Following this comprehensive review, Chapters 3-11 provide a carefully sequenced program of balanced skills instruction in the four areas of listening, speaking, reading, and writing. In addition, every chapter is rich in authentic language and culture.

Chapter 12 is a review of the third year's study of German. It provides an opportunity to reinforce skills and remediate deficiencies before the end of the school year. This opportunity to pause and reflect on what has been learned provides closure and gives students a sense of accomplishment and renewed purpose.

At the end of the *Pupil's Edition*, a Reference Section summarizes functions and grammar rules for quick reference. It also provides a list of Additional Vocabulary as well as German>English and English>German glossaries. Throughout the year, students are encouraged to consult the Reference Section to review and expand their choices of functional expressions, vocabulary, and structures.

Activity-Based Instruction

In *Komm mit!*, language acquisition is an active process. From the first day, students are using German. Within each lesson, a progression of activities moves students from discrete point use of language to completely open-ended activities that promote personalized expression and meaningful communication! This sequence allows students to practice receptive skills before moving on to language production. It is this carefully articulated sequence that ensures success.

A Guided Tour

On the next several pages, you will find a guided tour of *Komm mit!* On these pages we have identified for you the essential elements of the textbook and the various resources available. If, as you are using *Komm mit!*, you encounter any particular problems, please contact your regional office for information or assistance.

Location Openers

In *Komm mit!*, students visit four locations: the new states of Germany *(Brandenburg, Mecklenburg-Vorpommern, Sachsen, Sachsen-Anhalt,* and *Thüringen)* and three German cities: *Würzburg, Frankfurt,* and *Dresden.* The Location Opener pages introduce students to each of these locations with photographs and accompanying text.

The coats of arms for each location introduce the symbols identified with these regions. In the interleaf pages of the *Teacher's Edition,* the symbols of the coats of arms are explained and related to historical events. Teachers can then incorporate this information into the lesson.

Inset maps show the location within Germany and its relationship to neighboring countries. *The Teacher's Edition* suggests activities that strengthen students' understanding of the geography of the region.

The almanac information given for each location provides basic economic, demographic, political, and geographic facts about the region or city covered in the chapters that follow.

Four pages of photographs illustrate life in the cities, towns, and countryside of the region being targeted and provide both teachers and students with a background that makes the activities and readings in the chapter more meaningful. Suggestions in the *Teacher's Edition* provide teachers with ideas for incorporating the information on these pages into the lesson cycle.

KAPITEL 10, 11, 12

Komm mit nach

Dresden!

Dresden

Dresden, das weltberühmte „Elbflorenz", erlebte seine Glanzzeit unter den prunkliebenden Kurfürsten Friedrich August I. und seinem Sohn Friedrich August II., beide auch Könige von Polen. In diesem „Augustäischen" Zeitalter (1694-1783) entwickelte sich Dresden zu einer der schönsten barocken deutschen Residenzstädte.

② Der Goldene Reiter zeigt August I. — auch August der Starke genannt — in der Rüstung eines römischen Cäsaren.

③ Dresdens berühmtestes Baudenkmal ist der Zwinger, eine Perle des Barock von Baumeister Pöppelmann in den Jahren 1711 bis 1732 geschaffen. Der Zwinger beherbergt Dresdens einmalige Kunstsammlung, die „Gemäldegalerie Alte Meister", mit Meisterwerken europäischer Maler wie Rubens, Rembrandt, Dürer, Holbein, Cranach, Velázquez, Raffael, Giorgione, Correggio, Tintoretto und andere Meister.

④ Das Albertinum enthält die „Gemälde[...] Diese Kunstsammlung von Weltruf z[...] Romantik, des Biedermeier, des Expr[...] sionismus deutscher und europäische[...] befindet sich auch das „Grüne Gewölb[...] aus der kurfürstlichen Schatzkammer[...] Gefäße, Schmuck, Waffen und ander[...] aus Gold, Silber und kostbaren Edelst[...]

230 *zweihundertdreißig*

Dresden

Bundesland: Sachsen
Einwohner: 520 000
Fluß: Elbe
Sehenswürdigkeiten: Zwinger, Albertinum, Schloß, Semperoper
Berühmte Leute: Kurfürsten Friedrich August I. und II., Carl Maria von Weber (1786-1826), Richard Wagner (1813-1883)
Industrie: Maschinenbau, Elektronik, Arzneimittelproduktion, Genußmittelindustrie (Schokolade), optische Artikel
Bekannte Gerichte: Dresdener

⑤ Die ehemalige Katholische Hofkirche, die größte Kirche Sachsens, wurde vom römischen Architekten Gaetano Chiaveri zwischen 1739 und 1755 im Stil des römischen Barock errichtet.

⑥ Die Ruine der Frauenkirche. Hier stand einst Deutschlands bedeutendster protestantischer Kirchenbau und das Wahrzeichen Dresdens. Die Kirche, wie auch der größte Teil Dresdens, wurde im Februar 1945 durch Bombenangriffe total zerstört. Die Kirche wird zur Zeit wieder aufgebaut.

⑦ Die weltberühmte Semperoper, ein Bauwerk von Gottfried Semper im Stil der Hochrenaissance in den Jahren 1871 bis 1878 errichtet, ist Heimat der Dresdner Staatsoper.

Chapter Opener

Each chapter is organized around a topic of interest to teenagers. Some examples are rights and privileges, prejudice, the environment, and advertising. As the topic is developed through a variety of situations, students will learn and practice the functions, grammar, and vocabulary necessary for real-life communication.

LIVELY PHOTOGRAPHS
Colorful photos illustrate authentic scenes that are tied to the chapter theme. Most of the chapter opener photos also show people interacting with each other and involved in activities that will be introduced and discussed within the chapter. The photos offer both teachers and students a great deal of cultural information and provide an opportunity for discussions related to material that will be covered in the chapter.

REALISTIC SITUATIONS
Each chapter topic is immediately placed in a realistic context or situation. Through a series of questions, students are motivated to explore the topic within the context of the chapter and then to personalize the new material and relate it to their own lives.

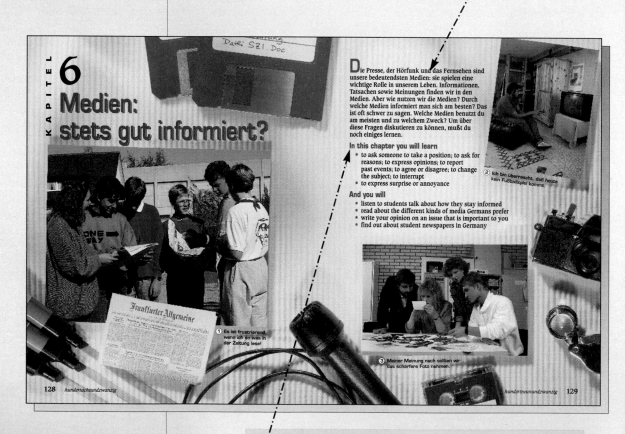

KAPITEL 6

Medien: stets gut informiert?

Die Presse, der Hörfunk und das Fernsehen sind unsere bedeutendsten Medien: sie spielen eine wichtige Rolle in unserem Leben. Informationen, Tatsachen sowie Meinungen finden wir in den Medien. Aber wie nutzen wir die Medien? Durch welche Medien informiert man sich am besten? Das ist oft schwer zu sagen. Welche Medien benutzt du am meisten und zu welchem Zweck? Um über diese Fragen diskutieren zu können, mußt du noch einiges lernen.

In this chapter you will learn
- to ask someone to take a position; to ask for reasons; to express opinions; to report past events; to agree or disagree; to change the subject; to interrupt
- to express surprise or annoyance

And you will
- listen to students talk about how they stay informed
- read about the different kinds of media Germans prefer
- write your opinion on an issue that is important to you
- find out about student newspapers in Germany

① Es ist frustrierend, wenn ich so was in der Zeitung lese!

② Ich bin überrascht, daß heute kein Fußballspiel kommt.

③ Meiner Meinung nach sollten wir das schärfere Foto nehmen.

128 *hundertachtundzwanzig*

hundertneunundzwanzig 129

FUNCTIONAL OUTCOMES
The functions and functional expressions practiced in the chapter are listed here as student outcomes. This is what students will be expected to know after they have completed the chapter. Stating the functional outcomes upfront helps students focus and organize and makes them feel more comfortable because they know what is expected of them.

Los geht's!

After students have been introduced to the location, situation, and functional outcomes of the chapter, the next step is to provide authentic cultural and linguistic input. This input at Level 3 takes the form of interviews or discussions that focus on the chapter theme and introduce students to language that they will practice as they go through the chapter.

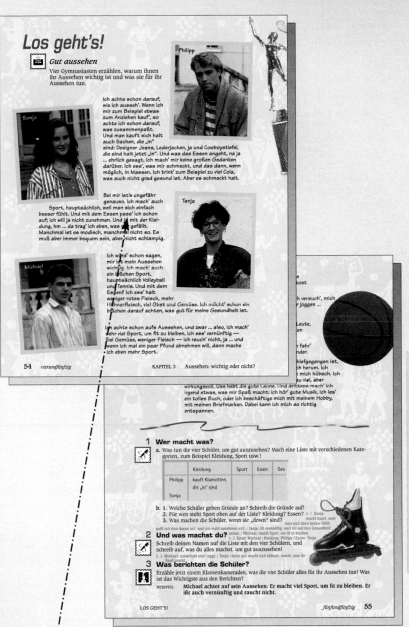

RECEPTIVE SKILLS

Activities following the **Los geht's!** interview enable students to respond to the interview or discussion at the recognition level. This is their first step in dealing with the new material in the chapter. Throughout the first **Stufe** and later in the **Anwendung,** they will continue to work with this material—first exploring the new language presented, then relating it to their own experiences, and finally making new combinations based on their accumulated language base.

AUTHENTIC INPUT

In the interviews and discussions on these pages, students are given both information and language models to enable them to discuss the topics with their classmates. Auditory learners also have access to audio recordings of the interviews and/or discussions that introduce each chapter.

Los geht's!

Gut aussehen

Vier Gymnasiasten erzählen, warum ihnen ihr Aussehen wichtig ist und was sie für ihr Aussehen tun.

Philipp

Sonja

Ich achte schon darauf, wie ich aussch'. Wenn ich mir zum Beispiel etwas zum Anziehen kauf', so achte ich schon darauf, was zusammenpaßt. Und man kauft sich halt auch Sachen, die "in" sind: Designer Jeans, Lederjacken, ja und Cowboystiefel, die sind halt jetzt "in". Und was das Essen angeht, na ja ... ehrlich gesagt, ich mach' mir keine großen Gedanken darüber. Ich ess', was mir schmeckt, und das dann, wenn möglich, in Massen. Ich trink' zum Beispiel zu viel Cola, was auch nicht grad gesund ist. Aber es schmeckt halt.

Bei mir ist's ungefähr genauso. Ich mach' auch Sport, hauptsächlich, weil man sich einfach besser fühlt. Und mit dem Essen pass' ich schon auf; ich will ja nicht zunehmen. Und ja, mit der Kleidung, hm ... da trag' ich eben, was mir gefällt. Manchmal ist es modisch, manchmal nicht so. Es muß aber immer bequem sein, aber nicht schlampig.

Tanja

Michael

Ich würd' schon sagen, mir ist mein Aussehen wichtig. Ich mach' auch ein bißchen Sport, hauptsächlich Volleyball und Tennis. Und mit dem Essen? Ich ess' halt weniger rotes Fleisch, mehr Hühnerfleisch, viel Obst und Gemüse. Ich möcht' schon ein bißchen darauf achten, was gut für meine Gesundheit ist.

Ich achte schon aufs Aussehen, und zwar ... also, ich mach' sehr viel Sport, um fit zu bleiben, ich ess' vernünftig — viel Gemüse, weniger Fleisch — ich rauch' nicht, ja ... und wenn ich mal ein paar Pfund abnehmen will, dann mache ich eben mehr Sport.

54 *vierundfünfzig* KAPITEL 3 Aussehen: wichtig oder nicht?

1 Wer macht was?

a. Was tun die vier Schüler, um gut auszusehen? Mach eine Liste mit verschiedenen Kategorien, zum Beispiel Kleidung, Sport usw.!

	Kleidung	Sport	Essen	Ges
Philipp	kauft Klamotten, die „in" sind			
Sonja				

b. 1. Welche Schüler geben Gründe an? Schreib die Gründe auf!
2. Für wen steht Sport oben auf der Liste? Kleidung? Essen?
3. Was machen die Schüler, wenn sie „down" sind?

2 Und was machst du?

Schreib deinen Namen auf die Liste mit den vier Schülern, und schreib auf, was du alles machst, um gut auszusehen!

3 Was berichten die Schüler?

Erzähle jetzt einem Klassenkameraden, was die vier Schüler alles für ihr Aussehen tun! Was ist das Wichtigste aus den Berichten?

BEISPIEL: Michael achtet auf sein Aussehen: Er macht viel Sport, um fit zu bleiben. Er ißt auch vernünftig und raucht nicht.

LOS GEHT'S! *fünfundfünfzig* 55

Weiter geht's!

Like the **Los geht's!** feature at the beginning of the **Erste Stufe**, these pages give students both the information and the authentic language models to practice new material and eventually to be able to discuss the chapter topic. The material in these two features (**Los geht's!** and **Weiter geht's!**) gives students a solid base for exploring the chapter topic at a level that is challenging but also motivating.

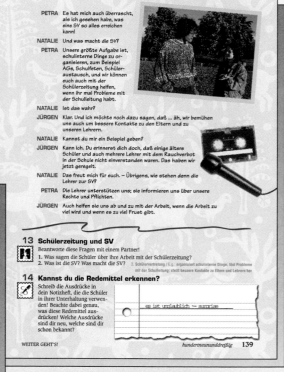

Stufen

Each chapter is divided into two **Stufen,** short manageable lessons that provide a carefully planned progression of activities. Within each **Stufe,** activities are sequenced from structured practice to open-ended communication in individual, pair, and group activities that accommodate many different learning styles.

VOCABULARY IN CONTEXT

Theme-related, functional vocabulary is presented in the **Wortschatz** and then re-entered as much as possible in the activities of the **Stufe.** In Level 3, the vocabulary is presented in two ways. In the **auf deutsch erklärt** column, German words are defined or explained in German. In the right-hand column, labeled **auf englisch erklärt,** vocabulary words are presented in a sentence and explained in English. The purpose of this system is to give students a context where one is needed in order to figure out the meaning of a new word but also to give them models for explaining difficult vocabulary in German.

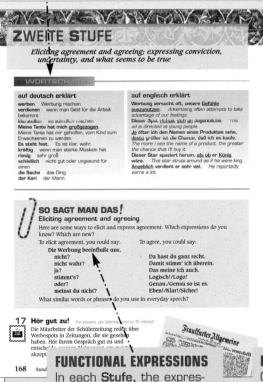

ZWEITE STUFE

Eliciting agreement and agreeing; expressing conviction, uncertainty, and what seems to be true

WORTSCHATZ

auf deutsch erklärt

werben Werbung machen
verdienen wenn man Geld für die Arbeit bekommt
klar stellen verständlich machen
Meine Tante hat mich großgezogen.
Meine Tante hat mir geholfen, vom Kind zum Erwachsenen zu werden.
Es steht fest. Es ist klar, wahr.
kräftig wenn man starke Muskeln hat
riesig sehr groß
schädlich nicht gut oder ungesund für einen
die Sache das Ding
der Kerl der Mann

auf englisch erklärt

Werbung versucht oft, unsere Gefühle auszunutzen. *Advertising often attempts to take advantage of our feelings.*
Dieser Spot richtet sich an Jugendliche. *This ad is directed at young people.*
Je öfter ich den Namen eines Produktes sehe, desto größer ist die Chance, daß ich es kaufe. *The more I see the name of a product, the greater the chance that I'll buy it.*
Dieser Star spaziert herum, als ob er König wäre. *This star struts around as if he were king.*
Angeblich verdient er sehr viel. *He reportedly earns a lot.*

SO SAGT MAN DAS!

Eliciting agreement and agreeing

Here are some ways to elicit and express agreement. Which expressions do you know? Which are new?

To elicit agreement, you could say:

Die Werbung beeinflußt uns, nicht?
nicht wahr?
ja?
stimmt's?
oder?
meinst du nicht?

To agree, you could say:

Da hast du ganz recht.
Damit stimm' ich überein.
Das meine ich auch.
Logisch!/Logo!
Genau./Genau so ist es.
Eben!/Klar!/Sicher!

What similar words or phrases do you use in everyday speech?

17 Hör gut zu! For answers, see listening script on TE Interleaf.

Die Mitarbeiter der Schülerzeitung reden über Werbespots in Zeitungen, die sie gesehen haben. Hör ihrem Gespräch gut zu und entscheide, wessen Meinung ... akzept...

168 *hundert...*

FUNCTIONAL EXPRESSIONS

In each **Stufe,** the expressions that students need in order to develop proficiency are summarized in **So sagt man das!** These functional expressions, supported by the necessary vocabulary and grammar, are the main focus of the lesson.

18 Einverstanden oder nicht?

Constance und Stefan äußern ihre Meinungen über die Werbung. Bist du einverstanden oder nicht mit dem, was sie sagen? Was sagst du dazu? Such dir eine Partnerin und reagiert zusammen auf die Aussagen! Versucht auch, Gründe anzugeben!

CONSTANCE **Die Werbung versucht nur, den Käufer zu beeinflussen, meinst du nicht?**
DU **Klar!** *oder*
  Das ist nicht ganz wahr. Es gibt Werbung, die auch informiert.
STEFAN „Die meisten Reklamen haben Frauen als Blickfang."
CONSTANCE „Viele Sportler verdienen mit der Werbung zu viel Geld."
STEFAN „Das Image der Frau wird weiterhin in einer traditionellen Rolle gezeigt."
CONSTANCE „Es gibt aber auch gute Werbung, die nicht so manipulativ ist."
STEFAN „Die meisten Werbespots für Kinder find' ich sehr blöd."
CONSTANCE „Die Werbung nutzt oft nur die Gefühle der Kinder aus."
STEFAN „Die Werbemacher brauchen immer wieder neue Ideen."
CONSTANCE „Die Werbung macht nur Appetit aufs Kaufen."
STEFAN „Je weniger Geld man hat, desto mehr sehnt man sich nach einem guten Leben."
CONSTANCE „Die Werbung verspricht, was sich die meisten nicht leisten können."

Schon bekannt
Ein wenig Grammatik

In Kapitel 4 you learned about relative clauses. Relative clauses are introduced by relative pronouns, the various forms of **der, die, das.**

Das ist ein Werbeslogan, den ich nicht kenne.

Identify the relative pronoun in this sentence. What does it refer to? What case is it in? Why?

Die bringen in der Werbung immer das, was wir schon haben.

Grammatik Introducing relative clauses with was and wo

1. The word **was** introduces a relative clause when it refers back to
   a. indefinite pronouns like **das, alles, etwas, nichts, wenig, viel.**
      Ich sehe **etwas, was** mir gefällt.
   b. the entire idea of the preceding clause.
      Ich kann es mir nicht leisten, **was** diese Leute anpreisen.

2. The word **wo** is used to refer to places, especially in a broader sense.
   Die Welt ist ein Kaufhaus, **wo** man sich alles kaufen kann.

Relative clauses are dependent clauses. Do you remember what happens to the ... uses?

hundertneunundsechzig 169

FORM FOLLOWS FUNCTION

Grammatical structures that support the communicative functions appear under the headings **Grammatik** and **Ein wenig Grammatik.** This carefully planned integration of grammar with a communicative purpose helps students communicate with increasing accuracy.

AUTHENTIC CULTURAL INPUT

In addition to the authentic materials found in a number of the **Los geht's!** and **Weiter geht's!** sections, realia is used throughout the chapter to provide authentic linguistic and cultural input. Students gain cultural insight and increasing confidence in their ability to read and comprehend authentic material.

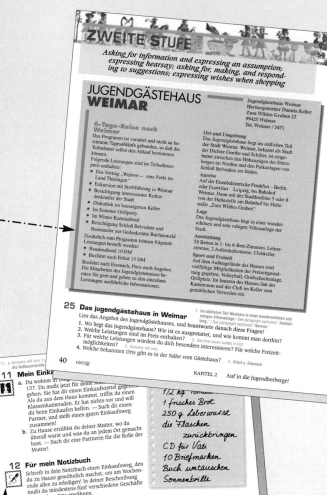

ZWEITE STUFE

Asking for information and expressing an assumption; expressing hearsay; asking for, making, and responding to suggestions; expressing wishes when shopping

JUGENDGÄSTEHAUS
WEIMAR

Jugendgästehaus Weimar
Herbergsmutter Danuta Keller
Zum Wilden Graben 12
99425 Weimar
Tel. Weimar / 3471

6-Tage-Reise nach Weimar

Das Programm ist variabel und nicht an bestimmte Tagesabläufe gebunden, so daß die Teilnehmer selbst den Ablauf bestimmen können.

Folgende Leistungen sind im Teilnehmerpreis enthalten:

- Dia-Vortrag „Weimar – eine Perle im Land Thüringen"
- Exkursion mit Stadtführung in Weimar
- Besichtigung interessanter Kulturdenkmäler der Stadt
- Diskothek im hauseigenen Keller
- Im Sommer Grillparty
- Im Winter Kaminabend
- Besichtigung Schloß Belvedere und Bustransfer zur Gedenkstätte Buchenwald

Zusätzlich zum Programm können folgende Leistungen bestellt werden:

- Badenabend 10 DM
- Busfahrt nach Eisenach 15 DM

Busfahrt nach Eisenach, Preis nach Angebot. Die Mitarbeiter des Jugendgästehauses beraten Sie gern und geben zu den einzelnen Leistungen ausführliche Informationen.

Ort und Umgebung
Das Jugendgästehaus liegt im südlichen Teil der Stadt Weimar. Weimar, bekannt als Stadt der Dichter Goethe und Schiller, ist eingebettet zwischen den Höhenzügen des Enersberges im Norden und den Parkanlagen von Schloß Belvedere im Süden.

Anreise
Auf der Eisenbahnstrecke Frankfurt – Berlin, oder Frankfurt – Leipzig, bis Bahnhof Weimar. Dann mit der Stadtbuslinie 5 oder 8 von der Haltestelle am Bahnhof bis Haltestelle „Zum Wilden Graben".

Lage
Das Jugendgästehaus liegt in einer wunderschönen und sehr ruhigen Villenanlage der Stadt.

Ausstattung
58 Betten in 1- bis 6-Bett-Zimmern. Lehrerzimmer, 2 Aufenthaltsräume, Clubkeller.

Sport und Freizeit
Auf dem Außengelände des Hauses sind vielfältige Möglichkeiten der Freizeitgestaltung gegeben: Volleyball, Großschachanlage, Grillplatz. Im Inneren des Hauses lädt der Kaminraum und der Club im Keller zum gemütlichen Verweilen ein.

25 Das Jugendgästehaus in Weimar
Lies das Angebot des Jugendgästehauses, und beantworte danach diese Fragen!
1. Wo liegt das Jugendgästehaus? *1. im südlichen Teil Weimars in einer wunderschönen und ruhigen Villenanlage / See paragraph captioned "Ausstat-*
2. Welche Leistungen sind im Preis enthalten? Wie ist es ausgestattet, und wie kommt man dorthin? *lung." / See paragraph captioned "Anreise".*
3. Für welche Leistungen würdest du dich besonders interessieren? Für welche Freizeitmöglichkeiten? *2. See first seven bullets in text.*
4. Welche bekannten Orte gibt es in der Nähe vom Gästehaus? *3. Answers will vary.* *4. Erfurt u. Eisenach*

40 vierzig KAPITEL 2 Auf in die Jugendherberge!

---

11 Mein Einkau[f]

a. Du wohnst in Ding[skirchen]... 137. Du mußt jetzt für deine alte... gehen. Sie hat dir einen Einkaufszettel gegeben... Als du aus dem Haus kommst, triffst du einen Klassenkameraden. Er hat nichts vor und will dir beim Einkaufen helfen. — Such dir einen Partner, und stellt einen guten Einkaufsweg zusammen!

b. Zu Hause erzählst du deiner Mutter, wo du überall warst und was du an jedem Ort gemacht hast. — Such dir eine Partnerin für die Rolle der Mutter!

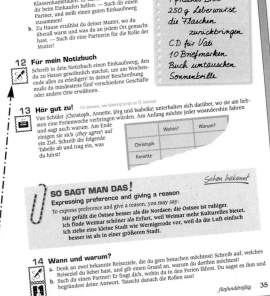

1/2 kg Tomaten
1 frisches Brot
250 g Leberwurst
die Flaschen
    zurückbringen
CD für Vati
10 Briefmarken
Buch umtauschen
Sonnenbrille

12 Für mein Notizbuch
Schreib in dein Notizbuch einen Einkaufsweg, den du zu Hause gewöhnlich machst, um am Wochenende alles zu erledigen! In deiner Beschreibung mußt du mindestens fünf verschiedene Geschäfte oder andere Orte erwähnen.

13 Hör gut zu! *For answers, see listening script on TE Interleaf.*
Vier Schüler (Christoph, Annette, Jörg und Isabella) unterhalten sich darüber, wo sie am liebsten eine Ferienwoche verbringen würden. Am Anfang möchte jeder woandershin fahren und sagt auch warum. Am Ende einigen sie sich (*they agree*) auf ein Ziel. Schreib die folgende Tabelle ab und trag ein, was du hörst!

	Wohin?	Warum?
Christoph		
Annette		

SO SAGT MAN DAS!
Schon bekannt

Expressing preference and giving a reason

To express preference and give a reason, you may say:

Mir gefällt die Ostsee besser als die Nordsee; die Ostsee ist ruhiger.
Ich finde Weimar schöner als Erfurt, weil Weimar mehr Kulturelles bietet.
Ich ziehe eine kleine Stadt wie Wernigerode vor, weil da die Luft einfach besser ist als in einer größeren Stadt.

14 Wann und warum?
a. Denk an zwei bekannte Reiseziele, die du gern besuchen möchtest! Schreib auf, welches Reiseziel du lieber hast, und gib einen Grund an, warum du dorthin möchtest!
b. Such dir einen Partner! Er fragt dich, wohin du in den Ferien fährst. Du sagst es ihm und begründest deine Antwort. Tauscht danach die Rollen aus!

ZWEITE STUFE fünfunddreißig 35

---

7 Wohin geht's?

a. Wie gut kennst du Deutschland schon? Schreib vier Orte oder Gegenden, die du gern besuchen möchtest, auf einen Zettel, und schreib daneben, was du dort gern machen möchtest!
b. Such dir eine Partnerin, mit der du gern reisen möchtest! Sie fragt dich nach deinen Vorschlägen. Gib zwei Alternativen, und sag in jedem Fall, warum du dieses Ziel vorschlägst!

8 Nö, da war ich schon!

Such dir einen Partner! Lad ihn ein, mit dir wegzufahren! Dein Partner ist aber ein Reisemuffel. Er sagt dir immer, daß er schon dort war, wo du hin willst, und er sagt dir auch, warum er nicht mitfahren will. Im Kasten unten stehen ein paar Ideen. Gebrauche aber auch deine eigenen!

BEISPIEL   DU   Du, ich möchte mal nach Thüringen fahren. Willst du mit?
   PARTNER   Nö, ich war schon mal in Thüringen. Es hat mir dort nicht gefallen.

11. a. Answers will vary. E... die Nußbaumstraße ...

9 Hör gut zu! *For answers, see listening script on TE Interleaf.*
Schüler erzählen, was sie in Dingskirchen machen. Schreib auf, wo jeder zuletzt hingeht oder zuletzt war!

wohin?/wo?		
Thüringen	Ostsee	Harz
Bodensee	Rhein	Alpen
Wernigerode	Zugspitze	Schweiz
Berge	Insel Rügen	Meer

10 In Dingskirchen
Kennst du dich in Dingskirchen aus? Ein Tourist stellt dir viele Fragen. Such dir einen Partner, der den Touristen spielt!

BEISPIEL   TOURIST   Entschuldigung, wo ist das Restaurant „Bella Italia"?
   DU   Das ist in der Uhlandstraße, an der Ecke Agnesstraße.

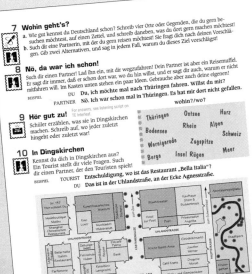

34 vierunddreißig KAPITEL 2 Auf in die Jugendherberge!

PERSONAL JOURNALS
Students practice new structures and vocabulary while reinforcing previously learned skills by keeping a **Notizbuch** or personal journal.

T54

Landeskunde

The information presented in the **Landeskunde** feature of the German 3 textbook covers a wide range of topics drawn from German life. Cultural information about German history and literature is included (such as a description of Weimar) as well as discussions on topics that relate to student life in Germany (such as **Die Schülerzeitung**). Other **Landeskunde** features focus on issues that students will be able to relate (and compare) to their own lives.

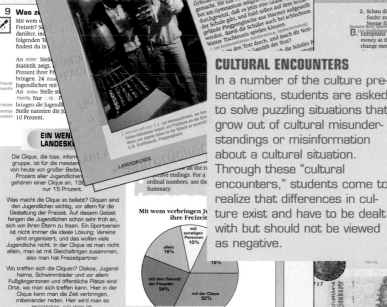

CULTURAL ENCOUNTERS

In a number of the culture presentations, students are asked to solve puzzling situations that grow out of cultural misunderstandings or misinformation about a cultural situation. Through these "cultural encounters," students come to realize that differences in culture exist and have to be dealt with but should not be viewed as negative.

CULTURAL AWARENESS

The **Ein wenig Landeskunde** are small cultural notes that appear wherever useful to explain some point of German culture that might be puzzling to an American teenager.

Zum Lesen

The reading selections in this book cover topics that will appeal to students. Even though some of the texts are challenging, they are also interesting and fun. Students will find many opportunities to apply the reading strategies they learned in the first two levels of *Komm mit!* Selections include a short piece by Kafka, Peter Bichsel's *Ein Tisch ist ein Tisch,* a Grimm's fairy tale, a modern fairy tale, a cartoon, and some articles related to issues, such as teenage slang, political suppression, and teenagers working for the environment.

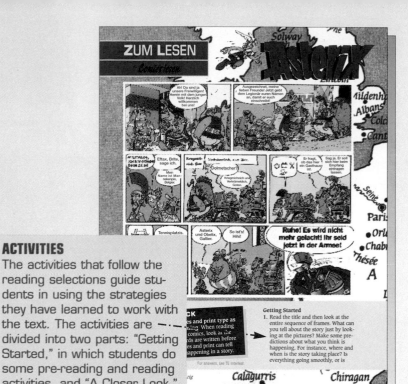

ACTIVITIES

The activities that follow the reading selections guide students in using the strategies they have learned to work with the text. The activities are divided into two parts: "Getting Started," in which students do some pre-reading and reading activities, and "A Closer Look," in which students work with the text both at the idea level and at the word level.

Getting Started

1. Read the title and then look at the entire sequence of frames. What can you tell about the story just by looking at the pictures? Make some predictions about what you think is happening. For instance, where and when is the story taking place? Is everything going smoothly, or is

For answers, see TE Interleaf.

READING STRATEGIES

Every reading is accompanied by a reading strategy (**Lesetrick**) that is practiced in the activities that follow. These strategies will help students read more effectively and go beyond the reading to such higher-order skills as identifying the main idea. Some of the strategies are recycled from the earlier levels (using pictures as clues to meaning) and expanded (using print type as clues to meaning).

ZUM LESEN
Moderne Literatur

Eine alltägliche Verwirrung von Franz Kafka

"Selbstporträt" von Karl Schmidt-Rottluff

LESETRICK
Using time lines for comprehension You don't need to know the exact meaning of every word to figure out what a story is about. By first taking a moment to discover how a story is organized you can make up for not knowing every word. Try to organize a text around a single guiding principle. For example, a narrative usually contains many words that indicate the sequence of events. You can use those words to construct a time line and better understand the flow of the story.

For answers, see TE Interleaf.

24 vierundzwanzig

in alltäglicher Vorfall: sein Ertragen eine alltägliche Verwirrung. A hat mit B aus H ein wichtiges Geschäft abzuschließen. Er geht zur Vorbesprechung nach H, legt den Hin- und Herweg in je zehn Minuten zurück und rühmt sich zu Hause dieser besonderen Schnelligkeit. Am nächsten Tag geht er wieder nach H, diesmal zum endgültigen Geschäftsabschluß. Da dieser voraussichtlich mehrere Stunden erfordern wird, geht A sehr früh morgens fort. Obwohl aber alle Nebenumstände, wenigstens nach A's Meinung, völlig die gleichen sind wie im Vortag, braucht er diesmal zum Weg nach H zehn Stunden. Als er dort ermüdet abends ankommt, sagt man ihm, daß B, ärgerlich wegen A's Ausbleiben, vor einer halben Stunde zu A in sein Dorf gegangen sei und sie sich eigentlich unterwegs hätten treffen müssen. Man rät A zu warten. A, in Angst wegen des Geschäftes, macht sich

sofort auf und eilt nach Hause.

Diesmal legt er den Weg, ohne besonders darauf zu achten, geradezu in einem Augenblick zurück. Zu Hause erfährt er, B sei doch schon gleich früh gekommen — gleich nach dem Weggang A's; ja, er habe A im Haustor getroffen, ihn an das Geschäft erinnert, aber A habe gesagt, er hätte jetzt keine Zeit, er müsse jetzt eilig fort.

Trotz diesem unverständlichen Verhalten A's sei aber B doch hier geblieben, um auf A zu warten. Er habe zwar schon oft gefragt, ob A nicht schon wieder zurück sei, befinde sich aber noch oben in A's Zimmer. Glücklich darüber, B jetzt noch zu sprechen und ihm alles erklären zu können, läuft A die Treppe hinauf. Schon ist er fast oben, da stolpert er, erleidet eine Sehnenzerrung und fast ohnmächtig vor Schmerz, unfähig sogar zu schreien, nur winselnd im Dunkel hört er, wie B — undeutlich ob in großer Ferne oder knapp neben ihm — wütend die Treppe hinunterstampft und endgültig verschwindet.

and B. Discuss any problems you notice with the rest of the class.

The endings -lich and -ig in German signal that a word is an adverb or adjective. When reading fiction, you can often use these words as clues to how people or things are.

6. Read the story again to find out how the characters act or react. Decide who or what is characterized by each of the following adverbs and adjectives:

wichtig	in Angst
ermüdet	eilig
ärgerlich	unverständlich
glücklich	undeutlich
ohnmächtig	wütend
unfähig	winselnd

7. Find the following words in the passage and, using context and familiar elements of compound words, try to derive their meanings: **Schnelligkeit, Nebenumstände, Ausbleiben,** and **Augenblick.**

8. What is A's problem? What is the cause? What is B's reaction? What does he do? How is the conflict resolved? Or is it?

9. Using the time line you created in Activity 5, reconstruct the story (in writing) using complete sentences. Your **Nacherzählung** should be one to two paragraphs.

10. Kafka's story depicts some rather bizarre events, yet the title seems to suggest the opposite — that the situation is commonplace. How can you reconcile or explain the apparent contradiction?

fünfundzwanzig 25

Zum Schreiben

A new feature at Level 3 is the writing page, **Zum Schreiben.** This feature challenges students to write in a systematic but creative way on topics related to the chapter themes and in a variety of styles and genres.

PERSONAL, CHAPTER-RELATED TOPICS

Each **Zum Schreiben** topic has been carefully chosen to relate to the theme and the functions of each chapter. In addition, the tasks encourage students to write about aspects of the topic that inspire or interest them personally.

PROCESS WRITING

In each chapter, students are given a writing topic and a series of tasks that guide them through the steps of prewriting, writing, and revising. In addition, each **Zum Schreiben** activity focuses on one **Schreibtip**, or writing strategy, that will help students develop their writing skills.

ZUM SCHREIBEN

In this chapter you have learned new ways to express feelings of fear, happiness, and sadness. The expression of feelings is central to some of the cultural activities you have discussed, as well as such works of art, poetry, and song. In this activity, you will write a poem or a song to express your feelings about a place, a memory, a person, or an image that had a strong impact on you.

Ein Gedicht — ein Bild mit Wörtern gemalt

Schreib ein Gedicht oder ein Lied über etwas (ein Erlebnis, einen Ort, eine Person, oder ein Bild), was dich tief beeindruckt hat! Drück in dem Gedicht ein bestimmtes Gefühl wie Furcht, Freude oder Traurigkeit in malerischer Sprache aus!

A. Vorbereiten
1. Such eine Idee für dein Gedicht oder Lied! Sieh dir alte Fotos an, und lies alte Tagebücher und Briefe, die du einmal geschrieben hast! Wähl einen Moment in deiner Vergangenheit, wo du ein starkes Gefühl erlebt hast!
2. Such ein Wort für das Gefühl, das du in dem Gedicht ausdrücken willst! Stell dir den Moment vor, und denk an die verschiedenen Empfindungen und Gefühle, die du mit dem Moment verbindest!
3. Schreib malerische Ausdrücke auf, die zu diesem Gefühl passen! Wähle Metaphern, Gleichnisse und Personifizierungen, um die Details zu beschreiben! Denk auch an den Klang der Sprache!
4. Mach einen Plan für das Gedicht oder Lied! Wie lang soll es sein? Wie viele Strophen soll es haben? Soll es einen bestimmten Rhythmus oder Reim haben?

SCHREIBTIP

Using figurative language and sound devices Different types of writing are distinguished in large part by the type of language used in them. Newspaper articles, critical reviews, and business letters are composed of matter-of-fact writing for the purpose of conveying information efficiently and clearly. But creative writing, especially poetry and song, is often composed of figurative language and sound devices. Use figurative language such as metaphors, similes, personification, and concrete imagery to evoke sensory images and to create an appropriate mood for the emotion you want to convey. Use sound devices such as rhyme, rhythm, assonance and alliteration to play with the musical sounds of language itself.

B. Ausführen
Benutze deinen Plan und die Ausdrücke, die du aufgelistet hast, und schreibe das Gedicht oder das Lied! Wenn du ein Lied schreibst, achte auf die Melodie und den Rhythmus der Musik, damit die Musik und die Wörter gut zusammenpassen!

C. Überarbeiten
1. Lies dein Gedicht oder Lied einem Partner vor! Kann sich der Partner die Gefühle vorstellen, die du ausdrückst? Rufen deine Wörter die richtige Wirkung hervor?
2. Lies das Gedicht noch einmal laut vor, und paß diesmal auf den Klang der Wörter auf! Verwende Stabreim und Assonanz, um die Sprache musikalischer zu machen!
3. Hör jetzt auf den Rhythmus der Wörter! Nimm Silben heraus oder setze Wörter ein, um den Rhythmus zu verbessern!
4. Hast du alles richtig buchstabiert? Hast du Präpositionen mit dem Akkusativ und Dativ richtig verwendet?
5. Schreib das verbesserte Gedicht oder Lied noch einmal ab!

zweihunderteinundfünfzig **251**

A system of icons is used throughout the *Pupil's Edition* to identify activities that are specifically designed to promote certain skills or that might be particularly useful in pair or group work.

Anwendung

The end-of-chapter review, Anwendung, offers the same level of interest and challenge as the instructional pages. Students are engaged in a series of activities that measure their ability to comprehend and generate language.

Listening

This icon indicates the listening activities that range from global comprehension to discrete tasks. Teachers can use the audiocassette for authentic input or read from the scripts available in the *Teacher's Edition* interleaf before each chapter.

Writing

Komm mit! offers a variety of writing activities, many of which are intended to be placed in the student's ***Notizbuch***. Teachers may decide how formal they wish the ***Notizbuch*** or journal to be, but students who are able to look back at their own writing periodically are reassured and encouraged by seeing their own growth and improvement.

Pair Work

Activities with this icon are ideal for pair work. It may be helpful to assign pairs for a certain period of time, preferably a week or two. This also promotes students' social growth as they learn to interact with a variety of people.

COMPLETE SKILLS REVIEW
Each **Anwendung** covers all four skill areas: listening, speaking, reading, and writing. These activities require students to recombine language and are a true measure of their growth in proficiency.

Group Work

Group activities are particularly successful in alleviating students' stress and inhibitions. Students will benefit from being assigned to groups at times and allowed to choose their own groups at others. The choice of how these groups will report is the teacher's, and direction lines may be varied so that groups report orally or in writing, or both.

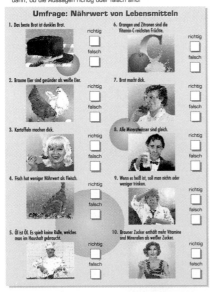

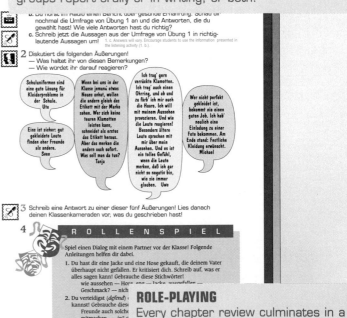

ROLE-PLAYING
Every chapter review culminates in a **Rollenspiel**. These dramatic activities encourage students to use language in imaginative and creative expression.

SPIRALED CHAPTER OBJECTIVES

Questions in the margins recall the communicative functions found at the beginning of each chapter. Each activity reveals students' strengths and points out areas for possible improvement.

Kann ich's wirklich?

This self-check page allows students to gauge their progress and gives them a true sense of accomplishment. After its successful completion, students can move ahead with confidence.

KANN ICH'S WIRKLICH?

Can you ask for and express opinions? (p. 57)

1 How would you ask for an opinion and give your own opinion of
a. Biokost? a. E.g.: Was hältst du von Biokost?; Ich halte viel davon.
b. eine Ernährung ohne Fleisch? b. E.g.: Was hältst du von einer Ernährung ohne Fleisch?; Ich halte nichts davon.
c. Bodybuilding? c. E.g.: Was würdest du zu Bodybuilding sagen?; Ich würde sagen, daß es Spaß macht.

Can you express sympathy and resignation? (p. 65)

2 How would you express sympathy or resignation in response to these statements?
a. Ich hab' jetzt schon die zweite Fünf in Geschichte. a. E.g.: Das ist ja schlimm!
b. Du hast wohl Probleme mit deiner Frisur! b. E.g.: Ja, was kann ich schon tun?
c. Stell dir vor, ich hab' meine Kamera verloren! c. E.g.: So ein Pech!
d. Meine beste Freundin hat mich zu ihrer Fete eingeladen.
e. Der Peter, der paßt sich seinen Freunden überhaupt nicht an.
d. E.g.: Na und! Wirklich? e. F.g.: Da kann man nichts machen. Er ist halt so.

Can you give advice? (p. 66)

3 What advice would you give to a friend who told you the following?
a. Meine Mutter sagt, ich zieh' mich zu schlampig an. a. E.g.: Warum ziehst du nicht mal was Konservatives an?
b. Sie sagt, meine Haare sind viel zu lang. b. E.g.: Laß dir doch die Haare schneiden!
c. Sie sagt, mein Zimmer ist nie aufgeräumt. c. E.g.: An deiner Stelle würde ich es mal aufräumen.
d. Sie sagt, daß ich zu viel fernsehe. d. E.g.: Versuch doch mal, etwas weniger fernsehen zu schauen!

Can you give a reason? (p. 67)

4 How would you complete these statements so that they tell why you do these things?
a. Ich ess' eigentlich keine Süßigkeiten, ... a. E.g.: weil es nicht gut für meine Zähne ist.
b. Mit dem Essen pass' ich schon auf, ... b. E.g.: damit ich nicht zunehme.
c. Ich treibe natürlich viel Sport, ... c. E.g.: um fit zu bleiben.
d. Ich beschäftige mich aber auch mit meinen Hobbys, ... d. E.g.: weil es mir Spaß macht.

Can you admit something and express regret? (p. 68)

5 How would you admit and express regret that you
a. paid too much for ...? a. E.g.: Ich geb's zu, daß ich zu viel Geld für (diese Jacke) ausgegeben habe. I wieder habe ich zu viel Geld für (diese Jacke) ausgegeben.
b. judge your friends by their clothes? b. E.g.: Ich muß zugeben, daß ich meine Freunde nach ihrer Kleidung beurteile. Ich bedauere es wirklich, daß ich meine Freunde nach ihrer Kleidung beurteile.
c. dress in a ... way (schlampig)? c. E.g.: Ich geb's zu, daß ich mich schlampig anziehe. Ich bedaure, daß ich mich schlampig anziehe.

74 vierundsiebzig   KAPITEL 3   Aussehen: wichtig oder nicht?

HELPFUL PAGE REFERENCES

Page numbers tell students where to find the essential functional expressions, grammar, and vocabulary they may need to complete each task.

VOCABULARY LISTS

The **Wortschatz** page provides a comprehensive list of the words and expressions targeted in the chapter. Divided by **Stufe** and arranged in semantic fields, this vocabulary list can be used for reference, review, or study.

WORTSCHATZ

ERSTE STUFE

GIVING OPINIONS
Du hältst viel von unserer Lehrerin, oder?
You think highly of our teacher, don't you?

OTHER USEFUL WORDS AND PHRASES
s. Gedanken machen über (acc)   *to think about*
s. entspannen   *to relax*
s. ablenken (sep)   *to divert oneself*

s. beschäftigen mit   *to keep busy with*
s. schminken   *to put on makeup*
achten auf (acc)   *to pay attention to*
zunehmen (sep)   *to gain weight*
abnehmen (sep)   *to lose weight*
übertreiben   *to exaggerate*
schiefgehen (sep)   *to go wrong*
treffen (sep)   *to meet*
zusammenpassen (sep)   *to go together, match*
aufpassen (sep)   *to pay attention*
was (das) angeht   *as far as (that) goes*
heben   *to lift*

hübsch   *pretty, handsome*
mickrig   *lousy*
schlampig   *sloppy*
vollwertig   *nutritious*
regelmäßig   *regularly*
hauptsächlich   *mainly*
wirkungsvoll   *effective*

die Kleidung   *clothing*
die Laune   *mood*
die Sache, -n   *thing*
die Biokost   *organic food*
das Krafttraining   *weight lifting*

ZWEITE STUFE

EXPRESSING SYMPATHY AND RESIGNATION
Das muß ja schlimm sein!   *That must be really bad!*
Wie schrecklich!   *How terrible!*
Ich hab' eben eine Pechsträhne.   *I'm just having a streak of bad luck.*
Da kann man nichts machen.   *There's nothing you can do.*
Was kann ich schon tun?   *Well, what can I do?*
Es ist halt so.   *That's the way it is.*

GIVING ADVICE
Komm, ich geb' dir mal einen guten Rat!   *Okay, let me give you some good advice.*
Versuch doch mal, etwas zu machen!   *Why don't you try to do something?*
Du solltest mal ins Kino gehen.   *You should go to the movies.*

An deiner Stelle würde ich mehr lernen.   *If I were you, I'd study more.*
Laß dir doch die Haare schneiden!   *Why don't you get your hair cut?*

OTHER USEFUL WORDS AND PHRASES
Das sagt etwas über dich aus.   *That says something about you.*
mitmachen mit (sep)   *to go along with*
beurteilen nach   *to judge according to*
ankommen bei (sep)   *to be accepted by*
s. anpassen (sep, dat)   *to conform to*
beeinflussen   *to influence*
ausdrücken (sep)   *to express*
zugeben (sep)   *to admit*
entwickeln   *to develop*
versuchen   *to attempt, try*

vorhaben (sep)   *to plan*
aushalten (sep)   *to endure, stand something*
nähen   *to sew*
sparen   *to save money*
herumblättern (sep)   *to leaf through (a newspaper)*

der Geschmack   *taste*
das Mitleid   *pity, sympathy*
der letzte Schrei   *the latest fashion*
Kleider (pl)   *clothes*

ausgefallen   *unusual*
verrückt   *crazy*

ohne   *without*
ohne weiteres   *easily, readily*
ohne ... zu machen   *without doing ...*
um ... zu machen   *in order to do ...*
damit (conj)   *so that, in order to*

WORTSCHATZ   fünfundsiebzig   75

T59

The Teacher's Edition

The Komm mit! *Teachers' Edition is designed to help you meet the increasingly varied needs of today's students by providing an abundance of suggestions and strategies. The Teacher's Edition includes the pages of the Pupil's Edition, with annotations, plus interleaf pages before each location and chapter opener.*

Using the Location Opener Interleaf

Preceding each Location Opener is a two-page interleaf section with specific background information on each photograph. In addition, teaching suggestions help you motivate students to learn more about the history, geography, and culture of German-speaking countries.

Using the Chapter Interleaf

The Chapter Interleaf includes background information, a list of resources, additional culture notes, and suggestions on how to motivate students, present material, and adapt activities to accommodate different learning styles.

Getting Started

At the beginning of each chapter you'll find a chapter overview chart, listening scripts, a suggested project, and games.

Chapter Overview outlines the chapter in a concise chart that includes the functions, grammar, and culture presented in each **Stufe,** as well as a list of corresponding resource materials. The re-entry column lists previously presented material that is recycled in the chapter.

Textbook Listening Activities Scripts provide scripts of the recorded chapter listening activities.

Project proposes an extended activity based on the theme of the Chapter or some special feature of the chapter.

Games allow students to apply and reinforce the functions, structures, vocabulary, and culture in an informal, non-threatening atmosphere.

Teaching Cycle

For each **Stufe,** a logical instructional sequence enables you to:

motivate students by personalizing and contextualizing the topic;

teach the functions, vocabulary, structures, and culture with a variety of approaches;

close each **Stufe** with activities that combine the communicative goals;

assess students' progress with a quiz and/or performance assessment.

The teaching cycle contains the following sections:

Meeting Individual Needs

The following features suggest alternate approaches to help you address the diverse needs and abilities of students.

Visual, Auditory, Tactile, Kinesthetic Learners benefit from activities that accommodate their unique learning styles.

A Slower Pace provides ideas to break the presentation of information into smaller steps to facilitate comprehension.

Challenge includes creative, open-ended activities that encourage students to extend their reach.

Making Connections

To help students appreciate their membership in a global community, suggestions for linking German with other disciplines and cultures appear under the following categories:

Math (History, . . .) Connections relate the chapter topic to other subject areas, making German relevant to the students' experiences.

Multicultural Connection compares and contrasts the language and culture of German-speaking countries with those of other parts of the world.

Community/Family Link encourages students to seek opportunities for learning outside of the classroom by interacting with neighbors and family members.

Developing Thinking Skills

Thinking Critically helps students develop their higher-order thinking skills by drawing inferences, comparing and contrasting, analyzing, and synthesizing.

Establishing Collaborative Learning

Cooperative Learning allows students to work in small groups to attain common goals by sharing responsibilities.

Actively Involving Students

Total Physical Response techniques visually and kinesthetically reinforce structures and vocabulary.

Teaching *Zum Lesen*

Prereading, reading, and post-reading activities in **Zum Lesen** help teachers show students how to use the reading strategies and activities in the *Pupil's Edition* to improve comprehension.

Teaching *Zum Schreiben*

Prewriting, writing, and post-writing activities and teaching suggestions lead teachers through the steps in the writing activity.

Komm mit! Ancillaries

The Komm mit! *Holt German program offers a state of the art ancillary package that addresses the concerns of today's teachers. Because foreign language teachers are providing for all types of students, our ancillaries are designed to accommodate all learners. The* Komm mit! *ancillary materials are innovative, relevant to students' lives, and full of variety and fun.*

Teaching Resources with Professional Organizer

HRW has taken an innovative approach to organizing our **Teaching Resources**. The *Komm mit!* ancillaries are conveniently packaged in time-saving **Chapter Resources** books with a **Teaching Resource Organizer**. Each Chapter Resources book puts a wealth of resources at your fingertips!

Chapter Resources, Books 1-4

◆ Oral communication is the language skill that is most challenging to develop and test. The *Komm mit!* **Situation Cards** and **Communicative Activities** are designed to help students develop their speaking skills and give them opportunities to communicate in a variety of situations.

◆ **Additional Listening Activities,** in combination with the textbook audiocassette program, provide students with a unique opportunity to actively develop their listening comprehension skills in a variety of authentic contexts.

◆ The *Komm mit!* **Realia** reproduce the real documents to provide your students with additional language practice in authentic cultural contexts. Included with the **Realia** are suggestions for their use.

◆ The **Student Response Forms** are provided for your convenience. These copying masters enable you to reproduce standard answer forms for the listening activities in the textbook.

◆ The *Komm mit!* **Assessment Program** responds to your requests for a method of evaluation that is fair to all students, and that encourages students to work toward realistic, attainable goals. The **Assessment Program** includes the following components:
  ◆ Two **Quizzes** per chapter (one per **Stufe**)
  ◆ One **Chapter Test** per chapter; each **Chapter Test** includes listening, speaking, reading, writing, and culture. Part of each test can be corrected on ScanTron®.

◆ Also included in the *Chapter Resources:*
  ◆ **Teaching Transparency Masters** for use in a variety of activities
  ◆ **Listening Scripts** for the Additional Listening Activities and the Assessment Program
  ◆ **Answer Key** for the *Practice and Activity Book*

Assessment Guide

The **Assessment Guide** describes various testing and scoring methods. This guide also includes:
  ◆ **Portfolio Assessment** suggestions and evaluation rubrics
  ◆ **Speaking Tests** to be used separately or as part of the Chapter Tests
  ◆ A cumulative **Midterm Exam** (Chapters 1-6)
  ◆ A **Final Exam** that focuses on Chapters 7-12

Teaching Resource Organizer

A tri-fold binder helps you organize the ancillaries for each chapter.

KAPITEL 6

Was tut dir weh?

Komm mit! Holt German Level 2

HRW material copyrighted under notice appearing earlier in this work.

Teaching Transparencies

The **Teaching Transparencies** benefit the visual learner as well as all students. These colorful, situational transparencies add variety and focus to your classroom. The **Chapter Resources** books include suggestions to help you integrate the 24 transparencies and two full-color map transparencies into your lesson plans.

Audiocassette Program

The listening activities in the **Audiocassette Program** help students develop their listening and pronunciation skills by providing opportunities to hear native speakers of German in a variety of authentic situations and to practice the sounds of the language.

Practice and Activity Book

The **Practice and Activity Book** is filled with imaginative, challenging activities that will motivate students to learn German. In addition, there are exercises that reinforce the grammatical structures. Extension activities allow students to explore culture and language in a personally relevant context.

Test Generator

The **Test Generator** is a software program that enables you to create customized worksheets, quizzes, and tests for each chapter in *Komm mit!* The **Test Generator** is available for IBM© PC and Compatibles and Macintosh © computers.

Komm mit! Video

The Komm mit! Video Program *brings the German-speaking world right into your classroom! The high interest authentic interviews and German television commercials and video clips offer students authentic language in a natural setting and introduce topics that encourage student discussion.*

Video is the ideal medium for providing authentic input and increasing proficiency in German. With the *Komm mit! Video Program*, students both see and hear speakers of German interacting with another naturally in realistic settings. Students' comprehension of authentic speech is enhanced by the visual cues in the video. Moreover, the video is entertaining as well as educational.

Komm mit! German 3 Video Program

The Level 3 video has a different structure and serves a different purpose than the Level 1 and Level 2 videos. The on-the-street interviews that are the core of the Level 3 Video Program cover questions and issues that reflect the challenges all Germans, both in the east and the west, are facing today in the aftermath of reunification. These issues touch almost every facet of life in the unified Germany: unemployment, housing, pollution, education, confusing new choices for con-

sumers, and the pain of facing the realities and consequences of the past. The interviews serve as a springboard for student discussions in German.

In addition to the interviews, the video contains numerous television commercials, many of which are thematically tied to the chapters of the Level 3 book. These commercials are entertaining and contain visual clues that will help students understand the language used in the commercials.

Chapter 4 Sample Lesson Plan

DAILY PLANS	RESOURCES

DAY 1

OBJECTIVE: To learn about the city of Würzburg and to listen to German youth talk about relationships with parents and friends

Location Opener—Würzburg, pp. 76-79
  Background Information and teaching suggestions, pp. 75A-B
  Present video; see *Video Guide* for suggestions
Chapter Opener, discussion, pp. 80-81;
  Motivating Activity and teaching suggestions, p. 79G
Los geht's! pp. 82-83:
  Motivating Activity, p. 79H
  Verhältnis zu Eltern und Freunden: present audio recording
    and use teaching suggestions, p. 79H
  Activity 1, p. 83 (chart of students' statements); p. 79H
  Activity 3, p. 83 (completion exercise—open-ended activity);
    p. 79H
  Optional: *Practice and Activity Book* (**Los geht's!** activity)
  Assignment: Activity 2, p. 83 (student charts on relationships)

Video Program, Videocassette 1
Video Guide
Textbook Audiocassette 2B
Chapter Resources, Book 2
Practice and Activity Book

DAY 2

OBJECTIVE: To talk about conflicts and learn to express agreement

Focus: Activity 2, p. 83
Closure: **Los geht's!** p. 79H
Erste Stufe, p. 84:
  Motivating Activity, p. 79I
  Presentation: **Wortschatz** (p. 84); 79I
  Activity 8, p. 85 (partners discuss statements about relation-
    ships with parents—open-ended activity);
    p. 79I;
  Activity 5, p. 85 (listening—specific and evaluative ques-
    tions); p. 79I
  Optional: Additional Listening Activities
  Activity 6, p. 85 (partners combine clauses—cause and effect)
  Presentation: **So sagt man das!** (agreeing) p. 85
  Activity 7, p. 85 (listening—notes and role-play)
  Optional: *Practice and Activity Book*
  Assignment: Activity 4, p. 84 (written activity about
    conflicts—completion); p. 79I; Activity 9, p. 86 (written—
    word completion using graph)

Chapter Resources, Book 2
Textbook Audiocassette 2B
Additional Listening Activities,
  Audiocassette 9B
Practice and Activity Book

DAY 3

OBJECTIVE: To learn about German students' *Cliquen* and activities and to report on your own

Focus: Activities 4 and 9, pp. 84 and 86
Presentation: **Ein wenig Grammatik** (ordinal numbers)
  (p. 86); p. 79I
Presentation: **Ein wenig Landeskunde** (**Cliquen**)
  (p. 86); p. 79J
Video clip: **Im Freizeitzentrum** (see *Video Guide* for
  suggestions)
Presentation: **Grammatik** (relative clauses) (p. 87); p. 79J
Activity 11, p. 87 (relative pronouns—completion)
Optional: Communicative Activities
Optional: Situation Card
Closure: game, pp. 79F and 79K
Performance Assessment: p. 79K
Assignment: Activity 10, p. 86 (journal entry); study for quiz;
  Practice and Activity Book (optional)

Video Program, Videocassette 1
Video Guide
Chapter Resources, Book 2
Practice and Activity Book

DAILY PLANS	RESOURCES

DAY 4   **OBJECTIVE:** To listen to German youth talk about relationships with other people

Focus: Activity 10, p. 86 (share entries with class)
Quiz: 4-1
Weiter geht's! pp. 88-89:
   Motivating Activity, p. 79K
   Verhältnis zu anderen Leuten: present audio
    recording and read pp. 88-89; p. 79K
   Activities 12-13, p. 89 (true, false—correction; checking
    for understanding); p. 79K
   Closure: p. 79K
Assignment: *Practice and Activity Book* (**Weiter geht's!**
activity)

Chapter Resources, Book 2
Assessment Items
   Audiocassette 7B
Textbook Audiocassette 2B
Practice and Activity Book

DAY 5   **OBJECTIVE:** To give advice and introduce another point of view

Focus: Summarize **Weiter geht's!**; *Practice and Activity
   Book* (discuss answers to **Weiter geht's!** activity)
Zweite Stufe, p. 90:
   Motivating Activity, p. 79L
   Activity 14, p. 90 (listening—decide which students fit in
    and which don't); p. 79L
   Activity 15, p. 90 (small groups discuss prejudices);
    p. 79L
   Presentation: **So sagt man das!** (giving advice and intro-
    ducing another point of view) (p. 91); p. 79L
   Activity 16, p. 91 (listening—find out what problem is and
    if advice is followed or not); Challenge, p. 79L
   Optional: Additional Listening Activities
   Activity 17a, p. 91 (describe persons of differing view-
    points)
   Optional: *Practice and Activity Book*
Assignment: Activity 17b, p. 91 (write conversation between
two groups of people); A Slower Pace or Challenge, p. 79L

Chapter Resources, Book 2
Textbook Audiocassette 2B
Additional Listening Activities,
   Audiocassette 9B
Practice and Activity Book

DAY 6   **OBJECTIVE:** To hypothesize about relationships

Focus: Activity 17b, p. 91; A Slower Pace or Challenge,
   p. 79L; Thinking Critically, p. 79M
   Activity 18, p. 91 (partners make observations and give
    advice—directed activity)
Presentation: **So sagt man das!** (hypothesizing) (p. 92);
   p. 79M
Presentation: **Ein wenig Grammatik,** (**hätte, wäre** with
   hypothesis) (p. 92); p. 79M
   Activity 19, p. 92 (listening—what is certain and what is
    speculative—listing), p. 79M
   Activity 20, p. 92 (writing—completion); Challenge, p. 79M
   Activity 21, p. 92 (group work—open-ended); Challenge,
    p. 79M
Presentation: **Grammatik** (genitive case), (p. 93); p. 79M
   Activity 22, p. 93 (discrete practice of genitive case); Teacher
    Note, p. 79M
   Optional: Communicative Activities
Assignment: Activity 23, p. 93 (journal entry)

Chapter Resources, Book 2
Textbook Audiocassette 2B

DAILY PLANS	RESOURCES

DAY 7   **OBJECTIVE:** To compare and contrast the German school system with the American school system

Focus: Activity 23, p. 93; Focusing on outcomes, (p. 81); p. 79P
Performance Assessment: p. 79O
Optional: Situation Card
Presentation: **Landeskunde,** (discussion of the German school system) p. 94; see p. 79N for suggestions and Background Information
  Optional: *Practice and Activity Book* (**Landeskunde** activities)
Zum Schreiben, p. 95 (a letter):
  Motivating Activity, p. 79O
  Pre-writing, suggestions p. 79O
  Schreibtip (determining the purpose), p. 95
Assignment: Activity A (**Vorbereiten**—deciding on problem and purpose of letter) p. 95; study for quiz; *Practice and Activity book* (optional)

Chapter Resources, Book 2
Practice and Activity Book

DAY 8   **OBJECTIVE:** To write a letter asking for advice

Quiz 4-2
Focus: Discuss **Schreibtip** and Activity A (**Vorbereiten**), p. 95
Zum Schreiben:
  Activity B (**Ausführen**), p. 95; see p. 79O for suggestions
  Activity C1-2-3. (**Überarbeiten**—partner corrections), p. 95; see p. 79O for suggestions
Assignment: Activity C4, p. 95; see p. 79O for suggestion

Chapter Resources, Book 2
Assessment Items
  Audiocassette 7B

DAY 9   **OBJECTIVE:** To determine the main idea of the reading selection

Focus: Activity C4, p. 95; **Lesetrick,** p. 96; p. 79P
Zum Lesen: *Ein Tisch ist ein Tisch*, pp. 96-99:
  Prereading: Motivating Activity, p. 79P
  Reading: Activities 1-10, pp. 96-99; Teacher Notes and suggestion, p. 79P
  Post-reading: Activities 11-12, p. 99; Thinking Critically, p. 79Q
  Project: (several day assignment—recreate story with illustrations), see p. 79F
  Closure: p. 79Q
Review: **Wortschatz,** p. 103; p. 79R; **Anwendung,** Activities 1-6, pp. 100-101; p. 79R
Optional: Situation Card
Assignment: **Kann ich's wirklich?**, p. 102; p. 79R; study for Chapter Test

Chapter Resources, Book 2
Textbook Audiocassette 2B

DAY 10   **OBJECTIVE:** To assess progress

Focus: **Kann ich's wirklich?**, p. 102
Kapitel 4 Chapter Test
Speaking Test

Chapter Resources, Book 2
Assessment Items,
  Audiocassette 7B
Assessment Guide

Location Opener

Die neuen Bundesländer, pages 1-3
Video Program, Videocassette 1

Brandenburg

**Mecklenburg-
Vorpommern**

Sachsen

**Sachsen-
Anhalt**

Thüringen

*U*sing the Photograph, *p. 1*

Background Information

- The cathedral pictured here, **Dom St. Stephanus,** was badly damaged in 1945. Restoration began in 1946 and was completed in 1960. The **Domschatz** contains the most significant collection of its kind in Germany, including medieval garments, original writings dating back to the Carolingian period, and the **Abrahamsteppich,** a nine-meter long tapestry from 1160.

- The **Gleimhaus,** pictured next to **Dom St. Stephanus,** was named after the writer Wilhelm Ludwig Gleim (1719-1803). His home at **Domplatz 31** became an intellectual meeting place for such renowned German literaries as Klopstock, Herder, and Jacobi. In 1862 the house was made into a memorial (**Gedenkstätte**) and now contains letters, art, and an extensive library.

*U*sing the Almanac and Map, *p. 1*

Brandenburg For a description of the coat of arms of Brandenburg, refer to Level 1 (p. 11A).

Mecklenburg-Vorpommern The crowned bull's head symbolizes Mecklenburg, where this coat of arms appeared in the 13th century; the griffin represents the rulers of Pomerania.

Sachsen The coat of arms of Saxony dates back to 1261 when the **Askanier** dynasty added the diagonal row of green diamonds to the existing black and gold bars. It symbolized the Saxon and Anhalt descendants.

Sachsen-Anhalt The shield of **Sachsen-Anhalt** that was created in 1991 unites elements of **Sachsen, Prussia,** and **Anhalt** to represent the new state. It reintroduces the diagonally divided black and gold bars used in the coat of arms of **Sachsen,** with the addition of a black Prussian eagle in the upper right corner. The bear walking on top of the wall comes from the former coat of arms of **Anhalt** and dates back to the 15th century.

Thüringen The lion on this coat of arms is the traditional symbol of the landgraves of Thuringia. The stars represent the seven small principalities from which the state of Thuringia was created after World War I, plus the formerly Prussian district of Erfurt which became part of the state in 1944.

For Individual Needs

Tactile Learners Have students draw the coats of arms on large poster board and display them in the classroom.

Terms in the Almanac

- **Potsdam:** The city began to flourish in the 17th century when various dukes and kings discovered the charm of the town and the surrounding areas and established their residences soon after. **Schloß Sanssouci,** the most famous residence, was built as a summer residence for **Friedrich der Große.** For more information, see Level 1: Brandenburg Location Opener, *Teacher's Edition,* pp. 11A-B, *Pupil's Edition,* pp. 12-15 and the Culture Note on p. 63I of the *Teacher's Edition.*

- **Theodor Fontane** (1819-1898): Writer famous for his *Wanderungen durch die Mark Brandenburg,* which he wrote between 1862 and 1889 and for the novel *Effi Briest* published in 1895.

- **Schwerin:** This city's history can be traced back as far as the eighth or ninth century. Schwerin was officially founded in 1160 by Duke Henry the Lion and later became home to the Dukes of Mecklenburg.

- **Dresden:** This city was introduced to students in Level 2 (p. 61). For more information, see Level 3, *Teacher's Edition,* pp. 227A-B and *Pupil's Edition,* pp. 228-231.

- **Meißen:** This town's history dates back to 929 when King Henry I built the castle Misni on the **Burgberg.** Meißen is also home to Europe's oldest porcelain factory, known for its famous **Meißner Porzellan.**

- **Magdeburg:** Located on the River Elbe, Magdeburg has a history dating back a thousand years. The name Magdeburg first appeared in official records in 805. Magdeburg was badly damaged during the Thirty Years' War and almost destroyed during World War II. It was rebuilt after 1945 under the communist regime.

- **Wittenberg:** Also referred to as **Lutherstadt Wittenberg,** this city became famous after Martin Luther posted his "95 Theses" on the door of the castle church.

- **Erfurt:** First mention of this city dates back to 729. As early as the 9th century, under **Karl der Große** (*Charlemagne*), Erfurt flourished as a trading center. Its first university was founded in 1379 and closed in 1816; Martin Luther taught there from 1501 to 1505. Today this state capital has a population of 220,000.

Using the Map

Have students identify the country or countries that share borders with Mecklenburg-Vorpommern (**Polen**), Brandenburg (**Polen**), and Sachsen (**Polen** and **Tschechische Republik**). You may also want to use Map Transparency 1.

*I*nterpreting the Photo Essay, *pp. 2-3*

② The Wartburg was built in 1067 by **Ludwig der Springer** and later became the seat of the Thuringian landgraves. (See Level 1, *Teacher's Edition,* p. T66 for further information.)

③ Johann Sebastian Bach, one of the greatest composers of all times, wrote more than two hundred church cantatas, including the **Weihnachtsoratorium** and the **Johannes- und Matthäuspassion,** as well as many secular works such as the six **Brandenburger Konzerte** and four **Orchesterzüge.**

④ Some of the first demonstrations leading to the fall of the Berlin Wall were held in Leipzig. Banners with slogans such as **Wir sind das Volk. Wir sind ein Volk!, Mauer ins Museum!,** and **Nie wieder selbsternannte Diktatur!** were some early public signs of dissatisfaction that ultimately led to the downfall of the communist regime.

⑤ Aside from being an important cultural city, Weimar has also played a significant role in history. In 1919, the German National Assembly met in Weimar to adopt a new constitution for the short-lived Weimar Republic.

⑥ The **Dom St. Maria** in Güstrow was built in several stages beginning in the early 13th century and continuing until the late 15th century. The interior reflects the changing styles of art from the two centuries during which it was built. Have students identify some gothic features in the architecture of the cathedral.

⑥ Born in Wedel, Ernst Barlach (1870-1938) was an expressionistic sculptor and writer whose works were simple yet revealed great depth. At the Ernst Barlach Memorial in Güstrow, located in the house the artist built in 1930, visitors can view over 100 sculptures, drawings, and several of his original manuscripts.

LOCATION OPENER

KAPITEL 1, 2, 3

Komm mit in die
neuen Bundesländer!

	Brandenburg	Mecklenburg-Vorpommern	Sachsen	Sachsen-Anhalt	Thüringen
Einwohner	2,6 Mio.	1,95 Mio.	4,9 Mio.	3,0 Mio.	2,6 Mio.
Fläche (qkm)	29 000	23 800	18 300	20 400	16 250
Hauptstadt	Potsdam	Schwerin	Dresden	Magdeburg	Erfurt
Sehenswerte Städte	Brandenburg Chorin	Stralsund Rostock	Meißen	Halberstadt Halle Wittenberg	Weimar Eisenach
Berühmte Leute	Fontane Kleist	Barlach Otto Lilienthal C.D. Friedrich	Lessing Karl May Schumann	Klopstock Luther Händel Nietzsche	Bach

Foto ① Der Dom St. Stephanus in Halberstadt, eine dreischiffige, gotische Basilika, 1235 begonnen und 1491 eingeweiht; rechts das Gleimhaus

Jahrelang war es fast unmöglich, die deutschen Kulturstätten in der ehemaligen DDR zu besuchen: sie lagen hinter Stacheldraht in einem anderen Land, dessen Grenze nur wenige überschreiten konnten. Seit Mitte November 1989, seit dem Fall der Mauer, ist es wieder möglich, die Schätze deutscher Kultur zu besuchen, zu bewundern. Leider wurde manches im Krieg zerstört, manches blieb erhalten und manches wurde auch restauriert. Das meiste aber ist in Zerfall geraten, und es wird einige Jahre dauern, bis diese Stätten wieder in alter Pracht erglänzen.

② Die Wartburg in Eisenach spiegelt 800 Jahre deutscher Kultur wider. Hier soll im Mittelalter der legendäre Sängerwettstreit stattgefunden haben, dem Richard Wagner im „Tannhäuser" ein musikalisches Denkmal gesetzt hat. In den Jahren 1521/22 hat hier Martin Luther als Junker Jörg das Neue Testament übersetzt und damit den Grundstein zur deutschen Schriftsprache gelegt.

③ Das Bachhaus in Eisenach, in dem einer der größten deutschen Komponisten, Johann Sebastian Bach, 1685 geboren wurde, ist heute ein Museum.

④ Die berühmte Stadt Leipzig, einst Zentrum des deutschen Buchhandels, war und ist eine deutsche Musikstadt: das Gewandhausorchester, der Thomaschor und die Hochschule für Musik sind hier zu Hause. In der berühmten Thomaskirche war J.S. Bach von 1723 bis zu seinem Tod 1750 Kantor der Kirche. Hier schrieb Bach die meisten seiner Werke. Seit 1950 ist die Thomaskirche auch Bachs Ruhestätte.

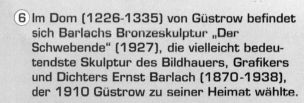

⑤ Weimar ist als „Stadt der deutschen Klassik" weltweit bekannt. Luther, Cranach und Bach wirkten hier. Im 18. Jahrhundert begann mit den großen deutschen Dichtern Wieland, Goethe, Herder und Schiller die bedeutendste Epoche Weimars. Im Stadtschloß befindet sich eine ständige Kunstausstellung, insbesondere die Cranach-Galerie mit 28 Bildern von Lucas Cranach d. Ä., sowie Gemälde von Dürer, Veronese, Tiepolo, Tintoretto, u.a.

⑥ Im Dom (1226-1335) von Güstrow befindet sich Barlachs Bronzeskulptur „Der Schwebende" (1927), die vielleicht bedeutendste Skulptur des Bildhauers, Grafikers und Dichters Ernst Barlach (1870-1938), der 1910 Güstrow zu seiner Heimat wählte.

Kapitel 1: Das Land am Meer *Wiederholungskapitel*

	REVIEW OF FUNCTIONS	REVIEW OF GRAMMAR	CULTURE
Los geht's! pp. 6-7	Zwei Freunde treffen sich, *p. 6*		
Erste Stufe pp. 8-12	•Reporting past events, *p. 9* •Asking how someone liked something; expressing enthusiasm or disappointment; responding enthusiastically or sympathetically, *p. 12*	•Prepositions followed by dative case forms, *p. 9* •Past tense, *p. 10* •Dative case forms, *p. 12*	Insel Rügen, *p. 8*
Zum Schreiben p. 13	Was ich in den Ferien gemacht habe. Writing Strategy: Brainstorming and freewriting		
Weiter geht's! pp. 14-15	Gregor besucht Johannes, *p. 14*		
Zweite Stufe pp. 16-21	•Asking and telling what you may or may not do, *p. 17* •Asking for information, *p. 18* •Inquiring about someone's health and responding; asking about and expressing pain, *p. 20* •Expressing hope, *p. 20*	•Forms of **dieser** and **welcher**, *p. 18* •Reflexive pronouns, *p. 20*	•Fit ohne Fleisch, *p. 16* •Landeskunde: Währungen und Geld wechseln, *p. 22*
Zum Lesen pp. 24-25	Moderne Literatur Reading Strategy: Using time lines for comprehension		
Review pp. 26-27	•Kann ich's wirklich? *p. 26* •Wortschatz, *p. 27*		

Assessment Options	**Stufe Quizzes**
	 •*Chapter Resources,* Book 1
	   Erste Stufe, Quiz 1-1
	   Zweite Stufe, Quiz 1-2
	 •*Assessment Items, Audiocassette* 7 A
			Kapitel 1 Chapter Test
			 •*Chapter Resources,* Book 1
			 •*Assessment Guide,* Speaking Test
			 •*Assessment Items,* Audiocassette 7 A
			
			 Test Generator, Kapitel 1

Chapter Overview

RESOURCES Print	RESOURCES Audiovisual
Practice and Activity Book	*Textbook Audiocassette* 1 A
Practice and Activity Book *Chapter Resources*, Book 1 •Communicative Activity 1-1 •Communicative Activity 1-2 •Additional Listening Activity 1-1 •Additional Listening Activity 1-2 •Additional Listening Activity 1-3 •Student Response Forms •Realia 1-1 •Situation Card 1-1 •Teaching Transparency Master 1-1 •Quiz 1-1	*Textbook Audiocassette* 1 A *Additional Listening Activities, Audiocassette* 9 A *Additional Listening Activities, Audiocassette* 9 A *Additional Listening Activities, Audiocassette* 9 A *Teaching Transparency* 1-1 *Assessment Items, Audiocassette* 7 A
Practice and Activity Book	*Textbook Audiocassette* 1 A
Practice and Activity Book *Chapter Resources*, Book 1 •Communicative Activity 1-3 •Communicative Activity 1-4 •Additional Listening Activity 1-4 •Additional Listening Activity 1-5 •Additional Listening Activity 1-6 •Student Response Forms •Realia 1-2 •Situation Card 1-2 •Teaching Transparency Master 1-2 •Quiz 1-2 *Video Guide*	*Textbook Audiocassette* 1 A *Additional Listening Activities, Audiocassette* 9 A *Additional Listening Activities, Audiocassette* 9 A *Additional Listening Activities, Audiocassette* 9 A *Teaching Transparency* 1-2 *Assessment Items, Audiocassette* 7 A *Video Program*, Videocassette 1
	Textbook Audiocassette 11
Chapter Resources, Book 1 •Realia 1-3 •Situation Card 1-3 *Video Guide*	*Video Program*, Videocassette 1

Alternative Assessment
•Performance Assessment
Teacher's Edition
  Erste Stufe, p. 3K
  Zweite Stufe, p. 3O

•Portfolio Assessment
  Written: **Zweite Stufe**, Activity 28, *Pupil's Edition*, p. 21;
  Assessment Guide, p. 14
  Oral: **Erste Stufe**, Activity 6, *Pupil's Edition*, p. 9;
  Assessment Guide, p. 14
•**Notizbuch**, *Pupil's Edition*, p. 12

Kapitel 1: Das Land am Meer
Textbook Listening Activities Scripts

For Student Response Forms, see *Chapter Resources,* Book 1, pp. 22-25.

Erste Stufe
Activity 5, *p. 9*

RÜDIGER Hallo, Heike! Na, bist du endlich aus dem Urlaub zurück?

HEIKE Hallo, Rüdiger! Hallo, Antje! Ja, wir sind gestern abend erst zurückgekommen, meine Eltern und ich. War echt toll. Wir waren fast drei Wochen lang weg. Wir sind schon in der ersten Augustwoche abgereist.

ANTJE Wo habt ihr denn dieses Jahr Urlaub gemacht?

HEIKE Dieses Jahr haben wir was ganz Neues ausprobiert. Wir waren auf Sylt, du weißt schon, an der Nordsee. Meine Mutter wollte schon immer mal auf diese Insel fahren, und dieses Jahr hat sie meinen Vater tatsächlich dazu überredet. Mir hat es dort wahnsinnig gut gefallen.

RÜDIGER Na, da hast du ja Glück gehabt. Wir waren auch in Urlaub, aber schon letzten Monat. Leider waren wir nur eine Woche lang weg. Wir sind nach Österreich in die Berge gefahren. War echt langweilig dort. Sogar meine Eltern waren von diesem Urlaub enttäuscht.

HEIKE Und warum seid ihr denn in die Berge gefahren, wenn es dir dort nicht gefallen hat?

RÜDIGER Na ja, das war so. Meine Großeltern sind dieses Jahr mitgefahren, und sie wollten auf jeden Fall in die Berge. Es hat aber fast jeden Tag geregnet, und wir haben die meiste Zeit im Hotel rumgesessen. Einfach scheußlich, sage ich euch.

ANTJE Und fahrt ihr nächstes Jahr wieder in die Berge oder nicht?

RÜDIGER Hoffentlich nicht! Ich möchte auch mal nach Amerika. Mensch du, Florida oder Kalifornien, da möchte ich gern mal hin.

HEIKE Und du, Antje? Seid ihr dieses Jahr in Urlaub gefahren?

ANTJE Nein, diesmal waren wir nicht weg. Aber letztes Jahr waren wir auf Ibiza. Das war echt toll dort. Ich war mit meiner Schwester dort, weil sie unbedingt ihre Spanischkenntnisse ausprobieren wollte. Bestimmt fahre ich nächstes Jahr wieder mit ihr in die Ferien.

Answers to Activity 5

Heike: erste Augustwoche; Sylt; Mutter wollte schon immer dorthin

Rüdiger: letzten Monat; Österreich; Großeltern wollten in die Berge

Antje: letztes Jahr; Ibiza; Schwester wollte Spanischkenntnisse ausprobieren

Activity 10, *p. 10*

VOLKER Hallo, Britta, wie geht's? Du siehst heute aber fesch aus!

BRITTA Danke! Ich war vorhin beim Friseur, weil ich mir die Haare schneiden lassen wollte. Danach bin ich noch schnell beim Juwelier Werner vorbeigegangen, weil ich ein neues Armband und eine Batterie für meine Uhr brauchte. Meine Uhr funktioniert jetzt wieder, nur leider gab es kein Armband, das mir gefallen hat. Aber dafür habe ich mir diese Ohrringe hier gekauft. Schau mal! Toll, nicht? Und was hast du heute in der Stadt zu erledigen, Volker?

VOLKER Ach, ich habe gerade ein paar Flaschen zum Getränkemarkt zurückgebracht, und dann war ich noch im Obstladen. Meine Mutter macht heute nachmittag nämlich Obstkuchen, und sie braucht halt Erdbeeren dazu. Jetzt war ich gerade im Reisebüro, weil mein Freund Uli da arbeitet und ich ihn fragen wollte, ob er heute abend ins Kino gehen will. Was hast du denn da in der Tasche?

BRITTA Ach, ich war heute morgen in der Bücherei. Ich habe mir mehrere Bücher über Amerika ausgeliehen, weil wir diesen Sommer in Urlaub dorthin fahren wollen. Du, schau mal, da ist der Thomas! He, Thomas!

THOMAS Hallo, Britta! Hallo, Volker! Puh, habt ihr heute auch so viel zu erledigen wie ich?

VOLKER Wieso, was mußt du denn heute alles machen?

THOMAS Na ja, ich hab' halt heute ein volles Programm! Das meiste hab' ich aber schon erledigt. Also zuerst war ich beim Lambert und habe die Fotos von unserem Urlaub in der Türkei abgeholt. Dann bin ich beim Musikladen vorbeigegangen und habe mir die neue CD von Sting und zwei Kassetten gekauft. Jetzt komme ich gerade aus der Bank. Ich mußte noch das restliche Geld von unserem Urlaub wechseln.

BRITTA Also, da hast du heute schon eine ganze Menge zu tun gehabt.

THOMAS Ach übrigens, ich will gleich ins Schwimmbad gehen. Wollt ihr mitkommen?

BRITTA Nein, danke. Diese Bücher hier sind echt schwer und ich muß nach Hause, um meinen Eltern im Garten zu helfen.

THOMAS Und du, Volker? Kommst du mit?

VOLKER Ja, gerne. Also, tschüs dann, Britta!

BRITTA Tschüs ihr zwei!

Answers to Activity 10

Britta: Friseur / hat sich die Haare schneiden lassen; Juwelier / hat Batterie für Uhr und Ohrringe gekauft; Bücherei / hat Bücher ausgeliehen

Volker: Getränkemarkt / hat Flaschen zurückgebracht; Obstladen / hat Erdbeeren gekauft; Reisebüro / hat Freund gefragt, ob er mit ins Kino will

Thomas: Fotogeschäft / Urlaubsfotos abgeholt; Musikladen / CD und Kassetten gekauft; Bank / Geld umgetauscht

Activity 14, p. 12

ULI Hallo, Sabine! Endlich treffen wir uns ja mal wieder!

SABINE Ach, hallo, Uli! Ja, seit du nicht mehr im Schwimmverein bist, sieht man dich ja kaum noch! Ach, übrigens, ich war gestern zum ersten Mal in dem neuen Freibad in Kreuzing.

ULI Wie war's denn? Ich habe gehört, das Freibad soll echt toll sein.

SABINE Also, mir hat es dort echt super gefallen, weil es ganz modern und funkelnagelneu ist. Ich war mit dem Tobias und der Valerie da. Wir sind den ganzen Vormittag geschwommen und haben uns so richtig schön fit gefühlt. Mittags haben wir dann im Stadtpark ein tolles Picknick gemacht. Es hat mir echt gut gefallen, weil ich gerne draußen an der frischen Luft bin.

ULI Also, ich gehe nächstes Wochenende auch mal ins neue Freibad. Du hast auf jeden Fall mehr Spaß gehabt als ich gestern.

SABINE Wieso? Was hast du denn gestern gemacht?

ULI Na ja, wir sind gestern gleich nach dem Frühstück in die Stadt gefahren. Im Deutschen Museum gab es eine neue Ausstellung, die mein Vater unbedingt sehen wollte.

SABINE Und, wie hat dir die Ausstellung gefallen?

ULI Sie war fürchterlich langweilig. Es war eine Sammlung von alten römischen Münzen und diese Ausstellung hat mich überhaupt nicht interessiert.

SABINE Das ist aber schade! Ich finde solche Sachen eigentlich sehr interessant.

ULI Ich aber nicht. Wir waren drei Stunden lang im Museum. Und dann am Nachmittag mußte ich zu Hause bleiben, um für eine Mathearbeit zu lernen. War ebenfalls langweilig, weil ich die meisten Aufgaben gar nicht verstanden habe. Aber am Abend war ich dann mit Heiko im Kino. Wir haben uns einen Thriller mit Steven Seagal angeschaut.

SABINE Und, wie hat dir der Film gefallen?

ULI War echt toll! Spannende Thriller sind meine Lieblingsfilme.

SABINE Ja, ich glaube ich gehe mir den Film nächstes Wochenende anschauen.

MANUELA Bernd, da bist du ja! Wir haben gestern versucht, dich anzurufen, aber du warst nicht zu Hause. Wo hast du denn nur gesteckt?

BERND Ach, hallo Manuela! Du, der Jörg und ich, wir haben gestern eine Fahrradtour nach Ising gemacht. Stell dir mal vor, wir haben über sechzig Kilometer zurückgelegt! Wir sind schon ganz früh morgens losgefahren. Es war echt super!

MANUELA Ach, ich wußte gar nicht, daß du so sportlich bist! Machst du gerne solche langen Radtouren?

BERND Und wie! Ich mache Sport überhaupt sehr gerne, aber radeln ist mir immer noch am liebsten. Wir sind übrigens bei der Stefanie vorbeigefahren und haben sie besucht. Sie wohnt doch jetzt in Ising.

MANUELA Wirklich? Und, hat sie sich über euren Besuch gefreut?

BERND Ja, ich glaub' schon. Es war echt nett, weil wir uns schon länger nicht gesehen haben. Ach übrigens, sie läßt dir schöne Grüße ausrichten. Wieso habt ihr denn eigentlich gestern versucht, mich anzurufen?

MANUELA Der Thomas und ich wollten dich zum Volleyball spielen auf dem Sportplatz einladen. Ich spiele doch so gerne Volleyball. Das hat echt Spaß gemacht. Nachher haben wir dann bei mir zu Hause das Fußballspiel angeschaut.

BERND Und, wie hat es euch gefallen? Muß doch echt aufregend gewesen sein.

MANUELA Nein, im Gegenteil! Es ist null zu null ausgegangen. Mir hat es eigentlich nicht so gut gefallen. Es war ein ziemlich langweiliges Spiel.

BERND Schade! Aber da habe ich ja nicht viel verpaßt. Na, vielleicht können wir uns ja heute abend treffen und Volleyball spielen!

MANUELA Ja, gerne! Ich ruf' nachher mal den Thomas an und sag' ihm, er soll noch ein paar Leute mitbringen.

BERND Super! Bis heute abend dann!

MANUELA Tschüs!

Answers to Activity 14

Sabine: im Freibad / ist geschwommen / ihr hat es gut gefallen / weil das Freibad modern und neu ist; im Stadtpark / hat Picknick gemacht / ihr hat es gut gefallen / weil sie gern draußen an der frischen Luft ist

Uli: in der Stadt / hat ein Museum besucht / es hat ihm nicht gefallen / weil er sich nicht für die Ausstellung interessiert; zu Hause / hat für eine Mathearbeit gelernt / es hat ihm nicht gefallen / weil er die Aufgaben nicht verstanden hat; im Kino / hat sich einen Thriller angeschaut / es hat ihm gut gefallen / weil spannende Thriller seine Lieblingsfilme sind

Bernd: in Ising / hat eine Fahrradtour gemacht / es hat ihm gut gefallen / weil er gern Sport macht und am liebsten radelt; in Ising / hat Stefanie besucht / es hat ihm gut gefallen / weil sie sich schon länger nicht gesehen haben

Manuela: auf dem Sportplatz / hat Volleyball gespielt / es hat ihr gut gefallen / weil sie gern Volleyball spielt; zu Hause / hat sich das Fußballspiel angeschaut / es hat ihr nicht gefallen / weil es ein langweiliges Spiel war

Zweite Stufe
Activity 21, p. 17

JULIA He, Franziska! Willst du heute abend mitkommen? Wir gehen ins argentinische Steakhaus. Die haben diese leckeren Rippchen da! Ich kann's kaum abwarten! Ich freu' mich schon auf diese leckere gemischte Fleischplatte für mehrere Personen.

FRANZISKA Ach, ich weiß nicht so recht, Julia! Mir schmeckt argentinisches Essen echt gut, aber ich esse überhaupt kein Fleisch mehr.

JULIA Wie, du ißt kein Fleisch mehr? Wieso denn nicht? Fleisch schmeckt doch fabelhaft!

FRANZISKA Also, ich habe vor einigen Monaten beschlossen, nur noch vegetarisch zu essen. Ich finde, das ist viel gesünder. Und außerdem fühle ich mich auch schon viel fitter, seit ich kein Fleisch mehr esse! Ich esse jetzt am liebsten Nudeln oder Reis mit viel Gemüse. Rosenkohl und Spargel mag ich besonders gern.

JULIA Ich bin gegen Spargel allergisch. Den darf ich nicht essen. Außerdem mag ich Gemüse überhaupt nicht gern. Aber dafür schmeckt mir Obst ganz gut, besonders Wassermelone. Aber am liebsten esse ich Fleisch und Wurst. Einmal in der Woche gibt es bei uns Innereien und ab und zu sogar mal Reh. Leber mag ich übrigens wahnsinnig gern.

FRANZISKA Igitt! Also, Leber, nein danke! Du, schau mal, da drüben ist der Mehmet. Der geht sicher gerne mit ins argentinische Restaurant.

JULIA Ja bestimmt! Komm, fragen wir ihn doch! He, Mehmet! Willst du heute abend mit uns essen gehen? Ich versuche gerade, Franziska dazu zu überreden, mitzukommen.

MEHMET Ja, ich komme gerne mit! Hauptsache, wir gehen irgendwohin, wo es nicht nur Schweinefleisch gibt. Das darf ich nämlich nicht essen.

JULIA Wieso denn nicht? Bist du etwa allergisch dagegen?

MEHMET Nein, das ist es nicht. Ich esse kein Schweinefleisch, weil ich Moslem bin.

SCRIPTS

JULIA   Ach ja, das hatte ich ganz vergessen! Na, kommt schon, ihr zwei. Ich bin sicher daß es im argentinischen Steakhaus etwas gibt, was ihr beide essen dürft. Wie wär's mit einem Salat oder einer Gemüseplatte?

MEHMET   Also, Salat mag ich eigentlich nicht so gerne, aber hoffentlich gibt es dort auch Lammfleisch mit grünen Bohnen. Das mag ich gerne.

FRANZISKA   Also gut! Dann treffen wir uns heute abend dort. So gegen sieben?

JULIA   Super! Tschüs!

MEHMET   Bis heute abend!

Answers to Activity 21

Franziska: mag argentinisches Essen, Nudeln, Reis, Gemüse (Rosenkohl, Spargel); mag kein Fleisch und keine Leber; ißt nur vegetarisch.

Julia: mag Wurst, Fleisch (Rippchen, Innereien, Leber, Reh) und Obst (Wassermelone); mag kein Gemüse; darf keinen Spargel essen; sie ist allergisch gegen Spargel.

Mehmet: mag Lamm und grüne Bohnen; mag keinen Salat; darf kein Schweinefleisch essen; er ist Moslem.

Activity 24, *p. 19*

MARKUS   Du, Jens, was hast du da auf deinem Pausenbrot?

JENS   Ach, das ist Quark mit Schnittlauch. Das esse ich am liebsten auf meinem Brot. Manchmal habe ich auch Tomaten und ein Blatt Salat drauf.

MARKUS   Na, also so was schmeckt mir nicht besonders gut. Quark esse ich zwar auch gern, aber nicht auf 'ner Scheibe Brot, sondern nur als Nachspeise mit Früchten. Ich habe lieber eine gute Portion Wurst oder Käse auf meinem Pausenbrot. Salami ist am besten, aber Schinken schmeckt auch nicht schlecht.

JENS   Nee, Markus! Sowas schmeckt mir eigentlich nicht so gut. Sag mal, Antje, was ißt du denn am liebsten auf deinem Pausenbrot?

ANTJE   Also, heute habe ich Erdnußbutter auf meinem Brot, aber sonst esse ich auch gerne Quark oder Naturjoghurt auf meinem Brot. Ab und zu schmeckt mir Leberwurst auch ganz gut. Und du Heike, was ißt du denn immer auf deinem Pausenbrot?

HEIKE   Mir ist Abwechslung am wichtigsten. Ich mag nicht immer nur das gleiche auf meinem Pausenbrot essen. Also, ich mag am liebsten Käse und Radieschen auf meinem Brot oder aber auch Leberwurst oder gekochten Schinken mit etwas Senf. Und ich esse außerdem auch gerne Honig auf meinem Pausenbrot.

Answers to Activity 24

Markus ißt viel Fleisch und Wurst; Jens ißt vegetarisch; Markus, Antje und Heike essen sowohl Tierprodukte als auch Pflanzenprodukte.

Activity 26, *p. 20*

ANNABELLA   He, Jungs! Darf ich euch für die Schülerzeitung interviewen? Also, das war ja diesmal wieder ein tolles Sportfest! Herzlichen Glückwunsch zu eurem Sieg! Das Fußballspiel war wirklich spitzenmäßig! Aber mir scheint, daß ihr eine ganze Menge Verletzungen davongetragen habt! Fangen wir mal mit dir an, Jürgen! Was hast du dir alles verletzt?

JÜRGEN   Ja, also, als ich auf dem nassen Gras ausgerutscht bin, habe ich mir meinen rechten Arm und auch mein linkes Knie verletzt. Aber es tut eigentlich nicht so sehr weh. Am wichtigsten ist für mich, daß wir das Spiel gewonnen haben. Aber leider habe ich noch ein bißchen Kopfschmerzen und sogar eine Beule am Kopf.

ANNABELLA   Ja, aber dafür hast du doch das phänomenale Tor mit diesem Kopfball geschossen! Alle Achtung! Und Markus, wie sieht's bei dir aus mit den Verletzungen?

MARKUS   Tja, ich glaube, daß ich heute ziemlich viel Glück hatte. Meine Verletzung hält sich in Grenzen. Als ich mit dem Uli zusammengestoßen bin, habe ich mir nur ganz leicht die Stirn verletzt, sonst nichts. Aber ich glaube, den Uli hat's schlimmer erwischt!

ANNABELLA   Dann fragen wir doch direkt mal den Uli! Uli, was ist dir beim Zusammenprall mit dem Markus passiert?

ULI   Also, wie du sehen kannst, habe ich ein Pflaster auf der Nase. Sofort nach dem Zusammenprall hat sie angefangen, fürchterlich zu bluten. Zuerst habe ich gedacht, sie ist gebrochen, aber zum Glück ist sie nur blau und grün. Sie tut aber doch ganz schön weh.

ANNABELLA   Das tut mir wirklich leid für dich! Kim, was hast du dir denn verletzt?

KIM   Ja, also mich hat es am linken Ellbogen erwischt. Er ist ein bißchen verstaucht. Aber sonst geht es mir gut.

ANNABELLA   Ja, also ich glaube, daß alle eure Fans sich freuen, daß ihr trotz den Verletzungen so gute Laune habt. Vielen Dank für das Interview. Ihr seid ein tolles Team.

Answers to Activity 26

Jürgen ist Nummer 7; Markus ist Nummer 1; Uli ist Nummer 3; Kim ist Nummer 2.

Kapitel 1: Das Land am Meer
Projects and Games

PROJECT

*Students will compose a letter to a company in a German-speaking country as if they were applying for a summer internship. Begin this project after students have worked through the **Zum Schreiben** section and are comfortable with the writing elements taught there. This project is intended to review vocabulary and grammatical structures from Level 2 and incorporate the writing skills introduced in **Zum Schreiben**.*

Materials Students will need paper, pens, and a small photograph of themselves.

Suggested Sequence

1. Students brainstorm as to what kind of information they could include in their letter. For what internship are they applying? Why? When would they like to begin? Why should they get the position? What information about themselves would help them be selected?
2. Students organize their notes and make an outline of their letter.
3. Students write their first draft and share it with classmates for peer input. At this point, you may also want to check students' drafts and make suggestions if necessary.
4. Students evaluate what they wrote, make changes as necessary, and rewrite the letter, attaching a small photo of themselves to the final copy.

Grading the Project

Suggested point distribution (total = 100 points)
Content   50
Organization 25
Accuracy   25

GAME

Das ist ja die Frage!

This game will help students review questions and vocabulary in a variety of categories.

Preparation Make a game grid on the board or on a transparency. The grid should have six columns, each labeled with a category, and five boxes below it containing the point values 100, 200, 300, 400, and 500. The example game grid shown below can be used for this chapter or modified for others. The words in parentheses should not be written on the grid that students see, rather they are given as potential answers.

Rügen		Tierprodukte		Körperteile		Pflanzenprodukte		Währungen		Hauptstädte	
(Badeort)	100	(Schweine-fleisch)	100	(die Ferse)	100	(Zwiebeln)	100	(D-Mark)	100	(Potsdam)	100
(Hansestadt)	200	(Leber)	200	(die Zehe)	200	(Mais)	200	(Schilling)	200	(Dresden)	200
(Caspar David Friedrich)	300	(Speck)	300	(das Handgelenk)	300	(Spargel)	300	(Franken)	300	(Erfurt)	300
(Rügendamm)	400	(Hasenfleisch)	400	(die Wade)	400	(Paprika)	400	(Lira)	400	(Magdeburg)	400
(926 km²)	500	(Rippchen)	500	(die Kniescheibe)	500	(Rosenkohl)	500	(Krone)	500	(Schwerin)	500

Procedure Divide the class into two or three teams. After deciding the order of play, have one player from the first team choose a category and a numerical value. Then, make a statement appropriate to the category. For example, if a student chooses the category **Hauptstädte** for 100 points, you might say **"Diese Stadt ist die Hauptstadt von Brandenburg."** The player must then respond in question form, **"Was ist Potsdam?"** If the player responds correctly, the answer is written in the box and the team receives the appropriate number of points. If the player responds incorrectly or is unable to respond accurately in question form, a player from the other team has the opportunity to answer the same question for the same number of points. You might want to have one student keep score and write the answers in the boxes, and another student act as an impartial judge in cases where an answer is close, pronounced incorrectly, or not given in appropriate question form. For example, **"Wer ist Potsdam?"** would not be an acceptable response.

PROJECTS AND GAMES

Kapitel 1: Das Land am Meer
Lesson Plans, pages 4-27

Teacher Notes

- Chapter 1 is a review chapter that reintroduces functions, grammar, and vocabulary from *Komm mit!* Levels 1 and 2.

- Before you begin the chapter, you may want to preview the *Video Program* and consult the *Video Guide*. Suggestions for integrating the video into each chapter are given in the *Video Guide* and in the chapter interleaf. Activity masters for video selections can be found in the *Video Guide*.

Using the Chapter Opener,
pp. 4-5

Motivating Activity

Ask students about a place or places they visited during the summer. Write the places on the board. Then ask the class what a visitor or tourist might find to do at some of the places listed. (**Was könnten Besucher oder Touristen in ... unternehmen?**) Once students have made a few suggestions about one of the locations, ask the student who visited that particular place what he or she did there.

Language Note

① **Radeln** is a term commonly used in southern Germany and is equivalent to the verb **radfahren**.

Teaching Suggestions

① Ask students if they have ever gone on an extended bike tour. When, with whom, and where did they go? (**Wer von euch hat schon mal eine längere Radtour unternommen? Wann war das, mit wem seid ihr gefahren, und wohin ging es?**)

② Ask students what they believe are some of the most common bike injuries that occur. (**Was, glaubt ihr, sind die häufigsten Verletzungen, die beim Fahrradfahren passieren können?**)

Thinking Critically

③ **Drawing Inferences** Have students locate Rügen on a map and brainstorm types of activities, scenery, weather, and food specialties a visitor could expect to find there based on what they can infer about the location.

Teaching Suggestion

To reacquaint students with one another as well as to introduce new students, have them ask a partner the following questions:
1. **Was hast du in den Ferien gemacht?**
2. **Ist etwas Interessantes oder Besonderes passiert?**
3. **Was hat dir im Sommer am besten gefallen?**
4. **Was war weniger schön?**
After students have asked each other these questions, have them summarize the information they got from their partner. Then call on several students to tell about their partners' summer activities.

Building on Previous Skills

In Levels 1 and 2 (Brandenburg and Berlin Location Openers), as well as the Location Opener on pp. 1-3, students were introduced to a number of historic areas and sights in the new **Bundesländer**. Can students recall some of those places?

Focusing on Outcomes

Have students preview the learning outcomes listed on p. 5. Then ask them to think of some questions they could use to ask a new student about his or her summer. How could they express enthusiasm or disappointment in response to the other student's account of his or her summer vacation? Examples:
Wirklich? Wie ist das denn passiert?
Kannst du mir mehr darüber erzählen?
Das tut mir aber leid. Schade, daß das nicht geklappt hat.
NOTE: These outcomes are modeled in **Los geht's!** (pp. 6-7) and **Weiter geht's!** (pp. 14-15) and evaluated in **Kann ich's wirklich?** (p. 26).

Teaching Los geht's!

pp. 6-7

Resources for Los geht's!

- *Textbook Audiocassette* 1 A
- *Practice and Activity Book*

Teacher Note

Los geht's! is recorded on audiocassette.

Los geht's! Summary

In **Zwei Freunde treffen sich**, Johannes and Gregor meet for the first time after their summer vacation. The following student outcomes listed on p. 5 are modeled in the conversation: reporting past events, asking how someone liked something, expressing enthusiasm or disappointment, and responding enthusiastically or sympathetically.

Motivating Activity

Ask students to discuss the chores and errands that must be taken care of when the family returns home after a vacation. (**Was müßt ihr alles zu Hause machen, wenn ihr aus den Ferien zurückkommt?**)

Teaching Suggestion

Have students read along as they listen to the audio recording of **Zwei Freunde treffen sich** at least two times. Ask students to make note of any words or expressions they don't know. Afterwards, they can use the context and other clues to help each other define or explain unfamiliar words and phrases.

Language Note

Johannes mentions the word **Hallenbad** *(indoor pool)*. You may want to explain the difference between these four types of pools.

das Hallenbad *indoor pool*
das Freibad *large outdoor pool*
der Swimmingpool *smaller private outdoor pool*
das Wellenbad *wave pool*

 Culture Note

On p. 7, Gregor mentions his grandmother's frugality (**Sie ist immer sehr sparsam**). His grandmother most likely grew up during World War II when staples were often scarce or rationed. This required people to develop thrifty habits that have remained with many of them ever since.

Thinking Critically

Comparing and Contrasting Ask students if they can think of a time period in U.S. history that required similar habits. (Example: the Great Depression beginning in 1929)

 For Individual Needs

1 A Slower Pace Ask students to work with a partner as they answer the eight questions in writing. As students refer back to the text, ask them to make note of where in the text they find each answer and what led them to the answer. When students have completed the activity, call on eight different students to share their answers with the rest of the class.

Building on Previous Skills

3 Before doing this activity, ask students what conjunctions they should use to introduce the clause that gives the reason. (**weil** or **denn**) Remind students of the differing word order when using **denn** and **weil**. Help students also with the prepositions and prepositional phrases they will need for expressing location for the places listed.

Closure

Ask pairs of students to come up with a scenario depicting what could happen next. Give students five minutes to write down some notes and a rough summary of what they predict as a continuation of the conversation between the two friends. (**Wie stellt ihr euch eine Fortsetzung dieser Unterhaltung vor? Macht euch einige Stichwörter, und schreibt eine kurze Zusammenfassung darüber.**)

LOS GEHT'S!

*T*eaching Erste Stufe,
pp. 8-12

► **page 8**

MOTIVATE
Teaching Suggestion
Ask students what kind of information is typically included in travel and guide books. Using their own city or town as an example, what information can students come up with that could or should be given to visitors in a short description? List ideas on a transparency or on the chalkboard.

TEACH
Teacher Notes
- Here is some additional vocabulary you may want to introduce prior to reading the text with the class.
  trutzig: mächtig, stark
  künden: von etwas berichten
  Hiddensee-Goldschmuck: *a prehistoric goldfind near the island of Rügen*
  die Mole: *pier*
  die Schlucht: *ravine, gorge*

- You may want to review reading strategies from Level 2, such as analyzing different types of texts, using grammatical and lexical clues to derive meaning, and predicting the context of a text to help students read this article about Rügen. Another reading strategy that will be helpful is finding the main clause before reading the many subordinate clauses used for describing places in this piece.

⬧ For Individual Needs
Visual Learners Ask students to read the text quietly to themselves while you prepare two columns on a transparency or on the board like the ones below.

Was wissen wir über ...?	
Stralsund	Saßnitz

Now ask students to scan the text again, extracting facts and information that will help them complete the chart. List their answers under the appropriate heading.

► **page 9**

PRESENTATION: So sagt man das!
Have students scan the **Los geht's!** conversation on pages 6-7 to identify the various verbs that are used to report past events. Then ask them to separate the verb forms into the following categories: conversational past formed with **haben**, conversational past formed with **sein**, and narrative past.

PRESENTATION: Ein wenig Grammatik
The three prepositions **an, auf,** and **in** indicate location and are therefore used with the dative case. Ask students when these same prepositions must be used with the accusative case. (when indicating direction) Ask students to come up with sample sentences using these prepositions with the accusative case.

🗀 Portfolio Assessment
6 You might want to suggest this activity as an oral portfolio item for your students. See *Assessment Guide,* p. 14.

▶ *page 10*

Total Physical Response

8 Review the vocabulary for chores by asking for help around the classroom.
Examples:
Paula, räum bitte den Tisch ab!
Ross, stell bitte das Geschirr in die Geschirr-spülmaschine!
Olivia, trockne bitte die Gläser ab!
Felix, saug im Wohnzimmer Staub!

PRESENTATION: Wortschatz

• Use props to present the new vocabulary. For example, you could use foreign money to pantomime the exchanging of money, use a phone and bring an old bill for the next expressions, and so on. Tell students what you did at the different places. Then ask: **Wo war ich, und was habe ich da gemacht?**

• Using the brief descriptions given in the **Wortschatz** as a starting point, ask students to tell what they did last time they were at the six places mentioned.
Example:
Ich war auf der Post. Dort habe ich Briefmarken gekauft und einen Brief nach Österreich geschickt.
Next have students ask each other: **Wo warst du denn?** and give their own answers.

Teaching Suggestions

10 Preview the map of **Dingskirchen** with students before they listen to the audiocassette. Make sure they are familiar with all the places in town.

10 When students report back on the activities of Britta, Volker, and Thomas, encourage them to tell you several things in sequence using appropriate sequencing words.

10 You may want to use the script for this activity (p. 3C) to prepare a **Lückentext**. For example, you could leave out all of the place names for students to fill in as they listen to the conversation.

▶ *page 11*

◆ For Individual Needs

11 Challenge If you would like students to go beyond listing the things that one can do, ask them to incorporate their ideas into an ad-like skit. One student is the store owner who tries to interview the other student for a part-time position and is telling him or her about all the jobs that are involved. The owner gets interrupted several times by the third student, who plays the role of a customer asking for service.

▶ *page 12*

PRESENTATION: So sagt man das!

After reviewing the expressions in the function box, have students respond to a number of questions and statements.
Examples:
Im Sommer habe ich mir das linke Bein gebrochen.
Wie hat euch das Konzert von ... gefallen?
Mike, wie war dein Fußballcamp diesen Sommer?
Ich war am ... beim ...spiel. Mir hat es gut gefallen.

Teaching Suggestion

14 Since the exchanges between Sabine and Uli and Bernd and Manuela are quite long, it might be best to play one scene at a time and repeat it if necessary. Check after each set of exchanges how much students understood and entered in the different columns.

For Additional Practice

15 After students have made their lists and reported to the class about their activities around **Dingskirchen**, ask students to each write a postcard to one of their relatives or friends as they take a break at a nearby **Konditorei**. Students can use their notes from part b of this activity to help them with the postcard.

ERSTE STUFE

Teacher Note

16 In Levels 1 and 2, **Für mein Notizbuch** pages were provided for the students in the *Practice and Activity Book*. Since students are expected to do more extensive writing in Level 3, you may want to ask them to keep a folder or a spiral notebook in which to write their **Notizbuch** entries.

PRESENTATION: Ein wenig Grammatik

After you have reviewed the list of verbs in the Grammar Summary, help students organize the different types of verbs used with the dative case into the following categories to help them remember them. Some of the verbs could fall into more than one category.
a) verbs that involve physical discomfort or comfort (Example: **mir tut der Kopf weh**)
b) verbs whose objects refer to people (Examples: **gefallen, glauben, gehören**)
c) verbs that express personal opinion and are used with the impersonal **es** (Examples: **es schmeckt mir gut, es tut mir leid**)
Students may want to keep this list in their notebooks and add to it as they learn about similar words.

CLOSE

Teaching Suggestion

Put the following topic on the board and ask students to discuss it: **Warum ich keine Postkarten aus den Ferien geschickt habe.** Have students write down their ideas, and then call on students to find out how they responded to the question. Ask them to give reasons for their opinion. (**Begründe deine Aussage.**)

Focusing on Outcomes

Refer students back to the learning outcomes listed on p. 5. They should recognize that they now know how to report past events, ask how someone liked something, express enthusiasm or disappointment, and respond enthusiastically or sympathetically.

ASSESS

- **Performance Assessment** Ask students to list at least five things they had to do to get ready for their last vacation. Remind them to use sequencing words such as **zuerst, dann, danach,** and **zum Schluß.** (**Was hattest du alles zu tun, um dich auf deinen letzten Urlaub vorzubereiten? Nenne mindestens fünf Sachen, die du machen mußtest.**)

- Quiz 1-1, *Chapter Resources,* Book 1

Teaching Zum Schreiben, p. 13

Teacher Notes

- There will be a **Zum Schreiben** exercise in each chapter of Level 3. These activities are intended to encourage students to use previously learned vocabulary and grammatical structures to create a cohesive composition.

- Encourage the process aspect of the **Zum Schreiben** activities by making sure students always do the entire writing assignment. Students need to work through all the steps of the assignments to become better writers. Some assignments may have to be started in class and completed as homework.

- You might want to consider selecting a few samples of students' final products from each of these major writing tasks with which to compile a class publication at the end of the term.

- You may want to use the portfolio evaluation forms *(Evaluating Written Activities, Forms A and B)* found in the *Assessment Guide* to help you evaluate students' final products.

- Remember to consider the **Zum Schreiben** activities as you and your students determine what they will include in their portfolios.

Writing Strategy

The targeted strategy in this writing activity is brainstorming and freewriting. Students should learn about this strategy before beginning the assignment.

PREWRITING

Motivating Activity

Ask students if they document their holidays and vacations. If so, how do they do it? Does the family buy postcards or souvenirs, take pictures, or make videos? Does anybody keep a travel journal to record the daily activities?

For Individual Needs

A Visual Learners Tell students to bring pictures, souvenirs, postcards, or maps from recent trips that will provide them with ideas for this activity.

A1 Auditory Learners Allow students to record their ideas on audiocassette. When students are finished, have them play back their ideas and transcribe them.

Teaching Suggestion

A3 After students have collected their ideas, remind them to think about the order in which they plan to present them. Organizing events in chronological order is one way students should already be familiar with. Review sequencing words if necessary.

WRITING

Teaching Suggestion

Turn students' desks to face away from each other so they can concentrate as they write. You may want to play Mozart or other classical music while they are writing.

POST-WRITING

Cooperative Learning

C After students have finished Activity C1, ask them to sit together with two other classmates. Students in each group exchange papers and proceed with Activities C2 and C3 as a cooperative learning activity. Peer evaluation should focus on content and organization as well as spelling and grammar. Peers should point out strengths and weaknesses and make specific suggestions to help the writer improve his or her text.

Closure

You may want to have students put their journal entries in a folder or a notebook which will become their writing journal for the term. This journal can be used for completing prewriting activities throughout the school year, and students may want to keep final versions of their writing in it as well.

*T*eaching Weiter geht's!
pp. 14-15

> **Resources for Weiter geht's!**
>
> - *Textbook Audiocassette* 1 A
> - *Practice and Activity Book*

Teacher Note

Weiter geht's! is recorded on audiocassette.

Weiter geht's! Summary

In **Gregor besucht Johannes**, Gregor stops by to visit Johannes and his family. The following student outcomes listed on p. 5 are modeled in the scene: asking and telling what you may and may not do, asking for information, inquiring about someone's health and responding, asking about and expressing pain, and expressing hope.

Motivating Activity

Ask students about their most recent visit to a friend's home. When did they go, whom did they visit, and why? What were some of the things they did? What did they eat? (**Berichte der Klasse über deinen letzten Besuch bei einem Freund oder einer Freundin. Wann war das und bei wem? Warum warst du da, und was habt ihr so gemacht? Was hast du gegessen?**)

17 Challenge Have students use the answers to the nine questions to help them write a summary of **Gregor besucht Johannes**. (**Benutzt die Antworten zu den neun Fragen, um eine Zusammenfassung von dem Inhalt dieser Unterhaltung zu schreiben!**) Tell students not to get lost in detail but to concentrate on the main points and major information.

Closure

Ask students what type of questions Johannes' parents might ask Gregor when he shares his **Rügen-Prospekte** with them. (**Könnt ihr an einige Fragen denken, die Johannes' Eltern dem Gregor stellen könnten, wenn er ihnen seine Rügen-Prospekte zeigt?**)

Teaching Zweite Stufe, pp. 16-21

Resources for Zweite Stufe

Practice and Activity Book
Chapter Resources, Book 1
- Communicative Activities 1-3, 1-4
- Additional Listening Activities 1-4, 1-5, 1-6
- Student Response Forms
- Realia 1-2
- Situation Card 1-2
- Teaching Transparency Master 1-2
- Quiz 1-2

Audiocassette program
- *Textbook Audiocassette* 1 A
- *Additional Listening Activities, Audiocassette* 9 A
- *Assessment Items, Audiocassette* 7 A

Video Program, Vidocassette 1
Video Guide

▶ **page 16**

MOTIVATE

Teaching Suggestion

Ask students if they or people they know follow a vegetarian diet. If so, why? Discuss the pros and cons of vegetarianism. (**Bist du Vegetarier? Kennst du Leute, die Vegetarier sind? Warum bist du/sind diese Leute Vegetarier? Was sind die Vorteile und die Nachteile?**)

TEACH

Thinking Critically

20 Drawing Inferences Ask students to scan the reading to identify what type of text it is. Then ask students if they generally read the Letters to the Editor section of magazines or newspapers. Can students think of the function that this section provides? (It is a forum for readers to voice their opinions.) (**Liest du gewöhnlich die Leserbriefe in Zeitschriften oder Zeitungen? Wozu dient dieser Teil einer Zeitung?**)

▶ *page 17*

PRESENTATION: Wortschatz

- Before introducing the new vocabulary, ask students to think of foods they already know that are either **Tierprodukte** or **Pflanzenprodukte** and make a list of them.
- To introduce the new vocabulary, use either food props or a transparency you have prepared ahead of time.
- To practice this and previously learned vocabulary, ask students to describe a dish that includes one of the featured products. (**In welchen Gerichten eßt ihr diese aufgelisteten Produkte? Könnt ihr diese Gerichte ein wenig beschreiben?**)

Teaching Suggestion

21 Stop the tape at logical points and check students' understanding of key information. When students are finished, have them report back on their findings. Then ask for a summary of the eating habits of each of the three students.

PRESENTATION: So sagt man das!

After reviewing the content of this function box, ask students for the meaning of the German modal verb **dürfen.** (expresses the idea of permission: *may, to be allowed to,* and *can* as in *What can't you eat? Can you eat everything?*)

▶ *page 18*

For Individual Needs

22 Visual Learners Once students have completed this partner activity, gather and record the information about students' eating and drinking habits. Make a simple chart to display the information on a transparency or on the board. Ask students to examine the information in the chart. Then ask them to analyze the data and give a brief summary of the class' eating habits. (**Schaut euch die Informationen an der Tafel näher an. Was sagen sie über die Eßgewohnheiten dieser Klasse aus?**)

PRESENTATION: So sagt man das!

After the initial presentation and review of phrases in this function box through question and answer practice, use visuals of foods—those in the textbook and others from magazines—to bring variety into asking and responding.

For Individual Needs

23 Kinesthetic Learners Ask students to follow the same directions but to role-play a conversation that takes place in the cafeteria line. You may provide some props such as trays and utensils. Students take turns performing their scenes in front of the class.

PRESENTATION: Wortschatz

- Prior to introducing the vocabulary, make a list of the items and bring them to class. Arrange them on a table and ask students to gather around as you introduce the foods and prepare a sandwich.
- Ask a couple of volunteers to take over and describe what they are doing as they each prepare a sandwich.

▶ *page 19*

For Additional Practice

24 Have students take notes while they listen to the four German students describe their **Pausenbrot.** Have them make a simple chart in their notebook with the following headings: 1) **wer** 2) **was für Pausenbrote.** Under 2) have students list all varieties of sandwiches that are mentioned by each speaker.

ZWEITE STUFE

PRESENTATION: Wortschatz

- Introduce the first four statements and phrases and provide immediate practice by asking students to take the roles of the people pictured and to respond accordingly when you ask: **Was ist passiert? Hast du dich verletzt?** Then ask students if they have ever suffered from any of these injuries and when, where, and how it happened. (**Ist euch so etwas Ähnliches schon mal passiert? Wann, wo und wie ist das passiert?**)
- To introduce the eight parts of the body, point them out on yourself. You may want to include other previously learned body parts by having students point to the place where it hurts as they answer your questions. (Examples: **Was tut dir weh, das Handgelenk? Was hast du dir verletzt, die Schulter? Hast du dich in den Daumen geschnitten?**)

📼 Video Program

In the video clip **Junge Sportler,** students from Dresden tell how their training program in sports has changed since the unification of Germany. See *Video Guide* for suggestions.

▶ page 20

PRESENTATION: So sagt man das!

To review these expressions, ask students to come up with questions a physician might ask a patient who is not feeling well. Make a list of the questions students suggest and then ask them to come up with possible answers for each of the physician's questions.

PRESENTATION: So sagt man das!

- Using the four pictures in the top row of the **Wortschatz** box on p. 19, have individual students tell what happened to them and have another student express hope that something isn't broken or that he or she will soon feel better.
- Ask students to react to you in a caring way when you tell them what happened to you. Students thus get practice with the polite form **Ich hoffe, daß Ihnen ...** or **Hoffentlich haben Sie sich nicht ....**

▶ page 21

📁 Portfolio Assessment

28 You might want to suggest this activity as a written portfolio item for your students. See *Assessment Guide,* p. 14.

▶ pages 22-23

PRESENTATION: Landeskunde

Teaching Suggestion

You might want to point out to students that the word **Franc** is pronounced the French way in German: [frã]. They use the nasal "an" and don't pronounce the "c."

Math Connection

B Ask students to imagine they are each preparing for a trip to five European countries of their choice. For their convenience, they will want to exchange $100 for each country's currency before the trip. Tell students to provide a table with the most recent exchange rates, locate the equivalent value of each of the five currencies they need to exchange, and show the total amount of each foreign currency that equals $100.

CLOSE

♖ Game

Play the game **Der besetzte Stuhl.** Choose one student to start the game. Seat him or her on a chair in front of the class (**der besetzte Stuhl**). The student must answer questions asked by his or her classmates. When the student on **der besetzte Stuhl** has answered three questions correctly, he or she may choose another student to sit in **der besetzte Stuhl.** While asking questions, students should use the function and vocabulary boxes as a point of departure, but questions can be related to any part of this **Stufe.**
Examples:
Nenne mindestens zwei Tierprodukte, die du neu gelernt hast!
Was ist Rote Grütze?
Wie kann man sich in der Küche verletzen?

Focusing on Outcomes

Refer students back to the learning outcomes listed on p. 5. Students should recognize that they now know how to ask and tell what they may or may not do, ask for information, inquire about someone's health and respond, ask about and express pain, and express hope.

ASSESS

• **Performance Assessment** Have students imagine they are planning to take a vegetarian German-speaking exchange student to a new restaurant in town. Ask each student to prepare at least five questions he or she plans to ask about the menu when calling to make a reservation. Perform the conversation with individual students while the rest of the class prepares quietly.

• Quiz 1-2, *Chapter Resources,* Book 1

*T*eaching Zum Lesen, *pp. 24-25*

Teacher Note

Eine alltägliche Verwirrung is recorded on *Textbook Audiocassette* 11.

Reading Strategy

The targeted strategy in this reading is using time lines for comprehension. Students should learn about this strategy before beginning Question 2.

PREREADING

Motivating Activity

Ask students to think about the concept of time. Time, as measured by our watches, is something that we usually think of as "objective"—that is, a kind of universal truth, quite independent of human thought. Do students ever think about how arbitrary our division of time into days, hours, minutes, and seconds truly is? Are five minutes spent talking to a good friend really the same as five minutes spent sleeping or five minutes spent waiting for a bus? Have they ever had the experience of dreaming about a seemingly endless event or series of events, only to wake up and find that only a few minutes have passed and that it's still a long way until morning?

Background Information

Many readers of Kafka have remarked on the "irrational and dreamlike quality" of his prose. Although we tend to think of him as a unique writer, the notion that dreams are a key to the understanding of the individual (or at least his or her repressed emotions) and of the collective unconscious was quite current among European intellectuals of Kafka's time. What is perhaps most unique about Kafka is that he presents such experiences in a very "unemotional" style, pretending to report them more or less objectively, rather than commenting on the intensity of feeling that underlies his writing. The words "repressed emotion" may come to mind when reading his short stories and novels.

Teacher Note

Activity 1 is a prereading activity.

READING

Teaching Suggestion

The first indirect quote in the text is short and is introduced by the verb **sagen** (... **sagt man ihm, daß B, ... gegangen sei ...**). Students should be able to at least skim over it without losing the thread of the narrative. However, the second, long indirect quote may cause them to entirely misread that part of the narrative. Tell students that everything between "**Zu Hause erfährt er**" and "**... noch oben in A's Zimmer**" is reported speech—from persons unknown. The forms **sei, habe,** and **befinde sich** in these three sentences come from the special pattern used in German to indicate indirect quotations, or reported speech. Another way to write this would have been: **Zu Hause erfährt er, daß B doch schon gleich früh gekommen ist ...** Kafka, however, chose to use the more formal, impersonal style of quotation.

Thinking Critically

2 Analyzing If students have trouble getting started on the "Why?" portion of this question, you might ask where else they could find this kind of representation of individuals. Are **A**, **B**, and **H** similar to the X, Y, and Z in math? Or to the John/Jane Doe in judicial warrants for unknown persons? Why did Kafka not choose the letters M, R, and W, for instance? How are these names different from the fictional ones used in reports with the disclaimer "Only the names have been changed to protect the innocent"?

Teaching Suggestion

3 You may want to draw students' attention to the indefinite **man** as the "other character or characters" in the story in addition to **A** and **B**. There are actually two settings in the story, the town or village of **H,** and **A**'s village and home. Also, students should note the discrepancy between **zehn Minuten** and **zehn Stunden**—this is crucial. Why, for example, did Kafka not make it ten minutes and *three* hours?

Teacher Note

4 The idea of "confusion" should be at the center of the summary statements.

8 Analyzing Students will need to take into consideration the concept of "human error" as opposed to some kind of cause outside the characters' control. Is **A**'s disorientation internally or externally caused? A key question is: what causes **A**'s incomprehensible behavior to **B** in the second paragraph? Does **A** later remember this episode? How do we know it happened? Why does Kafka use indirect quotes from an unidentified source? What is **A** planning to explain to **B** as he runs up the stairs?

Teaching Suggestion

9 You may want to point out to students that a **Nacherzählung** is a little different from an abstract or summary—more like a concise abridgement—but not more than half as long as the original.

Teacher Note

The **Selbstporträt** shown on p. 24 is that of Karl Schmidt-Rottluff who co-founded the group of expressionists in Dresden in 1905 called **Die Brücke.** The group was dissolved by 1913, and World War I halted most group activity.

Thinking Critically

Evaluating Kafka's story is not an "objective" report—for example, a police report or the kinds of facts that the emergency ambulance attendants might string together if called to assist **A** after his accident. The human portrait in the text is also quite obviously not the same as a photograph. But are they "subjective" in the same ways? To get students started on this discussion, ask them to think about some other portraits and some other short stories that everyone in the class is familiar with. (Examples: Mona Lisa, some of Picasso's paintings, one of Poe's "strange" stories, some contemporary science fiction or fantasy literature)

POST-READING

Teacher Note

Activity 10 is a post-reading task that will show whether students can apply what they have learned.

Closure

- As students look at the story again, ask them to draw a picture of **A**, **B**, or **H**. Ask them who the unnamed individuals are who tell **A** about **B**'s actions and reactions.

- Ask students to think about how they would make a short film of this story. How would they depict the characters? What film devices would they use to handle the time elements? Students should discuss their ideas with the class, using everyone's knowledge of the various film techniques currently available.

Answers to Activity 1

A common confusion, an ordinary occurrence

Answers to Activity 2

A and B designate the main characters, and H represents a town or a city; answers will vary, possible answer: the letters stress how generic or common the situation is.

Answers to Activity 3

A and B (two male adults); unnamed town where A resides and H. A goes to see B in H to do business. The next morning he makes the same journey, but arrives too late to speak with B. A hurries back home, but arrives too late because it took him ten hours to get to H.

Answers to Activity 4

A is doing business with B, but arrives too late to speak with him in H. He hurries home to catch B at his office, but falls as he runs up his stairs. B does not see him and leaves A's office.

Answers to Activity 5

Time lines will vary. The important thing students should notice is that time is distorted in the story, however they choose to depict it.

Answers to Activity 6

wichtig: the business deal; **ermüdet:** A; **ärgerlich:** B; **in Angst:** A; **eilig:** A; **unverständlich:** A's behavior; **glücklich:** A; **ohnmächtig:** A; **unfähig:** A; **winselnd:** A; **undeutlich:** B's distance from A; **wütend:** B

Answers to Activity 7

Schnelligkeit: *speed;* **Nebenumstände:** *minor circumstances;* **Ausbleiben:** *absence;* **Augenblick:** *moment*

Answers to Activity 8

A arrives too late to meet B; it takes him ten hours to get to H, instead of ten minutes; B is angry about A not showing up in H and (in the doorway at A's room) for being told by A that he has no time to talk; B first goes to A's town to see him, and then, after meeting him in the doorway, he decides to wait upstairs in A's room for A to return; the conflict is not resolved. When B decides to leave A's house and not wait for A, B does not see A lying on the stairs and never finds out what happened. The business deal is left unresolved.

Kann ich's wirklich?
p. 26

This page helps students prepare for the test. It is a brief checklist of the major points covered in the chapter. The students should be reminded that it is only a checklist and not necessarily everything that will appear on the test.

Using Wortschatz,
p. 27

♜ Game

Play the game **Ich glaub' dir nicht!** to review the vocabulary from this chapter. Divide the class into two teams. Students from one team must call out a word or phrase from the **Wortschatz** which must be used in a sentence by a member of the opposing team. The sentence must clearly illustrate the meaning of the word in order for the team to receive a point. For example, "**Ich habe einen Ausweis.**" would not count. An acceptable sentence for **Ausweis** might be "**Ich brauche einen Ausweis, um ins Ausland zu reisen.**" If a student does not know the meaning of a word, he or she can try to bluff the other team by making up a sentence. The other team can call the bluff by saying "**Ich glaub' dir nicht!**" If they are right, and the player does not know the word, the opposing team receives two points. On the other hand, if they are wrong, and if the player did know the word, the opposing team loses a point.

❖ For Individual Needs

Visual Learners Provide students with an illustration of a body with lines pointing to body parts you wish to review. Ask students to label the body parts.

Building On Previous Skills

Tell students to imagine they are having eight friends over after school and need to offer them something to eat. Ask pairs of students to come up with a menu using only vocabulary from the **Wortschatz**.

📼 Video Program

At this time, you might want to use the authentic advertising footage from German television. See *Video Guide* for suggestions.

Teacher Note

Give the **Kapitel 1** Chapter Test, *Chapter Resources, Book 1.*

1
Das Land am Meer

① Du, wir sind die Ostseeküste entlang geradelt. Prima war's!

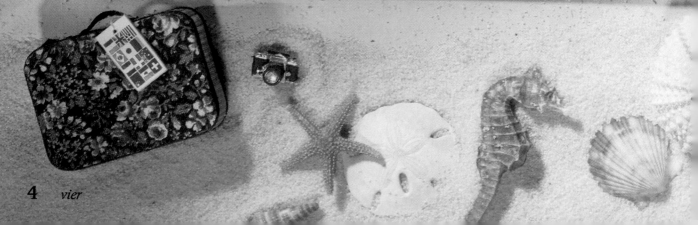

Wenn Schulfreunde sich nach den Sommerferien treffen, gibt es immer viel zu erzählen. Wo warst du und wie war's? Was hast du dort gemacht? Was ist alles passiert?

In this chapter you will review and practice

- reporting past events; asking how someone liked something; expressing enthusiasm or disappointment; responding enthusiastically or sympathetically
- asking and telling what you may or may not do; asking for information; inquiring about someone's health and responding; asking about and expressing pain; expressing hope

And you will

- listen to students talk about where they spent their vacations and what they did
- read about vacation spots in the new states of Germany that are once again accessible to everyone
- write about where you were during summer vacation and what you did
- find out about historic areas in the new states of Germany

② Mir tut immer noch der Knöchel weh.

③ Wie hat dir denn die Insel Rügen gefallen?

Los geht's!

 Zwei Freunde treffen sich

JOHANNES Hallo, Gregor!

GREGOR Hallo, Hannes! Schon lange nicht gesehen!

JOHANNES Stimmt! Ich find's toll, daß du auch mal wieder im Lande bist!

GREGOR Tja, du freust dich, daß ich wieder da bin, und ich find's schade.

JOHANNES Wirklich? Hat es dir auf Rügen so gut gefallen?

GREGOR Es war einsame Spitze! Wirklich Superferien!

JOHANNES Na, das freut mich.

GREGOR Was machst du denn jetzt? Du siehst so nach Arbeit aus.

JOHANNES Ich war gerade im Getränkemarkt, hab' Flaschen zurückgebracht. Bei uns ist heute großer Aufräumetag. Alle sind am Arbeiten. Ich hab' heute schon die Garage aufgeräumt, den Müll sortiert und weggebracht — ja, ich muß arbeiten, und du gehst spazieren.

GREGOR Du, bei uns ist Waschtag — wir müssen die ganze Ferienwäsche waschen. Ich war eben in der Bücherei und hab' unsere Ferienlektüre zurückgebracht. Und vorher war ich einkaufen. Übrigens, im Supermarkt hab' ich die Ulla getroffen. Sie war in Kalifornien; hat ihr echt prima gefallen. Sag, wie war's denn in den Bergen?

JOHANNES Nicht besonders! Da hat's dauernd geregnet. Wir sind kaum gewandert, und ich habe die meiste Zeit im Hallenbad verbracht. Na ja. Was kann man machen?

GREGOR Du, ich muß weiter. Ich muß vor zwölf noch was erledigen. Ich muß auf der Bank Geld wechseln für meine Oma. Sie war in Italien und hat die meisten Lire wieder zurückgebracht. Das kann auch nur die Oma! Sie ist immer sehr sparsam.

JOHANNES Meine aber auch! Ja, also ... du, komm doch mal rüber zu uns! Meine Eltern waren noch nie an der Ostsee, und sie würden sich bestimmt für Rügen interessieren. Bring deine Fotos mit!

GREGOR Mach' ich. Ich bring' auch ein paar Prospekte mit, da können sie sich schon mal etwas aussuchen.

JOHANNES Okay! Also, tschüs!

GREGOR Tschüs!

1 Was passiert hier?

1. auf der Straße
2. weil Gregor lange weg war

3. auf Rügen / mit seiner Familie; super
4. in den Bergen / es hat geregnet; sind kaum gewandert; war meistens im Hallenbad

Hast du das Gespräch verstanden? Dann beantworte die Fragen! 5. Gregor muß noch zur Bank.

1. Wo, glaubst du, treffen sich Johannes und Holger?
6. Sie war in Italien und hat die meisten Lire wieder zurückgebracht; weil er die Lire auf der Bank umtauschen muß
2. Warum findet es Johannes toll, daß Gregor wieder da ist?
3. Wo war Gregor? Mit wem war er weg, und wie hat es ihm gefallen? 7. weil Johannes' Eltern sich für Rügen interessieren würden
4. Wo war Johannes? Was erzählt er über seine Ferien?
5. Warum können die beiden Jungen nicht länger miteinander sprechen?
6. Was erzählt Gregor über seine Oma, und warum erzählt er das überhaupt?
7. Warum soll Gregor Johannes besuchen und Prospekte mitbringen?
8. Was haben die beiden Jungen heute schon alles getan?

8. Johannes: Flaschen in den Getränkemarkt zurückgebracht; Garage aufgeräumt; Müll sortiert und weggebracht / Gregor: Wäsche gewaschen; Ferienlektüre in die Bücherei zurückgebracht; war einkaufen

2 Genauer lesen For answers, see underlined words in text on page 6.

Read the text again, then answer these questions.

1. Which phrases express liking something or not?
2. Which ones express enthusiasm and disappointment?

a. Rügen: hat Ferien gemacht; Bücherei: hat Ferienlektüre zurückgebracht; Supermarkt: war einkaufen   b. in den Bergen: hat Ferien gemacht; Hallenbad: weil es meistens geregnet hat; Getränkemarkt: hat Flaschen zurückgebracht

3 Wer war wo?

Sag, wo jede von diesen vier Personen war und warum!

a. Gregor
b. Johannes
c. Ulla c. Kalifornien: hat Ferien gemacht
d. Gregors Oma
d. Italien: hat Urlaub gemacht

Italien   Rügen

Getränkemarkt

Berge   Hallenbad

Bücherei

Kalifornien   Supermarkt

Reporting past events; asking how someone liked something; expressing enthusiasm or disappointment; responding enthusiastically or sympathetically

RÜGEN

Die über 750 Jahre alte HANSESTADT STRALSUND liegt, vom Festland kommend, am Anfang und am Ende jeder Rügen-Reise. Der Rügendamm und viele geschichtliche Ereignisse verbinden die 926 km² große Insel mit dem Festland. Eine trutzige Stadtmauer, die prächtigen Giebel jahrhundertealter Kaufmannshäuser, hochhinaufragende Kirchen, das prunkvolle Rathaus am Alten Markt und schöne Klosteranlagen in mittelalterlicher Backsteingotik künden vom einstigen Reichtum der Stadt am Strelasund. Ein Bummel durch die alten Gassen, vorbei an bunten Geschäften der Fußgängerzone, Besuche des Kulturhistorischen Museums, wo der berühmte Hiddensee-Goldschmuck aufbewahrt wird und des Meeresmuseums mit Aquarien sind unvergeßliche Erlebnisse für jung und alt.

SASSNITZ, einst Badeort, später Stadt der Rügenfischer und Fährhafen nach Skandinavien, liegt am Tor zum Nationalpark Jasmund. Entlang der Mole im Fischerhafen riecht's nach Meer, Teer und Fisch. Saßnitz ist Ausgangspunkt für die romantische Tour auf den Spuren Caspar David Friedrichs[1], vorbei an den Wissower Klinken, den Tälern und Schluchten des Stubnitzwaldes bis zum 107m hohen Königsstuhl, dem magischen Anziehungspunkt aller Rügen-Besucher. Jedoch, wer das Auto benutzt, vermag den wahren Reiz dieser Landschaft nur zu ahnen.

Königsstuhl

Stralsunder Rathaus

4 Von Stralsund nach Saßnitz

Lies diesen Bericht über Rügen, und beantworte die Fragen!

1. Wo liegt Rügen, und wie kommt man auf diese Insel? 1. in der Ostsee / über den Rügendamm

2. Wie zeigt sich, daß Stralsund im Mittelalter sehr reich war? 2. hat trutzige Stadtmauer, Kaufmannshäuser mit prächtigen Giebeln, prunkvolles Rathaus, schöne gotische Klosteranlagen

3. Was kann man in Stralsund alles sehen? 3. see answer no. 2, alte Gassen, bunte Geschäfte, Kulturhistorisches Museum, Hiddensee-Goldschmuck, Meeresmuseum

4. Was für ein Ort ist Saßnitz? 4. früherer Badeort, Stadt der Rügenfischer, Fährhafen nach Skandinavien

5. Wofür ist Saßnitz bekannt? 5. Wissower Klinken, Stubnitzwald, Königsstuhl

1. Caspar David Friedrich wurde 1774 in Greifswald geboren und starb 1840 in Dresden. Er ist der bekannteste Meister der protestantischen-norddeutschen Landschaftsmalerei der Romantik.

SO SAGT MAN DAS!

Schon bekannt

Reporting past events

When asking someone about something in the past, you might ask:

Sag mal, was hast du denn am Sonntag gemacht?

And the response might be:

Du, ich bin mit meiner Fahrradclique in den Bergen gewesen. Wir waren auf dem Wallberg. Dort sind wir gewandert, und ich hab' viel fotografiert. Ach ja, am Abend waren wir noch im Kino.

Schon bekannt
Ein wenig *G*rammatik

You know sentences such as:

Gregors Familie war an der Ostsee.
Sie waren auf der Insel Rügen.
Johannes war mit den Eltern in den Bergen.
Aber die meiste Zeit war er im Hallenbad.

Point out the prepositions in these sentences. Which case form follows them? What do these phrases express? For more on this point see the Grammar Summary.

WORTSCHATZ

letzte Woche	**gerade** *just*	
letztes Wochenende	**vor kurzem**	
letzten Monat	*recently*	
letztes Jahr	**neulich** *the other day*	

What do the different endings of **letzt**- indicate? Which case are these time expressions in?[1] You may also use **dies**- and **nächst**- in the same way.

---

5 Hör gut zu! For answers, see listening script on TE Interleaf.

Schüler erzählen, wann sie Ferien gemacht haben und wo sie waren. Sie sagen auch, warum sie dort Ferien gemacht haben. Schreib ihre Aussagen auf unter den Rubriken (*columns*): Wann? Wo? und Warum?!

6 Wo warst du in den Ferien?

a. Schreib mehrere Ferienorte, die du schon kennst oder von denen du schon gehört hast, auf eine Liste! Dann stell eine kleine Ferienreise zusammen!
b. Such dir jetzt eine Partnerin! Erzähl ihr, wo du in den letzten Ferien überall warst! Gebrauch dabei die Adverbien: zuerst, dann, danach und zuletzt! Tauscht dann die Rollen aus!

7 Wo übernachtet und eßt ihr gewöhnlich?

a. Schreib auf, wo du gewöhnlich übernachtest und ißt, wenn du mit deinen Eltern unterwegs bist!
b. Sprich dann mit deinem Partner darüber! Gib auch Gründe dafür an!

> BEISPIEL   DU   **Wo übernachtet ihr gewöhnlich, wenn ihr unterwegs seid?**
>
>   PARTNER   **Wir übernachten gewöhnlich in einem Motel, weil es nicht so teuer ist.**

---

1. In German, definite time expressions involving nouns are always in the accusative case.

Schon bekannt
Ein wenig *Grammatik*

Read this paragraph:

Zuerst habe ich den Rasen gemäht. Dann habe ich meiner Mutter im Haus geholfen — ich habe für sie die Küchenfenster geputzt. Danach bin ich zum Bäcker gegangen und hab' ein paar Brötchen gekauft. Am Nachmittag bin ich noch im Schwimmbad gewesen, und am Abend war ich mit meinen Freunden im Kino.

Which tense is used in this paragraph? Name the verb forms used to express that tense. For more on this point, see the Grammar Summary.

WORTSCHATZ

Wo warst du, und was hast du dort erledigt?

Ich war auf der Bank. Ich hab' Geld umgewechselt, Dollar in D-Mark.

Ich war auf der Post. Dort hab' ich telefoniert und eine Rechnung bezahlt.

Ich war im Sportgeschäft Winkler. Da hab' ich eine Jacke umgetauscht, denn sie war zu klein.

Ich war in der Bücherei. Ich hab' Bücher zurückgebracht und einige ausgeliehen.

Ich war im Getränkemarkt. Ich hab' leere Flaschen zurückgebracht und vier Flaschen Limo gekauft.

Ich war im Musikladen. Dort hab' ich mir eine CD bestellt, eine neue CD von den „Prinzen".

8 Hast du zu Hause geholfen?

a. In der letzten Woche hast du bestimmt zu Hause geholfen. Schreib auf, was du alles getan hast und für wen!

b. Frag deinen Partner, was er in der letzten Woche zu Hause für seine Eltern, Geschwister oder andere Verwandte getan hat! Danach sagst du ihm, was du für deine Familie getan hast.

9 Wie aktiv warst du?

a. Schreib auf, was du in den letzten zwei Tagen alles gemacht hast, um dich körperlich fit zu halten! Schreib mindestens sechs Sätze auf!

b. Erzähl einer Partnerin, was du vorgestern alles gemacht hast! Sie erzählt dir dann, was sie gestern getan hat.

10 Hör gut zu! For answers, see listening script on TE Interleaf.

Schüler erzählen, was sie in der Stadt gemacht haben. Schau beim Zuhören auf den Stadtplan von Dingskirchen auf Seite 11! Schreib für jeden Schüler zuerst auf, wo er war und danach, beim zweiten Zuhören, was er dort gemacht hat! Vergleiche deine Notizen mit denen deines Partners! Habt ihr beiden wirklich alles verstanden und wißt, was diese Schüler alles gemacht haben? Wenn ihr nicht alles verstanden habt, müßt ihr euch die Übung zusammen noch einmal anhören.

11 Was kann man dort tun?

Bildet drei oder vier kleine Gruppen! Überlegt euch so viele Antworten wie möglich zu folgender Frage: Was kann man alles in den Geschäften und Institutionen tun, die auf dieser Skizze eingezeichnet sind? Ein Schriftführer von jeder Gruppe schreibt die Antworten auf.

BEISPIEL **In einem Buchladen kann man: Bücher kaufen, Bücher bestellen ...**

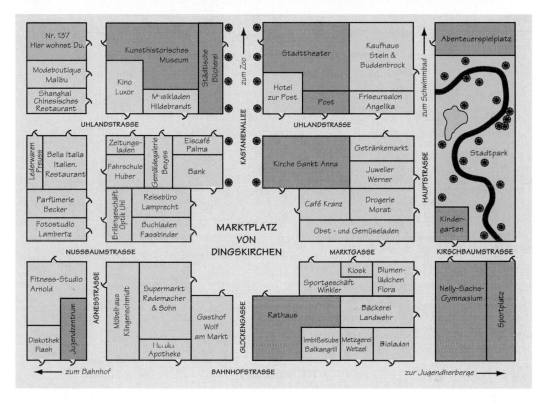

12 Überall in Dingskirchen

Frag deinen Partner, wo er etwas gemacht hat! Stellt euch abwechselnd diese Fragen!

BEISPIEL DU **Wo hast du die Äpfel gekauft?**

PARTNER **Im Obst- und Gemüseladen in der Nußbaumstraße.**

T-Shirt kaufen	Geburtstag feiern	Nußbaumstraße	Bank (auf der)
Limo kaufen	Taschenrechner kaufen	Brillengeschäft	Stadtpark
CD hören	Geld umwechseln	Supermarkt	Metzgerei
Hackfleisch holen	Lehrer treffen (meet)	Schul-Shop	Musikladen
Volleyball spielen	Geld abholen	Restaurant	Getränkemarkt
Brille bekommen	telefonieren	Post (auf der)	Sportgeschäft

13 Wo warst du, und was hast du dort gemacht?

a. Auf dem Weg zur Schule hast du an drei oder vier verschiedenen Stellen gehalten und dir etwas besorgt. Schreib auf, wo du überall warst und was du dort gekauft hast!

b. Auf dem Weg von der Schule nach Hause hast du an drei oder vier verschiedenen Stellen gestoppt, um etwas zu erledigen. Schreib auf, wo du warst und was du dort erledigt hast!

c. Lies deinem Partner vor, was du aufgeschrieben hast! Wenn er auch dort war, wo du warst, muß er es dir sagen. Tauscht dann die Rollen aus!

SO SAGT MAN DAS!

Schon bekannt

Asking how someone liked something; expressing enthusiasm or disappointment; responding enthusiastically or sympathetically

In order to find out how someone liked something or someplace, you might ask:

Wie hat dir der Film gefallen?
Hat euch Österreich gefallen?
Na, wie war's denn? Hat es euch gefallen?

If you liked it, you may say:

> **Er war super!**
> **Mir hat es gefallen.**
> **Also, uns hat's gut gefallen.**

If you didn't like it, you may say:

> **Er hat uns überhaupt nicht gefallen.**
> **Mir hat es nicht gefallen.**

The other person may respond enthusiastically or sympathetically:

> **Das freut mich!**
> **Na, super!**

> **Das tut mir leid.**
> **Das ist aber schade!**

---

14 Hör gut zu!

For answers, see listening script on TE Interleaf.

Vier Schüler erzählen, wo sie gestern gewesen sind, was sie dort gemacht haben, wie es ihnen gefallen hat und warum oder warum nicht. Übertrag die Tabelle rechts in dein Heft, und trag die Information ein, die du hörst!

wer?	wo?	was?	gefallen?	warum?

15 Was hat euch gefallen und warum?

a. Such dir eine Partnerin! Entscheidet euch (*decide on*) für einen Ort auf dem Stadtplan von Dingskirchen! Überlegt euch, was euch an diesem Platz gefallen oder nicht gefallen hat und warum! Denkt dabei an einen ähnlichen Platz in eurem Heimatort!

b. Schreibt eure Gedanken auf einen Zettel! Ordnet eure Gründe nach: was euch (gut, besonders gut) gefallen hat und was euch nicht (gar nicht, überhaupt nicht) gefallen hat!

c. Danach erzählt einer von euch der ganzen Klasse, wo ihr wart und was euch dort gefallen oder nicht gefallen hat. Der Rest der Klasse macht entsprechende Bemerkungen wie: Das freut uns! oder: Das tut uns aber leid!

16 Für mein Notizbuch

Schreib in dein Notizbuch, wann und wo du deine letzten Ferien verbracht hast, was du dort alles gemacht hast und wie dir alles gefallen oder nicht gefallen hat! Vergiß nicht, deine Aussagen zu begründen!

> Schon bekannt
> ### Ein wenig *Grammatik*
>
> There are some verbs that are always used with the dative case.
>
> **Der Urlaub hat meinen Eltern überhaupt nicht gefallen.**
> **Die Ferien haben mir gut gefallen.**
>
> For dative case forms and for verbs that are used with the dative case, see the Grammar Summary.

Vacationers very often like to keep a record of what they see and do. Some people take pictures or make videos, some buy postcards, and some record their activities in a journal. In this activity, you will choose an experience you had during your last vacation and write about it as though you were writing in your journal.

Was ich in den Ferien gemacht habe.

Mach eine Liste von allen Erlebnissen, die du in den Ferien gehabt hast! Dann wähl ein oder zwei von den interessantesten (oder lustigsten, traurigsten usw.) Erlebnissen aus, und schreib sie in dein Tagebuch!

A. Vorbereiten

1. Schreib eine Liste von allen Dingen, die du in den Ferien gemacht hast! (Was hast du alles gemacht? Bist du zu Hause geblieben, oder bist du verreist? Wohin bist du gereist? Wer war dabei? Was hast du dort gemacht? Was hast du gesehen? Wo hast du gewohnt? usw.)
2. Wähl jetzt eine oder zwei Ideen von der Liste, um dein Thema zu beschränken! Unterstreiche alle anderen Ideen, die auch mit deinem „Hauptthema" zusammenhängen!
3. Schreib jetzt über dieses Erlebnis! Wenn möglich, verwende auch die Ideen, die du unterstrichen hast — aber denk noch nicht an die Grammatik oder die Wortstellung!

> **SCHREIBTIP**
> **Brainstorming and freewriting**
> Whatever your purpose in writing — whether you are writing an assignment for one of your classes, for the school paper, or for yourself, as in your journal — you will write more effectively if you develop an idea of what you want to write about, then focus on that idea. A good way to develop ideas is to brainstorm and freewrite, writing down everything that comes to mind without worrying about grammar or sequencing. Once you have several ideas, narrow your focus to the one or two ideas that really convey what you want to say.

B. Ausführen

Verwende jetzt deine Liste und deinen frei geschriebenen Text, um eine geordnete und logische Tagebucheintragung zu schreiben! Vergiß nicht, das Datum zu notieren!

C. Überarbeiten

1. Lies deine Eintragung durch, und vergleiche sie mit dem frei geschriebenen Text und mit der Liste! Hast du alles geschrieben, was du schreiben wolltest, oder hast du etwas in der endgültigen Version ausgelassen? Wenn ja, trag diese Ideen jetzt ein!
2. Wie sieht dein Text jetzt aus? Hast du die Ideen logisch geordnet? Hast du dein Erlebnis ausführlich beschrieben, oder hast du nur eine Liste von Erlebnissen gemacht?
3. Lies die Eintragung noch einmal durch, und denk diesmal auch an Grammatik und Wortstellung! Hast du alles richtig geschrieben? Hast du die Zeitformen beachtet? Hast du die richtigen Fälle (Akkusativ oder Dativ) mit den richtigen Präpositionen verwendet?
4. Schreib jetzt den korrigierten Text noch einmal in dein Tagebuch ab!

Weiter geht's!

Gregor besucht Johannes

JOHANNES Hallo, Gregor! Prima, daß du uns besuchen kommst!

GREGOR Ich hab's dir doch versprochen, und versprochen ist versprochen!

JOHANNES Komm rein und setz dich! Meine Eltern kommen auch bald, und dann gibt's Kaffee und Kuchen. Sag, magst du etwas trinken? Oder möchtest du Obst? Du, wir haben ganz süße Erdbeeren aus unserem Schrebergarten — mit Sahne, ja? Lecker!

GREGOR Kann schon sein, aber ich darf das nicht essen. Ich bin nämlich allergisch gegen Erdbeeren.

JOHANNES Wirklich? Das hab' ich nicht gewußt. Tut mir leid.

GREGOR Du kannst wohl alles essen, ja?

JOHANNES Sicher! Ich hab' keine Allergien. Nur mag ich eben vieles nicht; ich mag zum Beispiel keinen Fisch.

GREGOR Und warum nicht?

JOHANNES Schmeckt mir einfach nicht.

GREGOR Dann ißt du wohl viel Fleisch, ja?

JOHANNES Nicht unbedingt. Wir essen viel Obst und Gemüse, Teigwaren, ja und, wie gesagt, auch Fleisch, Huhn und so.

GREGOR Weil du grad Teigwaren erwähnst: was ich gern mag, ist ein Gericht ... na ja, wie heißt es denn schnell ... hat was mit Salzburg zu tun.

JOHANNES Ach ja! Du meinst Salzburger Nockerln, ja?

GREGOR Genau! Ess' ich unwahrscheinlich gern.

JOHANNES Hab' ich auch ein paarmal in den Ferien gegessen. Wir waren ja gar nicht weit von Salzburg entfernt.

GREGOR Ja, erzähl doch mal was über deine Ferien!

JOHANNES Du, da gibt's nicht viel zu erzählen. Ich hab' dir ja schon gesagt, es hat fast nur geregnet. Wir sind kaum gewandert, und trotzdem hab' ich mir auf so einer kleinen Wanderung den Knöchel verstaucht.

GREGOR <u>So ein Pech! Geht's dem Knöchel wieder besser?</u>

JOHANNES <u>Klar, es geht wieder.</u> Ich muß nur noch ein bißchen vorsichtig sein.

GREGOR Übrigens, hier hab' ich ein paar Rügen-Prospekte für deine Eltern.

JOHANNES Prima! Sie werden sich bestimmt darüber freuen. — Ja, da kommen sie auch schon. Ich höre unser Auto!

17 Was passiert hier?

1. weil er es dem Johannes versprochen hat; weil er die Rügen Prospekte Johannes' Eltern zeigen will 2. Erdbeeren mit Schlagsahne / weil sie frisch aus dem eigenen Garten sind

Hast du das Gespräch verstanden? Beantworte die folgenden Fragen!

1. Warum besucht Gregor den Johannes? 3. Gregor sagt nein. / daß er gegen Erdbeeren allergisch ist
2. Was bietet Johannes seinem Freund an? Warum wohl? 4. Fisch. / Obst,
3. Wie reagiert Gregor darauf? Was sagt er? Gemüse, Teigwaren, Fleisch, Huhn
4. Was mag Johannes nicht essen? Was ißt er meistens?
5. Was für ein Gericht erwähnt Gregor, und warum erwähnt er es?
6. Kennt Johannes das Gericht? Woher? 5. Salzburger Nockerln; weil er das Gericht gern mag
7. Wie waren Johannes' Ferien? Was sagt er darüber?
8. Was ist dem Johannes passiert? Wie geht's ihm jetzt?
9. Was hat Gregor mitgebracht? Warum? 6. Ja. / Er hat es in den Ferien gegessen. 7. Nicht besonders. / Er sagt, daß es nicht viel zu erzählen gibt; daß es fast nur geregnet hat; daß sie kaum gewandert sind

18 Genauer lesen
8. Er hat sich den Knöchel verstaucht. / besser

Lies das Gespräch noch einmal, und beantworte diese Fragen auf deutsch! 9. Rügen-Prospekte / um sie Johannes' Eltern zu zeigen

1. Which phrases are used to ask and tell what you may or may not do?
2. Which phrases express concern about someone's health or are responses to such concern?

For answers, see underlined words in text on pages 14 and 15.

19 Wie steht's mit dir?

Beantworte diese Fragen!

1. Welche Gerichte magst du und welche nicht?
2. Was darfst du nicht essen? Warum nicht?
3. Was hast du dir schon einmal verletzt, und wie ist es passiert?

Asking and telling what you may or may not do; asking for information; inquiring about someone's health and responding; asking about and expressing pain; expressing hope

2. Fleisch, Käse, Honig (acc. to biological science), Schweinefleisch; Anti-Fleisch-Burger, Vollkornbrötchen, Naturjoghurt, Salatblätter, Gurken, Tomaten, Zwiebelringe, Paprika, Möhren, Gemüse, Honig (acc. to nutritional science), Tee, Brot

20 Gesund essen? Gesund leben?

Lies die Leserbriefe an die Jugendzeitschrift „Girl!", und beantworte danach die folgenden Fragen!   1. für Tierprodukte: Susi, Simone, Michaela; für Pflanzenprodukte: Vanessa, Melanie

1. Welche Schüler sind für Tierprodukte oder für Pflanzenprodukte?
2. Welche Tierprodukte und welche Pflanzenprodukte erwähnen die Mädchen?
3. Mit welchem Satz drückt jedes Mädchen ihre Meinung am besten aus?   3. Answers will vary.
4. Mit welcher Schülerin kannst du dich identifizieren? Warum?   4. Answers will vary.

Fit ohne Fleisch

Im Urlaub in Italien habe ich gemerkt, daß es auch ohne Fleisch geht. Seit einigen Wochen lebe ich nun schon vegetarisch. Am Anfang hatte ich noch unangenehme Hungergefühle, doch die habe ich mit der Zeit besiegt. Übrigens: Kennt Ihr schon den Anti-Fleisch-Burger? Das Rezept: Ein Vollkornbrötchen aufschneiden, beide Hälften mit Naturjoghurt bestreichen, dazwischen Salatblätter, eine Scheibe Käse, Gurken, Tomaten, Zwiebelringe, Paprika und Möhren packen. Ich sage Euch: ein Genuß!

Vanessa, Bielefeld

Wer weiß denn eigentlich genau, ob Vegetarier wirklich so viel gesünder leben als Fleischesser? Was, bitte schön, ist denn alles an Pflanzenschutzmitteln in unserem Gemüse drin? Oder denkt doch mal an den jüngsten Skandal mit den Tees, wo Unmengen von Schwermetallen und Pflanzenschutzmitteln drin gefunden wurden. An alle Vegetarier: Macht mal halblang!

Susi, München

An alle Veganer: Ihr könnt ruhig Honig essen, da er kein Tierprodukt ist. Die Bienen nehmen bei seiner Herstellung keinen Schaden, es ist sogar ihre Lebensaufgabe. Brot ist ja auch kein Menschenprodukt, nur weil ein Bäcker es herstellt, sondern ein Pflanzenprodukt.

Melanie, Dielheim-Balzfeld

Wir sind der Meinung, daß Nahrung, sorgfältig ausgesucht (nur ein- bis zweimal die Woche Schweinefleisch), die vernünftigste Form ist, sich zu ernähren. Als Voll-Vegetarier zu leben, würde für uns eine Einschränkung des alltäglichen Lebens bedeuten. Davon haben wir eigentlich schon genug (Eltern, Schule, Gesetze etc.). Wenn man alles zu negativ sieht, vermiest man sich das Leben. Da kann man ja gleich Schluß machen.

Simone und Michaela, Eisenberg

Was für Produkte essen wir?

Pflanzenprodukte

Zwiebeln

Paprika

Rosenkohl

Mais

Spargel

Wassermelone

Tierprodukte

Rippchen

Speck

Schweinefleisch

Innereien

Leber

Reh- und Hasenfleisch

Welche anderen Pflanzenprodukte kennst du? Welche anderen Tierprodukte? Welche Produkte ißt du gern oder überhaupt nicht gern? Warum?

---

21 **Hör gut zu!** For answers, see listening script on TE Interleaf.

Drei Schüler sprechen über ihre Eßgewohnheiten. Was mag jeder und was nicht? Wer darf etwas überhaupt nicht essen und warum nicht? Mach eine Tabelle mit diesen Kategorien: Wer? Mag was? Mag was nicht? Darf das nicht essen! Warum nicht? Schreib in die Tabelle die Information, die du hörst!

SO SAGT MAN DAS !

Schon bekannt

Asking and telling what you may or may not do

When asking someone what he or she may or may not do, you might ask:

> **Was darfst du essen und trinken?**
> **Darfst du alles essen?**
> **Was darfst du nicht essen?**
> **Was darfst du nicht tun?**

And the answer may be:

> Gemüse, Obst ... und so.
> Na klar!
> Ich darf keine Rosinen essen.
> Joggen darf ich jetzt nicht und auch nicht Tennis spielen.

When inquiring about the reason, you might ask:

> **Warum darfst du keine Rosinen essen?**
> **Warum darfst du nicht joggen?**

And the answer might be:

> Weil ich allergisch gegen Rosinen bin.
> Weil ich mir den Knöchel verstaucht habe.

22 Was darfst du essen und was nicht?

Such dir einen Partner! Frag ihn, was er nicht gern ißt oder trinkt, und ob es etwas gibt, was er nicht essen oder trinken darf! Warum oder warum nicht? Tauscht dann die Rollen aus!

SO SAGT MAN DAS!

Schon bekannt

Asking for information

You know many different ways to ask for information. For instance:

> **Sag mal, wie heißt dieses Gemüse?**
> **Welche Suppe magst du?**
> **Welchen Salat ißt du gern?**

And you know many different ways to respond. You might answer:

> **Das ist doch Spinat!**
> **Ich mag Nudelsuppe.**
> **Thunfischsalat.**

23 Was nimmst du?

Frag den Jens, deinen deutschen Gastbruder, welches von zwei Gerichten er mag! Er weiß es noch nicht und fragt dich, was du nimmst. Du sagst es ihm und auch, warum du dieses Gericht nimmst. Such dir einen Partner für die Rolle von Jens!

BEISPIEL DU **Nun, Jens, magst du diese(n) ... oder diese(n) ...?**

JENS **Ich weiß nicht. Welche Suppe nimmst du?**

DU **Also, ich nehme diese ...**

> Schon bekannt
> **Ein wenig Grammatik**
>
> For the forms of **dieser** and **welcher** see the Grammar Summary.

Nudelsuppe
Hähnchen
Speck
Bratkartoffeln
Nudeln
Rosenkohl
Tomatensalat
Äpfel

Gemüsesuppe
Fisch
Leber
Salzkartoffeln
Reis
Mais
Gurkensalat
Trauben

WORTSCHATZ

Was hast du alles auf dem Brot?

Ich habe es zuerst mit Naturjoghurt bestrichen.   **Darauf kommt ein Blatt Salat**   **und dann eine Scheibe Tomate**   **saure Gurken**

oder
ißt du
vielleicht
lieber ...

 oder oder

Radieschen   **Erdnußbutter**   **Thunfischsalat**

24 Hör gut zu! For answers, see listening script on TE Interleaf.

Vier Schüler erzählen, was sie auf ihrem Brot haben. Wer von diesen vier ißt viel Fleisch und Wurst? Wer ist wohl Vegetarier? Wer ißt sowohl Tierprodukte als auch Pflanzenprodukte?

25 Was für ein tolles belegtes Brot!

Bildet Gruppen zu sechs oder acht Schülern! Einer fängt an und sagt, was er auf seinem Brot hat. Der nächste wiederholt das und gibt etwas anderes dazu, bis alle etwas gesagt haben und euer belegtes Brot fertig ist. (Kann und will man das auch wirklich essen?)

WORTSCHATZ

Was ist passiert? Hast du dir weh getan?

Ich hab' mich verletzt, bin vom Rad gefallen.

Ich bin ausgerutscht und hingefallen. Ich hab mich aber nicht verletzt.

Ich hab' mich verbrannt, hab' mir die Hand verbrannt.

Ich hatte einen Unfall, einen kleinen Autounfall.

Was hast du dir verletzt? — Ich hab' mir ... verletzt.

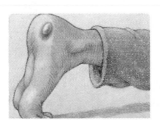
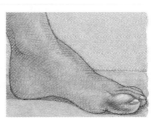

| die Kniescheibe | die Wade | die Ferse | die Zehe |

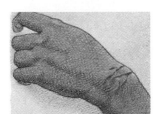

| den Ellbogen | das Handgelenk | den Daumen | den Fingernagel |

Was für andere Körperteile kann man sich verletzen? Wann hast du dir das letzte Mal weh getan? Was ist passiert? Wobei hast du dich verletzt?

    beim Fußballspielen?   beim Radfahren?
    beim Tennisspielen?   beim Joggen?

Und dann noch ...

Was hast du dir schon mal gebrochen?
den Kiefer   das Schlüsselbein
das Schulterblatt   eine Rippe

SO SAGT MAN DAS!

Inquiring about someone's health and responding; asking about and expressing pain

To inquire about someone's health, you might ask:

> **Wie fühlst du dich?**
> **Was fehlt dir?**

And the response might be:

> **Ich fühl' mich überhaupt nicht wohl.**
> **Mir fehlt nichts.**

To inquire about pain someone may be suffering, you might ask:

> **Tut dir etwas weh?**
> **Was tut dir weh?**

The response might be:

> **Ja, der Arm tut mir weh.**
> **Mir tut der Hals weh.**

For answers, see listening script on TE Interleaf.

26 Hör gut zu!

Es war ein ganz tolles Fußballspiel. Aber das Spiel war hart, und viele Spieler haben sich dabei verletzt. — Hör zu, wie jeder Spieler über seine Verletzung spricht, und identifiziere jeden Spieler an seiner Verletzung!

SO SAGT MAN DAS!

Expressing hope

To express hope, you might say:

> **Ich hoffe, daß** es dir bald wieder besser geht.
> **Hoffentlich** hast du dir nicht den Fuß gebrochen.

27 Was ist los mit euch?

Jeder von euch denkt sich eine Verletzung aus. Drückt diese Verletzung durch Gestik (*gestures*) und Mimik (*mime*) aus! — Fragt euch dann gegenseitig, was ihr euch verletzt habt, was passiert ist und wie, und ob es weh tut! Am Ende muß jeder die Hoffnung ausdrücken, daß es dem verletzten Schüler oder der verletzten Schülerin bald wieder besser geht.

> ### Schon bekannt
> ### Ein wenig *Grammatik*
>
> Look at the following sentences:
>
> **Ich hab' mich verletzt. Ich hab' mir die Hand verletzt.**
>
> How are the object pronouns different, and why? For the reflexive pronouns, see the Grammar Summary.

28 Eine Entschuldigung schreiben

Du bist Gastschüler an einem deutschen Gymnasium. Du hast dich am Wochenende verletzt und konntest deshalb am Montag nicht in die Schule gehen. Schreib eine Entschuldigung! Schreib, was du dir verletzt hast und wie es passiert ist! Deine Gasteltern unterschreiben die Entschuldigung, und du gibst sie in der Schule ab.

29 Was ist mit dir?

a. Such dir eine Partnerin! Sucht euch zwei von diesen Illustrationen aus, und erfindet ein Gespräch, das zwischen den zwei Leuten in beiden Bildern stattfindet!
b. Führt anschließend das Gespräch der Klasse vor! Eure Mitschüler müssen raten, welche Illustrationen ihr vorführt.

a.

b.

c.

d.

e.

f.

g.

h.

30

ROLLENSPIEL

Bereite eins von diesen beiden Rollenspielen mit zwei anderen Schülern vor!
a. Dein Klassenkamerad und du, ihr macht zweimal im Monat Sozialarbeit, das heißt, ihr geht gewöhnlich für eine kranke Person einkaufen und erledigt auch andere Botengänge (*errands*). Der dritte Partner spielt die kranke Person, die eine Liste vorbereitet, auf der mindestens sechs Dinge stehen, die ihr erledigen müßt. Ihr besprecht diese Liste mit der kranken Person und einigt euch auf die Route, die ihr nehmen wollt, um alles zu erledigen. Verwende dabei den Plan von Dingskirchen auf Seite 11!
b. Uli, der am Wochenende eine Bergtour machen wollte, ist am Montag nicht in die Schule gekommen. Am Nachmittag gehst du ihn mit einem Klassenkameraden besuchen. Er sieht schlecht aus und scheint sogar Schmerzen zu haben. Ihr fragt ihn, wie die Bergtour war. Uli erzählt euch dann, was passiert ist und was ihm fehlt.

Währungen und Geld wechseln

A. 1. EU member countries as of 10/94: **Belgien, Dänemark, Deutschland, Frankreich, Griechenland, Großbritannien, Irland, Italien, Luxemburg, Niederlande, Portugal, Spanien**

A. 1. No matter where you live in Europe, you're always just a short drive away from another country, and usually more than one. Find Europe on a world map and compare it to other continents. How large is it compared to the United States? Actually, continental Europe west of the former USSR is less than half the size of the United States, but within this area you'll find 32 different countries and almost as many languages and currencies.

The **Europäische Union (EU)** is an organization that promotes social, economic, and political unity among several European countries. Can you name the European countries that currently belong to the EU? In addition to other goals, the European Union plans to introduce among its member countries a single currency, called the ECU (pronounced ekü), by the year 1999.

EUROPÄISCHE WÄHRUNGEN

LAND	NAME DER WÄHRUNG
Deutschland	(der) Franken, Franken
Österreich	(die) Peseta, Peseten
Schweiz	(das) Pfund, Pfund
Frankreich	(der) Schilling, Schilling
Spanien	(die) Krone, Kronen
Italien	(der) Rubel, Rubel
Großbritannien	(der) Forint, Forints
Niederlande	(die) Deutsche Mark, Mark
Griechenland	(der) Gulden, Gulden
Rußland	(der) Zloty, Zlotys
Polen	(die) Drachme, Drachmen
Ungarn	(die) Lira, Lire
Tschechische Republik	(der) Franc, Francs

AA131

22 *zweiundzwanzig*

2. Schau die Liste der verschiedenen Währungen Europas an! Suche zuerst die Länder auf eine Landkarte Europas heraus! Nenne für jedes Land die richtige Währung! A. 2. Deutschland: Deutsche Mark; Österreich: Schilling; Schweiz: Franken; Frankreich: Franc; Spanien: Peseta; Italien: Lira; Großbritannien: Pfund; Niederlande: Gulden; Griechenland: Drachme; Rußland: Rubel;

B. Europeans visiting other countries usually exchange some money at their bank before leaving home. German banks will change money into almost any popular currency. You can also change money at border crossings and, of course, at banks in the country you are visiting. Polen: Zloty; Ungarn: Forint; Tschechische Republik: Krone

At every bank in Europe you'll find tables similar to this one. What kind of information does it provide? For how long is this information valid? (Think about what you learned in *Komm mit!, Level I,* about exchanging money.) B. Exchange rate from DM to $ and vice versa. / Valid only for a short period of time after the card is printed (see sentence at the bottom of the card).

C. Was ist los?

Lies die folgenden zwei Texte! Welches Problem wird in jeder Situation beschrieben?

1. Du wohnst als Austauschschüler(in) in Kiel. Deine Eltern schicken dir jeden Monat 50 Dollar. Mit diesem Geld willst du eine Stereoanlage für 300 DM kaufen. Vor vier Monaten hast du gesehen, daß der Wechselkurs 1,50 DM pro Dollar war. Du hast schon 200 Dollar gespart. Heute gehst du mit deinem Geld zur Bank. Du willst die Dollars in D-Mark umtauschen. Der Bankangestellte gibt dir aber nicht genug D-Mark, um die Anlage kaufen zu können! Was ist los? 1. The exchange rate changed (the value of the dollar went down).

2. Du hast dich ganz spontan entschieden, mit deiner Schulklasse eine Reise nach Italien zu machen. Du hast deine Tasche gepackt und einen Hundertmarkschein geholt und bist am späten Nachmittag mit dem Zug nach Italien gefahren. Am nächsten Morgen hält der Zug in einer kleinen italienischen Stadt. Du steigst aus, um dir am Bahnhof eine Tasse Tee zu kaufen. Die Verkäuferin sagt (auf italienisch, natürlich) „2 000 Lire, bitte". Du denkst dir „Ach, nein!" Was hast du vergessen?

2. You forgot to change your money into lire.

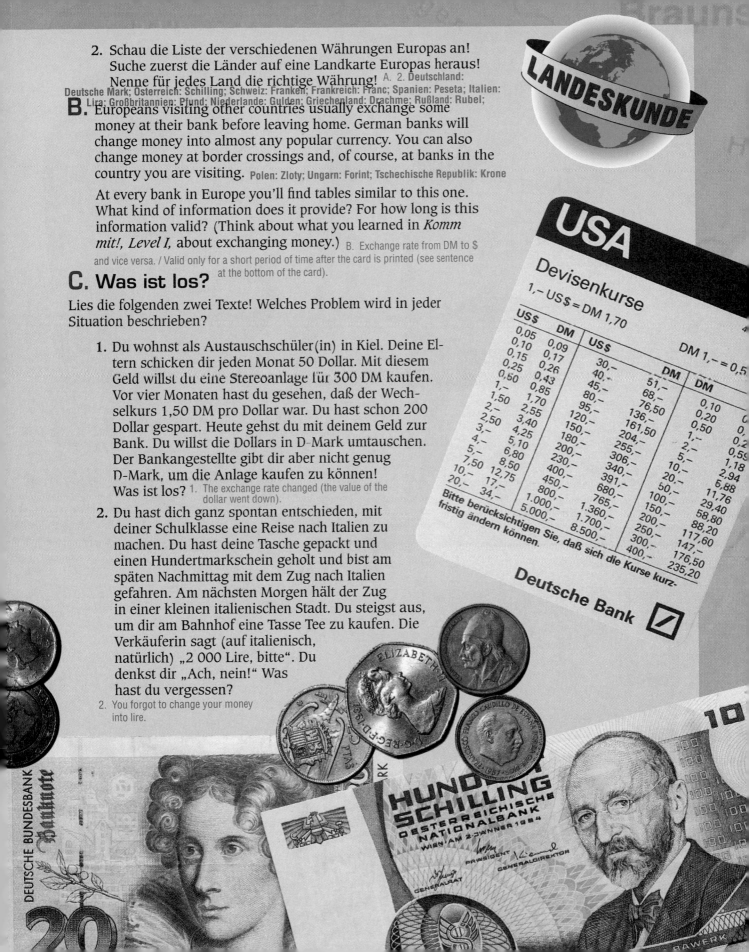

USA

Devisenkurse

1,– US$ = DM 1,70

US$	DM	US$	DM		DM 1,– = 0,5
					DM
0,05	0,09				0,10
0,10	0,17	30,–	51,–		0,20
0,15	0,26	40,–	68,–		0,50
0,25	0,43	45,–	76,50		1,–	0,59
0,50	0,85	80,–	136,–		2,–	1,18
1,–	1,70	95,–	161,50		5,–	2,94
1,50	2,55	120,–	204,–		10,–	6,88
2,–	3,40	150,–	255,–		20,–	11,76
2,50	4,25	180,–	306,–		50,–	29,40
3,–	5,10	200,–	340,–		100,–	58,80
5,–	6,80	230,–	391,–		150,–	88,20
7,50	12,75	400,–	680,–		200,–	117,60
10,–	17,–	450,–	765,–		250,–	147,–
20,–	34,–	800,–	1.360,–		300,–	176,50
		1.000,–	1.700,–		400,–	235,20
		5.000,–	8.500,–			

Bitte berücksichtigen Sie, daß sich die Kurse kurzfristig ändern können.

Deutsche Bank

Eine alltägliche Verwirrung

von Franz Kafka

„Selbstporträt" von Karl Schmidt-Rottluff

LESETRICK

Using time lines for comprehension You don't need to know the exact meaning of every word to figure out what a story is about. By first taking a moment to discover how a story is organized you can make up for not knowing every word. Try to organize a text around a single guiding principle. For example, a narrative usually contains many words that indicate the sequence of events. You can use those words to construct a time line and better understand the flow of the story.

For answers, see TE Interleaf.

Getting Started

1. Read the title of this selection. If **Alltag** means *everyday life* or *routine,* what kind of confusion is Kafka writing about?
2. Skim the story once. Scan for occurrences of the letters **A, B,** and **H.** Using context, try to determine what each letter represents. Why do you think the writer uses letters?
3. Read the first paragraph again. Who are the main characters? What is the setting? What happens in this paragraph? Why?
4. Reread the first paragraph and continue reading to the end of the story. Try to summarize the story in two or three sentences.

A Closer Look

5. Together with your partner, scan the story for any words that establish the sequence of events. Draw a time line of events that indicates time and place for both characters **A**

in alltäglicher Vorfall: sein Ertragen eine alltägliche Verwirrung. A hat mit B aus H ein wichtiges Geschäft abzuschließen. Er geht zur Vorbesprechung nach H, legt den Hin- und Herweg in je zehn Minuten zurück und rühmt sich zu Hause dieser besonderen Schnelligkeit. Am nächsten Tag geht er wieder nach H, diesmal zum endgültigen Geschäftsabschluß. Da dieser voraussichtlich mehrere Stunden erfordern wird, geht A sehr früh morgens fort. Obwohl aber alle Nebenumstände, wenigstens nach A's Meinung, völlig die gleichen sind wie am Vortag, braucht er diesmal zum Weg nach H zehn Stunden. Als er dort ermüdet abends ankommt, sagt man ihm, daß B, ärgerlich wegen A's Ausbleiben, vor einer halben Stunde zu A in sein Dorf gegangen sei und sie sich eigentlich unterwegs hätten treffen müssen. Man rät A zu warten. A aber, in Angst wegen des Geschäftes, macht sich so-

fort auf und eilt nach Hause.

Diesmal legt er den Weg, ohne besonders darauf zu achten, geradezu in einem Augenblick zurück. Zu Hause erfährt er, B sei doch schon gleich früh gekommen — gleich nach dem Weggang A's; ja, er habe A im Haustor getroffen, ihn an das Geschäft erinnert, aber A habe gesagt, er hätte jetzt keine Zeit, er müsse jetzt eilig fort.

Trotz diesem unverständlichen Verhalten A's sei aber B doch hier geblieben, um auf A zu warten. Er habe zwar schon oft gefragt, ob A nicht schon wieder zurück sei, befinde sich aber noch oben in A's Zimmer. Glücklich darüber, B jetzt noch zu sprechen und ihm alles erklären zu können, läuft A die Treppe hinauf. Schon ist er fast oben, da stolpert er, erleidet eine Sehnenzerrung und fast ohnmächtig vor Schmerz, unfähig sogar zu schreien, nur winselnd im Dunkel hört er, wie B — undeutlich ob in großer Ferne oder knapp neben ihm — wütend die Treppe hinunterstampft und endgültig verschwindet.

and **B.** Discuss any problems you notice with the rest of the class.

> The endings **-lich** and **-ig** in German signal that a word is an adverb or adjective. When reading fiction, you can often use these words as clues to how people or things are.

6. Read the story again to find out how the characters act or react. Decide who or what is characterized by each of the following adverbs and adjectives:

wichtig	in Angst
ermüdet	eilig
ärgerlich	unverständlich
glücklich	undeutlich
ohnmächtig	wütend
unfähig	winselnd

7. Find the following words in the passage and, using context and familiar elements of compound words, try to derive their meanings: **Schnelligkeit, Nebenumstände, Ausbleiben,** and **Augenblick.**
8. What is **A**'s problem? What is the cause? What is **B**'s reaction? What does he do? How is the conflict resolved? Or is it?
9. Using the time line you created in Activity 5, reconstruct the story (in writing) using complete sentences. Your **Nacherzählung** should be one to two paragraphs.
10. Kafka's story depicts some rather bizarre events, yet the title seems to suggest the opposite — that the situation is commonplace. How can you reconcile or explain the apparent contradiction?

Can you report past events? (p. 9)

1. Sag mal, wo warst du denn vorgestern? Was hast du dort gemacht? / Answers will vary. E.g.: **Du, ich war in der Stadt. Dort bin ich ins Kino gegangen. Danach war ich im Eiscafé. Und dann habe ich mir noch neue Schuhe gekauft.**

1 How would you ask someone where he or she was the day before yesterday, and what he or she did there? How would you answer the same question, mentioning at least three different things you did?

Can you ask how someone liked something? (p. 12)

2 How would you ask a friend how he or she liked the movie *Schindler's List* (**Schindlers Liste**)? 2. Wie hat dir „Schindlers Liste" gefallen?

Can you express enthusiasm or disappointment? (p. 12)

3 How would you respond if someone asked you if you liked a movie and
a. you loved it? a. E.g.: **Es war super!**
b. you didn't like it? b. E.g.: **Es hat mir überhaupt nicht gefallen.**

Can you respond enthusiastically or sympathetically? (p. 12)

4 How would you respond to the following statements?
a. Also, mir hat Weimar gut gefallen. a. E.g.: **Das freut mich!**
b. Ich hatte Fieber und mußte das ganze Wochenende im Bett bleiben. b. E.g.: **Das tut mir aber leid.**

Can you ask and tell what you may or may not do? (p. 17)

5 How would you ask a friend what he or she may not eat and why? How would your friend respond if he or she was allergic to chocolate?
5. Was darfst du nicht essen und warum nicht? / Ich darf keine Schokolade essen, weil ich allergisch dagegen bin.

Can you ask for information? (p. 18)

6 How would you ask someone
a. what a particular fruit is called? 6. a. Sag mal, wie heißt diese Frucht?
b. what dessert he or she likes? b. Welchen Nachtisch magst du?
c. what a particular dish is supposed to be? c. Sag mal, was soll denn dieses Gericht sein?
How would that person answer in each case?
E.g.: **Das ist doch eine Banane! / Ich mag Eis. / Das ist doch Paella!**

Can you inquire about s.o.'s health and respond? (p. 20)

7 How would you ask someone how he or she is feeling? How would that person respond if he or she was not feeling well?
7. E.g.: **Wie fühlst du dich? / Ich fühl' mich überhaupt nicht wohl.**

Can you ask about and express pain? (p. 20)

8 How would you ask a friend if he or she has pain? If your friend looks like he or she is in pain, how would you ask what hurts?
8. Tut dir was weh? / Was tut dir weh?

Can you express hope? (p. 20)

9 How would you respond if someone said the following things to you?
a. Ich habe hohes Fieber und Kopfweh und kann kaum schlucken.
b. Ich bin gerade vom Fahrrad gefallen. Mein Fuß tut mir furchtbar weh, und ich glaub', ich kann jetzt nicht mehr laufen.
9. a. E.g.: **Ich hoffe, daß es dir bald wieder besser geht.**
b. E.g.: **Hoffentlich hast du dir nicht den Fuß gebrochen.**

ERSTE STUFE

REPORTING PAST EVENTS

gerade *just*
vor kurzem *recently*
neulich *the other day*
letzt- *last*

OTHER USEFUL WORDS

dauernd *continually*
übrigens *by the way*
sparsam *frugal*
leer *empty*

die Bank, -en *bank*
die Bücherei, -en *library*

der Musikladen, ⸚ *music store*
die Post *mail; post office*
die Lektüre, -n *reading*
der Prospekt, -e *brochure, pamphlet*
die Flasche, -n *bottle*
die Rechnung, -en *bill, invoice*

bezahlen *to pay*
umwechseln (sep) *to change (money)*

ausleihen (sep) *to borrow, lend*
bestellen *to order*
umtauschen (sep) *to exchange*
zurückbringen (sep) *to bring back, return*
s. aussuchen (sep) *to pick out, choose*
erledigen *to take care of*

ZWEITE STUFE

PARTS OF THE BODY

der Daumen, - *thumb*
der Ellbogen, - *elbow*
die Ferse, -n *heel*
der Fingernagel, ⸚ *finger nail*
das Handgelenk, -e *wrist*
die Kniescheibe, -n *knee cap*
die Wade, -n *calf*
die Zehe, -n *toe*
der Unfall, ⸚e *accident*

s. verbrennen *to burn oneself*
ausrutschen (sep) *to slip*

FRUIT AND VEGETABLES

das Produkt, -e *product*
das Pflanzenprodukt, -e *vegetable produce*
die Erdnußbutter *peanut butter*

die Rosine, -n *raisin*
die saure Gurke, -n *pickle*
der Mais *corn*
der Paprika *bell pepper*
die Wassermelone, -n *watermelon*
die Zwiebel, -n *onion*
der Rosenkohl *Brussel sprouts*
das Radieschen, - *radish*
der Spargel, - *asparagus*
die Teigwaren (pl) *pasta*
die Scheibe, -n *slice*
das Blatt, ⸚er *leaf*
bestreichen *to spread, to butter*

MEAT PRODUCTS

das Tierprodukt, -e *animal product*

die Innereien (pl) *innards*
die Leber *liver*
das Schweinefleisch *pork*
der Speck *bacon*
das Rehfleisch *venison*
die Rippchen (pl) *ribs*
das Hasenfleisch *rabbit meat*
der Thunfischsalat *tuna fish salad*

OTHER USEFUL WORDS

erzählen *to tell*
versprechen *to promise*
erwähnen *to mention*

trotzdem *in spite of that*
vorsichtig *careful*

Kapitel 2: Auf in die Jugendherberge! *Wiederholungskapitel*

CHAPTER OVERVIEW

	REVIEW OF FUNCTIONS	REVIEW OF GRAMMAR	CULTURE
Los geht's! pp. 30-31	Auf nach Thüringen!, *p. 30*		
Erste Stufe pp. 32-37	•Asking for and making suggestions, *p. 33* •Expressing preference and giving a reason, *p. 35* •Expressing wishes, *p. 36* •Expressing doubt, conviction, and resignation, *p. 36*	•Two-way prepositions (**So sagt man das!**), *p. 33* •Word order in **daß**- and **ob**-clauses (**So sagt man das!**), *p. 36*	•Explanation of **Jugendherbergen**, *p. 32* •**Einkaufsliste**, *p. 35*
Weiter geht's! pp. 38-39	Auf nach Weimar!, *p. 38*		
Zweite Stufe pp. 40-44	•Asking for information and expressing an assumption, *p. 41* •Expressing hearsay, *p. 42* •Asking for, making, and responding to suggestions *p. 42* •Expressing wishes when shopping, *p. 44*	•Adjective endings, *p. 44* •The verb **hätte**, (**So sagt man das!**), *p. 44*	•**Programm für eine 6-Tage-Reise nach Weimar**, *p. 40* •**Landeskunde: Weimar im Blickpunkt** *p. 45*
Zum Lesen pp. 46-48	**Poesie** Reading Strategy: Deriving the main idea from supporting details		
Zum Schreiben p. 49	**... ist eine Reise wert!** Writing Strategy: Selecting information		
Review pp. 50-51	•**Kann ich's wirklich?** *p. 50* •**Wortschatz,** *p. 51*		

Assessment Options	**Stufe Quizzes**
	•*Chapter Resources*, Book 1
	   Erste Stufe, Quiz 2-1
	   Zweite Stufe, Quiz 2-2
	•*Assessment Items, Audiocassette* 7 A
			Kapitel 2 Chapter Test
			•*Chapter Resources*, Book 1
			•*Assessment Guide*, Speaking Test
			•*Assessment Items, Audiocassette* 7 A
			
			Test Generator, Kapitel 2

Chapter Overview

RESOURCES Print	RESOURCES Audiovisual
	Textbook Audiocassette 1 B
Practice and Activity Book	
	Textbook Audiocassette 1 B
Practice and Activity Book *Chapter Resources,* Book 1 • Communicative Activity 2-1 • Communicative Activity 2-2 • Additional Listening Activity 2-1 • Additional Listening Activity 2-2 • Additional Listening Activity 2-3 • Student Response Forms • Realia 2-1 • Situation Card 2-1 • Teaching Transparency Master 2-1 • Quiz 2-1 *Video Guide*	*Additional Listening Activities, Audiocassette* 9 A *Additional Listening Activities, Audiocassette* 9 A *Additional Listening Activities, Audiocassette* 9 A *Teaching Transparency* 2-1 *Assessment Items, Audiocassette* 7 A *Video Program,* Videocassette 1
Practice and Activity Book	Textbook Audiocassette 1 B
	Textbook Audiocassette 1 B
Practice and Activity Book *Chapter Resources,* Book 1 • Communicative Activity 2-3 • Communicative Activity 2-4 • Additional Listening Activity 2-4 • Additional Listening Activity 2-5 • Additional Listening Activity 2-6 • Student Response Forms • Realia 2-2 • Situation Card 2-2 • Teaching Transparency Master 2-2 • Quiz 2-2 *Video Guide*	*Additional Listening Activities, Audiocassette* 9 A *Additional Listening Activities, Audiocassette* 9 A *Additional Listening Activities, Audiocassette* 9 A *Teaching Transparency* 2-2 *Assessment Items, Audiocassette* 7 A *Video Program,* Videocassette 1
	Textbook Audiocassette 11
Chapter Resources, Book 1 • Realia 2-3 • Situation Card 2-3	

Alternative Assessment

• Performance Assessment
Teacher's Edition
  Erste Stufe, p. 27K
  Zweite Stufe, p. 27O

• Portfolio Assessment
  Written: **Zweite Stufe,** Activity 25, *Pupil's Edition,* p. 40;
  Assessment Guide, p. 15
  Oral: **Zweite Stufe,** Activity 25, *Pupil's Edition,* p. 40;
  Assessment Guide, p. 15
• **Notizbuch,** *Pupil's Edition,* pp. 35, 42, 44

CHAPTER OVERVIEW

Kapitel 2: Auf in die Jugendherberge!
Textbook Listening Activities Scripts

For Student Response Forms, see *Chapter Resources*, Book 1, pp. 82-85.

Erste Stufe
Activity 6, *p. 33*

USCHI Na, Herbert! Was machst du denn hier? Ich dachte, du bist die ganzen Sommerferien lang im Bayerischen Wald bei deiner Oma.

HERBERT Ach hallo, Uschi! Nein, doch nicht die ganzen sechs Wochen! Ich war nur in den ersten drei Wochen dort. Ich bin gestern erst zurückgekommen.

USCHI Erzähl' mal! Wie war's denn?

HERBERT Ach, es gefällt mir immer unheimlich gut bei meiner Oma. Sie kocht ganz tolle Sachen und ist immer guter Laune. Außerdem treffe ich immer dort den Martin. Er wohnt im Haus neben meiner Oma, und wir haben schon als Kinder zusammen gespielt, jedesmal wenn wir zu Besuch bei meiner Oma waren. Diesmal haben wir auch eine Menge zusammen unternommen. Martin ist echt ein super Kumpel. Er ist mit mir in der ganzen Gegend rumgefahren. Ich glaub', ich kenn' den Bayerischen Wald jetzt besser als unsere Gegend!

USCHI Meine Schwester war auch schon mal im Bayerischen Wald. Ihr hat es dort auch gut gefallen.

HERBERT Und du? Warst du denn schon weg?

USCHI Nein! Wir fahren erst am Samstag früh.

HERBERT Und wohin geht's diesmal?

USCHI Wir fahren nach Südfrankreich, nach Nizza, um genau zu sein!

HERBERT Nizza! Super! Warst du schon mal dort?

USCHI Nein, aber ich freu' mich schon wahnsinnig darauf! Dort soll es einen tollen Sandstrand geben und viele gute Restaurants, die frische Meeresfrüchte anbieten.

HERBERT Schau mal, da drüben kommt der Frank! He, Frank, komm, setz dich zu uns!

FRANK Hallo, ihr beiden!

USCHI Wir unterhalten uns gerade über unsere Ferien! Wie sieht's bei dir aus? Warst du schon weg?

FRANK Nein, leider noch nicht! Ich hab' die ersten drei Wochen der Sommerferien bei meinen Eltern im Supermarkt geholfen. Jetzt habe ich genug Taschengeld gespart, um mit dem Thorsten nach Thüringen zu fahren.

HERBERT Thüringen! Hört sich super an. Was wollt ihr denn da alles machen?

FRANK Ach, wir wollen verschiedene Orte besuchen und so eine Art Rundreise machen. Wir fangen in Eisenach an und weiter nach Gotha, über Erfurt bis nach Weimar. Dort bleiben wir dann eine Weile. Da gibt es kulturell 'ne Menge zu sehen. Ach, da ist Moni! Ich hab' mich hier mit ihr verabredet. Sie ist gestern aus den Ferien zurückgekommen und will mir erzählen, wie es war!

MONI Hallo, alle zusammen!

FRANK Hallo, Moni! Du bist ja richtig braun geworden! Wie war's auf Mallorca?

MONI Spitze! Sonne, Sand und Meer! Einfach sagenhaft! Ich wär' so gern noch länger dort geblieben.

Answers to Activity 6

Herbert: Bayern/war schon dort
Uschi: Nizza/fährt erst hin
Frank: Thüringen/fährt erst hin
Moni: Mallorca/war schon dort

Activity 9, *p. 34*

THOMAS Hallo, Uta. Warum hast du es denn so eilig?

UTA Ja, weißt du, ich fahre morgen früh mit meiner Klasse in den Harz. Ich komme gerade vom Fotostudio Lambertz, weil ich ein paar Filme für meine Kamera kaufen mußte. Dann muß ich noch in den Supermarkt, um Reiseverpflegung zu besorgen. Und was machst du hier, Thomas?

THOMAS Also, ich war vorhin im Getränkemarkt und hab' ein paar Flaschen zurückgebracht. Und jetzt gerade war ich im Sportgeschäft Winkler und habe mir meine neue Skiausrüstung für diesen Winter ausgesucht. Echt toll, sage ich dir.

UTA Du, schau mal, da drüben ist der Jürgen, der fährt auch morgen mit in den Harz. He, Jürgen!

JÜRGEN Hallo, Thomas! Hallo, Uta! Na, hast du schon alles für unsere Reise eingekauft?

UTA So ziemlich. Und du?

JÜRGEN Ich weiß nicht. Ich muß noch in den Obstladen, um mir ein bißchen Verpflegung für unterwegs einzukaufen. Vorhin war ich gerade bei Stein & Buddenbrock. Ich konnte meine Badehose nicht mehr finden, also habe ich mir noch schnell eine neue gekauft.

THOMAS Da drüben läuft meine Schwester. He, Angelika! Jürgen, Uta, kennt ihr meine Schwester Angelika?

UTA Also, ich habe sie noch nicht kennengelernt. Hallo!

ANGELIKA Hallo, Uta! Grüß dich Jürgen!

THOMAS Sag mal, Angelika, was machst du denn in der Stadt?

ANGELIKA Ich war gerade in der Parfümerie Becker und habe ein Parfüm für Oma gekauft. Sie hat doch morgen Geburtstag. Jetzt gehe ich ins Fitneß-Studio. Ich mach' dort einen Aerobic-Kurs.

THOMAS Ach so, ja. Mensch, ich muß noch schnell was für Oma besorgen. Ich glaub', ich hol' ihr ein neues Brillenetui. Ich lauf' mal schnell zu Optik Uhl. Tschüs!

UTA Tschüs, Thomas! Viel Spaß im Fitneß-Studio, Angelika!

ANGELIKA Danke! Tschüs!

Answers to Activity 9

Uta: geht zuletzt in den Supermarkt
Thomas: geht zuletzt zu Optik Uhl
Jürgen: geht zuletzt in den Obstladen
Angelika: geht zuletzt ins Fitneß-Studio

SCRIPTS

Activity 13, *p. 35*

CHRISTOPH Na, was meint ihr? Was sollen wir in den Ferien machen? Ich war noch nie an der Nordsee. Ich würde wahnsinnig gern dorthin fahren und ein bißchen segeln gehen. Und ihr? Wozu habt ihr denn Lust? Was meinst du, Annette?

ANNETTE Also, ich weiß nicht so recht. Ich war vor zwei Jahren in Bremerhaven, und ich fand es dort nicht so toll. Die Nordsee war ziemlich schmutzig, und es war kalt und sehr windig. Wenn wir schon an den Strand wollen, sollten wir lieber an die Ostsee fahren. Dort waren wir noch nie, und außerdem sind da nicht so viele Touristen. Was sagst du dazu, Isabella?

ISABELLA Wieso wollt ihr denn immer nur an den Strand? Also, ich war noch nie in Berlin. Das wäre doch toll, was meint ihr? Ich interessiere mich sehr für Kultur, und Berlin hat eben einfach alles: Denkmäler, Museen ... das ist eine richtig internationale Stadt. Jörg, du warst doch auch noch nie in Berlin. Was hältst du von der Idee?

JÖRG Ich weiß nicht so recht. So eine Großstadt ist mir einfach zu hektisch und voll. Ich habe keine Lust, dort meine Ferien zu verbringen. Außerdem hat mir meine Schwester erzählt, daß die Jugendherbergen dort meistens ausgebucht sind. Es wird schwierig sein, so kurzfristig zu reservieren. Ich finde, wir sollten irgendwohin fahren, wo wir wandern und schwimmen können. Was haltet ihr vom Schwarzwald?

ANNETTE Ja, das hört sich gut an, Jörg. Vielleicht können wir ja auch unsere Fahrräder mitnehmen.

ISABELLA Unbedingt! Dort können wir radeln, wandern und schwimmen, und Jugendherbergen gibt es dort sicherlich auch. Was hältst du davon, Christoph?

CHRISTOPH Das ist keine schlechte Idee. Im Schwarzwald war ich auch noch nie. Schau mal im Verzeichnis nach, Isabella, ob wir eine gute Jugendherberge finden!

ISABELLA Ja, in Freiburg ist bestimmt eine. Also, ich freu' mich schon auf den Schwarzwald.

Answers to Activity 13

Christoph: möchte an die Nordsee — war noch nie dort, möchte segeln gehen

Annette: möchte nicht an die Nordsee — war schon dort, fand es nicht toll, Nordsee ist schmutzig, es war kalt und windig; möchte an die Ostsee — war noch nie dort, es gibt dort nicht viele Touristen

Isabella: möchte nach Berlin — interessiert sich für Kultur

Jörg: möchte nicht nach Berlin — Großstadt ist zu hektisch und voll, Jugendherbergen sind meistens ausgebucht; möchte in den Schwarzwald — will wandern und schwimmen

Activity 18, *p. 37*

1. **ASSAM** Du, Werner, ich bin noch nicht sicher, ob ich dieses Wochenende mitkomme. Ich sollte eigentlich zu Hause bleiben und für die Biologiearbeit am Montag lernen.

   WERNER Ach was, Assam! Du kannst mir glauben, der Bio-Test wird total einfach sein. Der Hoffmann macht nie schwierige Prüfungen. Du mußt einfach mitkommen. Die Radtour wird ein Riesenspaß.

2. **ANJA** Elke, ich bezweifle, daß wir in Thüringen in der Jugendherberge noch Unterkunft bekommen. Da ist doch sicherlich alles voll.

   ELKE Mach dir nur keine Sorgen, Anja! Ich bin sicher, daß sie noch was freihaben. Die Jugendherberge dort ist ziemlich groß. Das dauert lange, bis da mal alle Betten voll sind.

3. **MARION** Du mußt einfach mit ins Rockkonzert kommen, Eva. Das gefällt dir ganz bestimmt, da bin ich mir sicher.

   EVA Ich weiß nicht, ob mir die Musik so liegt, Marion. Ich höre eigentlich lieber ruhige Musik.

4. **FRANK** Meinst du, daß Mutter das Geschenk gefallen wird, Claudia? Ich weiß nicht so recht. Ich bin mir nicht sicher, ob sie Blau gern hat.

   CLAUDIA Mach dir nur keine Sorgen, Frank! Du kannst mir glauben, daß ihr das gefallen wird. Sie mag Blau echt gern.

Answers to Activity 18

1. Assam bezweifelt etwas; Werner ist sicher.
2. Anja bezweifelt etwas; Elke ist sicher.
3. Eva bezweifelt etwas; Marion ist sicher.
4. Frank bezweifelt etwas; Claudia ist sicher.

Zweite Stufe
Activity 26, *p. 41*

1. **BRITTA** Was meinst du, Gerhard? Sollen wir in den Ferien lieber in einer Jugenherberge oder bei Verwandten und Bekannten bleiben?

   GERHARD Also, Britta, ich habe gehört, die Jugendherbergen sollen ganz toll sein. Der Werner hat gesagt, die Verpflegung soll hervorragend sein, und die Unterkünfte sollen sehr sauber und günstig sein.

   BRITTA Also, ich weiß nicht so recht. Jugendherbergen sind zwar billig und meistens auch in einer schönen Gegend, aber ich kann nicht gut schlafen, wenn zu viele Leute in einem Zimmer sind.

   GERHARD Also, Britta, ich finde Jugendherbergen einfach toll. Wo sonst kann man für ein paar Mark übernachten und essen?

   BRITTA Na ja, vielleicht sollten wir es mal ausprobieren.

2. **KLAUS** Du, Bruno, wenn wir nach Weimar fahren, sollten wir unbedingt in der Jugendherberge übernachten. Was meinst du?

SCRIPTS

BRUNO Von mir aus. Warst du denn schon mal dort in der Jugendherberge?

KLAUS Ja, wir sind letztes Jahr ganz kurz dort gewesen, nur ein Wochenende lang. Ich wär' gern noch länger geblieben, aber wir wollten ja weiter bis nach Dresden, und deshalb hab' ich nicht viel von Weimar gesehen. Aber ich erinnere mich, daß die Jugendherberge ein ganz tolles Programm angeboten hat.

BRUNO Tatsächlich? Was denn, zum Beispiel?

KLAUS Ja, also, es laufen dort Dia-Vorträge über Weimar, man kann eine Stadtführung machen oder Kulturdenkmäler besichtigen. Und stell dir vor, alles ist von der Jugendherberge aus organisiert!

BRUNO Super! Was wird sonst noch dort angeboten?

KLAUS Es gibt dort auch eine Diskothek und Grillabende und ...

BRUNO Fantastisch! Du, wenn in Weimar in der Jugendherberge so viel los ist, dann bin ich echt dafür, daß wir uns dort einquartieren!

Answers to Activity 26

1. Britta und Gerhard sprechen über Jugendherbergen im allgemeinen.
2. Klaus und Bruno sprechen über Jugendherbergen in Weimar.

Activity 30, p. 42

CLAUDIA Na, was sollen wir dieses Wochenende machen? Meine Kusine aus Düsseldorf kommt doch zu Besuch, und sie hat mich am Telefon gefragt, ob wir mal eine Radtour um den Chiemsee mit ihr machen würden. Ich finde die Idee toll! Und wie sieht's mit euch aus? Habt ihr auch Lust dazu? Was meinst du, Holger?

HOLGER Also, ich weiß nicht so recht, Claudia! Ich war erst letzte Woche mit meinen Eltern am Chiemsee. Ich würde lieber was anderes machen.

CLAUDIA Was schlägst du denn vor?

HOLGER Laßt uns doch ins Freibad gehen! Ich hab' Lust, mal wieder ein paar Sprünge vom Drei-Meter-Turm zu machen. Du nicht auch, Jens?

JENS Also, ich finde Claudias Vorschlag gut. Am Chiemsee gibt es ausgezeichnete Radwege, und ich würde gern mal wieder 'ne lange Radtour machen.

CLAUDIA Genau! Wir können uns doch was zu essen mitnehmen und den ganzen Tag am Chiemsee bleiben.

JENS Wie wär's mit einem Picknick? Ute, kannst du wieder deinen tollen Kartoffelsalat machen? Ich mach' dann die Frikadellen dazu.

UTE Ja also, eigentlich habe ich keine Lust, schon wieder eine Radtour zu machen. Ich fahr' halt jeden Tag mit dem Rad zur Schule, und würd' am Wochenende lieber mal das Rad im Keller lassen. Können wir nicht alle einfach nur so zum Bummeln in die Stadt gehen? Vielleicht läuft ja ein toller Film im Kino, und danach könnten wir doch ins Eiscafé gehen.

CLAUDIA Ach nein, das ist mir zu langweilig. Ich mache auf jeden Fall die Radtour um den Chiemsee mit meiner Kusine. Du kommst also mit, Jens?

JENS Ja, klar! Ich freu' mich schon.

Answers to Activity 30

Holger: ist nicht einverstanden
Jens: ist einverstanden; war erst letzte Woche am Chiemsee
Ute: ist nicht einverstanden; Chiemsee hat ausgezeichnete Radwege

Activity 33, p. 43

MARKUS Also, die belegten Brote sind fertig. Jetzt müssen wir nur noch die restlichen Sachen einpacken. Sag mal, Andreas, wo ist eigentlich unsere Kühlbox? Da müssen die ganzen Getränke rein.

ANDREAS Ist schon erledigt, Markus! Silvia hat gerade die Kühlbox und den Picknickkorb aus dem Keller geholt. Also, was kommt alles in den Korb? Ein Schneidebrett, drei Becher zum Trinken, drei Teller und drei Gabeln.

SILVIA Wieso nur Gabeln? Wir brauchen auch Messer und Löffel. Und vergiß nicht, dein Taschenmesser mit dem Flaschenöffner einzupacken, damit wir die Limoflaschen aufmachen können.

ANDREAS Gut. Also, das Besteck habe ich. Dann brauchen wir noch Servietten. Das wäre alles!

MARKUS Denkst du! Wir brauchen außerdem noch einen Salz- und einen Pfefferstreuer. Ich hab' doch auch Tomaten fürs Picknick gekauft. Silvia, hast du schon eine Abfalltüte für unseren Müll eingepackt?

SILVIA Ja, sie liegt ganz unten im Picknickkorb. Hier ist die Thermosflasche mit dem heißen Tee. Andreas, hast du schon den Erdbeerjoghurt in die Kühlbox getan?

ANDREAS Ja, klar! Ich hab' auch schon die Bananen dort reingelegt. Du, Markus, kannst du bitte die karierte Decke aus dem Schrank holen? Die nehmen wir natürlich auch noch mit.

MARKUS Okay, hier ist sie. Brauchen wir sonst noch was?

SILVIA Ich glaube, wir haben alles. Los geht's!

Answers to Activity 33

belegte Brote, Kühlbox, Getränke (Limo), Picknickkorb, Schneidebrett, Becher, Teller, Besteck (Gabeln, Messer, Löffel), Messer mit Flaschenöffner, Salz- und Pfefferstreuer, Tomaten, Abfalltüte, Thermosflasche mit heißem Tee, Erdbeerjoghurt, Bananen, karierte Decke

Kapitel 2: Auf in die Jugendherberge!
Projects and Games

PROJECT

In this activity students will write a letter requesting information about **Jugendherbergen** *in a town, city, or general area they would like to visit.*

Materials Students may need addresses for tourist information centers, travel agencies, and youth hostels, as well as writing paper, envelopes, and airmail stamps. Here are some addresses that might be helpful.

Deutsches Jugendherbergswerk, Hauptverband e.V., 32754 Detmold, Germany (Fax: 05231/740149)

Österreichischer Jugendherbergsverband, Schottenring 28, A-1010 Wien, Austria (Fax: 01/5350861)

Schweizer Jugendherbergen, Schaffhauserstr. 14, Postfach, 8042 Zürich, Switzerland (Fax: 01/3601460)

Suggested Sequence

1. Tell the class that they will be writing a letter to get information about **Jugendherbergen** in an area of the German-speaking world they would like to visit. Then have them brainstorm together what they would need to include in such a letter. (Examples: name of town, city, or general area to be visited, time of year of trip, age of those traveling, return address)
2. Have pairs of students decide what place they would like to visit. Students can refer back to the **Vorschau** from Level 1 or Location Openers from all levels for ideas.
3. Pairs outline their letters, including all important information.
4. Pairs write their letters in letter format with appropriate greetings and closings. You may want to remind students to use formal address and to date their letter using the German style. (Example: **Denver, den 31. Dezember 1999**)
5. Students exchange their letters with another pair for comments and corrections.
6. Pairs rewrite their letters and mail them to the appropriate agency in a German-speaking country.
7. As students receive responses from abroad, you may want to display them on a bulletin board in the classroom.

Grading the Project

Suggested point distribution (total = 100 points)
Content (clear and to the point)   50
Format and Style   25
Grammar and Usage   25

GAMES

Kettenspiel

This game will help auditory learners review vocabulary.

Procedure Make the following statement: **Wenn wir nach (New York) reisen wollen, müssen wir zuerst (Flugkarten kaufen).** The next student should repeat your sentence and add another part of the plan necessary to prepare for the trip. The game continues with each student repeating all the things that have to be done before the trip and then adding another. If a player leaves out any part of the plan or makes any other mistakes, he or she drops out of the game.

Tolle Reise

This game will help students review the geography of cities in German-speaking countries, as well as question formation and verbs in German.

Procedure Hang up a large map of the German-speaking countries. Divide the class into two teams. One student from Team A comes up to the map, locates a city on the map, and asks a student on Team B **Warum würdest du nach (Wien) reisen?** That student then tries to think of an activity or a sight that he or she would like to do or visit in that city. If the student's answer is appropriate, his or her team receives a point and continues the game. If the answer is incorrect, the other team gets a chance to answer, receives a point if the answer is correct, and gets another turn at the map.

Kapitel 2: Auf in die Jugendherberge!
Lesson Plans, pages 28-51

Teacher Notes

• Chapter 2 is a review chapter that reintroduces functions, grammar, and vocabulary from *Komm mit!* Levels 1 and 2.

• Before you begin the chapter, you may want to preview the *Video Program* and consult the *Video Guide*. Suggestions for integrating the video into each chapter are given in the *Video Guide* and in the chapter interleaf. Activity masters for video selections can be found in the *Video Guide*.

Using the Chapter Opener,
pp. 28-29

Motivating Activity

Ask students if they have gone on short trips with their friends. When did they go, where did they go, how long did they stay, and how did they plan for this trip? (**Bist du schon mal mit Freunden auf einer Kurzreise gewesen? Wann war das? Wohin ging es? Wie lange wart ihr dort? Wie habt ihr diese Reise geplant?**)

♜ Game

Play the game **Kettenspiel**. See p. 27F for the procedure.

Building on Previous Skills

Ask students to name examples of **öffentliche Verkehrsmittel** that they learned in Level 2. (Examples: **der Bus, die Straßenbahn, die U-Bahn, die S-Bahn**) In addition, you may ask them which types of public transportation are available in their area. (**Welche öffentlichen Verkehrsmittel gibt es in dieser Stadt? Könnt ihr die aufzählen?**)

Background Information

① Erfurt, is not only the state capital of **Thüringen** but also its largest city. Erfurt's history dates back to 729 when it was first mentioned in official records. The city is described as **turmreich** because of its large number of churches and monasteries (80 churches and 36 monasteries) dating back to the Middle Ages, many of which are still standing today.

Teaching Suggestion

① If available, show students a city map of Erfurt and ask them why people might be interested in visiting this historic city. (**Was gibt es für einen Besucher in Erfurt zu sehen und zu tun?**)

Thinking Critically

② **Drawing Inferences** Ask students about the various resources that are available to people planning a trip. Have students tell you what the people in the picture might be using to help them plan their vacation. (**Welche Materialien und Informationen brauchen Touristen, um eine Reise zu planen?**)

③ **Drawing Inferences** Ask students to imagine the conversation between the two students in the photo, incorporating the statement in the photo caption.

Focusing on Outcomes

To get students to focus on the chapter objectives, ask them what reasons they might give for wanting to travel with a group of friends rather than joining their family on their next trip. Then preview the learning outcomes listed on p. 29. **NOTE:** These outcomes are modeled in **Los geht's!** (pp. 30-31) and **Weiter geht's!** (pp. 38-39) and evaluated in **Kann ich's wirklich?** (p. 50).

Teaching Los geht's!
pp. 30-31

Resources for Los geht's!

- *Textbook Audiocassette* 1 B
- *Practice and Activity Book*

Teacher Note
Los geht's! is recorded on audiocassette.

Los geht's! Summary
In **Auf nach Thüringen!**, a group of friends talk about a trip they are planning together. The following functions listed on p. 29 are modeled in their conversation: asking for and making suggestions; expressing preference and giving a reason; expressing wishes; expressing doubt, conviction, and resignation.

Motivating Activity
Put students into pairs or small groups and ask them to share with their peers how their family goes about making a decision about where to go on vacation. Put some key questions on the board or on a transparency.
Examples:
Wie entscheidet deine Familie, wohin ihr in den Sommerferien fahrt?
Gibt es verschiedene Meinungen?

Background Information
Rennsteig is a famous German hiking trail that originates near Eisenach and ends in Bavaria, 15 km (9.3 miles) from the border. The first mention of it dates back to the early thirteen hundreds. The **Rennsteig** was used as a courier line and part of a shortcut to the Danube. The 170 km (105.4 miles) long trail takes at least five days to hike.

Teaching Suggestion
For teaching purposes, divide the text into three sections. Play the recording of the first part while students follow along in the book. Ask some questions to check for comprehension. Play the tape again. Follow the same procedure for parts 2 and 3. Then play the entire conversation and have students read along.

Teaching Suggestion
1 After students have listened to the recording of the conversation and have read it, ask these questions to check for comprehension. Allow students to look at the conversation while answering.

Building on Previous Skills
4 For this activity, ask students to look back at the information in the Location Opener on pp. 1-3. The Almanac as well as Photos 2, 3, and 5 provide some additional information on the state of **Thüringen**.

Closure
Ask students to review the conversation between the four students and then decide with whom they most identify based on their interests and statements. What made them decide on that person? (**Lest euch noch mal die Unterhaltung durch! Mit welchen von den vier Schülern identifiziert ihr euch am meisten? Warum?**)

Teaching Erste Stufe,
pp. 32-37

Resources for Erste Stufe

Practice and Activity Book
Chapter Resources, Book 1
- Communicative Activities 2-1, 2-2
- Additional Listening Activities 2-1, 2-2, 2-3
- Student Response Forms
- Realia 2-1
- Situation Card 2-1
- Teaching Transparency Master 2-1
- Quiz 2-1
Audiocassette Program
- *Textbook Audiocassette* 1 B
- *Additional Listening Activities, Audiocassette* 9 A
- *Assessment Items, Audiocassette* 7 A
Video Program, Videocassette 1
Video Guide

LOS GEHT'S!

ERSTE STUFE

▶ *page 32*

MOTIVATE

♖ Game

The game **Stadt, Land, Fluß** was introduced in Level 2 (p. 51F). You may want to play this game to review German geography as well as vocabulary from this and the previous chapter.

TEACH

Thinking Critically

Drawing Inferences Ask students to scan the text **Willkommen!** to identify what type of text it is, where one might see it printed, and what information one would expect to find in it. (**Was für ein Text ist das? Wo kann man so einen Text sehen? Was für Informationen gibt uns so ein Text gewöhnlich?**)

For Individual Needs

Challenge Read the text aloud as if you were speaking on the radio. After each of the six paragraphs, ask students to summarize what they have just read. Put the numbers 1 through 6 on the board or a transparency and make a list of the six summary statements.

Teaching Suggestion

5 Ask students to use the summary statements from the previous activity to help them answer these four questions in writing. Encourage students to paraphrase or answer the questions in their own words rather than simply copy the answers out of the text.

Culture Note

The text mentions that **Jugendherbergen** are for all kinds of groups including school groups. A **Klassenfahrt** is a yearly occurrence for most German students. The cost of such trips is kept low through inexpensive accomodations such as **Jugendherbergen**.

▶ *page 33*

PRESENTATION: Wortschatz

- After you have gone over the vocabulary with students, ask them to use the various words or phrases in a meaningful context by creating sentences. This can be done orally or in writing. Challenge students to incorporate more than one new word or phrase into a sentence. The sentences can be simple or complex.
- Make up statements or questions that paraphrase a word or phrase from the **Wortschatz** box. Students have to guess which one you mean and restate what you said.
  Example:
  Teacher: **Fast jeder weiß, wer ich bin.**
  Student: **Du bist/Sie sind berühmt.**

For Individual Needs

6 A Slower Pace Before students listen to the activity, ask them which time phrases they should be listening for in order to differentiate between **war schon dort** and **fährt erst dorthin**. What verb forms and tenses should they expect to hear? Ask students to give some examples.

PRESENTATION: So sagt man das!

Ask students to look back at the **Los geht's!** conversation and make a list of the expressions that are used to ask for and make suggestions. Then discuss the expressions in the **So sagt man das!** box. Ask students to find the key element in each of the choices for making suggestions.
Wir können mal ...
... wir doch mal ...
Ich schlage vor, daß ...
Then ask students for examples using each of the introductory phrases for making suggestions.

▶ *page 34*

 For Individual Needs

8 A Slower Pace Before students do the partner activity, practice with them the proper use of prepositions and cases for expressing motion towards a place and location at a place. Do this for all the places given in the suggestion box through quick question-answer practice.
Examples:
Teacher: **Wohin fährst du?**
Student: **Auf die Insel Rügen.**
Teacher: **Wo warst du?**
Student: **Auf der Insel Rügen.**

9 A Slower Pace Stop the tape after each exchange and play it again if necessary for students to understand where each of the four characters was last before running into his friends. Warn them to pay special attention to Thomas, who seems to have last been at the **Sportgeschäft** but later on in the conversation thinks of something else he needs to do.

▶ *page 35*

 For Individual Needs

11a Challenge When putting together a shopping route, ask students to disagree with some of their partner's suggestions and propose going to a different shop or doing the shopping in a different order.

13 A Slower Pace Stop the tape after each report and repeat if necessary. Since the key information is embedded each time in a rather lengthy monologue, students might need time to process each monologue before going on to the next.

PRESENTATION: So sagt man das!

To review and practice previously learned vocabulary and functions, encourage students to express preference in different contexts.
Examples:
Was ißt du lieber als Fisch? Warum?
Was ziehst du vor? An die See oder in die Berge fahren? Warum?

▶ *page 36*

PRESENTATION: So sagt man das!

Have students look back at the **Los geht's!** conversation and make a list of the expressions Uschi and Udo used to express wishes. Ask students to quote these expressions from the conversation and then restate them in different ways.

PRESENTATION: So sagt man das!

After reviewing the expressions, remind students that intonation plays a big role in the perception of what is being said. Then give students several statements to which they must react, expressing either doubt, conviction, or resignation.
Examples:
Du kannst mir glauben, es gibt heute Roast Beef in der Schulcafeteria.
Wir können dieses Jahr leider nicht in ein deutsches Restaurant essen gehen.

▶ *page 37*

Teaching Suggestion

18 Put the pairs of names for each exchange on the chalkboard or a transparency. Names should be in the same sequence in which they are heard on the audiocassette.

 For Individual Needs

18 Challenge Play the recording a second time and ask students about the context of each exchange. (**Worum geht es in jedem Gespräch?**) Ask students to write their ideas next to the number of each exchange.

 Video Program

In the video clip **Freizeit**, students of the **Drittes Gymnasium** in Prenzlauer Berg, talk about their leisure activities. See *Video Guide* for suggestions.

 For Individual Needs

20 Challenge Students may want to "leave a telephone message" and make their invitation orally on audiocassette. Let the other group listen to the message and give its response on tape as well.

ERSTE STUFE

Reteaching: Expressing Preference and Giving Reasons

Present pairs of students with the following situation: You have plans to visit **die neuen Bundesländer** together and have studied brochures and made plans that don't necessarily coincide. Tell each other why you prefer a particular place and give reasons with which you hope to change the other's mind.

CLOSE

Teaching Suggestion

Ask students to complete the following statement. **Ich hätte Lust, nächsten Sommer ..., weil ....**

Focusing on Outcomes

Refer students back to the learning outcomes listed on p. 29. They should recognize that they now know how to ask for and make suggestions; express preference and give a reason; express wishes; and express doubt, conviction, and resignation.

ASSESS

- **Performance Assessment** Present students with various situations (a list of statements and requests) that they try to avoid by using expressions of doubt and resignation.
  Examples:
  — **Debra wird heute beim Schachturnier bestimmt gewinnen!**
  — **Es tut mir leid, aber ich muß um 16 Uhr zum Zahnarzt.**

- Quiz 2-1, *Chapter Resources,* Book 1

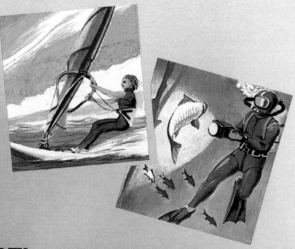

Teaching Weiter geht's!
pp. 38-39

Resources for Weiter geht's!

- *Textbook Audiocassette* 1 B
- *Practice and Activity Book*

Teacher Note

Weiter geht's! is recorded on audiocassette.

Weiter geht's! Summary

In **Auf nach Weimar!**, Frank, Udo, Uschi, and Sabine are making more detailed plans for their trip to Weimar. The following student outcomes listed on p. 29 are modeled in their conversation: asking for information and expressing an assumption; expressing hearsay; asking for, making, and responding to suggestions; expressing wishes when shopping.

Motivating Activity

Ask students to brainstorm things they need to do when planning a trip. (**Was müßt ihr alles machen, wenn ihr euch auf eine Reise vorbereitet?**)

Thinking Critically

Drawing Inferences Before students begin reading **Auf nach Weimar!**, ask them to predict what might happen next with the vacation plans the four classmates made. Write some of the students' ideas on the board.

Teaching Suggestions

- Ask students to scan the conversation to find out what the German students are talking about. Were their predictions accurate?

- Play the recording of the entire conversation while students follow along in their books. Then play the tape again, this time stopping it at brief intervals to ask some comprehension questions.

 Culture Note

Udo refers to his German teacher as **der Gleißner** instead of **Herr Gleißner.** It is common practice for secondary level and university students to refer to their teachers and professors that way.

For Individual Needs

22 Challenge Ask students to use their answers to the seven questions to help them compose a written summary of the **Weiter geht's!** conversation. This may be done for homework.

For Additional Practice

24 Ask students to imagine that they are providing information to a visitor to their area or town who would like some suggestions as to what to do and see.

Teaching Suggestion

After students have worked with the text in Activities 23 and 24, put them into groups of four with each student taking one of the four roles from the **Weiter geht's!** converation. Ask students to enact the conversation by speaking rather than reading their parts aloud, using a lot of expression to bring it alive.

 For Individual Needs

Challenge Ask pairs of students to rewrite the conversation (or part of it) using synonymous expressions, restatements, or by paraphrasing where they can, but keeping the exchanges essentially the same so that the content and the flow of the conversation does not change.

Closure

Ask students to make a list of information they can recall about **Thüringen** from the **Los geht's!** and **Weiter geht's!** conversations.

Teaching Zweite Stufe,
pp. 40-44

Resources for Zweite Stufe

Practice and Activity Book
Chapter Resources, Book 1
- Communicative Activities 2-3, 2-4
- Additional Listening Activities 2-4, 2-5, 2-6
- Student Response Forms
- Realia 2-2
- Situation Card 2-2
- Teaching Transparency Master 2-2
- Quiz 2-2

Audiocassette Program
- *Textbook Audiocassette* 1 B
- *Additional Listening Activities, Audiocassette* 9 A
- *Assessment Items, Audiocassette* 7 A

Video Program, Videocassette 1
Video Guide

▶ *page 40*

MOTIVATE
Thinking Critically

Drawing Inferences Ask students how they could find out about hotel accommodations in a city that they planned to visit. (**Wie würdest du dich über die Hotels in einer Stadt informieren, die du besuchen willst?**)

TEACH
Teaching Suggestion

Read the prospectus for **Jugendgästehaus Weimar** aloud to the class. Stop as needed to provide definitions for unfamiliar phrases or words, but refrain from using English.

Teacher Note

A **Baudenabend** is an evening of social interaction with refreshments and musical entertainment that usually takes place in a **Hütte** in the forest. **Baude** means **Hütte**.

ZWEITE STUFE

Cooperative Learning

25 Divide students into groups of three or four and have group members take the role of a reader, a writer/proofreader, a discussion leader (optional), or a reporter. Each group tries to answer Questions 1 through 4 within a set amount of time. Call on reporters to share their groups' responses with the class.

Portfolio Assessment

25 You might want to suggest this activity as a written and oral portfolio item for your students. See *Assessment Guide*, p. 15.

▶ *page 41*

PRESENTATION: Wortschatz

- Go over the words in the **Wortschatz** box with students.
- Have students identify the verbs from the **Wortschatz** that correspond to the following nouns.
  das Andenken (denken an)
  die Erinnerung (sich erinnern)
  der Streit (streiten)
- Finally, ask students to give definitions for the nouns based on the definitions for the verbs.

Teaching Suggestion

26 Ask students to listen to the two conversations again, this time listing all the positive things that are being said about youth hostels by any of the speakers.

Video Program

In the video clip **Ein neues Schulsystem**, students in Dresden talk about how school today compares with what it used to be in former East Germany. See *Video Guide* for suggestions.

PRESENTATION: So sagt man das!

- To review and practice the phrases in the function box, ask several questions incorporating **ob**-clauses and have students answer them.
  Examples:
  Michael, kannst du mir sagen, ob es heute Pizza in der Cafeteria zu kaufen gibt?
  Weißt du, ob unser Schuldirektor heute in der Schule ist?
- Ask simple yes/no questions that students have to change into questions with **ob**-clauses. Put several introductory clauses on the board or on a transparency.
  Examples:
  Weißt du,
  Wißt ihr, } ob ...
  Wissen Sie,
  Ich möchte wissen, ob ...
  Darf ich mal fragen, ob ...
  Kannst du
  Könnt ihr } mir sagen, ob ...
  Können Sie
  Have other students answer.

Teaching Suggestion

27 Students may refer to the text on p. 40 as they discuss their plans to visit Weimar with their partner. Monitor students' conversations as you walk around the classroom. Be available to answer specific questions about **Jugendherbergen**.

▶ *page 42*

PRESENTATION: So sagt man das!

- Present each of the statements and ask students immediately after each **Weiß ich das oder habe ich das nur so gehört?** to help students understand the idea of hearsay. You may want to add a few hearsay statements on your own.
- Next, present several factual statements that students have to change into hearsay. Use the context of Weimar.
  Examples:
  Weimar ist eine schöne Stadt.
  Es gibt dort einen Stadtpark.
- Ask students to share some news or gossip about an actor, musician, or other celebrity. You may want to begin by sharing your own bit of news.
  Example:
  Ich habe gehört, daß die David Letterman Sendung heute abend eine Wiederholung ist.

For Additional Practice

28 For further practice, you may want to add other topics such as **Pensionen, Sommercamps, Fahrschulen,** and **Campingplätze**. Students follow the directions for Activity 28 as they discuss the additional topics.

PRESENTATION: So sagt man das!

Ask students to use the different ways of making suggestions as they discuss the Location Opener on pp. 1-3. Students ask each other for suggestions, make suggestions, and respond to suggestions about what they would like to do and see in **die neuen Bundesländer**.

Teaching Suggestion

31 You may want to give students the option of writing about what they would like to see or do in other locations to appeal to all students' interests.

▶ *page 43*

PRESENTATION: Wortschatz

- Bring the utensils and other kitchen items presented in the **Wortschatz** box to class. Present the various items to students and have them repeat.
- Next, ask questions to which one or two of the utensils are the answer.
  Example:
  Was brauche ich zum Brotschneiden? (ein Messer und ein Schneidebrett)

▶ *page 44*

PRESENTATION: Ein wenig Grammatik

Remind students that unpreceded adjectives have to assume the role of an article; their endings have to indicate the gender, number, and case of the noun that follows.

PRESENTATION: So sagt man das!

- Remind students that the umlauts in **möchte** and **hätte** indicate the subjunctive mood. Subjunctive is used to express wishes or something that someone would like to do.
- Have students practice making requests with the **möchte**-forms and **hätte**-forms using the food vocabulary in the boxes above. Students work in pairs and role-play a conversation between vendor and customer at the **Marktplatz**.

Teacher Note

In the **So sagt man das!** box, **Schweizer** is used as an adjective. Unlike most other adjectives, **Schweizer** is always capitalized and never changes its endings.

Teaching Suggestion

Ask students to practice the adjective endings and food vocabulary as they prepare an order for their favorite sandwich they plan to phone in to a nearby deli.

Reteaching: Expressing Hearsay

To reteach the phrases used to express hearsay, ask students to look for one worthy piece of news from magazines, newspapers, radio, or TV the night before you do this activity. The next day, ask students to share what they read or heard with the rest of the class.

▶ *page 45*

PRESENTATION: Landeskunde

Background Information

- The Goethe-Schiller memorial is located near the entrance to the **Deutsches Nationaltheater**. It was erected in 1857 by the sculptor Ernst Rietschel, who is also known for his works around **Schloß Charlottenburg** in Berlin.

- **Goethes Gartenhaus** is located in the **Park an der Ilm**. The house was built in the 17th century. Goethe lived there between 1776 and 1782. It contains all the original furnishings and is open to the public.

Culture Note

On November 5, 1993, the Ministers of Culture of the European Community awarded Weimar the title of European City of Culture for 1999. During the year-long celebration, the city plans to honor the achievements of its classical past, recognizing such famous residents as Herder, Schiller, Goethe, Liszt, and Nietzsche. Other celebrations will also be linked to Weimar's history.

Teaching Suggestion

Remind students of the reading skills they have learned, such as reading for comprehension. Emphasize that they should try to focus on understanding ideas rather than isolated words. You may want to divide the text into the following five sections to help them.
1) **Weimar wird 1999 Kulturstadt Europas.**
2) **Wem hat Weimar das zu verdanken?**
3) **Das alte Weimar**
4) **Weimar heute**
5) **Zwei deutsche Städte als „Kulturstädte Europas"**

Teacher Note

Mention to your students that the **Landeskunde** will also be included in Quiz 2-2 given at the end of the **Zweite Stufe**.

CLOSE

 ## Total Physical Response

Prior to this activity, you may want to gather all the items from the **Wortschatz** on p. 43. Call on students to come to the front of the class. Give them specific instructions on what to do with the various items.
Examples:
Stell den Becher rechts neben den Teller!
Leg Messer, Gabel und Löffel auf den Teller!

Focusing on Outcomes

Refer students back to the learning outcomes listed on p. 29. Students should recognize that they now know how to ask for information and express an assumption; express hearsay; ask for, make, and respond to suggestions; and express wishes when shopping.

Video Program

At this time, you might want to use the authentic advertising footage from German television. See *Video Guide* for suggestions.

ASSESS

- **Performance Assessment** Prepare a class set of index cards by writing a question on each card that reflects the functions and phrases reviewed in this **Stufe**. Hand one card to each student. The first student calls on another student and reads the question to him or her. That student answers the question and then asks a third student the question on his or her card. This continues until all students have had a turn answering and asking a question.

- Quiz 2-2, *Chapter Resources,* Book 1

Teaching Zum Lesen,
pp. 46-48

Reading Strategy

The targeted strategy in this reading is deriving the main idea from supporting details. Students should learn about this strategy before beginning Question 3.

Teacher Notes

- You may want to remind students that the interpretation of poetry is very subjective; there is no single correct interpretation of the following poems.

- The following poems are recorded on *Textbook Audiocassette* 11: *Erlkönig, Der Panther, Der Radwechsel, ottos mops,* and *Kinderlied.*

PREREADING
Background Information

- *Erlkönig:* Like the English Romantic poets Wordsworth and Coleridge, many of the late 18th-century and 19th-century poets in Germany tried to revive old folk forms. The first poem students will read derives from that impulse, although Goethe later changed styles and went on, with Schiller, to develop the style known as German classicism.

- *Der Panther:* Rilke (1875-1926) was born and began writing in Prague, where he was a contemporary of Kafka's. Together with the sculptor Rodin, Rilke thought out his notion of the artist as a person who sees things purely and completely and depicts their true nature in precise, concrete form. *Der Panther* is from this genre.

- *Der Radwechsel:* Bertolt Brecht (1898-1956) went through several stages of lyric style during his lifetime, beginning as an expressionist, but later developing a starker, less emotional language.

- *ottos mops:* Ernst Jandl was born in Vienna in 1925. After the war, he studied English and German and taught at a **Gymnasium.** During the 1950s, Jandl developed a form of poetry he called **Sprechgedichte,** experimental texts characterized by the constant repetition of words and by playful distortions of sound. Jandl himself has become known for his lively recitations of these poems.

- *menschenskind* and *Apfel:* Reinhard Döhl (1934 -   ) was born in Wattenscheid and now lives in Stuttgart. The two pieces of Döhl's work included here are examples of concrete poetry. Among many other things, concrete poetry is a recognition of and an attempt to come to poetic terms with the fact that people no longer recite poetry orally in our culture.

- *Kinderlied:* Günther Grass (1927 -   ) was a stonecutter, sculptor, and painter before he began his career as poet, novelist, and playwright. In his novels and plays he purports to deal with man's existential guilt, a guilt which must be individually borne and reckoned with.

Motivating Activity

Before reading the poems, have students think about some poems they know in English or in English translation, including song lyrics. Which would they call *folk* poetry, and which would they call artistic poetry? If students can't think of many examples, you might ask them about some of the following: *Homer's Illiad, Beowulf, Milton's Paradise Lost,* Shakespeare's sonnets, and the songs *My Darling Clementine, Sweet Betsy from Pike, Blowing in the Wind,* and Stephen Foster's *Old Folks at Home.*

Teacher Note

Activity 1 is a prereading activity.

READING
Teaching Suggestion

2 In addition to playing the poem *Erlkönig* on audiocassette for the students, you might want to obtain a recorded version of Schubert's **Lied.** The Schubert version will give the students a feeling for the dramatic quality of the poem, even if they don't understand all the words.

3 You may want to give students the meaning of the following words in the poems.

Teaching Suggestions

- Ask students to describe the stanza form of the ballad *Erlkönig:* how many lines are in a stanza? Which lines rhyme? What is the rhythm? Compared with a genuine folk ballad like *Yankee Doodle,* in which there is usually one narrator or a dialogue between at most two singers, how does Goethe heighten the sense of drama?

9 Before students read *ottos mops,* you might want to point out that poetry isn't always earnest and intense. Ask them if they can think of some verses (including songs) that are just plain fun and some that are both fun and intended to make the listener or reader think. As students read the poem by Jandl, they should try to decide what his purpose was in writing it.

Teacher Note

The poem *menschenskind* is made up of one block of text in four different positions.

ZUM LESEN

Language Notes

11 Students should note that the only part of **menschenskind** that remains constant throughout the poem is **kind** = *kind.* All the other letters are shifted in various meaningless combinations until the English-German equation is reversed. Note that *kind* does not mean *kindly* in this poem. It is closer, instead, to *child of man,* i.e., *human.*

11 **Mensch!** or **Menschenskind!** is a fairly established colloquial expression which conveys surprise, often tinged with disapproval or dismay. However, it is likely in this poem to convey more of a sense of wonder similar to *gee whiz* or *man alive!*

POST-READING

Teacher Note

Activity 13 is a post-reading task that will show whether students can apply what they have learned.

Thinking Critically

Evaluating Looking at the poems presented in this chapter, do students feel that poetry is more successful and lasting when it is pure art for art's sake? Or do they feel that a poet has some obligation to entertain the public at the public's level? What about poetry that is primarily intended to teach the reader a particular philosophy or set of ideas? (Examples: Emerson and/or Alexander Pope) To what extent should a poet care about the audience, and to what extent should he or she create simply in order to please himself or herself? Which of the poems from this **Zum Lesen** selection do students think are the most successful, according to students' criteria?

Closure

Have students choose one of the poems to present in a different mode. For example, they could compose a melody to which they sing the poem, or sketch an illustration that fits the mood of the poem and illustrates some important feature of its content. They should each present their work to the class and discuss the various ways in which these presentations support certain interpretations of the poems.

Answers to Activity 1

Answers will vary. Students should notice that the *Apfel* and *menschenskind* poems look different from the others, more like pictures or geometric designs.

Answers to Activity 2

dramatic: *Erlkönig, Der Panther, Der Radwechsel, Kinderlied*
Lighthearted: *ottos mops*

Answers to Activity 3

Erlkönig: **Vater, Sohn, Erlkönig**; riding through the fields and forests, night; see Question 5. *Der Panther*: **Panther**; in a cage at the zoo in Paris; the panther is walking in circles in his cage. *Der Radwechsel*: **ich**; at the side of the street; the narrator is looking on as the driver changes a tire. *ottos mops*: Otto, **mops**; Otto is trying to train his dog. *Kinderlied*: no specific characters, time, or setting are mentioned

Answers to Activity 4

The quotes designate the lines spoken by the **Erlkönig,** and the dashes indicate a change of speaker (narrator, father, and son). The chart should help students see that the lines spoken by the narator form a frame for the poem.

stanza	1	2	3	4	5	6	7	8
narr.	1-4							29-32
father		5,8		15-16		23-24		
son		6-7		13-14		21-22	27-28	
elf king			9-12		17-20		25-26	

Answers to Activity 5

The father is taking his son somewhere to get help; the son dies at the end of the poem; the **Erlkönig** is trying to take the child away; answers will vary.

Answers to Activity 6

in captivity; the panther is looking through bars; the panther is tired, numb, hopeless, and tense; the image ceases to exist.

Answers to Activity 8

No, the narrator looks on passively as the driver changes the tire; they will continue on their journey; **herkomme>hinfahre**; no, it is a description of what is happening and how the narrator feels about his situation, but stated without any emotion until the last line; answers will vary.

Answers to Activity 9

beginning of direct speech; a dog

Answers to Activity 10

They let the reader know that the first line of each stanza is a question. The reader can assume that lines 2-4 of each stanza are the answers. Actions: laughing, crying, speaking, remaining silent, playing, and dying. Because the idea of *reason* is central to the poem; it ties the five stanzas together and brings closure to the poem. There's nothing child-like about the idea presented in the poem.

Answers to Activity 11
The poet relies on concrete visual images, as well as words, to convey his meaning.

Teaching Zum Schreiben,
p. 49

Writing Strategy
The targeted strategy in this writing activity is selecting information. Students should learn about this strategy before beginning the assignment.

PREWRITING

 ### For Individual Needs

A **Visual Learners** Tell students to carefully plan each step of the process of gathering, preparing, and organizing their materials. They can do this in the form of a chart which will help them organize their notes and visuals, as well as help them keep track of individual responsibilities.

WRITING

Teaching Suggestions

B You may want to set up research tables with books and pamphlets from travel agencies in the classroom to facilitate students' research.

B Remind students to use vocabulary that will be familiar to the rest of the class since too many unknown words from the dictionary might confuse readers. Each group should make a list of unfamiliar words and phrases and try to simplify them by paraphrasing or using synonyms.

POST-WRITING

Closure
After groups have completed the travel brochures, let students tour through the classroom to see the different brochures that were produced. Display them on a bulletin board. Afterwards, students can discuss in different groups which place they would most like to visit and why.

Kann ich's wirklich?
p. 50

This page helps students prepare for the test. It is a brief checklist of the major points covered in the chapter. The students should be reminded that it is only a checklist and not necessarily everything that will appear on the test.

Teaching Wortschatz,
p. 51

 ### For Individual Needs

Kinesthetic Learners Gather the items listed on the **Wortschatz** page and arrange them on a table in the front of the class. Have students set a table for two including all necessary utensils and dishes. Then tell them to set it up for a less formal setting like a picnic. Have students tell what they are doing as they do it.

Teaching Suggestion
Students should have their books closed for this activity. Ask individual students what specific items are used for.
Example:
Wozu braucht man einen Flaschenöffner?

Teacher Note
Give the **Kapitel 2** Chapter Test, *Chapter Resources, Book 1.*

REVIEW

Inter Rail -26

DM 630,00

2 Auf in die Jugendherberge!

① Ich schlage vor, daß wir mal nach Thüringen fahren, nach Erfurt!

Jugendliche reisen gern zusammen. In einem relativ kleinen Land wie Deutschland ist das auch kein großes Problem. Man kann fast jeden Ort mit öffentlichen Verkehrsmitteln erreichen, und die zirka 700 Jugendherbergen bieten jungen Leuten eine Möglichkeit, gut und billig übernachten und essen zu können.

In this chapter you will review and practice

- asking for and making suggestions; expressing preference and giving a reason; expressing wishes; expressing doubt, conviction, and resignation
- asking for information and expressing an assumption; expressing hearsay; asking for, making, and responding to suggestions; expressing wishes when shopping

And you will

- listen to students making travel plans and decisions
- read about youth hostels in Germany
- write about your own travel plans
- find out about some of Germany's most famous cultural landmarks

② Wie wär's denn mit einem Picknick?

③ Ich glaube schon, daß es in Weimar eine Jugendherberge gibt.

Los geht's!

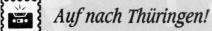

Auf nach Thüringen!

UDO So, Leute, ich hab' mir eben meinen Ferienpaß gekauft.

USCHI Das heißt also, du fährst mit, ja?

UDO Logo! Wohin geht's denn überhaupt?

FRANK Wir sind noch am Diskutieren. Ich bin dafür, daß wir an irgendeinen See in Mecklenburg fahren, zum Schwimmen und Windsurfen.

SABINE Das können wir ja auch bei uns, da brauchen wir nicht nach Mecklenburg zu fahren! Ich schlage vor, daß wir nach Thüringen fahren, zum Wandern. Dort gibt's doch diesen berühmten Wanderweg ... ja, wie heißt er denn noch?

USCHI Ich glaube, das ist der Rennsteig.

SABINE Stimmt, der Rennsteig.

FRANK Du willst wirklich wandern, Sabine?

SABINE Klar! Warum nicht?

FRANK Und du, Udo? Hast du Lust zum Wandern?

UDO Eigentlich schon. Ich hoffe nur, daß das Wetter schön bleibt.

USCHI Ja, sag uns mal, Udo, was du dir wünschst, was du gern unternehmen möchtest!

UDO Also, ich möchte auch lieber raus in die Natur, wandern, irgendwelche kleinen Städte ansehen und so.

USCHI Fahren wir doch mal in den Harz, in die Gegend von Wernigerode. Dort soll es sehr schön sein.

UDO Meine Eltern waren letztes Jahr in der Gegend, aber sie haben Thüringen interessanter gefunden, auch schöner.

SABINE Ja, ich ziehe Thüringen auch vor. Ich finde, da ist vom Kulturellen her mehr zu sehen, Weimar, Erfurt, Eisenach ...

USCHI Ich ziehe aber kleinere Städte vor, wo weniger Verkehr ist, wo die Luft besser ist.

SABINE Wir können ja beides machen: etwas Kultur und etwas für die Gesundheit, nämlich viel wandern.

UDO Wer weiß denn, wo es in Thüringen Jugendherbergen gibt?

FRANK	Ich hab' ein Verzeichnis zu Hause, ich seh' mal nach. In Eisenach gibt's eine, das weiß ich.
SABINE	Ich bezweifle aber, daß wir noch Unterkunft bekommen, jetzt in der ersten Ferienwoche.
FRANK	Ich kann ja mal anrufen. Übrigens, hat jeder von euch einen Jugendherbergsausweis?
UDO	Na klar!
SABINE	Nehmt euch aber ja nicht wieder so viele Klamotten mit wie letztes Mal!
USCHI	Keine Angst, Sabine! Aber du warst doch froh, daß ich damals ein extra Sweatshirt dabeihatte, weil du deins irgendwo verloren hattest.

1 Was passiert hier?

1. Sie sprechen darüber, wo sie ihre Ferien verbringen.

Hast du das Gespräch verstanden? Beantworte die folgenden Fragen!

1. Worüber sprechen die vier Klassenkameraden?
2. Woher weißt du, daß Udo bestimmt mitfährt?   2. Er hat sich einen Ferienpaß gekauft.
3. Warum will Sabine nicht nach Mecklenburg fahren?
4. Was schlägt Sabine vor?   4. Sie schlägt vor, zum Wandern nach Thüringen zu fahren.
5. Was möchte Udo unternehmen?   5. in der Natur wandern; sich Städte ansehen
6. Wohin möchte Uschi fahren? Warum?
7. Warum ist Udo nicht für Uschis Vorschlag?
8. Warum möchte Sabine nach Thüringen?
9. Wo wollen die Schüler übernachten?   9. in der Jugendherberge
10. Warum will Frank die Jugendherberge anrufen?

3. Sie meint, daß sie auch zu Hause schwimmen und windsurfen können.
6. Sie möchte in den Harz, in die Nähe von Wernigerode.   7. Er sagt, daß seine Eltern es in Thüringen interessanter fanden.
8. Sie findet, dort gibt es mehr Kulturelles zu sehen.
10. um zu sehen, ob sie noch Unterkunft bekommen

2 Wie gut bist du in Geografie?

Schreib alle Ortsnamen auf einen Zettel, die die vier Schüler erwähnen!
Sieh danach auf eine Landkarte und suche alle Ortsnamen, die du aufgeschrieben hast!

Mecklenburg, Thüringen, Harz, Wernigerode, Weimar, Erfurt, Eisenach

3 Was paßt zusammen?

Welche Ausdrücke rechts vollenden am besten die Satzanfänge auf der linken Seite?

1. Fahren wir doch mal an einen See   e   a. im Harz.
2. Ich möchte lieber nach Thüringen   g   b. eine Jugendherberge.
3. Dieser Wanderweg ist doch   d   c. in die Natur.
4. Ja, ich möchte auch am liebsten raus   c   d. der Rennsteig.
5. Wernigerode ist eine Stadt   a   e. zum Schwimmen.
6. Weimar und Erfurt sind Städte   f   f. in Thüringen.
7. In Eisenach gibt es ganz bestimmt   b   g. zum Wandern.

4 Wohin möchtest du fahren?

Du bist ein(e) Schulfreund(in) von Frank, Udo, Sabine und Uschi. Sag, wohin du fahren möchtest und warum!

Asking for and making suggestions; expressing preference and giving a reason; expressing wishes; expressing doubt, conviction, and resignation

Willkommen!

Deutschland hat seinen Gästen viel zu bieten: die Küsten der Nord- und Ostsee, die Lüneburger Heide, den Schwarzwald, die bayrischen Alpen, jahrhundertealte Städte, malerische Dörfer. Und überall, wo Deutschland am schönsten ist, finden Sie auch Jugendherbergen.

Sie können zwischen rund 700 Häusern wählen. Wollen Sie auf dem Lande in ruhiger Umgebung übernachten? Oder in einer romantischen Burg? Oder mitten in einer Stadt, hautnah zur Kunst- und Kulturszene?

Jugendherbergen sind nicht-kommerzielle Freizeiteinrichtungen, die vor allem Jugendlichen offenstehen. Sie fördern das gegenseitige Kennenlernen sowie die Toleranz gegenüber anderen Weltanschauungen und Gewohnheiten. Sie haben sich zu Stätten internationaler Begegnung entwickelt.

Wir bieten Ihnen saubere, freundliche Aufenthalts- und Schlafräume mit zwei bis sechs Betten. Die Gäste werden nach Geschlechtern getrennt untergebracht. Im Übernachtungspreis ist das Frühstück enthalten, auch Vollverpflegung wird angeboten. In fast allen Häusern sind Möglichkeiten für Spiel und Sport vorhanden. Die Jugendherbergen haben unterschiedliche Standards, allen gemeinsam sind jedoch die günstigen Preise.

Selbstbedienung und die Mithilfe der Gäste bei kleineren Arbeiten werden daher gern gesehen.

In der Regel sind die Jugendherbergen bis 22 Uhr geöffnet, Jugendherbergen in Großstädten schließen später.

Jugendherbergen sind ideal für Einzelreisende, Gruppen, Schulklassen sowie Familien. Viele Jugendherbergen sind behindertenfreundlich eingerichtet und auf Rollstuhlfahrer eingestellt.

5 Deutsche Jugendherbergen

Lies den Text über die Jugendherbergen, und beantworte die Fragen!

1. Was hat Deutschland seinen Gästen zu bieten?
2. Wo findet man Jugendherbergen?
3. Versuch, eine Jugendherberge zu beschreiben! Was sind Vorteile? Nachteile?
4. Würdest du gern mal in einer deutschen Jugendherberge übernachten? Gib drei Gründe für deine Entscheidung an! 4. Answers will vary.

1. die Küsten der Nord- und Ostsee; die Lüneburger Heide; den Schwarzwald; die bayerischen Alpen; jahrhundertealte Städte; malerische Dörfer

2. Dort, wo es in Deutschland am schönsten ist.

3. Answers will vary. / nicht-kommerzielle Einrichtungen; fördern das gegenseitige Kennenlernen und Toleranz; sind Stätten internationaler Begegnung; günstige Preise usw. / Selbstbedienung; Mithilfe bei kleineren Arbeiten; sind nur bis 22 Uhr geöffnet usw.

auf deutsch erklärt

Lust haben wenn man etwas gern machen will
die Gegend die Umgebung
die Jugendherberge ein Haus, wo Jugendliche für wenig Geld übernachten und essen können
die Unterkunft wo man übernachten kann
das Verzeichnis eine Liste mit Namen und Adressen
berühmt fast alle Leute kennen einen
unternehmen machen
der Ausweis ein Dokument mit Namen, Adresse und Geburtsdatum
verlieren Man wird es nicht mehr haben oder finden können.

auf englisch erklärt

Keine <u>Angst</u>! *Don't worry!*
Ich <u>seh'</u> mal <u>nach</u>. *I'll check it out.*
<u>Damals</u> war ich erst fünfzehn. *At the time I was only 15.*
Er ist <u>eben</u> zurückgekommen. *He just now got back.*
Wir wollen <u>beide</u> dahin. *Both of us want to go there.*

eine Burg

---

6 **Hör gut zu!** For answers, see listening script on TE Interleaf.

Schüler sprechen über Ferienorte. Wer war schon dort? Wer fährt erst dorthin? — Übertrag die Tabelle in dein Heft, und schreib den Ferienort, den du hörst, in die richtige Spalte!

Schüler	war schon dort	fährt erst hin

SO SAGT MAN DAS!

Schon bekannt

Asking for and making suggestions

If you need specific suggestions, you might ask:

> **Wohin fahren wir? Was schlägst du vor?**
> **Wohin geht's denn? Hast du eine Idee?**

When making suggestions, you might say:

> **Wir können mal an die Ostsee fahren.** *or*
> **Fahren wir doch mal in den Harz!** *or*
> **Ich schlage vor, daß wir nach Thüringen fahren.**

Identify the prepositional phrases used in these suggestions. What case follows the prepositions **an** and **in**? Why?[1]

---

1. These two-way prepositions get the accusative case because there is motion to a place.

7 Wohin geht's?

a. Wie gut kennst du Deutschland schon? Schreib vier Orte oder Gegenden, die du gern besuchen möchtest, auf einen Zettel, und schreib daneben, was du dort gern machen möchtest!

b. Such dir eine Partnerin, mit der du gern reisen möchtest! Sie fragt dich nach deinen Vorschlägen. Gib zwei Alternativen, und sag in jedem Fall, warum du dieses Ziel vorschlägst!

8 Nö, da war ich schon!

Such dir einen Partner! Lad ihn ein, mit dir wegzufahren! Dein Partner ist aber ein Reisemuffel. Er sagt dir immer, daß er schon dort war, wo du hin willst, und er sagt dir auch, warum er nicht mitfahren will. Im Kasten unten stehen ein paar Ideen. Gebrauche aber auch deine eigenen!

BEISPIEL   DU   **Du, ich möchte mal nach Thüringen fahren. Willst du mit?**

      PARTNER   **Nö. Ich war schon mal in Thüringen. Es hat mir dort nicht gefallen.**

9 Hör gut zu! For answers, see listening script on TE Interleaf.

Schüler erzählen, was sie in Dingskirchen machen. Schreib auf, wo jeder zuletzt hingeht oder zuletzt war!

wohin?/wo?

> Thüringen   Ostsee   Harz
>
> Bodensee   Rhein   Alpen
>
> Wernigerode   Zugspitze   Schweiz
>
> Berge   Insel Rügen   Meer

10 In Dingskirchen

Kennst du dich in Dingskirchen aus? Ein Tourist stellt dir viele Fragen. Such dir einen Partner, der den Touristen spielt!

BEISPIEL   TOURIST   **Entschuldigung, wo ist das Restaurant „Bella Italia"?**

      DU   **Das ist in der Uhlandstraße, an der Ecke Agnesstraße.**

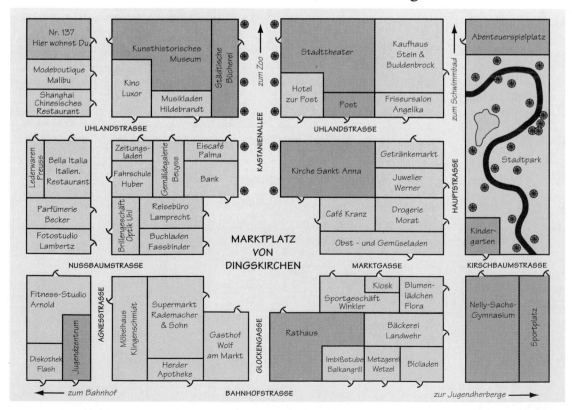

11. a. Answers will vary. E.g.: **Zuerst gehen wir ins Brillengeschäft in der Agnesstraße. Dann gehen wir nach links in die Nußbaumstraße bis zum Marktplatz. Dort gehen wir in den Buchladen usw.**

11 Mein Einkaufsweg

a. Du wohnst in Dingskirchen in der Agnesstraße 137. Du mußt jetzt für deine Mutter einkaufen gehen. Sie hat dir einen Einkaufszettel gegeben. Als du aus dem Haus kommst, triffst du einen Klassenkameraden. Er hat nichts vor und will dir beim Einkaufen helfen. — Such dir einen Partner, und stellt einen guten Einkaufsweg zusammen!

b. Zu Hause erzählst du deiner Mutter, wo du überall warst und was du an jedem Ort gemacht hast. — Such dir eine Partnerin für die Rolle der Mutter!

12 Für mein Notizbuch

Schreib in dein Notizbuch einen Einkaufsweg, den du zu Hause gewöhnlich machst, um am Wochenende alles zu erledigen! In deiner Beschreibung mußt du mindestens fünf verschiedene Geschäfte oder andere Orte erwähnen.

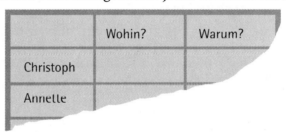

1 l Milch
5 kg Kartoffeln
1/2 kg Tomaten
1 frisches Brot
250 g Leberwurst
die Flaschen
    zurückbringen
CD für Vati
10 Briefmarken
Buch umtauschen
Sonnenbrille

13 Hör gut zu!   For answers, see listening script on TE Interleaf.

Vier Schüler (Christoph, Annette, Jörg und Isabella) unterhalten sich darüber, wo sie am liebsten eine Ferienwoche verbringen würden. Am Anfang möchte jeder woandershin fahren und sagt auch warum. Am Ende einigen sie sich (*they agree*) auf ein Ziel. Schreib die folgende Tabelle ab und trag ein, was du hörst!

	Wohin?	Warum?
Christoph		
Annette		

SO SAGT MAN DAS!

Schon bekannt

Expressing preference and giving a reason

To express preference and give a reason, you may say:

Mir gefällt die Ostsee besser als die Nordsee; die Ostsee ist ruhiger.
Ich finde Weimar schöner als Erfurt, weil Weimar mehr Kulturelles bietet.
Ich ziehe eine kleine Stadt wie Wernigerode vor, weil da die Luft einfach besser ist als in einer größeren Stadt.

14 Wann und warum?

a. Denk an zwei bekannte Reiseziele, die du gern besuchen möchtest! Schreib auf, welches Reiseziel du lieber hast, und gib einen Grund an, warum du dorthin möchtest!

b. Such dir einen Partner! Er fragt dich, wohin du in den Ferien fährst. Du sagst es ihm und begründest deine Antwort. Tauscht danach die Rollen aus!

15 Und in Dingskirchen?

Such dir eine Partnerin! Nenne ihr drei Geschäfte, wo du immer einkaufst! Nenne ihr auch Gründe dafür! Gebrauche in deiner Begründung Adjektive oder Komparative! Rechts stehen einige Anregungen.

Fleisch — gut
CDs — billig
Kleidung — schick
Brot — frisch

Answers will vary. E.g.: **Ich kaufe meine Sachen nur in der Modeboutique Malibu. Dort gibt es schickere Kleidung als im Kaufhaus.**

SO SAGT MAN DAS!

Schon bekannt

Expressing wishes

When asking someone about his or her wishes, you may ask:

Wohin möchtest du gern mal fahren?

Was wünschst du dir mal?

Was hättest du gern?

And the answer may be:

Ich möchte gern mal in den Harz fahren.

Ich wünsche mir mal einen schönen, langen Urlaub an der Ostsee.

Ich hätte gern viel Schnee im Winter.

---

16 Was für Wünsche hast du?

a. Schreib vier Dinge auf einen Zettel, die du dir einmal wünschst! Gebrauche die Kategorien Reisen, Schule, Freunde und Kleidung!

b. Such dir eine Partnerin, und frag sie nach ihren Wünschen!

17 Also, wohin geht's?

Setzt euch in Gruppen zu fünft oder zu sechst zusammen! Das Thema heißt: Wohin sollen wir fahren? Sprecht über eure Wünsche, diskutiert darüber, was euch gefällt, nicht gefällt oder besser gefällt, und macht verschiedene Vorschläge, bis (*until*) ihr euch auf ein gemeinsames Ziel geeinigt habt!

SO SAGT MAN DAS!

Schon bekannt

Expressing doubt, conviction, and resignation

When expressing doubt, you might say:

Ich weiß nicht, ob wir noch eine Unterkunft bekommen.
Ich bezweifle, daß es in der Jugendherberge einen Tennisplatz gibt.
Ich bin nicht sicher, daß wir am Ostseestrand tauchen können.

When expressing conviction, you might say:

Du kannst mir glauben, dort gibt es eine ganz tolle Jugendherberge.
Ich bin sicher, daß dir Thüringen gut gefallen wird.

What happens to the conjugated verb in **daß**- and **ob**-clauses?[1]

When faced with bad news you can express resignation. For example, if you hear:

Die Jugendherbergen sind überfüllt!
In dem See darf man nicht baden!

You might respond:

Da kann man nichts machen.
Schade. Das ist leider so.

---

1. The conjugated verb is in last position.

18 **Hör gut zu!** For answers, see listening script on TE Interleaf.

Du hörst als Kellnerin im Café verschiedene Gesprächs-fetzen (*scraps of conversation*). Wer von den Sprechenden bezweifelt etwas, und wer ist sicher?

	bezweifeln	sicher sein
1		
2		

19 **Bist du sicher?**

Such dir eine Partnerin! Sie ist sicher, daß es in dem Ferienort, den ihr euch ausgesucht habt, ganz bestimmte Einrichtungen gibt und daß ihr dort ganz bestimmte Sportarten ausüben könnt. Du bezweifelst das und gibst dafür deine Gründe an. Deine Partnerin ist ganz enttäuscht. — Benutzt die Illustrationen als Anregungen! Answers will vary. E.g.: **Ich bezweifle, daß man an der Nordsee segeln kann. Dort ist das Wetter immer sehr stürmisch und es regnet zu oft. / Schade. Da kann man nichts machen.**

20 **Eine Einladung schreiben — und eine Einladung beantworten**

Bildet Gruppen zu viert! Jede Gruppe wählt einen Schriftführer, also eine Person, die alles aufschreiben muß. Jede Gruppe schreibt einer anderen Gruppe eine informelle Einladung. Ihr macht zwei oder drei Vorschläge und schreibt, was ihr persönlich vorzieht. — Tauscht dann eure Einladungen aus, und beantwortet sie gegenseitig! Schreibt, daß ihr gern mitfahren wollt, aber daß ihr ganz bestimmte Wünsche habt. Ihr wollt an den vorgeschlagenen Orten bestimmte Dinge tun, bezweifelt aber, daß es dort alle Einrichtungen gibt, die ihr euch wünscht!

21

ROLLENSPIEL

Bereite eins von diesen beiden Rollenspielen mit drei anderen Schülern vor!

a. Du gehst mit drei Schülern in ein Reisebüro. Ihr sucht euch ein Reiseziel aus, das euch allen gefällt. Einer von euch spielt die Rolle des Angestellten im Reisebüro.

b. Du diskutierst mit deinen drei Freunden über ein Picknick, das du für die ganze Klasse organisieren mußt. Besprecht zuerst, was ihr alles braucht, und wer was zum Picknick mitbringen muß! Anschließend geht ihr Proviant fürs Picknick einkaufen. Einer von euch übernimmt die Rolle des Verkäufers.

Weiter geht's!

Auf nach Weimar!

Ein Plan verwirklicht sich.

FRANK Hallo, Leute! Glück gehabt! Die haben noch Platz für uns im Jugendgästehaus in Weimar.

USCHI Das ist ja unglaublich!

FRANK Hier ist das Fax.

UDO Laß mal sehen! — Ja, prima!

FRANK Aber nur für zwei Nächte.

UDO Das langt.

FRANK Da stimm' ich dir zu: zwei Tage Weimar genügt.

SABINE Ach, ihr beiden Kulturmuffel ihr! Aber wartet ab: Weimar wird euch schon gefallen! Übrigens soll Weimar im Jahr 1999 Kulturstadt Europas werden.

USCHI Woher weißt du denn bloß so viel über Weimar?

SABINE Ich hab' mich eben informiert.

FRANK Nun, kannst du mir vielleicht sagen, ob das Jugendgästehaus weit vom Bahnhof entfernt ist?

SABINE Blöde Frage! Bist du vielleicht fußkrank? Ich meine doch, daß es in Weimar einen Bus gibt!

USCHI Kommt, kommt, Leute! Jetzt nicht streiten!

UDO Nun, ich würde gern mal von der Sabine hören, was es so in Weimar zu sehen gibt.

USCHI Ich bin dafür, daß wir jetzt einen Plan machen, einen Plan, der uns allen gefällt.

FRANK Da hast du recht. Also, los!

UDO	Ja, ich kann mich noch an den Deutschunterricht erinnern, als uns der Gleißner von so einem Gartenhaus erzählt hat, wo der Goethe da ...
SABINE	Okay. Goethes Gartenhaus steht in einem schönen Park ...
FRANK	Da können wir bestimmt picknicken!
USCHI	Wie romantisch!
SABINE	<u>Das ist eine prima Idee!</u> Da kaufen wir uns frische Brötchen ...
UDO	<u>Wie wär's denn</u> mit einer Thüringer Wurst ...
USCHI	Schweizer Käse, süße Trauben ...
FRANK	Mir läuft jetzt schon das Wasser im Mund zusammen, wenn ich an unser Picknick denke!
SABINE	Also, ihr denkt doch wirklich nur ans Futtern!

22 Was passiert hier?

Hast du das Gespräch verstanden? Beantworte diese Fragen!

1. Worum geht es hier? Warum sind die Freunde zusammengekommen? 1. Es geht um die Fahrt nach Weimar. / Sie besprechen, was sie alles in Weimar unternehmen können.
2. Worüber ist Frank froh? 2. Darüber, daß sie noch einen Platz im Jugendgästehaus in Weimar bekommen haben.
3. Woher weiß Sabine so viel über Weimar? 3. Sie hat sich informiert.
4. Warum sagt Uschi: „Kommt, Leute! Jetzt nicht streiten!"?
5. Was haben die Freunde jetzt vor?
6. Wie kommen sie auf Goethes Gartenhaus zu sprechen?
7. Wie endet dieses Gespräch hier? Wie wird es wohl weitergehen?
For answers to exercises 4–7, see below.

23 Genauer lesen For answers, see underlined words in text on pages 38 and 39.

Lies das Gespräch noch einmal, und beantworte die Fragen auf deutsch!

1. Which phrases express surprise? Agreement?
2. Which phrases are used to ask for a suggestion? Make a suggestion?
3. Which phrases express hearsay?

24 Was würdest du dir gern ansehen?

Was würdest du dir gern in einer historischen amerikanischen Stadt ansehen, in einer Stadt wie Washington zum Beispiel?

4. Sabine ärgert sich über Franks Frage, ob das Jugendgästehaus weit vom Bahnhof entfernt ist.
5. Sie wollen einen Plan für ihre Unternehmungen in Weimar machen.
6. Udo erinnert sich daran, daß ihr Deutschlehrer davon gesprochen hat.
7. Es endet mit der Idee, ein Picknick zu machen. / Answers will vary. E.g.: Sie werden besprechen, was sie sonst noch alles in Weimar unternehmen können.

Asking for information and expressing an assumption; expressing hearsay; asking for, making, and responding to suggestions; expressing wishes when shopping

JUGENDGÄSTEHAUS
WEIMAR

Jugendgästehaus Weimar
Herbergsmutter Danuta Keller
Zum Wilden Graben 12
99425 Weimar
Tel. Weimar / 3471

6-Tage-Reise nach Weimar

Das Programm ist variabel und nicht an bestimmte Tagesabläufe gebunden, so daß die Teilnehmer selbst den Ablauf bestimmen können.

Folgende Leistungen sind im Teilnehmerpreis enthalten:

- Dia-Vortrag „Weimar — eine Perle im Land Thüringen"
- Exkursion mit Stadtführung in Weimar
- Besichtigung interessanter Kulturdenkmäler der Stadt
- Diskothek im hauseigenen Keller
- Im Sommer Grillparty
- Im Winter Kaminabend
- Besichtigung Schloß Belvedere und Bustransfer zur Gedenkstätte Buchenwald

Zusätzlich zum Programm können folgende Leistungen bestellt werden:

- Baudenabend 10 DM
- Busfahrt nach Erfurt 15 DM

Busfahrt nach Eisenach, Preis nach Angebot. Die Mitarbeiter des Jugendgästehauses beraten Sie gern und geben zu den einzelnen Leistungen ausführliche Informationen.

Ort und Umgebung

Das Jugendgästehaus liegt im südlichen Teil der Stadt Weimar. Weimar, bekannt als Stadt der Dichter Goethe und Schiller, ist eingebettet zwischen den Höhenzügen des Ettersberges im Norden und den Parkanlagen von Schloß Belvedere im Süden.

Anreise

Auf der Eisenbahnstrecke Frankfurt – Berlin, oder Frankfurt – Leipzig, bis Bahnhof Weimar. Dann mit der Stadtbuslinie 5 oder 8 von der Haltestelle am Bahnhof bis Haltestelle „Zum Wilden Graben".

Lage

Das Jugendgästehaus liegt in einer wunderschönen und sehr ruhigen Villenanlage der Stadt.

Ausstattung

58 Betten in 1- bis 6-Bett-Zimmern. Lehrerzimmer, 2 Aufenthaltsräume, Clubkeller.

Sport und Freizeit

Auf dem Außengelände des Hauses sind vielfältige Möglichkeiten der Freizeitgestaltung gegeben; Volleyball, Großschachanlage, Grillplatz. Im Inneren des Hauses lädt der Kaminraum und der Club im Keller zum gemütlichen Verweilen ein.

25 Das jugendgästehaus in Weimar

1. im südlichen Teil Weimars in einer wunderschönen und ruhigen Villenanlage / See paragraph captioned "Ausstattung." / See paragraph captioned "Anreise."

Lies das Angebot des Jugendgästehauses, und beantworte danach diese Fragen!

1. Wo liegt das Jugendgästehaus? Wie ist es ausgestattet, und wie kommt man dorthin?
2. Welche Leistungen sind im Preis enthalten?   2. See first seven bullets in text.
3. Für welche Leistungen würdest du dich besonders interessieren? Für welche Freizeitmöglichkeiten?   3. Answers will vary.
4. Welche bekannten Orte gibt es in der Nähe vom Gästehaus?   4. Erfurt u. Eisenach

auf deutsch erklärt

die Nacht die Zeit zwischen Abend und Morgen
fußkrank sein (ironisch) nicht gern zu Fuß gehen
futtern sehr viel essen
genügen genug sein
es langt das ist genug
streiten argumentieren
verweilen Zeit verbringen
der Kaminraum wo man sich vor ein schönes Feuer hinsetzen kann
die Großschachanlage wo man draußen Schach mit großen Spielfiguren spielen kann

auf englisch erklärt

Die Jugendherberge ist sicher <u>behindertenfreundlich</u>. *The youth hostel is surely accessible to the physically challenged.*
Sie ist 10 Kilometer <u>entfernt</u>. *It's 10 kilometers away.*
<u>Warte</u> nur <u>ab</u>! *Just wait and see!*
Ich kann <u>mich</u> noch <u>an</u> die Zeit <u>erinnern</u>. *I can still remember that time.*
Das Wasser läuft mir im Mund zusammen, wenn ich <u>an</u> das Picknick <u>denke</u>. *My mouth waters when I think of the picnic.*
Folgende <u>Leistungen</u> sind im Teilnehmerpreis <u>enthalten</u>. *The following services are included in the price for participants.*

For answers, see listening script in TE Interleaf.

26 Hör gut zu!

Schüler unterhalten sich über Jugendherbergen. Sprechen sie über Jugendherbergen im allgemeinen (*in general*) oder über Jugendherbergen in Weimar? Übertrag die Tabelle und hake ab, was du hörst!

	Jugendherbergen	
	im allgemeinen	in Weimar
1		
2		

SO SAGT MAN DAS !

Schon bekannt

Asking for information and expressing an assumption

When asking for information, you may ask:

Gibt es in Weimar eine Jugendherberge? *or*
Weißt du, ob es in Weimar eine Jugendherberge gibt? *or*
Kannst du mir sagen, ob die Herberge in der Stadt liegt?

As a response, you may express an assumption by saying:

Ich glaube schon, daß es dort eine Jugendherberge gibt. *or*
Ich meine doch, daß die Herberge in der Stadt liegt.

---

27 Ich will nach Weimar

Weil du eine Reise nach Deutschland und Weimar planst, hast du natürlich viele Fragen über Jugendherbergen in Deutschland im allgemeinen und ganz bestimmte Fragen über die Jugendherbergen in Weimar. Such dir eine Partnerin, und frag sie, was sie darüber weiß! Du hast bestimmt auch andere Fragen. Deine Partnerin glaubt schon, daß es gibt, wonach du sie fragst. Tauscht dann die Rollen aus!

Expressing hearsay

To express hearsay, you may want to say:

Ich habe gehört, daß es in Weimar zwei Jugendherbergen gibt.
Man hat mir gesagt, daß sie behindertenfreundlich eingerichtet sind.
Die Herbergen **sollen** gutes Essen **haben.**

How would you express these statements in English?

28 Weißt du auch etwas über Jugendherbergen?

Such dir einen Partner! Was weiß er über Jugendherbergen in deiner Stadt oder in einem Ort, den du kennst? Stell ihm mindestens vier Fragen darüber! In seiner Antwort kann er folgendes ausdrücken: er weiß es, er glaubt es oder er hat gehört, daß es so ist. Tauscht dann die Rollen aus! Answers will vary. E.g.: **Weißt du, ob die Jugendherberge hier einen Tennisplatz hat? / Ich habe gehört, sie soll einen Tennisplatz haben.**

29 Warum nach Weimar?

Schreib deinem Briefpartner in Deutschland, daß du gern mit ihm die Jugendherberge in Weimar besuchen möchtest, und gib mindestens fünf Gründe dafür an!

Asking for, making, and responding to suggestions

You could ask for a suggestion by saying:

Wo **sollen** wir denn unser Picknick **machen?**

And you could make a suggestion by saying:

Ich bin dafür, daß wir in den Park an der Ilm gehen.

When making suggestions, you might also say:

Würdest du gern mal in einer Jugendherberge übernachten?
Wie wär's denn mit einem Picknick?

When responding to a suggestion, you might say:

Ja schon, aber ich würde am liebsten mal zelten gehen.
Das wär' nicht schlecht!

How would you express these sentences in English?

30 Hör gut zu!   For answers, see listening script on TE Interleaf.

Claudia macht ihren Freunden einen Vorschlag. Wie reagieren sie darauf? Sind sie damit einverstanden oder nicht? Warum oder warum nicht?

31 Für mein Notizbuch

Schreib fünf Dinge in dein Notizbuch, die du in Deutschland gern einmal sehen oder machen möchtest! Gib auch jeweils einen Grund dafür an!

32 Also los! Was wollt ihr?

Setzt euch in kleinen Gruppen zusammen, und plant eure Klassenreise nach Deutschland! Jeder muß drei Vorschläge machen und jeweils einen Grund für seinen Vorschlag angeben. Die anderen müssen sagen, ob sie dafür oder dagegen sind und müssen ihre Antworten begründen.

BEISPIEL   DU   **Also, ich würde gern nach Weimar fahren, weil ich schon so viel über Weimar gelesen und gehört habe. Weimar soll ...**

     PARTNER   **Ich würde auch am liebsten nach Weimar fahren, denn dort ...**

WORTSCHATZ

Was man zum Picknick mitnimmt:

einen Teller   das Besteck   ein Messer   einen Löffel   eine Gabel

einen Becher   ein Schneidebrett   eine Serviette   einen Picknickkorb   eine Kühlbox

eine Thermosflasche   einen Salz- und Pfefferstreuer   ein Messer mit Flaschenöffner   eine Abfalltüte   eine Decke

Was nimmst du alles mit, wenn du picknickst? Was packst du in die Kühlbox ein?

---

33 Hör gut zu!   For answers, see listening script on TE Interleaf.

Drei Schüler planen ein Picknick. Hör ihrem Gespräch gut zu, und schreib auf, was sie alles mitnehmen wollen!

34 Picknick an der Ilm

Die Schüler planen ein Picknick im Park an der Ilm in Weimar. Was sollen sie alles mitnehmen? Was sollen sie sich zum Essen und zum Trinken kaufen? — Such dir eine Partnerin und plane das Picknick mit ihr! In den Kästen auf Seite 44 stehen ein paar Ideen für den Proviant.

     DU   **Also, ich würde dunkles Brot mitnehmen und ...**

     PARTNER   **Wie wär's denn mit ein paar saftigen Tomaten und ...**

ZWEITE STUFE   *dreiundvierzig*   **43**

Brot
Brötchen
Salami
Schinken
Gurken
Kartoffel-
salat

dunkel
frisch
hart
gekocht
sauer
würzig

Käse
Schafskäse
Tomaten
Trauben
Cola
Oliven

Schweizer
bulgarisch
italienisch
blau
eiskalt
griechisch

Schon bekannt

Ein wenig Grammatik

Look at these sentences:

Ich würde gern das dunkle Brot mitnehmen.
Ich würde gern dunkles Brot kaufen.

Can you explain why the adjective endings are different? For a table of the adjective endings, see the Grammar Summary.

SO SAGT MAN DAS!

Schon bekannt

Expressing wishes when shopping

When shopping for groceries, the clerk might ask you:

Was möchten Sie? *or* **Was hätten Sie gern?**

You may request the item by saying:

Ich möchte 250 Gramm Schweizer Käse. *or*
Ich hätte gern blaue Trauben. Ein Pfund, **bitte!**

What does the verb **hätte** express in these statements?

---

35 Fürs Picknick einkaufen

Such dir eine Partnerin und geh mit ihr fürs Picknick einkaufen! — Deine Partnerin spielt die Rolle der Verkäuferin. Tauscht dann die Rollen aus!

36 Für mein Notizbuch

Schreib in dein Notizbuch die Information, die du brauchst, um irgendwo in einer Jugendherberge zu übernachten und auch in diesem Ort zu picknicken! Schreib jetzt einen Brief an eine Jugendherberge, in dem du deine Fragen stellst und um weitere Informationen bittest!

37 Ein Brief nach Hause

Du bist mit Schülern eines deutschen Gymnasiums nach Weimar gefahren. Schreib deinen Eltern einen Brief über deine Reise! Erwähne folgendes:

1. Welche Reiseziele ihr gehabt habt, und warum ihr euch auf Weimar geeinigt habt.
2. Wie ihr nach Weimar gekommen seid.
3. Was ihr in Weimar alles gemacht habt, was dir besonders gut gefallen hat und warum.

Weimar im Blickpunkt:
Die deutsche Klassikermetropole wird 1999 Kulturstadt Europas

„Die Weimarer Bürger vollführten nach der Entscheidung regelrecht Luftsprünge", schildert Weimars Oberbürgermeister Klaus Büttner die Reaktion auf die gute Nachricht: Weimar wird Europas Kulturstadt 1999. Damit war nicht unbedingt zu rechnen. Unter den Bewerberstädten Avignon, Bologna, Istanbul, Graz, Prag und Stockholm war Weimar mit seinen 63 500 Einwohnern die kleinste. In erster Linie hat es die thüringische Stadt Johann

Wolfgang von Goethe zu verdanken, daß sie das Rennen machte. Denn 1999 jährt sich sein Geburtstag zum 250. Mal. Zwar ist Goethe nicht in Weimar geboren, doch lebte er 57 Jahre lang bis zu seinem Tod in der Stadt. Hier schrieb er seine großen Werke. Er war Minister, Theaterdirektor und trat auch als Stadtplaner auf (er hat — neben einem Gartenhaus für sich selbst — einen großen Park an der Ilm entworfen.) Zusammen mit anderen Größen der Geistesgeschichte, besonders mit Friedrich von Schiller, machte er das kleine Fürstentum zur „Hauptstadt des deutschen Geistes", die Dichter und Denker, später auch Musiker und Maler anlockte. Weimar heute steckt voller Sehenswürdigkeiten. Zu besichtigen sind das Goethehaus, Goethes Gartenhaus, das Schillerhaus, in dem der schwäbische Dichter sein Freiheitsdrama „Wilhelm Tell" schrieb, das Liszthaus, in dem Franz Liszt Klavierunterricht gab, und die Zentralbibliothek der Deutschen Klassik mit ihren rund 800 000 Büchern. Nach Berlin, das 1988 den Titel Kulturstadt Europas trug, ist Weimar die zweite deutsche Stadt, die ein Jahr kulturell im Mittelpunkt Europas stehen wird.

1. Wofür ist Weimar berühmt?   1. für die „Klassiker" Goethe und Schiller, die dort gelebt haben
2. Gibt es Städte in Amerika, die ähnliche Angebote haben?
3. Was muß eine Stadt haben, um als Kulturstadt bezeichnet zu werden?   3. kulturelle Sehenswürdigkeiten
4. Was wäre deine Wahl für eine amerikanische Kulturstadt des Jahres? Worauf würdest du die Wahl begründen?

ERLKÖNIG

Wer reitet so spät durch Nacht und Wind?
Es ist der Vater mit seinem Kind;
Er hat den Knaben wohl in dem Arm,
Er faßt ihn sicher, er hält ihn warm. —

Mein Sohn, was birgst du so bang dein Gesicht? —
Siehst, Vater, du den Erlkönig nicht?
Den Erlenkönig mit Kron und Schweif? —
Mein Sohn, es ist ein Nebelstreif. —

»Du liebes Kind, komm, geh mit mir!
Gar schöne Spiele spiel ich mit dir;
Manch bunte Blumen sind an dem Strand;
Meine Mutter hat manch gülden Gewand.«

Mein Vater, mein Vater, und hörest du nicht,
Was Erlenkönig mir leise verspricht? —
Sei ruhig, bleibe ruhig, mein Kind!
In dürren Blättern säuselt der Wind. —

»Willst, feiner Knabe, du mit mir gehn?
Meine Töchter sollen dich warten schön;
Meine Töchter führen den nächtlichen Reihn
Und wiegen und tanzen und singen dich ein.«

Mein Vater, mein Vater, und siehst du nicht dort
Erlkönigs Töchter am düstern Ort? —
Mein Sohn, mein Sohn, ich seh es genau;
Es scheinen die alten Weiden so grau. —

»Ich liebe dich, mich reizt deine schöne Gestalt;
Und bist du nicht willig, so brauch ich Gewalt.«
Mein Vater, mein Vater, jetzt faßt er mich an!
Erlkönig hat mir ein Leids getan! —

Dem Vater grauset's, er reitet geschwind,
Er hält in Armen das ächzende Kind,
Erreicht den Hof mit Mühe und Not;
In seinen Armen das Kind war tot.

Johann Wolfgang von Goethe

LESETRICK
Deriving the main idea from supporting details
Depending on what kind of passage you're reading, there are several strategies for identifying the main idea. When reading a poem, for example, you may first want to look at the supporting details, thinking about what the individual words, images, and symbols suggest. Then decide what the main idea is. Remember, there is no one "correct" interpretation.

For answers, see TE Interleaf.

Getting Started

1. Look at the different poems for a moment. Relying on visual cues alone, which poems look like they tell a story, and which look more like a poster or picture?

2. Read the title of each poem and then listen as the first five poems are read aloud. Judging by their intonation and rhythm, can you tell which poems are intended to be dramatic, and which are more lighthearted?

3. As you are reading and listening to each poem again, think about and try to answer the following questions:
   a. Wer sind die Hauptfiguren?
   b. Wo und wann finden die Ereignisse statt?
   c. Was passiert?

Der Panther
Im Jardin des Plantes, Paris

Sein Blick ist vom Vorübergehn der Stäbe
so müd geworden, daß er nichts mehr hält.
Ihm ist, als ob es tausend Stäbe gäbe
und hinter tausend Stäben keine Welt.

Der weiche Gang geschmeidig starker Schritte,
der sich im allerkleinsten Kreise dreht,
ist wie ein Tanz von Kraft um eine Mitte,
in der betäubt ein großer Wille steht.

Nur manchmal schiebt der Vorhang der Pupille
sich lautlos auf —. Dann geht ein Bild hinein,
geht durch der Glieder angespannte Stille —
und hört im Herzen auf zu sein.

Rainer Maria Rilke

Der Radwechsel

Ich sitze am Straßenhang.
Der Fahrer wechselt das Rad.
Ich bin nicht gern, wo ich herkomme.
Ich bin nicht gern, wo ich hinfahre.
Warum sehe ich den Radwechsel
Mit Ungeduld?

Bertolt Brecht

ottos mops

ottos mops trotzt
otto: fort mops fort
ottos mops hopst fort
otto: soso

otto holt koks
otto holt obst
otto horcht
otto: mops mops
otto hofft

ottos mops klopft
otto: komm mops komm
ottos mops kommt
ottos mops kotzt
otto: ogottogott

Ernst Jandl

POESIE

A Closer Look

4. Read the "Erlkönig" by Goethe and identify which lines are spoken by which person. Pay special attention to punctuation, such as quotation marks. Use a chart like the one below. The line numbers of the first two stanzas are already marked.

stanza	1		4
narrator	1-4		
father		5, 8	
son		6-7	
elf king			

5. What is the father trying to do? What happens to the son? What role does the **Erlkönig** play? What emotions does the poem evoke for you?

6. Read Rilke's poem "Der Panther." Is the animal in the wild or in captivity? How do you know? How has his situation affected him? When the panther looks at something, what happens to the image as it reaches his heart?

7. Try to sketch the world as the panther sees it.

8. In Brecht's "Radwechsel," is the person (**Ich**) in charge of his situation? What will happen when the driver finishes what he's doing? Look at lines 3 and 4. Which single word changes? Excluding the last line of the poem, does the language reflect any dramatic tension? How does the last line make you feel?

KINDERLIED

Wer lacht hier, hat gelacht?
Hier hat sich's ausgelacht.
Wer hier lacht, macht Verdacht,
daß er aus Gründen lacht.

Wer weint hier, hat geweint?
Hier wird nicht mehr geweint.
Wer hier weint, der auch meint,
daß er aus Gründen weint.

Wer spricht hier, spricht und schweigt?
Wer schweigt, wird angezeigt.
Wer hier spricht, hat verschwiegen,
wo seine Gründe liegen.

Wer spielt hier, spielt im Sand?
Wer spielt, muß an die Wand,
hat sich beim Spiel die Hand
gründlich verspielt, verbrannt.

Wer stirbt hier, ist gestorben?
Wer stirbt, ist abgeworben.
Wer hier stirbt, unverdorben
ist ohne Grund verstorben.

Günther Grass

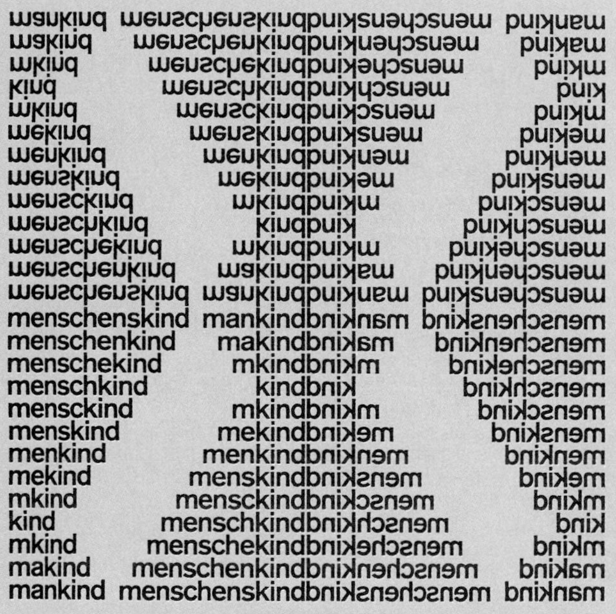

Reinhard Döhl

Reinhard Döhl

9. Read Jandl's poem "ottos mops," paying close attention to the colons. What do they indicate? Listen to the poem several times and add periods where you hear full stops. Can you guess what the word **Mops** refers to? See if your guess helps to explain what is going on in the poem.

10. Read "Kinderlied" by Grass. How do the question marks help you understand the organization of the poem? Which actions are mentioned? Why do you think some form of the word **Grund** is used in the last line of every stanza? What makes the title ironic?

11. Now look at the two selections of concrete poetry. Why do you think this is called concrete poetry? How does the poet convey his message? Through words alone or some other way?

12. Skim the seven poems you've just read again. What do all these poems have in common? In what ways are they different? Do you think all the poets had the same idea about the purpose of poetry? Support your answers, based on the poems.

13. Schreib jetzt dein eigenes Gedicht im Stil der konkreten Poesie. Denk zuerst daran, was diesen Stil von anderen Gedichten unterscheidet! Versuch, diese Eigenschaften in dein Gedicht zu integrieren!

Sometimes a spontaneous vacation can be a lot of fun — but more often, careful planning will reduce stress and make your vacation more enjoyable. Whichever approach you prefer, one important decision you will have to make is where to go; travel brochures are a good resource for ideas. In this activity you will work together with classmates to select a good vacation spot and write a travel brochure about that place.

... ist eine Reise wert!

Wähl zusammen mit einer Gruppe eine Stadt oder ein Land aus, und schreib ein Flugblatt darüber, damit die Leser Lust haben, dahin zu reisen! Jeder in der Gruppe soll ein Thema bearbeiten, zum Beispiel die Sehenswürdigkeiten, das kulturelle Angebot, das Wetter, die Einkaufsmöglichkeiten usw., die der Ort zu bieten hat. Illustriert eure Ideen mit Fotos!

SCHREIBTIP

Selecting information
In order to write effectively about an unfamiliar topic, you will have to do some research then select the appropriate information to include. You also need to be aware of your audience and the kinds of information they want or expect to read. Once you know that, you can focus on that particular information. When writing a travel brochure, for example, you'll want to select information that makes your destination appealing, such as a pleasant climate, fascinating local culture, or shopping and entertainment, while at the same time providing information about expenses and accommodations.

A. Vorbereiten

1. Wähl mit deiner Gruppe einen Ort aus, und mach eine Liste von wichtigen Themen, die ihr erforschen wollt! Teil die Arbeit ein, damit jeder genau weiß, worauf er achten muß!
2. Geh in eine Bücherei (*library*) oder auch in ein Reisebüro und erforsche dein Thema! Mach dir Notizen von wichtigen Fakten! Denk an Informationen, die den Leser zu einer Reise überzeugen werden! Sammle auch Fotos von zutreffenden Orten und Sehenswürdigkeiten!
3. Vergleicht eure Notizen und Fotos in der Gruppe! Macht zusammen ein Layout des Flugblatts, und wählt die Informationen und Fotos aus, die ihr verwenden wollt!

B. Ausführen

Schreib die ausgewählten Informationen für dein Thema in kurzen, überzeugenden und auch logischen Sätzen auf! Stellt dann alle Teile zusammen, und illustriert sie mit Fotos! Denkt an ein zutreffendes Schlagwort für das Flugblatt!

C. Überarbeiten

1. Vergleich deinen Teil des Flugblatts mit deinen Notizen! Hast du alle wichtigen Fakten mit einbezogen? Passen Text und Fotos zusammen?
2. Lest euer Flugblatt in der Gruppe laut vor, und zeigt die entsprechenden Fotos! Besprecht die ganze Wirkung des Flugblatts! Würdet ihr jetzt „euren Ort" gern besuchen? Verändert die Sprache und den Ton, wenn nötig!
3. Wenn ihr mit dem Flugblatt zufrieden seid, lest es noch einmal durch! Korrigiert die Schreibfehler! Achtet besonders auf die Buchstabierung der komparativen Adjektive! Habt ihr auch die Präpositionen mit den richtigen Dativ- oder Akkusativformen verwendet?
4. Schreibt das korrigierte Flugblatt noch einmal ab, und klebt die Fotos auf das Papier!

KANN ICH'S WIRKLICH?

Can you ask for and make suggestions? (p. 33)

1 How would you ask a friend to suggest a place where both of you might go on vacation? E.g.: Wohin fahren wir in den Ferien? Was schlägst du vor?

2 How would you respond if a friend asked you **Was schenken wir der Brigitte zum Geburtstag?** E.g.: Ich schlage vor, daß wir ihr eine CD schenken.

Can you express preference and give a reason? (p. 35)
Can you express wishes? (p. 36)

3 How would you respond if someone asked you what American city you prefer and why? E.g.: Ich ziehe eine große Stadt wie New York vor, weil dort mehr los ist.

4 How would a German-speaking genie ask you what your wishes are? How would you then make three wishes to be granted by the genie? E.g.: Was wünschst du dir mal? / Ich möchte gern mal nach Europa fliegen. Ich wünsche mir Gesundheit. Ich hätte gern ein Motorrad.

Can you express doubt, conviction, and resignation? (p. 36)

5 How would you say to a friend a. E.g.: Ich bezweifle, daß es ein Hotel in Dingskirchen gibt.
a. that you doubt there is a hotel in Dingskirchen?
b. that you're sure there is a youth hostel? b. E.g.: Ich bin sicher, daß es dort eine Jugendherberge gibt.

6 How would you respond if you were on vacation and someone said to you **Das Wetter soll diese Woche furchtbar sein**? E.g.: Schade. Da kann man nichts machen.

Can you ask for information and express an assumption? (p. 41)

7 How would you ask someone if there is a swimming pool in Dingskirchen? E.g.: Gibt es in Dingskirchen ein Schwimmbad?

8 How would you say that you assume your town has a youth hostel? E.g.: Ich glaube schon, daß es hier eine Jugendherberge gibt.

Can you express hearsay? (p. 42)

9 How would you say that a. E.g.: Ich habe gehört, daß die Deutschen sehr gesund leben.
a. you heard that German-speaking people live very healthfully?
b. German food is supposed to be very good? b. E.g.: Deutsches Essen soll sehr gut sein.

Can you ask for, make, and respond to suggestions? (p. 42)

10 How would you ask a friend a. E.g.: Was sollen wir denn für den Test lernen?
a. what you both should study for the test?
b. if he or she would like to study with you? b. E.g.: Würdest du gern mit mir zusammen lernen?
How would you say that you are in favor of studying in the park instead of at home? E.g.: Ich würde lieber im Park lernen als zu Hause.

11 How would you respond if a friend asked you **Würdest du gern mal in einer Jugendherberge übernachten?** E.g.: Ja. Das wär' nicht schlecht!

Can you express wishes when shopping? (p. 44)

12 How would a grocery store clerk ask you what you need? How would you respond if you needed a pound of blue grapes E.g.: Was möchten Sie? Was hätten Sie gern? / Ich möchte ein Pfund blaue Trauben, bitte.

ERSTE STUFE

WORDS USEFUL FOR TRAVELING

die Natur *nature*
die Burg, -en *castle*
die Gegend, -en *area*
die Jugendherberge, -n *youth hostel*
die Unterkunft, ¨e *accomodations*

das Verzeichnis, -se *listing*
der Ausweis, -e *identification*

OTHER USEFUL WORDS AND EXPRESSIONS

also (part) *well, okay*
eben (gerade) *just now*
damals *at that time*

beide *both*
berühmt *famous*
nämlich *namely*

Keine Angst! *Don't worry!*
Lust haben *to want to*
nachsehen (sep) *to check on*
unternehmen *to undertake*
verlieren *to lose*

ZWEITE STUFE

THINGS TO TAKE ON A PICNIC

das Picknick, -s *picnic*
die Decke, -n *blanket*
das Besteck *silverware*
die Gabel, -n *fork*
der Löffel, - *spoon*
das Messer, - *knife*
der Teller, - *plate*
der Becher, - *mug*
der Picknickkorb, ¨e *picnic basket*
die Kühlbox, -en *cooler*
der Salzstreuer, - *salt shaker*
der Pfefferstreuer, - *pepper shaker*

der Flaschenöffner, - *bottle opener*
das Schneidebrett, -er *cutting board*
die Serviette, -n *napkin*
die Thermosflasche, -n *thermos bottle*
die Abfalltüte, -n *trash bag*

OTHER USEFUL WORDS AND EXPRESSIONS

der Mund, ¨er *mouth*
die Nacht, ¨e *night*
der Plan, ¨e *plan*

entfernt *away, at a distance*
frisch *fresh*

behindertenfreundlich *accessible to the physically challenged*
fußkrank sein (ironic) *to be too lazy to walk*
abwarten (sep) *to wait and see*
futtern *to stuff oneself*
s. informieren *to inform oneself*
denken an (acc) *to think of or about*
s. erinnern an (acc) *to remember*
genügen *to be enough*
es langt *that's enough*
stehen *to stand, to be*
streiten *to quarrel*

Kapitel 3: Aussehen: wichtig oder nicht?

	FUNCTIONS	GRAMMAR	CULTURE	RE-ENTRY
Los geht's! *pp. 54-55*	Gut aussehen, *p. 54*			
Erste Stufe *pp. 56-59*	Asking for and expressing opinions, *p. 57*	**Da-** and **wo-**compounds (Summary), *p. 58*	Landeskunde: **Die deutsche Subkultur,** *pp. 60-61*	•Expressing interest, *p. 57* •Sequencing events, *p. 57* •Expressing opinions, *p. 57* •Verbs requiring prepositional phrases, *p. 58* •Hobby and clothing vocabulary, *p. 58* •**Wo-** and **da-**compounds, *p. 58*
Weiter geht's! *pp. 62-63*	Immer mit der Mode. Oder? *p. 62*			
Zweite Stufe *pp. 64-68*	•Expressing sympathy and resignation, *p. 65* •Giving advice, *p. 66* •Giving a reason, *p. 67* •Admitting something and expressing regret, *p. 68*	Infinitive clauses, *p. 67*	Teenagers talk about what they do to feel better, *p. 64*	•Responding sympathetically, *p. 65* •Asking for and giving advice, *p. 65* •Making suggestions, *p. 66* •Giving reasons, *p. 67* •Infinitives, *p. 67* •**Weil-**clauses, *p. 67*
Zum Schreiben *p. 69*	Personen beschreiben Writing Strategy: Organizing your ideas			
Zum Lesen *pp. 70-71*	Was ist „in"? Reading Strategy: Determining the main idea of an article			
Review *pp. 72-75*	•Anwendung, *p. 72* •Kann ich's wirklich? *p. 74* •Wortschatz, *p. 75*			

Assessment Options	**Stufe Quizzes**
	•*Chapter Resources,* Book 1
	  Erste Stufe, Quiz 3-1
	  Zweite Stufe, Quiz 3-2
	•*Assessment Items, Audiocassette* 7 A
				Kapitel 3 Chapter Test
				•*Chapter Resources,* Book 1
				•*Assessment Guide,* Speaking Test
				•*Assessment Items, Audiocassette* 7 A
				
				Test Generator, Kapitel 3

Chapter Overview

RESOURCES Print	RESOURCES Audiovisual
	Textbook Audiocassette 2 A
Practice and Activity Book	

	Textbook Audiocassette 2 A
Practice and Activity Book	
Chapter Resources, Book 1	
•Communicative Activity 3-1	
•Communicative Activity 3-2	
•Additional Listening Activity 3-1	*Additional Listening Activities, Audiocassette* 9 A
•Additional Listening Activity 3-2	*Additional Listening Activities, Audiocassette* 9 A
•Additional Listening Activity 3-3	*Additional Listening Activities, Audiocassette* 9 A
•Student Response Forms	
•Realia 3-1	
•Situation Card 3-1	
•Teaching Transparency Master 3-1	*Teaching Transparency* 3-1
•Quiz 3-1	*Assessment Items, Audiocassette* 7 A
Video Guide	*Video Program,* Videocassette 1

	Textbook Audiocassette 2 A
Practice and Activity Book	

	Textbook Audiocassette 2 A
Practice and Activity Book	
Chapter Resources, Book 1	
•Communicative Activity 3-3	
•Communicative Activity 3-4	
•Additional Listening Activity 3-4	*Additional Listening Activities, Audiocassette* 9 A
•Additional Listening Activity 3-5	*Additional Listening Activities, Audiocassette* 9 A
•Additional Listening Activity 3-6	*Additional Listening Activities, Audiocassette* 9 A
•Student Response Forms	
•Realia 3-2	
•Situation Card 3-2	
•Teaching Transparency Master 3-2	*Teaching Transparency* 3-2
•Quiz 3-2	*Assessment Items, Audiocassette* 7 A

Chapter Resources, Book 1
- •Realia 3-3
- •Situation Card 3-3

Video Guide ....*Video Program,* Videocassette 1

Alternative Assessment
- •Performance Assessment
Teacher's Edition
  Erste Stufe, p. 51L
  Zweite Stufe, p. 51O
- •Portfolio Assessment
  Written: **Anwendung,** Activity 1, *Pupil's Edition,* p. 72;
  Assessment Guide, p. 16
  Oral: **Anwendung,** Activity 1, *Pupil's Edition,* p. 72;
  Assessment Guide, p. 16
- •**Notizbuch,** *Pupil's Edition,* pp. 59, 68

Kapitel 3: Aussehen: wichtig oder nicht?
Textbook Listening Activities Scripts

For Student Response Forms, see *Chapter Resources,* Book 1, pp. 142-145.

Erste Stufe
Activity 4, p. 57

DR. BEHRENS Guten Tag, alle zusammen. Hier ist wieder Radio Pop-shop mit dem Kummerkasten. Wie immer warte ich, Dr. Uwe Behrens, auf eure Anrufe und freue mich, heute den ersten Zuhörer oder die erste Zuhörerin zu begrüßen. Bitte stell dich kurz vor, wenn du möchtest, und erzähl uns dann von deinem Problem!

KRISTINA Ja, hallo, Dr. Behrens. Also, ich bin die ... ach ... ich möcht' lieber nicht sagen, wie ich heiße ... oder ... na ja, eigentlich ist es auch egal. Also, ich bin die Kristina und bin 16 Jahre alt.

DR. BEHRENS Hallo, Kristina. Schön, daß du anrufst. Sag doch einfach, was du auf dem Herzen hast.

KRISTINA Ja, also, ich brauche einen Rat. Es ist nämlich so: Meine beste Freundin ist sauer auf mich. Wir waren verabredet und wollten ins Kino gehen. Und gerade, als ich losgehen wollte, hat mein kleiner Bruder gefragt, ob ich ihm bei seinen Matheaufgaben helfen könnte. Das habe ich natürlich gemacht. Und sofort danach hat ein Mädchen aus meiner Klasse angerufen, um zu fragen, ob ich ihr meine Jeansweste für die Fete am Samstag leihen könnte. Ich kann es selbst nicht glauben, daß ich ja gesagt habe. Ich wollte die Weste nämlich selber anziehen. Na ja, wie auch immer, ich bin zu spät ins Kino gekommen. Meine Freundin war natürlich echt sauer. Ja, und sowas passiert mir andauernd.

DR. BEHRENS Also, wenn ich dich recht verstanden habe, dann ist das eigentliche Problem nicht, daß deine Freundin sauer auf dich ist, sondern daß du nicht nein sagen kannst.

KRISTINA Ja, stimmt genau! Ich schaffe es einfach nicht, jemandem zu sagen, daß ich zum Beispiel gerade keine Zeit habe oder keine Lust habe, etwas zu tun. Also, ich mach' mir echt Gedanken darüber, wie ich das Problem lösen könnte. Aber ich weiß einfach nicht wie. Ich habe manchmal das Gefühl, alle nutzen mich aus. Was soll ich bloß machen?

DR. BEHRENS Kristina, hast du dir schon mal überlegt, warum es so schwer ist, nein zu sagen? Hast du vielleicht Angst, deine Freunde zu verlieren? Oder vielleicht glaubst du, daß man dich dann nicht mehr so gern mag.

KRISTINA Mhhm ... das kann schon sein.

DR. BEHRENS Also, Kristina, was hältst du davon, einmal auszuprobieren, wie deine Freunde und Geschwister auf ein Nein von dir reagieren? Wahrscheinlich ist es gar nicht so schlimm, wie du meinst. Im ersten Moment sind sie vielleicht enttäuscht oder sogar sauer, aber es ist ziemlich unwahrscheinlich, daß sie aufhören, dich zu mögen. Im Gegenteil, sie werden dich sogar sicher mehr respektieren, wenn du deine ehrliche Meinung sagst.

KRISTINA Wirklich?

DR. BEHRENS Ja, bestimmt! Vielleicht hilft es auch, einen kleinen Streit zu riskieren, damit die anderen wirklich merken, daß dir eine Sache wichtig ist und sie auch mal deine Wünsche akzeptieren müssen.

KRISTINA Ja, also, ich glaube, das ist ein guter Ratschlag. Vielen Dank, Herr Dr. Behrens, und auf Wiederhören!

DR. BEHRENS Viel Glück und auf Wiederhören, Kristina!

Answers to Activity 4

Soll ausprobieren, nein zu sagen; soll einen kleinen Streit riskieren, damit die anderen merken, daß ihr eine Sache wichtig ist.

Activity 7, p. 57

VANESSA Schau mal, Martin, da hinten geht die Claudia! Mensch, die sieht ja mal wieder toll aus! Total gestylt! Also, die hat ja echt eine super Figur! Und erstmal die Klamotten! Der letzte Schrei!

MARTIN Ja, stimmt! Sie sieht wirklich klasse aus!

VANESSA Ach, ich muß die Claudia unbedingt zu meiner Fete einladen. Aber guck doch mal, der komische Typ, der neben ihr geht. Ach du meine Güte! Wie sieht der denn aus? Potthäßlich! Und mit so einem Typ läßt die sich blicken!

MARTIN Also, hör mal Vanessa! Du tust ja so, als ob alles nur vom Aussehen abhängt! Ich wußte gar nicht, daß du so oberflächlich bist! Was hältst du davon, erstmal jemanden kennenzulernen, bevor du dir eine Meinung bildest?

VANESSA Ach was! Davon halte ich nichts! Ich kann meistens schon auf den ersten Blick erkennen, ob jemand toll oder langweilig ist. Menschenkenntnis nennt man das!

MARTIN Also, ich finde, du spinnst! Für mich sind zum Beispiel innere Werte und Charakter viel wichtiger als nur das Aussehen.

VANESSA Ja, aber ich hab' echt keine Lust, Leute großartig kennenzulernen, die mir äußerlich überhaupt nicht gefallen. Also, Leute, die sich schlampig anziehen und total häßlich aussehen.

MARTIN Aber deswegen können es doch trotzdem ganz tolle Menschen sein, die Eigenschaften und Talente haben, von denen man auf den ersten Blick gar nichts bemerkt!

VANESSA   Ja, aber ist es meine Schuld, wenn sie ihre Qualitäten verstecken? Bei gutaussehenden und attraktiven Leuten weiß man wenigstens sofort, woran man ist. Man kann auf den ersten Blick erkennen, daß sie Wert auf ihr Äußeres legen. Ich würde sagen, daß schöne Menschen sogar viel sympathischer sind.

MARTIN   Das würde ich eigentlich nicht sagen! Außerdem, was verstehst du denn unter „schön"?

VANESSA   Also schön ist, wer seine Haut pflegt, seine Haare stylt, einen sportlichen Body hat, Modetrends mitmacht ... im Prinzip kann jeder was aus seinem Aussehen machen!

MARTIN   Ja, klar kann man sein Äußeres mit Make-up, Haarfarbe, Kleidung und von mir aus sogar mit Schönheitsoperationen verändern. Aber ich finde, daß man dadurch seinen Charakter oder seine Persönlichkeit noch lange nicht verbessert. Und wenn man einen tollen Charakter hat, ist es völlig egal, wie man aussieht. Das ist jedenfalls meine Meinung.

Answers to Activity 7

Sie unterhalten sich übers Aussehen; Vanessa hält viel vom Aussehen; Martin hält mehr von inneren Werten.

Zweite Stufe

Activity 22, p. 66

1. BRITTA   Hallo, Susi! Na, hast du wieder mal dein Lieblings-T-Shirt an? Du scheinst es wirklich zu mögen. Jedesmal, wenn ich dich treffe, hast du es an!

SUSI   Ach, hallo Britta! Mein T-Shirt? Ja, da hast du recht. Ich ziehe es wirklich sehr gern an, weil es so ein auffälliges Motiv hat. Nur leider kann ich es am Samstag zur Fete nicht schon wieder anziehen. Ich habe es nämlich bereits auf der letzten Fete vom Klaus getragen.

BRITTA   Ja, also ich würde es auch nicht nochmal zur Fete anziehen. Sag mal, warum kaufst du dir nicht mal was Neues? Es ist doch gerade Schluß-verkauf. Da findest du bestimmt was. Sollen wir morgen zusammen in die Stadt gehen?

SUSI   Au ja, toll! Das machen wir!

2. BRITTA   Schau mal, da hinten an der Bushaltestelle steht der Hans-Jörg!

SUSI   Ach ja, und er liest natürlich, wie immer. Es ist schon echt komisch, daß er ständig liest, sei es nun an der Bushaltestelle oder in der Pause. Wenn er wenigstens nur Comics oder Zeitschriften lesen würde, aber stell dir mal vor, er nimmt manchmal sogar das Geschichtsbuch mit in die Pause und lernt daraus!

BRITTA   Ja, das ist eben typisch Hans-Jörg! Also, an seiner Stelle würde ich mich in der Pause mit den anderen unterhalten und mich nicht so von allen absondern.

SUSI   Ja, da hast du recht. Du, übrigens ich wollte gerade den Tobias abholen gehen. Wir wollen zusammen eine Radtour machen. Hast du Lust mitzukommen?

BRITTA   Ja, gerne! Also, ich geh' dann mal nach Hause und hol' mein Rad aus dem Keller.

SUSI   Gut! Wir kommen dich dann abholen! Bis nach-her!

BRITTA   Tschüs! Bis nachher!

3. *[Brief pause, doorbell rings]*

TOBIAS   Hallo, Susi. Ich hab' schon auf dich gewartet!

SUSI   Grüß dich, Tobias! Mensch, wie siehst du denn aus? Hast du gerade gepennt? Du siehst noch ganz verschlafen aus. Wir wollten doch heute die Radtour machen!

TOBIAS   Ja, äh, also, ich bin echt müde. Ich glaub', ich bin gestern zu spät ins Bett gegangen. Weißt du, da läuft seit ein paar Tagen nachts so eine unheimlich spannende Krimiserie. Die ersten drei Folgen hab' ich schon gesehen, und es kommen noch fünf weitere. Das Blöde ist, ich kann dann am nächsten Morgen kaum wach werden!

SUSI   Also, versuch doch mal, früher ins Bett zu gehen! Du wirst schon sehen, das du dich dann am nächsten Morgen viel besser fühlst! Die Krimiserie kannst du doch auf Video aufnehmen und tagsüber gucken. Also, was ist nun mit unserer Radtour?

TOBIAS   Äh ... Uaaahh [*Yawning*] ...

SUSI   Komm, hol deine Jacke und schmeiß dich aufs Rad! Wenn wir erst mal 'ne Weile geradelt sind, wirst du schon munter! Die Britta kommt übrigens auch mit. Wir müssen sie nur noch von zu Hause abholen.

TOBIAS   Was? Die Britta Zellmann? Du, der Uwe findet die echt nett, glaub' ich! Laß uns doch schnell mal beim Uwe vorbeifahren und ihn abholen!

SUSI   Kannst du ihn nicht einfach anrufen? Vielleicht hat er ja gar keine Lust! So wie ich ihn kenne, sitzt er doch eh' lieber vor der Glotze.

TOBIAS   Nee du, den Uwe, den muß man vor vollendete Tatsachen stellen. Wenn ich da erst anrufe und frage, ob er Lust hat, dann zögert er nur rum und kann sich nicht entscheiden. Aber wenn wir einfach vor der Tür stehen, kann er nicht so leicht nein sagen!

SUSI   Also, gut. Dann mal los!

4. *[Brief pause, doorbell rings]*

UWE   Hey! Hallo Tobias, hallo Susi! Was macht ihr denn hier?

TOBIAS   Tja, also, wir wollen dich zu 'ner Fahrradtour abholen. Wie sieht's aus? Hast du Lust?

UWE   Äh, also, ich guck' mir gerade das Fußballspiel zwischen Fortuna Düsseldorf und Kaiserslautern an ...

SUSI   Das gibt's doch wohl nicht! Soll das etwa heißen, daß du lieber vor dem Fernseher hängst als mit uns was zu unternehmen? Also, ich finde sowieso, du solltest etwas mehr Sport treiben! Na komm schon! Wir müssen uns beeilen. Die Britta wartet!

UWE   Die Britta? ... Äh, also gut ... ich komm ja schon!

Answers to Activity 22

1. c; 2. d.; 3. a; 4. b

Anwendung
Activity 1b., *p. 73*

RUNDFUNKMODERATOR	Und nun, liebe Zuhörer, möchten wir Sie mit den neuesten Erkenntnissen aus der Ernährungswissenschaft bekannt machen. Wir beginnen jeweils mit der Nennung einiger weitverbreiteter Annahmen über den Nährwert verschiedener Lebensmittel und lassen dann unsere Expertin Stellung dazu nehmen. Wir begrüßen heute hier bei uns im Studio die Leiterin des Ernährungswissenschaftlichen Institutes in Bonn, Frau Professor Doktor Lohmann. Herzlich Willkommen!
PROF. DR. LOHMANN	Danke schön!
RUNDFUNKMODERATOR	Erstens: Das beste Brot ist dunkles Brot. Richtig oder falsch, Frau Professor Doktor Lohmann?
PROF. DR. LOHMANN	Falsch! Dunkles Brot ist oft nur mit Zuckerfarbe gefärbtes Brot — aber es wird dunkel, weil es lange gebacken wird. Das beste Brot, weiß oder dunkel, ist das Brot, das aus Vollkorn hergestellt ist.
RUNDFUNKMODERATOR	Zweitens: Braune Eier sind gesünder als weiße Eier. Richtig oder falsch?
PROF. DR. LOHMANN	Ganz eindeutig falsch! Braune Eier haben nur eine dickere Schale als weiße Eier. Ansonsten haben sie den gleichen Nährwert wie weiße Eier.
RUNDFUNKMODERATOR	Drittens: Kartoffeln machen dick. Ja, das hat auch schon immer meine Großmutter gesagt. Was sagt die Ernährungswissenschaft dazu, Frau Professor?
PROF. DR. LOHMANN	Auch diese weit verbreitete Annahme ist falsch! Kartoffeln sind arm an Kalorien und haben viele Vitamine.
RUNDFUNKMODERATOR	Viertens: Fisch hat weniger Nährwert als Fleisch. Richtig oder falsch?
PROF. DR. LOHMANN	Wiederum falsch! Fisch hat im allgemeinen weniger Fett als Fleisch, aber fast so viele Proteine wie Fleisch. Außerdem ist Fisch reich an Vitamin D.
RUNDFUNKMODERATOR	Fünftens — und hier bin ich selbst neugierig: Öl ist Öl. Es spielt keine Rolle, welches man im Haushalt gebraucht. Frau Professor Doktor Lohmann, richtig oder falsch?
PROF. DR. LOHMANN	Auch diese Annahme ist falsch! Der Gesundheit zuliebe bitte nur Pflanzenöle verwenden, denn Pflanzenöle enthalten kein Cholesterin.
RUNDFUNKMODERATOR	Sechstens: Orangen und Zitronen sind die Vitamin-C-reichsten Früchte. Richtig oder falsch?
PROF. DR. LOHMANN	Falsch! Zitrusfrüchte enthalten pro 100 Gramm Fruchtgewicht nur 50 Milligramm Vitamin C. Kiwis enthalten dreimal so viel Vitamin C, nämlich 150 Milligramm.
RUNDFUNKMODERATOR	Siebtens: Brot macht dick. Wie sieht's hier aus, richtig oder falsch?
PROF. DR. LOHMANN	Falsch! Brot hat weniger Kalorien als Fett oder Zucker. Was auf dem Brot liegt, die Butter, die Wurst, der Käse, das macht dick!
RUNDFUNKMODERATOR	Achtens: Alle Mineralwässer sind gleich. Auch hier wieder die Frage: richtig oder falsch?
PROF. DR. LOHMANN	Falsch! Die Substanzen, die im Wasser sind, können sehr verschieden sein. In vielen Wässern ist sehr viel Salz, und Salz ist sowieso schon in vielen Lebensmitteln. Jeder weiß natürlich, daß zuviel Salz ungesund für den Körper ist.
RUNDFUNKMODERATOR	Neuntens: Wenn es heiß ist, soll man nichts oder nur wenig trinken. Oh, das hört sich sehr falsch an. Was sagt unsere Expertin dazu?
PROF. DR. LOHMANN	In der Tat: sehr falsch! Wenn es heiß ist, soll man besonders viel trinken, weil der Körper in der Hitze viel Flüssigkeit verliert.
RUNDFUNKMODERATOR	Zehntens: Brauner Zucker enthält mehr Vitamine und Mineralien als weißer Zucker. Richtig oder falsch?
PROF. DR. LOHMANN	Auch hier wieder lautet die eindeutige Antwort: falsch! Weder brauner noch weißer Zucker enthalten Vitamine oder Mineralien. Der braune Zucker ist heute meist gefärbt.
RUNDFUNKMODERATOR	Und damit sind wir am Ende der Sendung. Wir bedanken uns ganz herzlich bei Frau Professor Doktor Lohmann und möchten Sie, liebe Zuhörer, bitten, uns weitere Anfragen zuzuschicken, die wir gerne wieder von einem Experten im Studio beantworten lassen.

Kapitel 3: Aussehen: wichtig oder nicht?
Projects and Games

PROJECT

In this activity students will write and present a report on a current event from one of the German-speaking countries.

Materials Students may need newspapers from the school library such as *World Brief, World Events,* or *The Week in Germany*, local and national newspapers, and magazines that focus on news abroad.

NOTE Tell students about the project at the beginning of Chapter 3 but allow them time to follow the German-speaking countries in the news for at least two weeks before beginning the written part of the project.

Suggested Sequence

1. Have students monitor print and broadcast news media to collect information on current events in Austria, Germany, Liechtenstein, and Switzerland. They should be sure to note the source and date of any information they collect.
2. In class, have students share the information they have gathered and come up with a list of events currently taking place in the German-speaking countries.
3. Allow individuals or pairs of students to choose an event about which they will prepare an in-depth report. Also give students the opportunity to share with one another the information that they collected while monitoring the media.
4. Have students outline the order in which they plan to organize their reports. Review sequencing words with them if necessary.
5. Students write the first draft of their reports. You may want to evaluate students' first drafts or have them peer-edited before students revise them.
6. Students use their final drafts to present their reports to the class.

Grading the Project

Suggested point distribution (total = 100 points)

Content	25
Organization	25
Correct language usage	25
Oral presentation	25

GAME

Wörtersalat

This game will help students review the vocabulary they have learned thus far.

Preparation Prepare a list of words from the **Wortschatz** page. Give each student a copy of the list.

Procedure Tell students that you will call out one word at a time from the list. They will have thirty seconds to write down one word that starts with each letter of the word you called out. To make the game more challenging, limit acceptable words to certain categories such as nouns, verbs, or adjectives. See the examples below.

(verbs) **Z U N E H M E N**
zugeben umrühren nehmen essen holen mähen erhalten nennen

(adjectives) **M I C K R I G**
modisch italienisch chic kalt reich intelligent gut

Kapitel 3: Aussehen: wichtig oder nicht?
Lesson Plans, pages 52-75

Teacher Note

Before you begin the chapter, you may want to preview the *Video Program* and consult the *Video Guide*. Suggestions for integrating the video into each chapter are given in the *Video Guide* and in the chapter interleaf. Activity masters for video selections can be found in the *Video Guide*.

*U*sing the Chapter Opener, *pp. 52-53*

Motivating Activity

Here are two sayings related to appearance:
Kleider machen Leute.
Schönheit vergeht, Tugend besteht.
Write these statements on the board and give students a few minutes to think about what they mean. Divide students into two groups and have each group talk about one of the two sayings, discussing what it means and thinking of an example to which it would apply.

Thinking Critically

Comparing and Contrasting Ask students about sayings in English that are related to appearance. (Example: *Don't judge a book by its cover*.) Do any of the English sayings express the same ideas as those discussed in the Motivating Activity?

◆ For Individual Needs

① **Visual Learners** Ask students to comment in German on the similarities and the differences in hairstyle and clothing of the four students pictured. Then have students describe the group as a whole. Write some of the words and expressions brainstormed by students on the chalkboard or on a transparency.

Teaching Suggestion

② Put students in pairs and ask them to comment in German on the items shown in Photo 2. Then have partners ask each other how they choose their own clothing and shoes, as well as certain accessories. They should also discuss what they consider to be "in" at the moment. Get feedback from several groups.

Building on Previous Skills

③ Students were introduced to **Reformhäuser** in Level 2 (p. 96). Ask students if they can remember the difference between a **Reformhaus** and a regular grocery store or a supermarket. Do students know of such stores in their neighborhood or town? Can they think of specific items that would be sold there? How many items can they name in German?

Focusing on Outcomes

To help students focus on the learning outcomes listed on p. 53, ask them to tell the class in German what types of things they do to make themselves look and feel better. **NOTE:** These outcomes are modeled in **Los geht's!** (pp. 54-55) and **Weiter geht's!** (pp. 62-63) and evaluated in **Kann ich's wirklich?** (p. 74).

*T*eaching Los geht's!

pp. 54-55

Resources for Los geht's!

- *Textbook Audiocassette* 2 A
- *Practice and Activity Book*

Teacher Note

Los geht's! is recorded on audiocassette.

Los geht's! Summary

In **Gut aussehen**, four students explain how they feel about appearance and what they do to look their best. The following student outcome listed on p. 53 is modeled in the episode: asking for and expressing opinions.

Motivating Activity

Bring pictures of several different people to class. Ask students in German what kind of person each might be, based strictly on their appearance. (**Schaut euch diese Person an. Wie sieht die Person aus? Was meint ihr, was für eine Person ist das?**) Ask students if it is fair to judge people strictly on their appearance. (**Ist es fair oder unfair, eine Person nur nach dem Aussehen zu beurteilen? Warum oder warum nicht?**)

Language Note

In her last statement on p. 55, Tanja uses the words **mickrig** and **schiefgehen** (**schiefgegangen**). You might want to paraphrase these terms for students.

sich mickrig fühlen: sich überhaupt nicht gut fühlen

schiefgehen: wenn etwas nicht so geht, wie es geplant war

Teaching Suggestion

1 Before students make their lists, remind them of the strategy of note-taking they learned in Level 2 (p. 302). These notes will be helpful when students do Activity 3.

For Individual Needs

1 **A Slower Pace** Ask students to reread the interviews and to make a list of the words and expressions they don't understand. Write them on the chalkboard or on a transparency and ask for volunteers to explain the meaning of the terms in German.

Teaching Suggestions

2 Have students write their own narration in paragraph form rather than writing a series of disconnected sentences. Students should respond as if they too had been asked by an interviewer: **Warum ist dir dein Aussehen wichtig, und was tust du dafür?**

3 Ask students to use the notes they took in Activity 1. Students should avoid rereading the interviews and should instead rely on their notes.

Closure

Ask students with which of the four students interviewed they most closely identify and why. (**Schaut euch die vier Schüler noch einmal an. Mit welchem Schüler oder mit welcher Schülerin identifiziert ihr euch am meisten? Und warum?**)

Philipp

LOS GEHT'S!

*T*eaching Erste Stufe, *pp. 56-59*

Resources for Erste Stufe

Practice and Activity Book
Chapter Resources, Book 1
- Communicative Activities 3-1, 3-2
- Additional Listening Activities 3-1, 3-2, 3-3
- Student Response Forms
- Realia 3-1
- Situation Card 3-1
- Teaching Transparency Master 3-1
- Quiz 3-1

Audiocassette Program
- *Textbook Audiocassette 2 A*
- *Additional Listening Activities, Audiocassette 9 A*
- *Assessment Items, Audiocassette 7 A*

Video Program, Videocassette 1
Video Guide

▶ *page 56*

MOTIVATE

Teaching Suggestion

Ask students to define physical fitness and well-being. Ask them how they would rate themselves in these two categories. Then ask them about some physical activities in which they participate regularly.

TEACH

Teaching Suggestions

- The **Fitneßtest** at the top of p. 56 contains new vocabulary items. You might want to introduce them to students by paraphrasing them in question form.

  Allgemeines Wohlbefinden: Wie fühlt ihr euch generell?

  Körperliche Leistungsfähigkeit: Wie fit seid ihr?

  Ausdauer: Wie lange könnt ihr etwas machen?

  Konzentrationsfähigkeit: Wie gut könnt ihr euch konzentrieren?

  Lebensfreude, Spannkraft: Wieviel Spaß macht euch das Leben? Wie vital fühlt ihr euch?

- After finishing the test, students should form pairs and ask their partner about his or her fitness level according to the answers that were given on the test. Students could use the questions from the definitions or make up their own.

PRESENTATION: Wortschatz

Introduce the new vocabulary to students. Then ask them to work with a partner to write a series of short dialogues between two or more people containing at least one of the new expressions. Tell students that they can vary the expressions according to their needs and interests.

Example:
— **Wie entspannst du dich am besten?**
— **Durch Sport, besonders Jogging. Und du?**
— **Ich entspanne mich durch Lesen und Musik.**

▣ Video Program

In the video clip **Gesund essen**, the owner of a health food store talks about trends in health food consumption. See *Video Guide* for suggestions.

▶ *page 57*

❖ For Individual Needs

4 Challenge After students have listened to the **Höranruf**, ask them what advice they would give the caller. Do students agree or disagree with Dr. Behrens' advice? (**Was würdet ihr diesem Mädchen raten? Meint ihr, Dr. Behrens hat das Mädchen gut oder schlecht beraten? Warum?**)

For Additional Practice

5 Ask students to assume the role of a popular musician, actor or actress, or any celebrity of their choice. Partners should interview each other using questions similar to the ones in Activity 5.

Teaching Suggestion

6 Ask students to talk about what can make them feel down or unhappy. List their answers on one side of the board or a transparency. Once students have mentioned several things, start from the top of the list and ask the class about things that would make them feel better in each of the cases. Write the solutions in the other column.

PRESENTATION: So sagt man das!

Students learned ways to express opinions in Level 1 (pp. 55 and 232). Ask students to give you their opinions of the latest fashions, movies, or current events using the expressions they already know. Example:
— **Wie findest du den neuen Harrison Ford Film?**
— **Den finde ich ganz toll!** or
— **Ich glaube, daß der Film ein großer Hit wird!**
Then introduce the new expressions from the **So sagt man das!** box.

▶ *page 58*

For Additional Practice

8 Prepare a list of additional topics on a transparency and have students tell you or write their opinions of each of the listed items. (Examples: **Was hältst du von schnellen Wagen? ... von Schulklubs? ... vom Leben auf dem Land? ... von Telekommunikation? ... von einem Job nach der Schule? ... von Natursendungen?**)

PRESENTATION: Grammatik

Students learned about **da-** and **wo-**compounds in Level 2 (p. 241). To review them briefly, list the following prepositions on the board or on a transparency: **aus, an, auf, bei, mit, nach, von, zu, für, gegen, in, durch,** and **um.** Bring a few props to class such as a comb and a tooth brush. While combing your hair say **Ich kämme mir die Haare mit einem Kamm.** Put the comb down and ask **Womit kämme ich mir die Haare?** Pointing to the comb, say **mit einem Kamm.** Then ask **Womit?** Pointing to the comb, say **Damit!** Write the compounds **womit** and **damit** on the board or on a transparency to help visual learners. Give a few additional examples of compounds that do not require the addition of an "r." Next, review the compounds that require the "r." Put a book on your desk and say **Ich lege das Buch auf den Tisch.** Look at the class and ask **Worauf habe ich das Buch gelegt?** Point to the desk and say **auf den Tisch.** Then ask **Worauf?** Point to the desk and say **Darauf!** Write the compounds **worauf** and **darauf,** as well as other compounds that include an "r," on the board or a transparency. See if students can remember in what instances an "r" must be added to form the compound.

Teaching Suggestion

Ask students to find all the **wo-** and **da-**compounds contained in the interviews of the **Los geht's!** section on pp. 54 and 55. Students should also identify the part of the sentence the compound refers to. For example, in the sentence **Und was das Essen angeht, ... ich mach' mir keine großen Gedanken darüber,** the compound **darüber** refers to **das Essen.**

▶ *page 59*

Group Work

10 Divide the class into groups of three and assign one discussion topic to each group. Tell students that they should be ready to share their opinions with the rest of the class after the activity and that they will have to support each of their opinions. (Example: **Biokost ist zwar sehr gesund, aber nicht alle Leute sollten unbedingt Biokost essen, denn ...**)

For Individual Needs

11 Auditory Learners Write the six questions from this activity on as many index cards as there are students in the class. Give each student a card. Ask students to mingle with classmates and ask three different people the question on their index card. Tell students that they will have about five minutes before they must return to their seats. Then call on some students to report the responses they got to their questions.

Teaching Suggestions

12 You may want to record students' conversations. Afterwards, play some of the conversations for the class and ask students to take notes on how students supported their opinions. Students should decide whether the opinions stated were well supported or not. If they think an opinion was not well supported, they should offer an alternative.

13 Tell students to imagine they are writing for a teen magazine and that their piece will be read by German-speaking teenagers eager to find out more about young Americans' attitude toward appearance and fitness.

Reteaching: Vocabulary

Prepare a list of questions. Call on individual students to answer your questions. Here are a few examples you might want to use.
Wie entspannst du dich gewöhnlich?
Was hältst du von Biokost an Schulen?
Was hebt die Laune bei dir?
Was ist denn vollwertiges Essen?

▶ *pages 60-61*

PRESENTATION: Landeskunde

Motivating Activity

Have students think of certain teenage "happenings" in the past or present that elicit "cult"-like behavior. (Example: the viewing of the *Rocky Horror Picture Show* to which teens flocked week after week in strange outfits and where they exhibited certain group behaviors, such as chanting, clapping, getting up, or throwing things)

 ### Total Physical Response

Bring the following props to class to introduce the vocabulary of items teenagers take to **Tekkno-Parties**: hard hat, sunglasses, rubber gloves, surgical mask, plastic bag, and whistle. Ask one student to be a **Tekkno-Fan** and have other students tell him or her to put on the different items.

Cooperative Learning

A Divide the class into groups of three students. Assign each of the group members a specific task as reader, recorder, or reporter. Once the groups have completed their assignments, call on the reporters to present their answers. You may also want to collect the papers at the end to verify that the task has been completed by all groups.

Family Link

Have students interview their parents about expressions or words they used when they were teenagers. What do the expressions mean? Are they still around or are they now obsolete? Encourage students with parents who grew up in other countries to share their expressions with the class as well.

Thinking Critically

Analyzing After students complete the activities in the **Landeskunde** section, write the following statement on the board and ask students how it relates to the **Lexikon** at the end of the **Landeskunde: Sprache ist immer lebendig!** (*Language is a living thing!*).

Teacher Note

Mention to your students that the **Landeskunde** will also be included in Quiz 3-1 given at the end of the **Erste Stufe**.

CLOSE

 ### For Individual Needs

Challenge Ask students about their opinions of current fashions worn by actors and actresses on TV programs. Do these fashions influence the way students dress? (**Was hältst du von dem Kleidungsstil von ... in der Sendung ...?** or **Was hältst du von dem Kleidungsstil von Schauspielern im Fernsehen? Meinst du, ihr Stil beeinflußt dich?**)

Focusing on Outcomes

Refer students back to the learning outcomes listed on p. 53. They should recognize that they now know how to ask for and express opinions.

ASSESS

- **Performance Assessment** Make a list of at least ten questions that incorporate functions and vocabulary from the **Erste Stufe**. Give a copy to each student and ask them to move around the class asking as many students as possible the questions on their lists. Have students return to their desks and write down the answers they received from their classmates.
  Examples:
  Was hältst du vom Schminken?
  Wie entspannst du dich am Wochenende?
  Was denkst du über Krafttraining für Teenager?
  Was würdest du dazu sagen, wenn es nur noch Biokost in der Schulmensa geben sollte?

- Quiz 3-1, *Chapter Resources,* Book 1

*T*eaching Weiter geht's!
pp. 62-63

> ### Resources for Weiter geht's!
> - *Textbook Audiocassette* 2 A
> - *Practice and Activity Book*

Teacher Note

Weiter geht's! is recorded on audiocassette.

Weiter geht's! Summary

In **Immer mit der Mode. Oder?,** four students talk about what fashion means to them and how closely they follow trends. The following student outcomes listed on p. 53 are modeled in the reports: expressing sympathy and resignation, giving advice, giving a reason, admitting something and expressing regret.

Motivating Activity

Have students bring pictures from fashion magazines. Ask students what they think of fashion in general and what they think of the styles shown in the pictures. What do students think of designer clothes? How do students choose their clothes? (**Was haltet ihr von der derzeitigen Mode? Was denkt ihr über Designer-Kleidung? Wie entscheidet ihr euch für eure Klamotten? Was beeinflußt eure Wahl?**)

Teaching Suggestion

Have students listen to one report at a time, following along in the book. Then work through the text, asking questions to detect any problems in comprehension caused by new words and phrases. Use synonyms or paraphrasing to explain new words.
Example:
Philipp sagt: „Ich geb' zu, daß ich mich von der Mode beeinflussen lass'." Was meint er damit?
Once students have been given some examples showing how to get around new words, they should be able to do this on their own, using context to establish meaning.

Group Work

16 Divide the class into four or more groups and have each group work on one of the reports from p. 62. Ask groups to do tasks a and b. Students might need help with task b, finding the main point of each response. Have students quote the key sentence(s) and then identify the sentences that support each one.

Teaching Suggestion

17 Since matching the fifteen statements with people requires a lot of close reading, encourage students to look first for the most obvious ones, such as number 3 (Sonja) or number 14 (Tanja). After students have completed this activity, ask them which of the fifteen statements would best describe them. (**Welche dieser Aussagen trifft auf dich/euch zu?**)

WEITER GEHT'S!

For Individual Needs

18 Auditory Learners Have a student give an oral description of an imaginary outfit or an outfit in a picture. Each person in the group draws the outfit based on what he or she hears. Have students compare their drawings at the end.

Closure

Put students in pairs. Each pair should write down as many words as they can to fit the categories that you call out or write on the board or on a transparency. Give students three to four minutes per category. Then ask four or five pairs of students to share their lists with the rest of the class. Here are a few categories and some related words students might come up with.

ausgeflippte Klamotten: zerrissenes T-Shirt, verwaschene Jeans
Bodybuilding: Krafttraining, Anstrengung
Biokost: Tofu, Sojasprossen, gesund, umweltfreundlich
Aussehen: schminken, schön, mickrig
guter Geschmack: gutes Aussehen, gefallen
Diät ohne Fleisch: Vegetarier(in), gesund
To make the activity more challenging, you could ask students to use some of the words they thought of in sentences and then paragraphs. (Example: **Was ich über Biokost denke? Ja, ich glaube, daß Biokost sehr gesund und noch dazu umweltfreundlich ist, weil ...**)

Teaching Zweite Stufe, pp. 64-68

Resources for Zweite Stufe

Practice and Activity Book
Chapter Resources, Book 1
- Communicative Activities 3-3, 3-4
- Additional Listening Activities 3-4, 3-5, 3-6
- Student Response Forms
- Realia 3-2
- Situation Card 3-2
- Teaching Transparency Master 3-2
- Quiz 3-2
Audiocassette Program
- *Textbook Audiocassette* 2 A
- *Additional Listening Activities, Audiocassette* 9 A
- *Assessment Items, Audiocassette* 7 A

▶ **page 64**

MOTIVATE
Teaching Suggestion

Ask students whom they confide in most of the time when they need to talk to someone. (**Wem vertraust du dich an, wenn du Probleme hast? Deiner Freundin? Deinem Freund? Deinen Eltern?**)

TEACH
Teaching Suggestion

Ask two students to read the conversation between Elke and Tanja aloud in class. Then ask the class to tell you a) the gist of the problem b) Elke's reaction, and c) the way Tanja tries to help. (**Was ist mit Elke los? Wie reagiert sie? Was rät Tanja ihrer Freundin?**)

▶ **page 65**

PRESENTATION: Wortschatz

Introduce the new words and expressions. For each one, ask a question or make a statement to which students have to respond. Then ask students to write two related sentences or a question and a response incorporating at least one of the new vocabulary items.

ZWEITE STUFE

PRESENTATION: So sagt man das!

Ask students to reread the conversation between Elke and Tanja and identify all expressions of sympathy and resignation in the text. Ask students to quote these in the context in which they were used.

Language Note

You may want to point out to students that **eine Pechsträhne haben** has an equivalent in English: *to have a streak of bad luck.*

Building on Previous Skills

21 In Level 2 (p. 147) students learned expressions used to ask for and give advice. Review those expressions with students and ask them to give some advice to their partner responding to their partner's resignation.
Examples:
Geh doch mal früher zu Bett!
Du brauchst unbedingt Nachhilfe in Mathe!

▶ *page 66*

PRESENTATION: So sagt man das!

Present the new expressions, then ask students how the words **doch** and **mal** affect the meaning of the statements. What might be an equivalent for these words in English? (There is probably no single "right" translation, but expressions such as *why don't you* as in *Why don't you wear something stylish?* or *go ahead* as in *Go ahead and try wearing fashionable clothes!* or *just* as in *You should just wear something really cool!* might be feasible equivalents.)

❖ For Individual Needs

24 A Slower Pace Do this activity orally with the class. Have students come up with several different problems or situations, then let the whole class offer advice.

▶ *page 67*

PRESENTATION: Grammatik

Introduce the grammar box, focusing on one point at a time. Give special attention to each section by giving additional examples. Contrast modals with other verbs to give students practice using infinitives with and without **zu.**
Examples:
Wir wollen ins Kino gehen —> Wir haben vor, ins Kino zu gehen. or **Wir haben uns entschieden, ins Kino zu gehen.**
Ich möchte baden gehen. —> Ich werde versuchen, baden zu gehen.

PRESENTATION: So sagt man das!

- When presenting the phrases in the function box, ask students to pay special attention to the linking words **weil, damit,** and **um ... zu.** They all are used to introduce an explanation or expression of purpose. Their meanings, though, as in English, are slightly different. Can students guess what they mean? If not, put the English equivalents on a transparency or on the board in random order and have students match the meanings. (**weil** *because,* **damit** *so that,* **um ... zu** *in order to*)
- Point out to students that a subordinate clause with the conjugated verb in last position follows the conjunctions **weil** and **damit. Um ... zu** is followed by an infinitive construction.

▶ *page 68*

❖ For Individual Needs

26 Challenge Have the student who repeats his or her partner's statement give an additional reason why he or she does the same thing as the partner. (Example: **Ich zieh' mich auch nett an, um mich gut zu fühlen und auch, weil ich mit der Mode mitmachen will.**)

26 Challenge Have students initiate some statements with explanations on their own, talking about things they do frequently, referring to school, then job, then friends, then home life. (Examples: **Ich helfe zu Hause, damit ich ...; ich arbeite nach der Schule, um ... zu ...**)

ZWEITE STUFE

Teacher Note

27 Remind students to use the correct word order in **daß**-clauses and to use reflexive verbs and verbs with separable prefixes properly.

CLOSE

Thinking Critically

Drawing Inferences Discuss with students the saying **Freunde erkennt man in der Not** and determine how it applies to the functions presented in the **Zweite Stufe**.

Focusing on Outcomes

Refer students back to the learning outcomes listed on p. 53. They should recognize that they now know how to express sympathy and resignation, give advice, give a reason, and admit something and express regret.

ASSESS

- **Performance Assessment** Assuming the role of a caller to a radio talkshow, ask individual students to play the role of **Dr. Antwort** and give you advice for your problems. Here are some problems you could bring up.

  Meine Eltern lassen mich nicht meine Haare färben. Was soll ich tun?

  Mein Freund zieht sich einfach zu schlampig an, was mir oft peinlich ist. Können Sie mir raten, was ich tun soll?

  Ich bekomme nur wenig Taschengeld. Wie kann ich mich trotzdem hübsch anziehen?

- Quiz 3-2, *Chapter Resources,* Book 1

Teaching Zum Schreiben, *p. 69*

Writing Strategy

The targeted strategy in this writing activity is organizing your ideas. Students should learn about this strategy before beginning the assignment.

PREWRITING

Motivating Activity

On the board or on a transparency, write the name of a celebrity that students recognize. Give students one to two minutes to write down any physical features or other characteristics they associate with that person. Ask students to share their ideas with the class and write down any descriptive words or phrases they come up with. Ask students how one could group them to organize the ideas. Point out that although each student was focusing on the same person, not all of them used the same words to describe that person. Each student had a unique mental image associated with that person.

Teaching Suggestions

- You might want to bring magazine pictures to class and let students choose one of the people depicted in the photos for their written descriptions.

- Students should use the motivating activity as an example and jot down as many descriptive German words as they can to describe their subject before starting their **Ideenbaum**.

Teacher Note

To help students organize their **Ideenbaum**, you might want to show them a sample on the overhead projector.

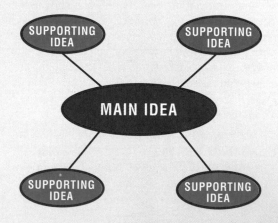

WRITING

Teaching Suggestion

Encourage students to use the German vocabulary, expressions, and constructions that they know, rather than trying to *translate* every thought into German. Students should feel free to consult the end-of-book vocabulary lists to reactivate vocabulary they might have forgotten or to spur their creativity, but should avoid relying heavily on a bilingual dictionary. You might want to tell them that the point of the exercise is not to translate their English ideas into German, but to actively communicate using the language they have acquired thus far.

POST-WRITING

Closure

Display the final drafts of students' descriptions along with the corresponding drawings in the classroom. This will reinforce student pride and will also serve to show first and second level students the tasks they will be able to carry out once they reach Level 3.

Teaching Zum Lesen, pp. 70-71

Reading Strategy

The targeted strategy in this reading is determining the main idea of an article. Students should learn about this strategy before beginning Question 2.

PREREADING

Motivating Activity

Have students ask an older person to tell them the meanings of some of the following slang expressions: *the bee's knees, fly boy, peachy keen, can you dig it?, square, flower power*. With the class, decide which terms belonged to which generations.
"Flapper" generation: *the bee's knees,* meaning *the best*
World War II generation: *fly boy,* meaning *pilot; peachy keen,* meaning *really good*
50s generation: *can you dig it?,* meaning *can you understand or accept it?; square,* meaning *old fashioned*
60s generation: *flower power,* meaning *persuasive power of gentleness and peacefulness*

READING

Teacher Note

The word **geil** means **toll** or **großartig** in teen language. It equivalates roughly to the American teen use of *cool!* or even *hot!*.

Teaching Suggestion

In order to complete Activities 4-9, students will first need to go systematically through the many quotes in this article and sort them into three sources: teens, parents, and experts. Within the teens category, they then should distinguish between a) citations of specific teens' statements and b) terms that have been put into quotes by the writer in order to indicate that they are slang. Students may need help with the quotes-within-a-quote ('**Ächz-Stöhn**' and '**Kotz-Würg**' from a woman's fifteen-year-old) and with determining the source of **Ich geb' dir 20 Pfennig ...**, a saying supposedly recommended by psychologists to exasperated parents for use on their complaining offspring. This activity lends itself well to cooperative learning with students in groups of three or four: one or two researchers, a recorder, and a reporter. Groups could "specialize" in finding the quotes made by teens, parents, and experts.

Teacher Note

You might want to point out to students after they've completed Activity 5 that the adults in this article use some relatively negative language. The 36-year-old mother's **bescheuert** *(stupid)* is a slang term which has somewhat replaced **blöd**. **Gymnasial-Pädagoge Kutschke** chooses to use **maulfaul** instead of **mundfaul**. And the advice, "**... erzähl's der nächsten Parkuhr!**" is the way many older Germans say *I don't want to hear about it!*

Thinking Critically

Analyzing The author of this article states that teen slang mixes a variety of areas of experience, including borrowings from English, technical German, and comic book language. Can students analyze the examples given in the text in terms of where they might have come from? Is this any different from the sources of the slang currently used by American teens? If so, how?

Teaching Suggestion

9 Presumably, the language expert is trying to reassure parents by saying that teen slang is "only a phase." Students need to know what kind of magazine this article appeared in, and who the intended audience must have been. (**Frauenzeitschrift**; parents)

POST-READING

Teacher Note

Activity 12 is a post-reading task that will show whether students can apply what they have learned.

Closure

Using the German slang they already know and the terms introduced in this article, pairs of students should try to carry on a conversation using as much slang as possible.

Answers to Activity 1

teen language/slang; teenagers and parents

Answers to Activity 2

teenage slang is just a phase; **Der Sprachforscher ... hält die Jugend-Sprüche lediglich für eine „Durchgangsstation"**

Answers to Activity 3

teenagers: Tanja, Uli, Olaf, Lilo; parents: mother of Tanja, mother of 15-year-old boy; experts: psychologists, educator (**Pädagoge**), language expert; a series of interviews in essay form

Answers to Activity 4

pfiff sich 'ne Mafia-Torte rein: hat eine Pizza gegessen; legte Emaille auf: hat sich geschminkt; Kalkleisten: Leute über 25; Grufties: Eltern/Erwachsene; Lappen: Geld; heavy: schwer
If the writer wants to be understood by her readers, she must make sure they know what the words mean.

Answers to Activity 5

Possible answers: **Die Sprüche klingen blöd. Die Teenagers sind einfach faul. Die Eltern können ihre Kinder nicht verstehen. Teenagers wollen miteinander über wichtige Sachen nicht reden oder diskutieren.**

Answers to Activity 6

Parents are no better, they only talk about the most essential things (**Die meisten Eltern sprechen zu Hause auch nur das Allernötigste**). They sit in front of the TV and don't say anything (**Die Alten sitzen doch nur stumm wie die Fische vor dem Fernseher**).

Answers to Activity 7

psychologists; Teenagers do talk and think about important issues (**Da sind Sachen dabei, die zeigen, daß die sich auf ihre Art ebenfalls Gedanken machen**). Their language shows they want to make things better (**Sie wollen ... etwas Eigenes, Besseres erfinden**).

Answers to Activity 8

Parents should avoid imitating their children (**Nicht nachaffen, nicht mitspielen!**).

Answers to Activity 9

The writer quotes the language expert in the final paragraph to support the idea that teenspeak is just a phase.

Answers to Activity 10

Die Sprache von der Jugend ist nur eine Phase.

Answers to Activity 11

Die Jugendlichen werden wieder normal sprechen, wenn die Clique sich auflöst und die Berufe beginnen. Die heutige Jugend ist wie frühere Generationen: Sie wollen einfach etwas Eigenes erfinden. Ihre Sprüche zeigen, daß sie sich Gedanken machen.

*U*sing Anwendung,
pp. 72-73

Resources for Anwendung

Chapter Resources, Book 1
- Realia 3-3
- Situation Card 3-3

Video Program, Videocassette 1

Video Guide

Video Program

At this time, you might want to use the authentic advertising footage from German television. See *Video Guide* for suggestions

Portfolio Assessment

1 You might want to suggest this activity as a written and oral portfolio item for your students. See *Assessment Guide,* p. 16.

Teaching Suggestion

2 Before starting the activity, brainstorm with students words and expressions that will help them discuss the statements. Write each word or expression on the board or on a transparency.

Examples:

Ich glaube, daß ...

Ich finde es ..., daß ...

Ja schon, aber ...

Ja, ich stimme da schon zu, aber ...

Ich finde das überhaupt nicht richtig, denn ...

Ich würde sagen, daß ...

Meiner Meinung nach ...

Multicultural Connection

2 Have students present these statements to students from other countries or various cultural backgrounds and report back to the class whether the opinions or reactions of those students differ from their own.

*K*ann ich's wirklich?
p. 74

This page helps students prepare for the test. It is a brief checklist of the major points covered in the chapter. The students should be reminded that it is only a checklist and not necessarily everything that will appear on the test.

*U*sing Wortschatz,
p. 75

♖ Game

Play the game **Wörtersalat** using the vocabulary from this chapter. See p. 51F for the procedure.

Teaching Suggestion

Ask students to complete the following statements.

... ist jemand, der gerade eine Pechsträhne hat.

... ist vollwertige Nahrung.

Ich ... und ..., um mich zu entspannen.

Ich mache mir oft Gedanken über ...

Ich habe vor, ...

Ich spare Geld, um ... zu ...

♖ Game

Play the game **Heiße Kartoffel.** See Level 2 (p. 233F) for the procedure. Here are some phrases or words you may want to use.

Biokost, Pechsträhne, herumblättern, vorhaben

Teacher Note

Give the **Kapitel 3** Chapter Test, *Chapter Resources,* Book 1.

3

Aussehen: wichtig oder nicht?

① Wir versuchen, uns so oft wie möglich zu treffen.

Wie man aussieht und wie man sich fühlt, trägt zum allgemeinen Wohlbefinden bei und stärkt damit das Selbstvertrauen des Menschen. Wie wichtig ist gutes Aussehen für Jugendliche? Was tun die jungen Deutschen für ihr Aussehen? Ernähren sie sich richtig? Machen sie genügend Sport? Wie kleiden sie sich? Und was machen sie, wenn sie sich innerlich mal nicht wohl fühlen? Um über diese Themen zu diskutieren, zu lesen und zu schreiben, müßt ihr noch einiges lernen.

In this chapter you will learn

- to ask for and express opinions
- to express sympathy and resignation; to give advice; to give a reason; to admit something and express regret

And you will

- listen to students talking about what contributes to their well-being
- read about ways young Germans make statements about themselves
- write a description of someone you know
- find out what German students do to look good and feel good about themselves

Top-Qualität zum klasse Preis

② Du solltest dir mal ein Paar modische Schuhe kaufen!

Alles Gute für Ihre Gesundheit neuform

neuform **Reformhaus**

Gesund, vital und dabei schlank!

③ Was hältst du von Biokost?

Los geht's!

Gut aussehen

Vier Gymnasiasten erzählen, warum ihnen ihr Aussehen wichtig ist und was sie für ihr Aussehen tun.

Philipp

Sonja

Ich achte schon darauf, wie ich ausseh'. Wenn ich mir zum Beispiel etwas zum Anziehen kauf', so achte ich schon darauf, was zusammenpaßt. Und man kauft sich halt auch Sachen, die „in" sind: Designer Jeans, Lederjacken, ja und Cowboystiefel, die sind halt jetzt „in". Und was das Essen angeht, na ja ... ehrlich gesagt, ich mach' mir keine großen Gedanken darüber. Ich ess', was mir schmeckt, und das dann, wenn möglich, in Massen. Ich trink' zum Beispiel zu viel Cola, was auch nicht grad gesund ist. Aber es schmeckt halt.

Bei mir ist's ungefähr genauso. Ich mach' auch Sport, hauptsächlich, weil man sich einfach besser fühlt. Und mit dem Essen pass' ich schon auf; ich will ja nicht zunehmen. Und ja mit der Kleidung, hm ... da trag' ich eben, was mir gefällt. Manchmal ist es modisch, manchmal nicht so. Es muß aber immer bequem sein, aber nicht schlampig.

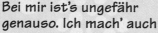

Tanja

Michael

Ich würd' schon sagen, mir ist mein Aussehen wichtig. Ich mach' auch ein bißchen Sport, hauptsächlich Volleyball und Tennis. Und mit dem Essen? Ich ess' halt weniger rotes Fleisch, mehr Hühnerfleisch, viel Obst und Gemüse. Ich möcht' schon ein bißchen darauf achten, was gut für meine Gesundheit ist.

Ich achte schon aufs Aussehen, und zwar ... also, ich mach' sehr viel Sport, um fit zu bleiben, ich ess' vernünftig — viel Gemüse, weniger Fleisch — ich rauch' nicht, ja ... und wenn ich mal ein paar Pfund abnehmen will, dann mache ich eben mehr Sport.

SONJA Meine Mutter achtet darauf, daß wir vollwertige Sachen essen, Gemüse, Obst und so. Aber Biokost machen wir nicht. Man soll's nicht übertreiben.

MICHAEL Wenn ich mal down bin, mach' ich halt Sport. Ich versuch', mich mit Sport abzulenken. Ich geh' schwimmen oder joggen ...

TANJA Das tun, glaub' ich, aber viele.

MICHAEL Ja schon, aber an der Schule gibt's halt einige Leute, die zweimal in der Woche ins Fitneß-Center gehen und ein regelmäßiges Krafttraining machen.

PHILIPP Ich halt' überhaupt nichts von Bodybuilding. Ich fahr' lieber Rad, oder ich geh' wandern. Das ist gesünder.

TANJA Wenn ich mich mal mickrig fühl', wenn etwas schiefgegangen ist, dann mach' ich erstens einmal Ordnung um mich herum. Ich räum' mein Zimmer auf. Und zweitens mach' ich mich hübsch. Ich zieh' mich nett an, ich schminke mich — nicht zu viel, aber wirkungsvoll. Das hebt die gute Laune. Und drittens mach' ich irgend etwas, was mir Spaß macht: ich hör' gute Musik, ich les' ein tolles Buch, oder ich beschäftige mich mit meinem Hobby, mit meinen Briefmarken. Dabei kann ich mich so richtig entspannen.

1 Wer macht was?

a. Was tun die vier Schüler, um gut auszusehen? Mach eine Liste mit verschiedenen Kategorien, zum Beispiel Kleidung, Sport usw.!

	Kleidung	Sport	Essen	Ges
Philipp	kauft Klamotten, die „in" sind			
Sonja				

b. 1. Welche Schüler geben Gründe an? Schreib die Gründe auf!
2. Für wen steht Sport oben auf der Liste? Kleidung? Essen?
3. Was machen die Schüler, wenn sie „down" sind?

b. 1. Sonja: macht Sport, weil man sich dann besser fühlt; paßt mit dem Essen auf, weil sie nicht zunehmen will. / Tanja: ißt vernünftig, weil sie auf ihre Gesundheit achtet. / Michael: macht Sport, um fit zu bleiben.

b. 2. Sport: Michael / Kleidung: Philipp / Essen: Tanja

2 Und was machst du?

Schreib deinen Namen auf die Liste mit den vier Schülern, und schreib auf, was du alles machst, um gut auszusehen!

b. 3. Michael: schwimmt oder joggt. / Tanja: räumt auf; macht sich hübsch; macht, was ihr Spaß macht.

3 Was berichten die Schüler?

Erzähle jetzt einem Klassenkameraden, was die vier Schüler alles für ihr Aussehen tun! Was ist das Wichtigste aus den Berichten?

BEISPIEL **Michael achtet auf sein Aussehen: Er macht viel Sport, um fit zu bleiben. Er ißt auch vernünftig und raucht nicht.**

Asking for and expressing opinions

Ein Fitneßtest

Machen Sie den Fitneßtest! Beurteilen Sie Ihre gegenwärtige Fitneß anhand der nebenstehenden fünf Punkte mit je einer Bewertung von 1 bis 10 (1 = ungenügend, 10 = ideal). Essen Sie während der nächsten 3 Monate täglich frisches Obst. Dann wiederholen Sie die Bewertung und stellen Sie fest, wie sich Ihre Fitneß verbessert hat!

Allgemeines Wohlbefinden	1	2	3	4	5	6	7	8	9	10
Körperliche Leistungsfähigkeit	1	2	3	4	5	6	7	8	9	10
Ausdauer	1	2	3	4	5	6	7	8	9	10
Konzentrationsfähigkeit	1	2	3	4	5	6	7	8	9	10
Lebensfreude, Spannkraft	1	2	3	4	5	6	7	8	9	10

WORTSCHATZ

Tanja schminkt sich ab und zu.

Sie ist schlampig angezogen.

Er fühlt sich mickrig.

Sie macht sich hübsch.

auf deutsch erklärt

sich entspannen relaxen
auf das Aussehen achten das Aussehen ist dir wichtig
mit dem Essen aufpassen darauf achten, daß man Gutes ißt
Was hältst du davon? Wie findest du das?
die Sache das Ding
zunehmen Wenn man zu viel ißt, nimmt man zu.
abnehmen Wenn man eine Diät macht, nimmt man ab.
vollwertig hat gute Nährstoffe
regelmäßig immer zur gleichen Zeit
wirkungsvoll effektiv
übertreiben schlimmer oder besser machen, als es wirklich ist
schiefgehen nicht gutgehen

auf englisch erklärt

Er macht sich Gedanken darüber. *He's thinking about it.*
Sie beschäftigt sich mit Umweltproblemen. *She is involved in environmental problems.*
Er lenkt sich mit Sport ab. *Sport is a diversion for him.*
Was das Essen angeht ... *As far as food goes ...*
Biokost schmeckt mir gut. *I like organic food.*
Das hebt die gute Laune. *That makes one feel better.*
Seine Kleidung paßt gut zusammen. *His clothes go together well.*

4 Hör gut zu! For answers, see listening script on TE Interleaf.

Zweimal in der Woche beantwortet Radio Pop-shop Höreranrufe junger Leute. Jungen und Mädchen können mit dem bekannten Jugend-Psychologen Dr. Uwe Behrens über ihre Probleme sprechen. — Hört euch das Problem eines Jugendlichen an und schreibt auf, was das Problem ist und was Dr. Behrens dem Jugendlichen rät (*advises*)!

5 Wie steht's bei dir?

Interessierst du dich dafür, wie deine Klassenkameraden leben? Such dir eine Partnerin und frag sie, wie es bei ihr mit dem Essen, dem Aussehen, der Gesundheit und der Freizeit steht!

richtig?   schlampig?   wohl?   Hobbys

gesund?   modisch?   krank?   Sport

falsch?   konservativ?   mickrig?   Fernsehen

> PARTNER   **Wie steht's bei dir mit dem Essen? Wie ernährst du dich?**
>
> DU   **Ich ernähr' mich falsch. Ich ess' zu viel ...**

1. Wie steht's mit dem Anziehen? Wie ziehst du dich an?
2. Wie steht's mit deiner Gesundheit? Wie fühlst du dich?
3. Wie steht's mit deiner Freizeit? Womit beschäftigst du dich?

6 Was hebt deine Laune?

Schreib alle Dinge auf, die deine Laune heben, wenn du einmal down bist! Erzähl dann der Klasse, was du machst! Sind folgende Dinge auf deiner Liste? Andere Dinge?

> DU   **Wenn ich einmal down bin, mache ich zuerst Ordnung. Dann ... danach ...**

Buch lesen
Musik hören
Zimmer aufräumen
Sport machen
spazierengehen
Ordnung machen
radfahren
Freund(in) anrufen

s. hübsch machen
s. modisch anziehen
s. beschäftigen mit ...
s. ablenken mit ...
s. hinlegen
s. etwas Nettes kaufen

SO SAGT MAN DAS!

Asking for and expressing opinions

To ask for someone's opinion, you might ask:

> **Was hältst du von Biokost?**
>
> **Was würdest du dazu sagen?**

To give your opinion, you could say:

> **Ich halte viel/wenig davon.**
> **Ich halte nichts davon.**
> **Ich würde sagen, daß ...**

How would you express these phrases in English? What case is used after **von**?[1]

---

7 Hör gut zu! For answers, see listening script on TE Interleaf.

Hör zu, wie verschiedene Schüler ihre Meinungen zu bestimmten Themen äußern! Worüber äußern sich die Schüler? Welche Meinung hat jeder Schüler? Ist sie positiv oder negativ? Mach dir Notizen!

1. the dative case

8 Und du? Was hältst du davon?

Du unterhältst dich mit einem Klassenkameraden. Er will wissen, was du meinst. Was würdest du zu diesen Themen sagen? Was hältst du davon — viel? wenig? nicht viel? nichts? Gib Gründe an!

PARTNER	**Was hältst du von Kleidung, die „in" ist?**
DU	**Ich halte ...** Answers will vary. E.g.: **Ich halte viel davon, weil man dann modisch aussieht.**

Kleidung, die „in" ist   Biokost

Bodybuilding   Designer Jeans

einer Diät ohne Fleisch

einem regelmäßigen Training

Grammatik   Da- and wo-compounds (Summary)

Read the following exchange:

HOLGER	**Worüber sprecht ihr?**
ANTJE	**Wir sprechen über die Schule.**
HOLGER	**Wir haben auch gerade darüber gesprochen.**

What would be the English equivalents of **worüber** and **darüber** in the sentences above? To what does **darüber** refer? Why does Holger say **darüber** rather than **über** followed by the pronoun **sie**?

Many verbs you know are paired with particular prepositions:

> Sie **spricht** gern **über** Politik, während sie **auf** den Bus **wartet.**

When you want to replace the nouns in those prepositional phrases with pronouns, you have to watch out for certain things.

1. When the object of the preposition is a person, use an appropriate pronoun to replace it. Always consider the case of the noun:

> Ich warte **auf Anja/sie. Auf wen** wartest du?
> Heiko kommt **mit Susi.** Wer kommt noch **mit ihr? Mit wem** kommst du?

2. However, when the object of the preposition is a thing, use the appropriate **da-** or **wo-**compound:

> **Worauf** wartest du? Ich warte **auf den Bus/darauf.**
> Ich weiß nicht, **worauf** sie warten.
> Wir reden **über die Hausaufgaben/darüber. Worüber** redet ihr?

3. You should also use a **da-**compound when the object of the preposition is an entire clause, rather than just a noun.

> **Woran** denkst du? Ich denke **daran, daß ich morgen zum Zahnarzt muß.**

---

9 Umfrage in der Klasse

Was machen deine Freunde? Frag sie mal! Benutze in jeder Frage eine wo-Konstruktion!

DU	**Also, ich beschäftige mich mit meinen Briefmarken. Und du?**
PARTNER	**Ich beschäftige mich ...**

1. Ich beschäftige mich mit ...
2. Ich interessiere mich nicht für ...
3. Ich lenke mich mit ... ab.
4. Ich halte nichts von ...

Fahrradfahren	Computerspielen
Kleidung	Briefmarken
Mode	gesunde Ernährung
Bodybuilding	Zukunft
Kunst	Beruf
Musik	regelmäßiges
Aussehen	Training

10 Klassendiskussion

Ein Klassenkamerad äußert die folgenden Meinungen. Was meint ihr dazu? Diskutiert darüber!

1. Es ist überhaupt nicht wichtig, wie man aussieht und was man anhat.
2. Alle Leute sollten nur Biokost essen!
3. Wenn man mal down ist, kann man überhaupt nichts machen. Da hilft nichts.

11 Was sagst du dazu?

Stell deiner Partnerin die folgenden Fragen! Reagiere auf das, was deine Partnerin sagt! Jedes Gespräch soll ein paar Mal hin- und hergehen.

Ist dir gutes Aussehen wichtig?

Ißt du immer alles, was auf den Tisch kommt?

Was willst du übers Wochenende machen?

Wie oft machst du Sport?

Willst du ab- oder zunehmen, oder so bleiben, wie du bist?

Wie geht's dir denn heute? Warum?

12 Wichtig oder nicht?

Jetzt sprecht ihr über Dinge, die euch wichtig sind! Was sagen deine Klassenkameraden? Was sagst du? Warum ist das so?

PARTNER	**Wie wichtig ist dir dein Aussehen?**
DU	**Ich würde sagen, mein Aussehen ist mir sehr wichtig.**
PARTNER	**Warum? Kannst du mir das erklären?**
DU	**(Wenn ich mich zum Beispiel modisch anziehe, fühl' ich mich wohl.)**

deine Hobbys   deine Ernährung
die Schule   deine Freunde
deine Gesundheit   dein Aussehen
Sport   deine Kleidung

13 Für mein Notizbuch

Schreib einen Kurzbericht zum Thema: „Mein Aussehen ist mir (nicht) wichtig". Schreib etwas über deine Ernährung, über Sport und über Kleidung!

14 Und deine Meinung über Kleidung?

Erzähl einer Partnerin, was du von Kleidung hältst! Wie wichtig sind dir neue Sachen? Was trägst du gern? Was nicht? Muß alles zusammenpassen? Wie finden die Eltern deine Kleidung?

15 Was hältst du von Kleidung?

Schreib einen Absatz zum Thema Kleidung! Hier sind ein paar Schreibhilfen.

Sachen tragen, die   halten von   was andere denken, ist   zusammenpassen

ist/sind mir wichtig   am liebsten tragen   darauf achten, daß

Die deutsche Subkultur

Lisa, 15

Ideologie

Gymnasiastin, 9. Klasse. Mutter Spanisch-Lehrerin an der Volkshochschule. Vater Internist. „Ich bin Punk, weil ich gegen die Ellenbogen-Gesellschaft rebelliere. Ich hab' mal einen Spruch gelesen, der mir sehr gut gefällt: ‚Ich fühle mich einsam, wenn ich eine Hand suche und nur Fäuste finde.'"

Je schlampiger, umso schöner! Zum Grunge-Look gehören strähnige Haare (einfach Haarwachs in die Spitzen kneten), lässig weite Opa-Hemden oder karierte Shirts.

Tekkno-Fieber

Tekkno-Parties locken tausende Jugendliche an. Kids in abenteuerlichen Verkleidungen warten vor den Discos auf Einlaß: Sie tragen Bauhelme, Sonnenbrillen, Gummihandschuhe, Mundschutz oder Plastiksäcke. Einer hat sogar einen Staubsauger auf dem Rücken.

Drinnen dröhnt die härteste Musik der Welt: Rhythmus ist alles, Melodie nichts. Die Tekkno-Fans begleiten das Ganze mit Trillerpfeifen.

Raver (engl. to rave = rasen) sind die Hippies der 90er — sanft, gegen Gewalt. Sie feiern die längsten Partys (24 Stunden), ihre Musik (Tekkno) zerreißt Eltern das Trommelfell, 220 Baßschläge in der Minute. Ihr Look: Latzhosen, Minikleider mit „adidas"® Streifen, Springer-Stiefel.

Raver Girls lieben Plüschtier Rucksäcke (z.B. Drache oder Dinosaurier)

Tom, 18

Liebe

„Ich habe gerade eine ewig lange Beziehung beendet. Wir haben uns auseinander entwickelt, weil ich Raver wurde und nicht wie sie Abi machen wollte. Mein Traum wäre es, eine Freundin zu finden, die mir ähnlich ist. Ich finde es schön, wenn es jemanden gibt, dem man vertrauen kann."

Sprache

„Im Raver-Slang bedeutet >>Chill-Out<<: sich ausruhen. >>Afterhour<<-Party: die Party nach der Party, morgens ab sechs Uhr bis mittags." A. 1. vier; Answers will vary; Punk: Weltanschauung / Grunge: Mode / Tekkno: Musik / Rave: Kombination von allem.

LEXIKON

Wörter, die voll im Trend liegen, und was sie bedeuten

DAS IST DURCHAUS
ich stimme total zu

END DIE MEILE
weit entfernt

ENTERGIGANT
mehr als gigant, gigantischer

GESCHMEIDIG DIE LORCHE
prima, stark, optimal

KRASS IN DER BIRNE SEIN
verrückte Ideen haben

PSEUDO
jemand, der so tut, als ob er etwas ist, was er in Wirklichkeit nicht ist

A. 1. Schau die Fotos an, und lies die verschiedenen Texte! Wie viele verschiedenen Trends kannst du feststellen? Beschreibe sie! Worauf beziehen sich die Trends hauptsächlich? Auf Mode? Musik? Sprache? Oder Weltanschauung?
2. Welche Trends sind dir schon bekannt? Gibt es ähnliche Trends in den USA? Was für Unterschiede gibt es?

B. Lies den Text links! Worum geht es? Was bedeuten die Ausdrücke? Wie sagt man sie auf englisch? Wie kann man sie anders auf deutsch ausdrücken?

B. **Umgangssprache der Jugend**; (see chart); I agree / very far away / humongous / fantastic / to be crazy / a wannabe; **einverstanden / ganz weit weg / ganz groß / toll; Spitze / komisch sein / ein Möchtegern.**

Weiter geht's!

Immer mit der Mode. Oder?

Unsere vier Freunde erzählen, was sie von der Mode halten.

PHILIPP

Ich geb' zu, daß ich mich von der Mode schon ein wenig beeinflussen lass'. Meine Mutter sagt schon manchmal: „Für diese Klamotten zahl' ich dir nichts dazu. Die sind mir viel zu ausgefallen. Was hast du denn bloß für einen Geschmack? Du hättest dir das nicht kaufen sollen!" Aber mir gefällt's eben.

TANJA

Ich mach' auch mit der Mode mit. Das geb' ich ohne weiteres zu. Mit der Mode kann man ausdrücken, wie man sich fühlt. Wie ich ausseh', ... das sagt auch etwas über mich aus, wie ich bin und so. Und das ist wichtig für mich. Ich zieh' mich also schon modisch an. Es macht Spaß, ja und ... äh ... ich fühle mich wohl. Ich bedaure nur, daß ich oft nicht genug Geld habe, um mir wirklich schicke Sachen kaufen zu können. Manche Sachen näh' ich mir auch selbst, um Geld zu sparen.

SONJA

Ich kenn' Leute, die wollen eben bei anderen immer gut ankommen. Und sie glauben, sie können das mit der Mode machen. Die tun mir leid, diese Leute, die ... die machen alles nur mit, weil es gerade „in" ist. Ich würde mich nie so ausgeflippt anziehen, wie es manche tun. Ich seh' halt, was mir gefällt, und das kauf' ich mir halt. Aber ich muß auch zugeben, ich pass' mich schon irgendwie meinen Freunden an. Man möchte sich nicht von andern beeinflussen lassen, aber man tut es halt doch. Man möchte auch andere nicht nach der Kleidung beurteilen. Aber leider tut man das auch oft, ohne es zu wollen. Wenn ich jemand seh', der sich ganz verrückt anzieht, na, da denk' ich, wie kann man nur so herumlaufen? Haben die Leute denn überhaupt keinen Geschmack? Die müssen ganz schön blöd sein!

MICHAEL

Ich finde, man sollte schon ein bißchen mit der Mode gehen, aber nicht unbedingt den letzten Schrei tragen. Vieles sieht echt dumm aus, wenn man da mal in einer Modezeitschrift herumblättert. Ich finde, man sollte seinen eigenen Stil entwickeln. Ich zieh' eigentlich nur das an, was mir gefällt. Zu Hause lauf' ich meist im Trainingsanzug herum. Ich könnte es den ganzen Tag in Jeans nicht aushalten.

16 Hast du alles verstanden?

a. Was für ein Text ist das? Ein Bericht? Ein Interview? Eine Erzählung? ein Interview

b. Lies den Text noch einmal, und stell für jeden Schüler fest, was der Hauptpunkt der Aussage ist! Welche Gründe geben die Schüler an, um den Hauptpunkt zu unterstützen?
P: läßt sich von der Mode beeinflussen. / T: drückt mit Mode Gefühle aus. / S: interessiert sich nicht für verrückte Mode. / M: findet, daß man seinen eigenen Stil entwickeln sollte.   P: Mode gefällt ihm. / T: Es ist ihr wichtig, daß Mode etwas über sie aussagt; Mode macht ihr Spaß, sie fühlt sich wohl. / S: Es ist nicht ihr Geschmack. / M: findet, daß vieles, was modisch ist, dumm aussieht.

17 Was halten die vier von Mode?

Lies die Aussagen der vier Schüler über Mode! Dann schreib auf, zu welchem Schüler jede Beschreibung paßt!

1. Hat eine Mutter, die die Klamotten von ihrem Kind kritisiert. Philipp
2. Will mit der Mode ausdrücken, wie er oder sie sich fühlt. Tanja
3. Zieht sich nie ausgeflippt an. Sonja
4. Möchte andere Leute nicht nach ihrer Kleidung beurteilen. Sonja
5. Glaubt, daß viele Leute keinen guten Geschmack haben. Sonja
6. Will schick sein, aber muß nicht den letzten Schrei tragen. Michael
7. Kauft sich manchmal sehr ausgefallene Sachen. Philipp
8. Bedauert, daß er oder sie nicht genug Geld für wirklich schicke Sachen hat. Tanja
9. Paßt sich mit der Kleidung den Freunden an. Sonja
10. Möchte sich nicht von anderen beeinflussen lassen, aber tut es doch. Sonja
11. Will einen eigenen Stil entwickeln. Michael
12. Kauft sich, was ihm oder ihr gefällt. Philipp; Sonja; Michael
13. Findet, daß vieles in Modezeitschriften dumm aussieht. Michael
14. Näht sich manche Sachen selbst. Tanja
15. Läuft zu Hause immer im Trainingsanzug herum. Michael

18 Jeder wird jetzt Designer

Wähl dir eine Schülerin oder einen Schüler in diesen Interviews aus, und zeichne ein tolles Outfit, das diese Person wahrscheinlich tragen würde! Zeig deine Zeichnung deinen Klassenkameraden! Können sie erraten (*guess*), zu wem das Outfit paßt?

19 Und du? Was sagst du dazu?

Überleg dir folgende Fragen, und stell sie einem Partner! Gib deinem Partner so viel Auskunft, wie du kannst! Tauscht dann die Rollen aus!

1. Machst du mit der Mode mit? Gib ein Beispiel dazu!
2. Was ist für dich wichtig, wenn du an Kleidung denkst?
3. Du möchtest bei deinen Freunden gut ankommen. Was tust du?
4. Würdest du dich ausgeflippt anziehen? Wann? Was würdest du tragen?
5. Wie läufst du gewöhnlich herum?
   In der Schule? Zu Hause?

Expressing sympathy and resignation; giving advice; giving a reason; admitting something and expressing regret

Eine Freundin gibt Rat

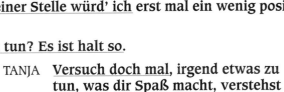

TANJA   Ja, Elke. Du bist's? Aber was ist denn los mit dir? Wie siehst du denn bloß aus?

ELKE   Warum, wie seh' ich denn aus?

TANJA   Ist alles in Ordnung mit dir? Wie geht's denn? Erzähl mal!

ELKE   Na ja, zur Zeit geht mal alles wieder schief bei mir.

TANJA   Das ist schlimm! Hast du Probleme zu Hause? In der Schule?

ELKE   Überall! In der Schule, zu Hause, mit meinem Freund ...

TANJA   Wie schrecklich! Kann ich dir irgendwie helfen?

ELKE   Nö. Ich hab' eben jetzt eine Pechsträhne, weißt du, und da kann man nichts machen.

TANJA   Das würd' ich nicht sagen. An deiner Stelle würd' ich erst mal ein wenig positiver denken.

ELKE   Ach, komm! Was kann ich schon tun? Es ist halt so.

TANJA   Versuch doch mal, irgend etwas zu tun, was dir Spaß macht, verstehst du? Du solltest ...

ELKE   Du hast gut reden! Du hast ...

TANJA   Laß mich mal ausreden! Du solltest mal etwas tun, was deine Laune hebt!

ELKE   Was denn?

TANJA   Warum gehst du nicht mal joggen? Oder spiel doch Volleyball draußen im Park!

ELKE   Ach, Quatsch! Und wer spielt denn schon mit?

TANJA   Du, kein Problem! Ich ruf' schnell mal einige Klassenkameraden an, und dann spielen wir! So was hebt meine Laune. Das hilft. Jedenfalls mir.

auf deutsch erklärt

__ausgefallen__ angezogen interessante Klamotten tragen, die nicht jeder hat

__bei__ anderen __gut ankommen__ wenn dich andere Leute mögen

Ich __pass' mich__ meinen Freunden an. Ich möchte so sein, wie meine Freunde, und machen, was sie machen.

Er trägt __den letzten Schrei__. Er trägt, was gerade Mode ist.

in der Zeitung __herumblättern__ die Zeitung nicht lesen, sondern nur Seite für Seite ansehen

auf englisch erklärt

Ich __lasse mich von__ der Mode __beeinflussen__. *I let myself be influenced by fashion.*

Aber ich __mache__ nicht __mit__ der Mode __mit__. *But I don't go along with fashion.*

Man __drückt__ sich durch Kleidung __aus__. *You can express yourself with clothes.*

Ich __gebe__ schon __zu__, daß ich einige Menschen __nach__ ihrer Kleidung __beurteile__. *I admit that I judge some people by their clothes.*

Sagt das etwas __über__ solche Leute __aus__? *Does that say something about such people?*

Sie näht gern.

Er spart Geld.

Sie zieht sich verrückt an.

SO SAGT MAN DAS!

Expressing sympathy and resignation

You have already learned some ways of expressing sympathy:

> **Es tut mir leid! Wirklich!**

Other ways of expressing sympathy are:

> **Das ist ja schlimm!**
> **Das muß schlimm sein!**
> **Wie schrecklich!**
> **So ein Pech!**

And resignation:

> **Da kann man nichts machen.**

To express resignation you could say:

> **Was kann ich schon tun?**
> **Es ist halt so.**
> **Ich hab' eben eine Pechsträhne.**

---

20 Wo sagen sie das? For answers, see underlined words in text on page 64.

Lest euch jetzt das Gespräch zwischen Tanja und Elke noch einmal durch! Sucht zusammen die Stellen heraus, die Mitleid (*sympathy*), Resignation und Rat ausdrücken!

21 Dein Freund hat Probleme

Dein Partner erzählt dir etwas über seine Probleme. Du drückst dein Mitleid aus, aber dein Freund ist resigniert. Vielleicht kannst du ihm auch einen Rat geben.

FREUND **Ich habe eine Fünf in Geschichte bekommen.**

DU **Das ist ja schlimm!**

FREUND **Was kann ich schon tun? Es ist halt so.** Answers will vary. E.g.: **Vielleicht solltest du mehr lernen.**

1. Ich bin immer müde.
2. Ich hab' mein Taschengeld verloren.
3. Meine Freundin mag mich nicht mehr.
4. In Mathe bin ich eine absolute Niete (*loser*).
5. Meine Eltern schimpfen (*scold*) die ganze Zeit mit mir.

SO SAGT MAN DAS!

Giving advice

Here are several ways of making suggestions and giving advice:

Warum machst du dich nicht mal hübsch?
Versuch doch mal, dich fesch anzuziehen!
Du solltest mal etwas Tolles tragen.
An deiner Stelle würde ich versuchen, positiver zu denken.
Laß dir doch die Haare schneiden!

22 Hör gut zu! For answers, see listening script on TE Interleaf.

Welche Ratschläge passen für wen?

a.   b.   c.   d.

23 Komm, ich geb' dir mal einen guten Rat!

Dein Partner ist heute etwas down. Rate ihm, was er tun soll! Er reagiert positiv oder negativ.

DU   **Warum liest du nicht mal ein Buch?**
PARTNER   **Tja, ich habe keine Lust dazu.**   *oder*
            Gute Idee!

Einige Ratschläge

sich mal hübsch machen
ein gutes Buch lesen
vernünftig essen
Sport machen
positiver denken
Ordnung schaffen
sich modisch anziehen
eine Reise machen

sich mit einem Hobby ablenken
sich die Haare schneiden lassen
mehr auf das Aussehen achten
sich etwas Modisches kaufen
einen Tag zu Hause bleiben

24 Hast du einen guten Rat?

Denk an fünf verschiedene Leute, die du gut kennst! Hast du einen guten Rat für sie?
Schreib auf einen Zettel, was du ihnen rätst!

BEISPIEL   **Meine Schwester ißt sehr viele Süßigkeiten. Ich rate ihr:**
               An deiner Stelle würd' ich nicht so viele Süßigkeiten essen!   *oder*
               Warum versuchst du nicht, mehr Obst zu essen!   *oder*
               Du solltest wirklich nicht so viele Süßigkeiten essen!

Grammatik Infinitive clauses

Compare the following sentences:

Ich versuche, dir zu helfen.   *I am trying to help you.*
Ich bin bereit, nach Hause zu gehen.   *I am ready to go home.*
Ich habe vor mitzumachen.   *I plan to participate.*

Find the verbs in the sentences above. Compare verb positions in English and German. What differences do you see? What do you notice about the verb **mitmachen** in the sentences above?

1. In infinitive clauses, the German infinitive is always preceded by **zu** and is placed at the end of the sentence. With separable-prefix verbs, **zu** is inserted between the prefix and the verb. **Zu** is never added in sentences when the conjugated verb is a modal, **werden** or **würde**!

2. A comma precedes the infinitive clause whenever anything is added to it, for example:

Ich versuche zu lernen.
Ich versuche, heute abend Deutsch zu lernen.

3. Certain prepositions can also introduce infinitive clauses. For example, **um zu** (*in order to*) and **ohne zu** (*without ...ing*).

Ich näh' mir Kleider selbst, um Geld zu sparen.
Man tut das oft, ohne es zu wollen.

25 Gute Vorsätze

Was haben deine Klassenkameraden vor? Jeder sagt, was für Vorsätze er oder sie hat.

BEISPIEL   DU   **Ich habe vor, weniger zu essen. Und du?**
PARTNER   **Ich habe vor, mehr Obst und Gemüse zu essen.**

gesund leben	nicht alles
etwas abnehmen	mitmachen
fit bleiben	sich nicht beein-
sich modisch	flussen lassen
anziehen	andere nicht nach
sich mit Sport	der Kleidung
ablenken	beurteilen
etwas zunehmen	seinen eigenen Stil
positiver denken	entwickeln

SO SAGT MAN DAS!

Giving a reason

There are different ways of expressing purpose and giving a reason. If someone asks you, for example: **Wozu machst du so viel Sport?**

You could answer:

Ich mache so viel Sport, { **weil ich mich nach dem Sport besser fühle.**
damit ich mich besser fühle.
um mich besser zu fühlen.

26 Warum machst du das?

Deine Partnerin sagt dir, warum sie verschiedene Sachen macht. Sag ihr, ob du das auch machst und wozu! Wenn du es nicht machst, sag warum!

PARTNER **Ich mach' viel Sport, damit ich fit bleibe.**

DU **Bei mir ist das auch so. Ich mach' auch viel Sport, um fit zu bleiben.**

1. Ich kauf' mir teure Klamotten, damit ich ...
2. Ich zieh' mich nett an, damit ich ...
3. Ich kauf' mir Modezeitschriften, damit ich ...
4. Ich geh' in Bioläden, damit ich ...
5. Ich ess' keine Süßigkeiten, damit ich ...
6. Ich mach' eine Diät, damit ich ...

SO SAGT MAN DAS!

Admitting something and expressing regret

To admit something, you might say:

> Ich geb's zu.
> Ich geb's zu, daß ich ...
> Ich muß zugeben, daß ...

To express regret, you have already learned:

> Leider!
> Ich bedaure, daß ...
> Ich bedaure es wirklich, daß ...

27 Mensch, gib's doch zu!

Du unterhältst dich mit einer Partnerin. Du fragst, ob sie folgende Sachen macht. Deine Partnerin gibt es zu und fragt dich auch. Was sagst du dazu? Bedauerst du das?

DU **Sag mal, machst du mit der Mode mit?**

PARTNERIN **Na ja, ich geb's zu, daß ich mit der Mode mitmache. Und du?**

DU **Ich eigentlich auch. Manchmal bedaure ich es, daß ...** *oder* **Nein. Das ...**

sich ab und zu ausgeflippt anziehen	zu viel Geld für Kleidung ausgeben
sich manchmal die Haare färben	zu kritisch sein
sich oft neue Klamotten kaufen	Leute nach der Kleidung beurteilen
sich zu sehr seinen Freunden anpassen	zu konservativ sein
	sich zu sehr beeinflussen lassen

28 Das bedaure ich aber ...

Denk an die Dinge in deinem Leben, die du bedauerst und schreib sie auf! Wie lang ist deine Liste? Vergleiche deine Liste mit der Liste eines Mitschülers!

BEISPIEL **Ich bedaure, daß ich mich nicht fit halte.**

29 Für mein Notizbuch

Schreib einen kurzen Aufsatz zu dem Thema Mode! Erwähne, was du von der Mode hältst, wie du dich anziehst, wieviel Geld du für modische Sachen ausgibst, ob du dich von der Mode beeinflussen läßt, ob du dich deinen Freunden anpaßt, usw.!

Have you ever read a text in which the characters were so vividly described that they seemed to be standing right in front of you? That is because the writer had carefully selected words that evoke strong visual images. In this activity, you will describe a person, either someone you know or a famous or fictional character, so that your classmates can visualize that person in their minds.

Personen beschreiben

Such dir eine Person aus, die du gut beschreiben kannst! Denk an das Aussehen dieser Person, zum Beispiel das Gesicht und die Kleidung! Wähl dann die wichtigsten Eigenschaften aus, und beschreib diese Person!

A. Vorbereiten

1. Mach einen Ideenbaum für deine Beschreibung! Auf den „Stamm" schreibst du ein Adjektiv oder eine Eigenschaft, die deiner Person am nächsten kommt! Das soll der Hauptpunkt deiner Beschreibung sein. Dann wähle Adjektive, Eigenschaften und Gewohnheiten, die diesen Hauptpunkt unterstützen, und schreib sie auf die „Zweige"!

2. Such jetzt ein Organisationsprinzip für deine Ideen! Sind sie sinnvoll, so wie du sie auf den „Baum" geschrieben hast, oder mußt du ein paar Ideen umstellen, um deine Beschreibung zu organisieren?

SCHREIBTIP

Organizing your ideas
No matter what you are writing, it is important to organize your thoughts around a main idea and choose details that support this main focus. There are many ways to organize your supporting details. For example, you can organize your ideas chronologically, spatially, or in order of importance. Always choose an organization pattern which fits your writing task.

B. Ausführen

Verbinde jetzt die Ideen auf deinem Ideenbaum zu einer fließenden Beschreibung! Paß gut auf, daß der Hauptpunkt im Mittelpunkt steht! Vergiß auch nicht: Man soll diese Person fast sehen können, wenn man deine Beschreibung liest!

C. Überarbeiten

1. Stell jetzt fest, ob deine Beschreibung die richtige Wirkung hat! Lies deine Beschreibung einem Partner vor! Dein Partner soll gleichzeitig versuchen, die Person zu zeichnen. Frag den Partner, was ihm an der Person auffällt! Was hält er von dieser Person?

2. Denk jetzt an die folgenden Fragen: Konnte dein Partner der Beschreibung folgen? Konnte er die Person gut zeichnen? Hat er den Hauptpunkt und die wichtigen Eigenschaften auch verstanden? Mach die nötigen Veränderungen, um deine Beschreibung zu verbessern!

3. Wenn du mit deiner Beschreibung und ihrer Wirkung zufrieden bist, lies den Text noch einmal durch! Hast du alles korrekt buchstabiert? Hast du auch Kommas und Punkte richtig gesetzt? Mach die nötigen Korrekturen!

4. Schreib jetzt deinen korrigierten Text auf ein reines Blatt Papier!

Das Thema, das uns alle angeht ...

Das macht viele Erwachsene richtig sprachlos

Unsere heutige Jugend und ihre Sprüche

Es begann harmlos, mit einem gedehnten „Ey, affengeil!" Von da an fing Tanja (16) jeden Satz mit „Ey ..." an. „Ey, Mom", „Ey, Dad" — und ihre Schulfreunde hießen alle „Ey, Alter!"

Sie aß keine Pizza mehr, sondern „pfiff sich 'ne Mafia-Torte rein". Wenn Tanja im Bad vor dem Spiegel stand, schminkte sie sich nicht, sondern „legte Emaille" auf.

„Sag mal, was sind denn das für Sprüche?" fragte ihre Mutter. „Reden die in deiner Klasse jetzt alle so?"

In der Tat — sie tun's.

„Die heutige Jugend will sich auf diese Art bewußt von der Sprache der Erwachsenen abheben", stellten Psychologen fest.

„Da kriegt Mama 'n Föhn!"

„Jede Clique hat ihre eigenen Sprüche, auf die sie stolz ist." Und die Begriffe wechseln so schnell, daß die „Kalkleisten" (Leute über 25) kaum mitkommen.

„Wenn ich richtig loslege", sagt Uli (14) lachend zur Reporterin, „dann brennt bei

LESETRICK

Determining the main idea of an article When reading magazine or newspaper articles, you can usually determine the main idea by reading the title, captions, and the first paragraph. In the case of a feature article, which is in essay form, you will also need to look carefully at the last paragraph.

For answers, see TE Interleaf.

Getting Started

1. Read the title, subtitle, and caption. In your opinion, what is this passage about? On what group of people does it focus?
2. Now read the first and last paragraphs. Based on this information, what would you say is the main idea? Support your answer with evidence from the passage.
3. Scan the article to see what types of people the writer quotes. How has the writer organized the article? Is it a story, a report, or something else?

A Closer Look

4. Now read the article once carefully. Find some examples of teenage slang. What do

Paps ein Chip durch, und Mama kriegt 'nen Föhn."

In der neuen Jugendsprache wird alles durcheinandergemischt: Technik, Englisch, Comic-Sprechblasen ...

„Sobald mein 15jähriger im Haushalt helfen muß", klagt eine Mutter (36), „ist alles ‚Ächz-Stöhn' oder ‚Kotz-Würg' — das klingt wirklich bescheuert".

Ganz unberechtigt sind die Sorgen vieler Eltern nicht.

Der Marburger Gymnasial-Pädagoge Joachim Kutschke (49) hält die heutige Generation für maulfaul. „Ihr fehlt das Bedürfnis, sinnvoll miteinander zu reden. Wozu lange Diskussionen, Begründungen, Erklärungen. Das stört doch nur."

Die Jugendlichen, mit denen er darüber sprach, sehen das anders. Olaf (17): „Was wollt ihr überhaupt? Die meisten Eltern sprechen zu Hause auch nur das Allernötigste." Und Lilo (16): „Die Alten sitzen doch nur stumm wie die Fische vor dem Fernseher."

Und umgekehrt. „Mein 15jähriger kommt heim, geht wortlos in sein Zimmer und dröhnt sich den ganzen Tag mit Musik voll."

Allerdings sehen viele Psychologen in den neuesten „Sprach-Schöpfungen" der Jugend auch Gutes. „Da sind Sachen dabei, die zeigen, daß sie sich auf ihre Art ebenfalls Gedanken machen."

Über das Waldsterben zum Beispiel. „Sauer macht lustig — der Wald lacht sich krank", geistert zur Zeit durch die Schulen. Sie wollen, wie frühere Generationen auch, die Welt der „Grufties" (Erwachsenen) entlarven, ablehnen und dafür etwas Eigenes, Besseres erfinden.

„Das war schon immer das Bedürfnis der Jugend", geben auch die Pädagogen zu.

... alles schon mal dagewesen

„Und dieses Gefühl finden die Kids dann eben oberaffen-megaturbo-geil. Aber sie sind dabei nicht anders als wir, als wir jung waren."

„Fetenmäßig" muß alles stimmen, „actionmäßig" der Tag in Ordnung sein, also immer was los sein.

Aber das kostet „Lappen" (Geld), und für die braucht man wieder die „Kalkleisten" (Eltern), und die haben da manchmal leider einen „Hörsturz", wenn's zuviel wird ...

Echt „heavy" (schwer), das Leben, hohl, gichtig, schlaff, abgefahren. Aber alles schon mal dagewesen.

Der einzige Rat, den Psychologen Eltern geben können, ist: Nicht nachaffen, nicht mitspielen! Wobei natürlich eigene Sprüche erlaubt sind wie „Ich geb' dir 20 Pfennig, erzähl's der nächsten Parkuhr!"

Der Sprachforscher Johannes Schwittalla hält die Jugend-Sprüche lediglich für eine „Durchgangsstation": „Wenn die Clique sich auflöst, der Beruf beginnt, sprechen die alle wieder ganz normal." Logisch, ey?

—Emily Reuter

they mean, according to the writer's "translations?" Do you think such translations are needed? Why or why not?

5. Write one to three sentences summarizing adults' complaints about teenage slang.

6. How do the teenagers in the article respond to those complaints?

7. Who comes to the defense of teenagers' language? What do these people have to say about the slang used by teens?

8. What advice do the psychologists give parents?

9. Why does the writer quote the language expert in the final paragraph?

10. Was meinst du jetzt, was der Hauptgedanke von diesem Artikel ist? Schau auf deine Antwort von Frage 2, und ändere deine erste Aussage, wenn nötig! Schreib deine Formulierung auf!

11. Welche Sätze oder Absätze unterstützen den Hauptgedanken des Textes? Schreib drei unterstützende Aussagen unter deine Formulierung des Hauptgedankens!

12. Schreib jetzt eine Zusammenfassung des Textes! Verwende dabei die Informationen von Fragen 10 und 11! Vergiß nicht, auch einen Schlußsatz zu schreiben!

1 **a.** Du möchtest dich mit richtiger Ernährung fit halten. Wieviel weißt du über den Nährwert von Lebensmitteln? Lies die Umfrage! Entscheide dann, ob die Aussagen richtig oder falsch sind!

Umfrage: Nährwert von Lebensmitteln

1. Das beste Brot ist dunkles Brot.

richtig ☐
falsch ☐

2. Braune Eier sind gesünder als weiße Eier.

richtig ☐
falsch ☐

3. Kartoffeln machen dick.

richtig ☐
falsch ☐

4. Fisch hat weniger Nährwert als Fleisch.

richtig ☐
falsch ☐

5. Öl ist Öl. Es spielt keine Rolle, welches man im Haushalt gebraucht.

richtig ☐
falsch ☐

6. Orangen und Zitronen sind die Vitamin-C-reichsten Früchte.

richtig ☐
falsch ☐

7. Brot macht dick.

richtig ☐
falsch ☐

8. Alle Mineralwässer sind gleich.

richtig ☐
falsch ☐

9. Wenn es heiß ist, soll man nichts oder weniger trinken.

richtig ☐
falsch ☐

10. Brauner Zucker enthält mehr Vitamine und Mineralien als weißer Zucker.

richtig ☐
falsch ☐

1. b. For answers, see listening script on TE Interleaf.

b. Du hörst im Radio einen Bericht über gesunde Ernährung. Schau dir nochmal die Umfrage von Übung 1 an und die Antworten, die du gewählt hast! Wie viele Antworten hast du richtig?

c. Schreib jetzt die Aussagen aus der Umfrage von Übung 1 in richtig-lautende Aussagen um!

1. c. Answers will vary. Encourage students to use the information presented in the listening activity (1. b.).

2 Diskutiert die folgenden Äußerungen!
— Was haltet ihr von diesen Bemerkungen?
— Wie würdet ihr darauf reagieren?

> Schuluniformen sind eine gute Lösung für Kleiderprobleme in der Schule.
> Ute

> Eins ist sicher: gut gekleidete Leute finden eher Freunde als andere.
> Sven

> Wenn bei uns in der Klasse jemand etwas Neues anhat, wollen die andern gleich das Etikett mit der Marke sehen. Wer sich keine teuren Klamotten leisten kann, schneidet als erstes das Etikett heraus. Aber das merken die andern auch sofort. Was soll man da tun?
> Tanja

> Ich trag' gern verrückte Klamotten. Ich trag' auch einen Ohrring, und ab und zu färb' ich mir auch die Haare. Ich will mit meinem Aussehen provozieren. Und wie die Leute reagieren! Besonders ältere Leute sprechen mit mir über mein Aussehen. Und es ist ein tolles Gefühl, wenn die Leute merken, daß ich gar nicht so negativ bin, wie sie immer glauben.
> Uwe

> Wer nicht perfekt gekleidet ist, bekommt nie einen guten Job. Ich hab' neulich eine Einladung zu einer Fete bekommen. Am Ende stand: Festliche Kleidung erwünscht.
> Michael

3 Schreib eine Antwort zu einer dieser fünf Äußerungen! Lies danach deinen Klassenkameraden vor, was du geschrieben hast!

4

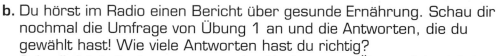

R O L L E N S P I E L

Spiel einen Dialog mit einem Partner vor der Klasse! Folgende Anleitungen helfen dir dabei.

1. Du hast dir eine Jacke und eine Hose gekauft, die deinem Vater überhaupt nicht gefallen. Er kritisiert dich. Schreib auf, was er alles sagen kann! Gebrauche diese Stichwörter!

wie aussehen — Hose, eng — Jacke, ausgefallen — Geschmack? — nicht kaufen sollen — nichts dazu zahlen

2. Du verteidigst (*defend*) dich. Schreib auf, was du alles sagen kannst! Gebrauche diese Stichwörter!

Freunde auch solche Klamotten haben — mit der Mode mitmachen — „in" sein — Aussehen wichtig — Sachen waren billig — nicht genug Geld für schicke Sachen

KANN ICH'S WIRKLICH?

Can you ask for and express opinions? (p. 57)

1 How would you ask for an opinion and give your own opinion of

a. **Biokost?** a. E.g.: **Was hältst du von Biokost?; Ich halte viel davon.**

b. **eine Ernährung ohne Fleisch?** b. E.g.: **Was hältst du von einer Ernährung ohne Fleisch?; Ich halte nichts davon.** c. E.g.: **Was würdest du zu Bodybuilding sagen?; Ich würde sagen, daß es Spaß macht.**

c. **Bodybuilding?**

Can you express sympathy and resignation? (p. 65)

2 How would you express sympathy or resignation in response to these statements?

a. **Ich hab' jetzt schon die zweite Fünf in Geschichte.** a. E.g.: **Das ist ja schlimm!**

b. **Du hast wohl Probleme mit deiner Frisur!** b. E.g.: **Ja, was kann ich schon tun?**

c. **Stell dir vor, ich hab' meine Kamera verloren!** c. E.g.: **So ein Pech!**

d. **Meine beste Freundin hat mich nicht zu ihrer Fete eingeladen.**

e. **Der Peter, der paßt sich seinen Freunden überhaupt nicht an.**

d. E.g.: **Das tut mir leid! Wirklich!** e. E.g.: **Da kann man nichts machen. Er ist halt so.**

Can you give advice? (p. 66)

3 What advice would you give to a friend who told you the following?

a. **Meine Mutter sagt, ich zieh' mich zu schlampig an.** a. E.g.: **Warum ziehst du nicht mal was Konservatives an?** b. E.g.: **Laß dir doch die Haare schneiden!** c. E.g.: **An deiner Stelle würde ich es mal aufräumen.**

b. **Sie sagt, meine Haare sind viel zu lang.**

c. **Sie sagt, mein Zimmer ist nie aufgeräumt.**

d. **Sie sagt, daß ich zu viel fernsehe.** d. E.g.: **Versuch doch mal, etwas weniger Fernsehen zu schauen!**

Can you give a reason? (p. 67)

4 How would you complete these statements so that they tell why you do these things?

a. **Ich ess' eigentlich keine Süßigkeiten, ...** a. E.g.: **weil es nicht gut für meine Zähne ist.** b. E.g.: **damit ich nicht zunehme.** c. E.g.: **um fit zu bleiben.**

b. **Mit dem Essen pass' ich schon auf, ...**

c. **Ich treibe natürlich viel Sport, ...** d. E.g.: **weil es mir Spaß macht.**

d. **Ich beschäftige mich aber auch mit meinen Hobbys, ...**

Can you admit something and express regret? (p. 68)

5 How would you admit and express regret that you

a. paid too much for ...? a. E.g.: **Ich geb's zu, daß ich zu viel Geld für (diese Jacke) ausgegeben habe. Leider habe ich zu viel Geld für (diese Jacke) ausgegeben.** b. E.g.: **Ich muß zugeben, daß ich meine Freunde nach ihrer Kleidung beurteile. Ich bedaure es wirklich, daß ich meine Freunde nach ihrer Kleidung beurteile.** c. E.g.: **Ich geb's zu, daß ich mich schlampig anziehe. Ich bedaure, daß ich mich schlampig anziehe.**

b. judge your friends by their clothes?

c. dress in a ... way (**schlampig**)?

ERSTE STUFE

GIVING OPINIONS

Du hältst viel von unserer Lehrerin, oder? *You think highly of our teacher, don't you?*

OTHER USEFUL WORDS AND PHRASES

s. Gedanken machen über (acc) *to think about*
s. entspannen *to relax*
s. ablenken (sep) *to divert oneself*

s. beschäftigen mit *to keep busy with*
s. schminken *to put on makeup*
achten auf (acc) *to pay attention to*
zunehmen (sep) *to gain weight*
abnehmen (sep) *to lose weight*
übertreiben *to exaggerate*
schiefgehen (sep) *to go wrong*
treffen *to meet*
zusammenpassen (sep) *to go together, match*
aufpassen (sep) *to pay attention*
was (das) angeht *as far as (that) goes*
heben *to lift*

hübsch *pretty, handsome*
mickrig *lousy*
schlampig *sloppy*
vollwertig *nutritious*
regelmäßig *regularly*
hauptsächlich *mainly*
wirkungsvoll *effective*

die Kleidung *clothing*
die Laune *mood*
die Sache, -n *thing*
die Biokost *organic food*
das Krafttraining *weight lifting*

ZWEITE STUFE

EXPRESSING SYMPATHY AND RESIGNATION

Das muß ja schlimm sein! *That must be really bad!*
Wie schrecklich! *How terrible!*
Ich hab' eben eine Pechsträhne. *I'm just having a streak of bad luck.*
Da kann man nichts machen. *There's nothing you can do.*
Was kann ich schon tun? *Well, what can I do?*
Es ist halt so. *That's the way it is.*

GIVING ADVICE

Komm, ich geb' dir mal einen guten Rat! *Okay, let me give you some good advice.*
Versuch doch mal, etwas zu machen! *Why don't you try to do something?*
Du solltest mal ins Kino gehen. *You should go to the movies.*

An deiner Stelle würde ich mehr lernen. *If I were you, I'd study more.*
Laß dir doch die Haare schneiden! *Why don't you get your hair cut?*

OTHER USEFUL WORDS AND PHRASES

Das sagt etwas über dich aus. *That says something about you.*
mitmachen mit (sep) *to go along with*
beurteilen nach *to judge according to*
ankommen bei (sep) *to be accepted by*
s. anpassen (sep, dat) *to conform to*
beeinflussen *to influence*
ausdrücken (sep) *to express*
zugeben (sep) *to admit*
entwickeln *to develop*
versuchen *to attempt, try*

vorhaben (sep) *to plan*
aushalten (sep) *to endure, stand something*
nähen *to sew*
sparen *to save money*
herumblättern (sep) *to leaf through (a newspaper)*

der Geschmack *taste*
das Mitleid *pity, sympathy*
der letzte Schrei *the latest fashion*
Kleider (pl) *clothes*

ausgefallen *unusual*
verrückt *crazy*

ohne *without*
ohne weiteres *easily, readily*
ohne ... zu machen *without doing ...*
um ... zu machen *in order to do ...*
damit (conj) *so that, in order to*

◼ Location Opener
Würzburg, pages 76-79
Video Program, Videocassette 1

*U*sing the Photograph,
pp. 76-77

Background Information

- The history of Würzburg can be traced back as far as the Celtic time (700 BC). In 741 AD Bonifatius, who soon after became archbishop of Mainz, founded the **Bistum** *(bishopric)* of Würzburg. The city was then ruled for centuries by **Fürst-bischöfe** *(prince-bishops)*, and the diets of the Holy Roman Empire sometimes met in Würzburg. Secularized in 1802, Würzburg became part of Bavaria in 1815.

- Würzburg is situated at the beginning of the **Ro-mantische Straße,** which follows the Tauber river, a tributary of the Main. The **Romantische Straße** then continues south to Rothenburg ob der Tauber, to Augsburg, and finally ends in Hohen-schwangau, near the Neuschwanstein Castle.

- The statue in the foreground of the photograph represents St. Kilian, the apostle of the Franks and patron saint of Würzburg. July 8th is celebrated in his honor in Würzburg.

- The building in the background is the **Festung Marienberg** *(Marienberg fortress.)* It sits 266 meters (872 feet) above the city. The fortress was originally a celtic **Fliehburg** *(refuge)*. In 706, **Herzog Heltan II.** commissioned a church to be built on the **Marienberg.** Today, it remains the oldest church building (**Rundkirchenbau**) east of the Rhine. Between 1253 and 1719, it became the residence of the **Fürstbischöfe.** After several fires, Julius Echter transformed it into a renaissance-style castle. Then, after the new **Residenz** was built in town, the fortress was used for military purposes through much of the 19th century. Today it houses the **Mainfränkisches Museum.**

Thinking Critically

Comparing and Contrasting Ask students if they can think of other German towns or cities that have a castle or a fortress located above the city. (Examples: Heidelberg—**Schloß**; Eisenach—**Wartburg**)

◈ For Individual Needs

Tactile Learners For extra credit or as a project, students could build a model of the **Festung Ma-rienberg.** For a detailed map of the fortress you may want to write to **Fremdenverkehrsamt, Am Congress Centrum, 97070 Würzburg.**

Geography Connection

Ask students to trace the path of the **Romantische Straße** in an atlas. Can students think of reasons why this stretch of road might have received its name? (Examples: beautiful landscape, picturesque towns)

*U*sing the Almanac and Map,
p. 77

Würzburg's coat of arms shows a tilted red and golden flag on a silver lance before a black background. This coat of arms is related to that of the former duchy of Franconia and has been used since the sixteenth century, when it replaced an older emblem displaying an image of St. Kilian. The colors red and gold are also found in the coat of arms of the modern district **Unterfranken** whose capital is Würzburg.

Terms in the Almanac

- **Tilman Riemenschneider:** He was the principal wood-carving artist of the German gothic period. He came to Würzburg in 1483 and created altars, statues, and sculptures that are now found throughout the region. Riemenschneider became a member of the Würzburg city council in 1509 and served as mayor from 1520 to 1521. During the **Bauernkriege,** he supported the farmers who fought against the **Kirchenfürst** Konrad von Thingen (*ecclesiastical prince*). After the defeat of the farmers at Marienberg, Riemenschneider was taken to prison and tortured for eight weeks. He died in 1531, a broken man and forgotten artist. The **Marienkapelle** in Würzburg features 14 **Riemenschneiderfiguren** as well as replicas of his famous carvings of Adam and Eve.

- **Mathias Grünewald:** Grünewald, whose real name was Mathis Gothardt Nithardt, was a major figure in a generation of great German Renaissance painters that also included Albrecht Dürer and Lucas Cranach. He remained relatively unknown until the 20th century. Today only about 13 of his paintings remain. His greatest masterpiece is the **Isenheimer Altar** (*Isenheim Altarpiece*), which is now in the Colmar Museum in Alsace.

- **Julius Echter:** Prince-bishop Julius Echter of Mespelbrunn was responsible for several noteworthy contributions to the city of Würzburg. Following two damaging fires to the Marienberg fortress and residence of the bishops in 1572 and 1600, he was largely responsible for the renovations that gave Marienberg a much more elegant and renaissance-style look. In 1576, Echter founded the **Juliusspital** that was built in the baroque style. Finally, in 1582, he founded the University of Würzburg.

- **Weinbau:** October, the month of wine harvesting, is one of the best times to be in Würzburg because of the many festivals. Between the Main and Danube rivers lies the heavily agricultural region of Franconia. *Stein* and *Leisten* are among the finest wines of this area. Their grapes grow in the vineyards on the slopes surrounding the Marienberg fortress.

- **Zwiebelkuchen:** This is a pastry dish in which browned onions are spread over a bread crust. A mixture of egg, cream, and spices is poured on top of the onions and baked. It is served hot with wine or beer.

Geography Connection

Can students think of other regions in Germany that are known for their quality wines? (Examples: the Rhine and Mosel river areas, Baden)

Thinking Critically

Drawing Inferences Discuss with students the relationship of the agricultural region, resources, and the navigable Main river to Würzburg's economy. (Examples: good conditions for growing grapes because of mild climate, fertility of land, and water from river; access to water ways to export goods)

Using the Map

Have students look at the map and infer why the location of Würzburg would be good for trade. You may also want to use Map Transparency 1.

*I*nterpreting the Photo Essay, *pp. 78-79*

② The **Alte Mainbrücke mit den Apostelfiguren** is shown in the foreground of this photograph. The **Alte Mainbrücke** was built as the first stone bridge in the 12th century. It was restored from 1473 to 1543 to its present form. In the 18th century, large statues of apostles were added to the bridge's pillars, including the one of St. Kilian.

② Rising in the background of the photo is **Dom St. Kilian.** Although construction of **Dom St. Kilian** began in 1045, the main building was not dedicated until 100 years later. During the 13th, 16th, and 17th centuries, the church was expanded and renovated. In 1945, it was heavily damaged, and reconstruction was not completed until 1967. Inside are several tombs, a christening font dating back to 1279, a renaissance-style pulpit from 1609, and a wood carving of Christ and two apostles from 1502-1506.

③ The **Residenz** was built under Balthasar Neumann from 1719 to 1744 and is considered one of the most significant palaces of Europe. This building took the place of Marienberg as residence of the **Fürstbischöfe.** The baroque building encompasses five large halls, more than 300 rooms, and a church. The cellar was built to hold 1.4 million liters (369,600 gallons) of wine. One of the most impressive features is a unique staircase designed by Balthasar Neumann with vaulted ceilings that were painted by the Italian artist Giovanni Battista Tiepolo.

④ **Das Haus zum Falken** is a former inn famous for its rich stucco work. The building was heavily damaged in 1945 during World War II, but was later rebuilt to its original form. It now houses the tourist office and the public library.

LOCATION OPENER

Komm mit nach

Würzburg!

Würzburg

Bundesland: Bayern

Einwohner: 128 000

Fluß: Main

Sehenswürdigkeiten: Festung Marienberg, Dom, Residenz, Haus zum Falken

Berühmte Künstler: Tilman Riemenschneider (1460-1531), Mathias Grünewald (ca. 1480-1529)

Fürstbischöfe: Rudolf von Scherenberg (1466-1495), Julius Echter (1545-1617), Franz von Schönborn (1674-1746)

Industrie: Weinbau, Textil, Elektronik, Tourismus

Bekannte Gerichte: Bratwürste, Zwiebelkuchen, Zwetschgenkuchen

Foto ① **St. Kilian, Frankenapostel und Schutzheiliger Würzburgs, mit Festung Marienberg, einst Residenz der Fürstbischöfe**

Würzburg

*Würzburg feierte 1992 seinen 1250. Geburtstag! Die
Geschichte dieser Stadt reicht bis in die keltische Zeit zurück.
Schon im 8. Jahrhundert erhob St. Bonifatius den damals
kleinen Ort zum Bistum. Im 12. Jahrhundert erhob Kaiser
Friedrich Barbarossa die Bischöfe von Würzburg zu Herzögen
von Franken. Damit begann eine Entwicklung, die in den
folgenden Jahrhunderten Würzburg zu einem kulturellen Zentrum Europas machte.*

*Im Zentrum steht der Dom St. Kilian, im Jahre 1045 begonnen.
Der Dom ist die viertgrößte romanische Kirche Deutschlands.
Im Innern befinden sich die Grabmäler von Bischöfen, u.a. die
Grabmäler von Rudolf von Scherenberg (gest. 1495) und
Lorenz von Bibra (gest. 1519), beide von Riemenschneider
aus Salzburger Rotmarmor geschaffen.*

(2) **Die Alte Mainbrücke mit den Apostelfiguren führt in die Innenstadt zum Dom.**

③ Die fürstbischöfliche Residenz, der bedeutendste Profanbau des deutschen Barocks, wurde 1719-1744 unter der Leitung von Balthasar Neumann errichtet. Im Innern ist das großartige Treppenhaus mit dem berühmten Freskogemälde von Tiepolo und der einzigartig dekorierte Kaisersaal, in dem jährlich die Konzerte des Mozartfestes stattfinden.

④ Das Haus zum Falken, das heute das Fremdenverkehrsamt beherbergt, hat die schönste Rokokofassade (1751) der Stadt.

Kapitel 4: Verhältnis zu anderen

	FUNCTIONS	GRAMMAR	CULTURE	RE-ENTRY
Los geht's! *pp. 82-83*	Verhältnis zu Eltern und Freunden, *p. 82*			
Erste Stufe *pp. 84-87*	Agreeing, *p. 85*	•Ordinal numbers, *p. 86* •Relative clauses, *p. 87*	**Ein wenig Landeskunde:** Importance of **Cliquen** for young people, *p. 86*	•Agreeing, *p. 85* •**Wenn-, weil-,** and **daß**-clauses, *p. 85* •Cardinal numbers, *p. 86* •Pronouns (nom., acc., and dat. case), *p. 87*
Weiter geht's! *pp. 88-89*	Verhältnis zu anderen Leuten, *p. 88*			
Zweite Stufe *pp. 90-93*	•Giving advice, *p. 91* •Introducing another point of view, *p. 91* •Hypothesizing, *p. 92*	•**Hätte** and **wäre,** *p. 92* •The genitive case, *p. 93*	**Landeskunde: Die verschiedenen Bildungswege in Deutschland,** *p. 94*	•Giving advice, *p. 91* •**Wenn**-phrases, *p.92* •Subjunctive (**würde-, hätte-, wäre-**forms), *p. 92* •The preposition **von** + dative, *p. 93*
Zum Schreiben *p. 95*	**Lieber Herr Weißalles!** Writing Strategy: Determining the purpose			
Zum Lesen *pp. 96-99*	**Eine Kurzgeschichte** Reading Strategy: Determining the main idea of a story			
Review *pp. 100-103*	•**Anwendung,** *p. 100* •**Kann ich's wirklich?** *p. 102* •**Wortschatz,** *p. 103*			

Assessment Options	**Stufe Quizzes**
	 •*Chapter Resources,* Book 2
	   Erste Stufe, Quiz 4-1
	   Zweite Stufe, Quiz 4-2
	 •*Assessment Items, Audiocassette* 7 B
			Kapitel 4 Chapter Test
			 •*Chapter Resources,* Book 2
			 •*Assessment Guide,* Speaking Test
			 •*Assessment Items, Audiocassette* 7 B
			
			 Test Generator, Kapitel 4	

RESOURCES Print	RESOURCES Audiovisual
Practice and Activity Book	*Textbook Audiocassette* 2 B

Textbook Audiocassette 2 B

Practice and Activity Book
Chapter Resources, Book 2
- Communicative Activity 4-1
- Communicative Activity 4-2
- Additional Listening Activity 4-1 ....*Additional Listening Activities, Audiocassette* 9 B
- Additional Listening Activity 4-2 ....*Additional Listening Activities, Audiocassette* 9 B
- Additional Listening Activity 4-3 ....*Additional Listening Activities, Audiocassette* 9 B
- Student Response Forms
- Realia 4-1
- Situation Card 4-1
- Teaching Transparency Master 4-1 ....*Teaching Transparency* 4-1
- Quiz 4-1 ....*Assessment Items, Audiocassette* 7 B
Video Guide ....*Video Program*, Videocassette 1

Practice and Activity Book

Textbook Audiocassette 2 B

Textbook Audiocassette 2 B

Practice and Activity Book
Chapter Resources, Book 2
- Communicative Activity 4-3
- Communicative Activity 4-4
- Additional Listening Activity 4-4 ....*Additional Listening Activities, Audiocassette* 9 B
- Additional Listening Activity 4-5 ....*Additional Listening Activities, Audiocassette* 9 B
- Additional Listening Activity 4-6 ....*Additional Listening Activities, Audiocassette* 9 B
- Student Response Forms
- Realia 4-2
- Situation Card 4-2
- Teaching Transparency Master 4-2 ....*Teaching Transparency* 4-2
- Quiz 4-2 ....*Assessment Items, Audiocassette* 7 B

Chapter Resources, Book 2
- Realia 4-3
- Situation Card 4-3
Video Guide ....*Video Program*, Videocassette 1

Alternative Assessment
- Performance Assessment
Teacher's Edition
  Erste Stufe, p. 79K
  Zweite Stufe, p. 79O
- Portfolio Assessment
  Written: **Anwendung,** Activity 5, *Pupil's Edition*, p. 101; *Assessment Guide*, p. 17
  Oral: **Anwendung,** Activity 2, *Pupil's Edition*, p. 100; *Assessment Guide*, p. 17
- **Notizbuch,** *Pupil's Edition*, pp. 86, 93

Kapitel 4: Verhältnis zu anderen
Textbook Listening Activities Scripts

For Student Response Forms, see *Chapter Resources,* Book 2, pp. 22-25.

Erste Stufe
Activity 5, *p. 85*

1. **MARITA** Du, Mutti! Ich hab' einen ganz tollen Pulli bei Malibu-Moden gesehen. Meinst du, ich kann ihn haben?

   MUTTER Ach, Marita! Schon wieder was Neues? Du hast doch schon so viele Sachen.

   MARITA Stimmt ja gar nicht! Außerdem habe ich schon so lange nichts Neues mehr bekommen!

   MUTTER Also, hör mal, hast du denn ganz vergessen, daß ich dir erst vor zwei Wochen das silberfarbene T-Shirt gekauft habe, das du unbedingt für die Fete haben wolltest?

   MARITA Ach, Mutti! Das T-Shirt hat doch kurze Ärmel. Das kann ich doch jetzt, wo es wieder kälter wird, nicht mehr anziehen. Aber der Pulli, der ist ganz weich und warm, aus reiner Schurwolle! Das ist genau das Richtige, jetzt für den Herbst!

   MUTTER Also Marita, du hast wirklich genug Pullover und Jacken im Schrank! Du brauchst einfach keinen neuen Pulli!

   MARITA Mutti, bitte! Er kostet doch nur 89 Mark!

   MUTTER Wie bitte? Ich hör' wohl nicht richtig! 89 Mark? Das kann ja wohl nicht dein Ernst sein. Also, nein, das ist viel zu teuer! Die Diskussion ist beendet!

2. **HERBERT** Also, tschüs dann! Frank, sag Mutti und Vati, daß ich so gegen zehn wieder zu Hause bin!

   FRANK He, Herbert! Moment mal! Wo willst du denn hin?

   HERBERT Ich geh' mit der Tina ins Kino. Hast du was dagegen?

   FRANK Allerdings! Du bist heute mit dem Geschirrspülen dran. Na los, mach schon, bevor die Mama zurückkommt! Vorher laß' ich dich nicht gehen!

   HERBERT Was soll das heißen, ich soll das Geschirr spülen?! Heute ist Montag, und Montag abends bist du mit dem Geschirrspülen dran, Brüderchen!

   FRANK Ja, normalerweise schon! Aber erinnere dich mal daran, wer denn am Samstag abend das Geschirr gespült hat! Du jedenfalls nicht, obwohl du an der Reihe warst!

   HERBERT Ach ja, da wollte ich ja unbedingt auf die Fete vom Klaus-Jürgen!

   FRANK Genau! Und was war, bevor du losgedüst bist? Du hast mir versprochen, ...

   HERBERT ... daß ich das Geschirr am Montag spüle, wenn du es am Samstag für mich spülst! Mensch, Frank, das hab' ich total vergessen! Tut mir echt leid!

   FRANK Ist schon gut! Hauptsache, du machst es überhaupt!

   HERBERT Kannst du schnell die Tina anrufen und ihr sagen, daß ich fünf Minuten später komme?

   FRANK Klar, mach' ich!

3. **ANDREAS** Du, Vati, ich hab' einen Job gefunden, wo ich mir nebenbei etwas Geld verdienen kann. Du weißt doch, daß das Taschengeld für mein Hobby nicht ausreicht.

   VATER Na, Andreas, ich weiß nicht, ob das so eine gute Idee ist. Deine Noten in der Schule, das weißt du ja selbst, dürfen nicht schlechter werden. Du hast doch neben den Hausaufgaben gar keine Zeit für einen Job.

   ANDREAS Doch! Ich hab' mir die Zeit schon genau eingeteilt. Nachmittags von zwei bis vier lerne ich für die Schule, und von halb fünf bis halb sieben gehe ich jobben.

   VATER Was? Nur zwei Stunden pro Tag willst du für die Schule lernen?

   ANDREAS Ach Vati! Dann mach' ich eben am Wochenende mehr für die Schule!

   VATER Sag mal, Andreas, was für ein Job soll das denn sein?

   ANDREAS Ach, weißt du, auf der Nievenheimer Dorfstraße ist doch dieser neue, große Supermarkt. Dort suchen sie Schüler, die die neuen Waren auspacken und in die Regale einordnen. Ich hab' mir gedacht, daß ich das doch ganz locker nebenbei machen könnte. Also, was sagst du dazu?

   VATER Hm ... also, die Schule ...

   ANDREAS Ja ja, ich weiß schon, was du sagen willst. Die Schule ist wichtiger. Also, ich versprech' dir, mit dem Job sofort aufzuhören, wenn meine Noten schlechter werden. Laß es mich doch probieren, bitte! Einverstanden?

   VATER Na gut, mein Sohn!

4. **ELKE** Also, Papa, ich hau' jetzt ab!

   VATER Warte mal, Elke! Wohin denn so eilig?

   ELKE Zum Tanzen. Das hab' ich dir doch schon gesagt.

   VATER Hm ... hab' ich nicht gehört. Du warst doch gestern abend erst weg. Und Mutti hat gesagt, daß du ganz schön spät nach Hause gekommen bist!

   ELKE Ja und?

   VATER Also, wenn du heute wieder weg willst, mußt du aber früher nach Hause kommen, hörst du?!

   ELKE Ach, wie gemein! Immer soll ich nach Hause kommen, wenn es erst richtig anfängt, Spaß zu machen. Kann ich nicht mal so lange wegbleiben, wie ich will?

   VATER Na sowas! Das kommt überhaupt nicht in Frage! Mit wem gehst du denn heute weg?

   ELKE Warum willst du das denn wissen?

   VATER Also, hör mal! Als Vater darf ich doch wohl fragen, mit wem meine Tochter ihre Zeit verbringt! Also, mit wem gehst du zum Tanzen?

   ELKE Weiß nicht! Da kommen ein paar aus der Klasse. Die Ulrike ist auch dabei.

   VATER Soso, die Ulrike ... und welche Jungs kommen mit?

   ELKE Ach Papa, die kennst du doch sowieso nicht! Aber wenn du's halt unbedingt wissen willst: der Uli, der Thomas und der Matthias. Sonst noch was?

   VATER Also, um halb elf bist du wieder zu Hause, hörst du?

   ELKE Waaas? Halb elf? Da kann ich ja gleich hier bleiben! Um zehn Uhr wird doch erst die Disko richtig voll! Papa, das kannst du mir nicht antun! Da mach' ich mich ja lächerlich vor den anderen. Die dürfen alle viel länger bleiben. Kann ich nicht bis zwölf Uhr bleiben?

   VATER Ich hab' halb elf gesagt, und dabei bleibt's! Verstanden?

   ELKE Ach, manno!

Answers to Activity 5

1. Marita will einen neuen Pulli. Der Streit endet schlecht für Marita, sie erreicht nichts.
2. Herbert hat das Geschirr nicht gespült. Der Streit endet gut/produktiv für Frank.
3. Andreas will jobben. Der Streit endet gut/produktiv für Andreas.
4. Elke will länger ausbleiben. Der Streit endet schlecht für Elke, sie erreicht nichts.

Activity 7, p. 85

PATRICK   Hallo, Claudia! Du siehst heute aber nicht besonders glücklich aus. Was hast du denn?

CLAUDIA   Ach, bei uns zu Hause hat es wieder Krach gegeben.

PATRICK   Hast du dich wieder mit deinem Vater gestritten?

CLAUDIA   Ja, ja, immer das alte Thema. Nie darf ich weg, wenn ich will! Er behandelt mich wie ein kleines Kind. Dabei werde ich schon bald siebzehn!

PATRICK   Was war denn diesmal los?

CLAUDIA   Ach, er hat mir gesagt, daß ich heute abend nicht ins Kino gehen darf, bevor ich mein Zimmer aufgeräumt habe. Kannst du das glauben? Ich habe ihn gefragt, wieso er sich plötzlich dafür interessiert, wie es in meinem Zimmer aussieht! Er kommt ja sonst auch nie zu mir ins Zimmer!

PATRICK   Ja, bei mir ist das auch so! So lange man zu Hause rumhängt, ist alles in Ordnung. Aber kaum will man mal weg, fangen die Eltern an zu meckern!

CLAUDIA   Da geb' ich dir recht. Sofort heißt es: „Hast du schon deine Schulaufgaben gemacht? Hast du schon das Geschirr gespült?" Bla bla bla ... Ich kann es schon wirklich bald nicht mehr hören!

PATRICK   Ganz meiner Meinung!

CLAUDIA   Und stell dir mal vor, ich muß nicht nur mein Zimmer aufräumen, sondern auch noch tausend Fragen beantworten! Mein Vater wollte wissen, mit wem ich weggehe, welchen Kinofilm wir uns anschauen wollen, wann der Film zuende ist ... und so weiter und so fort! So was Blödes!

PATRICK   Und hast du ihm mal gesagt, daß dich das nervt?

CLAUDIA   Ja, also, ich war ganz schön sauer und wollte eigentlich gar nicht mit ihm diskutieren. Aber dann habe ich ihm gesagt, daß ich nicht verstehe, warum er mich so kontrolliert! Ich finde, er hat nicht genug Vertrauen zu mir, wenn er denkt, daß ich schlimme Sachen mache oder was anstelle!

PATRICK   Und was hat er dazu gesagt?

CLAUDIA   Ach, er meint, das hat nichts mit Vertrauen zu tun, sondern mit Verantwortung. Ach, du weißt doch, typisch Eltern!

PATRICK   Ja, ich weiß genau, was du meinst!

Answers to Activity 7

Claudia darf nicht weg, wenn sie will. Sie findet, daß ihr Vater sie wie ein kleines Kind behandelt. Sie muß ihr Zimmer aufräumen, sonst darf sie nicht ins Kino. Sie muß ihrem Vater viele Fragen beantworten. Claudia findet, daß ihr Vater sie kontrolliert und nicht genug Vertrauen zu ihr hat. Answers will vary.

Zweite Stufe
Activity 14, p. 90

KALLE   Na, Hannes, hast du schon ein paar Worte mit unseren neuen Klassenkameraden gewechselt?

HANNES   Ja, ich hab' gestern nach der Schule im Bus neben dem Thomas gesessen. Weißt du, der große, dunkelhaarige Typ. Er ist vor ein paar Wochen mit seinen Eltern aus Gundersheim nach hier gezogen.

KALLE   Und, was hat er so gesagt? Wofür interessiert er sich?

HANNES   Ach, er hat sich beschwert, daß die Lehrer doof sind, und er meint, daß ihn keiner in der Klasse leiden kann.

KALLE   Also, woher will der das denn wissen? Er kennt uns alle doch noch gar nicht! Und außerdem hat er gestern noch nicht mal beim Fußballtraining mitgemacht. Er ist einfach nach der Schule abgehauen, obwohl er wußte, daß wir uns noch auf dem Sportplatz treffen wollten.

HANNES   Ja, er ist schon komisch! Auf der Schulfete haben wir uns alle verrückt angezogen, nur er nicht. Ich finde, er sollte mehr mit den anderen mitmachen und sich nicht nur beschweren. Die Silke, zum Beispiel, weißt du, die mit den ...

KALLE   Ach, meinst du die kleine Rothaarige?

HANNES   Ja, genau die! Also, die Silke hat uns alle am Samstag zu einer Gartenparty bei ihr zu Hause eingeladen. Das find' ich echt toll.

KALLE   Allerdings! Dabei ist sie doch ganz neu und kennt noch niemanden.

HANNES   Mensch, Kalle! Deswegen macht sie doch die Gartenparty! Damit sie die anderen alle kennenlernen kann, kapiert?

KALLE   Ach so, ja klar! Hör mal, da gibt es doch noch eine Neue, Renate heißt die, glaub' ich. Die Anne hat mir gestern erzählt, daß diese Renate ganz schön frech ist.

HANNES   Wieso das denn?

KALLE   Ach, die Anne hat diese Neue, also die Renate gefragt, ob sie bei der Umwelt-AG mitmachen will. Und stell dir mal vor, die Renate soll ganz schnippisch gesagt haben, daß sie keine Lust dazu hat, weil sie was Besseres vorhat.

HANNES   Mensch, wenn die immer so ist, dann macht sie sich aber ganz schön schnell unbeliebt.

KALLE   Stimmt! Du, hast du schon mal mit dem Joachim geredet?

HANNES   Ja, aber nur ganz kurz. Er ist von Düsseldorf nach hier gezogen, weil seine Mutter einen Job hier an der Uni in Tübingen bekommen hat. Aber sonst weiß ich nichts über ihn.

KALLE   Also, ich finde, er sondert sich immer von allen ab. In der Pause sitzt er irgendwo in einer stillen Ecke und liest. Er unterhält sich mit keinem und ist auch sonst ziemlich zugeknöpft.

HANNES   Ach, vielleicht vermißt er einfach nur seine Freunde in Düsseldorf.

KALLE   Ja, kann schon sein.

Answers to Activity 14

Thomas paßt sich nicht an.
Silke paßt sich an.
Renate paßt sich nicht an.
Joachim paßt sich nicht an.

Activity 16, p. 91

PAUL   Na, Ulf, was gibt's? Du siehst heute aber nicht gerade fröhlich aus!

ULF   Ach, Paul, ich hab' mich mal wieder mit meinem Bruder gestritten. Manchmal kann ich es gar nicht erwarten, bis der Jens anfängt zu studieren. Dann wohnt er wenigstens nicht mehr zu Hause. Er hilft nie und läßt immer alles rumliegen. Ich muß dann immer seine Sachen wegräumen. Und dazu noch das Geschirr spülen und den Rasen mähen, auch wenn er eigentlich dran ist. Das stinkt mir echt!

PAUL   Mensch, Ulf! Ich würde meinen Eltern sagen, daß dein Bruder seine Arbeit nicht macht. Sie werden sich dann schon darum kümmern.

ULF   Das glaube ich nicht! Du darfst nicht vergessen, daß meine Eltern beide arbeiten gehen. Sie wissen gar nicht, daß er tagsüber fast nie zu Hause ist und alles liegen läßt. Er hängt immer nur mit seiner Clique herum. Außerdem habe ich keine Lust, wie ein kleines Kind zu petzen!

PAUL Vielleicht kannst du einfach nur deinen Teil der Arbeit machen und den Rest liegen lassen. Dann sehen deine Eltern doch, wie faul er ist.

ULF Ach Paul, so einfach ist das nicht! Denk doch mal daran, daß meine Eltern abends total gestreßt von der Arbeit heimkommen. Wenn meine Mutter sieht, daß alles herumliegt, regt sie sich nur auf und räumt selber auf. Und dann wird sie meistens sauer.

PAUL Das mag schon sein, aber du kannst ja nichts dafür. Weißt du, ich finde es wichtig, daß du mal vernünftig mit dem Jens redest anstatt nur zu streiten. Vielleicht begreift er ja dann ja endlich mal, daß sein Verhalten dir gegenüber nicht fair ist.

ULF Ja, also ich glaube, du hast recht. Ich werde gleich mal mit ihm reden, wenn er nach Hause kommt. Danke für deinen Rat, Paul.

PAUL Ach, nicht der Rede wert, Kumpel!

Answers to Activity 16

Ulf hat sich mit seinem Bruder Jens gestritten, weil Jens nie zu Hause hilft und Ulf alles machen muß.

Paul rät Ulf, es seinen Eltern zu erzählen. Ulf will diesem Rat nicht folgen.

Paul rät Ulf, nur seinen Teil zu machen und den Rest liegen zu lassen. Ulf will diesem Rat nicht folgen.

Paul rät Ulf, mal vernünftig mit Jens zu reden anstatt zu streiten. Ulf will diesem Rat folgen.

Activity 19, p. 92

KERSTIN Puh! Also, ich freue mich schon wahnsinnig auf unsere Reise nach Amerika! Komm, Gertrud, laß uns mal überlegen, was wir uns alles anschauen wollen!

GERTRUD Ja, okay! Du, Kerstin, ich finde deine Idee wirklich prima, mit dem Campingwagen durchs Land zu reisen. Das mit dem Wagen geht doch klar, oder?

KERSTIN Ja, ist schon alles organisiert! Den Campingwagen kriegen wir ganz bestimmt. Meine Verwandten in Kalifornien leihen ihn uns gern. Als allererstes schauen wir uns San Francisco an. Meine Kusine Cindy kommt ja auch mit auf unsere Tour. Und sie will noch eine Freundin fragen. Dann wären wir zu viert.

GERTRUD Hm, hoffentlich wird das dann nicht zu schwierig, wenn wir uns entscheiden wollen, wohin wir fahren und was wir besichtigen wollen. Du weißt ja, viele Leute, viele verschiedene Interessen! Du, ich möcht' aber auf jeden Fall auch nach Los Angeles!

KERSTIN Ich weiß nicht, Gertrud, ich glaube, das liegt nicht auf unserer Tour. Von San Francisco aus fahren wir doch nach Nevada. Ich will unbedingt nach Las Vegas.

GERTRUD Nee, also Kerstin, das mit Las Vegas, das müssen wir aber noch mal besprechen. Da kann man doch nichts anderes tun als Geld verspielen. Dazu hab' ich nun wirklich keine Lust! Ich will lieber weiter nach Utah und mir den Bryce Canyon ansehen.

KERSTIN Ach Gertrud, ich würd' lieber direkt von Nevada nach Arizona weiterfahren. Bis zum Grand Canyon! Den müssen wir unbedingt sehen!

GERTRUD Ja, davon träum' ich schon ewig! Ich kann's kaum glauben, daß wir schon bald dort sein werden. Du, Kerstin, meinst du, wir könnten auch noch weiter bis nach New Mexico zu den Rocky Mountains fahren?

KERSTIN Ich weiß nicht, Gertrud. Bestimmt hat meine Kusine keine Lust dazu. Sie hat doch in New Mexico gewohnt und kennt dort doch schon die ganze Gegend. Laß uns lieber weiter runter nach Tucson fahren, wenn wir schon mal in Arizona sind.

GERTRUD Na gut! Aber nur, wenn wir dann auf dem Rückweg auch nach San Diego fahren! Okay?

KERSTIN Ja, San Diego liegt auf der Rücktour. Das schauen wir uns ganz bestimmt an.

GERTRUD Hm! Vielleicht schaffen wir es doch, uns auch noch Los Angeles anzuschauen.!

KERSTIN Also, ich glaube, daß wir dann wahrscheinlich keine Zeit mehr dazu haben!

GERTRUD Na ja, sehen wir mal!

Answers to Activity 19

Was Kerstin und Gertrud bestimmt machen: mit dem Campingwagen fahren; San Francisco anschauen; in Arizona den Grand Canyon ansehen; nach Tucson, Arizona fahren; nach San Diego fahren

Was spekulativ bleibt: Los Angeles anschauen; nach Las Vegas, Nevada fahren; Bryce Canyon in Utah ansehen; zu den Rocky Mountains nach New Mexico fahren

Anwendung
Activity 1, p. 100

1. MARTIN Also dieser Dieter ist schon komisch! Wie der sich anzieht! Und seine Haare sehen auch immer so ungepflegt aus! Typisch Punker! Bin ich froh, daß der nicht in unserer Clique ist!

2. EVA Also, mein Lieblingsfach in der Schule ist Erdkunde. Ich finde andere Kulturen und Völker einfach faszinierend. Ich möchte später mal unbedingt ein Jahr lang nach Afrika ziehen, am liebsten nach Namibia. Ich möchte alles über die Bantu-Völker lernen, sogar ihre Sprache. Sie haben ganz andere Sitten und Gebräuche als wir. Das find' ich toll!

3. BRITTA Ich verstehe einfach nicht, wieso die Tina nicht mit uns ins Konzert will! Also, solche Leute, die nur klassische Musik hören und keine Rockmusik mögen, sind einfach komisch! Wie kann sie nur daheimbleiben, wenn sie stattdessen mit uns mitgehen könnte! Na, vielleicht will sie nur nicht mit, weil sie nichts Besonderes zum Anziehen hat! Ich finde die Klamotten von der Tina echt altmodisch!

4. ANDREAS Also, ich verstehe mich ganz gut mit dem Herbert. Er ist in der Schule ziemlich unbeliebt, weil er sich immer von den anderen absondert. Aber er bleibt nun mal lieber allein, weil er sehr schüchtern ist. Außerdem liest er wahnsinnig gern. In der Pause nimmt er sich immer ein Buch mit und liest. Ich habe aber neulich mit ihm gesprochen, und er ist sehr gescheit. Er interessiert sich für Archäologie und war mit seinen Eltern schon auf vielen Reisen im Ausland.

Answers to Activity 1

1. Martin: nicht tolerant
2. Eva: tolerant
3. Britta: nicht tolerant
4. Andreas: tolerant

SCRIPTS

Kapitel 4: Verhältnis zu anderen
Projects and Games

PROJECT

*In this activity, students will recreate the story **Ein Tisch ist ein Tisch** by illustrating it with a captioned collage. Begin this project after students have completed the **Zum Lesen** section. This project is designed for students to do in small groups.*

Materials Students may need poster board, paper, catalogs, scissors, markers, and dictionaries.

Suggested Sequence

1. Discuss the project with students and divide the class into small groups.
2. Within their groups, students brainstorm and make an outline of what they feel should be included in their recreation of the story. Notes should include how certain parts can be illustrated and what types of pictures and sources could be useful.
3. Students plan the layout of the collage and begin with the artistic part of the project.
4. Students write a caption for each illustration.
5. Groups present their completed projects to the class.

Grading the Project

Suggested point distribution (total = 100 points)

Illustration/Creativity	40
Written information	30
Oral presentation	30

 GAME

Wort für Wort

*Playing this game will help students review the vocabulary of the **Erste Stufe** along with previously learned vocabulary.*

Preparation Divide the class into groups of three to four students. Each group assigns one member to be the writer/recorder and another student to be the reporter. Prepare a list of words you plan to review and make sure that each group has a piece of paper and something to write with.

Procedure The use of books is not allowed during this game. Call out a word from the list and signal the groups to begin writing down as many related words as they can within a set amount of time. All members should actively suggest vocabulary, which the writer records. When time is called, the writer transfers his or her group's list to the board. Go over each list, review the meanings, and verify spelling before awarding a point for the vocabulary item. The group with the most related words wins.

Examples:

reden	sprechen
	der Mund
	die Sprache
	diskutieren
angehören	die Clique
	die Familie
	die Gruppe
	der Klub

Kapitel 4: Verhältnis zu anderen
Lesson Plans, pages 80-103

Teacher Note

- Before you begin the chapter, you may want to preview the *Video Program* and consult the *Video Guide*. Suggestions for integrating the video into each chapter are given in the *Video Guide* and in the chapter interleaf. Activity masters for video selections can be found in the *Video Guide*.

*U*sing the Chapter Opener, *pp. 80-81*

Motivating Activity

Ask students about their families. How would they best describe their families? (**Erzähle ein bißchen über deine Familie! Wer gehört alles dazu? Wie kann man deine Familie am besten beschreiben?**)

Teaching Suggestion

Have students describe their close circle of friends. When and how often do they get together? What do they typically do? (**Beschreib deinen Freundeskreis! Wann und wie oft trefft ihr euch gewöhnlich, und was macht ihr so?**)

For Individual Needs

① **Visual Learners** Have students describe the young people in the photo. Where are they? What might some of their common interests be?

Teaching Suggestion

② Ask students about the advantages and disadvantages of "fitting in." What do they think is more important, fitting in or being an individual? Is it possible for someone to fit in and also retain individuality?

③ Ask students if there is anyone in their lives to whom they often turn for advice. Do they generally seek advice from peers, family members, or older friends?

For Individual Needs

Challenge To review vocabulary that might be useful in this chapter, ask students to write riddles in German for vocabulary items. Distribute one index card to each student. On one side write the word for which you want students to create a riddle. Let students write their riddle on the other side. When all students have finished, each gets to read his or her riddle and lets the rest of the class guess the word. Following is a list of words learned in Levels 1 and 2: **Halbbruder, Halbschwester, Clique, Fete, Eltern, Austauschschüler, Nachbar, Jugendzentrum, Mannschaft, Freizeit, Brieffreund(in)**.

Teaching Suggestion

Give students a few moments to think about how they would most like to spend their time outside of school and with whom. (**Wie würdest du deine Freizeit am liebsten verbringen? Wenn nicht allein, mit wem und warum gerade mit dieser Person?**)

Focusing on Outcomes

Have students preview the learning outcomes listed on p. 81. Ask them what the people in the three photographs might be talking about that would represent each function. **NOTE:** These outcomes are modeled in **Los geht's!** (pp. 82-83) and **Weiter geht's!** (pp. 88-89) and evaluated in **Kann ich's wirklich?** (p. 102).

Teaching Los geht's!
pp. 82-83

Resources for Los geht's!
- *Textbook Audiocassette* 2 B
- *Practice and Activity Book*

Teacher Note
Los geht's! is recorded on audiocassette.

Los geht's! Summary
In **Verhältnis zu Eltern und Freunden**, an interviewer talks to Sonja, Tanja, Michael, and Philipp about their relationships with their friends and families. The following outcome listed on p. 81 is modeled in the interviews: agreeing.

Motivating Activity
Discuss with students some of the typical things their parents ask of them or comment on. (**Könnt ihr einige typische Beispiele geben von Sachen, die ihr von euren Eltern zu hören bekommt? Worum bitten sie euch? Was sollt ihr zu Hause alles tun?**)

Teaching Suggestion
Divide the text into three sections, **Eltern, Freunde, frühere Klassenkameraden**, using the interviewer's key questions as the introduction to each part. Play the audiocassette of one section at a time and have students follow along in their books. Repeat and ask questions to check for comprehension. Rephrase or paraphrase new or difficult terms as you go to help students understand them. At the end, have students listen to the whole interview with their books closed.

Language Note
Azubi, used by the interviewer in his final question, is an abbreviated form of the word **Auszubildender** (*apprentice*) that has replaced **Lehrling**. The verb **ausbilden** means *to train*, or *to educate*. An **Auszubildender** is someone who is being trained in a profession.

Teaching Suggestion
In Level 2 (Chapter 7) students learned to use grammatical and lexical clues to derive meaning when reading a text. Remind them of this strategy and encourage them to use it to determine the meaning of new phrases and statements in the interview. For example, they might not understand the phrase **ein echter Kumpel**. They should read the preceding and following sentences: "**Ich verstehe mich jetzt mit meinen Eltern so prima.**" and "**Wir gehen zusammen Tennis spielen und so ...**" to help them determine the meaning.

✦ For Individual Needs
1 A Slower Pace Copy the chart on the chalkboard and write the phrases in as you go along. Have students find corresponding statements in the text and help them rephrase them to focus on main points. For example, they might read **Ich versteh' mich jetzt mit meinen Eltern so prima.** Students rephrase it and write alongside Philipp's name **versteht sich prima mit ihnen.**

2 Challenge To expand this activity, ask students to use the notes about their relationship with parents and friends to write a short cohesive paragraph for homework.

✦ Cooperative Learning
3 Ask students to work in cooperative learning groups to do this activity in writing. Then ask all group reporters to share their findings. You may also want to have students do the same for Tanja.

Closure
Have students take a close look at the photos accompanying the **Los geht's!** section. Ask students what impressions they have about the atmosphere and social interaction of the people in the photos based on the main theme of the interview (**Verhältnis zu Eltern und Freunden**). What might the people in each photograph be saying?

LOS GEHT'S!

Los geht's! **79H**

Teaching Erste Stufe, pp. 84-87

Resources for Erste Stufe

Practice and Activity Book
Chapter Resources, Book 2
- Communicative Activities 4-1, 4-2
- Additional Listening Activities 4-1, 4-2, 4-3
- Student Response Forms
- Realia 4-1
- Situation Card 4-1
- Teaching Transparency Master 4-1
- Quiz 4-1

Audiocassette Program
- *Textbook Audiocassette* 2 B
- *Additional Listening Activities, Audiocassette* 9 B
- *Assessment Items, Audiocassette* 7 B

Video Program, Videocassette 1
Video Guide

▶ *page 84*

MOTIVATE

Teaching Suggestion

Ask students to name two common situations that cause friction or conflict between them and their parents. (**Nennt zwei Situationen, die bei euch zu Hause gewöhnlich zu Problemen zwischen euch und euren Eltern führen!**)

TEACH

PRESENTATION: Wortschatz

To present the vocabulary in this box, do the following for each word or expression. First, read it to students. Then incorporate the item into statements about yourself and people in your life. Finally, use it in questions directed at individual students. Examples:

Brett, kommst du gut mit deinen Eltern aus?
Tommy, wie verstehst du dich mit deinen Geschwistern?
Cindy, gehörst du einer Clique an? Wenn ja, welcher? Wenn nicht, warum nicht?

Building on Previous Skills

4 After students have matched the phrases with the corresponding illustrations, ask them to come up with a reprimand that a parent would give to the teenager in each picture.

Thinking Critically

4 Comparing and Contrasting Discuss the situations with students and find out which ones they can relate to. Have students elaborate on the situation with a sentence or two.

▶ *page 85*

Teaching Suggestion

5 Play the conversation again and have students determine a reason for each of the four arguments. (**Hört noch einmal diesen vier Gesprächen zu, um herauszufinden, worüber sich die Leute streiten!**)

✦ For Individual Needs

8 Challenge To provide students with additional written practice, have them choose one of the five statements on which to express their opinion in three to five sentences.

▶ *page 86*

PRESENTATION: Ein wenig Grammatik

- Explain to students that if they want to express the ordinals in numerals, the number must be followed by a period as in **in der 10. Klasse.** Ordinal numerals are often used in dates. (Example: **3.10.1995**)
- Prepare a handout for practicing ordinal numbers as adjectives using sentences like the following:
Wir haben Deutsch in der ____ Stunde.
Meine Mutter feiert nächstes Jahr ihren ____ Geburtstag.
Neil Armstrong war der ____ Mann auf dem Mond.

PRESENTATION: Ein wenig Landeskunde

Briefly discuss the concept of cliques in German with your students, including both positive and negative aspects. You may want to direct the discussion with the following questions.

Gibt es in dieser Schule Cliquen?
Woher weißt du das?
Gehörst du einer Clique an?
Wo trefft ihr euch?
Was macht ihr gewöhnlich?

Teacher Note

As students look at the chart entitled **Mit wem verbringen Jugendliche ihre Freizeit?**, remind them to use the title to help them interpret the information.

🅣🅟🅡 Total Physical Response

Ask students to sit down. Then give them commands based on the chart **Mit wem verbringen Jugendliche ihre Freizeit?**
Examples:
Wenn du die meiste Freizeit allein verbringst, steh auf!
Wenn du die meiste Freizeit mit der Familie verbringst, steh auf!

After each command, count the number of students who have stood up. At the end, compare the class results with those of the German teenagers in the chart.

📼 Video Program

In the video clip **Im Freizeitzentrum,** some students from Würzburg talk about their friends and their activities at the youth center. See *Video Guide* for suggestions.

▶ *page 87*

PRESENTATION: Grammatik

- Tell students that one way to increase German writing proficiency is to use more complex sentence structures, such as relative clauses.
- Write several pairs of sentences on the board or a transparency and walk students through the steps involved in combining them into one sentence.
Example:
Ich habe am Samstag Milch gekauft. Sie war schon sauer.

Ich habe am Samstag Milch gekauft, die schon sauer war.

- Tell students that in German a relative clause is always introduced by a relative pronoun; in English the relative pronoun is often not used.
Example:
Die Milch, die ich am Samstag gekauft habe, war schon sauer.
The milk (that) I bought on Saturday was already spoiled.

- Point out also that a relative clause is a dependent clause; therefore, the verb must be the last element in the clause.

Reteaching: Relative Clauses

Tell students to imagine that they are looking through a catalog, and there are a lot of things they would like to have for one reason or another. Have them tell you or a partner what they want and why.

die CD von U2
die Armbanduhr
die Jeans
die Skiausrüstung
die Stiefel
die Stereoanlage
das Designer Sweatshirt
der Pullover
der Computer
das Armband
der Ring
die Kette

Example:
Da ist die Kette, die ich für die Fete am Samstag haben will.

ERSTE STUFE

CLOSE

♜ Game

Play the game **Wort für Wort** to review the vocabulary of the **Erste Stufe**. See p. 79F for the procedure.

Focusing on Outcomes

Refer students back to the learning outcomes listed on p. 81. They should recognize that they now know how to agree.

ASSESS

- **Performance Assessment** Ask students to describe orally or in writing a) their relationship with a family member of their choice, or b) their relationship with their best friend. Students should include the strong and weak points of their relationship.

- Quiz 4-1, *Chapter Resources,* Book 2

*T*eaching Weiter geht's!
pp. 88-89

> ### Resources for Weiter geht's!
> - *Textbook Audiocassette* 2 B
> - *Practice and Activity Book*

Teacher Note

Weiter geht's! is recorded on audiocassette.

Weiter geht's! Summary

In **Verhältnis zu anderen Leuten,** an interviewer talks with Sonja, Tanja, Michael, and Philipp about their relationships with different types of people. The following student outcomes listed on p. 81 are modeled in the interview: giving advice, introducing another point of view, and hypothesizing.

Motivating Activity

Have students take a look at the makeup of their class. How many different nationalities are represented? How many students speak a language other than English at home? Are there any foreign exchange students or other students from different countries living here temporarily?

Teaching Suggestions

- Divide the interview into its two parts and have students read along as they listen to the first segment. Repeat and ask some detailed questions to check comprehension. Work with the new vocabulary by paraphrasing, using synonyms, and asking either/or questions. Follow the same procedure for the second segment of the interview.
- After students have a good understanding of the interview, divide the class into groups of four and have each student assume one of the roles. Give the role of the interviewer who has only two questions to the student who plays Sonja. Tell students to practice reading the conversation until it sounds spoken not read, with typical hesitations, pauses, self-corrections, and repetitions one hears in natural speech.

Language Note

The abbreviation **AG** is an acronym for **Arbeitsgemeinschaft,** a group of students that meets after school to discuss and work on topics of common interest, similar to an American school club. An **Umwelt AG,** for example, is a group of students who want to know about and do more for the environment.

Teaching Suggestion

12 After students have agreed to or corrected each statement, ask them to explain it further, based on what they have read.

❖ For Individual Needs

13 Visual Learners Divide a transparency into three sections, one for each question. Ask students to scan the interview for all the phrases and statements that answer each question. Help students rephrase the quotes if necessary to get to the key information from the interviews and write that in the corresponding section of the transparency.

Closure

Have students brainstorm other ways to bridge the cultural differences between Germans and foreigners living in Germany.

Teaching Zweite Stufe,
pp. 90-93

Resources for Zweite Stufe

Practice and Activity Book
Chapter Resources, Book 2
- Communicative Activities 4-3, 4-4
- Additional Listening Activities 4-4, 4-5, 4-6
- Student Response Forms
- Realia 4-2
- Situation Card 4-2
- Teaching Transparency Master 4-2
- Quiz 4-2

Audiocassette Program
- *Textbook Audiocassette* 2 B
- *Additional Listening Activities, Audiocassette* 9 B
- *Assessment Items, Audiocassette* 7 B

▶ *page 90*

MOTIVATE
Teaching Suggestion
Ask students who they usually go to for advice. Does anyone ever ask them for advice? (**Wem vertraust du dich gewöhnlich an? Vertrauen sich andere Leute dir an?**)

TEACH
PRESENTATION: Wortschatz
Introduce the new vocabulary to students by using each item in context. Then ask students to respond to a statement or question you make, using the context of the interview in **Weiter geht's!** or the context of your students' lives.
Example:
Wir haben auch ein paar Ausländer an unserer Schule.
Ich finde, die sondern sich nicht von den anderen Schülern ab.

Teaching Suggestion
14 After students have decided which of the students new to the school are trying to fit in and which are not, have them give the facts on which they base their decision in each of the cases.

Teaching Suggestion
15 After students have completed their group work, ask for volunteers to report their findings. Put them on a transparency or on the chalkboard and use the ideas to discuss the problem of prejudices. You may want to provide students with the following additional vocabulary to help them discuss the pictures and answer the questions.
der Rollstuhl *wheelchair*
mit jemandem gehen *to go steady with someone*
der Haarschnitt *haircut*

▶ *page 91*

PRESENTATION: So sagt man das!
After introducing the first function, giving advice, ask students to come up with statements on their own in reaction to situations that you set up.
Examples:
Wir haben einen Punker in unserer Klasse. Er sondert sich ganz ab von uns. Sicher findet er uns sehr langweilig und altmodisch.
Ich kann mit meinen Eltern nicht reden. Es gibt nur Streit.
For practicing the second function, introducing another point of view, express opinions in different situations, and ask students to react.
Examples:
Ausländer haben es schwer, einen guten Job zu finden.
Wenn man in ein fremdes Land kommt, muß man sich vielen neuen kulturellen Dingen anpassen.

◆ For Individual Needs
16 Challenge Ask students to list the things that got Ulf into the situation he is in. Which character traits make him susceptible to being used by his brother? (**Wie kommt es, daß Ulf sich von seinem Bruder ausnutzen läßt?**)

17b A Slower Pace Help students get started by giving them the first line of the conversation.

17b Challenge Ask students to add comments, reactions, and questions to the eight statements given in order to bring the conversation alive and make it more real.

Thinking Critically

17 Comparing and Contrasting As an alternative or additional activity, ask students to adapt the group's statements to fit a social problem in their area, city, or state.

 For Individual Needs

18 A Slower Pace Review the different ways of giving advice and introducing another point of view listed in the function box on this page before starting on this activity. Students should use these expressions when playing the role of teacher, Markus, or friend.

▶ *page 92*

PRESENTATION: So sagt man das!

To help students understand the concepts of real versus unreal conditions, present several situations in both forms so students see the difference. Let them discover it.

Ich bin <u>nicht</u> in Deutschland. Ich bin in Amerika. Aber wenn ich in Deutschland wäre, würde ich aufs Oktoberfest gehen.

Ich habe <u>keine</u> schlechten Noten, nur Einsen und Zweien. Aber wenn ich schlechte Noten hätte, würde ich viel mehr für die Schule lernen.

PRESENTATION: Ein wenig Grammatik

- After students have reviewed these subjunctive verb forms, ask them what the expressions all have in common.
- Point out to students that the use of subjunctive makes questions, requests, and wishes somewhat more polite and more formal. (Examples: **Ich hätte gern ..., ich würde gern ..., ich wäre lieber ...**)
- Ask students how they would express the examples in English.

Geography Connection

19 To extend this activity, have students imagine that Kerstin and Gertrud are exchange students at your school. What advice would students give them as they prepare for their trip? Do they have any further suggestions as to what they might want to see and do along the way?

For Individual Needs

20 Challenge After students have correctly completed the activity, ask them to use the given clauses for making speculations on their own. Have them first work with the four conditions, then with the four solutions. Ask students to share their ideas with the class.

21 Challenge Have students follow the same format, but let them choose the country or place that they would like to visit as an exchange student. Example:
Wenn ich ein Austauschschüler in Spanien wäre, ...

▶ *page 93*

PRESENTATION: Grammatik

- Point out to students that the genitive case (**das Auto meines Vaters**) often indicates an "of-relationship" denoting possession. That is why it is also referred to as the possessive case. Can students recall another way of expressing the same idea? (**von** + dative as in **das Auto von meinem Vater**)
- Explain to students that in spoken German the genitive case is used less and less frequently. It shows that standard German, like English, is moving to a less formal way of expression.

Reteaching: Genitive Case

Ask students to use the genitive case to talk about people and things. Following are some examples that you can either do orally as a class activity or in writing.
Examples:
die Handtasche von der Austauschschülerin
das Problem von der türkischen Bevölkerung
die Eltern von dem Punker

Teacher Note

22 The **Grammatik** box states that the genitive case can replace **von** when showing possession. Point out to students that the genitive can also replace relative clauses.
Die Probleme, die unsere Schüler haben, werden immer schwieriger.
Die Probleme unserer Schüler werden immer schwieriger.

ZWEITE STUFE

▶ *page 94*

PRESENTATION: Landeskunde

Building on Previous Skills

In Levels 1 and 2, students were introduced to various aspects of school life in Germany. Before you begin the **Landeskunde,** ask students what they remember about the school system. Jot down students' ideas, then discuss some of the differences as well as the similarities between the German and American schools.

Teaching Suggestion

You may want to discuss the following vocabulary before students begin to read the text.
Bildungsweg: *schooling; course of instruction*
Kaufhof: *name of a large chain of German department stores*
Berufsschule: *trade school, vocational school*
ausbilden: *to train*
wird ausgebildet: *is being trained*
der Abteilungsleiter: *department supervisor*
der Krankenpfleger: *male nurse*
Bundeswehr: *Federal armed forces*
Zivildienst: *alternate service*

Teacher Note

Schools that provide education to students with special needs are called **Sonderschulen.** They are separate from other public schools and are staffed entirely by teachers with special education certification. For additional information on the German school system, refer to pp. 27L and 157I of the Level 2 *Teacher's Edition.*

Background Information

* School attendance is mandatory in Germany for everyone between the ages of six and eighteen. Students must attend school full-time for the first nine years, in some **Bundesländer** for ten years. Afterwards, part-time attendance is required at vocational schools.

* All men in Germany are expected to serve twelve months of basic military service. Exceptions are made when young men, for medical or moral reasons, cannot or choose not to enter the service. They then agree to **Zivildienst** (*alternate service*).

For Individual Needs

A Visual Learners Ask students to review each student's educational path. Have them read again what Hassan, Helga, and Klaus are doing. Each time, follow their educational career on the chart. Discuss with students how the three educational paths differ. Who will be the first one to finish training and get a job? Who has the longest training ahead? Which one has chosen a profession that is always in demand?

For Individual Needs

B Tactile Learners Ask students to prepare a chart of the American school system with a foreign audience in mind. This chart could be for a German pen pal who is unfamiliar with the American school system.

Multicultural Connection

B Ask students to interview foreign exchange students or other foreign people to gather information about the school system in their countries. Students should then prepare a short explanation of the school systems of those countries. Compare the various systems and discuss unfamiliar aspects of each.

Teacher Note

Mention to your students that the **Landeskunde** will also be included in Quiz 4-2 given at the end of the **Zweite Stufe.**

CLOSE

Game

To review the vocabulary of this **Stufe,** divide the class into two teams with each team sending one member to the front. Prepare a list of words and phrases ahead of time. Then write one vocabulary item on the board and give the first team 20 seconds to explain or define the word in German. If the explanation is unsatisfactory, the other team has a chance to define the word. If students from the first team successfully define the word, they score a point for their team and the other team gets a turn. If no team can explain or define the word, the teacher does it, and the word is used again at a later time.

Focusing on Outcomes

Refer students back to the learning outcomes listed on p. 81. They should recognize that they now know how to give advice, introduce another point of view, and hyphothesize.

ASSESS

- **Performance Assessment** Ask students to think about what they would do if they could be President of the United States for one day. Give students a few moments to think about this hypothetical situation and then call on several to find out about their plans. (**Was würdest du tun, wenn du einen Tag lang Präsident(in) der Vereinigten Staaten sein könntest?**)

- Quiz 4-2, *Chapter Resources*, Book 2

Teaching Zum Schreiben, *p. 95*

Writing Strategy

The targeted strategy for this writing activity is determining the purpose. Students should learn about this strategy before beginning the assignment.

PREWRITING

Motivating Activity

Ask students where one can typically find advice columns. Have students make a list of sources and come up with some problems people might write about in each publication.

Teaching Suggestion

Tell students that writing about a problem is not intended to put anyone on the spot. They should feel free to invent a problem if they choose.

Journalism Connection

A Ask the journalism teacher to come to your class and talk about the importance of readers' letters to a newspaper or a magazine. What makes letters so interesting and how do they differ, in terms of format and style, from articles?

WRITING

For Individual Needs

B **A Slower Pace** In Level 2 (p. 147) students first learned expressions used to ask for advice. Review those expressions if necessary with students to help them put their ideas into cohesive sentences.

Teaching Suggestion

B Remind students to double or triple-space their drafts to leave space for comments in the evaluating and revising stage.

POST-WRITING

Teaching Suggestions

C Help students understand the detailed instructions for revision by taking one point at a time and giving examples on the chalkboard or a transparency.

C You may want to suggest the following criteria guidelines for students to use as they evaluate each other's composition.
1. Content: Does everything make sense? Is the problem described clearly? Are the supporting details all directly related to the problem?
2. Organization: Is the problem the main idea of the letter? Are the details relevant and easy to follow?
3. Grammar and usage: Are there mistakes in grammar, spelling, or punctuation that need to be corrected?
4. Final thoughts/suggestions: What is your general impression of the text? What can the writer do to improve it?

C4 Have students type or neatly print their letters in columns so that they appear as in a newspaper. Post the best letters on a bulletin board or have students read them to the class.

Closure

Redistribute the completed letters and have students take on the role of **Herr Weißalles** as they write a response to a classmate's letter.

*T*eaching Zum Lesen,
pp. 96-99

Reading Strategy

The targeted strategy in this reading is determining the main idea of a story. Students should learn about this strategy before beginning Question 1.

PREREADING

Motivating Activity

In the course of their study of German, students might have asked themselves more than once why humans have evolved different natural languages and whether each language isn't purely arbitrary. In order to get students started thinking more critically about language, you might explain that even body language differs from one culture to another. For example, Germans, Americans, and Japanese all use slightly different ways of counting on their fingers; and the Japanese gesture for "come here" (waggling the fingers with the palm facing downward) can look to westerners like it should mean "go away!" or "get out of here!" Have students discuss the basic functions of human languages. Does Latin fulfill any of all of these functions? How about computer programming languages such as BASIC or FORTRAN? Is the periodic table in chemistry a universal language? What functions does it fulfill?

READING
Teacher Notes

1e It will probably be clear to students that the story is told in the third person, and that the opening "Ich will ... erzählen" is a similar convention to that used in oral story telling. The two instances of **vielleicht** in the second paragraph might suggest that the narrator is not omniscient. However, this assumption will not stand the test, as we later find the narrator reporting the man's thoughts. Later in the story, when the narrator tells his audience: "**Jetzt könnt ihr die Geschichte selbst weiterschreiben,**" we find confirmation that the narrator is fully in control of and stands above the character. If the students think of this as a children's story or as a fable told for adults they can easily understand the narrative conventions without much analysis.

4 Perhaps the students know the expression *calling a spade a spade*, meaning using the plain, ordinary name for a plain, ordinary thing. In German, this is **das Ding beim rechten Namen nennen.**

Teaching Suggestion

6 As they do this activity, students should look especially for the instances of the verb **sich ändern** in the central paragraphs of the story.

Teacher Note

The expression, **an die Füße frieren**, at the top of p. 98, would be **an den Füßen frieren** in modern standard German.

POST-READING
Teacher Note

Activities 11 and 12 are post-reading tasks that will show whether students can apply what they have learned.

Thinking Critically

Analyzing Tell students a little about Peter Bichsel: He was born (1935) in Lucerne, Switzerland, and was an elementary school teacher before becoming a writer. Does this deepen their understanding of the story in any way? The class should be aware that German Swiss people speak many different local dialects of **Schwyzerdütsch** but have to learn to write the standard version of German in school. Additionally, they are exposed to many influences from the French-Swiss and the Italian-Swiss and are aware of the existence of an almost extinct fourth language, Romansch. Would students argue that Bichsel's background would heavily influence what he has to say, or that it would, at most, suggest some choices of topic to him?

Closure

Ask students to think about the following questions:

If someone is bored and tired of life, which of the following would be good advice?

get a new hobby; take a class; learn a new skill; change jobs or schools; change hair styles or buy a new wardrobe; join a group and meet people; buy some new video games; get involved in a simulation; take a trip; go to a foreign country; move to a new place and start fresh; do some self analysis

Which of these might have worked for the man in Bichsel's story?

Answers to Activity 1

a. ein alter Mann; b. im obersten Stock eines Hauses in einer kleinen Stadt am Ende der Straße, nahe einer Kreuzung; c. müdes Gesicht, dünner Hals, trägt graue Kleider; d. geht morgens und nachmittags spazieren, spricht mit Nachbarn, sitzt abends am Tisch; e. iimited third person (see first sentence of story)

Answers to Activity 3

There was a special day, and everything was perfect; the weather was just right, people were friendly, the sun was shining, etc.; the man was suddenly happy.

Answers to Activity 4

The old man thinks things will be different, but when he gets home, he finds nothing has changed. His room is still the same, the table is still a table, etc.

Answers to Activity 5

The man gets angry that nothing changes. He begins to rename things and invents his own language. In the end, he can no longer understand people, and they can't understand him. He stops communicating with other people all together. Answers will vary.

Answers to Activity 6

Answers will vary.

Answers to Activity 7

paragraph 5; **dann** signals to the reader that something in the story is going to change; **jetzt** is used every time the man believes his life is going to change, and **aber** indicates a contrast: in contrast to what the man believes is going to happen, his life does not change.

Answers to Activity 8

He thought that renaming objects would change his life; he thought his new language was funny, and it kept him busy and amused; he could no longer communicate with other people.

Answers to Activity 10

Answers will vary.

Answers to Activity 11

Answers will vary. (possible answers: language is a social tool; at least two or more people have to understand it, for it to be a language. Language is by nature communicative.)

Answers to Activity 12

Answers will vary. (possible answers: similarity—both the teens and the old man invent their own language; difference—the teens' language is understood by more than one person (the whole group); consequence—the teens' language brings the group closer together, thus it serves as a social tool. However, for the old man it only serves to isolate him because no one else can understand him.

Using Anwendung,
pp. 100-101

Resources for Anwendung

Chapter Resources, Book 2
- Realia 4-3
- Situation Card 4-3

Video Program, Videocassette 2

Video Guide

 ## Video Program

At this time, you might want to use the authentic advertising footage from German television. See *Video Guide* for suggestions.

Teaching Suggestion

1 After students have listened to the statements and completed the activity, ask them how they would feel or react in each of the situations. (**Wie würdest du auf ... Aussage reagieren?**)

Cooperative Learning

2 Divide the class into four groups, assigning each group one of the questions. Each group then discusses the assigned question in detail, with the recorder taking notes as they go along. After a set amount of time, call on the reporter from each group to **a)** reread the question to the rest of the class, **b)** share how the group feels about the question and what its opinion is, and **c)** pose at least two questions to the rest of the class to elicit some reactions or opinions.

Portfolio Assessment

2 You might want to suggest this activity as an oral portfolio item for your students. See *Assessment Guide,* p. 17.

Teaching Suggestion

5 Divide the class into smaller groups of two or three students in order to get more than one response to each of the letters. This also helps the peer writing process which is easier in a smaller group. Have each group share its response letter with the rest of the class.

Portfolio Assessment

5 You might want to suggest this activity as a written portfolio item for your students. See *Assessment Guide,* p. 17.

Kann ich's wirklich?
p. 102

This page helps students prepare for the test. It is a brief checklist of the major points covered in the chapter. The students should be reminded that it is only a checklist and not necessarily everything that will appear on the test.

Using Wortschatz,
p. 103

 ## For Individual Needs

Visual Learners Look through the comics section of a newspaper for a scenario that involves or focuses on relationships. Cut out the comic strip, cover the text, enlarge the strip on the photocopier, and make a class set. Let students create an original story line using at least five expressions from the **Wortschatz** on this page. Let students role-play their story for the rest of the class.

Teaching Suggestion

To review and practice the vocabulary, call on several students to answer a question like one of the following.

Was würdest du tun, wenn du in einem fremden Land wärst?

Was findest du gut an deiner besten Freundin?

Teacher Note

Give the **Kapitel 4** Chapter Test, *Chapter Resources,* Book 2.

4

Verhältnis zu anderen

1 Du, ich geb' dir recht. Wir kommen alle gut miteinander aus.

Deutschen Teenagern ist es wichtig, bei anderen gut anzukommen, gute Freunde zu haben, vielleicht einer Clique anzugehören. Wie ist dein Verhältnis zu anderen Leuten? Kommst du mit deinen Eltern gut aus? Wer sind deine Freunde? Bist du anderen Leuten gegenüber tolerant, auch wenn sie anders sind als du? Um über diese Fragen diskutieren zu können, mußt du noch einiges lernen.

In this chapter you will learn

- to agree
- to give advice; to introduce another point of view; to hypothesize

And you will

- listen to students talk about their relationships with other people
- read about how different students get along with others
- write about the relationship you have with someone important to you
- learn more about the German school system

② Es ist schon wichtig, daß man sich nicht von den andern absondert.

Wintergrüße aus St. Jakob i. H., Tirol

MIT LUFTPOST PAR AVION

40 JAHRE EUR

5027

③ Also, wenn ich du wäre, würde ich das gleich erledigen.

Los geht's!

Verhältnis zu Eltern und Freunden

Über ihr Verhältnis zu Eltern und Freunden
sprach ein Interviewer mit vier Gymnasiasten.
Er unterhielt sich mit Sonja (17), Tanja (18),
Michael (17) und Philipp (17).

INTERVIEWER Wie kommt ihr mit euern Eltern aus?

MICHAEL Ja, bei mir läuft seit zwei Jahren
alles prima.

INTERVIEWER Was meinst du damit? War's vorher anders?

MICHAEL Na ja, bis vor zwei Jahren hat's ab und zu Streitigkeiten gegeben.

INTERVIEWER Kannst du mal ein Beispiel geben?

MICHAEL Es ist damals meistens um so kleine Alltäglichkeiten gegangen
— die Mutter will, daß man schnell noch aufräumt, bevor man
weggeht und so weiter.

TANJA Ja, bei mir ist es auch so: jetzt gibt's keine Streitigkeiten mehr.
Das Problem mit dem Weggehen, das
früher ein Streitpunkt war, hat
sich jetzt erledigt — ich bin ja
jetzt achtzehn — und ja, alles andere, darüber kann man ja reden,
da braucht man nicht streiten.

SONJA Da geb' ich dir recht, Tanja. Und ich
möchte dazu noch sagen, daß ...
also, es dauert eben auch eine
Zeitlang, bis sich die Eltern daran
gewöhnen, daß aus ihren Kindern
erwachsene Leute geworden sind.

PHILIPP Eben. Ich versteh' mich jetzt mit
meinen Eltern so prima. Mein Vater ist ein echter Kumpel. Wir
gehen zusammen Tennis spielen und so ... und ich frag' mich
oft, warum es früher nicht so gut geklappt hat.

INTERVIEWER Wer sind eure Freunde? Mit wem seid ihr gewöhnlich zusammen?

PHILIPP Unser Freundeskreis? Ja, das sind eigentlich die Leute aus der
letzten Klasse. Es ist ja so: in der Kollegstufe gibt es keine
festen Klassen, also man ist immer mit anderen Leuten zusammen. Aber im Jahr davor, da waren wir in der 10. Klasse und
eben schon seit der 5. Klasse mit den gleichen Leuten zusammen. Und da haben sich gewisse Cliquen gebildet, die eben
jetzt was zusammen machen.

INTERVIEWER Was macht ihr so? Geht ihr tanzen?

MICHAEL Nee, wirklich nicht!

SONJA	Wir gehen öfters weg, einfach so in ein Café, trinken irgendwas und unterhalten uns, oder wir schauen uns zusammen einen Videofilm an oder ...
MICHAEL	Ins Kino gehen wir auch ab und zu zusammen, manchmal sogar auch ins Theater.
TANJA	Besonders, wenn wir Freikarten kriegen.
PHILIPP	Und wir machen Sport zusammen, wir spielen Tennis, und im Sommer gehen wir halt oft zusammen schwimmen.
INTERVIEWER	Seid ihr auch mit anderen Leuten zusammen, mit denen ihr in der Grundschule wart?
SONJA	Kaum.
MICHAEL	Ich kenn' einen, der mit mir im Schwimmverein ist. Ich war mit dem in der Grundschule zusammen und hatte aber keinen Kontakt mehr zu ihm bis eben jetzt ... aber wir machen nichts zusammen. Er haut immer gleich ab und fährt zu seiner Clique.
SONJA	Man macht sicher auch etwas mit anderen Leuten, aber ich würd' auch sagen, daß man hauptsächlich mit den eigenen Leuten unterwegs ist. Mit der Zeit merkt man halt, mit was für Leuten man sich versteht, wer die gleichen Interessen hat, ja und demnach richtet man seinen Freundeskreis ein.
INTERVIEWER	Was machen denn die Azubis in ihrer Freizeit?
MICHAEL	Keine Ahnung. Weiß nicht.
TANJA	Ich hab' früher in einer Gegend gewohnt — da war ein Freizeitheim, in dem sich meistens Azubis getroffen haben. Aber ich weiß nicht, was die sonst so gemacht haben.

1 Verhältnis zu Eltern und Freunden

Welche Aussagen (*statements*) machen die vier Schüler zu den Fragen?

a. Wie ist euer Verhältnis zu den Eltern?
b. Wer sind eure Freunde, und was macht ihr mit ihnen?

NAME	ELTERN	FREUNDE
Michael	alles läuft prima	
Tanja	Es gibt keine Streitigkeiten mehr.	
Philipp		
Sonja		
————		

2 Und du? Wie steht's mit dir?

Trag deinen Namen in die Tabelle ein und berichte kurz, wie dein Verhältnis zu deinen Eltern und Freunden ist!

3 Was erzählt Philipp?

Erzähle, was Philipp über sein Verhältnis zu seinen Eltern und Freunden berichtet!

a. Philipp versteht sich mit seinen Eltern prima. Sein Vater ...
b. Die Freunde, die er hat, sind Leute aus der 10. Klasse. Er ist mit ihnen ...
c. Sie machen ...

WORTSCHATZ

auf deutsch erklärt

Ich komme gut mit ihnen aus. Wir haben keine Probleme miteinander.
Wir verstehen uns nicht so gut mit ihnen. Wir kommen nicht gut mit ihnen aus.
Wir richten uns nach euch. Wir machen gern, was ihr machen wollt.
der Kumpel ein guter Freund
der Freundeskreis die Gruppe von Freunden
erwachsen sein kein Kind mehr sein
reden sprechen

auf englisch erklärt

Wir haben ein problematisches Verhältnis.
We have a difficult relationship.
Wir haben aber wenig Krach miteinander. *We really don't argue much with one another.*
Meine Eltern schimpfen immer mit mir! *My parents are always scolding me!*
Das kann ich nicht leiden! *I can't stand that!*
der Streit *quarrel*
der Streitpunkt *point of contention*
Worum geht es? *What's it about?*
Sie gehört einem Volleyballclub an. *She belongs to a volleyball club.*

E.g.: **Es gibt Krach, wenn ich mein Zimmer nicht aufräume.**

4 Gibt es hier Konflikte?

Was können Eltern manchmal nicht leiden? Schau dir die Zeichnungen an und suche die Satzteile ganz unten, die zu den Zeichnungen am besten passen! Schreib dann die Sätze richtig ab, indem du sie mit den Konjunktionen verbindest!

Es gibt Krach, ...

Meine Eltern schimpfen, ...

Sie können es nicht leiden, ...

(wenn) ich räume mein Zimmer nicht auf

(wenn) ich komme zu spät nach Hause

(wenn) ich sehe zu viel fern

(daß) ich habe mir die Haare gefärbt

(weil) ich helfe nicht immer

(wie) ich ziehe mich an

(weil) meine Noten sind schlecht

(wenn) ich spiele die Musik laut

5 Hör gut zu! For answers, see listening script on TE Interleaf.

Ihr hört jetzt vier Gespräche. Die Leute, die sich unterhalten, streiten sich. Worüber streiten sie? Endet in jedem Fall der Streit gut, also produktiv, oder schlecht, d.h. die Personen erreichen nichts?

6 Die Eltern schimpfen so oft!

Erzähle deiner Partnerin, wann es bei dir zu Hause Krach gibt, und deine Partnerin erzählt dir dann, wie es bei ihr zu Hause ist!

DU **Es gibt Krach, wenn ich ...** *oder*
Meine Mutter schimpft immer, weil ... *oder*
Die Eltern können es nicht leiden, daß ...

Zimmer nicht aufräumen
einen Freund/eine Freundin haben
zu viel ausgehen
die Musik zu laut spielen
zu spät nach Hause kommen

schlechte Noten haben
zu viel Geld ausgeben
sich verrückt anziehen
sich die Haare färben
sich zu sehr schminken

SO SAGT MAN DAS!

Agreeing

You have learned a number of ways to express agreement. Here are a few more:

If your friend says:

Du sollst nicht so viel streiten.

Wir müssen unsere Hausaufgaben erledigen.

Bei uns ist der Streitpunkt das Geschirrspülen.

You may answer:

Da geb' ich dir recht.

Ganz meine Meinung.

Bei mir ist es auch so.

What are some other ways you have learned to express agreement?[1]

7 Hör gut zu! For answers, see listening script on TE Interleaf.

Claudia erzählt Patrick, daß sie Streit mit ihrem Vater hatte. Hör gut zu, und mach dir Notizen, worum es geht! Stimmt Patrick Claudias Meinung zu oder nicht? Anhand deiner Notizen spiel dann mit einem Partner die Rollen von Claudia und ihrem Vater!

8 Was sagst du dazu?

Diskutier über die folgenden Aussagen mit deinem Partner! Stimmst du diesen Aussagen ganz zu oder nur teilweise? Was kannst du noch dazu sagen?

1. Eltern sollen mehr Vertrauen zu ihren Kindern haben.
2. In unserem Alter braucht man nicht streiten. Über Probleme kann ich mit meinen Eltern immer reden.
3. Die meisten Streitigkeiten gehen nur um Alltäglichkeiten.
4. Eltern können sich nicht daran gewöhnen, daß aus ihren Kindern erwachsene Leute werden.
5. Man sollte ab und zu auch mal mit den Eltern ins Theater oder in ein klassisches Konzert gehen.

1. **Da hast du recht; Ich meine das auch; Stimmt!; Das finde ich auch.**

9 Was zeigt die Statistik?

Mit wem verbringen Jugendliche ihre Freizeit? Schreib einen kurzen Bericht darüber, indem du die Satzlücken in dem folgenden Text füllst! Die Information dafür findest du in der Grafik rechts unten.

An ~~erster~~ Stelle steht die Clique. Die Statistik zeigt, daß die Jugendlichen ~~32~~ Prozent ihrer Freizeit mit der Clique verbringen. 24 ~~Prozent~~ ihrer Freizeit sind die Jugendlichen mit ═════ zusammen. An ~~dritter~~ Stelle steht mit 18 Prozent die ~~Familie~~. Nur ~~16~~ Prozent ihrer Freizeit verbringen die Jugendlichen allein. An ═════ Stelle nannten die Jugendlichen ═════ mit 10 Prozent.

dem Freund/
der Freundin

fünfter/letzter
sonstige
Personen

EIN WENIG LANDESKUNDE

Die Clique, die lose, informelle Freundesgruppe, ist für die meisten Jugendlichen von heute von großer Bedeutung. Sechzig Prozent aller Jugendlichen sagen, sie gehören einer Clique an, 1962 waren es nur 15 Prozent.

Was macht die Clique so beliebt? Cliquen sind den Jugendlichen wichtig, vor allem für die Gestaltung der Freizeit. Auf diesem Gebiet fangen die Jugendlichen schon sehr früh an, sich von ihren Eltern zu lösen. Ein Sportverein ist nicht immer die ideale Lösung: Vereine sind organisiert, und das wollen viele Jugendliche nicht. In der Clique ist man nicht allein, man ist mit Gleichaltrigen zusammen, also man hat Freizeitpartner.

Wo treffen sich die Cliquen? Diskos, Jugendheime, Schwimmbäder und vor allem Fußgängerzonen und öffentliche Plätze sind Orte, wo man sich treffen kann. Hier in der Clique kann man die Zeit verbringen, miteinander reden. Hier wird man so genommen, wie man ist.

Mit wem verbringen Jugendliche ihre Freizeit?

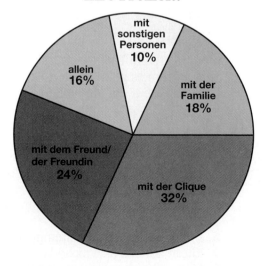

10 Für mein Notizbuch

Schreib, warum deine Eltern manchmal mit dir schimpfen, worüber sie sich freuen und wann oder warum es ab und zu Krach gibt!

Grammatik   Relative clauses

1. Sometimes you may want to say more than you can express in a simple sentence. One solution is to create a new sentence.

Ich kenne einen netten Jungen. Er ist in meinem Schwimmverein.

2. For a more fluid style you can also use a relative clause. A relative clause is introduced by a relative pronoun that refers back to the noun it replaces.

Ich kenne einen netten Jungen, **der in meinem Schwimmverein ist.**

Siehst du die Frau, **die da drüben steht?**

3. The gender of a relative pronoun depends on the word it refers back to.

Der Freundeskreis, der aus sieben Schülern besteht, trifft sich im Café.
Die Clique, die jedes Wochenende zusammenkommt, spielt gern Tennis.
Das Problem, das früher ganz groß war, ist jetzt gelöst.
Die Schüler, die jetzt von der Schule kommen, sind bei mir in der Klasse.

4. The case of the relative pronoun is determined by its *function in the relative clause* as a subject, direct object, indirect object, or object of a preposition.

Die Schüler, **die** sich immer treffen, ...	(subject)
Der Freundeskreis, **den** ich gern mag, ...	(direct object)
Die Clique, **der** ich angehöre, ...	(object of a verb taking the dative)
Die Frau, **über die** wir jetzt reden, ...	(object of an accusative preposition)
Die Leute, **mit denen** ich ausgehe, ...	(object of a dative preposition)

5. As relative clauses are dependent clauses, the conjugated verb in the relative clause is always in last position.

6. Here are the relative pronouns:

	masculine	feminine	neuter	plural
nominative	der	die	das	die
accusative	den	die	das	die
dative	dem	der	dem	denen

11 Ich verstehe mich schon ganz gut mit ihnen!

Eine Schülerin erzählt, wie ihr Verhältnis zu Eltern, Freunden und Lehrern ist. Füll die Satzlücken mit den richtigen Relativpronomen!

Mir geht's eigentlich sehr gut. Ich habe Eltern, ▭die▭ ganz vernünftig und tolerant sind. Ich habe Freunde, mit ▭denen▭ ich mich gut verstehe. Ich habe Lehrer, ▭die▭ sehr nett sind. Ein Lehrer, ▭den▭ wir alle furchtbar gern haben, trifft sich mit uns nach der Schule. Wir diskutieren über irgendein Problem, ▭das▭ einer von uns gerade hat. Meine Freundin Renate, mit ▭der▭ ich schon in der Grundschule war, ist auch immer dabei. Nach einer Diskussion, ▭die▭ besonders interessant war, sind wir in ein Café gegangen, ▭das▭ nicht weit von der Schule ist, und haben uns noch lange darüber unterhalten.

Weiter geht's!

Verhältnis zu anderen Leuten

Die deutschen Schulklassen sind längst nicht mehr so homogen wie früher. Heute gibt es nicht nur Randgruppen in den Klassen sondern auch viele ausländische Schüler. Was sagen unsere vier Gymnasiasten dazu?

INTERVIEWER Gehört ihr irgendwelchen Gruppen wie Punker, Raver oder sowas an? Kennt ihr vielleicht Leute aus solchen Gruppen?

MICHAEL Bei uns, also an unserer Schule, gibt es ein paar Punker, Grunger, Öko-Freaks und so ... , und die sondern sich schon ab von den andern. Die Punker zum Beispiel sind immer zusammen, aber sie unterhalten sich genauso mit andern Leuten wie untereinander. Und ich versteh' mich mit denen auch ganz gut, aber wir machen außerhalb der Schule nie etwas zusammen.

TANJA Ja, also ich bin in einer Raver-Clique. Wir ziehen uns gern anders an und hören Raver-Musik, aber ich habe auch Freunde, die keine Raver sind.

PHILIPP Also, was ich an den Randgruppen gut finde ist, die bringen die Interessen der anderen Schüler an die Lehrer. Manche sind eben doch aufsässig ...

SONJA Ja, und damit machen sie sich auch manchmal unbeliebt bei vielen Lehrern. Aber so mit den Punkern zum Beispiel gibt's keine Schwierigkeiten. Ich hab' da auch keine Vorurteile, und ich find' es okay, wenn man zu einer Gruppe gehört.

INTERVIEWER Wie ist euer Verhältnis zu ausländischen Schülern? Sind da welche an euerm Gymnasium?

PHILIPP Ja, wir haben schon einige Ausländer, aber fast alle von ihnen sind in Deutschland geboren und sprechen deutsch genau so gut wie wir, sogar besser als ihre Muttersprache.

TANJA Meine Schwester geht auf die Realschule, in die 7. Klasse, und da sind ein paar türkische Schüler mit ihr in der Klasse. Und die Elke, so heißt meine Schwester, sagt, daß sie meistens unter sich bleiben, also in der Pause und auch nach der Schule.

MICHAEL Die sind selber schuld daran. Sie versuchen oft gar nicht, sich in unserm Land anzupassen.

PHILIPP   Das stimmt aber so nicht! Auch wenn sie versuchen, sich anzupassen, werden sie oft von uns Deutschen nicht akzeptiert, weil sie Ausländer sind. Aber die Mädchen tun mir echt leid. Viele müssen sich hier so anziehen wie in der Türkei, ein Kopftuch tragen und so. Ihre Eltern wollen das so.

TANJA   Genau. Meine Schwester sagt zum Beispiel, daß einige Mädchen beim Sport überhaupt nicht mitmachen dürfen. Die Eltern verbieten das einfach.

SONJA   Die haben eben in der Türkei andere Sitten und Gebräuche. Ich finde, wir sollten nicht vergessen, daß sie sich nicht absichtlich absondern, sondern daß es kulturbedingt ist.

MICHAEL   Ja, klar. Aber wenn ich als Gast in einem anderen Land wohne, so muß ich doch versuchen, mich ein wenig anzupassen.

TANJA   Was würdest du denn einem ausländischen Schüler raten, der sich isoliert fühlt?

MICHAEL   Ja, ich würde ihm sagen, du, es ist wichtig, daß du mit uns Sport machst, oder vielleicht kannst du in unserer Umwelt AG mitmachen ...

TANJA   Sicher, aber denk doch mal daran, daß diese Leute oft ganz andere Interessen haben!

MICHAEL   Eine Möglichkeit wäre, mal mit ihnen was zu unternehmen, um ihre Kultur besser kennenzulernen.

SONJA   Das find' ich gut. Das machen aber viel zu wenig Deutsche. Warum organisieren wir nicht mal eine Fete für nächsten Samstag und laden Hassan und seine Clique dazu ein?

MICHAEL   Find' ich prima!

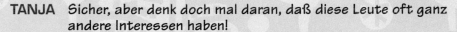

12 Stimmt oder stimmt nicht?

1. Stimmt nicht. Die Punker unterhalten sich auch mit anderen Leuten.

Wenn der Satz nicht stimmt, schreib die richtige Antwort!

1. Die Punker in dieser Schule sprechen nicht mit anderen Leuten.
2. Die Lehrer haben ab und zu Schwierigkeiten mit den Punkern.
3. Alle Ausländer an dieser Schule können nicht sehr gut Deutsch.
4. Einige ausländische Kinder dürfen sich nicht so kleiden wie die Deutschen.   4. Stimmt.
5. Die meisten ausländischen Schüler sind mit anderen Sitten und Gebräuchen aufgewachsen.   5. Stimmt.

2. Stimmt nicht. Mit den Punkern gibt es keine Schwierigkeiten.
3. Stimmt nicht. Die Ausländer an der Schule sprechen gut deutsch.

13 Was hast du verstanden?

1. Wie beschreiben die vier Schüler die Randgruppen an ihrer Schule?
2. Was ist anders bei türkischen Schülern als bei deutschen Schülern?
3. Wie könnten deutsche und ausländische Schüler vielleicht besser zusammenkommen?

ZWEITE STUFE

Giving advice; introducing another point of view; hypothesizing

WORTSCHATZ

auf deutsch erklärt

Was <u>an</u> dir <u>gut</u> <u>ist</u>, ist deine Toleranz.   Ich finde deine Toleranz gut.
Sie sind <u>anders</u>.   Sie sind nicht wie wir.
Wir <u>verbieten</u> es dir.   Wir sagen dir, daß du es nicht darfst.
Sie <u>bleiben</u> <u>unter</u> <u>sich</u>.   Sie gehen nicht mit anderen aus.
unbeliebt   Man mag ihn oder sie nicht.
der Ausländer   einer aus einem anderen Land
die Schwierigkeit   Problem

auf englisch erklärt

Sie haben andere <u>Sitten</u> und <u>Gebräuche</u>.   *They have different customs and traditions.*
Wir haben nicht die gleiche <u>Muttersprache</u>.   *We don't share the same native language.*
Das Mädchen dort <u>sondert</u> <u>sich</u> <u>von</u> den anderen <u>ab</u>.   *That girl there keeps to herself.*
Sie macht es nicht <u>absichtlich</u>.   *She doesn't do it on purpose.*
Es ist <u>kulturbedingt</u>.   *It is for cultural reasons.*
Sie gehören einer <u>Randgruppe</u> an.   *They belong to a fringe group.*
Wir <u>sind</u> ja selber <u>schuld</u> daran!   *It's our own fault!*
Aber <u>Vorurteile</u> haben, find' ich schlimm.   *But I think having prejudices is really bad.*

---

14 Hör gut zu!   For answers, see listening script on TE Interleaf.

Kalle und Hannes sind in der 10. Klasse. Es ist zu Anfang des Schuljahres, und sie sprechen über die neuen Schüler in der Klasse. Hör ihrem Gespräch gut zu und bestimme, welche von den neuen Schülern sich anpassen und welche nicht!

15 Hast du Vorurteile?

Setzt euch in kleinen Gruppen zusammen und seht euch die Illustrationen an! Überlegt euch folgendes und diskutiert darüber!

1. Was sind Vorurteile? Definiert dieses Wort auf deutsch!
2. Welche Vorurteile, die ihr kennt, gibt es gegen die Leute in den Illustrationen?
3. Welche Vorurteile gibt es gegen Leute in deiner Stadt? Welche Schwierigkeiten haben sie?
4. Was kann man diesen Leuten raten? Und den Leuten mit den Vorurteilen?

SO SAGT MAN DAS!

Giving advice; introducing another point of view

When giving advice, you could begin your sentence by saying:

Vielleicht kannst du dich anpassen.
Es ist wichtig, daß man frei von Vorurteilen bleibt.
Ich würde mit den anderen Sport machen.

When presenting another point of view, you might begin your sentence with:

Das mag schon sein, aber es ist schwerer, als du meinst.
Es kommt darauf an, ob deine Eltern es dir verbieten.
Aber denk doch mal daran, daß sie aus einer anderen Kultur kommen.
Du darfst nicht vergessen, daß jeder Mensch irgendwo Ausländer ist.

---

16 Hör gut zu!   For answers, see listening script on TE Interleaf.

Der Paul hat zu allem eine Meinung und gibt gern seinen Freunden Rat. Aber nicht alle akzeptieren blind, was er meint. Hör zu, wie er versucht, einem unglücklichen Kumpel Rat zu geben! Was ist das Problem? Welchem Rat will der Kumpel folgen, welchem nicht?

17 Was sagen die Gruppen?

Zwei verschiedene Gruppen von Schülern machen Aussagen rechts. Lies mit einer Partnerin die verschiedenen Aussagen und entscheide, wer wahrscheinlich diese Aussagen macht!

a. Beschreib diese Personen, wer sie sind, woher sie kommen, was sie machen, usw.!

b. Schreibt dann zusammen ein Gespräch, das zwischen den zwei Gruppen stattfindet! Wer gibt Rat? Wer akzeptiert ihn?

Die einen sagen:

> Ihr habt andere Sitten und Gebräuche.

> Ihr sondert euch ab.

> Ihr seid selber schuld daran, weil ihr euch nicht anpaßt.

> Ihr tut euch schwer.

Die anderen sagen:

> Wir haben Schwierigkeiten mit der Sprache.

> Wir fühlen uns isoliert.

> Ihr habt Vorurteile, weil wir anders sind.

> Wir sind hier fremd.

18 Der Markus tut sich schwer in der Schule

Markus' Freunde machen sich Sorgen um (*worry about*) ihn, weil der Lehrer meint, daß Markus Schwierigkeiten in der Schule hat. Markus selber ist natürlich unglücklich darüber. Such dir eine Partnerin! Hört euch Markus' Probleme an! Danach ratet ihm, was er tun soll!

a. Lest zuerst zusammen die Beobachtungen unten, die Markus' Lehrer gemacht hat! Spielt dann die Rollen von Lehrer und Markus! Der Lehrer sagt Markus, was er macht und nicht macht!

> BEISPIEL   **Markus, du kommst oft sehr spät in die Schule!**

> ist ziemlich aufsässig

> paßt sich nicht an

b. Dann tauscht die Rollen aus! Einer spielt die Rolle eines Freundes von Markus und gibt ihm Rat.

> BEISPIEL   **Markus, es ist wichtig, daß du pünktlich kommst.**

> sondert sich von den andern ab

> macht sich bei den Lehrern unbeliebt

SO SAGT MAN DAS!

Hypothesizing

People often make hypotheses about how things might or could be. In English, we often use an "if ..., then ..." statement to make a hypothesis. In German, „wenn ..., dann ..." statements express the same idea, although dann is often omitted.

When hypothesizing, you might say:

> **Wenn** du in einem fremden Land **wärst**, **(dann) würdest** du schon mit den andern **mitmachen**.
> **Wenn** sie Schwierigkeiten mit der Sprache **hätte**, **(dann) würde** sie sich isoliert **fühlen**.

What do you notice about the word order and punctuation in these statements?

19 Hör gut zu! For answers, see listening script on TE Interleaf.

Kerstin und Gertrud sprechen über ihre nächste Reise, die sie in den amerikanischen Westen machen wollen. Hör gut zu, wie sie über ihre Pläne spekulieren! Was werden sie bestimmt machen? Was bleibt spekulativ?

20 Wenn ich reich wäre ...

Füll die Satzlücken mit Formen von **hätte**, **wäre** und **würde**. Verbinde dann die Sätze, und paß auf die Wortstellung auf!

Wenn meine junge Schwester jetzt erwachsen *wäre*,
Wenn wir Krach mit unsren Eltern *hätten*,
Wenn er mein Kumpel *wäre*,
Wenn ich eine schlechte Note in Mathe *hätte*,

wir *würden* ruhig darüber reden.
wir *würden* zum Fußballspiel gehen.
mein Lehrer *würde* schimpfen.
sie *würde* auch Auto fahren dürfen.

Ein wenig *Grammatik*

When making hypotheses, German speakers use two very common verbs to shorten a phrase. As you already know, **hätte** means the same as **würde** plus **haben**.

> **Wenn ich Angst haben würde, (dann) würde ich nicht hingehen.**
> *or*
> **Wenn ich Angst hätte, ...**

Another is **wäre**, which is the same as **würde** plus **sein**.

> **Ich würde lieber in München sein.**
> *or*
> **Ich wäre lieber in München.**

The endings for **wäre** are the same as for **hätte** and **würde**.

21 Als Austauschschüler in Deutschland

Setzt euch in Gruppen zusammen und sagt, was ihr tun würdet, wenn ihr in einem anderen Land wärt, zum Beispiel als Austauschschüler an einem Gymnasium in Deutschland!

BEISPIEL   DU   **Was würdest du tun, wenn du als Austauschschüler an einem deutschen Gymnasium wärst?**

PARTNER 1   **Also, wenn ich an einem deutschen Gymnasium wäre, würde ich mich mit meinen Klassenkameraden unterhalten. Und du?**

PARTNER 2   **Wenn ich in Deutschland wäre, ...**

Grammatik The genitive case

You have learned to use phrases with **von** to show possession. For example: **Das ist das Auto von meinem Vater.** You can also use the genitive case to show possession: **Das ist das Auto meines Vaters.**

How would you say that in English? Notice also the difference between English and German word order.

Definite and indefinite articles as well as possessives have the following forms in the genitive case:

Das ist das Auto ...

	masculine	*feminine*	*neuter*
def. article	**des Jungen**	**der Chefin**	**des Geschäfts**
indef. article	**eines Freundes**	**einer Frau**	**eines Mädchens**
possessive	**meines Vaters**	**meiner Mutter**	**meines Kindes**

Definite articles and possessives have the same form in the plural as the feminine singular.

**Das sind die Autos der Schüler der dreizehnten Klasse,
und hier sind die Mofas meiner jüngeren Schüler.**

The following applies to the genitive:

• Most masculine nouns that end in **-e** add **-n**.
• Masculine and neuter nouns of one syllable add **-es**.
• Masculine and neuter nouns with two or more syllables add **-s**.
• Adjectives add **-en** regardless of the gender and number of the noun.

Prepositional phrases with **von** are more common in spoken than in written German. For example, **Das Haus von meinem Onkel ...,** is more common than **Das Haus meines Onkels ...** There are also some fixed expressions with the genitive which you will learn as you become more familiar with the language.

22 Die Arbeit dieses Lehrers wird zu viel!

Schreib die folgenden Sätze um, und verwende dabei Genitivformen!
1. Die Schüler vom Einstein-Gymnasium sind sehr gescheit (*clever*).
2. Die Leute von der letzten Klasse sind jetzt unsere Freunde.
3. Die Ziele von diesen Cliquen gefallen mir überhaupt nicht.
4. Die Mitglieder von diesem Schwimmverein treffen sich morgen.
5. Die Interessen, die ein Freund hat, können ganz anders sein.
6. Die Vorurteile, die unsere Schüler haben, sind oft groß.
7. Das Deutsch, das der türkische Schüler spricht, ist sehr gut.
8. Der Lehrer, den meine Schwester hat, ist aus Deutschland.

1. Die Schüler des Einstein-Gymnasiums sind sehr gescheit.
2. Die Leute der letzten Klasse sind jetzt unsere Freunde.
3. Die Ziele dieser Cliquen gefallen mir überhaupt nicht.
4. Die Mitglieder dieses Schwimmvereins treffen sich morgen.
5. Die Interessen eines Freundes können ganz anders sein.
6. Die Vorurteile unserer Schüler sind oft groß.
7. Das Deutsch des türkischen Schülers ist sehr gut.
8. Der Lehrer meiner Schwester ist aus Deutschland.

23 Für mein Notizbuch

Schreib in dein Notizbuch, wie du dich mit deinen Klassenkameraden verstehst! Hast du Vorurteile gegen Schüler, die anders sind als du? Kennst du Schüler, die sich isoliert fühlen? Hast du Kontakte zu ihnen?

Die verschiedenen Bildungswege in Deutschland

Helga, Klaus und Hassan sind im gleichen Alter und wohnen in derselben Nachbarschaft. Sie kennen sich schon Jahre lang. Als Kinder haben sie dieselbe Grundschule besucht, bis sie 10 Jahre alt waren. Danach hat jeder einen anderen Bildungsweg genommen. Jetzt sind sie 18 Jahre alt und sehen einander selten.

Hassan lernt jetzt für das Abitur. Er muß sehr gute Noten bekommen, weil er Psychologie an einer Universität studieren will.

Helga ist auch sehr fleißig und hat neulich ihre Lehre (*apprenticeship*) im Kaufhof als Verkäuferin begonnen. Sie geht zweimal die Woche in die Berufsschule; an den restlichen drei Tagen wird sie in den verschiedenen Abteilungen des Kaufhauses ausgebildet. Sie hat vor, eines Tages Abteilungsleiterin zu werden.

Klaus besucht jetzt die Fachoberschule und will danach eine Lehre als Krankenpfleger machen. Deshalb möchte er auch nach der Lehre nicht zur Bundeswehr, sondern Zivildienst in einem Krankenhaus machen.

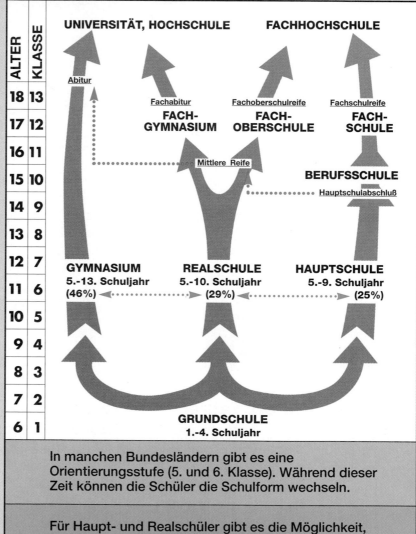

SCHEMATISCHE GLIEDERUNG DES BILDUNGSWESENS

In manchen Bundesländern gibt es eine Orientierungsstufe (5. und 6. Klasse). Während dieser Zeit können die Schüler die Schulform wechseln.

Für Haupt- und Realschüler gibt es die Möglichkeit, auf ein Gymnasium zu gehen, wenn sie beim Schulabschluß überdurchschnittliche Noten haben.

A. 1. Schau dir die Tabelle an!

2. Welche Bildungswege sind Hassan, Klaus und Helga gegangen? Was fällt dir am deutschen Schulsystem auf? Diskutier über die Hauptmerkmale mit einem Klassenkameraden!

3. Wodurch unterscheidet sich das deutsche Schulsystem von dem amerikanischen System? Mach eine ähnliche Tabelle vom amerikanischen System.

B. Vergleiche das deutsche Schulsystem mit dem amerikanischen Schulsystem! Was findest du besser oder schlechter?

As a teenager you have a lot of difficult decisions to make. Good advice can often help you make these decisions, and one place to get it is from advice columns. In this activity, you will ask for advice in a letter to an advice column.

Lieber Herr Weißalles!

Denk an ein Problem, das du hast oder das vielleicht deutsche Schüler haben! Schreib einen kurzen Brief an eine Zeitung, um Rat für dieses Problem zu holen!

A. Vorbereiten

1. Schreib das Problem auf, wofür du Rat suchst! Dann schreib alle Ideen auf, die mit diesem Problem zusammenhängen!
2. Denk an den Zweck (*purpose*) deines Briefes! Warum schreibst du den Brief? Was willst du damit erreichen? Wähl Ideen von der Liste aus, die diesen Zweck unterstützen und unterstreiche sie!

B. Ausführen

Verwende jetzt die Punkte, die du gewählt hast, und beschreib das Problem in einem kurzen Brief an Herrn Weißalles! Erfinde einen Namen und einen Ort für den Absender (dich)!

C. Überarbeiten

1. Lies deinen Brief einem Partner vor! Hat er dein Problem gut verstanden? Frag deinen Partner, welche Punkte geholfen haben, dein Problem klarzumachen, und streiche unnötige Punkte durch! Besprich die Wirkung der Sprache in deinem Brief!
2. Wenn dein Brief viele kurze Sätze enthält, mach ihn fließender mit Nebensätzen!
3. Wenn du mit dem Brief zufrieden bist, lies ihn noch einmal durch! Hast du alles richtig buchstabiert? Hast du Nebensätze durch Kommas getrennt?
4. Jetzt schreib deinen Brief sehr ordentlich in Spalten ab (du kannst auch einen Computer benutzen), damit er aussieht, wie ein Brief in einer Zeitung!

SCHREIBTIP

Determining the purpose
Before you begin to write, carefully consider the purpose of what you are writing. You may be writing to express yourself, to entertain, to persuade someone of something, to get or to give information, or for many other reasons. In fact, some writing may have more than one purpose. In a personal letter, for example, you may want to convey information but also entertain a friend. Thinking about the purpose(s) of your writing helps to clarify who your audience is and what tone of language you should choose.

Ein Tisch ist ein Tisch
von Peter Bichsel

Ich will von einem alten Mann erzählen, von einem Mann, der kein Wort mehr sagt, ein müdes Gesicht hat, zu müd zum Lächeln und zu müd, um böse zu sein. Er wohnt in einer kleinen Stadt, am Ende der Straße, nahe der Kreuzung. Es lohnt sich fast nicht, ihn zu beschreiben, kaum etwas unterscheidet ihn von andern. Er trägt einen grauen Hut, graue Hosen, einen grauen Rock und im Winter den langen grauen Mantel, und er hat einen dünnen Hals, dessen Haut trocken und runzelig ist, die weißen Hemdkragen sind ihm viel zu weit.

Im obersten Stock des Hauses hat er sein Zimmer, vielleicht war er verheiratet und hatte Kinder, vielleicht wohnte er früher in einer andern Stadt. Bestimmt war er einmal ein Kind, aber das war zu einer Zeit, wo die Kinder wie Erwachsene angezogen waren. Man sieht sie so im Fotoalbum der Großmutter. In seinem Zimmer sind zwei Stühle, ein Tisch, ein Teppich, ein Bett und ein Schrank. Auf einem kleinen Tisch steht ein Wecker, daneben liegen alte Zeitungen und das Fotoalbum, an der Wand hängen ein Spiegel und ein Bild.

Der alte Mann machte morgens einen Spaziergang und nachmittags einen Spaziergang, sprach ein paar Worte mit seinem Nachbarn, und abends saß er an seinem Tisch.

Das änderte sich nie, auch sonntags war das so. Und wenn der Mann am Tisch saß, hörte er den Wecker ticken, immer den Wecker ticken.

Dann gab es einmal einen besonderen Tag, einen Tag mit Sonne, nicht zu heiß, nicht zu kalt, mit Vogelgezwitscher, mit freundlichen Leuten, mit Kindern, die spielten — und das Besondere war, daß das alles dem Mann plötzlich gefiel.

Er lächelte.

„Jetzt wird sich alles ändern", dachte er. Er öffnete den obersten Hemdknopf, nahm den Hut in die Hand, beschleunigte seinen Gang, wippte sogar beim Gehen ein bißchen in den Knien und freute sich. Er kam in seine Straße, nickte den Kindern zu, ging vor sein Haus, stieg die Treppe hoch, nahm die Schlüssel aus der Tasche, freute sich über ihr Klingeln und schloß sein Zimmer auf.

Aber im Zimmer war alles gleich, ein Tisch, zwei Stühle, ein Bett. Und wie er sich hinsetzte, hörte er wieder das Ticken, und alle Freude war vorbei, denn nichts änderte sich.

Und den Mann überkam eine große Wut.

LESETRICK

Determining the main idea of a story Focusing on the main idea (or ideas) of a short story, rather than trying to understand every word, is a strategy that will make reading German more manageable and enjoyable. In a short story, the main idea is rarely stated explicitly, but rather illustrated through a series of events. As you read, ask yourself from time to time what point or statement the author is making.

Getting Started   For answers, see TE Interleaf.

1. Read the title and the first four paragraphs. Answer the following questions using words and phrases from the story.
   a. Wer ist die Hauptfigur?
   b. Wo wohnt er?
   c. Wie sieht er aus?
   d. Was macht der Mann an einem gewöhlichen Tag?

Er sah im Spiegel sein Gesicht rot anlaufen, sah, wie er die Augen zukniff; dann verkrampfte er seine Hände zu Fäusten, hob sie und schlug mit ihnen auf die Tischplatte, erst nur einen Schlag, dann noch einen, und dann begann er auf den Tisch zu trommeln und schrie dazu immer wieder:

„Es muß sich ändern, es muß sich ändern!"

Und man hörte den Wecker nicht mehr. Und dann begannen seine Hände zu schmerzen, seine Stimme versagte, dann hörte man den Wecker wieder, und nichts änderte sich. „Immer derselbe Tisch", sagte der Mann, „dieselben Stühle, das Bett, das Bild. Und dem Tisch sage ich Tisch, dem Bild sage ich Bild, das Bett heißt Bett, und den Stuhl nennt man Stuhl. Warum denn eigentlich?" Die Franzosen sagen dem Bett „li", dem Tisch „tabl", nennen das Bild „tablo" und den Stuhl „schäs", und sie verstehen sich. Und die Chinesen verstehen sich auch.

„Weshalb heißt das Bett nicht Bild", dachte der Mann und lächelte, dann lachte er, lachte, bis die Nachbarn an die Wand klopften und „Ruhe" riefen.

„Jetzt ändert es sich", rief er, und er sagte von nun an dem Bett „Bild".

„Ich bin müde, ich will ins Bild", sagte er, und morgens blieb er oft lange im Bild liegen und überlegte, wie er nun dem Stuhl sagen wolle, und er nannte den Stuhl „Wecker".

Er stand also auf, zog sich an, setzte sich auf den Wecker und stützte die Arme auf den Tisch. Aber der Tisch hieß jetzt nicht mehr Tisch, er hieß jetzt Teppich. Am Morgen verließ also der Mann das Bild, zog sich an, setzte sich an den Teppich auf den Wecker und überlegte, wem er wie sagen könnte.

Dem **Bett** sagte er Bild.
Dem **Tisch** sagte er Teppich.
Dem **Stuhl** sagte er Wecker.
Der **Zeitung** sagte er Bett.
Dem **Spiegel** sagte er Stuhl.
Dem **Wecker** sagte er Fotoalbum.
Dem **Schrank** sagte er Zeitung.
Dem **Teppich** sagte er Schrank.
Dem **Bild** sagte er Tisch.
Und dem **Fotoalbum** sagte er Spiegel.

e. Wer erzählt die Geschichte? Wie weißt du das?

2. Versuche jetzt, das Zimmer des alten Mannes zu zeichnen!

3. Read to the end of the sixth paragraph. Explain what happened one day. What was that day like? How was it different from any other day?

4. Read to the end of the eighth paragraph. How does this part of the story explain the title?

5. Continue reading to the end. Outline the plot by listing the main events of the story. In your opinion, what is the main idea?

Also:

Am Morgen blieb der alte Mann lange im Bild liegen, um neun läutete das Fotoalbum, der Mann stand auf und stellte sich auf den Schrank, damit er nicht an die Füße fror, dann nahm er seine Kleider aus der Zeitung, zog sich an, schaute in den Stuhl an der Wand, setzte sich dann auf den Wecker an den Teppich und blätterte den Spiegel durch, bis er den Tisch seiner Mutter fand.

Der Mann fand das lustig, und er übte den ganzen Tag und prägte sich die neuen Wörter ein. Jetzt wurde alles umbenannt. Er war jetzt kein Mann mehr, sondern ein Fuß, und der Fuß war ein Morgen und der Morgen ein Mann.

Jetzt könnt ihr die Geschichte selbst weiterschreiben. Und dann könnt ihr, so wie es der Mann machte, auch die andern Wörter austauschen:

läuten heißt stellen,
frieren heißt schauen,
liegen heißt läuten,
stehen heißt frieren,
stellen heißt blättern

So daß es dann heißt:

Am Mann blieb der alte Fuß lange im Bild läuten, um neun stellte das Fotoalbum, der Fuß fror auf und blätterte sich auf den Schrank, damit er nicht an die Morgen schaute.

Der alte Mann kaufte sich blaue Schulhefte und schrieb sie mit den neuen Wörtern voll, und er hatte viel zu tun damit, und man sah ihn nur noch selten auf der Straße.

Dann lernte er für alle Dinge die neuen Bezeichnungen und vergaß dabei mehr und mehr die richtigen. Er hatte jetzt eine neue Sprache, die ihm ganz allein gehörte.

Hie und da träumte er schon in der neuen Sprache, und dann übersetzte er die Lieder aus seiner Schulzeit in seine Sprache, und er sang sie leise vor sich hin. Aber bald fiel ihm auch das Übersetzen schwer, er hatte seine alte Sprache fast vergessen, und er mußte die richtigen Wörter in seinen blauen Heften suchen. Und es machte ihm Angst, mit den Leuten zu sprechen. Er mußte lange nachdenken, wie die Leute den Dingen sagen.

A Closer Look

6. Read the story again more carefully and, as you read, try to determine the main idea of each paragraph or each group of paragraphs. Based on the main ideas, divide the story into sections and supply a title for each section.

7. Scan to find the first use of **dann** in the story. What purpose does **dann** serve at that point? What does the word signal in the unfolding of the story? What about **jetzt** and **aber?** How do these words help to organize the story?

8. Rarely does an author want just to relate a sequence of events. Usually a more important idea is the cause or the effect of the events. What caused the man to rename everything? What effect did this have in the short run? And in the long run? Which sentences from the story

Seinem *Bild* sagen die Leute **Bett**.
Seinem *Teppich* sagen die Leute **Tisch**.
Seinem *Wecker* sagen die Leute **Stuhl**.
Seinem *Bett* sagen die Leute **Zeitung**.
Seinem *Stuhl* sagen die Leute **Spiegel**.
Seinem *Fotoalbum* sagen die Leute **Wecker**.
Seiner *Zeitung* sagen die Leute **Schrank**.
Seinem *Schrank* sagen die Leute **Teppich**.
Seinem *Tisch* sagen die Leute **Bild**.
Seinem *Spiegel* sagen die Leute **Fotoalbum**.

Und es kam so weit, daß der Mann lachen mußte, wenn er die Leute reden hörte.

Er mußte lachen, wenn er hörte, wie jemand sagte: »Jetzt regnet es schon zwei Monate lang.« Oder wenn jemand sagte: »Ich habe einen Onkel in Amerika.«

Er mußte lachen, weil er all das nicht verstand.

Aber eine lustige Geschichte ist das nicht. Sie hat traurig angefangen und hört traurig auf.

Der alte Mann im grauen Mantel konnte die Leute nicht mehr verstehen, das war nicht so schlimm.

Viel schlimmer war, sie konnten ihn nicht mehr verstehen.

Und deshalb sagte er nichts mehr.

Er schwieg,
sprach nur noch mit sich selbst,
grüßte nicht einmal mehr.

support your answers?

9. Look again at what you wrote about the main idea and revise your statement if necessary.

10. Discuss with your classmates some of the funny parts of the story and some of the sad parts. How do the funny parts actually make the story sad?

11. Think again about the results of the man's actions in the long run. What is the author saying about the nature and purpose of language?

12. Compare and contrast the points made about language in Bichsel's "Ein Tisch ist ein Tisch" with "Unsere heutige Jugend und ihre Sprüche" (pp. 70-71). What similarities or differences do you see between what teenagers do and what the old man does with language, especially in terms of consequences?

ANWENDUNG

 1 Manche Leute sind tolerant, manche nicht. Hör zu, was folgende Leute sagen! Wie würdest du jede Aussage bezeichnen — tolerant oder nicht tolerant? 1. For answers, see listening script on TE Interleaf.

 2 Schreib deine Meinung zu den folgenden Fragen! Diskutiere mit deinen Klassenkameraden das, was du geschrieben hast!

    a. Redet man mit einem Freund genauso wie mit einer Freundin?

    b. Ist es gut, viele Freunde oder Freundinnen zu haben?

    c. Was ist der Unterschied zwischen Freunden und Bekannten?

    d. Kennst du jemanden, der wirklich ganz anders ist als du und ganz andere Interessen hat? Sind Freundschaften zwischen Leuten möglich, die ganz verschieden sind?

 3 Was für Probleme haben diese Leute unten? Schreib die wichtigsten Punkte jedes Leserbriefes in dein Notizheft! Wähle dann einen Leserbrief aus und erzähle anhand deiner Notizen, was darin steht!

Ratgeber-Ecke

Mein Mann und ich stehen vor einem großen Problem. Unsere Heike ist jetzt 16 Jahre alt, und sie möchte mehr Taschengeld haben. Sie will auch am Abend länger wegbleiben. Sie meint, die andern in der Clique dürfen das auch. Das ist nun alles gut und schön, und wir freuen uns auch darüber. Aber etwas stört uns: unsere Tochter will weiterhin wie ein kleines Mädchen behandelt werden. Ich muß ihr Zimmer aufräumen, ihr Bett machen, ihre Wäsche waschen, ihre Schuhe putzen, und so weiter. Und sie benimmt sich wie eine kleine Prinzessin. Und mein Mann macht das mit. Er lacht sogar darüber. Aber ich finde das nicht richtig.
Regine Pfaff (38)

Wir sind verzweifelt! Unser Ältester hat vor fast zwei Jahren den Hauptschulabschluß nicht geschafft. Er hat dann doch noch eine Lehrstelle bekommen, ist aber nach einem halben Jahr abgehauen. Dann hat er als Hilfsarbeiter gearbeitet, wir glauben in einer Gärtnerei. Vor zwei Wochen, als Gerd 18 wurde, ist er ausgezogen. Wir wissen nicht wohin. Ein früherer Klassenkamerad hat Gerd jetzt einmal im Stadtpark gesehen — mit Punkern! Wir können es nicht glauben, daß unser Gerd mit Punkern herumläuft. Was haben wir falsch gemacht? Sind wir schuld an allem? Wir glauben, daß wir unser Bestes getan haben: wir haben uns früher mit Gerd immer verstanden. Jetzt haben wir keine Ruhe. Was können wir tun? Wir möchten unsern Jungen wiederhaben.
Elli und Hans Bauer

Vor zwei Monaten habe ich einen netten Jungen kennengelernt. Er ist drei Jahre älter als ich, und er ist Türke. Er sieht phantastisch aus. Seitdem das meine Eltern wissen, gibt es zu Hause wieder Streitigkeiten, auch um kleine Dinge. Dabei helfe ich zu Hause, halte mein Zimmer in Ordnung, gehe einkaufen. Nun, vor einer Woche bin ich erst um 22 Uhr nach Hause gekommen, und seitdem verbieten mir die Eltern, abends auszugehen. Achmed ist nett, so lustig — besonders wenn er deutsch spricht und Fehler macht! Ich sollte nächste Woche seine Eltern kennenlernen. Seine Schwester und seine Mutter hab' ich schon einmal in der Stadt gesehen: echte Türkinnen, Kleider über den Hosen und mit Kopftuch und so. Ich hatte mich schon auf den Besuch gefreut. Was soll ich tun? Soll ich mit Achmed abbrechen, damit zu Hause wieder Friede wird?
Julia (16)

4 Was meinst du dazu?

    a. Was nervt Frau Pfaff wirklich?

    b. Was ist Elli und Hans Bauers Problem?

    c. Was stört Julias Eltern? Was ist wohl der eigentliche Grund?

s. benehmen (wie)	*to behave (like)*
verzweifelt	*desperate*
ausziehen	*to move out*
die Ruhe	*peace and quiet*
abbrechen mit	*to break off with*
der Friede	*peace*

5 Bildet drei Gruppen! Jede Gruppe hat die Aufgabe, einen der drei Leserbriefe zu beantworten.

    a. Überlegt euch zuerst, welche Ratschläge ihr geben wollt! Benutzt dabei die Redemittel, die ihr in dieser Lektion gelernt habt!

    b. Formuliert dann eure Antwort! Seid höflich!

    c. Wählt dann einen in der Gruppe aus, der eure Antwort den andern vorliest!

    d. Wer hat die beste Antwort geschrieben? Diskutiert darüber!

6 # R O L L E N S P I E L

Such dir einen Partner! Zuerst interviewst du deinen Partner, dann interviewt dein Partner dich. Wenn ihr wollt, könnt ihr euer Interview auf eine Tonkassette aufnehmen. Hier sind die Interviewfragen:

1. Wie ist dein Verhältnis zu deinen Eltern? Geschwistern?

2. Mit wem unterhältst du dich am liebsten?

3. Worüber redet ihr am meisten?

4. Wofür interessiert ihr euch gemeinsam?

5. Mit wem verstehst du dich am besten?

6. Zu wem hast du keinen Kontakt? Warum nicht?

Es ist wichtig, daß euer Interview nicht nur aus Fragen und Antworten besteht, sondern daß es ein richtiges, natürliches Interview wird. Gebraucht deshalb zum Beispiel die Ausdrücke, die man benutzt, wenn man etwas nicht ganz versteht oder wenn man mehr Information braucht!

Can you agree?
(p. 85)

1 How would you agree with the following statements?
  a. Vorurteile zu haben, find' ich schlimm.   E.g.: Ganz meine Meinung.
  b. Bei uns ist der Streitpunkt das Aufräumen.   E.g.: Bei mir ist es auch so.
  c. Bevor wir ausgehen, müssen wir zuerst unsere Hausaufgaben erledigen.   E.g.: Da geb' ich dir recht.

Can you give advice?
(p. 91)

2 How would you give advice to a friend if he or she said the following things to you?   E.g.: Vielleicht kannst du mit ihnen darüber reden.
  a. Ich versteh' mich nicht mit meinen Eltern.
  b. Ich fühle mich isoliert.   E.g.: Ich würde mit den anderen ausgehen.
  c. Ich bekomme immer schlechte Noten. Ich glaub', der Lehrer mag mich nicht.   E.g.: Es ist wichtig, daß du mehr für die Schule lernst.

Can you introduce another point of view? (p. 91)

3 How would you introduce another point of view if someone said the following things to you?   a. E.g.: Das mag schon sein, aber es ist nicht so einfach.
  a. Ausländer sollen versuchen, sich in unserm Land anzupassen.
  b. Meine Eltern verstehen mich überhaupt nicht.   b. E.g.: Du darfst nicht vergessen, daß sie ganz anders denken als du.
  c. Ich finde die Punker zu aufsässig.
    c. E.g.: Es kommt darauf an, was sie machen.

Can you hypothesize?
(p. 92)

4 How would you make a hypothesis about what you would do
  a. if you were President of the United States?   a. E.g.: Wenn ich Präsident der Vereinigten Staaten wäre, (dann) würde ich mehr für die Umwelt tun.
  b. if you had ten million dollars?
  c. if you lived in Germany?   b. E.g.: Wenn ich zehn Millionen Dollar hätte, (dann) würde ich eine Weltreise machen.
    c. E.g.: Wenn ich in Deutschland leben würde, (dann) würde ich die deutsche Sprache viel schneller lernen.

ERSTE STUFE

WORDS USEFUL FOR TALK-ING ABOUT RELATIONSHIPS

Wir kommen gut miteinander aus. *We get along well with one another.*

Ich verstehe mich super mit ihr. *She and I really get along*

Wir richten uns nach euch. *We'll do whatever you want to do.*

Worum geht es? *What's it about?*

Das kann ich nicht leiden! *I can't stand that!*

der Kumpel, - *buddy*

der Freundeskreis, -e *circle of friends*
das Verhältnis *relationship*
der Krach *quarrel*
der Streit *quarrel, argument*
die Streitigkeit, -en *quarrel*
der Streitpunkt, -e *point of contention*
die Toleranz *tolerance*
gleich *immediately*
reden *to speak*
schimpfen *to scold*
angehören (sep, dat) *to belong to*
erwachsen sein *to be grown up*

AGREEING

Da geb' ich dir recht. *I agree with you about that.*
Ganz meine Meinung. *I completely agree.*
Bei mir ist es auch so. *That's the way it is with me, too.*

ORDINAL NUMBERS

erst- *first*
zweit- *second*
dritt- *third*

ZWEITE STUFE

GIVING ADVICE

Vielleicht kannst du ... *Perhaps you can ...*
Es ist wichtig, daß ... *It's important that ...*
Ich würde (ihr) sagen, ... *I would tell (her) ...*

INTRODUCING ANOTHER POINT OF VIEW

Das mag schon sein, aber ... *That may well be, but ...*
Es kommt darauf an, ob ... *It depends on whether ...*
Aber denk doch mal daran, daß ... *But just consider that ...*
Du darfst nicht vergessen, daß ... *You mustn't forget that ...*

HYPOTHESIZING

Wenn du ... wärst, dann würdest du ... *If you were ..., then you would ...*

Wenn sie ... hätte, würde sie ... *If she had ..., she would ...*

GETTING ALONG WITH OTHERS

Was an dir gut ist, ist deine Freundlichkeit. *What I like about you is your friendliness.*
die Sitten und Gebräuche (pl) *customs and habits*
das Vorurteil, -e *prejudice*
die Schwierigkeit, -en *difficulty*
die Randgruppe, -n *fringe group*
Ausländer(in), -/nen *foreigner*
geboren *born*
die Muttersprache, -n *native language*
anders *different*
aufsässig *rebellious*
kulturbedingt *for cultural reasons*
unbeliebt *unpopular*

untereinander *among one another*
unter sich bleiben *to keep to oneselves*
s. absondern von (sep) *to separate oneself from*
die Fete, -n *party*
raten (dat) *to give advice*
verbieten *to forbid*
schuld sein an etwas (dat) *to be at fault*
absichtlich *on purpose*
die Möglichkeit, -en *possibility*
außerhalb (gen) *outside of*
nicht nur ... sondern auch *not only ... but also*

Kapitel 5: Rechte und Pflichten

	FUNCTIONS	GRAMMAR	CULTURE	RE-ENTRY
Los geht's! pp. 106-107	Mit achtzehn darf man alles. Oder? *p. 106*			
Erste Stufe pp. 108-111	•Talking about what is possible, *p. 109* •Saying what you would have liked to do, *p. 110*	•The **könnte**-forms, *p. 109* •Further uses of **wäre** and **hätte**, *p. 110*	•Artikel 38/2. Absatz des Grundgesetzes, *p. 108* •Cartoon, *p. 108*	•The modal **können**, *p. 109* •**Hätte**-forms and **wäre**-forms, *p. 110* •**Weil**-clauses, *p. 111* •Giving reasons, *p. 111*
Weiter geht's! pp. 112-113	Die Wehrpflicht: dafür oder dagegen? *p. 112*			
Zweite Stufe pp. 115-119	•Saying that something is going on right now, *p. 115* •Reporting past events, *p. 116* •Expressing surprise, relief, and resignation, *p. 118*	•Use of verbs as neuter nouns, *p. 116* •The past tense of modals (the imperfect), *p. 117*	•Landeskunde: Gleichberechtigung im deutschen Militär? *p. 114* •Ein wenig Landeskunde: Wehrpflicht, *p. 116*	•The modals **können, wollen,** and **müssen,** *p. 116* •Reporting past events, *p. 116* •Expressing surprise, *p. 118* •Expressing resignation, *p. 118* •Expressing hearsay, *p. 118*

Zum Lesen pp.120-122
Nie wieder!
Reading Strategy: Determining purpose

Zum Schreiben p.123
Lerne Land und Leute durch ein Interview kennen!
Writing Strategy: Asking questions to gather ideas

Review pp. 124-127
•Anwendung, *p. 124*
•Kann ich's wirklich? *p. 126*
•Wortschatz, *p. 127*

Assessment Options

Stufe Quizzes
•*Chapter Resources,* Book 2
 Erste Stufe, Quiz 5-1
 Zweite Stufe, Quiz 5-2
•*Assessment Items, Audiocassette* 7 B

Kapitel 5 Chapter Test
•*Chapter Resources,* Book 2
•*Assessment Guide,* Speaking Test
•*Assessment Items, Audiocassette* 7 B

Test Generator, Kapitel 5

Chapter Overview

RESOURCES Print	RESOURCES Audiovisual
	Textbook Audiocassette 3 A
Practice and Activity Book	
	Textbook Audiocassette 3 A
Practice and Activity Book *Chapter Resources*, Book 2 • Communicative Activity 5-1 • Communicative Activity 5-2 • Additional Listening Activity 5-1 • Additional Listening Activity 5-2 • Additional Listening Activity 5-3 • Student Response Forms • Realia 5-1 • Situation Card 5-1 • Teaching Transparency Master 5-1 • Quiz 5-1 *Video Guide*	*Additional Listening Activities, Audiocassette* 9 B *Additional Listening Activities, Audiocassette* 9 B *Additional Listening Activities, Audiocassette* 9 B *Teaching Transparency* 5-1 *Assessment Items, Audiocassette* 7 B *Video Program*, Videocassette 1
	Textbook Audiocassette 3 A
Practice and Activity Book	
	Textbook Audiocassette 3 A
Practice and Activity Book *Chapter Resources*, Book 2 • Communicative Activity 5-3 • Communicative Activity 5-4 • Additional Listening Activity 5-4 • Additional Listening Activity 5-5 • Additional Listening Activity 5-6 • Student Response Forms • Realia 5-2 • Situation Card 5-2 • Teaching Transparency Master 5-2 • Quiz 5-2 *Video Guide*	*Additional Listening Activities, Audiocassette* 9 B *Additional Listening Activities, Audiocassette* 9 B *Additional Listening Activities, Audiocassette* 9 B *Teaching Transparency* 5-2 *Assessment Items, Audiocassette* 7 B *Video Program*, Videocassette 1
Chapter Resources, Book 2 • Realia 5-3 • Situation Card 5-3 *Video Guide*	*Video Program*, Videocassette 1

Alternative Assessment

• Performance Assessment
Teacher's Edition
Erste Stufe, p. 103K
Zweite Stufe, p. 103N

• Portfolio Assessment
Written: **Anwendung,** Activity 2, *Pupil's Edition,* p. 124;
Assessment Guide, p. 18
Oral: **Anwendung,** Activity 8, *Pupil's Edition,* p. 125;
Assessment Guide, p. 18
• **Notizbuch,** *Pupil's Edition,* pp. 111, 119

Kapitel 5: Rechte und Pflichten
Textbook Listening Activities Scripts

For Student Response Forms, see *Chapter Resources,* Book 2, pp. 82-85.

Erste Stufe

Activity 3, p. 109

1. Also, ich bin wahnsinnig froh, endlich 18 zu sein. Jetzt kann ich nämlich Verträge unterschreiben und bin natürlich auch selbst dafür verantwortlich, sie einzuhalten. Also, den ersten Vertrag, den ich selbst unterschrieben hab', war der Kaufvertrag mit dem Möbelhaus Wellenroth. Ich wollte nämlich unbedingt dieses kleine, schicke, schwarze Ledersofa für mein Zimmer haben. Meine Eltern wollten es mir nicht kaufen, weil sie meinten, ich würde ja bestimmt sowieso bald ausziehen, um in einer anderen Stadt zu studieren, oder so. Ja, und da haben sie gesagt, ich bräuchte in meinem Zimmer kein neues Sofa. Na ja, eigentlich haben sie ja auch recht. Aber ich fand das Sofa nun mal total scharf, und es hatte auch so einen günstigen Preis. Also habe ich es mir gekauft, und jetzt steht es bei mir im Zimmer. Das heißt, bezahlt habe ich es natürlich noch nicht ganz, weil ich ja so viel Geld auf einmal gar nicht hab'! Also, laut Vertrag muß ich jetzt jeden Monat 75 Mark ans Möbelhaus Wellenroth bezahlen, zwölf Monate lang. Tja, und dann gehört das Sofa mir! Und wenn ich mal von zu Hause ausziehe, dann nehm ich's natürlich mit! Das einzig Blöde ist, ich hab' jetzt halt nicht mehr so viel von meinem Taschengeld übrig!

2. Ja, also, was sich bei mir auf jeden Fall verändert hat, ist, daß ich am Wochenende länger ausbleibe. Früher mußte ich immer um zehn zu Hause sein. Seit ich 18 bin, bleibe ich halt auf den Partys so lange, wie es mir Spaß macht. Gestern bin ich bis kurz vor Mitternacht mit Freunden unterwegs gewesen. Wir waren halt auf 'nem Rockkonzert. Die Stimmung war super! Die Band hat eine Zugabe nach der anderen gespielt, einfach sagenhaft! Tja, da ist es halt fast Mitternacht geworden. Meine Eltern waren ja nicht sehr erfreut, als ich so spät heimkam. Aber was wollen sie machen — ich bin ja jetzt erwachsen. Na ja, ich weiß, daß es auch eine Menge Pflichten gibt, aber warum soll ich nicht auch mal meine Rechte genießen? Ich finde es toll, 18 zu sein.

3. Mir ist es sehr wichtig, daß ich jetzt wählen darf. Ich bin ja schon seit ein paar Jahren politisch aktiv. Ich bin Mitglied in der Jugendabteilung einer Partei seit meinem sechzehnten Lebensjahr. Letzten Monat bin ich zur Vorsitzenden gewählt worden. Außerdem bin ich Mitarbeiterin beim „Politischen Forum". Das ist eine Zeitung für Schüler und Jugendliche, die sich politisch informieren wollen. Tja, und natürlich schaue ich mir täglich die Nachrichten im Fernsehen an und lese die Tageszeitung. Wenn ich im Sommer mein Abi mache, melde ich mich an der Uni in Bochum an, um Politik und Soziologie zu studieren. Tja, also, wie gesagt, ich bin echt stolz darauf, daß ich im Oktober zum ersten Mal einen Stimmzettel ausfüllen darf! Auch wenn man nicht so politisch engagiert ist wie ich, finde ich es doch wichtig, wählen zu gehen. Für mich ist jede politische Wahl Recht und Pflicht zugleich!

4. Peter und ich, wir haben vor kurzem geheiratet. Als meine Eltern von unseren Hochzeitsplänen erfuhren, haben sie zuerst gemeint, wir sollen noch etwas warten. Sie fanden, wir sind noch zu jung. Aber wir sind ja beide volljährig und haben das selbst entschieden. Na ja, wir haben ja auch nicht Hals über Kopf geheiratet, sondern erst mal die Schule fertiggemacht. Peter und ich, wir kennen uns doch schon so lange. Wir sind schon ein Jahr lang, bevor wir geheiratet haben, miteinander ausgegangen. Meine Eltern haben sich auch Sorgen über unsere finanzielle Situation gemacht. Zuerst hatte ich auch große Angst davor, aber eigentlich klappt alles ganz gut. Peter macht zur Zeit Zivildienst in einem Krankenhaus, und ich habe eine Ausbildung als Fotografin angefangen.

5. Ich nehme seit zwei Monaten Fahrstunden bei der Fahrschule Drombusch. Die Fahrstunden und die theoretische Ausbildung sind ja nicht gerade billig, aber man muß diese gründliche Ausbildung auf jeden Fall haben. Die Prüfungen sind nämlich ganz schön streng! Wenn man nicht hundertprozentig aufpaßt, lassen manche Prüfer einen glatt durchrasseln! Mein Fahrlehrer ist echt okay. Er sagt immer ganz genau, worauf ich achten muß und läßt mich alles wiederholen, was ich beim Autofahren falsch mache. Für die Theorie muß man halt ziemlich viel büffeln und eine Menge auswendig lernen. Ich habe mich in vier Wochen zur Prüfung angemeldet. Hoffentlich klappt alles. Ich kann's kaum erwarten!

Answers to Activity 3
1. d 2. e 3. c 4. b 5. a

Activity 4, p. 109

MARTINA Du, Tobias, hast du dich schon um einen Studienplatz beworben, oder suchst du dir einen Job, wenn wir mit der Schule fertig sind?

TOBIAS Ja also, ich hab' mich schon vor ein paar Wochen bei der ZVS beworben. Ich möchte am liebsten Anglistik in Göttingen studieren. Weißt du, Martina, wenn ich nach Göttingen ziehe, suche ich mir als allererstes eine eigene Wohnung.

MARTINA Wieso das denn? Du könntest dir doch im Studentenwohnheim ein Zimmer nehmen.

TOBIAS Was? Du machst wohl Witze! Also, ich hab' keine Lust, in einem kleinen quadratischen Kasten zu hocken und die Küche und das Badezimmer mit zig Leuten zu teilen!

MARTINA Ja und? Das ist doch nicht so schlimm! Wenn ich einen Studienplatz in Berlin bekomme, dann will ich auf jeden Fall im Studentenwohnheim wohnen.

TOBIAS Nee, also das ist nichts für mich. Mensch, Martina, ich versteh' gar nicht, daß du so heiß darauf bist.

MARTINA Überleg doch mal, Tobias! Wenn man im Studentenwohnheim wohnt, lernt man doch am schnellsten neue Leute kennen.

CHRISTA Ja, die Martina hat recht! Ich finde es wichtig, mit den anderen Studenten zusammenzusein, besonders, wenn man doch sonst ganz fremd in der Stadt ist.

TOBIAS Ach Christa! Du hast gut reden. Du ziehst doch gar nicht woanders hin! Du bleibst doch nach der Schule hier in Düsseldorf, oder?

CHRISTA Ja, stimmt! Ich will auf jeden Fall hier bleiben. Ich werde mich bei der Firma Kallenbroich um einen Ausbildungsplatz zum Industriekaufmann bewerben.

SCRIPTS

MARTINA Spitze! Dann kannst du ja zu Hause wohnen bleiben und sparst dir das Geld für die Miete!

CHRISTA Ja! Und stellt euch mal vor! An der Straßenbahnhaltestelle vor unserem Haus hält die Linie 5, und die fährt direkt bis vor das Werkstor von Kallenbroichs! Ist das nicht super? Ich brauch' noch nicht mal umsteigen.

TOBIAS Mensch! Was heißt hier umsteigen? Ich werde mir bestimmt ein Auto kaufen, wenn ich nach Göttingen ziehe!

MARTINA Ja, aber dafür mußt du erst mal Geld verdienen! Studieren und dabei das große Geld machen, das geht ja wohl nicht alles auf einmal!

TOBIAS Wieso nicht? Ich werd' mir ganz locker neben meinem Studium Geld verdienen. Jobs für Studenten gibt's doch überall! Du, Christa, du kaufst dir doch bestimmt auch ein eigenes Auto, sobald du Geld verdienst, oder?

CHRISTA Nee, du, ganz bestimmt nicht. Das wäre zu schade ums Geld! Ich komm' prima überall mit dem Bus, der Bahn oder dem Rad hin. Ich werd' mein Geld für Reisen ausgeben.

MARTINA So? Wohin willst du denn?

CHRISTA Also, wenn ich Urlaub habe, fahr' ich mit der Bahn nach Frankreich. Ich will unbedingt mal nach Paris. Das habe ich mir schon immer gewünscht!

Answers to Activity 4

Tobias: Anglistik in Göttingen studieren; sich eine Wohnung suchen; sich ein Auto kaufen; neben dem Studium Geld verdienen

Martina: Studienplatz in Berlin bekommen; im Studentenwohnheim wohnen

Christa: um einen Ausbildungsplatz zum Industriekaufmann bewerben; zu Hause wohnen bleiben; Reise nach Paris machen

Tobias hat am meisten vor

Zweite Stufe
Activity 14, p. 117

— Ja guten Tag, Herr Heckel! Ich hab' Sie ja schon lange nicht mehr gesehen. Wie geht's denn heute?

— Ach, guten Tag, Frau Erhard! Ich hab' Sie fast gar nicht erkannt! Haben Sie eine neue Frisur?

— Ja. Das ist aber nett, daß Sie das bemerken! Ich komm' gerade vom Friseur. Stellen Sie sich vor, die ganze Prozedur hat fast zwei Stunden gedauert. Jetzt ist mir doch fast dadurch der ganze Vormittag verlorengegangen. Und dabei hab' ich noch so viel zu erledigen!

— Was haben Sie denn alles noch zu tun?

— Ach, wissen Sie, wir bekommen heute abend Besuch. Wir haben Freunde aus dem Kegelclub zum Abendessen eingeladen. Na, und ich muß noch alles aus dem Supermarkt besorgen. Mein Mann kocht seine Spezialität, Eisbein mit Sauerkraut und Semmelknödeln! Ach, zum Metzger muß ich ja auch noch, das hätte ich fast vergessen!

— Wenn ich das gewußt hätte! Ich komm' gerade vom Metzger. Zu dumm! Da hätte ich Ihnen doch das Fleisch mitbringen können. Und im Supermarkt war ich auch schon.

— Ja, also ich muß mich wirklich beeilen, damit ich alles noch rechtzeitig schaffe. Zum Glück habe ich heute früh schon die Fenster geputzt und Staub gesaugt. Meine Güte, heute ist aber wirklich ein hektischer Tag für mich. Und das dauert mal wieder so lange am Schalter.

— Frau Erhard, ich lasse Sie gern vor! Ich hab's nicht so eilig.

— Dankeschön, Herr Heckel! Wie gut, daß Sie schon alles besorgt haben.

— Na ja, alles hab' ich auch noch nicht erledigt. Ich muß noch zum Bäcker. Aber das kann warten. Ich wollte für heute nachmittag Kuchen besorgen. Meine Frau hat Geburtstag.

— Ach, dann richten Sie ihr doch bitte schöne Grüße aus und gratulieren ihr von mir!

— Ja, danke! Mach' ich gern.

— Ach! Endlich bin ich an der Reihe. Ich muß doch Geld abheben, weil ich gleich noch den Kindern neue Schuhe kaufen gehe, wenn sie aus der Schule kommen.

Answers to Activity 14

Answers will vary. E.g.: Heute vormittag habe ich ein Gespräch zwischen zwei Leuten in der Bank mitangehört. Die Frau ist gerade beim Friseur gewesen usw.

Activity 17, p. 118

INGO Du, Paul, ich bin eigentlich ganz froh, daß ich am 1. Juli zum Bund gehe.

PAUL Ach, seit wann das denn? Vor ein paar Monaten hast du aber noch ganz anders geredet, Ingo.

INGO Ach weißt du, ich bin ja jetzt bald mit meiner Lehre fertig, und ich hatte überhaupt keine festen Pläne für die Zeit danach.

PAUL Wieso? Kannst du denn nicht nach deiner Lehre dort weiter arbeiten?

INGO Nee, du! Die bauen gerade Personal ab, und keiner von uns Lehrlingen kann bleiben. Aber so schlecht find' ich das gar nicht.

PAUL Ach, deswegen willst du erst mal zum Bund.

INGO Ja, genau. Jetzt kann ich mir für 'ne Welle in Ruhe überlegen, was ich nach dem Bund machen will. Außerdem komme ich in eine technische Einheit, da lerne ich bestimmt etwas, was mir später beruflich hilft. Und du, Paul?

PAUL Mensch, Ingo, so froh wie du bin ich ja nicht. Weißt du, vorgestern, aus heiterem Himmel hab' ich plötzlich diesen Brief bekommen — „Kreiswehrersatzamt" stand da drauf. Ich war vielleicht überrascht, sag' ich dir!

INGO Und, wann mußt du zur Musterung?

PAUL Ich hab' in zwei Wochen einen Termin. Der Bund will mich haben, ich soll schon am ersten März eingezogen werden.

INGO Was? So früh schon?

PAUL Ja! Ich kann dir sagen, mir paßt das überhaupt nicht in den Kram. Ich wollte eigentlich noch jobben, und dann im Herbst mit dem Studium anfangen.

INGO Ja, das ist natürlich jetzt blöd für dich.

PAUL Ja, find' ich auch. Irgendwie habe ich gedacht, die ziehen mich erst später ein. Daß es so schnell gehen kann, das ist mir neu. Na, wie steht's bei dir, Alfred?

ALFRED Ich hab' auch einen Einberufungsbefehl bekommen. Am ersten Juli muß ich nach Ingolstadt zu einer Panzereinheit. Na ja, was soll's? Ich wollte eigentlich im Herbst Soziologie studieren, aber ich wußte, daß der Bund mir vielleicht dazwischenkommt. Jetzt muß die Uni eben ein paar Semester warten. Da kann man nichts machen. Und du? Was machst du jetzt, Gerd?

GERD Ich habe mich jetzt endgültig entschieden, Zivildienst zu machen und bin wirklich froh, daß das jetzt klar ist. Ich hab' auch schon eine Stelle im Städtischen Krankenhaus in Erlangen.

ALFRED Ja, Gerd, du hast dir ja lange hin und her überlegt, ob du zum Bund gehen sollst oder lieber Zivildienst machen sollst.

GERD Ja, stimmt! Ich muß schon sagen, ich habe mir die ganze Sache lange überlegt, aber ich kann einfach nicht mit der Waffe dienen. Daß alles mit der Zivi-Stelle so schnell geklappt hat, ist schon eine Riesenerleichterung.

PAUL Ich find's super, daß du deinen Zivildienst im Krankenhaus machst. Da kannst du doch bestimmt 'ne Menge lernen. Du willst doch Krankenpfleger werden, oder?

GERD Ja, auf jeden Fall! Ich glaube, nach dem Zivildienst mache ich auf jeden Fall 'ne Lehre als Krankenpfleger.

Answers to Activity 17

Überraschung: Paul war überrascht, als er einen Brief vom Bund bekommen hat, denn er wollte lieber zuerst studieren. Paul hat gedacht, daß er erst später eingezogen wird.

Resignation: Alfred wollte im Herbst anfangen zu studieren, hat aber gewußt, daß er vielleicht zuerst zum Bund muß.

Erleichterung: Ingo ist froh, daß er zum Bund geht, denn er hat noch keine festen Pläne, wenn er mit der Lehre fertig ist. Ingo meint, daß er beim Bund bestimmt etwas lernt, was ihm beruflich hilft. Gerd macht Zivildienst und ist erleichtert, daß er so schnell eine Stelle bekommen hat.

Anwendung
Activity 1, p. 124

— Ja, so eine Überraschung! Die Dagmar! Schön, daß du mich wieder mal besuchst.

— Hallo, Opa! Wie geht's? Du, ich will dich für ein Schulprojekt interviewen.

— Was? Mich interviewen? Ja, was willst du denn wissen, Kind?

— Also, wir machen eine Ausstellung mit dem Thema „Unsere Großeltern als Teenager". Jeder sammelt Kommentare von seinen Großeltern, und wir stellen dann Plakate, Collagen und Illustrationen her.

— Und wo macht ihr die Ausstellung, Dagmar?

— Die Ausstellung wird dann am „Tag der offenen Tür" gezeigt. In zwei Wochen ist es soweit.

— Na, da bin ich ja mal gespannt. Also, fang mal ruhig an mit deinen Fragen!

— Also, findest du, daß du es als Teenager leichter oder schwerer hattest, als die Teenager der neunziger Jahre?

— Ja, ich bin überzeugt, daß wir es in vielen Dingen schwerer hatten. Zunächst mal waren wir ja eine große Familie mit sechs Kindern. Da hatten wir nicht viel Geld übrig.

— Woran hast du denn gemerkt, daß das Geld bei euch zu Hause knapp war? Hast du weniger Taschengeld bekommen?

— Taschengeld? Taschengeld haben wir Kinder gar nicht bekommen! Du, damals war das nicht so wie heute, wenn du sagst: „Mutti, ich will die CD haben, oder Papa, gib mir mal Geld, ich will ins Kino!" Von wegen! Geschenke haben wir nur zum Geburtstag und zu Weihnachten bekommen. Und sonst nicht!

— Aber du hast mir doch mal erzählt, daß du so gern als Junge ins Kino gegangen bist. Woher hattest du denn das Geld?

— Tja, das Geld hab' ich mir erst verdienen müssen!

— Welche Jobs hast du denn so gemacht?

— Also, bei uns hatte jedes Kind eine Aufgabe zu Hause! Ich habe die Schuhe von der ganzen Familie geputzt. Für jedes Paar Schuhe habe ich von meinem Vater fünf Pfennig bekommen. Dann hab' ich morgens vor der Schule Milch und Zeitungen ausgetragen. Na ja, und das Geld hab' ich mir dann zusammengespart.

— Wofür hast du dein Geld denn noch ausgegeben?

— Hmm, laß mich mal überlegen. Ja, einmal, da war Tanz im Dorf. Da wollte ich so eine fesche Weste haben, wie sie in der Stadt modern waren. Weißt du, ich wollte doch der Elfriede aus meiner Klasse imponieren. Nun ja, aber die Weste war natürlich viel zu teuer. Da hab' ich in der Stadt den Stoff gekauft, und die Mutter hat die Weste dann für mich genäht!

— Mensch, Opi, das find' ich ja stark! Ich wußte gar nicht, daß du dich für Mode interessierst! Hat deine Mutter auch sonst alle Kleidung für euch genäht?

— Nein, dafür hatte sie gar keine Zeit. Die ältesten haben, wenn es nötig war, neue Sachen bekommen, aber wir Kleinen mußten immer die Klamotten und Schuhe der größeren Geschwister auftragen.

— Ach übrigens, Opa? Hast du denn mit deiner neuen Weste großen Eindruck auf die Elfriede aus deiner Klasse gemacht? Bist du dann mit ihr ausgegangen?

— [lacht] Was du dir so denkst! Na ja, getanzt habe ich an jenem Abend schon ein paar Mal mit ihr. Aber ausgegangen bin ich nicht mit ihr. Damals mußte man sich doch gleich mit dem Mädel verloben, wenn man mit ihr gehen wollte. Und dazu war ich ja noch viel zu jung, damals! Ach ja, damals ...

— Du, Opa, erzähl mir doch jetzt mal bitte was aus deiner Schulzeit! Hast du manchmal blau gemacht?

— Na, von wegen! Sowas konnten wir uns damals gar nicht leisten! Die Schule war ja viel strenger als heutzutage. Wir mußten noch viel auswendig lernen — Gedichte, Lieder, historische und geographische Daten. Ich kann dir heute noch alle Nebenflüsse der Donau aufzählen! Und den „Erlkönig" kann ich dir auch auswendig aufsagen!

— Ja ja, Opa. Ich glaub's dir ja! Wie waren denn die Lehrer so? Hattest du manchmal Streit mit denen?

— Ach was, wenn da mal in der Klasse einer von uns aus der Reihe getanzt ist, gab's direkt 'nen Tadel! Und du darfst auch nicht vergessen, damals war es den Lehrern noch erlaubt, die Schüler mit dem Stock auf die Finger zu hauen!

— Ach du meine Güte! Na ja, das gibt es ja heutzutage zum Glück schon lange nicht mehr!

— Ja, und die Lehrer waren auch strenger — der alte Oberlehrer Breitenbach sagte immer, „Eiserne Disziplin ist wichtig!" Weißt du, Dagmar, ich glaube, ihr habt jetzt viel mehr Freiheiten als wir damals.

— Ja, das glaub' ich auch. Mensch, danke Opi, für das klasse Interview. Du mußt unbedingt zum „Tag der offenen Tür" kommen und dir unsere Ausstellung anschauen.

— Na klar, das ist doch Ehrensache!

Answers to Activity 1

Großvater sagt, daß er es als Teenager schwerer hatte als die Teenager heutzutage; seine Familie hatte sechs Kinder und nicht viel Geld übrig; er hat kein Taschengeld bekommen; er hat Geschenke nur zum Geburtstag und zu Weihnachten bekommen; er ist gern ins Kino gegangen; er hat sein eigenes Geld verdient; hat die Schuhe von der Familie geputzt; er ist zum Tanz ins Dorf gegangen; er konnte sich keine modische Weste leisten, weil sie zu teuer war; er hat von seinem Geld Stoff gekauft; seine Mutter hat die Weste für ihn genäht; nur die älteren Geschwister haben manchmal neue Sachen bekommen; die jüngeren Kinder mußten die Klamotten und Schuhe der älteren auftragen; hatte keine Freundin, weil er zu jung war, um sich zu verloben; die Schule war strenger; er mußte vieles auswendig lernen; die Lehrer durften damals die Schüler mit dem Stock auf die Finger hauen.

Kapitel 5: Rechte und Pflichten
Projects and Games

PROJECT

In this project students will create an illustrated recruitment advertisement for either the **Bundeswehr** *or the* **Zivildienst**. *Students can work individually or with a partner.*

Materials Students may need poster board, paper, pens, and subject related materials such as photos, brochures, or magazine cutouts.

Suggested Topics
Bundeswehr
Zivildienst

Suggested Sequence

1. Individuals or pairs of students decide on the topic for the recruitment advertisement and make an outline showing how the project will be organized.
2. Students gather resources and prepare a convincing visual presentation. The project should include facts and data from the **Landeskunde** on pp. 114 and 116 of this chapter. Drawings, slogans, photos, or other eye catching materials should also be incorporated into the poster.
3. Students present their posters and give a brief (1 minute) statement to the rest of the class to convince them to join the service, whether it is the **Bundeswehr** or the **Zivildienst**.

Grading the Project

Suggested point distribution (total = 100 points)

Originality and Design	40
Language usage	30
Oral presentation / Sales pitch	30

GAME

Seeschlacht

This game allows students to review new words and phrases with a competitive and familiar game.

Preparation Prepare a grid on a sheet of paper that you copy for students. Also prepare a list of questions that are based on the **Wortschatz** on p. 127.

	A	B	C	D	E	F	G	H	I	J	K	L	M	N
1														
2														
3							U							
4							U							
5												Z		
6	S	S	S							K	Z			
7								K	Z					
8														
9				K										
10				K										
11						F	F	F	F					
12														

Procedure Divide the class into equally sized teams. Each team of students gets a sheet of paper with a grid. Teams then hide the following five ships on the grid: **das Schlachtschiff, der Flugzeugträger, der Kreuzer, der Zerstörer,** and **das U-Boot.** Each ship takes up a specific number of spaces on the grid, which you can change according to the size of the grid. Write the verbs **getroffen, verfehlt,** and **gesunken** on the board for teams to use during the game. Ask a member of the first team a question from the list you prepared ahead of time. If he or she answers correctly, he or she gets to guess a position of an opposing team's ship using German letters and numbers. The first team to knock out all of the other teams' ships wins.

NOTE: In a large class this game can be played in pairs. Each partner gets a copy of the grid, a separate list of questions, and the answers.

Kapitel 5: Rechte und Pflichten
Lesson Plans, pages 104-127

Teacher Note

Before you begin the chapter, you may want to preview the *Video Program* and consult the *Video Guide*. Suggestions for integrating the video into each chapter are given in the *Video Guide* and in the chapter interleaf. Activity masters for video selections can be found in the *Video Guide*.

*U*sing the Chapter Opener,
pp. 104-105

Motivating Activity

Go around the classroom and ask students how they are involved in their community. Do they take an interest or an active role in local politics, concerns, or interest groups? Are other members of their families involved? What are some of their concerns?

Teaching Suggestion

Read the introductory paragraph (**Mit dem Erreichen des 18. Lebensjahres ...**) to the class, stopping after each sentence and simplifying the style by paraphrasing. (Example: **Wenn man 18 wird, wird man volljährig. Man ist dann erwachsen. Ein Erwachsener hat bestimmte Rechte. Ein Recht ist, was man tun darf. Ein Erwachsener hat auch bestimmte Pflichten. Eine Pflicht ist, was man tun soll.**)

Thinking Critically

① **Drawing Inferences** Ask students to look at the photo and the different banners. What do the photos say about these teenagers' interests and concerns?

Teaching Suggestion

② After students have looked at this photo and read the accompanying caption, ask them where they typically hang out with their friends and what they usually talk about. Make a list of some of the topics. (**Wo trefft ihr euch gewöhnlich mit eurer Clique oder euren Freunden? Über welche Themen diskutiert ihr normalerweise?**)

Background Information

③ In Germany, all men are required to serve twelve months of compulsory military service; however, Article 4 of the **Grundgesetz** (*constitution*) states that men can be exempt from the service if it is against their conscience to make use of arms. In such a case the **Kriegsdienstverweigerer** (*conscientious objector*) must perform alternate service which is referred to as **Zivildienst**.

③ The Red Cross dates back to 1863 when it was established by the Swiss humanitarian Henri Dunant. Since 1986, it has officially been referred to as the International Movement of the Red Cross and Red Crescent. It is also organized into independent affiliates in most countries. (Examples: the American Red Cross and **das Deutsche Rote Kreuz**)

Community Link

Ask students to find out what services the Red Cross provides in their community. (Examples: training, maintaining blood banks, relief services)

For Individual Needs

③ **Visual Learners** Ask students to take a closer look at the photo. Have them describe the scene in German in as much detail as possible.

Focusing on Outcomes

To get students to focus on the chapter objectives, ask them which rights they consider most important when they reach legal maturity. Then preview the learning outcomes listed on p. 105. **NOTE:** These outcomes are modeled in **Los geht's!** (pp. 106-107) and **Weiter geht's!** (pp. 112-113) and evaluated in **Kann ich's wirklich?** (p. 126).

Teaching Los geht's!

pp. 106-107

Resources for Los geht's!

- *Textbook Audiocassette* 3 A
- *Practice and Activity Book*

Teacher Note

Los geht's! is recorded on audiocassette.

Los geht's! Summary

In **Mit achtzehn darf man alles. Oder?**, Julia, Angie, Stefan, and Martin talk about the rights and obligations that come with being and adult. The following student outcomes listed on p. 105 are modeled in the interviews: talking about what is possible and saying what you would have liked to do.

Motivating Activity

Have students make a list of things that will change for them when they reach legal maturity.

Teaching Suggestion

Play the tape of the interviews and have students follow along in the text. Stop the tape after each response and ask detailed questions to check for understanding. Explain new vocabulary in German through paraphrasing and synonyms. Be sure to clarify the time frames in which the interviews operate. Martin: present - past; Angie: present - past - present; Stefan: present - future; Julia: present. Finally, work with the last part of the interview in which all four German teenagers participate. Again, stop after each major point (costs, length of training, and comparison of the two driver education systems) and ask some quick questions to check comprehension.

 For Individual Needs

Challenge Ask students to make up a couple of sentences in German that summarize the main ideas of the first three interviews.(**Martin: Mit 18 darf man Auto fahren, aber sonst hat sich nicht viel geändert. Angie: Mit 18 darf man seine eigene Entschuldigung schreiben, aber man sollte die Schule nicht schwänzen. Jeder Tag ist wichtig. Stefan: Mit 18 kann man wählen, aber man sollte sich vorher gut informieren.**)

 Cooperative Learning

1 Have students work in groups of three to read the responses of Martin, Angie, and Stefan. Students should take on the role of group writer, proofreader, or reporter as they complete the activity. While students work in groups, go around the classroom to help clarify unfamiliar phrases or answer questions they might have. Upon completion, call on groups to discuss their notes.

 For Individual Needs

2 Visual Learners Make a chart on the board to compare and contrast the requirements for getting a driver's license in the United States and in Germany for Part 3 of this activity.

 Multicultural Connection

2 Have students find out what requirements and fees exist for getting a driver's license in other countries. If possible, obtain samples or copies of foreign licenses to compare. What information do all provide? Which ones differ slightly?

Closure

Ask students to take a moment to think about how they would complete the following statement. **Volljährigkeit wird für mich sehr wichtig sein, denn ...**

LOS GEHT'S!

ERSTE STUFE

*T*eaching Erste Stufe!
pp. 108-111

Resources for Erste Stufe

Practice and Activity Book
Chapter Resources, Book 2
- Communicative Activities 5-1, 5-2
- Additional Listening Activities 5-1, 5-2, 5-3
- Student Response Forms
- Realia 5-1
- Situation Card 5-1
- Teaching Transparency Master 5-1
- Quiz 5-1

Audiocassette Program
- *Textbook Audiocassette 3* A
- *Additional Listening Activities, Audiocassette 9* B
- *Assessment Items, Audiocassette 7* B

Video Program, Videocassette 1
Video Guide

▶ *page 108*

MOTIVATE
Teaching Suggestion

Ask students to imagine the day that they reach legal adulthood. How would they like that day to unfold? (**Wie stellst du dir den Tag vor, an dem du volljährig wirst?**)

TEACH

Video Program

In the video clip **In einer Fahrschule,** trainees in a driver's education class talk about their experiences. See *Video Guide* for suggestions.

Culture Note

The German **Grundgesetz** (*basic law or constitution*) came into effect on May 23, 1949.

Thinking Critically

Comparing and Contrasting Go over the list of changes that occur as a result of reaching legal adulthood (18) in Germany (See "**Was bedeutet das?**"). Then ask students to compare the required age in the United States for each of the nine points listed.

PRESENTATION: Wortschatz

After introducing the new vocabulary to the class, assign each word or phrase to individual students. Give them a few moments to come up with a brief scenario in which the word or phrase could be used. Have several students share their word or phrase with the class.
Example: **Ich schwänze heute; Prüfung:**
    Ich glaube, ich schwänze heute lieber nicht, denn wir haben eine wichtige Matheprüfung.

▶ *page 109*

 ### For Individual Needs

3 A Slower Pace Before listening to the audiocassette, go over Pictures a through e and ask students to describe each picture briefly in German.

3 Challenge After students have listened to the five narrations and completed the matching exercise, ask them to listen again, this time noting two or three things about each person and thus telling more about the situation pictured. (Example: for Picture c: **Jutta ist froh, daß sie jetzt wählen darf. Sie ist politisch sehr aktiv, ist Mitglied einer Partei. Sie arbeitet für eine politische Zeitung. Sie sieht sich täglich die Nachrichten an und ...**)

Teaching Suggestion

4 Replay the tape several times and have students list all the plans that the three German students talk about.

For Individual Needs

4 Challenge Have students listen for the reasons the three German teenagers give for their choices. They should tell why they want to do certain things and not others.

PRESENTATION: So sagt man das!

• Ask students to look back at the first caption in the chapter opener on p. 104: **"Du könntest dich wirklich ein bißchen für Politik interessieren!"** Why are the four students saying this to the student on the right, and what does it indicate about their interest in politics? Can students think of alternate ways to state this sentence? Examples:
Es ist wichtig, sich für Politik zu interessieren.
Du solltest mehr Interesse an Politik haben!

• Go over the explanation in the function box with students.

PRESENTATION: Ein wenig Grammatik

After introducing the **könnte**-forms, ask students to say what the people in Pictures a through e of Activity 3 will be able to do when they turn 18. Using the same pictures, ask students to give advice to the people shown.

▶ *page 110*

For Individual Needs

6 A Slower Pace Do the following activity in class before beginning Activity 6. Ask for suggestions and have students take notes. If students have trouble coming up with ideas, ask questions. Examples:
Kannst du jetzt ...
  jeden Tag arbeiten gehen?
  mit Freunden in den Ferien wegfahren?
  ein Auto haben?
After the discussion, have students write their own lists with reasons why they were not able or not allowed to do these various things.

PRESENTATION: So sagt man das!

• Review with students the previously introduced function of hypothesizing in which students used the forms **wäre** and **hätte**.

• Provide students with practice by having them complete the following statements:
Ich wäre letzten Sommer gerne ..., aber ...
Ich hätte gestern abend ..., aber ...

7 For Additional Practice

For further practice with this construction, have students give the answer using the **ich**-form and then have the next student report what the first student said. (Example: **Er/Sie hätte gern ...**) A third student could continue. (Example: **Wir hätten auch gern ...**)

▶ *page 111*

Teaching Suggestion

10 To give students time to think about these questions, you may want to assign them for homework.

Reteaching: The *könnte*-forms

Ask pairs of students to scan the two Location Openers (**die neuen Bundesländer** and **Würzburg**) for things they could do if they were to visit these places. Also what would they suggest that others go and see during a visit? Example:
Wir könnten uns das Bachhaus in Eisenach anschauen, denn das ist heute ein Museum.

CLOSE

 ## Multicultural Connection

Ask students to interview foreign exchange students, other foreign language teachers, or anybody else they know from a different country about how reaching legal adulthood is important to a young person of that country. What is the legal age in that country and in which way does it change a young person's status? Discuss students' findings in class.

Focusing on Outcomes

Refer students back to the learning outcomes listed on p. 105. They should recognize that they now know how to talk about what is possible and to say what they would have liked to do.

ASSESS

- **Performance Assessment** Ask students to think about three things they would have liked to do during the previous school year but didn't get to do. Call on several students to reflect upon those plans. (**Denkt zurück an das letzte Schuljahr! Welche drei Dinge hättet ihr gern gemacht, aber ihr seid nie dazu gekommen? Woran hat das gelegen?**)

- Quiz 5-1, *Chapter Resources,* Book 2

*T*eaching Weiter geht's!
pp. 112-113

> ### Resources for Weiter geht's!
>
> - *Textbook Audiocassette* 3 A
> - *Practice and Activity Book*

Teacher Note

Weiter geht's! is recorded on audiocassette.

Weiter geht's! Summary

In **Die Wehrpflicht: dafür oder dagegen?,** four young people are asked to talk about their opinions of military service. The following student outcomes listed on p. 105 are modeled in the interviews: saying that something is going on right now; reporting past events; and expressing surprise, relief, and resignation.

Motivating Activity

Ask students about their opinions of compulsory military service. Is it a good idea? In the United States military service is voluntary. Does the U.S. system work? Should women be allowed to fight in combat? Have students list some advantages and disadvantages to being in the armed forces.

Teaching Suggestion

Divide the interview into three sections. Play the audiocassette for each section as students read along in the text. Then ask questions to check for understanding and explain any unfamiliar terms in German, using synonyms or paraphrasing. Put the key terms on the chalkboard or a transparency to aid comprehension.
Examples: **Wehrpflicht, Wehrdienst, Bundeswehr (Bund), Streitkräfte, vermeiden, einziehen**

For Individual Needs

12 Auditory Learners Prepare a blank chart like the one suggested for this activity and make a copy for each student (see example below). Go over the activity with students, then have them listen to the continuation of the interview at least twice. As students listen, they should take notes and fill in the chart as best they can.

**Die Wehrpflicht: dafür oder dagegen?
Was sagen die folgenden Schüler dazu?**

Stefan	Martin	Angie	Julia
Wehrdienst soll freiwillig sein	Bundeswehr ist sinnlos	Streitkräfte sind nicht mehr wichtig	ist froh, daß sie als Mädchen nicht wehrpflichtig ist

Discuss the opinions of the four German teenagers with students.

Closure

Ask students if they know anyone who has served or is still serving in the United States military. Do they know what those people specifically did or do in the service and for how long they served or will serve?

▶ *page 114*

PRESENTATION: Landeskunde

Teaching Suggestion

You might want to introduce the following vocabulary to help students understand the text.

die Gleichberechtigung: eine Frau darf das gleiche machen wie ein Mann und hat die gleichen Rechte

der Dienst: die Arbeit

der Bundestagsabgeordnete: ein Politiker

verbieten: etwas nicht erlauben

die Streitkräfte: Truppen, das ganze Militär

die Kaserne: wo die Soldaten wohnen

der Stahlhelm: was Soldaten auf dem Kopf tragen

Ausschluß: Teilnahmeverbot

widersprechen: eine andere Meinung haben

der öffentliche Dienst: ein Beruf, in dem man für die Regierung arbeitet

Aufstiegsmöglichkeit: die Möglichkeit, schnell nach oben zu kommen, eine bessere Position zu bekommen oder beruflich Karriere zu machen

Teaching Suggestions

• After introducing the additional vocabulary, remind students of the reading strategy of scanning a text for specific information. (Level 1, Chapter 2, p. 58)

• Before reading the text, have students preview Questions 1-5 to determine what they should be looking for as they read. If they understand what is being asked, they can identify key information more easily.

Group Work

Divide the class into seven groups and assign each group a question. Ask each group to read the text to determine the answer to their question. For Questions 6 and 7, have the group discuss their opinions and come to a consensus. Call on all seven groups to share their answers or ideas with the rest of the class.

Teacher Note

Mention to your students that the **Landeskunde** will also be included in Quiz 5-2 given at the end of the **Zweite Stufe.**

Teaching Zweite Stufe
pp. 115-119

Resources for Zweite Stufe

Practice and Activity Book
Chapter Resources, Book 2
 • Communicative Activities 5-3, 5-4
 • Additional Listening Activities 5-4, 5-5, 5-6
 • Student Response Forms
 • Realia 5-2
 • Situation Card 5-2
 • Teaching Transparency Master 5-2
 • Quiz 5-2
Audiocassette Program
 • *Textbook Audiocassette* 3 A
 • *Additional Listening Activities, Audiocassette* 9 B
 • *Assessment Items, Audiocassette* 7 B
Video Program, Videocassette 1
Video Guide

▶ *page 115*

MOTIVATE
Teaching Suggestion

Ask students about their opinions of computer or video games that depict war themes. (**Was haltet ihr von Computer- und Videospielen, die mit Krieg zu tun haben? Begründet eure Meinung!**)

TEACH
Teaching Suggestion

Discuss with students any current conflicts around the world that involve military forces. What are the most recent images that they can recall? (**Gibt es zur Zeit Krisen, Konflikte oder Kriege in der Welt, an denen Militärstreitkräfte teilnehmen? Welche Bilder kommen dir in den Sinn?**)

PRESENTATION: Wortschatz

- To introduce the new vocabulary to students you could collect materials (posters, flyers, etc.) from military recruitment offices or the ROTC that show the various vocabulary items. Describe the realia, incorporating as much of the new vocabulary as possible.
- If you want students to produce the new vocabulary, ask either/or questions such as **Ist das ein Laster oder ein Panzer?** as well as open-ended questions such as: **Was machen diese jungen Leute beim Wehrdienst?**

PRESENTATION: So sagt man das!

- Have students point out the specific word(s) in each of the three sentences that express the idea of current action.
- Adverbs such as **gerade** or **eben** are often used as well as the prepositions **an** or **bei** together with a nominalized infinitive. (Example: **am** and **beim Diskutieren**) Have students create additional sentences from phrases you give them. (Examples: **Briefe schreiben, das Zimmer aufräumen, das Essen kochen, Geschenke kaufen**)

▶ *page 116*

❖ For Individual Needs

13 Kinesthetic Learners As a variation, have students take turns acting out what Martin is doing. Ask the class to describe what is being acted out using the expressions listed in the **So sagt man das!** box on p. 115. Have students do the same for additional actions such as **Hausaufgaben machen, den Koffer packen, den Tisch decken, Schuhe putzen, sich anziehen,** and **sich schminken.**

PRESENTATION: Ein wenig Landeskunde

After students have read the **ein wenig Landeskunde** segment, ask them to work with a partner to come up with at least three questions to check for comprehension of the text. Then have pairs direct their questions to other students. Examples:
Wie lange dauert die Wehrpflicht in der BRD?
Wie lange dauert der Grundwehrdienst in Österreich?
Woraus bestehen die Streitkräfte der Bundeswehr?

Video Program

In the video clip **Zivis in Würzburg,** four young men discuss their duties as community service workers. See *Video Guide* for suggestions.

PRESENTATION: So sagt man das!

After students have recognized that the past tense is expressed with a simple past tense form of the modal together with an infinitive, refer back to the pictures in Activity 13 and have students restate what Martin had to do.
Example: **Martin mußte zu Hause Staub saugen.**
Now have students imagine what he wanted to do but couldn't do because he had to do certain chores.
Example: **Martin wollte Tennis spielen gehen, aber er konnte nicht, denn er mußte Staub saugen.**

▶ *page 117*

❖ For Individual Needs

14 Challenge After students have completed Activity 14, have them listen to the conversation again, this time focusing on all the chores and errands that the speakers have already completed and those they are still planning to do. Have students make a simple chart to organize their notes.

	hat schon gemacht	muß noch tun
die Frau		
der Mann		

PRESENTATION: Grammatik

- Have students compare the imperfect modal forms with the forms in the present tense.
- Make a transparency with two columns showing verb forms in the present and past tense. Have students point out the differences between the forms.

▶ *page 118*

PRESENTATION: Wortschatz

- Use a large calendar to review previously introduced vocabulary as well as the new phrases. Talk about events in the past making specific references to them on the calendar.
  Example:
  Im vergangen Monat, also im Juni, hat die Rockgruppe Rolling Stones in der Konzerthalle gespielt. Wer von euch war denn da und hat sie spielen hören?
- Have students order the words and phrases according to how far they reach into the past. Have them start with **im vorigen Jahrhundert** and end with **heute.**

PRESENTATION: So sagt man das!

- In Level 2, (pp. 217 and 251) students learned some ways to express resignation and surprise. Review these before beginning this **So sagt man das!** box.
- Remind students that intonation plays a big role in the perception of what is being said.

Teaching Suggestion

17 Divide the conversation into four parts and play one part at a time, repeating if necessary. Then discuss students' findings immediately afterwards.

▶ *page 119*

✦ For Individual Needs

21 Challenge After the discussion, ask each pair to compose a letter to the editorial section of the school paper giving their opinions about one of the two issues.

Reteaching: Past Tense of Modals

Ask students to recall typical statements they often hear from older members of their family or families of their friends describing how different things were when they were teenagers. Students should use the past tense of the various modals in their statements.

CLOSE

✦ For Individual Needs

Visual Learners Bring to class old photos or magazines that depict life in your area or town several decades ago. Ask students how things must have been different then.

Focusing on Outcomes

Refer students back to the student outcomes listed on p. 205. They should recognize that they now know how to say that something is going on right now; report past events; and express surprise, relief, and resignation.

ASSESS

- **Performance Assessment** Ask students how they would advise a German pen pal who cannot decide between the **Bundeswehr** or the **Zivildienst.** Students should include at least three reasons for their opinion in their response.

- Quiz 5-2, *Chapter Resources,* Book 2

ZWEITE STUFE

Teaching Zum Lesen,
pp. 120-122

Reading Strategy

The targeted strategy in this reading is determining purpose. Students should learn about this strategy before beginning Question 4.

PREREADING

Motivating Activity

Discuss with students the basic rights guaranteed by the Constitution and ask them to imagine giving up these rights. Then discuss with them the following question: Which would be preferable: a party that promises to uphold basic rights for every individual—or a party that promises prosperity and national strength at the expense of certain basic rights?

Background Information

The Weimar Constitution (adopted in August, 1919 and officially in effect until March, 1933) was modeled after the U.S. Constitution and British law and included similar human rights provisions. But millions of Germans became unemployed during the time it was in effect, and inflation was rampant. Many Germans lost faith in the ability of a democratic government to provide political and economic solutions to their problems. When the National Socialists promised prosperity and national security, their promises fell on many receptive ears. Eventually, many Germans opted for the promise of prosperity and national strength, only to discover too late that they had lost most of their basic rights along the way.

3 The following background information will provide students with a context for the reading selections:

October 1929: Beginning of the Great Depression which brought widespread unemployment to the United States and Europe.

September 1930: National Socialist Party receives 6.5 million votes in the national election and becomes the second largest party in the **Reichstag**.

Summer 1932: Approximately 34% of the German work force is unemployed.

July 31, 1932: Nazi Party wins even more seats in the **Reichstag** with the promise that it will create jobs for everyone.

November 1932: In parliamentary elections, Nazis lose several seats while Communists gain additional seats. This loss of support among German voters convinces Nazi officials to take a more militant and aggressive stance in order to remain in power.

January 30, 1933: Hitler is named Chancellor by President Hindenburg.

February 27, 1933: Fire in the **Reichstag**. Hitler blames the Communists. Four thousand of his opponents are arrested.

March 1, 1933: Emergency decree suspends guarantee of all civil rights.

March 23, 1933: German Parliament votes 441-94 in favor of a law that will enable the executive branch to govern, to make new laws, and to revise the Constitution without consent of the **Reichstag**.

April 1, 1933: First (unsuccessful) boycott of Jewish businesses.

May 10, 1933: Students burn "undesirable" books at several universities

August 1934: Death of Hindenburg. Hitler becomes president and chancellor. He gives himself the official title "**der Führer.**"

Teacher Note

Activities 1-3 are prereading activities.

READING
Background Information

6 To fully understand what Hitler had in mind with these speeches, students need to know what was happening in Germany at the time each speech was given. In 1933, although France and Great Britain had agreed to stop their demands for World War I reparations payments, Germany broke the Versailles Treaty and walked out of the League of Nations. In 1937, when Hitler first proposed the **Lebensraum** policy to the military, Defense Minister von Blomberg, Foreign Minister von Neurath, and **Wehrmacht** General von Fritsch protested. Hitler eventually got rid of all three and put the War Department directly under his own command. Following its 1938 annexation of the border province of Sudetenland and the subsequent occupation of the remainder of Czechoslovakia in 1939, Germany bullied Lithuania into giving up the Memelland on the Baltic sea coast. Then Hitler made plans to invade and partition Poland with the help of the Soviet Union. In 1940, Nazi troops invaded France, and then in June, 1941, they invaded the Soviet Union itself, with the ultimate goal of subjugating all non-Aryan peoples in Europe.

Teaching Suggestion

8 Before students attempt to understand the **Flugblatt,** ask them to hypothesize about the main idea of the text based on what they know about the purpose of the text. Then ask students to read the text to confirm or refute their predictions. Students should apply the reading strategies of determining the main idea and reading to get the gist. Remind students that the main idea of each paragraph is usually stated in the first or second sentence of the paragraph. The first paragraph provides information about the occasion for which the Scholls wrote the **Flugblatt,** the German casualties in Russia. After students find the main idea(s), ask them to find two or three supporting details.

Background Information

9 The reference to Hitler as a **Dilettant** (*amateur*) in military strategy was most likely born of frustration at Hitler's disastrous policy on the Eastern Front and of anguish from having experienced the Russian campaign personally, as a number of the Munich White Rose group had done. When the Russian winter of 1941 slowed the troops' advance toward Moscow, Hitler fired several generals and personally took over command of the Eastern Front. It was as a result of his orders to hold Stalingrad at all costs through the winter of 1942/43 that the frozen, starving Sixth Army was encircled and defeated by Stalin's forces. Thus the writers of the **Flugblatt** felt justified in referring to Hitler as a **Dilettant** and in calling for passive resistance against his policies.

11 The article **"Verführt von dummen, mörderischen Sprüchen"** is based on an incident that took place in 1993 in Germany. A group of German young people in Solingen set fire to an apartment building inhabited primarily by Turkish families. Several people were killed in the fire. The exchange here between the judge (**Richter**) and Felix K. (**der Angeklagte** or *defendant*) took place at the trial following that incident.

POST-READING
Teacher Note

Activity 12 is a post-reading task that will show whether students can apply what they have learned.

Closure

From what students now know, do they think that student protests at that time made a difference? How would they have organized such protests? Was there a period in American history when similar student protests were significant in the outcome of events? (Examples: Vietnam war, civil rights movement of 1960s) What issues do students think could cause student protest today?

Answers to Activity 1

excerpts from speeches, political flyer, excerpt of an interview; Hitler, **Geschwister Scholl**, source: *Focus;* 1933-1942, 1943, 1994

Answers to Activity 2

Hans and Sophie, brother and sister, college students during World War II, founder/member of the resistance movement **Weiße Rose**

Answers to Activity 3

See Background Information.

Answers to Activity 4

Hitler: the German people (excerpts 2 and 3 directed to German military), Scholls: fellow students; Hitler: to convince the German population/military to support Hitler and the National Socialist agenda (war and expansionism) and ideology (anti-Semitism), Scholls: to convince others to join the fight against Hitler and the party, both are examples of political propaganda; inform readers of facts

Answers to Activity 5

anerkennen *to acknowledge;* **Gewaltanwendung** *use of force;* **ergreifen** *to take;* **Erkenntnis** *realization;* **vorbereiten** *to prepare for;* **hinwegströmen** *to stream forth;* **fürchten** *to fear*

Answers to Activity 6

victory, conqueror, conquering; the desire to feel superior, to conquer, and to take revenge on others for Germany's troubles

Answers to Activity 7

Die Welt ist gegen Deutschland; Die Regierung kann froh sein, daß die Leute nicht viel denken; Deutschland muß in die Offensive gehen und mehr Lebensraum gewinnen; Sieg ist wichtiger als das Recht; Die Bedeutung von Rasse ist eine unwiderstehliche Idee; Die Deutschen sollen ihre Minderwertigkeitsgefühle aufgeben, und sie sollen über andere Nationen siegen und von anderen gefürchtet sein; speeches evoke images of an embattled Germany, the importance of victory and power; the tone is aggressive and provocative, designed to evoke aggressive feelings in listeners.

Answers to Activity 8

fellow students; other college students; Hitler and his party (**Kampf gegen die Partei**); freedom and honor (**Freiheit und Ehre**)

Answers to Activity 9

amateur: he is an incompetent military leader responsible for the deaths of thousands of young Germans; Hitler and his party

Answers to Activity 11

seduced by dumb and deadly slogans; Felix K., by neo-Nazi slogans; National Socialism is still an ideology among right wing extremists in Germany today.

Teaching Zum Schreiben,
p. 123

Writing Strategy

The targeted strategy in this writing activity is asking questions to gather ideas. Students should learn about this strategy before beginning the assignment.

PREWRITING

Motivating Activity

Have students imagine that they are going to be interviewed by German students about life in the United States. What kind of questions would they anticipate? What would they like to talk about? What would they want to convey about life in America? What would be easy questions? Difficult ones? Have students brainstorm ideas in pairs or small groups and then share their responses with the class.

Teaching Suggestion

If students cannot find interviewees who grew up in another country and culture, you could invite several foreign-born guests to class and have group interviews for each person. Some sources might be local or state foreign language organizations, any local or regional agency working with immigrants, area universities or colleges, and civic and religious groups.

Teaching Suggestions

A1 Have pairs or small groups of students work together to brainstorm specific interview questions.

A2 In addition to the written statements, students may want to ask the person they plan to interview if they could take a picture of him or her or borrow some photos that would provide visual support for their reports.

◆ For Individual Needs

A3 Visual Learners You may want to remind students about the **Ideenbäume** they made for the **Zum Schreiben** activity in Chapter 3. Students may find it helpful to organize their report using an outline or **Ideenbaum**.

WRITING

Teaching Suggestion

B Remind students to double or triple-space their first drafts so they have room to make revisions during the **Überarbeiten** stage of the activity.

POST-WRITING

Teaching Suggestion

Students could post their reports along with pictures of their interviewees on bulletin boards in the classroom which should be organized according to geographical location.

Closure

After reports have been presented and displayed, have small groups of students discuss how their lives would be different if they lived or had lived in the native country of the interviewees.

Using Anwendung,
pp. 124-125

Resources for Anwendung

Chapter Resources, Book 2
- Realia 5-3
- Situation Card 5-3
Video Program, Videocassette 1
Video Guide

Video Program

At this time, you might want to use the authentic advertising footage from German television. See *Video Guide* for suggestions.

Portfolio Assessment

2 You might want to suggest this activity as a written portfolio item for your students. See *Assessment Guide*, p. 18

Total Physical Response

3 After students have completed the list of what students in **Oma**'s time had to do and what they were not allowed to do, ask them to make up commands that grandmother probably heard as a child. Example: **Leg die Hände auf den Tisch!**

For Individual Needs

5 **Challenge** Have students make up a chart like the one in this activity. They may choose their own topic and come up with phrases they like for the box on the right—funny or serious.

History Connection

6 If students are unable to interview an older person ask them to use an autobiography or biography of a historically significant person as the source for their report.

Portfolio Assessment

8 You might want to suggest this activity as an oral portfolio item for your students. See *Assessment Guide*, p. 18.

Kann ich's wirklich?
p. 126

This page helps students prepare for the test. It is a brief checklist of the major points covered in the chapter. The students should be reminded that it is only a checklist and not necessarily everything that will appear on the test.

Using Wortschatz,
p. 127

Game

Play the game **Seeschlacht** to review the Chapter 5 vocabulary. See p. 103F for the procedure.

Teaching Suggestion

With their books closed, ask individual students to give you a definition of words or expressions you call out.

Teacher Note

Give the **Kapitel 5** Chapter Test, *Chapter Resources*, Book 2.

Rechte und Pflichten

FÜHRERSCHEIN

D

Permis de conduire
Kòrekort
Άδεια Όδηγήσεως
Permiso de Conducción
Ceadúnas Tiomána
Patente di guida
Rijbewijs
Carta de Condução
Driving licence

Modell der
EUROPÄISCHEN GEMEINSCHAFT
C 1420746

POLITIK

UMWELT

① Du könntest dich wirklich ein bißchen für Politik interessieren!

Stimmzettel
für die Wahl zum Deutschen Bundestag im Wahlkreis 03 Bonn
am 16. Oktober 1994

Sie haben 2 Stimm

hier 1 Stimme
für die Wahl
eines/einer Wahlkreis-
abgeordneten

Erststimme

hier 1 Stimme
einer Landesliste (Partei
insgesamt auf die einzelnen

Zweitstimme

Mit dem Erreichen des 18. Lebensjahres, der Volljährigkeit, erwerben die jungen Erwachsenen bestimmte Rechte und Pflichten. Denk einmal daran, wie die Volljährigkeit dein Leben beeinflussen wird! Wirst du zur Wahl gehen? Wirst du eine Wohnung mieten? Welche anderen Rechte und Pflichten erwirbst du, wenn du achtzehn wirst? Um über diese Fragen diskutieren zu können, mußt du noch einige Ausdrücke lernen.

In this chapter you will learn

- to talk about what is possible; to say what you would have liked to do
- to say that something is going on right now; to report past events; to express surprise, relief, and resignation

And you will

- listen to students talk about their rights and obligations
- read a passage written during World War II by students involved in the Resistance
- write about someone's experiences in another country
- learn more about German teenagers' rights and responsibilities

② Was machen wir jetzt? — Wir sind grad am Diskutieren.

③ Ich bin froh, daß ich den Zivildienst beim Roten Kreuz machen kann.

Los geht's!

Mit achtzehn darf man alles. Oder?

Über dieses Thema haben wir mit Julia (17), Angie (18),
Stefan (fast 18) und Martin (18) gesprochen.

Das einzige, was sich wirklich mit meinem achtzehnten Geburtstag
geändert hat, ist, daß ich mich jetzt im Auto selbst hinters
Steuer setzen darf. Wenn man den Führerschein hat, ist man eben
unabhängiger. Man kann schnell mal ein paar Freunde besuchen
und kurzfristig zusammen wegfahren. Aber sonst hat sich an
meinem 18. Geburtstag überhaupt nichts geändert. Ich hatte
schon vorher ein gutes Verhältnis zu meinen Eltern, also da hat
sich auch in dieser Hinsicht nichts zu ändern brauchen. Für mich
war also der 18. Geburtstag ein Geburtstag wie jeder andere.

Martin, 18

Jetzt könnte ich die Schule schwänzen und meine eigene
Entschuldigung schreiben! Als ich 15 war, war das Schule-
schwänzen oft ein großes Problem. Da hätte ich oft gern
geschwänzt, weil ich die Hausaufgaben nicht gemacht hatte, weil
ich den Unterricht blöd fand, weil ich Angst vor der Prüfung
hatte und so weiter und so fort. Und heute? Die Schule ist weiterhin stressig, aber ich weiß, daß jede Schulstunde wichtig ist.
Ich kann es mir gar nicht erlauben zu fehlen. Ich muß das Abi
schaffen, sonst ist es aus mit dem Studieren.

Angie, 18

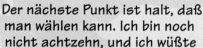

Der nächste Punkt ist halt, daß
man wählen kann. Ich bin noch
nicht achtzehn, und ich wüßte
auch heute gar nicht, wen ich wählen sollte.
Ich bin politisch überhaupt nicht aktiv. Ich kenn'
aber einige Schüler, die sich schon sehr politisch
engagieren. Die sind noch unter achtzehn und sind
schon Mitglied in der Jungen Union.[1] Übrigens, bei
meinen Eltern ist es lustig: wenn mein Vater CSU
wählt, dann wählt meine Mutter bestimmt SPD,
und auch umgekehrt. Vielleicht würd' ich meine
Stimme den Grünen[2] geben; die sind für die
Umwelt, sagen sie. Aber bevor ich wähle, werde
ich mich bestimmt besser informieren.

Stefan, fast 18

1. Die Junge Union ist die Jugendorganisation der CDU/CSU.
2. Die CDU (Christlich-Demokratische Union) und die SPD (Sozialdemokratische Partei Deutschlands)
sind die beiden größten Parteien. In Bayern gibt es die CSU (Christlich-Soziale Union); ihre Ziele stimmen
weitgehend mit denen der CDU überein. Ferner gibt es die FDP (Freie Demokratische Partei), die Grünen
(die Umweltpartei), die PDS (Partei des Demokratischen Sozialismus), die Nachfolgepartei der früheren
SED in der ehemaligen DDR, seit 1988 die Republikaner und noch einige andere, kleinere Parteien.

Bei mir ist es halt so, daß ich den Führerschein nicht gezahlt bekomm', und ich ihn also nicht machen kann. Ich würd' ihn zwar gern machen, aber er ist mir zu teuer. Und es ist mir zu schade um mein eigenes Geld.

Julia, 17

INTERVIEWER Und wie teuer ist der Führerschein?

JULIA Im Schnitt 1 500 Mark. Und wenn ich mich nicht irre, hat meine Schwester über 2 000 Mark gezahlt. Es kommt eben darauf an, wieviel Stunden man braucht.[3]

ANGIE Es dauert auch sehr lange. Also man kann durchaus ein halbes Jahr daran herummachen; drei Monate dauert's aber bestimmt.

MARTIN Ja, da zieh' ich das amerikanische System vor. Wir haben hier an der Schule ein paar Leute, die waren ein halbes Jahr oder ein Jahr in den Staaten und haben dort den Führerschein gemacht, und die fahren damit hier herum.

JULIA Mir scheint, drüben ist es einfacher.

MARTIN Der Jens hat mir gesagt, er hat nur ein paar Fragen beantworten müssen, ein paar Dollar gezahlt und ist einmal um den Block gefahren. Das war's.

STEFAN Soviel ich weiß, hat er sogar schlecht eingeparkt!

3. Seit 1986 gibt es in der Bundesrepublik den **Führerschein auf Probe**. Jeder Fahranfänger muß sich zwei Jahre im Straßenverkehr bewähren, bevor er die endgültige Fahrerlaubnis erhält. Im Jahr 1985 verursachten die 18- bis 24jährigen 39 Prozent aller Unfälle. Der Führerschein auf Probe soll dazu beitragen, die hohen Unfallquoten der jungen Leute zu verringern. Schon 1987 war die Unfallquote dieser Altersgruppe auf 33,3 Prozent gesunken. 1992 lag die Unfallquote nur noch bei 27 Prozent.

1 Der 18. Geburtstag: Was bedeutet er für diese Schüler?

Schreib in Stichworten die wichtigsten Dinge auf, die Martin, Angie und Stefan gesagt haben! Erzähle dann der Klasse, was einer von den vier deutschen Schülern erzählt hat!

Martin	
Angie	
Stefan	

2 Beantworte die Fragen!

1. Warum kann Julia den Führerschein nicht machen? bekommt ihn nicht gezahlt; ist zu teuer
2. Warum zahlt sie nicht selbst dafür? Das eigene Geld ist ihr zu schade.
3. Welche Unterschiede gibt es beim Führerscheinmachen zwischen der Bundesrepublik und den Vereinigten Staaten?

E.g.: **Preis; Dauer; Prüfung; Gültigkeit**

ERSTE STUFE

Talking about what is possible; saying what you would have liked to do

Artikel 38/2. Absatz des Grundgesetzes:
„Wahlberechtigt ist, wer das achtzehnte Lebensjahr vollendet hat; wählbar ist, wer das Alter erreicht hat, mit dem die Volljährigkeit eintritt."

Seit 1975 sind Jugendliche in der Bundesrepublik Deutschland mit dem vollendeten achtzehnten Lebensjahr volljährig.

WAS BEDEUTET DAS?

1. Man kann selbst bestimmen, wo man wohnen will.
2. Man kann nach Hause kommen, wann man will.
3. Man kann Ausbildungs- und Arbeitsverträge selbst unterschreiben.
4. Man kann Entschuldigungen für die Schule selbst schreiben.
5. Man kann Verträge über Käufe, Kredite, Mieten, usw. selbst abschließen.
6. Man kann heiraten.
7. Man kann selbst wählen und gewählt werden.
8. Man kann den Führerschein machen.
9. Man kann im Lokal alkoholische Getränke bestellen.

Wieso Führerschein? Ich denke, den bekommt man erst mit achtzehn Jahren!

WORTSCHATZ

auf deutsch erklärt

der Unterricht das Lernen eines Schulfaches, zum Beispiel Deutsch (der Deutschunterricht)
die Prüfung der Test
schwänzen nicht in die Schule gehen, weil man keine Lust hat
fehlen nicht da sein
Ich kann es mir nicht erlauben. Ich darf es nicht.
Du irrst dich. Du denkst falsch.
Das dauert lange. Das braucht eine lange Zeit.
wählen man sagt einem politischen Kandidaten offiziell ja
sich politisch engagieren politisch aktiv sein
kurzfristig nach wenig Zeit, schnell

auf englisch erklärt

Er ist Mitglied unseres Vereins. *He is a member of our club.*
Ich will von meinen Eltern unabhängig sein. *I want to be independent from my parents.*
Wir werden im Juni heiraten. *We're going to get married in June.*
Es scheint, du willst nicht. *It seems you don't want to.*
Das wäre zu schade ums Geld. *It wouldn't be worth the money.*
Unterschreiben Sie den Vertrag! *Sign the contract!*
In dieser Hinsicht ist es umgekehrt. *In this respect it's the other way around.*
Es ist schwer, sich zu ändern. *It's difficult to change yourself.*

For answers, see listening script on TE Interleaf.

3 Hör gut zu!

Schüler erzählen, was sich in ihrem Leben mit dem 18. Geburtstag geändert hat. Welche Aussagen passen zu den Illustrationen?

a.　　　　b.　　　　c.　　　　d.　　　　e.

SO SAGT MAN DAS!

Talking about what is possible

If you ask yourself **Was soll ich morgen machen?**, here is a way to say what you could possibly do:

> **Ich könnte die Schule schwänzen, aber ich kann es mir nicht erlauben.**

If your friend tells you **Ich habe Lust, Auto fahren zu lernen**, you can answer by saying:

> **Du könntest den Führerschein machen, weil du jetzt alt genug bist.**

How would you talk about what is possible in English?

For answers, see listening script on TE Interleaf.

4 Hör gut zu!

Drei Freunde sprechen über ihre Pläne. Hör zu und schreib auf, was die drei vorhaben! Wer scheint am meisten vorzuhaben?

5 Mit achtzehn könnte ich ...

Stellt euch vor, ihr wohnt in Deutschland und seid schon 18! Sag, was du jetzt alles tun könntest, und sag auch, warum du es nicht tust! Tauscht die Rollen aus!

DU　　Ich könnte jetzt ...

PARTNER　Ja, und warum tust du's nicht?

DU　　Weil ich ...

Ein wenig Grammatik

To express possibility, you need to know the **könnte**-forms. Of what verbs do these forms remind you?

Ich **könnte** das Abi schaffen.
Du **könntest** ausziehen.
Es **könnte** einfacher sein.
Wir **könnten** den Meier wählen.
Ihr **könntet** euch informieren.
Sie **könnten** jetzt heiraten.

---

wohnen, wo ich will

die eigene Entschuldigung schreiben, wenn ich die Schule schwänze

selbst eine Wohnung mieten

nach Hause kommen, wann ich will

heiraten

den Führerschein machen

wählen

von zu Hause ausziehen

allein wegfahren

---

6 Ich könnte, aber ich tu's nicht.

Denk an fünf Dinge, die du jetzt tun könntest, aber aus irgendeinem Grund nicht tust und schreib sie auf!

BEISPIEL   **Ich bin jetzt (16). Ich könnte abends bis elf Uhr wegbleiben, aber ich tu's nicht, weil ich früh aufstehen muß.**

SO SAGT MAN DAS!

Saying what you would have liked to do

Sometimes you have intentions that just don't get carried out. When you want to express these intentions, you can say:

Ich hätte gern die Schule **geschwänzt,** aber ich bin doch hingegangen.
Ich wäre gern zu Hause **geblieben,** aber wir hatten heute eine Prüfung.

How would you express these phrases in English?

Grammatik   Further uses of **wäre** and **hätte**

In the **So sagt man das!** box you learned that intentions that don't get carried out are expressed with **hätte** or **wäre.** In that case, **hätte** and **wäre** are auxiliary verbs, and are both used with a past participle.

Sie **hätten** gern **geheiratet,** aber die Eltern wollten es nicht.
Ich **hätte** meine Hausaufgaben **gemacht,** aber ich war krank.

The decision to use **hätte** or **wäre** as the auxiliary verb depends on the past participle. If it normally takes **sein** in the past tense (like **gekommen**), then **wäre** is correct.

Wir **wären** gestern nach Berlin **gefahren,** aber unser Auto ist kaputt.
Ich **wäre** heute schwimmen **gegangen,** aber es hat furchtbar geregnet.

7 Was hättest du gern getan?

Leider gehen nicht alle Wünsche in Erfüllung. Sag einer Klassenkameradin, was du alles gern getan hättest! Hier sind einige Wünsche. Hast du andere?

hätte	Freunde besuchen	(die CDU) wählen	hätte
hätte	den Führerschein machen	seine Stimme (den Grünen) geben	hätte
hätte	die Schule schwänzen	etwas für die Umwelt tun	hätte
hätte	die Hausaufgaben machen	mit Freunden wegfahren	wäre
hätte	die Fragen beantworten	länger im Urlaub bleiben	wäre
hätte	sich politisch engagieren	sich besser informieren	hätte
wäre	Mitglied im Fußballklub werden	nach (Österreich) fahren	wäre
hätte	eine tolle Sendung sehen	den Vertrag unterzeichnen	hätte
wäre	nach Deutschland fliegen	ins Kino gehen	wäre

8 Aber sag auch warum!

Setzt euch in kleinen Gruppen zusammen und erzählt, was ihr gern getan hättet! Ihr könnt die letzte Übung zu Hilfe nehmen. Gebt auch einen Grund dafür an!

DU **Ich hätte gern ...**

PARTNER **Und warum hast du das nicht getan?**

DU **Ja, weil ...**

PARTNER **Schade!** *oder* **Ja, wirklich?** *oder* **Zu dumm!**

Warum nicht?

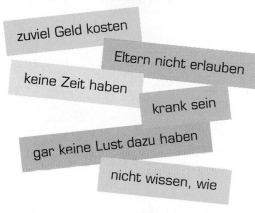

zuviel Geld kosten

Eltern nicht erlauben

keine Zeit haben

krank sein

gar keine Lust dazu haben

nicht wissen, wie

9 Für mein Notizbuch

Denk an drei Dinge, die du in letzter Zeit gern getan hättest! Gib Gründe an, warum du sie nicht getan hast!

BEISPIEL **Gestern abend hätte ich gern ferngesehen, aber leider war unser Fernseher kaputt, und ich hatte keine Lust, zu meiner Klassenkameradin zu gehen.**

10 Was hältst du davon?

Denk über folgende Fragen nach, und schreib die Antworten in Stichworten auf! Diskutiere darüber mit deinen Klassenkameraden!

1. Wie ist die Schule für dich? Leicht? Stressig? Warum?
2. Würdest du den Unterricht schwänzen, wenn du könntest?
3. Hast du schon einmal die Schule geschwänzt? Warum?
4. Was wird sich bei dir ändern, wenn du achtzehn wirst?
5. Was hat sich geändert, als du sechzehn geworden bist?
6. Freust du dich darauf, daß du mit achtzehn wählen darfst? Wen oder welche Partei würdest du wählen? Warum?
7. Bist du politisch aktiv oder wenigstens gut informiert? Kennst du Schüler, die sich politisch engagieren?
8. Wie wichtig ist für dich der Führerschein? Hast du schon den Führerschein? Wenn ja, was hast du alles machen müssen, um ihn zu bekommen?

11 Für mein Notizbuch

Wähle eins der beiden Themen unten, und schreib einen Kurzbericht darüber!

1. Der Führerschein auf Probe ist eine gute Idee.
2. Jeder Schüler sollte sich ein wenig politisch engagieren.

Weiter geht's!

Die Wehrpflicht: dafür oder dagegen?

Das Interview geht weiter. Die vier jungen Leute
unterhalten sich über das Thema „Wehrpflicht".

Artikel 12a des Grundgesetzes:
„Männer können vom vollendeten achtzehnten
Lebensjahr an zum Dienst in den Streitkräften,
im Bundesgrenzschutz oder in einem
Zivilschutzverband verpflichtet werden."

STEFAN   Eine Pflicht, die jeder Achtzehnjährige hat,
ist, zur Bundeswehr zu gehen. Und das ist
auch nicht gerade angenehm, weil man
fast zwei Jahre vom Studium oder von der Arbeit verliert.

INTERVIEWER   Habt ihr euch schon entschieden, ob ihr den Wehrdienst
oder den Zivildienst macht?

MARTIN   Ja, wir sind halt immer noch am Diskutieren. Ich, zum Beispiel ...

STEFAN   Darf ich dich schnell mal unterbrechen, Martin?

MARTIN   Bitte.

STEFAN   Es ist nämlich so: wir hatten vorigen Monat einen Bundeswehroffizier zu einer Fragestunde eingeladen. Die
Diskussion war sehr interessant, und wir konnten uns
dabei gut informieren.

ANGIE   Und was ist dabei herausgekommen?

MARTIN   Ja, für mich wenig.

STEFAN   Für mich auch nicht viel. Aber trotzdem!
Ich hab' die Diskussion prima gefunden.

MARTIN   Das ist mir neu, was du da sagst.

STEFAN   Ich hab' nur gesagt, die Diskussion war
prima, interessant. Es hat sich gelohnt,
ihn einzuladen. Das kannst du doch
nicht abstreiten.

MARTIN   Tu' ich auch nicht. Ich frag mich bloß, ob
jemand wirklich seine Meinung nach
dieser Diskussion geändert hat.

STEFAN   Das glaub' ich nicht. Die einen sind eben
für die Bundeswehr, die anderen sind
dagegen. Daran ändert sich nichts.
Jeder muß allein für sich entscheiden,
ob er zum Bund geht oder nicht.

ANGIE   Gehst du zum Bund, Martin?

MARTIN Also, ich sag's mal so: wenn ich's vermeiden kann, nicht. Weil ich's heutzutage für sinnlos halte. Und wenn ich muß, geh' ich halt hin.

JULIA Ich bin wahnsinnig froh, daß ich so eine Entscheidung nicht machen muß.

MARTIN Ja, ihr Mädchen habt's gut. Man sollte euch einziehen, wie in Israel.

ANGIE Meinst du das im Ernst?

MARTIN Ja, warum denn nicht? Ihr müßt nicht unbedingt ein Gewehr in den Kampf tragen. Es gibt viele Sachen, die Mädchen bei der Bundeswehr machen könnten. Sie sollten aber wenigstens den Zivildienst machen müssen!

STEFAN Das mag sein. Ich find' es aber wirklich schlecht, daß man in Deutschland Wehrdienst machen muß.

ANGIE Sonst würd's keiner machen.

MARTIN Ja, stimmt. Wir müssen aber Streitkräfte haben, auf die wir uns verlassen können!

ANGIE Das ist heutzutage nicht mehr so wichtig, wie es noch vor kurzem war.

STEFAN Immerhin — der Wehrdienst sollte freiwillig sein. In England klappt's, in den USA klappt's.

MARTIN Wir haben wenigstens noch einen Ersatzdienst.

STEFAN Ja, schon! Aber der Zivildienst kann noch anstrengender sein. Es kommt eben darauf an, was man machen muß.

ANGIE Ich hab' einen Bekannten, der gerade seinen Zivildienst in einem Altenheim macht. Er sagt, er kann es bald nicht mehr aushalten. Die alten Leute, die er betreuen muß, tun ihm so furchtbar leid: sie können sich nicht mehr selber helfen. Und das belastet ihn wahnsinnig.

STEFAN Und ich find' es ausgesprochen fies, daß es Firmen gibt, die keine Zivildienstleute einstellen.

MARTIN Andererseits nutzt dir der Zivildienst mehr als der Wehrdienst, wenn du zum Beispiel Arzt werden willst.

STEFAN Ja, schon. Aber was soll's! Ich nehm's, wie's kommt. Vielleicht mag mich der Bund gar nicht. Mit meinen Kontaktlinsen und meinem schwachen Kreuz werd' ich bei der Musterung bestimmt durchfallen.

12 Was haben die vier Schüler gesagt?

Macht eine Liste mit vier Spalten und tragt die wichtigsten Dinge ein, die die vier Schüler gesagt haben! Nehmt dann eure Notizen zur Hand und berichtet der Klasse, was die vier Schüler zum Thema „Wehrdienst" gesagt haben! Was fällt dir an Martins Aussagen auf?

Gleichberechtigung im deutschen Militär?

Deutschen Frauen ist der Dienst mit der Waffe noch immer offiziell verboten. Aber wie lange noch?

Die Stimmen vieler Bundestagsabgeordneter werden immer lauter, den deutschen Frauen künftig das Tor zur Bundeswehr zu öffnen. Noch immer verbietet Artikel 12a des Grundgesetzes den „Dienst mit der Waffe" für Frauen.

Seit 1975 dienen Frauen bei der Bundeswehr hauptsächlich in verwaltungstechnischen Berufen und im Pflegedienst (z.B. als Ärztinnen, Apothekerinnen). Damals wollten sich junge Männer für diese Berufe nicht verpflichten, denn die Wirtschaft zahlte mehr.

Frauen im Militärdienst sind nichts Neues. Israels Frauen müssen mit 18 Jahren für 20 Monate zur Armee. Sie leisten Wehrdienst wie ihre männlichen Kameraden. Sie werden an allen Waffen ausgebildet — sie sind Pilotinnen und kommandieren Kampfpanzer.

In den USA stellen Soldatinnen heute über zehn Prozent aller Streitkräfte, mehr als in jeder anderen Berufsarmee der Welt. Sie fliegen Transportflugzeuge, reparieren Panzer, fahren Armeelaster, bewachen Kasernen, bilden Rekruten aus und ziehen mit Stahlhelm und Maschinengewehr nicht nur ins Manöver, sondern setzen auch ihr Leben an der Front aufs Spiel. Frauen können Offizier werden und auch General.

Der Ausschluß von Frauen für den Dienst bei der Bundeswehr schränkt die Karrierechancen von Frauen ein. Das widerspricht dem Recht auf Gleichberechtigung aller Bürger. Der Ausschluß verbietet Frauen die Möglichkeit, in einem Zweig des öffentlichen Dienstes Arbeit und Aufstiegsmöglichkeiten zu finden.

Natürlich müßte das Grundgesetz geändert werden, bevor Frauen beim deutschen Militär in Panzern, Bombern und U-Booten Dienst leisten könnten. Viele Leute glauben, man sollte 52 Prozent der deutschen Bevölkerung diesen Weg nicht versperren.

1. daß Frauen in Deutschland im Militär nicht gleichberechtigt sind
2. Deutschland, Israel, USA / Deutschland: Wehrpflicht gilt nicht für

Kannst du das erklären?

Frauen, Dienst mit der Waffe ist Frauen gesetzlich verboten; Israel: Wehrpflicht und Dienst mit der Waffe gilt auch für Frauen; USA: keine Wehrpflicht

Beantworte die Fragen!

1. Wovon handelt der Artikel?
2. Welche Länder werden im Artikel verglichen? Wie unterscheidet sich das Militär in den verschiedenen Ländern? sondern Berufsarmee, Dienst mit der Waffe gilt auch für Frauen   3. weil das Grundgesetz es verbietet   4. verwaltungstechnische Berufe, Berufe im Pflegedienst
3. Warum dürfen deutsche Frauen nicht überall in der Bundeswehr dienen?
4. Welche Berufe üben (*perform*) seit 1975 einige Frauen in der Bundeswehr aus?
5. Was für Folgen (*consequences*) hat der Ausschluß (*exclusion*) von Frauen bei der Bundeswehr? 5. schränkt die Karrierechancen für Frauen ein
6. Sind Frauen für den Militärdienst geeignet? Was meinst du?
7. Sollte man das Grundgesetz in Deutschland ändern? Warum oder warum nicht?

ZWEITE STUFE

Saying that something is going on right now; reporting past events; expressing surprise, relief, and resignation

In der Bundeswehr kommandieren Frauen bestimmt einmal ...

einen Panzer

einen Bomber

einen Laster

ein Transportflugzeug

ein U-Boot

Was würdest du gern kommandieren?

auf deutsch erklärt

die Streitkräfte   das ganze Militär
die Bundeswehr   die deutsche Armee
der Bund   die Bundeswehr
die Wehrpflicht   wenn man in die Armee gehen muß, also nicht freiwillig
freiwillig   wenn man etwas nicht machen muß, aber machen will
der Frieden   wenn es keinen Krieg gibt
sich entscheiden   wenn man zwischen zwei Dingen wählt
ausgesprochen   ganz besonders

auf englisch erklärt

Er schießt mit dem Gewehr.   *He shoots the gun.*
Ein Panzer ist eine wichtige Waffe.   *A tank is an important weapon.*
Der Kampf war hart.   *The battle was heavy.*
Muß man bei euch Wehrdienst machen?   *Do you have to serve in the military where you're from?*
Wir dürfen auch den Zivildienst wählen.   *We can also choose community service.*
Unsere Demokratie hat ein Grundgesetz.   *Our democracy has a constitution.*
Gleichberechtigung für alle!   *Equality for all!*
Können wir uns auf dich verlassen?   *Can we rely on you?*
Aber im Ernst!   *But seriously!*

SO SAGT MAN DAS!

Saying that something is going on right now

Here are three ways of expressing that something is occurring at this moment:

> **Wir diskutieren gerade darüber.**
> **Wir sind dabei, dieses Thema zu besprechen.**
> **Wir sind am (beim) Überlegen.**

What common English form do these sentences express?

13 Was macht Martin gerade?

Michael möchte mit Martin Tennis spielen, aber Martin hat vorher noch viel zu tun. Michael ruft Martin an und will wissen, wie weit er ist und ob sie bald spielen können. Spiel die Rollen mit einem Partner!

MICHAEL **Hallo, Martin! Willst du Tennis spielen?**

MARTIN **Ich bin gerade am Fensterputzen. Vielleicht später.**

MICHAEL **Gut, bis später.**

Was Martin alles machen muß:

EIN WENIG LANDESKUNDE

In der Bundesrepublik besteht seit 1956 die allgemeine Wehrpflicht für Männer. Diese Wehrpflicht kann durch den 12monatigen Wehrdienst (ab 1996 zehn Monate) oder den 15monatigen Zivildienst (ab 1996 13 Monate) erfüllt werden. In Österreich dauert der Grundwehrdienst 6 Monate. In der Schweiz gibt es eine Rekrutenausbildung von 15 Wochen und alle zwei Jahre neunzehnwöchige Wehrübungen bis zum vollendeten 40. Lebensjahr.

Die Streitkräfte der Bundeswehr bestehen aus Armee, Luftwaffe und Marine. Viele junge Männer gehen zur Bundeswehr, weil sie Interesse am Soldatenberuf haben oder weil sie hoffen, später einen sicheren Arbeitsplatz zu finden. Soldaten haben nämlich die Möglichkeit — wenn sie längere Zeit beim Bund bleiben — sich während der Dienstzeit beruflich ausbilden zu lassen. Abiturienten können auch an den Bundeswehruniversitäten in Hamburg und München studieren. Ungefähr 30 Prozent der wehrpflichtigen Männer in Deutschland entscheiden sich für den Zivildienst.

SO SAGT MAN DAS!
Reporting past events

Here is a more expressive way to report something that happened in the past:

Wir haben letzten Monat einen Bundeswehroffizier eingeladen. Die Diskussion war sehr interessant, und wir konnten uns gut informieren. Wir wollten noch mehr hören, aber wir mußten zum Unterricht gehen.

What verb forms do you recognize? What are the infinitives of those verbs?

14 Hör gut zu! For answers, see listening script on TE Interleaf.

Du stehst in einer langen Schlange am Bankschalter. Zwei Leute vor dir sprechen darüber, was sie am Vormittag alles erledigt haben oder noch tun müssen. Hör ihrem Gespräch gut zu, und mach dir Notizen über die Besorgungen (*errands*)! Anhand der Notizen erzähl dann deinem Partner von dem Gespräch, das du mit angehört hast.

Grammatik The past tense of modals (the imperfect)

1. The modals have these forms in the imperfect:

dürfen	müssen	können	mögen	sollen	wollen
ich durf-t-e	mußte	konnte	mochte	sollte	wollte
du durf-t-est	mußtest	konntest	mochtest	solltest	wolltest
er durf-t-e	mußte	konnte	mochte	sollte	wollte
wir durf-t-en	mußten	konnten	mochten	sollten	wollten
ihr durf-t-et	mußtet	konntet	mochtet	solltet	wolltet
sie durf-t-en	mußten	konnten	mochten	sollten	wollten

  a. The modals in the imperfect do not carry over the umlaut of the infinitive.
  b. All modals are conjugated.
  c. The imperfect of **mögen** also has a consonant change.

2. In conversation, the imperfect forms of modals are almost always used rather than the present perfect.
  — Was ist bei eurer Diskussion herausgekommen?
  — Nichts. Aber wir **konnten** uns gut informieren.
  — Und wie hast du die Diskussion gefunden?
  — Sie **war** prima! Die Klassenkameraden **wollten** gar nicht nach Hause gehen. Sie **hatten** so viele Fragen.

---

15 Wie war's früher?

Sag einem Partner, wie's früher war und wie's heute ist!

BEISPIEL **Früher mußte ich eine Brille tragen, heute kann ich Kontaktlinsen tragen.**

früher:

Eltern die Entschuldigung schreiben

ein Zimmer teilen

radfahren

eine Brille tragen

mit den Eltern wegfahren

sich aufs Taschengeld verlassen

um 20 Uhr zu Hause sein

heute:

Kontaktlinsen tragen

Auto fahren

bis um 22 Uhr wegbleiben

selbst Geld verdienen

allein wegfahren

die Entschuldigung selbst schreiben

ein eigenes Zimmer haben

Schon bekannt	Neu	
gestern, gestern (vormittag)	vergangen-: vergangenes Jahr	früher
vorgestern, vorgestern (abend)	vergangenen Monat	
letzt-: letzte Woche, letztes Jahr	vorig-: vorige Woche	
	im vorigen Jahrhundert	

16 Als ich zwölf war ...

Denk an sechs Dinge, die du nicht tun konntest oder durftest, als du zwölf warst! Schreib sie auf und vergleiche deine Liste mit der Liste eines Partners!

BEISPIEL **Als ich zwölf war, mußte ich/konnte ich/durfte ich (nicht) ...**

SO SAGT MAN DAS!

Expressing surprise, relief, and resignation

If someone said something surprising to you, for example:

> **Also, bei uns dürfen die Hunde mit ins Restaurant gehen.**

You might answer:

> **Das ist mir (völlig) neu!**

If you heard reassuring news, for example:

> **Gestern ist Mari gesund aus dem Krankenhaus gekommen.**

You might express relief by saying:

> **Ich bin (sehr) froh, daß es ihr besser geht.**

If someone complained to you:

> **Ich mußte das ganze Wochenende mit dem Matheheft verbringen.**

You might express resignation about the plight of students by saying:

> **Ach, was soll's! Das ist leider so.**

---

17 Hör gut zu! For answers, see listening script on TE Interleaf.

Hör gut zu, wie einige Schüler darüber diskutieren, ob sie zum Bund gehen oder nicht! Welche Schüler drücken Überraschung aus? Resignation? Erleichterung?

18 Was für eine Reaktion hast du darauf?

Wie reagierst du auf folgende Aussagen? Lies einer Partnerin eine Aussage vor, und sie wird darauf reagieren! Gebrauch dabei die Ausdrücke, die du gelernt hast!

1. Ich hab' gehört, daß wir jetzt das ganze Jahr zur Schule gehen müssen und daß wir keine langen Sommerferien mehr haben.
2. Ich hab' gehört, daß Jungen zwischen 16 und 25 über $1 000 im Jahr für ihre Autoversicherung bezahlen müssen.
3. Ich hab' gehört, daß es jetzt auch bei uns einen Führerschein auf Probe geben soll.
4. Ich hab' gehört, daß Frauen in der amerikanischen Marine jetzt auf U-Booten dienen dürfen.

19 Reaktionen hervorrufen!

a. Schreib zuerst ein paar Situationen auf, auf die ein Partner mit Überraschung, Resignation oder Erleichterung reagieren könnte! Hier sind ein paar Anregungen, aber du kannst dir selber etwas ausdenken.

wie eine Sportmannschaft gespielt hat

monatliches Taschengeld von den Eltern

eine Prüfung in einem Schulfach

das kuriose Leben eines Film- oder Popstars

… oder anderes vom Leben!

b. Lies dann einem Partner die Situationen vor, und er muß jeweils darauf reagieren!

20 Vorteile und Nachteile

Der Militärdienst und der Zivildienst haben Vor- und Nachteile. Einige sind hier aufgelistet, andere kannst du dir selbst ausdenken. Du nimmst eine Position ein und ein Klassenkamerad eine andere. Diskutiert darüber!

Militärdienst

Vorteile	Nachteile
ein geregeltes Leben haben etwas lernen neue Leute kennenlernen Kameradschaft haben Karriere machen können	Zeit verlieren nicht viel lernen wenig Freiheit haben ein rauhes Leben haben Familie und Freunde verlassen müssen

Zivildienst

Vorteile	Nachteile
anderen Menschen helfen etwas Gutes tun etwas Nützliches lernen offen gegen Krieg sein können	lange Arbeitszeit haben oft deprimierende Arbeit haben berufliche Nachteile haben können wenig Geld verdienen

21 Was sagst du dazu?

Diskutier mit deinen Klassenkameraden über folgende Themen!

a. Die USA haben seit vielen Jahren keine allgemeine Wehrpflicht mehr. Sollte man die allgemeine Wehrpflicht wieder einführen — für Männer und für Frauen? Warum oder warum nicht?

b. Manche Schulen in den USA verlangen (*demand*), daß Schüler in ihrer Schulzeit etwas Zivildienst leisten. Wird sowas in eurer Schule verlangt? Was sind die Bedingungen (*conditions*)? Bist du dafür oder dagegen und warum oder warum nicht?

22 Für mein Notizbuch

Wenn du mit der Schule fertig bist, wirst du dann zum Militär gehen? Warum oder warum nicht? Möchtest du an einer Militärakademie studieren? An welcher? Schreib deine Gedanken dazu auf!

Auszüge aus Hitlers Reden

Die Welt, sie verfolgt uns. Wir wollen den Frieden. Sie wendet sich gegen uns. Sie will nicht unser Recht zum Leben anerkennen. Mein deutsches Volk, wenn so die Welt gegen uns steht, dann müssen wir umso mehr zu einer Einheit werden.

Aus einer Rede Hitlers im Mai 1933

Was für ein Glück für die Regierenden, daß die Menschen nicht denken!

Bemerkungen Hitlers bei einer Geheimkonferenz mit Generälen im Jahre 1937

Deutschland muß zusätzlichen Lebensraum gewinnen—und zwar in Europa. Ohne Gewaltanwendung geht das nicht. Wir können damit auch nicht mehr lange warten. Denn unser Rüstungspotential wird in den Jahren 1943 bis 45 seinen Höhepunkt erreicht haben. Wir müssen die Offensive ergreifen, bevor die übrige Welt unseren Vorsprung einholt.

Geheime Anweisung Hitlers an die Wehrmacht, sich auf einen Krieg mit Polen vorzubereiten. April 1939

Ich werde den propagandistischen Anlaß zur Auslösung des Krieges geben, gleichgültig, ob glaubhaft. Der Sieger wird später nicht danach gefragt, ob er die Wahrheit gesagt hat oder nicht. Bei Beginn und Führung des Krieges kommt es nicht auf das Recht an, sondern auf den Sieg.

Aus einer Rede Hitlers

Über einen humanen Weltbegriff erhebt sich heute die Erkenntnis von der Bedeutung des Blutes und der Rasse! Nichts kann das mehr aus der Welt schaffen. Das ist eine siegende Idee, die heute wie eine Welle über die ganze Erde hinwegströmt ...

Noch eine besondere Aufgabe haben wir: die Beseitigung all jener Minderwertigkeitsempfindungen, die in unserem Volk waren, da die früheren Regierungen sie notwendig benötigten und brauchten. Wir sind Todfeinde der sogenannten halben, weil falschen Bescheidenheit, die da sagt, wir wollen uns etwas zurückhalten, wir wollen nicht immer von uns reden und alles übertrumpfen, wir wollen bieder bleiben und nicht übel auffallen, man soll uns mehr lieben, die anderen sollen uns nicht mit schiefen Augen ansehen. Im Gegenteil; wir wollen unser Volk ganz nach vorne führen! Ob sie uns lieben, das ist uns einerlei! Wenn sie uns nur respektieren! Ob sie uns hassen, ist uns einerlei, wenn sie uns nur fürchten ...

Adolf Hitler am 18. Januar 1942

LESETRICK

Determining purpose
Determining the purpose of a text before you read allows you to read more critically. It will also help you guess the meaning of unfamiliar words as you read. Use your prereading strategies (looking at visual clues, titles, captions, and format) to hypothesize about the purpose for which a text was written. You'll also want to use any background knowledge you have about the author and the time in which he or she was writing.

Getting Started   For answers, see TE Interleaf.

1. Look at the photos and read the titles, captions, and source references for each reading selection. What kinds of texts are these? Who are the authors? When was each written?

2. Read the caption for the Geschwister Scholl again. Who were the Geschwister Scholl and why were they important?

3. Before reading further, find out as much as you can about German history before and during World War II and about Hitler and the resistance movement specifically. Together with your classmates, construct a time line of major events. What was hap-

GESCHWISTER SCHOLL

Hans, geb. 1918, Medizinstudent, Begründer der Widerstandsbewegung „Weiße Rose" im 2. Weltkrieg. Sophie, geb. 1921, Philosophiestudentin, Mitglied der „Weißen Rose". Beide 1943 zum Tode verurteilt und hingerichtet.

WIDERSTAND GEGEN DIE DIKTATUR:
DAS LETZTE FLUGBLATT

Kommilitonen! Kommilitoninnen!

Erschüttert steht unser Volk vor dem Untergang der Männer von Stalingrad. Dreihundertdreißigtausend deutsche Männer hat die geniale Strategie des Weltkriegsgefreiten sinn- und verantwortungslos in Tod und Verderben gehetzt. Führer, wir danken dir!

Es gärt im deutschen Volk: Wollen wir weiter einem Dilettanten das Schicksal unserer Armeen anvertrauen? Wollen wir den niederen Machtinstinkten einer Parteiclique den Rest der deutschen Jugend opfern? Nimmermehr! Der Tag der Abrechnung ist gekommen, der Abrechnung der deutschen Jugend mit der verabscheuungswürdigsten Tyrannis, die unser Volk je erduldet hat. Im Namen der deutschen Jugend fordern wir vom Staat Adolf Hitlers die persönliche Freiheit, das kostbarste Gut des Deutschen zurück, um das er uns in der erbärmlichsten Weise betrogen.

pening at the time Hitler was making his speeches? And at the time Hans and Sophie Scholl were writing?

4. Using what you've learned from questions 1-3, think about the occasions for which Hitler's speeches and **Das letzte Flugblatt** were written. Who was the intended audience in each case? Can you guess what the purpose of each text was? What is the purpose of the magazine interview?

A Closer Look

5. Read the excerpts from Hitler's speeches and try to determine the meaning of the following words using root words, context, and your understanding of the purpose of the text.

anerkennen	to stream forth
Gewaltanwendung	to acknowledge
ergreifen	to fear
Erkenntnis	realization
vorbereiten	to take
hinwegströmen	use of force
fürchten	to prepare for

6. Look for occurrences of the words **Sieg**, **Sieger**, and **siegend**. In your own words, state what you think Hitler had in mind when he used them. What emotions is he appealing to in his various audiences?

7. In one or two sentences, summarize the main idea of each excerpt from Hitler's speeches. Does the text confirm your hypothesis about the purpose of these

In einem Staat rücksichtsloser Knebelung jeder freien Meinungsäußerung sind wir aufgewachsen. HJ, SA, SS haben uns in den fruchtbarsten Bildungsjahren unseres Lebens zu uniformieren, zu revolutionieren, zu narkotisieren versucht. Weltanschauliche Schulung hieß die verächtliche Methode, das aufkeimende Selbstdenken in einem Nebel leerer Phrasen zu ersticken ...

Es gibt für uns nur eine Parole: Kampf gegen die Partei! ... Es geht uns um wahre Wissenschaft und echte Geistesfreiheit! Kein Drohmittel kann uns schrecken, auch nicht die Schließung unserer Hochschulen. Es gilt den Kampf jedes Einzelnen von uns um un-

sere Zukunft, unsere Freiheit und Ehre in einem seiner sittlichen Verantwortung bewußten Staatswesen ...

Freiheit und Ehre! Zehn Jahre lang haben Hitler und seine Genossen die beiden herrlichen deutschen Worte bis zum Ekel ausgequetscht, abgedroschen, verdreht, ... Studentinnen! Studenten! Auf uns sieht das deutsche Volk! Von uns erwartet es, wie 1813 die Brechung des Napoleonischen, so 1943 die Brechung des nationalsozialistischen Terrors aus der Macht des Geistes. Beresina und Stalingrad flammen im Osten auf; die Toten von Stalingrad beschwören uns!

1943

VERFÜHRT VON DUMMEN, MÖRDERISCHEN SPRÜCHEN

ANGEKLAGT: Felix K., 16

RICHTER: Wolfgang Steffen

Im Prozeß um den Solinger Brandanschlag gab einer der Angeklagten Auskunft über seine Ideologie

Richter: Was ist denn für Sie „rechts"?
Felix: Na ja, Störkraft*, dann halt Hitler und so.
Richter: Und weiter?
Felix: Na ja, Ausländer raus.
Richter: Und weiter?
Felix: Juden raus.
Richter: Und weiter?
Felix: Türken raus, und dann noch Sieg heil und Deutschland erwache.
Richter: Und weiter?
Felix: Das war's.

*Musikgruppe mit rechtsradikalen Texten
FOCUS 20/1994

speeches? Adjust your original statement, if necessary. What tone and what images does Hitler use to convince his audiences?

8. Read the passage by Hans and Sophie Scholl several times. What do you think **Kommilitonen** and **Kommilitoninnen** mean? Who were the intended readers? What were the Scholls fighting against? What were they fighting for? Support your answer with words and phrases from the passage.

9. In the second paragraph, the writer refers to Hitler as a **Dilettant**. What does the word mean, and why do the call him that? Read the fifth paragraph. Whom do the Scholls accuse of distorting the words **Freiheit und Ehre**?

10. Does the passage confirm your hypothesis about the author's purpose? Explain.

11. Read the interview with Felix K. What does the title mean? Who has been "seduced," and by what? What is the significance of this interview in relation to the other two texts? Is there any connection?

12. Wie würdest du jemanden überzeugen, mit dir gegen eine Ungerechtigkeit zu kämpfen? Schreib jetzt dein eigenes Flugblatt, um für deine Meinung zu einer bestimmten Ungerechtigkeit zu plädieren. Bevor du schreibst, denke daran, wer dein Flugblatt lesen wird, zum Beispiel andere Schüler, Erwachsene usw. Versuche, deine Ideen so überzeugend wie möglich zu machen!

In this chapter you have learned how life for German teenagers can be different from that of American teenagers. People who live or have lived in different places do things in a variety of ways that are new to us and sometimes hard for us to understand. In this activity, you will interview a person from another place to find out what life is like in his or her native country. You will write the results of your interview in a report to share with the class.

Lerne Land und Leute durch ein Interview kennen!

Denk an eine Person, die aus einem anderen Land kommt, und interview diese Person! Stell durch das Interview fest, wie das Leben in der Heimat dieser Person ist! Was habt ihr in eurem Leben gemeinsam, und was ist anders? Faß danach das Interview zu einem Bericht zusammen!

A. Vorbereiten

1. Was willst du wissen? Formuliere deine Fragen, und schreib sie auf ein Blatt Papier! Laß zwischen deinen Fragen genug Platz für deine Notizen!
2. Interview deine ausgewählte Person! Das Interview soll ganz informell sein. Wenn dich eine Antwort besonders interessiert, stell weitere Fragen!
3. Benutze deine Notizen, um eine Struktur für deinen Bericht zu schaffen! Welche Ideen tauchen immer wieder auf? Welche Antworten passen gut zusammen? Kannst du jetzt erkennen, welche Aussagen für deinen Bericht brauchbar sind und welche nicht?

B. Ausführen

Wähle die interessantesten Aussagen aus, und schreib einen Bericht über das Leben im anderen Land auf deutsch! Präsentiere Unterschiede und Gemeinsamkeiten, die zwischen dieser Person und dir bestehen!

C. Überarbeiten

1. Lies deinem Interviewpartner deinen Bericht vor, wenn er oder sie Deutsch spricht! Wenn nicht, erkläre, was du geschrieben hast! Wie findet diese Person deine Darstellung?
2. Hast du alle interessanten und wichtigen Punkte erwähnt? Vergleiche den Bericht mit deinen Notizen!
3. Lies den Bericht noch einmal durch! Hast du alles richtig geschrieben? Achte besonders auf die Modalverben!
4. Schreib den korrigierten Bericht noch einmal ab!

> **SCHREIBTIP**
>
> **Asking questions to gather ideas** You have already learned many ways to gather ideas for your writing, including brainstorming and freewriting. Another way is to ask people questions to find out what they know or about their experiences. When asking people questions, try to phrase them in a way that is specific enough to focus in on your topic, but also open-ended enough to allow people the freedom to answer as they please. You should have a plan for your questioning, but allow yourself the flexibility to follow up with unplanned questions as the interview leads in new directions.

ANWENDUNG

1 Eine Schülerin fragt ihren Großvater, wie das Leben war, als er jung war. Hör gut zu, und schreib in Stichworten auf, was der Großvater über seine Jugendzeit berichtet! For answers, see listening script on TE Interleaf.

2 Einige Schüler reden darüber, wie es früher war. Sabine erzählt von ihrer Oma. Lies, was sie berichtet!

Meine Oma hat einmal erzählt, wie es war, als sie ein Kind war. Morgens mußte sie immer sehr früh aufstehen, um zur Schule zu gehen. Sie mußte zu Fuß gehen, über drei Kilometer! Auch am Samstag mußte sie zur Schule. In der Klasse mußten die Schüler still sitzen und die Hände auf den Tisch legen. Sie durften keinen Krach machen, nicht miteinander sprechen. Wer etwas sagen wollte, mußte die Hand heben. Wenn ein Schüler frech war, durfte ihn der Lehrer schlagen. Die Schüler mußten auch auf ihre Kleidung achten. Alles mußte sauber sein, kein Knopf durfte fehlen! Ja, und die Mädchen durften auch keine Hosen tragen, nur Röcke. Nach der Schule mußte meine Oma immer gleich die Hausaufgaben machen, bevor sie mit ihren Freundinnen spielen durfte. Wenn ihre Mutter einkaufen gehen wollte, mußte meine Oma ihre Geschwister betreuen. Nur einmal im Monat durfte sie ins Kino gehen. Meine Oma meint, heute geht es den Kindern viel besser als früher. Sie müssen zwar mehr lernen, haben aber mehr Freizeit für sich.

3 Schreib auf, was die Schüler zu Omas Zeiten alles tun mußten und was sie nicht tun durften!

sie mußten:	sie durften nicht:
früh aufstehen	Hosen tragen (Mädchen)

4 Beschreibe das Foto auf Seite 124! Was ist in diesem Foto anders als heute?

 5 Was hat sich alles von früher geändert? Sag einer Partnerin, wie es früher war und wie es heute ist!

	durften	die Schüler	immer
Früher	konnten	die Mädchen	(fast) nie
	mußten	die Jungen	selten
	können	die Kinder	oft
Heute	dürfen	die Lehrer	manchmal

ihre Meinung frei sagen

auch samstags in die Schule gehen

anziehen, was sie wollen

die Schüler schlagen

sehr viel auswendig lernen

in der Klasse still sein

politisch aktiv sein

selber Vorschläge machen

6 a. Interview eine ältere Person, Bekannte oder Verwandte, über das Thema: Wie war das Leben, als du (Sie) sechzehn Jahre alt warst (waren)? Mach dir kurze Notizen!

 b. Schreib einen kurzen Bericht über das, was du erfahren hast! Lies deinen Bericht der Klasse vor!

c. Vergleiche das Leben, das in dem Bericht geschildert wird, mit deinem Leben heute!

 7 Ein Recht, das junge Leute mit der Volljährigkeit erwerben, ist das Recht, ihren Wohnsitz frei bestimmen zu können. — Stell dir vor, du möchtest jetzt von zu Hause ausziehen, oder du mußt ausziehen, weil du in einem anderen Ort zur Universität gehst! Denk über die Vorteile und Nachteile nach und schreib sie auf!

Vorteile: **Nachteile:**

Ich könnte jetzt …   Ich müßte (*would have to*) jetzt …

8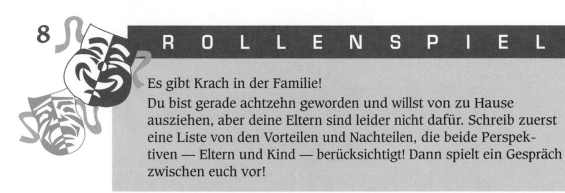

R O L L E N S P I E L

Es gibt Krach in der Familie!

Du bist gerade achtzehn geworden und willst von zu Hause ausziehen, aber deine Eltern sind leider nicht dafür. Schreib zuerst eine Liste von den Vorteilen und Nachteilen, die beide Perspektiven — Eltern und Kind — berücksichtigt! Dann spielt ein Gespräch zwischen euch vor!

KANN ICH'S WIRKLICH?

1 How would you respond if a friend said the following things to you?

a. Wen soll ich wählen? E.g.: Du könntest die (… Partei) wählen.

b. Ich weiß nicht, wem ich meine Stimme geben soll.

c. Der Führerschein ist mir zu teuer. b. E.g.: Du könntest deine Stimme der (… Partei) geben. c. E.g.: Du könntest dir das Geld für den Führerschein mit einem Job verdienen.

2 How would you say that

a. you would have liked to skip class, but you know you should never do that? Ich hätte gern die Schule geschwänzt, aber ich weiß, daß ich das niemals tun soll.

b. you would have liked to go to the movies but you had to help your parents? Ich wäre gern ins Kino gegangen, aber ich mußte meinen Eltern helfen.

3 How would you respond if your parents asked you when you were going to do the following things, and you were already doing them when they asked? a. E.g.: Ich bin dabei, diesen Artikel zu lesen.

a. Hast du den Artikel über den Zivildienst schon gelesen?

b. Überlegst du dir, ob du zur Bundeswehr gehst? b. E.g.: Ich bin am Überlegen.

c. Wann diskutierst du mit deinem Bruder darüber?
c. E.g.: Wir diskutieren gerade darüber.

4 How would you say that

a. you wanted to go out last Sunday, but you couldn't because you had too much to do? Ich wollte letzten Sonntag ausgehen, aber ich hatte zu viel zu tun.

b. your friends couldn't come along and had to stay home?
Meine Freunde konnten nicht mitkommen und mußten zu Hause bleiben.

5 How would you respond to the following statements? a. Das ist mir völlig neu!

a. Leute mit Kontaklinsen dürfen nicht in der Bundeswehr dienen.

b. In der Bundeswehr hatte ich mir den Fuß gebrochen, aber jetzt ist er wieder in Ordnung. b. Ich bin froh, daß es dir wieder besser geht.

c. Ich finde es nicht gut, daß wir eine Wehrpflicht in Deutschland haben.
c. Ach was soll's! Das ist leider so.

ERSTE STUFE

TALKING ABOUT WHAT IS POSSIBLE

**Ich könnte das machen, wenn
...** *I could do that, if ...*

SAYING WHAT YOU WOULD HAVE LIKED TO DO

**Ich hätte gern die Sendung
gesehen.** *I would have
liked to have seen the show.*
**Ich wäre gern nach München
gereist.** *I would have liked
to have traveled to Munich.*

OTHER USEFUL WORDS

der Unterricht   *class, school*
die Prüfung, -en   *test*
das Mitglied, -er   *member*
der Verein, -e   *club*
der Vertrag, ̈-e   *contract*
die Pflicht, -en   *duty*
das Recht, -e   *right*
in dieser Hinsicht   *as far as
that goes*

bevor (conj)   *before*
kurzfristig   *on short notice*
schade sein um   *to be a
shame about something*

umgekehrt   *vice-versa*
schwänzen   *to cut class*
fehlen   *to be missing*
s. erlauben   *to permit oneself*
dauern   *to last*
schaffen   *to achieve, make*
s. irren   *to be wrong*
scheinen   *to seem*
wählen   *to vote for*
s. engagieren   *to be active in*
unterschreiben   *to sign
(your name)*
heiraten   *to marry*
unabhängig sein   *to be independent*
s. ändern   *to change oneself*

ZWEITE STUFE

SAYING THAT SOMETHING IS GOING ON RIGHT NOW

Ich arbeite an dem Projekt.   *I'm
working on the project.*
**Ich bin dabei, am Projekt zu
arbeiten.**   *I'm getting
started on the project.*
Ich bin am Arbeiten.   *I'm
working.*

REPORTING PAST EVENTS

**Ich konnte gestern meine
Hausaufgaben erledigen.**
*I was able to finish my home-
work yesterday.*

EXPRESSING SURPRISE, RELIEF, AND RESIGNATION

Das ist mir neu!   *That's news
to me!*
Ich bin aber froh.   *I'm sure
happy about that.*
**Ach, was soll's? Das ist leider
so.**   *Well, what's the use?
That's the way it is.*

OTHER USEFUL WORDS

der Panzer, -   *tank*

der Laster, -   *truck*
das Transportflugzeug, -e
transport plane
der Bomber, -   *bomber*
die Streitkräfte (pl)   *armed
forces*
die Bundeswehr   *German
Federal Defense Force*
der Bund=die Bundeswehr
das U-Boot, -e   *submarine*
der Wehrdienst   *armed
forces*
die Wehrpflicht   *compulsory
service*
der Offizier, -e   *officer*
der Frieden   *peace*
das Gewehr, -e   *gun*
die Waffe, -n   *weapon*
der Kampf, ̈-e   *struggle, battle*
der Zivildienst   *community
service*
die Demokratie, -n   *democracy*
das Grundgesetz   *basic law*
die Gleichberechtigung
equality
die Entscheidung, -en   *decision*
das Studium   *university
studies*
im Ernst   *seriously*

das Thema, Themen   *theme,
matter*

abstreiten (sep)   *to argue
against*
belasten   *to weigh on, burden*
betreuen   *to care for*
einstellen (sep)   *to hire*
einziehen (sep)   *to draft*
s. entscheiden für   *to decide
on*
halten für   *to consider something as*
kommandieren   *to command*
s. lohnen   *to be worth it*
schießen   *to shoot*
unterbrechen   *to interrupt*
s. unterhalten über (acc)   *to
discuss*
s. verlassen auf (acc)   *to
count on*

angenehm   *pleasant*
fies   *awful*
anstrengend   *strenuous*
sinnlos   *senseless*
freiwillig   *voluntary*
vergangen-   *past*
vorig-   *last*
früher   *earlier*
ausgesprochen   *particularly*

Kapitel 6: Medien: stets gut informiert?

	FUNCTIONS	GRAMMAR	CULTURE	RE-ENTRY
Los geht's! pp. 130-131	Die Macht der Medien, *p. 130*			
Erste Stufe pp. 132-136	•Asking someone to take a position, *p. 133* •Asking for reasons, *p. 133* •Expressing opinions, *p. 133* •Reporting past events, *p. 134* •Agreeing or disagreeing, *p. 136* •Changing the subject, *p. 136* •Interrupting, *p. 136*	Narrative past (imperfect), *pp. 134, 135*	•Die TV-Kids, *p. 132* •Landeskunde: Die Schülerzeitung, *p. 137*	•Talking about favorites, *p. 133* •Leisure-time activities, *p. 133* •Expressing opinions, *p. 133* •The conversational past, *p. 135* •Agreeing and disagreeing, *p. 136* •Television vocabulary, *p. 136*
Weiter geht's! pp. 138-139	Unsere eigene Zeitung! *p. 138*			
Zweite Stufe pp. 140-143	Expressing surprise or annoyance, *p. 141*	Superlative forms of adjectives, *p. 142*	Leserbriefe an die Redaktion der Pepo, *p. 140*	•Expressing surprise, *p. 141* •The comparative forms of adjectives, *p. 142* •Time expressions, *p. 143* •Words of quantity, *p. 143*
Zum Lesen pp. 144-146	Ein Märchen Reading Strategy: Predicting outcomes			
Zum Schreiben p. 147	Ich nehme dazu Stellung. Writing Strategy: Using an outline			
Review pp. 148-151	•Anwendung, *p. 148* •Kann ich's wirklich? *p. 150* •Wortschatz, *p. 151*			

Assessment Options

Mid-term Exam, *Assessment Guide* Audiocassette 7 B

Stufe Quizzes
•*Chapter Resources*, Book 2
  Erste Stufe, Quiz 6-1
  Zweite Stufe, Quiz 6-2
•*Assessment Items, Audiocassette* 7 B

Kapitel 6 Chapter Test
•*Chapter Resources*, Book 2
•*Assessment Guide*, Speaking Test
•*Assessment Items, Audiocassette* 7 B

Test Generator, Kapitel 6

RESOURCES Print	RESOURCES Audiovisual
Practice and Activity Book	*Textbook Audiocassette* 3 B

	Textbook Audiocassette 3 B
Practice and Activity Book	
Chapter Resources, Book 2	
•Communicative Activity 6-1	
•Communicative Activity 6-2	
•Additional Listening Activity 6-1	*Additional Listening Activities, Audiocassette* 9 B
•Additional Listening Activity 6-2	*Additional Listening Activities, Audiocassette* 9 B
•Additional Listening Activity 6-3	*Additional Listening Activities, Audiocassette* 9 B
•Student Response Forms	
•Realia 6-1	
•Situation Card 6-1	
•Teaching Transparency Master 6-1	*Teaching Transparency* 6-1
•Quiz 6-1	*Assessment Items, Audiocassette* 7 B
Video Guide	*Video Program*, Videocassette 1

	Textbook Audiocassette 3 B
Practice and Activity Book	

	Textbook Audiocassette 3 B
Practice and Activity Book	
Chapter Resources, Book 2	
•Communicative Activity 6-3	
•Communicative Activity 6-4	
•Additional Listening Activity 6-4	*Additional Listening Activities, Audiocassette* 9 B
•Additional Listening Activity 6-5	*Additional Listening Activities, Audiocassette* 9 B
•Additional Listening Activity 6-6	*Additional Listening Activities, Audiocassette* 9 B
•Student Response Forms	
•Realia 6-2	
•Situation Card 6-2	
•Teaching Transparency Master 6-2	*Teaching Transparency* 6-2
•Quiz 6-2	*Assessment Items, Audiocassette* 7 B

	Textbook Audiocassette 11

Chapter Resources, Book 2	
•Realia 6-3	
•Situation Card 6-3	
Video Guide	*Video Program*, Videocassette 1

Alternative Assessment
•Performance Assessment
Teacher's Edition
Erste Stufe, p. 127K
Zweite Stufe, p. 127N

•Portfolio Assessment
Written: **Anwendung**, Activity 8, *Pupil's Edition*, p. 149; *Assessment Guide*, p. 19
Oral: **Anwendung**, Activity 8, *Pupil's Edition*, p. 149; *Assessment Guide*, p. 19
•**Notizbuch**, *Pupil's Edition*, p. 133

Kapitel 6: Medien: stets gut informiert?
Textbook Listening Activities Scripts

For Student Response Forms, see *Chapter Resources, Book 2*, pp. 142-145.

Erste Stufe
Activity 4, p. 133

KÄSSI Sagt mal, habt ihr gestern abend auch den Bericht über Serbien im Fernsehen gesehen?

ANTJE Nee. Du, Holger?

HOLGER Nein. Ich hab' gestern Radio gehört.

KÄSSI Also, der Bericht war wirklich interessant, muß ich sagen. Ich sehe mir sowieso gern die Nachrichten im ZDF an. Du etwa nicht, Antje?

ANTJE Nein, nicht so gern. Weißt du, Kässi, meiner Meinung nach sind die Nachrichten im Fernsehen ziemlich oberflächlich.

KÄSSI Finde ich aber nicht! Das reicht doch als Information aus.

ANTJE Hm! Also, ich brauche schon etwas mehr Information.

THOMAS Was genau meinst du denn? Ich finde, daß man durchs Fernsehen am besten informiert wird.

ANTJE Also, paß mal auf, Thomas! Es reicht mir nicht, wenn der Nachrichtensprecher im Fernsehen einfach nur sagt: Es gibt einen Konflikt im Land A und die Völker B und C streiten aus dem Grund D! Ich will mehr über die historischen, politischen und wirtschaftlichen Hintergründe wissen.

THOMAS Ja, aber das geht nun mal nicht in einer Nachrichtensendung, die nur kurze, sachliche Informationen herausbringt!

ANTJE Das stimmt! Deswegen lese ich eben lieber Zeitung!

KÄSSI Ach Antje! Viele Zeitungen und Magazine bringen doch nur Sensationsnachrichten und keine Tatsachen.

ANTJE Ich meine ja auch seriöse Zeitungen, so wie die *Frankfurter Allgemeine* oder die *Süddeutsche Zeitung*.

HOLGER Also, ich finde, wenn man sich schnell über Neuigkeiten informieren will, schaltet man am besten das Radio an. Dort kommen alle 30 Minuten Kurznachrichten.

THOMAS Dann lies doch einfach nur die Schlagzeilen!

KÄSSI Bloß nicht! So kann man sich auf keinen Fall informieren! Die Schlagzeilen sind doch meistens extra ganz provokativ formuliert und spiegeln nicht unbedingt Tatsachen wider!

ANTJE Ja, da hast du recht, Kässi. Deswegen ist es wichtig, den ganzen Artikel zu lesen.

Answers to Activity 4

Kässi: TV; Antje: Zeitung; Holger: Radio; Thomas: TV

Activity 5, p. 133

MARKUS He, Leute! In der letzten Ausgabe der *Frankfurter Allgemeinen Zeitung* gibt es einen tollen Artikel über Umweltprobleme. Hat den einer von euch gelesen? Du, Michaela?

MICHAELA Nein! Was für ein Artikel war denn das, Markus?

MARKUS Ja, also in dem Artikel steht, daß es verboten werden sollte, mit dem Auto zu fahren. Ich finde das auch.

RÜDIGER Kannst du das begründen?

MARKUS Mensch, Rüdiger, die Abgase werden doch zu einem immer größeren Problem für die Umwelt!

MICHAELA Das stimmt! Wenn wir nicht vorsichtig sind, werden wir bald überhaupt keine saubere Luft und kein sauberes Trinkwasser mehr haben.

MARKUS Ja, genau! Ich stimme der Michaela zu. Und deswegen bin ich heute auch gleich mit dem Fahrrad zur Schule gekommen, weil ich bei mir selbst anfangen möchte, die Umwelt zu schonen. Ich finde, du solltest auch nicht mehr mit deinem Moped kommen, Rüdiger.

RÜDIGER Ach, das ist doch völliger Quatsch! Ich fahre weiter mit dem Moped.

MARKUS Also, Rüdiger! Wieso ist das Quatsch? Dazu mußt du jetzt aber wirklich mal genauer Stellung nehmen.

RÜDIGER Ach, das ist doch ganz einfach! Ich finde, diese Nachrichten, die immer von den Umweltbelastungen reden, sind doch sowieso nur Sensationsmeldungen.

MICHAELA Na ja, also meiner Meinung nach sollte man vielleicht nicht ganz aufs Autofahren verzichten.

CORNELIA Wie meinst du das, Michaela?

MICHAELA Weißt du, Cornelia, ich finde, daß es okay ist, mit dem Auto zu fahren, wenn man einen Notfall hat. Also, wenn man zum Beispiel schnell ins Krankenhaus muß.

CORNELIA Also, Michaela, meinst du denn wirklich, daß die Leute in Deutschland nur noch in Notfällen mit dem Auto fahren? Das funktioniert niemals. Das kannst du mir glauben.

MARKUS Und wieso nicht, Cornelia?

CORNELIA Ich weiß nicht! Das kann ich mir halt einfach nicht vorstellen!

Answers to Activity 5

Grund: Markus, Michaela, Rüdiger; keinen Grund: Cornelia; Answers will vary.

Activity 11, p. 136

WOLFGANG Sagt mal, habt ihr gestern den Krimi im RTL gesehen? Der war echt toll! Du, Simone, du mußt deine Familie endlich mal dazu überreden, einen Fernseher zu kaufen. Sonst kannst du ja nie mitreden.

SIMONE Also, weißt du, Wolfgang, wir brauchen keinen Fernseher. Wir unternehmen lieber etwas zusammen als Familie.

DIRK Wirklich?

SIMONE Ja! Wir finden nämlich, daß die meisten Familien, die einen Fernseher haben, abends nur vor der Glotze sitzen und kaum miteinander reden. Ist dir das denn noch nie aufgefallen, Dirk?

DIRK Hm! Da ist schon was dran. Bei uns zu Hause ist das ähnlich. Bei euch doch bestimmt auch, oder, Beate?

BEATE Quatsch! Das stimmt gar nicht! Bei uns zu Hause wird viel geredet. Wir diskutieren oft über das, was wir im Fernsehen gesehen haben.

WOLFGANG Richtig! Außerdem kann man sich durchs Fernsehen viel leichter über alle wichtigen Ereignisse in der Welt informieren.

SIMONE Moment mal, Wolfgang! Das kann man auch wenn man Zeitung liest oder Radio hört. Ich finde außerdem, daß man in seiner Freizeit viel weniger aktiv ist, wenn man zu viel fernsieht.

DIRK Ja, da hat die Simone recht. Ich finde auch, daß man sich von anderen Menschen isoliert und nicht so viel unternimmt.

WOLFGANG Laß mich mal wieder zu Wort kommen, Dirk! Also, für mich ist das Fernsehen wichtig. Außer den Nachrichten oder Fernsehserien kann ich mir nämlich auch Opern, Theaterstücke und Konzerte sehen.

BEATE Ja! Finde ich auch, Wolfgang! Erstens ist das nicht so teuer wie Opern- oder Konzertkarten und zweitens kann man schön zu Hause die Aufführung genießen, ohne erst irgendwo hinfahren zu müssen.

WOLFGANG Eben! Und außerdem kann man eine Sendung aufnehmen. Dann kann man sich später das Video anschauen! Das ist doch total praktisch!

SIMONE Ach! Das kommt doch alles aufs gleiche raus! Tatsache ist, daß man vorm Fernseher hockt und nichts unternimmt! 75 Prozent aller Leute, die täglich vier oder mehr Stunden vor dem Fernseher sitzen, essen zu viel! Sie werden häufiger krank, beklagen sich über Müdigkeit und haben keine Energie!

DIRK Ja! Richtige Gesundheitsmuffel sind das!

Answers to Activity 11
Answers will vary.

Zweite Stufe
Activity 16, p. 141

BERNHARD He, Leute, denkt dran! Wir treffen uns heute abend bei mir zu Hause, damit wir noch mal das Layout für den Druck besprechen können!

REGINA Ja, in Ordnung, Bernhard! Ich hab' auch schon die Seite mit den Leserbriefen fertig gemacht.

BERNHARD Spitze, Regina! Du hast bestimmt stundenlang daran gesessen.

REGINA Ach was! Mir hat es echt Spaß gemacht. Und ich glaub', ich hab' die richtige Mischung aus guten und kritischen Leserbriefen zusammengestellt!

BERNHARD Gut! Wir müssen nur noch die Ergebnisse aus unserer letzten Umfrage in den Computer eintippen, damit wir eine tolle Grafik in der Zeitung abbilden können.

GERD Schon erledigt! Hab' ich gestern nachmittag gemacht.

REGINA Super, Gerd! Was gibt es sonst noch zu tun?

BERNHARD Tina hat ihren Artikel über die Schulfete noch nicht fertig geschrieben.

GERD Das ist ja unglaublich! Immer fängt sie alles an und macht es dann nie zu Ende!

BERNHARD Ja, leider! So ist sie nun mal. Da kann man nichts machen.

GERD Und wer schreibt ihren Artikel bis heute abend fertig?

BERNHARD Keine Panik! Ich schreib' den Artikel heute nachmittag zu Ende.

GERD Mensch, Bernhard! Auf dich kann man sich wirklich verlassen. Aber fair find' ich das nicht! Das ist jetzt schon das dritte Mal, daß du für die Tina einspringst. Stimmt's Regina?

REGINA Ja, leider, Gerd. Es überrascht mich wirklich, daß Tina so faul ist.

BERNHARD Ja, das ist echt schade, denn sie schreibt wirklich gute Artikel, wenn sie Lust hat.

REGINA Also, was müssen wir sonst noch alles bis heute abend erledigen?

GERD Wir müssen uns auf das Titelblatt einigen. Regina hat drei Vorschläge ausgearbeitet.

REGINA Ja, ich glaub', ich hab' drei super Ideen. Wir müssen nur noch die Heidi fragen, ob sie für uns die Illustration machen kann. Ach, da kommt sie ja! Hallo, Heidi!

HEIDI Hallo, alle zusammen! Was gibt's?

BERNHARD Du, Heidi, meinst du, du schaffst es, bis heute abend drei Illustrationen fürs Titelbild zu machen?

HEIDI Was? Fürs Titelbild? Heißt das etwa, daß wir noch kein Titelbild haben, obwohl die nächste Ausgabe morgen gedruckt werden soll? Das darf doch wohl nicht wahr sein!

REGINA Doch, leider! Also, was ist? Können wir mit dir rechnen?

HEIDI Also, es stört mich wirklich, daß alles immer bis auf die letzte Minute verschoben wird! Fragt doch jemand anders!

BERNHARD Ach, komm schon, Heidi! Wir sind doch alle unter Streß wegen dem Abi und den Noten und so!

HEIDI Ja, ja! Schon gut! Ich bring' heute abend die Illustrationen mit, okay?!

REGINA Klasse, Heidi!

Answers to Activity 16
gern: Bernhard, Regina, Gerd; nicht gern: Heidi, Tina

Activity 17, p. 141

ANGELIKA Also, Leute! Ich habe euch hierher gebeten, damit jeder seine Meinung zu unserer Schülerzeitung sagen kann ...

BODO Meine Meinung kann ich dir gern sagen, Angelika! Es ist wirklich frustrierend, wenn wir nichts als Kritik über ...

ANGELIKA Moment mal, Bodo! Laß mich kurz ausreden! Dann kommst du dran. Also, ich will mit euch über unseren nächsten Leitartikel sprechen und die Aufgaben neu verteilen. Aber als erstes sollten wir über unsere letzte Ausgabe diskutieren. Also, Bodo?

BODO Na ja, wie gesagt, ich habe halt echt hart an dem Artikel über die neue Umwelt AG gearbeitet. Und dann höre ich von den Schülern, daß ihnen alles mögliche nicht daran gefallen hat, oder daß der Artikel blöd war oder so! Stimmt's, Georg?

GEORG Da ist schon was dran, Bodo. Mich stört es auch, wenn ich viel Zeit in einen Artikel investiere, und dann nur kritisiert werde.

ANGELIKA Es überrascht mich, daß ihr so sauer seid! Überlegt doch mal, vielleicht ist es auch unsere eigene Schuld, wenn die Schülerzeitung nur kritisiert wird!

GEORG Wieso?

ANGELIKA Ganz einfach! Weil wir offensichtlich nicht das bringen, was den Schülern gefällt! Wir sollten eine Umfrage machen, um herauszufinden, für welche Themen sich die Schüler interessieren.

CLAUDIA Also, ich bin überrascht, daß du das vorschlägst, Angelika! Wir haben doch erst letzten Monat eine Umfrage gemacht, und kaum jemand hat sich daran beteiligt!

GEORG Eben! Den meisten Schülern ist es doch egal, was und worüber wir schreiben, stimmt's, Claudia?

CLAUDIA Ja, leider, Georg! Ich finde es einfach unglaublich, daß die meisten Schüler einfach nicht verstehen, wieviel Arbeit in so einer Schülerzeitung steckt!

BODO Ja, genau! Mich stört es wirklich, daß keiner Vorschläge macht, wie wir unsere Zeitung besser machen können!

CLAUDIA Genau! Was Bodo sagt, stimmt! Die letzten Leserbriefe waren voller Kritik! Kein einziger Verbesserungsvorschlag! Es ist wirklich frustrierend!

ANGELIKA Moment Mal, Claudia! Ich würde das alles nicht so pessimistisch sehen. Ich bin der Meinung, daß die Kritik doch gerade das ist, was uns weiter hilft!

CLAUDIA Wie meinst du das, Angelika?

ANGELIKA Paßt mal auf! Erstens müssen wir die kritischen Kommentare ganz genau durchlesen. Zweitens dürfen wir die Sachen, die kritisiert worden sind, nicht wieder machen. Und drittens fangen wir an, diese Sachen zu verbessern, so daß es jeder merkt.

GEORG Mensch, Angelika! Das ist ein super Vorschlag! Ich bin überrascht, daß wir nicht schon früher darauf gekommen sind.

CLAUDIA Ja! Dann hätten wir uns 'ne Menge Frust erspart!

Answers to Activity 17

Bodo: frustriert; Angelika: überrascht; Georg: frustriert und überrascht; Claudia: überrascht und frustriert

*A*nwendung
Activity 2, p. 148

— Also, Axel, hast du schon ein paar gute Ideen für die Artikel in unserer nächsten Ausgabe?

— Na klar, Michaela! Ich hab' da ganz verschiedene Vorschläge. Also, Umwelt ist immer ein gutes Thema! Viele Schüler interessieren sich dafür und ...

— Nun sag schon, worüber du berichten willst!

— Du läßt mich ja nicht ausreden! Also, paß auf! Die Verschmutzung der Mosel ist zur Zeit hier in der Stadt ein heißes Thema!

— Hm. Bist du sicher, daß sich die Schüler dafür interessieren?

— Ganz bestimmt! Ich wollte den Hans-Joachim fragen, ob er Lust hat, darüber zu schreiben. Seine Berichte zum Thema Umwelt kommen immer gut an!

— Da hast du recht, Axel! Was schlägst du noch vor?

— Wir könnten eine Kritik über den neuen Film mit Arnold Schwarzenegger schreiben.

— Gut! Ich hab' auch einen Vorschlag. Die Susanne Krämer aus der Theater AG hat mir von dem Theaterstück erzählt, das für die Weihnachtsfeier geprobt wird. Wir könnten einen Artikel über die ganzen Vorbereitungen schreiben.

— Das hört sich gut an. Du, Michaela, wie wär's denn außerdem mit einem Artikel über das neue Austauschprogramm mit der Schule in unserer Partnerstadt Austin in Texas?

— Hm. Nicht schlecht! Die Schüler wissen fast gar nichts darüber. Hast du sonst noch eine Idee?

— Klar, und das ist eigentlich mein bester Vorschlag: Ich finde, wir sollten einen Artikel über die ausländischen Schüler an unserer Schule schreiben. Die Raffaela und der Assam haben schon einige Vorschläge zu dem Artikel. Was hältst du davon?

— Klasse Idee! Vielleicht können wir daraus eine Serie machen und in jeder Ausgabe über einen anderen Schüler berichten!

— Spitze! Du, Michaela, ich würd' gern den Artikel über die ausländischen Schüler schreiben. Übernimmst du den Artikel über das amerikanische Austauschprogramm?

— Nee, Axel, keine Zeit! Ich muß noch das Interview mit der neuen Biologielehrerin machen.

— Ach ja, stimmt! Dann fragen wir eben die Steffi, ob sie den Artikel schreiben will.

— Hat Holger schon die Cartoons gezeichnet?

— Glaub' ich nicht! Er wollte warten, bis wir die Themen für die Artikel festgelegt haben.

— Logo! Ach übrigens, der Peter Hamacher aus der 12b macht für uns die Fotos auf der Schulfete!

— Spitze! Für die nächste Ausgabe scheint ja alles ziemlich gut organisiert zu sein!

— Ja! Wir müssen uns nur noch ein Thema für die Umfrage ausdenken.

— Vielleicht sollten wir diesmal keine Umfrage machen.

— Doch, doch! Auf jeden Fall! Die Schüler finden es toll, wenn wir sie nach ihrer Meinung fragen und dann das Ergebnis der Umfrage in der Schülerzeitung veröffentlichen.

Answers to Activity 2

Answers will vary.

Kapitel 6: Medien: stets gut informiert?
Projects and Games

PROJECT

In this activity students will design and plan the premier issue of a German language newspaper for their school. This project should start after the **Zum Schreiben** *and* **Anwendung** *sections where students receive many helpful suggestions for this project.*

Materials Students may need paper, pens, pencils, scissors, glue, and photos.

Suggested Sequence

1. Ask students to brainstorm about what this German paper should look like. What type of articles and features should be included?
2. Let the class choose a title and a masthead for the paper.
3. Students divide up the work, and each team works on a specific feature.
4. Students prepare drafts of the features or articles for which they are responsible.
5. Students peer edit each other's work and make necessary changes.
6. Students work together to design a layout and determine what types of illustrations should be included in the final copy. If possible, have students prepare the final layout using a computer.
7. Students evaluate the first proof and correct any errors.
8. The final copy is printed, copied, and distributed to all German students.

Grading the Project

Since the outcome of the newspaper is based on class cooperation and effort, you may want to assign one grade to the entire class.

Suggested point distribution (total = 100 points)

Content	25
Appearance of pages	25
Accurate language usage	25
Originality	25

GAME

Eine unmögliche Geschichte aus dem Schuhkarton

This game will help students review the vocabulary from this and previous chapters.

Preparation Write vocabulary words and phrases on small slips of paper and put them all in a shoebox. Here are some suggested vocabulary items.

vermissen	Schüleraustausch
besuchen	allein
erfahren	der Musikladen
die Wahrheit	die Jugendherberge

Procedure The first student takes a piece of paper from the shoebox and begins to tell a story incorporating the vocabulary item he or she has chosen. He or she then passes the box to another student in the class, who draws another slip of paper and continues the story by incorporating the word or phrase on his or her piece of paper. The story must end with the last piece of paper in the box.

NOTE: You may want to record the story on an audiocassette and then play it back to the class.

Kapitel 6: Medien: stets gut informiert?
Lesson Plans, pages 128-151

Teacher Note

Before you begin the chapter, you may want to preview the *Video Program* and consult the *Video Guide*. Suggestions for integrating the video into each chapter are given in the *Video Guide* and in the chapter interleaf. Activity masters for video selections can be found in the *Video Guide*.

*U*sing the Chapter Opener, *pp. 128-129*

Motivating Activity

Ask students how they usually get their news information. Do they prefer radio, television, or newspapers and magazines? Take a survey of the students' preferences.

Journalism Connection

Ask students about their school's newspaper. What is its name, how often is it published, and what type of information does it provide for the student body?

Teaching Suggestions

① Have students recall a news item that they recently discussed with friends. When was this, how did they find out about it, and what was it about? (**Könnt ihr euch an das letzte Thema in den Nachrichten erinnern, über das ihr mit Freunden diskutiert habt? Wann war das, und worum ging es?**)

① Have students think of several topics that might be covered in a newspaper. (Examples: a national event, a natural disaster, an election) Then have small groups of students choose one of the topics the class came up with and create possible conversations that the students in the photo might be having.

② Ask students how they find out what is on TV. What types of television programs do they prefer to watch? (**Wie erfahrt ihr gewöhnlich, was es im Fernsehen gibt? Was für Programme seht ihr euch am liebsten an?**)

Thinking Critically

• **Comparing and Contrasting** Have students research several different newspapers and/or news magazines and find an event that was covered by all of them. Have them read each article carefully and find similarities and differences in the coverage in each one. Can students draw conclusions about the way news events are treated in each of the publications? For example, are the facts presented objectively in all of the articles? Are some of them more sensationalist in their approach? (**Vergleicht den Bericht in ... mit dem Bericht in ... In welcher Hinsicht sind sich die Berichte ähnlich? In welcher Hinsicht sind sie verschieden? In welchem Artikel sind die Tatsachen am sachlichsten dargestellt? Was scheint die Absicht jedes Artikels zu sein?**)

• As a variation, have students compare the coverage of the same event in a daily newspaper (local or national) and on television. Are there differences in the way the event is presented in the two media? (**Vergleicht einen Bericht in der Zeitung mit einem Fernsehbericht. In welcher Hinsicht sind sich die Berichte ähnlich? In welcher Hinsicht sind sie verschieden?**)

③ **Drawing Inferences** Have students take a closer look at this photo and read the accompanying caption. Can they determine where these students are and what they might be doing?

Focusing on Outcomes

To get students to focus on the chapter objectives, ask them how they would like to stay informed if they had the time and means. Then have students preview the learning outcomes listed on p. 129. **NOTE:** These outcomes are modeled in **Los geht's!** (pp. 130-131) and **Weiter geht's!** (pp. 138-139) and evaluated in **Kann ich's wirklich?** (p. 150).

*T*eaching Los geht's!
pp. 130-131

Resources for Los geht's!

- *Textbook Audiocassette* 3 B
- *Practice and Activity Book*

Teacher Note

Los geht's! is recorded on audiocassette.

Los geht's! Summary

In **Die Macht der Medien,** some students talk about the German media and discuss how they prefer to inform themselves about what is happening in the world. The following student outcomes listed on p. 129 are modeled in the conversation: asking someone to take a position, asking for reasons, expressing opinions, reporting past events, agreeing or disagreeing, changing the subject, and interrupting.

Motivating Activity

Take a brief survey in class to find out how many hours per day students spend a) reading newspapers or magazines, b) watching news on TV, and c) listening to news on the radio. (**Wieviel Zeit pro Tag verbringt ihr mit a) Zeitung oder Zeitschrift lesen? b) Nachrichten im Fernsehen sehen? c) Nachrichten im Radio hören?**)

Teaching Suggestion

Play the tape of the interview and have students follow along in the text. Then divide the text into several sections, play one part at a time, and follow up with questions to check for comprehension. Explain new vocabulary and phrases in German using actions, synonyms, and paraphrasing. After working through the complete interview in such a fashion, play the entire conversation again, stopping repeatedly to check students' understanding of the main arguments.

Language Note

Nicole makes a reference to a particular newspaper using the acronym **SZ.** It stands for *Süddeutsche Zeitung,* which is published in Munich.

Cooperative Learning

1 Have students do this activity in cooperative groups. Ask one student to be the recorder and have the rest of the group scan the text to fill in each of the three columns. Call on the reporters of each group to give their findings as you check responses for each of the types of media.

Teaching Suggestion

2 Have pairs of students take turns asking each other the three questions. Then call on students to find out what their partners said.

Teacher Note

Newspapers like *Bild* and *Bild am Sonntag* are the largest circulating papers in Germany. They are quite sensational. Some of the newspapers that offer extensive coverage of national and international news, business, and the arts are *Die Zeit, Frankfurter Allgemeine Zeitung,* and the *Süddeutsche Zeitung. Der Spiegel* is the leading news magazine. Several **Programmzeitschriften** have information about TV and radio programming, articles about celebrities, and various other features.

For Individual Needs

Visual Learners If possible, bring in newspapers and magazines from German-speaking countries. Have students work in groups to determine what sections the papers contain and report on one article in a section of their choice.

Closure

Ask students to review the **Los geht's!** conversation and decide whose opinion they most identify with.

LOS GEHT'S!

*T*eaching Erste Stufe
pp. 132-136

▶ **page 132**

MOTIVATE

Teaching Suggestion

Survey students to find out about their reading habits. Ask them what other things they usually read besides what is required for school. Find out how much time they take to read for pleasure.

TEACH

▣ Video Program

In the video clip **Über Kinos und Videos,** young people in Würzburg talk about their preferences as to where they like to watch movies—on the big screen in a movie theater or at home, using a rental in their VCR. See *Video Guide* for suggestions.

Thinking Critically

Analyzing Have students look at the six slogans about TV and decide which of them are positive statements and which are negative. Then have small groups of students each look more closely at one of the six slogans and discuss possible reasons for the statement. One student should take notes for each group and share the outcome of their discussion with the rest of the class.

For Individual Needs

Challenge Have pairs or small groups of students read the article "**Die TV-Kids**" and give several reasons for calling the students in the survey "**TV-Kids.**"

Thinking Critically

Comparing and Contrasting Ask students to find recent statistics on the television viewing habits of young Americans aged 11-13, and then compare their findings to those in the German survey.

PRESENTATION: Wortschatz

Go over the new vocabulary with students. Then ask them to use at least three of the new words or phrases in sentences of their own. This can be done orally or in writing.

Language Note

The word **Glotze** in the **Wortschatz** box is a colloquial word referring to the television. An English equivalent to **die Glotze** might be *the tube.*

Teaching Suggestion

Have students group the new vocabulary under certain headings, such as **Zeitung** or **Fernsehen**, or build "webs" with one of these key words in the center.

▶ **page 133**

Teaching Suggestions

3 Use these questions to involve all students in a class discussion. One student can read each question to the rest of the class and another can initiate the discussion by giving his or her opinion.

- For part 3 of this activity, have students make their **positiv** and **negativ** list on butcher paper or on the chalkboard.

ERSTE STUFE

PRESENTATION: So sagt man das!

- Before you introduce these new expressions, review similar expressions students have already learned.
  Examples:

Wie findest du ...?	**Ich glaube, ...**
Wofür bist du?	**Ich meine, ...**
Was hält sie von ...?	
Was denkst du über ...?	

- After presenting the new phrases, have students review the **Los geht's!** interview and give the contexts in which the new expressions were used.

▶ *page 134*

For Individual Needs

7 A Slower Pace Review with students the various types of media that are available to them. Students may then refer to this list during the interview with their partner and for the group interview as well.

PRESENTATION: So sagt man das!

Students have seen the narrative past tense in previous reading selections. Have them first read the narrative for general comprehension and then find all the past tense forms. See if they recognize the past tense marker -**te**.

PRESENTATION: Grammatik

Present the three types of verbs to students: weak verbs, strong verbs, and hybrids. Each time, ask students to identify the critical element that makes the verb form a past tense form. Follow with some application exercises. For weak verbs, present other examples to check whether students understand the pattern. For strong verbs, give several additional examples that follow the same pattern to see if students can guess what the past tense will be.
Examples:

geben —> gab; sehen —> ?; essen —> ?
finden —> fand; singen —> ?; trinken —> ?
fahren —> fuhr; tragen —> ?; laden ein —> ?

▶ *page 135*

Teaching Suggestions

- Ask students to look back at the text in the **So sagt man das!** box on p. 134. Have them name all the verbs in the narrative past, including prefixes. Where appropriate, have students give the corresponding forms of conversational past. This exercise will show students how awkward and cumbersome the conversational past is in comparison to the imperfect for relating past events in a narrative.

9 This activity could be done orally in class and then as a written assignment for homework.

▶ *page 136*

Culture Note

10 While cable television, VCRs, CD players, and home computers are becoming more widespread in Germany, they are not yet quite as common as they are in the United States. The value added tax (VAT) and the smaller German market with less competition are two facts that make these items and services less affordable than comparable products in the United States.

Multicultural Connection

10 Have students use the format of this survey to interview someone from another country who might be familiar with the use of this equipment. Have them report their findings to the class.

For Additional Practice

Have pairs of students tell each other how they spent last weekend. Ask students to use the conversational past to tell each other what they did. Then call on several students and have them tell from memory what their partners did using the narrative past.

ERSTE STUFE

▶ *page 137*

PRESENTATION: Landeskunde

Motivating Activity

Ask students about their own school newspaper. Do they know students who are involved in producing the paper? Do they read the paper? What do they like or not like about it?

Teaching Suggestions

• The **Landeskunde** article has three parts. Although entitled "**Die Schülerzeitung,**" it also deals with student government in general and with student government at a specific high school in particular. To begin, read each section to the class and follow up with comprehension questions. Then have students work in pairs or small groups and do the same: read the text aloud, generate some questions, and respond to them. Finally, pairs or groups should answer Questions 1, 2, and 3. Have students share their responses with the class.

4 Ask students to solicit opinions and perspectives on Question 4 from members of their school paper as well as their student council. Students should report their findings to the class.

Thinking Critically

Drawing Inferences Ask students to look at the two pictures that accompany the text. Have them describe what the people in each photo are doing and determine what they could be discussing based on the context of this **Landeskunde** section.

Teacher Note

Mention to your students that the **Landeskunde** will also be included in Quiz 6-1 given at the end of the **Erste Stufe.**

CLOSE

Teaching Suggestion

Give students a few moments to think about what they would do with their time if they did not have access to television, VCR, or radio for a whole week. (**Wenn du eine Woche lange ohne Fernsehen, Videorekorder oder Radio wärst, was würdest du mit deiner Zeit machen?**)

Focusing on Outcomes

Refer students back to the learning outcomes listed on p. 129. They should recognize that they now know how to ask someone to take a position, ask for reasons, express opinions, report past events, agree or disagree, change the subject, and interrupt.

ASSESS

• **Performance Assessment** Ask students how they used the different types of media discussed in this **Stufe** during the past week. Have students use the narrative past as they recall each day. (**Welche Medien habt ihr in der vergangenen Woche benutzt, um euch zu informieren?**)

• Quiz 6-1, *Chapter Resources,* Book 2

Teaching Weiter geht's!
pp. 138-139

> ### Resources for Weiter geht's!
>
> • *Textbook Audiocassette* 3 B
> • *Practice and Activity Book*

Teacher Note

Weiter geht's! is recorded on audiocassette.

Weiter geht's! Summary

In **Unsere eigene Zeitung!**, some students talk about their involvement in the school newspaper and present an interview with representatives of the student government. The following student outcome listed on p. 129 is modeled in the conversations: expressing surprise or annoyance.

Motivating Activity

Briefly discuss the student government in your school. How is it set up? How does one become a representative? What is the function of the student government? (**Wie funktioniert die Schülervertretung an dieser Schule? Wie kann man Vertreter werden? Wozu gibt es eine Schülervertretung?**)

Background Information

Student government is a tradition in German schools that is supported by faculty and administration as well as the students, who can participate starting in the 5th grade. Each class chooses a **Klassensprecher** and a **Klassensprechervertreter** (*alternate*) who meet regularly with the **Schülervertretung** to discuss questions and problems of the student body. The student government elects an advisor from the faculty who serves as the liaison between faculty, parents, school administration, and student government.

Teaching Suggestion

Play the first part of **Unsere eigene Zeitung!** and have students follow along in the text. Stop at strategic points and ask comprehension questions and clarify new words and expressions using synonyms and paraphrasing. At the end, play the whole conversation again. Follow the same procedure for the second conversation.

Teacher Note

The **Weiter geht's!** text lends itself well to the review of the word order in dependent clauses.

 For Individual Needs

13 A Slower Pace Ask students to work in pairs or groups of three to create a chart with three columns summarizing the statements made by Guido, Rainer, and Natalie. In addition, ask them to elaborate on the function of the **SV** by noting its specific tasks. Call on students to share their information with the rest of the class. You may also want to collect each group's notes to check for completion or to assign a grade.

14 A Slower Pace Explain to students that **Redemittel** refers to functional expressions and, on a transparency, give several examples from the text. Ask students to give you the function or purpose of each of the expressions you picked out. Then put students in pairs and have them scan the text for all the other functional expressions used and, in each case, give the purpose for which the speaker uses it. Have students share their findings with the rest of the class.

Closure

Based on what they read in the **Landeskunde** section on p. 137 and the **Weiter geht's!** interview on pp. 138-139, ask students to compare their own school paper and student council to the way they are organized in German schools. (**Vergleicht die Schülerzeitung und die Schülervertretung an dieser Schule mit denen an deutschen Schulen.**)

Teaching Zweite Stufe, *pp. 140-143*

Resources for Zweite Stufe

Practice and Activity Book
Chapter Resources, Book 2
- Communicative Activities 6-3, 6-4
- Additional Listening Activities 6-4, 6-5, 6-6
- Student Response Forms
- Realia 6-2
- Situation Card 6-2
- Teaching Transparency Master 6-2
- Quiz 6-2

Audiocassette Program
- *Textbook Audiocassette* 3 B
- *Additional Listening Activities, Audiocassette* 9 B
- *Assessment Items, Audiocassette* 7 B

▶ **page 140**

MOTIVATE

Teaching Suggestion

Ask students about the strengths and weaknesses of their school paper. What would they like eliminated and what are some items they would like to have added? (**Wie findet ihr unsere Schülerzeitung? Was gefällt euch an der Zeitung und was nicht? Was würdet ihr darin gern lesen, was es bis jetzt noch nicht gibt?**)

TEACH

 For Individual Needs

Challenge After students have read the four letters to the editor, ask them to state the key idea in their own words. This can be done orally or in writing.

PRESENTATION: Wortschatz

Go over the new vocabulary with your students. Then ask students to think of a situation in which they might overhear a particular phrase or statement from this **Wortschatz** box.

▶ **page 141**

Teaching Suggestion

16 Ask students to go back to the **Landeskunde** section and review the different tasks involved in publishing a school paper.

PRESENTATION: So sagt man das!

Introduce the new expressions. Then provide students with practice by writing the bold-faced part of each sentence on a transparency or on the board and having students complete the sentences using different contexts.
Examples:
Es ist unglaublich, ...
... überrascht mich.
Ich bin überrascht, ...

Teaching Suggestion

18 These statements could be used as a basis for brief discussions. Students could react using one of the given phrases and then continue with a thought or two of their own.

▶ **page 142**

PRESENTATION: Grammatik

Remind students that adjectives enable them to express various levels of quality and degree. Students learned about the comparative forms of adjectives in Level 2 (Ch. 7, p. 166). The third and last of these forms is the superlative. To practice and review these adjective forms, direct questions such as the ones listed below to students.
Sag mal, was du gern ißt!
Was ißt du denn noch lieber?
Und was ißt du am liebsten?

For Additional Practice

Point out various items in the classroom that lend themselves to comparison and have students compare them. For example, you could show students three pieces of chalk: a short one, a shorter one, and one that is even shorter than the other two and say: **Das Stück Kreide hier ist kurz. Das Stück da ist kürzer. Das Stück dort ist am kürzesten.**

▶ **page 143**

Teacher Note

20 You might want to point out to students that the form of **dies-** in each sentence signals the gender and number of the noun.

Teaching Suggestion

22 You could prepare a list of topics to help students with this activity.
Examples:

Footballmannschaft	**Bücherei**
Orchester	**Schülerzeitung**
Lehrer	**Schülervertretung**
Cafeteriaessen	

To extend the activity, have students give one reason to support each of their claims.

ⓉⓅⓇ Total Physical Response

Bring a newspaper to class. If possible, make transparencies of some of the pages such as the front page or the weather report. Give students commands such as the following.
Zeig mir die Stadt, wo das Wetter am wärmsten/kältesten ist!
Zeig auf eine Schlagzeile über einen Autounfall!
Zeig auf die letzten Nachrichten aus dem Gebiet Schulsport!

PRESENTATION: Wortschatz

Introduce the words of quantity by talking about students in German class in general terms based on what you know about them.
Examples:
Alle Schüler in dieser Klasse lernen Deutsch.
Viele machen nach der Schule Sport.
Einige spielen ...

Reteaching: Superlative Forms of Adjectives

Ask students to create an original poster illustrating superlative forms of adjectives. For example they could show three generations of a family to illustrate the three degrees of quality using the adjective **alt**.

CLOSE

For Individual Needs

Tactile Learners Write a description of a fictitious person or animal incorporating as many positive, comparative, and superlative adjectives as possible. Read the description to the class and have students draw the person or animal being described. Let students share and compare their drawings.

Focusing on Outcomes

Refer students back to the learning outcomes listed on p. 129. They should recognize that they now know how to express surprise or annoyance.

ASSESS

• **Performance Assessment** Prepare a class set of 3 x 5 index cards by writing on each card one statement to which students have to react by expressing surprise or annoyance. Distribute the cards and ask students to direct the statement on their card to another student in class who then responds accordingly.
Examples:
Unsere Basketballmannschaft hat gestern wieder ihr Spiel verloren.
In der Cafeteria ist die Pizza heute schon alle!
Du hast ein A in deiner letzten Matheprüfung bekommen.

• Quiz 6-2, *Chapter Resources*, Book 2

Teaching Zum Lesen,
pp. 144-146

Teacher Note
Rumpelstilzchen is recorded on *Textbook Audiocassette* 11.

Reading Strategy
The targeted strategy in this reading is predicting outcomes. Students should learn about this strategy before beginning Questions 3 and 4.

PREREADING
Motivating Activity
Now that students have read some German short stories and poetry in the original, they may be interested in briefly discussing the following questions: Is there any particularly "German" literary form? Or is it more accurate to speak of "literature in the German language?" In thinking about what they know of German literature—including translations—is there any particular subject matter that seems to be typically German? How do they suppose the Nazis decided what to accept as "pure German" literature? You might want to mention to the class that the reading selection in this chapter has often been identified as being of a type that is "typically German."

Background Information
As early as the 1770s, J. G. Herder had drawn attention to folklore and myth as "primitive poetry" and inspired young German writers (including Goethe) to seek out "Germanic" sources, i.e. those not influenced by Latin or French literary traditions. The brothers Grimm—Jakob (1785-1863) and Wilhelm (1786-1859)—brought to this trend their own background in linguistics, particularly in Indo-European studies, and a conviction that European folk tales were descended from a common Indo-European mythology. Since their methods of gathering folk tales were not what modern anthropologists would consider "scientific," they saw no harm in mixing educated and uneducated sources and then doing a little polishing and ghost-writing of their own in the two-volume *Kinder- und Hausmärchen* (1812; 1815).

READING

Teacher Note

Rumpelstilzchen is a complex tale that includes at least three separate motifs:

- the impossible task (similar to slaying a dragon or finding a strange and unique item like the golden apples of the Hesperides),
- the lightly-given promise (compare the princess' promises in the "Frog Prince" story), and
- name-guessing, which has a superficial resemblance to the riddle motif in folklore (compare the episode of the Sphinx in the Oedipus story) but derives from an older layer of folklore in which knowledge of someone's name conferred power over that individual.

If students can find a copy of Stith Thompson's *Motif-Index of Folk-Literature* (Bloomington, 1955) in the local library, they can trace any of these motifs in world literature.

Teacher Notes

2 In other literatures, "once upon a time," can be "long, long ago," or "long ago in a faraway place," or "in the days of X."

6 Students will probably guess accurately that the king's demands will come in a sequence of three. They might be interested to know that not all world literatures agree upon 3 as the "magic number." In much Native American lore, the number 4 is crucial.

Thinking Critically

Analyzing This story will probably seem very simple and "artless" to students at first reading, partly because they are so familiar with its general form from their childhood. A closer look at how it is put together, especially the details, may show them that only a very experienced story teller or talented writer would come up with exactly this version. For example, they should look at the sets of names which the young woman offers near the end of the story. What must have been the source for the first set? What were the three men with those names famous for? (**Kaspar, Melchior,** and **Balzer** are versions of the names of the three kings from the Orient who brought fabulous gifts to the infant Jesus. These are not common names in Germany.) In the second set, what do the compound names actually mean? What kind of person do they suggest? (**Rippenbiest:** *rib-brute,* **Hammelswade:** *mutton-leg,* and **Schnürbein:** *cord-leg,* are ugly and dehumanising names.) If students know that **Hinz und Kunz** in the third set is the common German expression for "Tom, Dick and Harry" (i.e. any non-descript group of fellows), can they see how the young woman is teasing? Finally, what could **Rumpelstilzchen** mean? (Have students look up **Rumpel:** *rumbling.* **Stilzchen** might be the diminutive of **Stelz,** which means *stilt,* or *peg-leg.*) Does the combination conjure up any mental pictures of this character? (Think again about the scene in which the messenger observes him hopping around the fire.) Is the manner of his demise fitting?

POST-READING

Teacher Note

Activities 9 and 10 are post-reading tasks that will show whether students can apply what they have learned.

Closure

In contrast to fables, which usually have a moral, or myths, which attempt to explain some aspect of the natural world, **Märchen** use magical elements to exploit some of our most common human fears—of being orphaned, lost, threatened by monsters, and of things that go bump in the night. Aside from the happy ending, which is by no means guaranteed in Grimms' tales, how would students compare *Rumpelstilzchen* with the Kafka short story that they read in Chapter 1? Are the characters any more or less individual? Are the events any more or less unbelievable? Are students any more or less interested in the outcome?

Answers to Activity 1
Rumpelstilzchen, der Müller, seine Tochter, der König

Answers to Activity 2
Once upon a time ...; fairy tales; as with other Grimm fairy tales, the exact time and place are left undetermined, emphasizing the fantastic quality of the events; however, students could give answers such as in medieval times or in a kingdom somewhere in Germany.

Answers to Activity 3
She must turn a room full of straw into gold by morning. Rumpelstilzchen will spin the straw into gold in return for her necklace.

Answers to Activity 4
Answers will vary.

Answers to Activity 5
Answers will vary.

Answers to Activity 6
Time lines should include the three visits from **Rumpelstilzchen** to spin the gold and his three visits to the queen to let her guess his name.

Answers to Activity 7
a. es traf sich *es ist passiert;* die Kammer *das Zimmer;* das Männlein *der kleine Mann;* die Jungfer *das Fräulein;* das Rädchen *das kleine Spinnrad;* um das Leben keinen Rat wissen *nicht wissen, was man tun soll*
b. **Schnurr** is the sound of the spinning wheel. The naming of a thing or action by an imitation of the sound associated with it is called onomatopoeia.

Answers to Activity 8
a. er: der Müller; ihm: dem König; ihm: dem König; er: der König; es: das Mädchen; es: das Männlein (Rumpelstilzchen)
b. **darin** translates as *in it.* It refers back to **die Kammer; davon:** a **da**-compound is used because the object of **von** here is a clause: **wie man Stroh zu Gold spinnen konnte.**

*T*eaching Zum Schreiben,
p. 147

Writing Strategy
The targeted strategy in this writing activity is using an outline. Students should learn about this strategy before beginning the assignment.

PREWRITING
Motivating Activity
Ask students to think of an issue that they recently discussed with their parents, one where the parents disagreed and they had to support their point of view with detailed information. Then ask students how their arguments would have been different had they had to do it in writing.

Thinking Critically
Analyzing Bring samples of advertisements from German magazines to class. Discuss the purpose of the advertisements by addressing visual elements and focusing on word choice. Discuss the importance of an audience so that students understand that they also need to have a specific audience in mind when stating their arguments in their essay.

Teaching Suggestion
A2 If students are unsure about an appropriate subject, brainstorm with the class and make a list of possible topics.

WRITING

For Individual Needs
B A Slower Pace Have students recall the various phrases they have learned to express opinions. Review these phrases and, if necessary, compile a list that students can refer to as they write their essays.

REVIEW

POST-WRITING

Teaching Suggestion

C1 If several students in the class write about similar issues from opposite points of view, you might want to assign them to work together so that they can play devil's advocate for each other during the revising phase.

Closure

Have students with opposing essays read them to the class. Afterwards, the other students can debate the subject, deciding which position they most agree with and why.

*U*sing Anwendung, *pp. 148-149*

> ### Resources for Anwendung
>
> *Chapter Resources,* Book 2
> * Realia 6-3
> * Situation Card 6-3
> *Video Program,* Videocassette 1
> *Video Guide*

▣ Video Program

At this time, you might want to use the authentic advertising footage from German television. See *Video Guide* for suggestions.

Thinking Critically

1 Comparing and Contrasting Ask students to compare these suggestions for a school paper with the one published at their own school. Have several copies of a recent issue of the paper in your classroom and ask students to make an outline in German of the different features that are contained in that paper. (**Vergleicht den Aufbau und Inhalt unserer Schülerzeitung mit den Vorschlägen für die deutsche Schülerzeitung! Fehlt etwas in unserer Schülerzeitung? Gibt es etwas, was wir haben, aber was nicht in den Vorschlägen für die deutsche Schülerzeitung erwähnt wurde?**)

Teaching Suggestion

3 This activity could be done orally with a partner in class and then assigned as written homework.

Group Work

5 This project could be shared with other German classes. Students of all levels could contribute features, such as articles, cartoons, jokes, and reviews of books, movies, or TV shows. See the Project suggested on p. 127F for more ideas.

Teaching Suggestion

8 Put all the questions on a form labeled "**Umfrage über Medienbenutzung**" with enough space between the questions to record the answers. There should also be a line on the bottom to write in the name of the **Reporter** and the **Befragte(r)**. Give each student an interview form and have them interview one of their classmates. Collect all forms and summarize the results of each question. Give the summary to students and have them discuss the findings in small groups or as a class.

▉ Portfolio Assessment

8 You might want to suggest this activity as a written and oral portfolio item for your students. See *Assessment Guide,* p. 19.

*K*ann ich's wirklich?
p. 150

This page helps students prepare for the test. It is a brief checklist of the major points covered in the chapter. The students should be reminded that it is only a checklist and not necessarily everything that will appear on the test.

*U*sing Wortschatz,
p. 151

For Individual Needs

Challenge Ask students to categorize the verbs in the **Wortschatz** under the following headings: Reflexive; Separable Prefix; Stem-Vowel Change; Used with a Preposition. Some verbs will appear under several headings. Have students use each verb in a sentence orally or in writing.

For Additional Practice

Ask students to bring several eye-catching headlines from newspapers to class. Have them use the vocabulary from Chapter 6 to write their own humorous story to fit the headline.

Teaching Suggestion

Ask students to explain the difference between the following word pairs.
der Bericht / die Schlagzeile
vermissen / weglassen
Schülervertretung / Schulleitung

♜ Game
Play the game **Eine unmögliche Geschichte aus dem Schuhkarton** using the vocabulary from this and previous chapters. See p. 127F for the procedure.

Teacher Note

Give the **Kapitel 6** Chapter Test, *Chapter Resources,* Book 2.

6 Medien: stets gut informiert?

1 Es ist frustrierend, wenn ich so was in der Zeitung lese!

Die Presse, der Hörfunk und das Fernsehen sind unsere bedeutendsten Medien: sie spielen eine wichtige Rolle in unserem Leben. Informationen, Tatsachen sowie Meinungen finden wir in den Medien. Aber wie nutzen wir die Medien? Durch welche Medien informiert man sich am besten? Das ist oft schwer zu sagen. Welche Medien benutzt du am meisten und zu welchem Zweck? Um über diese Fragen diskutieren zu können, mußt du noch einiges lernen.

② Ich bin überrascht, daß heute kein Fußballspiel kommt.

In this chapter you will learn

- to ask someone to take a position; to ask for reasons; to express opinions; to report past events; to agree or disagree; to change the subject; to interrupt
- to express surprise or annoyance

And you will

- listen to students talk about how they stay informed
- read about the different kinds of media Germans prefer
- write your opinion on an issue that is important to you
- find out about student newspapers in Germany

③ Meiner Meinung nach sollten wir das schärfere Foto nehmen.

Los geht's!

Die Macht der Medien

Hier ist ein Ausschnitt aus einer Diskussion von Schülern einer 10. Klasse zum Thema „Medien."

Wie informiert ihr euch? Durch welche Medien erfahrt ihr, was in der Welt passiert?

SANDRA Ja, durch Zeitung, Radio und Fernsehen.

CHRISTOF Im Radio hört man meistens die Nachrichten; die kommen ja alle halbe Stunden. Und das Radio informiert eben am schnellsten über Neuigkeiten und wichtige Ereignisse.

FRANK Is' doch Quatsch! Solche Informationen bekommst du im Fernsehen genau so schnell!

CHRISTOF Aber nicht, wenn du im Auto unterwegs bist, oder wenn du ...

NICOLE Moment mal, Christof! Laß mich auch mal zu Wort kommen!

CHRISTOF Entschuldigung!

NICOLE Also, ich bekomm' meine Information meistens aus der Zeitung. Ich blättere alles mal durch, und was mich dann anspricht, das les' ich halt.

FRANK Viele Leute lesen nur die Sensationspresse und oft nur die Schlagzeilen.

NICOLE Ja schon, aber wenn man eine seriöse Tageszeitung liest, die Stuttgarter Nachrichten vielleicht oder sogar die SZ, da muß ...

ALEX Die liest du doch gar nicht! Das ist ...

CHRISTOF Mensch, laß die Nicole mal ausreden!

NICOLE Ja, wo war ich? Ach ja, wenn man so eine Zeitung liest, wie die Süddeutsche Zeitung vielleicht, da muß man sich schon aussuchen, was man lesen will. Da ist einfach zu viel da.

CHRISTOF Eben! Aber ich möcht' noch mal auf die anderen Medien zurückkommen, aufs Fernsehen zum Beispiel.

FRANK Richtig! Ich finde nämlich Zeitunglesen langweilig.

RALF Ja, weil Zeitunglesen für dich zu anstrengend ist. Du sitzt lieber vor der Glotze!

MARTINA Komm, Ralf, nicht gleich persönlich werden!

RALF	Na, okay. War nur Spaß. Mach weiter!
FRANK	Also, ich zum Beispiel bekomm' meine Information hauptsächlich durchs Fernsehen. Man kann sich alles viel besser vorstellen als beim Zeitunglesen. Und meiner Meinung nach trägt das Fernsehen am meisten zur Bildung einer eigenen Meinung bei.

CHRISTOF	Das ist doch alles Quatsch, was du da sagst! Beim Fernsehen bekommst du kurze, oberflächliche Berichte, und du erfährst nur das, was die Redakteure für wichtig halten. Deine Meinung wird also nur durch die Berichte und Bilder geformt, die gezeigt werden, und durch das, was weggelassen wird.
FRANK	Na ja, eine Zeitung beeinflußt die Leser auch.
CHRISTOF	Ja, schon. Aber eine Zeitung kann viel mehr bringen; sie kann auch gründlicher berichten. Du bekommst eher das gesamte Bild sozusagen: Tatsachen, Einzelheiten, Hintergrund und auch Kommentare.
NATALIE	Jetzt haben wir zwei verschiedene Meinungen gegenüberstehen. Wer nimmt mal dazu Stellung?
SANDRA	Ich finde, die Zeitung regt mehr zum Nachdenken an.
NICOLE	Meiner Meinung nach eignet sich das Fernsehen am besten zur Unterhaltung und Entspannung. Die Presse und das Radio informieren besser.
FRANK	Kannst du das begründen?
NICOLE	Ja, vielleicht so: Da gab's vor ein paar Jahren mal einen Druckerstreik, und viele Bundesbürger fanden sich nicht richtig informiert. Sie vermißten besonders die Lokalnachrichten und die Annoncen der örtlichen Geschäfte, die ja durchs Fernsehen nicht gesendet werden.
FRANK	Da ist schon was dran. Aber andererseits: Möchtest du ohne Fernseher sein? Ich nicht.

1 Zeitung, Radio, Fernsehen

Was haben die Schüler über die verschiedenen Medien gesagt? Mach eine Liste mit drei Spalten: Zeitung, Radio, Fernsehen! Schreib in Stichworten auf, was die Schüler gesagt haben!

2 Wie sieht's bei dir aus?

1. Welche Medien gebrauchst du am meisten? Gib Gründe dafür an!
2. Welche Teile der Tageszeitung interessieren dich am meisten?
3. Welche Radiosender hörst du am meisten? Warum?

Asking someone to take a position; asking for reasons; expressing opinions; reporting past events; agreeing or disagreeing; changing the subject; interrupting

Die TV-Kids

Das TV-Leben der 6b des Münchner Erasmus-Grasser-Gymnasiums (fünf Mädchen, neunzehn Jungen zwischen elf und dreizehn Jahren): Nur ein Schüler ohne TV-Gerät, sechs mit eigenem Fernseher, sechzehn mit Kabelanschluß. 50 Prozent sahen den Prügelstreifen „Rambo", 40 Prozent kannten den Horrorfilm „Alien". TV-Konsum täglich 30 bis 60 Minuten: 3 Schüler; bis zu 2 Stunden: 3 Schüler; bis 3 Stunden: 15 Schüler; bis 4 Stunden: 3 Schüler.

(aus FOCUS 11/1993)

Zahl des Tages

Von den Deutschen, die Bücher lesen, schaffen 38 Prozent fünf Bände pro Jahr, 26 Prozent lesen sechs bis zehn, 18 Prozent elf bis 20 und gut zehn Prozent 21 bis 50.

WORTSCHATZ

auf deutsch erklärt

Ich erfahre es durch das Radio. Ich höre es im Radio.
Romeo vermißt seine Julia. Er ist traurig, daß sie nicht bei ihm ist.
die Glotze der Fernseher
die Neuigkeit etwas Neues
das Ereignis das, was passiert
die Unterhaltung was man zum Spaß macht
die Schlagzeile die großgedruckten Wörter über einem Text
die Tatsache etwas, was geschehen ist
die Einzelheit das Detail
verdrängen den Platz von etwas oder jemandem einnehmen
unterwegs auf dem Weg, nicht zu Hause
gesamt total, alles
der Streik wenn Arbeiter nicht arbeiten

auf englisch erklärt

Zuviel Fernsehen trägt zur allgemeinen Volksverdummung bei. *Too much TV contributes to the general dumbing down of the people.*
In der Zeitung steht ein Bericht darüber. *There's a report about it in the paper.*
Ich will nur schnell mal die Zeitung durchblättern. *I just want to leaf through the paper real quick.*
Diese Sendung spricht mich an. *This program appeals to me.*
So stelle ich es mir vor. *That's the way I imagine it.*
Die Nachrichten regen mal zum Nachdenken an, mal sind sie oberflächlich. *Sometimes the news stimulates thought, sometimes it's superficial.*
Diese Situation eignet sich gut zu einem Spaß. *This situation is well suited to making a joke.*

3 Was sagst du dazu?

1. Was machen die Deutschen am liebsten in ihrer Freizeit? Was machst du am liebsten? Was steht bei dir ganz oben? Und unten?
2. Was ist ein TV-Kid?   Ein Kind, das in seiner Freizeit viel Fernsehen schaut.
3. Welche Aussagen über das Fernsehen auf Seite 132 sind positiv, welche negativ? Stimmst du damit überein? Kannst du noch einige Aussagen hinzufügen?

4 Hör gut zu! For answers, see listening script on TE Interleaf.

Wer von diesen Leuten informiert sich hauptsächlich durch Zeitunglesen, Fernsehen oder Radiohören? Hör gut zu, und schreib die Information in die entsprechende Spalte!

Schüler	Zeitung	TV	Radio
Kässi			

SO SAGT MAN DAS!

Asking someone to take a position; asking for reasons; expressing opinions

When having a discussion, you use certain communication strategies. Here are some ways to help you encourage a discussion in German.

To ask someone to take a position on a subject you could say:

Möchtest du mal dazu Stellung nehmen?
Wer nimmt mal dazu Stellung?

To ask for reasons you say:

Kannst du das begründen?

To express an opinion you may begin with:

Meiner Meinung nach soll man Zivi werden.
Ich finde, daß wir zuviel fürs Militär ausgeben.

5 Hör gut zu! For answers, see listening script on TE Interleaf.

Im Schulhof wird lebhaft diskutiert. Hör zu und schreib auf, wer von diesen Schülern seine Meinung begründet und wer nicht! Welcher Schüler begründet seine Meinung am besten und warum?

Schüler	Grund	keinen Grund
Markus		

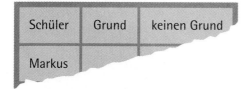

6 Für mein Notizbuch

Schreib in dein Notizbuch, welches Medium (z.B. Zeitung, Radio, Fernsehen) du vorziehst! Nimm zu deiner Aussage Stellung, indem du deine Meinung mit mehreren Punkten begründest!

7 Eure Meinung über die Medien, bitte!

Bildet Gruppen zu viert! Führt ein Gespräch über die Medien, indem ihr die verschiedenen Fragen unten behandelt! Die Gesprächspartner nehmen dann dazu Stellung.

> DU **Meiner Meinung nach trägt die Zeitung am besten zur Bildung einer eigenen Meinung bei.**
> PARTNER **Kannst du das mal begründen?**
> DU **Ja, man kann die Zeitung in Ruhe lesen, man kann ...**

Tageszeitung

Fernsehen

Radio

Welches Medium ...

berichtet am wahrheitsgetreusten (*closest to the truth*)?

regt am stärksten zum eigenen Nachdenken an?

trägt am besten zur Bildung einer eigenen Meinung bei?

berichtet am verständlichsten über (politische) Ereignisse?

informiert über Neuigkeiten und wichtige Ereignisse?

ist am besten zur Unterhaltung und Entspannung geeignet?

bietet den meisten Gesprächsstoff im Freundes- und Bekanntenkreis an?

8 Nacherzählen

Lies den folgenden Text, und erzähl ihn einem Partner wieder!

Was würden Sie ohne Fernseher machen?

Vor einiger Zeit führte ein Fernsehsender folgenden Test durch: Zwei Familien erklärten sich bereit, vier Wochen lang ohne Fernsehen zu leben. Und was passierte? In der einen Familie wußten die Leute einfach nicht mehr, was sie ohne Fernseher anfangen sollten! Sie saßen da und starrten sich an. Nichts fiel ihnen ein. Sie hatten vergessen, wie man sich unterhält, wie man sich amüsiert. Sie langweilten sich zu Tode — dann fingen sie sogar an zu streiten. In der anderen Familie fing man an zu reden. Man erzählte sich Witze und Geschichten. Die Familie hörte jetzt Musik, machte Spiele, sie luden wieder Freunde ein. — Nach vier Wochen bekamen beide Familien ihren Fernseher wieder. Das Ergebnis: Die eine Familie sitzt jetzt nach wie vor jeden Abend vor dem Bildschirm, die andere Familie macht jetzt lieber etwas zusammen, anstatt automatisch den Fernseher einzuschalten.

SO SAGT MAN DAS!

Reporting past events

Here is how you might narrate a long sequence of past events:

> Vor einiger Zeit **führte** ein Fernsehsender folgenden Test durch: Zwei Familien **erklärten** sich bereit, ... Und was **passierte**? Die Leute **wußten** einfach nicht mehr, was sie ohne Fernseher anfangen **sollten**. Sie **saßen** da und **starrten** sich an ...

Grammatik   Narrative past (imperfect)

1. When talking about or relating events that took place in the past, use the following general rules as a guide:

   a. When writing longer sequences, use the narrative past (imperfect).

   b. In conversation, use the conversational past (perfect).

2. Weak verbs and strong verbs form the imperfect as follows:

a. Weak verbs form the imperfect by adding the past tense marker **-te** to the verb stem.

	hören	**führen**	**erklären**
ich	hör**te**	führ**te**	erklär**te**
er, sie, es, man	hör**te**	führ**te**	erklär**te**
wir, sie, Sie	hör**ten**	führ**ten**	erklär**ten**

b. Strong verbs often have a vowel change in the imperfect: geben — **gab;** finden — **fand.** The imperfect of strong verbs that you had are listed in the Grammar Summary.

	geben	**finden**
ich	**gab**	**fand**
er, sie, es, man	**gab**	**fand**
wir, sie, Sie	**gaben**	**fanden**

Note: Second-person forms of the imperfect are rarely used and are therefore not given here.

3. There are a number of verbs in German that form the imperfect like weak verbs but also have a vowel change. Here are some you have had so far:

	kennen	**nennen**	**denken**	**bringen**	**wissen**
ich	**kannte**	**nannte**	**dachte**	**brachte**	**wußte**
er, sie, es, man	**kannte**	**nannte**	**dachte**	**brachte**	**wußte**
wir, sie, Sie	**kannten**	**nannten**	**dachten**	**brachten**	**wußten**

Look at the past tense forms of modals on page 117. How is the past tense formed? What observations can you make when comparing them to weak and strong verbs? How are they similar to the verbs listed above?

9 Wie war das denn?

Erzähle die folgenden Aussagen nach! Verwende dabei das Imperfekt!

a. Ich hab' gestern abend nicht fernsehen können, weil ich keine Zeit gehabt hab'. Ich hab' gehört, daß der Bericht über die wichtigsten Ereignisse in Südafrika ausgezeichnet gewesen ist. Ich hab' nicht gewußt, daß es große Demonstrationen gegeben hat, an denen Tausende teilgenommen haben.

b. Mein Vater hat früher seine Information gewöhnlich aus den Tageszeitungen bekommen. Wie er mir gesagt hat, hat er sich nur seriöse Zeitungen gekauft. Aber er hat ja nicht alles lesen können. Er hat erst alles mal durchgeblättert, und was ihn dann angesprochen hat, hat er gelesen.

ansprechen — sprach an (ansprach)

lesen — las   bekommen — bekam

teilnehmen — nahm teil (teilnahm)   können — konnte

„Kannst du mal schön ruhig den ‚Aus'-Knopf drücken?"

10 Klassenumfrage: Mediennützung

Macht in eurer Klasse eine Umfrage! Stellt fest, welche Medien ihr am meisten und welche ihr am wenigsten benutzt! Was könnt ihr noch hinzufügen? Kassetten, CDs hören? Videos sehen? Computer, CD-Rom spielen?

SO SAGT MAN DAS!

Agreeing or disagreeing; changing the subject; interrupting

Here are some more expressions you will find useful when you're having a discussion.

To accept a point someone makes, you can say:

Da ist schon was dran.   **Eben!**   **Richtig!**

To reject a point, you might say: (and informally:)

Das stimmt gar nicht!   **Das ist alles Quatsch!**

To change the subject, use these expressions:

Übrigens, ich wollte etwas anderes sagen.
Ich möchte nochmal (aufs Fernsehen) zurückkommen.

To interrupt someone, you can say:

Laß mich mal zu Wort kommen!
Moment mal! Laß (die Nicole) mal ausreden!

---

11 Hör gut zu!   <small>For answers, see listening script on TE Interleaf.</small>

Im Schulhof unterhalten sich einige Schüler über die Vorteile und Nachteile des Fernsehens. Schreib mindestens drei Vorteile und drei Nachteile auf, die du hörst! Stimmst du auch mit diesen Meinungen überein?

12 Was haltet ihr vom Fernsehen?

Ist Fernsehen nützlich oder schädlich? Diskutiert in der Klasse über diese Frage!

a. Lest die Aussagen übers Fernsehen unten und nehmt dazu Stellung! Verwendet dabei die Ausdrücke, die ihr in diesem Kapitel gelernt habt! Nehmt eure Diskussion auf eine Kassette auf!

b. Hört euch dann die Diskussion an, und diskutiert über die folgenden Fragen!
    1. Wer hat was gesagt?
    2. Wer hat seine Aussagen am besten begründet?
    3. Welche Ausdrücke habt ihr verwendet? Schreibt diese Ausdrücke in euer Notizheft!

Ist das Fernsehen **nützlich?**	Ist das Fernsehen **schädlich?**
Ja, schon. Denn …	Fernsehen kann dazu führen, daß man …
• man erhält eine Fülle von Informationen.	• in seiner Freizeit weniger aktiv ist.
• man hat ein „Fenster zur Welt".	• seine künstlerischen Talente vergißt.
• man wird über viele Probleme informiert und kann dann vielleicht helfen.	• weniger mit anderen Menschen zusammenkommt.
• man kann Filme und Theateraufführungen sehen, wozu man sonst keine Gelegenheit hätte.	• seine eigenen Ideen und Gefühle weniger ausdrücken kann.
	• zuviel ißt und zunimmt.

Die Schülerzeitung

Für manche Schüler ist die Mitarbeit an der Schülerzeitung nicht nur ein Hobby, sondern auch der Anfang einer Karriere im Journalismus. Wie bei einer Zeitung müssen die Schüler ihre Berichte recherchieren, Photos machen, Grafiken erstellen, Layouts vorbereiten, Platz für Anzeigen an Geschäftsleute verkaufen, den Text säuberlich tippen und für den Drucker vorbereiten — und dann die Zeitung an die Schüler verkaufen.

Eine andere Art, sich für die Schule zu engagieren, ist, in der Schülervertretung mitzuarbeiten. Gewöhnlich werden von jeder Schulklasse zwei Klassensprecher gewählt, die ein Jahr lang ihre Interessen in der SV vertreten. An der Spitze der SV stehen zwei Schulsprecher, die von den Klassensprechern gewählt werden. Schulsprecher dürfen Schulsprecherkonferenzen besuchen, bei denen Schülerprobleme des Bundeslandes diskutiert werden.

Die Schülervertretung am Markgräfler Gymnasium hat sich zum Beispiel sehr verdient gemacht. Sie hat an dem allgemeinen Rauchverbot am Gymnasium mitgearbeitet. Sie hat es durchgesetzt, daß es jetzt eine Graffitiwand an der Schule gibt, und bald sollen auf dem Schulgelände Pingpongtische aus Marmor aufgestellt werden, damit die Schüler auch bei schlechtem Wetter Tischtennis spielen können.

1. von Schülerinitiativen (Schülerzeitung, Schülervertretung)

1. Lies den Text durch, und mach dir Notizen! Wovon handelt der Text?

2. Warum interessieren sich die Schüler für die Schülerzeitung und Schülervertretung?

3. Habt ihr auch eine Schülerzeitung und Schülervertretung in eurer Schule? Wie unterscheiden sie sich von den deutschen Schülerorganisationen?

4. Findest du es wichtig, solche Schülerorganisationen zu haben? Was meinst du?

2. Answers will vary. E.g.: um herauszufinden, wo ihre beruflichen Interessen liegen; um Probleme an der Schule zu lösen; um eigene Ideen an der Schule zu verwirklichen (z.B. Graffitiwand, Pingpongtisch)

Weiter geht's!

Unsere eigene Zeitung!

An den meisten Realschulen und Gymnasien gibt es Schülerzeitungen. Da gibt es die „Glatze" am Schwann Gymnasium in Neuss, die „Meinung" am Gymnasium in Starnberg, den „List-Käfer" an der Wirtschafts-Schule in München oder die „Pepo" (*People's Post*) am Markgräfler Gymnasium in Müllheim, um nur einige Namen zu nennen. — Drei Redaktionsmitglieder unterhalten sich hier über ihre Arbeit mit der „Pepo".

GUIDO Es ist unglaublich, wieviel Arbeit wir mit der „Pepo" haben. Und das alles nach der Schule.

RAINER Da stimm' ich dem Guido zu. Manchmal frag' ich mich, ob sich die viele Arbeit lohnt.

NATALIE Es überrascht mich, daß du das sagst.

RAINER Die viele Arbeit macht mir nichts aus. Was mich stört ist, daß sich viele Schüler gar nicht für die Zeitung interessieren und die meisten fast gar nichts dazu beitragen. Und ich werde sauer, wenn sie unsere Arbeit bloß kritisieren!

NATALIE Ich kann dich verstehen, das ist frustrierend. Aber trotzdem, ich find' die Arbeit anregend.

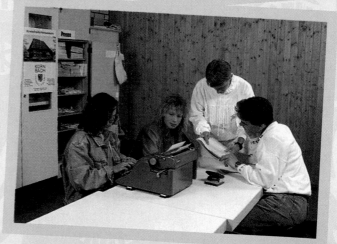

GUIDO Das ist wahr. Das find' ich auch. Übrigens, dein letztes Interview mit der SV war super, bestimmt das beste Interview in der *Pepo*.

Hier ist Natalies Interview mit der SV, der Schülervertretung. Sprecher: Jürgen und Petra.

NATALIE Warum macht ihr bei der SV mit?

JÜRGEN Mich hat gestört, daß einige Klassensprecher und viele Schüler am Gymnasium so ganz ohne Interessen waren. Und deshalb wollte ich mich mal selber um Rechte und Pflichten der SV kümmern.

PETRA Es hat mich auch überrascht, als ich gesehen habe, was eine SV so alles erreichen kann!

NATALIE Und was macht die SV?

PETRA Unsere größte Aufgabe ist, schulinterne Dinge zu organisieren, zum Beispiel AGs, Schulfeten, Schüleraustausch, und wir können euch auch mit der Schülerzeitung helfen, wenn ihr mal Probleme mit der Schulleitung habt.

NATALIE Ist das wahr?

JÜRGEN Klar. Und ich möchte noch dazu sagen, daß ... äh, wir bemühen uns auch um bessere Kontakte zu den Eltern und zu unseren Lehrern.

NATALIE Kannst du mir ein Beispiel geben?

JÜRGEN Kann ich. Du erinnerst dich doch, daß einige ältere Schüler und auch mehrere Lehrer mit dem Rauchverbot in der Schule nicht einverstanden waren. Das haben wir jetzt geregelt.

NATALIE Das freut mich für euch. – Übrigens, wie stehen denn die Lehrer zur SV?

PETRA Die Lehrer unterstützen uns; sie informieren uns über unsere Rechte und Pflichten.

JÜRGEN Auch helfen sie uns ab und zu mit der Arbeit, wenn die Arbeit zu viel wird und wenn es zu viel Frust gibt.

---

13 Schülerzeitung und SV

Beantworte diese Fragen mit einem Partner!

1. Was sagen die Schüler über ihre Arbeit mit der Schülerzeitung?
2. Was ist die SV? Was macht die SV? 2. Schülervertretung / E.g.: organisiert schulinterne Dinge; löst Probleme mit der Schulleitung; stellt bessere Kontakte zu Eltern und Lehrern her

14 Kannst du die Redemittel erkennen?

Schreib die Ausdrücke in dein Notizheft, die die Schüler in ihrer Unterhaltung verwenden! Beachte dabei genau, was diese Redemittel ausdrücken! Welche Ausdrücke sind dir neu, welche sind dir schon bekannt?

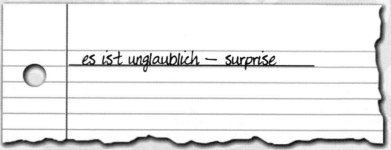

es ist unglaublich — surprise

ZWEITE STUFE

Expressing surprise or annoyance

Leserbriefe an die Redaktion der Pepo

Die Tatsache, daß in der „Meckerecke" auch anonyme Briefe erscheinen, finde ich schwach. Meiner Meinung nach sollte man zu seiner Meinung stehen. Wer Angst hat, was zu schreiben, der sollte es lassen!

Ursel Roth, 9a

Es überrascht mich wirklich, daß die Redaktion der Pepo Tatsachen und Meinungen nicht auseinanderhalten kann. Tatsache ist, daß wir das letzte Fußballspiel verloren haben. Meinung ist, daß wir nicht Fußball spielen können.

Bernd Rauh, 10b

Ich möchte mehr Berichte und Information über Veranstaltungen in der Schule!

Linda Schuster, 8b

Der Artikel im letzten Heft „Wie man sich in der Klasse gute Notizen macht" war sehr nützlich! Nur möchte ich dazu sagen, daß ich einige Vorschläge etwas unrealistisch fand. Die Lehrer zum Beispiel sprechen nicht immer sehr deutlich, und es ist schwer, ja manchmal unmöglich, alles mitzuschreiben!

Jochen Blick, 11a

WORTSCHATZ

auf deutsch erklärt

deutlich klar
sich um jemanden kümmern wenn man für jemanden alles tut, was man kann
der Schüleraustausch wenn Schüler von einer anderen Schule zu uns kommen, und Schüler von uns dorthin gehen
unterstützen einem Menschen helfen und Rat geben
nützlich man kann es gebrauchen
zustimmen zu etwas ja sagen
deshalb aus diesem Grund
die Schulleitung die Schuldirektion
anregend stimulierend

auf englisch erklärt

Die Schülervertretung (SV) regelt die Veranstaltung. *The student council takes care of the event.*
Wir haben eine schwere Aufgabe vor uns. *We have a difficult task in front of us.*
Das macht mir nichts aus. *That doesn't matter to me.*
Meckere nicht so! *Don't complain so much!*
Die Redaktion bemüht sich um Klarheit. *The editors strive for clarity.*
Du machst ihn sauer, wenn du ihn störst. *He'll get annoyed with you if you disturb him.*
Überraschen wir sie mit einer Fete! *Let's surprise her with a party!*

15 Was sagen die Schüler?

Diskutiert die Leserbriefe auf dieser Seite! Was sagen die Leserbriefe aus? Was ist der Hauptgedanke jedes Briefes? Wer drückt folgendes aus: Ärger (*annoyance*), Frust (*frustration*), Überraschung (*surprise*)?

16 Hör gut zu!

For answers, see listening script on TE Interleaf.

Ein paar Schüler arbeiten für eine Schülerzeitung und müssen morgen eine neue Ausgabe drucken. Hör ihrem Gespräch gut zu und entscheide, wer diese Arbeit gern macht und wer nicht!

SO SAGT MAN DAS!

Expressing surprise or annoyance

To express surprise you could say:

Es ist unglaublich, daß die Mannschaft verloren hat.
Das schlechte Spiel **überrascht mich.**
Ich bin überrascht, daß sie so miserabel gespielt haben.

To express annoyance or frustration you could say:

Was mich stört ist, daß wir besser spielen können.
Ich werde sauer, wenn die Spieler so oft meckern.
Es ist frustrierend, daß wir ihnen nicht helfen können.

17 Hör gut zu!

For answers, see listening script on TE Interleaf.

Die Mitglieder der Schülerzeitung haben dich zu ihrer Versammlung eingeladen. Hör gut zu, wie einige Schüler Überraschung und Frust ausdrücken! Notiere, wer wie reagiert!

		Überraschung	Frust
Bodo			

18 Bist du überrascht, oder stört es dich?

Such dir eine Partnerin! Sie spricht mit dir über einige Probleme an der Schule. Drück deine Überraschung oder deinen Ärger darüber aus! Wechselt einander ab!

1. Wir haben so viel Arbeit mit der Schülerzeitung.
2. Die meisten Schüler interessieren sich nicht einmal für die Zeitung.
3. Die Arbeit ist manchmal sehr frustrierend.
4. Wir haben leider auch keine gute Schülervertretung.
5. Wir haben auch keinen Schüleraustausch mit anderen Schulen.
6. Unsere Eltern haben wenig Kontakt zu den Lehrern.
7. ...

Das tut mir leid.

Das ist schade.

Da stimme ich dir zu.

Das ist frustrierend.

Das ist aber wahr!

Das stört mich auch!

Ja, das ist eben so.

Da kann man nichts machen.

Grammatik Superlative forms of adjectives

1. You have been using comparative forms of adjectives in sentences such as:

   Wir haben ein **größeres** Auto (als ihr).   Das ist eine **bessere** Kamera.

2. You have also been making equal and unequal comparisons like these:

   Das Fernsehen informiert **genau so schnell wie** das Radio.
   Das Radio informiert **schneller als** die Zeitung.

3. Superlative forms in German are similar to English superlative forms, for example fastest, smallest, most expensive, best. The superlative form in German is made by adding **-st** (sometimes **-est**) to the positive form. When used before a noun, the superlative form must have an adjective ending.

4. Most adjectives of one syllable take an umlaut in the comparative and superlative. Here are some examples. For a more complete listing, refer to the Grammar Summary at the end of this textbook.

Positive	*Comparative*	*Superlative*	*Positive*	*Comparative*	*Superlative*
alt	älter	ältest-	kurz	kürzer	kürzest-
arm	ärmer	ärmst-	lang	länger	längst-
groß	größer	größt-	oft	öfter	öftest-
hart	härter	härtest-	schwach	schwächer	schwächst-
jung	jünger	jüngst-	stark	stärker	stärkst-
kalt	kälter	kältest-	warm	wärmer	wärmst-

Note that adjectives that end in **-d**, **-t**, **-z** add **-est** in the superlative form.

5. Several adjectives have irregular comparative and superlative forms.

Positive	*Comparative*	*Superlative*	*Positive*	*Comparative*	*Superlative*
gern	lieber	liebst-	nah	näher	nächst-
gut	besser	best-	viel	mehr	meist-
hoch	höher	höchst-			

6. Superlative forms are often used in the following phrase:

   am *superlative form* + **en**   Was mich **am meisten** stört ist, ...

19 Unsere Schülerzeitung ist die beste!

Spiel mit einem Partner die Rollen von zwei Schülern, die für verschiedene Schülerzeitungen mitarbeiten! Ihr denkt natürlich, daß jeder die beste Zeitung hat. Macht Reklame für eure eigene Schülerzeitung, indem ihr nur in Superlativen redet! Was sagt ihr?
BEISPIEL **Wir haben die lustigsten Witze!**   *oder*   **Unsere Witze sind am lustigsten!**

Neuigkeiten	Leserbriefe	Witze
Interviews	Tips	Geschichten
Anekdoten	Cartoons	Artikel

seriös	spannend	gut	wichtig
witzig	toll	klug	lustig
faszinierend	komisch	schön	

20 Stimmst du dem Guido zu?

Guido hat ganz bestimmte Ansichten, und du, als sein bester Freund, stimmst ihm immer zu! Such dir eine Partnerin, und spielt zusammen die Rollen von Guido und seinem Freund! Tauscht oft die Rollen aus!

BEISPIEL   GUIDO **Keine Zeitung ist so interessant wie diese.**

DU **Da stimm' ich dir zu. Es ist die interessanteste Zeitung!**

1. Keine Arbeit ist so schwer wie diese.
2. Keine Schüler sind so faul wie diese.
3. Kein Interview ist so langweilig wie dieses.
4. Kein Beispiel ist so blöd wie dieses.
5. Keine Schule ist so gut wie diese.
6. Keine Lehrerin ist so nett wie diese.

21 Nicht gut, nicht besser, sondern das beste!

a. Such dir eine Partnerin, und sprecht einander die Sätze unten vor! Benutzt dabei aber die Superlative statt der Wörter in Klammern!   1. beste; nettesten; tollsten; neusten; wichtigsten
b. Schreibt dann die neuen Formen dieser Wörter in eure Notizbücher!

1. Der (gut) Radiosender, den wir haben, ist ... Dieser Sender hat den (nett) Discjockey, und der spielt die (toll) Hits. Für die (neu) Nachrichten unterbricht er jede Sendung und berichtet die (wichtig) Ereignisse.   2. älteste; größte; schönsten; lustigsten; beste
2. Die (alt) Zeitung in unserer Stadt ist ... Es ist die (groß) Zeitung im ganzen Staat. Die Zeitung hat die (schön) Sportartikel und die (lustig) Comics — ganze zwei Seiten! Meine Mutter sagt, die Zeitung hat auch die (gut) Reklame.
3. Im Sommer haben wir die (langweilig) Fernsehprogramme. Sie zeigen uns die (schlecht) Filme und die (alt) Krimis. Im Herbst haben wir das (gut) Fernsehen. Die (viel) Sendungen sind super, besonders die (neu) Shows.
   3. langweiligsten; schlechtesten; ältesten; beste; meisten; neusten

22 Wie ist es bei euch?

Such dir einen Partner, und spielt die Rollen von zwei Cousins! Dein Cousin besucht dich in seinen Ferien und fragt dich, wie es in deiner Schule ist. Natürlich habt ihr das beste von allem!

BEISPIEL   COUSIN **Habt ihr eine große Schule?**
DU **Wir haben die größte Schule!**

23 Über Massenmedien

Stellt in der Klasse eine Liste darüber zusammen, welche der drei wichtigen Medien ihr benutzt! Gebraucht die folgenden Hinweise als Hilfe!

1. Beobachtet euch selbst und schreibt auf, wann ihr die Medien benutzt und wie lange!
2. Schreibt auf, was ihr am liebsten in der Zeitung lest oder welche Sendungen ihr euch im Radio anhört und im Fernsehen anseht!
3. Schreibt auf, welche Medien ihr im Unterricht und zu Hause benutzt! Wie oft und wie lange benutzt ihr diese?

4. Stellt diese Fragen euren Eltern, Großeltern, Verwandten und Bekannten! Welche Medieninteressen haben Menschen verschiedenen Alters, Geschlechts und verschiedener Berufe?

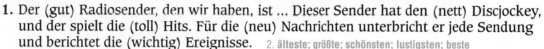

WORTSCHATZ

Words of quantity

Schon bekannt

wie viele

keine

ein paar

viele

alle

Neu

wenige

einige

5. Schreib dann einen Bericht über die Ergebnisse dieser Gruppenarbeit!

Rumpelstilzchen

Gebrüder Grimm

Es war einmal ein Müller, der war arm, aber er hatte eine schöne Tochter. Nun traf es sich, daß er mit dem König zu sprechen kam, und um sich ein Ansehen zu geben, sagte er zu ihm: „Ich habe eine Tochter, die kann Stroh zu Gold spinnen." Der König sprach zum Müller: „Das ist eine Kunst, die mir wohl gefällt; wenn deine Tochter so geschickt ist, wie du sagst, so bring sie morgen in mein Schloß, da will ich sie auf die Probe stellen."

Als nun das Mädchen zu ihm gebracht wurde, führte er es in eine Kammer, die ganz voll Stroh lag, gab ihr Rad und Haspel und sprach: „Jetzt mache dich an die Arbeit, und wenn du diese Nacht durch bis morgen früh dieses Stroh nicht zu Gold versponnen hast, so mußt du sterben!" Darauf schloß er die Kammer selbst zu, und sie blieb darin allein.

Da saß nun die arme Müllerstochter und wußte um ihr Leben keinen Rat; sie verstand gar nichts davon, wie man Stroh zu Gold spinnen konnte, und ihre Angst wurde immer größer, daß sie endlich zu weinen anfing. Da ging auf einmal die Tür auf, und trat ein kleines Männlein herein und sprach: „Guten Abend, Jungfer Müllerin, warum weinst du so sehr?" — „Ach", antwortete das Mädchen, „ich soll Stroh zu Gold spinnen und verstehe das nicht." Sprach das Männchen: „Was gibst du mir, wenn ich dir's spinne?" — „Mein Halsband", sagte das Mädchen. Das Männchen nahm das Halsband, setzte sich vor das Räd-chen, und schnurr, schnurr, schnurr, dreimal gezogen, war die Spule voll. Dann steckte es eine andere auf, und schnurr, schnurr, schnurr, dreimal gezogen, war auch die zweite voll; und so ging's fort bis zum Morgen, da war alles Stroh versponnen, und alle Spulen waren voll Gold.

Bei Sonnenaufgang kam schon der König, und als er das Gold erblickte, staunte er und freute sich. Aber sein Herz ward nur noch goldgieriger. Er ließ die Müllerstochter in eine andere Kammer bringen, die noch viel größer war, und befahl ihr, auch dieses Stroh in einer Nacht zu spinnen, wenn ihr das Leben lieb wäre.

Das Mädchen wußte sich nicht zu helfen und weinte. Da ging abermals die Tür auf, und das kleine Männchen erschien und sprach: „Was gibst du mir, wenn ich dir das Stroh zu Gold spinne?" — „Meinen Ring vom Finger", antwortete das Mädchen. Das Männchen nahm den Ring, fing wieder an zu schnurren mit dem Rade und hatte bis zum Morgen alles Stroh zu glänzendem Gold gesponnen.

LESETRICK

Predicting outcomes
Predicting what will happen in a story is a useful strat-egy. It helps you read more quickly and easily by focusing your attention on what you expect to happen. Making predictions requires both common sense and imagination.

For answers, see TE Interleaf.-

Getting Started

1. Read the title and the first paragraph of the reading selection. What characters are introduced?

2. What is the English equivalent of **Es war einmal ...** ? To which genre of literature does this story belong? When and where does the story take place?

3. Now read the first three paragraphs paying careful attention to the quotations. Make sure you know who is speaking at each point. What is the daughter's dilemma? How will it be resolved?

4. Before reading further, make some predic-tions about what might happen next.

er König freute sich über die Maßen bei dem Anblick, war aber noch immer nicht des Goldes satt, sondern ließ die Müllerstochter in eine noch größere Kammer voll Stroh bringen und sprach: „Die mußt du noch in dieser Nacht verspinnen! Gelingt dir's aber, so sollst du meine Gemahlin werden." — Wenn's auch eine Müllerstochter ist, dachte er, eine reichere Frau finde ich in der ganzen Welt nicht.

Als das Mädchen allein war, kam das Männlein zum drittenmal wieder und sprach: „Was gibst du mir, wenn ich dir noch diesmal das Stroh spinne?" — „Ich habe nichts mehr, das ich geben könnte", antwortete das Mädchen. „So versprich mir, wenn du Königin wirst, dein erstes Kind." — Wer weiß, wie das noch geht, dachte die Müllerstochter und wußte sich auch in der Not nicht anders zu helfen. Sie versprach also dem Männchen, was es verlangte, und das Männchen spann dafür noch einmal das Stroh zu Gold. Und als am Morgen der König kam und alles fand, wie er gewünscht hatte, so hielt er Hochzeit mit ihr, und die schöne Müllerstochter wurde eine Königin.

5. Reread the first three paragraphs and continue reading until the end of the fifth paragraph. Did the predictions you made in activity 4 prove correct? Continue reading until the end of the story, pausing every few paragraphs to make predictions. Check to see if your predictions were correct.

6. Now create a time line showing the order in which events occur. (*Hint:* In a European story of this genre, things often occur in sets of three. There are at least two sets of three things happening together in this story. Be sure to include these events in your time line.)

A Closer Look

7. a. Identify the following story-telling or antiquated words and phrases in the first three paragraphs and match each with a more common expression.

es traf sich	*der kleine Mann*
die Kammer	*das Fräulein*
das Männlein	*es ist passiert*
die Jungfer	*das kleine Spinnrad*
das Rädchen	*nicht wissen, was*
um das Leben	*man tun soll*
keinen Rat wissen	*das Zimmer*

äber ein Jahr brachte sie ein schönes Kind zur Welt und dachte gar nicht mehr an das Männchen. Da trat es plötzlich in ihre Kammer und sprach: „Nun gib mir, was du versprochen hast!" Die Königin erschrak und bot dem Männchen alle Reichtümer des Königreichs an, wenn es ihr das Kind lassen wollte. Aber das Männchen sprach: „Nein, etwas Lebendiges ist mir lieber als alle Schätze der Welt." Da fing die Königin so an zu jammern und zu weinen, daß das Männchen Mitleid mit ihr hatte. „Drei Tage will ich dir Zeit lassen", sprach es, „wenn du bis dahin meinen Namen weißt, so sollst du dein Kind behalten."

Nun besann sich die Königin die ganze Nacht über auf alle Namen, die sie jemals gehört hatte. Und sie schickte einen Boten über Land, der sollte sich erkundigen weit und breit, was es sonst noch für Namen gäbe. Als am andern Tag das Männchen kam, fing sie an mit Kaspar, Melchior, Balzer und sagte alle Namen, die sie wußte, der Reihe nach her. Aber bei jedem sprach das Männlein: „So heiß' ich nicht."

Den zweiten Tag ließ sie in der Nachbarschaft herumfragen, wie die Leute genannt würden, und sagte dem Männchen die ungewöhnlichsten und seltsamsten Namen vor:

„Heißt du vielleicht Rippenbiest oder Hammelswade oder Schnürbein?" Aber es antwortete immer: „So heiß' ich nicht."

Am dritten Tag kam der Bote wieder zurück und erzählte: „Neue Namen habe ich keinen einzigen finden können. Aber wie ich an einem hohen Berge um die Waldecke kam, wo Fuchs und Has' sich gute Nacht sagen, so sah ich da ein kleines Haus, und vor dem Haus brannte ein Feuer, und um das Feuer sprang ein gar zu lächerliches Männchen, hüpfte auf einem Bein und schrie:

‚Heute back' ich, morgen brau' ich,
übermorgen hol' ich der Königin ihr Kind;
ach, wie gut, daß niemand weiß,
daß ich Rumpelstilzchen heiß!'"

Da könnt ihr euch denken, wie die Königin froh war, als sie den Namen hörte. Und als bald danach das Männlein hereintrat und fragte: „Nun, Frau Königin, wie heiß' ich?" fragte sie erst: „Heißt du Kunz?" — „Nein." — „Heißt du Hinz?" — „Nein." — „Heißt du etwa Rumpelstilzchen?"

„Das hat dir der Teufel gesagt, das hat dir der Teufel gesagt!" schrie das Männlein und stieß mit dem rechten Fuß vor Zorn so tief in die Erde, daß es bis an den Leib hineinfuhr. Dann packte es in seiner Wut den linken Fuß mit beiden Händen und riß sich selbst mitten entzwei.

b. What does the word **schnurr** mean in the third paragraph? What is it the sound of? Explain what the author is doing here.

Writers use many kinds of cohesive devices (conjunctions, adverbs, and pronouns) to tie the elements of a story together. For example, **aber** lets you know to look for a contrast. Adverbs indicating time are clues to the sequence of events. When you see pronouns, including **da**-compounds, pay attention to the nouns they refer to in order to understand how individual sentences tie together.

---

8. Read the first three paragraphs again.

   a. Decide which characters the pronouns in the following sentences refer to:

- Und um sich ein Ansehen zu geben, sagte **er** zu **ihm**: …
- Als nun das Mädchen zu **ihm** gebracht wurde, führte **er es** in eine Kammer …
- Dann steckte **es** eine andere auf, …

   b. Identify the **da**-compounds **darin** and **davon** in the second and third paragraphs. What function does each compound serve?

9. Lies die Geschichte noch einmal! Erzähl die Geschichte mit eigenen Worten nach! Verwende dabei ordnende Zeitausdrücke!

10. Übernimm die Rolle von einer der Hauptfiguren, und erzähl die Geschichte aus ihrer Sicht, aber mit deinen eigenen Worten!

When people talk about their opinions they agree or disagree with one another and ask for clarification and support. When taking a position in writing, another person is not there to disagree or ask for clarification, so you need to state your argument clearly and address possible opposition. In this activity, you will select an issue of importance to you and write an essay about it, clearly stating and supporting your point of view.

Ich nehme dazu Stellung.

Schreib einen Aufsatz von fünf Abschnitten, in dem du Stellung zu einem wichtigen Thema nimmst! Schreib zuerst eine Inhaltsangabe (*outline*), um die Struktur des Aufsatzes im voraus zu planen!

A. Vorbereiten

1. Mach eine Inhaltsangabe für deinen Aufsatz! Schreib die römischen Zahlen I–V auf ein Blatt Papier, und laß viel Platz unter jeder Zahl! Schreib dann jeweils die Buchstaben A, B und C unter II, III und IV!
2. Denk an ein Problem, das dir wichtig ist! Nimm zu diesem Problem Stellung, und drück deine Stellungnahme in einem Satz aus! Schreib diesen Satz neben die Zahl I!
3. Begründe die Stellungnahme mit mindestens drei Punkten! Schreib diese stichwortartig (*in key words*) neben die Zahlen II–IV! Dann unterstütze diese Punkte mit zwei bis drei weiteren Ideen, und schreib diese wieder in Stichworten jeweils neben die Buchstaben A, B und C!
4. Lies dir die Inhaltsangabe durch, und schreib einen Satz, um den ganzen Aufsatz zusammenzufassen! Schreib diesen Satz als Schlußsatz unter die Zahl V!

SCHREIBTIP

Using an outline To write effectively, you need to organize your ideas before you begin. One way to do this is by using an outline. In an outline, you decide what general ideas you want to include as well as what order you want to discuss them in. Then you group more specific ideas together under your general headings. For a position paper, for example, your outline should include an introduction stating your position, followed by the main reasons for your position. Under each reason you should include supporting details. All of this is followed by a concluding section that ties the whole essay together.

B. Ausführen

Halte dich an deine Inhaltsangabe, und schreib den Aufsatz! Du mußt deine Ideen jetzt nur noch in ganze Sätze umwandeln! Gebrauche auch Nebensätze und Relativsätze, damit die Sprache fließend wirkt!

C. Überarbeiten

1. Such dir jemanden in der Klasse, der eine andere Stellung zu deinem Thema hat! Lies dieser Person deinen Aufsatz vor! Welche Gegenargumente äußert diese Person? Hast du diese Gegenargumente in deinem Aufsatz berücksichtigt? Wie kannst du deine Meinung gegen die Meinung deines Partners verteidigen?
2. Bist du deiner Inhaltsangabe gefolgt? Vergleich den Aufsatz mit dem Entwurf (*draft*)! Hast du etwas vergessen? Hast du überzeugend argumentiert?
3. Lies den Aufsatz noch einmal durch! Hast du alles richtig geschrieben? Gib besonders auf die komparativen und superlativen Adjektive acht!
4. Schreib den korrigierten Aufsatz noch einmal ab!

1 Einige Schüler möchten gern eine Schülerzeitung herausgeben. Mit einem Lehrer zusammen haben sie folgende Gedanken aufgeschrieben. Lies die Aufgaben durch! Welche Aufgaben findest du wichtig, welche nicht so wichtig? Gibt es einige Aufgaben, die du weglassen würdest? Möchtest du etwas hinzufügen? Schreib es auf!

Aufgaben einer Schülerzeitung

A. Anregungen und Information für alle Schüler
   1. Gute Schüleraufsätze abdrucken
   2. Interessante Bücher und neue Filme besprechen
   3. Tips geben, zum Beispiel, wie man vor einer Arbeit richtig lernt und wie man einen guten Aufsatz schreibt
   4. Über Berufe informieren
   5. Ratschläge geben über Geldverdienen, Taschengeld, usw.
   6. An wichtige Ereignisse und bedeutende Menschen erinnern
   7. Geschichten, Witze, Cartoons, lustige Anekdoten bringen

B. Berichte aus dem Schulleben
   1. Von Veranstaltungen und Ereignissen in der Schule berichten, zum Beispiel über Konzerte, Theaterspiele, Ausstellungen, Klassenreisen, Sport, usw.
   2. Neue Lehrer vorstellen
   3. Über allgemeine Schulfragen berichten, wie zum Beispiel Länge des Schultages, Wahl- und Pflichtfächer, Veränderungen im Schulgebäude oder im Verlauf des Schultages
   4. Deutsche und ausländische Schulen vergleichen

C. Sprachrohr der Schüler
   1. Fragen an die Schüler richten
   2. Meinungen der Schüler veröffentlichen
   3. Kritik und Vorschläge diskutieren
   4. Stellungnahmen der Lehrer und Schuldirektion bringen

2 Zwei Redaktionsmitglieder einer Schülerzeitung unterhalten sich über Themen, die in der nächsten Ausgabe erscheinen sollen, und danach sprechen sie über einige Arbeiten, die die Schüler noch machen müssen. Hör zu und schreib mindestens drei Themen auf, über die du auch gern in einer Schülerzeitung lesen möchtest! Dann schreib zwei Arbeiten auf, die du gern für deine Schülerzeitung machen möchtest! For answers, see listening script on TE Interleaf.

3 Wenn du an eurer Schule so eine Schülerzeitung hättest, was würde dich am meisten interessieren? Was würdest du regelmäßig lesen? Was interessiert dich nicht? Wenn du die Gelegenheit hättest, an so einer Zeitung mitzuarbeiten, für welche Artikel möchtest du verantwortlich sein?

4 Vergleicht eure Schülerzeitung mit der Liste von Aufgaben, die die Schüler in der ersten Übung aufgestellt haben! Was macht eure Zeitung alles? Was macht sie nicht? Könnt ihr an Hand eurer Zeitung Beispiele geben?

5 Gebt in eurer Deutschklasse eine Schülerzeitung heraus! Stellt zuerst eine Liste mit Aufgaben eurer Zeitung auf! Entscheidet euch, was für Artikel ihr schreiben wollt, und teilt die Arbeit unter den Klassenmitgliedern auf! Jeder bekommt eine Aufgabe.

6 Such dir einen Partner! Macht zusammen eine Umfrage für eure Schülerzeitung! Denkt an die Leute, die ihr in der Schule kennt oder von denen ihr etwas wißt! Seht euch die Kategorien an, und schreibt Sätze wie im Beispiel! Wen wählt ihr für die verschiedenen Kategorien? Vergleicht eure Umfrage mit denen eurer Klassenkameraden!

Kategorien:

sich schick anziehen	gute Noten haben	gescheit sein
tolle Witze erzählen	gut singen	sportlich sein
sich verrückt anziehen	viele Freunde haben	gut aussehen

Umfrage: 1. Wer zieht sich am schicksten an?
2. Wer erzählt die tollsten Witze?
3. Wer …

7 Nimm Stellung zu folgenden Aussagen, und schreib einen Leserbrief an die Schülerzeitung!
— Muß man immer sagen, was man denkt?
— Darf eine Schülerzeitung Lehrer kritisieren?

8

ROLLENSPIEL

Du bist Reporter oder Reporterin an einer Zeitung. Du interviewst einen Klassenkameraden oder eine Klassenkameradin über Medienbenützung. Stell folgende Fragen:

1. Warum liest du Zeitung?
2. Welche Zeitung(en) liest du?
3. Welche anderen Zeitungen kennst du?
4. Welches sind seriöse Zeitungen und welches Boulevardzeitungen?
5. Welche liest du intensiv? Welche blätterst du nur durch?
6. Welche Programmzeitschriften kennst du?
7. Was hörst du so alles im Radio?
8. Für welche Interessengruppen gibt es besondere Sendungen im Radio?
9. Welche TV-Sendungen sind besonders für Jugendliche geeignet?
10. Welche anderen Medien benützt du?

KANN ICH'S WIRKLICH?

Can you ask someone to take a position? (p. 133)

Can you ask for reasons? (p. 133)

1 How would you ask a friend to take a position on an issue or state his or her point of view?   Möchtest du mal dazu Stellung nehmen?

2 How would you ask someone for reasons that justify the way he or she feels about something?   Kannst du das begründen?

Can you express opinions? (p. 133)

3 How would you say that in your opinion we're not doing enough to protect the environment?   E.g.: Meiner Meinung nach tun wir nicht genug, um die Umwelt zu schützen.

Can you report past events? (p. 134)

4 How would you rewrite the following anecdote in a more formal style if a newspaper offered you to publish it?   For answers, see below.

Ich bin vier Jahre in der Redaktion der „Pepo" gewesen. Die viele Arbeit hat sich gelohnt, und es hat mir immer viel Spaß gemacht. Was mich ab und zu gestört hat, war, daß sich viele Schüler für die Zeitung nicht interessiert und sie nur kritisiert haben. Ich bin dann auch noch zwei Jahre in der SV gewesen. Wir haben Feten organisiert und unserer Schülerzeitung geholfen, wenn sie Probleme mit der Schulleitung gehabt hat.

Can you agree or disagree? (p. 136)

5 How would you respond if someone said the following things to you?
   a. Geld allein macht nicht glücklich. Hauptsache, man ist gesund.
   b. Was in der Zeitung steht, ist immer richtig.   5. a. E.g.: Da ist schon was dran.
   b. E.g.: Das stimmt gar nicht!

Can you change the subject? (p. 136)

6 How would you tell a friend with whom you're having a conversation that you would like to change the subject and go back to talking about the media?   Ich wollte etwas anderes sagen. Ich möchte nochmal auf die Medien zurückkommen.

Can you interrupt? (p. 136)

7 How would you tell a friend who is talking a lot that you want him or her to let you say something?   E.g.: Laß mich mal zu Wort kommen!

Can you express surprise or annoyance? (p. 141)

8 How would you express your surprise that your school's team didn't win the game?   E.g.: Ich bin überrascht, daß die Schulmannschaft das Spiel nicht gewonnen hat.

9 How would you express your annoyance if someone was constantly criticizing you?   E.g.: Was mich stört ist, daß ich immer kritisiert werde.

4. Ich war vier Jahre in der Redaktion der „Pepo". Die viele Arbeit lohnte sich, und es machte mir immer viel Spaß. Was mich ab und zu störte, war, daß sich viele Schüler nicht für die Zeitung interessierten und sie nur kritisierten. Ich war dann auch noch zwei Jahre in der SV. Wir organisierten Feten und halfen unserer Schülerzeitung, wenn sie Probleme mit der Schullleitung hatte.

ERSTE STUFE

ASKING SOMEONE TO TAKE A POSITION

Möchtest du mal dazu Stellung nehmen? *Would you like to take a position on that?*

ASKING FOR REASONS

Kannst du das begründen? *Can you give a reason for that?*

EXPRESSING OPINIONS

Meiner Meinung nach soll man sich besser informieren. *In my opinion one should get better informed*

AGREEING

Da ist schon was dran. *There's something to that.*
Eben! *Exactly!*
Richtig! *Right!*

DISAGREEING

Das stimmt gar nicht! *That's not true at all!*
Das ist alles Quatsch! *That's all a bunch of baloney!*

CHANGING THE SUBJECT

Ich möchte nochmal darauf zurückkommen. *I would like to get back to that.*

INTERRUPTING

Laß mich mal zu Wort kommen! *Let me get in a word!*
Moment mal, laß den Berti mal ausreden! *Hold on there, let Berti speak his mind!*

OTHER USEFUL WORDS

die Bildung *formation*
der Bericht, -e *report*
der Drucker, - *printer*
die Einzelheit, -en *detail*
das Ereignis, -se *event*
die Glotze, -n *television, idiot box*
der Hintergrund, ⸚e *background*
der Kommentar, -e *commentary*
die Medien (pl) *media*
das Nachdenken *reflection*
die Neuigkeit, -en *most recent event*
die Redaktion *editorial staff*

die Schlagzeile, -n *headline*
der Spaß *joke*
der Streik, -s *strike*
die Tatsache, -n *fact*
die Unterhaltung, -en *entertainment*
die Veranstaltung, -en *organized event*
die Wahrheit *truth*

anregen (sep) *to encourage, stimulate*
ansprechen (sep) *to appeal, speak to*
beitragen zu (sep) *to contribute to*
durchblättern (sep) *to page through*
s. eignen zu *to be suited to*
erfahren *to experience*
verdrängen *to displace, repress*
vermissen *to miss*
s. vorstellen (sep) *to imagine*
weglassen (sep) *to omit, drop*

oberflächlich *superficial*
gesamt *entire*
gründlich *thorough*
meist- *most*

ZWEITE STUFE

EXPRESSING SURPRISE

Es ist unglaublich, daß ... *It's unbelievable that ...*
Das überrascht mich. *That surprises me.*
Ich bin überrascht, daß ... *I'm surprised that ...*

EXPRESSING ANNOYANCE

Was mich stört, ist ... *What bothers me is ...*
Ich werde sauer, wenn ... *I get annoyed when ...*
Es ist frustrierend, wenn ... *It's frustrating when ...*

OTHER USEFUL WORDS AND EXPRESSIONS

die Aufgabe, -n *task*
der Schüleraustausch *student exchange*
die Schülervertretung *students' representatives*
die Schulleitung *school administration*

Das macht mir nichts aus. *That doesn't matter to me.*
Wie stehst du dazu? *What do you think of that?*
s. bemühen um *to strive for*
erreichen *to achieve*

s. kümmern um *to be concerned about*
meckern *to complain*
unterstützen *to support*

ab und zu *now and then*
anregend *stimulating*
deshalb *for this reason*
deutlich *clearly*
fast immer *almost always*
nützlich *useful*
selbst *oneself*
unterwegs *underway*
einige *some*
mehrere *several*
wenige *few*

📼 Location Opener
Frankfurt, pages 152-155
Video Program, Videocassette 2

𝒰sing the Photograph,
pp. 152-153

Background Information

First records refer to the city of Frankfurt in 794 as **Francono Furd** *(ford of the Franks).* Between 885 and 1792, thirty-six German rulers were elected here. The Golden Bull of 1356 designated Frankfurt as the seat for the election of the Holy Roman emperors. From 1562 on, the Holy Roman emperors were crowned in the **Kaiserdom,** the city's Gothic cathedral. Today this historic cathedral, the fair tower, and numerous bank buildings stand out in the city's skyline. Locals sometimes refer to the city as *Mainhattan* or *Bankfurt.*

Geography Connection

Ask students to refer to the map on p. 394 to find out what river runs through Frankfurt (Please note: the map is on p. 393 in the *Teacher's Edition.*). You may also want to use Map Transparency 1. Tell students the name of Germany's largest airport (**Rhein-Main-Flughafen**) and have them give an explanation for its name.

𝒰sing the Almanac and Map,
p. 153

The coat of arms of Frankfurt displays a white eagle on a red background. The eagle derives from the heraldic symbol of the medieval Holy Roman Empire. Frankfurt always had a close connection to the Empire, since it was both a Free Imperial City (i.e., not subject to a prince or bishop, but only to the Emperor) and the place where each newly elected emperor was crowned. Even after the end of the Holy Roman Empire in 1806, Frankfurt retained the eagle as its emblem.

Terms in the Almanac

- **Hessen:** The state Hessen covers an area of approximately 21,100 square kilometers (8,145 square miles) with most of its population living in the **Rhein-Main** region.

- **Main:** This river is the main tributary of the Rhine coming from the east. It is 524 kilometers (325.4 miles) long and ends at the city of Mainz. Only parts of it are navigable.

- **Römer:** See Level 2, *Teacher's Edition,* p. 51M and Level 3, *Teacher's Edition,* p. 151B.

- **Goethehaus:** See Level 2, *Teacher's Edition,* p. 51M and Level 3, *Teacher's Edition,* p. 151B.

- **Maria Sybilla Merian:** The Merians were a family of artists involved in engraving, publishing, and painting. Maria was a noted painter of flowers, insects, and animals.

- **J. W. von Goethe:** Goethe, who was born in 1749 in Frankfurt and died in 1832 in Weimar, is regarded as one of the greatest figures in German literary history. He first achieved international fame with his novel **Die Leiden des jungen Werthers** (1774) which describes a sensitive young man suffering because of unrequited love. In 1776, Goethe accepted a high position in the cabinet of the Duke of Sachsen-Weimar. Goethe spent most of his life in Weimar, a town that became the center of German literature. Among Goethe's greatest works are the novel **Wilhelm Meisters Lehrjahre,** volumes of poems such as **Wanderers Nachtlied** and **Der Erlkönig**, and the play **Faust.** Since 1961, the city of Frankfurt has awarded the **Goethepreis** in the amount of 50,000 marks to accomplished authors. Some of the best-known recipients have been Thomas Mann, Hermann Hesse, Max Planck, and Carl Zuckmayer.

- **Teaching Suggestion** Time permitting, you may want to introduce excerpts of some of Goethe's writings to your class.

- **Otto Hahn:** Hahn was a chemist and physicist whose discovery of the phenomenon of fission in 1938 led to the development of the atomic bomb. He received the Nobel Prize in Chemistry in 1944 for his discovery of the fission of heavy nuclei.

- **Bankwesen:** Frankfurt's connection to banking and finance dates back to the 16th century when the city was granted permission to mint money. Today the city is home to the **Deutsche Bundesbank** (*central bank of Germany*) as well as 400 other domestic and foreign banks. The **Frankfurter Börse** (*stock exchange*) is the largest in Germany.

- **Buchmesse:** The **Internationale Frankfurter Buchmesse** is one of the major trade fairs that take place in Frankfurt each year. Frankfurt has the third largest trade fair site in the world, after Hannover and Milan, Italy.

- **Handkäs mit Musik: Handkäs,** also referred to as **Mainzer** cheese, should be round and well-aged. The round cheese is cut into four sections and served with a marinade of vinegar, oil, salt, pepper, and onions. **Handkäs** is served on fresh bread with **Äppelwoi** as the beverage.

- **Äppelwoi:** This is one of the words used for **Apfelwein** in the Hessian dialect. In Level 2, students read about **Äbbewoi,** another word for **Apfelwein.**

Thinking Critically

Comparing and Contrasting Have students list ways in which Frankfurt and New York City are similar. (Examples: located on rivers, noted for their skylines, home of major stock exchanges, important financial centers) Can students tell why Frankfurt has the nicknames *Mainhattan* and *Bankfurt*?

Using the Map

Have students locate Frankfurt on a map. (You may want to use Map Transparency 1.) Then ask them to think about how Frankfurt's location has helped make it one of the most important industrial cities in central Europe. (Frankfurt is very centrally located in Europe, and many natural waterways, highways, and railways lead to and away from Frankfurt. The city also has one of the busiest airports in Europe. All of this makes Frankfurt an important crossroad between northern and southern Europe.)

*I*nterpreting the Photo Essay, *pp. 154-155*

② **Der Römer** (**Rathaus**) is located in the historic center of the city, the **Römerberg.** It got its name for being the oldest in the set of eleven **Giebelhäuser,** a complex of gabled buildings on the **Römerberg.** Pictured in the photo is a group of three buildings, the **Alt-Limpurg, Zum Römer,** and **Löwenstein.** The upper floor of the **Römer** was used for banquets following the coronation of kings or emperors. Today the **Römer** houses the city government.

③ The **Dom St. Bartholomäus,** also known as the **Kaiserdom,** was built during the 13th, 14th, and 15th centuries. It is made mostly of sandstone taken from the banks of the Main river.

- **Teaching Suggestion** Ask students to research and make a list of emperors who were crowned in the **Kaiserdom** starting in 1562. This could be done for extra credit.

④ The lower, rounded building of the **Paulskirche** was originally built as a Protestant church. The building was gutted during World War II and rebuilt through the help of private donations in 1948.

- **Drawing Inferences** Have students read the caption of Photo 4, then ask them to imagine that they are responsible for coordinating events at the **Paulskirche.** What types of programs might the **Paulskirche** be ideal for?

⑤ **Das Goethehaus** is the famous writer's birthplace and childhood home. It was destroyed in World War II and rebuilt between 1946 and 1951. It features the workroom where Goethe wrote *Werther, Götz von Berlichingen,* and parts of *Faust.* Today the house is also connected to the **Goethemuseum.**

⑥ The restoration of the group of **Fachwerkhäuser** on the east side of the **Römerberg** was completed in the early eighties. For information on **Fachwerk,** see Level 2, *Teacher's Edition,* p. 51M.

LOCATION OPENER

Komm mit nach

Frankfurt!

Frankfurt

DÄNEMARK
Ostsee
Nordsee
Kiel
Hamburg
NIEDERL.
POLEN
Berlin
Hessen
Frankfurt
BELG.
TSCHECH.
REPUBLIK
LUX.
München
FRANKR.
SCHWEIZ
ÖSTERREICH

Bundesland: Hessen

Einwohner: 650 000

Fluß: Main

Sehenswürdigkeiten: Römer, Paulskirche, Dom, Goethehaus

Berühmte Leute: Maria Sybilla Merian (1647-1717); J.W. von Goethe (1749-1832); Otto Hahn (1879-1968)

Industrie und Handel: Bankwesen, Buchmesse

Bekannte Gerichte: Rippchen mit Kraut, Handkäs mit Musik, Äppelwoi (Apfelwein)

Foto (1) Die Frankfurter Skyline

Frankfurt

Frankfurt feierte 1994 seinen 1200. Geburtstag! Der Ort wurde 794 zum ersten Mal erwähnt als einer der Sitze Karls des Großen, Kaiser des Fränkischen Reiches und seit 800 Kaiser des Heiligen Römischen Reiches Deutscher Nation. Heute ist Frankfurt eine moderne Großstadt, das Finanzzentrum der Bundesrepublik und seit 1994 auch geplante Finanzmetropole der Europäischen Union.

② Der Römer (in der Mitte), das alte Rathaus der Stadt, ist das Wahrzeichen Frankfurts. Im ersten Stock befindet sich der Kaisersaal mit Bildern der deutschen Kaiser, wo glanzvolle Krönungsfeierlichkeiten und Bankette stattfanden. Diese drei Häuser sind im gotischen Stil erbaut.

③ Der Dom St. Bartholomäus, im 13.-15. Jahrhundert erbaut, ist ein Wahrzeichen Frankfurts. Dieser Dom war von 1356 bis 1792 Wahlkapelle für die deutschen Könige und Kaiser, und seit 1562 fanden hier auch die Kaiserkrönungen statt.

(5) Das Goethehaus, Geburtshaus des großen deutschen Dichters Johann Wolfgang von Goethe (1749-1832) ist so eingerichtet, wie es einst war. Im Arbeitszimmer schrieb Goethe den „Götz", den „Werther" und Teile des „Faust". Nebenan ist das Goethemuseum mit über 100 000 Büchern und Manuskripten.

(4) Die Paulskirche (1787-1833) war in den Jahren 1848-1849 Tagungsort der ersten Deutschen Nationalversammlung. Die Kirche dient heute der Stadt zu repräsentativen Anlässen, wie zum Beispiel zur Verleihung des Goethepreises oder des Friedenspreises des Deutschen Buchhandels.

(6) Die schönen historischen Fachwerkbauten auf der Ostseite des Römerbergs gegenüber vom Römer wurden im Krieg total zerstört und erst 1984 wieder völlig aufgebaut. In zwei dieser Häuser befinden sich gemütliche Lokale, wo man im Sommer auch draußen sitzen und schmackhafte Frankfurter Spezialitäten probieren kann.

Kapitel 7: Ohne Reklame geht es nicht!

CHAPTER OVERVIEW

	FUNCTIONS	GRAMMAR	CULTURE	RE-ENTRY
Los geht's! pp. 158-159	Werbung—ja oder nein? *p. 158*			
Erste Stufe pp. 160-164	•Expressing annoyance, *p. 161* •Comparing, *p. 161*	•**Derselbe, der gleiche,** *p. 162* •Adjective endings following determiners of quantity, *p. 163*	•Werbung—pro und contra, *p. 160* •**Landeskunde: Warum so wenig Unterbrecherwerbung?** *p. 165*	•Expressing annoyance, *p. 161* •The conjunctions **wenn** and **daß,** *p. 161* •Comparative and superlative forms of adjectives, *p. 161* •Adjective endings, *pp. 162, 163*
Weiter geht's! pp. 166-167	Image-Werbung, *p. 166*			
Zweite Stufe pp. 168-171	•Eliciting agreement and agreeing, *p. 168* •Expressing conviction, uncertainty, and what seems to be true, *p. 170*	•Relative pronouns, *p. 169* •Introducing relative clauses with **was** and **wo,** *p. 169* •**Irgendein** and **irgendwelche,** *p. 171*	•Excerpt from *Frankfurter Allgemeine,* *p. 168* •Cartoon, *p. 169*	•Agreeing, *p. 168* •Relative pronouns, *p. 169* •Word order in dependent clauses, *p. 169* •Expressing conviction, *p. 170* •Expressing uncertainty, *p. 170* •Adjective endings, *p. 171*
Zum Lesen pp. 172-174	Comics lesen Reading Strategy: Using pictures and print type as clues to meaning			
Zum Schreiben p. 175	Es stört mich! Writing Strategy: Using tone and word choice for effect			
Review pp. 176-179	•Anwendung, *p. 176* •Kann ich's wirklich? *p. 178* •Wortschatz, *p. 179*			
Assessment Options	**Stufe Quizzes** •*Chapter Resources,* Book 3 Erste Stufe, Quiz 7-1 Zweite Stufe, Quiz 7-2 •*Assessment Items, Audiocassette* 8 A			**Kapitel 7 Chapter Test** •*Chapter Resources,* Book 3 •*Assessment Guide,* Speaking Test •*Assessment Items, Audiocassette* 8 A **Test Generator, Kapitel 7**

Chapter Overview

RESOURCES Print	RESOURCES Audiovisual
Practice and Activity Book	*Textbook Audiocassette* 4 A

Practice and Activity Book
Chapter Resources, Book 3
  •Communicative Activity 7-1
  •Communicative Activity 7-2
  •Additional Listening Activity 7-1
  •Additional Listening Activity 7-2
  •Additional Listening Activity 7-3
  •Student Response Forms
  •Realia 7-1
  •Situation Card 7-1
  •Teaching Transparency Master 7-1
  •Quiz 7-1
Video Guide
	Textbook Audiocassette 4 A
	
	Additional Listening Activities, Audiocassette 10 A
	Additional Listening Activities, Audiocassette 10 A
	Additional Listening Activities, Audiocassette 10 A
	
	Teaching Transparency 7-1
	Assessment Items, Audiocassette 8 A
	Video Program, Videocassette 2

Practice and Activity Book	*Textbook Audiocassette* 4 A

Practice and Activity Book
Chapter Resources, Book 3
  •Communicative Activity 7-3
  •Communicative Activity 7-4
  •Additional Listening Activity 7-4
  •Additional Listening Activity 7-5
  •Additional Listening Activity 7-6
  •Student Response Forms
  •Realia 7-2
  •Situation Card 7-2
  •Teaching Transparency Master 7-2
  •Quiz 7-2
Video Guide
	Textbook Audiocassette 4 A
	
	Additional Listening Activities, Audiocassette 10 A
	Additional Listening Activities, Audiocassette 10 A
	Additional Listening Activities, Audiocassette 10 A
	
	Teaching Transparency 7-2
	Assessment Items, Audiocassette 8 A
	Video Program, Videocassette 2

Chapter Resources, Book 3
- •Realia 7-3
- •Situation Card 7-3

Alternative Assessment

•Performance Assessment
Teacher's Edition
  Erste Stufe, p. 155L
  Zweite Stufe, p. 155O

•Portfolio Assessment
  Written: **Anwendung,** Activity 3, *Pupil's Edition,* p. 177;
  Assessment Guide, p. 20
  Oral: **Anwendung,** Activity 2, *Pupil's Edition,* p. 177;
  Assessment Guide, p. 20
•**Notizbuch,** *Pupil's Edition,* pp. 164, 171

Kapitel 7: Ohne Reklame geht es nicht!
Textbook Listening Activities Scripts

For Student Response Forms, see *Chapter Resources,* Book 3, pp. 22-25.

Erste Stufe
Activity 3, p. 161

UDO Hallo, Brigitte! Hallo, Rudi! Was macht ihr denn gerade?

RUDI Tag, Udo! Nichts Besonderes. Nur 'ne Kaffeepause.

UDO Du, Rudi, hast du neue Sportschuhe? Die sind aber schick. Wo hast du die denn her?

RUDI Tja, die hab' ich zum Geburtstag bekommen. Ich wollte diese Schuhe schon seit Monaten haben.

BRIGITTE Die Schuhe habe ich doch im Fernsehen gesehen, oder? In dieser Werbung mit dem Basketballspieler, der 10 Meter hoch springen kann, also durch die Decke und durch das Dach der Sporthalle oder sowas.

UDO Mensch! Die Werbung geht mir so auf die Nerven! Keiner kann doch so hoch springen!

RUDI Naja, Udo, bist du blöd? Das geht doch gar nicht darum, ob es realistisch ist oder nicht! Wichtig ist, daß die Zuschauer von dem Werbespot beeindruckt sind.

UDO Na ja, aber was mich aufregt, ist, daß die Werbung indirekt behauptet, daß man mit den Sportschuhen irgendwie stärker oder besser wäre. Oder zumindest, daß man gerade mit diesen Schuhen höher springen kann als die anderen Sportler.

BRIGITTE Genau! Versteckte Mitteilungen nennt man das! Mich regt sowas auch auf!

UDO Ja, es nervt mich halt, daß die Werbemacher versuchen, einen zu manipulieren.

RUDI Also mir ist das eigentlich egal. Ich lasse mich eben nicht manipulieren. Die Schuhe haben mir auch ohne Reklame gefallen.

BRIGITTE Na ja, aber ich glaube, daß wir in erster Linie erst durch die Werbung auf ein Produkt aufmerksam gemacht werden.

UDO Da stimme ich mit Brigitte überein. Mir geht es jedenfalls oft so.

BRIGITTE Also, ich habe festgestellt, daß ich mir eigentlich ganz gern Werbespots im Fernsehen, Reklamen an Plakatwänden oder in Zeitungsprospekten anschaue. Mir ist es echt egal, ob ich da beinflußt werde. Ich finde die meisten dieser Werbungen einfach bunt und witzig.

UDO Du gibst also zu, daß du dich manipulieren läßt?

BRIGITTE Wenn du es unbedingt so nennen willst! Guckt mal, hier! Meine Rudolfo-Carmanio-Bluse! Darauf wurde ich durch 'ne ganz bunte Reklame in einer Zeitschrift aufmerksam gemacht. Der Werbespruch war super: „Rudolfo — für die Frau, die sich selbst gefallen möchte!"

RUDI Und nur wegen des Slogans hast du die Bluse gekauft?

BRIGITTE Ach Quatsch, Rudi! Die Bluse habe ich gekauft, weil sie mir halt gefallen hat. Aber der Spruch, sag' ich euch, der hat mich beeindruckt!

UDO Mensch, die Rudolfo-Carmanio-Klamotten sind doch aber wahnsinnig teuer, oder?

BRIGITTE Ja schon! Aber der Preis ist mir egal, wenn die Werbung es geschafft hat, mich für ein Produkt zu interessieren.

UDO Ja, aber im Grunde genommen bezahlst du für den Namen und für die Werbung mit! Siehst du, das stört mich echt, und deswegen würde ich mir Produkte, für die die Firmen viel Geld für Werbung ausgegeben, nicht kaufen!

Answers to Activity 3

Udo: geht es auf die Nerven, wenn eine Werbung unrealistisch ist; regt sich über versteckte Mitteilungen auf; ärgert sich über Manipulation in der Werbung; stört es, wenn man beim Kauf eines Produktes die teuren Werbekosten mitbezahlt

Brigitte: regt sich über versteckte Mitteilungen auf; schaut sich gern Werbung an, und deshalb ist es ihr egal, ob sie beinflußt wird; ist der Preis eines Produktes egal, wenn die Werbung es geschafft hat, sie für das Produkt zu interessieren

Rudi: sind Manipulationen in der Werbung egal, weil er sich nicht manipulieren läßt

Activity 6, p. 161

FRAU W. Frau Gruber, haben Sie schon das neue Müsli probiert?

FRAU G. Welches meinen Sie denn, Frau Winter? Das von RITTERMANN mit den extra vielen Rosinen?

FRAU W. Ja, genau! Ich kaufe es jetzt immer, weil es neben den Rosinen auch noch vier verschiedene Sorten Trockenobst und viele Ballaststoffe hat. Ein richtig gesundes Müsli, sag' ich Ihnen!

FRAU G. Stimmt! Meinen Sie nicht auch, Herr Köhler?

HERR K. Hm ... haben Sie schon gesehen, wieviel es kostet?

FRAU W. 6 Mark 95 ist doch nicht so viel, wenn die Qualität wesentlich besser ist.

HERR K. Ich finde, das ist zu teuer für eine Packung Müsli. Da bleibe ich lieber bei meiner alten Marke.

FRAU G. Übrigens, haben Sie schon gesehen? Orangensaft ist diese Woche im Sonderangebot! Ich nehm' mir gleich einen ganzen Kasten mit!

FRAU W. Welchen meinen Sie denn, Frau Gruber, den aus Orangensaftkonzentrat oder den frischgepreßten?

FRAU G. Den frischgepreßten, natürlich. Von ORANSINA!

HERR K. Ja, der ist ausgezeichnet! Davon werde ich mir auch gleich mehrere Flaschen mitnehmen.

FRAU W. So, ich muß mal auf meine Einkaufsliste schauen! Ach, beinahe hätte ich den Kaffee vergessen!

FRAU G. Welchen nehmen Sie denn, Frau Winter?

FRAU W. Also, meine Familie mag nur den koffeinfreien von MOKKAROMA. Der ist am mildesten.

FRAU G. Ach, dann kaufen Sie also immer nur die eine Sorte?

FRAU W. Ja genau! Sie denn nicht, Frau Gruber?

FRAU G. Nein, ich kaufe jedesmal eine andere Marke. Dann haben wir im Geschmack mehr Abwechslung.

HERR K. Ja, da stimme ich Ihnen zu. Beim Kaffee unterscheidet sich das Aroma sehr zwischen den verschiedenen Sorten. Ich probiere auch immer wieder andere Marken aus.

FRAU W. So, was brauche ich noch? Ach, fast hätte ich das Waschpulver vergessen. Oh, ÖKOWEISS gibt's jetzt auch als Konzentrat in der Nachfüllpackung! Wie praktisch!

FRAU G. Haben Sie schon mal BLITZWASCH ausprobiert, Frau Winter? Da wird die Wäsche strahlend weiß und duftig! Hier, schauen Sie mal! Ich hab' mir gerade die 7,5-Kilo-Packung in den Einkaufswagen gelegt.

FRAU W. Ja, aber leider ist BLITZWASCH nicht biologisch abbaubar! Ich nehme lieber das umweltfreundliche ÖKOWEISS.

FRAU G. Tja, aber leider wäscht es die Flecken nicht so gut raus wie BLITZWASCH. BLITZWASCH hat eben eine stärkere Waschkraft.

FRAU W. Ach du liebe Zeit, es ist ja schon fast halb zwölf. Ich muß schnell heim. Auf Wiedersehen, Herr Köhler! Tschüs, Frau Gruber!

HERR K. Tschüs!

FRAU G. Schönen Tag noch, Frau Winter!

Answers to Activity 6

Frau Winter kauft: Müsli von RITTERMANN, weil es gesund ist; Kaffee von MOKKAROMA, weil er am mildesten ist; ÖKOWEISS-Waschpulver, weil es umweltfreundlich ist

Frau Gruber kauft: Müsli von RITTERMANN, weil es besser schmeckt; Orangensaft von ORANSINA, weil er im Angebot ist; immer andere Kaffeesorten, um mehr Abwechslung im Geschmack zu haben; BLITZWASCH-Waschpulver, weil es eine stärkere Waschkraft hat

Herr Köhler kauft: seine alte Müslimarke, weil sie billiger ist; Orangensaft von ORANSINA, weil er im Angebot ist; immer andere Kaffeesorten, um mehr Abwechslung im Geschmack zu haben

Activity 10, p. 163

1. KATZENSCHMAUS, aus reinem Fleisch und hochwertigen Vitaminen! Läßt Ihre Katze garantiert zum Feinschmecker werden!

2. Sehen, was man fühlt: Die einzigartige, neue Pflege von BIOWASCH, damit Ihre neuen Kleidungsstücke auch nach der Wäsche noch wie neu aussehen!

3. Natur pur: Sahnig-fein, cremig-schmelzend! Keine Butter ist besser im Geschmack als DEUTSCHE MARKENBUTTER!

4. Schützen Sie die Zukunft Ihres Haares mit dem Pflegeschampoo von LAREOL! Verwöhnen Sie Ihr Haar mit seidigem Glanz! Erleben Sie die neue Spannkraft in Ihrem Haar! Fühlen Sie die geschmeidige Fülle! Nur mit LAREOL!

5. Für den dynamischen, sportlichen Typ: Der neue AQUARIUS! Ein Wagen, der Sie nie im Stich läßt.

Answers to Activity 10

1. e; 2. b; 3. c; 4. d; 5. a

Activity 17, p. 168

ANDREA He, Leute, habt ihr gute Werbespots aus den Zeitungen gesammelt? Okay. Dann laßt mal sehen!

THOMAS Ich habe eine Werbung von einem Fitneßstudio gefunden, die ich ganz super fand. Schaut mal! Eine hübsche, schlanke Frau im Bodysuit und ein muskulöser Mann daneben. Darunter steht ein Slogan, mit dem das Fitneßstudio die Vorteile eines guttrainierten Körpers anpreist.

UTE Mensch, Thomas, das ist ja ekelhaft! Meint Ihr nicht, daß dieses Fitneßstudio ganz einfach versucht, die Leute zu beeinflussen?

ACHIM Na klar, Ute! Das ist doch der Sinn der ganzen Sache! Wenn Leute diese superathletischen Körper in den Zeitungen sehen, dann fühlen sie sich angesprochen und wollen auch so aussehen. Ich finde diese Werbung klasse!

ANDREA Eben! Achim hat recht!

UTE Ich mag diese Art von Werbung gar nicht, bei der versucht wird, den Leuten etwas vorzumachen, was eigentlich sehr unrealistisch ist.

ACHIM Ute, selbst wenn die Werbung etwas unrealistisch ist, appelliert sie doch an die Sportmuffel, mal endlich was für ihre Gesundheit zu tun.

UTE Na gut!

ANDREA Ich habe eine Anzeige für ein Blumengeschäft gefunden. Wie findet ihr die?

ACHIM Mensch, Andrea! So 'was Langweiliges! Wer kauft sich schon Blumen?

THOMAS Viele Leute mögen Blumen.

UTE Ich stimme ganz mit dir überein, Thomas.

ACHIM Wir suchen doch nach einem Werbespot, der die Schüler anspricht, oder?

ANDREA Achim hat recht. Blumen sind wahrscheinlich nicht so geeignet dafür.

UTE Aber hier ist ein toller Werbespot von einem Fahrradhändler. Der bietet Mountainbikes an.

THOMAS Na ja, Ute. Ich weiß nicht so recht! Heutzutage haben die meisten Schüler doch ein Mofa.

ACHIM Das stimmt doch gar nicht, Thomas! Die meisten Schüler und Studenten besitzen eher ein Fahrrad als ein Mofa.

UTE Das meine ich auch. Es gibt wahnsinnig viele Schüler, die mit dem Fahrrad zur Schule kommen, und deshalb finde ich den Werbespot auch besonders geeignet.

ACHIM Ja, also ich bin dafür, daß wir ihn nehmen.

UTE Hier ist noch eine gute Reklame vom Buchladen am Stadtbad.

ACHIM Ach, diese Werbung eignet sich doch gar nicht für unsere Schülerzeitung! Bücher erinnern die Schüler nur ans Lernen! Wir sollten eine Werbung nehmen, die in erster Linie Spaß suggeriert!

ANDREA Das ist eine gute Idee, Achim! Woran genau denkst du da?

ACHIM Wie wär's denn mit einer Reklame vom neuen Freizeitpark in Hermeskeil?

THOMAS Dafür interessieren sich die Schüler bestimmt!

UTE Das glaub' ich auch!

ACHIM Na prima! Dann hätten wir ja genügend Werbespots für die Schülerzeitung.

Answers to Activity 17

Achims Meinungen werden am meisten akzeptiert.

Activity 22, p. 170

CHRISTIAN Du, Sebastian, ich finde, daß der Werbespruch: „Weil Ihre Helden ganze Arbeit leisten" ein Versuch ist, die Konsumenten zu beeinflussen!

SEBASTIAN Das mag schon sein. Doch es scheint nicht der Fall zu sein, daß diese Werbung versucht, unsere Gefühle auszunutzen. Was meinst Du, Lisa?

LISA Ich meine, es sieht so aus, als ob in der Cowboywerbung und in diesem Werbespruch viele verborgene Mitteilungen stecken. Erstens will die Werbung sagen, wenn Ihr Kind diese Schokomilch trinkt, wird es sich gesund und kräftig entwickeln. Zweitens zeigt sie den Kindern, daß sie richtige Draufgänger sein können und das nur, wenn sie regelmäßig SCHOKO-SAM trinken. So ganz nach dem Motto: „Wenn ich SCHOKO-SAM trinke, bin ich auch ein Held."

CHRISTIAN Du meinst also, daß der Werbespruch etwas verspricht, was in Wirklichkeit nicht stimmt.

LISA Genau!

CHRISTIAN Das scheint mir auch so!

SEBASTIAN Und ich finde, daß Mädchen mit dieser Werbung überhaupt nicht angesprochen werden! Hier wird ganz eindeutig nur der kleine Junge als Held gezeigt.

CHRISTIAN Hm. Da bin ich mir nicht so sicher. Das würde ich nämlich nicht so eng sehen, Sebastian! Meine Schwester, zum Beispiel, mag diese Werbung sehr gern.

LISA Eben! Ich wäre mir da auch nicht so sicher! Meine kleinen Kusinen imitieren den Cowboy immer, wenn sie diese Werbung im Fernsehen sehen oder wenn sie SCHOKO-SAM trinken.

SEBASTIAN Aber darum geht es ja gerade! Hier werden doch ganz eindeutig die Gefühle der Eltern ausgenutzt, weil sie das Zeug wirklich für Ihre Kinder kaufen. Und die Gefühle der Kinder werden ebenfalls ausgenutzt, weil sie wie Helden sein wollen.

CHRISTIAN Das mag schon sein, Sebastian. Du kannst aber von Kindern nicht erwarten, daß sie die Werbesprüche im Fernsehen bereits analysieren können.

SEBASTIAN Ja, aber ich finde, die Eltern lassen sich auch von der Werbung beinflussen.

LISA Kann schon sein! Aber ich glaube, daß es genügend Eltern gibt, die sich für ein Produkt aus vernünftigeren Gründen entscheiden, und sich nicht nur an der Werbung orientieren.

SEBASTIAN Ich finde es außerdem auch unmoralisch, Kinder in der Werbung zu benutzen. Ich bin total dagegen!

CHRISTIAN Hm. Damit hab' ich kein Problem.

LISA Ja. Mich stört es eigentlich auch nicht, wenn Kinder in Werbespots mitmachen.

Answers for Activity 22

Konsumenten werden beinflußt: Christian ist überzeugt, daß er recht hat; Sebastian und Lisa sind nicht sicher.
Gefühle werden ausgenutzt: Christian ist nicht sicher; Sebastian ist überzeugt, daß er recht hat.
Werbung enthält verborgene Mitteilungen: Christian und Lisa sind überzeugt, daß sie recht haben.
Mädchen werden mit dieser Werbung nicht angesprochen: Christian und Lisa sind nicht sicher; Sebastian ist überzeugt, daß er recht hat.
Kinder in Werbung: Sebastian ist dagegen.

Anwendung, Activity 2, p. 177

1. POP-TEEN, die moderne Zeitschrift für junge Leute. Immer informiert, immer auf dem neusten Stand! POP-TEEN hat die heißesten Interviews, die größten Hits und die „coolsten" Tips zu allem, was Teenager der neunziger Jahre interessiert. Die neuste Ausgabe ist wieder vollgepackt mit Berichten über die größten Stars der Musikszene, mit einer exklusiven Fotoreportage über Madonna und mit der aktuellen Top-Ten Hitliste. Holt sie Euch, die neue POP-TEEN.

2. SPORT-AKTIV, das neue Fachgeschäft für Sportbekleidung und Sportausstattung bietet Ihnen eine riesige Auswahl an allem, was das Sportlerherz begehrt. Diese Woche ganz groß im Angebot: Tenniskleidung und Tennisschuhe von führenden Markenherstellern; dazu Stirnbänder mit feschem Design. Kommen Sie, und sehen Sie sich auch unsere enorme Auswahl an Tennisschlägern an! Bei SPORT-AKTIV gibt's garantiert für jeden etwas. Machen Sie auch mit bei unserer Verlosung! Gewinnen Sie eine Reise für zwei Personen nach Wimbledon! Sehen Sie ihre Stars live! Teilnahmebedingung: Kauf einer unserer Tennisartikel im Angebot. Lassen Sie sich diese Chance nicht entgehen! Kommen Sie noch heute zu SPORT-AKTIV!

3. Auch im Alter fit und aktiv mit BIOPUR. Eine spezielle Mischung aus essentiellen Vitalstoffen erhält Ihnen Gesundheit und jugendliche Frische. Konzentrierte, energiespendende Vitamine in BIOPUR helfen Ihnen, den Körper zu regenerieren und das Immunsystem zu stärken. Entdecken Sie die Welt mit neuem Schwung! Werden Sie wieder aktiv! BIOPUR macht einen neuen Menschen aus Ihnen.

4. Treffen Sie die richtige Entscheidung im Leben Ihres Kindes: Kaufen Sie BABYPLUS! Diese einzigartige Baby- und Kleinkindnahrung ist angereichert mit lebenswichtigen Vitaminen und Mineralstoffen, die Ihr Kind für eine gesunde und kräftige Entwicklung braucht. BABYPLUS gibt es in zehn verschiedenen Geschmacksrichtungen. Babys, Mütter und Väter lieben BABYPLUS!

5. Eine große Auswahl an lässiger, moderner Kleidung für junge Leute jetzt bei TOP-MODEN in der Innenstadt. TOP-MODEN hat alles, worauf es ankommt: schicke Hemden und Blusen aus reiner Baumwolle in fetzigen Farben; die neusten Designerjeans von bester Qualität; modische Lederjacken in den aktuellen Trendfarben, und vieles mehr. Die feschesten Outfits für junge Leute, nur bei TOP-MODEN in der Innenstadt!

Answers to Activity 2

1. b; 2. e; 3. d; 4. a; 5. c

Ganz schön lässig!

hier wird gezeigt, was „in" ist!

Für Sie u. für Ihn
- Stone-washed Jeans im Western-Style mit 5 Taschen Schwere Qualität, 13 Unzen Reine Baumwolle, überraschend cool
- Sweat-shirts, modisch und flott; auch mit tollem Schrift-Druck
- Für alle, die gern lässig gehen: Stiefelette aus Veloursleder

Kapitel 7: Ohne Reklame geht es nicht!
Projects and Games

PROJECT

In this activity students will create their own television commercials. This project can be done individually or in small groups.

Materials Students may need paper, pens, pencils, and props.

Suggested Sequence

1. Students brainstorm a list of products they might like to advertise and choose one for their commercial.
2. Students determine the format of their commercials.
3. Students write the script. They can treat their product seriously or make outrageous claims.
4. Students decide what props and sound effects they will need.
5. Students rehearse their commercials several times to make them convincing and easy to understand.
6. Students record their commercials on video or audio tape.
7. Broadcast the commercials in class. The class can judge them on a scale of 1 (lowest) to 5 (highest).

Grading the Project

Suggested point distribution (total = 100 points)

Presentation/Dramatization	60
Originality of idea	20
Accuracy of language	20

 GAME

Es war einmal ...

This game will help students review the vocabulary they have learned thus far.

Preparation Prepare a class set of index cards on which you write words and phrases you would like to review, including one card which says, "**Es war einmal ...**".

Procedure As students walk into the classroom, assign each a number from 1 up to the total number of students in your class. Distribute the cards randomly so that each student receives one card. The student with the "**Es war einmal ...**" card starts to tell a story, beginning with "**Es war einmal ...**" and adding to it. Next, call on the student who was assigned the number 2 to continue the story using the phrase on his or her card. Students with subsequent numbers add to the story until the last student ends the story incorporating the phrase on his or her card.

NOTE: You may want to record the story and play it back to the class afterwards.

PROJECTS AND GAMES

Kapitel 7: Ohne Reklame geht es nicht!
Lesson Plans, pages 156-179

Teacher Note

Before you begin the chapter, you may want to preview the *Video Program* and consult the *Video Guide*. Suggestions for integrating the video into each chapter are given in the *Video Guide* and in the chapter interleaf. Activity masters for video selections can be found in the *Video Guide*.

*U*sing the Chapter Opener,
pp. 156-157

Motivating Activity

Bring in a few ads for products that students in your class may have or even be wearing at the moment, such as sneakers, makeup, or designer clothing. Briefly discuss with your students what they think of the ads and whether they were influenced by them when they bought the specific items. Do they think the ads are informative, or do they just appeal to the eye and emotions?

Culture Notes

• Advertising in Germany is very much influenced by the United States. Slogans for American products sold in Germany are often taken over from the American ads, and many English words are used. Sometimes American ads are used with German texts. The jargon of the advertising profession includes many American expressions.

• Litfaßsäulen, mentioned in the introductory paragraph of the Chapter Opener, are round pillars on which ads and announcements are posted, particularly those for upcoming cultural events. Litfaßsäulen were named after Ernst Litfaß, a printer from Berlin who created this pillar in 1854.

Thinking Critically

① **Analyzing** Ask students to look at the photo and determine what this billboard is advertising. Can students determine the relationship between the design and colors used and the underlying message?

Thinking Critically

① **Drawing Inferences** Can students infer the meaning of the compound noun **Dosenmilch** in the ad? (Students might be able to infer that **Dosenmilch** is used in coffee.)

Teacher Note

① "Dallas" refers to the TV show that used to air on Tuesday nights in Germany.

Language Note

② The saying in the ad "**Da haben wir den Salat ...**" can be translated as "*now look at this mess.*"

Teaching Suggestion

② Ask students to describe the man in the ad and his expression. Can students interpret "**Etwas ist mißglückt,**" the underlying message in the ad?

Thinking Critically

③ **Drawing Inferences** Have students study the ad. Can they identify the speaker of the ad? (**wir**) What is the significance of the clocks in the background?

Focusing on Outcomes

Ask students what type of advertisements they think are most effective. Then have students preview the learning outcomes listed on p. 157.
NOTE: These outcomes are modeled in **Los geht's!** (pp. 158-159) and **Weiter geht's!** (pp. 166-167) and evaluated in **Kann ich's wirklich?** (p. 178).

*T*eaching Los geht's!
pp. 158-159

Resources for Los geht's!

- *Textbook Audiocassette* 4 A
- *Practice and Activity Book*

Teacher Note
Los geht's! is recorded on audiocassette.

Los geht's! Summary
In **Werbung — ja oder nein?**, two students are interviewed about how they feel they are influenced by advertising. The following student outcomes listed on p. 157 are modeled in the episode: expressing annoyance and comparing.

Motivating Activity
Ask individual students to describe their favorite TV commercial to the rest of the class in German. Do other students recognize it? If so, can they add to the description?

Teaching Suggestions
- Play the tape of the entire interview and have students follow along in the text. Then divide the text into several sections and play one part at a time. Follow each section with questions to check for comprehension. Explain new vocabulary, phrases, or constructions in German using actions, synonyms, and paraphrasing. After working through the interview in such a fashion, play the entire conversation again, stopping repeatedly to check students' understanding of the key points. End by playing the interview once again without stopping and have students listen with their books closed.

1 Help students get started finding key words and phrases. Ask for volunteers to suggest one or two ideas for each column before assigning the rest of the task to individuals.

For Individual Needs
1 Auditory Learners After students have jotted down notes, ask them to give a partner a brief oral summary of what Stefan and Constance said. Call on several students to share their synopses with the class. Students may want to record the summary on tape and play it back for self-evaluation. A written summary could be assigned for homework.

2 Analyzing As students work with the first part of this activity, have them think of words or phrases that indicate information or manipulation. Make a list with students. If possible, use German ads to find examples.

Teaching Suggestion
2 Have students give examples of products that are endorsed by high profile athletes in the United States.

Thinking Critically
Comparing and Contrasting If possible, bring in ads from a German magazine and an American magazine that advertise the same or similar products. Have students compare the ads.

Closure
Ask students what type of advertising they pay the most attention to and why. Does it come from television, radio, newspapers, or magazines? (**Was für Reklame wirkt am meisten bei euch? Die im Fernsehen, im Radio oder in Zeitungen und Zeitschriften?**)

ERSTE STUFE

Teaching Erste Stufe
pp. 160-164

Resources for Erste Stufe

Practice and Activity Book
Chapter Resources, Book 3
- Communicative Activities 7-1, 7-2
- Additional Listening Activities 7-1, 7-2, 7-3
- Student Response Forms
- Realia 7-1
- Situation Card 7-1
- Teaching Transparency Master 7-1
- Quiz 7-1

Audiocassette Program
- *Textbook Audiocassette* 4 A
- *Additional Listening Activities, Audiocassette* 10 A
- *Assessment Items, Audiocassette* 8 A

Video Program, Videocassette 2
Video Guide

▶ **page 160**

MOTIVATE

For Individual Needs

Visual Learners Record a series of commercials on videocassette or use some of the **Werbung** clips on the *Video Program* for this chapter and play them to the class without the sound. Have students think about what the characters or announcer might be saying. Call on volunteers to ad-lib the sound track or voice-over for each commercial.

TEACH
Group Work

Divide the class into groups of three to four students. Go over the eight statements in the **Werbung — pro und contra** section and explain in German any unfamiliar phrases or expressions. Write the following questions on the board for students to answer as they reread the eight statements.

1. **Von wem könnte diese Aussage stammen? Von der Werbeindustrie oder von Verbrauchern?**
2. **Welche Aussagen könnte man kombinieren, so daß sie einen Paragraphen bilden? Wenn nötig, fügt ein paar eigene Worte hinzu!**
3. **Welche Aussagen würden gute widersprechende Argumente abgeben? Schreibt für jedes Argument die beiden Nummern auf, und zwar in der Reihenfolge, wie man sie wiedergeben muß! Dann lest die Argumente laut vor!**

Thinking Critically

Comparing and Contrasting Have students try to arrange the statements in order from the strongest pro-opinion to the strongest con-opinion.

PRESENTATION: Wortschatz

- After going over the new vocabulary, ask students to come up with an example using words or phrases in the **auf deutsch erklärt** column. Example:
  (**Diesen Wagen kann ich mir nicht leisten.**)
  Ich kann mir diesen Monat keine Zeitschriften mehr leisten. Ich habe nämlich kein Taschengeld mehr.
- For the **auf englisch erklärt** column, ask students to describe contexts in which these phrases might be heard. Example:
  (**Lies mal, was auf der Plakatwand steht!**)
  Das sagt ein Freund zu einem anderen, als sie im Bus sitzen und an der Plakatwand vorbeifahren.

▶ *page 161*

PRESENTATION: So sagt man das!

- Ask students to review the **Los geht's!** section to find the expressions of annoyance that are used by the German students during the interview. Then have students make up additional expressions that Stefan or Constance could have used, based on what students know about their opinions about advertising.
- Ask students if they can think of other ways to express annoyance using phrases they already know. Make a list together.
Examples:
Ich find' es blöd, wenn/daß...
Was mich stört ist, wenn...

✦ For Individual Needs

4 Visual Learners Provide each group with a large piece of construction paper and a marker. Tell groups to divide the paper into six columns: **Schule, zu Hause, Sport, Fernsehen, Werbung,** and one additional topic of their choice. Group members discuss each topic and then write down three things that annoy them in each column. When all groups have finished, tape each paper on the wall and have the spokesperson for each group go over his or her group's list.

Teaching Suggestion

5 Students will need some data in order to answer Questions 2 and 3. Assign each student one hour of television to watch over the weekend. Each student should record all the products he or she sees advertised during the hour, as well as the slogans used to promote each one.

Community Link

5 Have students get in touch with local television or radio stations to help them gather supporting materials for this activity. They could inquire about the types of advertisements most frequently aired and also find out how time slots determine the types of products being advertised. Have students incorporate their findings in their answers to the three questions.

PRESENTATION: So sagt man das!

- Bring items such as youth magazines, different sized sweaters, two different types of sodas, or ads for different types of movies. Show these pairs of items to the class and ask them to compare them using expressions they already know.
Examples:
Dieser Pulli ist länger als der da.
Ich finde Film A besser als Film B.
- To introduce the new phrases, use additional items that would lend themselves for this demonstration.
Example:
Diese Jacke hier von C&A hat die gleiche Qualität wie die von Karstadt, aber die Preise sind sehr verschieden. Diese hier kostet ..., und diese hier von ... kostet ...

For Additional Practice

6 Ask students about their family members' preferences for certain types of products. How can they explain these preferences?

▶ *page 162*

PRESENTATION: Grammatik

Make statements that can be used to demonstrate the uses of **gleiche** and **-selbe.**
Example:
Sabine und Dieter benutzen das gleiche Deutschbuch.
Meine Schwester und ich sind in demselben Zimmer.

✦ For Individual Needs

7 A Slower Pace Help students with questions if necessary. Ask students if they and a friend go home the same way, ride the same bus, have the same kind of sneakers, read the same kind of books, or babysit for the same people.
Examples:
Habt ihr denselben Weg nach Hause?
Mögt ihr die gleichen Bücher?

Erste Stufe **155J**

ERSTE STUFE

Thinking Critically

8 Comparing and Contrasting Have students think of advertising slogans and give their opinions of them. Which ones do they like better than others? Have them compare ads for soft drinks, sneakers, and other types of products. Do they think one kind of ad is better or more effective than another?

▶ *page 163*

PRESENTATION: Grammatik

Give examples of each determiner of quantity or have students make up examples for each. Compare these and their endings with the normal plural adjective endings following **die, diese,** or **keine.**
Example: **diese ähnlichen Bücher/einige ähnliche Bücher**

◆ For Individual Needs

9 Challenge After students have created sentences that describe their town and its attributes, have them combine the sentences into a cohesive paragraph to persuade an exchange student to visit their town. This could be done in writing or orally, in which case partners could jointly record a convincing message on audiocassette. Remind students to use connectors.

Thinking Critically

10 Drawing Inferences Before students listen to the five advertisements, ask them to identify each product. Then have them brainstorm some of the words and phrases they think they will hear when they listen to each sales pitch. Make a list and compare it with the actual recording after listening to it with the class.

Teaching Suggestion

11 Have students decide if the commercial is meant for radio or television. Let students choose one or the other and plan their ad accordingly.

▶ *page 164*

Teaching Suggestion

12 If students enjoy this activity, bring in ads from magazines and newspapers published in German-speaking countries. Cut out or cover any direct references to the products so that students have to infer what is being advertised. Have students examine the ads and comment on them, using the suggested sequence of questions.

Building on Previous Skills

13 Ask students to think of additional adjectives to describe the four products listed. Which of the consumers' senses are being addressed with the adjectives (**hören, schmecken, sehen, fühlen,** or **riechen**)?

Group Work

14 Students may work in small groups to prepare for the discussion. Have them jot down ideas for each of the statements. Have students refer back to the function boxes on p. 161 if they need to.

Reteaching: *Derselbe* and *der gleiche*

Ask students to find at least three classmates with whom they have something in common. Students should write down the similarities and share them with the class at the end of the activity.

▦ Video Program

In the video clip **Ein großes Angebot,** consumers in a Berlin grocery store talk about the differences of consumer goods offered before and after German unification. See *Video Guide* for suggestions.

▶ *page 165*

PRESENTATION: Landeskunde

Teacher Note

The acronyms **ARD, ZDF,** and **RTL** stand for **Arbeitsgemeinschaft der öffentlich-rechtlichen Rundfunkanstalten Deutschlands, Zweites Deutsches Fernsehen,** and **Radio Télévision Luxembourg,** respectively.

Teaching Suggestions

- After students have read the first paragraph, ask them to summarize what was said in one or two sentences. Do the same for the second paragraph. Next have students guess the answers to Questions 1 and 2 with their books closed. Record their answers on a transparency.

- You may need to help students with words and phrases they are not able to guess from the context of the article.
  Examples:
  öffentlich-rechtlicher Sender: *state-regulated station*
  Fernsehgebühren: Geld, das man monatlich für den Fernsehempfang bezahlt
  Einblendung: ein Fernsehprogramm wird von Werbung unterbrochen.
  gesetzlich: vom Staat geregelt; *by law*
  Einnahmequelle: die Möglichkeit, Geld zu erhalten

- After students have worked with the text and can understand it, go back to Questions 1 and 2 and have students reconsider their answers. Were their guesses correct? Does anything need to be added?

Thinking Critically

Comparing and Contrasting Can students compare German networks with their American counterparts based on what they have learned so far?

Background Information

Currently the monthly subscription fee to have TV and radio in a German household is about 45 DM. Additional fees are required for the various private networks such as **RTL, SAT1, Tele 5,** and **RTL plus.**

Teacher Note

Mention to your students that the **Landeskunde** will also be included in Quiz 7-1 given at the end of the **Erste Stufe.**

CLOSE

Teaching Suggestion

Act out the following scene with students. In German, ask students to purchase some products that you are fond of, but they are not. Students then try to convince you to switch over to their favorite products. For example, if you tried to convince a student to buy a certain cola by saying: **Diese Cola schmeckt gut!**, he or she might respond with: **Ja schon, aber die Cola, die ich trinke, hat weniger Kalorien und ist billiger.** Try to get responses from several students for each item you show them, so that all students have a chance to participate.

Focusing on Outcomes

Refer students back to the learning outcomes listed on p. 157. They should recognize that they now know how to express annoyance and compare.

ASSESS

- **Performance Assessment** Prepare a class set of index cards by writing on each card a question reflecting the functions and phrases introduced in this **Stufe.** Give a card to each student. Student A calls on student B and reads the question to him or her. Student B answers the question and continues by reading his or her question to another student who has not yet been asked. All students should get a turn.
  Example:
  Wie würdest du die Qualität von Biokost mit Nahrungsmitteln von einem Supermarkt vergleichen?

- Quiz 7-1, *Chapter Resources,* Book 3

Teaching Weiter geht's!
pp. 166-167

Resources for Weiter geht's!

- *Textbook Audiocassette* 4 A
- *Practice and Activity Book*

Teacher Note

Weiter geht's! is recorded on audiocassette.

Weiter geht's! Summary

In **Image-Werbung**, some German students discuss a particular TV advertisement with their teacher. The following student outcomes listed on p. 157 are modeled in the conversation: eliciting agreement and agreeing and expressing conviction, uncertainty, and what seems to be true.

Motivating Activity

Ask students to describe a television commercial they dislike and explain why. Do they think that young people are more or less critical of television ads than adults are? Are adolescents more easily influenced by ads than adults?

✦ For Individual Needs

Auditory Learners Have students keep their books closed and listen as you read the commercial to them. Can they visualize the sequence of events? What is happening?

Thinking Critically

Drawing Inferences After students have heard or read the text of the commercial, help them to understand the slogan, **Weil Ihre Helden ganze Arbeit leisten!** Point out that **Ihre** is capitalized, that **ganze Arbeit** means **schwere Arbeit,** and that the slogan is only a partial sentence, a dependent clause; the main clause is not expressed but understood. What could the main clause be? Ask students to use the bar scene and the context of the ad to come up with some ideas.
Examples:
Kaufen Sie Schokomilch, ...
Schokogetränke sind das beste, ...

Teaching Suggestion

Have students follow the conversation on pp. 166-167 in their books as they listen to the audiocassette. As students listen to the conversation, they should make notes of words or phrases they are not familiar with. Call on students to find out what parts of the discussion seemed unclear and encourage other students to help out in giving definitions or paraphrasing.

Closure

Ask students to describe a popular commercial similar in form to the one described on p. 166. They should try not to reveal the product. Have the rest of the class guess what the commercial is advertising.

Teaching Zweite Stufe,
pp. 168-171

Resources for Zweite Stufe

Practice and Activity Book
Chapter Resources, Book 3
- Communicative Activities 7-3, 7-4
- Additional Listening Activities 7-4, 7-5, 7-6
- Student Response Forms
- Realia 7-2
- Situation Card 7-2
- Teaching Transparency Master 7-2
- Quiz 7-2
Audiocassette Program
- *Textbook Audiocassette* 4 A
- *Additional Listening Activities, Audiocassette* 10 A
- *Assessment Items, Audiocassette* 8 A
Video Program, Videocassette 2
Video Guide

▶ *page 168*

MOTIVATE

Teaching Suggestion

Ask students to name products that are of German origin. Which of these do they see advertised in the United States?

TEACH

PRESENTATION: Wortschatz

Go over the new vocabulary with students. Then incorporate various words and phrases from the box as you strike up conversations with individual students.

Examples:

Was haltet ihr von Kindern in der Werbung?

Könnt ihr an ein Beispiel denken, wo die Werbung die Gefühle der Leser oder Zuschauer ausnützt?

📼 Video Program

The authentic advertising clips in this section can be analyzed within the context of the chapter: advertising that offers facts (**Informationswerbung**) and advertising that appeals to the senses (**Image-Werbung**). See *Video Guide* for suggestions.

PRESENTATION: So sagt man das!

Ask students to work with a partner to write a statement that would precede or follow each functional expression. Then call on several pairs to role-play their exchanges using the expressions in the function box.

Example:

— **Werbung für Kriegsspielzeug ist für kleine Kinder schädlich, nicht wahr?**

— **Ja, damit stimm' ich überein.**

▶ *page 169*

✦ For Individual Needs

18 Challenge As students discuss each statement, they should try to support their opinions and give examples, perhaps describing an ad they have seen.

Teacher Note

You might want to point out to students that in the **Ein wenig Grammatik** box, **den** refers to **Werbeslogan.** It is used in the accusative case because of its function in the relative clause.

PRESENTATION: Grammatik

Have students compare the use of **was** and **wo** in relative clauses with the way *that, what,* and *where* are used in English relative clauses.

▶ *page 170*

✦ For Individual Needs

19 A Slower Pace To prepare students for the partner activity, have them first make up a number of sentences that incorporate the three different introductory clauses and the various ideas for relative clauses. Then, from the list they have created, have students create mini conversations, with student A not only asking questions but also reacting to what student B says.

20 Visual Learners Have students bring in ads in which the six comments are being applied. Discuss the ads in class.

Teaching Suggestion

Have students look for relative pronouns in the **Los geht's!** and **Weiter geht's!** conversations. Both episodes contain a variety of uses of relative pronouns. In each case, students need to find the antecedent and explain the form of the pronoun.

Example:

Ich trag' halt gern Sachen, die „in" sind.

relative pronoun: **die**

antecedent: **Sachen**

form: **plural**

PRESENTATION: So sagt man das!

Ask students to list all the expressions of conviction (**Du kannst mir glauben, ...; Ich bin sicher, daß ...**) and uncertainty (**Ich bin nicht sicher; ich weiß nicht, ...**) they have learned so far. Then ask them to study the new expressions in the function box, including those used for stating what seems to be true, and use them to comment on the statements studied in Activity 18 on p. 169. (Example: **Es steht fest, daß Werbung nur Appetit aufs Kaufen macht.**)

▶ *page 171*

PRESENTATION: Grammatik

Point out to students that the endings for **irgendein** are the same as for **ein, kein,** and possessives, and those for **irgenwelche** are the same as for **welcher** and the other **der**-words.

ZWEITE STUFE

For Individual Needs

24 Challenge When pairs have finished the activity, ask them to look again at the advertisement on p. 166. Have them come up with several other questions that they can pose to the rest of the class. In the responses students should again use the word **irgend-**. (Example: **Mit welchem Western-Star kann man den Jungen vergleichen?**)

PRESENTATION: Wortschatz

• Point out that these are some other word combinations using **irgend-** and tell students that here **irgend-** suggests randomness, or indefiniteness.
• Have students make up statements about themselves using these words. (Example: **Ich habe irgendwie keine Lust mitzukommen.**)

 For Individual Needs

25 A Slower Pace Before beginning the discussion, have students refer back to the function boxes of this **Stufe** to find some expressions they might use. Instead of discussing all four topics, have students choose one or two.

25 Challenge Have students think of and write down questions related to each of the statements that they could ask to stimulate and further the discussion.

Reteaching: *Irgendein* and *irgendwelche*

Prepare a list of advertisement slogans on a handout or a transparency. Students make suggestions as to what each slogan could be for, using a form of **irgend-**.
Examples:
... da kauf ich gern ein! (irgendein Kaufhaus oder Geschäft)
... löschen den Durst jedes Mal! (irgendwelche Getränke)

CLOSE

 Game

To review relative clauses with **was**, play the guessing game **Ich sehe was, was du nicht siehst.** One student secretly identifies an object in the classroom and then makes the statement: **Ich sehe was, was ihr nicht seht und das ist ...** (Example: **kaputt**). The rest of the class takes turns at guessing what the object in question could be. The student who guesses correctly starts the next round.

Focusing on Outcomes

Refer students back to the learning outcomes listed on p. 157. They should recognize that they now know how to elicit agreement and agree and express conviction, uncertainty, and what seems to be true.

ASSESS

• **Performance Assessment** Ask students to prepare a brief statement in which they express their conviction to the following statement: **Werbung verspricht oft mehr, als sie zu bieten hat!** Students should express their agreement or disagreement, using the functions introduced in this **Stufe**.

• Quiz 7-2, *Chapter Resources,* Book 3

Teaching Zum Lesen,
pp. 172-174

Reading Strategy

The targeted strategy in this reading is using pictures and print type as clues to meaning. Students should learn about this strategy before beginning Question 1.

PREREADING

Background Information

Asterix is a series created in France but quite popular in Germany. The clever **Asterix,** and his oafish sidekick, **Obelix,** are Gauls, i.e. "proto-Frenchmen," under the not-too-popular administration of the Roman colonial government (their village is the only remaining one that the Romans have not yet subdued). For the inhabitants of Roman Gaul, with its beautifully designed cities, roads, aquaducts, and other civilized features, the tax-levying conquerors were often a lesser evil than the barbarians pushing against the walls. Nevertheless, this comic strip is based on the idea that the Romans were oppressors and that the common folk of the provinces were underdogs to be cheered on in their efforts to make fools of them. The *Asterix* comics also contain many allusions to 20th-century culture and politics.

Motivating Activity

Have students think of comic strips and books that they enjoy reading. Ask them which ones they think would or would not be popular with German teens. Why? You might want to discuss what types of humor do and do not translate well. For example, puns, word plays, and humor based on "insider" knowledge of a popular culture are quite difficult for non-native speakers to understand in time to laugh.

Teaching Suggestions

1 Have students try to identify the hero(es) of this strip, based only on visual clues. Looking at the costumes (they are purposely clichéd and will help to identify the Romans and the representatives of the various provinces) might help students make predictions.

2 Larger type sizes used for emphasis are a familiar comic-strip device and will probably need no explanation. Students may be interested in checking a reference work to see how the artist has suggested "Greek" letters without actually using the Greek alphabet. Probably, they have seen **Fraktur** or the so-called "Gothic" letters which were used in German printing until well into this century and enjoyed a brief resurgence during the Third Reich.

Teacher Note

Activities 1 and 2 are prereading activities.

READING

Teacher Note

4 Students will probably recognize the "Egyptian pictographs" as clever variants on the international icons used in tourist spots.

POST-READING

Teacher Note

Activity 10 is a post-reading task that will show whether students can apply what they have learned.

Thinking Critically

Comparing and Contrasting Ask students how the details in *Asterix* hold the reader's attention. How would they compare this series to *the Flintstones*? In which series is the story line stronger and more important? In which is the humor more dependent on background knowledge and recognition of incongruent detail? (Students may want to look more carefully at the recruits' names and at the settings.) How would they compare *Asterix* to an action-packed series like *Batman* or to a heroic saga like *Prince Valiant*?

Closure

Ask the class to briefly discuss how they would account for the popularity of *Asterix* in Germany. Do they think the series would sell well in the United States? Why or why not? What sort of characters would be the American equivalents of **Asterix** and **Obelix**?

Answers to Activity 1

in the Roman Empire; Roman times, approximately the first century, A.D.; expressions of characters indicate conflict; for example, the Roman soldier is yelling.

ZUM LESEN

Answers to Activity 2

denotes tone of voice (e.g. large print indicates someone is yelling), other styles of print used to represent different languages or nationalities of the speakers

Answers to Activity 3

headquarters of the Roman army; time when Roman Empire was conquering other parts of Europe
Asterix: Gaul (France)
Obelix: Gaul (France)
Militaros: Greece
Eftax: Britain
Mannekenpix: Belgium
Kriegmichnich: Goth
Verkrümeldich: Goth
ein Ägypter: Egypt
die Römer: Rome

Answers to Activity 4

for the Egyptian; to caricature his speech

Answers to Activity 5

People from different conquered areas are being inducted into the Roman army; they are registered and then sent to have a physical; no; prisoners; answers will vary.

Answers to Activity 6

interpreter; the character "translates" everything the Egyptian says to the Roman soldier; he can't understand the Egyptian.

Answers to Activity 7

about the facilities; he thinks he's at an inn rather than being inducted into the army.

Answers to Activity 8

to the doctor; to have a physical; get undressed

Answers to Activity 9

skinny; the Goth is very thin.

Teaching Zum Schreiben,
p. 175

Writing Strategy

The targeted strategy in this writing activity is using tone and word choice for effect. Students should learn about this strategy before beginning the assignment.

PREWRITING
Teacher Notes

- This activity is a good opportunity to teach or review the correct form of business letters in German.
- Students may want to write about some of the products for which they created slogans in the chapter.

Motivating Activity

Ask students to think of one product they have bought recently that did not meet their expectations. What did they do about it?

Teaching Suggestion

As students plan their letters, remind them to distinguish between inferior quality of the product and their disappointment in the product. This will help them in their word choice. Remind them also to keep their audience in mind, i.e. the manufacturer of the product. What retribution do they want? A letter of apology? A refund?

WRITING
Teaching Suggestion

Encourage students to use as many of the new functions as possible including expressing annoyance, making comparisons with other, similar products, and expressing what they've heard in advertisements. Encourage them to use **der gleiche** and **derselbe** where appropriate.

✦ For Individual Needs

Challenge If available, have students look for the advertisements of the product with which they are unhappy. Have them pick out specific points in the ad that did not meet their expectations. Students should address these items in their letter.

POST-WRITING
Closure

As a follow-up activity, you may want to redistribute the letters and have each student write a response to another student's complaint.

Using Anwendung,
pp. 176-177

Resources for Anwendung

Chapter Resources, Book 3
• Realia 7-3
• Situation Card 7-3

Teaching Suggestions

1 Ask students to bring American advertisements that intentionally use incorrect language.

1 Ask students to identify the incorrect German in the text. Go over the list and have students first give an English equivalent of the word or phrase and then put each into correct German.

2 Before students listen to the radio ads, let them predict the type of slogans and phrases they expect to hear for each of the five ads based on the pictures (a-e). Make a list of students' ideas so they can later compare their predictions to the actual ads on audiocassette.

Portfolio Assessment

2 You might want to suggest this activity as an oral portfolio item for your students. See *Assessment Guide,* p. 20.

3 You might want to suggest this activity as a written portfolio item for your students. See *Assessment Guide,* p. 20.

Cooperative Learning

4 Divide the class into groups of three or four students. Each group should have two or three advertisements which they examine by answering the five questions. Call on the reporters of the groups to discuss their ads. Does the rest of the class agree with the responses?

Kann ich's wirklich?
p. 178

This page helps students prepare for the test. It is a brief checklist of the major points covered in the chapter. The students should be reminded that it is only a checklist and not necessarily everything that will appear on the test.

Using Wortschatz,
p. 179

Teaching Suggestion

Have students pick out all the adjectives on this page. Have them use as many as they can to describe advertisements with which they are familiar.

Game

Play the game **Es war einmal ...,** using the vocabulary from this and previous chapters. See p. 155F for the procedure.

Total Physical Response

Review the **Wortschatz** by physically polling the class about certain issues. For example, give a command such as the following.
Wenn es dich nervt, daß eine Reklame dein Lieblingsprogramm unterbricht, steh auf!
Ask some of the students standing to explain why it bothers them. (**Warum nervt es dich?**)
Now, have all the students sit back down and give another command.
Wenn du glaubst, daß die Werbung die Verbraucher ausnützt, steh auf!
Then, ask some of the students who remained seated to explain their opinion. (**Warum glaubst du das nicht?**)
Continue using other examples of functions and vocabulary from this chapter.

Teacher Note

Give the **Kapitel 7** Chapter Test, *Chapter Resources,* Book 3.

FAHRSCHULE HINZ

KAPITEL 7

Ohne Reklame geht es nicht!

① Mir gefällt dieser Werbeslogan am besten.

Werbung, in Zeitungen und Zeitschriften, im Radio und Fernsehen, an Plakatwänden und Litfaßsäulen ist ein unumgänglicher Teil unseres Lebens. Ist Werbung gut? Schlecht? Informativ? Überhaupt nötig? Um über diese Fragen diskutieren zu können, mußt du noch einiges lernen.

In this chapter you will learn

- to express annoyance; to compare
- to elicit agreement and agree; to express conviction, uncertainty, and what seems to be true

And you will

- listen to students talk about advertising in various media
- read various ads and a popular cartoon
- write your own ads
- learn about German advertising

② Diese Werbung ist sehr informativ. Glaubst du nicht?

③ Es nervt mich, daß mein Auto heute nicht fertig wird!

Los geht's!

Werbung — ja oder nein?

Constance und ihr Freund Stefan haben mit einem Herrn von einem Meinungsforschungs-Institut gesprochen. Er wollte wissen, ob und wie sie sich von der Werbung beeinflussen lassen.

INTERVIEWER Wie werden Sie zum Kaufen angeregt, und welche Rolle spielt dabei die Werbung?

STEFAN Ich trag' halt gern Sachen, die „in" sind.

INTERVIEWER Und woher wissen Sie, was „in" ist?

STEFAN Da seh' ich ja, was die andern tragen. Und dann les' ich auch die Reklame in Zeitschriften und so und an Plakatwänden.

CONSTANCE Ich kann nicht sagen, daß ich von der Werbung beeinflußt werde. Ich seh' eben etwas, was mir gefällt — im Fernsehen, in irgendwelchen Zeitschriften — und dann kauf' ich es mir eben. Aber zuvor vergleich' ich schon die Preise.

INTERVIEWER Nun, bitte: Sie sagen es ja selbst, daß Sie durch die Werbung zum Kaufen angeregt werden.

CONSTANCE Klar, aber das möchte ich nicht so einfach eingestehen. Es gibt heute so viele Sachen, die alle irgendwie die gleiche Qualität haben oder haben sollen, aber die eben doch verschieden sind. Und hier kann die Reklame informieren, das Produkt beschreiben, den Konsumenten aufklären.

STEFAN Das meine ich auch, aber ich möchte dazu etwas sagen: Oft beschreibt die Reklame das angepriesene Produkt gar nicht, sondern ... äh ... die Reklame zeigt Leute, die irgendwelche Eigenschaften haben, die der Käufer gern hätte. Er soll also glauben, wenn er dieses Produkt kauft, wird er auch diese Eigenschaften haben. Die Reklame manipuliert also den Käufer. Wer möchte nicht frei und fröhlich sein, nicht wahr? Oder etwas Gutes tun, ja?

INTERVIEWER Ja, logisch. Und können Sie mir auch ein Beispiel geben?

STEFAN Hm, da muß ich mal überlegen. Ach, ja! Da wird im Werbefunk zum Beispiel irgendein Fertiggericht angepriesen. Da sehen wir die hübsche Mutter in ihrer blitzblanken Küche stehen, im Hintergrund die glücklichen, guterzogenen Kinder und möglichst noch den gutmütigen Mann, der seine fabelhafte Frau stolz anstrahlt. Man hört überhaupt nichts vom Nährwert des Gerichts, sondern nur solche Werbesprüche wie „Eine weise Hausfrau denkt zuerst an ihre Kinder" oder „aus Liebe zur Familie", und dann kommt der Name des Produktes. Man kauft das Produkt, weil man im Unterbewußtsein glaubt, wenn ich dieses Fertiggericht meiner Familie gebe, wird mein Leben auch so perfekt sein.

CONSTANCE	Ja, das nervt mich auch immer, wenn ich so was höre und sehe — wie zum Beispiel mit der Autoreklame. Da werden immer nur Autos gezeigt in einer schönen Wiese, in den Bergen, wo alles heil ist, aber nie auf einer Straße im Stau. Die versteckte Mitteilung: Mit diesem Auto wirst du nie im Stau sitzen.
STEFAN	Genau! Da hast du ganz recht.
CONSTANCE	Und was mich noch aufregt ist die Werbung, wo irgendwelche Spitzensportler ein Produkt anpreisen ... und dann essen sie es selbst vielleicht überhaupt nicht. Und sie bekommen unheimlich viel Geld für so eine Reklame.
STEFAN	Eben! Und ich kann mir gar nicht leisten, was diese Leute ...
INTERVIEWER	Sie mögen also keine Statussymbole?
STEFAN	Mögen? Klar. Aber ich kann sie mir nicht leisten.
INTERVIEWER	Wie werden Sie denn auf ein bestimmtes Produkt aufmerksam gemacht?
CONSTANCE	Ach, ich würde sagen, da ist immer zuerst ein Bild, eine Bildreklame, häßlich oder schön ... und da schau ich eben hin.
STEFAN	Genau! Oft ist es ein Mädchen, ein Blickfang ...
CONSTANCE	Logo, im letzten Jahr zum Beispiel die Quark-Reklame, ein großer, roter Mund ...
STEFAN	Ja, daran erinnere ich mich auch. Diese Reklame war schon sehr raffiniert!
CONSTANCE	Was mich dabei nervt ist, daß die Reklame die Frau oft nur als Blickfang benutzt und daß sehr oft das Image der Frau weiterhin in einer traditionellen Rolle gezeigt wird. Es ist immer noch die Frau, die das Bad putzt — und die allwissende, männliche Stimme, die ihr sagt, welche Putzmittel sie dazu gebrauchen soll!
INTERVIEWER	Na, da ist schon was dran. Und zum Schluß ...
CONSTANCE	Ja, zum Schluß möchte ich sagen, daß ich ... ja, ich glaube wirklich, daß die Werbung in erster Linie das angepriesene Produkt in einem günstigen Licht zeigt und mit positiven Elementen in Verbindung bringt und weniger die Eigenschaften des Produkts dem Konsumenten beschreibt.
STEFAN	So ist es auch! Damit stimm' ich völlig überein!

1 Zusammenfassung

Schreib stichwortartig auf, was Stefan und Constance über die Werbung sagen! Schreib dann eine Zusammenfassung (*synopsis*) von dem, was jeder gesagt hat, und lies die Zusammenfassung der Klasse vor!

2 Was meinst du?

1. Informiert oder manipuliert Werbung die Konsumenten? Wie tut sie das?
2. Warum machen Spitzensportler Werbung für Produkte? Was soll damit erreicht werden?
3. Welche Werbung beeindruckt dich? Warum? Welche Werbung findest du wirklich blöd?
4. Vergleiche die Werbespots in diesem Kapitel mit denen, die du oft bei dir zu Hause siehst!

ERSTE STUFE

Expressing annoyance; comparing

Werbung — pro und contra

1 *„Werbung weckt verborgene Wünsche, verkauft Träume und macht den Verbraucher kritiklos."*

2 *„Werbung ist ein Motor der Wirtschaft, sorgt für Absatz und damit auch für Arbeitsplätze."*

3 *„Ohne Werbung wäre die Welt langweiliger. Werbung macht die Welt bunter."*

4 *„Werbung muß vielfältig sein. Es liegt allein am Verbraucher, sich von den Appellen an Gefühle nicht beeinflussen zu lassen und nur auf die Informationen zu achten."*

5 *„Werbung will den Verbraucher dazu verführen, Dinge zu kaufen, die er in Wirklichkeit nicht braucht."*

6 *„Werbung kostet viel Geld und verteuert dadurch die Waren."*

7 *„Nur durch Werbung werden Produkte bekannt. Dadurch erfährt der Verbraucher, wie er seine Bedürfnisse befriedigen kann."*

8 *„Wer Werbung als ‚Verführung' bezeichnet, überschätzt ihre Wirkung maßlos. Die Menschen sind viel zu kritisch: Es hat sich längst herumgesprochen, daß man nicht glücklich wird, nur weil man dieses oder jenes kauft."*

Mit welchen Aussagen stimmst du überein? Warum? Mit welchen stimmst du nicht überein? Warum nicht?

WORTSCHATZ

auf deutsch erklärt

die Reklame   Werbung
der Werbespruch   ein Slogan für ein Produkt
der Verbraucher   der Konsument, Käufer
aufklären   informieren
anpreisen   mit vielen Worten empfehlen
raffiniert   clever
verborgen   man kann es nicht sehen
die Wirtschaft   die Ökonomie
wahrnehmen   man hört oder sieht es
überlegen   über etwas nachdenken
glücklich   froh
fröhlich   gut gelaunt
das Putzmittel   ein Produkt, mit dem man etwas saubermacht
Wir stimmen miteinander überein.   Wir haben die gleiche Meinung.
Diesen Wagen kann ich mir nicht leisten. Ich habe nicht genug Geld für den Wagen.

auf englisch erklärt

Lies mal, was auf der Plakatwand steht!   *Read what's on the billboard.*
Vergleichen wir die Waren!   *Let's compare the goods.*
Ich möchte dich auf diese interessante Werbung aufmerksam machen.   *I would like to draw your attention to this interesting advertisement.*
Eine typische Eigenschaft von Werbung ist die versteckte Mitteilung.   *A typical characteristic of advertising is the hidden message.*
Ich gestehe es ein, daß günstige Preise ein echter Kaufreiz sind.   *I admit that favorable prices are a real enticement to buy.*
Wer weiß, was im Unterbewußtsein steckt. *Who knows what lurks in the subconscious.*

SO SAGT MAN DAS!

Expressing annoyance

Here are two useful expressions to help you convey annoyance or irritation:

> **Was mich aufregt ist, wenn** Leute ihre Fehler nie eingestehen.
> **Es nervt mich, daß** Anja sich von allen beeinflussen läßt.

You can use the conjunctions **wenn** and **daß** with both these phrases. How do you express annoyance in English?

3 Hör gut zu! For answers, see listening script on TE Interleaf.

Einige Freunde reden über Werbung, die sie im Fernsehen gesehen haben. Was regt sie auf? Was ist ihnen egal? Hör gut zu und schreib auf, wie diese Schüler reagieren!

4 Meckerecke

Was nervt euch alles — in der Schule, zu Hause, beim Sport, im Fernsehen, in der Werbung? Bildet eine größere Gruppe und sagt abwechselnd, was euch nervt oder aufregt!

5 Wie ist die Werbung bei euch?

Besprecht die folgenden Fragen gemeinsam in einer Gruppe!
1. Wo seht ihr die meiste Werbung?
2. Für welche Produkte wird die meiste Werbung gemacht?
3. Welche Werbung und welche Werbeslogans sind am effektivsten? Warum?

SO SAGT MAN DAS!

Comparing

When making statements about different things, we often compare them.
You've already learned to make comparisons using the following expressions:

> Ich kenne auch **so** einen Spitzensportler **wie** dich.
> Diese Werbung ist nicht **so gut wie** diese.
> Ich finde diesen Werbeslogan viel **besser als** den da.
> Und mir gefällt die Kinoreklame **am besten.**

What are some other comparative adjectives that you often use?
Here are some new ways to talk about comparisons:

> Bevor ich mir etwas kaufe, **vergleiche** ich die Preise.
> Manche Produkte haben die **gleiche** Qualität, aber die Preise sind oft sehr **verschieden.**
> Einige Leute kaufen sich immer **dieselben** Waren.

6 Hör gut zu! For answers, see listening script on TE Interleaf.

Du kaufst in einem deutschen Supermarkt ein und bleibst vor einigen Leuten stehen, die lebhaft einige Produkte vergleichen. Hör ihrem Gespräch gut zu und schreib auf, für welche Produkte sie sich entscheiden und warum!

*G*rammatik derselbe, der gleiche

The determiner **derselbe** is a combination of the definite article **der** and the word **selber**, and means *the very same.* The new word changes in form like any other adjective with a preceding definite article.

Ich habe **dieselben** Reklamen gesehen.
Wir haben **denselben** Preis dafür gezahlt.

	Masculine	Feminine	Neuter	Plural
Nominative	derselbe	dieselbe	dasselbe	dieselben
Accusative	denselben	dieselbe	dasselbe	dieselben
Dative	demselben	derselben	demselben	denselben

Der (die, das) gleiche means *similar, the same kind or type* and also functions like an adjective. Compare these sentences:

Wir tragen die **gleiche** Jacke und spielen die **gleichen** Kartenspiele.[1]
Mein Freund und ich gehen in **dieselbe** Schule und haben **denselben** Lehrer in Mathe.[2]

7 Was ist bei dir dasselbe oder das gleiche?

Such dir einen Partner und macht Vergleiche! Hier sind Beispiele.

BEISPIEL **Meine Schwester und ich, wir wohnen in demselben Haus.** *oder*
Mein Vater und mein Onkel fahren den gleichen Wagen, beide haben einen Opel. *oder*
Mein Freund und ich ...

8 Machen wir Vergleiche!

Was meint ihr? Stellt euch gegenseitig die folgenden Fragen, und besprecht sie dann zusammen! Sagt eure Meinungen frei und offen!

1. Welche Werbung ist effektiver, die Radiowerbung oder die Fernsehwerbung? Warum?
2. Welche Jeans sind deiner Meinung nach besser, einfache Jeans oder Designerjeans?
3. Welche Autos sind deiner Meinung nach besser, kleine oder große?
4. Welche Werbeslogans kennst du? Vergleiche sie!

---

1. We wear the same (type of) jacket and play the same (kinds of) card games.
2. My friend and I go to the (very) same school and have the (very) same teacher for math.

Grammatik Adjective endings following determiners of quantity

Determiners of quantity can be used as determiners before nouns or as pronouns.

1. Adjectives that follow determiners of quantity have the following endings in the nominative and accusative cases. What are the English equivalents of these words?

	alle, beide	**andere, ein paar, einige, mehrere, viele, wenige, zwei (drei, vier, usw.)**
Nom.	alle **-en** Häuser	mehrere **-e** Dörfer
Acc.	alle **-en** Häuser	mehrere **-e** Dörfer

2. In the dative case, the determiners of quantity (not the numerals) add the ending **-n,** and any following adjectives have the usual **-en** ending of the dative case.

An einig**en** groß**en** Plakatwänden hängen Poster.

9 Was gibt es alles in eurer Stadt?

Such dir eine Partnerin! Beschreibt einander eure Stadt oder eine Stadt, die ihr gut kennt! Wie viele Sätze könnt ihr machen?

| Es gibt | wenige
mehrere
ein paar
einige
etliche
viele
drei

keine | gut
schlecht
alt
neu
ausländisch
deutsch
interessant
modern
schön | Zeitungen
Schulen
Kinos
Museen
Diskotheken
Bücherläden
Videoläden
Restaurants
Parks
Universitäten
Kirchen |

10 Hör gut zu!

Hör jetzt einigen Werbeslogans gut zu! Welcher Werbeslogan, den du hörst, paßt zu welchem Produkt unten? For answers, see listening script on TE Interleaf.

a.   b.   c.   d.   e.

11 Schreiben wir auch einen Werbeslogan!

Experten in der Werbebranche benutzen viele Adjektive, die weniger das Produkt beschreiben als die Gefühle des Konsumenten ansprechen. Bildet Gruppen von vier Schülern und kreiert drei Werbeslogans für verschiedene Produkte! Dann lest euren besten Werbeslogan der Klasse vor! Diskutiert über eure Slogans und vergleicht sie miteinander! Welche findet ihr gut und welche nicht so gut? Warum?

märchenhaft   erstklassig
sensationell   super
                neu   modern
einmalig
        fabelhaft
atemberaubend   phantastisch

12 Kennst du die Sprache der Werbung?

In der Werbung benutzt man sehr viele Adjektive. Manche beschreiben das Produkt und informieren den Konsumenten. Natürlich stellt die Beschreibung das Produkt in ein schönes Licht. Wie beschreibt die Werbung die Produkte unten links? Such dir eine Partnerin, und versucht zusammen, die passenden Adjektive für jedes Produkt zu wählen!

BEISPIEL **In der Werbung sind Zigaretten gewöhnlich ... und ...**

Produkte

Zigaretten   Kaffee

Autos   Fruchtsaft

Adjektive

rostfrei   nikotinarm   tassenfertig   mild

superschnell   geräuscharm   vitaminreich   natürlich

13 Werbesprüche

Wie gut kannst du Werbung und Werbesprüche analysieren? Schau dir die Werbesprüche unten an, und diskutiere über diese Fragen mit einem Partner!

1. Welche Produkte werben mit diesen Werbesprüchen?
2. Versuche, diese vier Texte zu charakterisieren! Welcher Text informiert mehr? Welcher manipuliert mehr? Welcher diskriminiert? Welche Wörter im Text begründen deine Analyse?
3. Was für Konsumenten sollen diese Produkte kaufen? Wie weißt du das vom Text?

14 Zum Überlegen und Diskutieren

Diskutiert die folgenden Meinungen in der Klasse! Seid kritisch und gebt Beispiele!

1. Werbung hat die Aufgabe, uns über die Produkte zu informieren.
2. Die Werbung beeinflußt uns, auch wenn wir es nicht immer gleich eingestehen wollen.
3. Die meiste Werbung ist Image-Werbung; sie manipuliert den Käufer nur.
4. Manipulative Werbung sollte verboten werden.
5. Sportler in der Werbung? Nein!
6. Frauen werden in der Werbung oft nur als Blickfang benutzt.
7. Wir brauchen die Werbung überhaupt nicht; wir können auch ohne Werbung leben.

15 Für mein Notizbuch

Such dir zwei Themen von Übung 14 aus, und schreib deine eigene Meinung darüber! Gib mindestens drei Gründe für deine Meinung!

Warum so wenig Unterbrecherwerbung?

Michael ist seit einer Woche Austauschstudent in Deutschland. Seine Gasteltern sind ausgegangen, und er schaut allein zu Hause Fernsehen. Im ZDF läuft gerade der Film „Raumschiff Enterprise". Michael hat Hunger und möchte sich etwas aus dem Kühlschrank holen, aber er wartet auf einen Werbeblock. Nach zwanzig Minuten gibt es immer noch keine Pause. Wann kommt denn endlich die Reklame, fragt er sich. Er muß bis zum Ende der Sendung warten, bevor er sein Essen holen kann.

Danach schaltet er das Programm auf RTL um. In ein paar Minuten kommt ein Wildwestfilm mit Clint Eastwood. Diesmal holt er sich etwas zu essen, bevor die Sendung anfängt. Aber jetzt fällt ihm etwas auf. In der Mitte der Sendung kommen einige Reklamen. Bis zum Ende des Films gibt es zwei weitere Unterbrechungen (*interruptions*). Er versteht nicht, warum es im ZDF keine Unterbrecherwerbung und im RTL dreimal Unterbrecherwerbung gibt.

1. Warum gibt es bei der Unterbrecherwerbung einen Unterschied zwischen ZDF und RTL? Was meinst du?
2. Welches Programm ist ein Privatsender (*private station*)? Welches ist ein öffentlich-rechtlicher (*public*) Sender? Hast du eine Ahnung (*idea*), wie die Sender finanziert werden?
3. Wie ist die Werbezeit in den USA kontrolliert? Wie oft kommen Werbeblöcke?

For answers, see text below.

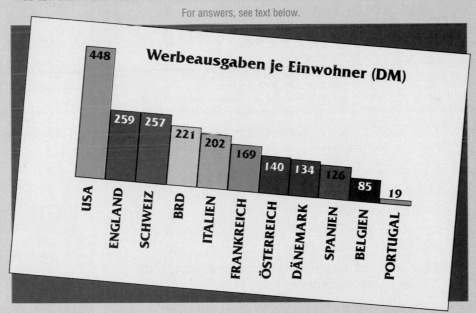

Werbeausgaben je Einwohner (DM)

USA	ENGLAND	SCHWEIZ	BRD	ITALIEN	FRANKREICH	ÖSTERREICH	DÄNEMARK	SPANIEN	BELGIEN	PORTUGAL
448	259	257	221	202	169	140	134	126	85	19

Erklärung zu Michaels Situation:

ARD und ZDF sind öffentlich-rechtliche Sender, die vorwiegend aus Fernsehgebühren finanziert werden. Werbeeinblendungen werden daher gesetzlich geregelt. Es dürfen nur 20 Minuten Werbung am Tag gesendet werden, davon dürfen zehn Minuten vor und zehn Minuten nach 20 Uhr laufen. Da RTL ein Privatsender ist, fällt er nicht unter diese Regelung. Für Privatsender, deren wichtigste Einnahmequelle die Werbewirtschaft ist, gelten andere Regeln. Ein Film bis zu 85 Minuten Länge darf nur einmal unterbrochen werden und ein Film von 90 Minuten Länge oder mehr zweimal. Privatsender dürfen täglich 20% ihres Programms mit Werbung füllen.

Weiter geht's!

Image-Werbung

Im Rahmen des Deutschunterrichts über aktuelle Themen hat Frau Klose ihren Schülern der 11. Klasse folgenden Werbespot gezeigt, der vor einiger Zeit im Werbefernsehen zu sehen war. Danach hat sie mit ihren Schülern über diesen Werbespot gesprochen.

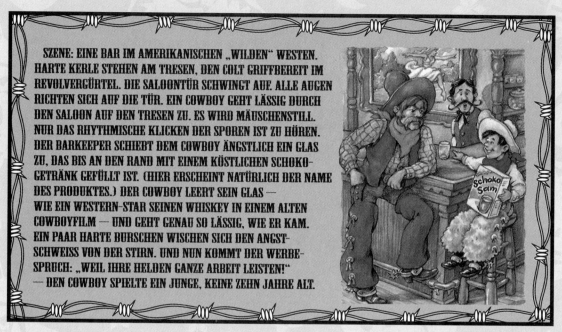

SZENE: EINE BAR IM AMERIKANISCHEN „WILDEN" WESTEN. HARTE KERLE STEHEN AM TRESEN, DEN COLT GRIFFBEREIT IM REVOLVERGÜRTEL. DIE SALOONTÜR SCHWINGT AUF. ALLE AUGEN RICHTEN SICH AUF DIE TÜR. EIN COWBOY GEHT LÄSSIG DURCH DEN SALOON AUF DEN TRESEN ZU. ES WIRD MÄUSCHENSTILL. NUR DAS RHYTHMISCHE KLICKEN DER SPOREN IST ZU HÖREN. DER BARKEEPER SCHIEBT DEM COWBOY ÄNGSTLICH EIN GLAS ZU, DAS BIS AN DEN RAND MIT EINEM KÖSTLICHEN SCHOKO-GETRÄNK GEFÜLLT IST. (HIER ERSCHEINT NATÜRLICH DER NAME DES PRODUKTES.) DER COWBOY LEERT SEIN GLAS — WIE EIN WESTERN-STAR SEINEN WHISKEY IN EINEM ALTEN COWBOYFILM — UND GEHT GENAU SO LÄSSIG, WIE ER KAM. EIN PAAR HARTE BURSCHEN WISCHEN SICH DEN ANGST-SCHWEISS VON DER STIRN. UND NUN KOMMT DER WERBE-SPRUCH: „WEIL IHRE HELDEN GANZE ARBEIT LEISTEN!" — DEN COWBOY SPIELTE EIN JUNGE, KEINE ZEHN JAHRE ALT.

LEHRERIN Nun, zuerst einmal, wer von euch kann sich noch an diesen Werbespot im Fernsehen erinnern?

CHRISTIAN Ich kann mich gut daran erinnern, oder besser gesagt, zu gut!

GABRIELE Logo! Weil dich deine Mutter mit diesem blöden Getränk großgezogen hat. Stimmt's?

CHRISTIAN Genau so ist es. Und schau, was aus mir geworden ist! Ich bin groß und kräftig.

ANNETTE Also, ich muß sagen, ich bin dagegen, daß man Kinder in der Werbung verwendet.

HANS-JÖRG Aber dieser Werbespot richtet sich an Kinder!

ANNETTE Eben! Aber Kinder wissen noch nicht, was wirklich gut ist für sie. Sie sind noch nicht kritisch genug; sie wollen halt alles, was sie sehen.

LEHRERIN Und was meinst du, Sebastian?

SEBASTIAN Es scheint, Christians Mutter hat das Getränk gekauft, weil es dem Christian geschmeckt hat.

KERSTIN Was mich eben nervt ist das Image. Wenn Ihr Kind, Ihr Sohn, dieses Getränk trinkt, so wird er einmal ein ganzer Kerl. Er wird ein Mann, der vor keinen anderen Männern Angst hat!

CHRISTIAN Du übertreibst, Kerstin.

KERSTIN Überhaupt nicht. Diese Werbung nützt die Gefühle von Eltern und Kindern aus. Und die Firma, die am besten wirbt, die verkauft ja auch leider am meisten, verdient das meiste Geld.

FLORIAN Genau! Im österreichischen Fernsehen sollen angeblich Werbespots mit Kindern und für Kinder verboten sein. Nicht wahr, Frau Klose?

LEHRERIN Es kann sein, aber ich weiß es nicht. Da bin ich überfragt.

WALTER Mir scheint, die Werbemacher haben's nicht einfach: sie müssen immer neue Ideen haben.

GABRIELE In der Werbung sieht es so aus, als ob sich jeder alles leisten kann und unbedingt haben muß. Viele Sachen braucht man doch gar nicht!

ANNETTE Eben! Ich möchte nur noch mal klarstellen, daß ich nicht gegen Werbung bin, nur gegen übertriebene Image-Werbung. Zigarettenmarken, Rasier- wasser, Sportwagen und so passen angeblich zur Männlichkeit, aber die Werbung sagt nicht, wie schädlich zum Beispiel Zigaretten sind.

HANS-JÖRG Da stimm' ich dir zu. Und mit der Werbung für Motorräder, Mode und auch Zigaret- ten wird uns „Freiheit" versprochen.

PETRA Da kann ich nur lachen. Und teure Parfüms und die neueste Mode passen nur zu schönen Frauen, was?

GÖTZ Na ja, eins steht fest: Wir haben uns an die Werbung gewöhnt.

USCHI Das mag schon sein. Was mich aber stört ist, daß ... äh, die Werbung macht uns Ap- petit aufs Kaufen. Sie zeigt die Welt als ein riesiges Kaufhaus, wo man sich alle Wünsche erfüllen kann.

GÖTZ Und warum nicht?

USCHI Weil man glaubt, man muß diese Sachen haben, um glücklich, zufrieden und beliebt zu sein. Das schlimme ist aber, daß es zu viele arme Menschen gibt. Und je weniger Geld man hat, desto mehr sehnt man sich nach einem guten, zufriedenstellenden Leben, nach einem Leben, das die Werbung verspricht, das sich aber die meisten doch nicht leisten können.

16 Was sagt der Text?

1. Adjektive: **amerikanisch**, **hart**, **rhythmisch**, **köstlich**, **alt** / Adverbien: **griffbereit**, **lässig**, **mäuschenstill**, **ängstlich**

1. Schreib alle Adjektive und Adverbien in dein Notizheft, die in der Barszene vorkommen!
2. Mach dein Buch zu! Erzähle die Barszene nach, so gut du kannst!
3. Jeder von euch übernimmt eine Rolle der Schüler von Frau Kloses Klasse. Lest das Klas- sengespräch dramatisch vor!
4. Welchen von den Aussagen im Text stimmst du am meisten zu?

ZWEITE STUFE

*Eliciting agreement and agreeing; expressing conviction,
uncertainty, and what seems to be true*

WORTSCHATZ

auf deutsch erklärt

werben Werbung machen
verdienen wenn man Geld für die Arbeit bekommt
klarstellen verständlich machen
Meine Tante hat mich großgezogen.
Meine Tante hat mir geholfen, vom Kind zum Erwachsenen zu werden.
Es steht fest. Es ist klar, wahr.
kräftig wenn man starke Muskeln hat
riesig sehr groß
schädlich nicht gut oder ungesund für einen
die Sache das Ding
der Kerl der Mann
Ich bin überfragt. Ich weiß die Antwort nicht.

auf englisch erklärt

Werbung versucht oft, unsere Gefühle auszunutzen. *Advertising often attempts to take advantage of our feelings.*
Dieser Spot richtet sich an Jugendliche. *This ad is directed at young people.*
Je öfter ich den Namen eines Produktes sehe, desto größer ist die Chance, daß ich es kaufe. *The more I see the name of a product, the greater the chance that I'll buy it.*
Dieser Star spaziert herum, als ob er König wäre. *This star struts around as if he were king.*
Angeblich verdient er sehr viel. *He reportedly earns a lot.*

SO SAGT MAN DAS!
Eliciting agreement and agreeing

Here are some ways to elicit and express agreement. Which expressions do you know? Which are new?

To elicit agreement, you could say:

Die Werbung beeinflußt uns,
   nicht?
   nicht wahr?
   ja?
   stimmt's?
   oder?
   meinst du nicht?

To agree, you could say:

   Da hast du ganz recht.
   Damit stimm' ich überein.
   Das meine ich auch.
   Logisch!/Logo!
   Genau./Genau so ist es.
   Eben!/Klar!/Sicher!

What similar words or phrases do you use in everyday speech?

17 Hör gut zu! For answers, see listening script on TE Interleaf.

Die Mitarbeiter der Schülerzeitung reden über Werbespots in Zeitungen, die sie gesehen haben. Hör ihrem Gespräch gut zu und entscheide, wessen Meinungen am meisten akzeptiert werden!

18 Einverstanden oder nicht?

Constance und Stefan äußern ihre Meinungen über die Werbung. Bist du einverstanden oder nicht mit dem, was sie sagen? Was sagst du dazu? Such dir eine Partnerin und reagiert zusammen auf die Aussagen! Versucht auch, Gründe anzugeben!

CONSTANCE **Die Werbung versucht nur, den Käufer zu beeinflussen, meinst du nicht?**
DU **Klar!** *oder*
Das ist nicht ganz wahr. Es gibt Werbung, die auch informiert.

STEFAN „Die meisten Reklamen haben Frauen als Blickfang."
CONSTANCE „Viele Sportler verdienen mit der Werbung zu viel Geld."
STEFAN „Das Image der Frau wird weiterhin in einer traditionellen Rolle gezeigt."
CONSTANCE „Es gibt aber auch gute Werbung, die nicht so manipulativ ist."
STEFAN „Die meisten Werbespots für Kinder find' ich sehr blöd."
CONSTANCE „Die Werbung nutzt oft nur die Gefühle der Kinder aus."
STEFAN „Die Werbemacher brauchen immer wieder neue Ideen."
CONSTANCE „Die Werbung macht nur Appetit aufs Kaufen."
STEFAN „Je weniger Geld man hat, desto mehr sehnt man sich nach einem guten Leben."
CONSTANCE „Die Werbung verspricht, was sich die meisten nicht leisten können."

Schon bekannt
Ein wenig *G*rammatik

In **Kapitel 4** you learned about relative clauses. Relative clauses are introduced by relative pronouns, the various forms of **der, die, das.**

Das ist ein Werbeslogan, den ich nicht kenne.

Identify the relative pronoun in this sentence. What does it refer to? What case is it in? Why?

Die bringen in der Werbung immer das, was wir schon haben.

*G*rammatik   Introducing relative clauses with **was** and **wo**

1. The word **was** introduces a relative clause when it refers back to
   a. indefinite pronouns like **das, alles, etwas, nichts, wenig, viel.**

      Ich sehe **etwas, was** mir gefällt.

   b. the entire idea of the preceding clause.

      Ich kann es mir nicht leisten, was diese Leute anpreisen.

2. The word **wo** is used to refer to places, especially in a broader sense.

   Die Welt ist ein Kaufhaus, **wo** man sich alles kaufen kann.

Relative clauses are dependent clauses. Do you remember what happens to the conjugated verb in dependent clauses?

19 Was möchtest du alles?

Frag einen Partner, was er möchte! Er antwortet dir, und dann fragt er dich.

1. Was kaufst du dir?   2. Was wünschst du dir?   3. Was gefällt dir?

BEISPIEL   DU   **Was wünschst du dir?**
PARTNER   **Ich wünsche mir nichts, was ich mir nicht leisten kann.**

das,   alles,   etwas,   nichts,   wenig,   viel,   **was**

s. (nicht) leisten können

irgendwie Qualität haben

im Fernsehen angepriesen werden

gebrauchen können

(nicht) viel Geld kosten

s. gefallen

20 Was regt dich auf?

Bist du aufgeregt? Such dir eine Partnerin und sag ihr, was dich alles aufregt! Sie sagt es dir dann auch. Stimmt ihr miteinander überein?

Mich regt Werbung auf, wo ...

Frauen dienen als Blickfang.

Die Gefühle der Leute werden ausgenutzt.

Werbung verspricht „Freiheit".

Die Werbesprüche sind besonders blöd.

Kinder werben für ein Produkt.

Die Image-Werbung ist übertrieben.

21 Das Analysieren ist eine Übung, die ...

Suche aus dem Text „Weiter geht's!" alle Relativsätze heraus! Analysiere die Relativpronomen! Was sind ihre Beziehungsworte (*antecedents*)? Sind sie spezifisch oder generell?

SO SAGT MAN DAS!

Expressing conviction, uncertainty, and what seems to be true

To express conviction, you may say:

Es steht fest, daß Werbung einen großen Einfluß auf uns ausübt.

To express uncertainty, you may say:

Es kann sein, daß ...   *oder*   **Das mag schon sein.**

You already know how to express what seems true to you:

Es scheint, daß Sportler immer mehr Geld durch Werbung verdienen.

You also may say:

Es sieht so aus, als ob sie das tun.

---

22 Hör gut zu!   For answers, see listening script on TE Interleaf.

Du hörst jetzt, wie Frau Kloses Schüler über den Werbespruch vom kleinen Cowboy sprechen. Welche Schüler sind überzeugt, daß sie recht haben? Welche sind nicht sicher oder sogar dagegen? Mach eine Tabelle und füll sie aus!

*G*rammatik irgendein and irgendwelche

Irgendein and **irgendwelche** mean *any (at all)*, or *some ... or another.*

Singular	Plural
Da liegt **irgendeine** Zeitung.	Da liegen **irgendwelche** Zeitungen.
Ich suche **irgendeinen** Spruch.	Ich suche **irgendwelche** Sprüche.
Das kommt in **irgendeiner** Werbung.	Das kommt in **irgendwelchen** Werbungen.

What do you notice about these words? What can you say about the endings?

23 Nein, irgendeine Antwort geht nicht!

1. irgendeine; 2. irgendeinen; 3. irgendwelche;
4. irgendein; 5. irgendwelche; 6. irgendeine;
7. irgendeiner; 8. irgendwelchen; 9. Irgendwelche;
10. irgendwelche

Welche Form von irgendein paßt in diese Lücken?

1. Das ist ... Reklame für Videos.
2. Er soll ... Werbeslogan schreiben.
3. Das sind ... Sachen für Kinder.
4. Das ist ... Fertiggericht.
5. Das sind ... Slogans für Bekleidung.
6. Ich suche ... Autoreklame.
7. Das Auto steht auf ... Wiese.
8. Die Wiese ist in ... Bergen.
9. ... Sportler preisen den Wagen an.
10. Ich kann nicht ohne ... Statussymbole sein.

24 Du warst irgendwo anders ...

Ein Klassenkamerad fragt dich über die Barszene, die Frau Klose in ihrer Klasse gezeigt hat. Du weißt aber sehr wenig darüber. Gebrauche deshalb das Wort „irgend" in deinen Antworten! Tauscht dann die Rollen aus! For answers, see below.

1. Wo spielt sich diese Szene mit dem Jungen ab?
2. Wer sind die Männer, die um den Tresen stehen?
3. Welche Tür schwingt auf?
4. Was für ein Cowboy geht durch den Saloon?
5. Was schiebt der Barkeeper dem Cowboy zu?
6. Wo hast du so einen Cowboy-Star schon gesehen?
7. Durch welche Tür geht dieser Cowboy raus?
8. Wann hat man diese Werbung gezeigt?

WORTSCHATZ

Words preceded by **irgend**

> **irgend etwas**
> **irgend jemand**
> **irgendwann**
> **irgendwie**
> **irgendwo**
> **irgendwohin**

25 Zum Überlegen und Diskutieren

Überlegt euch, was ihr zu folgenden Themen zu sagen habt, und diskutiert in der Gruppe darüber! Schreibt für jedes Thema die Argumente dafür und dagegen auf!

1. Werbespots für Kinder und mit Kindern sollten verboten werden.
2. Die Image-Werbung: dafür oder dagegen?
3. Die Werbung macht uns Appetit aufs Kaufen.
4. Werbung für gesundheitsschädliche Produkte wie Zigaretten und alkoholische Getränke sollte nicht erlaubt sein.

24. 1. In irgendeiner ...; 2. Irgendwelche ...; 3. Irgendeine ...; 4. Irgendein ...;
5. Irgendein ...; 6. Irgendwo ...; 7. Durch irgendeine ...; 8. Irgendwann ...

26 Für mein Notizbuch

Wähle eins der obigen Themen, und schreib deine Meinung darüber! Gebrauche mindestens sechs Sätze!

Ah! Da sind ja unsere Freiwilligen! Herein mit dem jungen Volk! Herzlich willkommen bei uns!

Ausgezeichnet, meine lieben Freunde! Jetzt gebt dem Legionär euren Namen an, damit er euch einschreibt!

MILITAROS, ICH BIN GRIECHE BEIM ZEUS!

Eftax, Brite, sage ich.

Mein Name ist Mannekenpix, Belgier.

Kriegmichnich, Gote

Verkrümeldich, auch Gote.

Dolmetscher?

Kriegmichnich und Verkrümeldich, Goten.

Er fragt, ob das hier ein Gasthaus ist.

Sag ja. Er soll sich hier beim Empfang eintragen lassen.

Tennisplatzis.

KLICK! KLICK! KLICK! KLICK!

Asterix und Obelix, Gallier.

So ist's! Hihi!

KLICK! KLICK! KLICK!

Ruhe! Es wird nicht mehr gelacht! Ihr seid jetzt in der Armee!

LESETRICK

Using pictures and print type as clues to meaning When reading cartoons and comics, look at the pictures and the way words are written before you begin to read. Pictures and print can tell you a lot about what is happening in a story.

For answers, see TE Interleaf.

Getting Started

1. Read the title and then look at the entire sequence of frames. What can you tell about the story just by looking at the pictures? Make some predictions about what you think is happening. For instance, where and when is the story taking place? Is everything going smoothly, or is

und OBELIX

there some kind of conflict?

2. Before you read the text, notice the different types of print in the bubbles. Looking only at the pictures and print, why do you think the cartoonist uses different types of print?

3. Skim the entire text twice. What is the setting? What is the approximate time period? How many different characters are introduced and where are they from?

A Closer Look

4. Look at the pictures again as you read the story. For which character does the writer use pictures instead of words in the bubbles? Why do you think he does that?

5. What, in general, is happening in the story? Are the characters who come in at the beginning really **Freiwillige**? What are they? Does the text confirm the predictions you made?

Bei den Legionären

Read the comic again more carefully and answer the following questions.

6. Based on the context, what do you think a **Dolmetscher** is? How do you know? Why does the Roman need a **Dolmetscher?**

7. What does the Egyptian want to know? What kind of mix-up has occurred?

8. Where does the Roman soldier take the men after signing them in? Why? What are they supposed to do when they get there?

9. What do you think **mager** means? How do you know?

10. Zeichne jetzt deinen eigenen Comic strip! Schreib auch die Sprechblasen dazu! Die Handlung darf komisch oder ernst sein, sogar belehrend, wie du willst.

*A*dvertisements can be very persuasive. They sometimes portray a product in such a way that you think you can't live without it. But, as we all know from experience, products are not always as good as they seem in the ads. In this activity, you will write a business letter complaining to a manufacturer about a product you have purchased.

Es stört mich!

Wähl ein nicht zufriedenstellendes Produkt, das du benutzt hast, und dessen Werbung du gesehen hast! Schreib einen Brief an den Hersteller, um deinen Ärger als Verbraucher des Produkts auszudrücken!

A. Vorbereiten

1. Mach zuerst eine Liste von allem, was dich an diesem Produkt stört!
2. Vergleich das Produkt mit anderen, ähnlichen Produkten! Ist es genau so gut? Schlechter? Teurer? Hat es die gleiche Wirkung? Schreib alles auf!
3. Hat dieses Produkt irgendwelche besonderen Qualitäten? Ist das Produkt so, wie es die Werbung verspricht? Mach dir Notizen!
4. Nimm jetzt deine Notizen zur Hand und suche Adjektive und Adverbien, die deinen Ärger gut ausdrücken!

SCHREIBTIP

Using tone and word choice for effect When you write you use words that convey how you feel. It is important to think about and choose words that will create the effect you want. This is exactly what advertisers do to get you to buy their products. Adjectives and adverbs are particularly effective for setting a tone. Different degrees of adjectives and adverbs can be used to intensify the strength of a given statement, such as **schlecht** vs. **schrecklich** or **gut** vs. **ausgezeichnet**. A person complaining about a product, for example, is likely to use strong adjectives to convey frustration.

B. Ausführen

Benutze jetzt deine Notizen, und schreib einen Brief an den Hersteller des Produktes! Vergiß nicht, die Adresse, Anrede und Schlußformulierung dazuzuschreiben!

C. Überarbeiten

1. Lies deinen Brief einem Partner vor und besprecht, ob der Brief den richtigen Ton hat, um deine Beschwerde (*complaint*) auszudrücken!
2. Besprecht die Adjektive! Was wolltest du mit ihnen ausdrücken? Wirken die Adjektive auf deinen Partner, wie du beabsichtigt hast?
3. Lies deinen Brief noch einmal durch! Hast du den Text in Briefform geschrieben? Hast du eine passende Anrede und eine geeignete Schlußformulierung benutzt? Hast du alles richtig buchstabiert?
4. Schreib den korrigierten Brief noch einmal ab!

ANWENDUNG

unkaputtbar: läßt sich nicht kaputt machen / BahnCard: Bahnkarte / Geschmackskraft der Natur: hat die Kraft der Natur im Geschmack / Schnupperpreise: Preise, nach denen man sonst suchen muß / Jugend froscht: Jugend forscht / aprilfrisch: so frisch, wie das Wetter im April / tiefenwirksam: eine tiefe, gründliche Wirkung haben / atmungsaktiv: ist lebendig und atmet

1 Lies den folgenden Text, und such dir die Wortkreationen der Werbetexter heraus! Bei allen Ausdrücken handelt es sich um erfundene Wörter. Versuch, diese Ausdrücke in gutes Deutsch zu übertragen! Zum Beispiel „Deutschlands meiste Kreditkarte" bedeutet: „Kreditkarte, die man in Deutschland am meisten benutzt."

Im kreativen Rausch
Zu kühn formuliert: Viele Werbeslogans stoßen bei Sprachexperten auf Kritik

Wenn Katrin M. Frank-Cyrus Schulkindern beim Pausenhofpalaver zuhört, befällt sie leichtes Unbehagen. Dann registriert die Geschäftsführerin der Wiesbadener Gesellschaft für deutsche Sprache (GfdS), daß die Kids gern Slogans aus der Fernsehwerbung nachplappern — nicht immer, aber immer öfter.

Pädagogen haben Bedenken, denn die Werbetexter gebrauchen in ihrem kreativen Rausch oft inkorrekte Formulierungen, also Sprache, die gegen die Normen von Grammatik und Semantik verstößt.

Der Sprach-TÜV der Wiesbadener Experten und Expertinnen findet viele Formulierungen einfach zu viel.

Ärgerlich: *„Deutschlands meiste Kreditkarte"* (Kampagne für Eurocard): absichtlicher Grammatikfehler, um mehr Aufmerksamkeit zu erregen — was auch funktioniert; *„unkaputtbar"* (Kampagne für Coca-Cola): raffinierte, aber sprachlich völlig unkorrekte Konstruktion; *„BahnCard"* (Deutsche Bahn): orthographisch (noch) nicht akzeptabel; *„Geschmackskraft der Natur"* (Food-Werbung): Natur kann weder uns schmecken noch selber schmecken — eine Unsinnsbildung.

Gefällig: *„Schnupperpreise"* (Kampagne für Bekleidung): werbewirksam, sprachlich in Ordnung; *„Jugend froscht"*[1] (Reiseveranstalter): platter Kalauer, erregt aber Aufmerksamkeit.

Originell: *„aprilfrisch"*, *„tiefenwirksam"*, *„atmungsaktiv"*: anschaulich witzig, einprägsam — und korrekt.

Rausch: *intoxication;* **stoßen:** *meet;* **Unbehagen:** *uneasiness;* **nachplappern:** imitieren; **Bedenken:** *concerns;* **Unsinn:** *nonsense;* **schnuppern:** *to sniffle out;* **Frosch:** *frog;* **Kalauer:** *word-play*

---

1. The slogan „Jugend froscht" alludes to „Jugend forscht", the title of a science contest for young people.

2 Du hörst jetzt einige Werbesendungen im Radio. Schau dir folgende Illustrationen an! Welche Zielgruppe soll mit jeder Werbung erreicht werden?

a.　　　　　b.　　　　　c.　　　　　d.　　　　　e.

3 Stellt euch vor, ihr seht die folgenden Reklamen ganz groß auf einer Litfaßsäule! Reagiert darauf! Was findet ihr gut, was nicht? Begründet eure Antworten!

4 Jeder von euch muß eine Werbeanzeige mit in die Klasse bringen. Sprecht darüber, und diskutiert dabei besonders über die folgenden Punkte:

   1. Ist das Informationswerbung oder Image-Werbung, oder beides?
   2. Mit welchen Worten werden die Produkte angepriesen?
   3. Hat die Werbung einen Blickfang? Welchen? Ist er wirkungsvoll?
   4. Würdet ihr dieses Produkt kaufen, so wie es beschrieben ist? Warum?
   5. Hat diese Werbung eine versteckte Mitteilung? Was für eine?

5 Schreib einen Bericht über „deine" Werbeanzeige! Halte dich dabei an die Diskussionsfragen von Übung 4!

6

ROLLENSPIEL

Gruppen spielen Mitglieder einer Werbeagentur, die einen wichtigen Werbespot fürs Fernsehen entwerfen muß.

Sucht ein Produkt aus, für das ihr werben wollt! Entwerft drei verschiedene Werbesprüche, und schreibt den Werbetext dazu! Einigt euch auf den besten Spruch, und verteilt Rollen an jedes Gruppenmitglied, um der Klasse den Spot vorzuspielen! Wenn möglich, macht auch ein Video davon!

Can you express annoyance? (p. 161)

1 How would you respond if a friend asked you **Was nervt dich alles?**
E.g.: Es nervt mich, daß ich für die Mathearbeit lernen muß.

2 How would you say

a. that it annoys you when commercials show women in traditional roles? Was mich aufregt, ist, wenn Werbungen die Frauen in traditionellen Rollen zeigen.

b. that it irritates you that commercials always try to manipulate consumers? Es nervt mich, daß die Werbung immer versucht, die Käufer/Konsumenten zu manipulieren.

Can you compare? (p. 161)

3 How would you compare a. E.g.: Werbung in Zeitschriften ist nicht so gut wie Werbung im Fernsehen.

a. magazine ads and TV ads?

b. your family and your best friend's family? b. E.g.: Meine Familie wohnt auf der gleichen Straße wie die Familie meines besten Freundes.

4 How would you say that you always compare products, and that you know that product 1 is not as good as product 2? How would you say that you find product 2 to be the best? Ich vergleiche immer Produkte, und ich weiß, daß (brand 1) nicht so gut wie (brand 2) ist. / Ich finde (brand 2) am besten.

Can you elicit agreement and agree? (p. 168)

5 How would you elicit agreement after making each one of the following statements? a. E.g.: ..., nicht wahr?; ..., stimmt's? b. E.g.: ..., oder?; ..., ja? c. E.g.: ..., meinst du nicht auch?; ... nicht?

a. **Die Werbung manipuliert den Konsumenten.**

b. **Die meisten Werbespots im Fernsehen sind blöd.**

c. **Wir haben uns an die Werbung gewöhnt.**

How would you agree with each of those statements?
E.g.: Da hast du ganz recht. / Genau. / Eben.

Can you express conviction, uncertainty, and what seems to be true? (p. 170)

6 How would you elaborate on the following statements, indicating that you are convinced, that you are uncertain, or that you feel the statement seems to be true? a. Es steht fest, daß die Werbung uns Appetit aufs Kaufen macht.

a. **Die Werbung macht uns Appetit aufs Kaufen.**

b. **Kinderwerbung ist unfair.** Das mag schon sein, daß Kinderwerbung unfair ist.

c. **Wir kaufen nur das, was wir brauchen.**
Es sieht so aus, als ob wir nur das kaufen, was wir brauchen.

ERSTE STUFE

EXPRESSING ANNOYANCE

Was mich aufregt ist, wenn ...
What annoys me is when ...
Es nervt mich, daß ... *It gets on my nerves that ...*

COMPARING

Bevor ich etwas kaufe, vergleiche ich die Preise. *Before I buy something I compare prices.*
das gleiche *the same*
derselbe, dieselbe, dasselbe *the same*

OTHER WORDS AND USEFUL EXPRESSIONS

aufmerksam machen auf (acc) *to draw attention to*
blitzblank *squeaky clean*
fröhlich *happy*
heil *whole, perfect*

raffiniert *clever*
weise *wise*
weiterhin *as before*

der Blickfang *eye-catcher*
die Eigenschaft, -en *characteristic*
der Kaufreiz *temptation to buy*
der Konsument, -en *consumer*
Linie: in erster Linie *primarily*
die Mitteilung, -en *message*
die Plakatwand, ¨e *billboard*
das Putzmittel, - *cleaning agent*
die Reklame, -n *advertisement*
Schluß: zum Schluß *finally*
der Stau, -s *traffic jam*
das Unterbewußtsein *subconscious*
der Verbraucher, - *consumer*

die Ware, -n *product, ware*
der Werbespruch, ¨e *advertising slogan*
die Werbung, -en *advertisement*
die Wiese, -n *meadow*
die Wirtschaft *economy*

anpreisen (sep) *to praise*
aufklären (sep) *to enlighten*
eingestehen (sep) *to admit*
s. leisten können *to be able to afford*
gebrauchen *to use*
überfluten *to flood*
überlegen *to consider*
verbergen *to hide*
verführen *to seduce*
vergleichen *to compare*
verstecken *to hide*
verursachen *to cause*
wahrnehmen (sep) *to perceive*

ZWEITE STUFE

AGREEING

Damit stimm' ich überein. *I agree with that.*
Logisch! Logo! *Of course!*
Klar! *Of course!*
Genau so ist es. *That's exactly right.*

EXPRESSING CONVICTION

Es steht fest, daß ... *It's certain that ...*

EXPRESSING UNCERTAINTY

Das mag schon sein. *That may well be.*

EXPRESSING WHAT SEEMS TO BE TRUE

Es sieht so aus, als ob ... *It looks as if ...*
angeblich *ostensibly, reported to be*

OTHER WORDS AND USEFUL EXPRESSIONS

glücklich *happy*
je mehr ... desto ... *the more ... the ...*
kräftig *strong*
riesig *huge*
schädlich *harmful*
überfragt sein *to not know*
irgend- *some-*

die Freiheit *freedom*
das Gefühl, -e *feeling*
der Kerl, -e *guy*
der König, -e *king*

ausnützen (sep) *to take advantage of*
erfüllen *to fulfill*
s. gewöhnen an (acc) *to get used to*
großziehen (sep) *to raise (a child)*
klarstellen (sep) *to make clear*
s. richten an (acc) *to be directed at*
s. sehnen nach *to long for*
verdienen *to earn*
verwenden *to use*
werben *to advertise*

Kapitel 8: Weg mit den Vorurteilen!

CHAPTER OVERVIEW

	FUNCTIONS	GRAMMAR	CULTURE	RE-ENTRY
Los geht's! pp. 182-183	Wie sehen uns die jungen Deutschen? *p. 182*			
Erste Stufe pp. 184-188	Expressing surprise, disappointment, and annoyance, *p.185*	•The conjunction als, *p. 187* •Coordinating conjunctions (Summary), *p 188*	•Cartoon, *p. 186* •Landeskunde: Verständnis für Ausländer? *p. 189*	•Expressing surprise, *p. 185* •Expressing disappointment, *p. 185* •Daß-clauses, *p. 185* •Narrative past, *p. 187* •Conversational past, *p. 187* •Coordinating conjunctions, *p. 188*
Weiter geht's! pp. 190-191	Wie sehen junge Amerikaner die Deutschen? *p. 190*			
Zweite Stufe pp. 192-195	•Expressing an assumption, *p. 193* •Making suggestions and recommendations; giving advice, *p. 195*	Verbs with prefixes (Summary), *p. 194*	Der sympathische Deutsche, *p. 192*	•Expressing an assumption, *p. 193* •Prepositions followed by dative case, *p. 194* •Separable prefix verbs, *p. 194* •Making suggestions, *p. 195* •Giving advice, *p. 195*
Zum Lesen pp. 196-198	**Stille Grenzen** Reading Strategy: Interpreting rhetorical devices			
Zum Schreiben p. 199	**Es waren einmal zwei Gruppen ...** Writing Strategy: Selecting a point of view			
Review pp. 200-203	•Anwendung, *p. 200* •Kann ich's wirklich? *p. 202* •Wortschatz, *p. 203*			

Assessment Options	**Stufe Quizzes**
	•*Chapter Resources*, Book 3
	  Erste Stufe, Quiz 8-1
	  Zweite Stufe, Quiz 8-2
	•*Assessment Items, Audiocassette* 8 A
			Kapitel 8 Chapter Test
			•*Chapter Resources*, Book 3
			•*Assessment Guide*, Speaking Test
			•*Assessment Items, Audiocassette* 8 A
			
			Test Generator, Kapitel 8	

Chapter Overview

RESOURCES Print	RESOURCES Audiovisual
Practice and Activity Book	*Textbook Audiocassette* 4 B

Practice and Activity Book
Chapter Resources, Book 3
- Communicative Activity 8-1
- Communicative Activity 8-2
- Additional Listening Activity 8-1 ....*Additional Listening Activities, Audiocassette* 10 A
- Additional Listening Activity 8-2 ....*Additional Listening Activities, Audiocassette* 10 A
- Additional Listening Activity 8-3 ....*Additional Listening Activities, Audiocassette* 10 A
- Student Response Forms
- Realia 8-1
- Situation Card 8-1
- Teaching Transparency Master 8-1 ....*Teaching Transparency* 8-1
- Quiz 8-1 ....*Assessment Items, Audiocassette* 8 A

Video Guide ....*Video Program*, Videocassette 2

Textbook Audiocassette 4 B

Practice and Activity Book — *Textbook Audiocassette* 4 B

Practice and Activity Book
Chapter Resources, Book 3
- Communicative Activity 8-3
- Communicative Activity 8-4
- Additional Listening Activity 8-4 ....*Additional Listening Activities, Audiocassette* 10 A
- Additional Listening Activity 8-5 ....*Additional Listening Activities, Audiocassette* 10 A
- Additional Listening Activity 8-6 ....*Additional Listening Activities, Audiocassette* 10 A
- Student Response Forms
- Realia 8-2
- Situation Card 8-2
- Teaching Transparency Master 8-2 ....*Teaching Transparency* 8-2
- Quiz 8-2 ....*Assessment Items, Audiocassette* 8 A

Video Guide ....*Video Program*, Videocassette 2

Textbook Audiocassette 11

Chapter Resources, Book 3
- Realia 8-3
- Situation Card 8-3

Video Guide ....*Video Program*, Videocassette 2

Alternative Assessment
- Performance Assessment
Teacher's Edition
  Erste Stufe, p. 179L
  Zweite Stufe, p. 179O

- Portfolio Assessment
  Written: **Anwendung,** Activity 6, *Pupil's Edition,* p. 201;
  Assessment Guide, p. 21
  Oral: **Anwendung,** Activity 6, *Pupil's Edition,* p. 201;
  Assessment Guide, p. 21
- **Notizbuch,** *Pupil's Edition,* pp. 186, 188, 195

Kapitel 8: Weg mit den Vorurteilen!
Textbook Listening Activities Scripts

For Student Response Forms, see *Chapter Resources,* Book 3, pp. 82-85.

Erste Stufe
Activity 2, p. 184

Also, ich bin gerade vor zweieinhalb Wochen aus den Vereinigten Staaten zurückgekommen. Wir haben von der Schule aus ein Austauschprogramm mit einer Schule in der Nähe von Dallas gemacht. Wir waren sechs Monate lang da und haben bei Familien mit Jugendlichen in unserem Alter gewohnt. Ich war vorher noch nie in Amerika, und ich hatte eigentlich keine Ahnung, was mich erwartete. In Deutschland denken viele, daß die Amerikaner alle nur Fast food essen. Das stimmt eigentlich gar nicht. Das war sogar die eine Sache, die mir in Amerika am besten gefallen hat. Ich war echt erstaunt, aber das Essen dort hat mir fantastisch geschmeckt. Meine Gastmutter hat eigentlich jeden Abend gekocht, und es gab oft mexikanisches Essen, und sogar ein- oder zweimal ein chinesisches Gericht. Wir sind auch öfters zum Essen ausgegangen, und die Gerichte in den Restaurants waren eigentlich immer frisch und sehr lecker. Eine andere Sache, die mir gefallen hat, war, daß die Amerikaner immer sehr hilfreich waren. Sie haben mich gleich akzeptiert und haben mir alles gezeigt. Die Gastfreundschaft der Amerikaner hat mich wirklich begeistert. Auch in der Schule waren alle viel offener als hier in Deutschland. Andererseits muß ich sagen, daß die Amerikaner eigentlich wenig über andere Länder wissen. Im Radio hört man nur selten Nachrichten, und auch die Zeitungen bringen meistens nur Lokalnachrichten. Das fand ich schade. Ich war auch ziemlich enttäuscht, daß es in Amerika viele Probleme mit Rassismus und Vorurteilen gegenüber Minoritäten gibt. Das hat mir dort nicht so gefallen, daß auch die Wohnviertel sehr getrennt sind. Was mir aber absolut super gefallen hat, war das warme, trockene Wetter dort. Seitdem ich wieder in Deutschland bin, regnet es nur. Ich bin aber trotzdem froh, daß ich wieder hier bin. Hier kann ich überall mit dem Fahrrad hinfahren. In Amerika benutzt man eigentlich immer nur das Auto. Die Leute laufen fast nie irgendwo hin, auch wenn es nicht sehr weit ist. Das hat mich irgendwie unheimlich gestört. Außerdem glaube ich, daß wir doch ein wenig vorsichtiger mit unserer Umwelt umgehen. Nicht sehr viele Amerikaner sortieren ihren Müll, und Verpackungen kann man dort auch nicht in den Supermärkten lassen. Außerdem wird viel Plastikgeschirr benutzt, das dann natürlich einfach weggeworfen wird. Da finde ich es schon wesentlich besser, wie wir das hier in Deutschland machen. Insgesamt würde ich sagen, daß jeder Schüler mal einen solchen Austausch machen sollte. Ich habe auf jeden Fall viel dazugelernt.

Answers to Activity 2

Gut: E.g.: Essen hat geschmeckt; Amerikaner sind hilfreich u. gastfreundschaftlich; sind offener in der Schule; warmes Wetter
Nicht gut: E.g.: Amerikaner wissen wenig über andere Länder; Medien bringen meistens Lokalnachrichten; Probleme mit Rassismus u. Vorurteilen; überall mit dem Auto hinfahren; Amerikaner sind nicht so umweltbewußt

Activity 5, p. 185

ELKE Ich würde gern auch mal von euch hören, was euch bei dem Austausch in Amerika am meisten gefallen hat, und auch, was euch eigentlich eher gestört hat. Gibt es zum Beispiel auch Sachen, die euch überrascht oder enttäuscht haben?

HEIDI Tja, also Elke, ich war sehr überrascht, wie hilfsbereit und offen die Leute zu mir waren. Ich dachte, daß es bestimmt Vorurteile gegenüber Ausländern dort gibt. Aber die Leute haben mich sofort akzeptiert und waren sehr nett.

FRANZ Ja, da stimme ich dir schon zu, Heidi, aber irgendwie hat es mich gestört, daß die vielen Einladungen, die wir bekommen haben, nicht immer ernst gemeint waren. Freundlich sind die Amerikaner schon, aber es scheint manchmal ein bißchen oberflächlich.

ELKE Meinst du, Franz? Also, ich finde das nicht! Was mich mehr gestört hat, war, daß wir eigentlich nie irgendwo zu Fuß hingegangen sind. Wir sind überall mit dem Auto hingefahren.

HEIDI Ja, ich war auch ein bißchen enttäuscht, daß meine Familie überhaupt kein Interesse am Fahrradfahren oder am Zelten hatte.

FRANZ Also, Heidi, ich muß sagen, da war ich eigentlich überrascht. Meine Familie hat viel draußen gemacht. Wir sind fast jedes Wochenende wandern und angeln gewesen. Das fand ich echt toll.

ELKE Also, ich war überrascht, wie gut das Essen dort war. Meine Vorstellung von Amerika war, daß alle Leute dort nur Fast food essen. Aber das stimmt überhaupt nicht. Meine Gastmutter hat immer gekocht, und auch in den Restaurants war das Essen lecker.

HEIDI Das stimmt schon, Elke. Aber in den Restaurants hat es mich immer gestört, daß die Portionen viel zu groß waren. Ich konnte immer nur die Hälfte essen, und alles andere wird weggeworfen. Das finde ich wirklich schlimm.

FRANZ Also, am meisten war ich eigentlich enttäuscht, wie wenig manche Amerikaner wirtschaftlich oder politisch über Deutschland informiert sind. Die einzigen Sachen, die sie mit Deutschland in Verbindung bringen, sind Sauerkraut, Autobahnen und das Oktoberfest.

ELKE Das stimmt aber auch nicht immer, Franz. Also, meine Gastfamilie war vor zwei Jahren in Europa im Urlaub, und sie wußten eigentlich viel über Deutschland!

FRANZ Na ja! Ausnahmen gibt es halt immer.

Answers to Activity 5

Elke: Es hat sie gestört, daß man überall mit dem Auto hinfährt und wenig zu Fuß geht. Sie war überrascht, daß es dort gutes Essen gab.
Heidi: Sie war überrascht, daß die Leute hilfsbereit, offen und nett sind. Sie war enttäuscht, daß ihre Familie kein Interesse am Fahrradfahren oder Zelten hatte. Es hat sie gestört, daß die Portionen in den Restaurants zu groß sind.
Franz: Es hat ihn gestört, daß Einladungen oft nicht ernst gemeint sind. Er war überrascht, daß seine Familie viel draußen war zum Wandern und Angeln. Er war enttäuscht, daß manche Amerikaner zu wenig wirtschaftlich und politisch über Deutschland informiert sind.

Zweite Stufe
Activity 19, p. 192

1. Also, bevor ich mit unserem Schüleraustausch nach Deutschland gefahren bin, dachte ich immer, daß die Deutschen nicht sehr freundlich sind und alles sehr genau nehmen. Meine Freundin, die einmal in den Ferien in Deutschland war, hatte mir erzählt, daß die Deutschen Hunde gern haben. Das stimmt wirklich! Meine Gastfamilie hatte zwei Hunde, einen Schäferhund und einen Dackel. Die durften überall mitfahren. Die Deutschen, die ich kennengelernt habe, sind sehr hundelieb.

2. Ich dachte immer, daß wir hier in Amerika sehr viel sportlicher sind als die Deutschen. Ich hatte mir vorgestellt, daß viele Deutsche sehr unsportlich sind. Jetzt weiß ich, daß das nicht stimmt. Meine Gastfamilie achtet sehr darauf, sich in der Freizeit sportlich zu betätigen. Jeden Sonntag nach dem Mittagessen gehen wir spazieren. Wir sind auch oft Wandern und Bergsteigen gewesen. Meine Gasteltern hatten eine kleine Hütte in den Alpen. Dort sind wir drei- oder viermal hingefahren und haben das Wochenende dort verbracht. Wir haben dann von der Hütte aus Tagestouren gemacht.

3. Also, bevor ich nach Deutschland ging, habe ich eigentlich nie viel über die Umwelt nachgedacht. Das war mir alles so ziemlich egal. Da habe ich in Deutschland viel dazugelernt. Die Deutschen achten sehr auf die Umwelt. In meiner Gastfamilie mußten wir den ganzen Abfall sortieren. Glasflaschen kamen in einen Korb, Plastik in einen andern, und das Papier haben wir gestapelt und zusammengebunden. Einmal in der Woche sind wir dann zu den Recycling-Containern gefahren und haben alles getrennt dort reingeworfen. Mit dem Auto sind wir nur gefahren, wenn wir weit weg mußten. Sonst sind wir meistens mit dem Rad oder mit dem Bus gefahren. Das fand ich echt toll, und ich werde jetzt auch hier in Amerika versuchen, mehr auf die Umwelt zu achten.

4. Ich war echt überrascht, als ich nach Deutschland kam. In meiner Gastfamilie ist es ganz anders als bei mir zu Hause. Meine Eltern haben beide einen Beruf und arbeiten sechzig Stunden in der Woche oder mehr. Ich sehe sie fast nie. Wenn wir zusammen essen, dann gehen wir in ein Restaurant. Sonst hole ich mir einfach etwas aus dem Kühlschrank. Meine Gastmutter in Deutschland hat nur am Vormittag gearbeitet. Jeden Abend haben wir alle zusammen gegessen. Sie hat immer ein sehr leckeres Abendessen gekocht. Am Wochenende gab es auch am Nachmittag Kaffee und selbstgebackenen Kuchen. Wir haben alle zusammen draußen im Garten gesessen und einfach nur geplaudert, manchmal zwei oder drei Stunden lang. Das war wirklich schön. Ich habe viel Deutsch gelernt und die deutsche Gemütlichkeit erlebt.

5. Also, ich bin ein richtiger Fleischfan. Gemüse und Obst, das mag ich nicht so gerne. Ich fand es nicht so gut, daß meine Gastfamilie in Deutschland so viel Gemüse und Obst gegessen hat. Sie waren richtige Fleischmuffel! Ich hatte immer gedacht, daß alle Deutschen jeden Tag Schweinefleisch essen. Das stimmt gar nicht. Einen Braten gab es eigentlich nur am Sonntag. Jeden Morgen gab es Müsli, und dann zum Mittagessen Suppe, Gemüse und Obst. Abends gab es dann belegte Brote und Salat.

Answers to Activity 19

1. d; 2. a; 3. c; 4. b; 5. e

Activity 22, p. 193

MANDY   Also, ich war noch nie in Deutschland, aber ich stelle mir vor, daß die Deutschen wahnsinnig genau sind und immer nur arbeiten.

JESSE   Ja, das kann schon sein, Mandy. Aber ich habe neulich einen Artikel gelesen, wo der Autor sagte, daß das gar nicht stimmt. Ich glaube, daß die Deutschen überhaupt keinen Sinn für Humor haben und immer furchtbar ernst sind. Das sieht man doch auch immer in den Filmen.

HAL   Ach komm, Jesse, was du in den Filmen siehst, das stimmt doch gar nicht.

MANDY   Mensch, hört doch auf zu streiten, Hal und Jesse! Jeder kann doch seine Meinung haben. Ich, zum Beispiel, vermute, daß viele Deutsche ziemlich dick sind, weil sie immer Schweinefleisch, Wurst und Knödel essen. Das ist doch alles sehr fett.

HAL   Ja, da hast du bestimmt recht, Mandy. Ich nehme an, daß die Deutschen oft in Lederhosen und Dirndln rumlaufen. Das sieht man ja immer auf den Postkarten aus Deutschland.

JESSE   Also, ich stelle mir vor, daß die meisten Deutschen sehr arrogant sind.

HAL   Ja, genau. Und ich meine auch, daß sie bestimmt unfreundlich sind.

MANDY   Also, so schlimm sind sie doch sicherlich nicht. Eigentlich wissen wir doch überhaupt nichts über die Deutschen.

HAL   Also, ich glaube schon, daß wir eine Menge über die Deutschen wissen.

MANDY   Hm. Da geb' ich dir aber nicht recht, Hal. Ich habe eher den Eindruck, daß dies alles Vorurteile sind.

HAL   Hm. Das kann natürlich sein. Eigentlich würde ich ganz gerne mal nach Deutschland, besonders weil die Deutschen alle schnelle Autos fahren. Das muß doch toll sein, mit einem Porsche oder Mercedes auf der Autobahn zu fahren.

MANDY   Ja, also ich würde auch gern mal nach Deutschland fliegen. Und du, Jesse?

JESSE   Ja, ich auch. Vor allen Dingen möchte ich herausfinden, ob die Deutschen wirklich so viel Bier trinken!

Answers to Activity 22

E.g.: Die Deutschen ...sind genau; arbeiten immer; haben keinen Sinn für Humor; sind ernst; sind dick; essen immer Schweinefleisch, Wurst und Knödel; tragen Lederhosen und Dirndl; sind arrogant; sind unfreundlich; fahren schnelle Autos auf der Autobahn; trinken viel Bier

SCRIPTS

Activity 25, *p. 194*

CHRISTIAN Hallo, Dorothee! Na, bist du froh, wieder zu Hause zu sein?

DOROTHEE Ja, also eigentlich schon. Es war schön, meine Familie und meinen Hund wiederzusehen. Und du, Christian? Seit wann bist du denn wieder da?

CHRISTIAN Ach, ich bin schon seit einer Woche aus Berlin zurück. Wie war's denn bei dir?

DOROTHEE Also, ich fand es in Deutschland einfach spitze. Ich kann nur jedem empfehlen, den Schüleraustausch mitzumachen. Man lernt wirklich soviel über ein Land, wenn man selbst dort hinfährt. Schau mal, da kommt die Lisa, die war letztes Jahr in Deutschland. Hallo, Lisa!

LISA Hallo, Dorothee! Hallo, Christian! Na, wie geht's euch?

DOROTHEE Wir haben uns gerade über unseren Austausch unterhalten. Christian war in Berlin und ich in München.

LISA Ja, also ich finde, es lohnt sich wirklich, ein Semester lang in Deutschland zu verbringen. Man lernt die Sprache viel schneller.

CHRISTIAN Ja, aber man lernt auch noch andere Sachen!

DOROTHEE Was meinst du denn?

CHRISTIAN Na ja, wirf zum Beispiel bloß nicht alles zusammen in den Abfall! Die Deutschen sind wahnsinnig umweltbewußt.

LISA Ja, das stimmt! Das habe ich auch festgestellt. Meine Familie hat den ganzen Müll sortiert und zum Recycling gebracht.

DOROTHEE Ach ja, und wißt ihr, wovon ich am meisten überrascht war? Ich dachte immer, daß die Deutschen sehr ausländerfeindlich sind, aber das stimmt gar nicht. Verbreite ja keine Klischees oder Vorurteile! Die meisten Deutschen können das überhaupt nicht leiden.

LISA Ja, also meine deutschen Freunde fanden das auch immer ganz schlimm.

CHRISTIAN Habt ihr auch so viel Sport in der Freizeit gemacht wie ich?

LISA Ja, als ich letztes Jahr dort war, habe ich erst richtig entdeckt, wieviel Spaß Fahrradfahren macht!

CHRISTIAN Genau! Ich bin in Deutschland auch überall mit dem Fahrrad hingefahren. Egal, was für ein Wetter es gab. Ich kann nur jedem den Tip geben: bring deine Sportkleidung mit.

DOROTHEE Nicht nur Sportkleidung, Christian! Es lohnt sich auch, warme Kleidung mitzubringen. Ich war mit der Claudia ein paar Mal wandern, und da war es ziemlich kalt.

CHRISTIAN Mein Bruder will nächstes Jahr auch beim Austausch mitmachen. Er hat so richtige Klischeevorstellungen von den Deutschen und wollte von mir wissen, ob das alles stimmt.

LISA Na, also ich würde ihm empfehlen, auf jeden Fall selbst dort hinzufliegen, damit er sich eine eigene Meinung bilden kann und nicht die Klischees von anderen verbreitet!

Answers to Activity 25

Dorothee: Empfehlung: Schüleraustausch mitmachen / Warnung: keine Vorurteile verbreiten; warme Kleidung mitbringen

Christian: Empfehlung: Sportkleidung mitbringen / Warnung: nicht alles zusammen in den Abfall werfen

Lisa: Empfehlung: ein Semester in Deutschland verbringen; selbst hinfliegen und eigene Meinung bilden

Anwendung
Activity 1, *p. 200*

1. Im Licht der Gastfreundschaft und des gegenseitigen Kennenlernens steht auch diesmal wieder das Austauschprogramm des Marie-Curie-Gymnasiums. Seit Jahren schon bemüht sich dieses Mädchengymnasium um einen regen Austausch mit mehreren Schulen in Chicago, Illinois. Die Mädchen, die die Gelegenheit haben, diese Reise anzutreten, wohnen direkt bei den Gastfamilien, die meistens auch Töchter im gleichen Alter haben. Teil des Programms sind außerdem intensive englische Sprachkurse und mehrere Reisen in verschiedene Gegenden der Vereinigten Staaten.

2. Eine erneute Umfrage des städtischen Arbeitsamtes hat auch für Januar wieder ergeben, daß deutsche Frauen im Gegensatz zu ihren männlichen Kollegen immer noch unterbezahlt sind. Das gilt auch, wenn sie die gleiche Arbeit erledigen. Im Durchschnitt erhalten Frauen für die gleiche Arbeit ungefähr 20% weniger Bezahlung als Männer. Außerdem arbeiten die meisten Frauen immer noch in herkömmlichen Frauenberufen, wie zum Beispiel als Krankenschwester, Sekretärin oder Lehrerin. Nur sehr wenige Frauen arbeiten als selbständige Geschäftsführerinnen. Demnach haben wir anscheinend nur wenig Fortschritt gemacht, was die Gleichberechtigung der Frau am Arbeitsplatz betrifft. Die Verteilung am Arbeitsmarkt ist immer noch sehr traditionell.

3. In der Kaserne haben alle Soldaten die Möglichkeit, ihre Wäsche kostenlos zu waschen. Die meisten Soldaten nehmen aber ihre schmutzige Wäsche am Wochenende mit nach Hause und lassen sie dort von der Mutter waschen. Auch die Anschaffung zusätzlicher Wasch- und Trockenautomaten in der Kaserne hat nichts geändert.

4. Immer wieder kann man in den Nachrichten hören und in den Zeitungen lesen, daß die Menschen in der modernen Gesellschaft immer weniger Kontakte zueinander haben. Familien unternehmen nur noch wenig, sondern sitzen jeden Abend vor dem Fernseher. Viele Menschen, die allein in der Großstadt leben, kennen nicht einmal ihre Nachbarn und haben kaum noch Freunde oder Bekannte. Um dieses wachsende Problem zu bekämpfen, gibt es jetzt einen neuen Freundeskreis, der sich mehrmals in der Woche trifft, um Ausflüge zu machen, zu radeln oder einfach miteinander zu reden. Die Menschen, die sich dort zusammenfinden, sagen, daß unsere Gesellschaft wieder partnerschaftlicher werden muß. „Die Menschen müssen wieder mehr miteinander reden. Technischer Fortschritt kann sehr positiv sein, aber er hat uns kontaktarm gemacht", meint ein Mitglied.

5. Im Altenheim Marienbad haben die Besitzer mit einer neuen Idee ihre Bewohner zu einem aktiveren Lebensstil angeregt. Das Altenheim hat in den letzten Monaten damit begonnen, eine Reihe von Sportveranstaltungen anzubieten. Die Bewohner des Hauses Marienbad bilden jetzt mehrmals im Monat Gruppen, um Tennis zu spielen, zu radeln oder Wanderausflüge zu machen. Auch einen Schwimmkurs gibt es inzwischen. Eine begeisterte Seniorin sagt darüber: „Ich finde das einfach toll. Man ist nie zu alt, um irgendeine Art von Sport zu treiben. Seit ich Tennisunterricht nehme, fühle ich mich viel besser, und ich habe auch viele andere Bewohner aus Marienbad näher kennengelernt."

Answers to Activity 1

Meldung 1: Amerika für junge Mädchen

Meldung 2: Jobs — immer noch nach traditioneller Manier

Meldung 3: Ohne Mutter geht es nicht

Meldung 4: Ein partnerschaftlicheres Leben im Kommen

Meldung 5: Wie alt ist zu alt?

Kapitel 8: Weg mit den Vorurteilen!
Projects and Games

PROJECT

In this activity, the class will work together to prepare a collage and letter representing their town or city to a prospective sister city in Germany. Their objective is to convince the German city to become their sister city.

Materials Students may need poster board, scissors, glue, and brochures or photos of their area.

Suggested Sequence

1. Students decide which city they would like to have as a sister city.
2. Students make an outline of what they will show and tell about their town or city and its people. They should try to view their town or city through the eyes of Germans. The local Chamber of Commerce and Tourism Bureau should be able to provide information and some materials.
3. Once students have collected their materials, including photos of their class, their school, and other points of interest, they should design the layout and arrange the various realia on the poster board. Each photo or piece of realia should have an accompanying caption.
4. For the writing component of this project, students should compose a letter to city officials in which they introduce themselves, briefly describe their town or city, and propose the city partnership program.
5. Before students write the final letter, they should collectively proofread what they have written and make necessary corrections.
6. Students send their collage and letter to the German town that they chose at the beginning of the activity and ask for a response.

Grading the Project

Since the outcome of the project is based on group cooperation and effort, one grade can be given to all students.
Suggested point distribution (total = 100 points)

Appearance of collage/Originality	30
Content/Representative examples of life in city or town	30
Quality of captions/Key descriptors used	20
Accurate language usage in captions and letter	20

 GAME

Genau das Gegenteil!

Playing this game will help students review the vocabulary of descriptive adjectives as well as previously learned expressions.

Procedure Divide the class into two teams. A player from Team A forms a sentence describing German or American people. The sentence must include a descriptive adjective such as the ones listed on p. 190. (Example: **Ich finde, daß die Deutschen, die ich kenne, immer sehr höflich sind.**) Then a player from Team B refutes the statement by saying: **Genau das Gegenteil! Ich finde, daß Deutsche eigentlich ziemlich unhöflich sind.** If the opposing team members use a correct contrasting adjective, they get to come up with a descriptive sentence that Team A must respond to. If an incorrect adjective is used, the team who made the initial statement gets a chance to respond and earn a point. The teacher acts as a monitor and determines the accuracy of statements and awards points accordingly.

Kapitel 8: Weg mit den Vorurteilen!
Lesson Plans, pages 180-203

Teacher Note

Before you begin the chapter, you may want to preview the *Video Program* and consult the *Video Guide*. Suggestions for integrating the video into each chapter are given in the *Video Guide* and in the chapter interleaf. Activity masters for video selections can be found in the *Video Guide*.

Using the Chapter Opener, pp. 180-181

Motivating Activity

Ask students to think of a specific incident which led them to falsely stereotype somebody. How and when did they realize that they had formed an opinion prematurely? (**Denkt mal an eine bestimmte Situation, in der ihr euch eine falsche Meinung über eine Person gebildet habt. Wie und wann habt ihr aber bemerkt, daß diese Meinung voreilig gemacht wurde?**)

Teacher Note

This chapter deals with prejudices, stereotypes, and clichés. The purpose is to help students realize how they view other people and to become critical of stereotypes. They should learn not to assume things just because they have heard them all their lives, but to think, observe, experience, and come to their own conclusions.

The **Los geht's!** section and **Erste Stufe** require students to stand back and view themselves and their country the way Germans do. As they read the comments of young Germans, they will experience firsthand how hard it is to make generalizations about a country and a people. Often, the impressions many people have of each other come from television, movies, and advertising, which can distort reality and promote stereotypes and clichés.

Teaching Suggestions

1. Ask students what this picture makes them think of. Do they think it represents a "typically" German scene? Why or why not? (Students may notice the mountainous background that is typical in southern Germany, but not northern Germany. They may realize, then, that the picture is typical of a specific region, but not of Germany in general.)

1. Ask students about the types of events at which they would expect a brass band such as this one to perform. Would it be at an "authentic" German party for Americans?

Thinking Critically

2. **Analyzing** Have students read the caption for this photo and determine what the statement suggests about the speaker's impression of Germany.

Teaching Suggestion

3. Have students examine the stickers on the bike. What messages do they convey?

Thinking Critically

Analyzing Ask students which of the three pictures best represents their image of Germany. Have them explain why.

Family Link

Have students survey family members about their image of Germany. What comes to their minds when they think of the country? What are their associations? Have students share the information with the class and compare with others.

Focusing on Outcomes

To get students to focus on the chapter objectives, have them give one misconception other people might have about them and explain what they would do or say to reverse it. Then have students preview the learning outcomes listed on p. 181. **NOTE:** These outcomes are modeled in **Los geht's!** (pp. 182-183) and **Weiter geht's!** (pp. 190-191) and evaluated in **Kann ich's wirklich?** (p. 202).

Teaching Los geht's!
pp. 182-183

Resources for Los geht's!

- *Textbook Audiocassette* 4 B
- *Practice and Activity Book*

Teacher Note

Los geht's! is recorded on audiocassette.

Los geht's! Summary

In **Wie sehen uns die jungen Deutschen?**, students are introduced to some perceptions young Germans have about the United States. Tanja, Sonja, Michael, and Phillip talk about how their own impressions changed after they visited the United States. The following student outcomes listed on p. 181 are modeled in the episode: expressing surprise, disappointment, and annoyance.

Motivating Activity

Discuss with students the various clichés that they have about German, Russian, French, British, and Chinese people. What do they consider typical of these groups? How did they form these opinions?

Teaching Suggestion

Before students begin the **Los geht's!** section, bring in the TV section of a German magazine, photocopy a class set, and ask students to scan the guide for all the American TV programs that are featured that day. What types of programs are they? Do those programs reflect an accurate image of the United States?

For Individual Needs

Auditory Learners With their books closed, have students listen to **Wie sehen uns die jungen Deutschen?** on audiocassette. Then have students recall as much as they can remember.

Cooperative Learning

1 After students have listened to the audiocassette and read along in their books once or twice, divide them into groups of three or four. Have students discuss the collage on p. 182, read the opinions of young Germans who visited the United States, and write them out in two columns. Then have the reporter of each group share his or her group's findings with the rest of the class.

Closure

Ask students to complete the following statement: **Nach Meinung dieser deutschen Schüler sind Amerikaner ..., weil ....**

Teaching Erste Stufe,
pp. 184-188

Resources for Erste Stufe

Practice and Activity Book
Chapter Resources, Book 3
- Communicative Activities 8-1, 8-2
- Additional Listening Activities 8-1, 8-2, 8-3
- Student Response Forms
- Realia 8-1
- Situation Card 8-1
- Teaching Transparency Master 8-1
- Quiz 8-1
Audiocassette Program
- *Textbook Audiocassette* 4 B
- *Additional Listening Activities, Audiocassette* 10 A
- *Assessment Items, Audiocassette* 8 A
Video Program, Videocassette 2
Video Guide

▶ **page 184**

MOTIVATE
Teaching Suggestion

Ask students what they would do if they had the opportunity to provide a German exchange student with a representative picture of the United States and its people. Where would they take that exchange student and why? (**Stell dir vor, du hättest die Möglichkeit einem deutschen Austauschschüler ein bißchen von Amerika und seinen Leuten zu zeigen. Was würdest du dem Schüler alles zeigen? Begründe deine Antwort!**)

TEACH

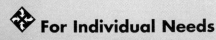 For Individual Needs

A Slower Pace Ask students to give examples for each of the following words: **Meinung, Vorurteil,** and **Klischee.**

PRESENTATION: Wortschatz

Work with the new vocabulary in three different ways. First, have students find the new word or expression used in the **Los geht's!** text. Then paraphrase the new vocabulary items in oral statements and have students tell you which word or expression you are referring to. Finally, create a cloze exercise by preparing a variety of written statements (in the context of this unit) in which you leave out the new word or phrase. Have students complete each sentence with the appropriate word or phrase.

Teaching Suggestion

3 Students may need help verbalizing their ideas. Help with vocabulary and allow students to work with a dictionary. Encourage them to express their agreement and disagreement with the opinions and suggestions of their classmates. Have them support what they say with examples.

▶ **page 185**

Thinking Critically

4 Analyzing After students have discussed the statements, ask them to examine each one and give possible reasons why Germans could have formed such opinions.

PRESENTATION: So sagt man das!

- Ask students to scan the **Los geht's!** section to find as many of the expressions listed in the function box as possible.
- On a transparency, provide a variety of dependent clauses for each function. Ask students to choose an introductory clause from the function box that would be suitable for each one. Examples:
  ..., **daß die Leute so kinderlieb und tierlieb sind.**
  ..., **wenn die Leute so dumme Vorurteile haben.**
- Have students choose one introductory statement per function (surprise, disappointment, annoyance) and use it in original sentences.

Thinking Critically

5 Drawing Inferences Once students have completed the chart, discuss each entry. Have them think about each statement and what it says about the German teenagers' lives.

▶ *page 186*

Teaching Suggestion

6 Remind students as they react to the statements here and throughout the unit how difficult it is to make generalizations about a group of people. Again, ask students how they think foreigners might have gotten these impressions of the United States. If students disagree with the opinions expressed in this activity, have them give reasons why they disagree and support them with examples.

Language Note

6 The expression used in the third statement **etwas hat Hand und Fuß** is equivalent to the English *something is done thoroughly or well.*

✦ For Individual Needs

8 A Slower Pace Help students brainstorm for additional ideas using their knowledge of problems and issues in American society as a basis. (Examples: too much rich food, not enough exercise, too much crime, people spending more money than they have, not doing enough for the environment)

8 Challenge Ask students to give an example to support each completed statement.
Example:
Die meisten Amerikaner sind äußerst nett.
Letzten Sommer, als ich mit meinen Eltern im Urlaub war, haben wir viele nette Leute kennengelernt.

▶ *page 187*

Building on Previous Skills

9 Have students continue this activity by making additional statements based on what they have previously learned.
Example:
Partner A: **In Amerika scheinen weniger Leute zu rauchen.**
Partner B: **Ich habe nicht gewußt, daß amerikanische Restaurants Raucher- und Nichtraucherecken haben. Das finde ich sehr gut.**

✦ For Individual Needs

10 Challenge After students have combined the sentences, have them write a cohesive letter from Hanno to his parents, incorporating all six sentences. This assignment could be started in class and continued as homework.

▣ Multicultural Connection

11 Have a group of students prepare a questionnaire, and then interview an exchange student in your school about his or her first experiences and impressions of the United States. Students should report their findings to the class.

▶ *page 188*

PRESENTATION: Grammatik

• To help students visualize the different uses of coordinating conjunctions and their effects on word order, compare and contrast them by showing examples on the board or a transparency.
• Let students explain how each conjunction is used, i.e. what type of clause it introduces and how it affects the word order.

Building on Previous Skills

12 In Chapter 7 (p. 168) students learned how to elicit agreement, to agree, and to express conviction, uncertainty, and what seems to be true (p. 170). Help students review the expressions by agreeing or disagreeing with the statements in this activity.
Example:
Ein Schüleraustausch ist ideal.
Damit stimm' ich überein. Durch einen Schüleraustausch lernt man das Land und die Leute viel genauer kennen.

Thinking Critically

14 Comparing and Contrasting Once students have completed their collages, have them compare their impressions with those of the German youth in the **Los geht's!** section. Together, identify cliches and stereotypes in both the **Los geht's!** section and the collages.

For Individual Needs

15 Challenge Have each group compose a letter to a German youth magazine in which they address the three questions. The purpose of their letter should be to clarify possible misconceptions Germans might have about Americans.

Teaching Suggestion

16 Before students begin this writing assignment, you may want to review vocabulary and expressions from this **Stufe** that will be helpful to students as they write.

Reteaching: Expressing Surprise, Disappointment, and Annoyance

List the functions from p. 185 on a transparency. Ask students to use them to react to statements German students have made in this **Stufe** about American people.
Example:
Ich war überrascht, daß die deutschen Teenager denken, daß wir wenig für die Umwelt tun.

 ▶ *page 189*

PRESENTATION: Landeskunde

Teaching Suggestion

Begin the **Landeskunde** page by asking students if any of them have ever been or plan to be an exchange student. What did they learn or do they hope to learn through an exchange?

Community Link

Have one or several students contact the local Chamber of Commerce to find out if their town or city has any sister cities. Have them find out when this relationship was established and what type of programs have been developed between the two places. Have students report back to class.

Geography Connection

1 Have students locate Passau, Soltau, and their respective sister cities in an atlas. Then have students compare each American city with its sister city in terms of size and geographic elements.

Social Studies Connection

4 Ask the social studies teacher to come to your class and talk about the number of foreigners residing in the United States.

Teaching Suggestion

4 Put students in groups to answer the last question (**Welche Klischees oder Stereotype hat man von diesen Gruppen?**). Assign one nationality to each group and have them come up with a list of positive and negative images people have of that group. Have each group present its list of stereotypes to the class.

Video Program

In the video clip **Asylanten in Frankfurt,** members of a family from Afghanistan talk about why they sought asylum in Germany. See *Video Guide* for suggestions.

Teacher Note

Mention to your students that the **Landeskunde** will be also included in Quiz 8-1 given at the end of the **Erste Stufe.**

CLOSE

Thinking Critically

Synthesizing Ask students the following question. If they had the opportunity to be an exchange student in Germany, what kind of questions would they ask their host family to get a more objective view of the German people?

Focusing on Outcomes

Refer students back to the learning outcomes listed on p. 181. They should recognize that they now know how to express surprise, disappointment, and annoyance.

ASSESS

• **Performance Assessment** Prepare the following chart for the day you plan to do this activity. Give students a few minutes to think of statements to complete the chart. Call on individual students and ask them to complete a specific part using vocabulary from this **Stufe.**

	über Deutsche	über Amerikaner
Meinung		
Vorurteil		
Klischee		

* Quiz 8-1, *Chapter Resources,* Book 3

Teaching Weiter geht's!
pp. 190-191

Resources for Weiter geht's!

• *Textbook Audiocassette* 4 B
• *Practice and Activity Book*

Teacher Note

Weiter geht's! is recorded on audiocassette.

Weiter geht's! Summary

In **Wie sehen junge Amerikaner die Deutschen?**, students are introduced to some perceptions young Americans have about Germany. The following student outcomes listed on p. 181 are modeled in the episode: expressing an assumption, making suggestions and recommendations, and giving advice.

Motivating Activity

Ask students what impressions they have of Germans and Germany. Discuss briefly with them what comes to their minds and how these impressions were formed.

Thinking Critically

Analyzing Ask students to write down those words from the box that they associate with their image of Germany and its people. Beside each word, ask them to give a reason or explanation for having chosen that characteristic. Discuss these associations briefly with students.

⊹ For Individual Needs

Visual Learners Ask students to study the collage on p. 190. Then have several students take turns interpreting and discussing how Germany and Germans are portrayed here.

Auditory Learners Ask students to keep their books closed as they listen to the statements. Then ask students to recall as many characteristics as they can remember. Have them listen a second time, but this time let them read along in their books.

Teaching Suggestion

Play the tape a third time stopping after each report and asking some key questions to see if students understand the main points in each one.

⊹ For Individual Needs

17 Challenge Ask students if they can think of other clichés they could add to this image of the German people.

Closure

Together, come up with a list of clichés about Germans and Germany. Then have students use what they know about the country and the people to refute some of these clichés in German.

ZWEITE STUFE

Teaching Zweite Stufe, pp. 192-195

Resources for Zweite Stufe

Practice and Activity Book
Chapter Resources, Book 3
- Communicative Activities 8-3, 8-4
- Additional Listening Activities 8-4, 8-5, 8-6
- Student Response Forms
- Realia 8-2
- Situation Card 8-2
- Teaching Transparency Master 8-2
- Quiz 8-2
Audiocassette Program
- *Textbook Audiocassette* 4 B
- *Additional Listening Activities, Audiocassette* 10 A
- *Assessment Items, Audiocassette* 8 A
Video Program, Videocassette 2
Video Guide

▶ page 192

MOTIVATE

Teaching Suggestion

Tell students that they have to plan a day for German visitors who want to tour their town. What would students want the German visitors to see that is representative of their area? What would they want them to know about the town and its people?

TEACH

Teaching Suggestion

After reading the article "**Der sympathische Deutsche,**" ask students to scan the text for positive and negative attributes. Make a list on the board.

Thinking Critically

Analyzing Have students determine what information they would need in order to carefully analyze the results of the study. For example, students might want to know which 17 countries were surveyed and what the ages of those surveyed were. Can students think of reasons why this information could be relevant?

PRESENTATION: Wortschatz

Ask students to think of a person they know who could be described with one or more of the listed adjectives in **auf deutsch erklärt.**

For Individual Needs

18 Challenge Once students have compiled a list, ask them to use some of the characteristics to describe a famous artist, actor, musician, scientist, or political figure. Do all students agree on the same adjectives? If not, why not?

Teaching Suggestion

19 As an advance organizer for this listening activity, ask students to predict phrases that they could expect to hear for each of the five photos.

▶ page 193

For Individual Needs

20 A Slower Pace Students should refer to the **Weiter geht's!** section and to the words listed on p. 190 to help them with this activity. Assist students with any other words they would like to use that are not on the list.

PRESENTATION: So sagt man das!

After you introduce the new expressions, have students look back at Activity 21. Ask students to use the new expressions to introduce their impression about the statements they came up with.
Examples:
Ich vermute, daß nicht alle Deutschen schnelle Autos haben.
Ich hatte mir vorgestellt, daß immer viel Bier in deutschen Haushalten getrunken wird.

Building on Previous Skills

23 Before students begin this partner activity, you may want to review the use of the subordinating conjunction **als** which was discussed on p. 187.

For Individual Needs

23 Challenge As students report to their partner about the various ways in which they had to change their opinions about the Germans, the partner should react to what he or she hears and ask questions so that the monologue becomes a dialogue.

Example:

A: **Ich habe immer geglaubt, daß die Deutschen nur Lederhosen und Dirndlkleider tragen. Aber das ist nicht wahr. Sie tragen alles, was wir tragen.**

B: **Ja, Jeans sind sehr beliebt, auch T-Shirts und Sweatshirts.**

A: **Woher weißt du das?**

B: **Oh, aus Zeitschriften, vom Fernsehen.**

▶ *page 194*

Thinking Critically

24 Analyzing Ask students to watch for news throughout the week that deals with Germany or Germans. Have students bring the article or share the news with the class. Then ask students to examine the news piece by deciding whether **Tatsachen, Vorurteile,** or **Klischees** are part of the information. What phrases or words helped them decide?

PRESENTATION: Grammatik

• Point out that separable prefixes are actual words that can stand by themselves. The inseparable verb prefixes, **be-, ver-, ge-, er-, ent-,** cannot stand alone. The past participles of verbs with inseparable prefixes do not add **ge-**. (Examples: **bekommen, enthalten, gewinnen, vergessen,** and **erraten**) Point out also that verbs with inseparable prefixes are stressed on the verb root, not on the prefix (See the following Teacher Note).

• As mentioned in this summary, there are certain verbs that look like they have separable prefixes, but actually do not. (Example: **überraschen**)

Teacher Note

One major difference between separable and inseparable prefix verbs is the spoken stress. For separable prefix verbs, the stress falls on the first syllable.

<u>an</u>kommen, <u>an</u>gekommen
<u>ein</u>laden, <u>ein</u>geladen
<u>mit</u>nehmen, <u>mit</u>genommen
<u>über</u>setzen, <u>über</u>gesetzt (what a ferry does with passengers)

For inseparable prefix verbs, the stress falls on the root verb.

über<u>rasch</u>en, über<u>rascht</u>
wieder<u>hol</u>en, wieder<u>holt</u>
unter<u>stütz</u>en, unter<u>stützt</u>
über<u>setz</u>en, über<u>setzt</u> (from one language into another)

▶ *page 195*

PRESENTATION: So sagt man das!

• Review some expressions students learned in Level 2 to make suggestions. Here are some expressions students should recognize.
  Ich schlage vor, daß ...
  Du solltest ...

• Ask students to use the new expressions by making a recommendation for their favorite restaurant, book, or movie. Then have students warn their classmates about a vacation destination, a musician, or a new store in town.

 For Individual Needs

26 A Slower Pace You may need to review the command forms of the verbs listed here before doing this activity. Students can also refer to the function box to use the different ways of suggesting, recommending, and warning. Help students find good reasons for doing or not doing the things their partners are trying to convince them to do. List these reasons on a transparency so students can refer to them when speaking with their partners.

ZUM LESEN

Multicultural Connection

27 Have students interview exchange students or go to other language classes to find out about prejudices that exist in other countries. What are some of these prejudices and who or what are they directed at? Have students report back to the class.

For Individual Needs

30 A Slower Pace Discuss the topic in class first, perhaps making a list on the board of ideas and images students now have about Germany.

Reteaching: Verbs with Prefixes

Ask students to illustrate the difference between the following word pairs by using them in sentences.

kaufen / einkaufen
kommen / bekommen
geben / zurückgeben
holen / wiederholen
sich setzen / übersetzen
nehmen / mitnehmen

CLOSE

Total Physical Response

Prepare a list of commands using separable and inseparable prefix verbs. Following are some suggestions.

Könntet ihr bitte diesen Satz mal schriftlich übersetzen!
Beginnt jetzt mit euren Hausaufgaben!
Verabschiedet euch von einer Person in der Klasse, bevor es klingelt!
Verlaßt diese Klasse ganz leise!
Craig, wisch die Tafel ab!
Hier sind Scheren und Lakritze! Kommt nach vorn und schneidet euch ein kleines Stück davon ab!
Wiederholt noch einmal eure Hausaufgaben!
Steck diese Papiere in den braunen Umschlag hinein!

Focusing on Outcomes

Refer students back to the learning outcomes listed on p. 181. They should recognize that they now know how to express an assumption, make suggestions and recommendations, and give advice.

ASSESS

• **Performance Assessment** In preparation for an exchange program with a German school, students are required to describe themselves to potential host families. Give students a few minutes to jot down some notes, then call on individual students to find out how they would describe themselves to a German family.

• Quiz 8-2, *Chapter Resources,* Book 3

Video Program

In the video clip **Ausländer in Berlin,** young Turkish people talk about their lives in Germany. See *Video Guide* for suggestions.

Teaching Zum Lesen,
pp. 196-198

Teacher Note

Sabines Eltern is recorded on *Textbook Audiocassette* 11.

Reading Strategy

The targeted strategy in this reading is interpreting rhetorical devices. Students should learn about this strategy before beginning Question 3.

PREREADING

Motivating Activity

From the byline, the students can see that the author of this selection has a foreign name. Help them see what possible assumptions can be made based on the author's name. (a. The author is a foreigner whose work has been translated into German. b. The author is bilingual or multilingual and has mastered German well enough to write it for publication. c. The author is a native speaker who has foreign relatives and a foreign name.) Ask students how the author's choice of subject matter could differ, depending upon whether the case is a, b, or c. Students can probably use their experiences reading American and world literature as a guide, although it's much more difficult to define what is a "foreign" name in the United States.

READING

Teacher Notes

1a Students should easily recognize that the narrative is in the first person, although the character, Ali, is not named until the sixth paragraph.

3 The rhetorical question **Wie ich bin?** following **Sie liebt mich, wie ich bin** is a repetition that introduces Ali's reflection on why it's so important that Sabine loves him as he is. His answer is somewhat defensive in tone.

4 It may not be obvious to the class that, for Ali, having potential in-laws who love him "as their own son" might be as important as having a girl friend who loves him for himself. You may want to explain this in terms of Ali's culture and the fact that in much of the world a marriage is still an alliance between two families and not just the union of two single people.

5 The narrator drops a number of hints, some of them by protesting too much in the fantasy sequence. (Example: **"Sie liebt mich und ich liebe sie. Nur das zählt und nichts anderes."**) He makes Sabine an only child with no threatening brothers. He and the fantasy parents agree to use the euphemism **nicht-einheimisch** and avoid the word **ausländisch.** The parents say they're ashamed at how kind people are to them when they visit Turkey, but that **"Es ist nicht so einfach"** when Ali criticizes German prejudices against foreigners in Germany; the fantasy is played out against the stark background of rejection.

6 Acceptance by Sabine's uncle completes Ali's "adoption" into this circle of kindly Germans. However, the students need to ask themselves why the uncle and aunt find it necessary to say that they **"bewundern sogar meine Freundin, Mut bewiesen zu haben mit mir [Ali.]"** Does this really lead to the conclusion that no one **"hierzulande"** has anything against foreigners?

Thinking Critically

Evaluating The class may be able to critique several aspects of the story, such as:
a) Ali's 100%-Swabian dream girl has a turned-up nose but Middle-Eastern almond eyes. Is this incongruity deliberate or a slip on the writer's part?
b) Ali says that his dream parents-in-law are particularly fond of vacationing in Turkey, **"das gelobte Land der Touristen."** Is this seeming sarcasm appropriate in the situation?
c) Why does Ali answer Onkel Peter's preferred **du** with the phrase-book response: **Es freut mich, Sie kennenzulernen.**? Are we to read the uncle's address as a put-down? In that case, why does Ali's response (using **Sie**) not bother the uncle?

POST-READING

Teacher Note

Activities 11 and 12 are post-reading tasks that will show whether students can apply what they have learned.

Closure

At the close of Paragraph 1, Ali asks: **"Was machen diese alles-Hasser, wenn Europa eins wird?"** What does a story like *Sabines Eltern* say about the future of the European Union? How would the class answer Ali's rhetorical question?

Answers to Activity 1
a. Ich-Erzähler; b. die Freundin des Erzählers; c. in Deutschland (Schwaben); 20. Jahrhundert (contemporary Germany)

Answers to Activity 2
The narrator is describing how he feels; he used to be a pessimist, but now he's an optimist (**grau, rosarot**); he's in love; **weil ich eben so glücklich bin. Und warum,** will ich auch verraten ...

Answers to Activity 3
She loves him for himself; he's not German, but Turkish.

Answers to Activity 4
Sabine's parents; friendly, he's respected.; they treat him like a son (**Sie lieben mich wie ihren eigenen Sohn.**); they like non-Germans.

Answers to Activity 5
Ali has been dreaming; answers will vary.

ZUM SCHREIBEN

Answers to Activity 6

That there's no such thing as prejudice or racism; the respect and friendship he receives from Sabine's parents and aunt and uncle

Answers to Activity 7

Casts doubt on his belief that there is no racism; answers will vary.

Answers to Activity 8

Cues the reader that something important is going to happen; the plot will take a new turn; Ali wakes up.

Answers to Activity 9

Answers will vary.

Answers to Activity 10

Answers will vary; the response of Sabine's father: her parents don't know him, but they don't like him because he's Turkish; the parents' feelings toward Ali play a central role in Ali's life; answers will vary.

Answers to Activity 11

Answers will vary.

Teaching Zum Schreiben
p. 199
Writing Strategy

The targeted strategy in this writing activity is selecting a point of view. Students should learn about this strategy before beginning the assignment.

PREWRITING
Teaching Suggestions

A1 Students might benefit from a class discussion to help them get ideas for their short story. Students should think of examples of groups that deal with prejudices or conflict due to a lack of knowledge and communication among a group of people.

- Before students start planning their stories, discuss with them the elements of a good story, such as a quickly developed plot and well developed characters.

For Individual Needs

A2 Visual Learners To help students practice describing characters and settings, bring to class several photos of different ethnic groups and their surroundings. Have students focus on observing details in each photo. Students can use similar details in their own descriptions.
Examples:
Die Frau/Der Mann scheint schüchtern und still zu sein.
Die Schlafstätte dieser Familie sieht ganz gemütlich aus.

WRITING
Teaching Suggestions

B Students will still need some guidance during the writing stage. Be available to answer questions and to check students' work informally as they work independently to arrange their notes.

B Remind students that using action verbs and descriptive adjectives can make their story more vivid.

POST-WRITING
Teaching Suggestions

C To help students understand the specific strengths and weaknesses of their final story you may want to use the following grading system.

Creativity	25%
Story development	25%
Consistent point of view	25%
Grammar, spelling, and punctuation	25%

- You may want to collect the final copies of students' stories and compile them in a class book to be displayed in the classroom for any students to read.

Closure

Assign one or two of the best stories for all students to read as homework, then have the class discuss the prejudices displayed in the story and the ways in which they were eliminated.

*U*sing Anwendung,
pp. 200-201

Resources for Anwendung

Chapter Resources, Book 3
- Realia 8-3
- Situation Card 8-3

Video Program, Videocassette 2
Video Guide

Video Program

At this time, you might want to use the authentic advertising footage from German television. See *Video Guide* for suggestions.

Thinking Critically

3 Drawing Inferences Ask students how they think the stereotypes listed in Activity 2 were formed. Why do these clichéd images of girls and boys persist? What are some "modern" stereotypes of girls and boys, women and men, and mothers and fathers?

For Individual Needs

6 A Slower Pace Ask students to read the letter again, this time focusing on Julia Bauer. Have them jot down notes that will give a good description of Julia. Then ask students to differentiate between things we know about Julia (**Tatsachen**) and things we might think about her (**Meinungen**).

Portfolio Assessment

6 You might want to suggest this activity as a written and oral portfolio item for your students. See *Assessment Guide,* p. 21.

Geography Connection

7 To find out if anybody would be interested in an exchange with Julia, ask students to locate Hagen in atlas. (Hagen is located in the **Bundesland** North Rhine-Westphalia, northeast of Düsseldorf and south of Dortmund. It has a population of around 214,000.)

*K*ann ich's wirklich?
p. 202

Teaching Suggestion

This page helps students prepare for the test. It is a brief checklist of the major points covered in the chapter. The students should be reminded that it is only a checklist and not necessarily everything that will appear on the test.

*U*sing Wortschatz,
p. 203

Teaching Suggestion

Ask students to list words from the **Wortschatz** that they might use to talk about their **Deutschlandbild**.

For Individual Needs

Challenge Ask students to work with a partner or in a small group. Have each group or pair of students write the words from this **Wortschatz** that are related to previously learned vocabulary or those for which they can find a synonym. The group with the most correct words wins.
Examples:
der Weg: die Straße, die Gasse
wiedergeben: wiederholen
still: ruhig, leise

For Additional Practice

Have students choose three or four incomplete statements from each **Stufe** and ask them to complete them in a meaningful way.
Example:
Es ärgert mich, wenn ...
... meine Schwester sich CDs von mir nimmt, ohne mich vorher zu fragen.

Game

Play the game **Genau das Gegenteil!** See p. 179F for the procedure.

Teacher Note

Give the **Kapitel 8** Chapter Test, *Chapter Resources,* Book 3.

REVIEW

8

Weg mit den Vorurteilen!

① Es lohnt sich, sich so eine Tiroler Blaskapelle im Gebirge anzuhören.

Was sind Vorurteile (*prejudices*)? Woher kommen sie? Wie kann man seine Vorurteile abbauen? In diesem Kapitel unterhalten sich junge Deutsche und junge Amerikaner über ihre Vorurteile, und wie sie diese teilweise oder sogar ganz abgebaut haben, als sie sich näher kennenlernten.

In this chapter you will learn

- to express surprise, disappointment, and annoyance
- to express an assumption; to make suggestions and recommendations; to give advice

And you will

- listen to students talk about their experiences in America
- read about stereotypes Germans and Americans have about each other's cultures
- write about what you think Germans and Americans are like, and examine those preconceptions
- learn more about how prejudices and stereotypes can be challenged through personal interaction and reflection

② Die meisten von uns hätten nicht gedacht, daß es in Deutschland so viele Blumen gibt.

③ Ich war erstaunt darüber, wie umweltbewußt die Deutschen sind.

Los geht's!

Wie sehen uns die jungen Deutschen?

Was die Deutschen über die Vereinigten Staaten wissen, erfahren sie gewöhnlich durch Presse, Film und Fernsehen, auch durch Reisen in Amerika oder durch Reiseberichte von Freunden und Bekannten. Was sind ihre Eindrücke?

Junge Deutsche, die noch nie in den Staaten waren, sehen die USA so:

Junge Deutsche, die in den Staaten waren, sagen:

„Ich hatte nicht gewußt, daß das Land so groß ist."

„Ich habe gestaunt, wie gut mir das Essen drüben geschmeckt hat — alles frisch und wenig aus Büchsen."

„Es hat mich furchtbar gestört, daß es dort keine Fahrradwege gibt, jedenfalls nicht dort, wo ich war."

„Die meisten Amerikaner sind äußerst hilfreich."

„Es ist unwahrscheinlich, wie wenig die Amerikaner lesen. Die Tageszeitung, ja, aber Bücher?"

„Es hat mich wahnsinnig gestört, daß meine Gastfamilie beim Abendessen ferngesehen hat."

„Mir haben die Lehrer gefallen: der Unterricht ist lockerer als bei uns, weniger stressig."

„Ich war schon etwas enttäuscht, daß viele Städte so schmutzig sind."

„Ich hatte immer gehört, die Amerikaner haben keinen Geschmack; alles ist aus Plastik, künstliche Blumen und so weiter. Aber das stimmt wirklich nicht."

„Ich war erstaunt, wie wenig die Amerikaner über die Bundesrepublik wissen."

„Ich bedaure, daß die Leute zu wenig für die Umwelt tun."

„Ich fand es unangenehm, wie so viele Leute ihren Kaugummi kauen — ich mein', so richtig kauen!"

„Als ich nach Amerika kam, hatte ich ein ganz anderes Amerikabild. Ich hatte starke Vorurteile gegen die Amerikaner, denn ich kannte sie nur als Touristen in Deutschland — laut angezogen, mit der Kamera um den Hals. Ich hatte angenommen, daß alle Amerikaner so sind."

Vier deutsche Schüler, Tanja, Sonja, Michael und Philipp erzählen, wie sie ihre Vorstellungen von den Vereinigten Staaten nach einem kurzen Besuch ändern mußten.

SONJA Also, ich war vier Wochen drüben, in der Nähe von Boston, und ich muß sagen, ich war wahnsinnig begeistert von den amerikanischen Jugendlichen. Sie sind viel herzlicher und offener als wir.

PHILIPP In diesem Punkt geb' ich dir recht. Aber sie wissen nur viel zu wenig über die Deutschen — sie wissen etwas über das Oktoberfest und unsere Autobahnen ...

MICHAEL Na, komm! Das stimmt aber auch nicht immer. Meine Gastfamilie, und insbesondere mein Gastbruder, wußte eine ganze Menge über Deutschland.

TANJA Ich hatte vorher überhaupt keinen Bezug zu Amerika. Ich hatte mir immer gedacht, da will ich überhaupt nicht hin, das interessiert mich gar nicht. Aber dadurch, daß ich einige Leute kennengelernt habe und die so wahnsinnig nett waren, hab' ich ein ganz anderes Verhältnis zu dem Land und zu den Leuten.

MICHAEL Ja, so ein Schüleraustausch ist schon ideal, weil man da mitten in die Familie hineinkommt. Und nur so kann man die Leute richtig kennenlernen, seine eigenen Vorurteile abbauen und seine eigene Meinung bilden.

PHILIPP Das möchte ich unterstützen. Man soll sich auf jeden Fall eine eigene Meinung bilden, bevor man eine fremde wiedergibt.

MICHAEL Ja, genau!

TANJA Ja, ich würd' auch sagen: nehmt keine Klischeevorstellungen an, und verbreitet auch keine! Fahrt in das Land und schaut euch die Leute an! So hab ich's gemacht und mußte sämtliche Meinungen überprüfen, die ich von dem Land und den Leuten hatte.

SONJA Also, hinfahren, alles gut beobachten, Leute kennenlernen! Nur so kann man sich das beste Urteil über ein Land bilden und nicht von dem, was man von andern hört oder im Fernsehen sieht.

TANJA Das ist auch meine Meinung.

1 Hast du alles verstanden?

1. Was meinen die Leute, die noch nie in den Staaten waren? Schaut euch die Collage auf Seite 182 an, und sprecht darüber! Welche sind Klischees, welche nicht?
2. Was meinen die jungen Deutschen, die schon in den Staaten waren?
3. Welche Eindrücke sind positiv, welche negativ? Wieso? Schreib sie in zwei Spalten auf!

6 Wie reagierst du darauf?

Die Deutschen interessieren sich sehr für Amerika, und jeder Deutsche scheint irgendeine Meinung über Amerika und die Amerikaner zu haben. Stimmen die Meinungen? Was überrascht dich, was enttäuscht dich und worüber regst du dich auf? Sag es deinem Partner!

1. Es gibt zu viele Amerikaner, die Vorurteile gegen andere Menschen haben.
2. Die Leute essen zu viel und haben zu wenig Bewegung.
3. Alles wird nur auf die Schnelle gemacht, nichts hat Hand und Fuß.
4. Die Regierung tut nichts für die Armen.
5. Viele Städte sind alt und sollten renoviert werden.
6. Die meisten Leute werden von der Werbung beeinflußt.
7. Die meisten Leute lesen nur den Sportteil in der Zeitung.
8. Das amerikanische Fernsehen bringt einfach zu viel Reklame!
9. Es gibt kein Familienleben.

— Sind diese Blumen künstlich?
— Natürlich!
— Natürlich?
— Nein, künstlich!

7 Für mein Notizbuch

Schreib in dein Notizbuch je drei Sätze über Dinge — in der Schule, zu Hause, auf der Reise — die dich in diesem Jahr überrascht haben, die dich enttäuscht haben und die dich aufgeregt haben! Gib Gründe dafür an!

8 Wie kann man alles beschreiben?

Wenn wir Leute oder Dinge beschreiben, können wir die Intensität unserer Beschreibung variieren. Hier sind einige Wörter links unten, mit denen wir das tun.

a. Such dir eine Partnerin, und füll die Lücke in diesem Satz!

**Die meisten Amerikaner sind ...
hilfreich/naiv.**

b. Frag jetzt deine Partnerin, was sie über Amerika sagen würde! Unten rechts stehen ein paar Ideen.

gar nicht nicht ziemlich
ein bißchen so
sehr besonders ganz
furchtbar zu äußerst
wahnsinnig irre
unheimlich
unwahrscheinlich

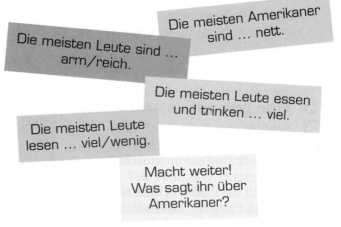

Die meisten Amerikaner sind ... nett.

Die meisten Leute sind ... arm/reich.

Die meisten Leute essen und trinken ... viel.

Die meisten Leute lesen ... viel/wenig.

Macht weiter! Was sagt ihr über Amerikaner?

9 Zwei Austauschschüler unterhalten sich

Zwei deutsche Austauschschüler sprechen über die USA. Spielt die beiden Rollen!

DU **Das Land ist so wahnsinnig groß!**

PARTNER **Das stimmt. Ich hätte ...** *oder*
Ich war sehr erstaunt, wie ...

> Der Unterricht in der Schule ist sehr locker.

> Das Land ist so wahnsinnig groß.

> Sie wissen schon eine ganze Menge über Deutschland.

> Sie haben wenige Klischeevorstellungen von den Deutschen.

> Sie interessieren sich für die Ereignisse in Deutschland.

> Mein Amerikabild hat sich schnell geändert.

> Mit 16 kann man schon den Führerschein bekommen.

Ein wenig *G*rammatik

The subordinating conjunction **als** is generally used with the narrative past (the imperfect) and has the meaning of *when, at the time when.* The **als**-clause can either follow or precede the main clause.

> Ich hatte ein ganz anderes Amerikabild, **als** ich nach Amerika **kam.**
> **Als** ich nach Amerika **kam,** hatte ich ein ganz anderes Amerikabild.

What do you observe about the word order in the main clause when it is preceded by a subordinate clause?

10 Bericht vom Austausch

Hanno schreibt seinen Eltern in Deutschland von seinem Austauschsemester in den USA. Was sagt er? Hilf ihm mit einem besseren Schreibstil, indem du die Sätze unten verbindest!

1. So ein Schüleraustausch ist ideal. (weil) Man kommt mitten in die Familie hinein.
2. Man lernt die Leute richtig kennen. (wenn) Man wohnt bei ihnen längere Zeit.
3. Meine Gasteltern sind erstaunt. (wie) Das Essen schmeckt mir hier gut.
4. Mir gefällt es so gut. (daß) Ich möchte noch ein Jahr da bleiben.
5. Ich seh' mir das Land noch besser an. (bevor) Ich fahre im Juni nach Hause.
6. Ich hatte es mir hier ganz anders vorgestellt. (als) Ich kam nach Amerika.

1. ..., weil man mitten in die Familie hineinkommt.
2. ..., wenn man bei Ihnen längere Zeit wohnt.
3. ..., wie gut mir hier das Essen schmeckt.
4. ..., daß ich noch ein Jahr da bleiben möchte.
5. ..., bevor ich im Juni nach Hause fahre.
6. ..., als ich nach Amerika kam.

11 Bei mir war es auch so

Zwei Austauschschüler unterhalten sich über ihre Amerikareise. Sie haben die gleichen Erfahrungen gemacht. Spielt die beiden Rollen, und gebraucht in jeder Wiederholung einen als-Satz!

PARTNER **Ich bin im August nach Amerika gekommen. Es war furchtbar heiß.**

DU **Stimmt. Als ich im August nach Amerika kam, war es auch furchtbar heiß.**

1. Meine Gastfamilie hat mich vom Flughafen abgeholt (*picked up*). Ich habe sie gleich erkannt (*recognized*).
2. Wir sind nach Hause gekommen, und sie wollten mir gleich alles zeigen.
3. Wir haben dann zu Abend gegessen. Es hat mir furchtbar gut geschmeckt.
4. Am nächsten Tag hab' ich die Umgebung gesehen. Ich war ganz begeistert.
5. Ich bin mit meinem Gastbruder in die Schule gegangen. Die Schüler waren alle sehr nett und freundlich zu mir.

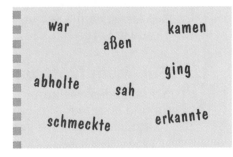

war   kamen
aßen
abholte   ging
sah
schmeckte   erkannte

Grammatik Coordinating conjunctions (Summary)

The conjunctions **denn, und, oder, aber,** and **sondern** are called coordinating conjunctions because they join two independent clauses.

> Ich hatte Vorurteile, **denn** ich kannte die Amerikaner nur als Touristen.
> Ich möchte meine Vorurteile abbauen, **aber** das ist nicht so einfach!

What do you notice about the word order in clauses introduced by coordinating conjunctions? You have also learned that both **weil** and **denn** can be used to introduce a clause expressing cause or reason. But they are significantly different in the kind of word order that follows each. What is this difference?[1]

12 Warum ist das so?

E.g.: 1. ..., weil man da mitten in die Familie hineinkommt.
..., denn da kommt man mitten in die Familie hinein.

Verbinde jedes der folgenden Satzpaare einmal mit „weil" und einmal mit „denn"!

1. Ein Schüleraustausch ist ideal. Man kommt da mitten in die Familie hinein.
2. Man kann die eigenen Vorurteile abbauen. Man lernt die Leute richtig kennen.
3. Man kann seine eigene Meinung bilden. Man macht genügend persönliche Erfahrungen.
4. Man sieht die Leute plötzlich ganz anders. Man hat ein anderes Verhältnis zu ihnen.
5. Man nimmt oft Klischeevorstellungen an. Man war selbst noch nie im anderen Land.
6. Der Unterricht in Amerika gefällt mir. Er ist lockerer und weniger stressig.

13 Gruppenprojekt: Wie sehen wir uns selbst?

Blättert durch eure eigenen Zeitungen und Zeitschriften, und sucht nach Artikeln und Illustrationen, die entweder ein positives oder ein negatives Amerikabild zeigen! Bringt eure Beispiele mit in die Klasse, und macht eine Collage mit diesen Artikeln und Illustrationen! Vielleicht kann einer von euch selbst einige passende Illustrationen machen.

14 Klassendiskussion

Diskutiert über eure Collagen! Was für ein Amerikabild stellen sie dar? Gebt Gründe an! Was zeigen sie, und was zeigen sie nicht? Wie könnten sie noch verbessert werden?

15 Was sagst du dazu?

Überleg dir folgende Fragen, und sag deiner Gruppe, was du dazu meinst!

1. Was sagst du zu Leuten, die nur Vorurteile über die Vereinigten Staaten haben?
2. Mit welchen Eigenschaften würdest du dich und deine Landsleute beschreiben?
3. Was ist deine eigene Meinung über die Amerikaner? Erwähne Tatsachen, Meinungen, sowie Vorurteile, die du gehört hast, aber an die du selbst nicht glaubst!

16 Für mein Notizbuch

Schreib deine Meinung zu dem Thema: „Wie sehe ich uns Amerikaner?"! Führe Tatsachen an und begründe sie! Baue Vorurteile ab, die andere Leute haben und die dich stören! Fang so an: Ich glaube, wir Amerikaner sind ...

---

1. As a subordinating conjunction, **weil** requires verb-last position in the clause. As a coordinating conjunction, **denn** requires verb-second position.

Verständnis für Ausländer?

Auch in einer Welt, die durch die Medien und durch Reisen kleiner geworden ist, gibt es noch immer viele Klischeevorstellungen über andere Länder.

Was kann man tun, um solche Klischees abzubauen? Es ist natürlich am besten, selbst in das andere Land zu fahren. Für junge Menschen bestehen viele Möglichkeiten, sich an Ort und Stelle zu informieren. Da gibt es eine Menge Schüleraustauschprogramme, wo junge Deutsche und junge Amerikaner die Lebensgewohnheiten ihrer Austauschpartner kennenlernen können.

Auch gibt es immer mehr Partnerstädte zwischen verschiedenen Ländern. Das Ziel der Städtepartnerschaften ist es, durch gegenseitiges Kennenlernen (z.B. in kulturellen Veranstaltungen, Sportwettkämpfen oder Jugendgruppen) das Verständnis für einander zu fördern (*encourage*) und alte Klischees abzubauen.

1. Schau die Abbildungen an! Mit welchen Städten haben Passau und Soltau eine Partnerschaft? Weißt du, ob die Schulen in deiner Stadt oder deinem Dorf auch ein Austauschprogramm mit ausländischen Schulen haben? Mit welchen Ländern sind diese Austauschprogramme?
2. Mit welcher Stadt im Ausland würdest du gern ein Austauschprogramm haben? Was würdest du gern über diese Stadt und die Menschen dieses Landes herausfinden?
3. Was für Folgen (*results*) würde ein Austauschprogramm haben? Was meinst du?
4. In der Bundesrepublik muß man nicht unbedingt ins Ausland reisen, um Ausländer kennenzulernen. Der Anteil der Ausländer an der Gesamtbevölkerung, der mit knapp acht Prozent zu den höchsten in Europa gehört, bereichert das kulturelle Spektrum. Millionen von Ausländern — Jugoslawen, Spanier, Italiener, Griechen und vor allem Türken — wohnen und arbeiten in Deutschland. Ihre Kinder gehen auf deutsche Schulen und sprechen Deutsch oft besser als ihre Muttersprache. Welche Klischees oder Stereotypen hat man von diesen Gruppen?

Weiter geht's!

Wie sehen junge Amerikaner die Deutschen?

Junge Amerikaner, die noch nie in Deutschland waren, sehen
die Deutschen gewöhnlich so:

**Die Deutschen werden oft so charakterisiert. Welche Wörter passen
zu deinem Deutschlandbild?**

groß   blond   blauäugig   gutmütig   ordentlich   ernst

freundlich   stolz   streng   stur   kameradschaftlich   stark

still   reserviert   materialistisch   arrogant   athletisch

nett   geduldig   unhöflich   snobistisch   pünktlich   höflich

gemütlich   vorsichtig   gründlich   verwöhnt   intolerant

intelligent   fleißig   musikalisch   ehrgeizig   egoistisch

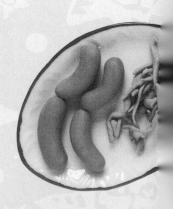

Hier sind einige Aussagen junger Amerikaner, die nach einem kurzen Besuch in den deutschsprachigen Ländern ihre Klischeevorstellungen relativieren mußten. Diese Aussagen wurden übersetzt, weil die meisten Schüler nur wenig oder gar kein Deutsch sprachen.

„Ich weiß nicht warum, aber ich hatte mir vorgestellt, daß die Deutschen in Lederhosen und Dirndlkleidern herumlaufen; aber das stimmt überhaupt nicht; sie sind meistens so angezogen wie wir."

John, 16

„Mir ist aufgefallen, daß die Deutschen die Natur sehr lieben. Überall sieht man Blumen und Pflanzen, drinnen und draußen. Die Deutschen gehen auch viel spazieren. Überall gibt es Spazierwege und Wanderwege!"

Kim, 17

„Ein Klischee ist, daß die Deutschen dick sind, weil sie sehr viel essen, besonders Knödel und Brezeln, auch Bratwurst und Sauerkraut. Ich hab' aber gesehen, daß die Leute auch nicht anders essen als wir; viele achten sogar sehr auf ihre schlanke Linie. Meine Gastfamilie ißt zum Beispiel sehr viel Obst, Gemüse und Joghurt — eine wirklich ausgewogene Kost."

Jessy, 16

„Es hat mich beeindruckt, daß die Deutschen sehr umweltbewußt sind. Sie bringen leere Flaschen in die Geschäfte zurück oder werfen sie in Container, und sie sammeln Papier."

Cathy, 17

„Ich dachte immer, daß die jungen Deutschen viel Bier trinken. Ich habe aber schnell meine Meinung geändert; sie trinken meistens Spezi, Apfelsaft oder Mineralwasser!"

Rich, 17

„Ich war überrascht, daß die Deutschen so tierlieb sind. Ich hab' nie so viele Hunde gesehen wie in Deutschland. Die dürfen sogar mit ins Restaurant gehen, und vor manchen Geschäften hab' ich Behälter mit Wasser gesehen für durstige Hunde. Das würde ich auch unseren Geschäftsleuten empfehlen."

Mandy, 15

„Ich war überrascht, wie friedliebend die Deutschen sind. Es gibt bei ihnen Großdemonstrationen gegen Gewaltanwendung, wenn in der Welt ein weiterer Krieg auszubrechen droht. Daran können sich viele ein Beispiel nehmen!"

Eric, 15

17 Klischees und Tatsachen

1. Was für Klischeevorstellungen haben viele junge Amerikaner, die noch nie in Deutschland waren? — Schreib auf, was für Klischeebilder in der Collage auf Seite 190 zu sehen sind.
2. Wie charakterisieren die jungen Amerikaner, die schon in Deutschland waren, die Deutschen? Stimmst du den Aussagen zu, oder hast du eine andere Meinung? Warum?
3. Was für Klischeevorstellungen hatten diese jungen Amerikaner und wie mußten sie diese nach ihrem Deutschlandbesuch revidieren (*revise*)? Mach deine eigene Liste!

Name	Klischee oder Vorurteil	„neue" Meinung
John, 16	Lederhosen, Dirndl	so angezogen wie wir
Rich, 17	trinken viel Bier	

ZWEITE STUFE

Expressing an assumption; making suggestions and recommendations; giving advice

Der sympathische Deutsche

1993 hat die deutsche Zeitschrift FOCUS eine weltweite Image-Studie gemacht. Mehr als 32 000 Erwachsene in 17 Ländern wurden gefragt, wie sympathisch oder unsympathisch ihnen die Deutschen sind. Das Ergebnis: ein durchweg freundliches Deutschlandbild! „Erfolgreich, fleißig, stark" lautet das Urteil der 17 befragten Nationen, ein Wirtschaftswunderland und Exportweltmeister. Lange stützte sich das deutsche Image einseitig auf diese industrielle Tatsache. Jetzt rundet sich das Bild: „Friedlich", „modern", „demokratisch" wirken die Deutschen der neunziger Jahre. Negative Eigenschaften gibt es jedoch auch. Die Deutschen werden auch von vielen als arrogant, humorlos, gefühlslos und intolerant bezeichnet. Resultat der Untersuchung: Die Welt sieht die Deutschen in weit besserem Licht, als die Deutschen selbst bislang geglaubt hatten.

WORTSCHATZ

auf deutsch erklärt

ehrgeizig wenn man viel plant und erreichen will
stark muskulös, kräftig, kann vieles machen
gutmütig freundlich und hilfsbereit
aufgeschlossen offen, freundlich
friedliebend wenn man keinen Krieg, sondern Frieden will
still ruhig, nicht laut
ordentlich wenn man immer Ordnung macht oder hat
umweltbewußt wenn man etwas zum Schutz der Umwelt tut

auf englisch erklärt

Es ist uns <u>aufgefallen</u>, wie <u>verwöhnt</u> diese Kinder sind. *We've noticed how spoiled these children are.*
Es <u>beeindruckt</u> mich, wenn Eltern <u>streng</u> aber auch <u>geduldig</u> sind. *It impresses me when parents are both strict and patient.*
Ich bin <u>stolz</u> <u>auf</u> meinen <u>höflichen</u> Sohn. *I am proud of my polite son.*
Du bist so <u>stur</u> wie ein Esel. *You're as stubborn as a mule.*

---

18 Eigenschaften — gute und schlechte

Macht in der Klasse eine Liste von Eigenschaften, guten und schlechten! Ihr könnt die aufschreiben, die auf diesen Seiten erscheinen und auch andere dazufügen.

19 Hör gut zu! For answers, see listening script on TE Interleaf.

Was sagen Jugendliche über die Deutschen? Hör gut zu, wie einige amerikanische Schüler ihre Erlebnisse in Deutschland besprechen! Welche Aussage paßt zu welchem Bild?

a.   b.   c.   d.   e.

20 Wie sehen wir die Deutschen?

Kommt jetzt wieder zu einer Brainstorming-Sitzung zusammen! Das Thema heißt diesmal: Wie sehen wir die Deutschen? Gebt Gründe an! Wählt wieder einen Schriftführer, der alle Aussagen aufschreibt. Verwendet Ausdrücke wie:

Die Deutschen sind ...   Ich glaube, daß die Deutschen ...
Nicht alle Deutschen sind ... Ich halte die Deutschen für ...
Einige/viele Deutsche sind ...

21 Tatsachen, Vorurteile, Klischees

Seht euch die Aussagen an, die ihr in der letzten Gruppenarbeit erarbeitet habt!

a. Ordnet jetzt diese Aussagen in drei Gruppen: Tatsachen, Vorurteile und Klischees! Die Deutschen haben/sind ...

Tatsachen	Vorurteile	Klischees
schnelle Autos	arrogant	tragen Lederhosen, Dirndl

b. Diskutiert jetzt darüber! Äußert eure Meinung und gebraucht dabei Ausdrücke wie:

Das stimmt (nicht). Ich glaube, daß ...   (Jessica) hat recht, wenn sie sagt, daß ...
Ich denke, daß ...   In diesem Punkt geb' ich dir (nicht) recht.

SO SAGT MAN DAS!
Expressing an assumption

To make an assumption or introduce an impression, you know these phrases:

   Ich glaube schon, daß ...
   Ich meine doch, daß ...

Other phrases you can use to make an assumption or introduce an impression are:

   Ich nehme an, daß ...
   Ich vermute, daß ...
   Ich hatte den Eindruck, daß ...
   Ich hatte mir vorgestellt, daß ...

22 Hör gut zu! For answers, see listening script on TE Interleaf.

Schüler erzählen, wie sie sich Deutschland und die Deutschen vorstellen. Schreib mindestens fünf Eindrücke auf, die diese Schüler erwähnen!

23 Hast du deine Meinung geändert?

Wie hast du dir am Anfang Deutschland und die Deutschen vorgestellt? Sag einem Partner deine Vorstellung! Dann sag ihm, ob du deine Meinung geändert hast! Erkläre ihm auch warum! Tauscht dann die Rollen aus!

BEISPIEL   **Ich hatte mir immer vorgestellt, daß die Deutschen ...**
                     Aber das stimmt überhaupt nicht. (Als ich in Deutschland war ...)

leben, um zu arbeiten   sind militaristisch   essen viel Fleisch und wenig Gemüse

sind nicht umweltbewußt   sind unfreundlich   tragen nur Lederhosen und Dirndl

haben keinen Humor   trinken immer nur viel Bier   mögen keine Hunde

24 Und du? Woher bekommst du deine Informationen?

Such dir eine Partnerin! Überlegt euch, wie man sich ein Bild von anderen Ländern und anderen Leuten macht, während ihr folgende Fragen beantwortet!

1. Woher bekommst du deine Informationen über die deutschsprachigen Länder? Unten sind einige Möglichkeiten aufgelistet.
2. Wie würdest du die Informationen charakterisieren, die du im Fernsehen über Deutschland erhältst?
3. Warum kommt es vor, daß Medien manchmal Vorurteile verstärken oder wenigstens nicht schwächen? Nenne Beispiele!

vom Fernsehen · vom Radio · von Zeitungen/Zeitschriften · aus Büchern · von Spielfilmen · aus dem Deutschunterricht · aus dem Geschichtsunterricht · von den Eltern · von Freunden/Bekannten · selbst dort gewesen

---

𝒢rammatik Verbs with prefixes (Summary)

1. Some of the most common separable prefixes are: **an, ab, ein, mit, zu, zurück;** also, the words that involve motion, **hin** and **her,** or combinations of these, such as **hinein, heraus, herum.** Compare and contrast the sentences. Explain the differences in the verb forms.

    (**ankommen**) Ich **kam** im August in den Vereinigten Staaten **an.**
    (**einladen**) Meine Gastfamilie **lädt** mich noch immer **ein.**
    (**abbauen**) **Bau** endlich mal deine Vorurteile **ab!**
    (**abholen**) Wer hat dich am Flugplatz **abgeholt?**
    (**mitnehmen**) Wir haben ihn doch auf die Reise **mitgenommen.**
    (**anrufen**) Mein Gastbruder hatte alle Freunde **angerufen.**

2. Of course, when such infinitives are used with **zu,** they get separated by **zu.**
    (**kennenlernen**) Ich hoffe, die Leute besser **kennenzulernen.**

3. There is another category of verbs with prefixes, called inseparable prefix verbs. Compare and contrast the sentences. How are the verb forms different?

    (**überraschen**) Das **überrascht** mich überhaupt nicht.
    (**wiederholen**) **Wiederhole** bitte deine Frage!
    (**übersetzen**) Das hast du wirklich prima **übersetzt!**
    (**unterstützen**) Versuch doch mal, mich zu **unterstützen.**

---

25 Hör gut zu!

For answers, see listening script on TE Interleaf.

Schüler erzählen von ihren Erfahrungen mit deutschen Jugendlichen in Deutschland. Welches sind Empfehlungen und welches sind Warnungen?

Name	Empfehlung	Warnung
Dorothee		
Christian		

SO SAGT MAN DAS!

Making suggestions and recommendations; giving advice

There are different ways to make suggestions and recommendations, and to give advice. Note how the command forms are used in these examples.

To make a suggestion or a recommendation, you can say:

Ich kann dir einen Tip geben: fahr nach Deutschland!
Ich empfehl' dir, selbst einmal nach Deutschland zu fahren.
Es lohnt sich, einen Schüleraustausch mitzumachen.
Fahr selbst mal hin! **Hinfahren!** **Leute kennenlernen!**

To give advice, you can say:

Verbreite keine Klischees!
Wiederhole bloß nicht eine fremde Meinung!

26 Was rätst du deinem Freund?

Ein guter Freund von dir will nach Deutschland fahren, aber du findest, daß er viele Vorurteile hat. Unten ist eine Liste mit Dingen, die dein Freund tun soll. Versuche, ihn zu überreden (*convince*), daß er deinem Rat folgt, bevor er wegfliegt!

> DU **Ich kann dir einen Tip geben, verbreite keine Klischees!**
> PARTNER **Ja, und warum denn (nicht)?**
> DU **Die Leute werden denken, daß alle Amerikaner Klischees verbreiten!**

keine Klischees verbreiten   sich eine eigene Meinung bilden   Vorurteile abbauen/haben

die Leute genau beobachten   einen Schüleraustausch mitmachen

27 Zum Überlegen und Diskutieren

Diskutiert mit euren Klassenkameraden über folgende Fragen!

1. Was für Vorurteile haben manche Deutsche gegen Ausländer und warum?
2. Wißt ihr von ähnlichen Situationen, vielleicht wo du wohnst, wo Vorurteile anderen Menschen gegenüber existieren? Was sind diese Vorurteile?
3. Warum bestehen Vorurteile? Was würdet ihr empfehlen, um Vorurteile abzubauen?

28 Klassenprojekt: Unser Deutschlandbild

Arbeitet an euerm Deutschlandbild! Sammelt Informationen aus Zeitungen und Zeitschriften, und fügt diese zu einer Collage zusammen! Wenn ihr wollt, könnt ihr euer Projekt erweitern und ein Österreichbild und ein Schweizbild erarbeiten.

29 Diskussion

Diskutiert über eure Collage, was sie zeigt, was sie nicht zeigt und wie sie noch verbessert werden könnte! Welche Images informieren? Welche Images verbreiten Klischees?

30 Für mein Notizbuch

Beschreibe dein jetziges Deutschlandbild! Überleg dir, was für Klischeevorstellungen und Vorurteile du hattest und warum du sie vielleicht geändert hast!

Sabines Eltern

O Mann, bin ich glücklich! Ich strahle im ganzen Gesicht. Könnte alle Menschen umarmen. Ja, ich würde sogar fliegen, wenn ich es nur könnte. Meine Freude kennt keine Grenzen, seit ein paar Wochen. Plötzlich entdecke ich meine Liebe für Blumen. Ich wußte gar nicht, daß sie so herrlich duften können. Die Welt sieht auf einmal auch ganz anders aus. Sie ist doch nicht grau in grau. Die Welt ist rosarot. Ich bin so unendlich glücklich. Pessimist bin ich nun auch nicht mehr. Seit vier Wochen bin ich ein großer Optimist geworden. Man muß einfach alles positiv sehen. Die Stadt stinkt nicht mehr nach Autoabgasen, und das Ozonloch wird schon wieder werden. Die Wälder, die werden mit Sicherheit wieder gesund — die Umweltheinis malen Bilder, die übertrieben sind. Diese unsere Welt ist noch so gut

intakt wie ein Mensch mit 17 Jahren. Wie gesagt, ich sehe alles positiv. Weil ich eben so glücklich bin. Und warum, will ich auch verraten: Ich bin verliebt. Jawohl. Ich habe jetzt eine Freundin, die mich liebt, wie ich bin. Wie ich bin? Eigentlich bin ich ein ganz normaler Mensch. Nur, ich bin kein Inländer. Dafür ist meine Freundin eine Deutsche. Und nicht nur das. Sie ist zudem noch Schwäbin. Durch und durch. Was aber nichts aussagt. Sie liebt mich und ich liebe sie. Nur das zählt und nichts anderes. Wir sehen uns fast jeden Tag. Wenn wir uns auch nur einen einzigen Tag nicht sehen, kommt es mir so vor, als ob ich sie eine kleine Ewigkeit nicht mehr gesehen hätte. Ich liebe sie über alles. So sehr, daß ich den ganzen Tag fast nur an sie denke. Sie ist so wunderschön. Die Mandelaugen schauen mich so an, daß ich beinahe ohnmächtig werde. Und ihre Stupsnase gibt es nur einmal. Diese Nase, diese Nase. Alles an ihr ist einmalig. Auch ihre Eltern! Wie jeder Mensch hat auch meine Freundin Eltern. Aber was für liebe Leute! Sie lieben mich wie ihren eigenen Sohn. Und vielleicht mehr. Wenn ich mit meiner Freundin zu ihren Eltern gehe, stehen sie sogar kurz auf, um mich zu begrüßen. Immer wieder laden sie mich zum Essen ein. Weil sie nur ein Kind haben, sitzen wir zu viert am Tisch. Nach dem Essen spielen wir verschiedene Spiele. Bei einem Pilsbier sprechen wir anschließend über die Probleme der nicht-

---

LESETRICK

Interpreting rhetorical devices When reading a story or essay that seems to be addressed directly to you — the reader — it's helpful to note rhetorical questions and exclamations. A question is *rhetorical* when it has no real answer or if its answer is obvious. Authors sometimes use rhetorical questions and exclamations to make their point more dramatically or to say something about their own doubts or prejudices. Think of these devices as invitations to get involved in the author's thought processes.

Getting Started

1. Read the title and the first paragraph, up to **Wir sehen uns fast jeden Tag.**
   a. In welcher Person wird die Geschichte erzählt?
   b. Schau den Titel an! Was meinst du, wer Sabine ist?
   c. Wann und wo spielt die Handlung ab? In welchem Land? In welchem Jahrhundert?
2. Read the first part again. What is happening? How has the narrator's view of the world changed in the previous few weeks? (Notice the colors he mentions.) What is the reason for this change? Identify the connecting

einheimischen Leute, um nicht Ausländer zu sagen. Es gibt jedesmal andere Themen. Wen wunderts? Die Eltern meiner Freundin mögen die Nicht-Einheimischen. Natürlich auch mich. Sie waren schon so oft im Ausland. Vor allem in meiner Heimat. In der Türkei. Das gelobte Land der Touristen. Sie erzählen, wie herzlich und freundlich sie empfangen wurden. Jedesmal. Immer wieder. Sie haben sich schämen müssen, sagen sie mir. Ich erwidere aber, daß sie sich nicht zu schämen brauchen. Ich sage, es sollen sich die schämen, die blind alles und jedes hassen, was nicht einheimisch ist. Ausländische Autos, ausländische Waren und auch ausländische Menschen. Es ist nicht so einfach, sagen sie mir. Sie haben recht, denke ich. Was machen diese alles-Hasser, wenn Europa eins wird?

Manchmal kommen Sabine, so heißt übrigens meine Freundin, und ihre Eltern zu uns nach Hause. Meine Eltern mögen sie auch sehr. Meine Mutter kocht türkisch. Das Essen ist für Sabines Eltern nichts Neues. Aber sie essen trotzdem gerne unsere Spezialitäten. Danach trinken sie natürlich Cay, also Tee. Es ist ein Muß. Meine Freundin und ich amüsieren uns unheimlich, wenn unsere Eltern versuchen, miteinander zu sprechen. Es ist ein wenig mühsam, aber zum Schluß verständigen sie sich doch. Ich wünsche mir, daß alle Menschen hier so miteinander leben. Nicht nur unsere Familien.

words which indicate the cause-and-effect relationship.

3. What does the narrator mention about the way his girlfriend loves him? Why would this be important?

4. Finish reading the first paragraph. On whom does the narrator focus? What kind of relationship does he have with these people? Support your answer with expressions from the text. What attitude do these people have toward non-Germans?

5. Finish reading the story. What is the unexpected twist? Were you surprised by the ending? If not, did you notice any clues that foreshadowed the ending?

A Closer Look

6. Read the story again more carefully. In the fourth paragraph, what does Ali become convinced of? What has led him to believe this?

7. Now read the fifth paragraph. What is the function of the rhetorical question here? What effect does repeating **nein** have? Are you convinced of what Ali is saying or made more skeptical?

8. What function does the word **plötzlich** serve at the beginning of the sixth paragraph? What happens at this point in the story?

9. Retell the story in your own words. Pay careful attention to how the plot develops. (Look at your answers to questions 2, 6, and 8.)

Wieder einmal bin ich bei ihren Eltern eingeladen. Mit leeren Händen will ich nicht hingehen. Ich kaufe einen schönen großen Strauß. Ich klingle, ihre Mutter macht die Tür auf. Wie immer, werde ich höflich hereingebeten. Wir essen, trinken und danach, auch wie fast immer, spielen wir etwas zusammen. Kaum haben wir angefangen, da klingelt es an der Haustür. Herein kommen Sabines Onkel und Tante, väterlicherseits. Als sie mich, zum erstenmal übrigens, sehen, sind sie sehr überrascht. So schauen sie mich jedenfalls an. Ich versuche, höflich zu wirken, stehe auf und grüße sie. Ich bin irgendwie unsicher. Was denken diese Leute über mich? Sind die Nicht-Einheimischen auch ihnen sympathisch? Oder mögen sie sie vielleicht gar nicht? Was wird nun geschehen? Was wird er sagen? »Guten Tag, ich heiße Peter. Wie heißt du?« fragt Sabines Onkel mich lächelnd. Ich bin sehr erleichtert.

»Mein Name ist Ali«, sage ich. »Es freut mich, Sie kennenzulernen«, füge ich hinzu.

Danach sitzen wir, diesmal zu sechst, am Tisch und spielen weiter. Sabines Onkel scheint ein sehr netter Mensch zu sein. Sie bewundern sogar meine Freundin, Mut bewiesen zu haben mit mir. Es ist spät in der Nacht, als sie gehen. Auch sie laden mich zu sich nach Hause ein. Ich freue mich unendlich. Langsam fange ich an zu glauben, daß eigentlich niemand hierzulande etwas gegen Ausländer hat. Sabines Eltern mögen mich, ihr Onkel konnte mich auf Anhieb leiden.

Also was soll das Gerede vom Rassismus? Sowas gibt es doch in meiner zweiten Heimat nicht. Ich lächle und sage immer wieder: nein, sowas gibt es hier nicht. Nein, Antisemitismus gibt es auch nicht. Nein, Herrgott nochmal, das gibt es nicht.

Plötzlich klingelt mein Wecker. Tut, tut, tut. Ich hatte einen schönen Traum. Ich habe von meiner Freundin Sabine geträumt. War irgend etwas passiert? Weil ich abergläubisch bin, rufe ich meine Freundin an. Es ist sieben Uhr morgens. Ihr Vater geht ans Telefon.
»Ich bin's, Ali. Ich möchte bitte mit Sabine sprechen«, sage ich.
Eine unfreundliche Stimme schreit mich an:
»Ich habe Ihnen doch schon einmal gesagt, daß Sie uns nicht anrufen sollen. Lassen Sie uns und meine Tochter in Ruhe.«
Ich habe eine Freundin. Sie heißt Sabine. Ihre Eltern habe ich noch nie gesehen ...

Mustafa S.

10. How do you think Ali feels after the telephone call? What causes him to feel this way? Why do you think the story is entitled *Sabines Eltern*? In your opinion, what is the main idea of the story?

11. Ergänze die Geschichte mit einem neuen Schluß, der der Wirklichkeit entspricht! Wo und wie oft treffen sich Ali und Sabine? Wissen ihre Eltern davon? Wie fühlt sich das junge Paar? Wie ist ihr Verhältnis zur Gesellschaft, in der sie leben?

12. Schreib nach dem folgenden Muster ein Gedicht darüber, wie man sich als Außenseiter fühlt!

a noun	(*the subject of poem*)
two adjectives	(*describing the subject*)
three verbs	(*actions associated with the subject*)
one sentence	(*expressing an emotion or idea about the subject*)
a noun	(*restating the subject in a different way*)

As you have seen in this chapter, prejudices can arise from a lack of knowledge about others. If we could know what others feel and think, we would probably be surprised at how much they are like us, and we would be better able to avoid prejudice. In this activity, you will write a fictional short story about an event that brought people in different groups together and changed their opinions of one another.

Es waren einmal zwei Gruppen …

Schreib eine fiktive Kurzgeschichte von zwei Gruppen, die eines Tages zusammenkommen und die durch diese Begegnung ein besseres Verständnis zueinander finden! Erzähl was passiert, was die Hauptfiguren denken und wie sie ihre Vorurteile abbauen!

A. Vorbereiten

1. Entwickle eine Idee für deine Geschichte! Denke an Gruppen, die traditionelle Vorurteile gegeneinander haben, wie zum Beispiel Männer und Frauen, Ausländer und Einheimische, Cowboys und Indianer, usw.
2. Erfinde Charakterrollen für die Geschichte! Wie heißen sie? Wie alt sind sie? Wie sehen sie aus? Was denken sie von den anderen? Wie sprechen sie? Stelle auch den Handlungsraum (*setting*) der Geschichte fest!
3. Überleg dir die Handlung und den Konflikt für die Geschichte!
4. Wähle jetzt eine Perspektive, aus der die Geschichte erzählt wird (erste Person oder dritte Person)! Denk an die verschiedenen Charakterrollen und an die Handlung, und entscheide dich, ob du die Gedanken von allen oder nur von einem wiedergeben willst!

B. Ausführen

Benutze deine Notizen, um einen ersten Entwurf der Geschichte abzufassen! Verwende sowohl Dialog als auch Beschreibung, um die Eigenschaften der Hauptfiguren zu entwickeln!

C. Überarbeiten

1. Lies deine Geschichte noch einmal durch! Hast du die Geschichte aus ein und derselben Perspektive erzählt? Streiche alle Sätzen durch, die die Erzählperspektive ändern!
2. Denk an die Handlung und die Charakterrollen! Ist die Handlung interessant? Hast du den Konflikt schnell entwickelt und in den Vordergrund gestellt? Bist du mit dem Schluß zufrieden? Paßt der Dialog der Hauptfiguren zu ihrer Wesensart?
3. Prüfe jetzt deinen Stil! Hast du die Zeitformen konsequent eingehalten? Wenn du die Vergangenheit gewählt hast, hast du „**als**" richtig benutzt? Hast du ab und zu Nebensätze verwendet, um den Satzbau zu variieren?
4. Hast du alles richtig buchstabiert? Hast du Kommas richtig gesetzt?
5. Schreib die korrigierte Geschichte noch einmal ab!

> **SCHREIBTIP**
>
> **Selecting a point of view** In most of what you have written so far, you have used the first person point of view, relating feelings and experiences from your personal vantage point. When writing fiction, however, you have more choices, including *first person,* in which the "I" of the story does not represent you; *third person limited,* in which the narrator focuses on the thoughts and feelings of one character; and *third person omniscient,* in which the narrator knows all the thoughts of all the characters. The point of view you choose to use affects the story because it establishes what can be perceived and determines which details can be included. Whichever point of view you select, be sure to remain consistent throughout your story.

1. For answers, see listening script on TE Interleaf.

1 Jeden Tag kann man im Radio die Sendung „Kurz notiert" hören. Man liest kurze Meldungen aus Zeitungen und Zeitschriften vor. Hör jetzt gut zu! Welche Schlagzeile unten paßt zu welcher Meldung? Schreib einige Notizen für jede Schlagzeile, damit du anschließend über die Meldungen diskutieren kannst. Welche Klischeevorstellungen sind zu erkennen? Diskutier mit deinen Klassenkameraden darüber!

Ohne Mutter geht es nicht   **Amerika für junge Mädchen**

Jobs — immer noch   **Ein partnerschaftlicheres**
nach traditioneller Manier   **Leben im Kommen**

Wie alt ist zu alt?

2 Es gibt viele Vorurteile, wenn es zum Thema Mädchen und Jungen kommt. Diese Wörter sollen zum Nachdenken und Diskutieren anregen. Sieh dir die Wörter im Kasten an, und schreib dann die Eigenschaften in zwei Spalten auf!

Mädchen/Jungen

3 Was ist typisch Mädchen? Was ist typisch Junge? Vergleiche deine Liste mit denen deiner Klassenkameraden! Denkt an andere Eigenschaften, die mit Mädchen und Jungen verbunden werden, und schreibt sie hinzu!

4 Mach eine Umfrage! Du kannst mit einem Partner arbeiten. Frag deine Klassenkameraden und auch Schulkameraden nach ihren Interessen und Hobbys! Schreib deine Ergebnisse in eine ähnliche Tabelle wie in Übung 2, Mädchen und Jungen, aber diesmal mit Tatsachen und nicht nur Stereotypen!

5 Kennst du Leute, die nicht zu den Klischeebildern von Mädchen/Jungen, Frauen/Männern passen? Beschreibe diese Personen!

6 Wer als Austauschschüler in ein anderes Land gehen will, muß nicht unbedingt an einem Austauschprogramm teilnehmen. Man kann sich auch an Verwandte oder Bekannte wenden. Anke Weber war im vorigen Jahr als Austauschschülerin in den USA. Von den Webers hat Julia Bauer die Adresse einer amerikanischen Bekannten, die auch Deutsch kann. Lies Julias Brief an Frau Weiß!

Hagen, den 3. April

Liebe Frau Weiß,

Vor ein paar Tagen fragten wir die Webers nach einer amerikanischen Familie, die eventuell ein deutsches Mädchen aufnehmen würde, da wir dachten, daß Anke uns vielleicht weiterhelfen könnte. Herr Weber gab uns dann Ihre Adresse, in der Hoffnung, daß Sie uns helfen könnten. Deshalb wende ich mich jetzt an Sie.

Ich heiße Julia und bin 16 Jahre alt. Da ich hier ziemlich weit von der Stadt entfernt lebe, würde ich es begrüßen, in den USA etwas näher an einer Stadt zu wohnen, wobei die Wohnlage eigentlich das Unwichtigste ist. Die Hauptsache für mich wäre eine nette Familie. Ganz toll fände ich es, wenn die Familie einen Teenager in meinem Alter hätte, damit ich leichten Anschluß zu Gleichaltrigen finden könnte.

Ich möchte entweder für 3 oder 6 Monate in den USA bleiben. Ich wäre sehr an einem Austausch interessiert. Wenn dies nicht möglich ist, würden wir meinen Aufenthalt natürlich bezahlen.

In meiner Freizeit spiele ich sehr gern Tennis. Außerdem mag ich auch Tiere unheimlich gern. Ich wäre sehr glücklich, wenn Sie eine nette Familie für mich ausfindig machen könnten. Im voraus bedanke ich mich schon recht herzlich bei Ihnen. Hoffentlich sind Sie erfolgreich!

Viele Grüße
Ihre Julia Bauer

7 Setzt euch in Gruppen zusammen und diskutiert Julias Brief! Kennt ihr eine Familie für Julia? Ist eine von euren Familien geeignet? Warum?

8 Du findest, daß deine Familie für die Julia geeignet ist, oder du kennst eine Familie für sie. Schreib einen Brief an Julia und erzähle davon! (Wenn du keine Familie kennst, erfinde eine!)

9

R O L L E N S P I E L

Zwei Klassenkameraden spielen die Rollen von deinen Eltern.
1. Du möchtest gern Julia zu euch einladen. Erzähle deinen Eltern davon und versuche, sie zu überzeugen! (*convince*)
2. Du möchtest gern ein Jahr als Austauschschüler in Deutschland verbringen. Du bittest deine Eltern um Erlaubnis. Sie stellen Fragen und du versuchst, sie zu überzeugen.

1 How would you express your surprise at hearing that a friend of yours wrote a novel?   E.g.: **Ich habe nicht gewußt, daß du einen Roman geschrieben hast.**

2 How would you express your disappointment
a. if your school's team didn't win?   E.g.: **Ich bedaure, daß unsere Mannschaft nicht gewonnen hat.**
b. if your teacher said to you **Wir haben keine Austauschschüler aus Deutschland bekommen**?   E.g.: **Ich bin enttäuscht, daß wir keine Austauschschüler aus Deutschland bekommen haben.**

3 How would you respond if someone annoyed or displeased you by reinforcing stereotypes?   E.g.: **Es ärgert mich, daß du denkst, Amerikaner essen nur Fast food.**

4 How would you express the following assumptions?   a. E.g.: **Ich vermute, daß deutsche Wagen alle sehr gut sind.**
a. **Deutsche Wagen sind alle sehr gut.**
b. **Viele Deutsche haben ihr Amerikabild vom Fernsehen.**
b. **Ich nehme an, daß viele Deutsche ihr Amerikabild vom Fernsehen haben.**

5 How would you say that before you started studying German, you had the impression all German people drank beer?
Ich hatte mir vorgestellt, daß alle Deutschen Bier trinken.

6 How would you recommend to someone
a. that he or she learn German?   a. E.g.: **Ich empfehl' dir, Deutsch zu lernen.**
b. that he or she visit Germany, Switzerland, and Austria?
b. E.g.: **Es lohnt sich, Deutschland, die Schweiz und Österreich zu besuchen.**

7 How would you advise a friend not to skip class?
E.g.: **Schwänz bloß nicht die Schule!**

ERSTE STUFE
EXPRESSING SURPRISE

Ich hätte nicht gedacht ...
I wouldn't have thought ...
Es ist unwahrscheinlich ...
It's improbable ...
Ich war erstaunt, ... *I was surprised ...*
Ich habe gestaunt, ... *I was amazed ...*
Ich habe nicht gewußt, ...
I didn't know ...
Ich war überrascht, daß ...
I was surprised that ...

EXPRESSING DISAPPOINT-MENT

Ich finde es schade, daß ...
I think it's too bad that ...
Ich bin enttäuscht, daß ...
I am disappointed that ...

EXPRESSING ANNOYANCE OR DISPLEASURE

Es regt mich auf, wenn ... *It irritates me when ...*

Es stört mich, daß ... *It disturbs me that ...*
Es ärgert mich, wenn ... *It annoys me when ...*
Ich finde es unangenehm, wenn ... *I think it's unpleasant when ...*

OTHER USEFUL WORDS

die Autobahn, -en *interstate highway*
Bezug haben zu *to have a connection to*
die Büchse, -n *can*
auf jeden Fall *in any case*
der, die Jugendliche, -n *teenager*
der Kaugummi *chewing gum*
das Klischee, -s *cliché*
Menge: eine ganze Menge *quite a lot*
in der Nähe von *in the vicinity of*
in diesem Punkt *in this matter*
das Urteil, -e *judgement*
die Vorstellung, -en *impression, image*

der Weg, -e *path*
als (conj) *when, at the time*
äußerst *highly*
herzlich *heartfelt*
hilfreich *helpful*
insbesondere *particularly*
jedenfalls *in any case*
künstlich *artificial*
laut *loud*
locker *easygoing*
nett *nice*
offen *open*
sämtlich *all*
stressig *stressful*
begeistert von *to be excited about*

abbauen (sep): **Vorurteile abbauen** *to overcome prejudices*
annehmen (sep) *to assume*
beobachten *to observe*
kauen *to chew*
überprüfen *to double-check*
verbreiten *to spread*
wiedergeben (sep) *to repeat*

ZWEITE STUFE
MAKING ASSUMPTIONS

Ich hatte den Eindruck ...
I had the impression ...
Ich hatte mir vorgestellt ...
I had imagined ...
Ich nehme an, daß ... *I assume that ...*
Ich vermute, daß ... *I suppose that ...*

MAKING SUGGESTIONS AND RECOMMENDATIONS

Ich kann dir einen Tip geben: ...
I can give you a tip: ...
Ich empfehl' dir ... *I recommend ...*
Mach das selbst! *Do that yourself!*
Es lohnt sich, das zu machen.
It's worth doing.

OTHER USEFUL WORDS

ausgewogen *well-balanced*
dick *fat*
durstig *thirsty*
ehrgeizig *ambitious*
friedliebend *peace-loving*
geduldig *patient*
gutmütig *good-natured*
höflich *polite*
kameradschaftlich *friendly*
ordentlich *orderly*
pünktlich *punctual*
stark *strong, robust*
still *quiet*
stolz sein auf (acc) *to be proud of*
streng *strict*
stur *stubborn*
tierlieb *animal-loving*
umweltbewußt *environmentally conscious*
im voraus *beforehand*

der Behälter, - *container*
der Container, - *recycling bin*
das Dirndl, - *traditional costume for females*
die Gewalt *violence*
die Pflanze, -n *plant*

abholen (sep) *to pick up*
auffallen (sep) *to be conspicuous*
beeindrucken *to impress*
empfehlen *to recommend*
drohen *to threaten*
relativieren *to qualify, make less absolute*
übersetzen *to translate*
verwöhnen *to spoil, pamper*

Kapitel 9: Aktiv für die Umwelt!

	FUNCTIONS	GRAMMAR	CULTURE	RE-ENTRY
Los geht's! pp. 206-207	Für eine saubere Umwelt, *p. 206*			
Erste Stufe pp. 208-211	•Expressing concern, *p. 208* •Making accusations, *p. 209* •Offering solutions, *p. 210* •Making polite requests, *p. 211*	Subjunctive forms of **können, müssen, dürfen, sollen,** and **sein,** *p. 210*	Environmental concerns, *pp. 208, 209*	•Adjective endings, *p. 208* •**Daß**-clauses, *p. 208* •**Wenn**-clauses, *p. 209* •**Weil**-clauses, *p. 209* •**Sollen,** *p. 209* •**Könnte**-forms, *p. 210* •**Würde**-forms, *p. 211*
Weiter geht's! pp. 212-213	Die Umwelt AG diskutiert: Umwelttips für Schüler, *p. 212*			
Zweite Stufe pp. 214-218	•Saying what is being done about a problem, *p. 215* •Offering solutions, *p. 216* •Hypothesizing, *p. 217*	•The passive voice, present tense, *p. 215* •Use of a conjugated modal verb in the passive, *p. 216* •Conditional sentences, *p. 217*	Landeskunde: Ein umweltfreundlicher Einkauf, *p. 219*	•**Würde**-forms, *p. 214* •**Könnte**-forms, *p. 214* •**Werden,** *p. 215* •Environment vocabulary, *p. 216* •Subjunctive forms, *p. 217*
Zum Lesen pp. 220-222	**Die Welt gehört allen!** Reading Strategy: Interpreting statistics			
Zum Schreiben p. 223	**Als Kanzler würde ich alles ändern!** Writing Strategy: Analyzing your audience			
Review pp. 224-227	•Anwendung, *p. 224* •Kann ich's wirklich? *p. 226* •Wortschatz, *p. 227*			
Assessment Options	**Stufe Quizzes** •*Chapter Resources,* Book 3 Erste Stufe, Quiz 9-1 Zweite Stufe, Quiz 9-2 •*Assessment Items, Audiocassette* 8 A			**Kapitel 9 Chapter Test** •*Chapter Resources,* Book 3 •*Assessment Guide,* Speaking Test •*Assessment Items, Audiocassette* 8 A **Test Generator, Kapitel 9**

Chapter Overview

RESOURCES Print	RESOURCES Audiovisual
	Textbook Audiocassette 5 A
Practice and Activity Book	
	Textbook Audiocassette 5 A
Practice and Activity Book *Chapter Resources*, Book 3 • Communicative Activity 9-1 • Communicative Activity 9-2 • Additional Listening Activity 9-1 .... • Additional Listening Activity 9-2 .... • Additional Listening Activity 9-3 .... • Student Response Forms • Realia 9-1 • Situation Card 9-1 • Teaching Transparency Master 9 1 .... • Quiz 9-1 .... *Video Guide*	*Additional Listening Activities, Audiocassette* 10 A *Additional Listening Activities, Audiocassette* 10 A *Additional Listening Activities, Audiocassette* 10 A *Teaching Transparency* 9-1 *Assessment Items, Audiocassette* 8 A *Video Program*, Videocassette 2
Practice and Activity Book	*Textbook Audiocassette* 5 A
Practice and Activity Book *Chapter Resources*, Book 3 • Communicative Activity 9-3 • Communicative Activity 9-4 • Additional Listening Activity 9-4 .... • Additional Listening Activity 9-5 .... • Additional Listening Activity 9-6 .... • Student Response Forms • Realia 9-2 • Situation Card 9-2 • Teaching Transparency Master 9-2 .... • Quiz 9-2 .... *Video Guide*	*Textbook Audiocassette* 5 A *Additional Listening Activities, Audiocassette* 10 A *Additional Listening Activities, Audiocassette* 10 A *Additional Listening Activities, Audiocassette* 10 A *Teaching Transparency* 9-2 *Assessment Items, Audiocassette* 8 A *Video Program*, Videocassette 2
Chapter Resources, Book 3 • Realia 9-3 • Situation Card 9-3 *Video Guide*	*Video Program*, Videocassette 2

Alternative Assessment

• Performance Assessment
Teacher's Edition
  Erste Stufe, p. 203K
  Zweite Stufe, p. 203N

• Portfolio Assessment
  Written: **Anwendung,** Activity 7, *Pupil's Edition*, p. 225; *Assessment Guide*, p. 22
  Oral: **Anwendung,** Activity 5, *Pupil's Edition*, p. 225; *Assessment Guide*, p. 22
• **Notizbuch,** *Pupil's Edition*, pp. 211, 218

Kapitel 9: Aktiv für die Umwelt!
Textbook Listening Activities Scripts

For Student Response Forms, see *Chapter Resources,* Book 3, pp. 142-145.

Erste Stufe
Activity 4, p. 208

JULIA Also, mir macht am meisten Angst, daß die Müllberge so wahnsinnig wachsen. Manchmal denke ich, daß wir eines Tages in unserem eigenen Müll ersticken! Ich finde es blöd, daß so viele Industrieländer heutzutage in einer Wegwerfgesellschaft leben. Vieles, was man in den Supermärkten kauft, ist zwei- oder dreimal verpackt. Das macht es sehr schwierig, den Müllberg zu verkleinern. Bei uns am Stadtrand gibt es eine riesige Müllkippe. Wenn man sieht, wie viele Lastwagen dort jeden Tag hinfahren, dann bekommt man es schon mit der Angst zu tun. Ich finde, jeder sollte versuchen, in seinem eigenen Haushalt den Müll zu reduzieren. In meiner Familie versuchen alle, möglichst wenig Müll zu produzieren. Wir kaufen nur Pfandflaschen und fast nur Produkte mit dem Grünen Punkt und dem Blauen Engel drauf. Außerdem nehmen wir immer einen Korb und ein paar Stoffbeutel zum Einkaufen mit, damit wir keine Plastiktüten beim Einpacken brauchen. Am Ausgang im Supermarkt schmeißen wir die extra Verpackungen von den Produkten, die wir gekauft haben, in die Tonnen. Dann brauchen wir nämlich den Müll erst gar nicht mit nach Hause zu schleppen. Ich find' das zwar gut, daß die Supermärkte gesetzlich verpflichtet sind, diese überflüssigen Verpackungen zurückzunehmen, aber der Müllberg wird dadurch noch lange nicht reduziert! Ich finde, die Regierung soll noch mehr und vor allem strengere Gesetze machen, damit die Müllberge verkleinert werden.

HELGA Ich fürchte, daß die Regierungen einfach zu wenig gegen die Umweltverschmutzung unternehmen. Die Industrien in der ganzen Welt tragen wahnsinnig zur Umweltverschmutzung bei, aber es gibt einfach nicht genug Gesetze, um das Problem zu lösen. Also, nehmen wir doch zum Beispiel mal die Produkte mit dem FCKW. Obwohl man wußte, daß sie umweltschädlich sind, hat es einige Jahre gedauert, bis die Produktion mit FCKW verboten wurde. Ich fürchte, daß die Industriekonzerne halt zu mächtig sind und einen zu großen Einfluß auf die Regierung haben. Die FCKW-Produktion wurde auch erst verboten, als die Industrien einen Ersatzstoff gefunden hatten. Da kann man mal sehen, was für eine politische Sache das Ganze ist! Ich fürchte wirklich, daß manchen Regierungen der industrielle Wohlstand wichtiger ist als die Umwelt! Ich habe in letzter Zeit sehr viel über das Ozonloch gelesen. Das wird immer größer. Ich finde, daß nicht nur ein paar Regierungen Gesetze zum Umweltschutz erlassen sollten, sondern es müßte Gesetze zum Umweltschutz geben, die weltweit gültig sind! Alle Regierungen müßten sich daran beteiligen! Ich würde dafür kämpfen, wenn ich Politikerin wäre.

PETER Ich möchte nach der Schule Forstwirtschaft studieren. Ich interessiere mich sehr für die Natur und gehe viel hier bei uns in Greifswald wandern. Also, mir macht das Waldsterben sehr große Sorgen. Wenn das so weitergeht, dann haben wir bald keine gesunden Bäume mehr in Deutschland! Neulich hat man untersucht, wie groß die Waldschäden in Deutschland sind. Es wurde festgestellt, daß es hier bei uns in Mecklenburg-Vorpommern die größten Waldschäden gibt. 62 Prozent der Bäume sind krank! Das macht mich selbst ganz krank, wenn ich das höre! Der saure Regen und die Luftverschmutzung sind hauptsächlich daran schuld. Wir wohnen ganz in der Nähe von einer Chemiefabrik, und ich könnte mir vorstellen, daß die bestimmt eine ganze Menge Gift in die Luft pumpen. Und das Gift wird von den Bäumen aufgenommen und verdrängt andere Nährstoffe, die lebenswichtig für die Erhaltung der Bäume sind. Eigentlich könnte man viel mehr unternehmen, um die Natur vor der Luftverschmutzung zu schützen. Als allererstes sollte man weniger Auto fahren und mehr Fahrgemeinschaften bilden. Außerdem sollte die Regierung die öffentlichen Verkehrsmittel viel billiger machen und das Benzin teurer machen.

Answers to Activity 4

Julia: Die wachsenden Müllberge machen ihr Angst. / Sie schlägt vor, daß jeder in seinem eigenen Haushalt den Müll reduzieren sollte und daß die Regierungen mehr Gesetze machen sollen, um die Müllproduktion zu verkleinern.

Helga: Fürchtet, daß die Regierungen zu wenig gegen Umweltverschmutzung tun; fürchtet, daß Industriekonzerne zu mächtig sind und großen Einfluß auf die Regierungen haben; fürchtet, daß manchen Regierungen der industrielle Wohlstand wichtiger ist als die Umwelt. / Schlägt vor, daß es Gesetze zum Umweltschutz geben sollte, die weltweit gültig sind.

Peter: Das Waldsterben macht ihm große Sorgen. / Er schlägt vor, daß man weniger Auto fahren sollte und mehr Fahrgemeinschaften bilden sollte; er schlägt vor, daß die Regierung die öffentlichen Verkehrsmittel billiger machen sollte und das Benzin teurer machen sollte.

Activity 8, p. 210

RADIOANSAGER Fühlen Sie sich öfters müde und schlapp? Merken Sie, wie häufig Sie das Auto nehmen, um zum Einkaufen zu fahren, auch wenn der Supermarkt gleich um die Ecke ist? In unserer modernen Industriegesellschaft treiben die Menschen immer weniger Sport. Es ist bekannt, daß man sich wenig leistungsfähig fühlt, wenn man sich nicht ausreichend körperlich bewegt. Der Deutsche Fahrradclub gibt Ihnen Anregungen, wie Sie sich und unsere Umwelt gesund erhalten können. Entdecken Sie Ihr Fahrrad wieder! Holen Sie es aus dem Keller, aus der Garage, aus dem Schuppen! Machen Sie mit bei einer der beliebtesten Sportarten der Deutschen: dem Radeln! Radeln Sie allein oder mit einem Freund auf dem Tandem! Radeln Sie im Verein oder mit der Clique! Sparen Sie Benzinkosten! Vermeiden Sie monatliche Gebühren für aerobische Fitneßkurse! Genießen Sie wieder die Natur! Vergessen Sie die ärgerliche Parkplatzsuche! Beteiligen Sie sich nicht an der Umweltverschmutzung, die durch Autoabgase verursacht wird! Tragen Sie zur Erhaltung der sauberen Luft bei! Erledigen Sie Ihre Besorgungen und Besuche im Umkreis mit dem Rad! Sie werden sich wundern, wie Sie sich schon nach kurzer Zeit wieder schwungvoll, fit und aktiv fühlen werden! Radeln ist angesagt!

Answers to Activity 8

Possible answers: weil man müde und schlapp ist; weil es eine der beliebtesten Sportarten der Deutschen ist; weil man Benzinkosten sparen kann; weil man keine monatlichen Gebühren für Fitneßkurse ausgeben muß; weil man die Natur genießen kann; weil man keinen Parkplatz suchen muß; weil man sich nicht an der Umweltverschmutzung beteiligt, die durchs Autofahren verursacht wird; weil man zur Erhaltung der sauberen Luft beiträgt; weil man sich wieder schwungvoll, fit und aktiv fühlen wird

Zweite Stufe
Activity 17, p. 215

1. Mehr Durst?—Mehr Flaschen!—Mehrwegflaschen!!!
2. Bilden Sie Fahrgemeinschaften! Damit Deutschlands Luft sauber bleibt!
3. Müllberge von heute sind die Zukunft von morgen!
4. Rauf aufs Rad! Rein in die Natur!
5. Haben Sie schon Bekanntschaft mit dem Blauen Engel gemacht?
6. Umweltbewußtsein und Verantwortung durch Recycling!

Activity 19, p. 215

MONI Du, Rolf, ich finde, wir haben schon eine ganze Menge in der Umwelt AG gelernt. Die Beckenbauer macht das wirklich gut!

ROLF Ja, auch mein Interesse an Umweltschutz ist deutlich gestiegen, seit ich in der Umwelt AG bin, Moni.

ULLA Tja, also ich bin erstaunt, wieviel wir hier in Deutschland schon für den Umweltschutz gemacht haben. Ich wußte gar nicht, daß wir ein Beispiel für andere Länder sind.

MONI Siehst du, Ulla! Und du hattest zuerst keine Lust, bei der Umwelt AG mitzumachen!

ULLA Na ja, aber ich bin echt geschockt, wie viele andere Länder einfach gar nichts für die Umwelt tun. Man sollte sich echt mal dafür engagieren, daß in diesen Ländern endlich was getan wird!

MONI Ja, Ulla, mich hat es auch geschockt, was wir da in der Umwelt AG gelernt haben. Aber weißt du, eigentlich bin ich der Meinung, daß man sich zuerst für seine eigene Umgebung einsetzen soll. Ich glaube, es gibt genug, was noch hier zu verbessern wäre.

ROLF Moni hat recht. Es reicht einfach nicht, nur Glas und Papier zum Container zu bringen.

ULLA Was meinst du, sollten wir noch tun?

ROLF Wir sollten darauf achten, daß wir hauptsächlich Sachen aus Recyclingmaterial kaufen! Hier, schaut mal! Meine Schulhefte zum Beispiel, die sind alle aus wiederverwertetem Altpapier. Viele Leute mögen keine recycelten Sachen, weil sie die Qualität nicht so gut finden. Ich finde, man kann der Umwelt zuliebe ruhig auf einiges verzichten.

ULLA Ja, ich bin deiner Meinung! Ich benutze auch nur Briefpapier, das recycelt ist.

MONI Also, mir ist die Verwendung von Mehrwegflaschen wichtig. Wenn ich unsere Einkäufe für zu Hause erledige, kaufe ich immer Milch in Mehrwegflaschen.

ULLA Ich kaufe immer Joghurt in Glasfläschchen. Ich finde die Plastikbecher verursachen einen zu großen Müllberg.

MONI Ja, und außerdem lassen sich nicht alle Plastiksorten recyceln. Bei Glas ist das kein Problem. Das bringt man einfach zum Container. Glas wird dann verflüssigt und zu neuen Produkten geformt.

ROLF Du mußt halt nur Joghurt kaufen, der in Plastikbehältern ist, die man recyceln kann. Die haben doch den Grünen Punkt drauf! Der ist ganz leicht zu erkennen. Zu Hause sammeln wir den Plastikmüll getrennt. Ich find's toll, daß man Plastik einschmelzen kann, um daraus wieder neue Produkte zu machen.

MONI Tja, also warum sprechen wir nicht das nächste Mal in der Umwelt AG darüber, was wir sonst noch alles außer recyceln tun könnten?!

ULLA Gute Idee!

Answers to Activity 19

Schulhefte: aus wiederverwertetem Altpapier
Briefpapier: recycelt
Milch: in Mehrwegflaschen
Joghurt: in Glasfläschchen (Glas kann man zum Container zum Recyclen bringen)
Joghurt: in Plastikbechern mit dem Grünen Punkt (wiederverwertbares Plastik kann man vom restlichen Müll sortieren, damit es recycelt werden kann)

Activity 23, p. 218

1. ARMIN Wir sortieren den Müll zu Hause und bringen Glas, Plastik und Papier in die Recycling-Container. Ja, und dann gehöre ich einer Umweltschutzgruppe an unserer Schule an. Wir haben uns dafür eingesetzt, daß Aluminium- und Altpapiercontainer auf dem Schulhof aufgestellt wurden. Außerdem haben wir den Hausmeister erfolgreich davon überzeugt, daß es umweltfreundlicher ist, Getränke in Mehrwegflaschen zu verkaufen und nicht mehr in einzelnen Dosen oder so. Er ist jetzt auch ganz umweltbewußt geworden und hat sogar vorgeschlagen, daß jedes Getränk zehn Pfennig weniger kostet, wenn die Schüler ihr eigenes Glas oder ihren eigenen Becher mitbringen.

2. MARIA Es macht mich echt immer traurig, wenn ich vom Waldsterben höre. Diese ganzen Autoabgase sind mit an der Luftverschmutzung schuld! Ich finde, man sollte nicht so viel Auto fahren. Ich hab' auch gar keine Lust, mir ein Auto zu kaufen oder den Führerschein zu machen, wenn ich 18 werde! Ich fahre weiterhin mit dem Fahrrad oder gehe zu Fuß. Nur wenn's regnet, dann nehme ich halt den Bus.

3. FELIX Ich gehöre einer Jugendgruppe an, die sich für den Umweltschutz engagiert. Einmal in der Woche sammeln wir Müll vom Straßenrand und von Kinderspielplätzen auf. Also, ich kaufe sehr viele Sachen aus recyceltem Papier, also Hefte und Schreibblöcke für die Schule, Briefpapier und natürlich auch Toilettenpapier und so.

4. TANJA Ich kaufe grundsätzlich nur Produkte mit dem Grünen Punkt oder dem Blauen Engel drauf. Außerdem achte ich darauf, daß ich solche Produkte, die einen wahnsinnigen Verpackungsmüll hinterlassen, erst gar nicht kaufe. Und wenn es sich nicht vermeiden läßt, also wenn ich doch mal was brauche, was tausendfach verpackt ist, dann lass' ich auf jeden Fall den Müll im Laden zurück.

Answers to Activity 23

1. Armin: sortiert Müll; bringt Glas, Plastik und Papier in Recycling-Container; gehört einer Umweltschutzgruppe an; hat sich mit der Gruppe dafür engagiert, daß der Schulhof Alu- und Altpapier-Container bekommen hat; hat mit der Gruppe den Hausmeister überzeugt, nur noch Mehrwegflaschen beim Getränkeverkauf zu benutzen
2. Maria: will kein Auto kaufen; fährt mit dem Rad oder geht zu Fuß
3. Felix: gehört einer Gruppe an, die sich für den Umweltschutz engagiert; sammelt mit der Gruppe Müll vom Straßenrand und von Kinderspielplätzen; kauft Sachen aus recyceltem Papier
4. Tanja: kauft nur Produkte mit dem Grünen Punkt oder dem Blauen Engel drauf; kauft keine Produkte, die eine große Verpackung haben; läßt Verpackungsmüll im Laden zurück

Anwendung
Activity 2, p. 224

THOMAS Hallo, alle zusammen! Ich heiße Thomas Burghofer und bin Mitglied der Umwelt AG hier an der Schule. Wir, das heißt ein Team von fünfzehn Schülern, treffen uns meistens ein- oder zweimal pro Woche, um Aktionen gegen Umweltverschmutzung zu besprechen, zu organisieren und durchzuführen. Manche von euch kennen uns sicherlich schon. Wir waren es, die vor einigen Monaten die Recycling-Container im Schulhof aufgestellt haben. Fast jeden Tag sehen wir im Fernsehen Berichte über Naturkatastrophen, verseuchte Landstriche, über das Waldsterben, über die Verschmutzung der Weltmeere und so weiter und so fort. Die Liste kann beliebig lang fortgesetzt werden. Oft fragen wir uns, was wir eigentlich dagegen tun könnten und sind ganz frustriert, wenn wir feststellen, wie wenig Einfluß wir auf den weltweiten Umweltschutz haben. Nun, es mag zwar sein, daß wir nichts gegen solche riesigen Umweltkatastrophen tun können. Aber ihr könnt sicher sein, daß jeder einzelne, der hier sitzt, einen Beitrag für die Umwelt leisten kann, der unser Umfeld und unsere Umgebung, in der wir leben, entscheidend verbessern kann!
Eins der schlimmsten Probleme ist die Luftverschmutzung durch Abgase von Autos und von der Industrie. Was könnt ihr dagegen tun? Fahrt mit dem Fahrrad oder geht zu Fuß! Öffentliche Verkehrsmittel sind eine andere gute Alternative.
Ein anderes Problem in unserer Gesellschaft ist der wachsende Müllberg. Nehmt Stoffbeutel und Körbe zum Einkaufen mit, und lehnt Plastiktüten an der Kasse ab! Schleppt Verpackungsmüll nicht mit nach Hause, sondern laßt ihn in den Läden! Die Industrie ist gesetzlich dazu verpflichtet, den Müll, den sie mit Verpackungsmaterial produziert, wieder zurückzunehmen.
Jeder von uns produziert Müll. Es ist fast unvermeidbar. Sortiert euren Müll! Bringt Glas, Altpapier, Plastik, Aluminium und Batterien in die entsprechenden Container, damit alles wiederverwertet oder fachgerecht entsorgt werden kann! Zeigt umweltfreundliches Verhalten bei eurem Pausensnack! Packt eure Pausenbrote nicht jeden Tag in Plastik- oder Aluminiumfolie ein! Nehmt Behälter, die sich auswaschen und wiederverwenden lassen! Kauft eure Getränke in Mehrwegflaschen, nicht in einzelnen Dosen, die weggeschmissen werden!
Vermeidet beim Einkauf umweltschädliche Produkte, die sich nicht im Hausmüll entsorgen lassen! Kauft, zum Beispiel, keine Tintenkiller, die mit gefährlichen Chemikalien getränkt sind!

Answers to Activity 2

Possible answers: mit dem Fahrrad fahren; zu Fuß gehen; öffentliche Verkehrsmittel benutzen; Stoffbeutel und Körbe zum Einkaufen nehmen; Plastiktüten ablehnen; Verpackungsmüll im Laden lassen; Müll sortieren; Müll in Container bringen; Pausensnack in wiederverwendbare Behälter einpacken; Getränke in Mehrwegflaschen kaufen; keine schädlichen Produkte kaufen

Kapitel 9: Aktiv für die Umwelt!
Projects and Games

PROJECT

Students will organize an Adopt-a-Classroom campaign for which they will initiate concrete tasks to help alleviate the environmental concerns with which a typical class might be faced on a daily basis. Students offer ideas through posters, slogans, and practical realia.

Materials Students may need poster board, scissors, markers, boxes, and glue or tape.

Suggested Sequence

1. Students decide to work in pairs or small groups.
2. Each pair or group approaches a teacher or class they would like to adopt. Students could also adopt a common area such as the cafeteria, the library, custodial services, or administrative offices.
3. Students take notes as they examine the problems and needs of the classroom or area on which they plan to work.
4. Students make an outline of the ideas they have for the room.
5. Students then prepare a plan of action which they discuss with the teacher of that class.
6. Students plan and lay out their posters, leaving space for catchy slogans.
7. After all projects are completed, students share and discuss them in class.
8. The final project is then taken to the designated classroom and presented to that teacher and class.

Grading the Project

Suggested point distribution (total = 100 points)
  Appearance of project/Originality 40
  Accuracy of language   30
  Oral presentation   30

GAME

Antworten jagen

This game, which was first introduced in Level 1 (Scavenger Hunt, p. 291F), can be easily adapted to this chapter and its vocabulary.

Preparation Compile a list of items or cues that will help students review the vocabulary from this chapter. This list will become the "scavenger list."

Procedure Give a copy of the list to each pair or group of students. Determine a time limit in which students can search for things or answer the questions on their lists. The group that has provided the most correct answers and gathered the most items when time is called wins.

Examples:
Wie viele Mülleimer gibt es in dieser Klasse?
Wo befindet sich der Container für Recyclingpapier auf dieser Etage?
Findet eine leere Aludose, und bringt sie zur Klasse!
Wo befindet sich der große Abfallcontainer der Schule?

Kapitel 9: Aktiv für die Umwelt!
Lesson Plans, pages 204-227

CHAPTER OPENER

Teacher Note

Before you begin the chapter, you may want to preview the *Video Program* and consult the *Video Guide*. Suggestions for integrating the video into each chapter are given in the *Video Guide* and in the chapter interleaf. Activity masters for video selections can be found in the *Video Guide*.

*U*sing the Chapter Opener,
pp. 204-205

Motivating Activity

Take a walk with students around school grounds and discuss in German how environmentally friendly the school is. In which areas does the school excel, and which areas could be improved? Have students take notes.

Community Link

① Have students find out where the recycling stations are in their area and what materials their neighborhoods recycle.

Thinking Critically

② **Drawing Inferences** Ask students what they think is meant by **Solarkaffee.** How might "solar" coffee be different from regular coffee?

Teaching Suggestions

② Ask students to think of some ways solar energy is or can be used as an energy source. (Examples: suntea, calculators, hot water and heating for homes)

③ Have students name the materials from the list in "**Mach mit!**" that are typically recycled in the United States.

③ Have students describe current environmental issues that concern them. (**Welche derzeitigen Umweltprobleme haltet ihr für wichtig?**)

Focusing on Outcomes

Have students preview the learning outcomes listed on p. 205. Ask them what the people in the photographs might be saying that represents each function. (Example: In Photo 1 the people might be talking about what is being done about a problem: "**Diese Flaschen werden mehrmals benutzt.**") **NOTE:** These outcomes are modeled in **Los geht's!** (pp. 206-207) and **Weiter geht's!** (pp. 212-213) and evaluated in **Kann ich's wirklich?** (p. 226).

*T*eaching Los geht's!
pp. 206-207

Resources for Los geht's!

• *Textbook Audiocassette* 5 A
• *Practice and Activity Book*

Teacher Note

Los geht's! is recorded on audiocassette.

Los geht's! Summary

In **Für eine saubere Umwelt,** adolescents talk about environmental concerns and offer some solutions to the problems. The following student outcomes listed on p. 205 are modeled in the episode: expressing concern, making accusations, offering solutions, and making polite requests.

Motivating Activity

Ask students to name one way they and their families help reduce air pollution. (**Was tut eure Familie gegen Luftverschmutzung?**)

Teaching Suggestion

Play the recording of the introduction and then of each report. Have students follow along in the text. Follow each segment with questions to check comprehension. Explain new vocabulary and concepts, including those given in the footnotes, by paraphrasing in German. After working through the four reports, play all of them again. Then ask what they all have in common. Continue with the two long reports on p. 207, again working on one at a time and checking students' understanding of the key points.

Background Information

In 1987, the *Montreal Protocol on Substances that Deplete the Ozone Layer* mandated that CFC use be reduced. In 1990, it was strengthened by requiring that CFCs be phased out completely by the year 2000.

Teaching Suggestion

FCKW (**Fluor-Chlor-Kohlenwasserstoff**), or CFCs are mentioned in Julia's statement. Can students think of some common uses for CFCs? (Examples: coolants for air conditioning and refrigerators, part of foam insulation, spray cans)

Cooperative Learning

Assign small groups of three or four students to do Activities 1 through 3 as a cooperative learning activity within a specific amount of time. Group members should be responsible for one of the three tasks: leader/reader, recorder, and reporter. Upon completion of the assignment, call on the reporters from each group to share their answers and ideas with the rest of the class.

For Individual Needs

A Slower Pace To help students get started doing the tasks, ask for volunteers to begin the list for Activities 1 and 2. Put answers on a transparency and discuss them with the class.

Closure

Ask students about ad campaigns that direct their attention toward environmental concerns. What are some of the slogans? (Example: *Don't be a litter bug!*)

Teaching Erste Stufe,
pp. 208-211

▶ *page 208*

MOTIVATE

Game

Prepare a **Kreuzworträtsel** for students using previously learned vocabulary that is related to the environment. Following is a list of words students should know.

Putzmittel *cleaning agent*
Müll *garbage*
wiederverwenden *to recycle*
Mehrwegflasche *refund bottle*
Altpapier *recycled paper*
Lärm *noise*
Luft *air*
sauber *clean*
schmutzig *dirty*
Umwelt *environment*

ERSTE STUFE

TEACH

Video Program

In the video clip **Umweltprobleme**, residents of Würzburg tell what they do for the environment. See *Video Guide* for suggestions.

PRESENTATION: Wortschatz

- Present some of the new vocabulary by bringing to class items such as detergent, a plastic bag, and a paper bag. Show these items as you present the words.
- Ask questions in which the new vocabulary is incorporated.
  Examples:
  Kennt ihr Leute, die in einer Fahrgemeinschaft sind?
  Was benutzt deine Familie beim Einkaufen, Papier- oder Plastiktüten?

PRESENTATION: So sagt man das!

Have students look over the **Los geht's!** reports on pp. 206-207 and find all phrases that express fear or concern. Then have them make up some additional sentences on their own, reporting what concerns young Germans have.

For Additional Practice

4 After students have listened to the conversations and made some notes, ask them if they agree or disagree with each suggestion and if they could offer other suggestions.

▶ *page 209*

Teaching Suggestion

5 Students may need help expressing the reasons given in the **warum?** box in complete sentences. You might first want to practice these with students.
Examples:
Es gibt zu wenige Fahrgemeinschaften.
Leute kaufen zu viele Produkte, die nicht abbaubar sind.

PRESENTATION: So sagt man das!

Present the new function to students. Make sure they recognize that the dative case is used in the idiomatic expression **schuld sein an**.

❖ For Individual Needs

6 Challenge See if students can come up with more excuses to explain why they don't do more to prevent pollution. Write the additional excuses on a transparency so students can include them in their conversations.
Examples:
Warum soll ich das machen? Andere Leute machen das auch nicht!
Dafür werden Leute bezahlt. Das mache ich nicht umsonst!

▶ *page 210*

Group Work

7 Divide students into groups of three and have each group chart or diagram the sources of the various environmental problems. Each group should work on a large piece of construction paper and write their ideas with markers. Then have each group share the information with the rest of the class.

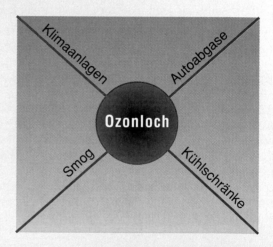

PRESENTATION: So sagt man das!

- Have students explain why modal verbs are used with this type of expression. (They help convey the speaker's feeling or attitude.)
- Remind students that modals have a range of meaning and that the meanings can be quite different from the way the corresponding English modal is used.
Examples:

Wenn wir nur Papierbeutel gebrauchen dürften!

If only we could use paper bags!

Man müßte nur noch Katautos bauen!

They should (would have to) only build cars with catalytic converters!

PRESENTATION: Grammatik

- Remind students that they have already learned the subjunctive forms **hätte** and **würde** in Level 2 (Chapter 11) and the **könnte**-forms in Level 3 (Chapter 5).
- The forms of these modals are the same as the narrative past forms except that **können, müssen,** and **dürfen** retain the umlaut from the infinitive. **Sein** adds an umlaut to the imperfect form and -**e** in the first and third person singular.

▶ **page 211**

For Individual Needs

9 A Slower Pace Have students respond using simple sentences.
Examples:
Wir müßten Fahrgemeinschaften bilden.
Wir sollten keine Plastiktüten benützen.

For Additional Practice

9 Encourage students to come up with additional suggestions to help improve the environment.
Examples:
Nur Produkte kaufen, die umweltfreundlich sind
Kein FCKW benutzen
Keine Aludosen kaufen

PRESENTATION: So sagt man das!

Remind students that they already know one way of expressing polite requests by using **möchte.** Explain that this is also a subjunctive form, stemming from **mögen.** On the board or a transparency, make a list of four sentences expressing polite requests. Ask students if they can detect different degrees of politeness or different "registers" of speech.
Examples:
Ich möchte bitte einen Papierbeutel.
Könnte ich bitte einen Papierbeutel haben?
Dürfte ich bitte einen Papierbeutel haben?
Würden Sie mir bitte einen Papierbeutel geben?

For Individual Needs

10 Kinesthetic Learners Have students role play this activity. They should use pictures or actual products as props. One student takes on the role of the salesperson who offers the products listed. Another student plays the customer who declines the product and requests one that is not harmful to the environment.

Teaching Suggestion

12 In preparation for the journal entry, ask students to complete the statement **Ich wünschte, ...,** using a modal verb in the subjunctive. Have them express their environmental concerns.
Examples:
Ich wünschte, man müßte mit dem Fahrrad zur Schule fahren.
Ich wünschte, die Cafeteria dürfte nur Gläser und Teller und kein Plastikgeschirr verwenden.

CLOSE

Multicultural Connection

Have students interview foreign exchange students or people they know from other countries. They should try to find out about the environmental problems that other countries face and the types of solutions that have been successful.

Focusing on Outcomes

Refer students back to the learning outcomes listed on p. 205. They should recognize that they now know how to express concern, make accusations, offer solutions, and make polite requests.

ERSTE STUFE

ASSESS

- **Performance Assessment** Ask students to come up with ideas to improve the environment in and around their school.

- Quiz 9-1, *Chapter Resources*, Book 3

*T*eaching Weiter geht's!
pp. 212-213

Resources for Weiter geht's!

- *Textbook Audiocassette 5 A*
- *Practice and Activity Book*

Teacher Note

Weiter geht's! is recorded on audiocassette.

Weiter geht's! Summary

In **Die Umwelt AG diskutiert: Umwelttips für Schüler,** students hold their weekly meeting for their environmental club. They discuss some articles they have brought to the meeting. The following student outcomes listed on p. 205 are modeled in the episode: saying what is being done about a problem, offering solutions, and hypothesizing.

Motivating Activity

Ask students if there are activities in their school in which students participate to help the environment. What do they do and what else could be done? (**Wie könnte man unsere Schule umweltfreundlicher machen? Könnte noch mehr getan werden?**)

Background Information

- Federal and state agencies, the community, and the schools in Germany are doing a great deal to educate people about the environment and encourage everyone to take part in protecting it. Students receive instruction, do projects, make posters, and organize events such as forest and river cleanups. Students are very conscious of such things as air and water pollution, damage to the ozone layer, and the impact of the vanishing rain forests.
- The political party **die Grünen** emerged in 1983 when it won seats in the German **Bundestag** for the first time. This political party's platform is based on environmental protection.

Teacher Note

Tintenkiller is a type of pen that students in Germany use to erase mistakes they make while writing with a fountain pen. After the **Tintenkiller** is used to erase a mistake, a special marker, usually on the other end of the **Tintenkiller,** is used to correct the mistake.

Thinking Critically

Comparing and Contrasting Ask students what types of tourist activities could be considered **Sanfter Tourismus.** (Examples: going on a bike tour, visiting a solar-powered resort) What types of activities could not be considered **Sanfter Tourismus?** (Examples: skiing, hunting, driving cross-country)

Building on Previous Skills

13 In Level 2, students learned several reading strategies to help them determine the meaning of a text. In this case, the titles of the three articles are very important, in that they give the main idea. Ask students to find supporting details for each title and to write them down. Then put students in pairs or groups of three and have them compare their findings.

For Individual Needs

14 Visual Learners Have students use their articles to make a bulletin board display. They could also bring in pictures of various environmentally friendly activities and intersperse the realia with environmental tips, slogans, or titles.
Examples:
Laß die Verpackung da, wo du sie gefunden hast: im Geschäft!
Sei nicht so dumm wie ein Esel, benutz den Drahtesel statt des Autos!

Teaching Suggestion

15 Have students do Activity 15 with a partner. They should make a chart with four columns to write down the suggestions made by the German students. Then call on pairs for their ideas and keep track of them on a transparency or on the board.

Closure

Ask each student to share with the rest of the class one new or interesting fact learned from the **Weiter geht's!** section.

Teaching Zweite Stufe,
pp. 214-218

Resources for Zweite Stufe

Practice and Activity Book
Chapter Resources, Book 3
- Communicative Activities 9-3, 9-4
- Additional Listening Activities 9-4, 9-5, 9-6
- Student Response Forms
- Realia 9-2
- Situation Card 9-2
- Teaching Transparency Master 9-2
- Quiz 9-2
Audiocassette Program
- *Textbook Audiocassette* 5 A
- *Additional Listening Activities, Audiocassette* 10 A
- *Assessment Items, Audiocassette* 8 A
Video Program, Videocassette 2
Video Guide

▶ **page 214**

MOTIVATE

♜ Game

Play the game **Assoziationsfeld** using lead words from this and previous chapters. See Level 1 (p. 91F) for the procedure. Following are some suggested topics for this **Stufe: Müll, Luftverschmutzung, Recycling, Umwelt.**

TEACH

🎦 Video Program

In the video clip **Die Umwelt in der Ex-DDR,** natives of Dresden talk about environmental problems in the former GDR. See *Video Guide* for suggestions.

ZWEITE STUFE

PRESENTATION: Wortschatz

- Go over the names of the creatures in th box. Ask students to think of other creatures that are threatened by environmental carelessness.
- Put students in pairs or small groups and have them make sentences with the vocabulary in **auf deutsch erklärt**.
- When working with the **auf englisch erklärt** section, ask students to replace one of the words in each sentence but keep the main idea the same.

Example: **Ich müßte mal ausrechnen, wieviel Benzin ich verbrauche.**

For Additional Practice

16 Use the art for further practice and review. Students could describe what is happening in each picture and say why it is good or bad. For example, for the first drawing, a student might say: **Die Person wirft die Zeitungen in den Container. Das ist natürlich gut für die Umwelt, denn das Papier wird wiederverwendet.**

▶ *page 215*

Teaching Suggestion

18 Have students refer to the notes they took for Activity 15. You might also ask some questions such as:

Wie könntest du Energie sparen?
Was könntest du mit alten Batterien tun?

PRESENTATION: So sagt man das!

Have students use the new expressions by stating what is currently being done to protect the environment in their home, town, and state.

PRESENTATION: Grammatik

- Point out to students that in contrast with the active voice where the subject is the agent, the subject is being acted upon in the passive voice. The performer of the action, if stated, is usually indicated by the preposition **von**.
- Have students give the English equivalents for the two examples not translated in this grammar box (**Das Licht wird ausgemacht. Alte autos werden wiederverwendet.**).

▶ *page 216*

For Individual Needs

20 Tactile/Visual Learners Ask students to work individually or with a partner to create a visual aid to represent each idea from this activity. Students title each piece with the corresponding phrase from the two boxes. This could be started in class and completed as a homework assignment.

PRESENTATION: So sagt man das!

Ask students to follow the structure of these three examples as they come up with additional statements using the suggestions from Activity 20.
Example: **Die Wälder müssen geschützt werden.**

For Individual Needs

22 Kinesthetic Learners Bring to class items or pictures of things to use for this activity. Place them where all students can see them. Have students work with a partner and role-play the functions to be practiced in this activity.
Example: *put out recyclable used items, such as paper, bottles, and batteries*
Student A: **Was soll ich mit diesem Müll hier tun?**
Student B: **Der muß sortiert werden.**
Student A: *sorts items and explains what he or she is doing*

▶ *page 217*

PRESENTATION: So sagt man das!

Ask students to compare the two statements. How does the one indicating a realizable condition differ from the one that cannot be realized or fulfilled?

PRESENTATION: Grammatik

- Have students observe the word order in the examples. What is the word order in the **wenn**-clauses? What can students observe about the word order in the conclusion when it follows the **wenn**-clause and when it precedes the **wenn**-clause?
- Have students look back at the **Weiter geht's!** section and the statements made by the four students. How many conditional sentences can students find?

▶ *page 218*

Teaching Suggestion

24 Divide the class into two teams and have each group come up with ideas about what they would do for the environment. Time the activity. Then have both teams read their ideas aloud. Count to see which group had more environmentally friendly ideas.

Reteaching: The Passive Voice

Make a list of statements that students can change from the active to the passive voice. Remind students to use a prepositional phrase with **von** to indicate the performer of the action.
Examples:
Die Schüler benutzen Recyclingpapier.
Wir sortieren bei uns zu Hause den Abfall.
Batterien wirft unsere Physiklehrerin nie weg.

▶ *page 219*

PRESENTATION: Landeskunde

Teaching Suggestions

• Have students take turns reading the **Landeskunde** text out loud. Stop after each paragraph and clarify new vocabulary by using synonyms or by paraphrasing.

• After reading the **Landeskunde** text, ask students what they found interesting or unusual about the way Germans do their grocery shopping. Make a list of students' comments.

• Have students work in groups to answer Questions 1 through 4. Have groups share their answers with the rest of the class.

Thinking Critically

Comparing and Contrasting Have students reverse the scenario of the **Landeskunde** reading. They should imagine an exchange student from Germany is staying with an American family. Put students into pairs or groups of three and have each group rewrite the story for the American setting. Have students share their versions with the class.

Multicultural Connection

If possible, have students find out how other countries deal with packing and handling grocery store purchases. Do stores provide bags, help the customer, or accept recyclable packing materials? Have students report their findings to the class.

Teacher Note

Mention to your students that the **Landeskunde** will be also included in Quiz 9-1 given at the end of the **Zweite Stufe**.

CLOSE

TPR Total Physical Response

Ask all students to stand up and follow you around the school. On the way, direct commands to individual students, asking them to perform tasks that incorporate some of the functions and vocabulary from the **Erste** and **Zweite Stufen**.
Examples:
Würdest du bitte das Licht in diesem leeren Klassenzimmer ausmachen!
Heb bitte das Butterbrotpapier auf, und wirf es in den Mülleimer!

Focusing on Outcomes

Refer students back to the learning outcomes listed on p. 205. Students should recognize that they now know how to say what is being done about a problem, offer solutions, and hypothesize.

ASSESS

• **Performance Assessment** Ask students to list (orally or in writing) five things they would do to improve the environment and explain why each would be effective.

• Quiz 9-2, *Chapter Resources,* Book 3

ZWEITE STUFE

Teaching Zum Lesen,
pp. 220-222

Reading Strategy

The targeted strategy in this reading is interpreting statistics. Students should learn about this strategy before beginning Question 5.

PREREADING

Motivating Activity

Put the following phrase on the board: "Scientific studies show that ..." and ask the class to quickly complete it in as many ways they can. (Example: "... brand X toothpaste prevents cavities.") Many of these will probably come from television advertising and be easily recognizable as somewhat extravagant claims. Then ask students to consider the following three completions in terms of what type of claim is expressed and what type of study must have been involved:

a) "... there are more overweight people in the United States now than there were twenty years ago."
b) "... German and Japanese students score much higher in math and science than U.S. students do."
c) "... Rap lyrics are the cause of much juvenile crime."

Help students see what groups (or statistics) are being compared in a) and b). Ask them why the third claim seems dubious. Why is it so difficult to prove a cause-and-effect relationship, where social trends are concerned?

Teaching Suggestion

Tell students that the article they will read is an interpretation of some studies and that they should pay careful attention to how the data is being evaluated.

Teacher Note

Activity 1 is a prereading activity.

READING

Teaching Suggestion

2 Make sure that the students notice that the article is divided into two parts. Point out the large-type **O** in the first paragraph and the large-type **W** in Paragraph 5.

Teacher Notes

3 The first part of the essay refers to the second part of the subtitle: *Nevertheless, there is growing ecological awareness and a readiness to make sacrifices for a cleaner environment.* This is implied in the title by "**mehr Bauch**" meaning "*more gut or feeling.*"

4 The second part of the essay contains the assertion that students are still undereducated about environmental issues. This idea is implied in the title by the image of "less **Kopf**."

Thinking Critically

Evaluation Ask the class what the reader knows about:
a) the researchers who gathered these statistics,
b) the sizes of the samples used (given in Paragraph 1, but not given in Paragraph 8),
c) the actual techniques used to gather and analyze data.

Some discussion questions are:
• Could you make any concrete educational decisions based on the claims made in Paragraph 6? Why or why not?
• Does the Bielefeld study actually show that schools play the most important role in promoting environmental awareness among teens? Does the article include the data needed to prove this implied cause-effect claim?

POST-READING

Teacher Note

Activities 9 and 10 are post-reading tasks that will show whether students can apply what they have learned.

Teaching Suggestion

10 Before the class designs the group projects, one or more students might want to go to a library and look at a few scientific journals to see how the reporting of statistical findings is handled when the audience is likely to want to replicate the study or base some actions on it. The questionnaires can then be designed to yield more "scientific" results.

Closure

In the final sentence of the article, **DGU-Geschäfts-führer**, Axel Beyer states that students can influence adults' behavior by serving as good examples, particularly in the area of energy-conservation (recycling, etc.). However, the illustrations give a different view of **Schüleraktionen**. Based on what they have read in this chapter, do students think that the image of dramatic protest or the image of teens working with and encouraging adults in small, every-day actions is more typical of this generation of German youth? How would students compare German and American youth in this respect?

Answers to Activity 1

the environment; teens

Answers to Activity 2

a magazine article about a survey; two

Answers to Activity 3

(**mehr ... als, dennoch**); Teens know too little about environmental issues, however, environmental awareness and activism are growing; the second part of the main idea

Answers to Activity 4

the first part of the main idea

Answers to Activity 5

The number of students in 1980 and in 1994 who were willing to make monetary sacrifices for the environment; the percent of students who answered yes to this survey question in 1980 and 1994; **Universität Bielefeld**; A few more teenagers today are willing to make sacrifices for the environment.

Answers to Activity 6

the percentage of students in 1980 and 1994 who took part in various programs to protect the environment (recycling/petitions); teens today are more environmentally active than they were in 1980.

Answers to Activity 7

während, eher, größer, eher, lieber; comparison and contrast

Answers to Activity 8

a. fear for the future
b. The students tested knew very little about current environmental problems.
c. Boys seem to know the facts, but girls tend to be more willing to make sacrifices and take individual action.
d. incorporating environmental education into the curriculum

Teaching **Zum Schreiben,** *p. 223*

Writing Strategy

The targeted strategy in this writing activity is analyzing your audience. Students should learn about this strategy before beginning the assignment.

PREWRITING

Motivating Activity

Ask students what they know about campaign speeches. How are they constructed? Make a list of student comments on the board.

Speech Connection

Ask a student who is taking a speech course to talk about the characteristics of persuasive speech to your class. The next day, model such a speech in German (on a topic other than the environment) that is of interest to students in the school.

Teaching Suggestion

Have students brainstorm German phrases and expressions that could be used to persuade someone of something. Compile a list for students to refer to as they outline their speeches.
Examples:
Wir müssen unbedingt ...
Wir sollten ...
Glauben Sie mir, wenn ich sage, daß ...

WRITING

Building on Previous Skills

Students have learned many words and phrases that help organize and shape a text. Remind students to incorporate connectors such as **zuerst, außerdem, erstens, zweitens, zum Schluß, zusammenfassend,** and **weiterhin** in their writing.

POST-WRITING

✦ For Individual Needs

Auditory Learners After students have prepared their speeches, have them record them on audiocassette. Then have students each listen to their own speech, determine the strengths and weaknesses, and make changes before they present their final speech to their audience.

Teaching Suggestion

After speeches have been presented, have the peer-editing groups discuss their effectiveness: Would they persuade audiences in Germany? Would they persuade Americans? How would they have to change their arguments to persuade either audience?

Closure

Let each peer-editing group select the best candidate as in a primary election. Then have the selected candidates give their speeches in front of the class. The class can elect a **Kanzler** based on these speeches. Afterwards, have students discuss their reasons for selecting the winner, including the content as well as the style and delivery of the speech.

℧sing Anwendung, *pp. 224-225*

Resources for Anwendung

Chapter Resources, Book 3
- Realia 9-3
- Situation Card 9-3
Video Program, Videocassette 2
Video Guide

▶ Video Program

At this time, you might want to use the authentic advertising footage from German television. See *Video Guide* for suggestions.

Teaching Suggestion

1 After students have read "**Das saubere Klassenzimmer,**" ask them to compile a list of the various projects that have been initiated at the **Regino-Gymnasium.** Which of the ideas would students like to try at their school?

Thinking Critically

2 Drawing Inferences After students have listened to the suggestions by the member of the **Umwelt-AG,** ask them which of his suggestions could be adopted by their school. Which ones would not seem necessary or useful. Why?

📁 Portfolio Assessment

5 You might want to suggest this activity as an oral portfolio item for your students. See *Assessment Guide,* p. 22.

Teacher Note

5 To analyze the chart, students should know that **Sammelquote** refers to the percentage of each material collected from the total amount that was produced in that year. **Recyclingquote** refers to the percentage of each material recycled from the total amount produced.

REVIEW

Teaching Suggestion

6 After students have compiled their own data (specific information on recycling might be available from the town's recycling center), ask them to compare their data with the German data.

Group Work

7 Divide the class into groups of three or four students and have each group come up with as many examples as possible. Time the activity and see which group comes up with the most ideas.

Portfolio Assessment

7 You might want to suggest this activity as a written portfolio item for your students. See *Assessment Guide*, p. 22.

*K*ann ich's wirklich?
p. 226

This page helps students prepare for the test. It is a brief checklist of the major points covered in the chapter. The students should be reminded that it is only a checklist and not necessarily everything that will appear on the test.

*U*sing Wortschatz,
p. 227

Thinking Critically

Analyzing Ask students to go over the list of words and determine which of them they consider positive or negative in regard to the environment.

Teaching Suggestion

Put pairs of students together and have them take turns giving each other definitions in German for specific vocabulary items. The other student tries to guess the correct word.

For Individual Needs

Challenge Ask students to write a story in which they describe an ideal town using as many words from the **Wortschatz** page as possible.

Game

Play the game **Antworten jagen.** See p. 203F for the procedure.

Teacher Note

Give the **Kapitel 9** Chapter Test, *Chapter Resources, Book 3.*

9

Aktiv für die Umwelt!

① Wenn wir Flaschen und Papier zu den Containern bringen würden, hätten wir weniger Müll zu Hause.

Der Schutz unserer Umwelt ist heute eines der Hauptziele unserer Gesellschaft geworden. Die Umweltprobleme wurden zwar schon vor vielen Jahren erkannt, und in den letzten Jahren ist schon viel getan worden. Es gibt aber noch viele Probleme, die auf eine Lösung warten. Es ist klargeworden, daß wir alle gemeinsam an der Lösung der Umweltprobleme arbeiten müssen, wenn wir in einer gesunden Umgebung leben und eine heile Welt hinterlassen wollen.

In this chapter you will learn

- to express concern; to make accusations; to offer solutions; to make polite requests
- to say what is being done about a problem; to offer solutions; to hypothesize

And you will

- read about environmental concerns
- listen to reports about environmental challenges
- write about your perceptions and opinions of environmentally responsible actions
- become aware of new ways to reduce pollution

② Wir könnten noch viel mehr Sonnenenergie benutzen!

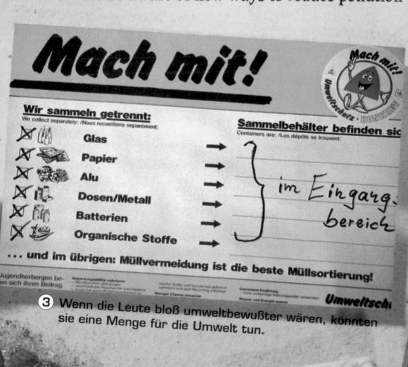

Mach mit!

Wir sammeln getrennt:
We collect separately: /Nous recueillons séparément:

- Glas
- Papier
- Alu
- Dosen/Metall
- Batterien
- Organische Stoffe

Sammelbehälter befinden sic
Containers are: /Les dépôts se trouvent:

im Eingang. bereich

... und im übrigen: Müllvermeidung ist die beste Müllsortierung!

③ Wenn die Leute bloß umweltbewußter wären, könnten sie eine Menge für die Umwelt tun.

Los geht's!

Für eine saubere Umwelt

Eine saubere Welt und der Umweltschutz sind nach Meinung der meisten Jugendlichen heute ganz besonders wichtig. Manche Jugendliche geben zu, daß sie selbst noch zu wenig für die Umwelt tun; aber die meisten engagieren sich schon aktiv für den Umweltschutz. Was sagen einige Schüler dazu?

Das größte Umweltproblem, glaub' ich, sind die Abgase. Die verpesten unsere Luft ganz schön. Und hier könnte man einiges tun, wenn nur alle mitmachen würden! Man könnte zum Beispiel Fahrgemeinschaften bilden, damit nicht jeder mit seinem Auto allein fährt. Und man sollte den VV[1] auch billiger machen; dann würden bestimmt mehr Leute mit dem Zug oder mit dem Bus fahren. Und man müßte jetzt nur noch Katautos[2] zulassen — dann könnte unsere Luft bestimmt wieder besser werden.

Mark, 18

Die Luftverschmutzung macht mir große Sorgen und ganz besonders das Ozonloch, das immer größer wird. Ich geh' schon gar nicht mehr gern in die Sonne, weil ich vor den UV-Strahlen Angst habe, die Hautkrebs auslösen können. Endlich haben unsere Politiker etwas Positives für die Umwelt getan, das FCKW[3] gesetzlich zu verbieten. FCKW wurde doch als Treibgas in Spraydosen benutzt, und das hat ja wesentlich mit zur Zerstörung der Ozonschicht beigetragen.

Julia, 17

Die Industrie verpestet die Luft immer mehr mit Schmutz. Die Fabriken blasen Schadstoffe und Chemikalien in die Luft, die dann mit dem Regen wieder zurück zur Erde kommen als saurer Regen.

Ulli, 16

Die Abgase von Autos und Lastwagen und die Schadstoffe der Industrie sind am großen Waldsterben schuld — nicht nur hier bei uns in Deutschland, sondern in der ganzen Welt.

Michaela, 17

---

1. VV ist die Abkürzung für Verkehrsverbund. In den Großstädten der Bundesrepublik darf man innerhalb einer bestimmten Zeit mit einem Fahrschein alle öffentlichen Verkehrsmittel benutzen, die man braucht, um ans Ziel zu gelangen.
2. Katautos sind Autos mit Katalysatoren, die die Luftverschmutzung reduzieren.
3. FCKW ist die Abkürzung für Fluor-Chlor-Kohlenwasserstoff, *chlorofluorocarbons (CFCs)*. Dieses Mittel wurde häufig als Treibgas in Spraydosen benutzt. Solche Spraydosen wurden mehr und mehr durch Pumpzerstäuber ersetzt. Die Verwendung von FCKW in Verbraucherprodukten wurde 1991 gesetzlich verboten. Bis 1995 soll die gesamte FCKW-Produktion in Deutschland eingestellt werden.

Wir zu Hause sortieren unseren Hausmüll. Einmal in der Woche bring' ich Papier, Flaschen und Aludosen zum Container.[4] Aber ich fürchte, daß viele Leute das nicht tun. Ein großer Teil des Hausmülls wäre überhaupt vermeidbar. Man müßte Getränke eben ausschließlich in Pfandflaschen kaufen und Einwegflaschen vermeiden. Und man sollte im Geschäft wirklich den Mut haben und sagen: „Dürfte ich bitte einen Papierbeutel haben?", wenn einem ein Plastikbeutel angeboten wird. Plastikbeutel müßte man überhaupt ganz durch Papierbeutel ersetzen.

Stefan, 18

Für mich ist die Verschmutzung des Wassers ein großes Umweltproblem. Durch den sauren Regen gibt es in vielen Seen schon keine Fische mehr, und wenn mal ein riesiger Öltanker irgendwo aufläuft und leck wird, dann verschmutzt das ausgelaufene Öl das Wasser und die Küste kilometerweit. Die Bilder aus Alaska mit den sterbenden Fischen und Vögeln werde ich nie vergessen! Aber ich glaube, jeder muß bei sich selbst anfangen, damit was verändert wird. Man müßte eben wirklich darauf achten, daß man Produkte kauft, die die Umwelt nicht belasten. Wir zu Hause kaufen zum Beispiel umweltfreundliche Wasch- und Spülmittel, die den Blauen Engel[5] draufhaben. Und wir benutzen Naturseife, die zu 99 Prozent biologisch abbaubar ist.

Angie, 18

4. In den meisten Dörfern und Städten stehen Container für Papier und Glas. Die Glascontainer sind oft dreigeteilt für Weiß-, Braun- und Grünglas. Auch gibt es heute schon genügend Annahmestellen für verbrauchte Batterien. Batterien gehören nicht in den Hausmüll. Sie enthalten Blei, Cadmium und Quecksilber, alle gefährliche Umweltgifte.

5. Der „Blaue Engel" ist ein Umweltzeichen, das Produkte haben, die umweltfreundlich oder weniger umweltschädlich als andere sind. Es gibt heute schon mehrere tausend Produkte mit diesem Zeichen.

1 Hast du alles verstanden?

Mach eine Liste mit Umweltwörtern und Begriffen! Weißt du, wie all diese Ausdrücke auf Englisch heißen? saubere Umwelt, Umweltschutz, Umweltproblem, Abgase, Luft verpesten, Luftverschmutzung, Ozonloch, Sonne, UV-Strahlen, FCKW, Zerstörung der Ozonschicht, Schmutz, Schadstoffe, Chemikalien, saurer Regen, Waldsterben, Hausmüll sortieren, Container, Pfandflaschen, Einwegflaschen

2 Die Umwelt verbessern

Die deutschen Schüler nennen in ihren Aussagen Probleme und auch konkrete Vorschläge zur Verbesserung der Umwelt. Schreib diese in Stichwörtern auf! Papierbeutel, Plastikbeutel, Verschmutzung des Wassers, Umwelt nicht belasten, umweltfreundliches Wasch- und Spülmittel, „Blauer Engel", Naturseife, biologisch abbaubar

3 Was läuft bei dir zu Hause?

Diskutiert die einzelnen Vorschläge zur Verbesserung der Umwelt, die die Schüler oben ausgeführt haben! Sind das praktische oder unpraktische Vorschläge? Warum? Wißt ihr, ob einige dieser Vorschläge in den USA schon praktiziert werden? Welche? Wo?

Expressing concern; making accusations; offering solutions; making polite requests

WORTSCHATZ

eine Pfandflasche

eine Plastiktüte

ein Pumpzerstäuber

ein Waschmittel

auf deutsch erklärt

verschmutzen schmutzig machen
der Schmutz das, was schmutzig ist
der Schadstoff Material, das schädlich ist
verpesten verschmutzen
die Autoabgase Gase, die aus dem Auto kommen und die Luft verschmutzen
eine Fahrgemeinschaft Leute, die gemeinsam mit nur einem Auto zur Arbeit fahren
herstellen produzieren
die Fabrik das Gebäude, wo Produkte hergestellt werden
das Spülmittel damit wäscht man Gläser, Teller und Tassen

auf englisch erklärt

<u>Giftige</u> <u>Treibgase</u> <u>vergrößern</u> das <u>Ozonloch</u>. *Poisonous gases enlarge the hole in the ozone layer.*
Ich <u>fürchte</u>, daß der <u>saure</u> <u>Regen</u> die Umwelt belastet und zum <u>Waldsterben</u> beiträgt. *I'm afraid that acid rain puts a load on the environment and contributes to the forests dying off.*
Das Gute an <u>Papierbeuteln</u> ist, daß sie <u>biologisch abbaubar</u> sind. *The good thing about paper bags is that they are biodegradable.*
Dem Umweltschutz zuliebe müßten wir <u>Einwegflaschen</u> mit <u>Pfandflaschen</u> <u>ersetzen</u>. *For the sake of environmental protection we should replace non-returnable bottles with returnable ones.*

SO SAGT MAN DAS!

Expressing concern

Many people are concerned about the environment and are apprehensive about the future. To express concern, you may say:

Ich habe Angst, daß das Ozonloch immer größer wird.
Ich fürchte, daß die Leute nicht viel für die Umwelt tun.
Die Luftverschmutzung **macht mir große Sorgen.**

How might you express similar things in English?

---

4 Hör gut zu! For answers, see listening script on TE Interleaf.

Verschiedene Leute drücken ihre Sorge zur Umweltverschmutzung aus. Schreib auf, welche Sorgen jeder hat, und was jeder vorschlägt, um die Umwelt zu verbessern!

5 Was macht dir Sorgen?

Wir haben schon viele Umweltprobleme und Gründe dafür erkannt (*recognized*). Einige sind hier aufgelistet. Sprich mit einem Partner darüber! Sag, was dir Sorgen macht und warum!

BEISPIEL	DU	**Wenn du an deine Umwelt denkst, was macht dir da Sorgen?**
	PARTNER	**Das Ozonloch über der Antarktis.**
	DU	**Mir auch. Und ich fürchte, daß die meisten Leute immer noch Spraydosen mit Treibgas benutzen.**
	PARTNER	**Da hast du ganz recht.** *oder* **Das glaub' ich nicht.**

was?

das Ozonloch über der Antarktis
die Autoabgase
die großen Müllberge
die Verschmutzung des Wassers
der saure Regen
die Industrieabgase

warum?

wenige Fahrgemeinschaften
Autos verpesten die Luft
Spraydosen mit Treibgas
Produkte nicht abbaubar
sortieren den Müll nicht
wenig gesetzliche Kontrolle

SO SAGT MAN DAS!

Making accusations

Who is to blame for our environmental problems? To make accusations, you can say:

> Du **bist** auch **schuld an** dem Problem, weil du ...
> Wir Verbraucher **sind schuld daran,** daß ... , wenn wir ...

An is a two-way preposition, and is used here in an idiomatic phrase. Note which case always follows this phrase!

6 Ihr Umweltverschmutzer!

Suse, eine engagierte Umweltschützerin und Mitglied der Umwelt AG, sagt anderen Klassenkameraden, daß sie auch an der Umweltverschmutzung schuld sind. Aber sie haben viele Ausreden! Spiel die Rolle der Suse, und unterhalte dich mit deinen Klassenkameraden!

BEISPIEL	SUSE	**Du bist auch schuld an der Umweltverschmutzung, weil du dich für die Umwelt nicht engagierst.**
	DU	**Ach du, ich habe einfach keine Zeit!**
	SUSE	**Das ist eine schlechte Ausrede. Für die Umwelt solltest du schon Zeit haben.**

Vorwürfe (*reproaches*):

den Hausmüll nicht sortieren

sich nicht für die Umwelt engagieren

die Flaschen nicht zum Container bringen

Getränke nur in Einwegflaschen kaufen

Ausreden:

keine Zeit haben

es einfach vergessen

es nicht für nötig halten

nicht daran denken

7 Schuld oder nicht?

Du und ein Partner, ihr unterhaltet euch darüber, wer oder was an unserer Umweltver-schmutzung schuld ist. Stimmst du deinem Partner zu? Begründe deine Antwort!

BEISPIEL   SUSE   **Woran sind die Autoabgase schuld?**
               UWE   **Am Waldsterben.**
               SUSE   **Genau! Denn ...**   *oder*   **Das stimmt eigentlich nicht, weil ...**

wer oder was?

der saure Regen?   viele Fabriken?

FCKW   die großen Öltanker?

schuld an

die Luftverschmutzung
die Wasserverschmutzung
das Ozonloch   das Waldsterben

SO SAGT MAN DAS !

Offering solutions

There are many ways to offer solutions to problems. Here are some ways to say what could or should be done:

Man **könnte** einiges für die Umwelt tun.
Man **müßte** nur noch Katautos bauen.
Man **sollte** den VV billiger machen.
Wenn wir nur Papierbeutel gebrauchen **dürften**!
Ein großer Teil des Mülls **wäre** vermeidbar.

8 Hör gut zu!   For answers, see listening script on TE Interleaf.

Der Allgemeine Deutsche Fahrradklub macht Werbung mit einem Bericht im Radio. Hör zu und schreib fünf Gründe auf, warum man öfters radfahren sollte!

Grammatik   Subjunctive forms of **können, müssen, dürfen, sollen,** and **sein**

You can use the subjunctive form to express a variety of attitudes. The subjunctive forms of the modals and **sein** can be used to express what could or should be done, or not be done. What similarities and differences can you observe between these forms and the imperfect forms?

	können	müssen	dürfen	sollen	sein
ich	könnte	müßte	dürfte	sollte	wäre
du	könntest	müßtest	dürftest	solltest	wärst
er, sie, es, man	könnte	müßte	dürfte	sollte	wäre
wir	könnten	müßten	dürften	sollten	wären
ihr	könntet	müßtet	dürftet	solltet	wärt
sie, Sie	könnten	müßten	dürften	sollten	wären

9 Was könnten wir tun?

Was könnten wir tun, um unsere Umwelt zu verbessern? Unterhaltet euch in der Klasse darüber! Frag deine Mitschüler, was man tun könnte, um verschiedene Umweltprobleme zu verbessern! Ein Mitschüler sagt jemandem, was diese Person nicht mehr machen sollte. Kann man noch etwas dazu sagen?

BEISPIEL	DU	**Was könnten wir denn tun, um (die Luft) zu verbessern?**
	PARTNER A	**He, du! Du solltest nicht mehr rauchen!**
	PARTNER B	**Das stimmt. (Aber wir müßten auch darauf achten, daß unsere Industrie keine Abgase in die Luft bläst — das trägt zum Waldsterben bei.)**

Vorschläge

nicht rauchen

keine Einwegflaschen kaufen

nur Produkte kaufen, die die Umwelt nicht belasten

Pfandflaschen zurückbringen

keine Industrieabgase in die Luft blasen

Fahrgemeinschaften bilden

keine Plastiktüten annehmen

SO SAGT MAN DAS!

Making polite requests

You can use subjunctive forms to make polite requests:

Könnte ich bitte einen Papierbeutel haben?
Dürfte ich bitte ein umweltfreundliches Waschmittel haben?
Würden Sie bitte den Motor abstellen?

10 Ein umweltfreundlicher Mensch   E.g.: Könnte ich bitte einen Solar-Taschenrechner haben?

Du bist in einem Geschäft, und deine Partnerin ist die Verkäuferin. Deine Partnerin bietet dir Produkte an, die du für umweltschädlich hältst. Du bist aber sehr umweltfreundlich, und du sagst der Verkäuferin, was du haben möchtest. Die Verkäuferin gibt dir ...

1. einen Taschenrechner mit Batterien.
2. einen Kaffee in einem Plastikbecher.
3. ein Getränk in einer Einwegflasche.
4. ein Waschmittel mit Phosphaten.
5. eine Seife, die die Natur belastet.
6. eine Plastiktüte für deine Einkäufe.

11 Klassenprojekt: Unsere Umwelt

Sammelt schriftliche Informationen und Bildinformationen, die folgendes zeigen:
1. die Belastung unserer Umwelt
2. was wir tun können, um unsere Umwelt zu schützen und zu verbessern

Macht eine Collage am Wandbrett, die Schüler an eurer Schule über Umweltprobleme und Lösungen informiert! Beschreibt die Collage und diskutiert darüber!

12 Für mein Notizbuch

Wähl eins der folgenden drei Umweltthemen: Luft, Wasser, Hausmüll! Schreib, warum du besonders an diesem Thema interessiert bist, wie du dich aktiv auf diesem Gebiet engagierst und was noch getan werden sollte, um die Umwelt in diesem Bereich zu verbessern!

Weiter geht's!

Die Umwelt AG diskutiert: Umwelttips für Schüler

Schon seit Jahren ist Umweltschutz ein Bestandteil der Lehrpläne an fast allen Schulen. Die Schüler handeln heute viel umweltbewußter als früher, doch gibt es noch immer eine Menge von Umweltsünden, gegen die man etwas tun könnte. Die Umwelt AG ist wie immer am Dienstagnachmittag mit ihrem Biolehrer zusammengekommen. Heute haben die Gymnasiasten Artikel aus Zeitungen und Zeitschriften mitgebracht, über die sie diskutieren wollen.

Energiesparen:
Papier wiederverwenden

Papier wird aus Holz gemacht. Für Papier müssen also Wälder abgeholzt werden. Aber Wälder sind wichtig, weil sie Sauerstoff produzieren und die Luft sauberhalten. Zur Herstellung von Papier braucht man Energie (Elektrizität oder Öl), viel Frischwasser und Chemikalien. Außerdem belasten die Abgase und Abwässer der Papierindu-strie die Umwelt. Es lohnt sich also, Papier zu sparen, und wiederzuverwerten. Man braucht zur Herstellung von Umweltschutzpapier 98% weniger Frischwasser und 60% weniger Energie!

Vorsicht mit Tintenkillern!

Tintenkiller enthalten das giftige Formaldehyd. Das ist sehr gefährlich! Es ist wichtig, daß man bei der Verwendung von Tintenkillern das Gesicht nicht zu nahe ans Papier bringt, daß man den Stift nicht in den Mund steckt und die Kappe immer sofort aufsteckt. Am besten ist es, solche Stifte nicht zu benutzen.

Die deutsche Industrie
sorgt für Sauberkeit!

- Die deutsche Papierindustrie basiert heute schon zu 43% auf Recycling!
- Die Wiederverwertung von Glas liegt heute bei 31%. (Vor fünf Jahren 5,5%)
- Alte Autos werden heute zu etwa 90% wiederverwertet!

Diesem Artikel nach bin ich ein großer Energiesparer. Das Papier und die Hefte, die ich benutze, sind alle aus Recyclingpapier. Aber natürlich könnten wir noch mehr für die Umwelt tun, wenn nur alle Schüler Recyclingpapier benutzen würden und wenn sie ihre Hefte nicht in Plastikumschläge stecken würden. Es wäre auch besser, wenn keiner mehr Kulis, Faserstifte und diese schädlichen Tintenkiller benützen würde! Das sind eben ein paar Vorschläge, die ich persönlich habe.

Sandra, 17

Ihr habt miterlebt, wieviel Müll in einer Woche an unserer Schule zusammenkommt. Freilich könnte dieser Müllberg kleiner werden, wenn jeder seinen Abfall nicht in den Papierkorb, sondern gleich in den Container werfen würde. Und wir alle müßten eben darauf achten, wie wir unsere Pausenbrote verpacken. Alu-Folie, PVC-Folie, Plastikbecher und Dosen müßten eben ganz verschwinden. Meine Mutter könnte mein Pausenbrot genau so gut in Butterbrotpapier einpacken. Ja, und wenn der Hausmeister die Milch in Mehrweg-flaschen verkaufen würde, hätten wir viel weniger Abfall.[1]

Gregor, 16

---

1. An vielen deutschen Schulen verkauft oft der Hausmeister Getränke und Eßwaren an Schüler.

Ich weiß nicht, wie das bei euch zu Hause ist, aber wir leben schon immer umweltbewußt. Solange ich lebe, höre ich schon immer: „Könntest du bitte das Licht in deinem Zimmer ausschalten!" oder: „Würdest du bitte die Tür schließen?" oder: „Würdest du bitte nicht so lange duschen und nicht so viel Shampoo benutzen?!" Und bei uns wird auch fast nichts weggeworfen, nichts verschwendet. Was zu reparieren ist, wird repariert. Wir haben zum Beispiel auch einen Sonnenkollektor auf unserm Dach. Mein Vater hat sich ausgerechnet, daß sich der Kollektor schon bezahlt gemacht hat.

Oliver, 17

Na ja, so umweltbewußt wie ihr leben wir wohl nicht. Es sieht so aus, als ob wir uns an euch ein Beispiel nehmen könnten. Wir leben mehr naturbewußt, und da tun wir schon einiges für die Umwelt. Meine Mutter liebt Tiere — Vögel, Bienen, Frösche, sogar Ameisen! — und deshalb benutzen wir in unserm Garten keinen Kunstdünger und keine Chemikalien. Und wir radeln viel. Mein Vater würde am liebsten jedes Wochenende nur radeln und lieber das Auto zu Hause lassen. Meine Eltern unterstützen den „sanften Tourismus".[2] Sie sind zum Beispiel letzten Winter mit ihren Freunden nicht zum Skilaufen gefahren. Sie wollten damit gegen den Bau neuer Skipisten protestieren. Und ich wäre so gern mitgefahren!

Viktoria, 17

2. Es hat sich gezeigt, daß längere Freizeit und aktiver Urlaub großen Schaden in der Natur angerichtet haben. Immer mehr Leute unterstützen deshalb die Aktion „Sanfter Tourismus", die sich für die Erhaltung der Natur für alle einsetzt.

13 Hast du alles verstanden?

Lies dir die Zeitungsartikel auf Seite 212 noch einmal durch! Es ist nicht notwendig, daß du jedes einzelne Wort verstehst. Schreib mit eigenen Worten die wichtigsten Punkte jedes Artikels auf!

14 Vergleiche mit anderen Texten

Such in amerikanischen oder deutschen Zeitungen und Zeitschriften nach einem ähnlichen Artikel wie auf Seite 212! Bring ihn in die Klasse mit und berichte darüber!

15 Wiederhole die Ansichten!

Schreib auf, was für umweltbewußte Vorschläge Sandra, Gregor, Oliver und Viktoria machen! Was machen die Eltern von Oliver und Viktoria, um Energie zu sparen und die Natur zu erhalten?

ZWEITE STUFE

Saying what is being done about a problem; offering solutions; hypothesizing

Was verschwindet, wenn wir zuviel Gift herstellen?

der Vogel

die Biene

der Frosch

die Ameise

auf deutsch erklärt

der Abfall   Sachen, die man wegwirft
wiederverwenden   nochmal gebrauchen
wiederverwerten   recyclen
die Mehrwegflasche   eine Flasche, die man zurückbringt und die dann wieder benutzt wird
verzichten auf   wenn man ohne etwas lebt
ausschalten   ausmachen
das Abwasser   schon gebrauchtes Wasser
die Herstellung   die Produktion
der Wald   wo viele Bäume sind
abholzen   wenn man Bäume aus dem Wald nimmt
der Sauerstoff   was wir in die Lungen einnehmen, um zu leben

auf englisch erklärt

Du mußt aufpassen, daß du beim <u>Duschen</u> nicht so viel Wasser <u>verschwendest</u>.
You should take care not to waste so much water when showering.
<u>Außerdem</u> sind <u>Kunstdünger</u> und <u>Tintenkiller</u> <u>giftig</u>.   *Besides that, artificial fertilizer and chemical erasers are poisonous.*
Ich müßte <u>ausrechnen</u>, wieviel <u>Strom</u> ich verbrauche.   *I would have to calculate how much electricity I use.*
Es ist <u>gefährlich</u>, wenn man keine <u>Vorsicht</u> üßt.
It's dangerous when you don't use caution.

16 Würdest du bitte ...

Was könnten deine Freunde für die Umwelt tun? Sag es ihnen!

BEISPIEL   **Würdet ihr bitte ...**
           Könntet ihr bitte ...

E.g.: **Würdet ihr bitte die Flaschen und die Zeitungen zum Container bringen?**

17 Hör gut zu!

For answers, see listening script on TE Interleaf.

Die Umwelt-AG möchte für jeden Slogan ein Poster entwerfen. Du hörst jetzt die Slogans. Zeichne einfache Skizzen (*sketches*), die die Slogans wiedergeben!

18 Was für Vorschläge hast du?

Schreib zehn Dinge auf, die du selbst tun könntest oder tun würdest, um deine Umwelt zu schützen!

Ich könnte ...   **Ich würde ...**

SO SAGT MAN DAS!

Saying what is being done about a problem

Many things are already being done to protect the environment. Here is how you can express what is being done:

> Batterien **werden** jetzt **gesammelt**.
> Recyclingpapier **wird benutzt**.
> Mehrwegflaschen **werden** schon oft **verkauft**.

How might you express similar intentions in English?

Grammatik   The passive voice, present tense

1. German often uses the passive voice for reporting that something generally is done, without telling who or what does it.

> **Papier wird jetzt aus Altpapier gemacht.**
> *Paper is now made from recycled paper.*

2. The present tense of the passive voice is formed by using a present-tense form of **werden** and the past participle of another verb.

	werden	*past participle*
Das Licht	wird	ausgemacht.
Alte Autos	werden	wiederverwertet.

3. If necessary, use the preposition **von** to indicate the performer of the action.

> **Die Flaschen werden von Schülern zum Container gebracht.**
> *The bottles are (being) brought by the students to the recycling bin.*

4. The passive voice is often used in German to make general statements.

> **Heute wird ein Film über Recycling gezeigt.**
> *A film about recycling is being shown today.*

19 Hör gut zu!

For answers, see listening script on TE Interleaf.

Schüler unterhalten sich über Umweltfragen. Über welche Produkte sprechen sie, und was erfährst du über diese Produkte? Mach dir Notizen!

20 Was wird alles für die Umwelt gemacht?

Sag verschiedenen Klassenkameraden, was für die Umwelt gemacht wird!

E.g.: **Mehrwegflaschen werden in unserer Familie benutzt.**

Dosen mein Sandwich Batterien Recyclingpapier PVC-Folie Mehrwegflaschen der Müll Energie die Wälder alte Fahrräder Alu-Dosen

wird
werden

benutzt gesammelt geschützt gespart in Butterbrotpapier eingepackt in den Container geworfen sortiert repariert vermieden zurückgebracht wiederverwendet

---

SO SAGT MAN DAS!

Offering solutions

To express what can, should, or must be done to protect the environment, you can say:

Der Abfall **kann** leicht **sortiert werden.**
Die Flaschen **sollen zurückgebracht werden.**
Alles **muß repariert werden.**

---

21 Deine Ideen zur Umweltverbesserung!

Schau dir die Bilder und Vorschläge in diesem Kapitel an! Schreib so viele Ideen und Vorschläge zur Umweltverbesserung, wie du kannst!

22 Was soll ich damit tun?

Du bist bei deinem Freund zu Hause und hilfst ihm aufräumen. Du fragst ihn, was du machen sollst. Stell ihm dann auch ein paar allgemeine Umweltfragen!

DU **Was soll ich mit dem Müll tun? Sortieren?**
FREUND **Ja, der muß sortiert werden.**

1. Was soll ich mit den Flaschen tun? Zurückbringen?
2. Was soll ich mit den Dosen tun? In den Container werfen?
3. Was soll ich mit dem Fahrrad tun? Reparieren?
4. Kann man Kunstdünger überhaupt ersetzen?
5. Kann man überhaupt umweltfreundliche Seife herstellen?
6. Kann man Mehrwegflaschen überhaupt richtig waschen?

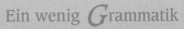

Ein wenig *Grammatik*

When expressing in German what can, should, or must be done about a problem, you use a conjugated modal verb along with a past participle and the infinitive **werden.**

Der Abfall **kann sortiert werden.**
The garbage can be sorted.
Die Umwelt **muß geschützt werden.** *The environment has to be protected.*

SO SAGT MAN DAS!

Hypothesizing

When making a hypothetical statement, the hypothetical condition can either be fulfilled or not (for example, if it's perhaps too late to do anything about it). If the hypothetical condition can be fullfilled, you say:

> **Wenn wir die Flaschen zurückbringen würden, hätten wir weniger Müll.**
>
> *If we returned the bottles, we would have less garbage.*

If the condition cannot be fulfilled, you use the past subjunctive:

> **Wenn wir die Flaschen zurückgebracht hätten, hätten wir weniger Müll gehabt.**
>
> *If we had returned the bottles, we would have had less garbage.*

Grammatik   Conditional sentences

Conditional sentences can be used to make hypothetical statements.

1. If the hypothesis can be realized or fulfilled, use subjunctive forms such as **hätte, wäre, könnte, dürfte,** or **würde** with the infinitive in both the conditional clause (the **wenn**-clause), and the conclusion.

> Wenn ich Zeit **hätte, würde** ich den Müll **sortieren.**
> *If I had time, I would sort the trash.*
> Wenn wir klug **wären, würden** wir uns um unsere Umwelt **kümmern.**
> *If we were smart, we would be concerned about our environment.*
> Wenn ich **könnte, würde** ich das Fenster **schließen.**
> *If I could, I would close the window.*
> Wenn der Hausmeister die Milch in Mehrwegflaschen **verkaufen würde, hätten** wir weniger Abfall.
> *If the custodian sold the milk in recyclable bottles, we would have less garbage.*

2. If the hypothesis can no longer be realized or fullfilled, the subjunctive forms are used in the compound tenses; that is, the forms of **hätte** and **wäre,** together with the past participle of the main verb.

> Wenn ich Zeit **gehabt hätte, hätte** ich den Müll **sortiert.**
> *If I had had time, I would have sorted the trash.*
> Wenn wir klug **gewesen wären, hätten** wir uns um die Umwelt **gekümmert.**
> *If we had been clever, we would have taken care of the environment.*
> Wenn der Hausmeister die Milch in Mehrwegflaschen **verkauft hätte, hätten** wir weniger Abfall **gehabt.**
> *If the custodian had sold the milk in recyclable bottles*
> *we would have had less garbage.*

3. Conditional sentences can also start with the conclusion, and then follow with the **wenn**-clause.

> Ich **würde** den Müll **sortieren,** wenn ich Zeit **hätte.**
> Ich **hätte** den Müll **sortiert,** wenn ich Zeit gehabt **hätte.**

23 Hör gut zu! For answers, see listening script on TE Interleaf.

Du hörst jetzt, was einige Mädchen und Jungen für die Umwelt tun. Schreib ein paar Sachen auf, die sie machen!

24 Jeder kommt zu Wort!

Du interviewst deine Klassenkameraden und fragst sie:

DU **Was würdest du für deine Umwelt tun, wenn du wirklich umweltbewußt leben würdest?**

PARTNER **Ich würde (unsern Müll sortieren und selbst zum Container bringen).**

25 Es ist leider schon zu spät!

Frag deine Klassenkameraden jetzt, was sie früher für den Umweltschutz getan hätten!

DU **Was hättest du alles für den Umweltschutz getan, wenn du mehr darüber gewußt hättest?**

PARTNER **Ich hätte (immer nur Mehrwegflaschen gekauft und Einwegflaschen vermieden).**

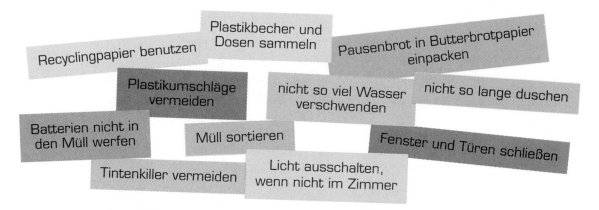

Recyclingpapier benutzen

Plastikbecher und Dosen sammeln

Pausenbrot in Butterbrotpapier einpacken

Plastikumschläge vermeiden

nicht so viel Wasser verschwenden

nicht so lange duschen

Batterien nicht in den Müll werfen

Müll sortieren

Fenster und Türen schließen

Tintenkiller vermeiden

Licht ausschalten, wenn nicht im Zimmer

26 Und du? Wie steht's mit dir?

Umweltschutz fängt bei jedem einzelnen an. Bilde eine größere Gruppe und beantwortet folgende Fragen!

1. Was tust du für deine Umwelt? Denk daran, daß auch ganz kleine Dinge wichtig sind!
2. Engagierst du dich aktiv in einer Umweltgruppe? Was machst du dort?
3. Was würdest du selbst gern für deine Umwelt tun, wenn du es könntest?
4. Was tut dein Heimatort für den Umweltschutz? Was macht deine Schule?
5. Was für Gesetze gibt es, die für die Erhaltung einer reinen und gesunden Umwelt sind?
6. Sollte es noch mehr Gesetze geben und welche, oder haben wir schon genügend Gesetze zum Schutz der Umwelt? Welche Gesetze sind überflüssig (*superfluous*) oder haben zu viele Nachteile?
7. Wenn du an die Umwelt denkst, siehst du optimistisch oder pessimistisch in die Zukunft?
8. Was wäre für dich eine ideale Umwelt?

27 Für mein Notizbuch

Schreib über das Thema „Was die Umwelt für mich bedeutet."! Halte dich an die Fragen in Übung 26!

Ein umweltfreundlicher Einkauf

Chelsea ist Austauschstudentin in Deutschland. Ihr deutscher Freund Martin und sie sind hungrig. Da es nichts Besonderes im Kühlschrank gibt, gehen die beiden einkaufen. Martin nimmt einen Korb und zwei Einkaufstaschen aus Baumwolle mit.

Draußen regnet es, und da Martin schon seinen Führerschein hat, erwartet Chelsea, daß sie mit dem Auto zum Supermarkt fahren. Aber statt dessen gehen die beiden zu Fuß mit Regenschirmen zum Supermarkt. Chelsea denkt, in Amerika würden wir ganz einfach mit dem Auto hinfahren, besonders wenn es regnet.

Im Supermarkt kaufen sie alles ein, was sie brauchen. Als sie an der Kasse stehen, merkt Chelsea, daß die Kassiererin ihnen keine Einkaufstaschen aus Papier oder Plastik gibt, sondern daß Martin die Sachen selber in den Korb und in die Baumwolltaschen einpackt. Bevor sie den Supermarkt verlassen, nimmt Martin das Verpackungsmaterial von verschiedenen Packungen, und wirft es in eine große Tonne vor dem Ausgang des Supermarkts. Chelsea fragt sich, warum ist das Einkaufen anders hier? For answers to questions 1 - 4, see text below.

1. Chelseas Erlebnis ist ein typischer Einkauf in Deutschland. Was ist beim Einkaufen in den USA anders? Beschreib die Unterschiede!
2. Warum bringt Martin Einkaufstaschen aus Stoff und einen Korb mit? Warum packt er alles an der Kasse selber ein? Warum läßt er das Verpackungsmaterial in der Tonne im Supermarkt?
3. Chelsea und Martin gehen zu Fuß einkaufen, obwohl es regnet. Was würdest du in diesem Fall machen? Warum?
4. Warum ist der Einkauf umweltfreundlich?

In Deutschland ist es üblich, Einkaufstaschen aus Stoff oder Körbe zum Einkaufen mitzubringen. Wenn man keine Taschen bei sich hat, kann man im Supermarkt Plastiktaschen für 20 Pfennig pro Stück kaufen. Um die zusätzlichen Kosten und den Gebrauch von Plastiktüten zu vermeiden, bringt man gewöhnlich seine eigenen Stofftaschen mit. Natürlich ist es auch umweltfreundlicher. Man darf auch Verpackungsmaterialien im Supermarkt lassen, denn Supermärkte sind gesetzlich verpflichtet, die sogenannten „Umverpackungen" zurückzunehmen und zu recyclen. Auch benutzen die Leute gewöhnlich nicht das Auto, um einkaufen zu gehen. In jeder Nachbarschaft gibt es genügend Lebensmittelgeschäfte, die man gut zu Fuß oder mit dem Rad erreichen kann. In der Großstadt ist es außerdem nicht leicht, einen Parkplatz zu finden.

Mit Gasmasken protestieren Berliner Schüler gegen die Luftverschmutzung. In den Greenteams von Greenpeace sind heute rund 10 000 Kinder für die Umwelt aktiv.

LESETRICK

Interpreting statistics

When you come across statistics in a text, use the following steps to help make sense of them. Find out 1) what is being compared, 2) what the numbers refer to, and 3) the source of the statistics. Most importantly, once you understand what the statistics represent, you'll want to draw conclusions based on them. Try to put your conclusions in your own words using phrases such as *more than, much less than*, etc., rather than numbers.

Getting Started

Identify the main idea by using the strategies you've learned. Remember that a main idea can be made up of several related ideas.

1. Look at the photo and then read the caption, the title, and subtitle of the reading. What is the topic? What group of people does it focus on?
2. What kind of text is this? Is it a narrative, a news report, or something else? Just by looking at the text, how many sections do you think it has? Can you identify them?

For answers, see TE Interleaf.

Mehr Bauch als Kopf

Eine Studie belegt: Jugendliche wissen zuwenig über Umweltfragen. Dennoch wachsen Ökobewußtsein und Opferbereitschaft

Ob sie bereit wären, für verbesserten Umweltschutz auch auf einen Teil ihres Taschengeldes zu verzichten, wollten Wissenschaftler der Universität Bielefeld kürzlich von 600 Schülern wissen. Viele sind es. Bei immerhin 30 Prozent macht das Umweltbewußtsein selbst vor dem eigenen Geldbeutel nicht halt. Dieselbe Frage hatten 1980 in einer gleich großen Gruppe noch geringfügig weniger (28 Prozent) bejaht.

Für den Leiter des Forscherteams, Professor Axel Braun, sind solche kleinen Fortschritte »ein Silberstreifen am Horizont«. Aus dem Vergleich der beiden Umfragen im Abstand von 13 Jahren zieht er den Schluß: »Es geht in die richtige Richtung, aber langsam.«

Besonders da, wo die Gesellschaft allgemein dazugelernt hat, ziehen die 15- bis 18jährigen verstärkt mit. So bringen heute 84 Prozent der Kids nach Partys ihre Flaschen zum Altglascontainer. 1980 machten sich nur 39 Prozent die Mühe. 70 Prozent verschmähen beim Einkaufen die Plastiktüte

(1980: 58 Prozent). Die Hälfte schreibt heute »Papier beidseitig voll« (1980: 37 Prozent), und 40 Prozent weisen aufwendig verpackte Ware zurück (1980: 15 Prozent).

Mehr als zwei Drittel sind bereit, für die Umwelt auf die Straße zu gehen, 41 Prozent haben schon an Unterschriftenaktionen teilgenommen, und 38 Prozent beteiligten sich an der Säuberung von Bächen und ähnlichen Einsätzen. Durchweg liegen diese Werte um zehn bis 20 Prozent über denen von 1980.

In **Kapitel 7** you learned that cohesive devices are words or phrases that help tie the individual ideas of a text together. Cohesive devices can be pronouns, including relative pronouns (**die, den, denen**), conjunctions (**aber, ob, wenn**), or adverbs (**dennoch, jetzt, im Vergleich**).

3. Scan the title and subtitle for cohesive devices indicating comparison or contrast. Using these words or phrases as clues, state what you think the main idea of the article is. Now read the first paragraph and decide which part of the main idea the first half of the essay must refer to.

4. Scan the first paragraph of the second part of the article for key words relating to or illus-

trating the title and subtitle of the article. Decide which part of the main idea this half of the essay refers to.

A Closer Look

Now that you have indentified the main idea, look at how the statistics support this point.

5. Look at the statistics given in the first paragraph. What facts are being compared? What do the numbers actually refer to? What is the source for these statistics? Based on the statistics, what conclusion can you draw about differences between teenagers today and those that answered the survey in 1980? Try to state your conclusion in terms that make sense to you.

Was die Jugendlichen bewegt, scheint vor allem Angst zu sein. Ob atomare Strahlung, Wasserverschmutzung, Klimaveränderung, Überbevölkerung oder Müll-Lawine, man sieht die Zukunft schwärzer als früher. Am Fachwissen mangelt es allerdings nach wie vor. Im Wissenstest erreichten Gymnasiasten nur rund die Hälfte der möglichen Punkte, Hauptschüler gut ein Drittel. Braun: »Glatt unbefriedigend.«

Während die Jungen eher sachlich Bescheid wissen, ist bei den Mädchen die persönliche Betroffenheit und die Handlungsbereitschaft größer. Jungen lasten die Umweltschäden eher Politik und Wirtschaft an, Mädchen kehren lieber vor der eigenen Haustüre.

Die wichtigste Rolle bei der Förderung des Umweltbewußtseins spielt nach den Bielefelder Erkenntnissen die Schule. Vor allem, wenn konkrete Probleme mit anschließenden Aktionen auf dem Stundenplan stehen, »bleibt bei den Schülern deutlich mehr hängen«.

Nach Umfragen des Kieler Instituts für Pädagogik in den Naturwissenschaften und der Deutschen Gesellschaft für Umwelterziehung (DGU) stieg in den letzten Jahren die Zahl der Schulen, die diesen Grundsatz beherzigen, von 15 auf 40 Prozent. DGU-Geschäftsführer Axel Beyer: »Da wird schon mal durch Schülereinsatz eine vierspurige Straße auf zwei Spuren verkleinert und Hausmeistern das Energiesparen vorgemacht.«

6. Continue reading the first part of the essay. What do the statistics in the third and fourth paragraphs refer to? What conclusions can you draw from these numbers? How do they fit with your original statement about the main idea of the article?

7. Read the entire second part of the article. In the sixth paragraph, identify cohesive devices and list them. Based on your list, what do you think the writer is showing in this paragraph? A sequence of events? Comparison and contrast? Cause and effect? Or something else?

8. Answer the following questions.

   a. What is the main reason teenagers try to protect the environment?

   b. Why did Herr Braun give the students mentioned in the fifth paragraph the grade **unbefriedigend**?

   c. In what ways do girls and boys differ in their involvement with the environment?

   d. Which single factor has helped most in promoting environmental awareness?

9. Schreib jetzt eine Zusammenfassung des Artikels! Verwende dabei deine Aussage über den Hauptgedanken (Frage 3)! Schließe mindestens drei unterstützende Aussagen von dem Text und einen Schlußsatz ein!

10. Bildet Gruppen von vier, und haltet jetzt eure eigene Umfrage, indem ihr zwei verschiedene Gruppen (zum Beispiel Mädchen und Jungen oder Schüler und Lehrer) vergleicht. Das Thema heißt Umwelt. Nachdem ihr die Statistiken gesammelt habt, müßt ihr logische Schlüsse daraus ziehen. Schreibt am Ende einen Bericht über die Ergebnisse!

As you have discussed in this chapter, you as an individual can do many different things to help protect the environment. Politicians, however, have even more potential to help the environment, since they determine policies for a whole country. In this activity, you will imagine that you are a candidate to become Chancellor of Germany. You will write a campaign speech outlining what you would do for the environment if elected.

Als Kanzler würde ich alles ändern!

Schreib eine Rede als Kanzlerkandidat! Erkläre in der Rede, was du als Kanzler für die Umwelt oder für andere wichtige Probleme der Gesellschaft machen würdest! Kritisiere die alten Politiker! Woran sind sie schuld? Erzähle auch deinem Publikum, was gemacht werden muß und soll!

A. Vorbereiten

1. Wer wird deine Rede hören? Wofür interessieren sich diese Leute, und was wissen sie schon über das Thema? Entwirf einen Fragebogen in der Klasse, um festzustellen, welche Probleme deinen Klassenkameraden besonders wichtig sind!
2. Wähle die Probleme aus, die du besprechen willst, und schreib sie auf Karteikarten (*index cards*)! Denk an die Details, die für die Zuschauer interessant wären, und schreib sie auch auf!
3. Wo hältst du die Rede? Wieviel Zeit hast du dazu? Wähle die geeigneten Karten aus, und ordne sie in der gewünschten Reihenfolge an!
4. Denk an die Ausführung der Rede! Willst du Diagramme oder Bilder benutzen?

> **SCHREIBTIP**
>
> **Analyzing your audience**
> Whenever you write, you are writing *for* someone — your intended audience. Analyzing who that audience is before you begin helps you determine the content as well as the style and tone of what you will write. To analyze your audience, first ask yourself what your intended readers or listeners know and what interests them. If they don't know much about your topic, include background details to inform them; if they already know a lot, focus on particular aspects of the topic that fit their interests. Select a style and tone, too, which are most appropriate to your audience. The more your audience knows, the more in depth your arguments can be.

B. Ausführen

Benutze deine geordneten Karten, um die Rede zu schreiben! Du mußt dich während der Rede nicht unbedingt an den geschriebenen Text halten, aber schreibe alles auf, damit du nichts vergißt!

C. Überarbeiten

1. Bildet Gruppen von jeweils vier Schülern und Schülerinnen! Jeder soll der Rede von den anderen zuhören. Hört einander sehr aufmerksam zu, und merkt euch die Fragen, die euch während der Rede einfallen!
2. Besprecht die Wirkung (*effect*) jeder Rede! Würdet ihr diesen Kandidaten jetzt wählen? Hat er euch mit seinen Gesichtspunkten überzeugt? Hat er seine Stimme und Gesten wirksam eingesetzt?
3. Habt ihr als Zuschauer die Rede interessant gefunden? Habt ihr etwas gelernt, oder habt ihr schon alles gewußt?
4. Lies deine eigene Rede noch einmal! Hast du alles richtig buchstabiert? Beachte besonders die Konjunktivformen der Modalverben! Hast du **konnte** und **könnte** richtig verwendet?
5. Schreib die korrigierte Rede noch einmal ab!

1 In vielen Orten und in vielen Schulen gibt es Umweltprojekte. Eine Schule in Prüm, eine kleine Stadt in der Eifel, hat zum Beispiel ein interessantes Projekt durchgeführt. Das Projekt wurde in einer Zeitschrift beschrieben. Lies zuerst den Artikel und versuche danach, dir ein interessantes Umweltprojekt für eure Schule auszudenken!

DAS SAUBERE KLASSENZIMMER

Die Schüler und Schülerinnen einer 11. Klasse am Regino-Gymnasium in Prüm haben sich eine tolle Projektwoche ausgedacht. Während der Projektwoche sollen alle Talente genutzt werden: eine „Müllband" will Instrumente aus Müll bauen und damit ein Konzert geben, Hobby-Köche wollen die Schüler mit Biokost versorgen, Rate-Füchse einen Müllquiz entwickeln, angehende Journalisten wollen Passanten über ihr Müllverhalten befragen, andere Schüler wollen „Kunst aus Müll" herstellen und die Fotogruppe will die Aktionen dokumentieren. Und am Ende wird's in der Schulturnhalle ein öffentliches Fest geben, bei dem die Ergebnisse präsentiert werden. „Natürlich soll nach einer Woche nicht alles vorbei sein", so die Klassenlehrerin Susanne Faschin, „deshalb möchten wir, daß jede Klasse einen festen Klassenraum erhält, für den sie verantwortlich ist und den sie auch selber reinigen muß. Dann würden viele Jugendliche nicht mehr alles so bedenkenlos wegschmeißen". Außerdem sollen ältere Schüler Patenschaften für jüngere übernehmen, um sie in die Geheimnisse des Müllsparens einzuweihen.

BRIGITTE 21/91

2 Hör gut zu!

For answers, see listening script on TE Interleaf.

Ein Mitglied der Umwelt-AG kommt in die Klasse und erzählt den Schülern, was sie alles für ihre Umwelt machen können. Hör seiner Rede zu und schreib acht Vorschläge auf, die er macht!

3 Teilt euch in zwei Gruppen auf! Sucht euch an eurer Schule oder in eurem Ort irgendein Umweltprojekt, an dem ihr aktiv arbeiten könnt. Schreibt eure Erfahrungen auf und macht Fotografien für euren Berich!. Jede Gruppe berichtet dann der anderen Gruppe, was sie gemacht hat und wie umweltbewußt ihre Arbeit war.

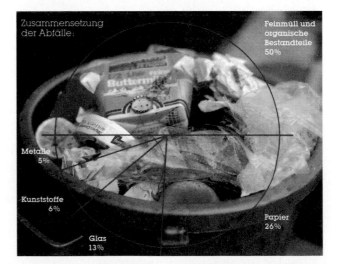

Zusammensetzung der Abfälle:
Feinmüll und organische Bestandteile 50%
Metalle 5%
Kunststoffe 6%
Glas 13%
Papier 26%

4 Du bist aktiv in der Umwelt-AG in deiner Schule. Du mußt morgen in eine Grundschulklasse gehen und mit den Kindern über Umweltschutz sprechen. Bereite eine kleine Rede vor, und übe sie mit deinen Klassenkameraden ein! Was halten sie von deiner Rede?

 5 Im deutschen Fernsehen gibt es ein Diskussionsprogramm: „Pro und Contra". Eure Klasse wurde dazu eingeladen. Teilt euch in zwei Gruppen auf und bereitet euch vor, eine von den zwei Ansichten zu argumentieren! Gruppe A ist der Ansicht, daß die Regierung mehr für die Umwelt machen muß; Gruppe B bereitet das Argument vor, daß die Regierung schon genug für die Umwelt macht — es kostet viel Geld und auch Jobs, und das können wir uns nicht leisten. Wählt abwechselnd Schüler von jeder Gruppe und diskutiert darüber!

Abfallvermeidung durch Recycling

Verpackungsstoffe	Sammelquoten (%)		Recyclingquoten (%)	
	1993	1995	1993	1995
Glas	60	80	42	72
Weißblech	40	80	26	72
Aluminium	30	80	18	72
Papier/Pappe	30	80	18	64
Kunststoffe	30	80	9	64
Verbund	20	80	66	4

Nach der Verpackungsverordnung von 1991 vorgeschrieben; Quelle: Verpackungsverordnung

6 Schau dir die Tabelle an! Welche Daten über Abfallvermeidung in Deutschland werden gezeigt? Welche Verpackungsstoffe werden am meisten gesammelt und wiederverwertet? Mach eine Umfrage in deiner Klasse oder in deiner Schule, und entwirf mit den Ergebnissen eine ähnliche Tabelle!

7 Die Grafik auf Seite 224 zeigt eine Zusammensetzung der gesamten Abfälle. Nenne für jede Kategorie konkrete Beispiele, und überlege dann, wie man diesen Müll wiederverwerten kann, anstatt ihn wegzuwerfen!

8

R O L L E N S P I E L

Du versuchst, deine Familie umweltbewußter zu machen. Du sprichst mit deinen Eltern und Geschwistern darüber, aber sie haben viele Ausreden. Du gibst dir Mühe, sie zu überzeugen. Deine Klassenkameraden spielen die Rollen von deinen Eltern und Geschwistern.

Can you express concern? (p. 208)

1 How would you express your fear that the hole in the ozone layer is getting larger?   1. Ich habe Angst, daß das Ozonloch immer größer wird.

2 How would you express your concern about air pollution?
2. Die Luftverschmutzung macht mir große Sorgen.

Can you make accusations? (p. 209)

3 How would you blame air pollution on people who always take their cars and never walk or take the bus?   3. Die Autofahrer sind schuld an der Luftverschmutzung, weil sie nie zu Fuß gehen oder den Bus nehmen.

Can you offer solutions? (p. 210)

4 How would you respond if someone asked you **Was könnte man für die Umwelt tun?**   4. E.g.: Man könnte einiges für die Umwelt tun.

Can you make polite requests? (p. 211)

5 How would you politely ask a salesperson for the following things?
a. a can without CFC   5. a. E.g.: Könnte ich bitte eine Dose ohne FCKW haben?
b. einen Papierbeutel b. E.g.: Dürfte ich bitte einen Papierbeutel haben?
c. ein Waschmittel ohne Phosphate
c. E.g.: Würden Sie mir bitte ein Waschmittel ohne   Phosphate geben?

Can you say what is being done about a problem? (p. 215)

6 How would you say that in Germany trash is always sorted?
6. In Deutschland wird Müll immer sortiert.

Can you offer solutions? (p. 216)

7 How would you respond if someone asked you what can, should, or must be done with the following things?
a. Müll (sortieren) 7. a. Müll kann sortiert werden.
b. Pfandflaschen (zurückbringen) b. Pfandflaschen sollen zurückgebracht werden.
c. alte Fahrräder (reparieren)
c. Alte Fahrräder müssen repariert werden.

Can you hypothesize? (p. 217)

8 How would you express the idea that we would have no air pollution if we all left our cars at home and rode bicycles?   8. E.g.: Wenn wir alle unsere Autos zu Hause lassen würden und Fahrrad fahren würden, hätten wir keine Luftverschmutzung.

9 How would you respond if a friend asked you **Was hättest du heute gemacht, wenn du nicht in der Schule gewesen wärst?**
9. E.g.: Wenn ich nicht in der Schule gewesen wäre, hätte ich heute meine Oma besucht.

ERSTE STUFE

EXPRESSING FEAR

Ich fürchte, daß ... *I am afraid that ...*
Das macht uns große Sorgen. *We are really worried about that.*

SAYING WHAT YOU COULD OR SHOULD DO ABOUT A PROBLEM

Wenn wir nur Naturprodukte benutzen dürften! *If only we were allowed to use natural products!*
Man müßte nur daran denken. *You would only have to think about it.*

OTHER USEFUL WORDS

das Abgas, -e *exhaust*
das Treibgas, -e *propulsion gas*
die Fabrik, -en *factory*

die Fahrgemeinschaft, -en *carpool*
das Katauto, -s *car with emission control*
das Öl, -e *oil*
die Luftverschmutzung *air pollution*
das Ozonloch *hole in the ozone layer*
der saure Regen *acid rain*
der Schadstoff, -e *pollutant*
der Schmutz *dirt*
das Waldsterben *the dying of the forests*
die Aludose, -n *aluminum can*
die Einwegflasche, -n *non-returnable bottle*
der Papierbeutel, - *paper bag*
die Pfandflasche, -n *deposit-only bottle*
die Plastiktüte, -n *plastic bag*
der Pumpzerstäuber, - *pump spray*

das Spülmittel, - *dishwashing liquid*
das Waschmittel, - *laundry soap*
der Mut *courage*
der Teil, -e *part*

s. Sorgen machen *to worry*
anbieten (sep) *to offer*
blasen *to blow*
ersetzen *to replace*
herstellen (sep) *to produce*
leck werden *to spring a leak*
sortieren *to sort*
vergrößern *to enlarge*
verpesten *to poison, pollute*
verschmutzen *to pollute*

biologisch abbaubar *biodegradable*
ausschließlich *exclusively*
umweltfreundlich *environmentally safe*
vermeidbar *avoidable*

ZWEITE STUFE

WORDS FOR TALKING ABOUT THE ENVIRONMENT

der Umweltschutz *environmental protection*
die Ameise, -n *ant*
die Biene, -n *bee*
der Frosch, ⸚e *frog*
der Vogel, ⸚ *bird*
der Wald, ⸚er *forest*
der Sauerstoff *oxygen*
der Schaden, ⸚ *damage*
die Skipiste, -n *ski run*
die Herstellung, -en *production*
die Vorsicht *caution*
der Abfall, ⸚e *trash, waste*
das Abwasser, ⸚ *wastewater*
die Batterie, -n *battery*
der Faserstift, -e *felt-tip pen*
der Kunstdünger, - *artificial fertilizer*

die Mehrwegflasche, -n *reusable bottle*
der Strom *electricity*
der Tintenkiller, - *chemical eraser*
das Gift, -e *poison*
das Dach, ⸚er *roof*

abholzen (sep) *to deforest*
ausrechnen (sep) *to calculate*
ausschalten (sep) *to switch off*
duschen *to shower*
miterleben (sep) *to experience*
radeln *to bicycle*
stecken *to put (into)*
verbessern *to improve*
verschwenden *to waste*
verzichten auf (acc) *to do without*

wiederverwenden (sep) *to use again*
wiederverwerten (sep) *to recycle*

außerdem *besides that*
gefährlich *dangerous*
giftig *poisonous*
nahe *near*
sogar *even*

📼 Location Opener
Dresden, pages 228-231
Video Program, Videocassette 2

*U*sing the Photograph,
pp. 228-229

Background Information

Dresden got its name from the old Sorbian (**altsorbisch**) word **drezd'ane** for the *forest people* who first settled the area around 600. Dresden was not documented until 1004 and is believed to have been officially founded around 1216. This view of the city shows several of its famous baroque buildings which led to its nickname *das Elbflorenz* (*Florence of the Elbe*). During World War II, Germans thought that Dresden would be spared from allied attacks because of its architectural and cultural treasures, but it was almost completely destroyed by an Allied air raid in February 1945. Rebuilding of the city started 40 years ago and is still not completed.

Geography Connection

Point out to students the boat landing pier along the river bank. This is called **Anlegestelle der Weißen Flotte** (*moorings of the white fleet*). It connects the city between spring and fall with Meißen and Bad Schandau. Have students identify the river Elbe, Meißen, and Bad Schandau on a detailed map of Germany.

Home Economics Connection

Have a student ask the home economics teacher about a popular quilting pattern called the "Dresden Plate." Have them find out what it looks like and how it got its name.

*U*sing the Almanac and Map,
p. 229

The coat of arms of Dresden depicts on one side a black lion on a golden background, and on the other side two black vertical bars on a golden background. While families of the nobility initiallly developed coats of arms out of military necessity—to distinguish friend from foe in battle—the heraldic symbols of medieval towns and cities generally evolved out of seals used on legal contracts. The first known occurence of the Dresden coat of arms is on a seal from 1309. The lion and the vertical bars refer to the crest of the Margrave of Meißen who ruled the city at that time. Since then, the coat of arms of Dresden has changed relatively little.

Terms in the Almanac

- **Schloß:** The **Dresdner Schloß** was built in the renaissance style in the 16th century. The castle was destroyed in 1945, and restoration did not begin until 1985.

- **Kurfürst Friedrich August I.:** Also referred to as **August der Starke,** he was the elector of Saxony from 1694 to 1733. He received the Polish crown after his conversion to Catholicism. He embellished the city of Dresden with ornate baroque buildings such as the **Zwinger** and the **Frauenkirche.**

- **Kurfürst Friedrich August II.:** He was the son of **August der Starke.**

- **Carl Maria von Weber:** He was a famous composer who created music for orchestra and piano, as well as for choir. He is best known for the operas *Euryanthe* (1823), *Oberon* (1826), and his most famous work *Freischütz* (1821).

- **Richard Wagner:** This composer was also the conductor of the Dresden symphony. He wrote such famous operas as *Der fliegende Holländer, Tannhäuser, Lohengrin, Tristan und Isolde,* and *Der Ring des Nibelungen.*

- **Genußmittelindustrie:** For many, the production of confection and pastries is synonymous with Dresden. Annual trade fairs for the baking and confectionary trade are held here.

- **Dresdener Stollen:** This traditional sweet Christmas bread is prepared four to six weeks before the holidays and stored in a cool place to develop its flavor. It is made of yeast, sugar, milk, flour, butter, eggs, almonds, almond paste, raisins, and a variety of spices. It is shaped into a loaf and baked. Then, powdered sugar is sprinkled on top.

Teacher Note

Recipes for **Dresdener Stollen** are available in many cookbooks. **Stollen** is also available in many American specialty stores during the holiday season.

Music Connection

Have a student check with the music teacher to learn more about Richard Wagner. Perhaps you can play some excerpts of his works.

Using the Map

Have students locate and trace the path of the Elbe river on the map on p. 394 (Please note: the map is on p. 393 in the *Teacher's Edition.*). You may also want to use Map Transparency 1.

*I*nterpreting the Photo Essay, *pp. 230-231*

② **Der Goldene Reiter** is a memorial to **August der Starke.** It is made of gold-plated copper and was put in its present location in 1736. The statue is located at the **Neustädter Markt.**

③ The **Zwinger** received its name from the original **Zwinger Garten** around which it was built.

④ Originally, in the 16th century, the **Albertinum** was a **Zeughaus** *(arsenal)*. It was later converted to a museum to hold the unique collection of the Saxon electors' treasures.

⑤ **Die ehemalige Katholische Hofkirche** was commissioned by **Friedrich August II.** and built from 1739 to 1755. Since 1980 it has also been referred to as the **Kathedrale Sanctissimae Trinitatis.** The church houses the largest organ designed by builder Gottfried Silbermann, who died shortly after having tuned this magnificent instrument.

⑥ The **Frauenkirche** was commissioned in 1726 and completed in 1738. The church with its 95-meter (311-foot) dome was once the best-known landmark of Dresden.

⑦ The **Staatsoper** or **Semperoper** has presented the premiere performances of many famous operas, including several by Richard Strauss. The facade is decorated with statues of Shakespeare, Molière, Schiller, and Goethe. In front of the opera stands a statue of King Johann as well as one of composer Carl Maria von Weber.

Thinking Critically

Analyzing Throughout the location openers in Levels 1, 2, and 3, students have learned about numerous buildings that were destroyed by war and have been or currently are being restored. Some people do not agree that spending millions on restoration is a good idea, in view of world hunger and other social problems. Why do students think the Germans have invested so much time and money in restoration of historical buildings? Is it worth it? If so, why?

Komm mit nach

Dresden!

Dresden

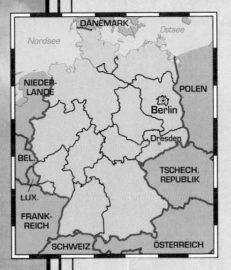

Bundesland: Sachsen

Einwohner: 520 000

Fluß: Elbe

Sehenswürdigkeiten: Zwinger, Albertinum, Schloß, Semper-oper

Berühmte Leute: Kurfürsten Friedrich August I. und II., Carl Maria von Weber (1786-1826), Richard Wagner (1813-1883)

Industrie: Maschinenbau, Elektronik, Arzneimittelpro-duktion, Genußmittelindustrie (Schokolade), optische Artikel

Bekannte Gerichte: Dresdener Stollen

Foto ① **Die bekannteste Stadtansicht, Schloß mit Hofkirche und Semperoper im Hintergrund**

Dresden

Dresden, das weltberühmte „Elbflorenz", erlebte seine Glanzzeit unter den prunkliebenden Kurfürsten Friedrich August I. und seinem Sohn Friedrich August II., beide auch Könige von Polen. In diesem „Augustäischen" Zeitalter (1694-1783) entwickelte sich Dresden zu einer der schönsten barocken deutschen Residenzstädte.

② Der Goldene Reiter zeigt August I. — auch August der Starke genannt — in der Rüstung eines römischen Cäsaren.

③ Dresdens berühmtestes Baudenkmal ist der Zwinger, eine Perle des Barock von Baumeister Pöppelmann in den Jahren 1711 bis 1732 geschaffen. Der Zwinger beherbergt Dresdens einmalige Kunstsammlung, die „Gemäldegalerie Alte Meister", mit Meisterwerken europäischer Maler wie Rubens, Rembrandt, Dürer, Holbein, Cranach, Velázquez, Raffael, Giorgione, Corregio, Tintoretto und andere Meister.

④ Das Albertinum enthält die „Gemäldegalerie Neue Meister". Diese Kunstsammlung von Weltruf zeigt Meisterwerke der Romantik, des Biedermeier, des Expressionismus und Impressionismus deutscher und europäischer Meister. Im Albertinum befindet sich auch das „Grüne Gewölbe", eine Kunstsammlung aus der kurfürstlichen Schatzkammer. Ausgestellt sind Gefäße, Schmuck, Waffen und andere Gegenstände, viele aus Gold, Silber und kostbaren Edelsteinen gefertigt.

⑥ Die Ruine der Frauenkirche. Hier stand einst Deutschlands bedeutendster protestantischer Kirchenbau und das Wahrzeichen Dresdens. Die Kirche, wie auch der größte Teil Dresdens, wurde im Februar 1945 durch Bombenangriffe total zerstört. Die Kirche wird zur Zeit wieder aufgebaut.

⑤ Die ehemalige Katholische Hofkirche, die größte Kirche Sachsens, wurde vom römischen Architekten Gaetano Chiaveri zwischen 1739 und 1755 im Stil des römischen Barock errichtet.

⑦ Die weltberühmte Semperoper, ein Bauwerk von Gottfried Semper im Stil der Hochrenaissance in den Jahren 1871 bis 1878 errichtet, ist Heimat der Dresdner Staatsoper.

Kapitel 10: Die Kunst zu leben

	FUNCTIONS	GRAMMAR	CULTURE	RE-ENTRY
Los geht's! *pp. 234-235*	Was tun für die Kultur? *p. 234*			
Erste Stufe *pp. 236-239*	•Expressing preference, given certain possibilities, *p. 236* •Expressing envy and admiration, *p. 237*	Prepositions with the genitive case, *p. 238*	Aphorismen, *p. 239*	•Expressing preference, *p. 236* •**Würde**-forms, *p. 236* •Genitive case forms, *p. 238* •Prepositions, *p. 238*
Weiter geht's! *pp. 240-241*	Zeitungsbericht: Schüler besuchen Staatstheater, *p. 240*			
Zweite Stufe *pp. 242-246*	•Expressing happiness and sadness, *p. 242* •Saying that something is or was being done, *p. 244*	•**Da-** and **wo-**compounds, *p. 243* •The passive voice (Summary), *p. 245*	Landeskunde: Kultur findet man überall! *p. 247*	•**Da-** and **wo-**compounds, *p. 243* •Past participles, *p. 245* •Subjunctive forms of modals, *p. 245* •**Von** + dative case, *p. 245*
Zum Lesen *pp. 248-250*	Eine Gruselgeschichte Reading Strategy: Reading for comprehension			
Zum Schreiben *p. 251*	Ein Gedicht — ein Bild mit Wörtern gemalt Writing Strategy: Using figurative language and sound devices			
Review *pp. 252-255*	•Anwendung, *p. 252* •Kann ich's wirklich? *p. 254* •Wortschatz, *p. 255*			

Assessment Options

Stufe Quizzes
•*Chapter Resources,* Book 4
  Erste Stufe, Quiz 10-1
  Zweite Stufe, Quiz 10-2
•*Assessment Items, Audiocassette* 8 B

Kapitel 10 Chapter Test
•*Chapter Resources,* Book 4
•*Assessment Guide,* Speaking Test
•*Assessment Items, Audiocassette* 8 B

Test Generator, Kapitel 10

Chapter Overview

RESOURCES Print	RESOURCES Audiovisual
	Textbook Audiocassette 5 B
Practice and Activity Book	

	Textbook Audiocassette 5 B
Practice and Activity Book *Chapter Resources*, Book 4 　●Communicative Activity 10-1 　●Communicative Activity 10-2 　●Additional Listening Activity 10-1 　●Additional Listening Activity 10-2 　●Additional Listening Activity 10-3 　●Student Response Forms 　●Realia 10-1 　●Situation Card 10-1 　●Teaching Transparency Master 10-1 　●Quiz 10-1	 *Additional Listening Activities, Audiocassette* 10 B *Additional Listening Activities, Audiocassette* 10 B *Additional Listening Activities, Audiocassette* 10 B *Teaching Transparency* 10-1 *Assessment Items, Audiocassette* 8 B

	Textbook Audiocassette 5 B
Practice and Activity Book	

	Textbook Audiocassette 5 B
Practice and Activity Book *Chapter Resources*, Book 4 　●Communicative Activity 10-3 　●Communicative Activity 10-4 　●Additional Listening Activity 10-4 　●Additional Listening Activity 10-5 　●Additional Listening Activity 10-6 　●Student Response Forms 　●Realia 10-2 　●Situation Card 10-2 　●Teaching Transparency Master 10-2 　●Quiz 10-2 *Video Guide*	 *Additional Listening Activities, Audiocassette* 10 B *Additional Listening Activities, Audiocassette* 10 B *Additional Listening Activities, Audiocassette* 10 B *Teaching Transparency* 10-2 *Assessment Items, Audiocassette* 8 B *Video Program*, Videocassette 2

	Textbook Audiocassette 11

Chapter Resources, Book 4 　●Realia 10-3 　●Situation Card 10-3 *Video Guide*	 *Video Program*, Videocassette 2

Alternative Assessment

●Performance Assessment
Teacher's Edition
　Erste Stufe, p. 231K
　Zweite Stufe, p. 231O

●Portfolio Assessment
　Written: **Anwendung,** Activity 3, *Pupil's Edition,* p. 252;
　Assessment Guide, p. 23
　Oral: **Anwendung,** Activity 6, *Pupil's Edition,* p. 253;
　Assessment Guide, p. 23
●**Notizbuch,** *Pupil's Edition,* pp. 239, 244

CHAPTER OVERVIEW

Kapitel 10: Die Kunst zu leben
Textbook Listening Activities Scripts

For Student Response Forms, see *Chapter Resources,* Book 4, pp. 22-25.

Erste Stufe
Activity 4, p. 236

ERWIN Hallo, Lise, hier ist Erwin! Du, wir wollten doch diese Woche mit der Clique was Kulturelles unternehmen. Hast du schon was aus dem Kulturkalender rausgesucht?

LISE Hallo, Erwin! Nee, du! Aber warte mal! Ich hole ihn sofort ... Also, hier ist er.

ERWIN Dann lies doch mal vor, was für Veranstaltungen so am Wochenende laufen!

LISE Also, da gibt es eine historische Ausstellung über das Leben der Juden im Deutschland des 19. Jahrhunderts.

ERWIN Interessiert dich denn sowas überhaupt?

LISE Ja, klar! Wir sprechen gerade im Geschichtsunterricht über den Holocaust zur Zeit des NS-Regimes. Da möchte ich schon etwas mehr Hintergrundwissen haben. Und du? Interessierst du dich denn dafür?

ERWIN Ja, schon! Aber ich würde lieber in ein Konzert gehen. Was läuft denn sonst noch?

LISE Also, den ganzen Samstag lang gibt's ein Jazzfestival im Stadtpark.

ERWIN Uii! Klasse! Dazu hätte ich auf jeden Fall Lust! Und du?

LISE Hmm. Mal sehen. Du, hör mal! Am Samstag gibt es auch eine Kunstausstellung mit Bildern von Andy Warhol ... und dann noch ein Konzert des evangelischen Jugendchors in der Sankt-Pius-Kirche.

ERWIN Hmm ... äh ...

LISE Also, mir fällt es echt schwer, mich zu entscheiden. Aber, ich glaub', daß ich am liebsten zur Ausstellung über das Leben der Juden gehen möchte! Tja, und dann würde ich eventuell noch zum Chorkonzert in die Sankt-Pius-Kirche gehen. Und du, Erwin?

ERWIN Also, wenn ich ehrlich sein soll, würde ich am liebsten tagsüber zum Jazzfestival gehen. Und dann, am Samstag abend würde ich vielleicht ins Kino gehen.

LISE Kino??? Ich denke, wir wollten was Kulturelles machen! Und jetzt schlägst du Kino vor!? Das ist ja wohl das Letzte!

ERWIN Was hast du denn, Lise? Seit wann haben Kinofilme nichts mit Kultur zu tun? Denk doch mal an all die alten Kultfilme mit Humphrey Bogart oder Clark Gable! Das sind echte Klassiker! Kultur pur, sag' ich dir!

LISE Na schön! Und in welchen Kultfilm möchtest du bitte gehen?

ERWIN Also, am Samstag ist die Premiere von dem neuen Action Thriller mit Arnold Schwarzenegger. Sagenhaft soll der sein!

LISE Soso, Arnold Schwarzenegger!

ERWIN Ja, wart's nur ab! In fünfzig Jahren oder so sind seine Filme richtige Klassiker! Das kannst du mir glauben!

LISE Also, paß mal auf, Erwin! Was hältst du davon, wenn wir zuerst aufs Jazzfestival gehen und abends dann zur historischen Ausstellung über die Juden?

ERWIN Hm. Okay, einverstanden! Ich ruf' die anderen an und sag' Bescheid, für welches Programm wir uns entschieden haben.

LISE Prima! Bis Samstag dann.

Answers to Activity 4

Lise: historische Ausstellung; Chorkonzert

Erwin: Jazzfestival; Kino

Sie entschließen sich, zum Jazzfestival und zur historischen Ausstellung zu gehen.

Zweite Stufe
Activity 17, p. 243

SUSI Hallo, Inge! Wie hat dir unser Klassenausflug gestern abend gefallen?

INGE Super! Das Ballett *Giselle* war echt beeindruckend. Außerdem war ich zum ersten Mal in der Staatsoper, du auch, Susi?

SUSI Ja! Schau mal, da kommen Ömur und Lutz. Ich möchte gern wissen, was sie über das Ballett denken. He, Lutz, Ömur, kommt doch mal hierher! Inge und ich haben uns gerade über die Aufführung gestern in der Staatsoper unterhalten. Was ist eure Meinung dazu?

LUTZ Also, zu Anfang war ich ja etwas skeptisch. Ich dachte immer, daß Ballett nur was für Mädchen ist.

INGE Wieso denn das, Lutz?

LUTZ Ach, das kann ich gar nicht begründen. Ich glaub', das war ein echtes Vorurteil von mir. Aber gestern, im Laufe der Vorstellung, habe ich meine Meinung allerdings geändert.

ÖMUR Ich war auch zuerst skeptisch. Ich habe nämlich gedacht, daß die Musik mir bestimmt nicht gefällt.

SUSI Und? Hast du deine Meinung geändert, Ömur?

ÖMUR Nee, eigentlich nicht! Wißt ihr, ich mag fetzige Musik, und diese Ballettmusik hat einfach zu wenig Power für mich.

INGE Das ist aber schade, Ömur. Für mich war es echt toll, mal was ganz anderes zu sehen und zu hören. Eben was Besonderes.

ÖMUR Das mag zwar sein, aber mir hat die Musik nun mal nicht gefallen. Ich kann's auch nicht ändern!

SUSI Wie fandet ihr denn die Kulissen? Ich glaube, die haben mich am meisten beeindruckt. Die erste Szene mit der Insel im Meer war doch spitze, meint ihr nicht?

ÖMUR Ja, das muß ich zugeben; mit den Kulissen haben sie sich echt Mühe gegeben.

INGE Da stecken wirkliche Künstler dahinter. Ich würde gern mal so eine Aufgabe im Kunstunterricht bei uns in der Schule machen.

LUTZ Gar keine schlechte Idee. Das würde mir auch Spaß machen. Übrigens war ich sehr begeistert von dem Schiff, das sie da auf der Bühne hatten.

ÖMUR Da stimme ich euch zu! Aber wißt ihr, was ich ganz toll fand?

INGE Na sag's schon!

ÖMUR Die Tänzer waren nicht nur gute Balletttänzer, son- dern meiner Meinung nach auch hervorragende Schauspieler!

SUSI Ja, da hast du recht! Vor allem der bärtige Hilarion, der vor lauter Eifersucht ganz wütend war.

INGE Der hat mir auch besser gefallen als der junge Maler Albrecht. Der sah zwar toll aus, aber er war gleich- zeitig auch ein bißchen langweilig.

LUTZ Ich fand sie alle gut. Immerhin gab es ja auch noch eine ganze Menge andere Tänzer, die nur in Nebenrollen auftraten, ohne die das Stück aber nicht möglich wäre.

ÖMUR Na ja, dafür war das Ende des Stückes aber etwas enttäuschend, genau wie die Musik.

LUTZ Nun hör schon auf mit deinen Beschwerden über die Musik, Ömur! Ich kann eigentlich nicht behaupten, daß ich vom Ende des Stückes enttäuscht war. Meiner Meinung nach muß es nicht immer ein Happy-End geben!

SUSI Hm. Also, ich stimme mit Ömur überein. Ich war auch etwas traurig darüber. Ein Happy-End hätte mir viel besser gefallen. Das hätte gut zu der märchenhaften Atmosphäre gepaßt.

INGE Eben! Ach übrigens, was ich noch toll fand, das waren die Kostüme!

SUSI Ja, stimmt, Susi! Waren die nicht prunkvoll und wunderschön?

INGE Genau! Also, ich hätte Lust, bald wieder in ein Ballett zu gehen.

Answers to Activity 17

Sie waren im Ballett *Giselle*.
Inge: gut / fand die Kostüme toll
Susi: gut / fand die Kulissen spitze
Lutz: gut / hatte zuerst Vorurteile
Ömur: nicht gut / ihm hat die Musik nicht gefallen; war vom Ende enttäuscht

Activity 23, *p. 244*

Guten Tag, sehr verehrte Zuhörer! Ich darf Sie herzlich zu unserem Sonntagskonzert begrüßen! Wir sind heute zu Gast in der Berliner Philharmonie. Das Konzert wird von dem weltberühmten Dirigenten Zubin Mehta dirigiert. Auf dem Programm stehen, wie bereits in unserem Vorspann angekündigt, Werke von Beethoven, Tschaikowski und Bach.

Da wir noch einige Minuten Zeit haben, bevor die Vorstellung beginnt, möchte ich Ihnen kurz beschreiben, was sich im Konzertsaal abspielt. Die Berliner Philharmoniker nahmen bereits vor einer halben Stunde ihre Plätze auf der Bühne ein. Das gesamte Ensemble ist mit den letzten Vorbereitungen beschäftigt. Die Instrumente werden von den Musikern gestimmt. Viele Zuschauer strömen in den Saal und werden zu ihren Sitzplätzen geführt.

Lassen Sie mich, liebe Freunde der klassischen Musik, die Gelegenheit nutzen, ein paar Worte über die Philharmonie einzuschieben. Für alle unsere Zuhörer, die den ungewöhnlichen Bau dieses Gebäudes nicht kennen, hier ein paar Details. Der Konzertsaal der Berliner Philharmonie ist asymmetrisch angelegt und sieht darum wie ein verschobenes Fünfeck aus. Ringsum steigen unregelmäßig angeordnete Logenterrassen an, die allen Zuschauern einen guten Blick auf die Bühne bieten. Die Akustik entfaltet sich dadurch äußerst wirkungsvoll.

Meine sehr verehrten Zuhörer, mittlerweile hat sich der Zuschauerraum fast gefüllt. Die letzten Gäste werden von den Platzanweisern zu ihren Plätzen gebracht. Das muntere Stimmengewirr des Publikums vermischt sich mit den Tönen der Geigen, Posaunen, Harfen und Kontrabässen. Die mei- sten Musiker sind nun bereit. Sie haben ihre Instrumente abgestellt, um noch ein letztes Mal ihre Noten auf den Notenständern zu überprüfen. Da betritt auch schon der Dirigent die Bühne. Maestro Mehta wird mit lautstarkem Beifall begrüßt. Er steht nun am Podest und erhebt seinen Dirigentenstab. Atemlose Stille füllt den Raum, bevor das Orchester unter Leitung des Maestros das Konzert beginnt. Meine lieben Zuhörer, ich verabschiede mich vorübergehend, damit Sie die harmonischen Klänge dieser wunderbaren Sinfonien genießen können.

Answers to Activity 23

die Musiker; die Zuschauer; den Konzertsaal; die Logen; die Akustik; die Instrumente; den Dirigenten / die Berliner Philharmoniker; Werke von Beethoven, Tschaikowski und Bach (klassische Musik)

SCRIPTS

Anwendung
Activity 1, p. 252

NICOLE   Hallo, Regina! Komm, setz dich zu uns!

REGINA   Ach, hallo Nicole! Hallo Sascha!

RAINER   Tag! Ich bin der Rainer. Kann ich dir was zu trinken bestellen?

REGINA   Tag, Rainer! Ja, gern. Ich nehm 'nen Cappuccino!

NICOLE   Du, Regina, hättest du nicht Lust, mit Rainer, Sascha und mir am Wochenende was zu unternehmen?

REGINA   Klar! Wofür interessiert ihr euch denn so?

RAINER   Also, wir überlegen gerade, ob wir zum B.B. King Konzert gehen sollen.

REGINA   Gibt es noch Karten?

RAINER   Ja, an der Abendkasse kriegt man immer noch welche! Das Konzert findet am Samstag in Karlsruhe statt. Wißt ihr, dieser Mann ist einfach spitze. Er ist ja bereits in den Sechzigern, geht aber trotzdem noch regelmäßig auf Tournee. Einfach sagenhaft!

REGINA   Du magst wohl Rhythm 'n Blues, was?

RAINER   Und wie! Du etwa nicht?

REGINA   Doch schon! Aber eigentlich gehe ich nicht so oft in Konzerte. Ich gehe lieber ins Ballett oder in die Oper!

NICOLE   Was? Das wußte ich ja gar nicht, daß du dich für sowas interessierst!

REGINA   Doch, leidenschaftlich! Am liebsten mag ich dramatische Opern mit einem tragischen Ende, so wie *La Traviata* zum Beispiel! Und du, Nicole? Was interessiert dich am meisten?

NICOLE   Tja, also ich bin ein Literaturfan!

SASCHA   Bücherwurm nennt man das!

NICOLE   Ha! Ha! Sehr witzig, Sascha! Ich les' halt gern; am liebsten Shakespeare. Und wenn sich die Gelegenheit ergibt, dann sehe ich mir auch gern Stücke im Theater an. Nächste Woche läuft im Landestheater *Andorra* von Max Frisch. Na, Sascha, gehst du mit mir dahin?

SASCHA   Nur wenn du mit mir in die Kunstausstellung im Stadtmuseum gehst!

NICOLE   Was wird denn ausgestellt?

SASCHA   Surrealistische Gemälde von Dali und Magritte. Einfach super! Ich steh' total darauf!

REGINA   Hmm. Es sieht so aus, als ob wir alle ziemlich verschiedene Interessen haben.

NICOLE   Willst du damit sagen, daß wir lieber doch nichts zusammen unternehmen sollten?

REGINA   Nein, im Gegenteil! Ich habe einen Vorschlag: warum machen wir nicht alles der Reihe nach? Zuerst gehen wir am Samstag ins B.B. King Konzert. Dann gehen wir nächste Woche ins Theater, dann in die Kunstausstellung und irgendwann auch mal ins Ballett oder in die Oper! Na, wie findet ihr das?

NICOLE   Klasse Idee! Das bringt auf jeden Fall mal was Abwechslung in unsere Unternehmungen! Ich bin dabei! Wie sieht's mit euch aus, Jungs?

SASCHA   Klar! Ich mach' mit! Und du Rainer?

RAINER   Ich bin auch dabei!

Answers to Activity 1

Rainer: Konzert; Sascha: Kunstausstellung; Regina: Ballett, Oper; Nicole: Literatur; Theater

Kapitel 10: Die Kunst zu leben
Projects and Games

PROJECT

In this activity, students will plan and coordinate a summer festival for their town. They should work in small groups. Each group should concentrate on one aspect of the festival.

Materials Students may need poster board, some photos or pictures, and markers.

Suggested Sequence

1. Ask students to write down their initial ideas of what they would like to include in the summer festival. Then narrow the events/exhibits/performances to a number which can be divided equally among groups of students.
2. Each group brainstorms and compiles information and materials for its part of the festival.
3. The groups work on a poster advertising their event.
4. After students have completed the artistic part of the project (designing and labeling), they must write a paragraph for the local paper advertising their event. The paragraph should describe the type of event, point out its uniqueness to the area, as well as reasons why it is worth attending.
5. Each group presents its contribution to the festival to the rest of the class. Display the entire program in the classroom.

Grading the Project

Suggested point distribution (total = 100 points)

Poster content and originality	30
Oral presentation	30
Written information	40

♜ GAME

Künstlerisch begabt

This game will help students review the new vocabulary by sketching a particular word or phrase from an oral description.

Procedure Ask students to choose a word or phrase from the **Wortschatz** page which will lend itself to being sketched. Each student sketches the word he or she chose, signs the paper, and returns it to the teacher. The teacher mixes up the papers, chooses one at a time, and calls on each student to describe his or her picture without telling what word or phrase it represents. The other students listen carefully and try to draw an identical picture and label it with its corresponding word.

PROJECTS AND GAMES

Kapitel 10: Die Kunst zu leben
Lesson Plans, pages 232-255

Teacher Note

Before you begin the chapter, you may want to preview the *Video Program* and consult the *Video Guide.* Suggestions for integrating the video into each chapter are given in the *Video Guide* and in the chapter interleaf. Activity masters for video selections can be found in the *Video Guide.*

Using the Chapter Opener, *pp. 232-233*

Motivating Activity

Ask students about their families' and their own artistic abilities. Do any of them play an instrument or have another artistic talent? (**Ist jemand in eurer Familie musikalisch begabt? Wenn ja, welches Instrument spielt er oder sie? Habt ihr in der Familie jemanden, der noch anders künstlerisch begabt ist?**)

Culture Note

① **Hausmusik** is not a specific genre, rather it refers to any type of music in which one or more family members participate at home. Popular instruments are **Blockflöte, Gitarre,** and **Klavier.**

Thinking Critically

② **Drawing Inferences** Ask students to take a closer look at the photograph and guess when in the course of the evening this scene is taking place. (**in der Pause**)

Drama Connection

② Have students find out about the most recent school play. What was the name of the play and what was it about? Perhaps students can obtain a poster or flyer from a performance and bring it to class.

 ### For Individual Needs

③ **Visual Learners** Bring to class a copy of the entertainment section of the local paper or that of a larger city. Let students go through it and discuss what types of cultural events or activities are offered that weekend. Have students make a list.

Teaching Suggestion

③ Ask students to recall a cultural event they attended in the past. What was it and what did they like or not like about it? (**Berichtet über eine kulturelle Veranstaltung, die ihr besucht habt! Hat euch die Veranstaltung gefallen oder nicht? Erzählt davon, und begründet eure Meinung!**)

Focusing on Outcomes

To get students to focus on the chapter objectives, ask them whose artistic abilities they admire and why. Then have students preview the learning outcomes listed on p. 233. **NOTE:** These outcomes are modeled in **Los geht's!** (pp. 234-235) and **Weiter geht's!** (pp. 240-241) and evaluated in **Kann ich's wirklich?** (p. 254).

*T*eaching Los geht's!

pp. 234-235

Resources for Los geht's!

- *Textbook Audiocassette* 5 B
- *Practice and Activity Book*

Teacher Note

Los geht's! is recorded on audiocassette.

Los geht's! Summary

In **Was tun für die Kultur?**, Philipp, Michael, Sonja, and Tanja talk about their cultural interests. The following student outcomes listed on p. 233 are modeled in the episode: expressing preference, given certain possibilities and expressing envy and admiration.

Motivating Activity

Ask students to name a cultural event they would not want to miss if it came to their area. (**Denkt an eine kulturelle Veranstaltung, die ihr auf keinen Fall verpassen würdet, wenn sie hier in ... stattfinden würde!**)

Teaching Suggestion

Divide the conversation into three parts. Play one portion at a time as students follow along in the text. Follow each partial playing with questions to check for comprehension. Explain any new terms, phrases, or constructions in German by paraphrasing or using synonyms. After working through all three segments, play the entire conversation again, stopping repeatedly to check for students' understanding of key points.

Thinking Critically

Drawing Inferences Ask students to think about the possible reasons why students' tickets to cultural events are discounted. Why do state supported cultural institutions and privately financed institutions do this? Do they have anything to gain from such a policy?

For Individual Needs

1 Challenge Ask students to work in pairs as they complete the chart with information about the cultural interests of the four German teenagers. Then prepare a blank chart on a transparency and elicit information from students to complete the chart.

Teaching Suggestions

2 This activity could also be used as a game, in which case each group that correctly answers a question from the opposing group receives a point. You can increase the number of questions to eight or ten to extend the game.

3 Expand this project by having one group do music, another art, and a third literature. Each group should take a section of the bulletin board to make a display. Provide a list of representative people from each field or have students make their own lists. Reports should include examples of these people's work.

3 Refer students to the Almanacs in the four Location Openers where **Berühmte Leute** are mentioned. Many of these people can be included in the group's projects.

Closure

Refer students back to the outcomes listed on p. 233. How would they describe the interest level of German students in cultural activities? How would they compare it to their own? (**Wie würdest du das Interesse deutscher Schüler an kulturellen Veranstaltungen beschreiben? Vergleich es mit deinem Interesse an kulturellen Veranstaltungen!**)

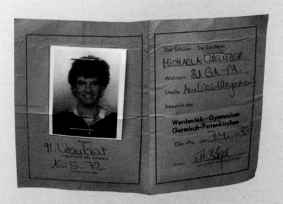

LOS GEHT'S!

Teaching Erste Stufe,
pp. 236-239

ERSTE STUFE

Resources for Erste Stufe

Practice and Activity Book
Chapter Resources, Book 4
  • Communicative Activities 10-1, 10-2
  • Additional Listening Activities 10-1, 10-2, 10-3
  • Student Response Forms
  • Realia 10-1
  • Situation Card 10-1
  • Teaching Transparency Master 10-1
  • Quiz 10-1
Audiocassette Program
  • *Textbook Audiocassette* 5 B
  • *Additional Listening Activities, Audiocassette* 10 B
  • *Assessment Items, Audiocassette* 8 B

▶ **page 236**

MOTIVATE

♜ Game

To play the game **Wer ist das?**, prepare a list of famous Germans. Write the names on separate pieces of paper. Then divide the class in two teams. Teams alternate picking a piece of paper and identifying the individual.
Examples:
Johann Sebastian Bach —-> war ein Komponist.
Wolfgang Borchert —-> war ein Schriftsteller.

TEACH
PRESENTATION: Wortschatz

• After introducing the new words from **auf deutsch erklärt,** make up sentences in which you circumlocute the word. Students have to restate each sentence using the new vocabulary.
• Ask students to use the new vocabulary from the **auf deutsch erklärt** section in sentences.
• Work with the new vocabulary in the **auf english erklärt** section. Read each sentence aloud and have students do the same. Then ask for variations of each sentence, keeping the structure the same but varying the context.
• Ask students to describe the difference between **Oper** and **Rockkonzert.**
• Have students give several examples of **Grimms Märchen.**

Teacher Note

The **Gebrüder Grimm** not only published numerous fairy tales but also published many reference works on language, such as the first German dictionary, *Deutsches Wörterbuch* and a book on German grammar, *Deutsche Grammatik.*

PRESENTATION: So sagt man das!

To practice the different phrases for expressing preference given in the **So sagt man das!** box, tell students to use the information provided in the Location Opener on pp. 228-231 to answer the following question: **Was würdest du gern in Dresden besuchen, wenn du genug Zeit hättest?**

▶ **page 237**

Teaching Suggestion

5 To prepare students for their partner work, go through all the phrases and elicit both singular and plural versions where appropriate. Students can use these phrases for general statements (plural) and a specific example (singular).
Examples:
sich eine Oper ansehen; sich viele Opern ansehen
in ein Kunstmuseum gehen; in Kunstmuseen gehen

For Individual Needs

5 Challenge Each time students respond, have them give an example of their main interest.
Example:
Ich würde hauptsächlich Comics lesen, so wie MAD, ja vielleicht auch mal Hemingway lesen.

Building on Previous Skills

6 Before you begin with this activity, compile a list of adverbial expressions with students. Here are some they should already know: **ab und zu, regelmäßig, immer, so oft wie möglich, am Wochenende, einmal im Monat, hin und wieder.**

PRESENTATION: So sagt man das!

- Point out to students that **der, die, das,** and their forms can be used as emphatic personal pronouns, replacing **er, sie, es,** and their forms.
- To practice the two new expressions, ask students to complete each of the following statements.
Ich beneide ..., weil ...
Ich bewundere Personen, die ...
- Make up some rumors or hearsay about people in your school and present them to the class. Have students react to what you tell them by telling you why they envy or admire that person.

▶ *page 238*

PRESENTATION: Grammatik

- Review with students the forms and uses of the genitive case (see p. 93).
- You may want to let students know that **anstatt** is considered slightly more formal than its short form **statt.**
- Before presenting the prepositional phrases in the grammar box, give students some sentences with prepositions taking the genitive. See if they can identify some the functions of the prepositions.
Examples:
Während des Sommers habe ich kaum Klavier geübt. Während is used to indicate the duration of an event.

Anstatt klassischer Musik höre ich Rockmusik. Anstatt indicates an alternative or reason.

 For Individual Needs

10 Challenge After students have worked through this activity, have them supply a **weil**-clause instead of a prepositional phrase. Then have them continue their sentence with a phrase using **wegen** or another **weil**-clause.
Examples:
..., weil es mir Spaß macht, nicht wegen ...
..., weil ich Musik gern habe, nicht weil, ...
..., weil ich Schauspieler werden möchte, nicht wegen ...

▶ *page 239*

Teaching Suggestion

11 This project could be done individually or in pairs. Have students mount their collages on poster board. Help students with names and titles of various events.

 For Individual Needs

12 Challenge Have students try to convince the others to attend the event they depicted in their collage. In Chapter 8 (p. 195) students learned to make suggestions and recommendations. Review these expressions with students prior to this activity.

Teaching Suggestions

13 Read the four quotes with students, modeling them first and helping students understand their meaning if necessary. Then ask each group to pick one of the aphorisms to discuss and paraphrase in German.

14 Question 7 asks about tradition. You may want to discuss the concept of tradition with your students. Ask the following questions.
Woran denkt ihr, wenn ihr das Wort Tradition hört?
Hat deine Familie bestimmte Traditionen, oder vielleicht deine Gemeinde oder Stadt?
Hat diese Schule Traditionen? Welche?

Reteaching: Expressing Preference

Ask students to make a list of eight things that are important to them, ranking these from most to least important. Have students write down their ideas and then share them with the class.

ERSTE STUFE

WEITER GEHT'S!

CLOSE

Thinking Critically

Analyzing The German language has a proverb that can be related to artistic abilities: **Es ist noch kein Meister vom Himmel gefallen.** (*Nobody is born a master of his craft.*) Ask students how expressions of admiration go hand in hand with the proverb. (We tend to admire people who have the dedication to develop skills and become masters of their crafts.)

Focusing on Outcomes

Refer students back to the learning outcomes listed on p. 233. They should recognize that they now know how to express preference, given certain possibilities and express envy and admiration.

ASSESS

• **Performance Assessment** Ask students to outline a weekend of activities for a group of German exchange students coming to visit their town or area. Using the functions and the vocabulary from this **Stufe**, have students elaborate on their plans for what they would like their visitors to do.

• Quiz 10-1, *Chapter Resources,* Book 4

*T*eaching Weiter geht's!
pp. 240-241

Resources for Weiter geht's!

• *Textbook Audiocassette* 5 B
• *Practice and Activity Book*

Teacher Note

Weiter geht's! is recorded on audiocassette.

Weiter geht's! Summary

In **Zeitungsbericht: Schüler besuchen Staatstheater,** students will read an article about a school class that went to the ballet. The following student outcomes listed on p. 233 are modeled in the episode: expressing happiness and sadness, and saying that something is or was being done.

Motivating Activity

Ask students if they have ever been to the ballet, and if so, what they have seen and where. Read a synopsis of the ballet *Giselle* in English or have students look up the story and report to the class.

Teaching Suggestion

Ask students to read the introductory paragraph. Then have them summarize the purpose of the weekly feature in the **Stuttgarter Zeitung** called **Zeitung in der Schule.**

Background Information

The role of Giselle is one that almost all ballerinas want to perform. The story was written by the French poet Théophile Gautier together with Marquis de Saint-Georges. It was inspired by a legend recorded in Heinrich Heine's *Zur Geschichte der neueren schönen Literatur in Deutschland* and set to music by the French composer Adolphe Adam. Adam was the first composer to use leitmotifs, short phrases of music repeated each time a particular character appears. In the ballet, the musical leitmotifs are accompanied by certain dance steps, which here, for example, vary as Giselle changes from a simple village girl to a mad creature and then to a wistful, loving spirit. The subtitle of the ballet, *Les Wilis,* refers to the ghostly spirits of young girls, who, according to the legend, die before their weddings.

Teaching Suggestion

Ask students to look back at Photo 3 in the Chapter Opener on p. 233. What information is given about the performance?

For Individual Needs

Auditory Learners Have students listen to the cassette segment of **Weiter geht's!.** Pause the tape at logical intervals and ask students to give the gist of what they have just listened to.

Teaching Suggestion

Play the tape again as students read along in their texts. Stop at shorter intervals and ask comprehension questions. Explain new vocabulary and difficult constructions in German by using gestures, drawings, and paraphrasing.

 Cooperative Learning

16 Divide students into groups of four. Instruct each group to choose a discussion leader, a recorder, a proofreader, and a reporter. Give students a specific amount of time to complete Part 1 of this activity (about 20 minutes). Monitor group work as you walk around, helping students with unfamiliar words or phrases. The recorder of each group can use a transparency or a large sheet of construction paper to write the group's answers. Call on a few group reporters to share their answers to the five questions in Part 1. You may want to do Parts 3 and 4 in the same way on another day.

Teaching Suggestion

16 Put students in pairs or small groups to do Part 2 (read the whole text in the present tense). Before they start, tell them to watch out for the following:
1) past perfect constructions which need to change to present perfect,
2) instances where the past must remain in order to show prior actions (Example: **Die Clowns, die anfangs so heiter und spaßig waren, bleiben ganz ratlos zurück.**),
3) passive voice when **wurde(n)** needs to be changed to **wird/werden**.

Game

16 After students have changed the text into the present, they can play the following game to check their work. Divide the class into two teams and have a member of Team A start reading the text in present tense. When a member of Team B thinks the reader has made a mistake in changing the verb form (or changed it when it shouldn't have been changed) the person calls out **Halt!** The reader from Team A must stop and the member of Team B gives what he or she believes to be the correct form of the verb. If the Team B member is correct, he or she continues reading the text until a member from Team A notices an error and calls out **Halt!** If a reader gets stopped but did not make an error, he or she can continue. The purpose of the game is to see how far students can go without making any errors.

Closure

If possible, play a piece of music from the ballet *Giselle* or show students a performance on video. Have students listen or watch for the leitmotifs.

WEITER GEHT'S!

ZWEITE STUFE

Teaching Zweite Stufe, pp. 242-246

▶ *page 242*

MOTIVATE

Teaching Suggestion

Ask students what they would like to see if they were offered a free ticket to any theatrical performance. In which theater would they like to see it, and with whom would they like to go?

TEACH

PRESENTATION: Wortschatz

- Teach the vocabulary in the **auf deutsch erklärt** section through pantomime, drawing, or by giving examples.
- For the **auf englisch erklärt** vocabulary, read through the new phrases, and then ask students related questions.
  Examples:
  Wann bekommst du Herzklopfen?
  Wann bekommst du eine Gänsehaut?
  Erinnerst du dich an das letzte Mal, an dem du dich bei Freunden oder Eltern über etwas beklagt hast?

PRESENTATION: So sagt man das!

- Ask students if they can think of synonyms for **froh** and **traurig**.
  Examples:
  froh: glücklich, fröhlich, zufrieden, erfreut
  traurig: enttäuscht, unglücklich, freudlos
- Ask students to complete the following phrases.
  Ich war wirklich froh, daß ...
  Ich war total traurig, weil ...

▶ *page 243*

Teaching Suggestion

17 After students have completed the listening activity, ask them to recall their most memorable field trip. Have them share their answers while the rest of the class takes notes.

✤ For Individual Needs

18 A Slower Pace Instead of using a **weil**-clause, have students give two sentences. **Ich bin froh. Ich habe eine Schülerkarte bekommen.** After they have practiced this way, they can do the activity using the **weil**-clause. Remind them that the **weil**-clause requires verb-last word order.

Teaching Suggestion

19 You may want to give students a starting point by providing them with a number of topics to discuss using the expressions **froh/traurig sein, daß ....**
Examples:
Familie
Freund(in)
Schule

PRESENTATION: Ein wenig Grammatik

- Students studied **da**- and **wo**-compounds in Chapter 3 (p. 58). If students need to review these materials, you may want to refer them to that page.
- Remind students that these two types of compounds are used only when reference is made to things and not to people.

▶ *page 244*

PRESENTATION: So sagt man das!

- Have students point out and explain how the two sets of sentences differ. Can students think of English equivalents for each of the four sentences?
- Have students go back to **Weiter geht's!** and point out all the sentences that tell what was being done.

For Individual Needs

23 Tactile Learners Let students listen to the description a second time with a pencil and paper in front of them. Have them imagine the concert hall and draw what they visualize. After students have completed their drawings, have them share their work with the rest of the class.

▶ *page 245*

PRESENTATION: Grammatik

- To review the difference between active and passive voice, ask students to change the sentences in the box to the active voice.
- Perform several activities around the classroom, tell students what you are doing, and let them say what is or was being done. (Example: clean the chalkboard and say **Ich wische die Tafel ab.** Students might say **Die Tafel wird/wurde abgewischt.**)
- Have students imagine they are planning a big party at their house this weekend. They must tell what needs to be done. When finished, have students share their ideas with the rest of the class.

▶ *page 246*

Teaching Suggestion

26 Encourage students to work this activity like a puzzle and to do the easier parts first, working up to the more difficult sentences with the past participles that are left.

For Individual Needs

26 Challenge Ask students to find different participles than those given for as many sentences as they can.
Examples:
Dann wurden wir auf unsere Plätze gebracht.
In der Pause wurde etwas zu essen gekauft.

Teaching Suggestion

28 To help students with the changes from active to passive, ask them first to find the object of each of the active sentences. Remind students that the object of the active sentence will become the subject of the passive sentence. Remind them also that the tense must remain the same. Have students work on one movie critique at a time. Then check their transformation into the passive.

Reteaching: Passive Voice

Ask students to help you describe in detail how to plan a costume party for a large group of friends. Make a list on the board.
Examples:
Zuerst wird das Datum festgelegt.
Dann wird eine Gästeliste gemacht.
Challenge students to be as detailed as possible.

▶ *page 247*

PRESENTATION: Landeskunde

Building on Previous Skills

Throughout their German studies, students have learned about famous German-speaking people who contributed to the arts, literature, and music. Let students brainstorm a list of famous German-speaking people and have them name at least one significant thing each person did. If students cannot come up with something specific a person has done, they should indicate the type of work the person is known for (Examples: **Dirigent, Dichter, Künstler, Komponist, Bildhauer**).

ZWEITE STUFE

ZWEITE STUFE

Teaching Suggestions

- Ask students how they were exposed to culture as children. Did they do special activities with their families? If so, what were they? How about now? How much of an interest in and exposure to cultural activities do they have now? Have students share their experiences with the class.

- Read the text out loud to students. Pause after each paragraph and have students summarize its content orally in English.

B Assign Activity B as an individual writing activity. Ask students for a paragraph of at least eight connected sentences.

Community Link

Have some students find out from the local Chamber of Commerce or Tourism Bureau what types of cultural activities are planned for their community this year. Students should make a list of the various programs and activities and report the information in class.

Background Information

In Germany, there is much state support for the arts. Federal, state, and local monies subsidize artists, musicians, writers as well as theater and ballet companies, orchestras, and various academies and professional schools for the arts. Reduced price tickets are available for students in order to make cultural experiences accessible to young people. In recent years, efforts have been made to increase museum attendance and make museums more attractive to the general public and young people in particular. A number of innovative ideas have come from museums in the United States. Most museums now have a cafeteria, evening hours, free tours, and some even have special children's sections.

Thinking Critically

Comparing and Contrasting Have students find out how many museums, theaters, symphonies, libraries, galleries, and special exhibits are located in their town or city.

Teacher Note

Mention to your students that the **Landeskunde** will be also included in Quiz 10-2 given at the end of the **Zweite Stufe**.

▣ Video Program

In the video clip, **Geld für Kultur?**, residents of East Berlin talk about whether public funds should be used for public housing or the restoration of monuments. See *Video Guide* for suggestions.

CLOSE
Group Work

Provide each group with a list of words and phrases. Students sit in a circle with the list in front of them and ask each other questions using the words from the list. (Examples: **die Eintrittskarte, die Aufführung, die Bühne, das Ballet, die Oper, das Theaterstück, die Abendvorstellung, das Instrument, atemlos, applaudieren**)
Example:
Weißt du, wieviel gute Eintrittskarten zu einem Theaterstück kosten?

Focusing on Outcomes

Refer students back to the learning outcomes listed on p. 233. They should recognize that they now know how to express happiness and sadness and say that something is or was being done.

ASSESS

- **Performance Assessment** Have students name five different types of cultural activities and tell why they would like to attend or not like to attend each.

- Quiz 10-2, *Chapter Resources,* Book 4

*T*eaching Zum Lesen,
pp. 248-250

Teacher Note

Die Nacht bei den Wachsfiguren is recorded on *Textbook Audiocassette* 11.

Reading Strategy

The targeted strategy in this reading is reading for comprehension. Students should learn about this strategy before beginning Question 1.

PREREADING
Motivating Activity

Ask students whether any of them have ever visited a wax museum. What kind of figures are usually depicted in a wax museum—characters from fairy tales, plays, movies, or real figures from history? Probably all the students will have an idea that wax museums are associated with "scary" figures in some way. Ask them what kind of pleasure people get from visiting such exhibits. How would they compare it to going to an art museum? Or to a historical museum? Tell them to think about this as they answer Questions 1 and 2.

READING
Teacher Note

8 **Deveroux, einer von Wallensteins Mördern,** would have both historical and literary associations for most Germans. The historical Albrecht von Wallenstein played a questionable role in the Thirty Years' War, first pushing his way up to the office of General of the Imperial (mercenary) Army, then entering into secret negotiations with the other side—the Protestant Swedes and Saxonians as well as with the French. He was finally relieved of his command, and assassinated in February 1634, by order of the Irish Colonel Buttler. Wallenstein's story inspired a 3-part epic drama by Schiller. Since its premiere in 1799, it has been standard fare in German theaters, and is required reading in high schools.

Teacher Note

9 In Europe, game poachers were historically viewed as desperate outlaws and depicted in much the same way as American western movies depict gangs of horse thieves or train robbers. Someone masquerading as a **Wilderer** would attempt to appear rough and threatening (see paragraph 4 of the reading passage).

POST-READING
Teacher Note

Activity 12 is a post-reading task that will show whether students can apply what they have learned.

Closure

Ask students the following questions: What kind of "horror" story is this? What do you think is the effect of finding out that it was just a nightmare? If someone wanted to film this story for American television, what kind of audience would it be suitable for? What time slots would be best? Would students make any changes in the story? What, exactly, would they change and why?

Answers to Activity 1

Answers will vary; horror

Answers to Activity 2

a. in der Nacht; b. ein Junge; c. in einem Wachsmuseum; d. die Hauptfigur schaut die Figuren an und wird müde; im dritten Stock setzt er sich hin.

Answers to Activity 3

Stock(werk) *floor*
gähnte *yawned*
dämmerig *dim*
Aufseher *guard*
anstrengend *exhausting*
Säle *rooms*

Answers to Activity 4

weil er müde ist; predictions will vary.

Answers to Activity 5

a. Hein; b. er schläft ein; c. irgend jemand hat ihm auf die Schulter getippt; d. eine Wachsfigur; e. aus dem Museum; f. unbehaglich

Answers to Activity 6

Answers will vary.

ZUM LESEN

Answers to Activity 7
ängstlich; er befürchtet, daß er im Museum eingesperrt ist.

Answers to Activity 8
ein Mörder

Answers to Activity 9
daß ihm jemand einen Streich spielt; nein

Answers to Activity 10
den Wilderer, dessen Kopf mit einem Messer auseinandergespalten ist; fast ohnmächtig vor Angst

Answers to Activity 11
Hein wacht vom Traum auf.

*T*eaching Zum Schreiben,
p. 251

Writing Strategy

The targeted strategy in this writing activity is using figurative language and sound devices. Students should learn about this strategy before beginning the assignment.

PREWRITING
Motivating Activity

Ask students about the last time they wrote or tried to write a poem. Can they recall any of the lines or why they wrote it?

Teaching Suggestion

To help students with the initial step into creative writing, show them a picture that lends itself to imaginative expression. (Examples: an idyllic landscape, the Berlin Wall coming down, a portrait or still life) Ask students to express their immediate thoughts and ideas about the picture(s).

✦ For Individual Needs

A Challenge Once students have chosen a topic, encourage them to make a list of antonyms and synonyms to increase the range of material for their poem.

Language Arts Connection

Have students find examples of forms for similes, metaphors, personification, and concrete imagery.

WRITING
Teaching Suggestions

B Using the figurative expressions they have gathered and the plan they have devised, have students write their poem from beginning to end. They should not worry too much about rhyme, and they should not translate poetic images directly from English. Once they have the thoughts and feelings on paper, they can go back and rearrange phrases for more effective visual or sound impressions.

B Encourage students to say their lines out loud as they write them and to listen to the melody of the language.

POST-WRITING

✦ For Individual Needs

Auditory Learners When students have completed their assignment, suggest that they record themselves on audiocassette. Then tell them to listen to their work and self-edit and evaluate it.

Teaching Suggestion

Have students put their poems on a transparency. Each student then delivers his or her poem or song orally.

Closure

Ask students to recall at least two issues that made a lasting impression on them about a particular poem that was read in class. (**Ihr habt jetzt viele Gedichte gehört. Könnt ihr zwei Themen nennen, die einen besonderen Eindruck auf euch gemacht haben?**)

Using Anwendung,
pp. 252-253

Video Program

At this time, you might want to use the authentic advertising footage from German television. See *Video Guide* for suggestions.

For Individual Needs

1 A Slower Pace Let students take notes as they listen for key words that indicate certain cultural interests.

Music Connection

2 If possible, play a recording by Nigel Kennedy in class after students have read the critique.

Portfolio Assessment

3 You might want to suggest this activity as a written portfolio item for your students. See *Assessment Guide,* p. 23.

For Individual Needs

4 Visual Learners Suggest that students use poster board and visuals such as brochures, flyers, and ads from the entertainment section of the local paper to illustrate their arts and entertainment calendar. They should be accompanied by brief descriptions of the events featured.

Building on Previous Skills

6 You might want to suggest that students use the four Location Openers from Level 3 to look up names of famous Germans.

Portfolio Assessment

6 You might want to suggest this activity as an oral portfolio item for your students. See *Assessment Guide,* p. 23.

Kann ich's wirklich?
p. 254

This page helps students prepare for the test. It is a brief checklist of the major points covered in the chapter. The students should be reminded that it is only a checklist and not necessarily everything that will appear on the test.

Teaching Wortschatz,
p. 255

Teaching Suggestions

- Have students list the words that are related to music or a musical performance. Which words refer to a theater production? Which words are related to museums? Some words may appear on more than one of the lists.

- Tell students to identify all the cognates from the **Wortschatz** and list them with their English equivalents.

Total Physical Response

Take students to the auditorium or theater. Give them commands to follow using the vocabulary presented in this chapter.
Example:
Stellt euch alle auf die Bühne!
Thomas, setz dich in die Ränge!

Game

 Play the game **Künstlerisch begabt** using the vocabulary from this chapter. See p. 231F for the procedure.

Teacher Note

Give the **Kapitel 10** Chapter Test, *Chapter Resources,* Book 4.

10
Die Kunst
zu leben

① Ich bewundere dich, daß du dich für Hausmusik interessierst.

Worin besteht die kulturelle Lebenswelt der deutschen Schüler? Was für Möglichkeiten gibt es für sie, sich kulturell zu bilden, und was für eine Rolle können Eltern und Lehrer dabei spielen? Um über diese Fragen diskutieren zu können, mußt du noch einige Ausdrücke lernen.

In this chapter you will learn

- to express preference, given certain possibilities; to express envy and admiration
- to express happiness and sadness; to say that something is or was being done

And you will

- listen to students talk about their cultural activities
- read about cultural life in German-speaking countries
- write about your own cultural interests
- learn more about the cultural activities being offered to German students

② Ich würde eventuell nächste Woche wieder ins Theater gehen.

③ Ich bin glücklich, daß Giselle wieder gezeigt wird.

Los geht's!

Was tun für die Kultur?

Wie sieht es mit dem kulturellen Leben bei deutschen Gymnasiasten aus? Interessieren sie sich für Kunst? Besuchen sie Theateraufführungen? Gehen sie in Konzerte? Hier unterhalten sich vier Gymnasiasten über ihre kulturellen Interessen außerhalb der Schule.

FRAGE Was sind eure kulturellen Interessen außerhalb der Schule?

PHILIPP Also, ich würd' sagen, hauptsächlich Theater, eventuell mal ein klassisches Konzert. Meine Eltern haben ein Konzertabonnement, und da kaufen sie ab und zu mal eine Karte für mich und nehmen mich mit. Aber sonst? Ich les' zum Beispiel ausgesprochen wenig. Ich hab' kaum Zeit dazu. Für den Deutschunterricht, ja da lesen wir Goethe, Schiller und wie sie alle heißen.[1] Das langt.

MICHAEL Bei mir ist es genau dasselbe. Ich konzentrier' mich so auf wissenschaftliche Werke, Informationen und so, aber Bücher ... so Philosophen lesen wie Nietzsche[2], ja, ich beneide alle, die so was lesen können. Aber ich hätt' nicht die Geduld dazu. Mich interessiert also mehr das Wissenschaftliche als das Literarische.

SONJA Also ich muß sagen, daß ich sehr viel lese und daß ich lieber lese als — meinetwegen — Hausaufgaben mache. Ich les' wahnsinnig gern Romane, historische Romane.

TANJA Musik ist mein Hobby. Ich könnte mir ein Leben ohne Musik nicht vorstellen. Also, ich selbst spiele Geige, schon zwölf Jahre lang, und hab' zweimal in der Woche Unterricht. Ich spiel' ganz gut; bin zwar keine Sophie Mutter und werde auch kaum in der Jungen Deutschen Philharmonie[3] spielen. Aber ich hab' viel Spaß daran. Ich mach' oft mit Freunden Hausmusik[4], klassische Musik von Bach, Beethoven und so. Aber ich mag auch Jazz, besonders New Orleans Jazz. Den find' ich stark, den find ich Spitze!

FRAGE Geht ihr in Museen und Ausstellungen?

MICHAEL Wenn ich in ein Museum gehe, dann nur ins Deutsche Museum. Das ist ein technisch-wissenschaftliches Museum und äh ... aber so Kunstausstellungen, nö.

---

1. An deutschen Gymnasien bestehen für alle Fächer feste Lehrpläne. Für den Deutschunterricht in allen Klassen gibt es Listen von Autoren und ihren Werken, aus denen die Deutschlehrer geeignetes Material für den Unterricht aussuchen können.
2. Friedrich Nietzsche (1844–1900), der als Philosoph und Kulturbeobachter großen Ruhm erlangt hat, zeichnete sich auch durch seinen gehobenen Schreibstil aus.
3. Die Junge Deutsche Philharmonie ist ein Orchester, das aus zirka 150 begabten Musikstudenten und -studentinnen zwischen 18 und 28 besteht. Zweimal im Jahr übt das Orchester mit berühmten Dirigenten zwei Wochen lang. Dann geht das Orchester auf Tournee und spielt in bekannten Konzerthallen der Welt.
4. Hausmusik ist beliebt. Rund eine Million Bundesbürger, so schätzt man, spielen zu Hause oder im Freundeskreis ein Instrument.

TANJA	Bei mir ist es gerade umgekehrt. Irgendwelche technisch-wissenschaftlichen Ausstellungen interessieren mich überhaupt nicht. Wenn, dann geh' ich eben in Galerien, Bilderausstellungen.
MICHAEL	Im technischen Museum blüh' ich auf! Wenn ich die Wunderwerke der Technik sehe und wenn man da so alles verstehen kann, aber nicht, wenn ich da so vor einem Bild stehe.
PHILIPP	Aber ich glaub', die meisten Museumsbesuche gehen doch von der Schule aus, daß man an irgendwelchen Schulausflugtagen eben in ein Museum geht.
SONJA	Für die Schüler wird schon wahnsinnig viel getan. Wenn man da mit seinem Schülerausweis an die Abendkasse geht, kann man sich für sechs Mark eine Oper oder ein schönes Theaterstück anschauen. Was da alles für die Schüler geboten wird! Man nützt es einfach zu wenig aus.
TANJA	Ist doch grotesk der Unterschied: wenn man in ein Café geht und sich etwas bestellt, da sind gleich so zehn Mark weg. Wenn man ins Theater oder ins Konzert geht, da kostet eine Karte nur sechs Mark, und man hat bestimmt mehr davon.
FRAGE	Wie sieht's bei euch mit dem Wort „Tradition" aus?
PHILIPP	Von Tradition ist wenig vorhanden bei uns.
FRAGE	Kennt ihr überhaupt noch Sagen und Märchen?
TANJA	Natürlich. Märchen haben mir unheimlich gut gefallen.
MICHAEL	Mir auch. Meine Mutter hat mir immer Märchen vorgelesen, als ich klein war ... ja, „Hänsel und Gretel" oder ...
SONJA	Teilweise hat man Märchen später auch selber gelesen. Ich, zum Beispiel, hab's getan.
FRAGE	Besucht ihr während des Jahres mal ein Volksfest?
PHILIPP	Schon, aber nur zum Vergnügen, nicht unbedingt wegen der Tradition.[5]

5. In den deutschsprachigen Ländern besteht eine große, regionale Tradition. Es gibt z. B. viele Theaterstücke bekannter Autoren, die im Dialekt geschrieben und auch im Dialekt aufgeführt werden. Auch gibt es Gesangsvereine und Volksfeste in jeder Region. Das größte und bekannteste Volksfest ist das Oktoberfest in München.

1 Was sind ihre Interessen?

Lies dir den Text noch einmal durch! Dann mach eine Tabelle mit vier Spalten! Schreib auf, was für Interessen jeder der vier Gymnasiasten hat!

2 Kannst du das beantworten?

Bildet zwei Gruppen! Jede Gruppe überlegt sich fünf Fragen zu dem Text, die die andere Gruppe beantworten muß. Zum Beispiel: Was ist ein Konzertabonnement? Warum spricht Tanja über die Violinistin Anne-Sophie Mutter?

3 Kennst du diese Personen?

Sammelt in kleinen Gruppen Informationen über die berühmten Personen, die im Text erwähnt werden! Berichtet der Klasse darüber!

ERSTE STUFE

Expressing preference, given certain possibilities; expressing envy and admiration

WORTSCHATZ

auf deutsch erklärt

das Vergnügen   etwas, was viel Spaß macht
vorlesen   lesen, so daß es alle hören können
die Hausmusik   Musik, die man zu Hause macht
die Geige   die Violine
die Abendkasse   wo man Karten für die Abendvorstellung verkauft
eventuell   vielleicht
teilweise   zum Teil
unheimlich   sehr groß, sehr viel

auf englisch erklärt

<u>Meinetwegen</u> brauchen wir nicht in die Oper zu gehen, ich gehe lieber ins Rockkonzert.   *As far as I'm concerned we don't need to go to the opera, I'd rather go to a rock concert.*
Es gibt riesige <u>Unterschiede</u> zwischen den Grimms <u>Märchen</u>.   *There are huge differences in the Grimms' fairy tales.*
Man braucht viel <u>Geduld</u>, wenn man die <u>wissenschaftlichen</u> <u>Werke</u> der Gebrüder Grimm durchlesen will.   *You need a lot of patience if you want to read through the research of the Grimm Brothers.*
Die Picasso <u>Ausstellung</u> wird <u>möglicherweise</u> <u>verlängert</u>.   *The Picasso exhibit will possibly be extended.*

SO SAGT MAN DAS!

Expressing preference, given certain possibilities

You have learned several ways to express preference. Here is another way to express general preference. If someone asks you

> **Welche kulturellen Veranstaltungen würdest du besuchen, wenn du genug Zeit hättest?**

You might say:

> **Ich würde mir hauptsächlich** ausländische Filme ansehen.

You could continue the thought by expressing specific possibility:

Und ich würde ⎰ **eventuell** / **vielleicht** / **möglicherweise** ⎱ auch mal in ein Konzert gehen.

---

 4 Hör gut zu!   For answers, see listening script on TE Interleaf.

Erwin hat Lust, mit einigen Klassenkameraden an diesem Wochenende irgendeine kulturelle Veranstaltung zu besuchen. Er ruft seine Klassenkameradin Lise an und bittet sie, ihm aus ihrem Kulturkalender vorzulesen. Hör gut zu, wie sie die Veranstaltungen besprechen! Welche kulturellen Interessen haben die beiden? Zu welchen Veranstaltungen entschließen sie sich? Mach dir Notizen, und vergleiche sie mit denen einer Klassenkameradin!

5 Und ihr? Wenn ihr viel Zeit hättet?

Was würdest du tun, wenn du viel Zeit für kulturelle Interessen hättest? Sag einem Partner, was du hauptsächlich — also generell — und was du möglicherweise — also spezifisch — tun würdest!

> DU   Ich würd' hauptsächlich Comics lesen, eventuell auch mal ein Märchen.
> PARTNER   Ich würd' ...

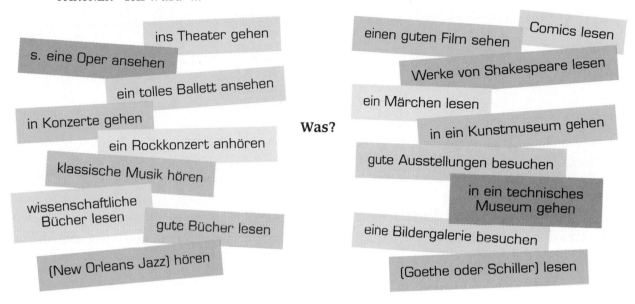

ins Theater gehen

s. eine Oper ansehen

ein tolles Ballett ansehen

in Konzerte gehen

ein Rockkonzert anhören

klassische Musik hören

wissenschaftliche Bücher lesen

gute Bücher lesen

(New Orleans Jazz) hören

Was?

einen guten Film sehen

Comics lesen

Werke von Shakespeare lesen

ein Märchen lesen

in ein Kunstmuseum gehen

gute Ausstellungen besuchen

in ein technisches Museum gehen

eine Bildergalerie besuchen

(Goethe oder Schiller) lesen

6 Was ist für euch wichtig?

Sagt jetzt einander, was für euch wichtig ist und was weniger wichtig ist!

> PARTNER   Es ist für mich wichtig, ab und zu mal in ein Museum zu gehen.
> DU   In ein Museum zu gehen, ist für mich weniger wichtig. Wichtig ist für mich, am Wochenende einen guten Film zu sehen.

7 Was könntet ihr euch nicht vorstellen?

Was möchtet ihr im Leben nicht vermissen? Ohne welche kulturellen Dinge könntet ihr euch das Leben nicht vorstellen?

> DU   Also, ich könnte mir ein Leben ohne klassische Musik nicht vorstellen.
> PARTNER   Tja, ich ...

Sport   Bücher   Filme

Fernsehen   Kunst

Musik   Reisen

SO SAGT MAN DAS!

Expressing envy and admiration

You can use the verb **beneiden** to express envy:

> **Ich beneide** meinen Freund. Der kann jeden Monat ins Theater gehen.

and the verb **bewundern** to express admiration:

> **Ich bewundere alle, die** sich für Philosophie interessieren.

8 Wen beneidest du? Wen bewunderst du?

Sag deinem Partner, wen du beneidest und wen du bewunderst und warum! Denk auch an berühmte Leute!

DU   **Ich beneide meine Schwester! Die fährt im Sommer nach England.**
PARTNER   **Ich bewundere meinen Freund! Er übt sehr viel und spielt gut Klavier.**

Grammatik   Prepositions with the Genitive Case

Certain prepositions are always followed by the genitive case.

anstatt eines Konzerts	*instead of a concert*
außerhalb der Schule	*outside of school*
innerhalb des Hauses	*inside the house*
während des Jahres	*during the year*
wegen der Tradition	*because of tradition*

---

9 Was sind Jörgs kulturelle Interessen?

Lies den folgenden Absatz, den der Realschüler Jörg über seine kulturellen Interessen für die Schule schreiben mußte! Da es leider auf sein Papier geregnet hat, fehlen jetzt einige Wörter. Setz die Wörter aus dem Kasten in die Lücken, damit er eine gute Note bekommt! Vergiß die richtigen Artikel nicht! Sag dann einem Partner, ob du ähnliche Interessen hast!

Meine kulturellen Interessen? Nun, ich mache oft während __des Winters__ Hausmusik, besonders Musik __des__ großen __Komponisten__ Beethoven, und ich gehe auch gern in Konzerte. Wenn das Wetter schlecht ist, besuche ich anstatt __eines Konzerts__ ein Museum, besonders das Museum __der Wissenschaft__ und Technik. In Kunstmuseen gehe ich weniger gern. Die meisten Gemälde __der__ alten __Meister__ langweilen mich. Moderne Kunst ist schon besser. Ja, außerdem lese ich ziemlich viel. Im Moment ist es Literatur __des__ neunzehnten __Jahrhunderts__, besonders Eichendorff und Keller, auch Werke __des Lyrikers__ Heinrich Heine.

10 Was besuchst du?

Sag einer Partnerin, was du besuchst und warum!

DU   **Besuchst du Volksfeste?**
PARTNER   **Ja, schon. Aber nur zum Vergnügen, nicht wegen der Tradition.**

des Jahrhunderts
des Komponisten   *der Meister*
des Lyrikers   *der Wissenschaft*
eines Konzerts   *des Winters*

was?	wozu/warum?	(nicht) wegen
Konzerte	zum Vergnügen	Tradition
Museen	zum Spaß	Musiker
Ausstellungen	zur Abwechslung	Schauspieler
Theateraufführungen	zum Zeitvertreib	Wissenschaft
Galerien	für die Schule	Gemälde
Volksfeste	für meine Eltern	Kunst

11 Klassenprojekt: Eine Collage machen

Sammelt Informationen über kulturelle Ereignisse, die zur Zeit in eurer Stadt stattfinden, und fertigt mit diesen Dokumenten eine Collage an!

12 Zeig mal deine Collage her!

Seht euch eure Collagen an und sprecht darüber! Wofür interessiert ihr euch? Welche Sachen würdet ihr gern besuchen? Welche habt ihr schon gesehen? Wie war's? Welche Aufführungen sind mehr für Erwachsene, welche mehr für Jugendliche oder Kinder geeignet?

13 Leseübung: Aphorismen

In der Schule müssen Schüler die Werke berühmter Autoren lesen. Dazu gehören auch Aphorismen und Sprüche. Lest die folgenden Zitate (*quotes*) und diskutiert darüber!

> „Zwei Dinge sollen Kinder von ihren Eltern bekommen: Wurzeln und Flügel."
> Johann Wolfgang von Goethe
> (1749–1832)

> „Es ist nicht genug zu wissen; man muß es auch anwenden; es ist nicht genug zu wollen; man muß es auch tun."
> Goethe

> „Was der Frühling nicht säte, kann der Sommer nicht reifen, der Herbst nicht ernten und der Winter nicht genießen."
> Johann Gotthelf Herder
> (1744–1803)

> „Kenntnisse kann jedermann haben, aber die Kunst zu denken ist das seltsamste Geschenk der Natur."
> Friedrich der Große
> (1712–1786)

14 Und du?

Was sind deine kulturellen Interessen? Überleg dir folgende Fragen und beantworte sie! Mach dir dabei stichwortartige Notizen!

1. Welche kulturellen Interessen hast du? Berichte deiner Gruppe darüber!
2. Welche Schriftsteller oder Dichter kennst du, und welche Werke von ihnen hast du schon gelesen?
3. Wie sieht es bei dir mit Musik aus? Bist du auch an klassischer Musik interessiert? Welche Werke bekannter Komponisten kennst du?
4. Spielst du ein Instrument und wenn ja, was für Musik spielst du? Spielst du in einer Gruppe? In welcher? Hast du auch andere musikalische Interessen?
5. Welche Museen hast du schon besucht? Welche Ausstellungen? Was hat dir besonders gut gefallen? Warum?
6. An welchen kulturellen Ereignissen würdest du gern mal teilnehmen, und warum hast du das bisher nicht getan?
7. Wie sieht es bei dir in der Familie mit „Tradition" aus?
8. Wer oder was trägt zu deiner kulturellen Erziehung am meisten bei? Erzähle darüber!

15 Für mein Notizbuch

Schreib einen Absatz darüber, welche kulturellen Interessen für dich wichtig sind! Hörst du lieber klassische Musik oder Pop und Rock? Welchen kulturellen Zeitvertreib (*pastime*) würdest du als dein Hobby bezeichnen?

Weiter geht's!

Zeitungsbericht: Schüler besuchen Staatstheater

Die Stuttgarter Zeitung druckt einmal in der Woche eine Seite „Zeitung in der Schule", die nur von Schülern für Schüler geschrieben wird. Hier haben junge Menschen die Möglichkeit, eine große Tageszeitung als Forum für ihre Ideen und Erfahrungen zu benutzen.

Ein kulturelles Erlebnis für die Schüler

Die 8b der Friedensschule beim „Musikunterricht" im Staatstheater

Für einen Ballettabend in das prächtige Reich der Wilis

Immer wieder mal zieht unser Klassenlehrer aus dem Schulhaus hinaus, und wir sind natürlich dabei! Diesmal verlegte er seinen Musikunterricht in die Staatsoper. Nach vielen vergeblichen Versuchen hatten wir endlich Glück: Schülerkarten für das Ballett „Giselle".[1] Das war schon etwas Besonderes! Die Buben waren skeptisch. Ballett, Theater, Großes Haus — das kannten die meisten kaum. Im Kino und auf dem Sportplatz waren sie eher zu Hause. Da es sich um eine richtige Abendvorstellung handelte, mußte auch die Kleiderfrage geklärt werden. Unser Lehrer erzählte uns einiges über Handlung, Musik und Tanz. Er sprach auch übers Große Haus mit seinen drei Rängen, übers Foyer, über Garderobe und Theke. Langsam wurden wir neugierig.

Am Tag der Aufführung wurden die Eintrittskarten verteilt, und irgendwie war der Nachmittag anders als sonst. Dauernd schaute ich auf die Uhr. Gegen Abend erwischte ich mich immer wieder vor dem Spiegel. Die meisten waren viel zu früh vor dem Theater. Die einen wurden zum zweiten Range hinaufbegleitet, andere hatten ihre Plätze in den Seitenlogen. Da öffneten sich die Türen des Zuschauerraums. Was für eine Pracht! Super, riesig, echt nobel, prunkvoll, großartig — so hörten wir uns sagen. Wir sahen uns in aller Ruhe um. Die meisten Zuschauer waren recht schick gekleidet, gut,

daß wir unsere besten Klamotten angezogen hatten. Unten stimmten die Musiker ihre Instrumente, die Bläser, die Streicher; nur Michael sah sie kaum, auch nicht die Pauken oder die Harfe, er saß nämlich genau hinter der großen Krone über der Königsloge.

Die Kronleuchter wurden hochgezogen, das letzte Klingelzeichen ertönte, einige Spätkommer suchten noch ihre Plätze. Das Licht ging ganz langsam aus, atemlose Stille! Vor lauter Spannung bekam Snjezana eine Gänsehaut, und ihre Nebensitzerin hatte sogar Herzklopfen vor lauter Aufregung.

Der Dirigent wurde mit Klatschen begrüßt. Nach einem kurzen Vorspiel der Instrumente ging der Vorhang auf: Eine Insel im Meer. Wir kamen aus dem Staunen nicht mehr heraus, denn dort landeten laufend neue Gäste mit einem Schiff. Im bunten Treiben auf dem Jahrmarkt erkannten wir die verträumte Giselle, die von zwei Männern geliebt wird. Der junge Maler Albrecht sah ganz toll aus, der bärtige Hilarion, wütend vor Eifersucht, gefiel uns besser. Sie alle tanzten und stellten ihre Pantomimen so gut dar, daß wir verstanden, um was es ging, obwohl weder gesprochen noch gesungen wurde. Das war besonders auch für die vielen ausländischen Schüler unserer Klasse leichter. Nur Serken beklagte sich über die Musik, sie hatte für ihn zu wenig Power. Dafür freute er sich auf die Pause. Hier schauten wir uns, nun schon sicherer geworden, überall um. Erdal aus der Türkei zeigte uns seine Loge. Ihm blieb beinahe die Spucke weg, als er erfuhr, daß sein Platz normalerweise 99 Mark gekostet hätte. Leider war der zweite Akt gar nicht mehr so lustig. Im romantischen Reich der Königin der Wilis mit ihren wunderschönen Kostümen war wohl alles recht märchenhaft, doch die meisten von uns waren traurig, weil es kein Happy-End gab. Die Clowns, die anfangs heiter und spaßig waren, blieben ganz ratlos zurück. Wir aber waren glücklich, weil wir einen so schönen Abend erlebt hatten. Alle fanden es toll; wir klatschten, bis uns die Hände weh taten, besonders, als die Blumensträuße für die Tänzer auf die Bühne flogen.

Der nächste Morgen — wieder im Schulalltag: Die einen träumten noch vom Balletterlebnis, andere diskutierten darüber. Wann gehen wir wieder ins Theater?

Sandra, Ralf, Manuela, Indir und die 8b der Friedensschule Stuttgart-West

1. „Giselle" (auch „Les Wilis" genannt) ist das Symbol des romantischen Balletts. Es beruht auf einem Gedicht von Heinrich Heine (1797–1856). Das Ballett wurde 1841 zum ersten Mal in Paris aufgeführt, wo Heine seit 1831 lebte. **1. a. in die Staatsoper   b. Weil die meisten Ballett, Theater und Oper nicht kannten.   c. Er hat der Klasse einiges über die Oper erzählt.   d. Snjezana: bekam eine Gänsehaut; Snjezanas Platznachbarin: hatte Herzklopfen; Erdal: „blieb die Spucke weg" (i.e. vor Staunen sprachlos sein)   e. Sie klatschten, bis ihnen die Hände weh taten.**

16 Arbeiten mit dem Text For answers see above.

1. Beantworte mit deinen Klassenkameraden folgende Fragen!
   a. Wohin hat der Lehrer den Musikunterricht verlegt?
   b. Warum sind besonders die Jungen skeptisch über den Besuch?
   c. Wie hat der Lehrer seine Klasse auf den Ballettbesuch vorbereitet?
   d. Für welche Schüler war der Besuch im Staatstheater ein besonderes Erlebnis? Wie zeigt sich das?
   e. Wie zeigt es sich, daß den Schülern die Aufführung gut gefallen hat?

2. Lest den Bericht euren Partnern vor, diesmal in der Gegenwart!

3. Schreib aus dem Text die Stellen heraus, die Enthusiasmus, Skepsis, Erwartung (*expectation*) und Bewunderung zeigen!

4. Schreib eine Liste mit Adjektiven, die in diesem Text erscheinen!

4. For answer see underlined words in text.

ZWEITE STUFE

Expressing happiness and sadness; saying that something is or was being done

Was findet man im Theater oder in der Oper?

einen Vorhang

eine Bühne

einen Rang

einen Dirigenten

auf deutsch erklärt

begrüßen jemanden grüßen, willkommen heißen
begleiten mit jemandem mitgehen
Zuschauer Besucher einer Veranstaltung, bei der es etwas zu sehen gibt
die Aufführung die Show
Handlung was passiert
aufführen im Theater etwas präsentieren
klatschen applaudieren
heiter gut gelaunt, froh
Bube (süddeutsch) Junge

auf englisch erklärt

Unser <u>Versuch</u>, Karten zu bekommen, war zuerst <u>vergeblich</u>. *Our attempt to get tickets was unsuccessful at first.*
Es <u>handelte sich um</u> eine Vorstellung, die <u>weder</u> ich <u>noch</u> mein Freund kannte. *It was about a performance that neither I nor my friend knew.*
Die Kleiderfrage <u>war geklärt worden</u>. *The issue of what to wear had been resolved.*
Ich war <u>atemlos</u> vor <u>lauter Aufregung</u>, bekam <u>Herzklopfen</u> und sogar eine <u>Gänsehaut</u>. *I was breathless from sheer excitement, my heart started pounding, and I even got goose bumps.*
Die Musiker <u>stimmten</u> ihre Instrumente. *The musicians tuned their instruments.*
Serken <u>beklagte sich</u> darüber. *Serken complained about that.*
Ich <u>erkannte</u> Giselle. *I recognized Giselle.*
Die Pantomimen der Tänzer waren so gut, daß wir verstanden, wor<u>um es ging</u>. *The pantomimes of the dancers were so good that we understood what it was all about.*

SO SAGT MAN DAS!
Expressing happiness and sadness

Here is one way to use **froh** for expressing happiness:

> (Erdal) war froh, daß er einen billigen Platz hatte.

And here is a way to express sadness using **traurig**:

> (Sie) waren traurig, weil es kein Happy-End gab.

17 Hör gut zu! For answers, see listening script on TE Interleaf.

Du hörst jetzt einen Bericht über einen Klassenausflug. Was haben die Freunde gemacht? Wie hat es ihnen gefallen? Schreib die wichtigsten Dinge auf, die sie sagen!

18 Froh oder traurig?

Worüber sind die Schüler, die das Ballett besucht haben, froh, und worüber sind sie traurig? Du und deine Klassenkameraden übernehmen die Rollen der verschiedenen Schüler.

PARTNER **Ja, ich bin die Sandra, und ich bin froh, daß ...**
DU **Gut, ich bin der Serken, und ich bin traurig, weil ...**

Gründe

Schülerkarten bekommen

der Vorhang endlich aufgehen

in die Oper gehen können

eine Abendvorstellung sein

die Pause so lange dauern

der 2. Akt nicht so lustig sein

die besten Klamotten anziehen können

kein Happy-End geben

die Handlung (nicht) kennen

(k)einen guten Platz haben

wieder in die Schule müssen

einen schönen Abend erleben

19 Erzähle mir, wie es dir geht!

Sag einer Partnerin, worüber du jetzt froh oder traurig bist und warum! Sie sagt es dir dann auch.

20 Wofür interessiert ihr euch?

Sag einem Partner, wofür du dich interessierst und warum! Dein Partner kann dir dann sagen, ob er sich auch dafür interessiert oder nicht.

DU **Ich interessiere mich für Musik, weil ich selbst ein Instrument spiele.**
PARTNER **Ich interessiere mich auch dafür, aber ich kann nur das Radio spielen.**
DU **Na prima!**

Schon bekannt
Ein wenig *Grammatik*

Do you remember how to form **da-** and **wo-**compounds? If someone said the following to you, but you didn't hear the last word well, how would you form a question to get the desired information?

Es handelt sich um eine Abendvorstellung.
DU **... handelt es sich?**[1]

If someone said something to you and you basically agreed with the statement, how might you restate it without being too redundant?

Ein Schüler beklagt sich über die Musik.
DU **Ich möchte mich auch ...**[2]

Musik — Instrument spielen

Ballett — gern tanzen

Oper — gern singen

Gemälde — gern malen

Bücher — gern lesen

Theater — Theater spielen

1. **Worum**
2. **darüber beklagen**

21 Verben mit Präpositionen

Lies dir die Texte **Los geht's!** and **Weiter geht's!** noch einmal durch und schreib alle Verben mit Präpositionen auf: teilnehmen an, sich unterhalten über, usw.! Schreib dann eine Frage mit jedem Verb, indem du ein Interrogativ mit „wo" gebrauchst!

22 Für mein Notizbuch

Wie ist es bei dir? Schreib deine Antworten in dein Notizbuch, und erkläre sie dann auch!
1. Worauf freust du dich?
2. Wofür interessierst du dich am meisten?
3. Wozu hast du keine Geduld?
4. Woran möchtest du auch gern mal teilnehmen?
5. Wovon träumst du manchmal?
6. Worüber beklagst du dich am meisten?

SO SAGT MAN DAS!

Saying that something is or was being done

In speaking, we often turn the sentence around to focus on the thing being done, for example:

> **Die Instrumente werden vor der Aufführung gestimmt.**
> **Die Musiker werden vom Dirigenten geleitet.**

Of course, you can also express something that was being done, i.e. in the past.

> **Die Schüler wurden auf ihre Plätze geführt.**
> **Das Ballett ist gestern nicht aufgeführt worden.**

23 Hör gut zu!   <small>For answers, see listening script on TE Interleaf.</small>

Du setzt dich in einen bequemen Sessel, um an einem ruhigen Sonntagnachmittag etwas Musik im Radio zu hören. Du hörst, wie der Ansager die Konzerthalle und die Vorbereitungen der Musiker auf das Konzert beschreibt. Was beschreibt er genau? Wer spielt, und was für Musik wird gespielt? Mach dir Notizen!

24 Was passiert hier?   <small>Hier werden Fotos entwickelt. Hier wird Schnitzel angeboten. Hier werden Aprikosen verkauft. Hier wird Basketball gespielt.</small>

Sieh dir die Illustrationen und die Verbformen im Kasten an! Sag dann deinen Partner, was hier passiert! Wechselt einander ab!

BEISPIEL   **Hier wird/werden …**

angeboten
entwickelt
gespielt
verkauft

*G*rammatik   The passive voice (Summary)

1. You have been using the passive voice in sentences to express that something is being done:

Der Tisch wird (eben/jetzt) gedeckt.

that something was being done:

Der Dirigent wurde mit Klatschen begrüßt.

or that something must still get done:

Der Wagen muß (noch) gewaschen werden.

2. The passive construction is very similar in English and in German. One construction, the impersonal passive, is different. It uses **es** as the subject:

Es wurde nicht **gesungen.**	*There was no singing.*
Es wird viel **geklatscht.**	*There is a lot of applause.*

When **es** is not used at the beginning of the sentence, it is omitted:

Nach der Aufführung wurde lange geklatscht.
..., obwohl weder gesprochen noch gesungen wurde.

3. The following is a summary of the tenses in the passive voice:

Present	Die Schülerkarten **werden verteilt.**
	The student tickets are being distributed.
Imperfect	Der Dirigent **wurde** vom Publikum **begrüßt.**
	The conductor was greeted by the audience.
Perfect	Ein Ballett **ist** gestern **aufgeführt worden.**
	A ballet has been performed yesterday.
Past Perfect	Eine Oper **war** am Abend vorher **gezeigt worden.**
	An opera had been performed on the previous evening.
Future	Ein Film **wird** von unserem Lehrer **gezeigt werden.**
	A movie will be shown by our teacher.

with modals:

Present	Dieses Museum **muß** von den Schülern **besucht werden.**
	This museum must be visited by the students.
Past	Die Kleiderfrage **konnte geklärt werden.**
	The question of what to wear could be cleared up.

with subjunctive forms:

Die Karten	könnten abgeholt werden.	*would be able to be picked up.*
	müßten abgeholt werden.	*would have to be picked up.*
	sollten abgeholt werden.	*ought to be picked up.*

Note:
a. The past participle is used in all tenses: even in the present!
b. In the perfect tenses, forms of **sein** are used with **worden** (which comes from **geworden**, the past participle of **werden**).
c. To also say who performed the action, you use **von** and the dative case.

25 Lese- und Schreibübung

Lies dir den Text auf Seite 240-41 noch mal durch! Achte beim Lesen besonders darauf, wie diese Schüler ihren Ballettbesuch in der Staatsoper beschrieben haben! Mach dann eine Liste von den Verbformen, die das Imperfekt und das Passiv zeigen!

Imperfekt	Passiv
er verlegte, wir hatten Glück, ...	geklärt werden, werden verteilt, ...

26 Wie war das?

Erzähle einem Partner, was alles am Ballettabend passiert ist! Benutze dabei das Passiv! 1. wurden/verteilt   2. wurden/geführt   3. wurden/gestimmt   4. wurde/ausgemacht/hochgezogen
5. wurde/begrüßt   6. wurde/gespielt/wurde/getanzt/gesprochen/gesungen   7. wurde/gegessen/getrunken   8. wurde/geklatscht

1. Zuerst ... die Eintrittskarten ...
2. Dann ... wir auf unsere Plätze ...
3. Die Instrumente ... noch ...
4. Dann ... das Licht ..., und der Kronleuchter ...
5. Der Dirigent ... mit Klatschen ...
6. Dann ... Musik ..., und es ... nur ..., nicht ... und nicht ...
7. In der Pause ... etwas ... und ...
8. Am Ende der Aufführung ... laut ...

27 Spielen wir Dramaturgen!

Entwickelt eine Idee für ein Theaterstück! Schreibt dazu in Stichwörtern folgendes auf: Zeit, Ort, Personen, Handlung und das Ende! Das Stück soll nicht in der Gegenwart spielen, und es soll in einem anderen Land stattfinden und auch ein Happy-End haben. Denkt euch dann einen Titel aus! Vergleicht, was sich jede Gruppe ausgedacht hat!

28 Rezensionen (*critiques*) in Schlagzeilen

Unten stehen Schlagzeilen über den Film „Der mit dem Wolf tanzt", den du vielleicht gesehen hast. Schreib mit Hilfe einer Partnerin diese Schlagzeilen ins Passiv um, soweit es geht!

Die Indianer werden von Costner einmal anders dargestellt: ...   **... Ein Meisterwerk wurde von einem Genie geschaffen.**

> „Costner stellt die Indianer einmal anders dar: als Menschen mit Gefühl. Endlich!"
> *Friesen Nachrichten*

> „Ich kann diesen Film nur jedem empfehlen. Ein Genie hat ein Meisterwerk geschaffen."
> **Frank Huebner**

> „Man hat den Film mit sieben Oscars ausgezeichnet! Sagenhaft!"
> **Süddeutsche Zeitung**

> „Hollywood glaubte nicht, daß man heutzutage einen Western mit Indianern vermarkten kann. Costner hat das Gegenteil bewiesen."
> Angelika Wertheimer

Der Film wurde mit sieben Oscars ausgezeichnet! ...   **... Das Gegenteil wurde von Costner bewiesen.**

Kultur findet man überall!

Die deutschsprachige Jugend hat sehr viele Möglichkeiten, am kulturellen Leben ihrer Stadt teilzunehmen. Sie brauchen diese Möglichkeiten nur zu nutzen. Wenn Kinder noch klein sind, lesen ihnen ihre Eltern die Sagen, Märchen und Geschichten vor, die schon seit Generationen erzählt werden.

Ein gutes Buch ist noch immer ein passendes Geschenk zu Weihnachten oder zum Geburtstag. Viele Eltern nehmen ihre Kinder zu kulturellen Veranstaltungen mit, in Konzerte, in die Oper, in Museen und zu Sonderausstellungen. In Deutschland gibt es heute rund 4000 Museen, 150 Theater, über 180 Orchester, 800 Musikschulen und mehr als 25 000 Bibliotheken.

Das Interesse der Jugendlichen an Musik ist groß. Die meisten Jugendlichen hören sich „ihre" Musik an, aber viele zeigen auch Interesse an klassischer Musik. Viele Jugendliche spielen selbst ein Instrument; sie spielen in irgendwelchen Gruppen in der Schule oder in der Gemeinde, oder sie machen Hausmusik mit Freunden und Bekannten. In der Schule selbst werden die Schüler mit Literatur, Philosophie, Musik und den bildenden Künsten vertraut gemacht. Die Unterrichtspläne für die verschiedenen Klassen beinhalten Museumsbesuche und Besuche zu anderen kulturellen Veranstaltungen. Für freiwillige Besuche zu kulturellen Veranstaltungen werden oft eine Anzahl von Freikarten für Schüler bereitgestellt, und die Schüler selbst können mit ihrem Schülerausweis die meisten kulturellen Veranstaltungen zu verbilligten Preisen besuchen.

A. 1. Wovon handelt der Text? Welche kulturellen Möglichkeiten werden genannt, an denen die Jugend teilnehmen kann? Mach eine Liste!

2. Warum interessiert man sich für solche kulturellen Veranstaltungen? Was meinst du?

3. Macht deine Klasse auch oft Besuche zu kulturellen Veranstaltungen? Zu welchen?

4. Findest du, daß es wichtig ist, solche Veranstaltungen zu besuchen oder daran teilzunehmen? Warum oder warum nicht?

B. Was ist Kultur für dich? Zum Beispiel, erlebt man Kultur nur, wenn man in die Oper, ins Theater oder ins Museum geht? Oder meinst du, daß man Kultur auch auf eine andere Art definieren kann? Gehören zum Beispiel Rockkonzerte und Kultfilme auch dazu?

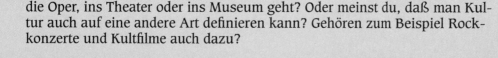

A. 1. **vom kulturellen Angebot / Bücher lesen; kulturelle Veranstaltungen besuchen (Konzerte, Opern, Museen, Sonderausstellungen, Theater); Instrument in einer organisierten Gruppe spielen; Hausmusik machen; kultureller Unterricht in der Schule (z. B. Museumsbesuche)**

ZUM LESEN

Eine Gruselgeschichte

DIE NACHT BEI DEN WACHSFIGUREN

LESETRICK

Reading for Comprehension

After reading the title and the first one or two paragraphs of a short story, always ask yourself the *who, when, where, what,* and *why* of the story. As you read the next few paragraphs, try to answer those questions completely. Focusing on those questions before reading further will aid comprehension and make reading German more fun.

Getting Started

1. Read the title of the story. What do you think the story might be about? What genre does it probably belong to?

2. Look at the title again and read the first paragraph. Try to answer the following questions.
   a. Wann spielt sich die Handlung ab?
   b. Wer ist die Hauptfigur?
   c. Wo findet die Handlung statt?
   d. Was passiert im ersten Absatz?

For answers, see TE Interleaf.

Als er das erste Stockwerk durchlaufen hatte, gähnte er lange und ausgiebig. Im zweiten Stock mußte er sich schon dreimal fünf Minuten auf einen der rotgepolsterten, leicht angestaubten Plüschsessel setzen. In der nächsten Etage aber drückte er sich in eine der dämmerigen Ecken, wo ihn kein Aufseher beobachten konnte, streckte genießerisch die Beine von sich und stellte zum soundsovieltenmal fest, daß es doch sehr anstrengend war, durch ein Museum zu gehen — auch wenn seine einzelnen Säle mit den interessantesten Wachsfiguren angefüllt waren, die man sich denken konnte: Kaiser, Wilderer und Mörder, Erfinder und Schwindler, Gauner und berühmte Künstler.

Hein fühlte, wie ihn der Schlaf überkam. Er stützte den rechten Ellenbogen aufs Knie und legte den schweren Kopf in die rechte Hand. So schlief er ein.

Er konnte noch nicht lange geschlafen haben — oder täuschte er sich? — da schreckte er zusammen. Irgend jemand hatte ihm auf die Schulter getippt.

Hein guckte sich um. Hinter ihm stand eine Wachsfigur in Lebensgröße; sie hielt die rechte Hand weit von sich gestreckt, und in dieser Hand trug sie — man sah ihn deutlich glänzen — einen Dolch. „Deveroux, einer von Wallensteins Mördern", entzifferte Hein auf dem Messingschildchen am Boden.

Der Junge beugte sich hinter die Figur, ob sich vielleicht dort jemand versteckt hielt. Niemand! Auch hinter den anderen Wachsplastiken niemand.

„Aber irgend jemand hat mich doch angestupst!" murmelte Hein und schritt auf den Zehenspitzen quer durch den Saal. Er wollte zum Ausgang zurück. Es bedrückte ihn, keinem Menschen zu begegnen. Und mit jedem Schritt wuchs dieses dumme Gefühl des Unbehagens noch mehr an.

Auch im nächsten Saal war Hein der einzige Besucher.

Im übernächsten wagte er leise „Hallo?" zu rufen. Doch niemand gab Antwort. Nur weiter vorne schien sich etwas bewegt zu haben: aber als Hein näher kam, war auch dort alles leblos und still.

Jetzt bekam es der Junge mit der Angst zu tun. „Ich werde doch nicht so lange geschlafen haben, daß das Museum inzwischen geschlossen worden ist?" stammelte er. „Das war — ja — nicht — auszudenken!" Halt! Waren das nicht Schritte gewesen? Hein erstarrte, als sei er selber aus Wachs.

Da kam doch wer? Ein Wärter vielleicht, der nochmals einen Rundgang machte? Hein hätte jubeln mögen — aber die Lippen blieben ihm geschlossen, als seien sie aufeinandergeklebt. Der da vorne um die Ecke bog, war doch — war doch — ja ganz gewiß: war niemand anders als Deveroux! Hein erkannte ihn

---

Weißt du noch? When using context to guess the meaning of unfamiliar words, it's helpful to look at grammatical and lexical clues. For example, ask yourself if the word is a noun, verb, adjective, conjunction, and so on. Then decide to which category the word belongs. For example, does the word represent a location, person, or object? If it is an object, to which class of objects does it belong?

3. Skim the first paragraph again, locating the following words: **Stock(werk)**, **gähnte**, **dämmerig**, **Aufseher**, **anstrengend**, and **Säle**. Using context, decide what these words might mean.

4. Reread the first paragraph and adjust your original answers to question 2, if necessary. Now answer the following question: **Warum setzt sich die Hauptfigur hin?** Before reading further, use what you know about stories of this genre to make predictions about what might happen.

A Closer Look

5. Lies die nächsten fünf Absätze, und beantworte die folgenden Fragen!
   a. Wer ist „er"?
   b. Was tut er im dritten Stock?
   c. Was erweckt ihn ganz plötzlich?

an dem dreieckigen Spitzhut und an der ausgestreckten Hand, die den Dolch hielt.

Dem Jungen setzte das Herz einen Schlag lang aus. Was war denn hier los? Ging denn das noch mit rechten Dingen zu? Plötzlich überfiel Hein ein Zittern. „Wenn mich der Wallenstein-Mörder nur nicht entdeckt!" flüsterte er. Und ohne sich recht bewußt zu werden, was er tat, drängte sich Hein unter die neben ihm stehende Gruppe. Wilderer stellten diese Wachsfiguren dar; sie trugen schwarze Bärte, dicke Rucksäcke und lange Flinten. Und als Hein sich jetzt in ihre Mitte schob, wichen — wichen — wichen sie ein paar Schritte zur Seite und machten dem Jungen bereitwillig Platz!

Der Junge wagte kaum zu atmen, als jetzt — wenige Meter von ihm entfernt — Wallensteins Mörder in einen anderen Raum hinüberschritt. Er ging, ohne den Kopf zu wenden, mit steifen Knien und hatte die Hand mit dem Dolch weit nach rechts ausgestreckt. Ganz deutlich hörte man es, wenn er die Füße aufsetzte. Tapp — tapp — tapp — tapp. Langsam ebbte das Geräusch ab und verwehte nun völlig. „Nur jetzt nicht schlappmachen", redete er sich ein, „sonst bin ich unter diesen unheimlichen Gesellen unweigerlich verloren!"

Am liebsten hätte er schnell einmal die Wilderer studiert, die neben ihm standen und ihm vorhin Platz gemacht hatten. Aber er traute sich nicht einmal die Pupillen zu bewegen; obgleich er fühlte, daß ihn jemand starr ansah. Endlich faßte er sich ein Herz und hob unmerklich den Blick. Und — sah einem der Wilderer direkt ins Gesicht.

War das wirklich noch eine Wachsfigur? Eine tote, zusammengebastelte Wachsfigur? Der Kerl lebte doch! Auch wenn er sich Mühe gab, geradeaus zu schauen! Freilich, man sah doch, wie seine Lippen ganz leicht bebten!

Hatten sich hier vielleicht ein paar übermütige Kerle maskiert, um Hein einen Schrecken einzujagen? Schon wollte Hein hell hinauslachen, um denen zu zeigen, daß er ihr Spiel durchschaut hatte, da sah er es.

Er sah es, und er dachte nur noch: Mensch, ich werde verrückt!

Er sah nämlich, daß eben diesem Wilderer der Hut mitsamt dem ganzen Kopf von einem furchtbaren Messerhieb auseinandergespalten war.

Hein fühlte, daß er jetzt gleich zusammensinken würde; da packte ihn der Wilderer vorne an der Jacke und schrie: „He, junger Mann! Aufwachen! Das Museum wird in zehn Minuten geschlossen!"

nach Thomas Burger

---

d. Was oder wen sieht er?

e. Wohin will er zunächst gehen?

f. Wie fühlt er sich dabei?

6. Lies die Erzählung zu Ende und versuche, die Ereignisse jedes Absatzes in Stichwörtern zusammenzufassen! Dann beantworte die folgenden Fragen!

7. Wie fühlt sich Hein, als er keine Besucher im Museum findet? Was befürchtet Hein?

8. Wer war Deveroux?

9. Im vierten Absatz vor dem Ende, was meint Hein, was passiert? Stimmt das?

10. Was sieht er plötzlich? Wie fühlt er sich?

11. Wie wird der Konflikt gelöst?

12. Bildet Gruppen zu dritt, und schreibt jetzt eure eigene Gruselgeschichte! Ein Schüler leitet die Gruppe, der zweite schreibt die Geschichte auf und der dritte liest sie nachher der Klasse vor. Einer fängt mit einem Satz an, der nächste ergänzt die Geschichte, indem er einen neuen Satz hinzufügt, usw. Macht weiter, bis ihr drei oder vier Absätze geschrieben habt! Versucht auch, eurer Gruselgeschichte eine überraschende Wende (*twist*) zu geben wie in „Die Nacht bei den Wachsfiguren"!

In this chapter you have learned new ways to express feelings of fear, happiness, and sadness. The expression of feelings is central to some of the cultural activities you have discussed, as well as such works of art, poetry, and song. In this activity, you will write a poem or a song to express your feelings about a place, a memory, a person, or an image that had a strong impact on you.

Ein Gedicht — ein Bild mit Wörtern gemalt

Schreib ein Gedicht oder ein Lied über etwas (ein Erlebnis, einen Ort, eine Person, oder ein Bild), was dich tief beeindruckt hat! Drück in dem Gedicht ein bestimmtes Gefühl wie Furcht, Freude oder Traurigkeit in malerischer Sprache aus!

A. Vorbereiten

1. Such eine Idee für dein Gedicht oder Lied! Sieh dir alte Fotos an, und lies alte Tagebücher und Briefe, die du einmal geschrieben hast! Wähl einen Moment in deiner Vergangenheit, wo du ein starkes Gefühl erlebt hast!

2. Such ein Wort für das Gefühl, das du in dem Gedicht ausdrücken willst! Stell dir den Moment vor, und denk an die verschiedenen Empfindungen und Gefühle, die du mit dem Moment verbindest!

3. Schreib malerische Ausdrücke auf, die zu diesem Gefühl passen! Wähle Metaphern, Gleichnisse und Personifizierungen, um die Details zu beschreiben! Denk auch an den Klang der Sprache!

4. Mach einen Plan für das Gedicht oder Lied! Wie lang soll es sein? Wie viele Strophen soll es haben? Soll es einen bestimmten Rhythmus oder Reim haben?

> ## SCHREIBTIP
> **Using figurative language and sound devices** Different types of writing are distinguished in large part by the type of language used in them. Newspaper articles, critical reviews, and business letters are composed of matter-of-fact writing for the purpose of conveying information efficiently and clearly. But creative writing, especially poetry and song, is often composed of figurative language and sound devices. Use figurative language such as metaphors, similes, personification, and concrete imagery to evoke sensory images and to create an appropriate mood for the emotion you want to convey. Use sound devices such as rhyme, rhythm, assonance and alliteration to play with the musical sounds of language itself.

B. Ausführen

Benutze deinen Plan und die Ausdrücke, die du aufgelistet hast, und schreibe das Gedicht oder das Lied! Wenn du ein Lied schreibst, achte auf die Melodie und den Rhythmus der Musik, damit die Musik und die Wörter gut zusammenpassen!

C. Überarbeiten

1. Lies dein Gedicht oder Lied einem Partner vor! Kann sich der Partner die Gefühle vorstellen, die du ausdrückst? Rufen deine Wörter die richtige Wirkung hervor?

2. Lies das Gedicht noch einmal laut vor, und paß diesmal auf den Klang der Wörter auf! Verwende Stabreim und Assonanz, um die Sprache musikalischer zu machen!

3. Hör jetzt auf den Rhythmus der Wörter! Nimm Silben heraus oder setze Wörter ein, um den Rhythmus zu verbessern!

4. Hast du alles richtig buchstabiert? Hast du Präpositionen mit dem Akkusativ und Dativ richtig verwendet?

5. Schreib das verbesserte Gedicht oder Lied noch einmal ab!

ANWENDUNG

For answers, see listening script on TE Interleaf.

1 Du hörst jetzt einige junge Leute über kulturelle Interessen sprechen. Schreib auf, wovon jeder spricht: von Literatur, von Kunst, von einem Konzert, von einer Oper oder von einem Ballett!

2 Der folgende Artikel ist eine typische Rezension eines Musikabends mit dem berühmten englischen Geiger Nigel Kennedy. Lies diese Rezension, und diskutier darüber mit deinen Klassenkameraden! Hast du Nigel Kennedy schon gesehen oder gehört? Was hältst du von ihm?

Super Geiger im Punk-Look

Die Presse hatte die Musikfanatiker schon genügend auf den jungen Super Geiger vorbereitet. Trotzdem schienen anfangs einige Musikliebhaber „schockiert". Er trug nämlich keinen schwarzen Frack. Die Haare hatte er punkig hochgekämmt. So präsentierte sich der junge englische Geiger Nigel Kennedy dem Frankfurter Musikpublikum. Ein Kulturschock? Überhaupt nicht! Der junge Geiger ist ein netter Kerl, der auf dem Klavier modernen Jazz genau so perfekt spielt wie klassische Musik auf seiner Guarnerius-Geige. Nigel Kennedy spielt nämlich in Stephane Grappellis Jazzgruppe mit — das ist lustig, aber noch kein Grund zur Panik. Kennedy ist auch ein Fußballfreak — so aber auch der berühmte Tenor Placido Domingo.

Die Freunde der ernsten Musik hörten gestern abend einen Musiker von großer Energie. Bachs a-Moll-Konzert wurde kraftvoll perfekt gespielt. Danach kamen Vivaldis „Vier Jahreszeiten" — exakt gegeigt, nicht besonders unorthodox oder sogar aufsässig, nein — nur etwas rigoros vielleicht. Der junge Geiger machte außerdem ein paar witzige Bemerkungen am Mikrofon, und das Publikum fand das prima. Demnächst will Kennedy in München spielen. Seine Fans in der bayrischen Hauptstadt warten schon eifrig auf ihn!

3 Schreib eine Rezension über ein Konzert, eine Theateraufführung oder einen Film, den du erlebt hast!

4 Entwerft in der Klasse einen kulturellen Veranstaltungskalender für diesen Monat! Was für Konzerte, Theateraufführungen, Kunstausstellungen werden angeboten? Wann finden sie statt, oder wann fanden sie statt? Welche Veranstaltungen habt ihr schon besucht? Was könnt ihr darüber berichten?

 5 Schau dir den Veranstaltungskalender an, den du mit deinen Klassenkameraden entworfen hast! Wähle eine Veranstaltung, die du noch nicht kennst! Besuche sie, schreib eine Rezension darüber, und lies sie der Klasse vor!

 6 Stellt mit Hilfe eures Lehrers oder eurer Lehrerin eine Liste zusammen mit Namen von berühmten Deutschen auf den Gebieten der Kunst, der Musik, der Literatur und der Philosophie! Teilt euch in vier Gruppen auf! Jede Gruppe ist für ein Gebiet verantwortlich und macht für dieses Gebiet eine Ausstellung. Die Ausstellung soll aus schriftlichen Berichten und visuellen Materialien bestehen. Die Mitglieder jeder Gruppe sollen dann ihre Ausstellung der Klasse zeigen und beschreiben.

 7 Macht jetzt ein „Kulturspiel"! Schreibt die Namen aus der Liste mit berühmten deutschen Frauen und Männern auf Zettel! Teilt euch in zwei Teams auf! Team A bekommt einen Zettel und muß die Person identifizieren: Maler, Komponisten, Sänger, Philosophen, Schriftsteller, Dichter, usw. Dann kommt Team B dran. Welches Team hat die meisten Personen richtig identifiziert?

8  R O L L E N S P I E L

Bereite eins von diesen beiden Rollenspielen mit drei anderen Schülern vor!

a. Du gehst mit drei Schülern in ein Reisebüro. Ihr sucht euch ein Reiseziel aus, das euch allen gefallen wird. Einer von euch spielt die Rolle des Angestellten im Reisebüro.

b. Du diskutierst mit deinen drei Freunden über ein Picknick, das du für die ganze Klasse organisieren mußt. Besprecht zuerst, was ihr alles braucht, und wer was zum Picknick mitbringen muß! Anschließend geht ihr Proviant fürs Picknick einkaufen. Einer von euch übernimmt die Rolle des Verkäufers.

Can you express preference, given certain possibilities? (p. 236)

1 How would you ask a friend what book he or she would read if he or she were on vacation? How would your friend respond if he or she wanted to read *It* by Stephen King? Welches Buch würdest du lesen, wenn du Ferien hättest? — Ich würde „It" von Stephen King lesen.

2 How would you respond if someone asked you **Welche kulturelle Veranstaltungen würdest du besuchen, wenn du genug Zeit hättest?** How would you then express specific possibility? Ich würde in ein Konzert gehen. / Ich würde eventuell/vielleicht/möglicherweise in ein Rockkonzert gehen.

Can you express envy and admiration? (p. 237)

3 How would you respond if a friend said to you **Ich hab' gerade einen neuen Wagen zum Geburtstag bekommen**? Ich beneide dich.

4 How would you say that you admire people who speak several languages? Ich bewundere Leute, die mehrere Sprachen sprechen.

Can you express happiness and sadness? (p. 242)

5 How would you say that you are happy about the following things?
a. **Ich darf ins Theater gehen.** Ich bin froh, daß ich ins Theater gehen darf.
b. **Die Plätze sind sehr gut.** Ich bin froh, daß die Plätze sehr gut sind.

6 How would you say that you are sad about the following things?
a. **Die Karten fürs Ballett waren ausverkauft.** For answers see below.
b. **Unsere Schulklasse darf keinen Ausflug machen.**

Can you say that something is or was being done? (p. 244)

7 How would you say that you and your classmates are taught (**unterrichtet**) by very good teachers? 7. Meine Klassenkameraden und ich werden von sehr guten Lehrern unterrichtet.

8 How would you say that *Cats* was performed in your town last year?
8. Voriges Jahr wurde „Cats" in unserer Stadt aufgeführt.

6. a. Ich bin traurig, daß die Karten fürs Ballett ausverkauft waren.
b. Ich bin traurig, daß unsere Schulklasse keinen Ausflug machen darf.

ERSTE STUFE

EXPRESSING PREFERENCE, GIVEN CERTAIN POSSIBILITIES

Ich höre mir hauptsächlich Jazz an.   *I listen mainly to Jazz.*

Ich würde mir möglicherweise auch klassische Musik anhören.   *I would possibly also listen to classical music.*

Und eventuell noch Country-Western.   *And perhaps also Country-Western.*

EXPRESSING ENVY AND ADMIRATION

Wir beneiden unseren Freund, weil ...   *We envy our friend because ...*

Ich bewundere Steffi Graf, da ...   *I admire Steffi Graf since ...*

OTHER USEFUL WORDS

die Abendkasse, -n   *ticket window*

die Ausstellung, -en   *exhibition*

das Abonnement, -s   *subscription*

die Geige, -n   *violin*

das Werk, -e   *work, achievement*

die Hausmusik   *house music*

die Sage, -n   *legend*

das Märchen, -   *fairy-tale*

der Philosoph, -en   *philosopher*

das Wunder, -   *wonder, miracle*

das Volksfest, -e   *regional festival*

die Geduld   *patience*

das Vergnügen, -   *pleasure*

der Unterschied, -e   *difference*

aufblühen (sep)   *to blossom, thrive*

ausgehen von (sep)   *to be initiated by*

vorhanden sein   *existing*

vorlesen (sep)   *to read aloud*

verlängern   *to extend*

grotesk   *grotesque*

unheimlich (gut)   *really (well)*

historisch   *historical*

wissenschaftlich   *scientific*

meinetwegen   *as far as I'm concerned*

zwar   *indeed*

teilweise   *partly*

PREPOSITIONS WITH THE GENITIVE CASE

während   *during*

wegen   *because of*

anstatt   *instead of*

innerhalb   *inside of*

ZWEITE STUFE

TELLING THAT SOMETHING IS OR WAS BEING DONE

Die Instrumente werden vor der Aufführung gestimmt.   *The instruments are being tuned before the performance.*

Die Tänzer sind kräftig applaudiert worden.   *The dancers were strongly applauded.*

OTHER USEFUL WORDS

die Aufführung, -en   *performance*

die Bühne, -n   *stage*

der Dirigent, -en   *conductor*

die Handlung, -en   *plot*

der Rang, ⸚e   *(theater) balcony*

der Vorhang, ⸚e   *curtain*

der Zuschauer, -   *spectator*

die Aufregung, -en   *excitement*

die Eifersucht   *jealousy*

die Gänsehaut   *goose bumps*

das Herzklopfen   *pounding heart*

die Spannung, -en   *tension, excitement*

der Bube, -n   *(southern German) boy*

die Königin, -nen   *queen*

die Pracht   *splendor*

der Spiegel, -   *mirror*

der Versuch, -e   *attempt*

aufführen (sep)   *to perform*

begleiten   *to accompany*

begrüßen   *to greet*

s. beklagen über (acc)   *to complain about*

darstellen (sep)   *to play (act)*

erkennen   *to recognize*

erleben   *to experience*

s. handeln um   *to be about*

klären   *to clear up*

klatschen   *to applaud*

stimmen   *to tune (an instrument)*

träumen   *to dream*

s. umsehen (sep)   *to look around*

verteilen   *to distribute*

atemlos   *breathless*

bärtig   *bearded*

heiter   *cheerful*

vergeblich   *futile*

weder ... noch   *neither ... nor*

Kapitel 11: Deine Welt ist deine Sache!

	FUNCTIONS	GRAMMAR	CULTURE	RE-ENTRY
Los geht's! pp. 258-259	Was kommt nach der Schule? *p. 258*			
Erste Stufe pp. 260-264	•Expressing determination or indecision, *p. 260* •Talking about whether something is important or not important, *p. 263*	The use of **wo**-compounds to ask questions, *p. 263*	•**Ein wenig Landeskunde:** German universities, *p. 262* •**Landeskunde: Wie findet man eine Arbeitsstelle in Deutschland?** *p. 265*	•Reflexive verbs, *p. 260* •Expressing indecision, *p. 260* •Conversational past, *p. 260* •Ob-clauses, *p. 260* •**Um ... zu,** *p. 262* •Conditional, *p. 262* •Daß-clauses, *p. 263* •Wo-compounds, *p. 263*
Weiter geht's! pp. 266-267	Wenn ich mal dreißig bin, ..., *p. 266*			
Zweite Stufe pp. 268-271	•Expressing wishes, *p. 269* •Expressing certainty and refusing or accepting with certainty, *p. 269* •Talking about goals for the future, *p. 270* •Expressing relief, *p. 271*	•Two ways of expressing the future tense, *p. 270* •The perfect infinitive with modals and **werden,** *p. 271*	Umfragen und Tests, *p. 268*	•Expressing wishes, *p. 269* •**Wäre,** *p. 269* •Conditional, *p. 269* •Determiners of quantity, *p. 269* •Negation with **kein,** *p. 269* •Future tense formation, *p. 270* •Daß-clauses, *p. 271*
Zum Lesen pp. 272-274	Literatur der Ex-DDR Reading Strategy: Interpreting symbols			
Zum Schreiben p. 275	Von einem Wendepunkt erzählen Writing Strategy: Writing drafts and revising			
Review pp. 276-279	•Anwendung, *p. 276* •Kann ich's wirklich? *p. 278* •Wortschatz, *p. 279*			

Assessment Options

Stufe Quizzes
•*Chapter Resources,* Book 4
  Erste Stufe, Quiz 11-1
  Zweite Stufe, Quiz 11-2
•*Assessment Items, Audiocassette* 8 B

Kapitel 11 Chapter Test
•*Chapter Resources,* Book 4
•*Assessment Guide,* Speaking Test
•*Assessment Items, Audiocassette* 8 B

Test Generator, Kapitel 11

Chapter Overview

RESOURCES Print	RESOURCES Audiovisual
Practice and Activity Book	*Textbook Audiocassette* 6 A

Practice and Activity Book
Chapter Resources, Book 4
  •Communicative Activity 11-1
  •Communicative Activity 11-2
  •Additional Listening Activity 11-1
  •Additional Listening Activity 11-2
  •Additional Listening Activity 11-3
  •Student Response Forms
  •Realia 11-1
  •Situation Card 11-1
  •Teaching Transparency Master 11-1
  •Quiz 11-1
Video Guide
	Textbook Audiocassette 6 A
	
	Additional Listening Activities, Audiocassette 10 B
	Additional Listening Activities, Audiocassette 10 B
	Additional Listening Activities, Audiocassette 10 B
	
	Teaching Transparency 11-1
	Assessment Items, Audiocassette 8 B
	Video Program, Videocassette 2

Practice and Activity Book	*Textbook Audiocassette* 6 A

Practice and Activity Book
Chapter Resources, Book 4
  •Communicative Activity 11-3
  •Communicative Activity 11-4
  •Additional Listening Activity 11-4
  •Additional Listening Activity 11-5
  •Additional Listening Activity 11-6
  •Student Response Forms
  •Realia 11-2
  •Situation Card 11-2
  •Teaching Transparency Master 11-2
  •Quiz 11-2
Video Guide
	Textbook Audiocassette 6 A
	
	Additional Listening Activities, Audiocassette 10 B
	Additional Listening Activities, Audiocassette 10 B
	Additional Listening Activities, Audiocassette 10 B
	
	Teaching Transparency 11-2
	Assessment Items, Audiocassette 8 B
	Video Program, Videocassette 2

	Textbook Audiocassette 11

Chapter Resources, Book 4
  •Realia 11-3
  •Situation Card 11-3
Video Guide
	Video Program, Videocassette 2

Alternative Assessment
- •Performance Assessment
Teacher's Edition
  Erste Stufe, p. 255L
  Zweite Stufe, p. 255O
- •Portfolio Assessment
  Written: **Anwendung,** Activity 7, *Pupil's Edition,* p. 277;
  Assessment Guide, p. 24
  Oral: **Anwendung,** Activity 9, *Pupil's Edition,* p. 277;
  Assessment Guide, p. 24
•**Notizbuch,** *Pupil's Edition,* pp. 262, 264, 270, 271

CHAPTER OVERVIEW

Kapitel 11: Deine Welt ist deine Sache!
Textbook Listening Activities Scripts

For Student Response Forms, see *Chapter Resources,* Book 4, pp. 82-85.

Erste Stufe
Activity 4, p. 261

GERD Hallo, Ulla! Hallo, Ralf! Stör' ich?

RALF Ach was, natürlich nicht! Wir haben uns gerade über unsere Pläne nach dem Schulabschluß unterhalten. Hast du schon darüber nachgedacht, was du nach der Schule machen willst, Gerd?

GERD Na klar! Ich weiß schon ziemlich genau, was ich machen werde.

ULLA Beneidenswert! Ich hab' mich noch nicht entschieden, ob ich studieren oder einen Beruf erlernen soll.

RALF Das klingt aber sehr allgemein. Weißt du denn wenigstens, was du studieren würdest, oder in welchem Beruf du später einmal arbeiten möchtest?

ULLA In den letzten Wochen habe ich mir darüber sehr viele Gedanken gemacht. Ich habe mich entschlossen, einen medizinischen Beruf zu erlernen. Aber ich weiß noch nicht, ob ich mir ein so schwieriges Studium zutraue. Ich könnte auch eine Ausbildung als Krankenschwester machen. Das dauert nur drei Jahre.

RALF Vielleicht solltest du dich mal mit einem Arzt oder einer Krankenschwester über diese Berufe unterhalten. Ich könnte mir vorstellen, daß es dir helfen würde, die richtige Entscheidung zu treffen.

ULLA Gute Idee! Daran habe ich noch gar nicht gedacht. Du, Gerd! Du hast gesagt, daß du schon ganz genau weißt, was du nach dem Abi machen wirst. Laß mal hören!

GERD Also, zuerst muß ich ja meinen Wehrdienst leisten. Danach fange ich ein Studium an. Ich habe mich entschieden, Englisch und Spanisch zu studieren.

ULLA Kein Wunder! Da hast ja auch immer Supernoten in den beiden Fächern.

GERD Ich hoffe, daß ich einen Studienplatz bekomme. Ich möchte Simultandolmetscher werden.

RALF Mensch, ich beneide dich, Gerd. Das stelle ich mir wahnsinnig schwierig vor.

GERD Ist es auch! Deshalb wird es auch nicht einfach sein, einen Studienplatz hier in Deutschland zu bekommen. Im Notfall werde ich eben ins Ausland gehen, wie zum Beispiel nach London oder auch nach New York. Ich muß mir das noch überlegen.

ULLA Klasse! Und wer finanziert deine Auslandspläne? Deine Eltern? Das muß doch ziemlich teuer sein.

GERD Wahrscheinlich würden sie mich schon finanziell unterstützen, aber eigentlich hoffe ich darauf, ein Stipendium zu bekommen.

RALF Ich bin echt beeindruckt, Gerd. Du hast wirklich an alles gedacht. Ich selbst hab' beschlossen, Maschinenbau zu studieren. Als Diplomingenieur kann ich mich später entweder selbständig machen, oder ich kann in die Industrie gehen.

ULLA Wo willst du denn Maschinenbau studieren?

RALF Ich weiß noch nicht, ob ich nach Braunschweig oder nach Kaiserslautern gehen soll. Beide Unis sollen ein ausgezeichnetes Studienprogramm für Maschinenbau haben. Wenn das Studium gut läuft, bin ich fest entschlossen, ein Jahr in den USA oder in Kanada einzuschieben. Aber das kommt erst später.

GERD Na ja, es scheint, als ob wir alle ziemlich genau wissen, was wir nach der Schule anfangen. Mensch, wenn doch bloß der Streß mit dem Abi schon vorbei wäre!

RALF He, Leute! Da fällt mir gerade was ein. Ich hab' gehört, daß der Geßner, der Klassenlehrer von der 13b, in zwei Wochen eine Party für alle gestreßten Abiturienten macht. Geht ihr hin?

ULLA Das kommt ja wie gerufen! Eine Party haben wir uns schon lange verdient. Find' ich toll, daß der Geßner uns alle einlädt. Also, ich muß jetzt los. Tschüs, ihr beiden!

GERD Tschüs, Ulla!

RALF Ciao!

Answers to Activity 4

feste Pläne: Gerd, Ralf
noch nicht sicher: Ulla

Activity 12, p. 263

HORST He, Steffi! Na, wie geht's?

STEFFI Hallo, Horst! Ich hab' dich gar nicht gesehen. Ist ja wieder mal ziemlich voll im Café Goethe.

HORST Sag mal, Steffi, hast du dir schon überlegt, was du nach dem Abitur anfangen willst?

STEFFI Ja, hab' ich! Ich bin nicht besonders interessiert daran zu studieren. Das steht auf jeden Fall fest.

HORST Wieso nicht? Was stört dich denn so sehr an einem Studium?

STEFFI Weißt du, ich lege einfach keinen großen Wert darauf, die nächsten fünf, sechs Jahre weiterhin nur lernen zu müssen.

HORST Das müßtest du doch auch, wenn du einen Beruf erlernen willst.

STEFFI Da gibt es aber einen großen Unterschied. Für mich ist es am wichtigsten, daß ich endlich mal etwas Praktisches tun werde. Ich habe es satt, ständig nur über den Büchern zu sitzen.

HORST Woran hast du denn gedacht?

STEFFI Am liebsten würde ich an einem Projekt von UNICEF arbeiten. Ich lege großen Wert darauf, daß den Menschen in den Entwicklungsländern und vor allem den Kindern dort geholfen wird. Mir ist weniger wichtig, daß ich gut verdiene. Menschen in Not zu helfen, ist mir mehr wert als eigener Luxus.

HORST Ich wußte gar nicht, daß du auf diesem Gebiet so engagiert bist.

STEFFI Ja, als mir klarwurde, wie wichtig diese Ziele für mich sind, habe ich mich entschieden, diesen Weg zu wählen. Aber wir reden ja die ganze Zeit nur von meinen Zukunftsplänen. Erzähl doch mal, was du so vorhast!

HORST Ich werde wahrscheinlich erst einmal meinen Zivildienst machen.

STEFFI   Zivildienst statt Wehrdienst?

HORST   Ausschlaggebend für mich ist, daß ich beim Zivildienst nicht mit Waffen umgehen muß. Lieber arbeite ich als Sozialarbeiter, Altenpfleger oder sonst etwas in der Richtung. Nach dem Zivildienst möchte ich am liebsten Jura studieren.

STEFFI   Jura! Da wirst du ewig an der Uni sein.

HORST   Es ist nicht entscheidend für mich, daß das Studium lang und hart ist. Ich finde es wichtig, daß das Gesetz vertreten wird.

STEFFI   Hast du dir schon überlegt, in welche Richtung du später einmal gehen möchtest?

HORST   Vielleicht Grundstücksrecht.

STEFFI   Wie kommst du denn ausgerechnet auf Grundstücke?

HORST   Tja, also ich glaube, daß die Spezialisierung auf Grundstücksrecht Zukunft hat. Nimm zum Beispiel mal die ganzen Grundstücke in der ehemaligen DDR. Die Rechtsfrage wird auch in den nächsten fünf bis zehn Jahren noch nicht geklärt sein.

STEFFI   Hm. Das mag schon sein. Ich wünsch' dir auf jeden Fall viel Spaß mit deinen Zukunftsplänen. Also, ich muß wieder los. Tschüs, Horst!

HORST   Tschüs, Steffi!

Answers to Activity 12

Wichtig für Steffi: etwas Praktisches tun; Menschen in Entwicklungsländern helfen / Wichtig für Horst: nicht mit Waffen umgehen müssen; daß das Gesetz vertreten wird / E.g.: Es macht Horst nichts aus, weiter zu studieren, aber Steffi will lieber etwas Praktisches tun, Steffi möchte sich mit Problemen in Entwicklungsländern beschäftigen, und Horst interessiert sich für Rechtsfragen in Deutschland.

Zweite Stufe

Activity 20, p. 269

MEIKE   Hallo, Conny! Toll, daß du kommen konntest. Felix und Harry sind schon da.

CONNY   Das war übrigens eine gute Idee von dir, Meike, zusammen für die nächste Englischarbeit zu lernen. Hallo, Felix! Hallo, Harry! Na, lernt ihr schon fleißig?

FELIX   Hi, Conny! Eigentlich haben wir uns gerade darüber unterhalten, was wir uns im Leben mal wünschen.

MEIKE   Interessant! Erzähl doch mal! Was wünschst du dir denn als erstes nach dem Schulabschluß, Felix?

FELIX   Also, am liebsten wäre mir, wenn es keine Wehrpflicht gäbe. Das ist doch alles bloß eine riesige Zeitverschwendung. Mit physischer Gewalt stimme ich sowieso nicht überein. Was meinst du, Harry?

HARRY   Du kannst ja auch verweigern und statt dessen Zivildienst machen.

FELIX   Dazu brauche ich aber auch mindestens eineinhalb Jahre. Gleich nach der Schule mit dem Studium anzufangen, wäre mir viel wichtiger.

CONNY   Das kann ich gut verstehen, Felix. Mir wäre es auch lästig, wenn ich so eine Verpflichtung hätte. Mein Wunschtraum wäre, genug Geld zu haben, um ein ganzes Jahr in der Welt herumzureisen.

MEIKE   Klingt super, Conny! Da würde ich garantiert mitkommen. Es gibt so viele interessante Sachen auf der ganzen Welt zu sehen. Es wäre nur schön, wenn es keine Umweltkatastrophen mehr gäbe.

HARRY   Da hast du recht, Meike. Bei all den Erdbeben und Wirbelstürmen, die die Welt in letzter Zeit erlebt hat, kann ich deinen Wunsch verstehen. Ich muß allerdings eingestehen, daß ich bei meinen Wünschen etwas egoistischer bin. Ein toller Beruf, der viel Geld, aber auch viel Freizeit bringt, wäre mir sehr wichtig.

FELIX   Nicht schlecht, Harry. Mir wäre außerdem noch wichtig, daß ich mal ein tolles Haus habe.

MEIKE   Ihr habt wirklich sehr materialistische Wünsche. Mir ist es ganz gleichgültig, ob ich mal reich werde oder ein tolles Haus habe. Viel wichtiger wären mir echte Freunde, denen man ein ganzes Leben lang vertrauen kann.

HARRY   Jeder wünscht sich eben etwas anderes, und das ist auch gut so, sonst wäre die Welt unheimlich langweilig.

MEIKE   He, es ist ja schon bald halb fünf! Jetzt müssen wir uns aber ganz schön beeilen, wenn wir überhaupt noch was für die Englischarbeit lernen wollen. Immerhin müssen wir erst einmal die Schule hinter uns bringen, sonst bleiben alle unsere Wünsche nur Träume!

Answers to Activity 20

Felix: keine Wehrpflicht; gleich nach der Schule mit dem Studium anfangen zu können; tolles Haus
Conny: genug Geld zu haben, um zu reisen
Meike: keine Umweltkatastrophen; echte Freunde
Harry: tollen Beruf mit viel Geld und viel Freizeit
Answers will vary.

Activity 26, p. 270

DANIEL   He, Jürgen! Was liest du denn so Spannendes? Du hast uns gar nicht kommen hören.

JÜRGEN   Hallo, Daniel! Ach, da kommen ja auch Sylvia und Sophie.

SYLVIA   Du bist ja ziemlich in dein Buch vertieft. Zeig doch mal, was du da liest, Jürgen?

JÜRGEN   Es ist eine Biographie über John F. Kennedy. Habt ihr überhaupt eine Ahnung, was der alles in seinem Leben erreicht hat? Schon als junger Mann hatte der was drauf, sag' ich euch. Mit 29 Jahren war er bereits Abgeordneter im Repräsentantenhaus in der amerikanischen Regierung. Ich möchte unbedingt auch eine politische Karriere begonnen haben, wenn ich dreißig bin.

DANIEL   In die Politik willst du?

JÜRGEN   Ja, ich möchte mich auch mal so für mein Land und das Volk engagieren, wie Kennedy das für sein Land getan hat.

SYLVIA   Du hast ja große Pläne, Jürgen.

JÜRGEN   Ach, komm, Sylvia! So wie ich dich kenne, hast du doch bestimmt große Ambitionen, oder?

SYLVIA   Ja, stimmt! Mit dreißig möchte ich in einer Karriere als Börsenmaklerin etabliert sein und bereits eine Menge Geld gespart haben. Für mich sind komfortable finanzielle Verhältnisse sehr wichtig. In zehn Jahren will ich mir jedenfalls keine Gedanken mehr um Geld machen müssen.

DANIEL Ihr wißt schon so genau, wie ihr euch euer Leben in zehn Jahren vorstellt, Jürgen und Sylvia. Ich weiß noch gar nicht, was ich einmal machen werde, wenn ich dreißig bin. Ziemlich sicher bin ich mir jedoch, daß ich irgendwann mal heiraten und eine Familie haben will. Vielleicht werde ich bis dahin ja meine Traumfrau gefunden haben.

SYLVIA Daniel, das finde ich toll. Wir haben alle nur an die berufliche Seite gedacht. Sophie, du hast noch gar nichts gesagt. Wie stellst du dir dein Leben mit dreißig vor?

SOPHIE Ich würde gern Schauspielerin werden, aber alle machen sich immer über meinen Berufswunsch lustig.

JÜRGEN Du mußt zugeben, daß die Chancen in dem Beruf nicht gerade rosig sind, weil es so viele Menschen gibt, die diesen Wunschtraum haben.

SOPHIE Trotzdem glaube ich, daß ich eine gute Schauspielerin wäre. Bis ich dreißig bin, will ich es geschafft haben, im Deutschen Theater oder im Berliner Schauspielhaus gespielt zu haben. Ich glaube jedenfalls an mein Talent und an meine Chancen.

JÜRGEN Ich wünsche dir viel Glück dabei. Wir sollten uns alle in zwölf Jahren wieder treffen, meint ihr nicht? Ich möchte wirklich mal sehen, ob wir unsere Träume verwirklichen können!

Answers to Activity 26

Jürgen: will sich politisch engagieren
Sylvia: will Karriere machen und viel Geld haben
Daniel: will heiraten und eine Familie haben
Sophie: will Schauspielerin werden
Answers will vary.

Anwendung
Activity 1, p. 276

CARMEN Martin, Simone, so ein Zufall, daß ich euch hier treffe!

SIMONE Hallo, Carmen! So ein Zufall ist das nun auch wieder nicht. Wir sind oft in diesem Eiscafé. Die haben hier das beste Eis in der ganzen Stadt.

MARTIN Stimmt! Setz dich doch, Simone! Wir haben uns gerade über unsere Berufswünsche unterhalten.

CARMEN Was möchtest du denn mal machen, Martin?

MARTIN Ich möchte gern Journalismus studieren. Am liebsten würde ich später mal als Journalist für eine große Zeitung oder für ein politisches Magazin arbeiten.

SIMONE Das ist sicher wahnsinnig interessant. Du kommst mit vielen wichtigen Leuten zusammen und wirst auf jeden Fall ein paar Politiker kennenlernen.

MARTIN Ja, Simone, das denke ich auch, und darauf freue ich mich ganz besonders.

CARMEN Wird deine Arbeitszeit aber nicht sehr unregelmäßig sein? Ich kann mir vorstellen, daß du zum Beispiel an einer heißen Story rund um die Uhr dranbleiben mußt.

MARTIN Na ja, Carmen, solche Fälle gibt es sicher hin und wieder, aber bestimmt nicht jeden Tag. Mir macht Journalismus einfach Spaß, und das ist es, worauf es mir ankommt. Was für eine Karriere hast du denn geplant, Carmen?

CARMEN Ich möchte gern Erzieherin werden.

SIMONE Du magst Kinder, nicht wahr? Wird es dir denn nicht zuviel werden, Tag für Tag mit kleinen Kindern umgehen zu müssen? Das ist doch sehr anstrengend.

CARMEN So sehe ich das eben nicht. Für mich gibt es viele positive Seiten an diesem Beruf. Ich mag Kinder sehr gern. Ich finde es faszinierend, mit so vielen kleinen Menschen umzugehen und zu sehen, wie sie sich kreativ entfalten. Außerdem macht es mir Spaß, bei der Erziehung der Kinder mitzuwirken.

MARTIN Mensch, Carmen, mir wäre diese Verantwortung viel zu groß. Die Kinder sind doch alle verschieden in ihren Charaktereigenschaften.

CARMEN Darin besteht eben die Herausforderung an mich. Ich muß einerseits Leitfigur sein, muß mich andererseits aber auch in die Kinder hineinversetzen können. Ich freue mich schon darauf.

MARTIN Viel Glück wünsche ich dir, Carmen. Sag mal, Simone, welchen Berufswunsch hast du eigentlich?

SIMONE Ich habe beschlossen, Zahnärztin zu werden.

CARMEN Zahnmedizin ist aber ein langes und hartes Studium. Außerdem kenne ich keinen, der sich darauf freut, zum Zahnarzt zu gehen. Meinst du, das wird dir auf Dauer Spaß machen?

SIMONE Mit dem Studium hast du recht, Carmen. Ich glaube allerdings, daß ich das schon schaffen werde. Und übrigens finde ich, daß die Angst vorm Zahnarzt ein Klischee ist. Nicht jeder macht schlechte Erfahrungen. Zum Teil hängt es ja auch von der mehr oder weniger guten Zahnpflege der Patienten ab, ob sie sich vorm Zahnarzt fürchten oder nicht.

MARTIN Ich kann mir vorstellen, daß du dich mal bemühen wirst, dieses Klischee aus der Welt zu räumen, Simone. Du wirst bestimmt mal eine gute Zahnärztin.

CARMEN Zahnärzte verdienen doch auch ganz gut, oder?

SIMONE Ja, das stimmt. Geldprobleme werde ich wohl keine haben, aber das ist nicht entscheidend für mich.

MARTIN Wenn du dich selbständig machst, kannst du dir auch deine Arbeitszeit einteilen, wie du willst.

SIMONE Richtig, Martin. Ich werde als Zahnärztin viel Urlaub machen können, ganz gut verdienen, und ich werde vor allem einen Beruf haben, der mir Spaß macht.

CARMEN Das freut mich für dich, Simone.

MARTIN Ich glaube, wir bestellen jetzt endlich unser Eis. Hallo, Bedienung! Wir möchten gern bestellen!

Answers to Activity 1

Martin: Journalist / interessanter Beruf; man lernt wichtige Leute kennen / unregelmäßige Arbeitszeit
Carmen: Erzieherin / macht Spaß, bei der Erziehung der Kinder mitzuwirken / anstrengender Beruf; große Verantwortung
Simone: Zahnärztin / langes, hartes Studium; viele Leute gehen nicht gern zum Zahnarzt / guter Verdienst; man kann sich selbständig machen; man kann sich die Arbeitszeit einteilen.

Kapitel 11: Deine Welt ist deine Sache!
Projects and Games

PROJECT

In this activity, students will create an extensive collage called **Karrieren mit Fremdsprachen.** *The project should be completed in German by individuals or pairs of students. Final projects should be presented and then displayed in the foreign language area.*

Materials Students may need poster board, paper, dictionaries, pencils, magazine cutouts, and materials from the counseling office.

Suggested Sequence

1. Have students make a list of professions that require a foreign language or are enhanced by one. Have them find information at the high school's career center, the local library, and in ads in newspapers such as the *Wallstreet Journal.*
2. From this list, students choose one profession they plan to research in detail.
3. Students make an outline of the information they plan to include in their presentation.
4. Students collect visual materials and design the layout of their collage.
5. For the written component, students should incorporate some of the new phrases and expressions they have learned in this chapter, particularly in the chart next to Activity 11 on p. 262.
6. The final product should include visuals, accompanied by a job description and the advantages of such a career.
7. Students present their collage to the rest of the class.

Grading the Project

Suggested point distribution (total = 100 points)
Accurate descriptions and
  correct language usage   50
Appearance   25
Oral presentation   25

♜ GAME

Erratet den Beruf!

This game tests students' knowledge of German professions and the skills necessary for these jobs.

Procedure Make a list of all the professions that students have learned thus far. Then divide the class into two teams. The first player on team A comes up to the front. You point to the first word on the list, and the student has to describe what this person does at his or her job without using the job title. The team that guesses the correct profession wins a point. Teams alternate giving job descriptions. The team with the most points at the end of the game wins.

Examples:
Er kümmert sich um Patienten, aber er ist kein Arzt. (Krankenpfleger)
Sie hackt und verkauft Fleisch. (Metzgerin)

Kapitel 11: Deine Welt ist deine Sache!
Lesson Plans, pages 256-279

Teacher Note

Before you begin the chapter, you may want to preview the *Video Program* and consult the *Video Guide.* Suggestions for integrating the video into each chapter are given in the *Video Guide* and in the chapter interleaf. Activity masters for video selections can be found in the *Video Guide.*

*U*sing the Chapter Opener, *pp. 256-257*

Motivating Activity

Ask students if they have ever had a job for which they got paid. When was this, what was the job, and what were some of the reasons students decided to work? (**Wer von euch hat schon mal eine Arbeit gehabt? Wann war das, was für Arbeit habt ihr gemacht, und warum habt ihr euch entschlossen zu arbeiten?**)

Background Information

① The German **Arbeitsamt** can be compared to an employment office in the United States. Its functions include job placement, vocational guidance, and promotion of vocational training. Furthermore, it provides financial assistance for retraining to people who need to adapt their skills to the changing demands of the labor market.

Thinking Critically

① **Drawing Inferences** Ask students to study the photo. Can they make out any of the notices and posters on the wall that might help them figure out where this scene is taking place? (**beim Arbeitsamt**) Students should then, with the help of the caption, describe the roles of these two people.

② **Analyzing** Ask students to interpret the statement in the caption. What does it reveal about what this student wants for her future?

Background Information

② The type of high school from which students graduate determines which diplomas they can earn. At the **Hauptschule,** the diploma is called **Hauptschulabschluß.** At the **Mittelschule** or **Realschule,** it is called **Mittlere Reife** or **Realschulabschluß.** At the **Gymnasium** or **Oberschule,** students graduate with the **Abitur** or **Reifeprüfung** referred to as **Matura** in Austria and Switzerland. The career path of a graduating student depends to a large degree on the type of secondary school he or she attended.

Building on Previous Skills

② To review some of the information related to German schools and jobs, have students look at the **Zum Lesen** section on pp. 110-111 in Level 1. Ask students to identify the different types of schools.

Teaching Suggestion

③ Have students think of a question or statement that could have triggered the caption of this photo.

Focusing on Outcomes

To get students to focus on the chapter objectives, ask them how much time they have spent thinking about what they will do after they graduate. Then have students preview the learning outcomes listed on p. 257. **NOTE:** These outcomes are modeled in **Los geht's!** (pp. 258-259) and **Weiter geht's!** (pp. 266-267) and evaluated in **Kann ich's wirklich?** (p. 278).

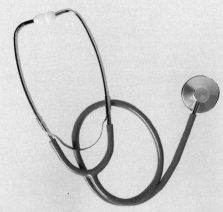

Teaching Los geht's!
pp. 258-259

Resources for Los geht's!

- *Textbook Audiocassette* 6 A
- *Practice and Activity Book*

Teacher Note

Los geht's! is recorded on audiocassette.

Los geht's! Summary

In **Was kommt nach der Schule?**, four students from a **Gymnasium** talk about what they plan to do after graduation. The following student outcomes listed on p. 257 are modeled in the episode: expressing determination or indecision and talking about whether something is important or not important.

Motivating Activity

Ask students what they plan to do immediately after graduation. Many older students will have definite plans. Younger students will probably be less definite but should be able to speculate. (**Was werdet ihr machen, wenn ihr mit der High School fertig seid?**)

Building on Previous Skills

Have students read the introductory paragraph. Based on what students know from previous learning, can they give examples of the kind of careers these four students can prepare for, knowing that they will graduate with the **Abitur**? Make a list of students' ideas. (**Auf welche Berufe können sich diese Gymnasiasten vorbereiten?**)

Teaching Suggestion

1 Let students listen to the taped statements as they read along in their textbooks. Stop the tape after each report and ask questions to check for understanding. Explain any new terms or phrases in German by paraphrasing or using synonymous expressions. Let students read Activity 1a. Have them read and listen to the statements again, one at a time, taking notes as they go along. This can be done individually or with a partner. Discuss students' findings with the entire class.

For Individual Needs

1b A Slower Pace Taking one of the four reports as an example, work with the whole class to summarize the report in students' own words. Put students into three groups, and have each group cover one of the three German students not discussed before.

2 A Slower Pace Help students verbalize the statistics in **Nach dem Abi?** (Examples: **51% der jungen Männer machen nach dem Abi den Wehr- oder den Zivildienst. 30% der jungen Frauen machen ein Studium.**) This is an excellent way to recycle the genitive case.

Thinking Critically

2 Analyzing Ask students to think of reasons why the percentage of young men planning to enter the university is only 21% compared to 30% for young women. (As students learned in Chapter 5, all young men in Germany are required to do military or alternate service, which accounts for the large percentage of those entering the **Wehr- oder Zivildienst.**)

Teaching Suggestions

2c On the day before starting Activity 2c, take a quick written survey of all students in your German classes. Ask them to write down their main interests, listing them in order of priority from 1 to 5. Summarize the survey in percentages for each of the main interest areas mentioned. Put the results on a transparency and use them to compare with the findings in **Information für junge Leute.**

3 If you do this as a class project, the questions should be asked in German. (Examples: **Was wirst du wahrscheinlich ein halbes Jahr nach deinem Schulabschluß machen? Wirst du studieren? Arbeiten? Eine Ausbildung machen? Zum Militär gehen?**) If you decide to do this activity as a school-wide project, the questions will be asked in English, but the results translated into German. You might choose to have students display the results in a chart like the one on p. 259.

Closure

Refer students back to the outcomes listed on p. 257. Ask them about their impressions of young German people's ideas about their future.

LOS GEHT'S!

ERSTE STUFE

*T*eaching Erste Stufe,
pp. 260-264

▶ *page 260*

MOTIVATE

♖ Game
Play charades to help kinesthetic learners review the vocabulary of professions. Prepare a set of index cards with a profession in German written on each. (Examples: **Dirigent, Komponist, Lehrer, Verkäufer, Arzt, Metzger, Bäcker**) Then divide the class into two teams. A member of Team A comes to the front and draws a card from the stack of index cards. This student must then try to act out the job to his or her own team within a set time. Members of Team A may ask yes/no questions as they try to guess the profession. If Team A is not able to guess the profession within the set time, Team B gets a chance to win the point. Teams alternate sending members to the front.

TEACH
PRESENTATION: Wortschatz

Introduce the new vocabulary in the **auf deutsch erklärt** section. Make up sentences using the definitions and ask students to restate your sentences using the new words.
Examples:
Hast du dich übers Wochenende gut entspannt?
Hast du dich übers Wochenende ausgeruht?
Ask students to use the new vocabulary in the **auf deutsch erklärt** section in sentences of their own. Then work with the new vocabulary in the **auf englisch erklärt** section. Model each sentence and have students repeat. Ask for variations of the sentences, keeping essentially the same context.
Examples:
Auf alle Fälle gibt es gute Gründe, Beamter zu werden.
Bestimmt hast du viele gute Gründe, Beamter zu werden.

PRESENTATION: So sagt man das!

After you have introduced the new expressions, call on individual students to personalize each statement by completing it.
Example:
Ich hab' beschlossen, heute ins Kino zu gehen.
Ich kann noch nicht sagen, ob ich dieses Wochenende Zeit habe.

▶ *page 261*

Teaching Suggestion

5 Before starting the activity, have students do two things. First, practice the section **Wünsche und Pläne** giving infinitive phrases with **zu**. Write on a transparency or on the chalkboard **Ich bin entschlossen, ...** and **Ich hab' mich entschieden, ...** and have students complete the sentence. Then brainstorm for additional reasons why your students would make certain choices for the future. Have students write these ideas in their notebooks.
Examples:
studieren: ein Stipendium haben; (Arzt) werden wollen
arbeiten: Geld brauchen; etwas Praktisches machen wollen
ins Ausland gehen: Freunde (Verwandte) dort haben; eine andere Kultur kennenlernen wollen

For Individual Needs

5 A Slower Pace Do two to three questions together with the whole class and practice giving reasons. Once students feel comfortable with the format, they should continue the activity with a partner. Remind students that the dependent clauses in the expressions of indecision require verb-last word order.

Teaching Suggestions

6 Do this activity as a chain around the room. Each student says something he or she has decided to do, expressing the decision in a different way than the preceding person. To help students out, put all starting phrases on a transparency or on the chalkboard.
Ich hab' mich entschieden, ...
Ich bin entschlossen, ...
Ich hab' beschlossen, ...
Ich weiß, daß ...
Ich werde bestimmt, ...

7 The reflexive makes constructing these sentences a little harder. Do two to three sentences orally with the class, including one in which the cue contains a **man**-construction that needs to be changed to **ich**. Then let students work in pairs, doing this activity orally and in writing. Call on pairs to read their roles.

 ▶ page 262

PRESENTATION: Ein wenig Landeskunde

Ask students why they think the leading fields of study listed in the chart are so popular. They might answer, for example: **Jura ist ein interessantes Studium, und man verdient später viel Geld.** You might also have students research some of the universities in Germany, Switzerland, and Austria to find out how old they are.

 ## Video Program

In the video clip **Neue Lehrpläne**, students talk about how their lives and especially their educational system have changed since unification. See *Video Guide* for suggestions.

 ## For Individual Needs

8 Challenge As students work in pairs, they should make notes about their partner's responses. Then call on several students and ask them how their partner responded to a certain question.
Example:
Emily sagte, daß sie noch nicht so genau weiß, ob sie studieren möchte.

For Individual Needs

11 A Slower Pace Be sure students understand what the terms in the chart mean. Explain difficult terms in German.
Example:
Einkommenshöhe: wieviel Geld man pro Monat oder pro Jahr verdient

 ▶ page 263

PRESENTATION: So sagt man das!

Model the phrases in the box, adding a short **daß**-clause after each. Have students repeat. Then have them express these phrases in English. To practice the expressions, ask students to answer your questions.
Example:
Was ist für dich am wichtigsten?
Für mich ist es am wichtigsten, daß ich gesund und fit bin.

Thinking Critically

12 Analyzing Have students take notes while they listen to Steffi and Horst, and then have them compare their responses to the survey on p. 259 (**Nach dem Abi?**). Are these statements representative of the results of the survey?

For Additional Practice

13 To continue this activity, have students add other things of importance to the ones already given.

ERSTE STUFE

▶ *page 264*

PRESENTATION: Wortschatz

To introduce the new vocabulary, model the words and have students repeat. (Although most of them are cognates, there is a shift in stress from the English.) Then have students give a brief description of the professions saying what people do or where they work.

Teaching Suggestion

15 Let students know that the suggested phrases are ideas to get them started. Encourage them to think of other reasons and give more detail.

 ## For Individual Needs

16 Challenge Have students write down their responses to each of the seven questions. Then tell students to arrange their notes into an outline and finally into a cohesive paragraph. They should refer back to the writing skills they have learned in the **Zum Schreiben** sections of the previous chapters.

Reteaching: Vocabulary

Ask students to assume the role of an interviewer who is making an outline of questions for a potential employee. Using the vocabulary of this **Stufe**, ask students to make a list of at least 10 questions they plan to ask. Allow students to work in pairs or small groups.

▶ *page 265*

PRESENTATION: Landeskunde

Teaching Suggestion

Survey students about their previous or current work experience. How did they find out about the job and how did they apply for it? (**Für diejenigen von euch, die schon mal berufstätig waren oder immer noch sind, möchte ich gern wissen, wie ihr über den Job gehört habt. Und wie habt ihr euch um den Job beworben?**)

Teaching Suggestion

Introduce some additional vocabulary to increase students' comprehension of the text.

sich bewerben/Bewerbung: eine Arbeit suchen
das Stellenangebot: die Stellenofferte
die Samstagsausgabe: die Zeitung, die am Samstag verkauft wird
der Sonderteil: ein Teil, den man nicht immer in der Zeitung findet
tabellarisch: in Form einer Tabelle
der Lebenslauf: die schriftliche Beschreibung des Lebens einer Person
der Absolvent: jemand, der seine Ausbildung beendet hat
gutdotierte Führungsposition: Managerstellung, in der man viel verdient
verfügen über: etwas tun können / eine Eigenschaft besitzen
gute Umgangsformen: gute Manieren / gutes Benehmen
eigenverantwortliche Führung: kann selbständig/allein arbeiten
die Einarbeitung: die ersten Wochen in der neuen Stelle

 ## Cooperative Learning

A/B Divide the class into groups of three or four students. Each group should have a writer, a discussion leader, a proofreader, and a reporter. Allow a whole class period for this activity. Before groups read the text, you will need to introduce the additional vocabulary. Then ask students to work through the text (article and ad), and answer the questions. When students have finished, ask groups to share their responses to questions A and B with the rest of the class.

 ## Multicultural Connection

Ask students to interview foreign exchange students, other foreign language teachers, or anyone else they know from a different country about seeking employment. What are the procedures in that particular country? Ask students to share their answers with the rest of the class.

Family Link

Have students interview their family members about their first jobs. How did they find out about the job? What did they have to do to apply? What did they have to do and how much did the job pay?

CLOSE

Thinking Critically

Drawing Inferences Ask students about their plans for their future. How are their parents involved in their decision making? What type of training and education will they need for their career choice? (**Inwiefern haben eure Eltern mit der Wahl eurer Zukunftspläne zu tun? Diskutiert ihr darüber in der Familie? Welche Ausbildung braucht ihr, um euer Berufsziel zu erreichen?**)

Focusing on Outcomes

Refer students back to the learning outcomes listed on p. 257. They should recognize that they now know how to express determination or indecision and to talk about whether something is important or not important.

ASSESS

- **Performance Assessment** Ask students to prepare a brief statement about their career goals. They should talk about their plans, the reasons for their choice, and what makes these plans important to them.

- Quiz 11-1, *Chapter Resources,* Book 4

Teaching Weiter geht's!
pp. 266-267

Resources for Weiter geht's!

- *Textbook Audiocassette* 6 A
- *Practice and Activity Book*

Teacher Note

Weiter geht's! is recorded on audiocassette.

Weiter geht's! Summary

In **Wenn ich mal dreißig bin, ...,** five teenagers talk about their plans for the future and the goals they want to have achieved by the age of thirty. The following student outcomes listed on p. 257 are modeled in the episode: expressing wishes, expressing certainty and refusing or accepting with certainty, talking about goals for the future, and expressing relief.

Motivating Activity

Ask students to picture their lives at age 30. What will they be doing? (**Wie stellt ihr euch das Leben vor, wenn ihr dreißig seid? Was werdet ihr dann tun?**)

Teaching Suggestion

17 With their books open, let students listen to the five interviews. Pause after each interview, ask questions to check for understanding, and explain any difficult words or passages in German. Ask students to take notes of key points made by each interviewee. Play the interviews at least twice.

Thinking Critically

18 Comparing and Contrasting After students have discussed their personal hopes and goals for their own futures, have them compare them to those of the five German students. With whom do they identify? Where do their goals differ? In which areas do they see similarities?

ZWEITE STUFE

Closure

Ask students to write a **Stellenangebot** for a job they would like to have. What would it have to offer? Have students share their job ad with a small group and have group members help each other with suggestions for improving wording and layout. Make a display of final **Stellenangebote**.

*T*eaching Zweite Stufe, *pp. 268-271*

Resources for Zweite Stufe

Practice and Activity Book
Chapter Resources, Book 4
- Communicative Activities 11-3, 11-4
- Additional Listening Activities 11-4, 11-5, 11-6
- Student Response Forms
- Realia 11-2
- Situation Card 11-2
- Teaching Transparency Master 11-2
- Quiz 11-2

Audiocassette Program
- *Textbook Audiocassette* 6 A
- *Additional Listening Activities, Audiocassette* 10 B
- *Assessment Items, Audiocassette* 8 B

Video Program, Videocassette 2
Video Guide

▶ *page 268*

MOTIVATE

Teaching Suggestion

Brainstorm with students about surveys typically conducted of young people. What kinds of questions are asked by newspapers or magazines? Have students think of questions other than those already discussed. (Examples: **wichtige Bedingungen am Arbeitsplatz, was man mit dreißig erreicht haben will**) Make a list of topics or questions in German.

TEACH

📼 Video Program

In the video clip **Azubis in Dresden,** young apprentices in Dresden talk about the apprenticeship program that is preparing them to become industrial mechanics. See *Video Guide* for suggestions.

Teaching Suggestion

Help students verbalize the statistics in the four charts.
Examples:
63% der Jugendlichen halten es für sehr wichtig, den richtigen Beruf zu wählen.
Für Jungen steht ein gesundes Leben an erster Stelle.

PRESENTATION: Wortschatz

- Present the new vocabulary in its original context. From the five reports in the **Weiter geht's!** section, write those sentences that contain the new vocabulary on a transparency. For each new word or phrase, provide as much context as necessary for students to be able to derive its meaning and to paraphrase it.
- Use the new words and phrases in statements of your own to which students have to react.
Examples:
Es ist gut, daß wir in der Schule geregelte Verhältnisse haben.
Weißt du schon, was auf dich zukommt, wenn du mit der High School fertig bist?

▶ *page 269*

Thinking Critically

19 Drawing Inferences Before students discuss Question 3 ask them to define a **Vorbild.** Does it have to be a known personality? Make a list of typical characteristics and attributes a **Vorbild** has to have. (**Wie charakterisiert ihr ein Vorbild?**)

PRESENTATION: So sagt man das!

- Refer students back to *Der Panther* in the Chapter 2 **Zum Lesen** section to see how the subjunctive is used.
- Ask students to complete the second sentence in the function box expressing their own wishes.
In meiner idealen Welt ...

For Individual Needs

21 Tactile Learners Have students use the suggestions in the box to illustrate their ideal world in a picture or a collage. This can be done in class or as a homework assignment. Students share their illustrations with the class and describe their visions.

PRESENTATION: So sagt man das!

- Present students with a situation in the form of a question or statement to which they must react with certainty.
  Examples:
  Weißt du schon, ob du einmal heiratest?
  Du wirst aufs College gehen, nicht wahr?
- Present situations to which students react with any phrase from the second set of expressions (refusing/accepting).
  Examples:
  Du mußt deine Autoversicherung selbst bezahlen?
  Du wirst sicher zu Hause wohnen, wenn du auf die Uni gehst.
- Ask students to think of other ways to express the phrases.

▶ *page 270*

Teaching Suggestions

22 Do this activity as a chain. Each student should ask a classmate about his or her future. That student answers and then asks another classmate a question, and so forth. To facilitate the conversations, write some other topics on the board which students can choose from. (Examples: **Familie, Umwelt, Politik, Beziehung zu Eltern, Freunde, Schule**) Help students formulate some sample statements and questions that bring about refusal or acceptance.

24 Prepare a list of phrases which can be used to give a reason (see Chapter 3, p. 67) Let students refer to this list as they justify the ranking of things on their list.

PRESENTATION: Ein wenig Grammatik

- Review the forms of the verb **werden** with the class.
- Have students compare the two sentences in the grammar box and review the two ways of expressing future time (with present or future tense). Discuss with them the questions in the box.

Teaching Suggestion

25 On a transparency or on the chalkboard, give students additional phrases for building sentences in the future tense.
Examples:
sehr gesund leben
eine gute Universität wählen
(Elektrotechnik) studieren
viel Geld verdienen
einen tollen Beruf ausüben
(meine) Lebensweise selbst bestimmen
in einem Vorort (in der Stadt, auf dem Land) wohnen
im Ausland leben

PRESENTATION: So sagt man das!

Present to students several sets of sentences that contrast the present or future with the perfect infinitive.
Example:
Ich möchte eine politische Karriere beginnen.
Ich möchte eine politische Karriere begonnen haben.
In English, ask students to explain how the different tenses affect the meaning of the sentences. Which sentence in each set expresses speculation that an action projected into the future will have been completed at a certain time?

▶ *page 271*

PRESENTATION: Grammatik

To practice these verb forms, have students predict the outcome of the following.
a) a family member having found a new job
b) additions/alterations made to the school building
c) an election (school, local, state, or federal) won or lost
d) a sport event won or lost

Teaching Suggestion

27 Before writing complete sentences, ask students to supply the perfect infinitive for each verb listed.

PRESENTATION: So sagt man das!

Ask students how they would express relief in English. Then present the expressions in the function box to students.

History Connection

29 Ask students to use the format of the activity to express relief about either a historical event they have studied or a current social or political event.

Reteaching: Perfect Infinitive with Modals and *werden*

Ask students to compile a list of at least five goals they will have accomplished by the year 2020. (**Macht eine Liste von mindestens fünf Zielen, von denen ihr glaubt, daß ihr sie im Jahr 2020 erreicht haben werdet.**)

CLOSE

Teaching Suggestion

Have students make predictions about what their classmates will have accomplished by the time they are 25, 50, and 75 years old.
Example:
Mit 25 wird Susi schon die ganze Welt gesehen haben.

Focusing on Outcomes

Refer students back to the learning outcomes listed on p. 257. They should recognize that they now know how to express wishes, express certainty and refuse or accept with certainty, talk about goals for the future, and express relief.

ASSESS

- **Performance Assessment** Let students choose one of the following questions and respond to it. Call on individual students. **Was gäbe es in deiner idealen Schule? In deinem idealen Beruf?**

- Quiz 11-2, *Chapter Resources,* Book 4

Teaching Zum Lesen, *pp. 272-274*

Teacher Note

Das Märchen vom kleinen Herrn Moritz is recorded on *Textbook Audiocassette* 11.

Reading Strategy

The targeted strategy in this reading is interpreting symbols. Students should learn about this strategy before beginning Questions 7 and 8.

PREREADING

Background Information

- Generally, literary theory makes a distinction between **Volksmärchen** and **Kunstmärchen:** respectively, folk tales that were passed down orally and tales intended for publication. Nineteenth-century German writers, particularly those of the Romantic school, consciously revived the **Märchen** in order to use the elements of fantasy and wonder in various ways, often playfully or ironically. Any contemporary writer can count on the reading public's familiarity with this tradition. Fairy tale and folk motifs and familiar symbols can thus be used to carry an implicit message, especially when they are combined with realistic settings or situations from contemporary everyday life.

- Wolf Biermann was born in Hamburg in 1936. His father, a stables foreman who was active in the Communist resistance movement, died in Auschwitz in 1943. Following his own political leanings, Biermann moved to the GDR in 1953, where he studied political economy, philosophy, and mathematics at Humboldt University in former East Berlin. Since then, he has written numerous poems, protest songs, ballads, chansons, narrative texts, and a play. As of 1965, he was no longer allowed to publish or perform his works in the GDR. During a concert tour in the West in November of 1975, he was suddenly expatriated from the GDR. Today, Biermann lives in Hamburg.

Motivating Activity

After presenting the background information to the class, ask the students to predict whether Biermann's **Märchen** is likely to be a children's story or a fable for adults. Explain that a fable differs from other kinds of tales in that it usually has a moral or a message that can be applied to everyday life. It doesn't matter whether the students predict correctly or not, since they will be reading to check their predictions and have plenty of opportunities to change their minds.

READING

Teacher Notes

6 Citizens of the former **DDR** were required to carry a **Personalausweis** to identify themselves at all times, even when they left their homes for a short walk (note that Moritz' I.D. case was worn out).

8 In answering this question, students can keep from going too far afield by asking themselves how the symbols they choose would fit into the motif of transformation, as it traditionally occurs in folklore. For example, the growth and wilting of the flowers, the change in the people's moods and **Herr Moritz**' hair loss are all part of that motif.

Thinking Critically

Analyzing One of the interesting features of this type of writing is that, while the story has a message of some kind, it is implicit rather than explicit. The students are probably familiar with other works, particularly science fiction and fantasy, in which the story carries a strong social or political message. Some examples might include *Brave New World, 1984,* and *Slaughterhouse-Five.* After the class has decided what the main ideas of Biermann's **Märchen** are, they may be interested in discussing how and why this form of presentation is more effective than writing an editorial about the same ideas. How does the literary form help make the ideas seem more current and present to readers in different countries and different eras?

POST-READING

Teacher Note

Activity 10 is a post-reading task that will show whether students can apply what they have learned.

Closure

In many places and at many different times, literature has been used as a vehicle for criticizing repressive regimes and disseminating "subversive" ideas. The students may already realize that if the censors catch on, the work may not get printed or performed, or the book may be seized and burned, or the play closed. Therefore, authors frequently try to avoid censorship by writing works that claim to be "pure fantasy." (Much pre-glasnost Russian science fiction is actually political protest literature.) Ask the students to decide whether Biermann's **Märchen** could be printed in countries such as North Korea, Singapore, or the Peoples' Republic of China.

Answers to Activity 1

Märchen; Answers will vary. Possible answers: characters with magical powers, fantastic events; a. **Herr Moritz**; b. **klein, große Schuhe, schwarzer Mantel, trägt Regenschirm**; c. **im Winter in der Großstadt Berlin**

Answers to Activity 2

The people of the city are very surly because of the long winter; supporting details: paragraphs 2 to 7 are all specific examples of how the long winter is making people angry.

Answers to Activity 3

Answers will vary. Possible answers: **Ein Mann will die Leute glücklich machen, indem er Blumen wachsen läßt. Ein Polizist aber macht ihm Angst, so daß die Blumen verschwinden und er seine Haare verliert.**

Answers to Activity 4

1st paragraph: **Eines Tages ...** , 8th paragraph: **An einem solchen kalten Schneetag ...** ; the first phrase introduces the general setting of the story, and the second phrase begins the actual narration of events.

Answers to Activity 5

a. **daß die Leute alle böse sind; Blumen wachsen aus seinem Kopf; Sie freuen sich;** b. **den Ausweis von Herrn Moritz; die Blumen schrumpfen zusammen und verschwinden;** c. **Er bekommt eine Glatze.**

Answers to Activity 6

Answers will vary. Possible answers: because **Herr Moritz** is doing something out of the ordinary, stands out, and is different; this attracts the policeman's attention; **Herr Moritz** becomes frightened, and the negative feelings make him unable to use his energy for the flowers and for making people happy.

Answers to Activity 7

Answers will vary. Possible answers: **Herr Klein** is essentially powerless; the average citizen; the police state, the repressive powers, the bureaucracy

Answers to Activity 8

Answers will vary.

Answers to Activity 9

Answers will vary. Possible answers: **Individualität wird manchmal in einer Gesellschaft unterdrückt. Die Gesellschaft erwartet von ihren Mitgliedern Anpassung und Beachtung der gesellschaftlichen Regeln.**

Teaching Zum Schreiben, *p. 275*

Writing Strategy

The targeted strategy in this writing activity is writing drafts and revising. Students should learn about this strategy before beginning the assignment.

PREWRITING

Motivating Activity

Ask students to think of TV shows or dramas which address typical situations of today's teenagers. Which of these shows are especially popular and why?

Theatre Connection

Have students check with the drama teacher to see if they can look at samples of scripts and how they are layed out. They should take notes of essential elements that are part of a script.

WRITING

For Individual Needs

B **A Slower Pace** Remind students to refer to the expressions in the function boxes on pp. 260, 263, 269, and 270 as they write.

POST-WRITING

Teaching Suggestion

Read the **Schreibtip** with students and point out to them that when they make changes to improve their writing, they can use four basic revision techniques: adding, cutting, replacing, and reordering (**hinzufügen, auslassen, ersetzen, umgestalten**). These steps are important to help clean up a piece of writing.

For Individual Needs

Auditory Learners You may want to videotape individual scenes and have the remaining students serve as a live audience, reacting to each scene after the performance with appropriate comments and questions.

Closure

Ask students to name the main topic or concern from each scene. In addition, students should be able to recall how at least two of the problems were resolved.

Using Anwendung, *pp. 276-277*

> ## Resources for Anwendung
>
> *Chapter Resources,* Book 4
> - Realia 11-3
> - Situation Card 11-3
> *Video Program,* Videocassette 2
> *Video Guide*

Video Program

At this time, you might want to use the authentic advertising footage from German television. See *Video Guide* for suggestions.

Teaching Suggestion

1 Have students review their notes from this listening activity. Do they agree with the **Vorteile** and **Nachteile**? Can they add at least two more **Vorteile** and **Nachteile** to each **Berufswunsch**?

Teaching Suggestions

2 Have students give examples of jobs which would correspond to the lists they have prepared. Help students with names for professions they might not know in German.
Examples:
Mit vielen Leuten zusammenkommen: Reise-führer(in), Flugpersonal, Verkäufer(in), Lehrer(in)
Anderen Menschen helfen: Krankenschwe-ster/Krankenpfleger, Arzt/Ärztin

4 Have each student design and write a brochure that addresses the questions indicated. At the end, all brochures can be duplicated to be handed out. You can also display them on a career board in the classroom.

5 Have students answer all ten questions individually in writing as a basis for the discussion and tabulation that follow in Activity 6.

6 Start the comparison of results and the discussion in small groups. Encourage students to ask each other why-questions and to give reasons for their own answers. Then complete a chart of responses to each question with the whole class. Have students discuss the findings.

 Portfolio Assessment

7 You might want to suggest this activity as a written portfolio item for your students. See *Assessment Guide,* p. 24.

9 You might want to suggest this activity as an oral portfolio item for your students. See *Assessment Guide,* p. 24.

Kann ich's wirklich?
p. 278

This page helps students prepare for the test. It is a brief checklist of the major points covered in the chapter. The students should be reminded that it is only a checklist and not necessarily everything that will appear on the test.

Using Wortschatz,
p. 279

 Game
Play the game **Erratet den Beruf!** to review the vocabulary of this chapter. See p. 255F for the procedure.

Teaching Suggestion

Have students close their books for this activity. Call out a male profession and ask students to give the corresponding word referring to the female profession.
Examples:
Der Mann ist Beamter. Die Frau ist Beamtin.
Die Frau ist Krankenschwester. Der Mann ist Krankenpfleger.

For Individual Needs

Challenge Ask students to complete all open ended phrases that are on this page in an original way. This can be done with a partner in writing or orally.

 Total Physical Response

Divide students into groups of three or four and have them develop their own TPR activities. They should use the vocabulary and functions from this chapter as the basis for their commands. Allow enough time for each group to try out their commands on their classmates.

Teacher Note

Give the **Kapitel 11** Chapter Test, *Chapter Resources, Book 4.*

REVIEW

11
Deine Welt ist deine Sache!

(1) Ich hab' mich entschieden, dieses Stellenangebot anzunehmen.

Was für Wünsche, Ziele, Vorstellungen, Hoffnungen und Erwartungen haben Jugendliche, die kurz vor ihrem Schulabschluß stehen? — Hast du dir schon einmal überlegt, was du werden möchtest? Ob oder was du studieren willst? Welchen Beruf du gern ausüben möchtest? Wie dein Leben in zehn Jahren sein wird? Werden sich dann deine Erwartungen erfüllt haben? Wirst du einen guten Job haben, verheiratet sein, eine Familie und vielleicht auch Kinder haben? Um über diese Dinge reden zu können, mußt du noch einiges lernen.

In this chapter you will learn

- to express determination or indecision; to talk about whether something is important or not important
- to express wishes; to express certainty and to refuse or accept with certainty; to talk about goals for the future; to express relief

And you will

- listen to other young people's ideas on their future
- read about the possibilities open to German youth after they graduate
- write about decisions you will make for your future
- discover, visualize, and refine your own plans

② Entscheidend für mich ist, daß ich einen guten Schulabschluß habe.

③ Mit dreißig möchte ich meinen Traumjob gefunden haben.

LEBENSLAUF

Name
Geburtsdatum und -ort   Hans-Jürge
Staatsangehörigkeit   27. Mai 19
Familienstand   deutsch
                               ledig

Schulbildung

August 1983 bis
Juli 1987

August 1987 bis   Städtische Grun
Juni 1996   Südpark in Neu

seit   Alexander-von-H
September 1996   Gymnasium in Ne

                              Studium der Anglis
                              Universität zu Köln

Interessen

Fußball (Mitglied im F.C. Novesia), Umv...
Modellflugzeugbau, Schach

Los geht's!

Was kommt nach der Schule?

Ein Schulabschluß ist wichtig für alle jungen Leute. Mit einem guten Schulabschluß haben sie eine bessere Möglichkeit, sich auf einen richtigen Beruf vorbereiten zu können. Hier unterhalten sich vier Gymnasiasten über ihre Wünsche und Vorstellungen für die Zukunft.

Ich will auf alle Fälle studieren; ich weiß nicht, warum. Ich kann dafür keinen konkreten Grund angeben. Ich wüßte gar nicht, was ich anderes machen sollte. Wir haben ja hier 13 Jahre nichts anderes getan als gelernt. — Was ich studieren möchte? Nun, ich kann mich noch nicht entscheiden. Wirtschaftswissenschaften vielleicht oder Jura. Ich muß mir das mal überlegen. Für mich spielt die größere Rolle, daß ich nach dem Studium wirklich etwas anfangen kann. Es kommt eben darauf an, ob es dann einen Job in meinem Fach gibt, wenn ich fertig bin. Ich muß mal zum Arbeitsamt gehen und mich erkundigen, wie es in fünf bis sechs Jahren aussehen wird. Aber erst mal mach' ich Ferien, ruh' mich von der Schule aus. Ich hab's nötig.

Sonja

Ich lege großen Wert darauf, an einer guten Universität zu studieren. Ich würde gern in den USA studieren, ja, weil die USA halt ... ja, erst mal wegen der Sprache. Ich mein', Englisch oder Amerikanisch ist nun mal Wissenschaftssprache, und zweitens: ich war in Amerika, und mir hat die Mentalität der Leute so wahnsinnig gut gefallen, und drittens, weil es eins der führenden Länder auf dem technologischen und wissenschaftlichen Sektor ist. Ja, für mich ist es am wichtigsten, daß ich wirklich etwas lerne und mich auf eine gute Karriere vorbereiten kann.

Michael

Ja, ich wollte mal studieren, aber jetzt bin ich nicht mehr besonders daran interessiert. Ich wüßte gar nicht, was ich studieren sollte. An der Uni beruht alles auf freiwilliger Basis, und ich bin zu undiszipliniert, ich würde das gar nicht schaffen. Entscheidend für mich ist, daß ich mal einen Beruf ausüben kann, der mir Spaß macht. Ich werd' also wahrscheinlich auf die Modehochschule gehen, weil ich an Mode besonders interessiert bin.

Tanja

Also, besonders vorbereiten tu' ich mich eigentlich nur durch die Schule, also dadurch, daß ich jetzt eben in der Schule die Kurse gewählt hab', die für mich im Studium am wichtigsten sein können. Ich mach' jetzt zum Beispiel einen Physik-Leistungskurs mit, denn Physik braucht man, wenn man Medizin studieren will. Ausschlaggebend ist für mich erst mal ein gutes Abi, denn nur so kann man überhaupt Medizin studieren. Zuerst aber werd' ich wohl zum Bund müssen. Ich werd' mal sehen, daß ich zum Sanitätskorps komme. Das ist eine gute, praktische Erfahrung für meinen späteren Beruf.

Philipp

Nach dem Abi?

Von je 100 Schulabgängern machen ein halbes Jahr nach dem Abitur	
junge Männer	junge Frauen
51% Wehrdienst/Zivildienst	30% ein Studium
21% ein Studium	29% eine Lehre
15% eine Lehre	13% eine Fachschule
3% eine Berufstätigkeit	9% ein Praktikum
2% eine Beamtenausbildung	4% eine Beamtenausbildung
1% ein Praktikum	2% eine Berufstätigkeit
5% Jobben, Ferien, usw.	13% Jobben, Ferien, usw.

Information für junge Leute

*** 71 Prozent aller Mädchen interessieren sich für Umweltschutz, danach folgen Mode (35%), dann Politik (26%), Religion (17%) und Wirtschaft (16%) *** Ein Drittel aller Abiturienten entscheidet sich für eine Lehre vor dem Studium *** Sechs Prozent aller Jugendlichen unter 18 sind auf Sozialhilfe angewiesen *** Mehr als eine halbe Million ausländischer Mädchen leben in der Bundesrepublik Deutschland ***

1 Hast du alles verstanden?

a. Mach eine Liste und schreib auf, was für Wünsche und Ziele diese vier jungen Leute haben!

b. Such dir einen von diesen vier Schülern aus, und berichte an Hand deiner Notizen über ihn oder über sie in der Klasse!

1. a. **Sonja:** Studium; Ferien / **Michael:** Studium in den USA; Karriere / **Tanja:** Beruf, der Spaß macht / **Philipp:** gutes Abi; Medizinstudium; Bundeswehr; Beruf

2 Genauer lesen

Schaut euch die beiden Grafiken an und sprecht darüber!

a. Welche Fakten stehen hinter folgenden Zahlen: 51%, 30%, 15%, 29%?
b. Was machen die jungen Leute ein halbes Jahr nach dem Abitur? Diskutiert über die Unterschiede zwischen jungen Männern und jungen Frauen!
c. Was für allgemeine Interessen haben deutsche Mädchen? Vergleicht diese mit euren eigenen Interessen!

2. a. **Wehrdienst/Zivildienst (junge Männer); Studium (junge Frauen); Lehre (junge Männer); Lehre (junge Frauen)**

2. c. **Umweltschutz; Mode; Politik; Religion; Wirtschaft**

3 Umfrage

Macht in eurer Klasse eine ähnliche Umfrage um festzustellen, was ihr ein halbes Jahr nach eurem Schulabschluß wahrscheinlich machen werdet! Vergleicht das Ergebnis mit dem Ergebnis der deutschen Umfrage! Diskutiert über die Unterschiede!

ERSTE STUFE

Expressing determination or indecision; talking about whether something is important or not important

auf deutsch erklärt

Schulabschluß das Ende der Schulzeit, wenn man das Diplom bekommt
fertig wenn man zu Ende gekommen ist
Zukunft zeitlich nicht jetzt, sondern alles das, was noch kommen wird
anfangen beginnen
Beruf der hauptberufliche Job
jobben arbeiten, aber nicht hauptberuflich
Arbeitsamt von der Stadt organisierte Stelle, wo man Arbeit suchen kann
s. ausruhen s. entspannen
nötig haben wenn man etwas sehr braucht
beschließen s. entscheiden
entschlossen man hat sich entschieden
auf etwas Wert legen wenn man etwas für wichtig hält

auf englisch erklärt

Ich möchte <u>mich nach</u> der <u>Möglichkeit erkundigen</u>, eine <u>Lehre</u> als Schreiner anzufangen. *I would like to get information on the possibility of beginning an apprenticeship as a carpenter.*
Andreas muß <u>sich auf</u> das Studium der Naturwissenschaft <u>vorbereiten</u>. *Andreas has to prepare himself for his studies in the natural sciences.*
<u>Auf alle Fälle</u> gibt es gute <u>Gründe</u>, Beamter zu werden. *In any case, there are good reasons to become a civil servant.*
Wenn man die <u>Sprache</u> eines Landes nicht kann, <u>ist</u> man <u>auf</u> Handbewegungen <u>angewiesen</u>. *When you can't speak the language of a country, you have to rely on gestures.*

SO SAGT MAN DAS!

Expressing determination or indecision

Sometimes, when you have made a firm decision, you'll want to express your determination. You can say:

> **Ich hab' beschlossen,** Jura zu studieren.
> **Ich hab' mich entschieden,** einen Beruf zu erlernen.
> **Ich bin fest entschlossen,** in den USA zu studieren.
> **Ich weiß jetzt, daß ...**

Of course, you may not be quite sure about something. This is the way you might express indecision:

> **Ich weiß nicht, ob** ich Musik studieren soll.
> **Ich hab' mich noch nicht entschieden, was/ob ...**
> **Ich kann (das) noch nicht sagen, was/ob ...**
> **Ich muß mir das überlegen.**
> **Es kommt darauf an, was/ob ...**
> **(Ich werde) mal sehen, ob ...**

4 Hör gut zu! For answers, see listening script on TE Interleaf.

Drei Schüler machen bald ihren Schulabschluß. Hör ihrem Gespräch gut zu und entscheide dich, wer schon feste Pläne hat und wer sich über seine Zukunft noch nicht so sicher ist!

5 Wie sieht's bei dir aus?

Sprich mit einer Partnerin über deine Pläne für die Zukunft! Wofür habt ihr euch entschieden? Was ist noch ungewiß? Was sind die Gründe?

PARTNER **Weißt du schon, ob oder was du studieren willst?**

DU **Ich bin fest entschlossen, Jura zu studieren. Rechtsanwalt ist ein Beruf mit Zukunft.**

Wünsche und Pläne

zuerst studieren
eine Lehre machen
einen Job suchen
nach der Schule nichts machen
im Ausland studieren
im Ausland arbeiten
auf die (Musikhochschule) gehen
Wehrdienst oder Zivildienst machen

Gründe

ein Beruf mit Zukunft sein
mit dem Studium etwas
    anfangen können
einen besseren Job nach
    dem Studium haben
erst einmal Ferien machen
wegen der Sprache
sich auf eine Karriere vorbereiten

6 Und du? Was möchtest du alles?

Sag einer Partnerin, was du alles machen möchtest, nachdem du deinen Schulabschluß hast!

DU **Ich möchte ...** *oder* **Ich hab' mich entschieden, ...** *oder* **Ich hab' beschlossen, ...**

Was?

die Universität besuchen   (Jura) studieren   einen Beruf erlernen   einen tollen Beruf ausüben

eine gute Allgemeinbildung haben   in (Deutschland) studieren   erst mal Ferien machen

7 Du machst dasselbe

Dein Partner sagt dir, was er macht. Sag ihm, daß du beschlossen hast, dasselbe zu tun!

PARTNER **Ich bereite mich auf eine gute Karriere vor.**

DU **Ich hab' auch beschlossen, mich auf eine gute Karriere vorzubereiten.**

s. auf eine gute Karriere vorbereiten   s. beim Arbeitsamt erkundigen, wie der Arbeitsmarkt aussieht

s. um ein Studium in Deutschland bewerben

s. zuerst mal umsehen, was man alles machen kann   s. gut überlegen, was man werden will

EIN WENIG LANDESKUNDE

Im Jahre 1386 wurde die älteste deutsche Hochschule, die Universität Heidelberg, gegründet. In Deutschland gibt es viele alte Universitäten und auch ganz junge. Seit 1960 sind mehr als zwanzig Universitäten gegründet worden. Immer mehr junge Deutsche wollen heute studieren. 1960 begannen nur fünf Prozent eines Altersjahrgangs ein Studium. Heute bewirbt sich fast jeder dritte Jugendliche um einen Studienplatz. Im Wintersemester 1992/93 studierten über 1,8 Millionen in Deutschland. Davon waren rund 122 000 Ausländer. Der Staat fördert nämlich das Studium von Ausländern an deutschen Hochschulen als Beitrag zur internationalen Verständigung.

Studienwünsche männlicher Abiturienten 1992		Studienwünsche von Abiturientinnen 1992	
Fach	Anteil (%)	Fach	Anteil (%)
Wirtschaft	14	Wirtschaft	11
Maschinenbau	13	Jura	7
Ellektrotechnik	11	Sozialwesen	6
Jura	5	Medizin	6
Informatik	5	Architekur	5
Bauinge-nieurwesen	4	Gestaltung	4
Architektur	4	Erziehungs-wissenschaft	4
Medizin	3	Germanistik	3
Physik	3	Biologie	3
Chemie	3	Psychologie	3

8 Fragen an dich

Sag einer Partnerin, wie du dich zu den folgenden Fragen stellst! Hast du zu diesen Fragen schon eine feste Meinung, oder kannst du dich noch nicht entscheiden? — Gebrauch in deiner Antwort die Ausdrücke, die auf Seite 260 aufgelistet sind!

1. Hast du schon feste Vorstellungen von deiner Zukunft?
2. Weißt du schon, was du nach der Schule machen willst?
3. Möchtest du studieren? — Wenn ja, was?
4. Welchen Beruf würdest du gern einmal ausüben?
5. Wirst du zum Arbeitsamt gehen, um dich nach Job-Möglichkeiten zu erkundigen?
6. Was machst du erst mal ganz bestimmt, wenn du mit der Schule fertig bist?
7. Würdest du gern in Deutschland oder anderswo im Ausland studieren oder arbeiten?
8. Möchtest du gleich nach der Schule heiraten und eine Familie gründen?

9 Für mein Notizbuch

Mach eine Liste mit fünf Dingen, für die du dich schon entschieden hast, und mit fünf Dingen, die du dir noch überlegen mußt!

10 Klassendiskussion

1. Vergleicht eure Listen in der Klasse und diskutiert über die Unterschiede in euren Wünschen und Zielen für die Zukunft!
2. Macht eine Klassenliste, die euch zeigt, wofür sich die meisten schon entschieden haben, und was sich die meisten von euch noch überlegen müssen!

11 Was ist am Arbeitsplatz wichtig?

Es gibt viele Gesichtspunkte, nach denen man einen Arbeitsplatz beurteilen kann. Hier ist das Ergebnis einer Umfrage. Es zeigt, was den Deutschen am wichtigsten ist und was ihnen weniger wichtig ist. (Die Nummern zeigen, wieviel Mal die einzelnen Gesichtspunkte erwähnt wurden.) Diskutiert über das Ergebnis der Umfrage! Was würde bei euch ganz oben stehen? Ganz unten? — Schreibt eure eigene Liste von Prioritäten am Arbeitsplatz!

Einkommenshöhe 53
Bedingungen am Arbeitsplatz 45
Inhalt der Arbeit 34
Kontakte mit Kollegen 34
Aufstiegschancen 23
Sicherheit vor Entlassung 22
Arbeitszeit 19
Verhältnis zum Boss 17
Sicherheit am Arbeitsplatz 15
Mitbestimmung im Betrieb 13
Angenehmes Arbeitstempo 9
Zugang zu Informationen 3

SO SAGT MAN DAS!

Talking about whether something is important or not important

To say what is important, you can use the following phrases:

> Ich lege großen Wert darauf, daß ...
> Ich bin interessiert daran, daß ...
> Für mich spielt die größte Rolle, daß ...
> Mir ist wichtig, daß ...
> Entscheidend für mich ist, daß ...
> Für mich ist es am wichtigsten, daß ...
> Ausschlaggebend ist für mich, daß ...

To say that something is not important, you can say:

> Ich lege keinen großen Wert darauf, daß ...
> Ich bin nicht besonders interessiert daran, daß ...
> Es ist nicht entscheidend für mich, daß ...
> Mir ist weniger wichtig, daß ...

12 Hör gut zu! For answers, see listening script on TE Interleaf.

Hör Steffi und Horst gut zu, wie sie über ihre Wünsche und Pläne für die Zukunft sprechen! Was für Dinge sind Steffi wichtig? Und Horst? Wie unterscheiden sich die zwei?

13 Kette: Worauf legt ihr großen Wert?

Wenn ihr an die Zukunft denkt, worauf legt ihr da großen Wert? — Drückt eure Meinungen auf verschiedene Arten aus! Jeder in der Gruppe kommt einmal dran.

FRAGE **Worauf legst du großen Wert?**

SCHÜLER 1 **Ich lege großen Wert auf eine gute Universität.**

SCHÜLER 2 **Entscheidend ist für mich, daß ich eine gute Universität besuche.**

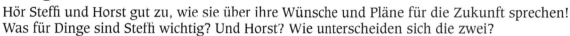

nette Mitarbeiter haben

gute Universität besuchen

viel Freizeit haben

vernünftige Arbeitszeit haben

Zugang zu Information haben

große Karriere vorbereiten

Sicherheit am Arbeitsplatz haben

Aufstiegschancen haben

gutes Gehalt bekommen

angenehmes Arbeitstempo haben

interessanten Beruf erlernen

Schon bekannt
Ein wenig Grammatik

Do you remember how to use **wo**-compounds to ask a question? If someone said **Wir interessieren uns für Politik** and you didn't hear the end of their sentence, how would you ask for clarification?[1]
Look at the following sentence:

> **Es kommt darauf an, ob ich einen guten Job finde.**

What does **darauf** anticipate?[2]

---

1. **Wofür interessiert ihr euch?**
2. It anticipates the entire clause that follows.

14 Und du? Wie steht's mit dir?

Denk an deine Wünsche und Ziele für die Zukunft, und beantworte die folgenden Fragen!

1. Woran denkst du schon mit (16) Jahren?
2. Worauf bereitest du dich vor?
3. Woran bist du am meisten interessiert?
4. Wofür wirst du dich entscheiden?
5. Worauf kommt es dir am meisten an?
6. Worauf legst du den größten Wert?

WORTSCHATZ

Tierärztin

Musiker

Biologe

Kauffrau

Und dann noch ...

Apotheker(in)	Journalist(in)	Professor(in)
Architekt(in)	Kaufmann, -frau	Rechtsanwalt, -anwältin
Biologe/Biologin	Krankenschwester, -pfleger	Reporter(in)
Computerspezialist(in)	Musiker(in)	Sekretär(in)
Diplomat(in)	Physiker(in)	Soldat(in)
Ingenieur(in)	Politiker(in)	Tierarzt, -ärztin

15 Was möchtest du mal werden?

Sag, was du mal werden möchtest und warum! Frag deine Klassenkameraden, was sie werden möchten! Jeder muß einen Grund angeben.

Talent dazu haben   (Kinder) gern haben   ein Beruf mit Zukunft   gut sein in ...

mein Vater/meine Mutter ist auch ...   interessante Arbeit   viel reisen können

16 Für mein Notizbuch

Schreib über deine eigenen Zukunftswünsche und Pläne! Folgende Fragen können dir dabei helfen.

1. Was möchtest du machen, wenn du mit der High School fertig bist?
2. Was für einen Beruf möchtest du einmal ausüben?
3. Was ist dir wichtig, wenn du an einen späteren Beruf denkst? Was ist dir weniger wichtig?
4. Mit wem besprichst du deine Zukunftspläne? Wer hilft dir bei deinen Entscheidungen?
5. Der zukünftige Beruf ist natürlich wichtig, aber was für andere Wünsche und Pläne hast du? Möchtest du zum Beispiel viel reisen oder eine Zeitlang im Ausland leben?
6. Möchtest du einmal heiraten und eine Familie gründen?
7. Wo möchtest du einmal wohnen?

Wie findet man eine Arbeitsstelle in Deutschland?

Wie bewirbt man sich um einen Job oder um eine Arbeitsstelle in Deutschland, wenn man mit der Schule fertig ist? Wer eine Arbeitsstelle sucht, sollte hauptsächlich die Stellenangebote in der Zeitung lesen. Alle Tageszeitungen in Deutschland haben in der Samstagsausgabe einen Sonderteil für Stellenangebote, den „Stellenmarkt". Hat man eine Anzeige gefunden, für die man sich interessiert, fertigt man eine schriftliche Bewerbung an. Zu den vollständigen Bewerbungsunterlagen gehören ein tabellarischer Lebenslauf, getippt oder handgeschrieben, ein Foto und Kopien von Schul- und Arbeitszeugnissen. Außerdem schreibt man einen Brief, in welchem man kurz erwähnt, warum man sich für diese Stelle interessiert.

Hier siehst du ein typisches Stellenangebot aus einer deutschen Tageszeitung.

A.

1. Lies zuerst den Text! Wie findet man eine Arbeitsstelle in Deutschland? Welche Unterlagen (*documents*) schickt man an die Firma?

2. Lies jetzt das Stellenangebot (*job offer*)! Wer würde sich für diese Anzeige interessieren? Welche Ausbildung ist für die angebotene Position nötig? Welche persönlichen Eigenschaften soll der Bewerber (*applicant*) haben? Was bietet die Firma dem Bewerber?

B.

1. Wie bewirbt man sich bei einer Firma in den USA? Was schickt man gewöhnlich an die Firma?

2. Wie unterscheidet sich das Bewerbungsverfahren in Deutschland von dem amerikanischen? Was schickt man in Deutschland, aber nicht hier? Welches Verfahren findest du besser? Warum?

3. Welche Fähigkeiten (*skills*) hast du, die eine Firma von einem Bewerber erwartet? Welche Leistungen (*benefits*) soll dir die Firma bieten?

WERTMARKT

Ihr steiler Weg nach oben

Wir suchen

Absolventen von Hoch- und Fachhochschulen der Studienrichtung Betriebswirtschaft

(mit Berufserfahrung)

SIE: suchen eine gutdotierte Führungsposition; sind bereit, Verantwortung zu tragen und selbständig Entscheidungen zu treffen; bringen die Fähigkeit mit, Mitarbeiter zu führen und zu motivieren; verfügen über gute Umgangsformen und ein gepflegtes Erscheinungsbild.

WIR: bieten Ihnen die eigenverantwortliche Führung eines Filialbereiches für eines der führenden Lebensmittel–Filialunternehmen in Deutschland als leitender Angestellter und Vorgesetzter; zahlen ein übertarifliches Gehalt bereits während der Einarbeitung; stellen Ihnen einen neutralen PKW zur Verfügung, den Sie auch privat nutzen können.

Ihre Bewerbung mit den üblichen Unterlagen wie handgeschriebenem Lebenslauf, Lichtbild, Zeugniskopien und Gehaltswunsch richten Sie bitte an:

WERTMARKT Lebensmittelfilialbetrieb GmbH
z. Hd. Herrn Reinke
Kaiserstraße 10
97070 Würzburg

A. 1. hauptsächlich durch Stellenangebote in der Zeitung / tabellarischen Lebenslauf; Foto; Kopien von Schul- und Arbeitszeugnissen; Brief

A. 2. jemand, der eine Führungsposition in einer Lebensmittelfirma sucht; der ein Studium der Betriebswirtschaft absolviert hat und Berufserfahrung hat / Studium der Betriebswirtschaft / soll bereit sein, Verantwortung zu tragen und selbständig Entscheidungen zu treffen; soll die Fähigkeit haben, Mitarbeiter zu führen und zu motivieren; soll gute Umgangsformen und ein gepflegtes Erscheinungsbild haben / eigenverantwortliche Führung eines Filialbereiches; übertarifliches Gehalt; PKW

Weiter geht's!

Wenn ich mal dreißig bin, ...

Fünf Jugendliche sprechen darüber, wie sie ihre Zukunft sehen und was sie mit dreißig Jahren erreicht haben möchten.

Bis vor kurzem hab' ich meine Zukunft ziemlich pessimistisch gesehen. Manchmal hatte ich richtige Angst, daß unsere Welt kaputtgeht an der Umweltverschmutzung und vor allem am Ost-West Konflikt: Panzer, Raketen, Krieg — vor einem Atomkrieg hab' ich mir große Sorgen gemacht. Gott sei Dank hab' ich diese Angst jetzt nicht mehr. Gut, daß der Osten vernünftig geworden ist. Was sich jetzt im Osten tut, gibt mir große Hoffnung für meine Zukunft. Jetzt will ich wirklich einen guten Schulabschluß machen, einen Beruf erlernen, Geld verdienen und reisen, in die ehemaligen Ostblockländer, vielleicht sogar dort arbeiten. Wer weiß?

Sandra, 16

Mit dreißig möchte ich eine politische Karriere begonnen haben. Mein Vater ist Politiker, und ich steh' auch auf Politik. Und was gerade in dieser Zeit auf uns zukommt, ist unbeschreiblich! Die Demokratisierung des Ostens und ein großes, vereintes Europa — da möchte ich auf jeden Fall einmal dabeisein. Ich bin froh, daß ich in der Schule gut bin, und ich werde das Abi ganz bestimmt schaffen. Nun, es steht fest, daß ich Politik und Sprachen studieren werde. Wer nämlich eine, zwei oder sogar mehrere Sprachen kann, der hat bessere Chancen im Beruf und im Leben überhaupt. Und ich mit dreißig? Vielleicht werd' ich bis dahin einen Traumjob gefunden haben oder im Bundestag sein, oder vielleicht werd' ich irgendwo in der Welt herumreisen oder sogar schon verheiratet sein und Kinder haben. Wer weiß? Es ist jedenfalls interessant, so viele Möglichkeiten vor sich zu haben.

Uta, 17

Wenn ich dreißig bin, möchte ich einen tollen Beruf ausüben — Raumfahrttechniker vielleicht, weil das ein Beruf mit Zukunft ist. Auf alle Fälle möchte ich keine materiellen Sorgen haben und ganz bestimmt viel reisen. Eine Familie haben? Kommt nicht in Frage! Nicht mit dreißig, vielleicht mit vierzig Jahren. Ich möchte ganz bestimmt erst mal viel mehr von der Welt sehen, einen weiteren Horizont kriegen.

Alexander, 17

Ich freu' mich direkt auf meine Zukunft. Mit dreißig möchte ich schon viel Geld verdienen, eine schöne Wohnung oder ein Haus haben, ich möchte verheiratet sein und Kinder haben, ja, natürlich auch ein tolles Auto fahren. Nun, das klingt wohl alles ziemlich materialistisch. Aber man muß Ziele im Leben haben und Sachen, an denen man sich freuen kann. Zum Glück bin ich gesund, und ich bin bereit, hart zu arbeiten, um das alles möglich zu machen.

Oliver, 16

Ich hab' noch keine großen Pläne für die Zukunft. Im Sommer werd' ich mit dem Real-gymnasium fertig, und dann werde ich bei einer Bank oder bei einer Versicherung eine Lehre anfangen. Bis ich mal Bankkaufmann bin, vergeht noch eine Weile. Ich werde weiterhin bei meinen Eltern wohnen; ausziehen kommt für mich nicht in Frage. Ich liebe geregelte Verhältnisse. Ich komm' mit meinen Eltern prima aus, und ich möchte weiterhin so leben wie jetzt und auch noch eine Weile so bleiben, wie ich bin. Angst vor der Zukunft hab' ich nicht.

Christian, 17

17 Was sagen die Jugendlichen?

Mach eine Liste und schreib auf, was für Wünsche und Ziele diese fünf Jugendlichen für ihre Zukunft haben! Sandra: guter Schulabschluß; Beruf; Geld; Reisen / Uta: politische Karriere; Studium; Reisen; Heirat; Kinder / Alexander: toller Beruf; keine materiellen Sorgen haben; viel reisen; Familie später / Oliver: Geld; Wohnung oder Haus; Heirat; Kinder; Auto

18 Brainstorming

Unterhaltet euch in der Klasse über eure Wünsche und Ziele für die Zukunft! Macht eine Liste, und schreibt sie in euer Notizheft!

22 Wie steht's mit euch?

Sagt, was bei euch feststeht, und was bei euch nicht in Frage kommt! Benutzt in euren Fragen und Antworten die Liste, die ihr in Übung 18 erstellt habt!

> PARTNER 1 **Hast du Angst vor der Zukunft?**
> DU **Ganz bestimmt. Ich weiß gar nicht, was kommt!** *oder*
> **Auf keinen Fall.**
> DU **Möchtest du in der Welt herumreisen?**
> PARTNER 2 **Ja! Ich möchte unbedingt einen Beruf erlernen, wo ich viel reisen kann.**
> *oder*
> **Kommt nicht in Frage, ich reise gar nicht gern.**

23 Für mein Notizbuch

Schreib zehn Sachen auf eine Liste, die dir für deine Zukunft sehr wichtig sind! Das wichtigste muß oben stehen.

24 Vergleicht eure Pläne!

Vergleicht jetzt eure Listen miteinander und sprecht über die Unterschiede, die ihr entdeckt! Denkt daran, daß ihr Gründe für eure Rangordnung angeben müßt!

25 Zukunftspläne

Was wirst du in der Zukunft machen? Was werden deine Freunde machen? Deine Geschwister? Deine Klassenkameraden? Bilde Sätze mit „werden"!

einen interessanten Beruf erlernen   Kinder haben

studieren   etwas für andere tun

politisch aktiv sein   verheiratet sein   viel reisen

Schon bekannt
Ein wenig *Grammatik*

Read the two sentences below. What do they mean? Is their meaning the same or different? What construction is used in the first sentence? In the second? How is the future tense formed? How else can future time be expressed?

> **Ich schaffe das Abi ganz bestimmt.**
> **Ich werde das Abi ganz bestimmt schaffen.**

SO SAGT MAN DAS!

Talking about goals for the future

When thinking about the future, you often speculate on what you would like to have accomplished by a certain time in your life. You could say:

> Mit dreißig **möchte ich** eine politische Karriere **begonnen haben.**
> Vielleicht **werde ich** bis dahin einen Traumjob **gefunden haben.**

How would you talk about your goals in English?

26 Hör gut zu!   For answers, see listening script on TE Interleaf.

Schreib auf, was diese Jugendlichen mit dreißig Jahren erreicht haben möchten! Wer von ihnen hat große Pläne?

27 Mit dreißig ...

Sagt euren Klassenkameraden, was ihr mit dreißig alles getan haben werdet, wenn es nach euren Wünschen geht!

DU   **Mit dreißig werd' ich viel von der Welt gesehen haben.**

PARTNER   **Mit dreißig ...**

Was?

viel von der Welt sehen

viel erleben

überallhin reisen

schon heiraten

schon viel Geld verdienen

ein Haus kaufen

das Studium abschließen

28 Was werde ich alles erreicht haben?

Schreib auf, was du mit 20 und mit 25 Jahren erreicht haben wirst, wenn alles so kommt, wie es du dir vorstellst!

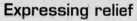

SO SAGT MAN DAS!

Expressing relief

These are some ways of saying that you are relieved about something:

Gut, daß ...   Zum Glück habe ich ...
Gott sei Dank, daß ... Ich bin froh, daß ...
Ein Glück, daß ...

29 Worüber seid ihr froh?

Jeder in der Klasse sagt, worüber er oder sie froh ist. Jeder muß der Reihe nach etwas anderes sagen!

DU   **Gut, daß ich meine Zukunft nicht so pessimistisch sehe.**
PARTNER 1   **Gott sei Dank, daß es keinen Ost-West Konflikt mehr gibt!**
PARTNER 2   **Zum Glück habe ich ...**

30 Für mein Notizbuch

Eine Bewerbung fürs College oder für die Universität verlangt häufig einen Aufsatz, in dem man einen Eindruck von sich gibt. Schreib einen solchen Aufsatz in dein Notizheft! Erwähne in deinem Aufsatz folgendes:

1. Was sind deine Wünsche und Ziele?   3. Was willst du mit 30 erreicht haben?
2. Wie bereitest du dich darauf vor?   4. Was würde dir Zufriedenheit geben?

Literatur der Ex-DDR

Das Märchen vom kleinen Herrn Moritz

von Wolf Biermann

Eines Tages geht ein kleiner älterer Herr spazieren. Er heißt Herr Moritz und hat sehr große Schuhe und einen schwarzen Mantel dazu und einen langen schwarzen Regenschirmstock, und damit geht er oft spazieren. Dann kommt nun der lange Winter, der längste Winter auf der Welt in Berlin, da werden die Menschen allmählich böse:

Die Autofahrer schimpfen, weil die Straßen so glatt sind, daß die Autos ausrutschen.

Die Verkehrspolizisten schimpfen, weil sie immer auf der kalten Straße rumstehen müssen.

LESETRICK

Interpreting symbols In works of fiction authors often use objects and characters as symbols that stand for something greater than themselves, usually something abstract. For example, objects and characters may symbolize emotions, ideas, or abstract concepts, such as good and evil; characters may represent particular groups of people or different aspects of society. A character's name is often a key to understanding what that character symbolizes.

Getting Started

1. Read the title and the first paragraph of the reading selection. To what genre of literature does this story belong? What elements are usually included in a **Märchen**? Answer the following questions:
   a. Wer ist die Hauptfigur?
   b. Wie sieht er aus?
   c. Wann und wo findet die Handlung statt?
2. Reread the first paragraph and continue reading to **An einem solchen ...** What is the main idea of that part of the story? Which statements support the main idea?
3. Lies die ganze Geschichte einmal! Schreib in zwei bis drei Sätzen, worum es in dieser Geschichte geht!

Die Verkäuferinnen schimpfen, weil ihre Verkaufsläden so kalt sind.

Die Männer von der Müllabfuhr schimpfen, weil der Schnee gar nicht alle wird.

Der Milchmann schimpft, weil ihm die Milch in den Milchkannen zu Eis friert.

Die Kinder schimpfen, weil ihnen die Ohren ganz rot gefroren sind, und die Hunde bellen vor Wut über die Kälte schon gar nicht mehr, sondern zittern nur noch und klappern mit den Zähnen vor Kälte, und das sieht auch sehr böse aus.

An einem solchen kalten Schneetag geht Herr Moritz mit seinem blauen Hut spazieren, und er denkt: „Wie böse die Menschen alle sind, es wird höchste Zeit, daß es wieder Sommer wird und die Blumen wachsen." Und als er so durch die schimpfenden Leute in der Markthalle geht, wachsen ganz schnell und ganz viele Krokusse, Tulpen, Maiglöckchen, Rosen und Nelken, auch Löwenzahn und Margeriten auf seinem Kopf. Er merkt es aber erst gar nicht, und dabei ist schon längst sein Hut vom Kopf hoch gegangen, weil die Blumen immer mehr werden und auch immer länger.

Da bleibt vor ihm eine Frau stehen und sagt: „O, Ihnen wachsen aber schöne Blumen auf dem Kopf!"

„Mir Blumen auf dem Kopf?" sagt Herr Moritz, „so was gibt es gar nicht!"

„Doch! Schauen Sie hier in das Schaufenster, Sie können sich darin spiegeln. Darf ich eine Blume abpflücken?"

Und Herr Moritz sieht im Schaufensterspiegelbild, daß wirklich Blumen auf seinem Kopf wachsen, bunte und große, und er sagt: „Aber bitte, wenn Sie eine wollen ..."

„Ich möchte gerne eine kleine Rose", sagt die Frau und pflückt sich eine.

„Und ich eine Nelke für meinen Bruder", sagt ein kleines Mädchen und Herr Moritz bückt sich, damit das Mädchen ihm auf den Kopf langen kann. Er braucht sich aber nicht so sehr tief zu bücken, denn er ist etwas kleiner als andere Männer. Viele Leute kommen und brechen sich Blumen vom Kopf des kleinen Herr Moritz, und es tut ihm nicht weh, und die Blumen wachsen immer gleich nach, und es kribbelt so schön am Kopf, als ob ihn jemand freundlich streichelte. Herr Moritz ist froh, daß er den Leuten mitten im kalten Winter Blumen geben kann. Immer mehr Menschen kommen zusammen und lachen und wundern sich und brechen sich Blumen vom Kopf des kleinen Herrn Moritz. Keiner, der eine Blume erwischt, sagt an diesem Tag noch ein böses Wort.

Aber da kommt auf einmal auch der Polizist Max Kunkel. Max Kunkel ist schon seit zehn Jahren in der Markthalle als Markthallenpolizist tätig, aber so was hat er nocht nicht gesehen! Mann mit Blumen auf dem Kopf! Er drängelt sich durch die vielen lauten Menschen, und als er

A Closer Look

4. Scan the first eight paragraphs to identify those that begin with sequencing expressions. Read the sentences or paragraphs that are introduced by those expressions. What different purposes do those expressions serve?

5. Lies die Geschichte noch einmal, und beantworte die folgenden Fragen!

   a. Woran denkt Herr Moritz, als er durch die Markthalle geht? Was passiert ihm dort? Wie reagieren die Leute darauf?

   b. Was will der Polizist sehen? Was geschieht, als Herr Moritz danach sucht?

   c. Was passiert dem Herrn Moritz am Ende der Geschichte?

Read the story again and discuss the following questions with a partner. Share your ideas with the rest of the class.

6. Why does the policeman want to see Herr Moritz's identification card? Why do you think the flowers wilt as Herr Moritz searches for his card?

7. Why do you think Herr Moritz is described as **klein**? What does the word **klein** suggest to you? Who or what might Herr Moritz represent? Think about his name, his appearance, and what you know about his character from his actions in the story. What might the policeman represent?

vor dem kleinen Herrn Moritz steht, schreit er: „Wo gibt's denn so was! Blumen auf dem Kopf, mein Herr. Zeigen Sie doch bitte mal sofort ihren Personalausweis!"

Und der kleine Herr Moritz sucht und sucht und sagt verzweifelt: „Ich habe ihn doch immer bei mir, ich habe ihn doch in der Tasche!" Und je mehr er sucht, um so mehr verschwinden die Blumen auf seinem Kopf.

„Aha", sagt der Polizist Max Kunkel, „Blumen auf dem Kopf haben Sie, aber keinen Ausweis in der Tasche!!"

Und Herr Moritz sucht immer ängstlicher seinen Ausweis und ist ganz rot vor Verlegenheit, und je mehr er sucht — auch im Jackenfutter — um so mehr schrumpfen die Blumen zusammen, und der Hut geht allmählich wieder herunter auf den Kopf! In seiner Verzweiflung nimmt Herr Moritz seinen Hut ab, und siehe da, unter dem Hut liegt in der abgegriffenen Gummihülle der Personalausweis. Aber was noch!? Die Haare sind alle weg! Kein Haar mehr auf dem Kopf hat der kleine Herr Moritz. Er streicht sich verlegen über den kahlen Kopf und setzt dann schnell den Hut darauf.

„Na, da ist ja der Ausweis", sagt der Polizist Max Kunkel freundlich, „und Blumen haben Sie wohl auch nicht mehr auf dem Kopf, wie?!"

„Nein", sagt Herr Moritz und steckt schnell seinen Ausweis ein und läuft, so schnell wie man auf den glatten Straßen laufen kann, nach Hause. Dort steht er lange vor dem Spiegel und sagt zu sich: „Jetzt hast du eine Glatze, Herr Moritz!"

8. There are many objects in this fairy tale that could be thought of as symbols, for example, the flowers or even the long, cold winter. What other symbols can you find in the story? What might they represent? Do your answers help to make the story more meaningful?

9. Was meinst du, was der Hauptgedanke der Geschichte ist? Schreib deine Idee in einem Satz auf!

10. Wähle zusammen mit einem Partner eine der folgenden Situationen, und entwickle ein passendes Gespräch dazu! Führ danach die Szene der Klasse vor!

a. Einige Reporter haben von den Ereignissen in der Markthalle gehört. Du bist ein Augenzeuge der Ereignisse. Mit deinem Partner übernimm die Rollen von Reporter und Zeuge! Erzähl dem Reporter alles, was passiert ist, damit er einen Bericht darüber schreiben kann!

b. Du bist Herr Moritz und triffst dich mit einem guten Freund einen Tag nach den Ereignissen in der Markthalle. Er will wissen, warum du ganz plötzlich eine Glatze hast. Erzähl ihm, was dir gestern alles passiert ist! Erzähl auch, wie du dich jetzt fühlst!

You have been reading about teenagers in Germany making career decisions that can be major turning points in their lives. Such pivotal moments are often the subject of TV shows and dramas. Imagine a show in which the characters must make a difficult decision which might result in arguments with parents or cause shifts in their relationships with others. In this activity you and your classmates will write a scene, as from a TV show or a movie, about such a turning point.

Von einem Wendepunkt erzählen

Bildet Gruppen von zwei bis vier Schülern, und schreibt zusammen eine Szene, in der jeder von euch eine Rolle hat! Die Szene soll von einer wichtigen Entscheidung und einem dadurch entstandenen Wendepunkt handeln.

A. Vorbereiten

1. Bildet eine Gruppe und besprecht eure Szene! Wer übernimmt welche Rolle? Was ist die wichtige Entscheidung? Was ist der Wendepunkt? Wo und wann spielt sich die Szene ab?
2. Jeder wählt eine Rolle und entwickelt seine Persönlichkeit. Was sind die Gefühle, Hoffnungen, Ziele und Erwartungen, die in dieser Rolle ausgearbeitet werden müssen?
3. Kommt zusammen und spielt eine Szene spontan vor! Schreibt alle guten Ideen auf, die während der Improvisation vorkommen! Denkt auch an die körperlichen Bewegungen, die die einzelnen Darsteller auf der Bühne ausführen sollen!

B. Ausführen

Verwendet eure Ideen von der Improvisation und den ausgearbeiteten Rollen, und schreibt zusammen die Szene! Paßt gut auf, daß die Rollen glaubhaft sind! Sie sollen schon in der geschriebenen Form einen lebendigen Charakter erhalten.

C. Überarbeiten

1. Spielt eure Szene als Gruppe unter euch vor! Denkt an die Rollen der anderen, und gebt einander nützliche Kritik!
2. Tauscht eure Rollen aus, damit ihr eine andere Perspektive gewinnt! Versteht ihr die Rollen der anderen? Müßt ihr irgendwelche Regie- oder Bühnenanweisungen hinzufügen, damit die anderen die Rollen überzeugend spielen können?
3. Verbessert die Szene, indem ihr eine neue Version schreibt! Spielt sie danach vor, und verbessert sie noch einmal, bis ihr alle damit zufrieden seid!
4. Lest eure Szene zusammen laut vor! Habt ihr alles richtig geschrieben?
5. Schreibt die endgültige Version der Szene auf ein reines Blatt Papier!

SCHREIBTIP
Writing drafts and revising When you first sit down to write, the task can seem overwhelming, so don't try to make your writing perfect the first time through. Instead, write several drafts following your outlines and plans, yet allowing yourself the freedom to be creative and add any new ideas that come to you. Between drafts, share your writing with friends to get constructive criticism. They can tell you what they don't understand so you'll know where you need to clarify your ideas. You may also want to wait a little while between drafts so that you can gain an objective perspective on what you have already written and improve upon it.

ANWENDUNG

1 Hör zu, wie einige Schüler sich über ihre Berufswünsche unterhalten! Was möchte jeder werden? Welche Vorteile und welche Nachteile erwähnen die Schüler? Mach dir Notizen! For answers, see listening script on TE Interleaf.

2 Wenn man einen Beruf wählt, muß man sich die Vorteile und die Nachteile überlegen. Was für den einen ein Vorteil ist, kann für den anderen ein Nachteil sein. Wie würdest du folgendes einschätzen? Ist das für dich ein Vorteil oder ein Nachteil? Mach zwei Listen, und besprich diese mit deinen Klassenkameraden!

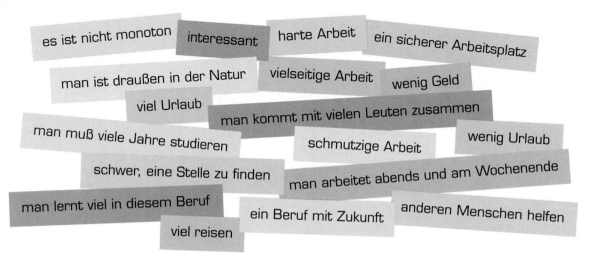

es ist nicht monoton   interessant   harte Arbeit   ein sicherer Arbeitsplatz

man ist draußen in der Natur   vielseitige Arbeit   wenig Geld

viel Urlaub   man kommt mit vielen Leuten zusammen

man muß viele Jahre studieren   schmutzige Arbeit   wenig Urlaub

schwer, eine Stelle zu finden   man arbeitet abends und am Wochenende

man lernt viel in diesem Beruf   ein Beruf mit Zukunft   anderen Menschen helfen

viel reisen

3 Was sind die Berufswünsche deiner Klassenkameraden? Stellt eine Liste auf! Wer will was werden? Wie viele von euch haben denselben Berufswunsch? Besprecht die Gründe für eure Berufswahl!

4 Klassenprojekt: Eure Schule hat vielleicht ein „Career Center". Dort findet ihr Information über die Ausbildung für alle Berufe. Jeder von euch wählt einen Beruf und sammelt darüber Information im „Career Center". Dann berichtet jeder der Klasse darüber — auf deutsch, natürlich! Ihr müßt Antworten auf Fragen haben, wie: Wie lange dauert die Ausbildung? Wie teuer ist sie? Welche Schulfächer braucht man für diesen Beruf? Hat dieser Beruf eine Zukunft? Wieviel kann man verdienen?

5 Ab und zu wird in einer Zeitung oder Zeitschrift die Frage gestellt: Hat die Familie als soziale Institution eine Zukunft? Was meinst du? Lies den folgenden Fragebogen! Überleg dir die Fragen, bevor du sie beantwortest!

Fragebogen

   1. Möchtest du einmal heiraten?
   2. Wie viele Kinder möchtest du haben?

3. Wo möchtest du leben?
4. Welchen Beruf möchtest du am liebsten haben?
5. Werden beide Eltern den Beruf ausüben, wenn Kinder kommen?
6. Sollten beide Ehepartner sich die tägliche Hausarbeit teilen?
7. Was findest du in deiner Familie gut? Weniger gut?
8. Findest du, daß deine Eltern Fehler in deiner Erziehung gemacht haben? Welche?
9. Was würdest du als Vater oder Mutter anders machen?
10. Möchtest du später einmal so leben wie deine Eltern?

 6 Diskutier die ausgefüllten Fragebögen mit deinen Klassenkameraden! — Wie sieht es aus? Stellt gemeinsam eine Tabelle auf, und füllt die Ergebnisse der Klassenumfrage ein! Sprecht dann über die Ergebnisse!

7 Nehmen wir an, du willst einmal heiraten! Welche Charakteristiken soll dein idealer Lebenspartner haben? Hier sind zwei Listen von Qualifikationen, die dich zu eigenen Wünschen und Vorstellungen anregen sollen. Wie wichtig sind dir zum Beispiel Geld und Statussymbole? — Was wäre für dich bei der Wahl eines Partners ausschlaggebend, und worauf legst du weniger Wert?

attraktiv	humorvoll
sportlich	reich
musikalisch	intelligent
unkompliziert	verständnisvoll
treu	fröhlich
tierlieb	kinderlieb
großzügig	witzig
zuverlässig	phantasievoll

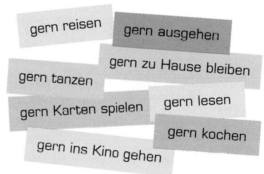

gern reisen · gern ausgehen · gern zu Hause bleiben · gern tanzen · gern Karten spielen · gern lesen · gern kochen · gern ins Kino gehen

 8 Schreib einen kurzen Brief an einen Briefpartner oder an eine Briefpartnerin! Berichte zuerst etwas über dich selbst, worauf du im Leben Wert legst und was für dich nicht so wichtig ist, und schreib dann, was du von deinem Lebenspartner erwartest!

9

R O L L E N S P I E L

Du bist Personalchef in einer Firma, und du interviewst einen Bewerber für einen Job.

Sucht euch ein Stellenangebot aus der Zeitung heraus, und bereitet euch auf das Interview vor, indem du einige Fragen dafür schreibst und dein Partner sich einige Dinge ausdenkt, die man bei so einer Situation vielleicht sagen müßte! Spielt dann das Interview!

KANN ICH'S WIRKLICH?

Can you express determination or indecision (p. 260)

1 How would you tell someone that you are determined to
  a. study at a university? a. E.g.: Ich hab' beschlossen, an einer Universität zu studieren.
  b. have an interesting profession? b. E.g.: Ich bin fest entschlossen, einen interessanten Beruf zu haben.

2 How would you say that you're undecided about the following things you might do after graduation? a. Ich weiß nicht, ob ich nach dem Schulabschluß erst einmal Ferien machen soll.
  a. **erst einmal Ferien machen**
  b. **im Ausland studieren** b. Ich hab' mich noch nicht entschieden, ob ich nach dem Schulabschluß im Ausland studieren soll.

Can you talk about whether something is important or not important? (p. 263)

3 How would you respond if a friend asked you what is important to you? E.g.: Ich lege großen Wert darauf, daß ich einen guten Schulabschluß mache.

4 How would you say what it is you find unimportant? E.g.: Es ist nicht entscheidend für mich, daß ich modische Klamotten habe.

Can you express wishes? (p. 269)

5 How would you respond if someone asked you what your ideal world would be like? E.g.: In meiner idealen Welt gäbe es keine Umweltverschmutzung.

Can you express certainty and refuse or accept with certainty? (p. 269)

6 How would you mention two things you are certain about? E.g.: Es steht fest, daß ich nächsten Monat meinen Führerschein mache. Es ist sicher, daß ich einen Studienplatz in Boston bekomme.

7 How would you tell someone that you absolutely refuse to take drugs (**Drogen**)? E.g.: Ich nehme auf keinen Fall Drogen!

8 How would you tell a friend that you certainly accept his or her invitation to see a movie? E.g.: Ja, natürlich!; Ganz bestimmt!

Can you talk about goals for the future? (p. 270)

Can you express relief? (p. 271)

9 How would you respond if someone asked you what your plans for the future are, and how you envision your life at age 30? E.g.: In der Zukunft werde ich eine Weltreise machen. Mit dreißig möchte ich eine eigene Firma haben.

10 How would you tell a friend you're relieved about the following things?
  a. **Es gibt keinen Ost-West Konflikt.**
  b. **Es gibt heute in Mathe keine Klassenarbeit.**
  a. E.g.: Gut, daß es keinen Ost-West Konflikt gibt.
  b. E.g.: Ein Glück, daß es heute in Mathe keine Klassenarbeit gibt.

ERSTE STUFE
EXPRESSING DETERMINATION

Ich hab' beschlossen, ... *I've decided ...*
Ich hab' mich entschieden, ... *I have decided ...*
Ich bin fest entschlossen, ... *I am determined ...*

EXPRESSING INDECISION

Ich hab' mich noch nicht entschieden, was/ob ... *I haven't decided yet what/whether ...*
Ich muß mir das überlegen. *I have to consider that.*

TALKING ABOUT WHETHER SOMETHING IS IMPORTANT

Ich lege großen Wert darauf, ... *I place great emphasis on ...*
Ich bin interessiert daran, ... *I am interested in ...*
Für mich spielt die größte Rolle, daß ... *What counts most for me is ...*

Mir ist wichtig, daß ... *Important to me is that ...*
Entscheidend für mich ist, ... *Decisive for me is ...*
Für mich ist es auch am wichtigsten,... *For me it's also most important ...*
Ausschlaggebend ist für mich, daß ... *The determining factor for me is that ...*

PROFESSIONS

der Beruf, -e *profession*
Biologe/Biologin, -n/nen *biologist*
die Kauffrau, -en *business woman*
Musiker(in), -/nen *musician*
Tierarzt, -ärztin *veterinarian*

OTHER WORDS

die Fachschule, -n *vocational school*
die Lehre, -n *apprenticeship*
der Abschluß, ¨sse *diploma*
das Arbeitsamt, ¨er *employment office*

die Erfahrung, -en *experience*
die Tätigkeit, -en *occupation*
die Karriere, -n *career*
die Zukunft *future*
Jura *(study of) law*
die Wissenschaft, -en *science*
die Mentalität *mentality*
die Möglichkeit, -en *possibility*
der Grund, ¨e *reason*
die Sprache, -n *language*

anfangen (sep) *to begin*
angeben (sep) *to indicate*
s. ausruhen (sep) *to rest*
ausüben (sep) *to practice (a profession)*
beruhen auf (acc) *to be based on*
s. erkundigen nach *to inquire about*
jobben *to have a job*
nötig haben *to require*
s. vorbereiten (sep) **auf** (acc) *to prepare for*

angewiesen sein auf (acc) *to be dependent on*
fertig *finished*

ZWEITE STUFE
EXPRESSING WISHES

Viele Freunde haben, wäre mir wichtig. *To have many friends would be important to me.*
In meiner idealen Welt gäbe es nur Frieden. *In my ideal world there would only be peace.*

REFUSING OR ACCEPTING WITH CERTAINTY

Kommt nicht in Frage! *It's out of the question!*
Auf keinen Fall! *No chance!*
Auf jeden Fall. *In any case.*
Auf alle Fälle. *By all means.*
Ganz bestimmt. *Certainly.*

EXPRESSING CERTAINTY

Es steht fest, ... *It's definite ...*

Ich möchte unbedingt ... *I certainly would like ...*

TALKING ABOUT GOALS FOR THE FUTURE

Mit dreißig möchte ich ... gemacht haben. *At thirty I would like to have done ...*

EXPRESSING RELIEF

Gott sei Dank, ... *Thank God!*
Ein Glück, daß ... *Lucky that ...*
Zum Glück ... *Luckily ...*

OTHER WORDS

die Versicherung, -en *insurance*
der Bundestag *German Federal Parliament*
der Ostblock *Eastern Bloc*
der Osten *east*
der Atomkrieg, -e *nuclear war*

die Hoffnung, -en *hope*
der Horizont *horizon*
die Raumfahrt *space travel*
der Traum, ¨e *dream*
das Verhältnis, -se *condition*
die Weile *while*
die Welt, -en *world*
das Ziel, -e *goal*

klingen *to sound*
stehen auf (acc) *to like*
vergehen *to pass (time)*
zukommen (sep) **auf** (acc) *to be in store for*
dabei sein *to take part*

bis (acc) *until*
bis dahin *by, until then*
vor allem *most of all*
geregelt *orderly*
vereint *unified*
ehemalig- *former*

Kapitel 12: Die Zukunft liegt in deiner Hand! *Wiederholungskapitel*

CHAPTER OVERVIEW

	REVIEW OF FUNCTIONS	REVIEW OF GRAMMAR	CULTURE
Los geht's! pp. 282-283	Mitgehört, *p. 282*		
Erste Stufe pp. 284-288	•Reporting past events, *p. 284* •Expressing surprise and disappointment, *p. 285* •Agreeing; agreeing with reservations; giving advice, *p. 285* •Giving advice and giving reasons, *p. 287*	•Narrative past, *p. 284* •The **würde**-forms, *p. 285* •Infinitive forms of verbs, *p. 287*	•Kummerkasten, *p. 288* •Landeskunde: Pauken allein reicht nicht, *p. 289*
Weiter geht's! pp. 290-291	Pläne für die Zukunft, *p. 290*		
Zweite Stufe pp. 292-296	•Expressing determination or indecision, *p. 293* •Talking about what is important or not important, *p. 294* •Hypothesizing, *p. 294*	•Direct and indirect object pronouns, *p. 294* •Subjunctive, *p. 294*	•Claudias Pläne für die Zukunft, *p. 292* •Textbilder, *p. 296*
Zum Schreiben p. 297	Eine Selbstbiographie schreiben Strategy: Evaluating your writing		
Zum Lesen pp. 298-301	Zeitgenössische Literatur Reading Strategy: Applying strategies on your own		
Review pp. 302-303	•Kann ich's wirklich? *p. 302* •Wortschatz, *p. 303*		

Assessment Options

Final Exam, *Assessment Guide Audiocassette* 8 B

Stufe Quizzes
•*Chapter Resources,* Book 4
 Erste Stufe, Quiz 12-1
 Zweite Stufe, Quiz 12-2
•*Assessment Items, Audiocassette* 8 B

Kapitel 12 Chapter Test
•*Chapter Resources,* Book 4
•*Assessment Guide,* Speaking Test
•*Assessment Items, Audiocassette* 8 B

Test Generator, Kapitel 12

Chapter Overview

RESOURCES Print	RESOURCES Audiovisual

Textbook Audiocassette 6 B

Practice and Activity Book

Textbook Audiocassette 6 B

Practice and Activity Book
Chapter Resources, Book 4
- Communicative Activity 12-1
- Communicative Activity 12-2
- Additional Listening Activity 12-1 ....*Additional Listening Activities, Audiocassette* 10 B
- Additional Listening Activity 12-2 ....*Additional Listening Activities, Audiocassette* 10 B
- Additional Listening Activity 12-3 ....*Additional Listening Activities, Audiocassette* 10 B
- Student Response Forms
- Realia 12-1
- Situation Card 12-1
- Teaching Transparency Master 12-1 ....*Teaching Transparency* 12-1
- Quiz 12-1 ....*Assessment Items, Audiocassette* 8 B

Textbook Audiocassette 6 B

Practice and Activity Book

Textbook Audiocassette 6 B

Practice and Activity Book
Chapter Resources, Book 4
- Communicative Activity 12-3
- Communicative Activity 12-4
- Additional Listening Activity 12-4 ....*Additional Listening Activities, Audiocassette* 10 B
- Additional Listening Activity 12-5 ....*Additional Listening Activities, Audiocassette* 10 B
- Additional Listening Activity 12-6 ....*Additional Listening Activities, Audiocassette* 10 B
- Student Response Forms
- Realia 12-2
- Situation Card 12-2
- Teaching Transparency Master 12-2 ....*Teaching Transparency* 12-2
- Quiz 12-2 ....*Assessment Items, Audiocassette* 8 B
Video Guide ....*Video Program*, Videocassette 2

Textbook Audiocassette 11

Chapter Resources, Book 4
- Realia 12-3
- Situation Card 12-3
Video Guide ....*Video Program*, Videocassette 2

Alternative Assessment
- Performance Assessment
  Teacher's Edition
  Erste Stufe, p. 279K
  Zweite Stufe, p. 279N

- Portfolio Assessment
  Written: **Zweite Stufe,** Activity 19, *Pupil's Edition,* p. 293; *Assessment Guide,* p. 25
  Oral: **Erste Stufe,** Activity 14, *Pupil's Edition,* p. 288; *Assessment Guide,* p. 25
- **Notizbuch,** *Pupil's Edition,* pp. 285, 295

CHAPTER OVERVIEW

Kapitel 12: Die Zukunft liegt in deiner Hand!
Textbook Listening Activities Scripts

For Student Response Forms, see *Chapter Resources,* Book 4, pp. 142-145.

Erste Stufe
Activity 3, p. 284

ARTHUR Hallo, Sabine! Ich habe dich ja schon lange nicht mehr gesehen. Wo hast du denn gesteckt?

SABINE Du, Arthur, ich bin erst vor kurzem aus Frankreich zurückgekommen.

ARTHUR Hast du Urlaub gemacht?

SABINE Nein, ich habe an einem Austauschprogramm teilgenommen. Ich war sechs Monate lang an der Sorbonne in Paris.

ARTHUR Mensch, Sabine! Das hört sich ja toll an. Erzähl doch mal!

SABINE Na ja, es war schon super. Ich habe 'ne Menge gelernt. Und mein Französisch hat sich enorm verbessert, sag' ich dir! Vor einem halben Jahr hatte ich noch richtige Hemmungen, Französisch zu sprechen. Aber du hättest mich mal in Paris hören sollen!

ARTHUR Das glaub' ich dir gern. Hast du auch nette Leute kennengelernt?

SABINE Ja, und stell dir vor, verliebt hab' ich mich auch in einen Franzosen. Jean-Luc heißt er. Ich bin richtig traurig, daß ich wieder hier bin. Ich war so glücklich in Frankreich.

ARTHUR Ja, das kann ich verstehen. Schau mal! Da kommt Markus. Aber ... was ist denn bloß mit ihm los? Er geht auf Krücken ... hallo, Markus!

MARKUS Ach, hallo, ihr beiden!

SABINE Was ist denn mit deinem Bein los, Markus?

MARKUS Tja, ich hatte vor einem halben Jahr einen Autounfall und bin ziemlich schwer verletzt worden. Drei Monate lang war ich im Krankenhaus.

ARTHUR Und wie geht's dir jetzt? Wird dein Bein wieder ganz gesund?

MARKUS Tja, das wissen die Ärzte noch nicht so genau. Ich mache nun schon seit drei Monaten Krankengymnastik, aber das Bein ist immer noch nicht ganz beweglich.

SABINE Ach, das tut mir leid, Markus. Ich hoffe, daß du bald Erfolg mit deiner Therapie hast.

MARKUS Ja, das hoffe ich auch. Und was ist bei euch so los? Seit unserer Abiturfeier haben wir uns ja gar nicht mehr gesehen.

ARTHUR Tja, ich hab' direkt nach dem Abitur angefangen zu jobben. Ich wollte mir so schnell wie möglich ein Motorrad kaufen und hatte auch schon die Hälfte des Geldes fürs Motorrad gespart.

MARKUS Und, was ist dir dazwischengekommen?

ARTHUR Tja, leider ist mir der Bund dazwischengekommen. Ich mußte den Job aufgeben. Das Motorrad kann ich erst mal vergessen. Seit einem halben Jahr bin ich nun schon beim Bund. Echt langweilig, sag' ich euch! Hoffentlich bekomme ich nach meiner Dienstzeit den Superjob in der Computerfirma wieder, den ich aufgeben mußte.

Answers to Activity 3

Sabine: hat ein Austauschprogramm in Frankreich gemacht; hat sich in Französisch verbessert; hat sich in einen Franzosen verliebt; ist traurig, wieder in Deutschland zu sein

Markus: hatte einen Autounfall; kann sein Bein kaum bewegen

Arthur: hat gejobbt, um sich ein Motorrad kaufen zu können; mußte den Job aufgeben, weil er zur Bundeswehr mußte

Answers will vary.

Activity 8, p. 285

SANDRA Gregor, du siehst richtig deprimiert aus. Was ist denn los?

GREGOR Ach, nichts, womit ihr mir helfen könntet.

BIRGIT Na, komm schon! Wozu sind denn Freunde da?

SANDRA Genau! Birgit hat recht. Komm, erzähl schon!

GREGOR Also, gut! Wenn ihr's unbedingt wissen wollt! Claudia und ich, wir hatten Streit. Ich glaub', es ist aus zwischen uns!

SANDRA Ach, ich hätte nicht geglaubt, daß ihr euch streitet. Claudia ist doch so nett. Was war denn los?

GREGOR Also, ich glaube, daß sie die Leute aus meiner Clique nicht mag. Sie hat sich beklagt, daß ich zu viel Zeit mit der Clique verbringe. Ich war wirklich überrascht, daß sie so etwas gesagt hat. Ich habe gedacht, daß sie gern mit den Leuten aus meiner Clique zusammen ist.

SANDRA Ach, Gregor! Ich glaube nicht, daß sie deine Freunde nicht leiden kann. Sie will bestimmt, daß du mehr Zeit mit ihr verbringst. Vielleicht kannst du mal etwas mehr Zeit mit ihr und ihrer Clique verbringen. Du wirst sehen, dann gibt es keinen Streit mehr zwischen euch.

GREGOR Hmm, ich weiß nicht. Also, ich bin enttäuscht von Claudia. Ich glaube nicht, daß wir uns so schnell wieder vertragen.

BIRGIT Ach, Gregor! Nun laß den Kopf nicht hängen! Andere Leute haben auch Probleme. Da bist du nicht der einzige!

SANDRA So? Hast du etwa auch Streit mit jemandem, Birgit?

BIRGIT Nein, eigentlich nicht. Ich habe Probleme mit Frau Wagner, meiner Deutschlehrerin. Sie mag meine Kommentare im Unterricht nicht. Ich glaube, sie findet, daß ich zu kritisch bin.

SANDRA Zu kritisch? Das gibt's doch gar nicht. Ich find's gut, wenn jemand mal eine andere Meinung äußert und nicht immer alles akzeptiert, was so gesagt wird.

BIRGIT Tja, sag das mal Frau Wagner! Ich finde es schade, daß sie nicht versteht, daß ich ihren Unterricht eigentlich ganz toll finde, mich aber kritisch mit der Thematik auseinandersetze. Ich befürchte, daß ich dieses Jahr eine schlechte Note in Deutsch bekomme.

GREGOR Hast du schon mal mit Frau Wagner darüber gesprochen?

BIRGIT Nein, eigentlich nicht! Ich habe einfach nur das Gefühl, daß sie meine Art nicht mag.

GREGOR Hm. Also, ich würde sagen, du gehst mal nach dem Unterricht zu ihr hin und redest mit ihr. Wenn du ihr ehrlich sagst, daß du ihren Unterricht magst und es toll findest, daß die Schüler im Unterricht offen ihre Meinung sagen dürfen, dann wird sie sich bestimmt nicht mehr durch deine kritischen Kommentare gestört fühlen.

BIRGIT Ja, vielleicht sollte ich wirklich mal mit ihr reden. Danke für deinen Rat, Gregor.

Answers to Activity 8

Gregor: hat Streit mit seiner Freundin / soll mehr Zeit mit ihr verbringen

Birgit: hat Probleme mit ihrer Deutschlehrerin / soll mit der Lehrerin darüber sprechen

Activity 11, p. 287

HANNES He, Stefan und Nicole, habt ihr Lust, mit zum Imbißstand zu kommen? Ich will mir was zu essen holen.

STEFAN Nee du, ich hab' keinen Hunger.

NICOLE Ach, komm doch, Stefan! Wir holen uns 'ne Kleinigkeit.

HANNES Ja, genau! Was ist denn mit dir los? Sonst hast du doch immer so einen Bärenhunger in der großen Pause.

STEFAN Tja, weißt du, Hannes, ich will ein bißchen abnehmen. Ich fühle mich in letzter Zeit so schlapp und ohne Energie. Ich glaube, ich esse zu viele ungesunde Sachen.

HANNES Hm. Ja, also wenn du wirklich mit Erfolg abnehmen willst, dann solltest du auf jeden Fall Sport machen. An deiner Stelle würde ich jeden Tag joggen gehen. Du wirst dich bestimmt dann auch viel fitter fühlen.

STEFAN Sport ... also, ich weiß nicht. Ich versuche lieber, weniger zu essen.

NICOLE Mensch, paß mal auf, Stefan! Damit erreichst du gar nichts! Du bekommst nur schlechte Laune, wenn du ständig Hungergefühle hast. Ich finde, du solltest lieber deine Ernährung ändern als weniger zu essen.

STEFAN Und was soll ich deiner Meinung nach tun?

NICOLE Also, du solltest viel Obst und Gemüse essen, viel Wasser trinken und zwischendurch nur fettreduzierte oder fettfreie Snacks zu dir nehmen. Einen Joghurt, zum Beispiel.

STEFAN Okay! Ich probiere es gleich aus. Also, kommt, laßt uns zum Imbißstand gehen! Ich hole mir einen gemischten Salat.

HANNES Das ist vernünftig! Wenn du was im Bauch hast, kannst du dich auch gleich viel besser auf die Mathearbeit konzentrieren und denkst nicht immer nur ans Essen.

NICOLE Apropos Mathearbeit! Ich hab' in der letzten Arbeit wieder nur 'ne Vier bekommen. Dabei hatte ich alle Formeln auswendig gelernt. Ich weiß einfach nicht mehr, was ich machen soll. In der Arbeit, die wir gleich schreiben, bekomme ich bestimmt auch wieder eine schlechte Note. Ich bewundere dich wirklich, Hannes. Du bist so ein Mathegenie!

HANNES Ach, nun übertreib mal nicht, Nicole! Mathe macht mir einfach Spaß. Weißt du, ich glaube es bringt nichts, wenn man die Matheformeln einfach nur auswendig lernt. Du mußt sie auch anwenden können. Versuch doch mal, die Formeln ganz systematisch in einer Aufgabe anzuwenden. Du wirst schon sehen, es ist alles total logisch!

NICOLE Tja. Das sagst du so einfach. Ich versteh' die Aufgaben aber nun mal nicht so schnell wie du.

STEFAN An deiner Stelle würde ich Nachhilfeunterricht nehmen. Du mußt jemanden finden, der dir die Aufgaben in aller Ruhe erklärt. Du wirst sehen, das hilft bestimmt.

NICOLE Ja, vielleicht hast du recht, Stefan. Ich häng' gleich nach der Pause einen Zettel ans Schwarze Brett.

Answers to Activity 11

Hannes rät Stefan, daß er Sport machen soll, um abzunehmen, damit er sich fitter fühlt.

Nicole rät Stefan, daß er lieber seine Ernährung ändern soll, anstatt gar nichts zu essen, damit er keine Hungergefühle hat.

Hannes rät Nicole, daß sie die Matheformeln systematisch anwenden soll, damit sie die Logik der Aufgaben versteht.

Stefan rät Nicole, daß sie Nachhilfeunterricht nehmen soll, damit sie die Matheaufgaben in Ruhe erklärt bekommt.

Zweite Stufe
Activity 20, p. 293

PETRA Du, Katja! Stell dir vor, ich weiß jetzt endlich, was ich studieren werde!

KATJA Na, sag's schon!

PETRA Also, ich hab' mich entschieden, Kunst zu studieren. Kunst ist schon immer in der Schule mein Lieblingsfach gewesen.

KATJA Hm. Klingt gut! Du hast ja auch immer gute Noten im Kunstunterricht bekommen. Und was willst du nach dem Studium machen?

PETRA Tja, eigentlich reicht mir das Kunststudium nicht aus. Ich muß mir überlegen, ob ich danach noch zusätzlich eine Ausbildung als graphische Designerin machen soll. Ich glaube, wenn man praktische Erfahrung hat, hat man bessere Chancen auf einen guten Job. Aber ich bin mir noch nicht sicher. Wie sehen denn deine Zukunftspläne aus?

KATJA Ach, weißt du, Petra, ich weiß noch gar nicht so genau, was ich mal machen will. Meine Eltern haben ein Schuhgeschäft in der Innenstadt und möchten, daß ich eine Ausbildung als Schuhverkäuferin mache. Wahrscheinlich wollen sie, daß ich später mal das Geschäft übernehme.

PETRA Hm. Es hört sich so an, als ob du gar nicht so begeistert bist von der Idee.

KATJA Ja, das kann man wohl sagen. Mich interessiert das Schuhgeschäft eben nicht so richtig. Ich bin mir nicht sicher, ob ich wirklich dort arbeiten will. Ach, schau mal! Da kommt Mario.

MARIO Hallo! Was habe ich da gehört? Du interessierst dich nicht fürs Schuhgeschäft? Mensch, wäre ich froh, wenn meine Eltern ein Geschäft hätten, wo ich einsteigen könnte.

KATJA   Was willst du denn nach der Schule machen?

MARIO   Ach, ich will erst mal ein paar Monate bei meinen Großeltern in Sizilien verbringen.

PETRA   Soso, einfach nur faulenzen willst du!

MARIO   Stimmt nicht! Ich hab' da schon eine Idee! Ich hab' nämlich beschlossen, mich in Italien nach Geschäftskontakten zu erkundigen.

PETRA   Das hört sich ja enorm wichtig an. Was hast du vor?

MARIO   Tja, ich will mir so schnell wie möglich hier ein kleines eigenes Unternehmen aufbauen. Mir ist es wichtig, selbständig und unabhängig zu sein.

KATJA   Hm. Was für Geschäftskontakte willst du denn knüpfen?

MARIO   Tja, ich will italienische Lebensmittel nach Deutschland importieren, also Pasta, Parmaschinken, Olivenöl und so. Ich muß in Italien nur gute Einkaufsquellen finden. Kunden in Deutschland zu finden, ist kein Problem.

PETRA   Klasse! Ich wünsch' dir viel Erfolg mit deiner Idee!

KATJA   Ja, ich dir auch! Wenigstens weißt du schon genau, wie deine Zukunftspläne aussehen. Ich hab' noch keine Idee!

MARIO   He, Katja! Du kannst meine Geschäftspartnerin werden!

KATJA   Nee, danke! Da kann ich ja gleich im Schuhgeschäft meiner Eltern anfangen. Mich interessiert Einkauf und Verkauf nun mal nicht.

MARIO   Na siehst du! Dann weißt du ja wenigstens, was du NICHT willst!

Answers to Activity 20

Petra: ist sich sicher, daß sie Kunst studieren will; es ist ihr Lieblingsfach / ist sich nicht sicher, ob sie eine zusätzliche Ausbildung machen soll; man hat bessere Jobchancen, wenn man praktische Erfahrung hat.

Katja: ist sich nicht sicher, ob sie eine Ausbildung als Schuhverkäuferin machen soll; interessiert sich nicht richtig dafür

Mario: ist sich sicher, daß er ein eigenes Unternehmen haben will; will selbständig und unabhängig sein

Activity 23, *p. 294*

ANDREAS   He, schaut mal! Hier in der Pop-Rocky gibt's ein Preisausschreiben. Man kann eine Reise nach Griechenland gewinnen!

HARTMUT   Und was soll man einsenden, Andreas?

ANDREAS   Ganz einfach: Pläne und Wünsche für die Zukunft. Wer den besten Wunsch oder Plan hat, gewinnt. Los, kommt, da machen wir mit! Also, Hartmut, du fängst an!

HARTMUT   Hm. Ich möchte mal gern wissen, wie die entscheiden wollen, welches der beste Wunsch oder Plan ist.

ANDREAS   Ach, ist doch egal! Es macht doch einfach nur Spaß, überhaupt mitzumachen.

HARTMUT   Also gut! Ich wünsche mir, daß ich mal ein weltberühmter Opernsänger an der Scala von Mailand werde. Ich will so berühmt werden wie Plácido Domingo oder Luciano Pavarotti!

VANESSA   Mensch, Hartmut. Du hast wirklich eine tolle Stimme. Du solltest mal irgendwo vorsingen, damit du entdeckt wirst!

HARTMUT   Tja, wenn meine Eltern nicht so dagegen wären, würde ich wirklich gern eine Gesangsausbildung machen. Aber leider meinen sie, ich sollte lieber was „Vernünftiges" lernen.

ANDREAS   Tja, typisch Eltern! Was sind denn deine Zukunftspläne, Vanessa?

VANESSA   Also, ich wünsche mir, eines Tages in Afrika zu leben. Ich möchte gern dort Entwicklungshilfe leisten. Wenn ich viel Geld hätte, würde ich ein Kinderhilfswerk gründen. Mir ist wichtig, Leuten, besonders Kindern, zu helfen. Ich lege keinen Wert auf ein großes Haus, ein teures Auto, schicke Klamotten und Schmuck oder so was.

ANDREAS   He, Vanessa, dieser Wunsch paßt wirklich sehr gut zu dir. Du bist fast die einzige aus unserer Clique, die sich immer überall freiwillig für eine gute Sache engagiert. Ich find's toll, daß du sowas in deiner Zukunft machen willst. Hoffentlich geht dein Wunsch in Erfüllung.

VANESSA   Martina, hast du dir schon einen Zukunftswunsch überlegt?

MARTINA   Mein Zukunftswunsch ist ganz einfach, daß ich einen der heiß umkämpften Studienplätze für Medizin bekomme. Wenn ich in Biologie und Mathe eine Eins bekommen würde, hätte ich ziemlich gute Chancen.

ANDREAS   Ach, Martina! Dieser Wunsch ist aber nicht sehr originell! Damit wirst du bestimmt nicht den Preis nach Griechenland gewinnen.

MARTINA   Ach, weißt du, Andreas, der Preis ist mir eigentlich ziemlich egal. Für meine Zukunft ist mir wirklich am wichtigsten, einen Studienplatz in Medizin zu bekommen, damit ich meinen Traumberuf als Ärztin verwirklichen kann.

HARTMUT   Jetzt bin ich aber mal gespannt, was dein Zukunftswunsch ist, Andreas. Laß mal hören!

ANDREAS   Also, ich möchte gern eine große Familie haben.

MARTINA   Waaas? Das ist dein Zukunftswunsch? Eine große Familie mit vielen Kindern?

ANDREAS   Ja, aber das ist noch nicht alles. Ich möchte am liebsten Kinder adoptieren, für die es so gut wie keine Zukunft gibt. Zum Beispiel Kinder aus Krisengebieten wie Bosnien, deren Eltern im Krieg gestorben sind. Mein Zukunftswunsch ist es, wenigstens ein paar Kindern ein schönes Leben zu ermöglichen, damit diese Kinder selber mal Pläne für die Zukunft schmieden können.

Answers to Activity 23

Hartmut: will ein weltberühmter Opernsänger werden

Vanessa: will in Afrika leben und in der Entwicklungshilfe arbeiten

Martina: will einen Studienplatz in Medizin bekommen, um Ärztin zu werden

Andreas: will eine große Familie haben und Kinder aus Krisengebieten adoptieren

Kapitel 12: Die Zukunft liegt in deiner Hand!
Projects and Games

PROJECT

Students will design and describe their own original games to review specific German language-related concepts.

Materials Students may need poster board, glue or masking tape, scissors, markers, their textbooks, or dictionaries.

Outline

This project should be started as soon as you begin Chapter 12. Students can work in pairs or individually.
The game should include
- a title,
- simple procedure written in German, and
- a sample of what the game looks like.

Suggested Sequence

1. Before students begin working on an original game, have them look through their German book(s) to identify a theme (Examples: vocabulary, grammar point).
2. Once students have decided on what they plan to address in their game, they should think of a creative way to review these materials.
3. Once the game has been designed, students should write directions, including an answer key if necessary.
4. Students test their game by explaining it to their classmates and then playing it in class.

Grading the Project

Suggested point distribution (total = 100 points)

Originality of the game	25
Completion of assignment requirements	25
Correct language usage in directions	25
Oral presentation of the game	25

GAME

Zeichenspiel

Play this game to review the profession vocabulary from this chapter.

Preparation On the chalkboard, make a list of the vocabulary you would like to review.

Procedure Divide the class into two teams and set up an overhead projector in front of the class. Have a member from Team A come to the overhead projector. Point to one of the professions listed on the chalkboard and give the signal to the student to make a drawing that represents the profession. While the student is sketching on the transparency, both teams try to guess the name of the profession. The first team that correctly identifies the profession gets a point. Teams alternate drawing on the transparency. The team with the most points wins.

PROJECTS AND GAMES

Kapitel 12: Die Zukunft liegt in deiner Hand!
Lesson Plans, pages 280-303

CHAPTER OPENER

Teacher Note

Before you begin the chapter, you may want to preview the *Video Program* and consult the *Video Guide*. Suggestions for integrating the video into each chapter are given in the *Video Guide* and in the chapter interleaf. Activity masters for video selections can be found in the *Video Guide*.

𝒰sing the Chapter Opener,
pp. 280-281

Motivating Activity

Ask students what they might be thinking about as they get ready for graduation. (**Worüber macht ihr euch Gedanken, wie ihr euch dem Schulabschluß nähert?**)

Teaching Suggestion

① Ask students if they have any concrete plans for the future. (**Habt ihr schon feste Pläne für eure Zukunft?**)

Thinking Critically

② **Drawing Inferences** Ask students to name several people who could have made the statement in the subtitle and to whom they could have made it. (**Wer könnte das gesagt haben? Und wem?**)

Teaching Suggestions

③ Have students think about where they would like to live if they had the choice. (**Wenn ihr die Wahl hättet, wo würdet ihr am liebsten leben? Warum da?**)

③ Ask students to describe the town pictured. Does this town fit their image of a typical German town? If yes, how? If no, why not? Can students rely strictly on their visual perception to form an objective opinion?

Focusing on Outcomes

To get students to focus on the chapter objectives ask them what advice they would give junior class students to prepare for their last year of high school. Then have students preview the learning outcomes listed on p. 281. **NOTE:** These outcomes are modeled in **Los geht's!** (pp. 282-283) and **Weiter geht's!** (pp. 290-291) and evaluated in **Kann ich's wirklich?** (p. 302).

Teaching Los geht's!
pp. 282-283

Teacher Note
Los geht's! is recorded on audiocassette.

Los geht's! Summary
In **Mitgehört**, we hear excerpts from conversations of different students discussing a variety of topics. The following student outcomes listed on p. 281 are modeled in the episode: reporting past events, expressing surprise and disappointment, agreeing, agreeing with reservations, giving advice, and giving reasons.

Motivating Activity
Ask students to talk about issues that they are most concerned about at this point in their lives. Have them write these down for comparison later. (**Worüber sorgt ihr euch zur Zeit am meisten?**)

Teaching Suggestions
• Ask students about resolutions they have made for themselves this past year. Which of these have they accomplished and which ones did they need to reevaluate? (**Welche Vorsätze habt ihr im letzten Jahr gefaßt? Welche davon habt ihr ausgeführt und welche mußtet ihr ändern?**)

• Ask students how they would dress for a job interview. (**Was würdet ihr zu einem Jobinterview anziehen?**)

• Ask students to look around the classroom and point out materials that can or should be recycled.

 ## For Individual Needs
Analyzing Ask students to discuss the advantages and disadvantages of mandatory military service in Germany. (**Welche Vor- oder Nachteile hat eurer Meinung nach der obligatorische Wehrdienst?**)

Thinking Critically
1 Comparing and Contrasting After students have read the statements and made a list of topics, have them compare these with their own concerns that they wrote down in the Motivating Activity. Are their concerns similar to or different from those of the German teenagers?

 ## For Individual Needs
2 Auditory Learners Put students in pairs and ask them to role-play two or three of the situations. One student reads the statement from the **Los geht's!** section, and the other responds to it. Have students share their exchanges with the class.

Closure
Refer students back to the outcomes listed on p. 281. Ask them to write down German phrases or words from the eight statements that correspond to each of the functions listed.

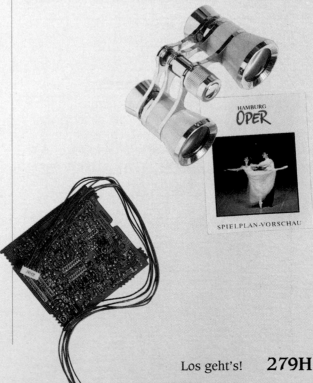

HAMBURG OPER

SPIELPLAN-VORSCHAU

LOS GEHT'S!

ERSTE STUFE

Teaching Erste Stufe
pp. 284-288

Resources for Erste Stufe

Practice and Activity Book
Chapter Resources, Book 4
- Communicative Activities 12-1, 12-2
- Additional Listening Activities 12-1, 12-2, 12-3
- Student Response Forms
- Realia 12-1
- Situation Card 12-1
- Teaching Transparency Master 12-1
- Quiz 12-1

Audiocassette Program
- *Textbook Audiocassette* 6 B
- *Additional Listening Activities, Audiocassette* 10 B
- *Assessment Items, Audiocassette* 8 B

▶ **page 284**

MOTIVATE

Teaching Suggestion

Ask students how they would react if they found out that they were accepted by the college of their choice. How would they react if they were turned down?

TEACH

 ### For Individual Needs

4 Challenge After the **Unzufriedenheiten** have been written on pieces of paper, put all the pieces into a hat. Let students pull out a piece of paper and read the **Unzufriedenheit** to the class. The rest of the students will try to give advice about how to overcome it.

PRESENTATION: So sagt man das!

- Read the text with students, and then have them identify all the verbs in the text. Have students continue the text with a few more statements in the narrative past.

Teaching Suggestion

5 Remind students to use the narrative past as they complete Elke's journal entry.

▶ **page 285**

PRESENTATION: So sagt man das!

After reviewing these expressions, ask students to talk about something that surprises or disappoints them. You may want to list some topics such as friends, politics, or TV shows.

For Individual Needs

6 Challenge In addition, have partners talk about what they would do if they were Elke. Ask students to share their ideas and suggestions for Elke with the rest of the class.

For Additional Practice

8 Have students add a piece of advice for each person in the listening activity.
Example:
Außerdem würde ich ihm/ihr noch vorschlagen, daß ...

PRESENTATION: So sagt man das!

In order for students to review the functions agreeing and giving advice, set up different situations to which students have to react.
Examples:
Ich finde, Zahnarzt ist ein langweiliger Beruf!
Ich brauche eine neue Kamera, aber ich habe nicht viel Geld!

▶ *page 286*

 For Individual Needs

9 A Slower Pace Instead of assigning the four scenes to pairs right away, first engage the whole class. Dramatize each statement and ask students to react to you. Follow up each student response with a reply of your own. Try to get several reactions to each statement so that all three functions can be modeled.

PRESENTATION: Wortschatz

- Have students give the female or male counterpart of each occupation illustrated (pay attention to the irregular change in **die Friseuse**).
- Put the class into two teams of boys and girls. Have the boys give the name of a profession and challenge the girls to quickly give the female counterpart. Reverse roles.
- Have students group the professions listed here and others they already know into four categories: **praktische Berufe, technische Berufe, soziale Berufe,** and **medizinisch-wissenschaftliche Berufe.**
- Have students identify the **Schulabschluß** that is required for each of the jobs listed. (Example: **Ein Friseur muß einen Hauptschulabschluß haben.**)
- Have students pick out at least three professions from the list and recommend a person of that profession to the rest of the class. (Example: **Ich kenne einen tollen Friseur. Der hat sein Geschäft in der ...straße, und der heißt ...**)

▶ *page 287*

Teaching Suggestion

10 Before students begin Activity 10, practice several genitive constructions. (Example: **Mich interessiert der Beruf eines Zahnarztes.**) Allow students to also express which occupations they are not interested in and give reasons. (Example: **Der Beruf eines Steuerberaters interessiert mich nicht, weil ich nicht gut in Mathe bin.**)

Community Link

10 Have students contact an employment office to find out about current job trends. What fields and professions are a lot of people entering now and why?

PRESENTATION: So sagt man das!

Review the expressions in the function box and then ask students to whom they have given advice recently. What were the circumstances and what kind of advice did they give?
Example:
Mein Bruder hilft zu Hause nie. Ich habe ihm gesagt: „Du solltest wirklich mithelfen: abwaschen, abtrocknen, den Tisch decken.“ Die Mutter wäre sehr froh.

▶ *page 288*

 For Individual Needs

13 A Slower Pace To help students get started, prepare a list on the board of suggested topics for giving advice. Solicit ideas from students.
Examples:
**Schularbeit
Sport
Freundschaften
Umwelt
Zukunftspläne**

Group Work

14 Divide the class into four groups and assign each group one letter from the **Kummerkasten** to which they respond in writing. After groups have outlined, revised, edited, and written a final draft of their responses, have them read their letters to the rest of the class.

📁 Portfolio Assessment

14 You might want to suggest this activity as an oral portfolio item for your students. See *Assessment Guide,* p. 25

Reteaching: Vocabulary for Professions

Use flash cards or pictures depicting all the professions students have learned thus far. Show each card briefly to the class. Have students write down the corresponding word. Quickly move through the set of cards or pictures. Finally, review all pictures to see if students correctly identified each profession.

ERSTE STUFE

▶ *page 289*

PRESENTATION: Landeskunde

Teaching Suggestion

Ask students to think of ways their community encourages involvement to improve social conditions in their area.

 For Individual Needs

A Challenge Ask students what would happen if graduating seniors were able to give their teachers a report card. If students wanted to undertake a project like this in their school, how would they go about it? What categories could the report card contain? Would they be the same categories as in Ingo's school or different ones?

A1 A Slower Pace Do this activity with the whole class and use a transparency or the chalkboard to gather and record students' findings.

Teaching Suggestions

A3 Have students ask this question of other students in the school and share their findings with the rest of the class.

B Before students discuss changes, have them name (possibly research) the various organizations involved in social projects. Where would they go to find out about such organizations, and what would they have to do to get involved?

CLOSE

Teaching Suggestion

Have students think of one piece of advice they would give to a person they are close to and then share it with the class.

Focusing on Outcomes

Refer students back to the learning outcomes listed on p. 281. They should recognize that they now know how to report past events, express surprise and disappointment, agree, agree with reservations, give advice, and give reasons.

ASSESS

- **Performance Assessment** Have students recall a situation from their childhood that taught them a lesson. Students should use the narrative past to retell the circumstances. (Example: **Als ich klein war, ...**)

- Quiz 12-1, *Chapter Resources*, Book 4

Teaching Weiter geht's!
pp. 290-291

> ### Resources for Weiter geht's!
> - *Textbook Audiocassette* 6 B
> - *Practice and Activity Book*

Teacher Note

Weiter geht's! is recorded on audiocassette.

Weiter geht's! Summary

In **Pläne für die Zukunft,** students talk about their plans for the future. The following student outcomes listed on p. 281 are modeled in the episode: expressing determination or indecision, talking about what is important or not important, and hypothesizing.

Motivating Activity

Have students recall the first time they thought about plans for their future. This can date back to their preschool or elementary school years. How have their plans and expectations changed over the years? What are their plans now?

Thinking Critically

Analyzing The interviews in this section were conducted with students in the tenth grade at a **Gymnasium**. Their average age is 15 to 16, and they are three years from graduation. Can students think of reasons why students would be so serious and concerned about their future plans at that early a point in their lives?

WEITER GEHT'S!

For Individual Needs

Auditory Learners Ask students to keep their books closed as they listen to the interviews on audiocassette. Pause after each interview and check students' comprehension by having them recall ideas, facts, and phrases from what they have heard.

Thinking Critically

Analyzing Have students read the individual interviews as they listen to the recording. Stop after each interview and have students give the key points made in each. (**Was sind die wichtigsten Punkte in dem (ersten) Interview?**)

Teaching Suggestions

15 Go over the four activities with students orally in class and discuss them. Students take notes for each of the activities. Then have them respond to the questions in writing. This can be assigned for homework. Students refer to their notes to complete the task.

16 Have students include several questions in their letter which they would like to ask the German student.

Closure

Ask student what tenth graders at their school are typically concerned about. Are their views similar to those of the German students in the interviews? What seems to be important to American tenth graders today?

*T*eaching Zweite Stufe,
pp. 292-296

Resources for Zweite Stufe

Practice and Activity Book
Chapter Resources, Book 4
- Communicative Activities 12-3, 12-4
- Additional Listening Activities 12-4, 12-5, 12-6
- Student Response Forms
- Realia 12-2
- Situation Card 12-2
- Teaching Transparency Master 12-2
- Quiz 12-2
Audiocassette Program
- *Textbook Audiocassette* 6 B
- *Additional Listening Activities, Audiocassette* 10 B
- *Assessment Items, Audiocassette* 8 B
Video Program, Videocassette 2
Video Guide

▶ *page 292*

MOTIVATE
Teaching Suggestion

The proverb **Die Glücklichen sind reich, die Reichen nicht immer glücklich** (similar to *Money can't buy you happiness*) often becomes an issue when making plans for the future. Ask students how important money is to them as they plan for the future. Discuss the underlying message of this proverb with your students.

TEACH

Cooperative Learning

17 Divide students into cooperative learning groups. Have them assume the roles of reader, recorder, and reporter as they complete the tasks in Activity 17.

▶ *page 293*

For Additional Practice

18 In addition to questioning Claudia's plans, have the partner think of at least three suggestions he or she would have for Claudia. At the end, call on students to find out what type of advice was offered.

For Individual Needs

19 A Slower Pace Before students begin the writing activity, you may want to review the functions of making recommendations (Chapter 8) and talking about goals for the future (Chapter 11).

Portfolio Assessment

19 You might want to suggest this activity as a written portfolio item for your students. See *Assessment Guide,* p. 25.

PRESENTATION: So sagt man das!

- After reviewing the expressions, ask students how various people could incorporate the phrases in a speech or discussion. (Examples: a politician giving a speech, an employment agent interviewing a prospective employee, a principal reprimanding a student, parents discussing a new curfew for their child)
- Ask students to look at the reports in the **Weiter geht's!** section. Have them restate what those five students said using expressions of determination or indecision, depending on how sure they are about their plans for the future.

PRESENTATION: Wortschatz

- Introduce the new vocabulary by describing what the individual jobs entail.
- For additional vocabulary, look through the classified ads of a recent German-speaking paper.
- Have student write out the names of other modern professions.

▶ *page 294*

PRESENTATION: So sagt man das!

Review the expressions by asking students questions to which they respond by completing the statements or varying those that are given in the box.
Examples:
Sag mal, was ist für dich wichtig?
Worauf legst du keinen großen Wert?

Teaching Suggestion

22 Expand the list in the box by brainstorming with students other positive attributes a person can have. Students should then use ideas from this list to create a detailed profile of their ideal partner. Remind students to use connectors in their descriptions.

For Individual Needs

23 Auditory Learners Plan to have a tape recorder on hand for this activity. Without much notice, ask students to use the same format as they talk about their future. Walk around the class and record these spontaneous interviews. Once you have completed the interviews, play them back to the entire class.

PRESENTATION: So sagt man das!

- To review and practice subjunctive forms, play **Kettenspiel** by having students complete the following phrase.
  Wenn ich reich wäre, würde ich ...
  Each students adds his or her own statement after repeating the ones previously mentioned.
- Have students look back at the Dresden Location Opener and talk about the things they would do and see in Dresden if they had a chance to visit the city. (**Wenn du Dresden besuchen könntest, was würdest du da alles besichtigen? Welche kulturellen Veranstaltungen würdest du besuchen?**)

▶ *page 295*

History Connection

27 Have students continue working with their partner. One of the students assumes the role of a historical figure who is discussing his or her future with a friend. Let students role-play this situation as they imagine what worries, concerns, and goals that person might have had.

▶ *page 296*

Teaching Suggestion

29 Encourage students to invent their own text pictures. Make it a competition with the whole class voting on the designs. Give out ribbons for **erster Platz, zweiter Platz,** etc. Display the finished products for other German classes to enjoy. You might want to enter winning designs in the school newspaper.

Reteaching: Vocabulary for *moderne Berufe*

Have students write a brief newspaper ad advertising a position for one of the **moderne Berufe** listed in the **Wortschatz** box on p. 293.

📠 Video Program

In the video clip **Wohnungsnot der Studenten,** students talk about their problems finding adequate housing at reasonable prices. See *Video Guide* for suggestions.

CLOSE
Teaching Suggestion

To review the vocabulary and expressions presented in the **Zweite Stufe,** design (or have students design) a crossword puzzle that contains words needed to complete some expressions. Here are a few examples:

Sie untersucht die Nahrungsmittel, die in Supermärkten verkauft werden. (die Lebensmittelkontrolleurin)

Steffi Graf hat viel _____ in ihrer sportlichen Karriere. (Erfolg)

Wenn man etwas zu tun versucht, muß man _____. (sich anstrengen)

Focusing on Outcomes

Refer students back to the learning outcomes listed on p. 281. They should recognize that they now know how to express determination or indecision, talk about what is important or not important, and hypothesize.

ASSESS

• **Performance Assessment** Ask students to imagine they are talking to a **Berufsberater(in)** who is visiting their school. Students tell the career counselor about their plans for the future so he or she can determine appropriate career choices for them.

• Quiz 12-2, *Chapter Resources,* Book 4

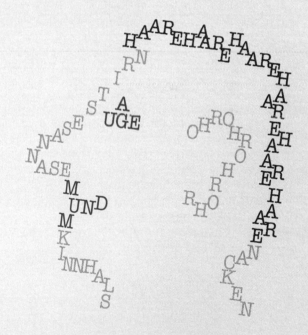

ZWEITE STUFE

ZUM SCHREIBEN

*T*eaching Zum Schreiben,
p. 297

Writing Strategy

The targeted strategy in this writing activity is evaluating your writing. Students should learn about this strategy before beginning the assignment.

PREWRITING

Motivating Activity

Have students review all eleven **Zum Schreiben** assignments they have completed in Level 3. Which was their favorite piece of writing and why?

Teaching Suggestion

You may want to model evaluating by having a student volunteer one of his or her previous assignments. Copy the piece of writing onto a transparency or make copies for all students. Show students how to analyze the writing, using specific examples to help them understand how certain parts can be improved. Encourage objective class input.

Building on Previous Skills

A Remind students to analyze their audience, as they did in the **Zum Schreiben** activity for Chapter 9 (p. 223). Their autobiography should be adapted to a specific audience as well. They should ask themselves the following questions.
Was weiß der Leser bereits über mich?
Was würde den Leser interessieren?
Was sollte ich genauer erklären?
Welchen Ton soll ich benutzen?

WRITING

 ### For Individual Needs

B **Visual Learners** Encourage students to accompany their writing with visuals. Remind students that the visuals should help organize their ideas and support their writing.

POST-WRITING

Teaching Suggestion

Have students post their autobiographies throughout the classroom on bulletin boards. If some students have home movies or slides they would like to show, they could present them in class along with their biographies.

Closure

Have students look back over evidence of the writing process for this piece. What parts of it were difficult to write about and why?

Teaching Zum Lesen, pp. 298-301

Teacher Note

Der hellgraue Frühjahrsmantel is recorded on *Textbook Audiocassette* 11.

Reading Strategy

The targeted strategy in this reading is applying strategies on your own. Students should learn about this strategy before beginning Question 1.

PREREADING

Background Information

Wolfgang Hildesheimer was born in Hamburg in 1916. He lived in Palestine, in England, and in Germany (Nürnberg) before moving to Switzerland in the fifties. He has published three novels, a collection of short stories, two collections of dramas, a biography of Mozart, and a fictitious "biography" called *Marbot.* He is also recognized as a painter and has had his work exhibited in Darmstadt, Bonn, Munich, Zurich, and Urbino.

Motivating Activity

After reading a number of contemporary authors, students may have noticed a trend in which the writer avoids explaining the psychological states or motivations of the characters and concentrates on simply describing their actions in concrete detail. The short story is an ideal vehicle for this kind of cool, terse style that leaves the interpretation of events up to the reader. As the students read Hildesheimer's story, they should be aware of how he maintains an objective distance from his characters—even from the first-person narrator. If a comparison is helpful, they could ask themselves while reading: How is this style different from the style of *Sabines Eltern?* Ask the class to watch for and flag instances in which characters act—or perhaps fail to react—in unexplained ways. Further, ask them to watch for moments at which there seems to be some kind of failure of language or communication breakdown going on within the world of the story.

Teacher Note

Activities 1-4 are prereading activities.

READING

Teaching Suggestion

2 If students have trouble getting started, ask them which of the other texts in Levels 2 and 3 they think this story resembles. They can think about the strategies they used with those texts. Make sure they have noticed the fact that, besides the narrative look of paragraph one, this text includes quotation marks—and therefore dialogue—and three personal letters that are given in full.

Teacher Notes

4 The class may want to refer to previous chapters in Level 3 and perhaps to reread some of the **Lesetrick** boxes to see how to apply various strategies that have been suggested by class members.

7 In addition to noting that Kolhaas is given cousin Eduard's coat as a replacement, students should probably notice that he doesn't complain or even seem very surprised at the loss of his own coat.

Teaching Suggestion

10 Help students recognize the **indirekte Rede** of Eduard's reply. You can restate "**Er habe nämlich in dem Mantel ...**" to "**Aber Blockflöten seien in Australien nicht erhältlich.**" in direct quote form in order to facilitate their comprehension.

Teacher Note

13 The students might need help recognizing what is odd about paragraph 3—that the wife is putting a heating coil in the flower vase in order to boil eggs—or the end of the story where she's taking the coffee grinder apart. They might also need help recognizing why it's comically in character for the wife to say that she wouldn't have been interested in seeing *Tannhäuser* anyway, but not to ask why the tickets are 12 years old.

Thinking Critically

Analyzing At first glance, this short story might seem like it would be much easier to film than the Kafka story the class read at the beginning of Level 3. Ask the students to use their answers to Questions 5 through 11 to make some story boards for a film of *Der hellgraue Frühjahrsmantel.* Next, ask them to consider how they would handle the letters in a film, and how they would handle such essentials as the narrator's description of his wife's character. Are there places where they would have to write their own material—dialogue lines or even whole scenes—in order to make the film coherent? How would they preserve the understated quality of the humor in a film version?

POST-READING

Teacher Note

Activity 14 is a post-reading task that will show whether students can apply what they have learned.

Closure

Have students write a review of the story as if for a newspaper or magazine.

Answers to Activity 5

Eduard ist vor zwölf Jahren nach Australien ausgewandert; Eduard hat neulich geschrieben; Eduard will seinen hellgrauen Frühjahrsmantel.

Answers to Activity 6

den Mantel von Herrn Kolhaas; der Erzähler hat den Mantel mit dem Mantel seines Cousins (Vetters) verwechselt.

Answers to Activity 7

Er bekommt den Mantel des Cousins.

Answers to Activity 8

Pilze; Herr Kolhaas will sich für das Buch für Pilzsammler bedanken.

Answers to Activity 9

Herr Kolhaas findet einen Brief; Der Brief war für einen Freund vom Cousin bestimmt; Der Cousin hatte vergessen, den Brief abzuschicken.

Answers to Activity 10

Der Mantel ist länger geworden; eine Tenorblockflöte

Answers to Activity 11

Sie reagiert ganz sachlich darauf.

*K*ann ich's wirklich?
p. 302

This page helps students prepare for the test. It is a brief checklist of the major points covered in the chapter. The students should be reminded that it is only a checklist and not necessarily everything that will appear on the test.

*U*sing Wortschatz,
p. 303

For Individual Needs

Challenge Ask students to choose one of the professions from the **Wortschatz** page. Tell them to imagine they are going to be interviewed about their field of work. They should be able to describe a typical day on the job and include some background information such as job requirements, training, and advantages of that particular job.

Game
Play the game **Zeichenspiel**. See p. 279F for the procedure.

For Individual Needs

Tactile Learners Give students each a 3 x 5 index card and ask them to make their own business card for one of the professions listed on the **Wortschatz** page. The business card should include their name, title, address of business, a catchy phrase, and the logo of their business.

Teaching Suggestion

Ask students to identify all professions on the **Wortschatz** page for which a foreign language would be useful. Students should also explain why they think foreign languages would be helpful for each of the professions they identify.

Total Physical Response

Divide students into groups of three or four and have them develop their own TPR activities. They should use the vocabulary and functions from this chapter as the basis for their commands. Allow enough time for each group to try out their commands on their classmates.

Video Program

At this time, you might want to use the authentic advertising footage from German television. See *Video Guide* for suggestions.

Teacher Note

Give the **Kapitel 12** Chapter Test, *Chapter Resources, Book 4.*

REVIEW

12

Die Zukunft liegt in deiner Hand!

(1) Ich hab' beschlossen, eine Lehre als Werkzeugmacherin zu beginnen.

Ein deutsches Sprichwort heißt „Wie man sich bettet, so schläft man". Das heißt, daß es von einem selbst abhängt, wie man sein Leben gestaltet. Jeder junge Mensch muß lernen, eigene Entscheidungen zu treffen und auch keine Angst davor zu haben, daß man ab und zu mal eine falsche Entscheidung trifft. Wer schlau ist, informiert sich genügend, befragt Eltern, Freunde, Lehrer und andere Personen, die ihre eigenen Erfahrungen mit Dingen gemacht haben, für die man sich entscheiden muß. Das schlimmste ist, nichts zu tun und den Kopf in den Sand zu stecken!

In this chapter you will learn

- to report past events; to express surprise and disappointment; to agree; to agree with reservations; to give advice; to give advice and give reasons
- to express determination or indecision; to talk about what is important or not important; to hypothesize

And you will

- listen to students make plans for their future
- read about some problems German teenagers face and how they deal with them
- write about your own expectations for the future
- find out how you can make your world a better one

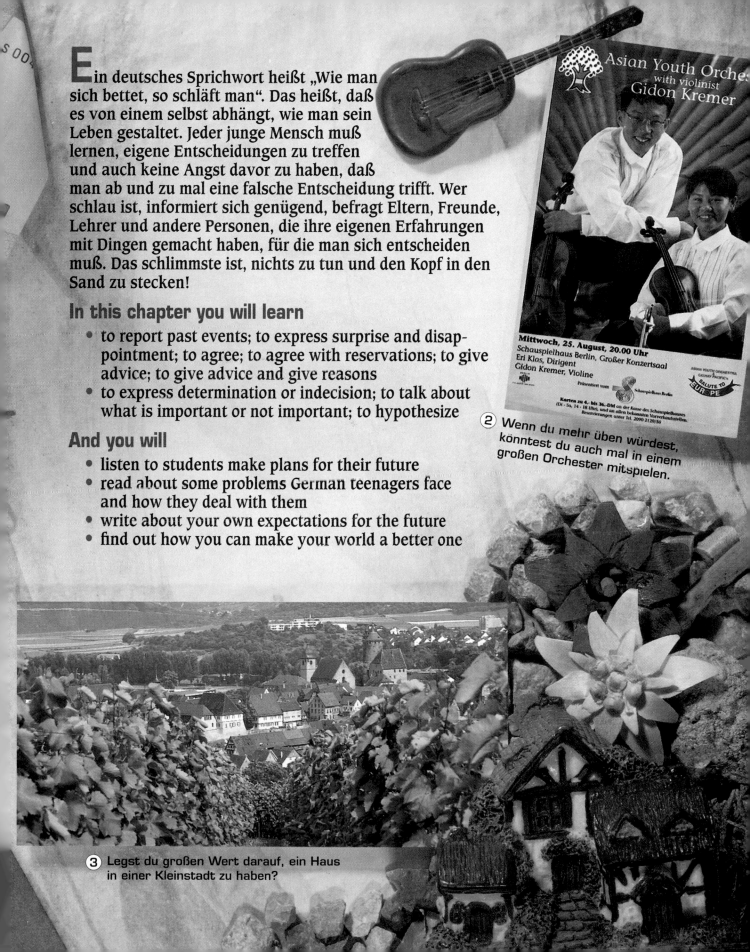

Asian Youth Orchestra with violinist Gidon Kremer

Mittwoch, 25. August, 20.00 Uhr
Schauspielhaus Berlin, Großer Konzertsaal
Eri Klas, Dirigent
Gidon Kremer, Violine

② Wenn du mehr üben würdest, könntest du auch mal in einem großen Orchester mitspielen.

③ Legst du großen Wert darauf, ein Haus in einer Kleinstadt zu haben?

Los geht's!

Mitgehört

Diese Gesprächsfetzen stammen aus diversen Gesprächen mit Schülern aus verschiedenen Realschulen und Gymnasien. Wovon handeln diese Aussagen?

„Für mich steht fest, daß ich nach dem Abitur erst einmal den Zivildienst mache, bevor ich studiere. Wenn ich mich nicht irre, dauert der Zivildienst ja nur 12 Monate."

Uwe

„Es ist wichtig, daß die Verbraucher ihre Getränke nur in Mehrwegflaschen kaufen; Einwegflaschen und vor allem Aludosen müßten eigentlich verboten werden."

Veronika

„Ich lege keinen großen Wert darauf, wie ich mich kleide, wie ich aussehe, und darüber bin ich sehr glücklich."

Hannes

„Ich weiß noch nicht, ob ich Kunst oder Sprachen studieren soll, denn ich bin gut in beiden Fächern. Fest steht jedoch, daß ich nicht Physik studiere, denn in diesem Fach bin ich eine absolute Niete."

Brigitte

„Ich habe beschlossen, meine Diät zu ändern und ein gesundes Leben zu führen. Und ich empfehle euch, dasselbe zu tun."

Jens

„Dein Husten macht mir aber langsam Sorgen, und ich bin wirklich sehr erstaunt, daß du noch nicht zum Arzt gegangen bist."

Katja

„Meiner Meinung nach solltest du mal diese Uhr reparieren lassen. Was mich stört ist, daß du alles immer gleich wegwerfen willst und dir was Neues kaufst."

Markus

HAMBURG
OPER

SPIELPLAN-VORSCHAU

„Ich geb' Ihnen recht, das Theaterstück war super. Als der Vorhang aufging und ich die bunten Kostüme der Schauspieler sah, bekam ich eine Gänsehaut."

Claudia

1 Hast du alles verstanden?

a. Über welche Themen sprechen diese Schüler? Mach eine Liste!
b. Was drückt jede dieser Aussagen aus? Diskutier darüber mit einem Partner! a. Zivildienst; Umwelt; Aussehen; Studium; Ernährung; Gesundheit; Umweltbewußtsein; Kultur

2 Und du?

Was würdest du diesen Schülern antworten, wenn sie diese Aussagen dir gegenüber gemacht hätten? Schreib zwei Antworten auf, und lies sie der Klasse vor!

ERSTE STUFE

Reporting past events; expressing surprise and disappointment; agreeing; agreeing with reservations; giving advice; giving advice and giving reasons

3 Hör gut zu!

For answers, see listening script on TE Interleaf.

Junge Leute erzählen, wie ihr Leben vor nur einem halben Jahr war, wie es jetzt ist und warum es sich geändert hat. Schreib die wichtigsten Tatsachen auf! Wer hat die größten Änderungen erlebt?

4 Unzufrieden? Worüber denn?

Setzt euch in kleinen Gruppen zusammen, und erzählt euch gegenseitig, worüber jeder von euch schon mal im Leben unzufrieden war und warum! Einer von euch muß dabei die einzelnen „Unzufriedenheiten" auf einen Zettel schreiben.

SO SAGT MAN DAS!

Schon bekannt

Reporting past events

What do you observe about the following text?

> Vor drei Wochen hatte ich eine schwere Erkältung. Ich fühlte mich gar nicht wohl und konnte nicht in die Schule gehen. Als es mir nach zwei Tagen noch immer nicht besser ging, rief meine Mutter unseren Hausarzt an. Der sagte, ...

What verb forms are used here? Why?

> Schon bekannt
> ## Ein wenig *Grammatik*
>
> For the forms of the narrative past (imperfect), used to report past events, see the Grammar Summary.

5 Worüber war Elke unzufrieden?

Elke war gerade dabei, etwas über sich selbst in ihr Tagebuch zu schreiben, als sie ans Telefon gerufen wurde. Schreib für sie die Eintragung fertig! Ein paar Ideen dafür stehen rechts unten. Lest danach eure Texte einander vor!

> Datum: Mittwoch, den 10. Mai
>
> Es gab mal eine Zeit bei mir, so ungefähr vor drei Monaten, da fühlte ich mich ziemlich

sich nicht wohl fühlen

schlechte Noten haben

keine tollen Klamotten haben

es gibt zu viel Schmutz und Lärm

kein Geld für Konzertkarten haben

keine Zukunft sehen

mit jemandem Streit haben

SO SAGT MAN DAS!

Schon bekannt

Expressing surprise and disappointment

When expressing surprise, you may begin your statement by saying:

Ich bin/war überrascht, daß Elke Streit mit ihrem Freund hat/hatte.
Ich war erstaunt, daß sie so schlechte Noten hatte.
Ich hätte nicht geglaubt, daß sie überhaupt Probleme hat.

When expressing disappointment, you may begin your statement
by saying:

Ich bin enttäuscht, daß Elke mir nichts gesagt hat.
Ich bedaure, daß sie sich keine neuen Klamotten leisten kann.
Ich finde es schade, daß wir ihr nicht helfen können.

What would you tell a beginning German student about the position of the conjugated verb in **daß**-clauses?

6 Arme Elke!

Such dir eine Partnerin, und schaut euch Übung 5 noch mal an! Sprecht über Elkes Probleme der letzten drei Monate, und drückt dabei eure Überraschung und Enttäuschung aus!

7 Für mein Notizbuch

Womit warst du in der letzten Zeit nicht zufrieden? Schreib einen kurzen Bericht darüber!

8 Hör gut zu!

For answers, see listening
script on TE Interleaf.

Junge Leute unterhalten sich über verschiedene Probleme. Hör gut zu und schreib auf, was die einzelnen Probleme sind und welcher Rat gegeben wird, wie man das Problem vielleicht lösen könnte!

wer?	Problem?	was tun?

SO SAGT MAN DAS!

Schon bekannt

Agreeing; agreeing with reservations; giving advice

When agreeing, you may say:

Da geb' ich dir recht, ... *or*
Bei uns ist es auch so; wir ...

When agreeing, but with reservations, you may say:

Das stimmt zwar, aber ... *or*
Es kommt darauf an, ob ...

When giving advice, you may say:

Vielleicht kannst du ... *or*
Es ist wichtig, daß ... *or*
Ich würde sagen, du gehst ...

> Schon bekannt
> Ein wenig *G*rammatik
> For the **würde**-forms, see the
> Grammar Summary.

9 Was meinst du?

Such dir eine Partnerin! — Die Aufgabe ist, jede der folgenden Aussagen zu diskutieren. Deine Partnerin liest zuerst eine der aufgelisteten Aussagen vor, als ob diese von ihr wäre. Du nimmst dazu Stellung: du gibst ihr recht und sagst warum, oder du machst Einwände (*express reservations*). Darauf rät dir deine Partnerin, was du tun sollst.

BEISPIEL   PARTNERIN   **Also, ich stehe auf Country Western: die Musik ist immer super, und die Texte sind immer aktuell.**

DU   **Da geb' ich dir recht. Ich ...**   *oder*
Na ja, aber es kommt doch darauf an, wer oder welche Gruppe singt, denn ...

PARTNERIN   **Ich würde sagen, daß du dir mal die (...) anhören solltest, denn die sind wirklich fetzig.**

1. „Also, ich stehe auf Country Western: die Musik ist immer super, und die Texte sind immer aktuell."
2. „Es hat keinen Sinn für mich, Kunst zu studieren, weil ich später damit wenig anfangen kann — davon kann ich nicht leben."
3. „Ich weiß nicht, ob ich als zweite Fremdsprache Italienisch oder Spanisch lernen soll. Meine Freunde meinen, ich soll Japanisch lernen."
4. „Meiner Meinung nach tun wir bei uns zu Hause noch nicht genug für die Umwelt. Wir sortieren oft unseren Müll nicht, und wir benutzen meistens nur Einwegflaschen."

WORTSCHATZ

Welche Berufe interessieren dich? Vielleicht der ...

eines Schornsteinfegers

eines Steuerberaters

einer Rundfunkmoderatorin

einer Toningenieurin

eines Friseurs

einer Schweißerin

eines Schreiners

einer Glasbläserin

Und dann noch ...

Anästhesist(in)
Elektroinstallateur(in)
Fotograf(in)
Koch/Köchin
Optiker(in)
Schuhmacher(in)
technische(r) Zeichner(in)
Winzer(in)
Zahnarzt/Zahnärztin
Zimmermann

10 Was willst du werden?

Sag einigen Klassenkameraden, welche von den oben aufgelisteten Berufen dich interessieren und warum! Kennst du auch Leute, die diese Berufe ausüben?

11 Hör gut zu!

For answers, see listening script on TE Interleaf.

Schüler unterhalten sich. Was raten einige Schüler ihren Klassenkameraden, und welche Gründe geben sie dafür an? Mach dir Notizen! Welcher Rat, findest du, paßt am besten zu welchem Schüler?

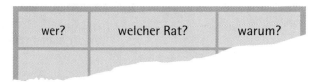

wer?	welcher Rat?	warum?

SO SAGT MAN DAS!

Giving advice and giving reasons

Schon bekannt

When giving advice, you may say:

Versuch doch mal, etwas gesünder zu leben!
An deiner Stelle würde ich nicht rauchen.
Und du solltest wirklich auch mehr schlafen.

When giving reasons for others to do something, you may say:

Du solltest mehr Fisch als Fleisch essen, **weil Fisch gesünder ist.**
Du solltest mehr Sport treiben, **damit du dich besser fühlst.**

When giving your own reasons for doing something, you may say:

Ich treibe viel Sport, **um wirklich fit zu bleiben.**

What words are used to introduce the clauses stating the reasons?
How do they differ in meaning?

12 Was ich alles tun sollte und warum!

Denk an fünf verschiedene Dinge, die du für dich selbst tun sollst, und schreib sie auf! Schreib auch einen Grund daneben!

Schon bekannt
Ein wenig *G*rammatik

For infinitive forms of verbs, see the Grammar Summary.

13 Rat geben

Such dir eine Partnerin! — Sag ihr drei Dinge, die du tun solltest, und nenne einen Grund dafür! Sie gibt dir Rat und begründet ihren Rat.

BEISPIEL   DU   **Ich sollte erst mal mehr Zeit für Deutsch verwenden, um eine bessere Note zu bekommen. Und zweitens ...**

PARTNERIN   **An deiner Stelle würde ich versuchen, alle Noten zu verbessern, damit du einen guten Schulabschluß machst und ...**

14 Leserbriefe beantworten

Lies die Leserbriefe im Kummerkasten! — Als Jugendpsychologe der Kummerkasten-Seite eines Jugendmagazins hast du die Aufgabe, solche Briefe zu beantworten. Such dir einen der vier Briefe aus und beantworte ihn! Drück in deiner Antwort Verständnis für die Probleme aus, und gib den Leuten einen guten Rat, den sie auch befolgen können! Lies dann deine Antwort einem Partner vor!

KUMMERKASTEN

Meine Eltern fahren dieses Wochenende weg, und ich muß auf das Haus achten. Ich würde in dieser Zeit gern meine Clique einladen zum Musikhören oder Videoschauen. Ich weiß aber, daß meine Eltern dagegen wären. Soll ich meine Freunde trotzdem einladen?

Haussitter Tobias

Ich habe vier Wochen „Hausarrest", weil ich letzten Samstag erst um Mitternacht nach Hause gekommen bin anstatt, wie fest versprochen, um 22.30 Uhr. Ich darf jetzt in den nächsten vier Wochen das Haus nach 19.00 Uhr nicht mehr verlassen. In zwei Wochen hat nun mein bester Freund eine Fete, zu der ich eingeladen bin. Die Fete geht bis 23.00 Uhr, und ich möchte gern dabei sein, kann es aber nicht. Was soll ich tun?

„Arrestant" Michael

Ich habe Probleme in der Schule, und meine Eltern werden deshalb bestimmt bald einen blauen Brief[1] erhal-

ten. Soll ich meine Eltern darauf vorbereiten? In zwei Wochen wird es sich entscheiden. Meine einzige Chance ist, eine gute Lateinarbeit zu schreiben, aber dafür müßte ich jetzt jeden Tag 3-4 Stunden und noch länger lernen. Ich habe aber wenig Lust, so viel Zeit mit Latein zu verbringen.

Antje, ein Lateinmuffel

Ich war mit meiner besten Freundin beim Einkaufen. In einem großen Bekleidungsgeschäft hat sie ein Halstuch gesehen, das ihr so gut gefallen hat. Sie hat es sich umgebunden, wir haben noch andere Sachen angeschaut — und plötzlich waren wir draußen auf der Straße. Ich habe meiner Freundin geraten, zurückzugehen und das Halstuch zu bezahlen. Aber das wollte sie nicht. Sie hatte Angst, daß man denkt, sie wollte es stehlen. Jetzt will ich mit meiner Freundin nie wieder einkaufen gehen!

Monika

1. Ein blauer Brief ist ein Mahnschreiben der Schule an die Eltern, wenn die Versetzung des Schülers in die nächste Klasse gefährdet ist.

Pauken allein reicht nicht

Für den Schulabschluß braucht man gute Noten und muß sehr fleißig lernen. Doch wo bleibt das soziale Lernen? Wer engagiert sich für seine Mitmenschen? Wie engagiert man sich? Zwei Schüler haben dazu Stellung genommen. Lies, auf welche Arten sie sich sozial engagieren!

„Man muß sich einmischen", meint Judith. Die Abiturientin hat oft nach diesem Motto gehandelt. Als Schulsprecherin versuchte sie immer „in Erfahrung zu bringen, was die Mitschülerinnen bedrückte". Sie vermittelte bei Konflikten und organisierte Feten und Konzerte für die Schulgemeinde. Der Schulkiosk verkauft dank ihrer Initiative statt „Süßkram" jetzt Biobrötchen. Judith setzte eine Mülltrennaktion an der Schule durch und engagierte sich für eine Kroatienhilfe. „Wenn ich mich über etwas aufrege, werde ich aktiv", erklärt die Schülerin, die am liebsten im Team arbeitet. Ihrer Meinung nach erzieht das Gymnasium heute zu viele „Einzelkämpfer": „Später im Beruf arbeitet man doch meistens in Gruppen."

Judith

„Man kann etwas verändern", weiß Ingo. Das hat der Abiturient eines Wirtschaftsgymnasiums selbst erfahren. Mit einem Freund sammelte er Kleidung und Nahrung für Menschen im ehemaligen Jugoslawien. Der Erfolg war groß. „Die anderen Schüler konnten sehen, daß sich Engagement lohnt", sagt Ingo heute. Etwas Besonderes haben sich Ingo und seine Mitschüler zum Abitur einfallen lassen: Es gibt Zeugnisse für Lehrer. Bewertet werden zum Beispiel Unterrichtsgestaltung, Toleranz, Charisma, Stärken und Schwächen. Besonders viel Lob hat Ingo für seinen Deutschlehrer: „Ein echter Pädagoge, wie es ihn nur selten gibt. Er hat Zeit für die Probleme der Heranwachsenden, nimmt uns als Schüler ernst und stellt dafür auch mal den Unterrichtsstoff zurück."

Ingo

A. 1. Mach dir Notizen darüber, was jeder Schüler für seine Mitmenschen macht! Wie unterscheiden sich die Schüler voneinander?
2. Welche Gründe geben die Schüler an, sich für andere zu engagieren?
3. Glaubst du, daß man die Verantwortung hat, sich für seine Mitmenschen zu engagieren? Was meinst du dazu?
4. Wie engagiert sich deine Klasse oder Schule auf sozialer Ebene? Habt ihr schon mal was verändert oder verbessert? A. 1. Judith: vermittelte bei Konflikten; organisierte Feten und Konzerte; hat durch ihre Initiative bewirkt, daß es Biobrötchen am Pausenstand gibt; setzte eine Mülltrennaktion an der Schule durch;

B. Welche Veränderungen könnte man erreichen (*achieve*), wenn man an sozialen Projekten teilnimmt? Wie würde die Welt deiner Meinung nach dann aussehen? engagierte sich für Kroatienhilfe. Ingo: sammelt Kleidung und Nahrung für Menschen im ehemaligen Jugoslawien; stellte Zeugnisse für Lehrer aus. Unterschiede zwischen beiden Schülern: Judith engagiert sich hauptsächlich für ihre Umgebung; ihr ist es wichtig, daß ihre Mitschüler sich gesund ernähren und umweltbewußt sind. Ingo ist es wichtig, welchen Eindruck Lehrer auf Schüler ausüben.

Weiter geht's!

Pläne für die Zukunft

Gymnasiasten einer 10. Klasse erzählen von ihren Zukunftsplänen.

1. Ich möchte Jura studieren und Strafverteidigerin werden. Erst dann möchte ich heiraten und eine Familie gründen, denn ich möchte immer unabhängig von meinem Mann sein (finanziell) im Fall einer Scheidung, damit ich meine Kinder auch alleine ernähren kann. Trotzdem wünsche ich mir ein Haus, eine gute und glückliche Ehe, zwei bis drei Kinder und Erfolg im Beruf.

2. Ich möchte später Zahntechniker werden, gut verdienen und eine Familie mit zwei Kindern haben. Und ein Haus wäre nicht schlecht. Ich würde vielleicht gern im Ausland arbeiten, weil man dort besser verdienen kann und die Menschen vielleicht nicht so kalt sind wie hier.

3. Wenn ich 35 bin, möchte ich einen Mann haben und vielleicht auch schon ein Kind — und gesund und glücklich sein. Natürlich einen guten Job und viel Geld. Ich möchte in Deutschland leben bleiben, weil ich es hier ganz schön finde. In anderen Ländern, mit anderen Glauben, gibt es nur Konflikte und oft auch Kriege; das wäre nichts für mich. Aber nach Frankreich oder England zu ziehen, könnte ich mir schon vorstellen. In anderen Ländern werden Frauen immer noch zu stark unterdrückt.

4. Nach meinem Schulabschluß habe ich mir schon mal leise überlegt, ob ich nicht vielleicht Jura studieren sollte. Durch das Jurastudium habe ich natürlich auch gute Chancen auf einen guten Beruf, viel Geld und ein Häuschen. Ich würde gerne heiraten und auch ein oder mehrere Kinder haben.

5. Sicherlich möchte ich später einmal einen guten Job und viel Geld haben. Ich weiß aber auch, daß ich mich sehr anstrengen muß, denn wie auch in Amerika ist es hier schwer, eine Arbeit zu finden, die einem wirklich gefällt. Ich glaube nicht, daß ich heiraten werde, denn ich habe es gern, unabhängig zu sein und machen zu können, was ich will. Durch meine Arbeit und andere Pflichten werde ich sowieso schon genug eingeengt sein.

15 Was sagst du zu diesen Aussagen?

1. Welche von diesen Aussagen stammen von einem Jungen und welche von einem Mädchen? Welche können von beiden sein? Wie weißt du das? 1. Mädchen; 2. Junge; 3. Mädchen; 4. beide; 5. beide
2. Welche Aussagen haben etwas gemeinsam (*in common*), und welche sind verschieden? Begründe deine Antwort!
3. Wer von diesen Gymnasiasten hat sich deiner Meinung nach die meisten Gedanken über die Zukunft gemacht? Warum meinst du das?
4. Was für einen allgemeinen Eindruck hast du von diesen Aussagen?

16 Eine Antwort

Mit welchem von diesen Gymnasiasten kannst du dich am besten identifizieren? — Schreib ihm oder ihr einen kurzen Brief, und berichte von deinen eigenen Plänen für die Zukunft!

Expressing determination or indecision; talking about what is important or not important; hypothesizing

In einer Zeit, in der es für Jugendliche nicht so einfach ist, Pläne für die Zukunft zu machen, hat die 16jährige Claudia aus Hamburg jedoch feste Pläne für ihre Zukunft. Lies, was sie geschrieben hat!

> *Pläne für die Zukunft*
>
> Nachdem ich die Schule mit einem Abi-Durchschnitt von 2,5 oder besser beendet habe, studiere ich Betriebswirtschaftslehre.
>
> Nach meinem Studium werde ich eine Lehre in einem großen, berühmten Hotel machen.
>
> Dann möchte ich für einige Zeit im Ausland arbeiten, am liebsten in Frankreich oder in den USA.
>
> Wenn ich so zwischen 25 und 30 Jahre alt bin, ziehe ich nach Frankreich, um dort ein eigenes Hotel zu bauen, oder ein anderes, gutlaufendes Hotel zu übernehmen.
>
> Dort werde ich meinen zukünftigen Mann kennenlernen und ihn heiraten. In den Flitterwochen fahren wir nach Hawaii.
>
> Dann möchte ich 2 Kinder kriegen. Es sollen Zwillinge sein (ein Mädchen und ein Junge).
>
> Wenn die beiden etwas älter sind, so etwa 14/15/16, sollen sie im Hotel mithelfen, soweit die Schule es ermöglicht.
>
> Claudia Müller (16)

by Claudia Müller, student in Herr Boelicke's class at Johann-Rist-Gymnasium in Wedel, Germany

17 Claudias Pläne

1. Wie viele konkrete Pläne hat Claudia erwähnt? Liste sie auf!
2. Welche Ausdrücke gebraucht Claudia, wenn sie über ihre Pläne spricht? Was drückt sie damit aus?
3. Was ist dein Eindruck von Claudia? Begründe deine Meinung!

18 Bist du so sicher, Claudia?

Such dir eine Partnerin! Sie übernimmt die Rolle von Claudia. Versuche nun, die einzelnen Pläne in Claudias Brief in Frage zu stellen! Claudia muß ihre Pläne verteidigen oder eine andere Möglichkeit erwähnen.

19 Eine Antwort an Claudia

Schreib Claudia einen Brief! Schreib ihr, was du von ihren Plänen hältst und was für Pläne du für deine Zukunft hast!

20 Hör gut zu!

For answers, see listening script on TE Interleaf

Schüler sprechen über ihre Zukunftspläne. Einige von ihnen haben schon feste Pläne, andere wissen noch nicht genau, was sie machen wollen. Schreib auf, was jeder vorhat, und schreib auch die Gründe auf, die jeder für seine Entscheidung angibt!

wer?	sicher	nicht sicher

SO SAGT MAN DAS!

Schon bekannt

Expressing determination or indecision

When expressing determination, you may say:

Ich weiß jetzt, daß ich Jura studieren werde.
Ich hab' beschlossen, Strafverteidigerin zu werden.
Ich hab' mich entschieden, finanziell unabhängig zu sein.

When expressing indecision, you may say:

Ich weiß nicht, ob ich studieren soll.
Ich kann noch nicht sagen, wann ich nach England ziehe.
Ich muß mir überlegen, wo ich einmal arbeiten werde.

---

21 Deine Pläne

Frag eine Partnerin, was für Pläne sie für die Zukunft hat, und ob sie sich schon für etwas fest entschieden hat oder noch nicht ganz sicher ist! Frag sie auch nach den Gründen! — Erzähl ihr danach von deinen eigenen Plänen!

einige Gründe:

unabhängig sein
viel Geld verdienen
Familie
Haus
guter Job
im Ausland arbeiten
nicht eingeengt sein

WORTSCHATZ

Moderne Berufe

Gesundheitswissenschaftler(in)
Sportökonom(in)
Umweltökonom(in)
Mediaplaner(in)
Kommunikationselektroniker(in)
Industriedesigner(in)
PR-Berater(in)
Touristikfachwirt(in)
Lebensmittelkontrolleur(in)

SO SAGT MAN DAS!

Talking about what is important or not important

Schon bekannt

To talk about what is important to you, you may say:

> **Ich lege großen Wert darauf, daß ...**
> **Mir ist wichtig, daß ...**
> **Entscheidend für mich ist, daß ...**

To talk about what is not important to you, you may say:

> **Ich lege keinen großen Wert auf** ein
> großes Haus.
> **Ich lege keinen Wert darauf, daß** das
> Haus einen Pool hat.
> Ein großer Wagen **ist mir überhaupt
> nicht wichtig.**

22 Partner für die Zukunft

Was wäre für dich bei der Wahl eines Partners sehr wichtig, und worauf legst du keinen Wert?

a. Mach zuerst eine Liste mit Qualifikationen, die dein Partner oder deine Partnerin haben sollte!

b. Diskutier dann mit einem Klassenkameraden deine Vorstellungen von einem idealen Partner! Im Kasten rechts stehen ein paar Ideen.

humorvoll   kinderlieb

Nichtraucher   sportlich

gern reisen   s. für Musik interessieren

23 Hör gut zu!

For answers, see listening script on TE Interleaf.

Hör diesen Leuten zu, wie sie über ihre Zukunft reden! Welche Wünsche drücken sie aus? Was würden sie gern tun? Mach dir Notizen!

SO SAGT MAN DAS!

Hypothesizing

Schon bekannt

When making hypotheses, you can say:

> **Wenn ich** in Deutsch fleissiger **wäre, würde ich** eine Eins **bekommen.**
> **Wenn ich** mehr Geld **hätte, würde ich** nach Deutschland **ziehen.**
> **Wenn ich könnte, würde ich** gern
> Jura **studieren.**

What do these sentences mean? What does each one express?

24 Wenn das Wörtchen wenn nicht wär', ...

Ein deutsches Sprichwort heißt: „Wenn das Wörtchen wenn nicht wär', wär' mein Vater Millionär." — Nun, setzt euch alle zusammen, und sucht so viele Möglichkeiten wie ihr könnt, um folgende Sätze zu vollenden! Wenn möglich, gebt auch einen Grund für eure Antworten an!

BEISPIEL **Also, wenn ich gut fotografieren könnte, würde ich Werbefotograf werden, weil man dann viel Geld verdient.**

1. Also, wenn ich viel Geld hätte, ...
2. Wenn ich mehr Zeit hätte, ...
3. Wenn ich in (Mathe) eine Eins hätte, ...
4. Wenn ich zwei Fremdsprachen könnte, ...
5. Wenn ich einen guten Beruf hätte, ...
6. Wenn ich nicht so müde wäre, ...
7. Wenn ich jetzt nicht so schlampig angezogen wäre, ...
8. ...

25 Wenn ich ...

Welche Vorteile und welche Nachteile hättest du deiner Meinung nach, wenn du:
a. studieren würdest?
b. schon sehr jung heiraten würdest?
c. in ein anderes Land ziehen würdest?

Denk über diese Fragen nach, und mach dir Notizen! Such dir dann einen Partner, und diskutiert darüber, was jeder von euch aufgeschrieben hat! (Ihr dürft euch auch andere Themen aussuchen.)

ES IST DER GESCHMACK, DER DAS EINFACHE BESONDERS MACHT.

GEROLSTEINER · DER STERN GUTEN GESCHMACKS

Fotograf: Thomas Balzar

26 Für mein Notizbuch

Mach dir kurze Notizen über deine Zukunft! Was hast du schon beschlossen, und was weißt du noch nicht? Worauf legst du großen Wert und worauf weniger oder keinen Wert? Was würdest du gern tun, wenn du deine Zukunft so einrichten könntest, wie du möchtest?

27 Pläne diskutieren

Such dir einen Partner! Diskutiert eure Pläne für die Zukunft, und gebraucht dabei die Notizen, die ihr in eure Notizbücher geschrieben habt!

28

ROLLENSPIEL

Die Klasse soll sich in vier Gruppen teilen. Eine Gruppe spielt Berater an eurer Schule, die zweite Gruppe spielt Studenten im ersten Jahr (*freshmen*), die dritte Gruppe spielt Eltern, und der Rest spielt Schüler, die bald ihren Schulabschluß machen. Die Schüler sollen Fragen über ihre Zukunft vorbereiten, die anderen sollen sich typische Ratschläge ausdenken, die sie den Schülern geben können. Jeder Schüler geht dann zu einer Person in jeder der drei Gruppen und holt sich Rat. Wie unterscheiden sich die Ratschläge?

29 Textbilder

Seht euch diese Textbilder an! Experimentiert danach mit Buchstaben, und entwerft eure eigenen Textbilder!

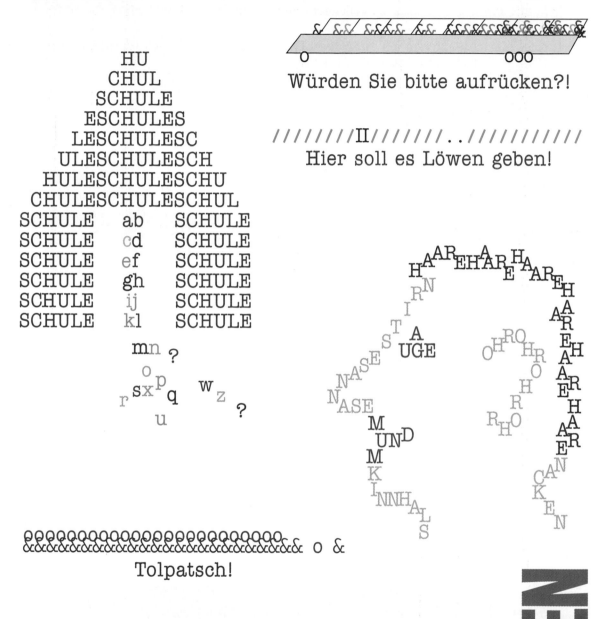

```
            HU
           CHUL
          SCHULE
         ESCHULES
        LESCHULESC
       ULESCHULESCH
      HULESCHULESCHU
     CHULESCHULESCHUL
SCHULE     ab     SCHULE
SCHULE     cd     SCHULE
SCHULE     ef     SCHULE
SCHULE     gh     SCHULE
SCHULE     ij     SCHULE
SCHULE     kl     SCHULE
           mn  ?
            o
           sx p     w
          r    q      z
              u          ?
```

Würden Sie bitte aufrücken?!

////////////II//////// ..///////////
Hier soll es Löwen geben!

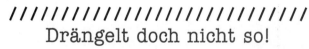

&&&&&&&&&&&&&&&&&&&&&&&&&&&&&&&&& o &
Tolpatsch!

//////////////////////////////
Drängelt doch nicht so!

Throughout this book you have been learning how to express yourself in German in more and more sophisticated and personal ways. You have also learned how to write in many different genres including journals, short stories, poems and songs, letters, speeches, and many others. In this activity, you will select the genre you enjoy the most and write a short autobiographical piece expressing something important about yourself.

Eine Selbstbiographie schreiben

Wähle ein Genre, das du gern hast, und schreib etwas Selbstbiographisches. Denk an etwas (an ein Ereignis, eine bestimmte Zeit, eine Person, ein Ding), was irgendwie in deinem Leben wichtig ist! Versuche, nicht nur Daten und Fakten aus deinem Leben aufzulisten, sondern beschreib auch deine Gefühle, Reaktionen, usw.!

SCHREIBTIP

Evaluating your writing
After you have conceived a plan and written several drafts, you should evaluate your writing by asking yourself questions which address many of the points you have learned throughout this book. Ask yourself, for example, whether the writing achieves a clear purpose, whether you have arranged your ideas in a coherent and effective way, and whether the tone and the choice of words is appropriate for your purpose and your audience. Don't worry about mechanical aspects of writing such as spelling, grammar and punctuation until you are satisfied with the content and structure of your writing. When you do finally proofread, focus carefully on each line and use reference guides to check your work.

A. Vorbereiten

1. Wähle ein Genre, das am besten zu deiner Persönlichkeit paßt!
2. Denk an dein Leben! Sieh dir alte Fotos, Dias, Tagebücher, persönliche Dokumente und Videos an! Welche wichtigen Ereignisse und Personen haben in deinem Leben eine bedeutende Rolle bei deiner persönlichen Entwicklung gespielt?
3. Mach eine Stichwortsammlung für deine Selbstbiographie, zum Beispiel in Form einer Inhaltsangabe oder einer Skizze! Wähle ein Organisationsprinzip! Willst du deine Biographie chronologisch oder thematisch organisieren?

B. Ausführen

Benutze die Stichwortsammlung, die Fotos und deine Erinnerungen, und schreib jetzt deine Selbstbiographie!
Vergiß nicht, daß du nicht nur persönliche Daten und Ereignisse wiedergeben sollst, sondern auch ein Porträt deiner Persönlichkeit vermitteln sollst. Beschreib dich, damit dich Unbekannte erkennen oder verstehen können!

C. Überarbeiten

1. Tausch deine Selbstbiographie mit der Biographie eines Klassenkameraden aus, ohne deinen Namen auf das Papier zu schreiben! Kann der Klassenkamerad dich in deiner Selbstbiographie erkennen? Kannst du ihn erkennen? Hast du dich treffend beschrieben?
2. Besprich deine Selbstbiographie mit einigen Klassenkameraden! Glauben sie, daß du ein passendes Genre gewählt hast?
3. Stell dir die folgenden Fragen: Hast du ein zentrales Thema deines Lebens dargestellt? Hast du die Ideen gut organisiert und einen geeigneten Ton gefunden? Ist die Sprache auf dem richtigen Niveau?
4. Wenn du mit dem Inhalt zufrieden bist, überprüfe Rechtschreibung und Grammatik!
5. Schreib deine korrigierte Selbstbiographie noch einmal auf ein reines Blatt Papier! Füge Fotos oder sonstige Illustrationen hinzu, die zu deiner Selbstbiographie passen!

Der hellgraue Frühjahrsmantel
von Wolfgang Hildesheimer

Vor zwei Monaten — wir saßen gerade beim Frühstück — kam ein Brief von meinem Vetter Eduard. Mein Vetter Eduard hatte an einem Frühlingsabend vor zwölf Jahren das Haus verlassen, um, wie er behauptete, einen Brief in den Kasten zu stecken, und war nicht zurückgekehrt. Seitdem hatte niemand etwas von ihm gehört. Der Brief kam aus Sydney in Australien. Ich öffnete ihn und las:

> Lieber Paul!
> Könntest Du mir meinen hellgrauen Frühjahrsmantel nachschicken? Ich kann ihn nämlich brauchen, da es hier oft empfindlich kalt ist, vor allem nachts. In der linken Tasche ist ein „Taschenbuch für Pilzsammler." Das kannst Du herausnehmen und behalten. Eßbare Pilze gibt es hier nämlich nicht. Im voraus vielen Dank.
>
> Herzlichst Dein Eduard

Ich sagte zu meiner Frau: „Ich habe einen Brief von meinem Vetter Eduard aus Australien bekommen." Sie war gerade dabei, den Tauchsieder in die Blumenvase zu stecken, um Eier darin zu kochen, und fragte: „So? Was schreibt er?"

Daß er seinen hellgrauen Mantel braucht und daß es in Australien keine eßbaren Pilze gibt. — „Dann soll er doch etwas anderes essen", sagte sie. — „Da hast du recht", sagte ich.

Später kam der Klavierstimmer. Er war ein etwas schüchterner und zerstreuter Mann, ein wenig weltfremd sogar, aber er war sehr nett, und natürlich sehr musikalisch. Er stimmte

nicht nur Klaviere, sondern reparierte auch Saiteninstrumente und erteilte Blockflötenunterricht. Er hieß Kolhaas. Als ich vom Tisch aufstand, hörte ich ihn schon im Nebenzimmer Akkorde anschlagen.

In der Garderobe sah ich den hellgrauen Mantel hängen. Meine Frau hatte ihn also schon vom Speicher geholt. Das wunderte mich, denn gewöhnlich tut meine Frau die Dinge erst dann, wenn es gleichgültig geworden ist, ob sie getan sind oder nicht. Ich packte den Mantel sorgfältig ein, trug das Paket zur Post und schickte es ab. Erst dann fiel mir ein, daß ich vergessen hatte, das Pilzbuch herauszunehmen. Aber ich bin kein Pilzsammler.

Ich ging noch ein wenig spazieren, und als ich nach Hause kam, irrten der Klavierstimmer und meine Frau in der Wohnung umher und schauten in die Schränke und unter die Tische.

„Kann ich helfen?" fragte ich.

„Wir suchen Herrn Kolhaas' Mantel", sagte meine Frau.

„Ach so", sagte ich, meines Irrtums bewußt, „den habe ich soeben nach Australien geschickt." — „Warum nach Australien?" fragte meine Frau. „Aus Versehen", sagte ich. „Dann will ich nicht weiter stören", sagte Herr Kolhaas, etwas betreten, wenn auch nicht besonders erstaunt, und wollte sich entschuldigen, aber ich sagte: „Warten Sie, Sie können dafür den Mantel von meinem Vetter bekommen."

Ich ging auf den Speicher und fand dort in einem verstaubten Koffer den hellgrauen Mantel meines Vetters. Er war etwas zerknittert — schließlich hatte er zwölf Jahre im Koffer gelegen — aber sonst in gutem Zustand.

Meine Frau bügelte ihn noch ein wenig auf, während ich mit

3. Before you make your final choice of strategies, discuss some of your ideas with your classmates and find out which strategies they find useful.

4. Before reading, make sure you understand how to apply the stategies you've chosen and what kind of information you will gain from each.

A Closer Look

After you have worked with the story, check your comprehension by answering the following questions.

5. Was hat Eduard vor zwölf Jahren getan? Warum erwähnt der Erzähler ihn überhaupt? Was will Eduard?

6. Was schickt der Erzähler nach Australien und warum?

Herrn Kolhaas ein Glas Sherry trank und er mir von einigen Klavieren erzählte, die er gestimmt hatte. Dann zog er ihn an, verabschiedete sich und ging.

Wenige Tage später erhielten wir ein Paket. Darin waren Steinpilze, etwa ein Kilo. Auf den Pilzen lagen zwei Briefe. Ich öffnete den ersten und las:

Lieber Herr Holle, (so heiße ich) da Sie so liebenswürdig waren, mir ein „Taschenbuch für Pilzsammler" in die Tasche zu stecken, möchte ich Ihnen als Dank das Resultat meiner ersten Pilzsuche zuschicken und hoffe, daß es Ihnen schmecken wird. Außerdem fand ich in der anderen Tasche einen Brief, den Sie mir wohl irrtümlich mitgegeben haben. Ich schicke ihn hiermit zurück.

Ergebenst Ihr A. M. Kolhaas

Der Brief, um den es sich hier handelte, war also wohl der, den mein Vetter damals in den Kasten stecken wollte. Offenbar hatte er ihn dann mitsamt dem Mantel zu Hause vergessen. Er war an Herrn Bernhard Haase gerichtet, der, wie ich mich erinnerte, ein Freund meines Vetters gewesen war. Ich öffnete den Umschlag. Eine Theaterkarte und ein Zettel fielen heraus. Auf dem Zettel stand:

Lieber Bernhard! Ich schicke Dir eine Karte zu „Tannhäuser" nächsten Montag, von der ich keinen Gebrauch machen werde, da ich

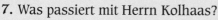

7. Was passiert mit Herrn Kolhaas?

8. Was schickt Herr Kolhaas dem Erzähler und seiner Frau? Warum?

9. Was findet Herr Kolhaas noch im Mantel? Für wen war das bestimmt? Warum war es noch im Mantel?

10. Was meint Eduard über den Mantel, den er bekam? Was will er noch von seinem Cousin haben?

11. Wie reagiert die Frau des Erzählers auf die Briefe?

12. Discuss the story with your classmates. Find out what they thought it was about. Which strategies did they find useful? Which strategies allowed each of you to enjoy the story most and get the most out of it?

verreisen möchte, um ein wenig auszuspannen. Vielleicht hast Du Lust, hinzugehen. Die Schmidt-Hohlweg singt die Elisabeth. Du schwärmst doch immer so von ihrem hohen Gis.

Herzliche Grüße, Dein Eduard

Zum Mittagessen gab es Steinpilze. „Die Pilze habe ich hier auf dem Tisch gefunden. Wo kommen sie eigentlich her?" fragte meine Frau. „Herr Kolhaas hat sie uns geschickt." — „Wie nett von ihm. Es wäre doch gar nicht nötig gewesen."

„Nötig nicht", sagte ich, „aber er ist eben sehr nett."

„Hoffentlich sind sie nicht giftig. — Übrigens habe ich auch eine Theaterkarte gefunden. Was wird denn gespielt?"

„Die Karte, die du gefunden hast", sagte ich, „ist zu einer Aufführung von ‚Tannhäuser', aber die war vor zwölf Jahren!" — „Na ja", sagte meine Frau, „zu ‚Tannhäuser' hätte ich ohnehin keine große Lust gehabt."

Heute morgen kam wieder ein Brief von Eduard mit der Bitte, ihm eine Tenorblockflöte zu schicken. Er habe nämlich in dem Mantel (der übrigens seltsamerweise länger geworden sei, es sei denn, er selbst sei kürzer geworden) ein Buch zur Erlernung des Blockflötenspiels gefunden und gedenke, davon Gebrauch zu machen. Aber Blockflöten seien in Australien nicht erhältlich.

„Wieder ein Brief von Eduard", sagte ich zu meiner Frau. Sie war gerade dabei, die Kaffeemühle auseinanderzunehmen und fragte: „Was schreibt er?" — „Daß es in Australien keine Blockflöten gibt." — „Dann soll er doch ein anderes Instrument spielen", sagte sie.

„Das finde ich auch", meinte ich.

Meine Frau ist von erfrischender, entwaffnender Sachlichkeit. Ihre Repliken sind zwar nüchtern aber erschöpfend.

13. Reread the story with the following question in mind: Which actions or dialogues deviate from what you would consider to be "normal" reactions or responses? For example, what do you expect to be in the first letter from the cousin? Are your expectations met? How do these instances make the story humorous?

14. Erzähl die Geschichte zusammen mit deinen Klassenkameraden nach! Fang die Geschichte mit einem Satz an, und eine Klassenkameradin erzählt weiter, indem sie einen neuen Satz hinzufügt. Jeder kommt einmal dran, bis die Geschichte zu Ende ist. Verwende ordnende Zeitausdrücke (**zuerst, dann usw.**) in der Nacherzählung!

KANN ICH'S WIRKLICH?

1 How would you respond if someone said to you **Erzähl mir alles, was du in den letzten Ferien gemacht hast!**? E.g.: In meinen letzten Ferien hatte ich einen Ferienjob im Supermarkt.

2 How would you respond if
a. a friend said **Meine Tante Anna hat mir 20 000 Mark zum Geburtstag geschenkt**? E.g.: Ich bin überrascht, daß sie dir so viel Geld geschenkt hat.
b. you heard that one of your friends takes drugs (**Drogen**)? E.g.: Ich bin enttäuscht, daß er/sie Drogen nimmt.

3 How would you agree with someone who said **Wir schauen zuviel Fernsehen, anstatt zu lesen**? E. g.: Bei uns ist es auch so.

4 How would you agree, but with reservations, if someone said **Wer Geld hat, hat auch Freunde**? E.g.: Es kommt darauf an. Manchen Freunden ist Geld egal.

5 How would you respond if a friend said to you **Ich weiß nicht mehr, was ich machen soll; ich bekomme immer schlechte Noten**? E.g.: Vielleicht kannst du etwas mehr lernen.

6 How would you tell someone that he or she should exercise and why? How would you give your own reason for exercising regularly? E.g.: Du solltest mehr Sport treiben, weil er dich fit hält.; Ich treibe viel Sport, um wirklich fit zu bleiben.

7 How would you say
a. what you're determined to do after high school? a. E.g.: Ich hab' mich entschieden, nach der Schule Biologie zu studieren.
b. that you're not yet sure what you'll do? b. E.g.: Ich weiß noch nicht, was ich nach der Schule machen soll.

8 How would you tell a friend
a. what is important to you? E.g.: Mir ist wichtig, gesund zu essen.
b. what is not important? E.g.: Ich lege keinen großen Wert auf modische Klamotten.

9 How would you respond if someone asked you **Was würdest du tun, wenn du Millionär wärst?** E.g.: Wenn ich Millionär wäre, würde ich eine Weltreise machen.

ERSTE STUFE
PROFESSIONS

Schornsteinfeger(in), -/nen
chimney sweep
Steuerberater(in), -/nen
tax consultant
Rundfunksprecher(in), -/nen
radio announcer
Toningenieur(in), -e/nen
sound engineer
Friseur/Friseuse, -e/n *hair stylist*
Schweißer(in), -/nen
welder
Schreiner(in), -/nen
cabinet maker

Glasbläser(in), -/nen *glass blower*
Anästhesist(in), -en/nen
anesthesiologist
Elektroinstallateur(in), -e/nen
electrician
Fotograf(in), -en/nen
photographer
Koch (Köchin), ⁼e/nen *chef*
Optiker(in), -/nen *optician*
Schuhmacher(in), -/nen
shoemaker
technische(r) Zeichner(in),
-/nen *technical designer*
Winzer(in), -/nen *vintner*

der Zahnarzt, ⁼e *dentist*
die Zahnärztin, -nen (female)
dentist
der Zimmermann, -leute
carpenter

OTHER USEFUL WORDS

die Niete, -n *failure (in a subject)*
die Diät, -en *diet*
das Kostüm, -e *costume*

führen *to lead*

ZWEITE STUFE
MODERN PROFESSIONS

Zahntechniker(in), -/nen
dental technician
Strafverteidiger(in), -/nen
lawyer for the defense
Gesundheitswissenschaftler(in),
-/nen *nutritional scientist*
Sportökonom(in), -en/nen
sports scientist
Umweltökonom(in), -en/nen
environmental scientist
Mediaplaner(in), -/nen
media planner
Kommunikationselektroniker
(in), -/nen *communications engineer*

Industriedesigner(in), -/nen *industrial designer*
PR-Berater(in), -/nen
PR-consultant
Touristikfachwirt(in), -e/nen
tourism specialist
Lebensmittelkontrolleur(in),
-e/nen *health inspector*

OTHER USEFUL WORDS

die Ehe, -n *marriage*
die Scheidung, -en *divorce*
der Erfolg, -e *success*

der Konflikt, -e *conflict*
die Chance, -n *chance*

ziehen *to move (residence)*
unterdrücken *to oppress*
gründen *to found*
s. anstrengen (sep) *to make an effort*
einengen (sep) *to confine*

finanziell *financially*
im Fall *in the case (of)*
sicherlich *certainly*

SUMMARY OF FUNCTIONS

Functions are probably best defined as the ways in which you use a language for specific purposes. When you find yourself in specific situations, such as in a restaurant, in a grocery store, or at school, you will want to communicate with those around you. In order to do that, you have to "function" in the language so that you can be understood: you place an order, make a purchase, or talk about your class schedule.

Such functions form the core of this book. They are easily identified by the boxes in each chapter that are labeled SO SAGT MAN DAS! These functions are the building blocks you need to become a speaker of German. All the other features in the chapter—the grammar, the vocabulary, even the culture notes—are there to support the functions you are learning.

Here is a list of the functions from Levels 1, 2, and 3 accompanied by the German expressions you will need in order to communicate in a wide range of situations. The level of the book is indicated by a Roman numeral I, II, or III. The chapter and page on which the expressions were introduced is also indicated.

You have learned to communicate in a variety of situations. Using these expressions, you will be able to communicate in many other situations as well.

SOCIALIZING

Saying hello
I, Ch. 1, p. 21

Guten Morgen!
Guten Tag!
Morgen! ⎤
Tag! ⎦ *shortened forms*
Hallo! ⎤
Grüß dich! ⎦ *informal*

Saying goodbye
I, Ch. 1, p. 21

Auf Wiedersehen!
Wiedersehen! *shortened form*
Tschüs! ⎤
Tschau! ⎥ *informal*
Bis dann! ⎦

Offering something to eat and drink
I, Ch. 3, p. 70

Was möchtest du trinken?
Was möchte *(name)* trinken?
Was möchtet ihr essen?

Responding to an offer
I, Ch. 3, p. 70

Ich möchte *(beverage)* trinken.
Er/Sie möchte im Moment gar nichts.
Wir möchten *(food/beverage)*, bitte.

Saying please
I, Ch. 3, p. 72

Bitte!

Saying thank you
I, Ch. 3, p. 72

Danke!
Danke schön!
Danke sehr!

Saying you're welcome
I, Ch. 3, p. 72

Bitte!
Bitte schön!
Bitte sehr!

Giving compliments
I, Ch. 5, p. 127

Der/Die/Das *(thing)* sieht *(adjective)* aus!
Der/Die/Das *(thing)* gefällt mir.
II, Ch. 8, p. 194
Dein/Deine *(clothing item)* sieht echt fetzig aus.
Sie/Er/Es paßt dir auch echt gut.
Und dieser/diese/dieses *(clothing item)* paßt dir prima!
Sie/Er/Es paßt gut zu deiner/deinem *(clothing item)*.

Responding to compliments
I, Ch. 5, p. 127

Ehrlich?
Wirklich?
Nicht zu *(adjective)*?
Meinst du?
II, Ch. 8, p. 193
Meinst du wirklich?
Ist er/sie/es mir nicht zu *(adjective)*?
Das ist auch mein/meine Lieblings*(clothing item)*.
Echt?

Starting a conversation
I, Ch. 6, p. 145

Wie geht's?	
Wie geht's denn?	*Asking how someone is doing*
Sehr gut!	
Prima!	
Danke, gut!	
Gut!	
Danke, es geht.	
So lala.	*Responding to* **Wie geht's?**
Nicht schlecht.	
Nicht so gut.	
Schlecht.	
Sehr schlecht.	
Miserabel.	

Making plans
I, Ch. 6, p. 150

Was willst du machen?	Ich will *(activity)*.
Wohin will *(person)* gehen?	Er/Sie will in/ins *(place)* gehen.

Ordering food and beverages
I, Ch. 6, p. 154

Was bekommen Sie?	Ich bekomme *(food/beverage)*.
Ja, bitte?	
Was essen Sie?	Einen/Eine/Ein *(food)*, bitte.
Was möchten Sie?	Ich möchte *(food/beverage)*, bitte.
Was trinken Sie?	Ich trinke *(beverage)*.
Was nimmst du?	Ich nehme *(food/beverage)*.
Was ißt du?	Ich esse *(food)*.

II, Ch. 11, p. 274

Haben Sie schon gewählt?	Ja, bringen Sie mir bitte den/die/das *(menu item)*.
Und was hätten Sie gern?	Ich hätte gern den/die/das *(menu item)*.

Talking about how something tastes
I, Ch. 6, p. 156

Wie schmeckt's?	Gut!
	Prima!
	Sagenhaft!
	Der/Die/Das *(food/beverage)* schmeckt lecker!
	Der/Die/Das *(food/beverage)* schmeckt nicht.
Schmeckt's?	Ja, gut!
	Nein, nicht so gut.
	Nicht besonders.

Paying the check
I, Ch. 6, p. 156

Hallo! Ich will/ möchte zahlen.	Das macht (zusammen) *(total)*.
Stimmt schon!	

Extending an invitation
I, Ch. 7, p. 174; Ch. 11, p. 277

Willst du *(activity)*?
Wir wollen *(activity)*. Komm doch mit!
Möchtest du mitkommen?
Ich habe am *(day/date)* eine Party. Ich lade dich ein. Kannst du kommen?

Responding to an invitation
I, Ch. 7, p. 174; Ch. 11, p. 277

Ja, gern!	
Toll!	
Ich komme gern mit.	*accepting*
Aber sicher!	
Natürlich!	
Das geht nicht.	*declining*
Ich kann leider nicht.	

Accepting with certainty
III, Ch. 11, p. 269

Ja, natürlich!
Ganz bestimmt.
Auf jeden Fall.
Auf alle Fälle.

Refusing with certainty
III, Ch. 11, p. 269

Nein, tut mir leid.
Kommt nicht in Frage!
Auf keinen Fall.

Expressing obligations
I, Ch. 7, p. 175

Ich habe keine Zeit. Ich muß *(activity)*.

Offering help
I, Ch. 7, p. 179

Was kann ich für dich tun?	
Kann ich etwas für dich tun?	*asking*
Brauchst du Hilfe?	
Gut! Mach' ich!	*agreeing*

Asking what you should do
I, Ch. 8, p. 198

Was soll ich für dich tun?	Du kannst für mich *(chore)*.
Wo soll ich *(thing/things)* kaufen?	Beim (Metzger/Bäcker). In der/Im *(store)*.
Soll ich *(thing/things)* in der/im *(store)* kaufen?	Nein, das kannst du besser in der/im *(store)* kaufen.

Getting someone's attention
I, Ch. 9, p. 222

Verzeihung!
Entschuldigung!

Offering more
I, Ch. 9, p. 230

> Möchtest du noch etwas?
> Möchtest du noch einen/eine/ein *(food/beverage)*?
> Noch einen/eine/ein *(food/beverage)*?

Saying you want more
I, Ch. 9, p. 230

> Ja, bitte. Ich nehme noch einen/eine/ein
> *(food/beverage)*.
> Ja, bitte. Noch einen/eine/ein *(food/beverage)*.
> Ja, gern.

Saying you don't want more
I, Ch. 9, p. 230

> Nein, danke! Ich habe keinen Hunger mehr.
> Nein, danke! Ich habe genug.
> Danke, nichts mehr für mich.
> Nein, danke, keinen/keine/kein *(food/beverage)* mehr.

Using the telephone
I, Ch. 11, p. 274

> Hier *(name)*.
> Hier ist *(name)*.
> Ich möchte bitte *(name)*
> sprechen.   *starting a conversation*
> Kann ich bitte *(name)*
> sprechen?
> Tag! Hier ist *(name)*.
> Wiederhören!
> Auf Wiederhören! *ending a conversation*
> Tschüs!

Talking about birthdays
I, Ch. 11, p. 278

> Wann hast du Geburtstag?   Ich habe am *(date)*
>   Geburtstag.
>   Am *(date)*.

Expressing good wishes
I, Ch. 11, p. 278

> Alles Gute zum/zur *(occasion)*!
> Herzlichen Glückwunsch zum/zur *(occasion)*!

II, Ch. 11, p. 275

> Zum Wohl!
> Prost!
> Auf dein/euer/Ihr Wohl!
> Guten Appetit!
> Mahlzeit!

Changing the subject
III, Ch. 6, p. 136

> Ich möchte noch mal auf *(topic)* zurückkommen.
> Übrigens, ich wollte etwas anderes sagen.

Interrupting
III, Ch. 6, p. 136

> Laß mich mal zu Wort kommen!
> Moment mal! Laß *(person)* mal ausreden!

Making polite requests
III, Ch. 9, p. 211

> Könnte ich bitte ...?
> Dürfte ich bitte ...?
> Würden Sie bitte ...?

EXCHANGING INFORMATION

Asking someone his or her name and giving yours
I, Ch. 1, p. 22

> Wie heißt du?   Ich heiße *(name)*.
> Heißt du *(name)*?   Ja, ich heiße *(name)*.

Asking and giving someone else's name
I, Ch. 1, p. 22

> Wie heißt der Junge?   Der Junge heißt *(name)*.
> Heißt der Junge *(name)*? Ja, er heißt *(name)*.
> Wie heißt das Mädchen?   Das Mädchen heißt
>   *(name)*.
> Heißt das Mädchen *(name)*? Nein, sie heißt *(name)*.

Asking and telling who someone is
I, Ch. 1, p. 23

> Wer ist das?   Das ist der/die *(name)*.

Asking someone his or her age and giving yours
I, Ch. 1, p. 25

> Wie alt bist du?   Ich bin *(number)* Jahre alt.
>   Ich bin *(number)*.
>   *(Number)*.
> Bist du schon *(number)*? Nein, ich bin *(number)*.

Asking and giving someone else's age
I, Ch. 1, p. 25

> Wie alt ist der Peter?   Er ist *(number)*.
> Und die Monika? Ist
> sie auch *(number)*?   Ja, sie ist auch *(number)*.

Asking someone where he or she is from and telling where you are from
I, Ch. 1, p. 28

> Woher kommst du?   Ich komme aus *(place)*.
> Woher bist du?   Ich bin aus *(place)*.
> Bist du aus *(place)*? Nein, ich bin aus *(place)*.

Asking and telling where someone else is from
I, Ch. 1, p. 28

> Woher ist *(person)*?   Er/Sie ist aus *(place)*.
> Kommt *(person)* aus *(place)*? Nein, sie kommt aus
>   *(place)*.

Talking about how someone gets to school
I, Ch. 1, p. 31

Wie kommst du
zur Schule?   Ich komme mit der/dem
(mode of transportation).

Kommt Ahmet zu Fuß
zur Schule?   Nein, er kommt auch mit
der/dem *(mode of
transportation)*.

Wie kommt Ayla
zur Schule?   Sie kommt mit der/dem
(mode of transportation).

Talking about interests
I, Ch. 2, p. 46

Was machst du in
deiner Freizeit?   Ich *(activity)*.
Spielst du *(sport/
instrument/game)*?   Ja, ich spiele *(sport/
instrument/game)*.
Nein, *(sport/instrument/
game)* spiele ich nicht.
Was macht *(name)*?   Er/Sie spielt *(sport/
instrument/game)*.

Asking about interests
II, Ch. 8, p. 193; Ch. 10, p. 240

Interessierst du dich für *(thing)*?
Wofür interessierst du dich?
Was für Interessen hast du?

Expressing interest
II, Ch. 8, p. 193; Ch. 10, p. 240

Ja, *(thing)* interessiert mich.
Ich interessiere mich für *(thing)*.

Expressing disinterest
II, Ch. 8, p. 193

(Thing) interessiert mich nicht.
Ich hab' kein Interesse an *(thing)*.

Expressing indifference
II, Ch. 8, p. 193

(Thing) ist mir egal.

Saying when you do various activities
I, Ch. 2, p. 53

Was machst du nach
der Schule?   Am Nachmittag *(activity)*.
Am Abend *(activity)*.
Und am Wochenende?   Am Wochenende *(activity)*.
Was machst du im
Sommer?   Im Sommer *(activity)*.

Talking about where you and others live
I, Ch. 3, p. 69

Wo wohnst du?   Ich wohne in *(place)*.
In *(place)*.

Wo wohnt
der/die *(name)*?   Er/Sie wohnt in *(place)*.
In *(place)*.

Describing a room
I, Ch. 3, p. 75

Der/Die/Das *(thing)* ist alt.
Der/Die/Das *(thing)* ist kaputt.
Der/Die/Das *(thing)* ist klein,
aber ganz bequem.
Ist *(thing)* neu?   Ja, er/sie/es ist neu.

Talking about family members
I, Ch. 3, p. 78

Ist das dein/deine
(family member)?   Ja, das ist mein/
meine *(family
member)*.

Und dein/deine *(family
member)*? Wie heißt er/sie?   Er/Sie heißt *(name)*.
Wo wohnen deine
(family members)?   In *(place)*.

Describing people
I, Ch. 3, p. 80

Wie sieht *(person)* aus?   Er/Sie hat *(color)* Haare und
(color) Augen.

Talking about class schedules
I, Ch. 4, p. 98

Welche Fächer hast du?   Ich habe *(classes)*.
Was hast du am *(day)*?   *(Classes)*.
Was hat die Katja am *(day)*?   Sie hat *(classes)*.
Welche Fächer habt ihr?   Wir haben *(classes)*.
Was habt ihr nach der Pause?   Wir haben *(classes)*.
Und was habt ihr am Samstag?   Wir haben frei!

Using a schedule to talk about time
I, Ch. 4, p. 99

Wann hast du *(class)*?   Um *(hour)* Uhr *(minutes)*.
Was hast du um
(hour) Uhr?   *(Class)*.
Was hast du von *(time)*
bis *(time)*?   Ich habe *(class)*.

Sequencing events
I, Ch. 4, p. 101

Welche Fächer hast
du am *(day)*?   Zuerst hab' ich *(class)*, dann
(class), danach *(class)*, und
zuletzt *(class)*.

Talking about prices
I, Ch. 4, p. 107

Was kostet *(thing)*?   Er/Sie kostet nur *(price)*.
Was kosten *(things)*?   Sie kosten *(price)*.
Das ist (ziemlich) teuer!
Das ist (sehr) billig!
Das ist (sehr) preiswert!

Pointing things out
I, Ch. 4, p. 108

Wo sind die *(things)*? Schauen Sie!
Dort!
Sie sind dort drüben!
Sie sind da hinten.
Sie sind da vorn.

Expressing wishes when shopping
I, Ch. 5, p. 122

Was möchten Sie?	Ich möchte einen/eine/ein *(thing)* sehen, bitte.
	Ich brauche einen/eine/ein *(thing)*.
Was bekommen Sie?	Einen/Eine/Ein *(thing)*, bitte.
Haben Sie einen Wunsch?	Ich suche einen/eine/ein *(thing)*.

Describing how clothes fit
I, Ch. 5, p. 125

Es paßt prima.
Es paßt nicht.

Talking about trying on clothes
I, Ch. 5, p. 131

Ich probiere den/die/das *(item of clothing)* an.
Ich ziehe den/die/das *(item of clothing)* an.

If you buy it:	*If you don't:*
Ich nehme es.	Ich nehme es nicht.
Ich kaufe es.	Ich kaufe es nicht.

Telling time
I, Ch. 6, p. 146

Wie spät ist es jetzt?	Es ist *(time)*.
Wieviel Uhr ist es?	Es ist *(time)*.

Talking about when you do things
I, Ch. 6, p. 146

Wann gehst du *(activity)*?	Um *(time)*.
Um wieviel Uhr *(action)* du?	Um *(time)*.
Und du? Wann *(action)* du?	Um *(time)*.

Talking about how often you do things
I, Ch. 7, p. 178

Wie oft *(action)* du?	(Einmal) in der Woche.
Und wie oft mußt du *(action)*?	Jeden Tag.
	Ungefähr (zweimal) im Monat.

Explaining what to do
I, Ch. 7, p. 179

Du kannst für mich *(action)*.

Talking about the weather
I, Ch. 7, p. 183

Wie ist das Wetter heute?	Heute regnet es.
	Wolkig und kühl.
Wie ist das Wetter morgen?	Sonnig, aber kalt.

Regnet es heute?	Ich glaube schon.
Schneit es am Abend?	Nein, es schneit nicht.
Wieviel Grad haben wir heute?	Ungefähr 10 Grad.

Talking about quantities
I, Ch. 8, p. 202

Wieviel *(food item)* bekommen Sie?	500 Gramm *(food item)*.
	100 Gramm, bitte.

Asking if someone wants anything else
I, Ch. 8, p. 203

Sonst noch etwas?
Was bekommen Sie noch?
Haben Sie noch einen Wunsch?

Saying you want something else
I, Ch. 8, p. 203

Ich brauche noch einen/eine/ein *(food/beverage/thing)*.
Ich bekomme noch einen/eine/ein *(food/beverage/thing)*.

Telling someone you don't need anything else
I, Ch. 8, p. 203

Nein, danke.
Danke, das ist alles.

Giving a reason
I, Ch. 8, p. 206

Jetzt kann ich nicht, weil ...
Es geht nicht, denn ...

III, Ch. 3, p. 67

..., weil ich ...
..., damit ...
..., um ... zu ...

Saying where you were
I, Ch. 8, p. 207

Wo warst du heute morgen?	Ich war in/im/an/am *(place)*.
Wo warst du gestern?	Ich war in/im/an/am *(place)*.

Saying what you bought
I, Ch. 8, p. 207

Was hast du gekauft?	Ich habe *(thing)* gekauft.

Talking about where something is located
I, Ch. 9, p. 222

Verzeihung, wissen Sie, wo der/die/das *(place)* ist?	In der Innenstadt.
	Am *(place name)*.
	In der *(street name)*.
Wo ist der/die/das *(place)*?	Es tut mir leid. Das weiß ich nicht.
Entschuldigung! Weißt du, wo der/die/das *(place)* ist?	Keine Ahnung! Ich bin nicht von hier.

Asking for directions
I, Ch. 9, p. 226

> Wie komme ich zum/zur *(place)*?
> Wie kommt man zum/zur *(place)*?

II, Ch. 9, p. 222

> Entschuldigung! Wo ist bitte *(place)*.
> Verzeihung! Wissen Sie vielleicht, wie ich zum/zur
> *(place)* komme?

Giving directions
I, Ch. 9, p. 226

> Gehen Sie geradeaus bis zum/zur *(place)*.
> Nach rechts/links.
> Hier rechts/links.

II, Ch. 9, p. 222

> Sie biegen hier *(direction)* in die *(streetname)* ein.
> Dann kommen Sie zum/zur *(place)*.
> Das ist hier *(direction)* um die Ecke.
> Ich weiß es leider nicht. Ich bin nicht von hier.

Talking about what there is to eat and drink
I, Ch. 9, p. 229

> Was gibt es hier zu essen?   Es gibt *(foods)*.
> Und zu trinken?   Es gibt *(beverage)* und
>   auch *(beverage)*.

Talking about what you did in your free time
I, Ch. 10, p. 260

> Was hast du *(time
>   phrase)* gemacht?   Ich habe ...
>   *(person/thing)* gesehen.
>   *(book, magazine, etc.)*
>   gelesen.
>   mit *(person)* über *(subject)*
>   gesprochen.

Discussing gift ideas
I, Ch. 11, p. 282

> Schenkst du *(person)*
>   einen/eine/ein *(thing)*
>   zum/zur *(occasion)*?   Nein, ich schenke ihm/ihr
>   einen/eine/ein *(thing)*.
>
> Was schenkst du *(person)*
>   zum/zur *(occasion)*?   Ich weiß noch nicht. Hast
>   du eine Idee?
>
> Wem schenkst du
>   den/die/das *(thing)*?   Ich schenke *(person)*
>   den/die/das *(thing)*.

Asking about past events
II, Ch. 3, p. 57; Ch. 3, p. 62

> Was hast du *(time phrase)* gemacht?
> Was hat *(person)* *(time phrase)* gemacht?

Asking what someone did
II, Ch. 3, p. 57

> Was hast du *(time phrase)* gemacht?
> Was hat *(person)* *(time phrase)* gemacht?

Telling what someone did
II, Ch. 3, p. 57

> Ich habe *(activity + past participle)*.
> Er/Sie hat *(activity + past participle)*.

Asking where someone was
II, Ch. 3, p. 63

> Wo bist du gewesen?
> Und wo warst du?

Telling where you were
II, Ch. 3, p. 63

> Ich bin in/im/an/am *(place)* gewesen.
> Ich war in/im/an/am *(place)*.
> Ich war mit *(person)* in/im/an/am *(place)*.

Asking for information
II, Ch. 4, p. 95; Ch. 10, p. 248

> Ich habe eine Frage: ...?
> Sag mal, ...?
> Wie steht's mit *(thing)*?
> Darf ich dich etwas fragen? ...?
> Wissen Sie, ob ...?
> Können Sie mir sagen, ob ...?

Stating information
II, Ch. 10, p. 248

> Ich glaube schon, daß ...
> Ich meine doch, daß ...

Responding emphatically
II, Ch. 4, p. 95

> Ja, natürlich!
> Na klar!
> Aber sicher!

Agreeing with reservations
II. Ch. 4, p. 95

> Ja, das kann sein, aber ...
> Das stimmt, aber ...
> Eigentlich schon, aber ...

Asking what someone may or may not do
II, Ch. 4, p. 98

> Was darfst du (nicht) tun?
> Was darfst du (nicht) essen/trinken?
> Darfst du *(activity)*?

Telling what you may or may not do
II, Ch. 4, p. 98

> Ich darf (nicht) *(activity)*.
> Ich darf *(food/drink)* (nicht) essen/trinken.

Expressing skepticism
II, Ch. 5, p. 114

> Was soll denn das sein, dieser/diese/dieses *(thing)*?

Making certain
II, Ch. 5, p. 113

Du ißt nur vegetarisch, was?	Ja/Nein.
Du ißt wohl viel Fleisch, ja?	Nicht unbedingt!
Du magst Joghurt, oder?	Na klar!
Du magst doch Quark, nicht wahr?	Sicher!

Calling someone's attention to something and responding
II, Ch. 5, p. 118

Schau mal!	Ja, was denn?
Guck mal!	Ja, was bitte?
Sieh mal!	Was ist denn los?
Hör mal!	Was ist?
Hör mal zu!	Was gibt's?

Asking for specific information
II, Ch. 5, p. 123

Welchen/Welche/Welches (thing) magst du?	Ich mag (thing).
Welchen/Welche/Welches (thing) willst du?	Diesen/Diese/Dieses (thing), bitte!

Inquiring about someone's health
II, Ch. 6, p. 137

Wie fühlst du dich?
Wie geht es dir?
Ist dir nicht gut?
Ist was mit dir?
Was fehlt dir?

Responding to questions about your health
II, Ch. 6, p. 137

Ich fühl' mich wohl!
Es geht mir (nicht) gut!
Mir ist schlecht
Mir ist nicht gut.

Responding to statements about someone's health
II, Ch. 6, p. 137

Ach schade!
Gute Besserung!
Hoffentlich geht es dir bald besser!

Asking about pain
II, Ch. 6, p. 143

Tut's weh?
Was tut dir weh?
Tut dir was weh?
Tut dir (body part) weh?

Expressing pain
II, Ch. 6, p. 143

Au!
Aua!
Es tut weh!
Der/Die/Das (body part) tut mir weh.
Ja, ich hab' (body part) schmerzen.

Expressing wishes
II, Ch. 7, p. 168

Was möchtest du gern mal haben?	Ich möchte gern mal einen/eine/ein (thing)!
Was wünschst du dir mal?	Ich wünsche mir mal ...
Und was wünscht ihr euch?	Wir wünschen uns ...

III, Ch. 11, p. 269

(Thing) wäre mir (nicht) wichtig.
In meiner idealen Welt gäbe es (kein/en/e) (thing).

Talking about plans
II, Ch. 10, p. 252

Ich werde (activity).
(Time phrase) werde ich (activity).

Expressing hearsay
II, Ch. 11, p. 270

Ich habe gehört, daß ...
Man hat mir gesagt, daß ...
(Thing) soll (adjective) sein.

Admitting something
III, Ch. 3, p. 68

Ich geb's zu.
Ich geb's zu, daß ich ...
Ich muß zugeben, daß ...

Reporting past events
III, Ch. 5, p. 116; Ch. 6, p. 134

Wir haben letzten Monat einen Bundeswehroffizier eingeladen. Die Diskussion war sehr interessant, und wir konnten uns gut informieren. Wir wollten noch mehr hören, aber wir mußten zum Unterricht gehen.

Vor einiger Zeit führte eine Fernsehstation folgenden Test durch: Zwei Familien erklärten sich bereit, ... Und was passierte? Die Leute wußten einfach nicht mehr, was sie ohne Fernseher anfangen sollten. Sie saßen da und starrten sich an ...

Saying that something is going on right now
III, Ch. 5, p. 115

Wir (action) gerade.
Wir sind dabei, (peron/place/thing) zu (action).
Wir sind am (beim) (action).

Comparing
III, Ch. 7, p. 161

Ich kenne auch so einen/eine (*type of person*) wie dich.
Dieser/Diese/Dieses (*thing*) ist nicht so gut wie
dieser/diese/dieses.
Ich finde diesen/diese/dieses (*thing*) viel besser als
den/die/das da.
Und mir gefällt der/die/das (*thing*) am besten.

Saying what is being done about a problem
III, Ch. 9, p. 215

(*Things*) werden jetzt (*past participle*).
(*Thing*) wird (*past participle*).
(*Things*) werden schon oft (*past participle*).

Saying that something is being done
III, Ch. 10, p. 244

Die (*people/places/things*) werden (*past participle*).
Die (*people/places/things*) werden vom (*person*) (*past participle*).

Saying that something was being done
III, Ch. 10, p. 244

Die (*people/places/things*) wurden (*past participle*).
Der/Die/Das (*person/place/thing*)ist (nicht) (*past participle*) worden.

Talking about goals for the future
III, Ch. 11, p. 270

Mit dreißig möchte ich ...
Vielleicht werde ich bis dahin ...

EXPRESSING ATTITUDES AND OPINIONS

Asking for an opinion
I, Ch. 2, p. 55; Ch. 9, p. 232

Wie findest du (*thing/activity/place*)?
III, Ch. 3, p. 57
Was hältst du von (*person/place/thing*)?
Was würdest du dazu sagen?

Expressing your opinion
I, Ch. 2, p. 55; Ch. 9, p. 232

Ich finde (*thing/activity/place*) langweilig.
(*Thing/Activity/Place*) ist Spitze!
(*Activity*) macht Spaß!
Ich finde es toll, daß ...
Ich glaube, daß ...
III, Ch. 3, p. 57; Ch 6, p. 133
Ich halte viel/wenig davon.
Ich halte nichts davon.
Ich würde sagen, daß ...
Meiner Meinung nach ...
Ich finde, daß ...

Asking for reasons
III, Ch. 6, p. 133

Kannst du das begründen?

Eliciting agreement
III, Ch. 7, p. 168

..., nicht?
..., nicht wahr?
..., ja?
..., stimmt's?
..., oder?
..., meinst du nicht?

Agreeing
I, Ch. 2, p. 56

Ich auch!
Das finde ich auch!
Stimmt!
II, Ch. 10, p. 251
Da stimm' ich dir zu!
Da hast du (bestimmt) recht!
Einverstanden!
II, Ch. 4, p. 85; Ch. 6, p. 136; Ch. 7, p. 168
Da geb' ich dir recht.
Ganz meine Meinung.
Bei mir ist es auch so.
Da ist schon was dran.
Eben!
Richtig!
Da hast du ganz recht.
Damit stimm' ich überein.
Das meine ich auch.
Logisch! Logo!
Genau. Genau so ist es.
Eben!
Klar!
Sicher!

Disagreeing
I, Ch. 2, p. 56

Ich nicht!
Das finde ich nicht!
Stimmt nicht!
II, Ch. 10, p. 251
Das stimmt (überhaupt) nicht!
III, Ch. 6, p. 136
Das stimmt gar nicht!
Das ist alles Quatsch!

Agreeing with reservations
II, Ch. 7, p. 175

Ja, schon, aber ...
Ja, aber ...
Eigentlich schon, aber ...
Ja, ich stimme dir zwar zu, aber ...

Commenting on clothes
I, Ch. 5, p. 125

Wie findest du
den/die/das
(clothing item)?   Ich finde ihn/sie/es *(adjective)*.
Er/Sie/Es gefällt mir (nicht).

Expressing uncertainty
I, Ch. 5, p. 125; Ch. 9, p. 222

Ich bin nicht sicher.
Ich weiß nicht.
Keine Ahnung!
III, Ch. 7, p. 170
Es kann sein, daß ...
Das mag schon sein.

Expressing what seems to be true
III, Ch. 7, p. 170

Es scheint, daß ...
Es sieht so aus, als ob ...

Expressing certainty
III, Ch. 11, p. 269

Es steht fest, daß ...
Es ist sicher, daß ...
Ich möchte unbedingt ...

Expressing regret
I, Ch. 9, p. 222

Es tut mir leid.
II, Ch. 5, p. 113
Ich bedaure, ...
Was für ein Pech, ...
Leider, ...
III, Ch. 3. p. 68
Leider!
Ich bedaure, daß ...
Ich bedaure es wirklich, daß ...

Downplaying
II, Ch. 5, p. 113

Das macht nichts!
Schon gut!
Nicht so schlimm!
Dann *(action)* ich eben *(alternative)*.
Dann *(action)* ich halt *(alternative)*.

Asking how someone liked something
II, Ch. 3, p. 68

Wie war's?
Wie hat dir Dresden gefallen?
Wie hat es dir gefallen?
Hat es dir gefallen?

Responding enthusiastically
II, Ch. 3, p. 68

Na, prima!
Ja, Spitze!
Das freut mich!

Responding sympathetically
II, Ch. 3, p. 68

Schade!
Tut mir leid!
Das tut mir aber leid!

Expressing enthusiasm
II, Ch. 3, p. 68

Phantastisch!
Es war echt super!
Es hat mir gut gefallen.
Wahnsinnig gut!

Expressing sympathy
III, Ch. 3, p. 65

Es tut mir leid! Wirklich!
Das ist ja schlimm!
Das muß schlimm sein!
Wie schrecklich!
So ein Pech!

Expressing disappointment
II, Ch. 3, p. 68

Na ja, soso!
Nicht besonders.
Es hat mir nicht gefallen.
Es war furchtbar!
III, Ch. 8, p. 185
Ich bedaure, daß ...
Ich finde es schade, daß ...
Ich bin enttäuscht, daß ...

Expressing approval
II, Ch. 4, p. 88

Es ist prima, daß ...
Ich finde es toll, daß ...
Ich freue mich, daß ...
Ich bin froh, daß ...

Expressing disapproval
II, Ch. 4, p. 88

Es ist schade, daß ...
Ich finde es nicht gut, daß ...

Expressing indecision
II, Ch. 9, p. 213

Was machen wir jetzt?
Was sollen wir bloß machen?

Expressing an assumption
II, Ch. 10, p. 248

> Ich glaube schon, daß ...
> Ich meine doch, daß ...

III, Ch. 8, p. 193

> Ich nehme an, daß ...
> Ich vermute, daß ...
> Ich hatte den Eindruck, daß ...
> Ich hatte mir vorgestellt, daß ...

Introducing another point of view
III, Ch. 4, p. 91

> Das mag schon sein, aber ...
> Es kommt darauf an, ob ...
> Aber denk doch mal daran, daß ...
> Du darfst nicht vergessen, daß ...

Hypothesizing
III, Ch. 4, p. 92; Ch. 9, p. 217

> Wenn du ... wärest, dann würdest ...
> Wenn sie ... hätte, dann würde sie ...
> Wenn wir *(activity)* würden, hätten wir ...
> Wenn wir *(activity + past participle)* hätten,
>   hätten wir ...

Talking about what is possible
III, Ch. 5, p. 109

> Ich könnte *(action)*.
> Du könntest *(action)*.

Saying what you would have liked to do
III, Ch. 5, p. 110

> Ich hätte gern *(activity + past participle)*.
> Ich wäre gern *(activity + past participle)*.

Asking someone to take a position
III, Ch. 6, p. 133

> Möchtest du mal dazu Stellung nehmen?
> Wer nimmt mal dazu Stellung?

Talking about whether something is important
III, Ch. 11, p. 263

> Ich lege großen Wert darauf, daß ...
> Ich bin interessiert daran, daß ...
> Für mich spielt die größte Rolle, daß ...
> Mir ist wichtig, daß ...
> Entscheidend für mich ist, daß ...
> Für mich ist es am wichtigsten, daß ...
> Ausschlaggebend ist für mich, daß ...

Saying something is not important
III, Ch. 11, p. 263

> Ich lege keinen großen Wert darauf, daß ...
> Ich bin nicht besonders interessiert daran, daß ...
> Es ist nicht entscheidend für mich, daß ...
> Mir ist weniger wichtig, daß ...

EXPRESSING FEELINGS AND EMOTIONS

Asking about likes and dislikes
I, Ch. 2, p. 48; Ch. 4, p. 102; Ch. 10, p. 250

> Was *(action)* du gern?
> *(Action)* du gern?
> Magst du *(things/activities)*?
> Was für *(things/activities)* magst du?

Expressing likes
I, Ch. 2, p. 48; Ch. 4, p. 102; Ch. 10, p. 250

> Ich *(action)* gern.
> Ich mag *(things/activities)*.
> *(Thing/Activities)* mag ich (sehr/furchtbar) gern.

Expressing dislikes
I, Ch. 2, p. 48; I, Ch. 10, p. 250

> Ich *(action)* nicht so gern.
> Ich mag *(things/action)* (überhaupt) nicht.

Talking about favorites
I, Ch. 4, p. 102

> Was ist dein
>   Lieblings*(category)*?   Mein Lieblings*(category)*
>   ist *(thing)*.

Responding to good news
I, Ch. 4, p. 104

> Toll!
> Das ist prima!
> Nicht schlecht.

Responding to bad news
I, Ch. 4, p. 104

> Schade!
> So ein Pech!
> So ein Mist!
> Das ist sehr schlecht!

Expressing familiarity
I, Ch. 10, p. 252

> Kennst du *(person/*
>   *place/thing)*?   Ja, sicher!
>   Ja, klar! *or*
>   Nein, den/die/das kenne ich nicht.
>   Nein, überhaupt nicht.

Expressing preferences
I, Ch. 10, p. 253

> (Siehst) du gern ...?   Ja, aber ... (sehe) ich lieber.
>   Und am liebsten (sehe) ich ...
>
> (Siehst) du lieber ...
>   oder ...?   Lieber ...

II, Ch. 5, p. 123; Ch. 7, p. 165

Welche *(thing)* magst du lieber?
(Thing) oder *(thing)*?   *(Thing)* mag ich lieber.
Welchen/Welche/Welches
(food item) schmeckt dir
besser? *(Food item)* oder
(food item)?   *(Food item)* schmeckt
mir besser.

Mir gefällt *(person/place/
thing)* besser als
(person/place/thing).
Ich finde die *(person/place/
thing)* schöner.
Ich ziehe *(person/place/
thing)* vor.

Expressing strong preference and favorites
I, Ch. 10, p, 253

Was (siehst) du am liebsten?   Am liebsten (sehe) ich ...
II, Ch, 5, p. 123

Welches *(thing)* magst
du am liebsten?   Am liebsten mag ich
(thing).

Welche *(food item)* schmeckt
dir am besten?   *(Food item)* schmeckt
mir am besten.

Expressing preference given certain possibilities
III, Ch. 10, p. 236

Ich würde (hauptsächlich) *(activity)*.
... eventuell mal ...
... vielleicht ...
... möglicherweise ...

Expressing hope
II, Ch. 6, p. 148

Ich hoffe, ...
Wir hoffen, ...
Hoffentlich ...

Expressing doubt
II, Ch. 9, p. 217

Ich weiß nicht ob ...
Ich bezweifle, daß ...
Ich bin nicht sicher, ob ...

Expressing resignation
II, Ch. 9, p. 217

Da kann man nichts machen.
Das ist leider so.
III, Ch. 3, p. 65; Ch. 5, p. 118

Was kann ich schon tun?
Es ist halt so.
Ich habe eben eine Pechsträhne.
Ach, was soll's! Das ist leider so.

Expressing conviction
II, Ch. 9, p. 217

Du kannst mir glauben: ...
Ich bin sicher, daß ...

III, Ch. 7, p. 170

Es steht fest, daß ...

Expressing determination
III, Ch. 11, p. 260

Ich habe beschlossen, ...
Ich habe mich entschieden, ...
Ich bin fest entschlossen, ...

Expressing indecision
III, Ch. 11, p. 260

Ich weiß nicht, ob ich ...
Ich habe mich noch nicht entschieden, was/ob ...
Ich kann noch nicht sagen, ob ...
Ich muß mir das überlegen.
Es kommt darauf an, was/ob ...
Ich werde mal sehen, ob ...

Expressing surprise
II, Ch. 10, p. 251

Das ist ja unglaublich!
(Das ist) nicht möglich!
Das gibt's doch nicht!
III, Ch. 5, p. 118; Ch. 6, p. 141; Ch. 8, p. 185

Das ist mir (völlig) neu!
Es ist unglaublich, daß ...
... überrascht mich.
Ich bin überrascht, daß ...
Ich war überrascht, daß ...
Ich habe gestaunt, ...
Ich habe nicht gewußt, daß ...
Ich hätte nicht gedacht, daß ....
Es ist unwahrscheinlich, daß ...
Ich war erstaunt, ...

Expressing relief
III, Ch. 5, p. 118

Ich bin (sehr) froh, daß ...

Expressing annoyance
III, Ch. 6, p. 141; Ch. 7, p. 161; Ch. 8, p. 185

Was mich stört ist, daß ...
Ich werde sauer, wenn ...
Es ist frustrierend, daß ...
Was mich aufregt ist, wenn ...
Es nervt mich, daß ...
Es regt mich auf, wenn/daß ...
Es stört mich, wenn/daß ...
Es ärgert mich, wenn/daß ...
Ich finde es unangenehm, wenn/daß ...

Expressing concern
III, Ch. 9, p. 208

Ich habe Angst, ...
Ich fürchte, daß ...
... macht mir große Sorgen.

Expressing envy
III, Ch. 10, p. 237

Ich beneide *(people)*.

Expressing admiration
III, Ch. 10, p. 237

Ich bewundere ...

Expressing happiness
III, Ch. 10, p. 242

(*Person*) war froh, daß ...

Expressing sadness
III, Ch. 10, p. 242

(*People*) waren traurig, weil ...

Expressing relief
III, Ch. 11, p. 271

Gut, daß ...
Gott sei Dank, daß ...
Ein Glück, daß ...
Zum Glück habe ich ...
Ich bin froh, daß ...

PERSUADING

Telling someone what to do
I, Ch. 8, p. 199

Geh bitte *(action)*!
(Thing/Things) holen, bitte!

Asking for suggestions
II, Ch. 9, p. 213; Ch. 11, p. 266

Hast du eine Idee?
Was schlägst du vor?
Was sollen wir machen?
Wofür bist du?

Making suggestions
II, Ch. 6, p. 138; Ch. 9, p. 213; Ch. 11, p. 266

Möchtest du *(activity)*?
Willst du *(activity)*?
Du kannst für mich *(activity)*.
(Activity) wir mal!
Sollen wir mal *(activity)*?
Wir können mal *(activity)*.
Ich schlage vor, ...
Ich schlage vor, daß ...
Ich bin dafür, daß ...
Wie wär's mit *(activity/place)*?
III, Ch. 8, p. 195
Ich kann dir einen Tip geben: ...!
Ich empfehl' dir, ...
Es lohnt sich, ..

Responding to suggestions
II, Ch. 11, p. 266

Das wäre nicht schlecht.

Asking for advice
II, Ch. 6, p. 147

Was soll ich machen?
Was soll ich bloß tun?

Giving advice
II, Ch. 6, p. 147

Am besten ...
Du mußt unbedingt ...
III, Ch. 3, p. 66; Ch. 4, p. 91; Ch. 8, p. 195
Warum machst du nicht ... ?
Versuch doch mal ... !
Du solltest mal ...
An deiner Stelle würde ich versuchen, ...
Laß dir doch ... !
Vielleicht kannst du ...
Es ist wichtig, daß ...
Ich würde ...

Persuading someone to buy or wear something
II, Ch. 8, p. 189

Warum kaufst du dir keinen/keine/kein *(thing)*?
Kauf dir doch diesen/diese/dieses *(thing)*!
Trag doch mal etwas *(adjective)*!

Persuading someone not to buy something
II, Ch. 8, p. 189

Kauf dir ja keinen/keine/kein *(thing)*!
Trag ja nichts aus *(material)*!

Asking for permission
II, Ch. 10, p. 247

Darf ich (bitte) *(activity)*?
Kann ich bitte mal *(activity)*?
He, du! Laß mich mal *(activity)*!

Giving permission
II, Ch. 10, p. 247

Ja, natürlich!
Bitte schön!
Bitte!
Gern!

Making accusations
III, Ch. 9, p. 209

Du bist auch schuld an dem Problem, weil du ...
Wir Verbraucher sind schuld daran, daß ...,
   wenn wir ...

Offering solutions
III, Ch. 9, p. 210; Ch. 9, p. 216

Man könnte *(action)*.
Man müßte *(action)*.
Man sollte *(action)*.
Wenn wir nur *(action)* dürften!
(Thing) kann leicht *(past participle)* werden.
(Things) sollen *(past participle)* werden.
Alles muß *(past participle)* werden.

ADDITIONAL VOCABULARY

This list includes additional vocabulary that you may want to use to personalize activities. If you can't find the words you need here, try the German-English and English-German vocabulary sections beginning on p. 342.

SPORT UND INTERESSEN
(SPORTS AND HOBBIES)

Aerobic machen *to do aerobics*
amerikanischen Fußball spielen *to play football*
Baseball spielen *to play baseball*
bergsteigen *to go mountain climbing*
Bodybuilding machen *to lift weights*
Handball spielen *to play handball*
Kajak fahren *to go kayaking*
Kanu fahren *to go canoeing*
malen *to paint*
Münzen sammeln *to collect coins*
nähen *to sew*
reiten *to ride (a horse)*
Rollschuh laufen *to roller-skate*
rudern *to row*
schnorcheln *to snorkle*
Skateboard fahren *to skateboard*
Ski laufen *to (snow) ski*
sticken *to embroider*
stricken *to knit*
Tischtennis spielen *to play table tennis*
Videospiele spielen *to play video games*
zelten *to go camping*

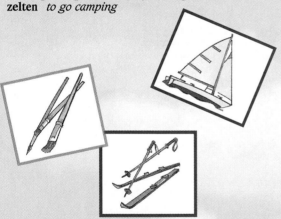

FAMILIE   (FAMILY)

der Enkel, - *grandson*
die Enkelin, -nen *granddaughter*
der Halbbruder, ⸚ *half-brother*
die Halbschwester, -n *half-sister*
der Neffe, -n *nephew*
die Nichte, -n *niece*
der Schwager, ⸚ *brother-in-law*
die Schwägerin, -nen *sister-in-law*
die Schwiegermutter, ⸚ *mother-in-law*
der Schwiegervater, ⸚ *father-in-law*

der Stiefbruder, ⸚ *stepbrother*
die Stiefmutter, ⸚ *stepmother*
die Stiefschwester, -n *stepsister*
der Stiefvater, ⸚ *stepfather*
die Urgroßmutter, ⸚ *great-grandmother*
der Urgroßvater, ⸚ *great-grandfather*

ZUM DISKUTIEREN
(TOPICS TO DISCUSS)

der Präsident *president*
die Reklame *advertising*
das Verbrechen *crime*
der Wehrdienst *military service*
der Zivildienst *community service*
die Drogen *drugs*
Gewalt im Fernsehen *violence on TV*

TIERE
(ANIMALS)

der Affe, -n *monkey*
der Bär, -en *bear*
der Büffel, - *buffalo*
der Bulle, -n *bull*
die Eidechse, -n *lizard*
die Ente, -n *duck*
der Frosch, ⸚e *frog*
der Fuchs, ⸚e *fox*
die Gans, ⸚e *goose*
die Giraffe, -n *giraffe*

der Hahn, ¨e *rooster*
der Hamster, - *hamster*
der Hase, -n *hare*
die Henne, -n *hen*
das Huhn, ¨er *chicken*
der Kanarienvogel, ¨ *canary*
das Kaninchen, - *rabbit*
die Klapperschlange, -n *rattlesnake*
die Kuh, ¨e *cow*
der Löwe, -n *lion*
die Maus, ¨e *mouse*
das Meerschweinchen, - *guinea pig*
das Nashorn, ¨er *rhinoceros*
das Nilpferd, -e *hippopotamus*
der Ochse, -n *ox*
der Papagei, -en *parrot*
das Pferd, -e *horse*
die Robbe, -n *seal*
der Seelöwe, -n *sea lion*
das Schaf, -e *sheep*
die Schildkröte, -n *turtle*
die Schlange, -n *snake*
der Schmetterling, -e *butterfly*
das Schwein, -e *pig*
der Stier, -e *steer*
der Tiger, - *tiger*
der Truthahn, ¨e *turkey*
der Vogel, ¨ *bird*
der Wal, -e *whale*
das Walroß, (pl) **Walrosse** *walrus*
der Waschbär, -en *racoon*
der Wolf, ¨e *wolf*
die Ziege, -n *goat*

GETRÄNKE *(BEVERAGES)*

der Grapefruitsaft *grapefruit juice*
der Kakao *cocoa*
der Kirschsaft *cherry juice*
der Kräutertee *herbal tea*
das Leitungswasser *tap water*
das Malzbier *(sweet, non-alcoholic beverage)*
der Milkshake *milkshake*
der Tomatensaft *tomato juice*

SPEISEN *(FOODS)*

die Ananas, - *pineapple*
der Apfelstrudel, - *apple strudel*
der Chip, -s *potato chip*
der Eintopf *stew*
die Erdbeere, -n *strawberry*
die Erdnußbutter *peanut butter*
das Gebäck *baked goods*
das Gulasch *goulash*
der Hamburger, - *hamburger*
die Himbeere, -n *raspberry*
die Karotte, -n *carrot*
der Ketchup *ketchup*
die Magermilch *low-fat milk*
die Mayonnaise *mayonnaise*
die Melone, -n *melon*
die Nuß, (pl) Nüsse *nut*
die Orange, -n *orange*
das Plätzchen, - *cookie*
der Pudding, -s *or* -e
  pudding
die Sahne *cream*
die Vollmilch *whole milk*

FARBEN *(COLORS)*

beige *beige*
golden *gold*
lila *purple*
orange *orange*
rosa *pink*
silbern *silver*
türkis *turquoise*

KLEIDUNGSSTÜCKE
(CLOTHING)

der Badeanzug, ¨e *swimsuit*
das Halstuch, ¨er *scarf*
der Handschuh, -e *glove*
der Mantel, ¨ *coat*
der Minirock, ¨e *miniskirt*
der Parka, -s *parka*
der Rollkragenpullover, - *turtleneck sweater*
die Sandalen (pl) *sandals*
die Strumpfhose, -n *panty hose*
die Weste, -n *vest*

KÖRPERTEILE
(PARTS OF THE BODY)

die Augenbraue, -n *eyebrow*
das Augenlid, -er *eyelid*
die Faust, ¨e *fist*
die Ferse, -n *heel*
das Gesicht, -er *face*
die Handfläche, -n *palm of the hand*
das Handgelenk, -e *wrist*
die Hüfte, -n *hip*
der Kiefer, - *jaw*
das Kinn *chin*
die Lippe, -n *lip*
der Magen *stomach*
der Nacken, - *neck*
die Nase, -n *nose*
das Ohr, -en *ear*
der Schenkel, - *thigh*
das Schienbein, -e *shin*
die Stirn *forehead*
die Wade, -n *calf*
die Wange, -n *cheek*
die Wimper, -n *eyelash*
der Zahn, ¨e *tooth*
der Zeh, -en *toe*
der Zeigefinger, - *index finger*
die Zunge, -n *tongue*

STOFFE (MATERIALS)

Acryl *acrylic*
Kaschmir *cashmere*
Kunstfasern *synthetic fibers*
Kunstseide *rayon*
Nylon *nylon*
Polyacryl *acrylic*
Polyester *polyester*

INSTRUMENTE
(MUSICAL INSTRUMENTS)

die Blockflöte, -n *recorder*
die Bratsche, -n *viola*
das Cello (Violoncello), -s *cello*
die elektrische Gitarre, -n *electric guitar*
die Flöte, -n *flute*
die Geige, -n *violin*
die Harfe, -n *harp*
das Horn, ¨er *French horn*
die Klarinette, -n *clarinet*
der Kontrabaß, (pl) Kontrabässe *double bass*
die Mandoline, -n *mandolin*
die Mundharmonika, -s *harmonica*
die Oboe, -n *oboe*
die Posaune, -n *trombone*
das Saxophon, -e *saxophone*
das Schlagzeug, -e *drums*
die Trompete, -n *trumpet*
die Tuba, (pl) Tuben *tuba*

FÄCHER (SCHOOL SUBJECTS)

Algebra *algebra*
Chemie *chemistry*
Chor *choir*
Französisch *French*
Hauswirtschaft *home economics*
Informatik *computer science*
Italienisch *Italian*
Literatur *literature*
Orchester *orchestra*
Philosophie *philosophy*
Physik *physics*
Politik *political science*
Russisch *Russian*
Spanisch *Spanish*
Sozialkunde *social studies*
Werken *shop*
Wirtschaftslehre *economics*

HAUSARBEIT   *(HOUSEWORK)*

den Fußboden kehren   *to sweep the floor*
saubermachen   *to clean*
die Wäsche aufhängen   *to hang clothes up*
die Wäsche einräumen   *to put clothes away*
die Wäsche zusammenlegen   *to fold clothes*

MÖBEL   *(FURNITURE)*

das Bild, -er *picture*
der Kleiderschrank, ¨e *wardrobe*
die Kommode, -n *chest of drawers*
der Nachttisch, -e *night stand*
der Vorhang, ¨e *curtain*

IN DER STADT
(PLACES AROUND TOWN)

die Brücke, -n *bridge*
die Bücherei, -en *library*
der Flughafen, (pl) Flughäfen *airport*
das Fremdenverkehrsamt, (pl) Fremdenverkehrsämter
  tourist office
der Frisiersalon, -s *beauty shop*
das Krankenhaus, (pl) Krankenhäuser *hospital*
der Kreis, -e *district, county*
die Minigolfanlage *mini-golf course*
die Polizei *police*
das Stadion, (pl) Stadien *stadium*
der Stadtrand, ¨er *outskirts*
der Stadtteil, -e *urban district*
das Stadtzentrum, (pl) Stadtzentren *downtown*

AUF DEM LAND
(IN THE COUNTRY)

auf dem Land wohnen   *to live in the country*
Tiere haben/züchten/füttern   *to have/raise/feed animals*
pflügen   *to plow*
der Bauernhof, ¨e   *the farm*
das Feld, -er   *field*
das Korn/Getreide   *grains*
die Landschaft, -en   *countryside*
der Mais   *corn*
die Scheune, -n   *barn*
die Sojabohnen (pl)   *soybeans*
der Weizen   *wheat*
die Wiese, -n   *meadow*

KULTURELLE VERANSTALTUNGEN
(CULTURAL EVENTS)

die Ausstellung, -en *exhibit*
das Chorkonzert, -e *choir concert*
das Kabarett *cabaret*
das Symphoniekonzert, -e *symphony*
der Vorverkauf, ̈e *advance ticket sales*
der Zirkus, (pl) Zirkusse *circus*

GESCHENKIDEEN
(GIFT IDEAS)

das Bild, -er *picture*
die Kette, -n *chain, necklace*
die Puppe, -n *doll*
das Puppenhaus, ̈er *doll house*
das Spielzeug, -e *toy*

AUTO (AUTOMOBILES)

die Alarmanlage, -n *alarm system*
die Alufelge, -n *aluminum rim, mag wheel*
der Aufkleber, - *(bumper) sticker*
die Automatik, -en *automatic transmission*
das 5-Gang-Getriebe *five speed
   (standard) transmission*
das Kabriolett, -s *convertible*
der Kassettenspieler, - *cassette player*
der Kombiwagen, - *station wagon*
die Lautsprecherbox, -en *speaker*
der Rallyestreifen, - *racing stripe*
die Servolenkung *power steering*
die Servobremsen (pl) *power brakes*
der Sitzschoner, - *seat cover*
das Stereo-Radio, -s *stereo*
die Zentralverriegelung, -en *power locks*

IM HAUSHALT
(HOUSEHOLD UTENSILS)

die Bratpfanne, -n *frying pan*
die Butterdose, - *butter dish*
der Deckel, - *lid*
der Herd, -e *stove*
die Kaffeekanne, -n *coffee pot*
der Kamin *fireplace*
der Kaffeelöffel, - *coffee spoon*
der Kochtopf, ̈e *large pot*
der Korkenzieher, - *corkscrew*
die Kuchenplatte, -n *cake plate*
die Lampe, -n *lamp*
die Müslischüssel, -n *cereal bowl*
das Salatbesteck, -e *salad server*
die Schöpfkelle, -n *ladle*
die Schüssel, -n *serving dish*
der Spiegel, - *mirror*
das Spülbecken, - *sink*
die Tasse, -n *cup*
der Teekessel, - *tea kettle*
das Tischtuch, ̈er *table cloth*
der Topf, ̈e *pot*
die Untertasse, -n *saucer*
die Zuckerdose, -n *sugar dish*

AUSSEHEN (APPEARANCE)

zum Friseur gehen *to go to a barber shop/hairdresser*
zur Friseuse gehen *to go to a hairdresser*
der Haarschnitt/die Frisur *haircut*
sich die Haare schneiden lassen *to get a haircut*
die Dauerwelle, -n *permanent wave*
sich eine Dauerwelle machen lassen *to get a perm*
sich maniküren lassen *to get a manicure*
die Nagelschere, -n *manicure scissors*
die Wimperntusche *mascara*
der Lippenstift, -e *lipstick*
der Augenbrauenstift, -e *eyebrow pencil*
der Fön *blow dryer*
sich das Haar fönen *to blow-dry one's hair*
der Handspiegel , - *hand mirror*
die Haarbürste, -n *hairbrush*
der Rasierapparat *electric razor*
der Lockenstab, ̈e *curling iron*
die Lockenwickler (pl) *curlers*
das Deodorant *deodorant*

FESTE   *(HOLIDAYS)*

Advent   *Advent (the four Sundays before Christmas)*
Allerheiligen   *All Saint's Day (Nov. 1)*
Chanukka   *Hanukkah*
Christi Himmelfahrt   *Ascension*
Erntedankfest   *Thanksgiving*
Heiligabend   *Christmas Eve*
Karneval   *Carnival, Mardi Gras*
Karfreitag   *Good Friday*
Martinstag   *St. Martin's Day (Nov. 11)*
Muttertag   *Mothers' Day*
Neujahr   *New Year*
Nikolaus   *St. Nicholas' Day (Dec. 6)*
Ostern   *Easter*
Silvester   *New Year's Eve*
Tag der Arbeit/Maifeiertag   *May Day (Labor Day)*
Tag der Deutschen Einheit   *Day of German Unity*
Vatertag   *Fathers' Day*
Weihnachten   *Christmas*

DAS WETTER   *(WEATHER)*

bedeckt   *cloudy*
feucht   *wet*
gewittrig   *stormy*
halbbedeckt   *partially overcast*
heiter   *sunny*
neblig   *foggy*
trüb   *hazy*
schwül   *humid*
windig   *windy*
es blitzt   *there is lightning*
es donnert   *it is thundering*
es nieselt   *it is drizzling*
es regnet   *it is raining*
es schneit   *it is snowing*
der Blitz, -e   *lightning*
der Donner   *thunder*
der Regen   *rain*
der Schnee   *snow*

BERUFE   *(CAREERS)*

Anästhesist(in), -en/innen   *anesthesiologist*
Apotheker(in), -/innen   *pharmacist*
Architekt(in), -en/innen   *architect*
Beamte/Beamtin, -n/innen   *civil servant*
Computerspezialist(in), -en/innen   *computer specialist*
Diplomat(in), -en/innen   *diplomat*
Elektroinstallateur(in) ,-/innen   *electrician*
Fotograf(in), -en/innen   *photographer*
Friseur/Friseuse, -e/n   *hair stylist*
Gesundheitswissenschaftler(in), -/innen   *nutritional scientist*
Industriedesigner(in), -/innen   *industrial designer*
Ingenieur(in), -e/innen   *engineer*
Kaufmann/Kauffrau, -leute   *merchant*
Koch/Köchin, ¨e/innen   *chef*
Kommunikationselektroniker(in), -/innen   *communications engineer*
die Krankenschwester, -n   *nurse*
der Krankenpfleger, -   *(male) nurse*
Mediaplaner(in), -/innen   *media planner*
Lebensmittelkontrolleur(in), -e/innen   *health inspector*
Lehrer(in), -/innen   *teacher*
Optiker(in), -/innen   *optician*
Physiker(in), -/innen   *physicist*
Politiker(in), -/innen   *politician*
PR-Berater(in), -/innen   *PR consultants*
Professor(in), -en/innen   *professor*
Rechtsanwalt/Rechtsanwältin, ¨e/innen   *lawyer*
Reporter(in), -/innen   *reporter*
Rundfunksprecher(in), -/innen   *radio announcer*
Schreiner(in), -/innen   *cabinet maker*
Schweißer(in), -/innen   *welder*
Steuerberater(in), -/innen   *tax consultant*
Sckretär(in), -e/innen   *secretary*
Soldat(in), -en/innen   *soldier*
Sportökonom(in), -en/innen   *sports scientist*
Srrafverteidiger(in), -/innen   *lawyer for the defense*
technischer Zeichner, -   *(male) drafter*
technische Zeichnerin, -nen   *(female) drafter*
Toningenieur(in), -e/innen   *sound engineer*
Touristikfachwirt(in), -e/innen   *tourism specialist*
Unternehmer(in), -/innen   *entrepreneur*
Winzer(in), -/innen   *vintner*
Zahnarzt(¨in), ¨e/innen   *dentist*
Zahntechniker(in), -/innen   *dental technician*
der Zimmermann, -leute   *carpenter*

ERDKUNDE *(GEOGRAPHY)*

Here are some terms you will find on German-language maps.

LÄNDER   *(STATES)*

Most of the states in the United States (**die Vereinigten Staaten**) have the same spelling in German that they have in English. Listed below are those states that have a different spelling.

Kalifornien	*California*
Neumexiko	*New Mexico*
Nordkarolina	*North Carolina*
Südkarolina	*South Carolina*
Süddakota	*South Dakota*

KONTINENTE   *(CONTINENTS)*

Afrika	*Africa*
die Antarktik	*Antarctica*
Asien	*Asia*
Europa	*Europe*
Nordamerika	*North America*
Südamerika	*South America*

MEERE   *(BODIES OF WATER)*

der Atlantik	*the Atlantic*
der Golf von Mexiko	*the Gulf of Mexico*
der Indische Ozean	*the Indian Ocean*
das Mittelmeer	*the Mediterranean*
der Pazifik	*the Pacific*
das Rote Meer	*the Red Sea*
das Schwarze Meer	*the Black Sea*

GEOGRAPHISCHE BEGRIFFE
(GEOGRAPHICAL TERMS)

der Breitengrad	*latitude*
die Ebene, -n	*plain*
der Fluß, (pl) Flüsse	*river*
das ... Gebirge	*... mountains*
die Grenze, -n	*border*
die Hauptstadt, ¨e	*capital*
der Kontinent, -e	*continent*
das Land, ¨er	*state or country*
der Längengrad	*longitude*
das Meer, -e	*ocean, sea*
der Nordpol	*the North Pole*
der See, -n	*lake*
der Staat, -en	*country or state*
der Südpol	*the South Pole*
das Tal, ¨er	*valley*

LAND UND LEUTE

STAAT		Adjektiv	Bewohner	Währung
Argentinien	*Argentina*	argentinisch	Argentinier	Peso
Australien	*Australia*	australisch	Australier	Dollar
Brasilien	*Brazil*	brasilianisch	Brasilianer	Cruzeiro
Haiti	*Haiti*	haitianisch	Haitianer	Gourde
Indien	*India*	indisch	Inder	Rupie
Indonesien	*Indonesia*	indonesisch	Indonesen	Rupie
Israel	*Israel*	israelisch	Israeli	Schekel
Jamaika	*Jamaica*	jamaikanisch	Jamaikaner	Dollar
Kolumbien	*Columbia*	kolumbisch	Kolumbianer	Peso
Korea	*Korea*	koreanisch	Koreaner	Won
Kuba	*Cuba*	kubanisch	Kubaner	Peso
Mexiko	*Mexico*	mexikanisch	Mexikaner	Peso
Neuseeland	*New Zealand*	neuseeländisch	Neuseeländer	Dollar
Norwegen	*Norway*	norwegisch	Norweger	Krone
Panama	*Panama*	panamaisch	Panamaner	Balboa
Phillipinen	*Phillipines*	phillipinisch	Phillipiner	Peso
Puerto Rico	*Puerto Rico*	puertoricanisch	Puertoricaner	Dollar
Schweden	*Sweden*	schwedisch	Schweden	Krone
Südafrika	*South Africa*	südafrikanisch	Südafrikaner	Rand
Vietnam	*Vietnam*	vietnamesisch	Vietnamesen	Dong

GRAMMAR SUMMARY
NOUNS AND THEIR MODIFIERS

In German, nouns (words that name a person, place, or thing) are grouped into three classes or genders: masculine, feminine, and neuter. All nouns, both persons and objects, fall into one of these groups. There are words used with nouns that signal the class of the noun. One of these is the definite article. In English there is one definite article: *the*. In German, there are three, one for each class: **der, die,** and **das**.

THE DEFINITE ARTICLE

SUMMARY OF DEFINITE ARTICLES

	NOMINATIVE	ACCUSATIVE	DATIVE	GENITIVE
Masculine	der	den	dem	des
Feminine	die	die	der	der
Neuter	das	das	dem	des
Plural	die	die	den	der

When the definite article is used with a noun, a noun phrase is formed. Noun phrases that are used as subjects are in the nominative case. Nouns that are used as direct objects or the objects of certain prepositions (such as **für**) are in the accusative case. Nouns that are indirect objects, the objects of certain prepositions (such as **mit, bei**), or the objects of special verbs (see page 335) are in the dative case. Below is a summary of the definite articles combined with nouns to form noun phrases.

SUMMARY OF NOUN PHRASES

	NOMINATIVE	ACCUSATIVE	DATIVE	GENITIVE
Masculine	der Vater der Ball	den Vater den Ball	dem Vater dem Ball	des Vaters des Balls
Feminine	die Mutter die Kassette	die Mutter die Kassette	der Mutter der Kassette	der Mutter der Kassette
Neuter	das Mädchen das Haus	das Mädchen das Haus	dem Mädchen dem Haus	des Mädchens des Hauses
Plural	die Kassetten die Häuser	die Kassetten die Häuser	den Kassetten den Häusern	der Kassetten der Häuser

DIESER-WORDS

The determiners **dieser, jeder, welcher,** and **alle** are called **dieser**-words. Their endings are similar to those of the definite articles. Note that the endings of the **dieser**-words are very similar to the definite articles.

SUMMARY OF DIESER-WORDS

dieser	*this, that, these*	welcher	*which, that*
jeder	*each, every*	mancher	*many, many a*
alle	*all*	solcher	*such, such a*

	NOMINATIVE		ACCUSATIVE		DATIVE		GENITIVE	
Masculine	dieser	jeder	diesen	jeden	diesem	jedem	dieses	jedes
Feminine	diese	jede	diese	jede	dieser	jeder	dieser	jeder
Neuter	dieses	jedes	dieses	jedes	diesem	jedem	dieses	jedes
Plural	diese	alle	diese	alle	diesen	allen	dieser	aller

DERSELBE

	NOMINATIVE	ACCUSATIVE	DATIVE	GENITIVE
Masculine	derselbe	denselben	demselben	desselben
Feminine	dieselbe	dieselbe	derselben	derselben
Neuter	dasselbe	dasselbe	demselben	desselben
Plural	dieselben	dieselben	denselben	derselben

THE INDEFINITE ARTICLE

Another type of word that is used with nouns is the *indefinite article:* **ein, eine, ein** in German, *a, an* in English. There is no plural form of **ein.**

SUMMARY OF INDEFINITE ARTICLES

	NOMINATIVE	ACCUSATIVE	DATIVE	GENITIVE
Masculine	ein	einen	einem	eines
Feminine	eine	eine	einer	einer
Neuter	ein	ein	einem	eines
Plural	—	—	—	—

THE NEGATING WORD KEIN

The word **kein** is also used with nouns and means *no, not,* or *not any*. Unlike **ein**, **kein** has a plural form.

	NOMINATIVE	ACCUSATIVE	DATIVE	GENITIVE
Masculine	kein	keinen	keinem	keines
Feminine	keine	keine	keiner	keiner
Neuter	kein	kein	keinem	keines
Plural	keine	keine	keinen	keiner

THE POSSESSIVES

These words also modify nouns and tell you *whose* object or person is being referred to (*my* car, *his* book, *her* mother). These words have the same endings as **kein**.

SUMMARY OF POSSESSIVES

	BEFORE MASCULINE NOUNS				BEFORE FEMININE NOUNS		
	NOM	ACC	DAT	GEN	NOM & ACC	DAT	GEN
my	mein	meinen	meinem	meines	meine	meiner	meiner
your	dein	deinen	deinem	deines	deine	deiner	deiner
his	sein	seinen	seinem	seines	seine	seiner	seiner
her	ihr	ihren	ihrem	ihres	ihre	ihrer	ihrer
our	unser	unseren	unserem	unseres	unsere	unserer	unserer
your	euer	eueren	euerem	eueres	euere	euerer	euerer
their	ihr	ihren	ihrem	ihres	ihre	ihrer	ihrer
your	Ihr	Ihren	Ihrem	Ihres	Ihre	Ihrer	Ihrer

	BEFORE NEUTER NOUNS			BEFORE PLURAL NOUNS		
	NOM & ACC	DAT	GEN	NOM & ACC	DAT	GEN
my	mein	meinem	meines	meine	meinen	meiner
your	dein	deinem	deines	deine	deinen	deiner
his	sein	seinem	seines	seine	seinen	seiner
her	ihr	ihrem	ihres	ihre	ihren	ihrer
our	unser	unserem	unseres	unsere	unseren	unserer
your	euer	euerem	eueres	euere	eueren	euerer
their	ihr	ihrem	ihres	ihre	ihren	ihrer
your	Ihr	Ihrem	Ihres	Ihre	Ihren	Ihrer

Commonly used short forms for unseren: unsren *or* unsern   *for* unsere: unsre
   eueren: euren *or* euern   euere: eure
for unserem: unsrem *or* unserm   *for* unserer: unsrer
   euerem: eurem *or* euerm   euerer: eurer
for unseres: unsres
   eueres: eures

DETERMINERS OF QUANTITY

alle	*all*	manche	*some*
andere	*other*	mehrere	*several*
beide	*both*	solche	*such*
ein paar	*a few*	viele	*many*
einige	*a few, some*	wenige	*few*

NOUN PLURALS

Noun class and plural forms are not always predictable. Therefore, you must learn each noun together with its article (**der, die, das**) and with its plural form. As you learn more nouns, however, you will discover certain patterns. Although there are always exceptions to these patterns, you may find them helpful in remembering the plural forms of many nouns.

Most German nouns form their plurals in one of two ways: some nouns add endings in the plural; some add endings and/or change the sound of the stem vowel in the plural, indicating the sound change with the umlaut (¨). Only the vowels **a, o, u,** and the diphthong **au** can take the umlaut. If a noun has an umlaut in the singular, it keeps the umlaut in the plural. Most German nouns fit into one of the following five plural groups.

1. Nouns that do not have any ending in the plural. Sometimes they take an umlaut.
   NOTE: There are only two feminine nouns in this group: **die Mutter** and **die Tochter**.

der Bruder, die Brüder	der Schüler, die Schüler	das Fräulein, die Fräulein
der Lehrer, die Lehrer	der Vater, die Väter	das Mädchen, die Mädchen
der Onkel, die Onkel	die Mutter, die Mütter	das Poster, die Poster
der Mantel, die Mäntel	die Tochter, die Töchter	das Zimmer, die Zimmer

2. Nouns that add the ending **-e** in the plural. Sometimes they also take an umlaut.
   NOTE: There are many one-syllable words in this group.

der Bleistift, die Bleistifte	der Sohn, die Söhne	das Jahr, die Jahre
der Freund, die Freunde	die Stadt, die Städte	das Spiel, die Spiele

3. Nouns that add the ending **-er** in the plural. Whenever possible, they take an umlaut, i.e., when the noun contains the vowels **a, o,** or **u,** or the diphthong **au**. **NOTE:** There are no feminine nouns in this group. There are many one-syllable words in this group.

das Buch, die Bücher	das Haus, die Häuser
das Fach, die Fächer	das Land, die Länder

4. Nouns that add the ending **-en** or **-n** in the plural. These nouns never add an umlaut.
   NOTE: There are many feminine nouns in this group.

der Herr, die Herren	die Frau, die Frauen	die Küche, die Küchen
der Junge, die Jungen	die Klasse, die Klassen	die Schwester, die Schwestern
die Briefmarke, die Briefmarken	die Karte, die Karten	die Tante, die Tanten
die Familie, die Familien	der Name, die Namen	die Wohnung, die Wohnungen
die Farbe, die Farben	der Vetter, die Vettern	die Zahl, die Zahlen

   Feminine nouns ending in **-in** add the ending **-nen** in the plural.

die Freundin, die Freundinnen	die Verkäuferin, die Verkäuferinnen

5. Nouns that add the ending **-s** in the plural. These nouns never add an umlaut.
   NOTE: There are many words of foreign origin in this group.

der Kuli, die Kulis	das Auto, die Autos
die Kamera, die Kameras	das Hobby, die Hobbys

SUMMARY OF PLURAL ENDINGS

Group	1	2	3	4	5
Ending:	-	-e	-er	-(e)n	-s
Umlaut:	sometimes	sometimes	always	never	never

MASCULINE NOUNS WITH THE ENDINGS -N OR -EN IN THE SINGULAR

	NOMINATIVE	ACCUSATIVE	DATIVE	GENITIVE
Singular	der Name der Polizist	den Namen den Polizisten	dem Namen dem Polizisten	des Namen des Polizisten

Some other nouns that add -n: **der Achtzehnjährige, der Auszubildene, der Bekannte, der Deutsche, der Erwachsene, der Gedanke, der Herr, der Junge, der Nachbar, der Reisende, der Verwandte, der Vorfahre**

Some other nouns that add **en**: **der Astronaut, der Dirigent, der Gymnasiast, der Held, der Klassenkamerad, der Konsument, der Mensch, der Philosoph, der Planet, der Tourist**

PRONOUNS

PERSONAL   REFLEXIVE

	NOMINATIVE	ACCUSATIVE	DATIVE	ACCUSATIVE	DATIVE
Singular					
1st person	ich	mich	mir	mich	mir
2nd person	du	dich	dir	dich	dir
3rd person *m.*	er	ihn	ihm		
f.	sie	sie	ihr	sich	sich
n.	es	es	ihm		
Plural					
1st person	wir	uns	uns	uns	uns
2nd person	ihr	euch	euch	euch	euch
3rd person	sie	sie	ihnen	sich	sich
you (formal, sing. & pl.)	Sie	Sie	Ihnen	sich	sich

DEFINITE ARTICLES AS DEMONSTRATIVE PRONOUNS

The definite articles can be used as demonstrative pronouns, giving more emphasis to the sentences than the personal pronouns **er, sie, es**. Note that these demonstrative pronouns have the same forms as the definite articles, with the exception of the dative plural form, which is **denen**.

Wer bekommt *den* Cappucino? *Der* ist für mich.
Wer sagt es *den* Schülern? *Denen* sag' ich es nicht.

	NOMINATIVE	ACCUSATIVE	DATIVE
Masculine	der	den	dem
Feminine	die	die	der
Neuter	das	das	dem
Plural	die	die	denen

DEFINITE ARTICLES AS RELATIVE PRONOUNS

The definite articles can be used as relative pronouns. Relative pronouns introduce relative clauses. Note that **was** is used as a relative pronoun after **alles, das, etwas, nichts, viel, wenig,** and when referring to a whole clause. **Wo** is used as a relative pronoun to refer to places, literally or in a broader sense.

	NOMINATIVE	ACCUSATIVE	DATIVE
Masculine	der	den	dem
Feminine	die	die	der
Neuter	das	das	dem
Plural	die	die	denen

INTERROGATIVES

INTERROGATIVE PRONOUNS

	PEOPLE		THINGS	
Nominative	**wer?**	*who?*	**was?**	*what?*
Accusative	**wen?**	*whom?*	**was?**	*what?*
Dative	**wem?**	*to, for whom?*		

OTHER INTERROGATIVES

wann? *when?* **warum?** *why?* **wie?** *how?* **wieviel?** *how much? how many?*	**wie viele?** *how many?* **wo?** *where?* **woher?** *from where?* **wohin?** *to where?*	**welch-?** *which?* **was für (ein)?** *what kind of (a)?*

WAS FÜR (EIN)?

	NOMINATIVE	ACCUSATIVE	DATIVE
Masculine *Feminine* *Neuter*	**Was für ein** Lehrer ist er? **Was für eine** Uhr ist das? **Was für ein** Buch ist das?	**Was für einen** Lehrer hast du? **Was für eine** Uhr kaufst du? **Was für ein** Buch liest du?	**Mit was für einem** Lehrer? **Mit was für einer** Uhr? **Mit was für einem** Buch?
Plural	**Was für Bücher** sind das?	**Was für** Bücher hast du?	**Mit was für Büchern?**

PREPOSITIONS

Accusative	durch, für, gegen, ohne, um
Dative	aus, bei, mit, nach, seit, von, zu

Two-Way:
    *Dative–**wo?***
    *Accusative–**wohin?***
	an, auf, hinter, in, neben, über, unter,
	vor, zwischen

Genitive	(an)statt, außerhalb, innerhalb, trotz, während, wegen

CONJUNCTIONS

COORDINATING CONJUNCTIONS

Coordinating conjunctions join independent or main clauses — clauses that can stand alone as complete sentences. When independent clauses are joined together by a coordinating conjunction, both clauses maintain verb-second word order.

aber	*but, (however)*	**oder**	*or*	**und**	*and*
denn	*because, for*	**sondern**	*but (on the contrary)*		

SUBORDINATING CONJUNCTIONS

Subordinating conjunctions introduce dependents or subordinating clauses — clauses that cannot stand alone because they do not make complete sense without the main clause. Dependent clauses may either follow or precede the main clause, but they always require verb-last position.

als	*(at the time) when*	**daß**	*that*	**seit(dem)**	*since (that time)*
als ob	*as if*	**bevor**	*before*	**während**	*while*
bis	*until*	**indem**	*while, as, by*	**weil**	*because*
damit	*in order (so) that*	**ob**	*whether*	**wenn**	*if, when, whenever*

WORD ORDER

POSITION OF VERBS IN A SENTENCE

The conjugated verb is in *first* position in:	yes/no *questions (questions that do not begin with an interrogative)* **Trinkst du Kaffee?** **Spielst du Tennis?** **Möchtest du ins Konzert gehen?** *both formal and informal commands* **Kommen Sie bitte um 2 Uhr!** **Geh doch mit ins Kino!**
The conjugated verb is in *second* position in:	*statements with normal word order* **Wir spielen heute Volleyball.** *statements with inverted word order* **Heute spielen wir Volleyball.** *questions that begin with an interrogative* **Wohin gehst du?** **Woher kommst du?** **Was macht er?** *sentences connected by* **und, oder, aber, denn** **Ich komme nicht, denn ich habe keine Zeit.**
The conjugated verb is in *second* position and the infinitive or past participle is *final* in:	*statements with modals* **Ich möchte heute ins Kino gehen.** *statements in conversational past* **Ich habe das Buch gelesen.** *statements with* **werde** *and* **würde** **Ich werde im Mai nach Berlin fliegen.** **Die Oma würde gern ins Theater gehen.**
The conjugated verb is in *final* position in:	*clauses that begin with interrogatives (***wo, wann, warum,*** etc.)* **Ich weiß, wo das Hotel ist.** **Ich weiß nicht, wer heute morgen angerufen hat.** *clauses that begin with* **weil, daß,** *or* **ob** **Ich gehe nicht ins Kino, weil ich kein Geld habe.** **Ich glaube, daß er Rockmusik gern hört.** **Ich komme morgen nicht, weil ich zu Hause helfen muß.** **Ich weiß nicht, ob er den Film schon gesehen hat.**

POSITION OF NICHT IN A SENTENCE

To negate the entire sentence, as close to end of sentence as possible:	Er fragt seinen Vater	nicht.
Before a separable prefix:	Ich rufe ihn	nicht	an.
Before any part of a sentence you want to negate, contrast, or emphasize:	Er kommt	nicht	heute. (Er kommt morgen.)
Before part of a sentence that answers the question **wo?**	Ich wohne	nicht	in Berlin.

ADJECTIVES

ENDINGS OF ADJECTIVES AFTER DER- AND DIESER-WORDS

	NOMINATIVE	ACCUSATIVE	DATIVE	GENITIVE
Masculine	der -e Vorort	den -en Vorort	dem -en Vorort	des -en Vororts
Feminine	die -e Stadt	die -e Stadt	der -en Stadt	der -en Stadt
Neuter	das -e Dorf	das -e Dorf	dem -en Dorf	des -en Dorfes
Plural	die -en Vororte	die -en Vororte	den -en Vororten	der -en Vororte

NOTE: 1. Names of cities used as adjectives always have the ending -er: **der Frankfurter Zoo, das Münchner Oktoberfest**

2. Adjectives such as **super, klasse, spitze,** and **rosa, lila, beige,** and **orange** never take endings.
Das ist ein klasse Wagen. Möchtest du auch so einen klasse Wagen?
Ich möchte auch so ein schönes rosa Hemd.

ENDINGS OF ADJECTIVES AFTER EIN AND KEIN

	NOMINATIVE	ACCUSATIVE	DATIVE	GENITIVE
Masculine	ein -er Vorort	einen -en Vorort	einem -en Vorort	eines -en Vororts
Feminine	eine -e Stadt	eine -e Stadt	einer -en Stadt	einer -en Stadt
Neuter	ein -es Dorf	ein -es Dorf	einem -en Dorf	eines -en Dorfes
Plural	keine -en Vororte	keine -en Vororte	keinen -en Vororten	keiner -en Vororte

ENDINGS OF ADJECTIVES AFTER THE POSSESSIVES

	NOMINATIVE	ACCUSATIVE	DATIVE	GENITIVE
Masculine	mein -er Vorort	meinen -en Vorort	meinem -en Vorort	meines -en Vororts
Feminine	meine -e Stadt	meine -e Stadt	meiner -en Stadt	meiner -en Stadt
Neuter	mein -es Dorf	mein -es Dorf	meinem -en Dorf	meines -en Dorfes
Plural	meine -en Vororte	meine -en Vororte	meinen -en Vororten	meiner -en Vororte

ENDINGS OF UNPRECEDED ADJECTIVES

	NOMINATIVE	ACCUSATIVE	DATIVE
Masculine	-er Salat	-en Salat	-em Salat
Feminine	-e Suppe	-e Suppe	-er Suppe
Neuter	-es Eis	-es Eis	-em Eis
Plural	-e Getränke	-e Getränke	-en Getränken

ENDINGS OF ADJECTIVES AFTER DETERMINERS OF QUANTITY

	NOMINATIVE	ACCUSATIVE	DATIVE
alle, beide, solche, manche	alle -**en** Häuser	alle -**en** Häuser	allen -**en** Häusern
andere, ein paar, einige, mehrere, viele, wenige, etc.	mehrere -**e** Dörfer	mehrere -**e** Dörfer	mehreren -**en** Dörfern

MAKING COMPARISONS

	Positive	Comparative	Superlative
1. *All comparative forms end in* -**er**.	schnell	schneller	am schnellsten
2. *Most one-syllable forms have an umlaut.*	alt	älter	am ältesten
3. *Exceptions must be learned as they appear.*	dunkel gut	dunkler besser	am dunkelsten am besten

Equal Comparisons:	Er spielt **so gut wie** ich (spiele). *He plays as well as I (do).*	
Unequal Comparisons:	Sie spielt **besser als** ich (spiele). *She plays better than I (do).*	
Comparative and superlative adjectives before nouns:	der **bessere** Wagen ein **schöneres** Auto	der **beste** Wagen mein **schönstes** Kleid.

NOTE: Comparative adjectives before nouns have the same endings as descriptive adjectives (see page 332).

ORDINAL NUMBERS

1. Ordinal numbers are formed by adding -**t** or -**st** to the cardinal numbers. They are used to express a place in a series. Irregular ordinal numbers are printed in boldface below.

eins	der, die, das **erst**-	sieben	der, die, das **siebt**-
zwei	zweit-	acht	acht-
drei	**dritt**-	neun	neunt-
vier	viert-	zehn	zehnt-
fünf	fünft-	zwanzig	zwanzigst-
sechs	sechst-	dreißig	dreißigst-

2. Ordinal numbers are most often used as adjectives. They take regular adjective endings.

> Heute ist der erst**e** Mai.
> Tu das nicht ein zweit**es** Mal!
> In der dritt**en** Stunde haben wir Deutsch.
> Ostern ist dieses Jahr am fünft**en** April.
> Wann hat Heinrich der Acht**e** gelebt?

VERBS

PRESENT TENSE VERB FORMS

		REGULAR	-eln VERBS	STEM ENDING WITH t/d	STEM ENDING WITH s/ß
INFINITIVES		spiel -en	bastel -n	find -en	heiß -en
PRONOUNS		stem + ending	stem + ending	stem + ending	stem + ending
I	ich	spiel -e	bastl -e	find -e	heiß -e
you	du	spiel -st	bastel -st	find -est	heiß -t
he	er				
she	sie	spiel -t	bastel -t	find -et	heiß -t
it	es				
we	wir	spiel -en	bastel -n	find -en	heiß -en
you (plural)	ihr	spiel -t	bastel -t	find -et	heiß -t
they	sie	spiel -en	bastel -n	find -en	heiß -en
you (formal)	Sie	spiel -en	bastel -n	find -en	heiß -en

NOTE: There are important differences between the verbs in the above chart:

1. Verbs ending in **-eln** (**basteln, segeln**) drop the **e** of the ending **-eln** in the ich-form: **ich bastle, ich segle** and add only **-n** in the wir-, sie-, and Sie-forms. These forms are always identical to the infinitive: **basteln, wir basteln, sie basteln, Sie basteln.** Similarly, verbs ending in **-ern**, (**wandern**) drop the **e** of the ending **-ern** in the ich-form: **ich wandre** and add only **-n** in the wir-, sie-, and Sie-forms. These forms are always identical to the infinitive: **wandern.**

2. Verbs with a stem ending in **d** or **t**, such as **finden**, add an **e** before the ending in the du-form (**du findest**) and the er- and ihr-forms (**er findet, ihr findet**).

3. All verbs with stems ending in an **s**-sound (**heißen**) add only **-t** in the du-form: **du heißt.**

VERBS WITH A STEM-VOWEL CHANGE

There are a number of verbs in German that change their stem vowel in the **du**- and **er/sie**-forms. A few verbs, such as **nehmen** (*to take*), have a change in the consonant as well. You cannot predict these verbs, so it is best to learn each one individually. They are usually irregular only in the **du**- and **er/sie**-forms.

		e → i			e → ie		a → ä	
		essen	geben	nehmen	lesen	sehen	fahren	einladen
ich		esse	gebe	nehme	lese	sehe	fahre	lade ein
du		ißt	gibst	nimmst	liest	siehst	fährst	lädst ein
er, sie		ißt	gibt	nimmt	liest	sieht	fährt	lädt ein
wir		essen	geben	nehmen	lesen	sehen	fahren	laden ein
ihr		eßt	gebt	nehmt	lest	seht	fahrt	ladet ein
sie		essen	geben	nehmen	lesen	sehen	fahren	laden ein
Sie		essen	geben	nehmen	lesen	sehen	fahren	laden ein

SOME IMPORTANT IRREGULAR VERBS: HABEN, SEIN, WISSEN, AND WERDEN

	haben	sein	wissen	werden
ich	habe	bin	weiß	werde
du	hast	bist	weißt	wirst
er, sie	hat	ist	weiß	wird
wir	haben	sind	wissen	werden
ihr	habt	seid	wißt	werdet
sie	haben	sind	wissen	werden
Sie	haben	sind	wissen	werden

VERBS FOLLOWED BY AN OBJECT IN THE DATIVE CASE

antworten, *to answer*	gratulieren, *to congratulate*
danken, *to thank*	helfen, *to help*
gefallen, *to like*	passen, *to fit*
glauben, *to believe*	

Es geht (mir) gut.	Es steht (dir) gut.
Es schmeckt (mir) nicht.	Es macht (mir) Spaß.
Es tut (mir) leid.	Es tut (mir) weh.
Was fehlt (dir)?	

MODAL (AUXILIARY) VERBS

The verbs **dürfen, können, müssen, sollen, wollen, mögen** (and the **möchte**-forms) are usually used with an infinitive at the end of the sentence. If the meaning of that infinitive is clear, it can be left out: **Du mußt sofort nach Hause!** (**Gehen** is understood and omitted.)

	dürfen	können	müssen	sollen	wollen	mögen	möchte
ich	darf	kann	muß	soll	will	mag	möchte
du	darfst	kannst	mußt	sollst	willst	magst	möchtest
er, sie	darf	kann	muß	soll	will	mag	möchte
wir	dürfen	können	müssen	sollen	wollen	mögen	möchten
ihr	dürft	könnt	müßt	sollt	wollt	mögt	möchtet
sie	dürfen	können	müssen	sollen	wollen	mögen	möchten
Sie	dürfen	können	müssen	sollen	wollen	mögen	möchten

VERBS WITH SEPARABLE PREFIXES

Some verbs have separable prefixes: prefixes that separate from the conjugated verbs and are moved to the end of the sentence.

Present:		
	einladen	Meine Gastfamilie **lädt** mich immer noch **ein.**
	abbauen	**Bau** endlich mal deine Vorurteile **ab!**
Narrative Past (Imperfect):		
	ankommen	Ich **kam** in August in den Vereinigten Staaten **an.**
	hingehen	Er **ging** sofort **hin** und **holte** sein Gepäck **ab.**
	abholen	Wir **holten** die Kinder am Flugplatz **ab.**
Conversational Past:		
	abholen	Wer **hat** dich am Flughafen **abgeholt?**
Past Perfect:		
	mitnehmen	Mein Vater **hatte** alle Kinder **mitgenommen.**
Infinitives used with zu:		
	kennenlernen	Ich hoffe, die Leute besser **kennenzulernen.**
Certain prefixes are never separated from the verb:		
	überraschen	Das **überrascht** mich überhaupt nicht.
	wiederholen	**Wiederhole** bitte deine Frage!
	übersetzen	Das hast du wirklich prima **übersetzt.**

COMMAND FORMS

Regular Verbs	gehen	spielen
with **du** (singular)	Geh!	Spiel!
with **ihr** (pl)	Geht!	Spielt!
with **Sie** (sing & pl)	Gehen Sie!	Spielen Sie!
"let's" form	Gehen wir!	Spielen wir!

Separable-prefix Verbs	mitkommen	anrufen	aufräumen	anziehen	ausgehen
	Komm mit!	Ruf an!	Räum auf!	Zieh an!	Geh aus!
	Kommt mit!	Ruft an!	Räumt auf!	Zieht an!	Geht aus!
	Kommen Sie mit!	Rufen Sie an!	Räumen Sie auf!	Ziehen Sie an!	Gehen Sie aus!
	Kommen wir mit!	Rufen wir an!	Räumen wir auf!	Ziehen wir an!	Gehen wir aus!

Stem-changing Verbs	essen	nehmen	geben	sehen	fahren
	Iß!	Nimm!	Gib!	Sieh!	Fahr!
	Eßt!	Nehmt!	Gebt!	Seht!	Fahrt!
	Essen Sie!	Nehmen Sie!	Geben Sie!	Sehen Sie!	Fahren Sie!
	Essen wir!	Nehmen wir!	Geben wir!	Sehen wir!	Fahren wir!

NOTE: The vowel changes e → i and e → ie are maintained in the **du**-form of the command. The vowel change a → ä does not occur in the command form.

EXPRESSING FUTURE TIME

In German, there are three ways to express future time:

1. present tense verb forms	Ich **kaufe** eine Jeans. Ich **finde** bestimmt etwas.	*I'm going to buy a pair of jeans.* *I will surely find something.*
2. present tense verb forms with words like *morgen, später*	Er kommt **morgen.** Elke ruft **später** an.	*He's coming tomorrow.* *Elke will call later.*
3. **werden,** *will,* plus infinitive	Ich **werde** ein Hemd **kaufen.** Er **wird** bald **gehen.**	*I'll buy a shirt.* *He'll go soon.*

To express that something will have happened or be completed in the future, you can use the perfect infinitive with a modal or with **werden:**

Ich möchte eine politische Karriere begonnen haben.
Ich werde einen Traumjob gefunden haben.

THE CONVERSATIONAL PAST

German verbs are divided into two groups: weak verbs and strong verbs. Weak verbs usually follow a regular pattern, such as the English verb forms *play — played — has played*. Strong verbs usually have irregularities, like the English verb forms *run — ran — has run* or *go — went — has gone*.

The conversational past tense of weak and strong verbs consists of the present tense of **haben** or **sein** and a form called the past participle, which is usually in last position in the clause or sentence.

Die Schüler Sabine	**haben** **ist**	ihre Hausaufgaben schon gestern zu Hause	**gemacht.** **geblieben.**

FORMATION OF PAST PARTICIPLES

Weak Verbs	spielen	(er) spielt	gespielt	Er hat gespielt.
with inseparable prefixes	besuchen	(er) besucht	besucht	Er hat ihn besucht.
with separable prefixes	aufräumen	(er) räumt auf	aufgeräumt	Er hat aufgeräumt.
Strong Verbs	kommen	(er) kommt	gekommen	Er ist gekommen
with inseparable prefixes	bekommen	(er) bekommt	bekommen	Er hat es bekommen.
with separable prefixes	mitkommen	(er) kommt mit	mitgekommen	Er ist mitgekommen.

NOTE: For past participles of strong verbs and irregular verbs, see pages 340–341.

WEAK VERBS FORMING THE PAST PARTICIPLE WITH SEIN

bummeln, *to stroll*	ist gebummelt	**surfen,** *to surf*	ist gesurft
reisen, *to travel*	ist gereist	**wandern,** *to hike*	ist gewandert

THE NARRATIVE PAST (IMPERFECT)

When relating a longer sequence that took place in the past, the narrative past is generally used.
NOTE: The **du-** and **ihr-**forms are rarely used in the narrative past.

Weak verbs add the past tense marker **-te** to the verb stem:

	hören	führen	sagen
ich	hörte	führte	sagte
du	hörtest	führtest	sagtest
er, sie	hörte	führte	sagte
wir	hörten	führten	sagten
ihr	hörtet	führtet	sagtet
sie, Sie	hörten	führten	sagten

Strong verbs often have a vowel change in the imperfect:

	haben	sein	werden	geben	finden
ich	hatte	war	wurde	gab	fand
du	hattest	warst	wurdest	gabst	fandest
er, sie, es	hatte	war	wurde	gab	fand
wir	hatten	waren	wurden	gaben	fanden
ihr	hattet	wart	wurdet	gabt	fandet
sie, Sie	hatten	waren	wurden	gaben	fanden

The modals in the imperfect do not have the umlaut of the infinitive:

	dürfen	können	mögen	müssen	sollen	wollen
ich	durfte	konnte	mochte	mußte	sollte	wollte
du	durftest	konntest	mochtest	mußtest	solltest	wolltest
er, sie	durfte	konnte	mochte	mußte	sollte	wollte
wir	durften	konnten	mochten	mußten	sollten	wollten
ihr	durftet	konntet	mochtet	mußtet	solltet	wolltet
sie, Sie	durften	konnten	mochten	mußten	sollten	wollten

There are some verbs in German that form the imperfect like weak verbs but also have a stem vowel change:

	kennen	nennen	denken	bringen	wissen
ich	kannte	nannte	dachte	brachte	wußte
du	kanntest	nanntest	dachtest	brachtest	wußtest
er, sie	kannte	nannte	dachte	brachte	wußte
wir	kannten	nannten	dachten	brachten	wußten
ihr	kanntet	nanntet	dachtet	brachtet	wußtet
sie, Sie	kannten	nannten	dachten	brachten	wußten

THE SUBJUNCTIVE FORMS

	haben	sein	werden	wissen
ich	hätte	wäre	würde	wüßte
du	hättest	wärst	würdest	wüßtest
er, sie, es	hätte	wäre	würde	wüßte
wir	hätten	wären	würden	wüßten
ihr	hättet	wäret	würdet	wüßtet
sie, Sie	hätten	wären	würden	wüßten

	können	müssen	dürfen	sollen	wollen
ich	könnte	müßte	dürfte	sollte	wollte
du	könntest	müßtest	dürftest	solltest	wolltest
er, sie, es	könnte	müßte	dürfte	sollte	wollte
wir	könnten	müßten	dürften	sollten	wollten
ihr	könntet	müßtet	dürftet	solltet	wolltet
sie, Sie	könnten	müßten	dürften	sollten	wollten

CONDITIONAL SENTENCES

Conditional sentences can be used to make hypothetical statements.

fulfillable	Wenn ich Zeit **hätte, würde** ich den Müll **sortieren.** Wenn wir **könnten, würden** wir dir **helfen.** Sie **würde kommen,** wenn sie nicht so viel zu **tun hätte.**
unfulfillable	Wenn ich Zeit **gehabt hätte, hätte** ich den Müll **sortiert.** Wenn du **gekommen wärst, hättest** du auch Spaß **gehabt.** Ich **wäre gekommen,** wenn du mich **eingeladen hättest.**

PASSIVE VOICE

The passive voice is used to express that something is being done or that something has to be done. It can also describe customary occurrence. The following is a summary:

Present Imperfect Perfect Past Perfect Future	Die Karten **werden verteilt.** Der Dirigent **wurde begrüßt.** Ein Ballett **ist aufgeführt worden.** Eine Oper **war gezeigt worden.** Ein Film **wird gezeigt werden.**	*The tickets are being distributed.* *The conductor was greeted.* *A ballet has been performed.* *An opera had been shown.* *A movie will be shown.*
with modals: Present Past	Dieses Museum **muß renoviert werden.** Die Kleiderfrage **konnte geklärt werden.**	*This museum must be renovated.* *The question of what to wear was* *able to be cleared up.*
with subjunctive *forms* Die Karten {	**könnten abgeholt werden.** **müßten abgeholt werden.** **sollten abgeholt werden.**	The tickets { *could be picked up.* *need to be picked up.* *should be picked up.*

PRINCIPAL PARTS OF VERBS

This list includes the strong verbs listed in the **Wortschatz** sections of Level 1, Level 2, and Level 3. Weak verbs with stem vowel changes and other irregularites are also listed. Past participles formed with **sein** are indicated. All other past participles on the list are formed with **haben**. Usually, only one English meaning of the verb is given. Other meanings may be found in the German-English Vocabulary.

INFINITIVE	PRESENT	IMPERFECT	PAST PARTICIPLE	MEANING
abnehmen	nimmt ab	nahm ab	abgenommen	*to lose weight*
anbieten	bietet an	bot an	angeboten	*to offer*
anfangen	fängt an	fing an	angefangen	*to begin*
angeben	gibt an	gab an	angegeben	*to indicate*
anpreisen	preist an	pries an	angepriesen	*to praise*
abheben	hebt ab	hob ab	abgehoben	*to lift*
annehmen	nimmt an	nahm an	angenommen	*to assume*
anrufen	ruft an	rief an	angerufen	*to call up*
ansprechen	spricht an	sprach an	angesprochen	*to address, speak to*
anziehen	zieht an	zog an	angezogen	*to put on (clothes)*
auffallen	fällt auf	fiel auf	aufgefallen	*to be conspicuous*
aushalten	hält aus	hielt aus	ausgehalten	*to endure*
ausleihen	leiht aus	lieh aus	ausgeliehen	*to borrow, lend*
aussehen	sieht aus	sah aus	ausgesehen	*to look, appear*
beitragen	trägt bei	trug bei	beigetragen	*to contribute*
bekommen	bekommt	bekam	bekommen	*to get, receive*
beschreiben	beschreibt	beschrieb	beschrieben	*to describe*
bestreichen	bestreicht	bestrich	bestrichen	*to spread, to butter*
blasen	bläst	blies	geblasen	*to blow*
bleiben	bleibt	blieb	(ist) geblieben	*to stay*
brechen	bricht	brach	gebrochen	*to break*
denken	denkt	dachte	gedacht	*to think*
eingestehen	gesteht ein	gestand ein	eingestanden	*to admit*
einladen	lädt ein	lud ein	eingeladen	*to invite*
einziehen	zieht ein	zog ein	eingezogen	*to draft*
erfahren	erfährt	erfuhr	erfahren	*to experience*
erkennen	erkennt	erkannte	erkannt	*to recognize*
essen	ißt	aß	gegessen	*to eat*
fahren	fährt	fuhr	(ist) gefahren	*to drive, ride*
fernsehen	sieht fern	sah fern	ferngesehen	*to watch TV*
finden	findet	fand	gefunden	*to find*
geben	gibt	gab	gegeben	*to give*
gefallen	gefällt	gefiel	gefallen	*to like, be pleasing to*
gehen	geht	ging	(ist) gegangen	*to go*
gießen	gießt	goß	gegossen	*to pour, to water*
großziehen	zieht groß	zog groß	großgezogen	*to raise (a child)*
haben	hat	hatte	gehabt	*to have*
halten	hält	hielt	gehalten	*to keep*
heben	hebt	hob	gehoben	*to lift*
heißen	heißt	hieß	geheißen	*to be called*
helfen	hilft	half	geholfen	*to help*
herausnehmen	nimmt heraus	nahm heraus	herausgenommen	*to take out*
kennen	kennt	kannte	gekannt	*to know*
klingen	klingt	klang	geklungen	*to sound*
kommen	kommt	kam	(ist) gekommen	*to come*

INFINITIVE	PRESENT	IMPERFECT	PAST PARTICIPLE	MEANING
lassen	läßt	ließ	gelassen	*to let*
laufen	läuft	lief	(ist) gelaufen	*to run*
lesen	liest	las	gelesen	*to read*
messen	mißt	maß	gemessen	*to measure*
nachsehen	sieht nach	sah nach	nachgesehen	*to check*
nehmen	nimmt	nahm	genommen	*to take*
radfahren	fährt Rad	fuhr Rad	(ist) radgefahren	*to bicycle*
scheinen	scheint	schien	geschienen	*to shine*
schiefgehen	geht schief	ging schief	(ist) schiefgegangen	*to go badly*
schießen	schießt	schoß	geschossen	*to shoot*
schlafen	schläft	schlief	geschlafen	*to sleep*
schlagen	schlägt	schlug	geschlagen	*to hit; to slam*
schreiben	schreibt	schrieb	geschrieben	*to write*
schwimmen	schwimmt	schwamm	(ist) geschwommen	*to swim*
sehen	sieht	sah	gesehen	*to see*
sein	ist	war	(ist) gewesen	*to be*
sprechen	spricht	sprach	gesprochen	*to speak*
stehen	steht	stand	gestanden	*to stand*
streiten	streitet	stritt	gestritten	*to quarrel*
tragen	trägt	trug	getragen	*to wear; to carry*
trinken	trinkt	trank	getrunken	*to drink*
tun	tut	tat	getan	*to do*
übertreiben	übertreibt	übertrieb	übertrieben	*to exaggerate*
s. umsehen	sieh s. um	sah s. um	umgesehen	*to look around*
umziehen	zieht um	zog um	(ist) umgezogen	*to move (residence)*
unterbrechen	unterbricht	unterbrach	unterbrochen	*to interrupt*
s. unterhalten	unterhält s.	unterhielt s.	unterhalten	*to discuss*
unternehmen	unternimmt	unternahm	unternommen	*to undertake*
unterschreiben	unterschreibt	unterschrieb	unterschrieben	*to sign*
verbergen	verbirgt	verbarg	verborgen	*to hide*
verbieten	verbietet	verbot	verboten	*to forbid*
s. verbrennen	verbrennt s.	verbrannte s.	verbrannt	*to burn oneself*
vergehen	vergeht	verging	(ist) vergangen	*to pass (time)*
vergleichen	vergleicht	verglich	verglichen	*to compare*
s. verlassen	verläßt s.	verließ s.	verlassen	*to count on*
verlieren	verliert	verlor	verloren	*to lose*
vermeiden	vermeidet	vermied	vermieden	*to avoid*
vorlesen	liest vor	las vor	vorgelesen	*to read aloud*
vorschlagen	schlägt vor	schlug vor	vorgeschlagen	*to suggest*
versprechen	verspricht	versprach	versprochen	*to promise*
vorhaben	hat vor	hatte vor	vorgehabt	*to plan*
vorziehen	zieht vor	zog vor	vorgezogen	*to prefer*
wahrnehmen	nimmt wahr	nahm wahr	wahrgenommen	*to perceive*
waschen	wäscht	wusch	gewaschen	*to wash*
weggeben	gibt weg	gab weg	weggegeben	*to give away*
weglassen	läßt weg	ließ weg	weggelassen	*to omit, to drop*
wegtragen	trägt weg	trug weg	weggetragen	*to take away*
wegwerfen	wirft weg	warf weg	weggeworfen	*to throw away*
werben	wirbt	warb	geworben	*to advertise*
wiedergeben	gibt wieder	gab wieder	wiedergegeben	*to repeat*
wissen	weiß	wußte	gewußt	*to know*
zugeben	gibt zu	gab zu	zugegeben	*to admit*
zukommen	kommt zu	kam zu	(ist) zugekommen	*to be in store for*
zunehmen	nimmt zu	nahm zu	zugenommen	*to gain weight*
zurückbringen	bringt zurück	brachte zurück	zurückgebracht	*to bring back*

GERMAN-ENGLISH VOCABULARY

This vocabulary includes almost all the German words in the textbook, both active (for production) and passive (for recognition only). Active words and phrases, indicated by bold faced type, are practiced in the chapter and are listed in the Wortschatz section at the end of each chapter. You are expected to know and be able to use active vocabulary. All other words are for recognition only and can often be understood from the context.

With some exceptions, the following are not included: proper nouns, verb conjugations, and forms of determiners. You will find irregular forms of past participles and the narrative past.

Nouns are listed with definite article and plural form, where applicable. The numbers after the entries refer to the level and chapter where the word or phrase first appears or where it becomes an active vocabulary word. Vocabulary from the location openers is followed by a "Loc" and the chapter number directly following the location spread.

The following abbreviations are used in this list: acc (accusative case), adj (adjective), coll (colloquial), conj (conjunction), dat (dative case), gen (genitive case), pl (plural), poss adj (possessive adjective), pp (past participle), prep (preposition), s. (*sich,* or reflexive), sep (separable-prefix verb), and sing (singular).

A

ab (dat prep) *down, off,* III 1
ab und zu *now and then,* III6
abbaubar *degradable,* III9
abbauen (sep): **Vorurteile abbauen** *to overcome prejudices,* III8
abbilden (sep) *to depict, draw,* III1
die Abbildung, -en *drawing, picture,* III8
abbrechen (sep) *to break off,* III4
abdrucken (sep) *to print, reprint,* III6
der Abend, -e *evening,* I; **am Abend** *in the evening,* I
das Abendessen, - *dinner, evening meal,* II
die Abendkasse, -n *ticket booth,* III10
das Abendkleid, -er *evening gown,* II
abends *evenings,* III4
die Abendvorstellung, -en *evening performance,* III10
der Abenteuerfilm, -e *adventure film,* I
abenteuerlich *adventurous,* III3
aber (conj) *but,* I; **aber sicher!** *but of course!,* II
abermals *over and over again,* III7
der Abfall, -̈e *trash, waste,* III9
die Abfalltüte, -n *trash bag,* III2
das Abgas, -e *exhaust,* III9
abgedroschen *trite, hackneyed,* III5
abgefahren (slang) *worn out,* III3
abgegriffen *well-worn, shabby,* III11
abgeschlossen *finished,* III11
abgeschnitten *cut-off,* II
abgeworben *enticed away,* III2
abhängen von (sep) *to be dependent on,* III12
abhauen (sep) (coll) *to leave,* III4
abheben (sep) *to pick up,* I; **den Hörer abheben** *to pick up the receiver,* I

abholen (sep) *to pick up,* III8
abholzen (sep) *to deforest,* III9
das Abi=Abitur, III3
das Abitur (*final exam and diploma from a German high school*), III4
Abiturient(in), -en/nen *student studying for the Abitur,* III5
die Abkürzung, -en *abbreviation,* III9
das Ablagefach, -̈er *storage shelf,* II
ablehnen (sep) *to turn down, reject,* III3
s. ablenken mit (sep) *to divert oneself with,* III3
abnehmen (sep) *to lose weight,* III3
das Abonnement, -s *subscription,* III10
abpflücken (sep) *to pick (from a plant),* III11
abräumen (sep) *to clean up, clear off,* I
die Abrechnung, -en *deduction, settlement of an account,* III5
der Absatz, -̈e *paragraph,* III3; *sales,* III7; *shoe heel,* II
abschließen (sep) *to lock up,* III1
der Abschluß, -̈sse *end, conclusion; diploma,* III11
der Abschnitt, -e *paragraph,* III6
abschreiben (sep) *to copy,* III4
absichtlich *on purpose,* III4
absolut *absolute(ly), unconditional(ly),* III3
der Absolvent, -en *graduate,* III11
s. absondern von (sep) *to separate oneself from,* III4
abstellen (sep) *to switch off,* II
abstreiten (sep) *to dispute, contest,* III5
die Abteilung, -en *division, department,* III4
die Abteilungsleiterin, -nen *head of a*

department, III4
abwarten (sep) *to wait and see,* III2
das Abwasser, -̈ *wastewater,* III9
abwechselnd *alternating, one after the other,* III1
die Abwechslung, -en *change, variety,* III10
abwechslungsreich *varied, diversified,* II
Ach *Oh!,* I; **Ach ja!** *Oh yeah!,* I
Ach schade! *That's too bad.,* II
achten auf (acc) *to pay attention to,* III3
ächzend *groaning,* III2
der Actionfilm, -e *action movie,* I
die Adresse, -n *address,* III2
ägyptisch (adj) *Egyptian,* II
ahnen *to suspect, surmise,* III1
ähnlich *similar,* III3
die Ahnung, -en *idea, notion,* III4; **Keine Ahnung!** *I have no idea!,* I
der Akkord, -e *agreement,* III12
der Akt, -e *act, action,* III10
die Aktion, -en *activity, initiative,* III9
aktiv *active,* III1
aktuell *current, contemporary,* III7
akzeptabel *acceptable,* III7
akzeptieren *to accept,* III4
der Alkohol, -e *alcohol,* II
all- *all,* II
allein *alone,* III5
allerdings *certainly, by all means,* III3
die Allergie, -n *allergy,* III1
allergisch (gegen) *allergic (to),* II
allerkleinst- *the littlest,* III2
allernötigst- *indispensible,* III3
allgemein *general,* III5
die Allgemeinbildung *all-round education, general knowledge,* III11
allmählich *gradually,* III11

der Alltag, -e *weekday, workday routine,* III1

alltäglich *daily,* III1

allwissend *omniscient,* III7

als *than,* II; **als** (conj) *when, at the time,* III8

als ob (conj) *as if, as though,* III7

also (part) *well, okay,* III2

alt *old,* I

das Altenheim, -e *home for the elderly,* III5

älter *older,* II

die Altersgruppe, -n *age group,* III5

der Altersjahrgang, -̈e *year of birth,* III11

das Altpapier *recyclable paper,* III9

das Alu=Aluminium *aluminum,* III9

die Aludose, -n *aluminum can,* III9

am=an dem *at the,* I; **am Abend** *in the evening,* I; **am ersten (Juli)** *on the first (of July),* I; **am letzten Tag** *on the last day,* I; **am liebsten** *most of all,* I; **am Tag** *during the day,* II

die Ameise, -n *ant,* III9

das Amerikabild *impression of America,* III8

die Ampel, -n *traffic light,* I; **bis zur Ampel** *until you get to the traffic light,* I

s. amüsieren *to have a good time,* III6

an (acc, dat prep) *to; at,* II; **an der Schule** *at school,* II

an: Was an dir gut ist, ist ... *What I like about you is ...,* III4

die Analyse, -n *analysis,* III7

analysieren *to analyse,* III7

Anästhesist(in), -en/nen *anesthesiologist,* III12

anbieten (sep) *to offer,* III9

der Anblick, -e *view, sight, look,* III7

ander- *other,* I; **ein(-) ander-** *another (a different) one,* II

andererseits *on the other hand,* III5

s. **ändern** *to change oneself,* III5

anders *different,* III4

anderswo *elsewhere,* III11

die Änderung, -en *change,* III12

die Anekdote, -n *anecdote,* III6

anerkennen (sep) *to recognize, acknowledge,* III5

der Anfang, -̈e *beginning,* III1

anfangen (sep) *to begin,* III11

der Anfänger, - *beginner,* II

anfangs *in the beginning,* III10

anfüllen (sep) *to fill up,* III10

angeben (sep) *to indicate, state,* III11

angeblich *ostensibly, reported to be,* III7

das Angebot, -e *offer,* I; **Angebot der Woche** *weekly special,* I

angeboten *offered,* III2

angehören (sep, dat) *to belong to,* III4

angeht: was (das) angeht *as far as (that) goes,* III3

angeln *to fish,* II

angenehm *comfortable, pleasant,* III5

angenommen *accepted, assumed,* III8

angepriesen *praised,* III7

angespannt *tense,* III2

angesprochen *spoken to,* III6

angestaubt *old, dusty,* III10

Angestellte, -n *employee,* III11

angewiesen sein auf (acc) *to be dependent on,* III11

angezogen *dressed,* III3

Angst haben vor (dat) *to be afraid of,* III2

ängstlich *anxious,* III7

anhaben (sep) *to have on,* III3

der Anhaltspunkt, -e *guiding principle, deciding factor,* III7

anhand *based on,* III3

anhören (sep) *to listen to,* III1

ankommen (sep) *to arrive,* III1; **Es kommt darauf an, ob ...** *It depends on whether ...,* III4; **ankommen bei** (sep) *to be accepted by,* III3

ankreuzen (sep) *to cross, mark off,* III3

die Anlage, -n *grounds, site,* II; *system, installation,* II

anlaufen: rot anlaufen *to blush,* III4

der Anlaß, (pl) Anlässe *occasion,* III5

die Anleitung, -en *direction, introduction,* III3

anlocken (sep) *to lure,* III2

die Annahmestelle, -n *receiving area,* III9

annehmen (sep) *to assume,* III8

die Annonce, -n *ad, announcement,* III6

anonym *anonymous,* III6

der Anorak, -s *parka,* II

s. **anpassen** (sep) *to conform to,* III3

anpreisen (sep) *to praise,* III7

anprobieren (sep) *to try on,* I

die Anrede, -n *speech, address,* III7

anregen (sep) *to encourage, stimulate,* III6

anregend *stimulating, exciting,* III6

die Anregung, -en *stimulation, incitement,* III2

die Anreise, -n *arrival,* III2

anrichten (sep) *to produce, cause, prepare,* III9

anrufen (sep) *to call (on the phone),* I

der Ansager, - *announcer,* III10

ansah (*imperfect of* ansehen), III10

anschauen (sep) *to look at,* III4

anschaulich *clear, vivid,* III7

der Anschlag, -̈e *announcement,* II

anschlagen (sep) *to strike; to post,* III12

anschließend *following, adjacent,* III1

s. ansehen (sep) *to have a look at,* III2

die Ansicht, -en *view, point of view,* III9

ansprechen (sep) *to talk to,* III1

anstatt (gen prep) *instead of,* III10

anstrahlen (sep) *to shine on; to smile at,* III7

s. **anstrengen** (sep) *to make an effort,*

III12

anstrengend *strenuous,* III5

anstupsen (sep) *to nudge,* III10

der Anteil, -e *portion, share,* III8

die Antwort, -en *answer,* III2

antworten (dat) *to answer,* III1

anvertrauen (sep, dat) *to entrust to,* III5

der Anwalt, -̈e *lawyer,* III11

die Anwältin, -nen *lawyer,* III11

die Anweisung, -en *order, instruction,* III5

anwenden (sep) *to make use of,* III10

die Anwendung, -en *application, use,* III3

die Anzahl *number, quantity,* III10

die Anzeige, -n *ad,* III6

anziehen (sep) *to put on, wear,* I

der Anziehungspunkt, -e *center of attraction,* III1

der Anzug, -̈e *suit,* II

der Apfel, -̈ *apple,* I

der Apfelkuchen, - apple cake, I

der Apfelsaft, -̈e *apple juice,* I; **ein Glas Apfelsaft** *a glass of apple juice,* I

die Apotheke, -n *pharmacy,* II

der Apotheker, - *pharmacist,* III5

der Apparat, -e *telephone,* I

der Appell, -e *appeal,* III7

der Appetit: Guten Appetit! *Bon appétit!,* II

applaudieren *to applaud,* III10

die Aprikose, -n *apricot,* II

der April *April,* I

die Arbeit, -en *work,* III1

arbeiten *to work,* II

der Arbeiter, - *worker,* III6

das Arbeitsamt, -̈er *employment office,* III11

der Arbeitsmarkt, -̈e *job market,* III11

die Arbeitsstelle, -n *job position,* III11

das Arbeitstempo, -s *work rate,* III11

der Arbeitsvertrag, -̈e *work contract,* III5

das Arbeitszeugnis, -se *work performance review,* III11

der Architekt, -en *architect,* III11

die Architektur *architecture,* III11

der Ärger *irritation, annoyance,* III6

ärgerlich *annoying,* III1

s. **ärgern** *to get annoyed,* III8

argumentieren *to argue,* III2

der Arm, -e *arm,* II

das Armband, -̈er *bracelet,* II

die Armbanduhr, -en *wristwatch,* I

die Armee, -n *army,* III5

der Armeelaster, - *army truck,* III5

ärmellos *sleeveless,* II

die Armen (pl) *poor,* III8

die Armut *poverty,* II

der Arrestant, -en *prisoner,* III12

die Art, -en *kind, sort,* III11; **auf ihre Art** *in their own way,* III3

der Artikel, - *article, commodity,* III3

die Arzneimittelproduktion *pharmaceutical production,* Loc10

der Arzt, -̈e *doctor,* II

aßen (*imperfect of* essen), III8

atemberaubend *breathtaking,* III7

atemlos *breathless*, III10
athletisch *athletic*, III8
atmen *to breathe*, III10
der **Atomkrieg**, -e *nuclear war*, III11
attraktiv *attractive*, III11
Au!, Aua! *Ouch!*, II
auch *also*, I; **Ich auch.** *Me too.*, I;
 auch noch *also*, II; **auch schon**
 also, II
auf (acc, dat prep) *on, onto, to*, II;
 Auf dein/Ihr/euer Wohl! *To your
 health!*, II; **auf dem Land** *in the
 country*, I; **Auf Wiederhören!**
 Goodbye!, I; **auf einer Fete** *at a
 party*, II
aufbauen (sep) *to construct*, Loc7
aufbewahren (sep) *to preserve, store*,
 III1
aufblühen (sep) *to blossom*, III10
aufeinanderkleben (sep) *to stick, glue
 together*, III10
der **Aufenthaltsraum**, ̈e *waiting room*,
 III2
auffallen (sep) *to be conspicuous*, III8
aufführen (sep) *to perform*, III10
die **Aufführung**, -en *performance*, III10
die **Aufgabe**, -n *assignment*, III6
aufgehen (sep) *to rise, expand*, III10
aufgeschlossen *open, friendly*, III8
aufgeschrieben *written down*, III1
aufging (*imperfect of* aufgehen), III12
aufkeimend *budding, dawning*, III5
aufklären (sep) *to enlighten*, III7
auflaufen (sep) *to run aground*, III9
auflegen (sep) *to hang up (the telephone)*, I
auflisten (sep) *to list*, III8
auflösen (sep) *to solve*, III3
aufmerksam machen auf (acc) *to
 draw attention to*, III7
die **Aufmerksamkeit**, -en *attention*, III7
aufnehmen (sep) *to take, pick up*, III4
aufpassen (sep) *to pay attention*, III3
aufräumen (sep) *to clean up*, I
aufregen (sep) *to excite*, III7
die **Aufregung**, -en *excitement*, III10
aufsässig *rebellious*, III4
der **Aufsatz**, ̈e *essay*, III3
aufschieben (sep) *to push open*, III2
aufschneiden (sep) *to cut open*, III1
der **Aufschnitt** *cold cuts*, III
aufschreiben (sep) *to write down*, III2
der **Aufseher**, - *supervisor*, III10
aufsetzen (sep) *to put or place on*,
 III10
aufstand (*imperfect of* aufstehen),
 III12
aufstecken (sep) *to put up*, III9
aufstehen (sep) *to get up*, III5
die **Aufstiegschance**, -n *chance for promotion*, III11
die **Aufstiegsmöglichkeit**, -en *possibility
 for promotion*, III5
aufwachen (sep) *to wake up*, III10
aufwachsen (sep) *to grow up*, III4
aufzeigen (sep) *to show, exhibit*, III10

das **Auge**, -n *eye*, I
der **Augenblick**, -e *moment*, III1
der **August** *August*, I
aus (dat prep) *from, out of*, II; **aus
 Baumwolle** *made of cotton*, I; **aus
 dem (16.) Jahrhundert** *from the
 (16th) century*, II
ausarbeiten (sep) *to work out in
 detail*, III1
ausbilden (sep) *to educate*, III4
die **Ausbildung**, -en *education*, II
ausbleiben (sep) *to stay out*, III1
ausbrechen (sep) *to break out*, III8
die **Ausdauer** *perseverance, endurance*,
 III3
ausdenken (sep) *to think, work out*,
 III10
der **Ausdruck**, ̈e *expression*, III4
ausdrücken (sep) *to express*, III3
auseinander *from each other*, III3
auseinanderhalten (sep) *to hold, keep
 apart*, III6
auseinandernehmen (sep) *to take
 apart*, III12
auseinanderspalten (sep) *to split
 apart*, III10
der **Ausflug**, ̈e *excursion*, II
das **Ausführen** *development*, III1
ausführlich *detailed*, III1
ausfüllen (sep) *to fill out*, III11
die **Ausgabe**, -n *edition*, III6
der **Ausgangspunkt**, -e *point of departure*,
 III1
ausgeben (sep) *to give out; to spend
 (money)*, III3
ausgedacht *thought up*, III10
ausgefallen *unusual*, III3
ausgeflippt (slang) *flipped-out*, III3
ausgegangen *gone out*, III7
ausgehen (sep) *to go out*, III4
ausgehen von (sep) *to be initiated
 by*, III10
ausgelassen *boisterous*, III1
ausgeliehen *borrowed, checked out*,
 III1
ausgerechnet *just, of all*, III9
ausgesprochen *distinct*, III5
ausgewogen *well-balanced*, III8
ausgezeichnet *excellent, outstanding*,
 II
ausgezogen *moved out*, III4
ausgiebig *extensive, exhaustive*, III10
aushalten (sep) *to endure, stand
 something*, III3
**auskommen: Wir kommen gut mit
 ihm aus.** *We get along well with
 him.*, III4
auslachen (sep) *to laugh (at someone)*, III2
das **Ausland** *foreign country*, III8
Ausländer(in), -/-nen *foreigner*, III4
ausländisch *foreign*, II
ausleihen (sep) *to borrow, lend*, III1
auslösen (sep) *to trigger, cause*, III9
die **Auslösung**, -en *cause*, III5
s. **ausmachen** (sep) *to make up, consti-*

tute, III9; **Das macht mir nichts
 aus.** *That doesn't matter to me.*,
 III6
ausnutzen (sep) *to take advantage
 of*, III7
ausquetschen (sep) *to squeeze out*,
 III5
ausrechnen (sep) *to calculate*, III9
die **Ausrede**, -n *excuse*, III9
ausreden (sep) *to finish speaking*,
 III6
s. **ausruhen** (sep) *to relax, rest*, III11
ausrutschen (sep) *to slip*, III1
die **Aussage**, -n *statement*, III1
**aussagen: Das sagt etwas über mich
 aus.** *That says something about
 me.*, III3
ausschalten (sep) *to switch off*, III9
ausschlaggebend *decisive*, III11
ausschließlich *exclusively*, III9
der **Ausschluß**, ̈sse *exclusion*, III5
der **Ausschnitt**, -e *excerpt*, III6
aussehen (sep) *to look like, to
 appear*, I; **der Rock sieht ... aus.**
 The skirt looks..., I; **Wie sieht er
 aus?** *What does he look like?*, I
das **Außengelände** *surroundings*, III2
außerdem *besides that*, III9
außerhalb (gen prep) *outside of*, III4
äußern *to express*, III3
äußerst *highly*, III8
die **Äußerung**, -en *comment, remark*, III3
ausspannen (sep) *to spread, stretch
 out*, III12
ausstatten (sep) *to equip*, III2
die **Ausstattung**, -en *equipment, furnish-
 ing*, III2
aussteigen (sep) *to get off (a train)*,
 III1
ausstellen (sep) *to exhibit, display*,
 Loc10
die **Ausstellung**, -en *exhibition*, III10
ausstrecken (sep) *to stick out*, III10
s. **aussuchen** (sep) *to pick out, select*,
 III1
der **Austausch**, -e *exchange*, III4
austauschen (sep) *to exchange*, III4
die **Auster**, -n *oyster*, II
ausüben (sep) *to practice, pursue*,
 III11
auswählen (sep) *to choose from*,
 III2
der **Ausweis**, -e *identification*, III2
auswendig *by heart, rote*, III5
auswickeln (sep) *to unwrap, undo*,
 III10
ausziehen (sep) *to move out, away*,
 III4
der **Auszug**, ̈e *excerpt*, III5
das **Auto**, -s *car*, I; **mit dem Auto** *by car*,
 I
die **Autobahn**, -en *interstate highway*,
 III8
der **Autofahrer**, - *driver*, III11
automatisch *automatic*, III6
Autor(in), -en/-nen *author*, III10

Azubi(=Auszubildende), -s *trainee, apprentice*, III4

B

der **Bäcker**, - *baker*, I
die **Bäckerei**, -en *bakery*, I
die Backsteingotik *gothic architecture style with red brick*, III1
   baden *to swim*, I; **baden gehen** *to go swimming*, I
der Badeort, -e *swimming resort*, III1
das **Badezimmer**, - *bathroom*, II
die **Bahn**, -en *train*, II
der **Bahnhof**, ⁼e *train station*, I
das **Ballett**, -e *ballet*, II
die **Banane**, -n *banana*, II
   bang, *anxious*, III2
die **Bank**, -en *bank*, III1
   Bankangestellte, -n *bank employee*, III1
das Bankett, -e *banquet*, Loc7
die Bankkauffrau, -en *banker*, III11
der Bankkaufmann, -leute *banker*, III11
der Bankschalter, - *bank window*, III5
das Bankwesen *banking*, Loc7
das Barock *baroque style*, Loc4
   barock *baroque*, Loc10
   bärtig *bearded*, III10
   basieren auf (acc) *to establish, base on*, III9
   Basketball *basketball*, I
die Baßschläge (pl) *bass beats*, III3
   basteln *to do crafts*, I
die **Batterie**, -n *battery*, III9
der Bau *construction*, III8
der **Bauch**, ⁼e *stomach*, II
die **Bauchschmerzen** (pl) *stomachache*, II
der Baudenabend, -e *folkloristic evening entertainment at a cabin*, III2
das **Baudenkmal**, ⁼er *monument*, II
   bauen *to build*, III8
der Bauhelm, -e *hardhat*, III3
der **Baum**, ⁼e *tree*, II
der Baumeister, - *architect*, Loc10
die **Baumwolle** *cotton*, I
das Bauwerk, -e *structure, building*, Loc10
   beabsichtigen *to intend*, III7
   beachten *to notice, heed, regard*, III6
der Beamte, -n *offical, civil servant*, III11
die Beamtin, -nen *offical, civil servant*, III11
   beantworten *to answer*, III1
   bearbeiten *to work at, process*, III2
   beben *to shake, tremble*, III10
der **Becher**, - *mug*, III2
   bedauern *to be sorry about*, II
die Bedenken (pl) *misgivings*, III7
   bedeuten *to mean*, III1
die Bedeutung, -en *meaning*, III4
   bedienen: die Kamera bedienen *to operate the camera*, II
die Bedingung, -en *condition*, III11

   bedrücken *to press; to oppress*, III10
das Bedürfnis, -se *need*, III3
   beeindrucken *to impress*, III8
   beeinflussen *to influence*, III3
   beenden *to end*, III3
   befahl (*imperfect of* befehlen), III7
   befallen *to befall*, III7
   befehlen *to command*, III7
s. **befinden** *to find oneself, to be*, Loc1
   befolgen *to obey, follow*, III12
   befragen *to ask questions*, III8
   befriedigen *to satisfy*, III7
   befürchten *to fear, suspect*, III10
   begabt *gifted*, III10
   begann (*imperfect of* beginnen), III3
   begegnen (dat) *to run into, meet*, III10
die Begegnung, -en *meeting, encounter*, III2
   begeistert sein von *to be excited about*, III8
der Beginn *beginning*, III5
   beginnen *to begin*, III11
   begleiten *to accompany*, III10
   begonnen *begun*, III4
der Begriff, -e *concept, idea*, III9
   begründen *to found; to give a reason for*, III6
der Begründer, - *founder*, III5
die Begründung, -en *reason; foundation*, III2
   begrüßen *to greet*, III10
   behalten *to keep*, III7
der Behälter, - *container*, III8
   behandeln *to handle, treat*, III4
   behaupten *to claim, assert*, III12
   beherbergen *to shelter*, Loc4
   beherrschen *to rule*, III7
   behindertenfreundlich *accessible to the physically challenged*, III2
   bei (dat prep) *by, near, at*, II; **beim Bäcker** *at the baker's*, I; **Bei mir ist es auch so.** *That's the way it is with me, too.*, III4
   beide *both*, III2
   beidseitig *on both sides, mutual*, III9
die **Beilage**, -n *side dish*, II
das **Bein**, -e *leg*, II
   beinahe *almost*, III8
   beinhalten *to contain*, III10
das **Beispiel**, -e *example*, III1
der **Beitrag**, ⁼e *contribution*, III11
   beitragen zu (sep) *to contribute to*, III6
   bejahen *to concur, agree*, III9
   bekam (*imperfect of* bekommen), III6
   bekannt *known*, III1
der Bekanntenkreis, -e *circle of acquaintances*, III6
s. **beklagen über** (acc) *to complain about*, III10
die Bekleidung, -en *clothes*, III7
   bekommen *to get, receive*, I
   bekömmlich *wholesome, beneficial*, III10
   belasten *to weigh on, burden*, III5

die Belastung, -en *burden*, III9
   belegen *to cover; to register for*, III1
   beliebt *popular*, III4
   bellen *to bark, howl*, III11
die Bemerkung, -en *comment, remark*, III1
s. **bemühen um** *to strive for*, III6
s. **benehmen** *to behave*, III4
   beneiden *to envy*, III10
   benötigen *to need*, III5
   benutzen *to use*, III4
   beobachten *to observe*, III8
die Beobachtung, -en *observation*, III4
   bequem *comfortable*, I
   beraten *to advise*, III2
der Berater, - *advisor*, III12
der Bereich, -e *area, field, region*, III9
   bereichern *to enrich*, III8
   bereit *willing, prepared*, III3
   bereits *already*, III11
   hereitstellen (sep) *to make ready*, III10
   bereitwillig *willing*, III10
der **Berg**, -e *mountain*, II
die Bergtour, -en *tour or trip in the mountains*, III1
der **Bericht**, -e *report*, III6
   berichten *to report*, III3
   berücksichtigen *to take into consideration*, III5
der **Beruf**, -e *profession*, III11
   beruflich *professional(ly)*, III5
die Berufserfahrung, -en *professional experience*, III11
die Berufstätigkeit, -en *occupation*, III11
die Berufswahl, -en *choice of profession*, III11
   beruhen auf (acc) *to be founded on*, III11
   berühmt *famous*, III2
   besann (*imperfect of* besinnen), III7
s. **beschäftigen mit** *to keep busy with*, III3
die Bescheidenheit, -en *modesty*, III5
   bescheuert *dumb*, III3
   beschleunigen *to accelerate*, III4
   beschließen *to decide*, III11
   beschlossen *decided*, III11
   beschränken *to limit*, III1
   beschreiben *to describe*, II
die Beschreibung, -en *description*, III2
   beschrieben *described*, III1
die Beschwerde, -n *trouble, complaint*, III7
   beschwören *to implore*, III5
die Beseitigung, -en *removal, elimination*, III5
   besetzt *busy (on the telephone)*, I
   besichtigen *to sightsee, visit a place*, II
die Besichtigung, -en *sightseeing, visit*, III2
   besiegt *defeated*, III1
   besinnen *to think about, consider*, III7
   besonders *especially*, I

besorgen *to provide*, III1
die Besorgung, -en *worry*, III5
besprechen *to discuss*, III5
besser *better*, I
die **Besserung**, -en *improvement*, II; **Gute Besserung!** *Get well soon!*, II
der Bestandteil, -e *part, component*, III9
das **Besteck** *silverware*, III2
bestehen aus *to consist of*, III5
bestellen *to order*, III1
besten: am besten *the best*, II
bestimmen *to determine*, III2
bestimmt *certainly, definitely*, I
bestreichen *to spread, to butter*, III1
der Besuch, -e *visit*, III4
besuchen *to visit*, I
betäuben *to stun, anesthetize*, III2
betrachten *to observe*, III11
betreten *to step on; to enter*, III12
betreuen *to take care of*, III5
der Betrieb, -e *business, firm*, Loc 10
die Betriebswirtschaft *business administration*, III11
betrogen *deceived, defrauded*, III5
das **Bett**, -en *bed*, I
betten *to rest*, III12
beugen *to bend*, III10
beurteilen nach *to judge according to*, III3
der Beutel, - *bag, pouch, sack*, III9
die Bevölkerung *population, inhabitants*, III5
bevor (conj) *before*, III5
bewachen *to guard*, III5
s. **bewähren** *to prove oneself*, III5
bewegen *to move*, III10
die Bewegung, -en *movement, motion*, III8
beweisen *to prove*, III10
s. **bewerben** *to apply*, III11
der Bewerber, - *applicant*, III2
die Bewerbung, -en *application*, III11
die Bewerbungsunterlage, -n *application material*, III11
das Bewerbungsverfahren *process of making an application*, III11
bewerten *to assess*, III12
die Bewertung, -en *assessment*, III3
bewiesen *proven*, III10
bewundern *to admire*, III10
die Bewunderung *astonishment, marvel*, III10
bewußt *conscious(ly)*, III3
bezahlen *to pay*, III1
bezeichnen *to indicate*, III2
die Bezeichnung, -en *indication, description*, III4
s. **beziehen auf** (acc) *to refer to*, III3
die Beziehung, -en *relationship*, III3
das Beziehungswort, ¨er *antecedent*, III7
Bezug haben zu *to have a connection to*, III8
bezweifeln *to doubt*, II
die Bibliothek, -en *library*, III10
bieder *upright, bourgeois*, III5
biegen *to bend, curve, turn*, II; ein-

biegen (sep): **Biegen Sie hier ein!** *Turn here!*, II
die **Biene**, -n *bee*, III9
bieten *to offer*, III1
das **Bild**, -er *picture*, III2
bilden *to form, construct*, III1
bildend: die bildenden Künste *the visual arts*, III10
der Bildhauer, - *sculptor*, Loc1
bildreich *rich in imagery*, III10
der Bildschirm, -e *display screen*, III6
die **Bildung**, -en *formulation*, III6
der Bildungsweg, -e *educational path*, III4
billig *cheap*, III2
die **Biokost** *organic food*, III3
Biologe/Biologin -n/nen, *biologist*, III11
die **Biologie=Bio** *biology*, I
die **Biologielehrerin**, -nen *biology teacher*, I
biologisch abbaubar *bio-degradable*, III9
birgst (*from* bergen) *to hide*, III2
die **Birne**, -n *pear*, II
bis (acc prep) *until*, III11; **Bis dann!** *Till then! See you later!*, I; **bis dahin** *until then*, III11
der Bischof, ¨e *bishop*, Loc4
bisher *up to now*, III10
bislang *up to now*, III8
das Bistum, ¨er *episcopate, diocese*, Loc4
bitte *please*, I; **Bitte (sehr/schön)!** *You're (very) welcome!*, I; **Bitte! Hier!** *Here you go!*, II
bitten *to request*, III1
bitter *bitter*, II
bißchen: ein bißchen *a little*, I
blasen *to blow*, III9
der Bläser, - *wind instrument player*, III10
die Blaskapelle, -n *brass-band*, III8
das **Blatt**, ¨er *leaf*, III1
blau *blue*, I
die Blaubeere, -n *blueberry*, II
der **Blazer**, - *blazer*, II
das Blei *lead*, III9
bleiben *to stay, remain*, II
der **Bleistift**, -e *pencil*, I
der Blick, -e *glance, view*, III2
der **Blickfang** *eye-catcher*, III7
der Blickpunkt, -e *point of view*, III2
blieb (*imperfect of* bleiben), III4
blitzblank *squeaky clean*, III7
die Blockflöte, -n *recorder (flute)*, III12
blöd *dumb*, I
blond *blonde*, I
der Blouson, -s *bomber jacket*, II
bloß *only*, I; **Was soll ich bloß machen?** *Well, what am I supposed to do?*, II
blühen *to flower, blossom*, III10
die **Blume**, -n *flower*, I
der **Blumenkohl** *cauliflower*, II
der **Blumenstrauß**, ¨e *flower bouquet*, I
die **Bluse**, -n *blouse*, II
das Blut *blood*, III5
der Boden *floor, ground*, III10

das **Bogenschießen** *archery*, II
die **Bohne**, -n *bean*, II
der Bombenangriff, -e *bomb attack*, Loc10
der **Bomber**, - *bomber*, III5
das **Boot**, -e *boat*, II; **Boot fahren** *to go for a boat ride*, II
böse *angry, evil*, III4
der **Bote**, -n *messenger*, III7
der Botengang, ¨e *errand*, III1
die Boulevardzeitung, -en *tabloid newspaper*, III6
brachte (*imperfect of* bringen), III6
brannte (*imperfect of* brennen), III7
der **Braten** *roast*, II
die **Bratkartoffeln** (pl) *fried potatoes*, II
brauchen *to need*, I
braun *brown*, I
s. **brechen (etwas)** *to break (something)*, II; **er/sie bricht** *he/she breaks*, II
die Brechung, -en *breaking*, III5
breit *large, wide*, III7
die **Bremse**, -n *brake*, II
brennen *to burn*, III3
das **Brettspiel**, -e *board game*, I; **ein Brettspiel spielen** *to play a board game*, I
die **Brezel**, -n *pretzel*, I
der **Brief**, -e *letter*, III10
die **Briefmarke**, -n *postage stamp*, I
der Briefpartner, - *pen pal*, III2
die **Brille**, -n *a pair of glasses*, I
bringen *to bring*, III1
der **Brokkoli** *broccoli*, II
die Bronzeskulptur, -en *bronze sculpture*, Loc1
das **Brot**, -e *bread*, I
das Brötchen, - *breakfast roll*, III1
der **Bruder**, ¨ *brother*, I
der **Brunnen**, - *fountain*, II
brutal *brutal, violent*, I
der **Bube**, -n (southern German) *boy*, III10
das **Buch**, ¨er *book*, I
die **Bücherei**, -en *lending library*, III1
der Buchhandel *book trade*, Loc1
der Buchladen, ¨ *bookstore*, III1
die Buchmesse, -n *book trade fair*, Loc7
die **Büchse**, -n *can*, III8
der Buchstabe, -n *letter (of the alphabet)*, III6
buchstabieren *to spell*, III7
die **Bucht**, -en *bay*, II
bücken *to bend*, III11
bügeln *to iron*, II
die **Bühne**, -n *stage*, III10
die Bühnenanweisung, -en *stage instruction*, III11
der **Bummel** *stroll*, III1
der **Bund=Bundeswehr**, III5
der Bundesbürger, - *citizen of the Federal Republic*, III6
der Bundesgrenzschutz *Federal Border Defense*, III5
das **Bundesland**, ¨er *(German or*

Austrian) federal state, I

der **Bundestag** *German Federal Parliament*, III11

Bundestagsabgeordnete, -n *parliamentarian*, III5

die **Bundeswehr** *German Federal Defense Force*, III5

bunt *colorful*, II

die **Burg, -en** *castle*, III2

der **Bürger, -** *citizen*, III2

bürgerlich *civic, civil*, II; **gut bürgerliche Küche** *good home-cooked food*, II

der **Bursche, -n** *young man*, III7

der **Bus, -se** *bus*, I

die **Busfahrt, -en** *bus trip*, III2

die **Butter** *butter*, I

das **Butterschmalz** *shortening*, I

bzw.=beziehungsweise *respectively*, III5

C

das **Café, -s** *café*, I

der **Camembert Käse** *Camembert cheese*, II

der **Cäsar, -en** *Caesar*, Loc10

Ćevapčići *(Serbocroat: rolled spicy ground meat)*, II

die **CD, -s** *compact disc*, I

die **Chance, -n** *chance*, III12

Chanukka *Hanukkah*, I; **Frohes Chanukka-Fest!** *Happy Hanukkah!*, I

der **Charakter** *character, personality, quality*, III10

charakterisieren *to characterize*, III7

die **Charakteristik, -en** *characteristic*, III11

der **Chefkoch, ¨e** *head chef*, II

der **Chef, -s** *boss*, III4

die **Chemie** *chemistry*, III11

die **Chemikalie, -n** *chemical*, III9

chic *smart (looking)*, I

chinesisch (adj) *Chinese*, II

das **Chlor** *chlorine*, III9

die **Chronologie, -n** *chronology*, III7

die **Clique, -n** *clique*, II

das **Cola, -s** *cola (also: die Cola)*, I

die **Comics** (pl) *comic books*, I

Computerspezialist(in), -en/nen *computer specialist*, III11

der **Container, -** *recycling bin*, III8

cool (adj) *cool*, II

die **Couch, -en** *couch*, I

der **Court, -s** *court*, II

der **Couscous=Kuskus** *couscous*, II

der **Cousin, -s** *cousin (male)*, I

die **Creme, -s** *cream*, II

die **Crêpes** (pl) *crepes*, II

D

da *there*, II; **Da hast du (bestimmt) recht!** *You're right about that!*, II;

da hinten *there in the back*, I; **da vorn** *there in the front*, I; **Da stimm' ich dir zu!** *I agree with you about that!*, II

da (conj) *since*, (part) *there*, III1

dabeisein (sep) *to take part*, III11

das **Dach, ¨er** *roof*, III9

dachte *(imperfect of denken)*, III4

dafür *for it*, II; **Ich bin dafür, daß ...** *I am for doing...*, II

dagewesen *been there*, III3

daher (conj) *for this reason*, III2

dalli *schnell*, III7

damals *at that time*, III2

damit (conj) *so that, in order to*, III3

dämmerig *dim, shadowy, vague*, III10

danach *after that*, I

Danke (sehr/schön)! *Thank you (very much)!*, I; **Danke! Dir/Ihnen auch!** *Thank you! Same to you!*, II; **Danke gleichfalls!** *Thank you and the same to you!*, II

danken (dat) *to thank*, III3

dann *then*, II; **Dann nehm' ich eben ...** *In that case I'll take...*, II; **Dann trink' ich halt ...** *I'll drink instead...*, II

Darf ich (bitte) ...? *May I (please)...?*, II

darstellen (sep) *to play (act)*, III10

der **Darsteller, -** *actor*, III11

die **Darstellung, -en** *depiction, performance*, III5

darüber *over it*, II

darunter *under it, underneath*, II

daß (conj) *that*, I

dauern *to last*, III5

dauernd *continually*, III1

der **Daumen, -** *thumb*, III1

dazu *in addition*, III4

dazufügen (sep) *to add to*, III8

die **Decke, -n** *blanket*, III2

decken *to cover*, II; **den Tisch decken** *to set the table*, I

definieren *to define*, III4

deftig *robust*, II

dein (poss adj) *your*, I

die **Delikatesse, -n** *delicacy*, II

demnach *accordingly*, III4

demnächst *before long*, III10

die **Demokratie, -n** *democracy*, III5

demokratisch *democratic*, III8

die **Demokratisierung, -en** *democratization*, III11

die **Demonstration, -en** *demonstration*, III6

denken an (acc) *to think of or about*, III2; **Aber denk doch mal daran, daß ...** *But just consider that ...*, III4

der **Denker, -** *intellectual*, III2

das **Denkmal, ¨er** *monument*, III2

denn (conj) *because, for*, I; **denn** (particle), I

dennoch *however*, III9

derselbe *the same*, III7

deshalb *therefore*, III6

dessen *of him, it; of whose*, III4

desto: je mehr ... desto ... *the more ... the ...*, III7

deutlich *clear*, III6

das **Deutsch** *German* (language), I; (school subject), I

der **Deutschlehrer, -** *German teacher*, I

die **Deutschlehrerin, -nen** *German teacher*, I

deutschsprachig *German-speaking*, III8

der **Deutschunterricht, -e** *German instruction*, III2

der **Dezember** *December*, I

das **Dia, -s** *slide*, II

der **Dialekt, -e** *dialect*, III10

der **Dialog, -e** *dialogue*, III3

die **Diät, -en** *diet*, III12

der **Dichter, -** *writer, poet*, III2

dick (adj) *fat*, III8; **dick machen** *to be fattening*, II

dienen (dat) *to serve*, III5

der **Dienst, -e** *service*, III5

der **Dienstag** *Tuesday*, I

dienstags *Tuesdays*, II

dies- *this*, II

diesmal *this time*, III1

der **Dilettant, -en** *dilettante, amateur*, III5

das **Ding, -e** *thing*, II; **vor allen Dingen** *especially*, III1

der **Dinosaurier, -** *dinosaur*, III3

der **Diplomat, -en** *diplomat*, III11

dir *to you*, II

direkt *direct*, III10

der **Dirigent, -en** *conductor*, III10

das **Dirndl, -** *traditional costume for females*, III8

die **Disko, -s** *disco*, I; **in eine Disko gehen** *to go to a disco*, I

die **Diskothek, -en** *discotheque*, II

diskriminieren *to discriminate*, III7

die **Diskussion, -en** *discussion*, II

das **Diskuswerfen** *discus throw*, II

diskutieren *to discuss*, III2

diszipliniert *disciplined*, III11

divers *sundry, diverse*, III12

DM=Deutsche Mark *German mark* (monetary unit), I

doch (particle) *yes, it is!*, I; **Ich meine doch, daß ...**, *I really think that...*, II

das **Dokument, -e** *document*, III2

der **Dolch, -e** *dagger*, III10

der **Dolmetscher, -** *interpreter*, III6

der **Dom, -e** *cathedral*, II

der **Donnerstag** *Thursday*, I

donnerstags *Thursdays*, II

doof *dumb*, I

das **Dorf, ¨er** *village*, II

dort *there*, I; **dort drüben** *over there*, I

dorthin *to there*, III2

die **Dose, -n** *can*, III9

dramatisch *dramatic*, III7

der **Dramaturg, -en** *theatrical producer*,

III10

dran=daran, III10

drängeln *to jostle, shove,* III11

drängen *to push, crowd,* III10

draußen *outside,* III8

drehen *to turn,* III2

dreieckig *triangular,* III10

dreischiffig *with three naves,* Loc1

drin=darin, III1

drinnen *inside,* III3

dritt- *third,* III4

das Drittel: ein Drittel *one third,* III11

drittens *thirdly,* III3

die Drogerie, -n *drugstore,* II

drohen (dat) *to threaten,* III8

die Drohmittel (pl) *threatening measures,* III5

dröhnen *to roar, boom,* III3

drüben *over there,* III4

drücken *to press, squeeze,* III1

der Drucker, - *printer,* III6

der Druckerstreik, -s *print workers' strike,* III6

der Druckknopf, ⁻e *snap,* II

duften *to be fragrant, smell sweet,* III8

dumm *dumb, stupid,* I

die Dummheit, -en *stupidity,* III10

dunkel *dark,* II

dünn *thin,* III4

durch (acc prep) *through,* II

durchaus *thoroughly,* III5

durchblättern (sep) *to page through,* III6

durchfallen (sep) *to fail,* III5

die Durchgangsstation, -en *intermediate station,* III3

durchlaufen (sep) *to run through,* III10

durchlesen (sep) *to read through,* III10

durchschauen (sep) *to see through,* III10

durchsetzen (sep) *to achieve,* III6

durchweg *throughout,* III8

dürfen *to be allowed to,* II; **er/sie/es darf** *he/she/it is allowed to,* II

dürfte: Wenn wir nur Naturprodukte benutzen dürften! *If only we were allowed to use natural products!,* III9

dürr *barren, dry,* III2

durstig *thirsty,* III8

duschen *to shower,* III9

düster *dark, sinister,* III2

E

ebben *to subside,* III10

eben (gerade) *just now,* III2; **eben** (particle), II; **Dann nehm' ich eben ...** *In that case I'll take...,* II; **eben nicht** *actually not,* II

die Ebene, -n *plain,* III12

ebenfalls *likewise,* III3

echt *real(ly),* II; *genuine,* II

die Ecke, -n *corner,* II

eckig *with corners,* I

der Edelstein, -e *precious stone,* Loc10

effektiv *effective,* III3

egal *alike, equal,* II; **egal sein: Mode ist mir egal.** *I don't care about fashion.,* II

egoistisch *egoistic,* III8

die Ehe, -n *marriage,* III12

ehemalig *former,* III11

der Ehepartner, - *spouse,* III11

eher *sooner; rather,* III3

die Ehre, -n *honor,* III5

ehrgeizig *ambitious,* III8

ehrlich *honestly,* III3

das Ei, -er *egg,* I

die Eifersucht *jealousy,* III10

eifrig *eager,* III10

eigen *(one's) own,* II

die Eigenschaft, -en *characteristic,* III7

eigentlich *actual(ly),* III1; **Eigentlich schon, aber ...** *Well yes, but...,* II

eigenverantwortlich *solely responsible,* III11

s. eignen zu *to be suited to,* III6

eilen *to hurry,* III1

eilig *quick, hurried,* III1

ein(-) ander- *another (a different) one,* II

einander *one another,* III3

die Einarbeitung, -en *familiarization,* III11

einbiegen (sep) *to turn,* II

der Eindruck, ⁻e *impression,* III8

einengen (sep) *to confine,* III12

einerlei *the same (to me, him),* III5

einfach *simple, simply,* III1

Einfach! *That's easy!,* I

einfallen (dat, sep) *to occur to,* III12

der Einfluß, (pl) Einflüsse *influence,* III7

eingebettet *embedded,* III2

eingestehen (sep) *to admit,* III7

eingestellt sein auf (acc) *to be set up for,* III2

eingeweiht *dedicated,* Loc1

eingezeichnet *written in, indicated,* III1

einheimisch *local, native,* III8

die Einheit, -en *unity, unit,* III5

einholen (sep) *to catch up with,* III5

einige *some,* III6

s. einigen auf (acc) *to agree,* III1

einjagen: ihm einen Schrecken einjagen (sep) *to scare him,* III10

einkaufen (sep) *to shop,* I; **einkaufen gehen** *to go shopping,* I

der Einkaufsweg *shopping route,* III2

der Einkaufszettel, - *shopping list,* III2

das Einkommen, - *income,* II

die Einkommenshöhe *earnings, income level,* III11

einladen (sep) *to invite,* I; **er/sie lädt ... ein** *he/she invites,* I

die Einladung, -en *invitation,* III2

der Einlaß *admission,* III3

einlegen (sep): **ein Video einlegen** *to insert a video,* II

einmal *once,* I; **einmal am Tag** *once a day,* II

einmalig *unique,* III7

s. einmischen (sep) *to get involved,* III12

die Einnahmequelle, -n *source of income,* III7

einnehmen (sep) *to take,* III6

einpacken (sep) *to pack up,* III9

einprägsam *easily remembered, impressive,* III7

einrichten (sep) *to furnish, arrange,* III2

die Einrichtung, -en *arrangement,* III2

einsam *lonely,* III3

einsame Spitze! *simply fantastic!,* III1

der Einsatz, ⁻e *effort,* III9

einschalten (sep) *to switch on,* III6

einschätzen (sep) *to estimate,* III11

die Einschränkung, -en *limitation,* III1

einschreiben (sep) *to enroll,* III7

einseitig *one-sided,* III8

einsetzen (sep) *to put, fill in,* III9

einst *once, formerly,* III1

einstellen (sep) *to hire,* III5

einstig *former, one-time,* III1

eintragen (sep) *to enter,* III1

s. eintragen lassen *to register,* III7

die Eintragung, -en *entry,* III1

eintreten (sep) *to enter,* III5

eintritt (*imperfect of* eintreten), III5

die Eintrittskarte, -n *admission ticket,* III10

Einverstanden! *Agreed!,* II

der Einwand, ⁻e *objection,* III12

die Einwegdose, -n *non-returnable can,* III9

die Einwegflasche, -n *non-returnable bottle,* III9

der Einwohner, - *resident,* III7

die Einzelheit, -en *detail,* III6

der Einzelkämpfer, - *lone fighter,* III12

einzeln *single, individual,* III2

Einzelreisende, -n *lone traveler,* III2

einziehen (sep) *to move in,* III5

einzig *only; unique,* III3

einzigartig *unique,* Loc4

das Eis *ice cream,* I

der Eisbecher, - *a dish of ice cream,* I

die Eisenbahnstrecke, -n *train route,* III2

eiskalt *ice cold,* II

der Ekel *loathing, nausea,* III5

elegant *elegant,* II

die Elektrizität *electricity,* III9

Elektroinstallateur(in), -e/nen *electrician,* III12

die Elektronik *electronic industry,* Loc4

die Elektrotechnik *electrical engineering,* III11

das Element, -en *element,* III7

der Ellbogen, - *elbow,* III1

Ellenbogen=Ellbogen, III3

die Eltern (pl) *parents,* I

die Emaille *nail polish,* III3

der Empfang, ⁻e *reception,* III7

empfangen *to greet, receive,* III8

empfehlen *to recommend,* III8
die Empfehlung, -en *recommendation,*
    III8
empfindlich *sensitive,* III12
die Empfindung, -en *sensation, feeling,*
    III10
das Ende, -n *end,* III1
enden *to end,* III2
endgültig *final(ly), last(ly),* III1
endlich *at last,* III7
die Energie, -n *energy,* III9
eng *tight,* I
s. engagieren *to be active in,* III5
der Engel, - *angel,* III9
das Englisch *English* (school subject), I;
    (language), I
entdecken *to discover,* III8
entfernt *away, at a distance,* III2
enthalten *to contain,* III2
der Enthusiasmus *enthusiasm,* III10
entlang *along,* III1
entlarven *to uncover,* III3
die Entlassung, -en *dismissal,* III11
s. entscheiden *to decide,* III5
die Entscheidung, -en *decision,* III5
entschieden *decided,* III1
s. entschließen *to decide,* III11
entschlossen *decided,* III11
entschuldigen *to excuse,* III12
Entschuldigung! *Excuse me!,* I
s. entspannen *to relax,* III3
die Entspannung, -en *relaxation,* III6
entsprechen (dat) *to correspond to, to*
    agree with, III1
entstanden *originated,* III11
enttäuschen *to disappoint,* III8
die Enttäuschung, -en *disappointment,*
    III12
entwaffnen *to disarm,* III12
entweder: entweder ... oder *either ...*
    or, III8
entwerfen *to draw up, design,* III7
entwickeln *to develop,* III3
die Entwicklung, -en *development,* Loc4
entworfen *sketched, outlined,* III10
der Entwurf, ⸚e *sketch, outline,* III6
entziffern *to decipher,* III10
entzwei *in two,* III7
die Epoche, -n *epoch,* Loc1
er *he,* I; *it,* I
erarbeiten *to gain by working for,* III8
erbärmlich *pitiful,* III5
erbaut *built, constructed,* Loc7
erblicken *to catch sight of,* III7
die Erbse, -n *pea,* II
die Erdbeere, -n *strawberry,* II
die Erde, -n *earth,* III5
die Erdkunde *geography,* I
die Erdnußbutter *peanut butter,* III1
erdulden *to suffer, endure,* III5
das Ereignis, -se *event,* III6
erfahren *to experience,* III6
Erfahrene, -n *experienced (person),*
    II
die Erfahrung, -en *experience,* III11
erfinden *to invent,* III1

der Erfinder, - *inventor,* III10
der Erfolg, -e *success,* III12
erfolgreich *successful,* III8
erfordern *to demand, require,* III1
erfrischen *to refresh, revive,* III12
erfuhr (*imperfect of* erfahren), III10
erfüllen *to fulfill,* III7
die Erfüllung, -en *fulfillment,* III5
erfunden *invented,* III7
ergänzen *to add to, complete,* III10
ergebenst *respectfully,* III12
das Ergebnis, -se *result,* III6
erglänzen *to shine,* Loc1
ergreifen *to seize, take,* III5
erhalten *to get, receive,* III5; **gut**
    erhalten *well maintained,* II
erhältlich *obtainable,* III12
die Erhaltung *preservation,* III9
erheben *to raise, edify,* III5
erhielt (*imperfect of* erhalten), III12
erhob (*imperfect of* erheben), Loc4
s. erinnern an (acc) *to remember,* III2
die Erkältung, -en *cold (illness),* II
erkannte (*imperfect of* erkennen), III10
erkennen *to recognize,* III10
die Erkenntnis, -se *knowledge,* III5
erklären *to explain,* III1
die Erklärung, -en *explanation,* III3
s. erkundigen nach *to inquire about,*
    III11
erlangen *to attain,* III10
s. erlauben (dat) *to permit,* III5
erleben *to experience,* III10
das Erlebnis, -se *experience,* III1
erledigen *to take care of,* III1
die Erleichterung *relief,* III5
erleiden *to suffer,* III1
erlernen *to learn,* III11
die Erlernung *learning,* III12
der Erlkönig *elf-king,* III2
ermüdet *exhausted,* III1
s. ernähren *to feed, nourish,* II
die Ernährung *food,* III3
ernst *serious,* III5
ernten *to harvest,* III10
erregen *to excite,* III7
erreichen *to reach,* III6
errichten *to construct,* Loc4
der Ersatzdienst *alternative service to*
    military service, III5
erscheinen *to appear,* III6
das Erscheinungsbild, -er *manifestation,*
    III11
erschien (*imperfect of* erscheinen), III7
erschöpfend *exhausting,* III12
erschrak (*imperfect of* erschrecken),
    III7
erschrecken *to be frightened,* III7
erschüttert *shaken,* III5
ersetzen *to replace,* III9
erst- *first,* III4
erstarren *to freeze up,* III10
erstaunt sein *to be astonished,* III8
erstellen *to make available,* III6
ersten: am ersten *on the first,* I
erstens *in the first place,* III3

ersticken *to suffocate,* III5
erstklassig *first-class,* III7
erstmal *first of all,* III12
erteilen (dat) *to give, grant,* III12
ertönen *to make a sound,* III10
das Ertragen *existence,* III1
erwachsen sein *to be grown up,* III4
Erwachsene, -n *adult,* III3
erwähnen *to mention,* III1
erwarten *to expect,* III5
die Erwartung, -en *expectation,* III10
erwecken *to waken,* III10
erweitern *to expand,* III8
erwerben *to obtain,* III5
erwidern *to reply,* III8
erwischen *to catch,* III10
erwünscht *desirable,* III3
erzählen *to tell,* III1
Erzähler(in), -/nen *story-teller, writer,*
    III12
die Erzählung, -en *story,* III10
erziehen *to raise,* III12
die Erziehung *upbringing, education,*
    III10
der Esel, - *donkey,* III8
eßbar *edible,* III12
essen *to eat,* I; **er/sie ißt** *he/she*
    eats, I
die Eßgewohnheit, -en *eating habit,* III1
der Eßtisch, -e *dining table,* I
die Eßwaren (pl) *food,* III9
das Eßzimmer, - *dining room,* II
die Etage, -n *floor, story,* III10
das Etikett, -e *label,* III3
etlich- *some, a certain,* III7
etwa *about, more or less,* III7
etwas *something,* I; **Noch etwas?**
    Anything else?, I
euch (pl, acc case) *you,* I; (pl, dat
    case) *to you,* II; (reflexive) *your-*
    selves, II
euer (poss adj) *your,* II
eventuell *possibly,* III10
ewig *eternal,* III3
die Ewigkeit, -en *eternity,* III8

F

fabelhaft *fabulous, amazing,* III7
die Fabrik, -en *factory,* III9
das Fach, ⸚er *school subject,* I
das Fachabitur *vocational degree,* III4
die Fachhochschule, -n *vocational college,*
    III11
die Fachoberschule, -n *vocational school,*
    III4
die Fachoberschulreife *(degree from a*
    vocational school), III4
die Fachschule, -n *vocational school,*
    III11
die Fachschulreife *(degree from a voca-*
    tional school), III4
das Fachwerkhaus, ⸚er *cross-timbered*
    house, II
die Fähigkeit, -en *ability,* III11
fahren *to go, ride, drive,* I; **er/sie**

fährt *he/she drives*, I; **Fahren wir mal nach ... !** *Let's go to... !*, II

die Fahrerlaubnis, -se *permission to drive*, III5

die Fahrgemeinschaft, -en *carpool*, III9

der Fährhafen, ⸚ *ferry port*, III1

das Fahrrad, ⸚er *bicycle*, II

das Fahrrad-Depot, -s *bicycle racks*, II

der Fahrschein, -e *ticket*, III9

das Fahrzeug, -e *vehicle*, III7

der Fakt, -en *fact*, III1

der Falke, -n *falcon*, Loc4

der Fall, ⸚e *case*, III1; **im Fall** *in the case (of)*, III12; **auf alle Fälle** *by all means*, III11; **auf jeden Fall** *in any case*, III8; **Auf keinen Fall!** *No chance!*, III11

fallen *to fall*, III5

falsch *false, wrong*, III3

der Faltenrock, ⸚e *pleated skirt*, II

die Familie, -n *family*, I

fand (*imperfect of* finden), III4

der Fantasyroman, -e *fantasy novel*, I

das Farbbild, -er *color photograph*, II

die Farbe, -n *color*, I

färben *to color, paint*, III3

das Farbfernsehgerät, -e *color TV set*, II

die Faser, -n *thread, material*, II

der Faserstift, -e *felt-tip pen*, III9

faßte: s. ein Herz fassen *to gather courage*, III10

fast *almost*, III6

faszinierend *fascinating*, III6

faul *lazy*, II

faulenzen *to be lazy*, II

die Faust, ⸚e *fist*, III3

der Februar *February*, I

fechten *to fence*, II

fehlen *to be missing*, III5; **Was fehlt dir?** *What's wrong with you?*, II

der Fehler, - *mistake*, III1

feiern *to celebrate*, III1

der Feiertag, -e *holiday*, I

fein *fine, exquisite*, II

das Fenster, - *window*, I

die Ferien (pl) *vacation (from school)*, II

die Ferienlektüre, -n *vacation reading*, III1

die Fernbedienung, -en *remote control*, II

die Ferne *distance*, III1

ferner *further*, III5

Fernseh gucken (colloquial) *to watch TV*, II

der Fernseh- und Videowagen *TV and video cart*, II

das Fernsehen *the medium of television*, III3

fernsehen (sep) *to watch TV*, II

Fernsehen schauen *to watch TV*, I

der Fernseher, - *television set*, II

das Fernsehgerät, -e *television set*, II

der Fernsehraum, ⸚e *TV room*, II

der Fernsehsender, - *television station*, III6

die Ferse, -n *heel*, III1

fertig *finished*, III11

fertigen *to finish*, Loc10

das Fertiggericht, -e *frozen food*, III7

fesch *stylish, smart*, I

fest *firm*, III3

das Festland *mainland*, III1

festlich *festive*, III3

feststehen (sep) *to be certain*, III7; **Es steht fest, daß ...** *It's certain that ...*, III7

feststellen (sep) *to determine*, III3

die Festung, -en *fortress*, Loc4

die Fete, -n *party*, III4

fetenmäßig *partywise*, III3

fett *fat, greasy*, II

das Fett: hat zu viel Fett *has too much fat*, II

fetzig *really sharp (looking)*, II

das Feuer, - *fire*, III7

das Fieber, - *fever*, II

fiel (*imperfect of* fallen), III4

fies *awful*, III5

die Figur, -en *figure, character*, III10

der Filialbereich, -e *subsidiary region*, III11

das Filialunternehmen, - *subsidiary operation*, III11

der Film, -e *movie*, I; *roll of film*, II

filmen *to film, videotape*, II

finanziell *financially*, III12

finanzieren *to finance*, III7

die Finanzmetropole, -n *financial center*, Loc7

finden *to think about*, I; **Das finde ich auch.** *I think so, too.*, I; **Ich finde es gut/schlecht, daß ...** *I think it's good/bad that ...*, I; **Ich finde den Pulli stark!** *The sweater is awesome!*, I

fing an (*imperfect of* anfangen), III3

der Fingernagel, ⸚ *finger nail*, III1

die Firma, (pl) Firmen *firm, business*, III5

der Fisch, -e *fish*, I

der Fischerhafen, ⸚e *fishing harbor*, III1

das Fischstäbchen, - *fish stick*, II

die Fitneß *fitness*, III3

der Fitneßraum, ⸚e *training and weight room*, II

flach *flat*, II

die Fläche, -n *flat area, surface*, Loc1

flammen *to burn*, III5

die Flasche, -n *bottle*, III1

der Flaschenöffner, - *bottle opener*, III2

das Fleisch *meat*, I

fleißig *hard-working*, II

die Fliege, -n *bow tie*, II

fliegen *to fly*, III5

fließend *running (water)*, III3

die Flinte, -n *shot-gun, musket*, III10

flogen (*imperfect of* fliegen), III10

das Flugblatt, ⸚er *pamphlet, flyer*, III5

der Flügel, - *wing*, III10

der Flughafen, ⸚ *airport*, III8

der Flugplatz, ⸚e *municipal airport*, III8

das Flugzeug, -e *airplane*, II

flüstern *to whisper*, III10

der Fluß, (pl) Flüsse *river*, II

Föhn: Mama kriegt 'nen Föhn. *Mom's going crazy.*, III3

folgen (dat) *to follow*, III4

folgend- *following*, III1

die Folie, -n *foil*, III9

fördern *to encourage*, III2

die Forelle, -n *trout*, II

formen *to form*, III4

formulieren *to formulate*, III4

die Formulierung, -en *formulation*, III3

forschen *to research*, III7

der Forscher, - *researcher*, III9

die Forschung *research*, III7

Fortgeschrittene, -n *advanced (person)*, II

der Fortschritt *progress*, III9

das Foto, -s *photo*, III11

das Fotoalbum, -alben *photo album*, III4

Fotograf(in), -en/nen *photographer*, III12

fotografieren *to photograph*, II

der Frack, ⸚e *tails*, III10

die Frage, -n *question*, II; **Das kommt nicht in Frage!** *It's out of the question!*, III11

der Fragebogen, ⸚ *questionnaire*, III11

fragen *to ask*, II

französisch (adj) *French*, II

die Frau, -en *woman; Mrs.*, I

frech *fresh, insolent*, III5

frei *free*, III11; **Wir haben frei.** *We have off (from school).*, I

die Freiheit *freedom*, III7

die Freikarte, -n *free ticket*, III4

freilich *to be sure, quite so*, III9

der Freitag *Friday*, I

freitags *Fridays*, II

freiwillig *voluntary*, III5

die Freizeit *free time, leisure time*, I

die Freizeiteinrichtung, -en *leisure area*, III2

die Freizeitgestaltung *leisure planning*, III2

das Freizeitheim, -e *leisure center*, III4

fremd *foreign; strange*, III4

die Fremdsprache, -n *foreign language*, III8

das Freskogemälde, - *fresco painting*, Loc4

die Freude *happiness*, III4

s. freuen auf (acc) *to look forward to*, III1

s. **freuen über** (acc) *to be happy about*, II; **Ich freue mich, daß ...** *I am happy that...*, II

der Freund, -e *friend*, I

der Freundeskreis, -e *circle of friends*, III4

freundlich *friendly*, II

die Freundlichkeit *friendliness*, III4

die Freundschaft, -en *friendship*, III4

der Frieden *peace*, III5

der Friedenspreis *Medal of Freedom*, Loc7

friedlich *peaceful*, II

friedliebend *peace-loving*, III8

frieren *to freeze*, III4
frisch *fresh*, III2
Friseur/Friseuse,
　　-e/n *hair stylist*, III12
die Frisur, -en *hair style*, III3
froh *happy*, II
fröhlich *happy*, III7
fror *(imperfect of* frieren*)*, III4
der **Frosch,** ⁼e *frog*, III9
die Frucht, ⁼e *fruit*, III3
fruchtbar *productive*, III5
früh *early*, III1
früher *earlier*, III5
der **Frühjahrsmantel,** ⁼ *light coat*, III12
der **Frühling** *spring* (season), I
das **Frühstück,** -e *breakfast*, II
die Frust *frustration*, III6
frustrierend *frustrating*, III6
s. **fühlen** *to feel*, II; **Ich fühle mich**
　　wohl! *I feel great!*, II
fuhr *(imperfect of* fahren*)*, III10
führen *to lead*, III12
der Führer, - *leader*, III5
der **Führerschein, -e** *driver's license*, II
die Führung *leadership*, III5
füllen *to fill*, III4
funktionieren *to function*, III7
für (acc prep) *for*, I
die Furcht *fear, terror*, III10
furchtbar *terrible, awful*, I; **furchtbar**
　　gern haben *to like a lot*, I
fürchten *to fear*, III9
fürs=für das, II
der Fürstbischof, ⁼e *prince bishop*, Loc4
der **Fuß,** ⁼e *foot*, II
Fußball *soccer*, I
die **Fußbremse, -n** *foot brake*, II
der Fußgänger, - *pedestrian*, III4
die Fußgängerzone, -n *pedestrian zone*,
　　III1
fußkrank sein *too lazy to walk*, III2
füttern *to feed*, I
futtern *to stuff oneself*, III2

G

gab *(imperfect of* geben*)*, III6
gäbe=würde geben, III7
die **Gabel, -** *fork*, III2
gähnen *to yawn*, III10
die Galerie, -n *gallery*, III10
die **Gänsehaut** *goose bumps*, III10
ganz *all, whole*, III1; **Ganz klar!** *Of*
　　course!, I; **ganz wohl** *extremely*
　　well, II; **Ganz meine Meinung.** *I*
　　completely agree., III4; **Ganz be-**
　　stimmt. *Certainly*, III11
gar nicht gern haben *not to like at*
　　all, I
die **Garage, -n** *garage*, II; **die Garage**
　　aufräumen *to clean the garage*, II
die Garderobe, -n *coat check-room*, III10
gären *to ferment*, III5
der **Garten,** ⁼ *garden, yard*, II
das Gartenhaus, ⁼er *garden house*, III3

die Gärtnerei, -n *gardening, nursery*, III4
das Gas, -e *gas*, III9
die Gasse, -n *alley*, III1
der Gast, ⁼e *guest*, III2
das Gästehaus, ⁼er *hotel*, III2
der **Gasthof,** ⁼e *restaurant, inn*, II
der Gauner, - *cheat, rogue*, III10
das Gebäude, - *building*, III9
　　geben *to give*, I; **er/sie gibt** *he/she*
　　　　gives, I; **Das gibt's doch nicht!**
　　　　There's just no way!, II
　　gebeten *asked*, II
das Gebiet, -e *area*, III4
　　gebildet *educated*, III4
das Gebirge, - *mountains*, III8
　　geblieben *remained, stayed*, II
　　geblümt *flowery*, II
　　geboren *born*, III4
　　geboten *offered*, III10
　　gebracht *brought*, III1
　　gebraten *fried*, II
der **Gebrauch,** ⁼e *custom*, III4
　　gebrauchen *to use*, III7
　　gebrochen *broken*, II
die Gebrüder (pl) *brothers*, III10
die Gebühr, -en *fee*, III7
　　gebunden an (acc) *connected with*,
　　　　III2
das Geburtsdatum, -daten *birthdate*, III2
der **Geburtstag, -e** *birthday*, I; **Alles Gute**
　　　　zum Geburtstag! *Best wishes on*
　　　　your birthday!, I; **Herzlichen**
　　　　Glückwunsch zum Geburtstag!
　　　　Best wishes on your birthday!, I;
　　　　Ich habe am ... Geburtstag. *My*
　　　　birthday is on..., I
　　gedacht *thought*, III8
der **Gedanke, -n** *thought, idea*, III1
　　s. **Gedanken machen über** (acc) *to*
　　　　think about, III3
　　gedenken *to consider*, III12
die Gedenkstätte, -n *monument*, III2
das Gedicht, -e *poem*, III10
die **Geduld** *patience*, III10
　　geduldig *patient*, III8
　　geeignet *suitable*, III10
　　gefährdet *endangered*, III12
　　gefährlich *dangerous*, III9
　　gefallen *to like*; **Wie hat es dir**
　　　　gefallen? *How did you like it?*, II
　　gefällig *agreeable*, III7
　　gefangen *captured*, III4
das Gefäß, -e *container (for liquid)*,
　　　　Loc10
　　gefiel *(imperfect of* gefallen*)*, III4
　　gefroren *frozen*, III11
das **Gefühl, -e** *feeling*, III7
　　gefühllos *insensitive, without feel-*
　　　　ings, III8
　　gefüllt: das gefüllte Ei, -er *deviled*
　　　　egg, II
　　gefunden *found, discovered*, III1
　　gefüttert *padded*, II
　　gegangen *gone*, II
　　gegen (acc prep) *against*, III1
die **Gegend, -en** *area*, III2

　　gegenseitig *mutual(ly)*, III1
der **Gegenstand,** ⁼e *object*, Loc10
das **Gegenteil, -e** *opposite*, III5
　　gegenüber (dat prep) *across from*, II
　　gegenüberstehen (dat, sep) *to stand*
　　　　across from, oppose, III6
die Gegenwart *present*, III10
　　gegenwärtig *current*, III3
　　gegessen *eaten*, II
　　gegrillt *grilled*, II
das Gehalt, ⁼er *salary*, III11
der Gehaltswunsch, ⁼e *desired income*,
　　　　III11
　　geheim *secret*, III5
der **Geheimtip, -s** *secret tip*, II
　　gehen *to go*, I; **Das geht nicht.** *That*
　　　　won't work, I; **Es geht.** *It's okay*, I;
　　　　Wie geht's (denn)? *How are*
　　　　you?, I; **Gehen wir mal auf den**
　　　　Golfplatz! *Let's go to the golf*
　　　　course!, II
　　gehoben *elevated*, III10
　　geholfen *helped*, II
　　gehören (dat) *to belong to*, III1
die **Geige, -n** *violin*, III10
　　geigen *to play the violin*, III10
　　Geigenbaumeister(in), /nen *master*
　　　　violin maker, III10
　　geil *great*, III3
　　geistern *to wander*, III3
die Geistesfreiheit *freedom of ideas*, III5
　　gekauft *bought*, I
　　gekleidet *dressed*, III3
　　gelangen *to acquire*, III9
　　gelaunt: gut gelaunt *in a good*
　　　　mood, II
　　gelb *yellow*, I
das **Geld** *money*, I
　　gelegen *appropriate*, III12
die **Gelegenheit, -en** *opportunity*, III6
　　gelesen (pp) *read*, I
　　gelingen (dat) *to succeed*, III7
　　gelten *to mean, count*, III7
　　gemacht *done*, I; **Was hast du am**
　　　　Wochenende gemacht? *What did*
　　　　you do on the weekend?, I
die Gemahlin *wife*, III7
das **Gemälde, -** *painting*, II
　　gemein *mean*, III9
die Gemeinde, -n *community*, III10
　　gemeinsam *in common; joint, togeth-*
　　　　er, III2
die Gemeinsamkeit, -en *common interest*,
　　　　III5
das **Gemüse** *vegetables*, I; **im Obst- und**
　　　　Gemüseladen *at the produce store*,
　　　　I
der **Gemüseladen,** ⁼ *produce store*, I
　　gemütlich *comfortable*, II
　　genannt *named*, III7
　　genau *exact(ly)*, III1
　　genau: **Genau so ist es.** *That's exactly*
　　　　right., III7
　　genauso *just so*, III3
die Generation, -en *generation*, III3
　　generell *generally*, III7

genial *ingenious*, III5
genießen *to enjoy*, III10
genommen *taken*, III4
der Genosse, -n *comrade*, III5
genug *enough*, I
genügen *to be enough*, III2
genügend *enough*, II; **genügend schlafen** *to get enough sleep*, II
der Genuß, (pl) Genüsse *pleasure*, III1
die Genußmittelindustrie *industry producing luxury articles*, Loc10
die Geografie *geography*, III2
gepflegt *well cared-for, well-groomed*, III11
gepunktet *polka-dotted*, II
gerade *just*, III1; *straight*, II; **Das ist gerade passiert.** *It just happened.*, II
geradeaus *straight ahead*, III10
geradezu *outright*, III1
das Gerät, -e *appliance*, III6
geraten *to get into*, III12
geräuchert *smoked*, II
das Geräusch, -e *sound*, III10
geräuscharm *low-noise*, III7
geregelt *ordered, fixed*, III11
das Gericht, -e *meal, entrée*, III1
geringfügig *negligible, trivial*, III9
die Germanistik (sing) *German studies*, III11
gern (machen) *to like (to do)*, I; **gern haben** *to like*, I; **Gern geschehen!** *My pleasure!*, I; **besonders gern** *especially like*, I; **Gern! Hier ist es!** *Here! I insist!*, II
gesamt *entire, whole*, III6
die Gesamtbevölkerung *total population*, III8
der Gesangsverein, -e *choral society*, III10
die Gesäßtasche, -n *back pocket*, II
das Geschäft, -e *store; business*, III1
geschehen *to happen*, III6
gescheit *smart, clever*, III4
das Geschenk, -e *gift*, I
die Geschenkidee, -n *gift idea*, I
die Geschichte *history*, I; Geschichte, -n *story*, III3
geschichtlich *historical*, III1
geschickt *skillful*, III7
das Geschirr *dishes*, I; **Geschirr spülen** *to wash the dishes*, II
das Geschlecht, -er *gender*, III2
geschlossen *closed*, III10
der Geschmack *taste*, III3
die Geschmackskraft *power of taste*, III7
geschrieben *written*, II
die Geschwister (pl) *brothers and sisters*, I
geschwommen *swum*, II
der Geselle, -n *fellow*, III10
die Gesellschaft, -en *social group; society*, III3
das Gesetz, -e *law*, III1
gesetzlich *legal*, III7
das Gesicht, -er *face*, III3
der Gesichtspunkt, -e *point of view*, III11

gesponnen *spun*, III7
das Gespräch, -e *conversation*, III1
die Gesprächsfetzen (pl) *scraps of conversation*, III2
der Gesprächsstoff *topic, subject of conversation*, III6
gesprochen *spoken*, I; **Worüber habt ihr gesprochen?** *What did you talk about?*, III1
gestalten *to form, arrange*, III4
die Gestaltung *arrangement, formation*, III11
gestern *yesterday*, I; **gestern abend** *yesterday evening*, I
gestiegen *climbed*, II
gestreift *striped*, II
gesund *healthy*, II
die Gesundheit *health*, II
gesundheitsschädlich *injurious to health*, III7
Gesundheitswissenschaftler(in), -/nen *nutritional scientist*, III12
gesungen *sung*, III10
gesunken *sunk*, III5
getan *done*, III1
das Getränk, -e *drink*, II
getroffen *met*, III1
getrunken *drunk*, III10
die Gewalt *violence*, III8
die Gewaltanwendung *use of force*, III8
das Gewehr, -e *gun, rifle*, III5
gewesen *been*, II
gewinnen *to win*, III5
gewiß *certain(ly)*, III4
das Gewitter, - *storm*, I
s. gewöhnen an (acc) *to get used to*, III7
die Gewohnheit, -en *habit*, III2
gewöhnlich *usually*, II
das Gewölbe *archway, vault*, Loc10
geworden *became*, II
geworfen *thrown*, III9
gewußt *known*, III1
gezogen *pulled*, III7
gichtig *arthritic*, III3
der Giebel, - *gable*, III1
gießen *to water*, I
das Gift, -e *poison*, III9
giftig *poisonous*, III9
gigantisch *gigantic*, III3
ging (*imperfect of* gehen), III4
Gis *g-sharp*, III12
die Gitarre, -n *guitar*, I
glänzen *to shine*, III10
glänzend *sparkling*, III7
glanzvoll *magnificent, glorious*, Loc7
die Glanzzeit *golden age*, Loc10
das Glas, -er *glass*, I; **ein Glas Apfelsaft** *a glass of apple juice*, I
Glasbläser(in), -/nen *glas blower*, III12
glatt *slick*, III9
die Glatze, -n *bald head*, III6
glauben *to believe*, I; **Ich glaube nicht, daß ...** *I don't think that...*, II

glaubhaft *believable*, III5
gleich *immediately*, III4; *same*, III7
gleichaltrig *of the same age*, III4
die Gleichberechtigung *equality (of rights)*, III5
gleichen (dat) *to be equal to, be alike*, III3
gleichfalls: Danke, gleichfalls! *Thank you and the same to you!*, II
gleichgültig *no matter*, III5
das Gleichnis, -se *simile*, III10
gleichzeitig *at the same time*, III3
die Glotze, -n *television, idiot box*, III6
das Glück *luck*, I; **So ein Glück!** *What luck!*, I; **Ein Glück, daß ...** *Lucky that ...*, III11; **Zum Glück habe ich ...** *Luckily I have ...*, III11
glücklich *happy*, III7
das Goethehaus *(Goethe's birthplace)*, II
das Gold *gold*, III7
goldgierig *lusting for gold*, III7
der Goldschmuck *gold jewelry*, III1
Golf *golf*, I
der Golfplatz, ⸚e *golf course*, II
der Gott, ⸚er *God*, III11; **Gott sei Dank, daß ...** *Thank God that ...*, III11
der Graben, ⸚ *ditch*, III2
das Grabmal, ⸚er *tomb*, Loc4
der Grad *degree(s)*, I; **zwei Grad** *two degrees*, I; **Wieviel Grad haben wir?** *What's the temperature?*, I
der Graf, -en *count*, III10
die Grafik, -en *illustration, grid*, III6
der Grafiker, - *graphic artist*, Loc1
das Gramm *gram*, I
grau *gray*, I; **in Grau** *in gray*, I
grausam *cruel*, I
die Grenze, -n *border*, Loc1
griechisch (adj) *Greek*, II
griffbereit *handy*, III7
groß *big*, I
großartig *wonderful*, II
die Größe, -n *size*, I
die Großeltern (pl) *grandparents*, I
größer *bigger*, II
großgedruckt *in capital letters*, III6
großgezogen *raised (a child)*, III7
die Großmutter, ⸚ *grandmother*, I
die Großschachanlage, -n *gigantic chess board*, II
die Großstadt, ⸚e *big city*, II
der Großvater, ⸚ *grandfather*, I
großziehen (sep) *to raise (a child)*, III7
großzügig *generous*, III11
grotesk *grotesque*, III10
grün *green*, I; **in Grün** *in green*, I
der Grund, ⸚e *reason*, III11
gründen *to found*, III12
das Grundgesetz *basic law, constitution*, III5
gründlich *thorough(ly)*, III6
die Grundschule, -n *grade school*, III4
der Grundstein, -e *corner stone*, Loc1
der Grundwehrdienst *basic military training*, III5

die **Gruppe, -n** *group*, I
die Gruppierung, -en *grouping*, III8
die Gruselgeschichte, -n *horror story*, III10
der **Gruselroman, -e** *horror novel*, I
der Gruß, -̈e *greeting*, III12
   grüßen *to greet* III4; **Grüß dich!** *Hi!*, I
   gucken *to look*, II; **Guck mal!** *Look!*, II; **Fernseh gucken** *to watch TV* (colloquial), II
der Gummihandschuh, -e *rubber glove*, III3
die Gummihülle, -n *rubber covering*, III11
   günstig *favorable*, III2
die **Gurke, -n** *cucumber*, II; **die saure Gurke** *pickle*, III1
der **Gürtel, -** *belt*, I
   gut *good*, I; **gut gelaunt** *good-tempered*, II; **Gut! Mach' ich!** *Okay, I'll do that!*, I; **gut sein: Ist dir nicht gut?** *Are you not feeling well?*, II
   gutdotiert *well funded*, III11
   guterzogen *well behaved*, III7
   gutgehen (sep) *to go well*, III3
   gutmütig *good-natured*, III8
   Gymnasiast(in), -en/nen *student in Gymnasium*, III3
das Gymnasium, (pl) Gymnasien *(German academic) high school*, III6
die **Gymnastik** *exercise, calisthenics*, II; **Gymnastik machen** *to exercise*, II
das **Gyros** *gyros*, I

H

das **Haar, -e** *hair*, I
das Haarwachs *hair wax*, III3
   haben *to have*, I; **er/sie hat** *he/she has*, I; **Haben Sie das auch in Rot?** *Do you also have that in red?*, I
das **Hackfleisch** *ground meat*, I
der Hafen, -̈ *harbor*, III1
das **Hähnchen, -** *chicken*, I
   halb *half*, I; **halb (eins, zwei, usw.)** *half past (twelve, one, etc.)*, I
   halblang: **Mach halblang!** *Don't exaggerate!*, III1
die Hälfte, -n *half*, III1
die **Halle, -n** *hall*, I
das **Hallenbad, -̈er** *indoor pool*, II
   Hallo! *Hi! Hello!*, I
der **Hals, -̈e** *throat*, II
das Halsband, -̈er *necklace*, III7
die **Halskette, -n** *necklace*, II
die **Halsschmerzen** (pl) *sore throat*, II
das Halstuch, -̈er *kerchief*, III12
   halt (particle), I; **Die Kleinstadt gefällt mir gut, weil es da halt ruhiger ist.** *I like a small town because it's just quieter there.*, II
   halten *to stop, hold*, III1; **halten für** *to consider as*, III5; **s. fit halten** *to keep fit*, II; **halten von** *to think of*, III3
die Haltestelle, -n *(bus) stop*, III2

die **Hand, -̈e** *hand*, II
die Handbewegung, -en *hand movement*, III11
die **Handbremse, -n** *emergency brake*, II
die **Handcreme** *hand cream*, II
 s. **handeln um** *to be about*, III10
   handeln von *to deal with, be about*, III5
das **Handgelenk, -e** *wrist*, III1
die **Handlung, -en** *plot*, III10
die **Handtasche, -n** *handbag*, II
   hängen *to hang*, III4
die Hansestadt, -̈e *Hanseatic city*, III1
die Harfe, -n *harp*, III10
   harmlos *harmless*, III3
   hart *hard, tough*, III7
das **Hasenfleisch** *rabbit meat*, III1
die Haspel, -n *reel*, III7
   hassen *to hate*, III5
   häßlich *ugly*, I
   hätte: Ich hätte gern ... *I would like...*, II
   häufig *frequent(ly)*, III9
   hauptberuflich *as a main profession*, III11
die Hauptfigur, -en *leading character*, III10
der Hauptgedanke, -n *main idea*, III3
das **Hauptgericht, -e** *main dish*, II
das Hauptmerkmal, -e *main characteristic*, III4
der **Hauptpunkt, -e** *main point*, III3
   hauptsächlich *mainly*, III3
der Hauptschulabschluß *degree (from a Hauptschule)*, III4
die **Hauptstadt, -̈e** *capital*, I
die **Hauptstraße, -n** *main street*, II
das **Hauptthema, -themen** *main theme*, III1
das Hauptziel, -e *primary destination*, III9
das **Haus, -̈er** *house*, II; **zu Hause bleiben** *to stay at home*, II
die Hausarbeit, -en *housework*, III11
der Hausarrest *house arrest*, III12
die **Hausaufgaben** (pl) *homework*, I; **Hausaufgaben machen** *to do homework*, I
das Häuschen, - *small house*, III12
   hauseigen *belonging to the house, in-house*, III2
der Haushalt, -e *household*, III3
der Hausmeister, - *janitor*, III9
der Hausmüll *garbage*, III9
die **Hausmusik** *house music*, III10
das **Haustier, -e** *pet*, I
das Haustor, -e *gate*, III1
die **Haut, -̈e** *skin*, II
der Hautkrebs *skin cancer*, III9
   hautnah *very close*, III2
   heben *to lift*, III3
das **Heft, -e** *notebook*, I
   heil *whole, perfect*, III7
der **Heilbutt** *halibut*, II
   heilig *holy*, Loc7
   heim *home*, III3
die **Heimat** *homeland*, III5

der Heimatort, -e *native place*, III1
   heiraten *to marry*, III5
   heiter *cheerful*, III10
   heiß *hot*, I
   heißen *to be called*, I; **er heißt** *his name is*, I
der **Held, -en** *hero*, III7
   helfen (dat) *to help*, I
   hell *bright*, II
   hellgrau *light gray*, III12
das **Hemd, -en** *shirt*, I
der Hemdknopf, -̈e *shirt button*, III4
der Hemdkragen, - *shirt collar*, III4
   heranwachsen (sep) *to grow up*, III12
   heraus *out*, III1
   herausbringen (sep) *to publish*, III6
   herausfinden (sep) *to find out*, III8
   herausgeben (sep) *to publish*, III6
   herausnehmen (sep) *to take out*, II
   heraussuchen (sep) *to pick out, select*, III1
die Herberge, -n *hostel*, III2
der **Herbst** *fall* (season), I; **im Herbst** *in the fall*, I
der **Herd, -e** *stove*, I
   hereingebeten *asked in*, III8
   hereintrat *(imperfect of hereintreten)*, III7
   hereintreten (sep) *to enter*, III7
   hergehen: hin- und hergehen *to go back and forth*, III3
der **Herr** *Mr.*, I
   herrlich *fantastic*, III5
   herstellen (sep) *to produce*, III9
der Hersteller, - *manufacturer*, III7
die **Herstellung, -en** *production*, III9
   herum *around; about*, III3
   herumblättern (sep) *to leaf through* (a newspaper), III3
   herumlaufen (sep) *to run around*, III4
   herumreisen (sep) *to travel around*, III11
   herunter *down*, III11
   hervor *out of*, III10
das **Herz, -en** *heart*, III7
   herzhaft *hearty*, II
das **Herzklopfen** *pounding heart*, III10
   herzlich *heartfelt*, III8; **Herzlichen Glückwunsch zum Geburtstag!** *Best wishes on your birthday!*, I
der Herzog, -̈e *duke*, Loc4
   hetzen *to chase, harass*, III5
   heute *today*, I; **heute morgen** *this morning*, I; **heute nachmittag** *this afternoon*, I; **heute abend** *tonight, this evening*, I
   heutig *of today, today's*, III3
   heutzutage *nowadays*, III5
   hielt *(imperfect of halten)*, III7
   hier *here*, I; **Hier bei ...** *The ... residence.*, I; **Hier ist ...** *This is...*, I
   hiermit *with this, herewith*, III12
   hieß *(imperfect of heißen)*, III3
die **Hilfe, -n** *help*, III5
   hilfreich *helpful*, III8
der Hilfsarbeiter, - *temporary worker*, III4

hilfsbereit *helpful, cooperative*, III8
die **Himbeermarmelade, -n** *raspberry marmalade*, II
hin *to*, III2
hinaufbegleiten (sep) *to take up, upstairs*, III10
hinaus *out*, III10
hinauslachen (sep) *to laugh at*, III10
hingehen (sep) *to go to*, III4
s. hinlegen (sep) *to lie down*, III3
hinrichten (sep) *to execute*, III5
s. hinsetzen (sep) *to sit down*, III4
Hinsicht: in dieser Hinsicht *as far as that goes*, III5
hinten *at the back*, II; **da hinten** *there in the back*, I
der **Hintergrund, ⁻e** *background*, III6
hinterlassen *to leave behind*, III9
hinüberschreiten (sep) *to walk across*, III10
hinüberschritt *(imperfect of* hinüberschreiten*)*, III10
hinunterstampfen (sep) *to stomp downstairs*, III1
hinwegströmen (sep) *to flow away*, III5
hinzufügen (sep) *to add to*, III6
historisch *historical*, III10
hob *(imperfect of* heben*)*, III4
das **Hobby, -s** *hobby*, II
hoch *high*, III4
hochgezogen *pulled up*, III10
hochhinaufragend *reaching high up*, III1
hochkämmen (sep) *to comb up*, III10
die Hochschule, -n *university*, III3
höchst *highest, greatest*, III8
die Hochzeit, -en *wedding*, III7
hoffen *to hope*, II
Hoffentlich ... *Hopefully...*, II; **Hoffentlich geht es dir bald besser!** *I hope you'll get better soon.*, II
die **Hoffnung, -en** *hope*, III11
die Hofkirche, -n *church of the royal court*, Loc10
höflich *polite*, III8
hoh- *high*, III1
die Höhenzüge (pl) *hills*, III2
der Höhepunkt, -e *highlight*, III5
hohl *hollow, empty*, III3
holen *to get, fetch*, I
das **Holz, ⁻er** *wood*, I; **aus Holz** *out of wood*, I
homogen *homogenous*, III4
der Honig *honey*, III1
hören: Hör mal zu! *Listen to this!*, II; **Hör mal!** *Listen!*, II; **Musik hören** *to listen to music*, I; **Hör gut zu!** *Listen carefully.*, I
der **Hörer, -** *listener; receiver*, I; **den Hörer abheben** *to pick up the receiver*, I; **den Hörer auflegen** *to hang up (the telephone)*, I
der Hörfunk *radio*, III6
der **Horizont** *horizon*, III11
der **Horrorfilm, -e** *horror movie*, I

der Hörsturz *hearing failure*, III3
die **Hose, -n** *pants*, I
das **Hotel, -s** *hotel*, II
hübsch *pretty, handsome*, III3
die **Hüfte, -n** *hip*, II
das **Huhn, ⁻er** *chicken*, II
das Hühnerfleisch *chicken meat*, III3
der **Hummer, -** *lobster*, II
humorlos *humorless*, III8
humorvoll *humorous*, III11
der **Hund, -e** *dog*, I
der Hundertmarkschein *hundred mark bill*, III1
der **Hunger** *hunger*, I; **Ich habe Hunger.** *I am hungry.*, II
hungrig *hungry*, III9
hupen *to honk the horn*, II
hüpfen *to hop, jump*, III7
der **Hürdenlauf, ⁻e** *hurdling*, II
der **Husten** *cough*, II
der **Hut, ⁻e** *hat*, II

I

ich *I*, I; **Ich auch.** *Me too.*, I; **Ich nicht.** *I don't.*, I
ideal *ideal*, III4
die **Idee, -n** *idea*, II; **Gute Idee!** *Good idea!*, II; **Hast du eine Idee?** *Do you have an idea?*, II
der Ideenbaum *tree of ideas*, III3
identifizieren *to identify*, III1
ihm *to, for him*, I
ihn *it, him*, I
ihnen *to them*, II
Ihnen (formal) *to you*, II
ihr (poss adj) *her, their*, I; *to, for her*, I; (pl) *you*, I
Ihr (poss adj, formal, pl, sing) *your*, II
die Illustration, -en *illustration*, III1
illustrieren *to illustrate*, III1
im=in dem; im Frühling *in the spring*, I; **im Januar** *in January*, I; **(einmal) im Monat** *(once) a month*, I
die **Imbißstube, -n** *snack bar*, II
imitieren *to imitate*, III7
immer *always*, I
immerhin *nevertheless, at least*, III5
in (acc, dat prep) *into, in*, II; **in Blau** *in blue*, I; **in der (Basketball) Mannschaft** *on the (basketball) team*, II; **in die Apotheke gehen** *to go to the pharmacy*, II
indem (conj) *in that*, III8
indisch (adj) *(Asian) Indian*, II
die Industrie, -n *industry*, III9
Industriedesigner(in), -/nen *industrial designer*, III12
die Informatik *computer science*, III11
die Information, -en *information*, III2
informativ *informative*, III7
informell *informal*, III2
s. **informieren** *to inform oneself*, III2
Ingenieur(in), -e/nen *engineer*, III11
das Ingenieurwesen *engineering*, III11

der **Inhalt** *content*, III11
die Inhaltsangabe, -n *table of contents*, III6
die Initiative, -n *initiative*, III12
inkorrekt *incorrect*, III7
der Inländer, - *native* III8
die **Innenstadt, ⁻e** *downtown*, II
inner *interior*, III2
die **Innereien** (pl) *innards*, III1
innerhalb (gen prep) *within, on the inside*, III10
innerlich *on the inside*, III3
insbesondere *particularly*, III8
die **Insel, -n** *island*, II
insgesamt *altogether*, III11
das **Institut, -e** *institute* III7
das **Instrument, -e** *instrument*, I
intakt *intact*, III8
intelligent *intelligent*, II
die Intensität *intensity*, III8
interessant *interesting*, III1
das **Interesse, -n** *interest*, I; **Hast du andere Interessen?** *Do you have any other interests?*, I; **Ich habe kein Interesse an Mode.** *I am not interested in fashion.*, II
s. **interessieren für** *to be interested in*, II; **Interessierst du dich für Mode?** *Are you interested in fashion?*, II
interessiert sein an (dat) *to be interested in*, III11
international *international*, III2
interviewen *to interview*, III4
inzwischen *in the meantime*, III10
irgend- *some-*, III7
ironisch *ironic*, III2
s. **irren** *to be mistaken*, III5
der **Irrtum, ⁻er** *error, misunderstand*ing, III12
irrtümlich *erroneous(ly), mistaken(ly)*, III12
isoliert *isolated*, III4
ist: sie ist aus ... *she's from...*, I; **Ist was mit dir?** *Is something wrong?*, II
italienisch (adj) *Italian*, II

J

das **Jahr, -e** *year*, I; **Ich bin ... Jahre alt.** *I am... years old.*, I
ja *yes*, I; **Ja klar!** *Of course!*, I; **Das ist ja unglaublich!** *That's really unbelievable!*, II; **Ja, kann sein, aber ...** *Yes, maybe, but...*, II; **Ja, natürlich!** *Certainly!*, II; *Yes, of course!*, II; **Ja, schon, aber ...** *Well yes, but...*, II; **Ja? Was denn?** *Okay, what is it?*, II
die **Jacke, -n** *jacket*, I
das **Jackenfutter** *jacket lining*, III11
jahrelang *for years*, Loc1
jähren: das jährt sich *it's been a year (ago) since*, III2
die **Jahreszeit, -en** *season*, III10

das **Jahrhundert**, -e *century*, II; **aus dem 17. Jahrhundert** *from the 17th century*, II
jahrhundertealt *centuries old*, III1
jährig *year-old*, III3
jährlich *yearly, annual*, Loc4
der **Jahrmarkt**, ¨e *annual fair* III10
jammern *to mourn, lament*, III7
der **Januar** *January*, I; **im Januar** *in January*, I
je *each, every*, III1; **je ... desto** *the more ... the*, III7
die **Jeans** (mostly sing) *jeans*, I
die **Jeansweste**, -n *jeans vest*, II
jed- *every*, II; **jede Woche** *every week*, II; **jeden Tag** *every day*, I
jedenfalls *in any case*, III8
jedermann *everyone*, III10
jedoch *however, nevertheless*, III1
jemals *ever*, III7
jemand *someone, somebody*, III3
jener *that one*, III5
jetzig *present, current*, III8
jetzt *at present, now*, I
jeweils *in each case, respectively*, III2
der **Job**, -s *job*, II
jobben *to have a job*, III11
joggen *to jog*, I
der **Jogging-Anzug**, ¨e *jogging suit*, I
das **Joghurt**, -s (or der) *yogurt*, II
der **Journalismus** *journalism*, III6
Journalist(in) -en/nen *journalist*, III11
jubeln *to rejoice*, III10
die **Jugend** *youth*, III3
das **Jugendgästehaus**, ¨er *youth hostel* III2
das **Jugendheim** *youth center*, III4
die **Jugendherberge**, -n *youth hostel*, II
der **Jugendherbergsausweis**, -e *youth hostel I.D.*, III2
Jugendliche, -n *teenager*, III8
der **Jugendpsychologe**, -n *psychologist for young people*, III12
die **Jugendsprache** *youth language*, III3
der **Juli** *July*, I
jung *young*, II
der **Junge**, -n *boy*, II
jünger *younger*, II
die **Jungfer**, -n *maiden* III7
der **Juni** *June*, I
Jura *law*, III11
das **Jurastudium** *study of law*, III12

K

der **Kabelanschluß**, ¨sse *cable connection*, III6
der **Käfer**, - *bug, beetle*, III6
der **Kaffee** *coffee*, I
die **Kaffeemühle**, -n *coffee grinder*, III12
kahl *bald*, III11
die **Kaiserkrönung**, -en *coronation of an emperor*, Loc7
der **Kaisersaal** *emperial banquet hall*, Loc4
der **Kakao** *chocolate milk*, II

der **Kalauer** *dumb joke*, III7
der **Kalender**, - *calendar*, I
die **Kalkleisten** (pl) *(ironic) parents*, III3
kalt (adj) *cold*, III4
die **Kälte**, -n *cold, coldness*, III11
kam (*imperfect of* kommen), III4
die **Kamera**, -s *camera*, II
kameradschaftlich *friendly*, III8
der **Kaminabend**, -e *evening by the fireplace*, III2
der **Kaminraum**, ¨e *room with a fireplace*, III2
s. **kämmen** *to comb one's hair*, II
die **Kammer**, -n *chamber*, III7
die **Kampagne**, -n *campaign*, III7
der **Kampf**, ¨e *struggle, battle* III5
kämpfen *to fight*, III5
der **Kampfpanzer**, - *battle tank*, III5
der **Kandidat**, -en *candidate*, III5
kannten (*imperfect of* kennen), III10
der **Kantor**, -en *choirmaster, organist*, Loc1
das **Kapitel**, - *chapter*, III1
die **Kappe**, -n *cap*, III9
das **Käppi**, -s *(baseball) cap*, II
kaputt *ruined, broken*, I
kaputtgehen (sep) *to go to pieces*, III11
die **Kapuze**, -n *hood*, II
kariert *checked*, II
das **Karo**, -s *(pattern) check, diamond*, II
der **Karpfen**, - *carp*, II
die **Karriere**, -n *career*, III11
die **Karte**, -n *card; ticket*, I
die **Kartoffel**, -n *potato*, I
der **Käse**, - *cheese*, I
das **Käsebrot**, -e *cheese sandwich*, I
die **Kaserne**, -n *barracks*, III5
die **Kasse**, -n *cash register*, III9
die **Kassette**, -n *cassette*, I
die **Kassiererin**, -nen *cashier*, III9
der **Kasten**, ¨ *box*, III2
der **Katalysator**, -en *catalytic converter*, III9
das **Katauto**, -s *car with emission control*, III9
die **Kategorie**, -n *category*, III1
die **Katze**, -n *cat*, I
kauen *to chew*, III8
der **Kauf**, ¨e *purchase*, III5
kaufen *to buy*, I
die **Kauffrau**, -en *saleswoman*, III11
das **Kaufhaus**, ¨er *department store*, III4
der **Kaufmann**, (pl) **Kaufleute** *salesman*, III11
das **Kaufmannshaus**, ¨er *commercial building*, III1
der **Kaufreiz** *temptation to buy*, III7
der **Kaugummi** *chewing gum*, III8
kaum *barely, hardly*, II
kein *no, none, not any*, I; **Ich habe keine Zeit.** *I don't have time.*, I; **Ich habe keinen Hunger mehr.** *I'm not hungry any more.*, I; **Keine Ahnung!** *I have no idea!*, I
der **Keks**, -e *cookie*, I

der **Keller**, - *cellar*, III2
der **Kellner**, - *waiter*, III2
kennen *to know, be familiar or acquainted with*, I
kennenlernen (sep) *to get to know*, III2
die **Kenntnis** *knowledge*, III10
der **Kerl**, -e *fellow*, III7
die **Kette**, -n *chain*, III11
der **Kiefer**, - *jaw*, III1
das **Kilo=Kilogramm**, - *kilogram*, I
kilometerweit *for kilometers*, III9
das **Kind**, -er *child*, I
kinderlieb *fond of children*, III8
das **Kinderlied**, -er *children's song*, III2
das **Kino**, -s *cinema*, I; **ins Kino gehen** *to go to the movies*, I
die **Kirche**, -n *church*, I
die **Kirsche**, -n *cherry*, II
klagen *to lament*, III3
die **Klamotten** (pl) *(casual term for) clothes*, I
der **Klang**, ¨e *sound, ring*, III10
klappen *to go smoothly, work*, III4
klappern *to rattle, clatter*, III11
Klar! *Of course!*, III7
klären *to clarify*, III10
die **Klarheit** *clarity*, III6
klarstellen (sep) *to make clear*, III7
klarwerden (sep) *to become clear*, III9
Klasse! *Great!; Terrific!*, I
die **Klasse**, -n *grade level*, I; *class*, II
der **Klassenausflug**, ¨e *class trip*, III10
Klassenkamerad(in), -en/nen *classmate*, III11
die **Klassenliste**, -n *class roster*, III11
der **Klassensprecher**, - *class representative*, III6
die **Klassik** *classical period*, III2
die **Klassikermetropole** *capital of the classicists*, III2
klassisch *classic(al)*, III4
klatschen *to applaud*, III10
das **Klavier**, -e *piano*, I; **Ich spiele Klavier.** *I play the piano.*, I
der **Klavierstimmer**, - *piano tuner*, III12
kleben *to glue, stick*, III2
das **Kleid**, -er *dress*, I
s. **kleiden** *to dress, get dressed*, III3
die **Kleider** (pl) *clothes*, III3
die **Kleidung** *clothing*, III3
klein *small*, I
die **Kleinstadt**, ¨e *town*, II
die **Klimaanlage**, -n *air conditioning*, II
klingeln *to ring*, III4
das **Klingelzeichen**, - *reminder bell*, III10
klingen *to sound*, III11
die **Klinke**, -n *door handle*, III1
die **Klippe**, -n *cliff*, II
das **Klischee**, -s *cliché*, III8
das **Klischeebild**, -er *clichéd image*, III8
die **Klischeevorstellung**, -en *clichéd image, impression*, III8
klopfen *to knock, pound*, III2
die **Klosteranlage**, -n *monastery grounds*, III1

der Kloß, ⸚e *dumpling*, II
klug *intelligent*, III6
der Knabe, -n *(small) boy*, III2
knapp *scarce(ly)*, III1
die Knebelung *gagging*, III5
kneten *to knead*, III3
das Knie, - *knee*, II
die Kniescheibe, -n *knee cap*, III1
knistern *to rustle, crackle*, III10
der Knoblauch *garlic*, II
der Knöchel, - *ankle*, II
der Knödel, - *dumpling*, III8
der Knopf, ⸚e *button*, II
Koch/Köchin, ⸚e/nen *chef*, III12
kochen *to cook*, II
der Koffer, - *suitcase*, III12
der Kofferraumdeckel, - *trunk lid*, II
der Kohlenwasserstoff *hydrocarbon*, III9
der Koks *degassified coal, coke*, III2
die Kollegstufe *(last three years at a Gymnasium)*, III4
der Kollektor, -en *collector*, III9
die Kombination, -en *combination*, III3
kombinieren *to combine*, III7
komisch *funny; strange*, III6
kommandieren *to command*, III5
kommen *to come*, I; **er kommt aus** *he's from*, I; **Komm doch mit!** *Why don't you come along?*, I; **Wie komme ich zum (zur) ... ?** *How do I get to...?*, I
der Kommentar, -e *commentary*, III6
kommerziell *commercial*, III2
der Kommilitone, -n *fellow-student* (university), III5
die Kommilitonin, -nen *fellow-student* (university), III5
Kommunikationselektroniker(in), -/nen *communications engineer*, III12
die Komödie, -n *comedy*, I
der Komponist, -en *composer*, III10
der Konflikt, -e *conflict*, III12
der König, -e *king*, III7
die Königin, -nen *queen*, III10
das Königreich, -e *kingdom*, III7
die Königsloge *royal box* (theater), III10
konkret *concrete*, III9
können *to be able to*, I; **Kann ich bitte Andrea sprechen?** *Could I please speak with Andrea?*, I
könnte *could*, III5
konservativ *conservative*, II
der Konsum *consumption*, III6
der Konsument, -en *consumer*, III7
der Kontakt, -e *contact*, III4
die Kontaktlinse, -n *contact lense*, III5
kontrollieren *to control, check*, III7
die Konzentrationsfähigkeit *ability to concentrate, focus*, III3
konzentrieren *to concentrate*, III10
das Konzert, -e *concert*, I; **ins Konzert gehen** *to go to a concert*, I
das Konzertabonnement, -s *concert subscription*, III10
die Konzerthalle, -n *concert hall*, III10

der Kopf, ⸚e *head*, II
der Kopfhörer, - *headphones*, II
die Kopfschmerzen (pl) *headache*, II
das Kopftuch, ⸚er *head scarf*, III4
das Kopfweh *headache*, III1
die Kopie, -n *copy*, III11
der Korb, ⸚e *basket*, III9
körperlich *physical(ly)*, III1
der Körperteil, -e *part of the body*, III1
korrekt *correct, proper*, III3
die Korrektur, -en *correction*, III3
korrigieren *to correct*, III1
kostbar *precious, valuable*, III5
die Kosten (pl) *costs*, III9
kosten *to cost*, I; *to taste*, II
köstlich *delicious, charming*, III7
die Köstlichkeit, -en *delicacy*, II
das Kostüm, -e *costume*, III12
kotzen *to vomit*, III2
die Krabbe, -n *crab*, II
der Krach *quarrel*, III4
kräftig *strong*, III7
das Krafttraining *weight lifting*, III3
kraftvoll *powerful, vigorous*, III10
krank *sick*, III3
das Krankenhaus, ⸚er *hospital*, III4
der Krankenpfleger, - *male nurse*, III4
die Krankenschwester, -n *female nurse*, III11
die Krankheit, -en *illness, disease*, III11
die Krawatte, -n *tie*, II
kreativ *creative*, III7
der Kredit, -e *credit*, III5
kreieren *to create*, III7
der Kreis, -e *circle; district*, III2
das Kreuz, -e *cross, check mark*, III5
die Kreuzung, -en *crossing, junction*, III4
kribbeln *to tickle*, III11
der Krieg, -e *war*, II
kriegen *to get, receive*, III3
der Kriegsfilm, -e *war movie*, I
der Krimi, -s *detective movie*, I
die Kritik, -en *criticism, critique*, III6
kritiklos *uncritical*, III7
kritisch *critical*, III3
kritisieren *to criticize*, III3
die Kroatienhilfe *support for Croatia*, III12
die Kroketten (pl) *potato croquettes*, II
der Krokus, -se *crocus*, III11
die Krone, -n *crown*, III1
der Kronleuchter, - *chandelier*, III10
die Krönungsfeierlichkeit, -en *coronation festivity*, Loc7
die Küche, -n *kitchen*, I; *cuisine*, II
der Kuchen, - *cake*, I
das Kugelstoßen *shot put*, II
kühl *cool*, I
die Kühlbox, -en *cooler*, III2
der Kühlschrank, ⸚e *refrigerator*, I
kühn *bold, brave*, III7
der Kuli, -s *ballpoint pen*, I
die Kultur, -en *culture*, III2
kulturbedingt *having to do with the culture*, III4
der Kulturbeobachter, - *observor of the*

cultural scene, III10
kulturell *cultural*, III2
der Kulturkalender, - *calendar of cultural events*, III10
der Kulturmuffel, *a person who ignores cultural events*, III2
das Kulturspiel, -e *cultural event*, III10
die Kulturstadt, ⸚e *city of great cultural significance*, III2
die Kulturstätte, -n *cultural sight*, Loc1
die Kulturszene *culture scene, art scene*, III2
der Kummerbund, -e *cummerbund*, II
der Kummerkasten *grief column* (in a newspaper), III12
s. kümmern um *to be concerned about*, III6
der Kumpel, - *buddy*, III4
künden *to tell (of), herald*, III1
künftig *future, next*, III5
die Kunst, ⸚e *art*, I
die Kunstausstellung, -en *art exhibition*, III10
der Kunstdünger, - *artificial fertilizer*, III9
Künstler(in), -/nen *artist*, III10
künstlerisch *artistic*, III6
künstlich *artificial*, III8
die Kunstsammlung, -en *art collection*, Loc10
der Kunststoff, -e: **aus Kunststoff** *made of plastic*, I
der Kurfürst, -en *Elector* (of a king), Loc10
der Kurs, -e *course*, III11
die Kurve, -n *curve*, II
kurz *short*, I
kurzfristig *on short notice*, III5
kürzlich *recently*, III9
die Kusine, -n *cousin* (female), I
die Küste, -n *coast*, II

L

lächeln *to smile*, III4
lachen *to laugh*, III3
lächerlich *ridiculous*, III7
der Lachs, -e *salmon*, II
der Lackschuh, -e *patent leather shoe*, II
der Laden, ⸚ *store*, I
lag (*imperfect of* liegen), Loc1
die Lage, -n *setting, place*, III2
das Lammfleisch *lamb*, II
die Lampe, -n *lamp*, I
das Land, ⸚er *country*, I; **auf dem Land** *in the country*, I
landen *to land*, III10
die Landkarte, -n *map of the country*, III1
die Landschaft, -en *countryside*, III1
die Landschaftsmalerei *landscape painting*, III1
die Landsleute (pl) *compatriots*, III8
lang *long*, I
langsam *slow(ly)*, II
längst *long ago, since*, III4

der **Langstreckenlauf**, -e *long distance run*, II
langt: das langt *that's enough*, III2
s. **langweilen** *to be bored*, II
langweilig *boring*, I
der **Lappen**, - (coll) *money*, III3
der **Lärm** *noise*, II
las (*imperfect of* lesen), III6
lassen *to let, allow*, II; **er/sie läßt** *he/she lets*, II; **Laß mich mal ...** *Let me...*, II
lässig *casual*, I
der **Laster**, - *truck*, III5
der **Lastkraftwagen (Lkw)**, - *truck*, II
der **Lastwagen**, - *truck*, III9
Latein *Latin*, I
der **Lateinmuffel**, - *a person who does not like Latin*, III12
die **Latzhose**, -n *bib pants*, III3
der **Lauf**, -e *run*, II; **der 100-Meter-Lauf** *the 100 meter dash*, II
laufen *to run*, II; **er/sie läuft** *he/she runs*, II; **Was läuft im Fernsehen?** *What's on TV?*, II
die **Laune** *mood*, III3
laut *loud*, III8
lauten *to sound, read*, III3
läuten *to ring*, III4
lauter: vor lauter ... *because of pure...*, III5
lautlos *soundless, silent*, III2
der **Lautstärkeregler**, - *volume control*, II
das **Leben** *life*, II
lebendig *lively*, III7
die **Lebensaufgabe**, -n *life-work*, III1
die **Lebensgewohnheit**, -en *lifelong habit*, III8
die **Lebensgröße** *life-size, actual-size*, III10
der **Lebenslauf**, -e *curriculum vitae*, III11
die **Lebensmittel** (pl) *groceries*, I
der **Lebensmittelfilialbetrieb**, -e *grocery store branch*, III11
Lebensmittelkontrolleur(in), -e/nen *health inspector*, III12
der **Lebenspartner**, - *partner* (to share one's life with), III11
der **Lebensraum** *living space*, III5
die **Lebensweise** *way of life*, III11
die **Lebenswelt** *world one lives in*, III10
die **Leber** *liver*, III1
der **Leberkäs** (*a Bavarian specialty*), I
lebhaft *lively*, III6
leblos *lifeless, inanimate*, III10
leck werden *to spring a leak*, III9
lecker *tasty, delicious*, I
das **Leder** *leather*, I
die **Lederhose**, -n *leather pants*, III8
die **Lederjacke**, -n *leather jacket*, II
leer *empty*, III1
legen *to lay*, Loc1; **Wert legen auf** (acc) *to consider important*, III11
die **Lehre** *instruction*, III11
Lehrer(in), -/nen *teacher*, I
der **Lehrplan**, -e *teaching curriculum*, III9
die **Lehrstelle**, -n *apprenticeship*, III4

der **Leib**, -er *body*, III7
leicht *easy, simple*, II; *light*, II
die **Leichtathletik** *track and field*, II
das **Leid** *harm, injury*, III2
leid: Es tut mir leid. *I'm sorry.*, I
leiden: Das kann ich nicht leiden! *I can't stand that!*, III4
leider *unfortunately*, I; **Ich kann leider nicht.** *Sorry, I can't.*, I; **Das ist leider so.** *That's the way it is unfortunately.*, II; **Ich hab' leider nur ...** *I only have...*, II
das **Leinen**, - *linen*, II
leise *soft, lightly*, III2
s. **leisten können** *to be able to afford*, III7
die **Leistung**, -en *effort*, III2
die **Leistungsfähigkeit** *efficiency*, III3
der **Leistungskurs**, -e *special courses* (at a Gymnasium), III11
leiten *to guide, lead*, III10
der **Leiter**, - *leader*, III9
die **Leitung**, -en *direction*, Loc4
die **Lektion**, -en *lesson*, III4
die **Lektüre**, -n *reading*, III1
lenken *to steer*, III3
lernen *to learn, study*, III3
lesen *to read*, I; **er/sie liest** *he/she reads*, I
Leser(in), -/nen *reader*, III2
letzt- *last*, I; **letztes Wochenende** *last weekend*, I
die **Leute** (pl) *people*, I
das **Licht**, -er *light, lamp*, III8
das **Lichtbild**, -er *photograph*, III11
der **Lichtschutzfaktor**, -en *sun protection factor*, II
lieb *dear*, III2
lieben *to love*, III3
liebenswürdig *charming, kind*, III7
lieber: lieber mögen *to prefer*, I
der **Liebesfilm**, -e *romance*, I
der **Liebesroman**, -e *romance novel*, I
Lieblings- *favorite*, I
liebst: Ich würde am liebsten ... *I would rather...*, II
das **Lied**, -er *song*, I
liegen *to lie (on)*, III1
liegen an (dat) *to depend on*, III1
die **Liegewiese**, -n *lawn for relaxing and sunning*, II
die **Limo**, -s (**Limonade**, -n) *lemon drink*, I
die **Linie**, -n *line*, III2; **Linie: in erster Linie** *primarily*, III7
link-, *left*, III2
die **Lippe**, -n *lip*, III10
die **Liste**, -n *list*, III1
der **Liter**, - *liter*, I
literarisch *literary*, III10
die **Literatur** *literature*, III10
die **Litfaßsäule**, -n *advertising column*, III7
der **Lkw=Lastkraftwagen**, - *truck*, II
loben *to praise*, III8
das **Loch**, -er *hole*, II

locken *to lure, tempt*, III3
locker *easy-going*, III8
der **Löffel**, - *spoon*, III2
die **Loge**, -n *(theater) box*, III10
Logisch! Logo! *Of course!*, III7
s. **lohnen** *to be worth it*, III5; **Es lohnt sich, das zu machen.** *It's worth doing.*, III8
das **Lokal**, -e *small restaurant*, II
los *detached*, III1; **Was ist los? What's going on?**, III3
lösen *to solve*, III4
loslegen (sep) *to get going*, III3
die **Lösung**, -en *solution*, III3
der **Löwenzahn** *dandelion*, III11
die **Lücke**, -n *blank*, III7
die **Luft** *air*, II
der **Luftsprung**, -e *jump*, III2
die **Luftverschmutzung** *air pollution*, III9
die **Lunge**, -n *lung*, III9
Lust haben *to want to, to feel like*, III2
lustig *funny*, I
Lyriker(in), -/nen *lyricist*, III10

M

machen *to do*, I; **Das macht (zusammen) ...** *That comes to...*, I; **Gut! Mach' ich!** *Okay, I'll do that!*, I; **Machst du Sport?** *Do you play sports?*, I; **Hausaufgaben machen** *to do homework*, I; **macht dick** *is fattening*, II; **Macht nichts!** *That's all right*, II
das **Mädchen**, - *girl*, I
mager *meager, scrawny*, III6
magisch *magic(al)*, III11
mähen *to mow*, I; **den Rasen mähen** *to cut the grass*, III1
die **Mahlzeit** *meal, mealtime*, III10; **Mahlzeit!** *Bon appétit*, II
das **Mahnschreiben**, -n *reminder notice*, III12
der **Mai** *May*, I; **im Mai** *in May*, I
das **Maiglöckchen**, - *lily of the valley*, III11
der **Mais** *corn*, III1
mal (particle), I
das **Mal**, -e *time*, III1
malen *to paint*, III8
der **Maler**, - *painter*, III2
malerisch *picturesque*, III2
man *one, you* (in general), *people*, I; **Man hat mir gesagt, daß ...** *Someone told me that...*, II
manch- *some*, III2
manchmal *sometimes*, I
die **Mandelaugen** (pl) *almond-shaped eyes*, III8
manipulativ *manipulative*, III7
manipulieren *to manipulate*, III7
der **Mann**, -er *man*, I
das **Männchen**, - *little man*, III7
das **Männlein**, - *little man*, III7

männlich *male,* III7

die Männlichkeit *masculinity,* III7

die **Mannschaft, -en** *team,* II

das Manöver, - *maneuver,* III5

das **Märchen, -** *fairy tale,* III10

märchenhaft *legendary, fairy-tale like,* III7

die **Margarine** *margarine,* II

die Margeriten (pl) *daisies,* III11

mariniert *marinated,* II

die **Mark, -** *mark* (German monetary unit), I

die Marke, -n *emblem,* III7

der Markt, ⁻e *market,* III1

die Markthalle, -n *indoor market,* III11

der **Marktplatz, ⁻e** *market square,* I

die **Marmelade** *marmalade,* II

der Marmor *marble,* III6

der **März** *March,* I

der Maschinenbau *mechanical engineering,* III11

das Maschinengewehr, -e *machine gun,* III5

maskieren *to mask,* III10

die Masse, -n *mass (of people),* III3

maßlos *boundless(ly),* III7

die **Mastente, -n** *fattened duck,* II

die Materialien (pl) *materials,* III10

materialistisch *materialistic,* III8

materiell (adj) *material,* III11

die **Mathematik=Mathe** *math,* I

die Mauer, -n *wall,* Loc1

maulfaul *reserved, tight-lipped,* III3

mäuschenstill *very quiet,* III7

die Meckerecke, -n *complaint column (newspaper),* III7

meckern *to complain, nag,* III6

Mediaplaner(in), -/nen *media planner,* III12

die **Medien** (pl) *media,* III6

mediterran *Mediterranean,* II

die Medizin *medicine,* III11

das Meer, -e *ocean,* III1

der Meeresduft, ⁻e *fragrance of the sea,* III7

das **Mehl** *flour,* I

mehr *more,* I; **Ich habe keinen Hunger mehr.** *I'm not hungry anymore.,* I

mehrere *several,* III6

die **Mehrwegflasche, -n** *reusable bottle,* III9

mein (poss adj) *my,* I

meinen: Meinst du? *Do you think so?,* I

meinetwegen *as far as I'm concerned,* III10

die **Meinung, -en** *opinion,* III4; **Meiner Meinung nach ...** *In my opinion...,* III6

die Meinungsäußerung, -en *expression of opinion,* III5

meist- *most,* III6

meistens *most of the time,* II

der **Meister, -** *master, champion,* III1

das Meisterwerk, -e *masterpiece,* III10

die Melodie, -n *melody,* III3

die **Menge, -n** *a lot,* III8: **eine ganze Menge** *quite a lot,* III8

der **Mensch, -en** *human, person,* III3

das Menschenprodukt *human product,* III1

die **Mentalität** *mentality,* III11

merken *to notice, pay attention to,* III1

messen: Fieber messen *to take someone's temperature,* II; **er/sie mißt** *he/she measures,* II

das **Messer, -** *knife,* III2

der Messerhieb, -e *knife blow,* III10

das Messingschildchen, - *brass tag,* III10

die Metapher, -n *metaphor,* III10

die Methode, -n *method,* III5

der **Metzger, -** *butcher,* II

die **Metzgerei, -en** *butcher shop,* I

mexikanisch (adj) *Mexican,* II

mich *me, myself,* I

mickrig *lousy,* III3

mieten *to rent,* III5

das Mikrofon, -e *microphone,* III10

die **Milch** *milk,* I

die Milchkanne, -n *milk jug,* III11

mild *mild,* II

das Militär *military, armed forces,* III5

der Militärdienst *military service,* III5

militaristisch *militaristic,* III8

die Million, -en *million,* III11

der Millionär, -e *millionaire,* III12

die Minderwertigkeit *inferiority,* III5

mindestens *at least,* III1

die Mineralien (pl) *minerals,* III3

das **Mineralwasser** *mineral water,* I

das Minikleid, -er *mini-dress,* III3

die Minute, -n *minute,* III6

mir *to, for me,* II; **Mir gefällt ...** *I like...,* II

mischen *to mix,* III3

miserabel *miserable,* I

mit (dat prep) *with, by,* I; **mit dem Auto** *by car,* I

die Mitarbeit *cooperation,* III6

mitarbeiten (sep) *to cooperate,* III6

der Mitarbeiter, - *co-worker, colleague,* III2

die Mitbestimmung *co-determination,* III11

mitbringen (sep) *to bring along,* III1

miteinander *with one another,* III11

miterleben (sep) *to experience,* III9

mitfahren (sep) *to go along, come along,* III2

mitgeben (sep) *to give (to),* III12

mitgebracht *brought along,* III1

mitgehen (sep) *to go along,* III10

mitgehört *overheard,* III12

das **Mitglied, -er** *member,* III5

die Mithilfe *cooperation,* III2

mitkommen (sep) *to come along,* I

das **Mitleid** *pity,* III3

mitmachen mit (sep) *to go along with,* III3

die Mitmenschen (pl) *fellow-men, neigh-*

bors, III12

mitnehmen (sep) *to take along,* III2

mitsamt *including,* III10

mitschreiben (sep) *to write down,* III6

Mitschüler(in), -/nen *schoolmate,* III1

mitspielen (sep) *to play along, take part in,* III3

mittag: **heute mittag** *this noon,* III1

das **Mittagessen** *lunch,* II

mittags *at noon,* III3

die Mitte *middle,* III2

die **Mitteilung, -en** *message,* III7

das Mittel, - *means, method,* III9

das Mittelalter *the Middle Ages,* III1

mittelalterlich *medieval,* III1

der Mittelpunkt *center,* III2

die Mitternacht *midnight,* III12

der Mittwoch *Wednesday,* I; **am Mittwoch** *on Wednesday,* I

mittwochs *Wednesdays,* II

die **Möbel** (pl) *furniture,* I

möchten *would like to,* I; **Ich möchte noch ein ...** *I'd like another...,* I; **Ich möchte kein ... mehr.** *I don't want another...,* I

die **Mode, -n** *fashion,* I

die Modehochschule *fashion school,* III11

das **Modell, -e** *model,* III7

modern *modern,* I

die Modezeitschrift, -en *fashion magazine,* III3

modisch *fashionable,* II

das **Mofa, -s** *moped,* III4

mögen *to like, care for,* I; **Ich mag kein ...** *I don't like...,* II; **Das mag schon sein, aber ...** *That may well be, but...,* III4

möglich *possible,* II

möglicherweise *possibly,* III10

die **Möglichkeit, -en** *possibility,* III4

die **Möhre, -n** *carrot,* II

Moll (musical key) *minor,* III10

der **Moment, -e** *moment,* I; **Einen Moment, bitte!** *Just a minute, please.,* I; **im Moment gar nichts** *nothing at the moment,* I

der **Monat, -e** *month,* I; **einmal im Monat** *once a month,* I

monoton *monotonous,* III11

der **Montag** *Monday,* I; **am Montag** *on Monday,* I

montags *Mondays,* II

das **Moped, -s** *moped,* I

der **Mörder, -** *murderer,* III10

morgen *tomorrow,* I

der **Morgen, -** *morning,* I; **Guten Morgen!** *Good morning!,* I; **morgens** *in the mornings,* III1

motivieren *to motivate,* III11

der **Motor, -en** *motor,* II

das **Motorrad, ⁻er** *motorcycle,* II

müde *tired,* II

die **Mühe** *trouble, pains,* III2

mühsam *with difficulty,* III8

der **Müll** *trash,* I; **den Müll sortieren** *to sort the trash,* I

die Müllabfuhr *garbage collection*, III11
der Müller, - *miller*, III7
die Mülltrennaktion *separation of garbage campaign*, III12
der Mund, ̈-er *mouth*, III2
der Mundschutz *mouth protection*, III3
die Münze, -n *coin*, I; Münzen einstecken *to insert coins*, I
murmeln *to murmer, mutter*, III10
das Museum, (pl) Museen *museum*, II
das Musical, -s *musical*, II
die Musik *music*, I; klassische Musik *classical music*, I
musikalisch *musical(ly)*, III8
Musiker(in), -/nen *musician*, III11
die Musikhochschule, -n *music conservatory*, III11
der Musikladen, ̈- *music store*, III1
der Musikliebhaber, - *music fan*, III10
das Musikpublikum *music audience*, III10
der Musikunterricht *music instruction*, III10
der Muskel, -n *muscle*, III7
muskulös *muscular*, III8
müssen *to have to*, I; ich muß *I have to*, I
müßte: Man müßte nur daran denken. *You would only have to think about it.*, III9
das Muster, - *pattern*, II
die Musterung, -en *recruitment physical*, III5
der Mut *courage*, III9
die Mutter, ̈- *mother*, I
die Muttersprache, -n *native language*, III4
der Muttertag *Mother's Day*, I; Alles Gute zum Muttertag! *Happy Mother's Day!*, I
die Mütze, -n *cap*, II

N

Na ja, soso. *Oh, all right.*, II
Na klar! *Of course!*, II
nach (dat prep) *after*, I; nach der Schule *after school*, I; nach links (rechts) *to the left (right)*, I; nach Hause gehen *to go home*, I; nach dem Mittagessen *after lunch*, II
nachaffen (sep) *to imitate, ape*, III3
der Nachbar, -n *neighbor*, I
die Nachbarschaft *neighborhood*, III4
nachdem (conj) *after*, III11
das Nachdenken *reflection, thinking over*, III6
nacherzählen (sep) *to retell*, III6
die Nacherzählung, -en *retelling*, III1
nachher *afterwards*, II
der Nachmittag, -e *afternoon*, I
nachmittags *in the afternoon*, III4
nachplappern (sep) *to parrot, imitate*, III7
die Nachricht, -en *message*, III2
die Nachrichten (pl) *the news*, III10

nachschicken (sep) *to send on, forward*, III12
nachsehen (sep) *to check on*, III2
die Nachspeise, -n *dessert*, II
nächst- *next*, II; die nächste Straße *the next street*, I
die Nacht, ̈-e *night*, II2
der Nachteil, -e *disadvantage*, II
der Nachtisch, -e *dessert*, II
nächtlich *nocturnal*, III2
nachts *nights, at night*, III12
nahe *near*, III9
Nähe: in der Nähe von *near to*, III8
nähen *to sew*, III3
nahm (*imperfect of* nehmen), III4
der Nährstoff, -e *nutrient*, III3
die Nahrung *nutrition*, III1
der Nährwert *nutritional value*, III3
naiv *naive*, III8
der Name, -n *name*, III2
nämlich *namely*, III2
nannte (*imperfect of* nennen), III4
narkotisieren *to drug*, III5
die Nase, -n *nose*, III8
naß *wet*, I
die Nation, -en *nation*, III8
die Nationalversammlung *National Assembly*, Loc7
die Natur *nature*, III2
naturbewußt *nature conscious*, III9
Natürlich! *Certainly!*, I; natürlich *natural*, II8
die Natursendung, -en *nature program*, II
der Nebel *fog*, III5
der Nebelstreif *streak of mist*, III2
neben (acc, dat prep) *next to*, II
nebenan *close by*, Loc7
der Nebensatz, ̈-e *dependent clause*, III6
Nebensitzer(in), -/nen *neighbor*, III10
nebenstehend *accompanying*, III3
die Nebenumstände (pl) *minor details*, III1
das Nebenzimmer, - *adjoining room*, III12
negativ *negative*, III1
nehmen *to take*, I; er/sie nimmt *he/she takes*, I; Ich nehme ... *I'll take...*, I
nein *no*, I
die Nelke, -n *carnation*, III11
nennen *to name*, III1
nerven: Es nervt mich, daß ... *It gets on my nerves that...*, III7
nett *nice*, III8
neu *new*, I
neugierig *curious*, II
die Neuigkeit, -en *most recent event*, III6
neulich *the other day*, III1
nicht *not*, I; Nicht besonders. *Not really (especially).*, I; nicht gern haben *to dislike*, I; Ich nicht. *I don't.*, I
nicht nur ... sondern auch *not only... but also*, III4
Nichtraucher(in), -/nen *non-smoker*, II

nichts *nothing*, I; Nichts mehr, danke! *Nothing else, thanks!*, I
nicken *to nod*, III4
nie *never*, I
nieder *down*, III5
niemand *no one*, III10
die Niete, -n *failure* (in a subject), III12
nikotinarm *low in nicotine*, III7
nimmermehr *by no means, never-again*, III5
nobel *noble*, III10
noch *yet, still*, I; Haben Sie noch einen Wunsch? *Would you like anything else?*, I; Ich brauche noch ... *I also need...*, I; Möchtest du noch etwas? *Would you like something else?*, I; Noch einen Saft? *Another glass of juice?*, I; noch höher *still higher*, II; noch nie *not yet, never*, II
nochmal *again*, III3
nochmals *once more, a second time*, III10
der Norden *north*, III2
die Norm, -en *norm, standards*, III7
normalerweise *normally, usually*, II
die Note, -n *grade*, I
notieren *to note, jot down*, III1
nötig *necessary*, III2
nötig haben *to need, require*, III11
die Notiz, -en *note*, III4
notwendig *necessary*, III5
der November *November*, I
nüchtern *sober*, III12
die Nudel, -n *noodle*, III1
die Nudelsuppe, -n *noodle soup*, I
die Nuklearwaffen (pl) *nuclear weapons*, III11
null *zero*, I
die Nummer, -n *number*, III11
nur *only*, II
nützen *to make use of, use*, III5
nützlich *useful*, III6
die Nützung *utilization*, III6

O

die Oase, -n *oasis*, II
ob (conj) *whether*, II
oben *above*, III1
ober- *upper*, III4
der Oberbürgermeister, - *Lord Mayor*, III2
oberflächlich *superficial*, III6
obgleich *although*, III10
das Obst *fruit*, I
der Obst- und Gemüseladen, ̈- *fresh produce store*, I
obwohl (conj) *although*, III1
oder (conj) *or*, II
der Ofen, ̈- *oven*, I
offen *open*, III8
offenbar *obviously*, III12
offenstehen (sep, dat) *to be open*, III2
öffentlich *public*, III2
öffentliche Verkehrsmittel (pl) *pub-*

lic transportation, II
offiziell *official*, III5
der Offizier, -e *officer*, III5
öffnen *to open*, III2
oft *often*, I
öfters *quite often*, III4
ohne (acc prep) *without*, III3; ohne weiteres *easily, readily*, III3; ohne ... zu machen *without doing ...*, III3
ohnehin *in any case*, III12
ohnmächtig *passed out*, III1
das Ohr, -en *ear*, III11
die Ohrenschmerzen (pl) *earache*, II
der Ohrring, -e *earring*, II
das Ökobewußtsein *environmental consciousness*, III9
die Ökonomic *economy*, III7
der Oktober *October*, I
das Öl, -e *oil*, III9
die Olive, -n *olive*, III2
der Olympiasieger, - *olympic champion*, II
die Oma, -s *grandmother*, I
der Onkel, - *uncle*, I
der Opa, -s *grandfather*, I
die Oper, -n *opera*, I
die Operette, -n *operetta*, II
die Opferbereitschaft *readiness for sacrifice*, III9
opfern *to sacrifice*, III5
Optiker(in), -/nen *optician*, III12
optimistisch *optimistic*, III9
die Orange, -n *orange*, III3
das Orchester, - *orchestra*, III10
ordentlich *orderly*, III8
ordnen *to put into sequence, order*, III1
die Ordnung *order*, III1
das Organisationsprinzip *organizational principle*, III3
organisieren *to organize*, III2
die Orientierungsstufe *(beginning years of the Gymnasium)*, III4
originell *original*, III7
der Ort, -e *place; location*, III1
orthographisch *orthographic*, III7
örtlich *local*, III6
der Ostblock *Eastern Bloc*, III11
der Osten *east*, III11
das Ostern *Easter*, I; Frohe Ostern! *Happy Easter*, I
das Ozonloch *hole in the ozone layer*, III9
die Ozonschicht *ozone layer*, III9

P

paar: ein paar, *a few*, III 1
paarmal: ein paarmal *a few times*, III1
packen *to pack, grab*, III1
die Packung *packaging*, III9
der Pädagoge *teacher*, III3
das Paket, -e *package*, III12
die Panik *panic*, III10
der Pantomime, -n *mimic*, III10

der Panzer, - *tank*, III5
das Papier, -e *paper*, III2
der Papierbeutel, - *paper bag*, III9
der Papierkorb, ¨e *paper basket, waste basket*, III9
der Paprika *bell pepper*, III1
das Parfüm, -e *perfume*, I
parfümiert *perfumed*, II
der Park, -s *park*, I; in den Park gehen *to go to the park*, I
die Parkanlage, -n *park*, III2
der Parkplatz, ¨e *parking spot, lot*, II
die Parkuhr, -en *parking meter*, III3
das Parlament, -e *parliament*, III11
die Partei, -en *(political) party*, III5
Partner(in), -/nen *partner*, I
die Partnerschaft -en *partnership*, III8
die Party, -s *party*, III3
passen *to fit*, I; Der Rock paßt prima! *The skirt fits great!*, I
passend *fitting*, III7
passieren *to occur*, III1; Das ist gerade passiert. *It just happened.*, II
Paßt auf! *Pay attention!*, I
pauken (coll) *to study*, III10
die Pause, -n *break*, I
das Pausenbrot, -e *sandwich (a school snack)*, II
das Pausenhofpalaver *schoolyard chatting*, III7
das Pech *bad luck*, I; So ein Pech! *Bad luck!*, I; Was für ein Pech! *That's too bad!*, II
die Pechsträhne, -n *streak of bad luck*, III3
die Peking Ente, -n *Peking duck*, II
die Pension, -en *inn, bed and breakfast*, II
perfekt *perfect*, III3
die Person, -en *person*, III1
der Personalausweis, -e *identity card*, III11
der Personalchef, -s *director of personnel*, III11
persönlich *personal(ly)*, III2
die Persönlichkeit, -en *personality*, III11
die Perspektive, -n *perspective*, III5
pessimistisch *pessimistic*, III9
die Pfandflasche, -n *deposit-only bottle*, III9
das Pfannengericht, -e *pan-cooked entrée*, II
das Pfd.=Pfund *pound*, I
der Pfefferstreuer, - *pepper shaker*, III2
der Pfennig, - *(smallest unit of German currency; 1/100 of a mark)*, I
pfiff rein *(imperfect of reinpfeifen)*, III3
der Pfirsich, -e *peach*, II
die Pflanze, -n *plant*, III8
das Pflanzenprodukt, -e *vegetable produce*, III1
das Pflanzenschutzmittel, - *herbicide*, III1
die Pflicht, -en *obligation*, III5
das Pflichtfach, ¨er *obligatory subject*, III6
pflücken *to pick* (fruit), III11

das Pfund, - (Pfd.) *pound*, I
phantasievoll *imaginative*, I
Phantastisch! *Fantastic!*, II
die Philharmonie *philharmonic orchestra*, III10
Philosoph(in), -en/nen *philosopher*, III10
das Phosphat, -e *phosphate*, III9
die Phrase, -n *expression*, III5
die Physik *physics*, III11
Physiker(in), -/nen *physicist*, III11
das Picknick, -s *picnic*, III2
picknicken *to picnic*, III2
der Picknickkorb, ¨e *picnic basket*, III2
die Pilotin, -nen *pilot*, III5
der Pilz, -e *mushroom*, II
die Pizza, -s *pizza*, I
der Pkw, -s *car*, II
plädieren *to plea*, III5
die Plakatwand, ¨e *billboard*, III7
der Plan, ¨e *plan*, III2
planen *to plan*, III2
die Plastik *plastic*, III8
der Plastikbecher, - *plastic mug*, III9
der Plastikbeutel, - *plastic bag*, III9
der Plastiksack, ¨e *plastic bag*, III3
die Plastiktüte, -n *plastic bag*, III9
der Plastikumschlag, ¨e *plastic envelope*, III9
der Platz, ¨e *place, site*, II
plötzlich *sudden(ly)*, III4
der Plüschsessel, - *club chair*, III10
das Plüschtier, -e *stuffed animal*, III3
polieren *to polish*, II
die Politik (sing) *politics*, I
Politiker(in), -/nen *politician*, III11
politisch *political*, III5
der Polizist, -en *policeman*, III8
die Pommes (frites) (pl) *French fries*, II
der Pool, -s *swimming pool*, II
positiv *positive*, III3
die Post *post office*, I; *mail*, III1
das Poster, - *poster*, I
PR-Berater(in), -/nen *PR-consultant*, III12
die Pracht *splendor*, III10
prächtig *magnificent*, III1
prägen *to leave a mark*, III4
das Praktikum *apprenticeship, in-service training*, III11
praktisch *practical(ly)*, III11
praktizieren *to practice*, III9
die Praline, -n *fancy chocolate*, I
präsentieren *to present*, III10
der Preis, -e *price*, III2
preisen *to praise*, III7
preisgünstig *cheap*, III7
preiswert *reasonably priced*, I; Das ist preiswert. *That's a bargain.*, I
die Presse *(news) press*, III6
Prima! *Great!* I
der Prinz, -en *prince*, III1
die Prinzessin, -nen *princess*, III4
die Priorität, -en *priority*, III11
privat *private*, III11

das **Privathaus**, ¨er *private home*, II
probieren *to try*, Loc7
das **Problem**, -e *problem*, III3
problematisch *problematic*, III4
das **Produkt**, -e *product*, III1
die Produktion, -en *production*, III9
produktiv *productive*, III4
produzieren *to produce*, II
der Profanbau, -ten *secular building*, Loc4
Professor(in), -en/nen *professor*, III11
das **Programm**, -e *schedule of shows*, II
das Projekt, -e *project*, III12
propagandistisch *propagandistic*, III5
der **Prospekt**, -e *brochure, pamphlet*, III1
Prost! *Cheers!*, II
protestantisch (adj) *Protestant*, III1
protestieren *to protest*, III9
der Proviant *provisions, food*, III2
provozieren *to provoke*, III3
das Prozent *percent*, III4
die **Prüfung**, -en *exam*, III5
der Prügelstreifen, - *brutal flick*, III6
prunkliebend *loving splendor*, Loc10
prunkvoll *stately, grand*, III1
der Psychologe, -n *psychologist*, III3
die Psychologie *psychology*, III4
das Publikum *public; audience*, III10
der **Pulli**, -s *pullover, sweater*, I
der **Pullover**, - *sweater*, I
der **Pumpzerstäuber**, - *pump spray*, III9
der Punker, - *punker*, III3
punkig *punk-like*, III10
Punkt: in diesem Punkt *in this matter*, III8
pünktlich *punctual*, III8
die Pupille, -n (eye) *pupil*, III2
putzen *to clean, shine*, I; **Fenster putzen** *to wash the windows*, I
das **Putzmittel**, - *cleaning agent*, III7

Q

die Qualität *quality*, III7
der **Quark** (a soft cheese similar to ricotta or cream cheese), II
Quatsch! *Baloney*, III6
das Quecksilber *quicksilver, mercury*, III9
quer *across*, III10

R

das **Rad**, ¨er *bike; wheel*, II; **mit dem Rad** *by bike*, I
das Rädchen, - *little wheel*, III7
radeln *to bicycle*, III9
radfahren (sep) *to ride a bike*, II
der **Radiergummi**, -s *eraser*, I
das **Radieschen**, - *radish*, III1
radikal *radical*, III11
das **Radio**, -s *radio*, II
der Radwechsel, - *tire change*, III2
raffiniert *clever*, III7
der Rahmen, - *frame, framework*, III7
die Rakete, -n *rocket*, III11

die **Randgruppe**, -n *fringe group*, III4
der **Rang**, ¨e (theater) *balcony*, III10
die Rangordnung *pecking order*, III11
der **Rasen**, - *lawn*, I; **den Rasen mähen** *to mow the lawn*, I
das Rasierwasser, - *shaving lotion*, III7
die Rasse, -n *race*, III5
der **Rat** *advice*, III3; **Komm, ich geb' dir mal einen guten Rat!** *Okay, let me give you some good advice.*, III3
raten (dat) *to give advice*, III4
die **Ratesendung**, -en *quiz show*, II
der Ratgeber, - *advisor, advice column*, III4
das **Rathaus**, ¨er *city hall*, I
ratlos *perplexed*, III10
der Ratschlag, ¨e *piece of advice*, III3
rauchen *to smoke*, II
das Rauchverbot *no-smoking regulation*, III6
rauh *rough*, III6
die **Raumfahrt** *space travel*, III11
der Raumfahrttechniker, - *space technician*, III11
das Raumschiff, -e *spaceship*, III7
raus=heraus *out, away*, III2
der Rausch, ¨e *intoxication*, III7
reagieren auf (acc) *to react to*, III1
die Reaktion, -en *reaction*, III2
das Realgymnasium, -gymnasien (type of a German highschool), III11
realistisch *realistic*, III11
die Realität *reality*, III8
rebellieren *to rebell*, III3
recherchieren *to do research, collect facts*, III6
rechnen *to tabulate, calculate*, III2; **rechnen mit** *to reckon with*, III2
die **Rechnung**, -en *bill, invoice*, III1
das **Recht** *law, right*, III5
recht haben *to be right*, II
recht geben: Da geb' ich dir recht. *I agree with you about that.*, III4
recht- *right, right-hand*, I; **nach rechts** *to the right*, I
rechtlich *lawful*, III7
Rechtsanwalt(-anwältin), ¨e/nen *lawyer*, III11
recyclen *to recycle*, III9
der Redakteur, -e *editor*, III6
die **Redaktion**, -en *editorial office*, III6
die Rede, -n *speech*, III4
das Redemittel, - (communicative) *expression*, III4
reden *to speak*, III4
reduzieren *to reduce*, III9
das **Regal**, -e *bookcase*, I
die Regel, -n *rule*, III2
regelmäßig *regularly*, III3
regeln *to arrange*, III6
regelrecht *regular, regularly*, III2
die Regelung, -en *ruling*, III7
der **Regen** *rain*, I
der Regenschirm, -e *umbrella*, III9
der Regenschirmstock, ¨e *walking umbrella*, III11

die Regieanweisung, -en *artistic direction*, III11
regieren *to rule*, III5
die Regierung, -en *government*, III5
regional *regional*, III10
registrieren *to register*, III7
regnen *to rain*, III1; **Es regnet.** *It's raining.*, I
das **Rehfleisch** *venison, deer meat*, III1
reich *rich*, III3
reicht: **Es reicht.** *That's enough.*, III12
das **Reichtum**, ¨er *wealth*, III1
Reife: **die Mittlere Reife** (name of a highschool diploma), III4
reifen *to ripen, become mature*, III10
Reih: **in Reih und Glied** *in rank and file*, III7
die Reihe, -n *row; line*, III7
der Reihn (poetic for Reigen) *circle dance*, III2
der Reim, -e *rhyme*, III10
rein *pure*, III3
die **Reinigung**, -en *cleaners*, II
reinpfeifen (sep) *to toss down*, III3
der **Reis** *rice*, II
die Reise, -n *trip, voyage*, III1
das Reisebüro, -s *travel office*, III2
der Reisemuffel, - *person who does not like to travel*, III2
reisen *to travel, take a trip*, III1
das Reiseziel, -e *travel destination*, III2
reißen *to tear*, III7
der **Reißverschluß**, (pl) **Reißverschlüsse** *zipper*, II
reiten *to ride a horse*, III2
der Reiz, -e *charm*, III1
reizen *to entice, charm*, III2
die **Reklame**, -n *advertisement*, III7
der Rekrut, -en *recruit*, III5
relativ *relative(ly)*, III2
relativieren *to qualify, make less absolute*, III8
relaxen *to relax*, III3
die **Religion**, -en *religion* (school subject), I
Rennen: **das Rennen machen** *to compete*, III2
renovieren *to renovate*, III8
reparieren *to repair*, III5
die Replike, -n *answer, reply*, III12
Reporter(in), -/nen *reporter*, III3
die Republik, -en *republic*, III1
reservieren *to reserve*, III8
die Residenz, -en *prince's residence*, Loc4
resigniert *resigned to, depressed*, III2
respektieren *to respect*, III5
das **Restaurant**, -s *restaurant*, II
restlich *remaining*, III4
das Resultat, -e *result*, III8
revidieren *to revise*, III8
revolutionieren *to revolutionize*, III5
die Rezension, -en *critique*, III10
das Rezept, -e *recipe*, III1
rhythmisch *rhythmic*, III7
der Rhythmus *rhythm*, III3
richten *to direct*, III12

s. **richten an** (acc) *to be directed at*, III7
richten: Wir richten uns nach euch.
We'll do whatever you want to do.,
III4
richtig *correct, proper*, III1
die **Richtung**, -en *direction*, III9
riechen *to smell*, III1
rief an (*imperfect of* anrufen), III4
riesig *huge*, III7
rigoros *rigorous*, III10
das **Rindersteak** (beef) *steak*, II
das **Rindfleisch** *beef*, II; **Rind schmeckt
mir besser.** *Beef tastes better to
me.*, II
der **Ring**, -e *ring*, II
der **Ringel**, - *ringlet*, II
die **Rippchen** (pl) *ribs*, III1
die **Rippe**, -n *rib* III1
riß (*imperfect of* reißen), III7
der **Rock**, ⸚e *skirt*, I
rodeln *to sled*, II
roh *raw*, II
die **Rolle**, -n *role*, III1
der **Rollstuhlfahrer**, - *person in a wheelchair*, III2
der **Roman**, -e *novel*, I
romanisch *Romanic*, Loc4
die **Romantik** *Romantic period*, III1
romantisch *romantic*, III1
der **Römer** (name of the city hall in
Frankfurt), II
römisch *Roman*, III6
rosarot *rose-colored*, III8
der **Rosenkohl** *Brussel sprouts*, III1
die **Rosine**, -n *raisin*, III1
rostfrei *free of rust*, III7
rot *red*, I; **in Rot** *in red*, I
Rote Grütze (red berry dessert), II
rotgepolstert *upholstered in red*, III10
der **Rotkohl** *red cabbage*, II
der **Rotmarmor** *red marble*, Loc4
rüber=herüber *from there to here*, III1
die **Rubrik**, -en *column* III1
der **Rücken**, - *back*, II
der **Rucksack**, ⸚e *knapsack, backpack*, III3
rücksichtslos *ruthless*, III5
rufen *to call*, III12
die **Ruhe** *calm, quiet*, III4
die **Ruhestätte**, -n *place of rest*, Loc1
ruhig *calm(ly)*, II
der **Ruhm** *fame*, III10
rühmen *to praise*, III1
die **Ruine**, -n *ruin*, Loc10
rumstehen=herumstehen (sep) *to
stand around*, III11
rund *round*, I
runden *to round (out)*, III8
Rundfunkmoderator(in), -en/nen
moderator on the radio, III12
Rundfunksprecher(in), -/nen *radio
announcer*, III12
der **Rundgang**, ⸚e *tour, walk*, III10
runzelig *wrinkled*, III4
russisch (adj) *Russian*, II
die **Rüstung**, -en *armor*, III5

S

der **Saal**, (pl) **Säle** *(large) room*, III10
das **Sachbuch**, ⸚er *non-fiction book*, I
die **Sache**, -n *thing*, III3
die **Sachlichkeit** *factuality*, III12
säen *to sow*, III10
der **Saft**, ⸚e *juice*, I
saftig *juicy*, III2
die **Sage**, -n *legend*, III10
sagen *to say*, I; **Sag mal ...** *Tell me...*,
II; **Was sagt der Wetterbericht?**
What does the weather report say?,
I
sagenhaft *great*, I
sah (*imperfect of* sehen), III4
die **Sahne**, -n *cream*, III1
das **Saiteninstrument**, -e *string instrument*, III12
der **Sakko**, -s *business jacket*, II
der **Salat**, -e *lettuce; salad*, I
das **Salatblatt**, ⸚er *lettuce leaf*, III1
die **Säle** (pl) *(large) rooms*, III10
salopp *casual*, II
das **Salz** *salt*, I
salzig *salty*, II
der **Salzstreuer**, - *salt shaker*, III2
sammeln *to collect*, I
der **Samstag** *Saturday*, I
samstags *Saturdays*, II
die **Samstagsausgabe** *Saturday edition*,
III11
sämtlich *all*, III8
der **Sandstrand**, ⸚e *sand beach*, II
sanft *soft*, III3
Sänger(in), -/nen *singer*, I
der **Sängerwettstreit** *contest of the min-
strels*, Loc1
das **Sanitätskorps** *medical unit*, III11
saß (*imperfect of* sitzen), III4
satt *full*, III7
der **Satz**, ⸚e *sentence*, III1
der **Satzanfang**, ⸚e *beginning of a sentence*, III2
die **Satzlücke**, -n *blank*, III4
der **Satzteil**, -e *part of a sentence*, III4
sauber *clean*, II
sauberhalten (sep) *to keep clean*, III9
die **Sauberkeit** *cleanliness*, III9
säuberlich *neat(ly)*, III6
sauer werden *to get annoyed*, III6
das **Sauerkraut** *sauerkraut*, II
der **Sauerstoff** *oxygen*, III9
saugen: Staub saugen *to vacuum*, I
die **Sauna**, -s *sauna*, II
die **saure Gurke**, -n *pickle*, III1
der **saure Regen** *acid rain*, III9
säuseln *to rustle*, III2
das **Schach** *chess*, I
schade sein um *to be a shame about*,
III5
Schade! *Too bad!*, I
der **Schaden**, ⸚ *damage*, III9
schädlich *harmful*, III7
der **Schadstoff**, -e *pollutant*, III9
schaffen *to accomplish, do, create*,

III5
der **Schafskäse** *goat cheese*, III2
der **Schal**, -s *scarf*, II
s. **schämen** *to be ashamed of*, III8
scharf *sharp*, II; *spicy, hot*, II
der **Schatz**, ⸚e *treasure*, III7
schätzen *to estimate*, III10
die **Schatzkammer**, -n *royal treasury*,
Loc10
schauen *to look*, I; **Schau mal!**
Look!, II
das **Schaufenster**, - *display window*, III11
das **Schaufensterspiegelbild**, -er *image in
the display window*, III11
das **Schauspiel**, -e *play*, II
Schauspieler(in), -/nen *actor*, I
die **Scheibe**, -n *slice*, III1
der **Scheibenwischer**, - *windshield wiper*,
II
die **Scheidung**, -en *divorce*, III12
der **Schein**, -e (money) *bill*, III1
scheinen *to seem*, III5; *to shine*, I; **Die
Sonne scheint.** *The sun is shin-
ing.*, I
der **Scheinwerfer**, - *headlight*, II
schenken *to give (a gift)*, I; **Was
schenkst du deiner Mutter?** *What
are you giving your mother?*, I
scheußlich *hideous*, I
schick *smart (looking)*, I
schicken *to send*, III11
das **Schicksal** *fate*, III5
das **Schiebedach**, ⸚er *sun roof*, II
schief *suspicious*, III5
schiefgegangen *went wrong*, III3
schiefgehen (sep) *to go wrong*, III3
schien (*imperfect of* scheinen), III10
schießen *to shoot*, III5
das **Schiff**, -e *ship*, II
schildern *to tell, report, describe*, III2
schimpfen mit *to scold*, III4
der **Schinken**, - *ham*, II
das **Schisch-Kebab** *shish kebab*, II
der **Schlaf** *sleep*, III2
schlafen *to sleep*, II
schlaff *slack, lax*, III3
das **Schlafzimmer**, - *bedroom*, II
der **Schlag**, ⸚e *blow, knock*, III4
schlagen *to strike*, III5
das **Schlagwort**, ⸚er *key-word*, III2
die **Schlagzeile**, -n *headline*, III6
schlampig *sloppy*, III3
die **Schlange**, -n *line*, III5
schlank *slim*, II
schlappmachen (sep) *to quit, lose it*,
III10
schlau *smart*, III12
die **Schlaufe**, -n *belt loop*, II
schlecht *bad(ly)*, I; **schlecht gelaunt**
in a bad mood, II; **Mir ist schlecht.**
I feel sick., II
die **Schleife**, -n *loop, bow*, II
schlief (*imperfect of* schlafen), III10
schließen *to close*, III2
schließlich *at the end, after all*, III12
die **Schließung** *closing*, III5

schlimm *bad*, II
Schlittschuh laufen *to ice skate*, I
das Schloß, (pl) Schlösser *castle*, III2
die Schlucht, -en *ravine*, III1
schlucken *to swallow*, II; **Ich kann kaum schlucken.** *I can barely swallow.*, II
schlug (*imperfect of* schlagen), III4
der Schluß *end*, III1; **zum Schluß** *finally*, III7; **Schluß machen** *to end one's life*, III1
der Schlüssel, - *key*, III4
das Schlüsselbein *collarbone*, III1
der Schlußsatz, ¨-e *final, crowning sentence*, III3
schmackhaft *tasty*, Loc7
schmalzig *corny, mushy*, I
schmecken *to taste*, III12; **Schmeckt's?** *Does it taste good?*, I; **Wie schmeckt's?** *How does it taste?*, I; **schmeckt mir nicht** *doesn't taste good*, II; **schmeckt mir am besten** *tastes best to me*, II
der **Schmerz**, -en *pain*, II
s. **schminken** *to put on makeup*, III3
der **Schmuck** *jewelry*, I
der **Schmutz** *dirt*, III9
schmutzig *dirty*, II
der **Schnee** *snow*, I
das **Schneidebrett**, -er *cutting board*, III2
schneiden: s. die Haare schneiden lassen *to get your hair cut*, III3
schneien: Es schneit. *It's snowing.*, I
schnell *fast*, II
die Schnelligkeit *speed*, III1
Schnitt: im Schnitt *on average*, III5
der **Schnittlauch** (sing) *chives*, II
das **Schnitzel**, - *cutlet (pork or veal)*, II
der **Schnupfen** *runny nose*, II
schnuppern *to sniff, detect*, III7
Schnupperpreise *prices for careful shoppers*, III7
schnurren *to whir*, III7
schob (*imperfect of* schieben), III10
schockiert *shocked*, III10
die **Schokolade**, -n *chocolate*, II
schon *already*, I; **Schon gut!** *It's okay!*, II; **schon oft** *a lot, often*, II; **Ich glaube schon, daß ...** *I do believe that...*, II
schön *pretty, beautiful*, I
die Schöpfung *creation*, III3
Schornsteinfeger(in), -/nen *chimney sweep*, III12
der **Schrank**, ¨-e *cabinet*, I
der **Schrebergarten**, ¨- *a leased garden*, III1
schrecken *to scare*, III5
schrecklich: Wie schrecklich! *How terrible!*, III3
Schrei: der letzte Schrei *the latest fashion*, III3
schreiben *to write*, I
der Schreibfehler, - *spelling mistake*, III2
die Schreibhilfe, -n *writing aid*, III3
der Schreibstil *writing style*, III10
der **Schreibtisch**, -e *desk*, I

die Schreibübung, -en *writing activity*, III10
schreien *to scream*, III1
Schreiner(in), -/nen *cabinet maker*, III12
schreiten *to step*, III10
schrie (*imperfect of* schreien), III4
schrieb (*imperfect of* schreiben), III2
der Schriftführer, - *recorder, note-taker*, III1
schriftlich *written*, III9
die Schriftsprache, -n *written language*, Loc1
Schriftsteller(in), -/nen *author*, III4
schritt (*imperfect of* schreiten), III10
der Schritt, -e *step*, III2
schrumpfen *to shrink*, III11
schüchtern *shy*, III12
der **Schuh**, -e *shoe*, II
Schuhmacher(in), -/nen *shoemaker*, III12
der Schulabschluß *degree, diploma from school*, III4
der Schulalltag *daily school routine*, III10
der Schulausflug, ¨-e *school trip*, III10
schuld sein an (dat) *to be guilty of*, III4
die **Schule**, -n *school*, I
Schüler(in), -/nen *student, pupil*, III1
der **Schüleraustausch** *student exchange program*, III6
der Schülerausweis, -e *student I.D.*, III10
die Schülerkarte, -n *student pass, ticket*, III10
die **Schülervertretung**, -en *student representation*, III6
das Schulfach, ¨-er *school subject*, III5
die Schulfete, -n *school party*, III6
das Schulgebäude, - *school building*, III6
das Schulgelände *school property*, III6
die Schulgemeinde *school community*, III12
der Schulhof, ¨-e *schoolyard*, III6
schulintern *in-school*, III6
der Schulkiosk, -e *kiosk, snack stand*, III12
die **Schulleitung** *school administration*, III6
die **Schulsachen** (pl) *school supplies*, I
Schulsprecher(in), -/nen *student representative*, III6
die **Schultasche**, -n *schoolbag*, I
die **Schulter**, -n *shoulder*, II
das Schulterblatt, ¨-er *shoulder blade*, III1
die Schulung *schooling*, III5
der Schutz *protection*, III9
schützen *to protect*, III9
der **Schutzfaktor**, -en *protection factor*, II
der Schutzheilige, -n *patron saint*, Loc4
schwach *weak*, III6
die Schwäche, -n *weakness*, III12
schwänzen *to cut class*, III5
schwärmen *to rave*, III12
schwarz *black*, II
schwebend *suspended*, Loc1
der Schweif *tail, train*, III2

schweigen *to be silent*, III2
das Schwein, -e *pig, pork*, III1
das **Schweinefleisch** *pork*, III1
das Schweinekotelett, -s *pork chop*, II
das **Schweinerückensteak**, -s *pork loin steak*, II
der Schweiß *sweat*, III7
Schweißer(in), -/nen *welder*, III12
der **Schweizer Käse** *Swiss cheese*, II
schwer *heavy; difficult*, III3
das Schwermetall, -e *heavy metal*, III1
die **Schwester**, -n *sister*, I
schwieg (*imperfect of* schweigen), III4
die **Schwierigkeit**, -en *difficulty*, III4
das **Schwimmbad**, ¨-er *swimming pool*, I
schwimmen *to swim*, I
der Schwimmverein, -e *swim club*, III4
der Schwindler, - *cheater*, III10
schwingen *to swing*, III7
der **Science-fiction-Film**, -e *science fiction movie*, I
der **See**, -n *lake*, II
die **See**, -n *ocean, sea*, II
segeln *to sail*, II
sehen *to see*, I; **er/sie sieht** *he/she sees*, I
sehenswert *worth seeing*, Loc1
die **Sehenswürdigkeit**, -en *place of interest*, III2
s. **sehnen nach** *to long for*, III7
die Sehnenzerrung, -en *torn tendon*, III1
sehr *very*, I; **Sehr gut!** *Very well!*, I; **sehr gesund leben** *to live in a very healthy way*, II
seid: ihr seid *you* (pl) *are*, I
die **Seide**, -n *silk*, I
das **Seidenhemd**, -en *silk shirt*, II
die **Seife**, -n *soap*, II
sein *to be*, I; **er ist** *he is*, I
sein (poss adj) *his*, I
seit (dat prep) *since*, III1
seitdem (*ever) since*, III4
die Seite, -n *page*, III1
die Seitenloge, -n *side balcony*, III10
Sekretär(in), -/nen *secretary*, III11
der Sektor, -en *sector*, III11
die Sekunde, -n *second*, III12
selber *self*, III4
selbst *self*, III6
selbständig *independent*, III11
die Selbstbedienung *self-service*, III2
das **Selbstdenken** *independent thinking*, III5
das Selbstporträt, -s *self-portrait*, III1
das Selbstvertrauen *self-confidence*, III3
selten *seldom*, II
seltsam *strange*, III10
seltsamerweise *strangely*, III12
die **Semmel**, -n *roll*, I
senden *to send*, III7
der **Sender**, - *station, transmitter, channel*, II
die **Sendung**, -en *show, program*, II
der **Senf** *mustard*, I
sensationell *sensational*, I
die Sensationspresse *tabloid press*, III6

der **September** *September,* I
seriös *sound, reliable,* III6
servierfähig *ready to be served,* III7
die **Serviette, -n** *napkin,* III2
der **Sessel, -** *armchair,* I
setzen *to put,* Loc1
das **Shampoo, -s** *shampoo,* II
die **Shorts** (sing or pl) *pair of shorts,* I
sich *herself, himself, itself, yourself, themselves, yourselves,* II
sicher *secure,* II
Sicher! *Certainly!,* I; **Ich bin nicht sicher.** *I'm not sure.,* I; **Aber sicher!** *But of course!,* II; **Ich bin sicher, daß ...** *I'm certain that...,* II
die **Sicherheit** *security, safety,* III8
sicherlich *certainly,* III12
die **Sicht** *visibility,* III7
sie *she; it; they; them,* I
Sie *you* (formal), I
der **Sieg, -e** *victory,* III5
siegend *victorious,* III5
der **Sieger, -** *victor,* III5
die **Silbe, -n** *syllable,* III10
das **Silber** *silver,* II; **aus Silber** *made of silver,* II
der **Silberstreifen, -** *silver lining,* III9
sind: sie sind *they are,* I; **Sie** (formal) **sind** *you are,* I; **wir sind** *we are,* I
singen *to sing,* III2
der **Sinn** *sense,* III12
sinnlos *senseless,* III5
sinnvoll *sensible,* III3
die **Sitten und Gebräuche** (pl) *customs and habits,* III4
sittlich *moral, ethical,* III5
die **Situation, -en** *situation,* III11
der **Sitz, -e** *seat,* Loc7
sitzen *to be sitting,* III2
die **Sitzung, -en** *meeting,* III8
der **Skandal, -e** *scandal,* III1
die **Skepsis** *scepticism, doubt,* III10
skeptisch *skeptical,* III10
skilaufen (sep) *to ski,* III9
die **Skipiste, -n** *ski run,* III9
die **Skizze, -n** *sketch,* III1
der **Smoking, -s** *tuxedo,* II
snobistisch *snobbish,* III8
so *so, well, then,* I; **so lala** *so so,* I; **So sagt man das!** *Here's how to say it!,* I
so ... wie *as ... as,* II
sobald *as soon as,* III3
die **Socke, -n** *sock,* I
soeben *right now,* III12
das **Sofa, -s** *sofa,* I
sofort *immediately,* III1
sogar *even,* III9
sogenannt *so-called,* III5
der **Sohn, -̈e** *son,* II
die **Sojasprossen** (pl) *bean sprouts,* II
solange *as long as,* III9
solch- *such,* III3
Soldat(in), -en/nen *soldier,* III5
sollen *should, to be supposed to,* I
sollten *should,* III3

der **Sommer, -** *summer,* I
der **Sonderteil, -e** *special part,* III11
die **Sonne** *sun,* II
der **Sonnenaufgang, -̈e** *sunrise,* III7
die **Sonnenbrille, -n** *sunglasses,* III3
die **Sonnencreme** *sun tan lotion,* II
die **Sonnenmilch** *sun tan lotion,* II
der **Sonnenstich, -e** *sunstroke,* II
sonnig *sunny,* I
der **Sonntag, -e** *Sunday,* I
sonntags *Sundays,* II
sonst *otherwise,* III4; **Sonst noch etwas?** *Anything else?,* II
die **Sorge, -n** *worry,* III3
sorgen für *to make sure that,* III9
s. Sorgen machen *to worry,* III9
sorgfältig *careful(ly),* III1
sortieren *to sort,* III9
soundsovieltenmal *for the umpteenth time,* III10
der **Souverän** *king,* III7
soviel *as much,* II
sowas *the like; like that,* III4
soweit *as far as,* III10
sowie *and,* III2
sowieso *in any case, anyhow,* III12
sowohl ... als auch ... *...as well as...,* III1
sozial *social,* III11
die **Sozialarbeit** *social work,* III1
die **Sozialhilfe** *welfare,* III11
das **Sozialwesen** *social system,* III11
sozusagen *so to speak,* III6
die **Spalte, -n** *column,* III2
spanisch (adj) *Spanish,* II
spann (*imperfect of* spinnen), III7
spannend *exciting, thrilling,* I
die **Spannkraft** *vitality,* III3
die **Spannung, -en** *tension, excitement,* III10
sparen *to save money,* III3
der **Spargel, -** *asparagus,* III1
sparsam *frugal,* III1
der **Spaß, -̈e** *joke,* III6; *fun,* I; (Tennis) **macht keinen Spaß** *(Tennis) is no fun,* I
spaßig *funny,* III10
spät *late,* III2
spazieren *to walk, stroll,* II
spazierengehen (sep) *to go for a walk,* III3
der **Spaziergang, -̈e** *stroll,* III4
der **Speck** *bacon,* III1
das **Speerwerfen** *javelin throw,* II
der **Speicher, -** *attic,* III12
die **Speise, -n** *food,* II
das **Spektrum** *spectrum,* III8
spekulativ *speculative,* III4
spekulieren *to speculate,* III4
spezifisch *specific,* III7
der **Spiegel, -** *mirror,* III10
spiegeln *to mirror,* III11
das **Spiel, -e** *game,* III2
spielen *to play,* I
die **Spielshow, -s** *game show,* II

der **Spinat** *spinach,* II
spinnen *to spin,* III7
das **Spinnrad, -̈er** *spinning wheel,* III7
Spitze! *Super!,* I
der **Spitzensportler, -** *top athlete,* III7
der **Spitzhut** *pointed hat,* III10
spontan *spontaneous,* III1
die **Spore, -n** *spur,* III7
der **Sport** *sports,* I; *physical education,* I
die **Sportanlage, -n** *sport facility,* II
die **Sportart, -en** *type of sport,* III2
sportlich *sporty,* II
Sportökonom(in), -en/nen *sports scientist,* III12
der **Sportplatz, -̈e** *sports field,* III10
die **Sportübertragung, -en** *sports telecast,* II
der **Sportverein, -e** *sports club,* III4
sprach (*imperfect of* sprechen), III3
die **Sprache, -n** *language,* III11
der **Sprachexperte, -n** *linguist,* III7
der **Sprachforscher, -** *linguist,* III3
der **Sprachführer, -** *dictionary, phrase book,* III3
sprachlich *linguistic,* III7
sprachlos *speechless,* III3
das **Sprachrohr** *mouthpiece,* III6
die **Sprachschule, -n** *language school,* III11
die **Spraydose, -n** *spray can,* III9
die **Sprechblase, -n** *speech bubble,* III3
sprechen *to speak,* II; **er/sie spricht über** *he/she talks about, discusses,* I; **Kann ich bitte Andrea sprechen?** *Could I please speak with Andrea?,* I
das **Sprichwort, -̈er** *saying,* III12
der **Spruch, -̈e** *saying, proverb,* III3
Spucke: Ihm blieb die Spucke weg. *He was dumbfounded.,* III10
das **Spülbecken, -** *sink,* I
die **Spule, -n** *spool,* III7
spülen *to wash,* I
das **Spülmittel, -** *dishwashing liquid,* III9
die **Spur, -en** *track, trail,* III1
der **Staat, -en** *country, state,* III5
das **Staatswesen** *political system,* III5
der **Stab, -̈e** *bar,* III2
der **Stabhochsprung** *pole vault,* II
der **Stabreim, -e** *alliteration,* III10
der **Stacheldraht, -̈e** *barbed wire,* Loc1
die **Stadt, -̈e** *city,* I; **in der Stadt** *in the city,* I; **in die Stadt gehen** *to go downtown,* I
die **Stadtansicht, -en** *view of the city,* Loc10
die **Stadtführung, -en** *guided city tour,* III2
die **Stadtmauer, -n** *city wall,* III1
der **Stadtplan, -̈e** *city map,* III1
der **Stadtplaner, -** *city planner,* III2
die **Stadtrundfahrt, -en** *city sightseeing tour,* II
das **Stadttor, -e** *city gate,* II
der **Stahlhelm, -e** *steel helmet,* III5
der **Stamm, -̈e** *trunk, stem,* III3

stammeln *to stammer,* III10
stammen *to stem (from),* III12
stand *(imperfect of* stehen), III10
ständig *constant(ly),* Loc1
der Standpunkt, -e *standpoint,* III8
starb *(imperfect of* sterben), III1
stark *strong, robust,* III8
die Stärke, -n *strength,* III12
stärken *to strengthen,* III3
starr *staring,* III10
starren *to stare,* III6
die Statistik (sing) *statistics,* III4
statt (gen prep) *instead of,* III10
stattdessen *in place of which,* III9
die Stätte, -n *place, sight,* III2
stattfand *(imperfect of* stattfinden), Loc7
stattfinden (sep) *to take place,* III1
stattgefunden *taken place,* Loc1
das Statussymbol, -e *status symbol,* III11
der Stau, -s *traffic jam,* III7
der Staub *dust,* I; Staub saugen *to vacuum,* I; Staub wischen *to dust,* II
der Staubsauger, - *vacuum cleaner,* III3
staunen *to marvel (at),* III8
stecken *to put (into),* III9
die Steghose, -n *stirrup pants,* II
stehen *to stand, be,* III2; Das steht dir prima! *That looks great on you!,* II; Wie steht's mit ... *So what about...?,* II; stehen auf (acc) *to like,* III11; Wie stehst du dazu? *What do you think of that?,* III6; Wie steht's? *How's it going?,* III3
stehlen *to steal,* III12
steif *stiff,* III10
steigen *to climb,* II
steil *steep,* III11
der Steinpilz, -e *an edible mushroom,* III12
die Stelle, -n *position; job,* III1; an deiner Stelle *if I were you,* III3
stellen *to put,* III1; Stell deinem Partner Fragen! *Ask your partner questions.,* III1
das Stellenangebot, -e *job offer,* III11
der Stellenmarkt *job market,* III11
die Stellung, -en *position,* III12; Stellung nehmen *to take a position,* III6
die Stellungnahme *point of view,* III6
sterben *to die,* III7
das Stereo-Farbfernsehgerät, -e *color stereo television set,* II
die Stereoanlage, -n *stereo,* I
der Stereotyp, -en *stereotype,* III8
stets *always,* III6
das Steuer *steering wheel,* III5
Steuerberater(in), -/nen *tax consultant,* III12
das Stichwort, -er *key word,* III3
stichwortartig *using key words,* III6
der Stiefel, - *boot,* I
stieg *(imperfect of* steigen), III4
stieß *(imperfect of* stoßen), III7
der Stift, -e *pencil,* III9
der Stil, -e *style,* II

still *quiet,* III8
die Stille *quietness,* III2
die Stimme, -n *vote; voice,* III4
stimmen *to be correct,* II; Stimmt (schon)! *Keep the change.,* I; Stimmt! *That's right! True!,* I; Stimmt (überhaupt) nicht! *That's not right (at all)!,* II; Stimmt, aber ... *That's true, but...,* II
stimmen *to tune* (an instrument), III10
stimulierend *stimulating,* III6
stinken *to stink,* III8
die Stirn, -en *forehead,* III7
das Stirnband, -er *head band,* II
das Stockwerk, -e *floor,* III10
der Stoff, -e *material,* III9
stöhnen *to moan, groan,* III3
stolpern *to stumble, trip,* III1
stolz sein auf (acc) *to be proud of,* III8
stören *to bother,* III6
stoßen *to push, shove,* III7
Strafverteidiger(in), -/nen *lawyer for the defense,* III12
der Strahl, -en *ray,* III9
strahlen *to beam,* III8
strähnig *in strands,* III3
der Strand, -e *beach,* II
die Straße, -n *street,* I; bis zur ...straße *until you get to ... Street,* I; in ...straße *on ... Street,* I
der Straßenhang *(street) shoulder,* III2
der Straßenverkehr *street traffic,* III5
die Strategie, n *strategy,* III5
der Strauch, -er *bush,* II
der Strauß, -e *bouquet,* II
strecken *to stretch,* III10
streicheln *to pet,* III11
streichen *to paint; to cross out,* III11
der Streicher, - *stringed instrument player,* III10
der Streifen, - *stripe,* II
der Streik, -s *strike,* III6
der Streit *quarrel, argument,* III4
streiten *to quarrel,* III2
die Streitigkeit, -en *quarrel,* III4
die Streitkräfte (pl) *armed forces,* III5
der Streitpunkt, -e *point of controversy,* III4
streng *strict,* III8
stressig *stressful,* III8
das Stroh *straw,* III7
der Strom *electricity,* III9
die Strophe, -n *stanza,* III10
die Struktur *structure,* III5
der Strumpf, -e *stocking,* II
das Stück, -e *piece,* I; ein Stück Kuchen *a piece of cake,* I
Student(in), -en/nen *(college) student,* III5
die Studie *study, essay,* III8
der Studienplatz, -e *enrollment slot,* III11
die Studienrichtung *course of study,* III11
studieren *to study, to attend a university,* III4

das Studium *college education, program of studies,* III5
die Stufe, -n *step,* III1
der Stuhl, -e *chair,* I
stumm *silent,* III3
die Stunde, -n *hour,* III1
der Stundenplan, -e *class schedule,* I
die Stupsnase, -n *snub-nose,* III8
stur *stubborn,* III8
stützen auf (acc) *to prop up* (one's arms), III4
suchen *to look for, search for,* I
der Süden *south,* III2
südlich *southern,* III2
super *super,* I
der Supermarkt, -e *supermarket,* I
supertoll *really great,* II
die Suppe, -n *soup,* II
süß *sweet,* II
die Süßigkeiten (pl) *sweets,* III3
der Süßkram *sweet junk,* III12
die Süßwaren (pl) *sweets,* III10
sympathisch *nice, pleasant,* II
die Synagoge, -n *synagogue,* II
die Szene, -n *scene,* III7

T

das T-Shirt, -s *T-shirt,* I
tabellarisch *in tabular form,* III11
die Tabelle, -n *table, grid,* III1
der Tag, -e *day,* I; eines Tages *one day,* I
das Tagebuch, -er *diary,* III1
die Tagebucheintragung, -en *diary entry,* III1
der Tagesablauf *daily routine,* III2
täglich *daily,* III1
der Tagungsort, -e *meeting place,* Loc7
das Tal, -er *valley,* III1
das Talent, -e *talent,* III6
die Talkshow, -s *talk show,* II
die Tante, -n *aunt,* I
der Tanz, -e *dance,* III2
tanzen *to dance,* I; tanzen gehen *to go dancing,* I
Tänzer(in), -/nen *dancer,* III10
die Tasche, -n *bag; pocket,* II
das Taschenbuch, -er *pocket book,* III12
das Taschengeld *allowance,* III4
der Taschenrechner, - *pocket calculator,* I
das Taschentuch, -er *handkerchief,* III1
die Tasse, -n *cup,* III1
tassenfertig *ready to be served in a cup,* III7
tat *(imperfect of* tun), III10
tätig sein *to be busy, employed,* III11
die Tätigkeit, -en *activity,* III11
die Tatsache, -n *fact,* III6
tauchen *to dive,* II
der Tauchsieder, - *immersion heater,* III12
tausend *thousand,* III2
die Technik *technology,* III3
technisch *technical,* III10
technische(r) Zeichner(in), -/nen *technical artist,* III12

technologisch *technological,* III11

der **Tee** *tea,* I; **ein Glas Tee** *a glass of tea,* I

das **Teer** *tar,* III1

die **Teigwaren** (pl) *pasta,* III1

der **Teil, -e** *part,* III9

teilen *to divide, share,* III5

teilgenommen *taken part,* III6

teilnahm (*imperfect of* teilnehmen), III6

teilnehmen an (sep, dat) *to participate in,* III6

der **Teilnehmer, -** *participant,* III2

der **Teilnehmerpreis** *price for each participant,* III2

teilweise *partly,* III10

das **Telefon, -e** *telephone,* I

telefonieren *to call,* I

die **Telefonnummer, -n** *telephone number,* I

die **Telefonzelle, -n** *telephone booth,* I

der **Teller, -** *plate,* III2

das **Tellergericht** *meal,* III10

die **Temperatur, -en** *temperature,* II

Tennis *tennis,* I

der **Tennisplatz, ⸚e** *tennis court,* II

der **Tennisschläger, -** *tennis racket,* II

die **Tenorblockflöte, -n** *recorder,* III12

der **Teppich, -e** *carpet,* I

die **Terrasse, -n** *terrace, porch,* II

teuer *expensive,* I

der **Teufel, -** *devil,* III7

der **Text, -e** *text,* III1

das **Theater, -** *theater,* I; **ins Theater gehen** *to go to the theater,* I

die **Theateraufführung, -en** *theatrical performance,* III10

die **Theaterkarte, -n** *theater ticket,* III12

das **Theaterstück, -e** *play,* II

die **Theke, -n** *counter, bar,* III10

das **Thema, (pl) Themen** *subject, topic,* III5

die **Thermosflasche, -n** *thermos bottle,* III2

der **Thunfischsalat** *tuna fish salad,* III1

tief *deep,* III7

das **Tier, -e** *animal,* III9

Tierarzt(-ärztin) ⸚e/nen *veterinarian,* III11

tierlieb *animal-loving,* III8

das **Tierprodukt, -e** *animal product,* III1

die **Tiersendung, -en** *animal documentary,* II

der **Tilsiter Käse** *Tilsiter cheese,* II

der **Tintenkiller, -** *chemical eraser,* III9

der **Tip, -s** *tip,* III8

tippen *to type,* III6

der **Tisch, -e** *table,* I

die **Tischplatte, -n** *table top,* III4

der **Titel, -** *title,* III2

Tja ... *Well...,* I

die **Tochter, ⸚** *daughter,* II

der **Tod** *death,* III2

der **Todfeind, -e** *arch enemy,* III5

das **Tofu** *tofu,* II

die **Toilette, -n** *bathroom, toilet,* II

die **Toleranz** *tolerance,* III4

toll *great, terrific,* I

die **Tomate, -n** *tomato,* I

Toningenieur(in), -e/nen *sound engineer,* III12

die **Tonkassette, -n** *audio cassette,* III4

die **Tonne, -n** *drum, container,* III9

das **Tor, -e** *gate,* III1

die **Torte, -n** *layer cake,* I

Tote, -n *dead person,* III5

der **Tourismus** *tourism,* III9

der **Tourist, -en** *tourist,* III2

Touristikfachwirt(in), -e/nen *tourism specialist,* III12

die **Tournee: auf Tournee gehen** *to tour,* III10

traditionell *traditional,* III7

traf (*imperfect of* treffen), III7

tragen *to wear; to carry,* II; **er/sie trägt zu** *he/she wears with,* II

der **Träger, -** *strap,* II

das **Trägerhemd, -en** *camisole,* II

trank (*imperfect of* trinken), III12

das **Transportflugzeug, -e** *transport plane,* III5

trat auf (*imperfect of* auftreten), III2

die **Traube, -n** *grape,* I

trauen (dat) *to trust,* III10

der **Traum, ⸚e** *dream,* III11

träumen *to dream,* III10

traurig *sad,* I

die **Traurigkeit** *sadness,* III10

treffen *to meet,* III3

das **Treiben** *activity,* III10

treiben: **Sport treiben** *to do sports,* III3

das **Treibgas, -e** *propulsion gas,* III9

die **Treppe, -n** *staircase,* III1

das **Treppenhaus, ⸚er** *well of a staircase,* Loc4

der **Tresen, -** *counter, bar,* III7

treu *faithful,* III11

die **Trillerpfeife, -n** *whistle,* III3

trinken *to drink,* I

trocken *dry,* I

das **Trommelfell** *ear drum,* III3

trommeln *to drum,* III4

trotz (gen prep) *in spite of, despite,* III1

trotzdem *in spite of that,* III1

trotzen *to be obstinate,* III2

trug (*imperfect of* tragen), III2

trutzig *defiant,* III1

Tschau! *Bye! So long!,* I

Tschüs! *Bye! So long!,* I

das **Tuch, ⸚er** *towel, rag,* III1

die **Tulpe, -n** *tulip,* III11

tun *to do,* I; **leid tun: Es tut mir leid.** *I'm sorry.,* I; **Tut mir leid. Ich bin nicht von hier.** *I'm sorry. I'm not from here.,* II; **weh tun: Tut dir was weh?** *Does something hurt?,* II; **Tut's weh?** *Does it hurt?,* II

die **Tür, -en** *door,* III10

türkisch (adj) *Turkish,* II

der **Turnschuh, -e** *sneaker, athletic shoe,* I

der **TÜV=Technischer Überwachungsverein** *motor vehicle inspection agency,* III7

typisch *typical,* III10

U

die **U-Bahn=Untergrundbahn, -en** *subway,* I

die **U-Bahnstation, -en** *subway station,* I

das **U-boot, -e** *submarine,* III5

übel *evil, bad,* III5

üben *to practice,* III4

über (acc, dat prep) *over; about; above,* III1

überall *everywhere; all over,* III1

überallhin *everywhere, in all directions,* III11

das **Überarbeiten** *revising,* III1

überdurchschnittlich *above-average, outstanding,* III4

übereinstimmen (sep) *to agree,* III7

überfallen *to overcome,* III10

überfiel (*imperfect of* überfallen), III10

überflüssig *superfluous,* III9

überfluten *to flood,* III7

überfragt sein *to not know,* III7

überfüllt *overcrowded,* III2

überhaupt *generally; absolutely,* III1; **überhaupt nicht** *not at all,* I; **überhaupt nicht gern haben** *to strongly dislike,* I; **überhaupt nicht wohl** *not well at all,* II

überkam (*imperfect of* überkommen), III10

überkommen *to come over,* III10

überlegen *to consider,* III7

übermäßig *excessive,* III8

übermorgen *the day after tomorrow,* III7

übermütig *playful,* III10

übernächst- *the (one) after,* III10

übernachten *to spend the night,* II

der **Übernachtungspreis** *room rate,* III2

übernehmen *to take over,* III7

überprüfen *to reexamine,* III8

überraschen *to surprise,* III6

die **Überraschung, -en** *surprise,* III5

überreden *to persuade,* III8

überschätzen *to overestimate,* III7

überschreiten *to cross over,* Loc1

übersetzen *to translate,* III8

übertragen *to transfer,* III1

die **Übertragung, -en** *telecast, transmission,* II

übertreiben *to exaggerate,* III3

übertrieben *exaggerated,* III7

übertrumpfen *to surpass,* III5

überzeugen *to convince,* III2

üblich *usual,* III9

übrig sein *to be left over,* III5

übrigens *by the way,* III1

die **Übung, -en** *exercise,* III1

die **Uhr, -en** *watch, clock,* III2; **um ein Uhr** *at one o'clock,* I; **Wieviel Uhr ist es?** *What time is it?,* I; **Um**

wieviel Uhr? *At what time?,* I
um (acc prep) *at; around,* II
um ... zu machen *in order to do ...,* III3
umarmen *to embrace,* III8
umbenannt *renamed,* III4
die Umfrage, -n *survey, poll,* III3
die Umgangsform, -en *manners,* III11
umgebunden *tied around,* III12
die Umgebung, -en *surrounding area,* II
umgekehrt *vice-versa,* III5
umher *around, on all sides,* III12
umschalten (sep) *to switch over,* III7
der Umschlag, ¨e *envelope,* III12
umschreiben (sep) *to rewrite, rework,* III3
s. umsehen (sep) *to look around,* III10
umso *see* je
umstellen (sep) *to transpose,* III3
umtauschen (sep) *to exchange,* III1
die Umverpackung *outer wrappings,* III9
umwandeln (sep) *to change,* III6
umwechseln (sep) *to change* (money), III1
die **Umwelt** *environment,* II
umweltbewußt *environmentally conscious,* III8
das Umweltbewußtsein *environmental consciousness,* III9
umweltfreundlich *environmentally safe,* III9
das Umweltgift *environmental poisoning,* III9
der Umweltheini, -s *environmental fanatic,* III8
Umweltökonom(in), -en/nen *environmental scientist,* III12
umweltschädlich *harmful to the environment,* III9
der **Umweltschutz** *environmental protection,* III9
die Umweltsünde, -n *sin against the environment,* III9
der Umweltverschmutzer, - *polluter,* III9
die Umweltverschmutzung *pollution,* III9
das Umweltzeichen *environmental logo,* III9
unabhängig sein *to be independent,* III5
unangenehm *unpleasant,* III1
unbedingt *absolutely, by all means,* III1; **Nicht unbedingt!** *Not entirely! Not necessarily!,* II
unbefriedigend *unsatisfactory,* III9
unbegrenzt *unlimited,* III8
das Unbehagen *discomfort,* III7
unbeliebt *unpopular,* III4
unbequem *uncomfortable,* I
unberechtigt *unjustified,* III3
unbeschreiblich *indescribable,* III11
und (conj) *and,* I
undeutlich *unclear,* III1
unendlich *infinite,* III8
unentschieden *undecided,* III11
unfähig *incapable,* III1
der **Unfall,** ¨e *accident,* III1

unfreundlich *unfriendly,* II
die Ungeduld *impatience,* III2
ungefähr *about, approximately,* I
ungenügend *insufficient,* III3
die Ungerechtigkeit, -en *injustice,* III5
ungewiß *uncertain,* III11
unglaublich *unbelievable,* II
unheimlich *weird, creepy,* III10
die Uni, -s=Universität *university,* III11
die Universität, -en *university,* III4
Unmenge: eine Unmenge *quite a lot,* III1
unmerklich *unnoticable,* III10
uns *us,* I; **ourselves,** II; *to us,* II
unser (poss adj) *our,* II
der Unsinn *nonsense,* III7
die Unsinnsbildung, -en *nonsense word,* III7
unsympathisch *unfriendly, unpleasant,* II
unten *underneath, below,* III1
unter (acc, dat prep) *under,* III1
unter sich bleiben *to keep to oneselves,* III4
das **Unterbewußtsein** *subconscious,* III7
unterbrechen *to interrupt,* III5
die Unterbrecherwerbung *interruption by advertising,* III7
die Unterbrechung *interruption,* III7
unterbrochen *interrupted,* III7
unterdrücken *to oppress,* III12
untereinander *among one another,* III4
der Untergang *decline, ruin,* III5
untergebracht *quartered, housed,* III2
s. unterhalten über (acc) *to talk about,* III5
die **Unterhaltung, -en** *conversation; entertainment,* III6
unterhielt (*imperfect of* unterhalten), III4
die **Unterkunft,** ¨e *accomodations,* III2
die Unterlage, -n *document,* III11
unternehmen *to undertake,* III2
der **Unterricht** *class, lesson,* III5
unterrichten *to teach,* III10
die Unterrichtsgestaltung *way of teaching,* III12
der Unterrichtsplan, ¨e *lesson plan,* III10
der Unterrichtsstoff *subject matter,* III12
unterscheiden *to distinguish,* III4
der **Unterschied, -e** *difference,* III10
unterschiedlich *distinct, different,* III2
unterschreiben *to sign,* III5
unterstreichen *to underscore,* III1
unterstrichen *underscored,* III1
unterstützen *to support,* III6
die Untersuchung, -en *inspection, examination,* III8
unterwegs *on the way, underway,* III6
unterzeichnen *to sign,* III5
unumgänglich *unavoidable,* III7
unverdorben *unspoiled,* III2
unweigerlich *without fail, inevitable,* III10

unwirksam *ineffective,* III8
unzufrieden *dissatisfied,* III12
die Unzufriedenheit *dissatisfaction,* III12
der **Urlaub, -e** *vacation* (time off from work), II
das **Urteil, -e** *judgement,* III8
usw.=und so weiter *et cetera, and so on,* III1

V

die **Vanillemilch** *vanilla-flavored milk,* II
variabel *variable,* III2
variieren *to vary,* III8
der **Vater,** ¨ *father,* I
väterlicherseits *on the father's side,* III8
der **Vatertag** *Father's Day,* I; **Alles Gute zum Vatertag!** *Happy Father's Day!,* I
der Veganer, - *complete vegetarian,* III1
der Vegetarier, - *vegetarian,* III1
vegetarisch (adj) *vegetarian,* III1
verabscheuungswürdig *detestable,* III5
s. verabschieden *to say goodbye,* III12
verächtlich *scornful,* III5
verändern *to modify, change,* III2
die Veränderung, -en *change,* III3
der Veranstalter, - *organizer,* III7
die **Veranstaltung, -en** *performance, show,* III6
verantwortlich *responsible,* III6
die Verantwortung, -en *responsibility,* III5
verantwortungslos *irresponsible,* III5
verbergen *to hide,* III7
verbessern *to improve,* III9
die Verbesserung, -en *improvement,* III9
verbieten (dat) *to forbid,* III4
verbilligen *to make cheaper,* III10
verbinden *to connect,* III1
die Verbindung, -en *connection,* III7
verborgen *hidden,* III7
verboten *forbidden,* III5
verbracht *spent,* III1
verbrannt *burned,* III2
verbrauchen *to consume, use up,* III9
der **Verbraucher,** - *consumer,* III7
das Verbraucherprodukt, -e *consumer product,* III9
verbreiten *to spread,* III8
s. verbrennen *to burn oneself,* III1
verbringen *to spend (time),* I
der Verdacht *suspicion,* III2
verdanken (dat) *to owe, be indebted,* III2
verderben *to spoil,* III5
verdienen *to earn,* III7
verdrängen *to displace, repress,* III6
verdrehen *to twist,* III5
der **Verein, -e** *association, club,* III5
vereinigen *to unite,* III8
vereint *unified,* III11
das Verfahren, - *method, procedure,* III11
verfolgen *to persecute, haunt,* III5
verfügen über (acc) *to have some-*

thing at one's disposal, III11
die Verfügung, -en *decree*, III11
verführen *to seduce*, III7
die Verführung, -en *temptation, entice-ment*, III7
vergangen- *past*, III5
die Vergangenheit *past*, III10
vergaß *(imperfect of* vergessen), III4
vergeblich *futile*, III10
vergehen *(time) passes*, III11
vergessen *to forget*, III4
vergleichen *to compare*, III7
verglichen *compared*, III5
das **Vergnügen**, - *pleasure, fun*, III10
vergrößern *to enlarge*, III9
das Verhalten, - *behavior*, III1
das **Verhältnis**, -se *relationship*, III4; *sit-uation*, III11
verheiratet sein *to be married*, III4
verkaufen *to sell*, III6
Verkäufer(in), -/nen *salesperson*, III1
der **Verkehr** *traffic*, II
das **Verkehrsmittel**, - *means of trans-portation*, II
der Verkehrsverbund *local transportation organisation*, III9
die Verkleidung *disguise*, III3
verkleinern *to make smaller*, III9
verkrampft *tense, rigid*, III4
verlangen *to demand*, III7
verlängern *to lengthen*, III10
s. **verlassen auf** (acc) *to count on*, III5
der Verlauf *course*, III6
verlegen *embarrassed, self-conscious*, III11
die Verlegenheit *embarrassment*, III11
verlegte *shifted*, III10
die Verleihung, -en *bestowal, award*, Loc7
s. **verletzen** *to injure (oneself)*, II
die Verletzung, -en *injury*, III1
verliebt *in love*, III8
verlieren *to lose*, III2
verließ *(imperfect of* verlassen), III4
verloren *lost*, III2
vermarkten *to market*, III10
vermeidbar *avoidable*, III9
vermeiden *to avoid*, II
vermiesen *to spoil, ruin*, III1
vermissen *to miss*, III6
vermitteln *to mediate*, III12
vermögen *to be able to*, III1
vermuten *to suppose*, III8
vernünftig *reasonable, sensible*, III1; **vernünftig essen** *to eat sensibly*, II
veröffentlichen *to publish*, III6
verpacken *to wrap*, III9
die Verpackung, -en *wrapping*, III9
verpesten *to poison, pollute*, III9
verpflichten *to enlist*, III5
verquer *against the grain*, III3
verraten *to disclose, betray*, III8
verreisen *to leave on a trip*, III1
verringern *to diminish*, III5
verrückt *crazy*, III3

versagen *to fail*, III4
die Versammlung, -en *assembly, meeting*, III6
verschieden *different*, I
verschmutzen *to pollute*, III9
verschwenden *to waste*, III9
verschwiegen *kept secret*, III12
verschwinden *to disappear*, III1
das Versehen *mistake*, III12
die Versetzung *promotion*, III12
die **Versicherung**, -en *insurance compa-ny*, III11
versperren *to block*, III5
verspielen *to lose*, III2
verspinnen *to use up by spinning*, III7
versponnen *spun*, III7
versprach *(imperfect of* versprechen), III7
versprechen *to promise*, III1
versprochen *promised*, III1
verstand *(imperfect of* verstehen), III7
verstanden *understood*, III1
verständigen *to communicate*, III8
die Verständigung *communication*, III11
verständlich *understandable*, III6
das Verständnis, -se *comprehension; sym-pathy*, III8
verständnisvoll *understanding, sym-pathetic*, III11
verstärken *to reinforce*, III8
verstaubt *dusty*, III12
s. **verstauchen** *to sprain*, II
verstecken *to hide*, III7
verstehen *to understand*, III3; **Ich verstehe mich super mit ihr.** *She and I really get along.*, III4
verstorben *late, deceased*, III2
verstoßen *to give offense*, III7
der **Versuch**, -e *attempt*, III10
versuchen *to attempt, try*; **Versuch doch mal, etwas zu machen!** *Why don't you try to do something?*, III3
verteidigen *to defend*, III3
verteilen *to distribute*, III10
verteuern *to raise the price*, III7
der **Vertrag**, ¨e *contract, agreement*, III5
vertrauen (dat) *to trust*, III3
verträumt *dreamy, sleepy*, III10
vertraut *familiar, intimate*, III10
vertreten *to represent*, III6
verursachen *to cause*, III7
verurteilen *to condemn*, III5
Verwandte, -n *relative*, III1
verwehen *to die out*, III10
verwehren *to deny, prevent*, III10
das Verweilen *staying, lingering*, III2
verwenden *to use*, III7
die Verwendung, -en *use, application*, III9
verwirklicht *realized*, III2
die Verwirrung, -en *confusion*, III1
verwöhnen *to spoil, pamper*, III8
das **Verzeichnis**, -se *listing*, III2
Verzeihung! *Excuse me!*, I; *Pardon me!*, II
verzichten auf (acc) *to do without*, III9

verzweifeln *to despair*, III4
die Verzweiflung *despair*, III11
der Vetter, -n *male cousin*, III12
das **Video**, -s *video cassette*, I
die **Videocassette**, -n *video cassette*, II
die **Videokamera**, -s *camcorder*, II
der **Videorecorder**, - *video cassette recorder*, II
der **Videowagen**, - *VCR cart*, II
viel *a lot*, I; **viel zu** *much too*, I; **viel Obst essen** *to eat lots of fruit*, II
viele *many*, I; **Vielen Dank!** *Thank you very much!*, I
vielfältig *various*, III2
vielleicht *maybe, perhaps*, I
vielseitig *versatile*, III11
vicrspurig *four-lane*, III9
das **Viertel: Viertel nach** *a quarter after*, I; **Viertel vor** *a quarter till*, I
die Villenanlage, -n *area of expensive homes*, III2
die Violine, -n *violin*, III10
Violinist(in), -en/nen *violinist*, III10
visuell *visual*, III10
das Vitamin, -e *vitamine*, III3
der **Vogel**, ¨ *bird*, III9
das Vogelgezwitscher *bird chirping*, III4
das Volk, ¨er *people*, III3
das **Volksfest**, -e *festival*, III10
voll *full*, III1
vollenden *to complete*, III2
Volleyball *volleyball*, I
vollführen *to carry out*, III2
völlig *completely*, III1
volljährig *of age*, III5
die Volljährigkeit *majority, full-age*, III5
die **Vollkornsemmel**, -n *whole wheat roll*, I
vollständig *complete*, III11
die Vollverpflegung *all meals included*, III2
vollwertig *nutritious*, III3
von (dat prep) *from, of*, II; **von 8 Uhr bis 8 Uhr 45** *from 8:00 until 8:45*, I; **von hinten** *from behind*, II
vor (acc, dat prep) *before, in front of*, II; **zehn vor ...** *ten till...*, I; **vor allem** *most of all*, III11; **vor kurzem** *recently*, III1
voraus: im voraus *beforehand*, III8
voraussichtlich *probable, probably*, III1
vorbei *along, by, past*, III1
s. **vorbereiten auf** (sep, acc) *to pre-pare for*, III11
die Vorbereitung, -en *preparation*, III10
die Vorbesprechung, -en *preliminary dis-cussion*, III1
das Vorbild, -er *model, idol*, III11
der **Vorfall**, ¨e *incident, event*, III1
vorführen (sep) *to present, show*, III1
Vorgesetzte, -n *boss*, III11
vorgestern *day before yesterday*, I
vorhaben (sep) *to plan*, III3
vorhanden sein *to be existent*, III10
der **Vorhang**, ¨e *curtain*, III10

vorher *before, beforehand*, III1
vorhin *before, a short time ago*, III10
vorig- *last*, III5
vorkommen (sep) *to happen*, III7
vorlesen (sep) *to read aloud*, III10
vormachen (sep) *to present, model*, III9
der Vormittag, -e *morning*, III5
vorne: von vorne *from the beginning*, III5
der **Vorort**, -e *suburb*, I
der Vorsatz, ⸗e *intention*, III3
der **Vorschlag**, ⸗e *suggestion, proposition, proposal*, II; **Das ist ein guter Vorschlag.** *That's a good suggestion.*, II
vorschlagen (sep) *to suggest*, II
die **Vorsicht** *caution*, III9
vorsichtig *careful(ly)*, III1
die **Vorspeise**, -n *appetizer*, II
das Vorspiel, -e *prelude, overture*, III10
vorspielen (sep) *to act out*, III7
der Vorsprung *lead, advantage*, III5
s. **vorstellen** (sep) *to present, introduce; to imagine*, III6
die **Vorstellung**, -en *impression, image*, III8; *performance*, III10
der Vortag *the day before*, III1
der **Vorteil**, -e *advantage*, II
der Vortrag, ⸗e *lecture, presentation*, III2
vorübergehen (sep) *to pass by, go past*, III2
das **Vorurteil**, -e *prejudice*, III4
vorwiegend *primarily, prevailing*, III7
der Vorwurf, ⸗e *reproach*, III9
vorziehen (sep) *to prefer*, II

W

das Wachs *wax*, III10
wachsen *to grow*, III9
die Wachsfigur, -en *wax statue*, III10
die Wachsplastik, -en *wax sculpture*, III10
die **Wade**, -n *calf*, III1
die **Waffe**, -n *weapon*, III5
wagen *to risk*, III10
der **Wagen**, - *car, truck, wagon*, II
wählbar *electable*, III5
wahlberechtigt *entitled to vote*, III5
wählen *to choose; elect*, III5
die Wahlkapelle, -n *chapel where the emperors were elected*, Loc7
wahnsinnig *insanely, extremely*, III5; **Wahnsinnig gut!** *Extremely well!*, II
wahr *true*, III1
während (gen prep) *during*, III10
die **Wahrheit**, -en *truth*, III6
wahrheitsgetreu *faithful, true*, III6
wahrnehmen (sep) *to perceive*, III7
wahrscheinlich *probably*, I
die Währung, -en *currency*, III1
das Wahrzeichen, - *landmark, symbol*, Loc7
der **Wald**, ⸗er *forest*, III9

das **Waldsterben** *the dying of the forests*, III9
das Wandbrett, -er *poster board*, III9
wandern *to hike*, I
die Wanderung, -en *hike*, III1
der Wanderweg, -e *hiking trail*, III2
wann? *when?*, I
die Wanne, -n *bathtub*, III12
war: ich war *I was*, I
ward/wurde, III7
wäre: Das wäre toll! *That would be great!*, II; **Das wär' nicht schlecht.** *That wouldn't be bad.*, II; **Viele Freunde haben, wäre mir wichtig.** *To have many friends would be important to me.*, III11
die **Ware**, -n *product, ware*, III7
warm *warm*, I
die Warnung, -en *warning*, III8
warten auf (acc) *to wait for*, III1
der Wärter, - *attendant, guard*, III10
warum? *why?*, I
was für? *what kind of?*, I; **Was für ein Pech!** *That's too bad!*, II
was=etwas *something*, II; **Ist was mit dir?** *Is something wrong?*, II
was? *what?*, I; **Was noch?** *What else?*, I; **Was gibt's?** *What is it?*, II; **Was ist?** *What is it?*, II
die **Wäsche** *laundry, clothes*, II
waschen *to wash*, II
s. **waschen** *to wash oneself*, II
das **Waschmittel**, - *laundry soap*, III9
das **Wasser** *water*, I
die **Wassermelone**, -n *watermelon*, III1
der Wechselkurs *exchange rate*, III1
wechseln *to exchange*, III1
wecken *to awaken*, III7
der **Wecker**, - *alarm clock*, II
weder ... noch *neither ... nor*, III10
der **Weg**, -e *path*, III8
wegbleiben (sep) *to stay away*, III4
wegen (gen prep) *because of*, III10
wegfahren (sep) *to go, drive away*, III2
der **Weggang** *departure*, III1
weggebracht *taken away, removed*, III1
weggehen (sep) *to go away*, III4
weggeworfen *thrown away*, III9
weglassen (sep) *to omit, drop*, III6
weh tun (sep) *to hurt*, II
der **Wehrdienst** *armed service*, III5
die **Wehrmacht** (sing) *armed forces*, III5
die **Wehrpflicht** *compulsory military service*, III5
wehrpflichtig *liable to military service*, III5
die **Wehrübung**, -en *military maneuver*, III5
weich *soft*, II
weichen (dat) *to give way, recede*, III10
die **Weide**, -n *willow tree*, III2
Weihnachten *Christmas*, I; **Fröhliche Weihnachten!** *Merry Christmas!*, I

weil (conj) *because*, I
die **Weile** *while*, III11
der **Weinbau** *wine growing*, Loc4
weinen *to cry*, III2
weise *wise*, III7
weiß *white*, I
die **Weißwurst**, ⸗e (southern German sausage specialty), I
weit *far; wide*, I; **weit von hier** *far from here*, I
weiter *further*, III1
weitergehen (sep) *to continue on*, III2
weiterhin *as before*, III7
weitgehend *extensive, largely*, III5
der **Weitsprung** *long jump*, II
welch-? *which?*, I; **Welche Fächer hast du?** *Which subjects do you have?*, I
die **Welle**, -n *wave*, III5
die **Welt**, -en *world*, III11
weltanschaulich *ideological*, III5
die **Weltanschauung**, -en *world view*, III2
der **Weltbegriff** *understanding of the world*, III5
weltfremd *innocent, starry-eyed*, III12
der **Weltkrieg**, -e *world war*, III5
der **Weltkriegsgefreite** *private first-class in a world war*, III5
der **Weltruf** *international reputation*, Loc10
weltweit *worldwide, global*, III8
wem? *to whom?, for whom?*, I
wen? *whom?*, I
wenden *to turn*, III5
der **Wendepunkt**, -e *turning point*, III11
wenige *few*, III6
wenigstens *at least*, III1
wenn (conj) *whenever*, II
wer? *who?*, I; **Wer ist das?** *Who is that?*, I
die **Werbeagentur**, -en *advertising agency*, III7
die **Werbeanzeige**, -n *advertisement*, III7
die **Werbeausgaben** (pl) *advertising expenditures*, III7
der **Werbeblock**, ⸗e *block of advertising*, III7
die **Werbebranche**, -n *advertising industry*, III7
die **Werbeeinblendung**, -en *advertisement fade-in*, III7
der **Werbemacher**, - *advertisement creator*, III7
werben *to advertise*, III7
die **Werbesendung**, -en *commercial*, II
der **Werbeslogan**, -s *advertising slogan*, III7
der **Werbespot**, -s *commercial spot*, III7
der **Werbespruch**, ⸗e *advertising slogan*, III7
der **Werbetexter**, - *advertisement writer*, III7
werbewirksam *effective advertising*, III7
die **Werbewirtschaft** *advertising industry*, III7

die Werbung *advertising*, III7
werden *will*, II; er/sie wird *he/she will*, II; Ich werde mir ... kaufen. *I'll buy myself...*, II
werfen *to throw*, III8
das Werk, -e *work; factory*, III10
Werkzeugmacher(in), -/nen *tool maker*, III12
Wert: Ich leg' viel Wert darauf. *That's real important to me.*, III11
wesentlich *substantial(ly)*, III9
weshalb? *for what reason?*, III4
wessen *whose*, III7
der Westen *the west*, III7
der Western, - *western (movie)*, I
das Wetter *weather*, I
der Wetterbericht, -e *weather report*, II
die Wetterjacke, -n *rain jacket*, II
der Wettkampf, ⁻e *contest, competition*, III8
der Whirlpool, -s *whirlpool*, II
wichen (*imperfect of* weichen), III10
wichtig *important*, III1
widersprechen *to contradict, oppose*, III5
die Widerstandsbewegung, -en *resistance movement*, III5
wie lange *how long*, II
wie? *how?*, I; wie oft? *how often?*, I; Wie spät ist es? *What time is it?*, I; Wie steht's mit ...? *So what about...?*, II; Wie wär's mit ...? *How would... be?*, II; Wie war's? *How was it?*, II
wieder *again*, I
wiedergeben (sep) *to repeat*, III8
wiederholen *to repeat*, III1
die Wiederholung, -en *repetition*, III8
Wiederhören *Bye!* (on the telephone), I; Auf Wiederhören! *Goodbye!* (on the telephone), I
Wiedersehen! *Bye!*, I; Auf Wiedersehen! *Goodbye!*, I
wiederverwenden (sep) *to use again*, III9
wiederverwerten (sep) *to recycle*, III9
die Wiederverwertung, -en *recycling*, III9
wiegen *to weigh*, I
das Wiener Schnitzel, - *breaded veal cutlet*, II
die Wiese, -n *meadow*, III7
wieso? *why?; how?*, III8
wieviel? *how much?*, I; Wieviel Grad haben wir? *What's the temperature?*, I; Wieviel Uhr ist es? *What time is it?*, I
der Wilderer, - *poacher*, III10
die Wildlederjacke, -n *suede jacket*, II
der Wildwestfilm, -e *wild west film*, II
der Wille *will, volition*, III2
willig *willing*, III2
willkommen *welcome*, III2
die Windjacke, -n *windbreaker*, II
windsurfen *to wind surf*, II
winselnd *whimpering*, III1
der Winter *winter*, I

Winzer(in), -/nen *vintner*, III12
wippen *to rock*, III4
wir *we*, I
wirken *to cause, effect*, III6
wirklich *really*, I
die Wirklichkeit, -en *reality*, III7
wirksam *effective*, III7
die Wirkung, -en *effect, consequence*, III2
wirkungsvoll *effective*, III3
die Wirtschaft *economy*, III7
die Wirtschaftswissenschaft *applied study of business*, III11
wischen *to wipe*, III7
wissen *to know* (a fact, information, etc.), I; Das weiß ich nicht. *That I don't know.*, I; Ich weiß nicht, ob ... *I don't know whether...*, II
die Wissenschaft, -en *science*, III11
Wissenschaftler(in) -/nen *scientist*, III9
wissenschaftlich *scientific*, III10
die Wissenschaftssprache, -n *scientific language*, III11
der Witz, -e *joke*, III6
witzig *fun, witty*, II
wo? *where?*, I
woandershin *to somewhere else*, III2
wobei *whereby*, III1
die Woche, -n *week*, I; (einmal) in der Woche *(once) a week*, I
das Wochenende, -n *weekend*, I
wofür? *for what?*, III1; Wofür interessierst du dich? *What are you interested in?*, II
woher? *from where?*, I; Woher bist du? *Where are you from?*, I; Woher kommst du? *Where are you from?*, I
wohin? *where (to)?*, I; Wohin fahren wir? *Where are we going?*, II
wohl *well*, III1; Ich fühle mich wohl. *I feel great.*, II
das Wohlbefinden *good health, well-being*, III3
wohnen *to live*, I
das Wohnhaus, ⁻er *residence*, II
der Wohnsitz, -e *place of residence*, III5
die Wohnung, -en *apartment*, II
das Wohnzimmer, - *living room*, II
wolkig *cloudy*, I
die Wolle *wool*, II
wollen *to want (to)*, I
das Wollhemd, -en *wool shirt*, II
das Wort, ⁻er *word*, III4
das Wörterbuch, ⁻er *dictionary*, I
wortlos *speechless*, III3
der Wortschatz *vocabulary*, III1
die Wortstellung *word order, syntax*, III1
worum: Worum geht es? *What's it about?*, III4
wozu? *why?; to what purpose?*, III3
wuchs (*imperfect of* wachsen), III10
das Wunder, - *wonder, miracle*, III10
wunderbar *wonderful*, III10
wundern *to be amazed*, III8

wunderschön *incredibly beautiful*, III2
der Wunsch, ⁻e *wish*, I; Haben Sie einen Wunsch? *May I help you?*, I; Haben Sie noch einen Wunsch? *Would you like anything else?*, I
s. wünschen *to wish*, II; Ich wünsche mir ... *I wish for...*, II
würde *would*, II; Würdest du gern mal ...? *Wouldn't you like to...?*, II
würgen *to choke*, III3
die Wurst, ⁻e *sausage*, I
das Wurstbrot, -e *bologna sandwich*, I
die Wurzel, -n *root*, III10
würzig *spicy*, II
die Wut *rage*, III4
wütend *furious*, III1

Z

die Zahl, -en *number*, III6
zahlen (dat) *to pay*, III3; Ich möchte/will zahlen! *The check please!*, I
zahlreich *countless*, II
der Zahn, ⁻e *tooth*, II
Zahnarzt(⁻in), ⁻e/nen *dentist*, III12
die Zahnpasta *toothpaste*, II
die Zahnschmerzen (pl) *toothache*, II
Zahntechniker(in), -/nen *dental technician*, III12
die Zehe, -n *toe*, III1
die Zehenspitze, -n *tip-toe*, III10
der Zehnkämpfer, - *decathlete*, II
das Zeichen, - *sign*, III9
zeichnen *to draw*, I
Zeichner: technische(r) Zeichner(in), -/nen *technical artist*, III12
die Zeichnung, -en *drawing*, III4
zeigen *to show*, III1; es zeigt sich, daß ... *it appears that...*, III1
die Zeit *time*, I; zur Zeit *right now*, II
das Zeitalter *age, era*, Loc10
die Zeitausdrücke (pl) *time expressions*, III12
die Zeitform *grammatical tense*, III1
zeitgenössisch *contemporary*, III12
Zeitlang: eine Zeitlang *for a while*, III4
zeitlich *temporal, time*, III11
die Zeitschrift, -en *magazine*, I
die Zeitung, -en *newspaper*, I
der Zeitvertreib *diversion, amusement*, III10
zelten *to camp out*, III2
das Zentrum, (pl) Zentren *center*, Loc1
der Zerfall *ruin, decay*, Loc1
zerknittert *wrinkled, crumpled*, III12
zerreissen *to tear apart*, III3
zerstört *destroyed*, Loc1
die Zerstörung, -en *destruction*, III9
zerstreut *absentminded*, III12
der Zettel, - *note*, III1
der Zeuge, -n *witness*, III11
das Zeugnis, -se *report card*, III12
die Zeugniskopie, -n *copy of report card*,

III11
ziehen *to move* (residence), III12
das **Ziel**, -e *goal,* III11
die **Zielgruppe**, -n *target group,* III7
ziemlich *rather,* I
das **Zimmer**, - *room,* I; **mein Zimmer aufräumen** *to clean my room,* I
die **Zimmerantenne**, -n *indoor antenna,* II
der **Zimmermann**, -leute *carpenter,* III12
der **Zimt** *cinnammon,* I
zirka *approximately,* III2
das **Zitat**, -e *quotation,* III10
die **Zitrone**, -n *lemon,* I
zittern *to tremble,* III10
der **Zivildienst** *community service,* III5
der **Zivilschutzverband** *national guard,* III5
zog (*imperfect of* ziehen), III4
der **Zoo**, -s *zoo,* I
der **Zorn** *anger,* III7
zu *too; to,* I; **zu Fuß** *on foot,* I; **zu Hause helfen** *to help at home,* I; **zu bitter** *too bitter,* II; **zu viel** *too much,* II; **zu viele** *too many,* II
der **Zucker** *sugar,* I
zuerst *first,* I
zufrieden *satisfied,* III2
die **Zufriedenheit**, -en *satisfaction,* III11
zufriedenstellend *satisfactory,* III7
der **Zug**, ⁻e *train,* III1
der **Zugang** *access,* III11
zugeben (sep) *to admit,* III3

zuhören (sep) *to listen to,* II; **Hör gut zu!** *Listen carefully!,* I
zukam (*imperfect of* zukommen), III11
zukneifen (sep) *to squeeze shut,* III4
zukniff (*imperfect of* zukneifen), III4
zukommen auf (sep, acc) *to be in store for,* III11
die **Zukunft** *future,* III11
zukünftig *(in) future,* III11
zulassen (sep) *to admit, approve,* III9
zuletzt *last of all,* I
zuliebe: der Umwelt zuliebe *for the love of the environment,* III9
zum=zu dem: zum Abendessen *for dinner,* II; **Zum Wohl!** *To your health!,* II 1
zunächst *for the time being,* III10
zunehmen (sep) *to gain weight,* III3
zunicken (sep) *to nod to,* III4
zurück *back,* III5
zurückbringen (sep) *to bring back, return,* III1
zurückgebracht *brought back,* III1
zurückhalten (sep) *to hold back, retain,* III5
zurückkehren (sep) *to return,* III12
zurückkommen auf (sep, acc) *to get back to,* III6
zusammen *together,* III1
zusammenbasteln (sep) *to rig together,* III10
zusammenfassen (sep) *to summarize,* III6

die **Zusammenfassung**, -en *synopsis,* III3
zusammenhängen (sep) *to be connected,* III1
zusammenkommen (sep) *to come together,* III2
zusammenpassen (sep) *to go together, match,* III3
zusammensinken (sep) *to collapse,* III10
zusammenstellen (sep) *to compile,* III1
zusätzlich *additionally,* III2
der **Zuschauer**, - *spectator,* III10
zuschicken (sep) *to send to,* III12
zuschlagen (sep) *to slam,* II
der **Zustand**, ⁻e *state, condition,* III12
zustimmen (sep, dat) *to agree,* II
die **Zustimmung**, -en *consent, agreement,* III3
zutreffend *correct, applicable,* III2
zuverlässig *dependable,* III11
zuvor *before,* III7
zwar *indeed,* III10
der **Zweck**, -e *purpose, object,* III6
der **Zweig**, -e *branch,* III3
zweimal *twice,* I
zweit- *second,* III4
zweitens *secondly,* III11
die **Zwetschge**, -n *plum,* II
die **Zwiebel**, -n *onion,* I
der **Zwilling**, -e *twin,* II
zwischen (acc, dat prep) *between,* II

ENGLISH-GERMAN VOCABULARY

This vocabulary includes all of the words in the **Wortschatz** sections of the chapters. These words are considered active—you are expected to know them and be able to use them.

Idioms are listed under the English word you would be most likely to look up. German nouns are listed with the definite article and plural ending, when applicable. The number after each German word or phrase refers to the chapter in which it becomes active vocabulary. To be sure you are using the German words and phrases in the correct context, refer to the book and chapter in which they appear.

The following abbreviations are used in the vocabulary: acc (accusative), adj (adjective), dat (dative), gen (genitive), masc (masculine), pl (plural), poss adj (possessive adjective), pp (past participle), sep (separable-prefix verb), and sing (singular).

A

a few *wenige*, III6
a, an *ein(e)*, I
able: to be able to *können*, I
about *ungefähr*, I
accept: to be accepted by *ankommen bei* (sep), III3
accessible to the physically challenged *behindertenfreundlich*, III2
accident *der Unfall, ⸚e*, III1
accomodations *die Unterkunft, ⸚e*, III2
accompany *begleiten*, III10
achieve *erreichen*, III6; *schaffen*, III5
achievement *das Werk, -e*, III10
acid rain *der saure Regen*, III9
across from *gegenüber*, II
action movie *der Actionfilm, -e*, I
active: to be active in *s. engagieren für*, III5
actor *der Schauspieler, -*, I
actress *die Schauspielerin, -nen*, I
address *ansprechen* (sep), III6
administration: school administration *die Schulleitung*, III 6
admire *bewundern*, III10
admit *eingestehen* (sep), III7; *zugeben* (sep), III3
advanced: to be advanced (person) *der Fortgeschrittene, -n*, II
advantage *der Vorteil, -e*, II; **to take advantage of** *ausnützen* (sep), III7
advertise *werben*, III7
advertisement *die Reklame, -n*, III7; *die Werbung, -en*, III7
advertising slogan *der Werbespruch, ⸚e*, III7
advice *der Rat*, III3; **to give advice** *raten* (dat), III4
afford: to be able to afford *s. leisten können*, III7
afraid: to be afraid *Angst haben*, III2; *fürchten*, III9

after *nach*, I; **after that** *danach*, I
afternoon *der Nachmittag, -e*, I; **in the afternoon** *am Nachmittag*, I
afterward *nachher*, II
again *wieder*, I
agree: to agree with *übereinstimmen mit* (sep), III7; *recht geben* (dat), III4; **I agree with you on that!** *Da stimm' ich dir zu!*, II; **Yes, I do agree with you, but...** *Ja, ich stimme dir zwar zu, aber ...*, II
Agreed! *Einverstanden!*, II
air *die Luft*, II; **air conditioning** *die Klimaanlage, -n*, II; **air pollution** *die Luftverschmutzung*, III9
airplane *das Flugzeug, -e*, II
alarm clock *der Wecker, -*, II
alcohol: to not drink alcohol *keinen Alkohol trinken*, II
all *all-*, II; *sämtlich*, III8
all right: Oh, (I'm) all right. *Na ja, soso!*, II
allergic: I am allergic to... *Ich bin allergisch gegen ...*, II
allowed: to be allowed to *dürfen*, II
almost always *fast immer*, III6
along: Why don't you come along! *Komm doch mit!*, I
aloud: to read aloud *vorlesen* (sep), III10
already *schon*, I
also *auch*, I; *auch schon*, II; **I also need...** *Ich brauche noch ...*, I
alternate: alternate service *der Zivildienst*, III5
aluminum can *die Aludose*, III9
always *immer*, I
amaze: to be amazed *staunen*, III8
ambitious *ehrgeizig*, III8
among one another *untereinander*, III4
and *und*, I

anesthesiologist *Anästhesist(in), -en/nen*, III12
animal product *das Tierprodukt, -e*, III1
animal-loving *tierlieb*, III8
ankle *der Knöchel, -*, II
announcement *der Anschlag, ⸚e*, II
annoy: to get annoyed *s. ärgern*, III8; *s. aufregen* (sep), III7; *sauer werden*, III6
another *noch ein*, I; **I don't want any more...** *Ich möchte kein(e)(en) ... mehr.*, I; **I'd like another...** *Ich möchte noch ein(e)(en) ...*, I
another (a different) one *ein(-) ander-*, II
ant *die Ameise, -n*, III9
antenna: indoor antenna *die Zimmerantenne, -n*, II
anything: Anything else? *Sonst noch etwas?*, I, II
apartment *die Wohnung, -en*, II
appear *aussehen* (sep), I
appetizer *die Vorspeise, -n*, II
applaud *klatschen*, III10
apple *der Apfel, ⸚*, I
apple cake *der Apfelkuchen, -*, I
apple juice *der Apfelsaft, ⸚e*, I
apprenticeship *die Lehre, -n*, III11
approximately *ungefähr*, I
apricot *die Aprikose, -n*, II
April *der April*, I
archery *das Bogenschießen*, II
area *die Gegend, -en*, III2
argue against *abstreiten* (sep), III5
argument *der Streit*, III4
arm *der Arm, -e*, II
armchair *der Sessel, -*, I
armed: armed service *der Wehrdienst*, III5; **armed services** *die Streitkräfte* (pl), III5
around *um*, II
art *die Kunst*, I

artificial *künstlich*, III8
artificial fertilizer *der Kunstdünger,
-*, III9
as ... as *so ... wie*, II
as: as if *als ob*, III7
asparagus *der Spargel, -*, III1
assume *annehmen* (sep), III8
at *an, in*, II
at: at 8 o'clock *um 8 Uhr*, I; at one
o'clock *um ein Uhr*, I; at the
baker's *beim Bäcker*, I; At what
time? *Um wieviel Uhr?*, I
athletic *sportlich*, II
attempt *der Versuch, -e*, III10; to
attempt, try *versuchen*, III3
attention: to draw attention to
aufmerksam machen auf (acc), III7;
to pay attention *aufpassen* (sep),
III3; to pay attention to *achten auf*
(acc), III3
August *der August*, I
aunt *die Tante -n*, I
avoid *vermeiden*, II
avoidable *vermeidbar*, III9
away, at a distance *entfernt*, III2
awesome *stark*, I; The sweater is awesome! *Ich finde den Pulli stark!*, I
awful *fies*, III5; *furchtbar*, I

B

back *der Rücken, -*, II
background *der Hintergrund, -̈e*,
III6
bacon *der Speck*, III1
bad *schlecht*, I; **badly** *schlecht*, I; Bad
luck! *So ein Pech!*, I; It's too bad
that... *Es ist schade, daß ...*, II;
That's not so bad. *Nicht so
schlimm!*, II; That's too bad! *Was
für ein Pech!*, II; *Ach schade!*, II
bad: a streak of bad luck *die
Pechsträhne*, III3
badly: to go badly *schiefgehen* (sep),
III3
bag: paper bag *der Papierbeutel, -*,
III9; plastic bag *die Plastiktüte, -n*,
III9
baker *der Bäcker, -*, I; at the baker's
beim Bäcker, I
bakery *die Bäckerei, -en*, I
balanced: well-balanced *ausgewogen*, III8
bald: to be bald *eine Glatze haben*, I
ballet *das Ballett, -e*, II
ballpoint pen *der Kuli, -s*, I
banana *die Banane, -n*, II
bank *die Bank, -en*, I
bargain: That's a bargain. *Das ist
preiswert.*, I

base: to be based on *beruhen auf*
(acc), III11
basket: picnic basket *der
Picknickkorb, -̈e*, III2
basketball *Basketball*, I
bathroom *das Badezimmer, -*, II; toilet *die Toilette, -n*, II
battery *die Batterie, -n*, III9
battle *der Kampf, -̈e*, III5
bay *die Bucht, -en*, II
be *sein*, I
be: to be, stand *stehen*, III2; to be
about *s. handeln um*, III10
beach *der Strand, -̈e*, II; sand beach
der Sandstrand, -̈e, II
bean (green) *die (grüne) Bohne, -n*,
II
bearded *bärtig*, III10
beautiful *schön*, I
because *denn, weil*, I
because of *wegen*, III10
become *werden*, II
bed *das Bett, -en*, I
bed and breakfast *die Pension, -en*, II
bedroom *das Schlafzimmer, -*, II
bee *die Biene, -n*, III9
beef *das Rindfleisch*, II
before *bevor* (conj), III5
before: as before *weiterhin*, III7
beforehand *im voraus*, III8
begin *anfangen* (sep), III11
beginner *der Anfänger, -*, II
behind: from behind *von hinten*, II
believe *glauben*, I; You can believe
me on that! *Das kannst du mir
glauben!*, II; I do believe that... *Ich
glaube schon, daß ...*, II
bell pepper *der Paprika*, III1
belong to *angehören* (sep, dat), III4
belt *der Gürtel, -*, I; belt loop *die
Schlaufe, -n*, II
besides that *außerdem*, III9
best: Best wishes on your birthday!
*Herzlichen Glückwunsch zum
Geburtstag!*, I
better *besser*, I
between *zwischen*, II
bicycle *radeln*, III9; *radfahren* (sep),
II; *das Fahrrad, -̈er*, I; by bike *mit
dem Rad*, I
bicycle racks *das Fahrrad-Depot, -s*,
II
big *groß*, I; *weit*, II
bigger *größer*, II
bill, invoice *die Rechnung, -en*, III1
billboard *die Plakatwand, -̈e*, III7
bio-degradable *biologisch abbaubar*,
III9
biologist *Biologe/Biologin, -n/nen*,
III11

biology *Bio (die Biologie)*, I
biology teacher *die Biologielehrerin,
-nen*, I
bird *der Vogel, -̈*, III9
birthday *der Geburtstag, -e*, I; Best
wishes on your birthday!
*Herzlichen Glückwunsch zum
Geburtstag!*, I; Happy Birthday!
Alles Gute zum Geburtstag!, I; My
birthday is on... *Ich habe am ...
Geburtstag.*, I; When is your birthday? *Wann hast du Geburtstag?*, I
bitter: too bitter *zu bitter*, II
black *schwarz*, I
blanket *die Decke, -n*, III2
blazer *der Blazer, -*, II
blossom *aufblühen* (sep), III10
blouse *die Bluse, -n*, I
blow *blasen*, III9
blower: glass blower *Glasbläser(in),
-/nen*, III12
blue *blau*, I; blue eyes *blaue Augen*,
I; in blue *in Blau*, I
blueberry *die Blaubeere, -n*, II
board game *das Brettspiel, -e*, I
board: cutting board *das
Schneidebrett, -er*, III2
boat *das Boot, -e*, II; to go for a boat
ride *Boot fahren*, II
bologna sandwich *das Wurstbrot, -e*,
I
bomber *der Bomber, -*, III5
bomber jacket *der Blouson, -s*, II
Bon appétit *Mahlzeit!*, II; *Guten
Appetit!*, II
book *das Buch, -̈er*, I
bookcase *das Regal, -e*, I
boot *der Stiefel, -*, I
bored: to be bored *sich langweilen*, II
boring *langweilig*, I
born *geboren*, III4
borrow, lend *ausleihen* (sep), III1
both *beide*, III2
bother, disturb *stören*, III6
bottle *die Flasche, -n*, III1; deposit-
only bottle *die Pfandflasche, -n*,
III9; non-returnable bottle *die
Einwegflasche, -n*, III9
bottle opener *der Flaschenöffner, -*,
III2
bought *gekauft*, I
bouquet of flowers *der
Blumenstrauß, -̈e*, I
bow *die Schleife, -n*, II
bow tie *die Fliege, -n*, II
boy *der Junge, -n*, I; (southern
German) *der Bube, -n*, III10
bracelet *das Armband, -̈er*, II
brake: (foot, hand) brake *die (Fuß-,
Hand)bremse, -n*, II

bread *das Brot, -e,* I

break *die Pause, -n,* I; **after the break** *nach der Pause,* I; **to break something** *sich etwas brechen,* II

breakfast *das Frühstück,* II; **For breakfast I eat...** *Zum Frühstück ess' ich ...,* II

breathless *atemlos,* III10

bright *hell,* II

bring back *zurückbringen* (sep), III1

bring: **Please bring me...** *Bringen Sie mir bitte ...,* II

broad *weit,* II

broccoli *der Brokkoli, -,* II

brochure *der Prospekt, -e,* III1

broken *kaputt,* I

brother *der Bruder, -̈,* I; **brothers and sisters** *die Geschwister* (pl), I

brown *braun,* I; **in brown** *in Braun,* I

brush one's teeth *sich die Zähne putzen,* II

Brussel sprouts *der Rosenkohl,* III1

brutal *brutal,* I

buddy *der Kumpel, -,* III4

bumps: **goose bumps** *die Gänsehaut,* III10

burden *belasten,* III5

burn oneself *s. verbrennen,* III1

bus *der Bus, -se,* I; **by bus** *mit dem Bus,* I

bush *der Strauch, -̈er,* II

businesswoman *die Kauffrau, -en,* III11

busy (telephone) *besetzt,* I

busy: **to keep busy with** *s. beschäftigen mit,* III3

but *aber,* I; **not only ... but also** *nicht nur ... sondern auch,* III4

butcher shop *die Metzgerei, -en,* I; **at the butcher's** *beim Metzger,* I

butter *die Butter,* I

button *der Knopf, -̈e,* II

buy *kaufen,* I; **Why don't you just buy...** *Kauf dir doch ...!,* I, II

buy: **temptation to buy** *der Kaufreiz,* III7

by *bei,* II; **by bike** *mit dem Rad,* I; **by bus** *mit dem Bus,* I; **by car** *mit dem Auto,* I; **by moped** *mit dem Moped,* I; **by subway** *mit der U-Bahn,* I

by the way *übrigens,* III1

Bye! *Wiedersehen! Tschau! Tschüs!,* I; (on the telephone) *Wiederhören!,* I

C

cabinet *der Schrank, -̈e,* I

cabinet: **cabinet maker** *Schreiner(in), -/nen,* III12

café *das Café, -s,* I; **to the café** *ins Café,* I

cake *der Kuchen, -,* I; **a piece of cake** *ein Stück Kuchen,* I

calculate *ausrechnen* (sep), III9

calendar *der Kalender, -,* I

calf *die Wade, -n,* III1

call *anrufen* (sep), *telefonieren,* I

called: **be called** *heißen,* I

calm *ruhig,* II

calories: **has too many calories** *hat zu viele Kalorien,* II

camcorder *die Videokamera, -s,* II

Camembert cheese *der Camembert Käse,* II

camera *die Kamera, -s,* II

camisole *das Trägerhemd, -en,* II

can *die Büchse, -n,* III8; **aluminum can** *die Aludose, -n,* III9

can *können,* I; **Can I please...?** *Kann ich bitte ...?,* II; **Can I ask (you) something?** *Kann ich (euch) etwas fragen?,* II; **Can you tell me whether...?** *Können Sie mir sagen, ob ...?,* II

cap *die Mütze, -n,* II; **(baseball) cap** *das Käppi, -s,* II

capital *die Hauptstadt, -̈e,* I

car *das Auto, -s,* I; *der Wagen, -,* II; **by car** *mit dem Auto,* I; **He's slamming the car door (the trunk)!** *Er schlägt die Autotür (den Kofferraumdeckel) zu!,* II; **to polish the car** *das Auto polieren,* II

card *die Karte, -n,* I

care for *mögen,* I; *betreuen,* III5

care: **I don't care about fashion.** *Mode ist mir egal.,* II

career *die Karriere, -n,* III11

careful *vorsichtig,* III1

carp *der Karpfen, -,* II

carpenter *der Zimmermann, -leute,* III12

carpet *der Teppich, -e,* I

carpool *die Fahrgemeinschaft, -en,* III9

carrot *die Möhre, -n,* II

case: **in any case** *auf jeden Fall,* III8; *jedenfalls,* III8; **in the case (of)** *im Fall,* III12

cassette *die Kassette, -n,* I

castle *die Burg, -en,* III2

casual *lässig,* I; *salopp,* II

cat *die Katze, -n,* I; **to feed the cat** *die Katze füttern,* I

cathedral *der Dom, -e,* II

cauliflower *der Blumenkohl,* II

cause *verursachen,* III7

caution *die Vorsicht,* III9

cellar *der Keller, -,* II

century *das Jahrhundert, -e,* II

certain: **I am certain that...** *Ich bin sicher, daß ...,* II; **It's certain.** *Es steht fest.,* III7

Certainly! *Natürlich!,* I; *Sicher!,* I; *Ja, natürlich!,* II; *Ganz bestimmt.,* III11; *sicherlich,* III12

chair *der Stuhl, -̈e,* I

challenged: **accessible to the physically challenged** *behindertenfreundlich,* III2

chance *die Chance, -n,* III12; **No chance!** *Auf keinen Fall!,* III11

change (money) *umwechseln* (sep), III1; **to change oneself** *s. ändern,* III5

change: **Keep the change!** *Stimmt (schon)!,* I

channel *der Sender, -; das Programm, -e,* II

characteristic *die Eigenschaft, -en,* III7

cheap *billig,* I

check on *nachsehen* (sep), III2

check: **The check please!** *Ich möchte/will zahlen!,* I

checked *kariert,* II

cheerful *heiter,* III10

Cheers! *Prost!,* II

cheese *der Käse, -,* I; **Swiss cheese** *der Schweizer Käse,* II; **cheese sandwich** *das Käsebrot, -e,* I

chef *Koch/Köchin, -̈e/nen,* III12

chemical eraser *der Tintenkiller, -,* III9

cherry *die Kirsche, -n,* II

chess *Schach,* I

chew *kauen,* III8

chicken *das Hähnchen, -,* I; *das Huhn, -̈er,* II

child *das Kind, -er,* II

chimney sweep *Schornsteinfeger(in), -/nen,* III12

Chinese *chinesisch* (adj), II

chives *der Schnittlauch,* II

chocolate *die Schokolade,* II; **chocolate milk** *der Kakao,* II; **fancy chocolate** *die Praline, -n,* I

choose *s. aussuchen* (sep), III1

Christmas *das Weihnachten, -,* I; **Merry Christmas!** *Fröhliche Weihnachten!,* I

church *die Kirche, -n,* I

cinema *das Kino, -s,* I

cinnammon *der Zimt,* I

circle of friends *der Freundeskreis, -e,* III4

city *die Stadt, -̈e,* I; **in the city** *in der Stadt,* I; **city gate** *das Stadttor, -e,* II; **in a big city** *in einer Großstadt,* II city hall *das Rathaus, ¨-er,* I

class *die Klasse, -n;* in class *in der Klasse,* II; class, school *der Unterricht,* III5

class schedule *der Stundenplan, ¨-e,* I

classical music *klassische Musik,* I

clean *(sich) putzen,* II

clean *sauber* (adj), II; squeaky clean *blitzblank,* III7

cleaner: cleaning agent *das Putzmittel, -,* III7

clear: to clear the table *den Tisch abräumen* (sep), I; to clear up *klären,* III10; to make clear *klarstellen* (sep), III7

clearly *deutlich,* III6

clever *raffiniert,* III7; clever(ly) *witzig,* II

cliché *das Klischee, -s,* III8

cliff *die Klippe, -n,* II

climb *steigen,* II

clique *die Clique,* II

clothes *Kleider* (pl), III3; (casual term for) *die Klamotten* (pl), I; to pick up my clothes *meine Klamotten aufräumen* (sep), I

clothing *die Kleidung,* III3

cloudy *wolkig,* I

club *der Verein, -e,* III5

coast *die Küste, -n,* II

coffee *der Kaffee,* I; a cup of coffee *eine Tasse Kaffee,* I

coin *die Münze, -n,* I

cold *kalt,* I

cold cuts *der Aufschnitt,* I

collect *sammeln,* I

color *die Farbe, -n,* I

colorful *bunt,* II

comb *(sich) kämmen,* II

come *kommen,* I; That comes to... *Das macht (zusammen) ...,* I; to come along *mitkommen* (sep), I

comedy *die Komödie, -n,* I

comfortable *bequem,* I; *gemütlich,* II

comics *die Comics,* I

command *kommandieren,* III5

commentary *der Kommentar, -e,* III6

communications engineer *Kommunikationselektroniker(in), -/nen,* III12

compact disc *die CD, -s,* I

compare *vergleichen,* III7

complain *meckern,* III6; to complain about *s. beklagen über* (acc), III10

compulsory service *die Wehrpflicht,* III5

concern: to be concerned about *s. kümmern um,* III6; as far as I'm concerned *meinetwegen,* III10

concert *das Konzert, -e,* I; to go to a concert *ins Konzert gehen,* I

conductor *der Dirigent, -en,* III10

confine *einengen* (sep), III12

conflict *der Konflikt, -e,* III12

conform to *s. richten nach,* III4; *s. anpassen* (sep, dat), III3

connection: to have a connection to *Bezug haben zu,* III8

conscious: environmentally conscious *umweltbewußt,* III8

conservative *konservativ,* II

consider *überlegen,* III7; to consider something as *halten für,* III5

conspicuous: to be conspicuous *auffallen* (sep), III8

constitution: basic law (constitution) *das Grundgesetz,* III5

consultant: PR-consultant *PR-Berater(in), -/nen,* III12; tax consultant *Steuerberater(in), -/nen,* III12

consumer *der Konsument, -en,* III7; *der Verbraucher, -,* III7

container *der Behälter, -,* III8

contention: point of contention *der Streitpunkt, -e,* III4

continually *dauernd,* III1

contract *der Vertrag, ¨-e,* III5

contribute: to contribute to *zu etwas beitragen* (sep), III6

cook *kochen,* II

cookie *der Keks, -e,* I; a few cookies *ein paar Kekse,* I

cool *kühl,* I, II

cooler *die Kühlbox, -en,* III2

corn *der Mais,* III1

corner *die Ecke, -n,* II; That's right around the corner. *Das ist hier um die Ecke.,* II; with corners *eckig,* I

corny *schmalzig,* I

cost *kosten,* I; How much does... cost? *Was kostet ...?,* I

costume *das Kostüm, -e,* III12

cotton *die Baumwolle,* I; made of cotton *aus Baumwolle,* I

couch *die Couch, -en,* I

cough *der Husten,* II

could *könnte,* III5

count on *s. verlassen auf* (acc), III5

countless *zahlreich,* II

country *das Land, ¨-er,* I; in the country *auf dem Land,* I

courage *der Mut,* III9

course: of course *klar,* III7; *logisch,* III7; *logo,* III7

court *der Court, -s,* II

cousin (female) *die Kusine, -n,* I; cousin (male) *der Cousin, -s,* I

cozy *gemütlich,* II

crab *die Krabbe, -n,* II

crafts: do crafts *basteln,* I

crazy *verrückt,* III3

cream: hand cream *die Handcreme,* II

crime drama *der Krimi, -s,* I

cross-timbered house *das Fachwerkhaus, ¨-er,* II

cruel *grausam,* I

cucumber *die Gurke, -n,* II

culture: for cultural reasons *kulturbedingt,* III4

cummerbund *der Kummerbund, -e,* II

curious *neugierig,* II

curtain *der Vorhang, ¨-e,* III10

curve: You're taking the curve too fast! *Du fährst zu schnell in die Kurve!,* II

customs and habits *die Sitten und Gebräuche* (pl), III4

cut class *schwänzen,* III5

cut-off *abgeschnitten,* II

cut: cutting board *das Schneidebrett, -er,* III2

cutlet *das Schnitzel, -,* II

D

damage *der Schaden, ¨-,* III9

dance *tanzen,* I; to go dancing *tanzen gehen,* I

dangerous *gefährlich,* III9

dark *dunkel,* II

dark blue *dunkelblau,* I; in dark blue *in Dunkelblau,* I

dash: 100 meter dash *der 100-Meter-Lauf,* II

daughter *die Tochter, ¨-,* II

day *der Tag, -e,* I; day before yesterday *vorgestern,* I; every day *jeden Tag,* I; on the last day *am letzten Tag,* II; the other day *neulich,* III1

decathlete *der Zehnkämpfer, -,* II

December *der Dezember,* I

decide *beschließen,* III11; *s. entschließen,* III11; to decide on *s. entscheiden für,* III5

decision *die Entscheidung, -en,* III5

defense: German Federal Defense Force *die Bundeswehr,* III5

definite: It's definite. *Es steht fest.,* III11

definitely *bestimmt,* I

deforest *abholzen* (sep), III9

degree *der Grad, -,* I

delicacy *die Delikatesse, -n,* II; *die Köstlichkeit, -en,* II

Delicious! *Lecker!,* I

democracy *die Demokratie, -n,* III5

dental technician *Zahntechniker(in)*, -/nen, III12

dentist *Zahnarzt, ¨e, Zahnärztin*, -nen, III12

depend on *auf etwas ankommen* (sep, acc), III4

dependent: to be dependent on *angewiesen sein auf* (acc), III11

describe *beschreiben*, II

designer: industrial designer *Industriedesigner(in)*, -/nen, III12

desk *der Schreibtisch, -e*, I

dessert *die Nachspeise, -n*, II

detail *die Einzelheit, -en*, III6

detective movie *der Krimi, -s*, I

determining: to be the determining factor *ausschlaggebend sein*, III11

develop *entwickeln*, III3

dial *wählen*, I; to dial the number *die Nummer wählen*, I

diamonds: check, diamond (pattern) *das Karo, -s*, II

dictionary *das Wörterbuch, ¨er*, I

diet *die Diät, -en*, III12

difference *der Unterschied, -e*, III10

different *anders*, III4; *verschieden*, I

difficulty *die Schwierigkeit, -en*, III4

dining room *das Eßzimmer, -*, II

dining table *der Eßtisch, -e*, I

dinner *das Abendessen*, II; For dinner we are having... *Zum Abendessen haben wir ...*, II

diploma *der Abschluß*, (pl) *Abschlüsse*, III11

direct: to be directed at *s. richten an* (acc), III7

directly *direkt*, I

dirt *der Schmutz*, III9

dirty *schmutzig*, II

disadvantage *der Nachteil, -e*, II

disagree: I disagree. *Das finde ich nicht.*, I

disappoint: to be disappointed *enttäuscht sein*, III8

disco *die Disko, -s*, I; to go to a disco *in eine Disko gehen*, I

discothek *die Diskothek, -en*, II

discus throw *das Diskuswerfen*, II

discuss *s. unterhalten über* (acc), III5

discussion *die Diskussion, -en*, II

dish: main dish *das Hauptgericht, -e*, II

dishes *das Geschirr*, I; to wash the dishes *das Geschirr spülen*, I

dishwashing liquid *das Spülmittel, -*, III9

dislike *nicht gern haben*, I; strongly dislike *überhaupt nicht gern haben*, I

displace, repress *verdrängen*, III6

distance: away, at a distance *entfernt*, III2

distribute *verteilen*, III10

disturb, bother *stören*, III6

dive *tauchen*, II

diverse *abwechslungsreich*, II

divert oneself *s. ablenken* (sep), III3

divorce *die Scheidung, -en*, III12

do *machen*, I; *tun*, I; to do crafts *basteln*, I

doctor *der Arzt, ¨e*, II

documentary: animal documentary *die Tiersendung, -en*, II

dog *der Hund, -e*, I

don't you: You like quark, don't you? *Du magst doch Quark, nicht wahr?*, II; You like yogurt, don't you? *Du magst Joghurt, oder?*, II

done *gemacht* (pp), I

doubt: I doubt that... *Ich bezweifle, daß ...*, II

downtown *die Innenstadt, ¨e*, I, II; to go downtown *in die Stadt gehen*, I

draft *einziehen* (sep), III5

draw *zeichnen*, I

dream *der Traum, ¨e*, III11; *träumen*, III10

dress *das Kleid, -er*, I

drink *trinken*, I; *das Getränk, -e*, II

drive *fahren*, I

drop, omit *weglassen*, III6

drugstore *die Drogerie, -n*, II

dry *trocken*, I

dry clothes *die Wäsche trocknen*, II

duck: fattened duck *die Mastente, -n*, II; Peking duck *die Peking Ente, -n*, II

dumb *blöd*, I; *doof, dumm*, I

dumpling *der Kloß, ¨e*, II

during *während*, III10

dust *Staub wischen*, II

duty *die Pflicht, -en*, III5

E

each, every *jed-*, II

earache *die Ohrenschmerzen* (pl), II

earlier *früher*, III5

earn *verdienen*, III7

earring *der Ohrring, -e*, II; a pair of earrings *ein Paar Ohrringe*, II

easily, readily *ohne weiteres*, III3

east *der Osten*, III11; Eastern Bloc *der Ostblock*, III11

Easter *das Ostern, -*, I; Happy Easter! *Frohe Ostern!*, I

easy *einfach*, I; That's easy! *Also, einfach!*, I

easy-going *locker*, III8

eat *essen*, I; to eat sensibly *vernünf-tig essen*, II; eat and drink *sich ernähren*, II

emissions: car with emission control *das Kat-auto, -s*, III9

emphasis: to place emphasis on *Wert legen auf* (acc), III11

employment office *das Arbeitsamt, ¨er*, III11

empty *leer*, III1

encourage *anregen* (sep), III6

endure *aushalten* (sep), III3

engineer: communications engineer *Kommunikationselektroniker(in)*, -/nen, III12; sound engineer *Toningenieur(in)*, -e/nen, III12

enlarge *vergrößern*, III9

enlighten *aufklären* (sep), III7

enough *genug*, I; that's enough *es langt*, III2; to be enough *genügen*, III2

entertainment *die Unterhaltung, -en*, III6

entire *gesamt*, III6

entranceway *der Flur, -e*, II

environment *die Umwelt*, I; environmental scientist *Umweltökonom (in)*, -en/nen, III12; environmentally conscious *umweltbewußt*, III8; environmentally safe *umweltfreundlich*, III9

envy *beneiden*, III10

equality *die Gleichberechtigung*, III5

eraser *der Radiergummi, -s*, I; chemical eraser *der Tintenkiller, -*, III9

especially *besonders*, I; to especially like *besonders gern haben*, I; Not especially. *Nicht besonders.*, II

even *sogar*, III9

evening *der Abend, -e*, I; in the evening *am Abend*, I

event *das Ereignis, -se*, III6

event: organized event *die Veranstaltung, -en*, III6

every day *jeden Tag*, I

exactly *eben*, III6

exaggerate *übertreiben*, III3

excellent *ausgezeichnet*, II

exchange *umtauschen* (sep), III1

excited: to be excited *begeistern*, III8

excitement *die Aufregung, -en*, III10; *die Spannung, -en*, III10

exciting *spannend*, I

exclusively *ausschließlich*, III9

excursion *der Ausflug, ¨e*, II

Excuse me! *Entschuldigung!, Verzeihung!*, I, II

exercise *Gymnastik machen*, II

exhaust *das Abgas, -e*, III9

exhibition *die Ausstellung, -en*, III10

existing *vorhanden sein*, III10

expensive *teuer*, I

experience *die Erfahrung, -en*, III11; *erfahren*, III6; *erleben*, III10; *miterleben (sep)*, III9

experienced (person) *der, die Erfahrene, -n*, II

express *ausdrücken (sep)*, III3

exquisite *fein*, II

extend *verlängern*, III10

eye *das Auge, -n*, I; **blue eyes** *blaue Augen*, I

eye-catcher *der Blickfang*, III7

F

fact *die Tatsache, -n*, III6

factory *die Fabrik, -en*, III9

failure (in a subject) *die Niete, -n*, III12

fairy-tale *das Märchen, -*, III10

fall *der Herbst*, I; **in the fall** *im Herbst*, I

family *die Familie, -n*, I

famous *berühmt*, III2

fancy chocolate *die Praline, -n*, I

Fantastic! *Phantastisch!*, II

fantasy novel *der Fantasyroman, -e*, I

far *weit*, I; **far from here** *weit von hier*, I; **as far as (that) goes** *was (das) angeht*, III3; **as far as this goes** *in dieser Hinsicht*, III5

fashion *die Mode*, I; **the latest fashion** *der letzte Schrei*, III3

fashionable *modisch*, II

fast *schnell*, II

fat *dick*, III8; **has too much fat** *hat zu viel Fett*, II; **It is fattening.** *Es macht dick.*, II

father *der Vater, ∺*, I; **Father's Day** *der Vatertag*, I; **Happy Father's Day!** *Alles Gute zum Vatertag!*, I

fault: to be at fault *schuld sein an etwas (dat)*, III4

favorite *Lieblings-*, I; **Which vegetable is your favorite?** *Welches Gemüse magst du am liebsten?*, II

February *der Februar*, I

feed *füttern*, I

feel *sich fühlen*, II; **How do you feel?** *Wie fühlst du dich?*, II; **I feel great!** *Ich fühle mich wohl!*, II; **Are you not feeling well?** *Ist dir nicht gut?*, II

feeling *das Gefühl, -e*, III7

felt-tip pen *der Faserstift, -e*, III9

fence *fechten*, II

fertilizer: artificial fertilizer *der Kunstdünger, -*, III9

festival: regional festival *das Volksfest, -e*, III10

fetch *holen*, I

fever *das Fieber*, II; **to take one's temperature** *Fieber messen*, II

few: a few *ein paar*, I; **a few cookies** *ein paar Kekse*, I

fibers: made from natural fibers *aus Naturfasern*, II

film, videotape *filmen*, II; **adventure film** *der Abenteuerfilm, -e*, II

finally *zum Schluß*, III7

financially *finanziell*, III12

fine *fein*, II

fingernail *der Fingernagel, ∺*, III1

finished *fertig*, III11

first *erst-*, I; **first of all** *zuerst*, I; **on the first of July** *am ersten Juli*, I

fish *angeln*, II; **fish stick** *das Fischstäbchen, -*, II

fit *passen*, I; **The skirt fits great!** *Der Rock paßt prima!*, I; **to keep fit** *sich fit halten*, II

flats *Schuhe mit flachen Absätzen*, II

flood *überfluten*, III7

flower *die Blume, -n*, I

flowery *geblümt*, II

food *die Speise, -n*, II

foods: to only eat light foods *nur leichte Speisen essen*, II

foot: to walk on foot *zu Fuß gehen*, I

for *für*, I; *denn (conj)*, I; **I am for doing...** *Ich bin dafür, daß ...*, II; **for whom?** *für wen?*, II

forbid *verbieten (dat)*, III4

foreign *ausländisch*, II

foreigner *Ausländer(in), -/-nen*, III4

forest *der Wald, ∺er*, III9; **the dying of the forests** *das Waldsterben*, III9

forget *vergessen*, III4

fork *die Gabel, -n*, III2

former *ehemalig*, III11

formulation *die Bildung*, III6

found *gründen*, III12

fountain *der Brunnen, -*, II

free time *die Freizeit*, I

freedom *die Freiheit*, III7

French *französisch (adj)*, II

fresh *frisch*, I

fresh produce store *der Obst- und Gemüseladen, ∺*, I

Friday *der Freitag*, I; **Fridays** *freitags*, II

fried *gebraten*, II; **fried potatoes** *die Bratkartoffeln (pl)*, II

friend (male) *der Freund, -e*, I; (female) *die Freundin, -nen*, I; **to visit friends** *Freunde besuchen*, I; **circle of friends** *der Freundeskreis, -e*, III4

friendliness *die Freundlichkeit*, III4

friendly *freundlich*, II; *kameradschaftlich*, III8

fries: french fries *die Pommes frites (pl)*, II

fringe group *die Randgruppe, -n*, III4

frog *der Frosch, ∺e*, III9

from *aus*, I; *von*, I; **from 8 until 8:45** *von 8 Uhr bis 8 Uhr 45*, I; **from the fifteenth century** *aus dem fünfzehnten Jahrhundert*, II

from where? *woher?*, I; **I'm from...** *ich bin (komme) aus ...*, I; **Where are you from?** *Woher bist (kommst) du?*, I

front: in front of *vor*, II; **there in the front** *da vorn*, I

frugal *sparsam*, III1

fruit *das Obst*, I, II; **a piece of fruit** *ein Stück Obst*, I; **to eat lots of fruit** *viel Obst essen*, II

frustrating *frustrierend*, III6

fulfill *erfüllen*, III7

fun *der Spaß*, I; **(Tennis) is fun.** *(Tennis) macht Spaß.*, I; **(Tennis) is no fun.** *(Tennis) macht keinen Spaß.*, I

funny *lustig*, I, II

furniture *die Möbel (pl)*, I

futile *vergeblich*, III10

future *die Zukunft*, III11

G

gain weight *zunehmen (sep)*, III3

garage *die Garage, -n*, II

garbage *der Müll*, II

garden *der Garten, ∺*, I

garlic *der Knoblauch*, II

gas: propulsion gas *das Treibgas, -e*, III9

geography *die Erdkunde*, I

German mark (German monetary unit) *DM = die Deutsche Mark*, I

German teacher (male) *der Deutschlehrer, -*, I; (female) *die Deutschlehrerin, -nen*, I

get *bekommen*, I; *holen*, I; **Get well soon!** *Gute Besserung!*, II

get along *auskommen (sep)*, III4; *s. verstehen mit*, III4

gift *das Geschenk, -e*, I

gift idea *die Geschenkidee, -n*, I

girl *das Mädchen, -*, I

give *geben*, I; **he/she gives** *er/sie gibt*, I

give (a gift) *schenken*, I

glad: I'm really glad! *Das freut mich!*, II

glass *das Glas, ∺er*, I; **a glass of tea** *ein Glas Tee*, I

glasses: a pair of glasses *eine Brille,*
-n, I

go *gehen,* I; **to go home** *nach Hause*
gehen, I; **goes with: The pretty**
blouse goes (really) well with the
blue skirt. *Die schöne Bluse paßt*
(toll) zu dem blauen Rock., II

go: to go along with *mitmachen mit*
(sep), III3

goal *das Ziel, -e,* III11

God: Thank God! *Gott sei Dank!,*
III11

Goethe's birthplace *das Goethehaus,*
II

gold: made of gold *aus Gold,* II

golf *Golf,* I; **golf course** *der Golfplatz,*
-e, II

good *gut,* I; **Good!** *Gut!,* I; **good:**
what's good about someone *an*
jemandem gut sein, III4

Good morning! *Guten Morgen!,*
Morgen!, I

Goodbye! *Auf Wiedersehen!,* I; (on
the telephone) *Auf Wiederhören!,* I

goose bumps *die Gänsehaut,* III10

gown: evening gown *das Abendkleid,*
-er, II

grade *die Note, -n,* I

grade level *die Klasse, -n,* I

grades: a 1, 2, 3, 4, 5, 6 *eine Eins,*
Zwei, Drei, Vier, Fünf, Sechs, I

gram *das Gramm, -,* I

grandfather *der Großvater -,* I; *Opa,*
-s, I

grandmother *die Großmutter, -,* I;
Oma, -s, I

grandparents *die Großeltern* (pl) I

grape *die Traube, -n,* I, II

gray *grau,* I; **in gray** *in Grau,* I

great: It's great that... *Es ist prima,*
daß ..., II; **really great** *supertoll,* II;
Echt super!, II; **Great!** *Prima!,* I;
Sagenhaft!, I; *Klasse!, Toll!,* I

H

hair: hair stylist *Friseur/Friseuse,*
-e/n, III12; **to get your hair cut** *s. die*
Haare schneiden lassen, III3

half *halb,* I; **half past (twelve, one,**
etc.) *halb (eins, zwei, usw.),* I

halibut *der Heilbutt,* II

hall *die Halle, -n,* II

hallway *der Flur, -e,* II

ham *der Schinken, -,* II

hand cream *die Handcreme,* II

handbag *die Handtasche, -n,* II

hang up (the telephone) *auflegen*
(sep), I

Hanukkah *Chanukka,* I; **Happy**

Hanukkah! *Frohes Chanukka Fest!,*
I

happy *fröhlich,* III7; *glücklich,* III7; **I**
am happy that... *Ich freue mich,*
daß ..., II; *Ich bin froh, daß ...,* II

hard-working *fleißig,* II

harmful *schädlich,* III7

hat *der Hut, -e,* II

have *haben,* I; **I have no classes on**
Saturday. *Am Samstag habe ich*
frei., I; **I'll have...** *Ich bekomme ...,* I

have to *müssen,* I

he *er,* I; **he is** *er ist,* I; **he's from** *er*
ist (kommt) aus, I

head *der Kopf, -e,* II; **headband** *das*
Stirnband, -er, II; **headache** *die*
Kopfschmerzen (pl) II

headlight *der Scheinwerfer, -,* II

headline *die Schlagzeile, -n,* III6

headphones (stereo) *der (Stereo)*
Kopfhörer, -, II

health: To your health! *Auf*
dein/Ihr/euer Wohl!, Zum Wohl!, II;
to do a lot for your health *viel für*
die Gesundheit tun, II; **health**
inspector *Lebensmittelkontrolleur*
(in) -e/nen, III12

hear *hören,* I

heard: I heard that... *Ich habe gehört,*
daß ..., II

heart: pounding heart *das*
Herzklopfen, III10

heartfelt *herzlich,* III8

hearty *herzhaft, deftig,* II

heel *die Ferse, -n,* III1

heel (shoe) *der Absatz, -e,* II; **flats**
Schuhe mit flachen Absätzen, II;
high heel shoe *Schuh mit hohen*
Absätzen, II

Hello! *Guten Tag!, Tag!, Hallo!, Grüß*
dich!, I

help *helfen,* I

helpful *hilfreich,* III8

Here you go! *Bitte! Hier!,* II; **Here! I**
insist! *Gern! Hier ist es!,* II

herself *sich,* II

hide *verbergen,* III7; *verstecken,* III7

hideous *scheußlich,* I

highly *äußerst,* III8

highway: interstate highway *die*
Autobahn, -en, III8

hike *wandern,* I

him *ihn,* I

himself *sich,* II

hip *die Hüfte, -n,* II

hire *einstellen* (sep), III5

historical *historisch,* III10

history *die Geschichte,* I

hobby *das Hobby, -s,* II

hobby book *das Hobbybuch, -er,* I

hole *das Loch, -er,* II

holiday *der Feiertag, -e,* I

home: good home cooked food *gut*
bürgerliche Küche, -n, II; **private**
home *das Privathaus, -er,* II; **to**
stay at home *zu Hause bleiben,* II

homework *die Hausaufgabe, -n,* I

honk (the horn) *hupen,* II

hood *die Kapuze, -n,* II

hope *die Hoffnung, -en,* III11

hope: I hope that... *Ich hoffe, daß ...,*
II; **I hope you'll get better soon.**
Hoffentlich geht es dir bald besser!,
II

hopefully *hoffentlich,* II

horizon *der Horizont,* III11

horror movie *der Horrorfilm, -e,* I

horror novel *der Gruselroman, -e,* I

hostel: youth hostel *die*
Jugendherberge, -n, III2

hot *heiß,* I; **hot (spicy)** *scharf,* II

hotel *das Hotel, -s,* I

house *das Haus, -er,* II

how much? *wieviel?,* I; **How much**
does... cost? *Was kostet ...?,* I

how often? *wie oft?,* I

how? *wie?,* I; **How are you?** *Wie*
geht es dir?, I, II; **How do I get**
to...? *Wie komme ich zum (zur)*
...?, I; **How does it taste?** *Wie*
schmeckt's?, I; **How's the weather?**
Wie ist das Wetter?, I; **How was it?**
Wie war's?, II; **How about...?** *Wie*
wärs mit ...?, II

huge *riesig,* III7

hunger *der Hunger,* I

hungry: I'm hungry. *Ich habe*
Hunger., I; **I'm not hungry any**
more. *Ich habe keinen Hunger*
mehr., I

hurdling *der Hürdenlauf,* II

hurt: Does it hurt? *Tut's weh?,* II;
Does your... hurt? *Tut dir ... weh?,*
II; **It hurts!** *Es tut weh!,* II; **My...**
hurts. *... tut mir weh.,* II; **What**
hurts? *Was tut dir weh?,* II

I

I *ich,* I; **I don't.** *Ich nicht.,* I

ice cream *das Eis,* I; **a dish of ice**
cream *ein Eisbecher,* I

ice skate *Schlittschuh laufen,* I

idea: I have no idea! *Keine Ahnung!,*
I; **Do you have an idea?** *Hast du*
eine Idee?, II; **Good idea!** *Gute*
Idee!, II

identification *der Ausweis, -e,* III2

if I were you *an deiner Stelle,* III3

image *die Vorstellung, -en,* III8

imaginative *phantasievoll*, I

imagine: to imagine something *s. etwas vorstellen* (sep), III6

immediately *gleich*, III4

impossible: (That's) impossible! *(Das ist) nicht möglich!*, II

impress *beeindrucken*, III8

impression *der Eindruck*, III8; *die Vorstellung, -en*, III8

improve *verbessern*, III9

in *in*, I; in the afternoon *am Nachmittag*, I; in the city *in der Stadt*, I; in the country *auf dem Land*, I; in the evening *am Abend*, I; in the fall *im Herbst*, I; in the kitchen *in der Küche*, I

in spite of that *trotzdem*, III1

income *das Einkommen*, II

indeed *zwar*, III10

independent: to be independent *unabhängig sein*, III5

Indian: (Asian) Indian *indisch* (adj), II

indicate *angeben* (sep), III11

industry: industrial designer *Industriedesigner(in), -/nen*, III12

influence *beeinflussen*, III3

inform: to inform oneself *s. informieren*, III2

initiate: to be initiated by *ausgehen von* (sep), III10

injure (oneself) *sich verletzen*, II

inn *die Pension, -en*, II

innards *die Innereien* (pl), III1

inquire: to inquire about *s. erkundigen nach*, III11

insert *einstecken* (sep), I; to insert coins *Münzen einstecken*, I

inspector: health inspector *Lebensmittelkontrolleur(in), -e/nen*, III12

instead of *anstatt* (gen), III10

instead: I'll drink... instead *Dann trink' ich halt ...*, II

instrument *das Instrument, -e*, I; Do you play an instrument? *Spielst du ein Instrument?*, I

insurance company *die Versicherung, -en*, III11

intelligent *intelligent*, II

interest *das Interesse, -n*, I; Do you have any other interests? *Hast du andere Interessen?*, I; I'm not interested in fashion. *Ich hab' kein Interesse an Mode.*, II; to be interested in *s. interessieren für*; Fashion doesn't interest me. *Mode interessiert mich nicht.*, II; Are you interested in fashion? *Interessierst du dich für Mode?*, II; What are you interested in? *Wofür interessierst*

du dich?, II; to be interested in *interessiert sein an* (dat), III11

interesting *interessant*, I

interrupt *unterbrechen*, III5

into *in*, II

invite *einladen* (sep), I

island *die Insel, -n*, II

Italian *italienisch* (adj), II

J

jacket *die Jacke, -n*, I; business jacket *der Sakko, -s*, II; leather jacket *die Lederjacke, -n*, II; bomber jacket *der Blouson, -s*, II

jam: traffic jam *der Stau, -s*, III7

January *der Januar*, I; in January *im Januar*, I

javelin throw *das Speerwerfen*, II

jealousy *die Eifersucht*, III10

jeans *die Jeans, -*, I

jewelry *der Schmuck*, I

job *der Job, -s*, II; to have a job *jobben*, III11

jog *joggen*, I, II

jogging suit *der Jogging-Anzug, ̈e*, I

joke *der Spaß*, III6

judge: to judge according to *beurteilen nach*, III3

judgement *das Urteil, -e*, III8

juice *der Saft, ̈e*, I

July *der Juli*, I

jump: long jump *der Weitsprung*, II

June *der Juni*, I

just *gerade*, III1; Just a minute, please. *Einen Moment, bitte!*, I; Just don't buy... *Kauf dir ja kein ...!*, II; That just happened. *Das ist gerade passiert.*, II

K

Keep the change! *Stimmt (schon)!*, I

keep to oneselves *unter sich bleiben*, III4

kilogram *das Kilo, -*, I

king *der König, -e*, III7

kitchen *die Küche, -n*, I; in the kitchen *in der Küche*, I; to help in the kitchen *in der Küche helfen*, II

knee *das Knie, -*, II

knee cap *die Kniescheibe, -n*, III1

knife *das Messer, -*, III2

know (a fact, information, etc.) *wissen*, I; Do you know whether...? *Weißt du, ob ...?*, II

know (be familiar or acquainted with) *kennen*, I

know: to not know *überfragt sein*, III7

L

lake *der See, -n*, II

lamb *das Lammfleisch*, II

lamp *die Lampe, -n*, I

language *die Sprache, -n*, III11

last *dauern*, III5

last *letzt-*, I; *vorig-*, III5; last of all *zuletzt*, I; last week *letzte Woche*, I

latest: the latest fashion *der letzte Schrei*, III3

Latin *Latein*, I

laundry *die Wäsche*, II

laundry soap *das Waschmittel, -*, III9

law: (study of) law *Jura*, III11

lawn *der Rasen, -*, I; to mow the lawn *den Rasen mähen*, I; lawn for relaxing and sunning *die Liegewiese, -n*, II

lawyer for the defense *Strafverteidiger(in), -/nen*, III12

layer cake *die Torte, -n*, I

lazy *faul*, II; to be lazy *faulenzen*, II; (ironic) to be too lazy to walk *fußkrank sein*, III2

lead *führen*, III12

leaf *das Blatt, ̈er*, III1

leak: to spring a leak *leck werden*, III9

leather *das Leder*, I

left: to the left *nach links*, I

leg *das Bein, -e*, II

legend *die Sage, -n*, III10

lemon *die Zitrone, -n*, I

lemon drink *die Limo, -s*, I

let, allow *lassen*, II; Let me... *Laß mich mal ...*, II; Let's go to the golf course! *Gehen wir mal auf den Golfplatz!*, II; Let's go to...! *Fahren wir mal nach ...!*, II

lettuce *der Salat, -e*, I

library: lending library *die Bücherei, -en*, III1

license: driver's license *der Führerschein, -e*, II

life *das Leben*, II

lift *heben*, III3

light blue *hellblau*, I

like *gefallen, mögen, gern haben*, I, II; like *stehen auf* (acc), III11; I like it. *Er/Sie/Es gefällt mir.*, I; I like them. *Sie gefallen mir.*, I; Did you like it? *Hat es dir gefallen?*, II; to like an awful lot *furchtbar gern haben*, I; to not like at all *gar nicht gern haben*, I; to not like very much *nicht so gern haben*, I; I don't like... *Ich mag kein ...*, II; I like to go to the ocean. *Ich fahre gern ans Meer.*, II; I would like... *Ich hätte gern ...*, II; like (to do) *gern*

(machen), I; **to not like (to do)** *nicht gern (machen)*, I
linen *das Leinen*, II
listen (to) *hören*, I; *zuhören*, (sep), I; Listen! *Hör mal!*, II; **Listen to this!** *Hör mal zu!*, II
listing *das Verzeichnis, -se*, III2
liter *der Liter, -*, I
little *klein*, I; **a little** *ein bißchen*, I
live *wohnen*, I; *leben*, II
liver *die Leber*, III1
living room *das Wohnzimmer, -*, II; **in the living room** *im Wohnzimmer*, I
lobster *der Hummer, -*, II
long *lang*, I
long for *s. sehnen nach*, III7
look *schauen*, I; **Look!** *Schauen Sie!*, I; *Guck mal!, Schau mal!, Sieh mal!*, II; **That looks great on you!** *Das steht dir prima!*, II; **look for** *suchen*, I; **look like** *aussehen* (sep), I; **look around** *s. umsehen* (sep), III10
lose *verlieren*, III2
lose weight *abnehmen* (sep), III3
lot: quite a lot *eine ganze Menge*, III8; **a lot** *viel*, I
loud *laut*, III8
lousy *mickrig*, III3
luck: Bad luck! *So ein Pech!*, I; **What luck!** *So ein Glück!*, I; **Luckily** *Zum Glück*, III11; **Lucky that...** *Ein Glück, daß ...*, III11
lunch *das Mittagessen*; **For lunch there is...** *Zum Mittagessen gibt es ...*, II

M

made: made of cotton *aus Baumwolle*, I
magazine *die Zeitschrift; -en*, I
mail, post office *die Post*, III1
mainly *hauptsächlich*, III3
make *machen*, I; **make, achieve** *schaffen*, III5
makeup: to put on makeup *s. schminken*, III3
man *der Mann, ¨er*, I
many *viele*, I
March *der März*, I
margarine *die Margarine*, II
marinated *mariniert*, II
mark *die Mark, -*, I
market square *der Marktplatz, ¨e*, I
marmalade *die Marmelade, -n*, II
marriage *die Ehe, -n*, III12
marry *heiraten*, III5
math *Mathe (die Mathematik)*, I
matter: in this matter *in diesem Punkt*, III8; **to not matter** *s. nichts*

ausmachen (sep), III6
May *der Mai*, I
may: May I help you? *Haben Sie einen Wunsch?*, I; **May I (please)...?** *Darf ich (bitte) ...?*, II; **That may well be.** *Das mag schon sein.*, III4
maybe *vielleicht*, I; **Yes, maybe, but...** *Ja, das kann sein, aber ...*, II
me *mich, mir*, I; **Me too!** *Ich auch!*, I
meadow *die Wiese, -n*, III7
means: By all means. *Auf alle Fälle.*, III11
measure *messen*, II; **he/she measures** *er/sie mißt*, II
meat *das Fleisch*, I; **You eat a lot of meat, right?** *Du ißt wohl viel Fleisch, ja?*, II
media planner *Mediaplaner(in), -/nen*, III12
meet *treffen*, III3
member *das Mitglied, -er*, III5
mentality *die Mentalität*, III11
mention *erwähnen*, III1
mess: What a mess! *So ein Mist!*, I
message *die Mitteilung, -en*, III7
miracle, wonder *das Wunder, -*, III10
mirror *der Spiegel, -*, III10
miss *vermissen*, III6
missing: to be missing *fehlen*, III5
mood *die Laune*, III3
moped *mit dem Moped*, I
more *mehr*, I; **the more ... the** *je mehr ... desto*, III7
morning *der Morgen*, I; **Morning!** *Morgen!*, I
most *meist-*, III6; **most of all** *am liebsten*, I; *vor allem*, III11; **most of the time** *meistens*, II
mother *die Mutter, ¨*, I; **Mother's Day** *der Muttertag*, I; **Happy Mother's Day!** *Alles Gute zum Muttertag!*, I
motor *der Motor, -en*, II
motorcycle *das Motorrad, ¨er*, II
mountain *der Berg, -e*, II; **in the mountains** *in den Bergen*, II
mouth *der Mund, ¨er*, III2
move (residence) *ziehen*, III12
movie *der Film, -e*, I; **to go to the movies** *ins Kino gehen*, I
movie theater *das Kino, -s*, I
mow *mähen*, I; **to mow the lawn** *den Rasen mähen*, I
Mr. *Herr*, I
Mrs. *Frau*, I
much *viel*, I; **much too** *viel zu*, I
mug *der Becher, -*, III2
museum *das Museum, (pl) Museen*, I
mushroom *der Pilz, -e*, II

music *die Musik*, I; **to listen to music** *Musik hören*, I
music store *der Musikladen, ¨*, III1
music: house music *die Hausmusik*, III10
musical *das Musical, -s*, II
musician *Musiker(in), -/nen*, III11
mustard *der Senf*, I
my *mein* (poss adj), I; **my name is** *ich heiße*, I
myself *mich*, II

N

name *der Name, -n*, I; **her name is** *sie heißt*, I; **What's the boy's name?** *Wie heißt der Junge?*, I
namely *nämlich*, III2
napkin *die Serviette, -n*, III2
native language *die Muttersprache, -n*, III4
nature *die Natur*, III2
nature: good-natured *gutmütig*, III8
nauseated: I'm nauseated. *Mir ist schlecht.*, II
near *nahe*, III9
near to *in der Nähe von*, III8
nearby *in der Nähe*, I
necklace *die Halskette, -n*, II
need *brauchen*, I
neither ... nor *weder ... noch*, III10
nerves: to get on the nerves *nerven*, III7
never *nie*, I; **not yet** *noch nie*, II
new *neu*, I
news: the news *die Nachrichten* (pl), II
newspaper *die Zeitung, -en*, I
next to *neben*, II
next: the next street *die nächste Straße*, I
nice *nett*, III8
night *die Nacht, ¨e*, III2
night: to spend the night *übernachten*, II
no *kein*, I; **No more, thanks!** *Nichts mehr, danke!*, I
no way: There's just no way! *Das gibt's doch nicht!*, II
noise *der Lärm*, II
non-fiction book *das Sachbuch, ¨er*, I
none *kein*, I
nonsense, baloney *Quatsch*, III6
noodle soup *die Nudelsuppe, -n*, I
nor: neither ... nor *weder ... noch*, III10
normally *normalerweise*, II
North: the North Sea *die Nordsee*, II
nose: runny nose *der Schnupfen*, II
not *nicht*, I; **not at all** *überhaupt*

nicht, I; **to not like at all** *gar nicht gern haben*, I; **Not really.** *Nicht besonders.*, I; **not any** *kein*, I; **Not entirely! / Not necessarily!** *Nicht unbedingt!*, II; **actually not** *eben nicht*, II

notebook *das Notizbuch*, ̈*er*, I; *das Heft*, *-e*, I

nothing *nichts*, I; **nothing at the moment** *im Moment gar nichts*, I; **Nothing, thank you!** *Nichts, danke!*, I; **There's nothing you can do.** *Da kann man nichts machen.*, II

notice: on short notice *kurzfristig*, III5

novel *der Roman*, *-e*, I

November *der November*, I

now *jetzt*, I; **just now** *eben, gerade*, III2; **now and then** *ab und zu*, III6

nuclear war *der Atomkrieg*, *-e*, III11

number *die (Telefon)nummer*, I; **to dial the number** *die Nummer wählen*, I

nutritional scientist *Gesundheitswissenschaftler(in)*, *-/nen*, III12

nutritious *vollwertig*, III3

O

o'clock: at 1 o'clock *um 1 Uhr*, I

oasis *die Oase*, *-n*, II

observe *beobachten*, III8

occupation *die Tätigkeit*, *-en*, III11

ocean *das Meer*, *-e*; *die See*, *-n*, II

October *der Oktober*, I

of *von*, II; **made of wool** *aus Wolle*, II

Of course! *Ja klar!*, I; *Ganz klar!*, I; *Na klar!*, II; **Yes, of course!** *Ja, natürlich!*, II

offer *anbieten* (sep), III9; *das Angebot*, *-e*, I

office: employment office *das Arbeitsamt*, ̈*er*, III11

officer *der Offizier*, *-e*, III5

often *schon oft*, I

Oh! *Ach!*, I; **Oh yeah!** *Ach ja!*, I

oil *das Öl*, *-e*, I

Okay! I'll do that! *Gut! Mach' ich!*, I; **It's okay.** *Es geht.*, I; *Schon gut!*, II; **well, okay** *also* (part), III2

old *alt*, I; **How old are you?** *Wie alt bist du?*, I; **older** *älter*, II

olympic champion *der Olympiasieger*, *-*, II

omit, drop *weglassen* (sep), III6

on: on ... Square *am ...platz*, I; **on ... Street** *in der ...straße*, I; **to walk on foot** *zu Fuß gehen*, I; **on**

Monday *am Montag*, I; **on the first of July** *am ersten Juli*, I; **on a lake** *an einem See*, II; **on a river** *an einem Fluß*, II

once *einmal*, I; **once a month** *einmal im Monat*, I; **once a week** *einmal in der Woche*, I; **once a day** *einmal am Tag*, II

oneself *selbst*, III6

onion *die Zwiebel*, *-n*, I

only *bloß*, I; *nur*, II

onto *auf*, II

open *offen*, III8

opener: bottle opener *der Flaschenöffner*, *-*, III2

opera *die Oper*, *-n*, I; **opera house** *die Oper*, *-n*, II

operetta *die Operette*, *-n*, II

opinion: in my opinion *meiner Meinung nach*, III6

oppress *unterdrücken*, III12

optician *Optiker(in)*, *-/nen*, III12

orange juice *der Orangensaft*, ̈*e*, I

order *bestellen*, III1

order: in order to do... *um ... zu machen*, III3

orderly *geregelt*, III11; *ordentlich*, III8

organic food *die Biokost*, III3

ostensibly *angeblich*, III7

other *andere*, I

other: the other day *neulich*, III1

Ouch! *Au!, Aua!*, II

ourselves *uns*, II

out of *aus* (dat), II

outside of *außerhalb* (gen), III4

outstanding *ausgezeichnet*, II

oven *der Ofen*, ̈*-*, I

over it *darüber*, II

over there *dort drüben*, I; **over there in the back** *da hinten*, I

overcast *trüb*, I

own: (one's) own *eigen-* (adj), II

oxygen *der Sauerstoff*, III9

oyster *die Auster*, *-n*, II

ozone: hole in the ozone layer *das Ozonloch*, III9

P

padded *gefüttert*, II

page through *durchblättern* (sep), III6

pain *der Schmerz*, *-en*, II

painting *das Gemälde*, *-*, II

pair *das Paar*, *-e*, II

pan dish *das Pfannengericht*, *-e*, II

pants *die Hose*, *-n*, I

Pardon me! *Verzeihung!*, II

parents *die Eltern* (pl), I

park *der Park*, *-s*, I, II; **to go to the park** *in den Park gehen*, I

parka *der Anorak*, *-s*, II

parking place/lot *der Parkplatz*, ̈*e*, II

parliament: German Federal Parliament *der Bundestag*, III11

part *der Teil*, *-e*, III9

part: to take part *dabeisein* (sep), III11

particularly *ausgesprochen*, III5; *insbesondere*, III8

partly *teilweise*, III10

party *die Fete*, *-n*, III4

pass: time passes *vergehen*, III11

past *vergangen-*, III5

pasta *die Teigwaren* (pl), III1

path *der Weg*, *-e*, III8

patience *die Geduld*, III10

patient *geduldig*, III8

pattern *das Muster*, *-*, II

pay *bezahlen*, III1

pea *die Erbse*, *-n*, II

peace *der Frieden*, III5

peace-loving *friedliebend*, III8

peaceful *friedlich*, 7

peach *der Pfirsich*, *-e*, II

peanut butter *die Erdnußbutter*, III1

pencil *der Bleistift*, *-e*, I

people *die Leute* (pl), I

pepper shaker *der Pfefferstreuer*, *-*, III2

perceive *wahrnehmen* (sep), III7

perch: filet of perch *das Seebarschfilet*, *-s*, II

perfect, whole *heil*, III7

perform *aufführen* (sep), III10

performance *die Aufführung*, *-en*, III10

perfume *das Parfüm*, *-e* or *-s*, I

perfumed *parfümiert*, II

perhaps *eventuell*, III10

permit oneself *s. erlauben*, III5

pet *das Haustier*, *-e*, I

pharmacy *die Apotheke*, *-n*, II

philosopher *der Philosoph*, *-en*, III10

photograph *fotografieren*, II; **color photograph** *das Farbbild*, *-er*, II

photographer *Fotograf(in)*, *-en/nen*, III12

physical education *der Sport*, I

physically: accessible to the physically challenged *behindertenfreundlich*, III2

piano *das Klavier*, *-e*, I; **I play the piano.** *Ich spiele Klavier.*, I

pick out *s. aussuchen* (sep), III1

pick up *aufräumen* (sep), I; *abholen* (sep), III8; **to pick up the telephone** *den Hörer abheben* (sep), I

pickle *die saure Gurke*, *-n*, III1

picnic *das Picknick, -s,* III2
picnic basket *der Picknickkorb, ⸚e,* III2
piece *das Stück, -e,* I; a piece of cake *ein Stück Kuchen,* I
pity, sympathy *das Mitleid,* III3
pizza *die Pizza, -s,* I
place *der Platz, ⸚e,* II
plan *der Plan, ⸚e,* III2; *vorhaben (sep),* III3
plant *die Pflanze, -n,* III8
plastic *der Kunststoff, -e,* I; made of plastic *aus Kunststoff,* I
plate *der Teller, -,* III2
play *spielen,* I to play a board game *ein Brettspiel spielen,* I; *das Schauspiel, -e,* II; *das Theaterstück, -e,* II
play (act) *darstellen (sep),* III10
pleasant *angenehm,* III5; *sympathisch,* II
please *bitte,* I
pleasure *das Vergnügen, -,* III10; My pleasure! *Gern geschehen!,* I
plot *die Handlung, -en,* III10
plum *die Zwetschge, -n,* II
pocket *die Tasche, -n,* II; back pocket *die Gesäßtasche, -n,* II
pocket calculator *der Taschenrechner, -,* I
poison *das Gift, -e,* III9; to poison, pollute *verpesten,* III9
poisonous *giftig,* III9
pole vault *der Stabhochsprung,* II
polite *höflich,* III8
political discussion *eine Diskussion über Politik,* II
politics *die Politik (sing),* I
polka-dotted *gepunktet,* I
pollutant *der Schadstoff, -e,* III9
pollute *verschmutzen,* III9
pollution: air pollution *die Luftverschmutzung,* III9
pool *der Pool, -s,* II; indoor pool *das Hallenbad, ⸚er,* II
porch *die Terrasse, -n,* II
pork *das Schweinefleisch,* III1
pork chop *das Schweinekotelett, -s,* II; pork loin steak *das Schweinerückensteak, -s,* II
position: to take a position *Stellung nehmen,* III6
possibility *die Möglichkeit, -en,* III4
possible *möglich,* II
possibly *möglicherweise,* III10
post office, mail *die Post,* II
poster *das Poster, -,* I
potato *die Kartoffel, -n,* I; fried potatoes *die Bratkartoffeln (pl),* II; potato croquettes *die Kroketten (pl),* II

pound *das Pfund, -,* I
pounding heart *das Herzklopfen,* III10
poverty *die Armut,* II
practice (a profession) *ausüben (sep),* III11
praise *anpreisen (sep),* III7
prefer *lieber (mögen),* I; *vorziehen (sep),* II; I prefer... *Ich ziehe ... vor,* II; I prefer noodle soup. *Nudelsuppe mag ich lieber.,* II; I prefer that... *Ich bin dafür, daß ...,* II
prejudice *das Vorurteil, -e,* III4
prepare for *s. vorbereiten (sep) auf (acc),* III11
pretty *hübsch,* I; *schön,* I
pretzel *die Brezel, -n,* I
primarily *in erster Linie,* III7
printer *der Drucker, -,* III6
probably *wahrscheinlich,* I
produce *herstellen (sep),* III9; *produzieren,* II
produce store *der Obst- und Gemüseladen, ⸚,* I
product *das Produkt, -e,* III1; product, ware *die Ware, -n,* III7
production *die Herstellung, -en,* III9
profession *der Beruf, -e,* III11
program (TV) *die Sendung, -en,* II; family program *die Familiensendung, -en,* II; nature program *die Natursendung, -en,* II
promise *versprechen,* III1
protection: environmental protection *der Umweltschutz,* III9
proud: to be proud of *stolz sein auf (acc),* III8
pullover *der Pulli, -s,* I
pump spray *der Pumpzerstäuber, -,* III9
punctual *pünktlich,* III8
purpose: on purpose *absichtlich,* III4
put (into) *stecken,* III9
put on *anziehen (sep),* I

Q

qualify, make less absolute *relativieren,* III8
quark *der Quark,* II
quarrel *der Krach,* III4; *die Streitigkeit, -en,* III4; *streiten,* III2; argument *der Streit,* III4
quarter: a quarter after *Viertel nach,* I; a quarter to *Viertel vor,* I
queen *die Königin, -nen,* III10
question *die Frage, -n,* II; It's out of the question! *Kommt nicht in Frage!,* III11
quiet *still,* III8

quiz show *die Ratesendung, -en,* II

R

rabbit meat *das Hasenfleisch,* III1
radio *das Radio, -s,* II
radio announcer *Rundfunksprecher (in), -/nen,* III12
radish *das Radieschen, -,* III1
railroad station *der Bahnhof, ⸚e,* I
rain *der Regen,* I; It's raining. *Es regnet.,* I
rain: acid rain *der saure Regen,* III9
rainy *regnerisch,* I
raise (a child) *großziehen (sep),* III7
raisin *die Rosine, -n,* III1
raspberry marmalade *die Himbeermarmelade, -n,* II
rather *ziemlich,* I
raw *roh,* II
read *lesen,* I
read aloud *vorlesen (sep),* III10
reading *die Lektüre, -n,* III1
really *ganz,* I; *wirklich,* I; *echt,* II; Not really. *Nicht besonders.,* I
really (well) *unheimlich (gut),* III10
reason *der Grund, ⸚e,* III11; for this reason *deshalb,* III6; to give a reason *begründen,* III6
rebellious *aufsässig,* III4
receive *bekommen,* I
receiver *der Hörer, -,* I
recent: most recent event *die Neuigkeit, -en,* III6
recently *vor kurzem,* III1
recognize *erkennen,* III10
recommend *empfehlen,* III8
recycle *wiederverwerten (sep),* III9
recycling bin *der Container, -,* III8
red *rot,* I; in red *in Rot,* I
red berry dessert *Rote Grütze,* II
red cabbage *der Rotkohl,* II
reduce *abbauen (sep),* III8
reexamine *überprüfen,* III8
refrigerator *der Kühlschrank, ⸚e,* I
regularly *regelmäßig,* III3
relationship *das Verhältnis,* III4
relax *s. entspannen,* III3
religion *die Religion, -en,* I
remember *s. erinnern an (acc),* III2
remote control *die Fernbedienung, -en,* II
repeat *wiedergeben (sep),* III8
replace *ersetzen,* III9
report *der Bericht, -e,* III6
reported to be *angeblich,* III7
require *nötig haben,* III11
residence *das Wohnhaus, ⸚er,* II; the ... residence *Hier bei ... ,* I
rest *s. ausruhen (sep),* III11

ENGLISH-GERMAN VOCABULARY

restaurant *das Restaurant, -s,* II; *der Gasthof, ̈-e,* II; **small restaurant** *das Lokal, -e,* II

return: to come back to (a topic) *zurückkommen auf* (sep, acc), III6

returnable: non-returnable bottle *die Einwegflasche, -n,* III9

reusable bottle *die Mehrwegflasche, -n,* III9

ribs *die Rippchen* (pl), III1

rice *der Reis,* II

right *das Recht, -e,* III5

right: That's all right. *Macht nichts!,* II; **That's not right (at all)!** *Das stimmt (überhaupt) nicht!,* II; **You're right about that!** *Da hast du recht!,* II

right: to the right *nach rechts,* I

ring *der Ring, -e,* II

ringlet *der Ringel, -,* II

river *der Fluß,* (pl) *Flüsse,* II; **on a river** *an einem Fluß,* II

roast *der Braten,* II

robust, strong *stark,* III8

role *die Rolle, -n,* III11

roll *die Semmel, -n,* I

roll of film *der Film, -e,* II

romance *der Liebesfilm, -e,* I; **romance novel** *der Liebesroman, -e,* I

roof *das Dach, ̈-er,* III9

room *das Zimmer, -,* I; **to clean up my room** *mein Zimmer aufräumen* (sep), I

round *rund,* I

ruined *kaputt,* I, II

run *laufen,* II; **long distance run** *der Langstreckenlauf,* II

run: ski run *die Skipiste, -n,* III9

runny nose *der Schnupfen,* II

Russian *russisch* (adj), II

S

sad *traurig,* I

safe: environmentally safe *umweltfreundlich,* III9

sail *segeln,* II

salmon *der Lachs, -e,* II

salt *das Salz,* I

salt shaker *der Salzstreuer, -,* III2

salty: too salty *zu salzig,* II

same: the same *das gleiche,* III7; *derselbe,* III7

sandwich *das Sandwich, -es,* II; **What do you have on your sandwich?** *Was hast du denn auf dem Brot?,* II

Saturday *der Samstag,* I; **Saturdays** *samstags,* II

sauerkraut *das Sauerkraut,* II

sauna *die Sauna, -s,* II

sausage *die Wurst, ̈-e,* I

save money *sparen,* III3

say *sagen,* I; **Say!** *Sag mal!,* I **to say something about** *aussagen über* (sep), III3

scan (a newspaper) *herumblättern* (sep), III3

scarf *der Schal, -s,* II

schedule of shows *das Programm, -e,* II

school *die Schule, -n,* I; **after school** *nach der Schule,* I; **How do you get to school?** *Wie kommst du zur Schule?,* I; **at school** *an der Schule,* II

school administration *die Schulleitung,* III6

school subject *das Fach, ̈-er,* I

school supplies *die Schulsachen* (pl), I

school, class *der Unterricht,* III5

schoolbag *die Schultasche, -n,* I

science *die Wissenschaft, -en,* III11

science fiction movie *der Science-fiction-Film, -e,* I

scientific *wissenschaftlich,* III10

scold *schimpfen,* III4

sea *die See, -n; das Meer, -e,* II

search (for) *suchen,* I

second *zweit-,* I; **the second street** *die zweite Straße,* I

secret tip *der Geheimtip, -s,* II

secure *sicher,* II

seduce *verführen,* III7

see *sehen,* I; **See you later!** *Bis dann!,* I; **to see a movie** *einen Film sehen,* I

seem *scheinen,* III5

seldom *selten,* II

sensational *sensationell,* I

senseless *sinnlos,* III5

separate oneself from *s. absondern von* (sep), III4

September *der September,* I

seriously *im Ernst,* III5

services: armed services *die Streitkräfte,* III5

set the table *den Tisch decken,* I

several *mehrere,* III6

sew *nähen,* III3

shaker: salt and pepper shaker *der Salz- und Pfefferstreuer,* III2

shame: to be a shame about something *schade um etwas sein,* III5

shampoo *das Shampoo, -s,* II

sharp (clothing) *scharf,* II; **really sharp** *fetzig,* II

shine: the sun is shining *die Sonne scheint,* I

ship *das Schiff, -e,* II

shirt *das Hemd, -en,* I

shish kebab *das Schisch Kebab,* 11

shoe: patent leather shoe *der Lackschuh, -e,* II

shoemaker *Schuhmacher(in), -/nen,* III12

shoot *schießen,* III5

shop *einkaufen* (sep), I; **to go shopping** *einkaufen gehen,* I

short *kurz,* I

short: on short notice *kurzfristig,* III5

shortening *das Butterschmalz,* I

shorts: pair of shorts *die Shorts, -,* I

shot put *das Kugelstoßen,* II

should *sollen,* I

shoulder *die Schulter, -n,* II

show *die Sendung, -en,* II

shower *duschen,* III9

side dish *die Beilage, -n,* II

sightsee *etwas besichtigen,* II

sign *unterschreiben,* III5

silk *die Seide,* I; **made of silk** *aus Seide,* I; **silk shirt** *das Seidenhemd, -en,* II; **real silk** *echte Seide,* II

silver: made of silver *aus Silber,* II

silverware *das Besteck,* III2

singer (female) *die Sängerin, -nen,* I; singer (male) *der Sänger, -,* I

sink *das Spülbecken, -,* I

sister *die Schwester, -n,* I; **brothers and sisters** *die Geschwister* (pl), I

site *die Anlage, -n,* II

situation *das Verhältnis, -se,* III11

size *die Größe, -n,* I

ski run *die Skipiste, -n,* III9

skin *die Haut,* II

skirt *der Rock, ̈-e,* I; **pleated skirt** *der Faltenrock, ̈-e,* II

sledding *rodeln,* II

sleep: to get enough sleep *genügend schlafen,* II

sleeveless *ärmellos,* II

sleeves: with long sleeves *mit langen Ärmeln,* II; **with short sleeves** *mit kurzen Ärmeln,* II

slender *schlank,* II

slice *die Scheibe, -n,* III1

slide *das Dia, -s,* II

slip *ausrutschen* (sep), III1

slogan: advertising slogan *der Werbespruch, ̈-e,* III7

sloppy *schlampig,* III3

slow(ly) *langsam,* II

small *klein,* I

smart (looking) *fesch, schick, chic,* I

smoke *rauchen,* II

smoked *geräuchert,* II

snack bar, stand *die Imbißstube, -n,* I

snap *der Druckknopf, ⁻e*, II
sneaker *der Turnschuh, -e*, I
snow *der Schnee*, I; It's snowing. *Es schneit.*, I
so *so*, I; So long! *Tschau! / Tschüs!*, I; so so *so lala*, I
so that, in order to *damit* (conj), III3
soap *die Seife, -n*, II
soap: laundry soap *das Waschmittel, -*, III9
soccer *Fußball*, I
sock *die Socke, -n*, I
soda: lemon-flavored soda *die Limo, -s (die Limonade, -n)*, I; cola and lemon soda *das Spezi, -s*, II
sofa *das Sofa, -s*, I
soft *weich*, II
some *einige*, III6; some- *irgend-*, III7
Someone told me that... *Man hat mir gesagt, daß ...*, II
something *etwas*, I
sometimes *manchmal*, I
son *der Sohn, ⁻e*, II
song *das Lied, ⁻er*, I
sorry: to be sorry *bedauern*, II; *leid tun*, II; I'm sorry. *Es tut mir leid.*, I; Sorry, I can't. *Ich kann leider nicht.*, I; Sorry, but unfortunately we're all out of couscous. *Tut mir leid, aber der Couscous ist leider schon alle.*, II; I'm so sorry. *Das tut mir aber leid!*, II
sort *sortieren*, I
sound *klingen*, III11
sound engineer *Toningenieur(in), -e/nen*, III12
soup *die Suppe, -n*, II
space travel *die Raumfahrt*, III11
Spanish *spanisch* (adj), II
speak *reden*, III4; to speak one's mind *ausreden* (sep), III6
specialist: tourism specialist *Touristikfachwirt(in), -e/nen*, III12
spectator *der Zuschauer, -*, III10
spend (time) *verbringen*, I; spend (the night) *übernachten*, II
spicy *würzig*, II; spicy, hot *scharf*, II
spinach *der Spinat*, II
splendor *die Pracht*, III10
spoil, pamper *verwöhnen*, III8
spoon *der Löffel, -*, III2
sport(s) *der Sport*, I; sport facility *die Sportanlage, -n*, II; sports telecast *die Sportübertragung, -en*, II; Do you play sports? *Machst du Sport?*, I
sports scientist *Sportökonom(in), -en/nen*, III12
sporty *sportlich*, II

sprain (something) *sich (etwas) verstauchen*, II
spray: pump spray *der Pumpzerstäuber, -*, III9
spread *verbreiten*, III8; spread, to butter *bestreichen*, III1
spring *der Frühling*, I; in the spring *im Frühling*, I
spring a leak *leck werden*, III9
sprouts (bean) *die Sojasprossen*, II
square *der Platz, ⁻e*, I; on ... Square *am ...platz*, I
stage *die Bühne, -n*, III10
stamp *die Briefmarke, -n*, I; to collect stamps *Briefmarken sammeln*, I
stand, to be *stehen*, III2; to not be able to stand something *etwas nicht leiden können*, III4
state: German federal state *das Bundesland, ⁻er*, I
station *der Sender, -*, II
stay, remain *bleiben*, II
steak (beef) *das Rindersteak, -s*, II
stereo *die Stereoanlage, -n*, I
stimulate, encourage *anregen* (sep), III6
stimulating *anregend*, III6
stinks: That stinks! *So ein Mist!*, I
stirrup pants *die Steghose, -n*, II
stocking *der Strumpf, ⁻e*, II
stomach *der Bauch, ⁻e*, II; stomachache *die Bauchschmerzen* (pl), II
storage shelf *das Ablagefach, ⁻er*, II
store *der Laden, ⁻*, I
store: to be in store for *zukommen auf* (sep, acc), III11
storm *das Gewitter, -*, I
stove *der Herd, -e*, I
straight ahead *geradeaus*, I
strange, silly *grotesk*, III10
strawberry *die Erdbeere, -n*, II; strawberry marmalade *die Erdbeermarmelade*, II
street *die Straße, -n*, I; on ... Street *in der ...straße*, I; main street *die Hauptstraße, -n*, II
stressful *anstrengend*, III5; *stressig*, III8
strict *streng*, III8
strike *der Streik, -s*, III6
stripe *der Streifen, -*, II
striped *gestreift*, I
stroll *spazieren*, II
strong *kräftig*, III7; *stark*, III8
struggle, battle *der Kampf, ⁻e*, III5
stubborn *stur*, III8
student exchange *der Schüleraustausch*, III6
students' representatives *die Schülervertretung*, III6

studies: university studies *das Studium*, III5
study *lernen*, III3
stuff oneself *futtern*, III2
stupid *blöd*, I
style *der Stil, -e*, II
stylist: hair stylist *Friseur/Friseuse, -e/n*, III12
subconscious *das Unterbewußtsein*, III7
subject (school) *das Fach, ⁻er*, I
submarine *das U-Boot, -e*, III5
subscription *das Abonnement, -s*, III10
suburb *der Vorort, -e*, I; in a suburb *in einem Vorort*, II
subway *die U-Bahn*, I; by subway *mit der U-Bahn*, I
subway station *die U-Bahnstation, -en*, I
success *der Erfolg, -e*, III12
suede jacket *die Wildlederjacke, -n*, II
sugar *der Zucker*, I
suggest *vorschlagen*, II; I suggest that... *Ich schlage vor, daß ...*, II
suggestion *der Vorschlag, ⁻e*, II
suit *der Anzug, ⁻e*, II
suit: to be suited to *s. eignen zu*, III6
summer *der Sommer*, I; in the summer *im Sommer*, I
sun *die Sonne*, I
sun protection factor *der Lichtschutzfaktor, -en*, II
sun tan lotion *die Sonnenmilch*, II; *die Sonnencreme*, II
Sunday *der Sonntag*, I; Sundays *sonntags*, II
sunny *sonnig*, I
sunroof *das Schiebedach, ⁻er*, II
sunstroke *der Sonnenstich, -e*, II
Super! *Spitze!, Super!*, I
superficial *oberflächlich*, III6
supermarket *der Supermarkt, ⁻e*, I; at the supermarket *im Supermarkt*, I
support *unterstützen*, III6
suppose *vermuten*, III8
suppose: I suppose so, but... *Eigentlich schon, aber ...*, II
supposed to *sollen*, I; The fish is supposed to be great. *Der Fisch soll prima sein.*, II; Well, what am I supposed to do? *Was soll ich bloß machen?*, II; What's that supposed to be? *Was soll denn das sein?*, II
sure: I'm not sure. *Ich bin nicht sicher.*, I
surprise *überraschen*, III6; to be surprised *erstaunt sein*, III8

surrounding area *die Umgebung, -en,* II

swallow: I can hardly swallow. *Ich kann kaum schlucken.,* II

sweater *der Pulli, -s,* I

sweet *süß,* II

swim *schwimmen,* I; **to go swimming** *baden gehen,* I

swimming pool *das Schwimmbad, ̈-er,* I; *der Pool, -s,* II; **to go to the (swimming) pool** *ins Schwimmbad gehen,* I

switch off *abstellen* (sep), II; *ausschalten* (sep), III9

sympathy, pity *das Mitleid,* III3

synagogue *die Synagoge, -n,* II

T

T-shirt *das T-Shirt, -s,* I

table *der Tisch, -e,* I; **to clear the table** *den Tisch abräumen* (sep), I

take *nehmen,* I

take care of *erledigen,* III1

take part *dabeisein* (sep), III11

talk about *sprechen über,* I; **What did you (pl) talk about?** *Worüber habt ihr gesprochen?,* I

tank *der Panzer, -,* III5

task *die Aufgabe, -n,* III6

taste *der Geschmack,* III3; *schmecken,* I; **Does it taste good?** *Schmeckt's?,* I; **How does it taste?** *Wie schmeckt's?,* I; **doesn't taste good** *schmeckt mir nicht,* II; **Beef tastes better to me.** *Rind schmeckt mir besser.,* II; **Which soup tastes best to you?** *Welche Suppe schmeckt dir am besten?,* II

Tasty! *Lecker!,* I

tax consultant *Steuerberater(in), -/nen,* III12

tea *der Tee,* I; **a glass of tea** *ein Glas Tee,* I

teacher (male) *der Lehrer, -,* I; (female) *die Lehrerin, -nen,* I

team *die Mannschaft, -en,* II; **on the (basketball) team** *in der (Basketball) mannschaft,* II

technical designer *technische(r) Zeichner(in), -/nen,* III12

teenager *der, die Jugendliche, -n,* III8

telecast, transmission *die Übertragung, -en,* II

telephone *das Telefon, -e, der Apparat, -e,* I; **to pick up the telephone** *den Hörer abheben* (sep), I

telephone booth *die Telefonzelle, -n,* I

telephone number *die Telefonnummer, -n,* I

television (medium of) *das Fernsehen,* I; **TV set** *der Fernseher, -,* II; **idiot box** *die Glotze, -n,* III6; **to watch TV** *Fernsehen schauen,* I; *fernsehen* (sep), *Fernseh gucken,* II; **color stereo television set** *das Stereo-Farbfernsehgerät, -e,* II; **TV and video cart** *der Fernseh- und Videowagen, -,* II; **What's on TV?** *Was läuft im Fernsehen?,* II

tell *erzählen,* III1

temptation to buy *der Kaufreiz,* III7

tension *die Spannung, -en,* III10

terrible *schrecklich,* III3

test *die Prüfung, -en,* III5

Thank you (very much)! *Danke (sehr/schön)!,* I; *Vielen Dank!,* I; **Thank you and the same to you!** *Danke gleichfalls!,* II; *Danke! Dir/Ihnen auch!,* II

that *daß* (conj), I; **That's all.** *Das ist alles.,* I; **That's...** *Das ist ...,* I

theater *das Theater, -,* I; (theater) **balcony** *der Rang, ̈-e,* III10

theme *das Thema, Themen,* III5

then *dann,* I

there *dort,* I

there: to be there, take part *dabeisein* (sep), III5

thermos bottle *die Thermosflasche, -n,* III2

thing *die Sache, -n,* III3

think: Do you think so? *Meinst du?,* I; **I think** *ich glaube,* I; **I think (tennis) is...** *Ich finde (Tennis) ...,* I; **I think so too.** *Das finde ich auch.,* I; **I don't think that...** *Ich glaube nicht, daß ...,* II; **I really think that...** *Ich meine doch, daß ...,* II; **I think I'm sick.** *Ich glaube, ich bin krank.,* II; **I think it's great that...** *Ich finde es toll, daß ...,* II

think a lot of *halten von,* III3; **to think about** *s. Gedanken machen über* (acc), III3; **to think of or about** *denken an* (acc), III2; **thinking over** *das Nachdenken,* III6

think: What do you think of that? *Wie stehst du dazu?,* III6

third *dritt-,* I

thirsty *durstig,* III8

this *dies-,* II; **this afternoon** *heute nachmittag,* I; **This is...** (on the telephone) *Hier ist ...,* I; **this morning** *heute morgen,* I

thorough *gründlich,* III6

threaten *drohen* (dat), III8

three times *dreimal,* I

thrilling *spannend,* I

thrive *aufblühen* (sep), III10

throat *der Hals, ̈-e,* II; **sore throat** *die Halsschmerzen* (pl), II

through *durch,* II

thumb *der Daumen, -,* III1

Thursday *der Donnerstag,* I; **Thursdays** *donnerstags,* II

ticket window *die Abendkasse, -n,* III10

tie *die Krawatte, -n,* II; **bow tie** *die Fliege, -n,* II

tight *eng,* I; **It's too tight on you.** *Es ist dir zu eng.,* II

till: ten till two *zehn vor zwei,* I

Tilsiter cheese *der Tilsiter Käse,* II

time *die Zeit,* I; **At what time?** *Um wieviel Uhr?,* I; **I don't have time.** *Ich habe keine Zeit.,* I; **What time is it?** *Wie spät ist es?, Wieviel Uhr ist es?,* I; **(time) passes** *vergehen,* III11; **at that time** *damals,* III2

tip *der Tip, -s,* III8

tire: wide tire *der Breitreifen, -,* II

tired *müde,* II

to *an, auf, nach,* II; **Let's drive to the ocean.** *Fahren wir ans Meer!;* **Are you going to the golf course?** *Gehst du auf den Golfplatz?;* **We're going to Austria.** *Wir fahren nach Österreich.,* II

today *heute,* I

toe *die Zehe, -n,* III1

tofu *der Tofu,* II

together: to go together (clothing) *zusammenpassen* (sep), III3

toilet *die Toilette, -n,* II

tolerance *die Toleranz,* III4

tomato *die Tomate, -n,* I

tomorrow *morgen,* I

tonight *heute abend,* I

too *zu,* I; **Too bad!** *Schade!,* I

toothache *die Zahnschmerzen* (pl), II

toothpaste *die Zahnpasta,* II

tour *besichtigen,* I; **to tour the city** *die Stadt besichtigen,* I; **city tour** *die Stadrundfahrt, -en,* II

tourism specialist *Touristikfachwirt(in), -e/nen,* III12

toward *nach,* II

town *die Kleinstadt, ̈-e,* II; **in a town** *in einer Kleinstadt,* II

traffic *der Verkehr,* II

traffic jam *der Stau, -s,* III7

train *die Bahn, -en,* II

train station *der Bahnhof, ̈-e,* I

training and weight room *der Fitneßraum, ̈-e,* II

translate *übersetzen,* III8

transmitter *der Sender, -,* II

transport plane *das Transportflugzeug, -e,* III5

transportation *das Verkehrsmittel, -,* II; **public transportation** *öffentliche Verkehrsmittel (pl),* II

trash *der Müll,* I; **trash, waste** *der Abfall, ⁼e,* III9

trash bag *die Abfalltüte, -n,* III2

tree *der Baum, ⁼e,* II

trout *die Forelle, -n,* II

truck *der Laster, -,* III5; *der Lastkraftwagen, -, (LKW, -s),* II

true: **Not true!** *Stimmt nicht!,* I; **That's right!** *Stimmt!,* I; **That's true, but...** *Das stimmt, aber ...,* II

truth *die Wahrheit,* III6

try hard *s. bemühen um,* III6

try on *anprobieren (sep),* I

Tuesday *der Dienstag,* I; **Tuesdays** *dienstags,* II

tuna fish salad *der Thunfischsalat,* III1

tune (an instrument) *stimmen,* III10

Turkish *türkisch (adj),* II

turn *einbiegen (sep);* **Turn in here!** *Biegen Sie hier ein!,* II

tuxedo *der Smoking, -s,* II

twice *zweimal,* I

twin *der Zwilling, -e,* II

type *der Typ, -en,* II

U

ugly *häßlich,* I

unbelievable *unglaublich;* **That's really unbelievable!** *Das ist ja unglaublich!,* II

uncle *der Onkel, -,* I

uncomfortable *unbequem,* I

under it, underneath *darunter,* II

undertake *unternehmen,* III2

underway *unterwegs,* III6

unfortunately *leider,* I; **Unfortunately I can't.** *Leider kann ich nicht.,* I; **That's the way it is, unfortunately.** *Das ist leider so.,* II

unfriendly *unsympathisch,* II

unhealthy *ungesund,* II; *nicht gut für die Gesundheit,* II

unified *vereint,* III11

university studies *das Studium,* III5

unpleasant *unsympathisch,* II

unpopular *unbeliebt,* III4

until *bis (acc),* III11; **from 8 until 8:45** *von 8 Uhr bis 8 Uhr 45,* I; **until you get to ... Square** *bis zum ...platz,* I; **until you get to ... Street** *bis zur ... straße,* I; **until you get to the traffic light** *bis zur Ampel,* I; **until then** *bis dahin,* III11

unusual *ausgefallen,* III3

use *gebrauchen,* III7; *verwenden,* III7;

use again *wiederverwenden (sep),* III9

used: **to get used to** *s. gewöhnen an (acc),* III7

useful *nützlich,* III6

usually *gewöhnlich,* II

V

vacation (from school) *die Ferien (pl),* II; **vacation (from work)** *der Urlaub, -e,* II; **What did you do on your vacation?** *Was hast du in den Ferien gemacht?,* II

vacuum *Staub saugen,* I

vanilla-flavored milk *die Vanillemilch,* II

varied *abwechslungsreich,* II

vegetable produce *das Pflanzenprodukt, -e,* III1

vegetables *das Gemüse,* I

vegetarian *vegetarisch;* **You're vegetarian, right?** *Du ißt wohl vegetarisch, was?,* II

venison *das Rehfleisch,* III1

very *sehr,* I; **Very well!** *Sehr gut!,* I

vest: **jeans vest** *die Jeansweste, -n,* II

veterinarian *Tierarzt, -ärztin,* III11

vice-versa *umgekehrt,* III5

video cassette *das Video, -s,* I; *die Videocassette, -n,* II; **insert a video cassette** *ein Video einlegen (sep),* II; **take out the video cassette** *das Video herausnehmen (sep),* II

video: **use a video camera/a camera** *die Videokamera/die Kamera bedienen,* II

village *das Dorf, ⁼er,* II; **in a village** *in einem Dorf,* II

vintner *Winzer(in), -/nen,* III12

violence *die Gewalt,* III8

violent *brutal,* I

violin *die Geige, -n,* III10

visit *besuchen,* I

visit (a place) *besuchen, besichtigen,* II; **I visited (the cathedral).** *Ich habe (den Dom) besichtigt.,* II

vocational school *die Fachschule, -n,* III11

volleyball *Volleyball,* I

volume control *der Lautstärkeregler,* II

voluntary *freiwillig,* III5

vote for *wählen,* III5

W

wait and see *abwarten (sep),* III2

walk *spazieren,* II

want (to) *wollen,* I; *Lust haben,* III2;

What do you want to do? *Was willst du machen?,* II

war *der Krieg, -e,* II; **war movie** *der Kriegsfilm, -e,* I

warm *warm,* I

wash *spülen,* I; **to wash the dishes** *das Geschirr spülen,* I; **to wash (sich) waschen,** II; **to wash clothes** *die Wäsche waschen,* II

waste *verschwenden,* III9

wastewater *das Abwasser, ⁼,* III9

watch *schauen,* I; **to watch TV** *Fernsehen schauen,* I; *fernsehen (sep),* II; (colloquial) *Fernsehen gucken,* II

water *das Wasser,* I; **a glass of (mineral) water** *ein Glas (Mineral-) Wasser,* I

water the flowers *die Blumen gießen,* I

watermelon *die Wassermelone, -n,* III1

weapon *die Waffe, -n,* III5

wear *anziehen (sep),* I; *tragen,* II; **Don't wear anything made of...** *Trag ja nichts aus ...!,* II; **Go ahead and wear...** *Trag doch mal ...!,* II

weather *das Wetter,* I; **How's the weather?** *Wie ist das Wetter?,* I

weather report *der Wetterbericht, -e,* II

Wednesday *der Mittwoch,* I; **Wednesdays** *mittwochs,* II

week *die Woche, -n,* I; **every week** *jede Woche,* II

weekend *das Wochenende, -n,* I; **on the weekend** *am Wochenende,* I

weekly special *das Angebot der Woche,* I

weigh *wiegen,* I

weigh on, burden *belasten,* III5

weight lifting *das Krafttraining,* III3

welder *Schweißer(in), -/nen,* III12

well, okay *also (part),* III2

well: **Well yes, but...** *Eigentlich schon, aber ...,* II; *Ja, schon, aber ...,* II; **extremely well** *ganz wohl,* II; **Get well soon!** *Gute Besserung!,* II; **I'm (not) doing well.** *Es geht mir (nicht) gut!,* II; *Mir ist (nicht) gut.,* II; **not well at all** *überhaupt nicht wohl,* II

were: **Where were you?** *Wo bist du gewesen?,* I

western (movie) *der Western, -,* I

wet *naß,* I

what *was;* **What are we going to do now?** *Was machen wir jetzt?,* II; **What is it?** *Was gibt's?,* II; *Was ist?,* II; **Okay, what is it?** *Ja? Was denn?,* II; **So what about...?** *Wie steht's mit ...?,* II; **Yes, what?** *Ja,* *was bitte?*, II; **What can I do for you?** *Was kann ich für dich tun?*, I; **What else?** *Noch etwas?*, I

what kind of? *was für?*, I; **What kinds of music do you like?** *Was für Musik hörst du gern?*, I

What's it about? *Worum geht es?*, III4

when, at the time *als* (conj), III8

when? *wann?*, I

whenever *wenn* (conj), II

where (from)? *woher?*, I

where (to)? *wohin?*, I; **Where are we going?** *Wohin fahren wir?*, II

where? *wo?*, I

whether *ob* (conj), II

which *welch-*, I

while *die Weile*, III11

whirlpool *der Whirlpool*, *-s*, II

white *weiß*, I; **in white** *in Weiß*, I

who? *wer?*, I

whole wheat roll *die Vollkornsemmel*, *-n*, I

whole, perfect *heil*, III7

whom *wen*, I; **to, for whom** *wem*, I

why? *warum?*, I; **Why don't you come along!** *Komm doch mit!*, I

wide *weit*, I

will *werden*, II

wind surf *windsurfen*, II

windbreaker *die Wind-, Wetterjacke*, *-n*, II

window *das Fenster*, *-*, I; **to clean the windows** *die Fenster putzen*, I

windshield wiper *der Scheibenwischer*, *-*, II

winter *der Winter*, I; **in the winter** *im Winter*, I

wise *weise*, III7

wish *sich wünschen;* **I wish for...** *Ich wünsche mir ...*, II; **What would you wish for?** *Was wünschst du dir (mal)?*, II

with *mit*, I; **with corners** *eckig*, I

without *ohne* (acc), III3; **without doing...** *ohne ... zu machen*, III3; **to do without** *verzichten auf* (acc), III9

witty *witzig*, II

woman *die Frau*, *-en*, I

wonder, miracle *das Wunder*, *-*, III10

wonderful *großartig*, II

wood: made of wood *aus Holz*, I

wool *die Wolle*, II

wool shirt *das Wollhemd*, *-en*, II

work *arbeiten*, II; **That won't work.** *Das geht nicht.*, I; **work, achievement** *das Werk*, *-e*, III10

world *die Welt*, *-en*, III11

worry *s. Sorgen machen*, III9

worse than *schlechter als*, II

worth: to be worth it *s. lohnen*, III5

would have (been) *wäre*, III5

would have (had) *hätte*, III5

wrist *das Handgelenk*, *-e*, III1

wrong: to be wrong *s. irren*, III5

Y

yard *der Garten*, *⸗*, II

year *das Jahr*, *-e*, I; **I am... years old.** *Ich bin ... Jahre alt.*, I

yellow *gelb*, I; **in yellow** *in Gelb*, I

yes *ja*, I; **Yes?** *Bitte?*, I; **Yes, I do!** *Doch!*, II

yesterday *gestern*, I; **yesterday evening** *gestern abend*, I; **the day before yesterday** *vorgestern*, I

yogurt *der Joghurt*, *-*, II

you're (very) welcome! *Bitte (sehr/schön)!*, I

younger *jünger*, II

youth hostel *die Jugendherberge*, *-n*, III2

Z

zero *null*, I

zipper *der Reißverschluß*, *-verschlüsse*, II

zoo *der Zoo*, *-s*, I; **to go to the zoo** *in den Zoo gehen*, I

GRAMMAR INDEX

This grammar index includes grammar topics introduced in **Komm mit!** Levels 1, 2, and 3. The Roman numeral I following the page number(s) indicates Level 1; the Roman numeral II indicates Level 2; the Roman numeral III indicates Level 3.

NOTE: For a summary of the grammar presented in this book see pages 388-392.

ABBREVIATIONS

acc	*accusative*	gen	*genitive*	prep	*preposition*
adj	*adjective*	indef art	*indefinite article*	pres	*present*
art	*article*	indir obj	*indirect object*	pron	*pronoun(s)*
comm	*command*	inf	*infinitive*	ques	*question(s)*
cond	*conditional*	interr	*interrogative*	reflex	*reflexive*
conv past	*conversational past*	narr past	*narrative past*	rel	*relative*
dat	*dative*	nom	*nominative*	sep pref	*separable prefix*
def	*definition*	pass	*passive*	sing	*singular*
def art	*definite article*	pers	*person*	subj	*subject*
dir obj	*direct object*	plur	*plural*		

A

accusative case: def art, p. 123 (I); indef art, p. 123 (I); p. 230 (I); third pers pron, sing, p. 128 (I); third pers pron, plur, p. 180 (I); first and second pers pron, p. 180 (I); following **für**, p. 180 (I); p. 297 (I); following **es gibt**, p. 229 (I); of reflex pron, p. 90 (II); of **jeder**, p. 94 (II); of **kein**, p. 98 (II); of possessives, p. 120 (II); adj following **der**- and **dieser**-words, p. 189 (II); following **durch** and **um**, p. 222 (II); rel pron, p. 87 (III)

adjectives: comparative forms of, p. 166 (II); endings following **ein**-words, p. 170 (II); endings of comparatives, p. 176 (II); endings following **der**- and **dieser**-words, p. 189 (II); endings of unpreceded adj, p. 271 (II); use of numbers as, p. 86 (III); superlative forms of, p. 142 (III); **derselbe** and **gleiche** p. 162 (III); determiners of quantity, p. 163 (III); **irgendein** and **irgendwelche**, p. 171 (III)

als: in a comparison, p. 166 (II); with narrative past, p. 187 (III)

am: contraction of **an dem**, p. 65 (II)

am liebsten: use of with **würde**, p. 267 (II)

an: followed by dat (location), p. 65 (II); followed by acc (direction), p. 214 (II)

ans: contraction of **an das**, p. 214 (II)

anstatt: followed by gen, p. 238 (III)

anziehen: pres tense forms of, p. 131 (I)

article: *see* definite article, indefinite article

auf: followed by dat (location), p. 119 (II); followed by acc (direction), p. 214 (II); use of with **s. freuen**, p. 241 (II); use of with **warten**, p. 58 (III)

aufs: contraction of **auf das**, p. 214 (II)

aus: followed by dat, p. 222 (II)

aussehen: pres tense forms of, p. 132 (I)

außerhalb: followed by gen, p. 238 (III)

B

bei: followed by dat, p. 222 (II)

beim: contraction of **bei dem**, p. 222 (II)

s. brechen: pres tense of, p. 145 (II)

C

case: *see* nominative case, accusative case, dative case

class: def of, p. 24 (I)

command forms: **du**-commands, p. 200 (I); p. 297 (I); **Sie**-commands, p. 227 (I); inclusive commands, p. 139 (II)

comparatives: *see* adjectives

conditional: p. 217 (III); *see also* subjunctive forms

conjunctions: **denn** and **weil**, p. 206 (I); **daß**, p. 232 (I); **wenn**, p. 199 (II); **ob**, p. 218 (II); coordinating conjunctions, **denn**, **und**, **oder**, **aber** and **sondern**, p. 188 (III)

conversational past: p. 58-59 (II); pass voice, p. 245 (III); *see also* perfect

contractions: of **in dem**, **im**, p. 65; of **an dem**, **am**, p. 65; of **zu dem**, **zum**, p. 125; of **zu der**, **zur**, p. 125; of **an das**, **ans**, p. 214; of **auf das**, **aufs**, p. 214; of **in das**, **ins**, p. 214; of **bei dem**, **beim**, p. 222; of **von dem**, **vom**, p. 222 (II)

D

da-compounds: p. 241 (II); p. 58 (III); p. 243 (III)

daß-clauses: p. 232 (I); verb in final position, p. 89 (II); with reflex verbs, p. 90 (II)

dative case: introduction to, p. 283 (I); following **mit,** p. 283 (I); word order with, p. 284 (I); following **in** and **an** when expressing location, p. 65 (II); with **gefallen,** p. 69 (II); of personal pron, p. 69 (II); plural of def art, p. 69 (II); of **ein**-words, p. 71 (II); following **auf** when expressing location, p. 119 (II); of possessives, p. 120 (II); verbs used with dat forms, **gefallen, schmecken,** p. 123 (II); following **zu,** pp. 125, 195 (II); use of to talk about how you feel, p. 137 (II); verbs requiring dat forms, p. 143 (II); reflex verbs requiring dat forms, p. 144 (II); reflex pron, p. 144 (II); use of to express idea of something being too expensive/large/small, p. 149 (II); plur endings of adj, p. 170 (II); endings of adj, p. 189 (II); further uses of, p. 195 (II); preps followed by, p. 222 (II); rel pron, p. 87 (III); *see also* indirect objects

definite article: to identify class, p. 24 (I); p. 74 (I); acc, p. 123 (I); dat, p. 283 (I); nom and acc, p. 305 (I); dat summary, p. 69 (II); dat plur, p. 69 (II); gen, p. 93 (III)

demonstratives: p. 114 (II)

den: dat plur of def art, p. 69 (II)

derselbe: p. 162 (III)

determiners of quantity: p. 163 (III)

dich: as a reflex pron, p. 90 (II)

dieser-words: demonstratives, p. 114, (II); adj following **dieser**-words, p. 189 (II)

dir: dat personal pron, p. 69 (II); reflexive personal pron, p. 144 (II)

direct object: def, p. 123 (I); *see also* accusative case

direct object pronouns: p. 128 (I); p. 180 (I)

direction: expressed by **nach, an, in** and **auf,** p. 214 (II); use of preps to express, p. 218 (II)

du-commands: p. 200 (I); p. 297 (I); of **messen,** p. 148 (II); of **tragen,** p. 194 (II)

durch: followed by acc, p. 222 (II)

dürfen: present tense of, p. 99 (II); past tense of, p. 117 (III)

E

ein: nom, p. 72 (I); acc, p. 123 (I); p. 230 (I); dat, p. 283 (I); p. 71 (II)

ein-words: **mein(e), dein(e),** p. 78 (I); **sein(e), ihr(e),** p. 79 (I); **kein,** p. 231 (I); p. 307 (I); dat, p. 283 (I); adj endings following, p. 170 (II)

-er: ending in place names, p. 213 (II)

es gibt: p. 229 (I)

essen: pres tense forms of, p. 155 (I)

euch: dat personal pron, p. 69 (II); as a reflex pron, p. 90 (II)

F

fahren: pres tense forms of, p. 227 (I)

fehlen: use of dat with, p. 143 (II)

s. fithalten: reflex verb, p. 90 (II)

s. freuen: reflex verb, p. 90 (II); **s. freuen auf,** p. 241 (II)

s. fühlen: reflex verb, p. 90 (II)

für: followed by acc, p. 180 (I); p. 297 (I); p. 89 (II); use of with **s. interessieren,** p. 194 (II);

future: use of **morgen** and present tense for, p. 183 (I); **werden,** p. 253 (II); pass voice, p. 245 (III); p. 270 (III)

G

gefallen: p. 125 (I); p. 132 (I); use of dat with, p. 69, (II); p. 123 (II); p. 143, (II)

gegenüber: followed by dat, p. 222 (II)

gehen: use of with dat forms, p. 143 (II)

genitive case: p. 93 (III); preps followed by, p. 238 (III)

gern: use of with **würde,** p. 267 (II); use of with **hätte,** p. 274 (II)

gleiche: p. 162 (III)

H

haben: pres tense forms, p. 100 (I); use of in conv past p. 58 (II); past participle of, p. 59 (II); simple past tense forms of, p. 64 (II)

hätte: forms of, p. 274 (II); p. 92 (III); further uses of, p. 110 (III)

helfen: use of dat with, p. 143 (II)

I

ihm: dat personal pron, p. 69 (II)

Ihnen, ihnen: dat personal pron, p. 69 (II)

ihr: dat personal pron, dat case, p. 69 (II)

im: contraction of **in dem,** p. 65 (II)

imperfect: simple past of **haben** and **sein,** p. 64 (II); of modals, p. 117 (III); pp. 134-135 (III); pass voice, p. 245 (III); *see also* narr past

in: followed by dat (location), p. 65 (II); followed by acc (direction), p. 214 (II)

indefinite article: **ein,** nom, p. 72 (I); acc, p. 123 (I); p. 230 (I), nom and acc, p. 303 (I); dat, p. 71 (II); gen, p. 93 (III)

indirect object: def of, p. 283 (I); *see also* dative case

verbs: p. 90 (II); used with dat, **gefallen, schmecken,** p. 123 (II); verbs requiring dat case forms, p. 143 (II); reflex verbs requiring dat case forms, p. 144 (II); **s. wünschen,** p. 169 (II); **passen** and **stehen** with dat, p. 195 (II); verbs requiring prep phrase, **sprechen über, s. freuen auf, s. interessieren für,** p. 241 (II); as neuter nouns, p. 116 (III); past tense of modals, p. 117 (III); narrative past (imperfect), pp. 134-135 (III); verbs with prefixes, p. 194 (III)

verb-final position: in **weil**-clauses, p. 206 (I); p. 165 (II); in clauses following **wissen,** p. 222 (I); in **daß**-clauses, p. 232 (I); p. 89 (II); in **wenn**-clauses, p. 199 (II); in **ob**-clauses, p. 218 (II); with **werden** in clauses beginning with **daß, ob, wenn, weil,** p. 253 (II); in rel clauses, p. 87 (III)

verb-second position: p. 54 (I); p. 151 (I); p. 309 (I)

vom: contraction of **von dem,** p. 222 (II)

von: followed by dat, p. 222 (II); use of in pass voice, p. 215 (III), p. 245 (III)

vor: followed by acc (direction) or dat (location), p. 223 (II)

W

wäre: p. 92 (III); further uses of, p. 100 (III)

während: followed by gen, p. 238 (III)

waschen: pres tense of, p. 145 (II)

wegen: followed by gen, p. 238 (III)

weh tun: as a sep pref verb, p. 143; use of dat with, p. 143 (II)

weil-clauses: verb in final position, p. 165 (II)

welcher: forms of, p. 124 (II)

wenn-clauses: verb in final position, p. 199 (II); in cond sentences, p. 217 (III)

werden: use of to express future, forms of, p. 253 (II); use of in pass voice, p. 215 (III); use of with a conjugated modal, p. 216 (III)

wissen: pres tense forms of, p. 222 (I); p. 299 (I)

wo-compounds: p. 241 (II); p. 58 (III); p. 243 (III); p. 263 (III)

wollen: pres tense forms of, p. 150 (I); p. 302 (I); past tense of, p. 117 (III)

word order: ques beginning with a verb, p. 23 (I); ques beginning with a ques word, p. 23 (I); verb in second position, p. 54 (I); p. 151 (I); p. 309 (I); in **denn**- and **weil**-clauses, p. 206 (I); verb-final in clauses following wissen, p. 222 (I); p. 299 (I); verb-final in **daß**-clauses, p. 232 (I); with dat case, p. 284 (I); in **weil**-clauses, p. 165 (II); in **wenn**-clauses, p. 199 (II); in **ob**-clauses, p. 218 (II); with **werden** in clauses beginning with **daß, ob, wenn, weil,** p. 253 (II); in relative clauses, p. 87 (III); in main clause preceded by a subordinate clause, p. 187 (III)

s. wünschen: with dat reflex pron, p. 168 (II)

würde: forms of, p. 267 (II)

Z

zu: p. 125 (II); prep followed by dat, p. 195 (II); in inf phrases, 67 (III)

zum: contraction of **zu dem,** p. 125 (II)

zur: contraction of **zu der,** p. 125 (II)

zwischen: followed by acc (direction) or dat (location), p. 223 (II)

Map of the Federal Republic of Germany

DÄNEMARK

Nordsee

Ostsee

Kiel

SCHLESWIG-HOLSTEIN

Rostock

Lübeck

MECKLENBURG-VORPOMMERN

HAMBURG

Neubrandenburg

Schwerin

Ems

Elbe

BREMEN

BRANDENBURG

POLEN

NIEDERSACHSEN

Weser

Havel

Oder

BUNDESREPUBLIK

BERLIN

TEUTOBURGER WALD

Hannover

Frankfurt a.d. O.

NIEDERLANDE

Potsdam

Magdeburg

Rhein

Münster

Braunschweig

Spree

NORDRHEIN-WESTFALEN

SACHSEN-ANHALT

Cottbus

Essen

Dortmund

HARZ

RUHRGEBIET

DEUTSCHLAND

Halle

Neisse

Neuss

Düsseldorf

Kassel

Erfurt

Leipzig

SACHSEN

Köln

THÜRINGEN

Dresden

Aachen

THÜRINGER WALD

Saale

Gera

Chemnitz

Elbe

Bonn

WESTERWALD

HESSEN

BELGIEN

EIFEL

ERZGEBIRGE

LUXEM-
BURG

Koblenz

TAUNUS

Suhl

RHEINLAND-PFALZ

Frankfurt a. M.

OBERPFÄLZER WALD

TSCHECHISCHE
REPUBLIK

Mosel

Wiesbaden

Main

BÖHMERWALD

Mainz

Würzburg

SAARLAND

Mannheim

Nürnberg

BAYERISCHER WALD

Saarbrücken

Heidelberg

BADEN-
WÜRTTEMBERG

BAYERN

Regensburg

FRANKREICH

Karlsruhe

Donau

Rhein

Stuttgart

SCHWÄBISCHE ALB

Isar

Inn

Neckar

Ulm

Augsburg

SCHWARZWALD

München

Freiburg

Rhein

BAYERISCHE ALPEN

SALZBURGER
ALPEN

SCHWEIZ

Rhein

Zugspitze

ÖSTERREICH

Map of Liechtenstein, Switzerland, and Austria

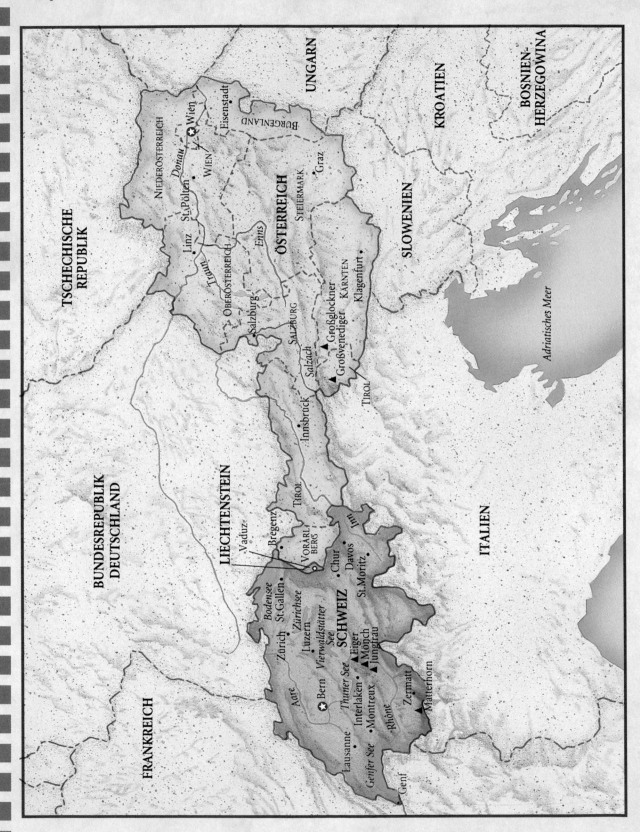

ACKNOWLEDGMENTS (continued from page T6)

Gruner & Jahr AG & Co.: "Mehr Bauch als Kopf" by Georg Wedemeyer from *stern,* no. 22, May 26, 1994, p. 96. Copyright © 1994 by Gruner & Jahr AG & Co.

Harenberg Lexikon-Verlag: Table, "Abfallvermeidung durch Recycling," from *Harenberg Lexikon der Gegenwart '94,* p. 416. Copyright © 1993 by Harenberg Lexikon-Verlag in Harenberg Kommunikation Verlags and Mediengesellschaft mbH & Co. KG, Dortmund.

Luchterhand Literaturverlag GmbH: "Ein Tisch ist ein Tisch" from *Kindergeschichten* by Peter Bichsel. Copyright © 1969 by Hermann Luchterhand Verlag Neuwied und Berlin. "ottos mops" from *Der künstliche Baum* by Ernst Jandl. Copyright © 1970 by Verlag Hermann Luchterhand, Neuwied.

Prälat Berthold Lutz: "Die Nacht bei den Wachsfiguren" by Thomas Burger from *Das Gespenstergespenst.*

MVG Medien Verlagsgesellschaft mbH & Co.: Excerpt, "Je schlampiger, umso schöner!..." from *Mädchen,* No. 13, June 2, 1993, p. 11. Copyright © 1993 by MVG Medien Verlagsgesellschaft mbH & Co.

Sanacorp eG: Advertisement, "Reisefieber?" from *stern,* no. 22, May 26, 1994, p. 179.

Schocken Books, published by Pantheon Books, a division of Random House, Inc.: "Eine alltägliche Verwirrung" from *Franz Kafka: The Complete Stories* by Franz Kafka, edited by Nahum N. Glatzer. Copyright © 1946, 1947, 1948, 1949, 1954, 1958, 1971 by Schocken Books Inc.

Staatsoper Hamburg: Cover page of brochure, *Hamburg Oper: Spielplan-vorschau, April 1993.*

Steidl: "Kinderlied" by Günter Grass from *Gedichte und Kurzprosa (Studienausgabe Band 11).* Copyright © 1994 by Steidl Verlag, Göttingen.

Suhrkamp Verlag, Frankfurt am Main: "Der hellgraue Frühjahrsmantel" by Wolfgang Hildesheimer from *Lieblose Legenden.* Copyright © 1962 by Suhrkamp Verlag, Frankfurt am Main.

Thames and Hudson Ltd.: Map of the Roman World by John Woodcock from *The Birth of Western Civilization: Greece and Rome* by George Huxley et al. Copyright © 1964 by Thames and Hudson Ltd.

Tiefdruck Schwann-Bagel GmbH: From "Tekkno-Fieber" from *JUMA: das Jugendmagazin,* 2/93, p. 4, April 1993. Copyright © 1993 by Tiefdruck Schwann-Bagel GmbH. From "Ingo," from "Judith," and from "Peter" from "Pauken allein reicht nicht" from *JUMA: das Jugendmagazin,* 3/94, pp. 23, 24, 26. Copyright © 1994 by Tiefdruck Schwann-Bagel GmbH.

Verlag Kiepenheuer & Witsch GmbH, Köln: "Das Märchen vom kleinen Herrn Moritz" by Wolf Biermann.

Verlag Moritz Diesterweg GmbH & Co., Frankfurt am Main: From pp. 102-103 from "Wortspiele" from *Texte und Fragen,* edited by Siegfried Buck and Wenzel Wolff. Copyright © 1977 by Verlag Moritz Diesterweg GmbH & Co., Frankfurt am Main. All rights reserved.

Verlag Neues Leben GmbH: Front cover from *Schiller: Hundert Gedichte.* Copyright © 1987 by Verlag Neues Leben, Berlin.

PHOTOGRAPHY CREDITS

Abbreviations used: (t) top, (c) center, (b) bottom, (l) left, (r) right, (bckgd) background, (bdr) border.

FRONT COVER: (l), HRW Photo/George Winkler; (r), Michelle Bridwell; (b), HRW Photo/Sam Dudgeon; (bckgd), HRW Photo/Andrew Yates/map courtesy of Bartholomew.

BACK COVER: (t), HRW Photo/Sam Dudgeon; (tl), Chad Ehlers/Tony Stone Worldwide; (tr) HRW Photo/George Winkler; (bl), (bc), (cl), HRW Photo/Sam Dudgeon; (bckgd), HRW Photo/Andrew Yates/map courtesy of Bartholomew.

FRONTISPIECE: HRW Photo/Sam Dudgeon.

TABLE OF CONTENTS: All photos HRW Photo/Sam Dudgeon, except: page v, HRW Photo/Kevin Galvin; vi(tl), Michelle Bridwell/Frontera Fotos; vii(br), HRW Photo/George Winkler; viii(tl), HRW Photo/George Winkler; ix(br), HRW Photo/Thomas Stephen; x(tl), HRW Photo/George Winkler; xi(br), HRW Photo/Kevin Galvin; xii(tl),(br), HRW Photo/George Winkler.

Chapter Opener Background: Scott Van Osdol.

UNIT ONE: **Chapter One:** Page xviii, 2, 3(tc), (tr), (bl), HRW Photo/George Winkler; 3(bc), (br), courtesy Dom Zu Güstrow; 4- 5(t), Thomas Kanzler/Viesti Associates; 5(b), HRW Photo/George Winkler; 6(t), (c), (b), Thomas Kanzler/Viesti & Associates; 7(t), Thomas Kanzler/Viesti & Associates; 7(b), HRW Photo/Sam Dudgeon; 8, HRW Photo/George Winkler; 13(bckgd), HRW Photo/Sam Dudgeon; 14(t), (c), (b), Thomas Kanzler/Viesti & Associates; 15(c), Thomas Kanzler/Viesti & Associates; 15(b), 22, 23, HRW Photo/Sam Dudgeon; 24, Bettmann Archive; 27, HRW Photo/Sam Dudgeon. **Chapter Two:** Page 28, HRW Photo/ George Winkler; 29, 30, 31(t), Michelle Bridwell/Frontera Fotos; 31(c), (b), HRW Photo/Sam Dudgeon; 32(r) courtesy DJH; 32(t),(b), HRW Photo/George Winkler; 38, 39 (tl), Michelle Bridwell/Frontera Fotos; 39(tr), (b), 41, HRW Photo/ Sam Dudgeon; 45(l), Tourist Office of Weimar; 45(r), HRW Photo/George Winkler; 49(bckgd), 51, HRW Photo/Sam Dudgeon. **Chapter Three:** Page 52, HRW Photo/Kevin Galvin; 53, HRW Photo/George Winkler; 54(tl), (tr), HRW Photo/Kevin Galvin; 54(r), HRW Photo/Sam Dudgeon; 54, HRW Photo/Kevin Galvin; 55(b), HRW Photo/Sam Dudgeon; 60(tl), *JUMA,* April, 1993 edition; 60(r), Frank Lange/*JUMA,* February, 1992 edition; 60(bl), Arno Al Doori/*Mädchen Magazin;* 61(tl), (r) *Bunte* Magazine, May 26, 1994 edition; 61(bl), Volker Wenzlawski/*JUMA,* April, 1994 edition; 62, HRW Photo/Kevin Galvin; 63, HRW Photo/Sam Dudgeon; 64, HRW Photo/Kevin Galvin; 69(bckgd), 74, HRW Photo/Sam Dudgeon.

UNIT TWO: **Chapter Four:** Page 76-77, Steve Vidler/Superstock; 78, Superstock; 79(tl), HRW Photo/George Winkler; 79(tr), HRW Photo/George Winkler; 79(c), Foto Marburg; 79(b), J. Messerschmidt/ Bruce Coleman, Inc.; 80, 81, HRW Photo/George Winkler; 82(l), HRW Photo/Sam Dudgeon; 82(tr), (br), HRW Photo/Kevin Galvin; 83(t), HRW Photo/Kevin Galvin; 83(b), HRW Photo/Sam Dudgeon; 88(t), Ed Kashi; 88(b), HRW photo/George Winkler; 89(t),

Thomas Mayer/Fotoarchiv/Black Star; 89(b), HRW Photo/Sam Dudgeon; 90(l), AP/Wide World Photos; 90(cl), HRW Photo/George Winkler; 90(cr), Harald Thiessen/Bavaria Bildagentur; 90(r), HRW Photo/Lisa Davis; 95(bckgd), HRW Photo/Sam Dudgeon; 97, HRW Photo/Gscheidle; 99, HRW Photo/Russell Dian; 101, 102, HRW Photo/Sam Dudgeon. **Chapter Five**: Page 104, 105, HRW Photo/George Winkler; 106(tl), HRW Photo/Sam Dudgeon; 106(tr), (c), (b), HRW Photo/Kevin Galvin; 107(t), HRW Photo/Kevin Galvin; 107(b), HRW Photo/Sam Dudgeon; 112(t), (b), HRW Photo/George Winkler; 113(t), Thomas Stephan/Fotoarchiv/Black Star; 113(c), HRW Photo/Sam Dudgeon; 113(b), Fritz Lang/Bavaria Bildagentur Gmbh; 114, Herman Kokojan/Black Star; 119, HRW Photo/Sam Dudgeon; 120, 121(bdr), 122(bdr), AP/Wide World Photos; 120, 122(bdr), Heinrich Hoffman; 121(c), Archiv/Interfoto; 121(bdr), 121(bckgd),122(bckgd), Ullstein Bilderdienst; 122(bckgd), Pierre Zucca; 123(bckgd), HRW Photo/Sam Dudgeon; 124, Archiv für Kunst and Geschichte, Berlin; 126, HRW Photo/Sam Dudgeon. **Chapter Six**: Page 129(t), HRW Photo/Thomas Stephen; 129(c), HRW Photo/George Winkler; 129(b), HRW Photo/Thomas Stephen; 130(t), (c), (b), HRW Photo/Thomas Stephen; 131(t), HRW Photo/Thomas Stephen; 131(b), HRW Photo/Sam Dudgeon; 137, HRW Photo/Thomas Stephen; 138(t), HRW Photo/Sam Dudgeon; 138(c), (b), 139(t), HRW Photo/Thomas Stephen; 139(c), (b), HRW Photo/Sam Dudgeon; 145(bckgd), From *Rumpelstiltskin* by Paul O. Zelinsky. ©1986 by Paul O. Zelinsky. Used by permission of Dutton Children's Books, a division of Penguin Books USA Inc.; 147(bckgd), 150, HRW Photo/Sam Dudgeon.

UNIT THREE: Chapter Seven: Page 152-153, 154, 155, HRW Photo/George Winkler; 156, Margot Granitsas/Image Works; 157(b), 158(t), (br), HRW Photo/George Winkler; 158(bl), HRW Photo/Sam Dudgeon; 159(t), HRW Photo/George Winkler; 159(b), 167(t), HRW Photo/Sam Dudgeon; 172, 173, 174, ©1994 Les Editions Albert René/Goscinny-Uderzo; 178, HRW Photo/Sam Dudgeon. **Chapter Eight**: Page 180(c), 181, HRW Photo/George Winkler; 182(t), HRW Photo/Sam Dudgeon; Collage: 182(l), HRW Photo/Stock Editions; 182(tl), HBJ Photo/Lance Shriner; 182(tr), Photo courtesy of Monsanto; 182(tr), HRW Photo/John Kelly; 182(r), HRW Photo/Russell Dian; 182(bl), HRW Photo/Stock Editions; 182(lc), courtesy U.S. Air Force; 182(bc), HRW Photo/Claude Poulet; 182(br), courtesy Architect of the Capitol; 183, HRW Photo/Sam Dudgeon; 189, HRW Photo/George Winkler; 190(t), HRW Photo/Sam Dudgeon; 190 (tl), (l), (tc), (lc), HRW Photo/George Winkler; 190(tr), (bc), HRW Photo; 191, HRW Photo/Sam Dudgeon; 196(bckgd), Kuchlbauer/H. Armstrong Roberts; 197, 199(bckgd), 202, HRW Photo/Sam Dudgeon. **Chapter Nine**: Page 204, HRW Photo/Kevin Galvin; 205, HRW Photo/George Winkler; 206(t), HRW Photo/Sam Dudgeon, 206(c), (b), HRW Photo/ George Winkler; 207(l), (tr), HRW Photo/Kevin Galvin; 207(br), HRW Photo/Sam Dudgeon; 212(l), (br), HRW Photo/Kevin Galvin; 212(tr), HRW Photo/Sam Dudgeon; 213(l), (tr), HRW Photo/George Winkler; 213(br), 216, 219, HRW Photo/Sam Dudgeon; 220, Peter Herbster/Greenpeace Germany; 220-222(bckgd), HBJ Photo/Mark Antman; 223(bckgd), HRW Photo/ Sam Dudgeon; 224, Staatsministerium für Landesentwicklung und Umweltfragen, München.

UNIT FOUR: Chapter Ten: Page 228-229, Joachim Messerschmidt/Bruce Coleman, Inc; 230(t), (bl), HRW Photo/George Winkler; 230(br), Wolfgang Staiger/Visum; 231(tl), Fotex/S.Brehm/Nawrocki Stock; 231(tr), HRW Photo/George Winkler; 231(b), Fotex/I. Wandmacher/Nawrocki Stock; 232(l), HRW Photo/George Winkler; 233(t), HRW Photo/Kevin Galvin; 233(b), HRW Photo/George Winkler; 234(t), HRW Photo/Kevin Galvin; 234(b), Jorg Reichardt/DGG; 235(t), HRW Photo/Kevin Galvin; 235(b), 240(tl), (tr), HRW Photo/Sam Dudgeon; 240(b), Otto/Bavaria Bildagentur GmbH; 241(t), J. Alexandre/Bavaria Bildagentur; 241(b), HRW Photo/Sam Dudgeon; 244, HRW Photo/George Winkler; 247, Beryl Goldberg; 248(c), HRW Photo/Sam Dudgeon/courtesy of Molly & George Winkler; 248-250(bckgd), 251(bckgd), HRW Photo/Sam Dudgeon; 252,Tim Hall/Redferns/Retna; 253, 254, HRW Photo/Sam Dudgeon. **Chapter Eleven**: Page 256, HRW Photo/Kevin Galvin; 257(t), HRW Photo/Sam Dudgeon; 257(b), HRW Photo/George Winkler; 258(t), HRW Photo/Sam Dudgeon; 258(l), (r), HRW Photo/Kevin Galvin; 259, 266(t), (b), HRW Photo/Sam Dudgeon; 266(l), 267(tl), (tc), (cl), (c), (cr), (bl), (bc), HRW Photo/George Winkler; 267(tr), Lufthansa Bildarchiv; 267(br), HRW Photo/C. von der Goltz; 275(bckgd), 276, 278, HRW Photo/Sam Dudgeon. **Chapter Twelve**: Page 280, 281, HRW Photo/George Winkler; 282(r), HRW Photo/Sam Dudgeon; 282(cl), (cr), (bl), (br), 283, 289, HRW Photo/George Winkler; 290(t), HRW Photo/Sam Dudgeon; 290(cl), HRW Photo/George Winkler; 290(c), HRW Photo/Sam Dudgeon; 290(cr), (b), 291(t), (c), HRW Photo/George Winkler; 291(b), HRW Photo/Sam Dudgeon; 295,Thomas Balzer/courtesy Gerolsteiner Brunnen; 297(bckgd), 298-299(bckgd), 300-301(bckgd), 302, 303, HRW Photo/Sam Dudgeon.

ILLUSTRATION AND CARTOGRAPHY CREDITS

Böhm, Eduard: 16, 21, 44, 65, 108, 316, 317, 318, 319, 320

Cooper, Holly: 163, 318

Enthoven, Antonia: 18, 43, 208

Henderson, Meryl: 56, 177, 286

Hildreth Debora: 156, 157, 178

Krone, Michael: 19, 33, 111, 166, 272, 274, 321

Lyle, Maria: 17

McLeod, George: 37, 320

Mizzi, Giorgio: 16, 20, 66, 84, 116, 177, 264, 319

Pichler, Peter: 115, 177, 192, 214

Reppel, Aletha: 37

Rosenzweig, Frank: 72, 109, 135

Rummonds, Tom: 10, 320

Sayer, Jon: 133, 141, 169, 186

Schöol, Biruta: 19

Tillmann, Jutta: 17, 177, 214, 242, 322